- **1,197 Respondents:** Instructors illuminated us about course dynamics in two national surveys.
- **114 Symposium Attendees:** Some of the brightest minds in the discipline created solutions to address core course needs.
- **76 Regional Focus-group Participants:** These faculty deeply informed the organization of Connect as well as created guidelines for training and implementation.
- **172 Editorial Reviewers:** Introductory Spanish instructors from around the country directly informed the development of the content of *Puntos.*
- **10 Digital Board of Advisors Members:** This board reviewed digital content and functionality, contributing invaluable expert input.
- **8 *Mundo interactivo* Consultants:** Each consultant vetted the content for and class tested **Mundo interactivo** with both undergraduate and graduate students.
- **3 Implementation Consultants:** These professors blazed the trail to create materials to help you move from the previous edition to the new edition of *Puntos.*
- **1,633 Beta Testers:** In the spring of 2011, this group of students tested every prompt of LearnSmart!
- **34 Beta-testing Institutions:** These schools successfully integrated LearnSmart into their curriculums as a diagnostic, a new learning module, or a revie
- **36 Graduate Student Bo ite Student Board of Advisors.** on the beta test that helped us refine the final product.
- **17 Class-testing Institutions:** For each class test, instructors swapped out a chapter of the previous edition for the new and shared the results of their hands-on experience with us.
- **22 Cultural Ambassadors:** Each ambassador, representing a different Spanish-speaking country, provided cultural content corresponding to each chapter's topic and theme.

Puntos helps ***you*** administer ***your*** course more **efficiently** and **effectively.**

"The time-saving facets of having seamless coordination of online work and Blackboard are an excellent improvement, especially as we are offering *Puntos* online now . . . The new digital offerings for the ninth edition are a necessary and welcome improvement as Web and hybrid classes increase in number, and also to keep up with a technological medium that students can relate to more easily."

Catherine Ortiz, *University of Texas at Arlington*

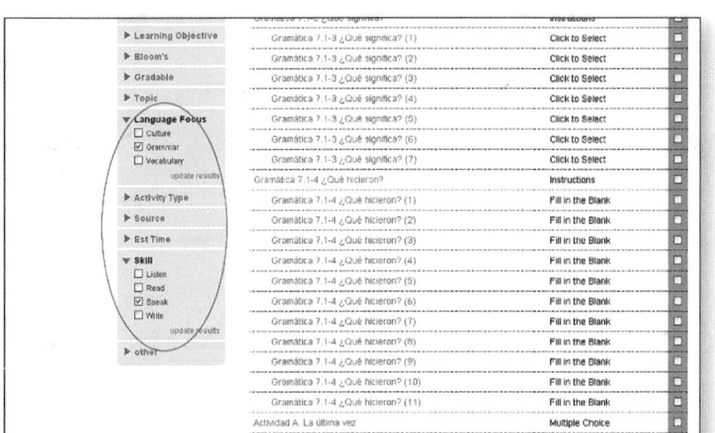

Puntos helps ***you*** achieve **consistent learning outcomes** across diverse instructional settings.

"Students also have an opportunity to put different skills into practice: listening, speaking, writing, and reading, sometimes within one single task. Connect is flexible enough to be used . . . in an F2F [face-to-face] course . . . being the sole teaching and learning tool for an online course."

Nuria López-Ortega, *University of Cincinnati*

PUNTOS—IT *WILL* TAKE YOU THERE!

Puntos de partida

Thalia Dorwick

Ana M. Pérez-Gironés
WESLEYAN UNIVERSITY

Anne Becher
UNIVERSITY OF COLORADO, BOULDER

Casilde A. Isabelli
UNIVERSITY OF NEVADA, RENO

Instructor's Edition

Ana M. Pérez-Gironés
WESLEYAN UNIVERSITY

A. Raymond Elliott
UNIVERSITY OF TEXAS AT ARLINGTON

McGraw Hill
Connect Learn Succeed™

The McGraw-Hill Companies

Mc Graw Hill Connect Learn Succeed™

Published by McGraw-Hill, an imprint of The McGraw-Hill Companies, Inc., 1221 Avenue of the Americas, New York, NY 10020.

This book is printed on acid-free paper.

2 3 4 5 6 7 8 9 0 DOW/DOW 1 0 9 8 7 6 5 4 3 2

ISBN: 978-0-07-338541-9 (Student Edition)
MHID: 0-07-338541-7

ISBN: 978-0-07-751172-2 (Instructor's Edition, **not for resale**)
MHID: 0-07-751172-7

Vice President Editorial: *Michael Ryan*
Editorial Director: *William R. Glass*
Senior Director of Development: *Scott Tinetti*

Publisher and Sponsoring Editor: *Katie Stevens*
Executive Marketing Manager: *Craig Gill*
Development Editor: *Allen J. Bernier*
Editorial Coordinators: *Sara Jaeger, Erin Blaze, and Laura Chiriboga*
Production Editor: *Brett Coker*
Production Service: *Aaron Downey, Matrix Productions, Inc.*
Manuscript Editor: *Danielle Havens*
Cover Designer: *Preston Thomas*
Interior Designer: *Elise Lansdon*
Art Editor: *Patti Isaacs*
Illustrators: *Harry Briggs, Patti Isaacs, Dartmouth Publishing, Inc.*
Photo Researchers: *Jennifer Blankenship and Sonia Brown*
Senior Buyer: *Tandra Jorgensen*
Media Project Manager: *Sarah B. Hill*
Digital Product Manager: *Jay Gubernick*
Composition: *10/12 Palatino by Aptara®, Inc.*
Printing: *45# Influence Soft Gloss by R.R. Donnelley*

Credits: The credits section for this book begins on page C-1 and is considered an extension of the copyright page.

Library of Congress Cataloging-in-Publication Data

Dorwick, Thalia, 1944–
Puntos de partida : an invitation to Spanish / Thalia Dorwick ... [et al.]. — 9th ed.
p. cm.
Previous ed.: 2009.
ISBN 978-0-07-338541-9 (Student edition) — ISBN 978-0-07-751172-2 (Instructor's edition)
1. Spanish language—Textbooks for foreign speakers—English. I. Title.
PC4129.E5P86 2011
468.2'421—dc23

2011040555

Printed in the USA

www.mhhe.com

Muchas gracias to the many *students* who have learned Spanish with *Puntos.* It is you who make this text meaningful. We hope we have inspired you to make the Spanish language and Hispanic cultures a meaningful part of your lives. What you say and do in Spanish is what ultimately matters most.

«Cada maestrillo tiene su librillo», as the Spanish **refrán** says. This **librillo** (which is really a complete learning program, not just a book) would not be what it is without the many *instructors* who have used it and given us suggestions and direction. **Nuestro libro es su libro. ¡Muchas gracias!**

Preface

As one of the best-selling introductory Spanish titles, *Puntos de partida,* or *Puntos,* as it is commonly referred to, has offered over a million students a starting place for their language studies. Today, the Spanish classroom is changing as are the teaching and learning experiences. Professors are offering more hybrid and online courses, technology is providing functionality we could only dream about a few years ago, and the students we teach are ever-changing. To complement the changing environment, materials for inside and outside the classroom must change and evolve as well. By employing a wide array of research tools including surveys, focus groups, symposia, and ethnographic studies, we listened to our customers—students and professors—to determine the most effective components of *Puntos* and to take an important leap forward in digital innovation.

WHAT DID WE LEARN FROM THE RESEARCH?

Introductory Spanish instructors want to motivate students to develop confidence and ownership of their communication skills.

- **40%** of faculty said they are dissatisfied with their students' ability to communicate in Spanish when they complete the introductory course. For this reason, instructors would like a tool that helps their students gain the confidence they need to communicate successfully in Spanish beyond the classroom.

Introductory Spanish classrooms consist of students with varying levels of language proficiency.

- **48%** of faculty said they spend more time than they would like dealing with variation in student preparedness and would like a tool that helps them mitigate these differences.

Instructors strive for consistent learning outcomes across classroom settings, whether their courses are face-to-face, hybrid, or fully online.

- **60%** of faculty said they find it difficult to achieve consistent course outcomes across different course formats and would like a tool that helps them deliver a seamless learning experience regardless of how the class is delivered.

Many instructors would like to handle issues of course administration more efficiently.

- **43%** of faculty said they are spending more time than they would like on administrative tasks related to delivering their courses and would like a tool that helps them better manage their workload.

THE RESULT?

The result is, simply put, *Puntos*. Take a fresh look at *Puntos*—it's everything you wanted.

Puntos . . .

- breaks new ground to meet the changing needs of face-to-face, hybrid, and online Spanish programs.
- offers students more opportunities to develop their communication skills via **TelePuntos,** a new integrated video section with corresponding in-text and digital activities.
- innovates through LearnSmart, a first-of-its-kind adaptive learning system within Connect Spanish that adjusts to the learning needs of *every* student in *every* classroom.

Puntos—it WILL take you there!

Puntos motivates ***students*** to develop their **communication skills.**

In national surveys and through symposia, we've listened to over a thousand instructors and professors speak about their experiences and challenges in teaching introductory Spanish. 84% stated that developing communication skills in Spanish is a top goal for the course. 79% indicated that the development of cultural competence was a "very important" or "extremely important" course outcome, but only 49% of professors are satisfied with how their current program integrates culture. This research, in addition to anecdotes from the classroom, reveals that students with a positive attitude toward the target culture are more motivated to participate in class, continue their language study beyond the required sequence, and retain their language skills longer after finishing their language study.

"[Connect Spanish] is a pioneering program that will take the teaching to a new amazing level in which the learning will be easier to evaluate by both the student and the teacher. It will also allow the student to feel less fear when speaking, which is the most difficult skill to acquire—due to inhibition. It could be revolutionary."

Lucero Tenorio,
Oklahoma State University

Relying upon the power of digital solutions, we introduce **Mundo interactivo,** task-based scenarios available in Connect Spanish. In these scenarios, students play the role of a television production assistant as they prepare the reporting segments for *Salu2,* a morning talk show based on our new video program.

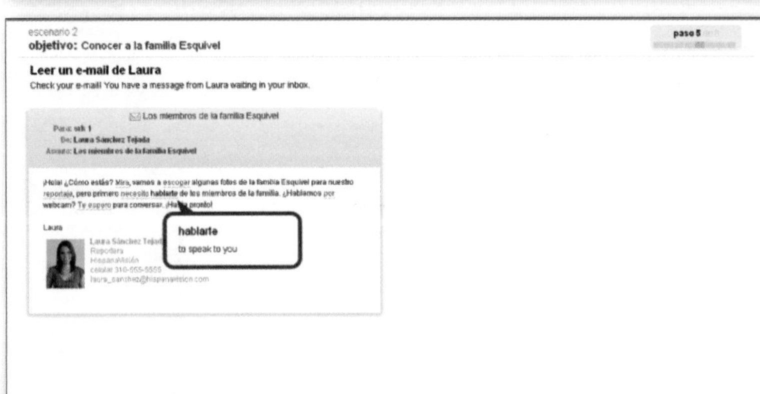

Students are transported into an immersive, story-based world where they experience the thrill of mastering relevant, task-based communication scenarios in real-world contexts. With functionality like synchronous and asynchronous video chat, students engage in communication practice online. This experience helps students gain the confidence to use their Spanish skills in the classroom and in their communities. Professors have access to a suite of media-rich content and tools to structure their students' experience and provide targeted feedback at just the right moments to maximize learning.

Professors also asked for more activities devoted to the four skill areas, and we responded. Within the text, *Puntos* offers instructors the necessary tools to help their students develop communicative proficiency in all four skill areas: listening and reading comprehension, and written and oral production. In each chapter, the new **A leer, A escuchar,** and **A escribir** sections expose students to written and aural language, drawing attention to reading, listening, and writing skills.

"I am pleased to see that there are more communicative activities in place and that instructors have more tools and options to work with."

Martha Guerrero-Phlaum,
Santa Ana College

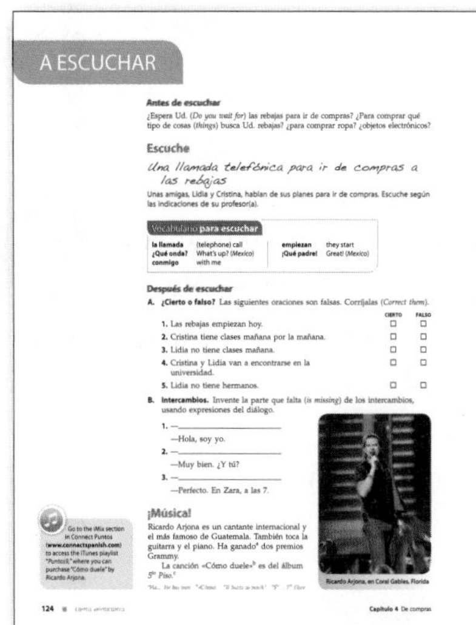

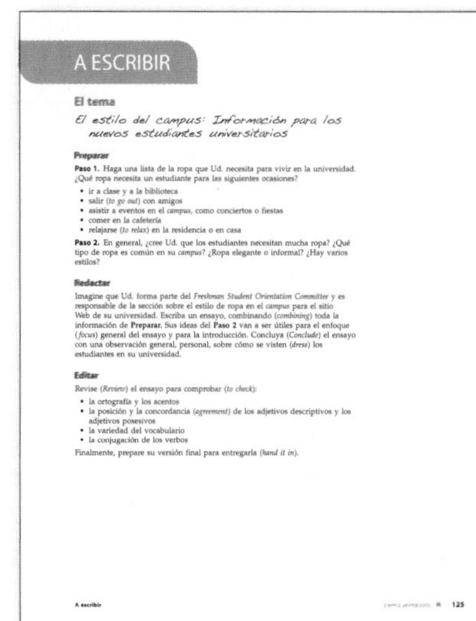

To give students more opportunities to communicate and thus improve their communicative proficiency, we've added new communicative objectives in the **En este capítulo** section of the chapter openers to let students know what they should be able to do by the end of the chapter. The new **En su comunidad** activity at the end of the **Un poco de todo** section asks students to interact and communicate directly with a Spanish speaker from their community about some cultural topic and then report their findings. The new two-page **TelePuntos** spread gives students opportunities to interact and communicate about each accompanying *Salu2* video segment, and the **Producción personal** feature prompts students to go out into their communities and create their own video segments, based on the topics presented in the *Salu2* segments.

"You blow my mind with how well you have integrated the personal and the '3Ps' of the National Standards! Products and Practices are clearly linked to Perspectives and/or the environments of the featured countries."

Janet Burke Norden,
Baylor University

Puntos addresses *students'* varying levels of **language proficiency.**

Introductory Spanish classrooms typically contain a mix of true beginners, false beginners, and even heritage speakers in the same classroom. Based on our research, we learned that the varying levels of language proficiency among students represent one of the greatest course challenges for the majority of introductory Spanish instructors.

"The adaptive diagnostic tool is very promising. It could be fruitfully added as a review tool, as tutoring support, or if sold as a free-standing item might even be used to place out of courses or to provide online testing. It provides the individualized feedback students need to take responsibility for their own learning and it stresses mastery."

Sandra Watts, *University of North Carolina, Charlotte*

Puntos offers LearnSmart, a powerful adaptive learning system, beta-tested by over 1,600 students. As the student completes each chapter's grammar and vocabulary modules, LearnSmart identifies the main grammatical structures and vocabulary words that warrant more practice, based on student performance, and provides an individualized study program.

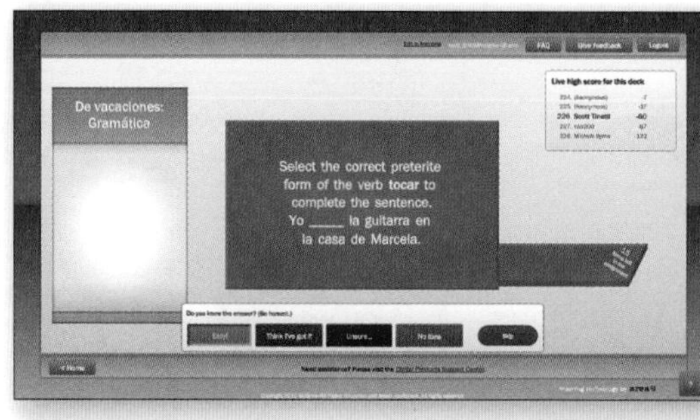

As the professor you can assign LearnSmart or you can simply say, "Go to LearnSmart and work on preterite vs. imperfect"—and off they go! LearnSmart allows you to quickly and easily choose how much content is covered within each module and to dig into very specific aspects of each grammar point rather than testing on an overall grammar point.

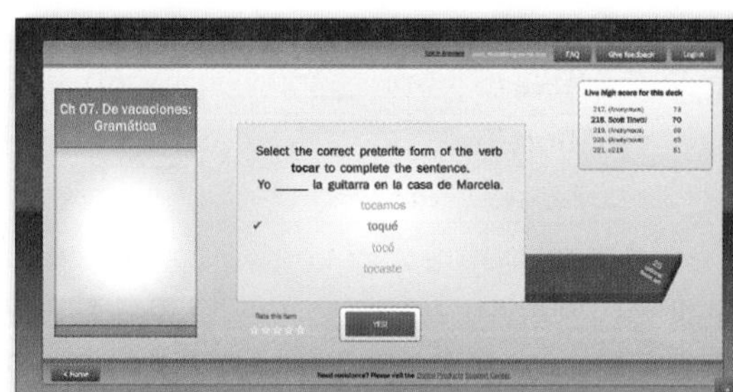

You will know exactly what your students know and where they continue to struggle.

What did we learn from our beta test students?

- **68%** agree or strongly agree that they were actively engaged in the LearnSmart activities.
- **75%** agree or strongly agree that LearnSmart increased their comprehension by studying vocabulary and grammar outside of the classroom.
- **93%** believe LearnSmart to be an effective way to review and learn concepts.
- **90%** would recommend LearnSmart to a friend.

In addition to addressing the variety of student levels in your classes, the *Puntos* program also appeals to students with diverse study habits. According to ethnographic research conducted by McGraw-Hill, four student types have emerged across disciplines.

Forward Learners

Interrupted Learners

Short-Term Learners

Delayed Learners

We took into consideration the diversity of student populations across the country and even within a single classroom when we designed *Puntos*. For example, for the Forward Learners, we provide a wealth of practice activities online and guide their workflow with options for additional practice. For the Interrupted Learners, we offer content downloadable to a laptop, iPod, or iPad, giving them the ability to study anywhere, anytime. Short-Term Learners can utilize LearnSmart to hone their weak areas so that they can use their study time more efficiently. And when Delayed Learners are cramming at the last minute, they will find all the study tools they need in one convenient location.

Puntos appeals to the individual needs of a wide variety of students by presenting interactive content and diagnostic tools that bring everyone to the same level of mastery.

"It suddenly started making sense when I started to use LearnSmart. I received a 95 on the essay after I started using LearnSmart, it is very helpful!"

Aaron De La Garza, Student, *Portland Community College*

Puntos helps **you** administer **your** course more **efficiently** and **effectively.**

Syllabus creation. Communicating with students outside of class. Assigning and grading homework. These are just a few of the administrative tasks that occupy instructors' time and diminish valuable opportunities to enrich teaching and learning experiences. Imagine a resource that efficiently handles these tasks and does so in a way that also allows you to easily administer your course to your goals and needs. Nearly half of the instructors surveyed told us that course administration issues are a huge obstacle to effective teaching. 91% of instructors stated that digital tools should save time in administering the course, but only 61% are satisfied with their current solution. 83% of instructors stated that they rely upon reporting features to manage their course, but only 60% are satisfied with their program.

Connect Spanish, as part of the *Puntos* program, provides online tools to reduce the amount of time and energy that instructors have to invest in administering their course. For example, when creating assignments, instructors can easily sort according to a variety of parameters that are important to their course in particular.

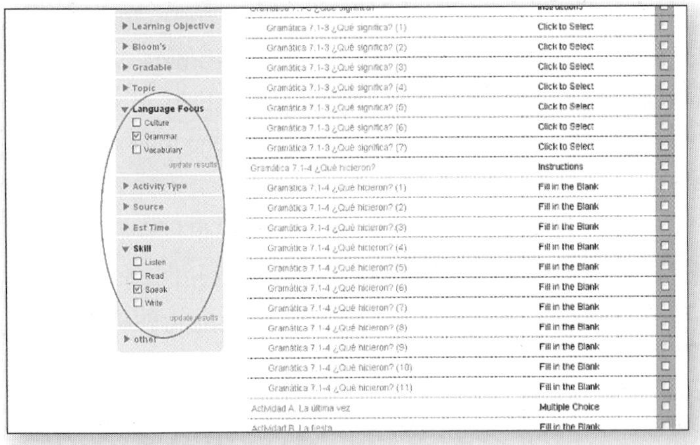

You can sort and assign based on language skill, grammar structure, vocabulary theme, the amount of time the activity takes, or the activity type (multiple choice, fill-in-the-blank, and so on). Once you create your section assignments, you can easily share your course with your colleagues, and as a course coordinator you can quickly see how all sections are progressing through the course assignments.

Do More

As a complement to Connect Spanish, McGraw-Hill and Blackboard have teamed up. What does this mean for your introductory Spanish course?

1. **Your life, simplified.** Now you and your students can access all McGraw-Hill Connect content directly from within your Blackboard course. Say good-bye to the days of logging in to multiple applications, and say hello to true, single sign-on.

2. **Deep integration of content and tools.** Not only do you get single sign-on with Connect, you also get deep integration of McGraw-Hill content and content engines right in Blackboard. Whether you're choosing a book for your course or building Connect assignments, all the tools you need are right where you want them—inside Blackboard.

3. **Seamless gradebooks.** Are you tired of keeping multiple gradebooks and manually synchronizing grades into Blackboard? We thought so. When a student completes an integrated Connect assignment, the grade for that assignment automatically (and instantly) feeds into your Blackboard grade center.

4. **A solution for everyone.** Whether your institution is already using Blackboard or you just want to try Blackboard on your own, we have a solution for you. McGraw-Hill and Blackboard can now offer you easy access to industry-leading technology and content, whether your campus hosts it or we do. Be sure to ask your local McGraw-Hill representative for details.

"The time-saving facets of having seamless coordination of online work and Blackboard are an excellent improvement, especially as we are offering *Puntos* online now . . . The new digital offerings are a necessary and welcome improvement as Web and hybrid classes increase in number, and also to keep up with a technological medium that students can relate to more easily."

Catherine Ortiz, *University of Texas at Arlington*

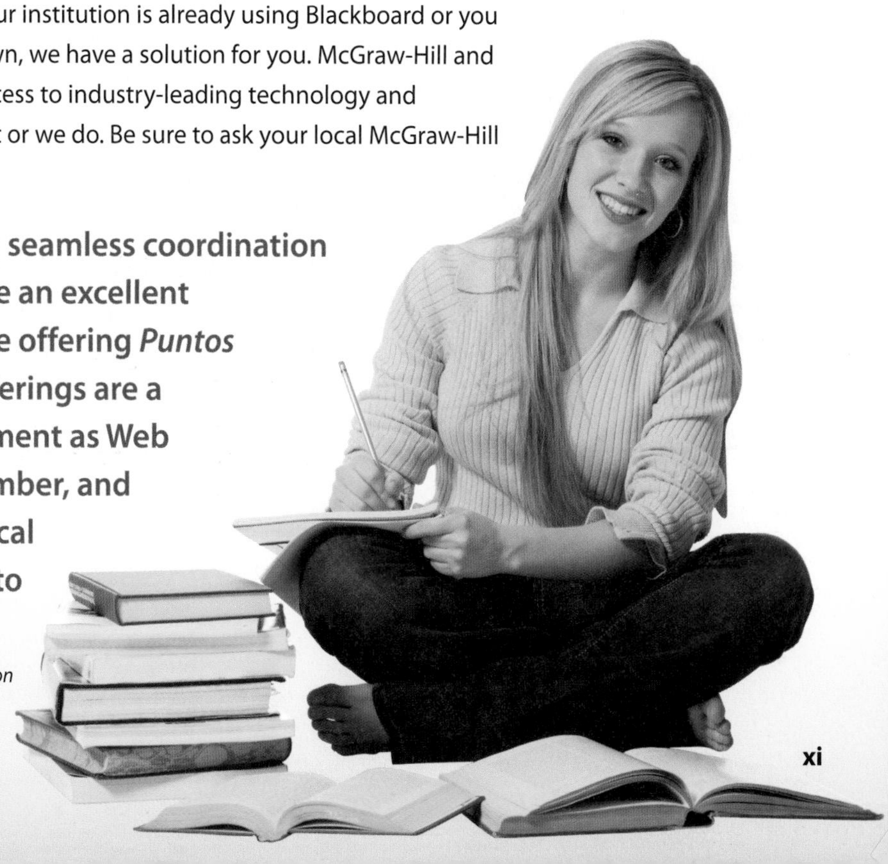

Puntos helps ***you*** achieve **consistent learning outcomes** across diverse instructional settings.

The context for teaching and learning can take many forms in today's world, including traditional face-to-face courses, fully online courses, and hybrid offerings. Nearly one-third of programs across the country are now offering hybrid or online sections. Given these trends, we created a unique online delivery of the *Puntos* program to provide consistent outcomes no matter which of these formats is used.

The content of *Puntos* is comprised of an array of integrated print and digital offerings, giving you the maximum flexibility to choose the most appropriate format for your courses. At the same time, you can be assured that regardless of the format, all content is directly tied to course learning objectives that are consistent across all components of the program.

Can students in an online course attain the same level of oral proficiency as those in a traditional classroom setting? With *Puntos*, the answer is yes! For example, in-class communicative activities are replicated in the online environment, allowing students to pair up with virtual partners for communication practice.

"I am very pleased with your continuous innovations and improvement of this program. Detecting needs, asking instructors, keeping updated with technology are all pluses . . . It's the very best program out there."

Lucero Tenorio,
Oklahoma State University

The video program is another example of flexibility: whether you have your students view the video online or you prefer to show the video in class, you can incorporate it into your face-to-face or online sections, depending on what works for you. Related activities can be done in class or online, so students receive the same amount of exposure and practice no matter what the class format.

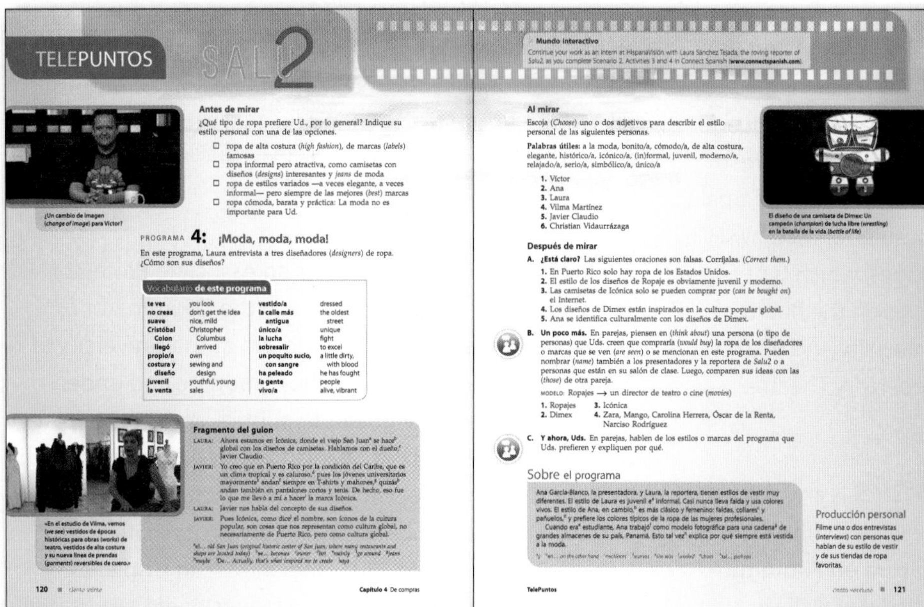

TELEPUNTOS SALU2

Antes de mirar

¿Qué tipo de ropa prefiere Ud., por lo general? Indique su estilo personal con una de las opciones.

- ☐ ropa de alta costura (*high fashion*), de marcas (*labels*) famosas
- ☐ ropa informal pero atractiva, como camisetas con diseños (*designs*) interesantes y *jeans* de moda
- ☐ ropa de estilos variados —a veces elegante, a veces informal— pero siempre de las mejores (*best*) marcas
- ☐ ropa cómoda, barata y práctica: La moda no es importante para Ud.

¿Un cambio de imagen (*change of image*) para Víctor?

PROGRAMA **4:** **¡Moda, moda, moda!**

En este programa, Laura entrevista a tres diseñadores (*designers*) de ropa. ¿Cómo son sus diseños?

Vocabulario de este programa

te ves	you look	**vestido/a**	dressed
no creas	don't get the idea	**la calle más antigua**	the oldest street
suave	nice, mild	**único/a**	unique
Cristóbal Colon llegó	Christopher Columbus arrived	**la lucha**	fight
propio/a	own	**sobresalir**	to excel
costura y diseño	sewing and design	**un poquito sucio, con sangre**	a little dirty, with blood
juvenil	youthful, young	**ha peleado**	he has fought
la venta	sales	**la gente**	people
		vivo/a	alive, vibrant

Fragmento del guion

LAURA: Ahora estamos en Icónica, donde el viejo San Juan[a] se hace[b] global con los diseños de camisetas. Hablamos con el dueño,[c] Javier Claudio.

JAVIER: Yo creo que en Puerto Rico por la condición del Caribe, que es un clima tropical y es caluroso,[d] pues los jóvenes universitarios mayormente[e] andan[f] siempre en T-shirts y mahones,[g] quizás[h] andan también en pantalones cortos y tenis. De hecho, eso fue lo que me llevó a mí a hacer[i] la marca Icónica.

LAURA: Javier nos habla del concepto de sus diseños.

JAVIER: Pues Icónica, como dice[j] el nombre, son íconos de la cultura popular, son cosas que nos representan como cultura global, no necesariamente de Puerto Rico, pero como cultura global.

[a]*el... old San Juan (original historic center of San Juan, where many restaurants and shops are located today)* [b]*se... becomes* [c]*owner* [d]*hot* [e]*mainly* [f]*go around* [g]*jeans* [h]*maybe* [i]*De... Actually, that's what inspired me to create* [j]*says*

«En el estudio de Vilma, vemos (*we see*) vestidos de épocas históricas para obras (*works*) de teatro, vestidos de alta costura y su nueva línea de prendas (*garments*) reversibles de cuero.»

120 ■ ciento veinte — **Capítulo 4** De compras

Mundo interactivo

Continue your work as an intern at HispanaVisión with Laura Sánchez Tejada, the roving reporter of Salu2, as you complete Scenario 2, Activities 3 and 4 in Connect Spanish (**www.connectspanish.com**).

Al mirar

Escoja (*Choose*) uno o dos adjetivos para describir el estilo personal de las siguientes personas.

Palabras útiles: a la moda, bonito/a, cómodo/a, de alta costura, elegante, histórico/a, icónico/a, (in)formal, juvenil, moderno/a, relajado/a, serio/a, simbólico/a, único/a

1. Víctor
2. Ana
3. Laura
4. Vilma Martínez
5. Javier Claudio
6. Christian Vidaurrázaga

El diseño de una camiseta de Dimex: Un campeón (*champion*) de lucha libre (*wrestling*) en la batalla de la vida (*battle of life*)

Después de mirar

A. **¿Está claro?** Las siguientes oraciones son falsas. Corríjalas. (*Correct them.*)

1. En Puerto Rico solo hay ropa de los Estados Unidos.
2. El estilo de los diseños de Ropaje es obviamente juvenil y moderno.
3. Las camisetas de Icónica solo se pueden comprar por (*can be bought on*) el Internet.
4. Los diseños de Dimex están inspirados en la cultura popular global.
5. Ana se identifica culturalmente con los diseños de Dimex.

B. **Un poco más.** En parejas, piensen en (*think about*) una persona (o tipo de personas) que Uds. creen que compraría (*would buy*) la ropa de los diseñadores o marcas que se ven (*are seen*) o se mencionan en este programa. Pueden nombrar (*name*) también a los presentadores y la reportera de *Salu2* o a personas que están en su salón de clase. Luego, comparen sus ideas con las (*those*) de otra pareja.

MODELO: Ropajes → un director de teatro o cine (*movies*)

1. Ropajes
2. Dimex
3. Icónica
4. Zara, Mango, Carolina Herrera, Óscar de la Renta, Narciso Rodríguez

C. **Y ahora, Uds.** En parejas, hablen de los estilos o marcas del programa que Uds. prefieren y expliquen por qué.

Sobre el programa

Ana García-Blanco, la presentadora, y Laura, la reportera, tienen estilos de vestir muy diferentes. El estilo de Laura es juvenil e[a] informal. Casi nunca lleva falda y usa colores vivos. El estilo de Ana, en cambio,[b] es más clásico y femenino: faldas, collares[c] y pañuelos,[d] y prefiere los colores típicos de la ropa de las mujeres profesionales.

Cuando era[e] estudiante, Ana trabajó[f] como modelo fotográfica para una cadena[g] de grandes almacenes de su país, Panamá. Esto tal vez[h] explica por qué siempre está vestida a la moda.

[a]*y* [b]*en... on the other hand* [c]*necklaces* [d]*scarves* [e]*she was* [f]*worked* [g]*chain* [h]*tal... perhaps*

Producción personal

Filme una o dos entrevistas (*interviews*) con personas que hablan de su estilo de vestir y de sus tiendas de ropa favoritas.

TelePuntos — ciento veintiuno ■ 121

Just like the video, each component of *Puntos* ensures a seamless transition from the face-to-face classroom to the virtual classroom and everything in between.

"Students also have an opportunity to put different skills into practice: listening, speaking, writing, and reading, sometimes within one single task. Connect is flexible enough to be used . . . in a F2F [face-to-face] course, . . . being the sole teaching and learning tool for an online course."

Nuria López-Ortega,
University of Cincinnati

ABOUT THE AUTHORS

Thalia Dorwick has retired as McGraw-Hill's Editor-in-Chief for Humanities, Social Sciences, and Languages. For many years she was also in charge of McGraw-Hill's World Languages college list in Spanish, French, Italian, German, Japanese, and Russian. She has taught at Allegheny College, California State University (Sacramento), and Case Western Reserve University, where she received her Ph.D. in Spanish in 1973. She has been recognized as an Outstanding Foreign Language Teacher by the California Foreign Language Teachers Association. Dr. Dorwick is the coauthor of several textbooks and the author of several articles on language teaching issues. She is a frequent guest speaker on topics related to language learning, and was an invited speaker at the **II Congreso Internacional de la Lengua Española,** in Valladolid, Spain, in October 2001. In retirement she consults for McGraw-Hill, especially in the area of world languages, which is of personal interest to her. She also serves on the Board of Trustees of Case Western Reserve University and on the Board of Directors of the Berkeley Repertory Theatre.

Ana María Pérez-Gironés is an Adjunct Professor of Spanish at Wesleyan University, Middletown, Connecticut. She received a **Licenciatura en Filología Anglogermánica** from the Universidad de Sevilla in 1985, and her M.A. in General Linguistics from Cornell University in 1988. Her professional interests include second language acquisition and the integration of cultural competence and technology in language teaching. She has published a variety of pedagogical material, and is co-author of the programs *A otro nivel, Apúntate, Más,* and *Puntos en breve.* At Wesleyan, she teaches and coordinates Spanish language courses at all levels, including Spanish for heritage speakers, and she has directed the university's Program in Madrid.

Anne Becher received her M.A. in Hispanic Linguistics in 1992 from the University of Colorado, Boulder, where she coordinates Beginning Spanish and teaches pedagogy and methods courses for the Department of Spanish and Portuguese. She has taught beginning through advanced levels of Spanish since 1996, including several years teaching Modified Spanish classes for students with difficulty learning languages. She has published several reviews in *Hispania,* presents frequently at the Colorado Congress of Foreign Language Teachers (CCFLT) conferences, and has served on the boards of CCFLT and the Colorado chapter of American Association of Teachers of Spanish and Portuguese. She co-edited the bilingual literary journal *La selva subterránea* from 1987–1996.

Casilde A. Isabelli is an Associate Professor of Spanish Linguistics and formerly the Coordinator of the Basic Spanish Language Program at the University of Nevada, Reno, where she teaches graduate and undergraduate courses in language, linguistics, and methodology. She received her Ph.D. in Spanish Applied Linguistics with a concentration in Second Language Acquisition and Teacher Education (SLATE) at the University of Illinois at Urbana-Champaign in 2001, and an M.A. in Hispanic Literature and Linguistics at the University of Iowa in 1994. Dr. Isabelli's research and publications focus on the effects of immersion experiences and formal instruction on SLA and psycholinguistically motivated theories behind SLA (processing instruction and language transfer). She also served as a World Languages Training Advisory Board Member for the eighth edition of *Puntos de partida.*

ACKNOWLEDGMENTS

We would like to thank the overwhelming number of friends and colleagues who served on boards of advisors or as consultants, completed reviews or surveys, and attended symposia or focus groups. Their feedback was indispensible in creating the *Puntos* program. The appearance of their names in the following lists does not necessarily constitute their endorsement of the program or its methodology.

Digital Board of Advisors

Susann Davis
Western Kentucky University

Luis Latoja
Columbus State Community College

Jeffery Longwell
New Mexico State University, Las Cruces

Nuria López-Ortega
University of Cincinnati

Andrea Petri
Miracosta College

Victoria Russell
Valdosta State University

Rosalinda Sandoval
San Diego City College

Adriana Vega-Hidalgo
University of North Carolina, Charlotte

Sandra Watts
University of North Carolina, Charlotte

Mundo interactivo Consultants

Yuly Asención-Delaney
Northern Arizona University

Flavia Belpoliti
University of Houston

Esther Castro
San Diego State University

Ronna Feit
Nassau Community College

Theresa Minick
Kent State University

Christine Sabin
Sierra College

Bruce Williams
William Patterson University

Susanna Williams
Macomb Community College

Special Consultants

Timothy Foxsmith
University of Texas at Arlington

Melissa Logue
Columbus State Community College

Janet Norden
Baylor University

Justin White
Florida Atlantic University

Cultural Ambassadors

Roberto Arroyo, Chile
University of Oregon

Alicia María Barrón López, Spain
University of Colorado, Boulder

Alejandra Bonifacino, Uruguay
Wichita State University

Delna Bryan, Panama

Alessandra Chiriboga Holzheu, Guatemala
University of Pittsburgh

Mayra Cortés-Torres, Puerto Rico
Pima Community College

Emilio del Valle Escalante, Guatemala
University of North Carolina, Chapel Hill

Max Ehrsam, Mexico
Massachusetts Institute of Technology

Carlos Gómez Florentín, Paraguay
Stony Brook University

Talia González, U.S. Hispanics
Columbia University

Flor Cecilia Gutiérrez, Colombia
University of Nevada, Reno

Antonio Iacopino, Argentina
Harper College

Jazmina Johnston, Nicaragua

Wladimir Yllich Márquez, Venezuela
University of Colorado, Boulder

Chris Ashton Monge, Costa Rica

Olga Moran, Honduras
Saddleback College

Ana Ozuna, Dominican Republic
Indian River State College

Yansi Pérez, El Salvador
Carleton College

Alonso María Rabi Do Carmo, Peru
University of Colorado, Boulder

Edison Robayo, Ecuador

Estrella C. Rodríguez, Cuba
Florida State University

Verónica Saunero-Ward, Bolivia
New Mexico Highlands University

Symposia

Amelia Island, FL

Flavia Belpoliti
University of Houston

Sarah Bentley
Portland Community College

Sara Casler
Sierra College

Jorge Cubillos
University of Delaware

Paul Larson
Baylor University

María Elizabeth Mahaffey
University of North Carolina, Charlotte

Leticia McGrath
Georgia Southern University

Catherine Ortiz
University of Texas at Arlington

Yanira Paz
University of Kentucky

Carlos Ramírez
University of Pittsburgh

Carmen Sotolongo
El Camino College

Edda Temoche-Weldele
Grossmont College

Amy Uribe
Lone Star College

Karen Zetrouer
Santa Fe Community College

Key West, FL

Michelle Cipriano
Wright State University

Edward Erazo
Broward College–Central

Cindy Espinosa
Central Michigan University

Vanessa Lazo-Wilson
Austin Community College–Round Rock

Kathy Leonard
University of Nevada, Reno

Melissa Logue
Columbus State Community College

Germán Negrón
University of Nevada, Las Vegas

Sylvia Nikopoulos
Central Piedmont Community College

Isabel Parra
University of Cincinnati, Batavia

Carlos Pedroza
Palomar College

Beatriz Potter
Valdosta State University

Latasha Russell
Florida State College, South Campus

Nancy Stucker
Cabrillo College

Lucero Tenorio
Oklahoma State University, Stillwater

Lilia Vidal
Miracosta College

Spring 2011 Focus Groups

Orlando, FL

Rosalina Collins
Polk State College

Elizabeth Dowdy
State College of Florida Manatee

Dina Fabery
University of Central Florida

Roxana Levin
St. Petersburg College

Mónica Montalvo
University of Central Florida

Dora Romero
Broward College

Alicia J. von Lehe
Santa Fe College

Houston, TX

Flavia Belpoliti
University of Houston

Encarna Bermejo
Houston Baptist University

Rosa Dávila
Austin Community College

Silvia Huntsman
Sam Houston State University

Sheila Jones
Sam Houston State University

Alejandro Latínez
Sam Houston State University

María López
Houston Community College

Lizette Moon
Houston Community College

Norma Mouton
Sam Houston State University

Carmen Parrón
Sam Houston State University

David Quintero
Seattle Community College

Amy Uribe
Lone Star College

Dana Point, CA

Verónica Álvarez
Golden West College

Valeria Barragán
Saddleback College

Marius Cucurny
Golden West College

David Detwiler
Miracosta College

Martha Guerrero-Phlaum
Santa Ana College

Vanessa Gutiérrez
Palomar College

Carmenmara Hernández-Bravo
Saddleback College

Leticia López-Jaurequi
Santa Ana College

Verónica Pizano
Golden West College

Dora Schoenbrun-Fernández
San Diego Mesa College

Maribel Villaseñor
Santiago Canyon College

Dallas, TX

Bill Dooley
Baylor University

Raymond Elliott
University of Texas at Arlington

José Luis Escorcia
Baylor University

Christina Fox-Ballí
Eastfield College

Ann Ortiz
Campbell University

Jaime Palmer
Tarrant Community College

Natalia Verjat
Tarrant Community College

Natalie Wagener
University of Texas at Arlington

Kim White
El Centro College

New York, NY

Silvia Álvarez-Olarra
Borough of Manhattan Community College

María Cabrera
Westchester University of Pennsylvania

María Enrico
Borough of Manhattan Community College

Eda Henao
Borough of Manhattan Community College

Richard McCallister
Delaware State University

Abigail Méndez
Borough of Manhattan Community College

Celinés Villalba
Rutgers University

Fall 2011 Focus Groups

Dallas, TX

Flavia Belpoliti
University of Houston

Rosa Chávez
Tarrant County College

Darren Crasto
Houston Community College

Bill Dooley
Baylor University

Timothy Foxsmith
University of Texas at Arlington

César Grisales
Broward Community College

Leticia McDoniel
Southern Methodist University

Janet Norden
Baylor University

Dennis Pearce
McLennan Community College

Isaac Rivera
Tarrant County College

Margarita Rodríguez
Lone Star College

Susana Solera-Adoboe
Southern Methodist University

Kerri Stephenson
Johnson County Community College

Amy Uribe
Lone Star College

Laguna Beach, CA

Valeria Barragán
Saddleback College

Graciela Boruszko
Pepperdine University

Mayra Cortés-Torres
Pima Community College

Jaime Estrada-Olalde
San Diego City College

Juan Carlos Gallego
California State University, Fullerton

Javier Galván
Santa Ana College

Elena Grajeda
Pima Community College

Lynda Graveson
Saddleback College

Martha Guerrero-Phlaum
Santa Ana College

Debbie Kaaikiola Strohbusch
University of Wisconsin, Madison

Silvia López
Santiago Canyon College

Sara Lotz
Northern Arizona University

Andrea Petri
Miracosta College

Beatriz Robinson
University of Nevada, Reno

Jared White
University of California, Irvine

Fall 2011 Class Testers

Verónica Álvarez
Golden West College

Claudia Behnke
Northern Arizona University

Sara Casler
Sierra College

Ed Erazo
Broward Community College

Jaime Estrada-Olalde
San Diego City College

Anna Kalminskaia
University of Nevada, Reno

Constance Kihyet
Saddleback College

Kathleen Leonard
Unversity of Nevada, Reno

Catherine Ortiz
University of Texas at Arlington

Lynne Overesch-Maister
Johnson County Community College

Beatriz Potter
Valdosta State University

Fran Raucci
Dutchess Community College

Beatriz Robinson
University of Nevada, Reno
Dora Romero
Broward Community College
Rosalinda Sandoval
San Diego City College
Sam Sommerville
Johnson County Community College
Kerri Stephenson
Johnson County Community College
Lucero Tenorio
Oklahoma State University, Stillwater
Amy Uribe
Lone Star College
Amber Williams-Lara
Lone Star College
Melissa Ziegler
University of Wisconsin, Madison

LearnSmart

Beta Testing Instructors

María Amores
University of West Virginia
Sarah Bentley
Portland Community College
Graciela Boruszko
Pepperdine University
Sara Casler
Sierra College
Christopher DiCapua
Community College of Philadelphia
Bill Dooley
Baylor University
Donna Factor
El Camino College
Max Gartman
Chattanooga State Community College
Elena Grajeda
Pima County Community College
Vanessa Gutiérrez
Palomar College
Constance Kihyet
Saddleback College
Luis Latoja
Columbus State Community College
Roxana Levin
St. Petersburg College
Nuria López-Ortega
University of Cincinnati
Robert Martinsen
Brigham Young University
Ornella Mazzuca
Dutchess Community College
Bryan McBride
Eastern Arizona College
Libardo Mitchell
Portland Community College
Javier Morín
Delmar College
Ann Ortiz
Campbell University
Catherine Ortiz
University of Texas at Arlington
Lynne Overesch-Maister
Johnson County Community College
David Quintero
Seattle Central Community College
Carlos Ramírez
University of Pittsburgh
Beatriz Robinson
University of Nevada, Reno
Dora Romero
Broward College
Irene Schmitt
Johnson County Community College
Louis Silvers
Monroe Community College
Craig Stokes
Dutchess Community College
Patricia Tello
University of Oklahoma
Edda Temoche-Weldele
Grossmont College
Verónica Tempone
Indian River State College
Amy Uribe
Lone Star College
Justin White
Florida Atlantic University

Graduate Teaching Assistant Board of Advisors

Under the direction of Flavia Belpoliti—University of Houston
María Álvarez
Mónica Barba
Emily Bernate
Eloisa Blum
Sofía Gellon
Diana Hernández
Aaron Madson
Carlos Martínez
Sara Mason
Burcu Mutlu
María Pérez
Luna Rubén
Eugenia Ruiz
Vivian Santana
Edna Velázquez
Joseph Yoo
Laura Zubiate

Under the direction of Anne Becher—University of Colorado, Boulder
Alicia María Barrón López
Mariana Bolívar Rubín
Joseph Haymaker
Ximena Keogh
Katherine Meis

Under the direction of Muriel Gallego—Ohio University, Athens
Allison Buzzelli
Stephanie Creighton
Carolyn Crowner
Ericha Franke
Cherita King
Irene Ramos

Under the direction of Nuria López-Ortega—University of Cincinnati
Lia Buitrago
Derek Furnish
María Carmen Hernández
Patricia Marín Cepeda
Juliana Martínez
Milton Medellín
Miguel Ángel Rodríguez-Dávila
Milton Romero

Undergraduate Student Board of Advisors

Under the direction of Christopher DiCapua—Community College of Philadelphia

Cinquetta Brown
Nylz Childs
Lauren Danella
Simone Maitland
Nina Poltoranina
Rashni Stanford

Under the direction of Edda Temoche-Weldele—Grossmont College

Heather Burdett
Claudia Connors
Lacey Cool
Mireya Cortez
Breanna Durant
Casey Flannery
Sandra Gracia de León
Angela Hinton
Brittany Huffman
Anna Le
Betheny Lel
John Nicholson
Tensai Ocbmichael
Breanna Parton
Fernando Ramírez
Vonna Redmond
Natalie Relph
Golan Silverman
Frank Valdez
María Villegas
Matthew Wadsworth
Isaura Yánez

Under the direction of Amy Uribe—Lone Star College

Al Ali Bayan
Natalie Henry
Travis Hines
Lauren Hopkins
Taylor Lewis
Brandon Postell
Austin Powell
Anna Rashe
Kristen Risley
Sharon Siman-Toy
Kristen Troxler

Reviewers

Melania Aguirre-Rabón
Wake Technical Community College
Matthew Alba
Brigham Young University, Idaho
Verónica Álvarez
Golden West College
Davila Anderson
Kankakee Community College
Daniel Arroyo-Rodríguez
Colorado College
Yuly Asención-Delaney
Northern Arizona University
Lisa Barboun
Coastal Carolina University
Hilary Barnes
Fayetteville State University
Valeria Barragán
Saddleback College
Alicia María Barrón López
University of Colorado, Boulder
Luis Bejarano
Valdosta State University
Clare Bennett
University of Alaska, Southeast Ketchikan
Barbara Bessette
Cayuga Community College
Tomás Beviá
Cornell University
Kathleen Bizzarro
Colorado College
Graciela Susana Boruszko
Pepperdine University
Jesús Bottaro
Medgar Evers College
Patrick Brady
Tidewater Community College
Luisa Briones
Hamilton College
Mónica J. Brito
Pima Community College, Northwest
Suzanne Buck
Central New Mexico Community College
Bryan Byrd
College of Charleston
Eduardo Cabrera
Millikin University
Lina Callahan
Fullerton College
Mayra Camacho Cummings
Paris Junior College
Sarah Campbell
Montgomery College, Rockville Campus
Martín Camps
University of the Pacific
Irene M. Caridi-De Barraicua
Sierra College
Sara K. Casler
Sierra College
Obdulia Castro
Regis University
Elena Cataldo
Lone Star College, Kingwood
Marco Tulio Cedillo
Lynchburg College
Alberto Chamorro
Drury University
Matthieu Chan Tsin
Coastal Carolina University
Sharon Chesser
Truett McConnell College
Rosa María Chism
Pennsylvania State University, Abington
Joseph Collentine
Northern Arizona University
Carmen Collins
Lake Michigan College
Robert Colvin
Brigham Young University, Idaho
Cristina Cordero
Lone Star College, CyFair
Mayra Cortés-Torres
Pima Community College
Sister Angela Cresswell
Holy Family University
Haydn Tiago de Azevedo Mafra Jones
Campbell University
María L. De Panbehchi
Virginia Commonwealth University
Carol de Rosset
Berea College
María Lorena Delgadillo
University of North Carolina, Charlotte
John Deveny
Oklahoma State University
Kent Dickson
California State Polytechnic University, Pomona
Tracy Dinesen
Simpson College
Debbie DiStefano
Southeast Missouri State University
Bill Dooley
Baylor University
María Enciso
Saddleback College
Eddy Enríquez Arana
Penn State University, Mont Alto
Edward Erazo
Broward College
José Luis Escorcia
Baylor University
Kristin Fletcher
Santa Fe College

Diana Frantzen
University of Wisconsin, Madison
Ellen Lorraine Friedrich
Valdosta State University
Muriel Gallego
Ohio University
Heidi Gehman-Pérez
Southside Virginia Community College
Stephanie Gerhold
Washington College
Ransom Gladwin
Valdosta State University
Juan M. González
Northern State University
Elena Grajeda
Pima Community College
Margarita R. Groeger
Massachusetts Institute of Technology
Gail Grosso
Central New Mexico Community College
Betty Gudz
Sierra College
Martha Guerrero-Phlaum
Santa Ana College
María D. Guzmán de Atherley
Sierra College
Angela Haensel
Cincinnati State Technical and Community College
Karen V. Hall Zetrouer
Santa Fe College
Sarah Harmon
Cañada College
Lucy Harney
Texas State University, San Marcos
Alan Hartman
Mercy College, Dobbs Ferry
William Hernández
Los Angeles Harbor College
Donna Hodkinson
Oklahoma City University
Milena M. Hurtado
Fayetteville State University
John J. Ivers
Brigham Young University, Idaho
William James
Cosumnes River College
Frank Johnson
Southern Nazarene University
Sheila B. Jones
Sam Houston State University
Alfred Keller
Broward College
Curtis Kleinman
Yavapai College
Alberto Landaveri
University of California, Irvine

Wayne Langehennig
South Plains College
Jeremy Larochelle
University of Mary Washington
Kajsa Larson
Northern Kentucky University
Kathleen Leonard
University of Nevada, Reno
Frederic Leveziel
Augusta State University
Lucía Llorente
Berry College
Melissa Logue
Columbus State Community College
Steve Lombardo
Purdue University, Calumet
María Helena López
Northwest Florida State College
Eder Maestre
Western Kentucky University
María Elizabeth Mahaffey
University of North Carolina, Charlotte
Monica Malamud
Cañada College
Dora Y. Marrón Romero
Broward College
María Isabel Martínez-Mira
University of Mary Washington
Thomas J. Mathews
Weber State University
Eric Mayer
Central Washington University
Ornella L. Mazzuca
Dutchess Community College
Bryan McBride
Eastern Arizona College
Dawn Meissner
Anne Arundel Community College
Marco Mena
MassBay Community College
José Mendoza
University of San Diego
Timothy B. Messick
Mohawk Valley Community College
William Miller
Indiana Wesleyan University
Ljiljana Milojevic
Ocean County College
Theresa Minick
Kent State University
José Luis Mireles
Coastal Carolina University
Rosa-María Moreno
Cincinnati State Technical and Community College
Olga M. Muniz
Hillsdale College

Jerome Mwinyelle
East Tennessee State University
Ruth F. Navarro
Grossmont College
Louise Neary
Wesleyan University
Elizabeth Nichols
Drury University
Sylvia Juana Nikopoulos
Central Piedmont Community College
Gustavo Adolfo Obeso
Western Kentucky University
Dale Omundson
Anoka-Ramsey Community College
Michelle Orecchio
University of Michigan, Ann Arbor
Martha Oregel
University of San Diego
Catherine Ortiz
University of Texas at Arlington
Jodie Parys
University of Wisconsin, Whitewater
Dennis Pearce
McLennan Community College
Luis Peralta
Millikin University
Federico Pérez-Pineda
University of South Alabama
María E. Pérez-Sanjurjo
County College of Morris
Inmaculada Pertusa
Western Kentucky University
Harold Pleitez
Beverly Hills Lingual Institute
Sarah Pollack
College of Staten Island, CUNY
Beatriz Potter
Valdosta State University
Johanna Ramos
Florida A & M University
María D. Ramos
Macomb Community College
Frances Raucci
Dutchess Community College
Kay E. Raymond
Sam Houston State University
Julie Resnick
Nashua Community College
Elena Retzer
California State University, Los Angeles
María Rodríguez-Cintrón
Tallahassee Community College
Christine Sabin
Sierra College
Rosa Salinas Samelson
Palo Alto College

José Alejandro Sandoval
Coastal Carolina Community College
Roman C. Santos
Mohawk Valley Community College
Nidia A. Schuhmacher
Brown University
Gilberto Serrano
Columbus State Community College
Louis Silvers
Monroe Community College
Martha Slayden
Colorado College
Matthew Smith
Pima Community College
Natalie Sobalvarro-Butler
Merced College
Lissette Soto
Massachusetts Institute of Technology
Stacy Southerland
University of Central Oklahoma
Kerri Stephenson
Johnson County Community College
Craig Stokes
Dutchess Community College
Nancy Stucker
Cabrillo College
Georgette Sullins
Lone Star College, Montgomery
Lucero Tenorio
Oklahoma State University, Stillwater
Gigi Terminel
Fullerton College
Brisa Teutli
Cornell University
Katheryn A. Thompson
Chattanooga State Technical Community College
Gheorghita Tres
Oakland Community College
John Twomey
University of Massachusetts, Dartmouth
Amy Uribe
Lone Star College
Mavel Velasco
Virginia Wesleyan College
Patricia Villegas-Bonno
Fullerton College
Alicia J. von Lehe
Santa Fe College
Natalie S. Wagener
University of Texas at Arlington
Sandra Watts
University of North Carolina, Charlotte
Christopher Weimer
Oklahoma State University
Amber Williams-Lara
Lone Star College, Kingwood
Elizabeth Willingham
Calhoun Community College
Íñigo Yanguas
San Diego State University
Amina Yassine
University of California, Irvine
María Zielina
California State University, Monterey Bay

The authors wish to thank the following friends and professional colleagues. Their feedback, support, and contributions are greatly appreciated.

- Dulce Aldama, Alicia Barrón López, Beatriz Builes Gómez, Shauna Polson, Scott Spanbauer, and Matthew B. Troxel, for their work as user diarists
- The Teaching Assistants and colleagues of Anne Becher at the University of Colorado, Boulder, whose thought-provoking conversations and annotations truly shaped the revision of the grammar, vocabulary, and activities. "Their work was perhaps the single most important kind of input that I received for this edition."—Thalia Dorwick
- Dora Y. Marrón Romero and Claudia Sahagún (Broward Community College), for their helpful comments about culture
- Alejandro Lee (Central Washington University), for the many comments and suggestions on the eighth edition
- Laura Chastain, for her meticulous work on the language and linguistic accuracy of the manuscript, over many editions but especially this one

Finally, the authors would like to thank their families and close personal friends for all of their love, support, and patience throughout the creation of this edition. **¡Los queremos mucho!**

Contributing Writers

Janet Banhidi, Rodney Bransdorfer, Sara Casler, Mayra Cortés-Torres, Mar Freire-Hermida, Danielle Havens, Jane Johnson, Constance Kihyet, Lynne Lemley, Eileen Locke, Misha MacLaird, Leticia McGrath, Ann Morrill, Kimberley Sallee, Jan Underwood, Susanna Williams

Product Team

Editorial and Marketing: Hector Alvero, Jorge Arbujas, Allen J. Bernier, Susan Blatty, Erin Blaze, Meghan Campbell, Laura Chastain, Laura Chiriboga, Laura Ciporen, Craig Gill, William R. Glass, Kirsten Gokay, Helen Greenlea, Suzanne Guinn, Sara Jaeger, Jennifer Kirk, Pennie Nichols, Alexa Recio, Kimberley Sallee, Katie Stevens, Scott Tinetti, Nina Tunac-Basey

Digital: Nathan Benjamin, María Betancourt, Jennifer Blankenship, Kyle Constance, Kirk DouPonce, Jay Gubernick, Elise Lansdon, Dennis Plucinik, Jenny Pritchett, Stephen Singerman

Art, Design, and Production: Nora Agbayani, Harry Briggs, Sonia Brown, Brett Coker, Aaron Downey, Anne Fuzellier, Sarah B. Hill, Patti Isaacs, Tandra Jorgensen, Robin Mouat, Terri Schiesl, David Staloch, Preston Thomas

Media Partners: Aptara, BBC Motion Gallery, Dartmouth Publishing, Inc., Eastern Sky Studios, Hurix, Inkling, Klic Video Productions, Inc., Laserwords, LearningMate, Strategic Content Imaging

CONTENTS

Capítulo

VOCABULARY & PRONUNCIATION

GRAMMAR

VIDEO, LISTENING, AND WRITING

READING AND CULTURE

Capítulo | VOCABULARY & PRONUNCIATION | GRAMMAR

VIDEO, LISTENING, AND WRITING

READING AND CULTURE

Capítulo

VOCABULARY & PRONUNCIATION

GRAMMAR

VIDEO, LISTENING, AND WRITING

READING AND CULTURE

VIDEO, LISTENING, AND WRITING

READING AND CULTURE

Capítulo | VOCABULARY & PRONUNCIATION | GRAMMAR

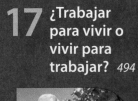

VIDEO, LISTENING, AND WRITING

READING AND CULTURE

What's New for the Ninth Edition?

There have been many changes made for this edition. However those changes were not made lightly, nor without extensive feedback and confirmation from you, our clients, as evidenced by the lists of reviewers presented earlier in this front matter. Here are some of the highlights of this revision. For specific details, especially an exhaustive list of chapter-by-chapter changes, please see the Instructor's Manual (IM), available online at **www.connectspanish.com.**

General Details

- New interior design
- Larger trim size for the Instructor's Edition, allowing for a larger image of the Student Edition pages
- All new drawings and many new photos, and a greater use of photos (rather than drawings) whenever feasible
- The optional **Un paso más** section from the eighth edition (8e) has been replaced by the following "skills" sections, which appear before the end-of-chapter **En resumen: En este capítulo** section.
    - New two-page reading (**A leer**) spread, which includes **Lectura cultural** and **Del mundo hispano. Lectura cultural** offers many smaller chunks of cultural content, with comprehension and discussion questions. **Del mundo hispano** is a more traditional reading presentation with pre- and post-reading activities and discussion questions. The **Del mundo hispano** readings are author-written or based on authentic materials (e.g., ads, brochures) in the first ten chapters, and poems or short literary selections in **Capítulos 11–18.**
    - New listening (**A escuchar**) section with audio activity and **¡Música!** feature
    - New writing (**A escribir**) section
- Answers to all activities are in new on-page annotations (light blue text) or in the annotations wrap
- New "pointer boxes" help explain the text's features to students.
- Introduction of active vocabulary other than in **Vocabulario: Preparación** or in grammar paradigms is noted for instructors in the annotations wrap. (This is not a change; the system is just more salient now.)
- Exciting new technology: Connect Spanish, LearnSmart, Blackboard
- New DVD, with activities support in the text (**TelePuntos**) and IM
- Revised and combined Workbook and Laboratory Manual (one product, two volumes: Vol. 1 = **Capítulos 1–9;** Vol. 2 = **Capítulos 10–18**), available in print or online as part of Connect Spanish.

Organizational Changes

- 18 chapters: The preliminary chapter (**Ante todo**) from the 8e is now **Capítulo 1,** most other chapters have shifted forward, and **Capítulo 18** content from the 8e has been incorporated into **Capítulos 17** and **18.**
- The regional focus has changed for six chapters for a more logical organization, with corresponding changes to activities and readings.
- See the IM for detailed charts of the new organization.

Culture

- Virtually all new cultural content is based on information from the cultural ambassadors, natives of each country of focus, who sent us key phrases and cultural tidbits to be woven into the fabric of *Puntos.* Additional basic information about each country of focus has been added to the annotations wrap and IM.
- The new **Lectura cultural** feature gives students some highlights about each country of focus and a "feeling" for it, rather than encyclopedic knowledge.
- **Nota cultural** features are now all in Spanish and have been rewritten, with a personal question at the end.
- See "Cultural Content" in the "Using *Puntos* in the Classroom" section later in this front matter.

Vocabulary

- Many **Vocabulario: Preparación** presentations have been revised, with some adjustment of individual vocabulary items to reflect current usage and a major revision of technology vocabulary in **Capítulo 12.**

Grammar

- Grammar explanations have been revised to include more charts and summaries, more bullet-point explanations, and better-focused examples; many **Gramática en acción** presentations have been rewritten, and internal repetition within grammar sections helps to reinforce learning. (See "Grammar Explanations" in the "Using *Puntos* in the Classroom" section later in this front matter.)
- Spanish grammar terms are more salient throughout for those instructors who prefer to present grammar in Spanish.

Activities

- Activities thoroughly revised for relevance and for clarity to students
- Additional scaffolding provided for many activities in general and in the new **Estrategia** feature
- Many completely new activities
- Dehydrated activities (with slashes) largely recast or simplified
- More integration of culture into activities when feasible (not to excess)
- The **En su comunidad** feature added to each **Un poco de todo** offers interview activities for students to use with native speakers

Using *Puntos* in the Classroom

Developing Language Proficiency

The authors believe that students' (and instructors') class time is best spent using Spanish: listening to and speaking with their instructor and classmates, listening and viewing audiovisual materials of many kinds, and reading in-text and supplementary materials. For that reason, grammar explanations have been written to be self-explanatory, and sample answers for many activities are provided for students online at **www.connectspanish.com** so that they can check their work before going to class. Thus, instructors can spot-check homework as needed in class but devote more time to the multitude of extensions, follow-up suggestions, and special activities offered in the Instructor's Edition and Instructor's Manual. Consequently, class time can be focused on new material and novel language experiences that will maintain student interest and provide more exposure to spoken and written Spanish. Research in second language acquisition has revealed that environments that offer learners opportunities to use the language in meaningful ways provide an optimal learning situation. Students make few gains in language learning when all of their class time is spent correcting homework.

The preceding comments underscore the authors' conceptualization of *Puntos* throughout its many editions as a text that fosters students' proficiency in Spanish. The following features help realize this objective:

- a focus on the acquisition of vocabulary during the early stages of language learning (**Capítulo 1: Ante todo**) and then in each chapter throughout the text
- an emphasis on meaningful and creative use of language
- careful attention to skills development rather than grammatical knowledge alone
- a cyclical organization in which vocabulary, grammar, and language functions are consistently reviewed and reentered
- an integrated cultural component that embeds practice in a wide variety of culturally significant contexts
- content that aims to raise student awareness of the interaction of language, culture, and society

The overall text organization progresses from a focus on formulaic expressions, to vocabulary and structures relevant to the here and now (student life, family life), to survival situations (ordering a meal, travel-related activities), and to topics of broader interest (current events, social and environmental issues). This breadth of thematic diversity—coupled with the focus on vocabulary, grammatical structures, and language functions—helps develop students' language proficiency, thus preparing them to function in Spanish in situations that they are most likely to encounter outside the classroom.

Grammar Explanations

Many people say that students don't read. We think that that's not completely accurate. They read a lot, though it tends to be in the form of online articles, e-mail, updates on Facebook and Twitter, and so on. Students are therefore used to getting information in bits and pieces, not to reading lengthy technical explanations.

Recognizing that fact, the authors have tried to make the grammar explanations (dense, technical by their very nature) more accessible. The first major attempt to do something in this vein came in the fifth edition, when the grammar explanations were recast into a two-column format: left-hand column for prose explanations, right-hand column for charts, tables, and paradigms. The approach was field-tested with students, in focus groups, with students saying that the design was clearer to them and that it enabled them to scan more easily for important information.

In the ninth edition, revisions to the grammar explanations have been extensive. They were driven in large part by very detailed, on-page comments written by instructors and teaching assistants who created user diaries for the authors, and also by comments from co-authors who activity teach with the text. The salient features of the revisions to the grammar include:

- A reduction in overall length of explanations whenever possible
- A reduction in the number of words in explanations overall, to make them less dense
- The inclusion of information in bulleted lists whenever possible
- The introduction of more redundancy into explanations, so that the same information is conveyed in a number of ways within a given grammar explanation: in prose explanations, in bullet points, in charts and tables, in summary form (sometimes twice in a given explanation: once at the beginning of the explanation, once at the end). This happens most frequently with important grammar topics.
- The alignment of information in grammar displays so that important information "pops" more visually
- The recasting of examples in such a way as to make the grammar point more salient
- The use of "pointer boxes" to remind students about features of the text that help them learn, like the use of red highlighting and parenthetical information for verbs

Cultural Content

Historically in the evolution of *Puntos*, cultural materials have been rewritten every few editions. Initially the program did not have a large amount of cultural content, the thinking being that the teaching of language and culture should be done separately and that it was "too much" for students to absorb not only information about the language but also information about the culture. This (perhaps artificial) separation of language and culture eventually fell away, and the authors began to search for optimal ways to select what kinds of cultural information to include and how best to integrate it with the vocabulary and grammar content.

For this edition, about 90% of the cultural content of the text has been rewritten. The following principles guided our work.

- *Less is more.* = Do not attempt to convey in-depth cultural information about all of the countries of the Spanish-speaking world. Rather, try to convey a smaller number of facts about each country and try to convey a sense of the "spirit" of the country, what natives think is representative and important about it.
- *Get information from natives of the countries in question.* = The contributions of the cultural ambassadors guided us in selecting what information to include.
- *Integrate culture.* = Include cultural information in exercises, activities, and **Gramática en acción** features whenever possible, keeping in mind that students should not have to process unfamiliar cultural information and grammar at the same time.
- *Keep cultural information short.* = This led to the rewriting of most **Nota cultural** features into very short, sometimes bullet-organized paragraphs. It meant that the **Lectura cultural** feature also conveys information in small chunks rather than in extended readings. We feel that this approach is particularly appropriate for a first-year program.

- *Ask questions about cultural content.* = The **Nota cultural** and **Lectura cultural** features are followed by questions that relate the cultural content to students' own culture, to help them expand their cross-cultural competence and recognize their own cultural patterns.

Instructors will find explicit cultural content in the following places.

- In the new chapter-opening two-page spreads: The left-hand page has a photo from the country of focus and related to the chapter's theme. Questions on this page allow instructors to start a whole-class discussion about the theme. The right-hand page has a map of the country (or countries) with geographical context, as well as population figures and three bullet points of interest about the country (or countries).
- In **Nota cultural** features: Comprehension questions are in the annotations wrap.
- In some **Gramática en acción** features
- In some **Práctica** and **Conversación** activities, and in **Un poco de todo** sections
- In all **Lengua y cultura** activities (in **Un poco de todo**)
- In the all-new **En su comunidad** activities (in **Un poco de todo**)
- In the new two-page **A leer** reading spreads
- In the new **A escuchar** listening passage
- In the new DVD Program and accompanying activities in the **TelePuntos** section
- In photographs and realia throughout the text

Program Materials

Whether you're using the *Puntos de partida* program in print form or in the new exciting Connect Spanish platform, a variety of additional components are available to support the needs of your students and you. Many are free to adopting institutions. Please contact your local McGraw-Hill representative for details on policies, prices, and availability.

Connect Spanish: Used in conjunction with *Puntos de partida,* Connect Spanish brings the *Puntos* program into the twenty-first century by providing a digital solution for schools with online programs, whether they be 100% online or hybrid. Some of the key features and capabilities of Connect Spanish include:

- complete integration of text, workbook / laboratory manual, audio, and video material
- additional practice with key vocabulary, grammar, and cultural material
- interactive, task-based scenarios (**Mundo interactivo**) that explore a wide variety of topics within a cultural framework
- LearnSmart adaptive learning system that offers individualized study plans to suit individual students' needs
- fully integrated gradebook
- ability to customize a syllabus and assignments to fit the needs of individual programs

Connect Spanish Instructor's Guide: A helpful guide for adopters of Connect Spanish, available online at **www.connectspanish.com.**

Annotated Instructor's Edition: The Instructor's Edition, which has always been regarded as a principal teaching resource for both novice and experienced instructors, provides an enlarged trim size with a wide variety of additional instructional notes, suggestions, and activities. This very useful supplement contains suggestions for implementing activities, supplementary exercises for developing listening and speaking skills, and abundant variations and follow-ups on student text materials. A special feature of the *Instructor's Edition* is the **Bright Idea** suggestions, which were provided by instructors from across the country who use *Puntos de partida* on a daily basis. We are grateful for their wonderful ideas and suggestions. In addition, special features found in the annotations wrap space include Resources notes that identify digital transparencies and other key resources, notes and suggestions for adapting certain activities to accommodate Heritage Speaker students, Culture notes, and notes that identify activities that support the National Standards.

Workbook / Laboratory Manual: Written by Alice and Oswaldo Arana and María Sabló-Yates, the newly revised and combined Workbook and Laboratory Manual is offered in two volumes: **Capítulos 1–9** in Volume 1; **Capítulos 10–18** in Volume 2. Both volumes are available in print or as part of Connect Spanish.

DVD Program: The all-new two-disc DVD Program contains the *Salu2* video segments that correspond to the **TelePuntos** sections of each chapter. *Salu2* (short for **Saludos,** or *Greetings*) is a fictitious morning news show based in Los Angeles and hosted by two anchors, a Mexican-American man (Víctor) and a Panamanian woman (Ana). Their reports, based on chapter themes, are augmented by additional live reports from a roving field reporter from Mexico named Laura and in some cases by fans of the show that have sent in footage on a specific topic. Students will see footage from around the Spanish-speaking world, including from countries such as Argentina, Costa Rica, the Dominican Republic, Ecuador, Mexico, Peru, Puerto Rico, Spain, and the United States. There are pre-, during, and post-viewing activities in the **TelePuntos** sections as well as a **Producción personal** section that will prompt students to film related topics outside of the classroom environment and then share those video segments with others.

Audio Program: The Audio Program provides the audio content for the following program features and is available on audio CDs or in downloadable format (mp3 files) at **www.connectspanish.com.**

- Listening activities in the Workbook / Laboratory Manual
- Words and phrases from the vocabulary presentations
- **Gramática en acción** segments that introduce each grammar topic

Supplemental Materials to accompany Puntos de partida, *by Sharon Foerster and Jean Miller:* Comprising worksheets and a teacher's guide, these two supplements are a compilation of materials that include short pronunciation practice, listening exercises, grammar worksheets, integrative communication-building activities, comprehensive chapter reviews, and language games.

Instructor's Manual: Available electronically at **www.connectspanish.com,** the IM offers an extensive introduction to teaching techniques, general guidelines for instructors, suggestions for lesson planning in semester and quarter schedules, detailed chapter-by-chapter suggestions, and much more, thus making it an indispensible resource for any adopter of the *Puntos* program.

Testing Program (print): The print Testing Program, available in downloadable Word files from **www.connectspanish.com,** contains five different tests for each chapter, as well as sample mid-term and final exams.

EZ Test Test Generator (online): McGraw-Hill's EZ Test is a flexible and easy-to-use electronic testing platform that allows instructors to create tests from publisher-provided items. It accommodates a wide range of question types, and instructors may add their own questions. Multiple versions of a test can be created.

Digital Transparencies: PDF files of all **Vocabulario: Preparación** art and any art that is not permissions-restricted are available to instructors at **www.connectspanish.com.**

Online Resources (*instructors only*): The following resources are available only to instructors at **www.connectspanish.com.**

- Connect Spanish Instructor's Guide
- Instructor's Manual
- Testing Program (print and digital)
- Testing Audio Program (mp3s)
- Audioscript
- Videoscript
- Digital Transparencies (for the text)
- Image Bank
- Cultural PowerPoint Presentations
- Grammar PowerPoint Presentations

Online Resources (*instructors and students*): The following resources are available to both instructors and students at **www.connectspanish.com.**

- Textbook Answer Key
- Audio Program (mp3s)
- Grammar Tutorials
- Interactive Verb Charts
- iTunes Playlist (for **¡Música!** sections)

An Invitation to…

Puntos de partida

Puntos de partida means *points of departure* in Spanish. This program will be your point of departure for learning Spanish and for learning about Hispanic cultures. With *Puntos de partida* you will get ready to communicate with Spanish speakers in this country and in other parts of the Spanish-speaking world. To speak a language means much more than just learning its grammar and vocabulary. To know a language is to know the people who speak it. *Puntos de partida* will provide you with cultural information to help you understand and appreciate the traditions and values of Spanish-speaking people all over the world. Get ready for the adventure of learning Spanish!

Chapter Opening Photo

Notes

- Every chapter begins with a photo or photos that introduce the theme of the chapter and place it within the context of students' knowledge of their own culture *vis-à-vis* Hispanic cultures.
- Point out the chapter opening photos. Ask students to talk about the ethnic makeup of their own campus. Encourage them to consider whether the proportion of students of diverse backgrounds is ideal. Ask what opportunities the campus offers for language learners to meet and talk to Heritage Speakers from this country and to native speakers from abroad. Request and offer information about available Spanish clubs and Spanish "houses" or "tables" where participants speak only Spanish.
- Use the questions that accompany the photo(s) to start a dialogue about the presence of Spanish in the United States and Canada and about the importance of Spanish in the history of the United States.
- Point out that *México, D.F.*, is Mexico City and that *D.F.* (*Distrito Federal*) is like D.C. in Washington, D.C.

Suggestion

After covering parts or all of *Capítulo 1* in class, return to this chapter opener and work with the photos as follows.

General Questions for Each Photo

1. *¿En que ciudad* (new word) *están las personas en la foto?* (Encourage a phrase answer: *En…*)
2. *¿En qué país* (new word) *están?* (*En…*)

1 Ante todo°

Ante… *First of all*

Zócalo (*Main Plaza*), México, D.F., México

- Have you ever visited a Spanish-speaking country? Which one(s)?
- Where can you go in your country to hear Spanish spoken around you?
- Why do you want to learn Spanish?

Plaza de España, Sevilla, España

connect SPANISH

www.connectspanish.com

Resources

For Students

- Connect Spanish (**www.connectspanish.com**), which contains all content from the following resources, as well as the *Mundo interactivo* scenarios, the LearnSmart adaptive learning system, and more!
- **Physical Resources:** Workbook / Laboratory Manual, Laboratory Audio Program, DVD

For Instructors

- Connect Spanish (**www.connectspanish.com**), which contains access to all student sections of Connect Spanish, as well as helpful time-saving tools and resources such as an integrated gradebook, Instructor's Manual, Testing Program, digital transparencies, Audioscript, Videoscript, and more!

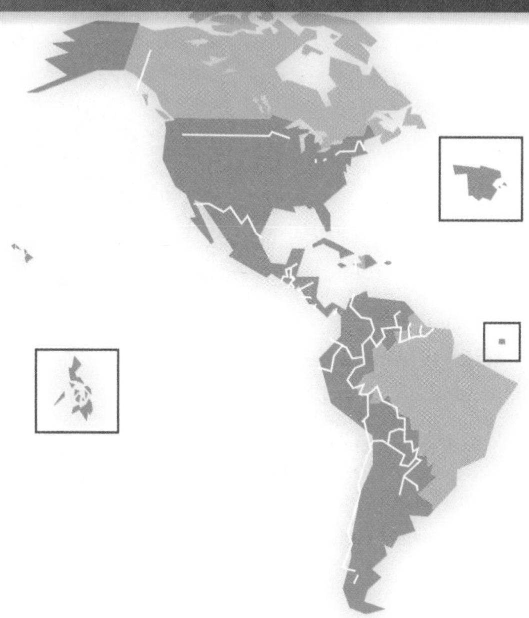

El mundo hispanohablante*

- El español es la lengua oficial en aproximadamente 21 (veintún) países (*countries*) del mundo (*in the world*).
- El español ocupa el segundo lugar (*second place*) entre las lenguas más habladas (*most widely spoken*) del mundo: 450 millones (cuatrocientos cincuenta millones) de hablantes (*speakers*).

*El… *The Spanish-speaking world*

En este capítulo°

En… *In this chapter*

CONTENT / **CONTENIDO**	OBJECTIVES / **OBJETIVOS**
Greetings and courtesy 4	To say hello and good-bye, meet others, and be polite
The Spanish alphabet 7, Spanish vowels 18	To spell in Spanish and learn the basics of Spanish pronunciation
Describing yourself and others 8	To tell what you and others are like
Numbers 0–30 12	To count in Spanish
Likes and dislikes 14	To express what you like and don't like
Telling time 16	To tell time in Spanish
¡Aquí se habla español! 10, La geografía del mundo hispano 20	To learn about the global importance of Spanish and about the geography of Spanish-speaking areas

3

El mundo hispanohablante

Notes

- The total number of countries in which Spanish is an official language is given as 21. That includes *Puerto Rico* (an *Estado Libre Asociado* of the United States). It does not include the United States or *las Islas Filipinas* because Spanish is not an official language in those countries.
- Even true beginning students should be able to understand the very basic Spanish used in the map caption.

En este capítulo

Notes

- The purpose of this map is to give students an overall sense for the large number of places in which Spanish is spoken around the world. (The countries are labeled on the map that is on page 11 of this chapter.) You may wish to use this unlabeled, stylized map to ask students how many of these places they can name right now. Locations that will be particularly difficult for students include *la Guinea Ecuatorial, las Filipinas,* and many of the Central American countries.
- The *En este capítulo* feature introduces the main cultural content, vocabulary, and grammar points of the chapter. It is intended to serve as an advance organizer.
- The language of *En este capítulo* is informal, reflecting the language students and instructors really use to refer to sections of the book rather than actual section titles.

Multimedia

The *Instructor's Manual* (IM) provides suggestions for using the multimedia materials in the classroom.

PRIMERA° PARTE

First

Saludos° y expresiones de cortesía

Greetings

Here are some words, phrases, and expressions for meeting and greeting others in Spanish. Can you tell the difference between those that are formal and those that are more informal or familiar (as on a first-name basis)?

Situaciones formales

1. ELISA VELASCO: Buenas tardes, señor Gómez.
MARTÍN GÓMEZ: Muy buenas, señora Velasco. ¿Cómo está?
ELISA VELASCO: Bien, gracias. ¿Y usted?
MARTÍN GÓMEZ: Muy bien, gracias. Hasta luego.
ELISA VELASCO: Adiós.

2. LUPE: Buenos días, profesor.
MARTÍN GÓMEZ: Buenos días. ¿Cómo se llama usted, señorita?
LUPE: Me llamo Lupe Carrasco.
MARTÍN GÓMEZ: Mucho gusto, Lupe.
LUPE: Igualmente.

Situaciones informales

3. VERÓNICA: ¡Hola, Carmen!
CARMEN: ¿Qué tal, Verónica? ¿Cómo estás?
VERÓNICA: Muy bien. ¿Y tú?
CARMEN: Regular. Nos vemos mañana, ¿eh?
VERÓNICA: Bien. Hasta mañana.

4. MIGUEL RENÉ: Hola. Me llamo Miguel René. ¿Y tú? ¿Cómo te llamas?
KARINA: Me llamo Karina. Mucho gusto.
MIGUEL RENÉ: Encantado, Karina. Y, ¿de dónde eres?
KARINA: Soy de Venezuela. ¿Y tú?
MIGUEL RENÉ: Yo soy de México.

Translations of short dialogues like these will always be at the foot of the page, but you should try to read them without the translations first!

---

1. *EV: Good afternoon, Mr. Gómez. MG: Afternoon, Mrs. Velasco. How are you? EV: Fine, thank you. And you? MG: Very well, thanks. See you later. EV: Bye.*
2. *L: Good morning, professor. MG: Good morning. What's your name, miss? L: My name is Lupe Carrasco. MG: Nice to meet you, Lupe. L: Likewise.*
3. *V: Hi, Carmen! C: How's it going, Verónica? How are you? V: Very well. And you? C: OK. See you tomorrow, OK? V: Fine. Until tomorrow.*
4. *MR: Hello. My name is Miguel René. And you? What's your name? K: My name is Karina. Nice to meet you. MR: Nice to meet you, Karina. And where are you from? K: I'm from Venezuela. And you? MR: I'm from Mexico.*

Saludos y expresiones de cortesía

Note

- The word *usted* appears in its unabbreviated form in this chapter and at the beginning of *Capítulo 2*. It will appear as *Ud.* in *Gramática 3*, where the abbreviation is introduced.
- All material in this section is active vocabulary unless otherwise noted, such as in *Así se dice*.

Suggestions

- See the model for vocabulary presentation and other material in the *Capítulo 1* "Chapter-by-Chapter Supplementary Materials" in the IM.
- Model pronunciation for each dialogue. Use multiple choral repetitions followed by individual repetitions. See "Teaching Techniques: IM, *GEA (Gramática en acción)*."
- Act out dialogues with several students.
- Have students use their own names in the exchanges. See "Teaching Techniques: Small Groups," IM.
- Emphasize that English equivalents of model dialogues will always appear at the foot of the page.
- For *Dialogue 1*, discuss the use of courtesy titles and formal forms: first-name-basis vs. last-name-basis relationships.
- Emphasize that *muy buenas* (or just *buenas*) can be used at any time of the day, instead of *buenos días, buenas tardes,* or *buenas noches.*
- For *Dialogue 2,* emphasize the formal *¿Cómo se llama usted?* vs. familiar *¿Cómo te llamas?* Have students use the familiar form with other students.
- *Dialogue 3* models the use of *regular*, which in real conversation (like *más o menos*) would stimulate a discussion about what was wrong. Students cannot do that at this point, but *regular* is presented to give them an option for answering honestly if things aren't fine. The simple use of *bien* can convey that as well.
- Offer this optional vocabulary for *Dialogue 3: más o menos, hasta pronto.*
- For *Dialogue 4,* have students practice the exchange using *usted.*
- Have students practice questions with a chain drill:

  Student 1 asks: *¿Cómo te llamas?*
  Student 2 answers and asks the same question of Student 3, and so on.
- Emphasize that *encantado* is used by males and *encantada* is used by females.
- Model *mucho gusto* and *encantado/a* in exchanges with several students, reversing roles. Have students practice the exchange.
- See suggestions in the IM for using this chapter of *Puntos de partida* with video supplements.

Resources: Transparencies 1–3

Transparencies 1–3 are maps of the Spanish-speaking world.

Note the use of red to highlight aspects of Spanish that you should pay special attention to.

¡OJO!* There is no Spanish equivalent for *Ms.*; use **Sra.** or **Srta.**, as appropriate.

¡OJO! Note the accent marks on Spanish words that ask questions.

	formal		informal	
títulos	**señor (Sr.)** **señora (Sra.)** **señorita (Srta.)** **profesor** (*for a man*) **profesora** (*for a woman*)	Mr. Mrs., ma'am Miss		
saludos	**buenos días** **buenas tardes** **buenas noches** **(muy) buenas**	good morning good afternoon/evening good evening/night good day (*any time*)	**hola**	
preguntas (*questions*)	**¿Cómo está?** **¿Y usted?**	How are you? And you?	**¿Cómo estás?** **¿Qué tal?** **¿Y tú?**	How are you? And you?
	—¿Cómo se llama (usted)? **—Me llamo…** "What's your name?" "My name is . . ."		**—¿Cómo te llamas (tú)?** **—Me llamo…** "What's your name?" "My name is . . ."	
	—¿De dónde es (usted)? **—(Yo) Soy de…** "Where are you from?" "I'm from . . ."		**—¿De dónde eres (tú)?** **—(Yo) Soy de…** "Where are you from?" "I'm from . . ."	

Nota cultural

Los saludos en el mundo° hispano — °world

Hispanics all over the world hug and kiss when they are greeting each other a lot more frequently than do non-Hispanics in this country. Younger people especially greet in this way, even when they have just met. Two men will typically hug or pat each other on the back, and if they are family, they will sometimes give a kiss on the cheek and embrace, just like women do.

How do you greet your friends? Your relatives?

¿Qué pasa, hombre?

Así se dice (*That's how it's said*) introduces optional vocabulary from the Spanish-speaking world.

Así se dice

The following greetings express *What's up?, What's happening?,* or *How's it going?*

¿Qué hay? ¿Qué pasa? ¿Qué hubo? ¿Qué onda? (*Mexico*)

The phrase **por nada** is an alternative to **de nada.**

Nota comunicativa

Más expresiones de cortesía

—Encantado. (*for a man*) **—Encantada.** (*for a woman*) **—Mucho gusto.**	"Nice to meet you."
—Igualmente.	"Likewise."
Gracias.	Thanks. Thank you.
Muchas gracias.	Thank you very much.
De nada. / No hay de qué.	You're welcome.
por favor	please (*also used to get someone's attention*)
perdón	pardon me, excuse me (*to ask forgiveness or to get someone's attention*)
(con) permiso	pardon me, excuse me (*to request permission to pass by or through a group of people*)

*¡**Ojo!** *means* watch out! *or* pay attention! *in Spanish.*

Formal/Informal

Suggestions

- Students should be able to see the differences between the formal and informal language presented in the chart, especially with the red highlighting of linguistic elements.
- Model phrases in brief conversational exchanges with students. Help students use the appropriate title for you, and be clear about whether you want them to address you as *usted* or *tú*.
- Call students' attention to the accents on interrogative words. That concept will be presented more formally in *Pronunciación* (*Cap. 4*).
- Point out that titles of respect are not capitalized when spelled out. When abbreviated, they *are* capitalized: *señor Sánchez* versus *Sr. Sánchez*.
- Optional: Introduce *don* and *doña* as titles of respect used only before the first name, as in *don José* or *doña Ana*. These terms are not capitalized, nor do they have standard abbreviations.
- Point out that lunchtime is often around 2 P.M. in Hispanic countries; the evening meal may be as late as 10 or 11 P.M. For this reason, one may hear Spanish speakers say *Buenas tardes* as late as 9 or 9:30 P.M.

Follow-up

Have students work in pairs to practice the four dialogues on page 4, using their own names. Use the phrase *trabajen en parejas* to cue students.

Así se dice

- Material from *Así se dice* boxes is not considered to be active.
- Additional greetings that contain object pronouns: *¿Cómo te/le va? (Mucho) Gusto (en) verte/lo/la. Me alegro de verte/lo/la.* You may wish to only introduce the familiar (*tú*) forms, which avoid the issues of *lo/la* agreement and *leísmo*.
- Offer any other regional expressions you're familiar with.
- Discuss with students the question of how they will know which words to use when traveling abroad or talking to native speakers. Students should listen carefully to what *they* say or ask direct questions about usage: **¿Cómo se dice… ?** (*How do you say . . . ?*)

Nota comunicativa

Suggestions

- Material from all *Nota comunicativa* boxes is considered to be active unless otherwise noted.
- Model phrases of thanks, creating situations in which these expressions are appropriate. For example, give a student a book and elicit *gracias.* You respond *de nada,* and so on.
- Provide optional vocabulary. Model the use of *con permiso* to take leave of someone, *cómo no* (as a rejoinder), *perdone* (in addition to *perdón*), *perdón* (to request permission to pass by or through), *disculpe, oiga.*

Con. A: Suggestion

Conduct a rapid response drill with students' books closed. See "Teaching Techniques," IM.

Con. B: Extension

5. you and your Spanish professor, at 11 A.M.
6. you and your cousin, at 10 P.M.
7. you and the president/rector of your university, at 4 P.M.

Con. E: Notes

- For use of the *Pasos* organization in this and subsequent activities, see "Using *Pasos* Activities," IM.
- The word *paso* in the headers *Paso 1* and *Paso 2* means "step." The word *paso* in the place name *El Paso* refers to a pass or a passageway.

Con. E: Suggestions

- Model an interview with two or three students before asking others to form pairs and follow your example.
- Remind students to use informal expressions in student exchanges, but formal expressions when addressing you, the instructor, if that is your preference.
- This activity presents an excellent opportunity for you to present and practice with students the *Mandatos y frases comunes en el salón de clase* that are presented on the last few pages of *Puntos de partida*. Doing so will allow you to communicate more with students in Spanish from the beginning of the course. Direction lines will gradually transition into all Spanish (except for complicated directions) by *Cap. 5*.

El alfabeto español

Notes

- The *Real Academia Española,* which establishes many of the guidelines for the use of Spanish throughout the world, published its latest edition of the *Ortografía de la Real Academia Española* in December 2010. At that time, it officially standardized several issues regarding the Spanish alphabet. Among those rulings were:
  - The *ch* and *ll* are no longer considered letters or even *diágrafos* (*signos ortográficos de dos letras*). That is, they have been officially eliminated from the Spanish alphabet, which now consists of just 27 letters: the same 26 letters of the English alphabet plus the *ñ*.

Conversación

Possible answers: 1. *Muy buenas.* **2.** *Adiós. Hasta luego.* **3.** *Muy bien. ¿Y tú?* **4.** *¡Hola!* **5.** *Bien. ¿Y usted?* **6.** *Buenas noches.* **7.** *De nada. No hay de qué.* **8.** *Adiós.* **9.** *Me llamo…* **10.** *De nada.* **11.** *Soy de…* **12.** *Buenos días.*

A. Expresiones de cortesía. How many different ways can you respond to the following greetings and phrases?

1. Buenas tardes.
2. Adiós.
3. ¿Qué tal?
4. ¡Hola!
5. ¿Cómo está?
6. Buenas noches.
7. Muchas gracias.
8. Hasta mañana.
9. ¿Cómo se llama usted?
10. Mucho gusto.
11. ¿De dónde eres?
12. Buenos días.

B. Situaciones. If the following people met or passed each other at the times given, what might they say to each other? Role-play the situations with a classmate.

1. Mr. Santana and Miss Pérez, at 5:00 P.M.
2. Mrs. Ortega and Pablo, at 10:00 A.M.
3. Ms. Hernández and Olivia, at 11:00 P.M.
4. you and a classmate, just before your Spanish class

C. Situaciones. What would you say in Spanish in the following situations?

1. Your classmate passes you a handout from the professor. Gracias.
2. You need to be excused from class to go to the restroom. Por favor. Perdón.
3. You just dropped your drink on a friend's book. Perdón.
4. Your professor thanks you for opening the door for her. De nada.
5. You need your professor's attention. Por favor. Perdón.

D. Más (*More*) **situaciones.** Are the people in this drawing saying **por favor, con permiso,** or **perdón? ¡OJO!** More than one response is possible for some items.

Possible answers: **1.** *Perdón.* **2.** *Perdón. Por favor.* **3.** *(Con) Permiso.*

E. Entrevista (*Interview*)

Paso (*Step*) **1.** Turn to a person sitting next to you and do the following.

- Greet him or her appropriately, that is, with informal forms.
- Ask how he or she is.
- Find out his or her name.
- Ask where he or she is from.
- Conclude the exchange.

Paso 2. Now have a similar conversation with your instructor, using the appropriate formal or familiar forms, according to your instructor's request.

NATIONAL STANDARDS: Comparisons

The annotations in the *A leer: Lectura cultural* feature of each subsequent chapter of *Puntos de partida* will present greetings and other common expressions specific to the country of focus for that chapter. To make comparisons now, look ahead to those sections and present some greetings from a variety of countries at this time.

Heritage Speakers

Los títulos *don* y *doña* no tienen equivalente en inglés. Cuando se traduce, por ejemplo, *don Tomás,* se dice simplemente *Tomás* o *Mr. Tomás.* Pídales a los estudiantes hispanohablantes de la clase que le den ejemplos a la clase de algunas personas a las cuales ellos se refieren con estos títulos.

El alfabeto español

The Spanish *alphabet* (**el alfabeto** or **el abecedario**) is slightly different from the English alphabet.

- It has 27 letters (not 26).
- The extra letter is **ñ.***
- The letters **k** and **w** appear only in words borrowed from other languages.

You will learn more about and practice the sounds of these and other letters whose pronunciation is different from English in **Práctica A.**

Letters	Names of Letters	Examples		
a	a	Antonio	Ana	(la) Argentina
b	be	Benito	Blanca	Bolivia
c	ce	Carlos	Cecilia	Cáceres
d	de	Domingo	Dolores	Durango
e	e	Eduardo	Elena	(el) Ecuador
f	efe	Felipe	Francisca	Florida
g	ge	Gerardo	Gloria	Guatemala
h	hache	Héctor	Hortensia	Honduras
i	i	Ignacio	Inés	Ibiza
j	jota	José	Juana	Jalisco
k	ca (ka)	(Karl)	(Karina)	(Kansas)
l	ele	Luis	Lola	Lima
m	eme	Manuel	María	México
n	ene	Nicolás	Nati	Nicaragua
ñ	eñe	Íñigo	Begoña	España
o	o	Octavio	Olivia	Oviedo
p	pe	Pablo	Pilar	Panamá
q	cu	Enrique	Raquel	Quito
r	ere	Álvaro	Rosa	(el) Perú
s	ese	Salvador	Sara	San Juan
t	te	Tomás	Teresa	Toledo
u	u	Agustín	Úrsula	(el) Uruguay
v	uve	Víctor	Victoria	Venezuela
w	doble uve	(Oswaldo)	(Wilma)	(Washington)
x	equis	Xavier	Ximena	Extremadura
y	ye	Pelayo	Yolanda	(el) Paraguay
z	ceta (zeta)	Gonzalo	Zoila	Zaragoza

¡OJO!

The **rr** combination occurs frequently in Spanish, but it is not a separate letter.

Práctica

A. ¡Pronuncie! The following letters and letter combinations represent the Spanish sounds that are the most different from English. Can you match the Spanish letters with their equivalent pronunciation?

EXAMPLES/SPELLING

1. __c__ mucho: **ch**
2. __e__ Geraldo: **ge** (also: **gi**); Jiménez: **j**
3. __i__ hola: **h**
4. __a__ gusto: **gu** (also: **ga, go**)
5. __f__ me llamo: **ll**
6. __h__ señor: **ñ**
7. __b__ profesora: **r**
8. __g__ Ramón: **r** (to start a word); Monterrey: **rr**
9. __d__ nos vemos: **v**

PRONUNCIATION

a. like the *g* in English *garden*
b. similar to *tt* of *butter* when pronounced very quickly
c. like *ch* in English *cheese*
d. like Spanish **b**
e. similar to a "strong" English *h*
f. like *y* in English *yes* or like the *li* sound in *million*
g. a trilled sound, several Spanish **r**'s in a row
h. similar to the *ny* sound in *canyon*
i. never pronounced

*The **ñ** is similar to the sound of *ny* in English *canyon*.

- The *be* (or *be larga, be grande,* and so on) is now called *be.*
- The *ve* (or *ve corta, ve baja,* and so on) is now called *uve.*
- The *doble ve* (or *ve doble, uve doble,* and so on) is now called *doble uve.*
- The *i griega* is now called *ye.*

The chart reflects these new rulings of the *RAE.* However feel free to share some of the old names of some of the letters with your students, as they will undoubtedly hear them for years to come, while the Spanish-speaking world adjusts to the new system.

- The website of the *Real Academia Española* has other useful teaching resources. It can be found at **www.rae.es.**
- *Prác. A* presents a brief explanation of the pronunciation of the sounds of Spanish letters that are most different from their English equivalents.

Pronunciación

Notes

- *Pronunciación* sections appear in *Cap. 1* as well as in *Caps. 2–4* of this edition of *Puntos de partida.* Vowel sounds are presented at the end of *Segunda parte* (*Cap. 1*). *Prac. A* is intended only for immediate practice with sounds and letters that may be strange to true beginning students of Spanish.
- Beginning in *Cap. 5, Pronunciación* sections appear only in the Workbook / Laboratory Manual and Audio Program. Notes in the ATE of each chapter will tell you which sound(s) are presented in that program.

Heritage Speakers

Invite a los estudiantes hispanohablantes de la clase a pronunciar estas palabras. Pregúnteles a los otros estudiantes si ellos oyen alguna diferencia entre el modo en que los hispanohablantes pronuncian los sonidos, especialmente la *j* y la *ll.*

NATIONAL STANDARDS: Connections

Have students ask Spanish-speaking children in the community to recite the alphabet in Spanish. If students have a hand-held recording device, they can record the children's recitals and play them in class.

Resources: Transparency 4

(Cont.)

Prác. B: Note

The state name Florida is given here without the article *la* because the context is English place names. Most Hispanic Americans would call the state *la Florida.* People from Spain would just call it *Florida.*

Prác. B: Suggestions

- Introduce the phrase *¿Cómo se escribe... ?*
- Explain that *acentuada* means "stressed" and that in Spanish the stressed vowel in some words must carry a written accent mark so that the word can be read correctly. Accent marks are presented in *Caps. 3* and *4.*

Prác. B: Follow-up

Have students think of other place names of Hispanic origin and spell them aloud in Spanish as other students pronounce them.

Nota comunicativa

Note

This *Nota* offers opportunities for pronunciation practice as well as being a vehicle for helping students feel comfortable with Spanish and encouraging self-expression.

Suggestions

- Interview students in the classroom, asking them to indicate whether the following statements are *cierto* (true) or *falso* (false).
  1. *Jennifer López es muy elegante.*
  2. *El presidente de los Estados Unidos no es muy importante.*
  3. *Homer Simpson es muy inteligente.*
  4. *El español es muy interesante.*

  Have students provide corrections for the statements they feel are false.
- Emphasize that words in English and in Spanish may look alike but will not sound alike.
- Tell students that they need not try to memorize all words in this *Nota.*
- Model pronunciation of adjectives in brief sentences about yourself: *cruel... No soy cruel* (pointing to yourself), and so on.

B. ¿Cómo se escribe... ? (*How do you write . . . ?*)

Paso 1. Pronounce these U.S. place names in Spanish. Then spell the names aloud in Spanish. All of them are of Hispanic origin: **Toledo, Los Ángeles, Texas, Montana, Colorado, El Paso, Florida, Las Vegas, Amarillo, San Francisco.**

Paso 2. Spell your own name aloud in Spanish, and listen as your classmates spell their names. Try to remember as many of their names as you can.

MODELO: Me llamo María: **M** (eme) **a** (a) **r** (ere) **í** (i acentuada) **a** (a).

Nota **comunicativa**

Los cognados

As you study Spanish, note that many Spanish and English words are similar or identical in form and meaning. These related words are called *cognates* (**los cognados**). It's useful to begin recognizing and using cognates immediately; they will help you enrich your Spanish vocabulary and develop language proficiency more quickly. Here are some examples.

TO DESCRIBE PEOPLE		TO NAME PLACES AND THINGS	
cruel	paciente	banco	hotel
elegante	pesimista	bar	museo
importante	responsable	café	oficina
inteligente	sentimental	diccionario	parque
interesante	terrible	estudiante	teléfono
optimista	tolerante	examen	televisión

¿Cómo es usted?° (Part 1)°

¿Cómo... *What are you like?*

Ángela Suárez Del Pino

Ismael Figueroa García

1. —¿Quién **es usted** y cómo **es**?
   —**Soy** Ángela Suárez Del Pino. **Soy** optimista y tolerante.

2. —¿Quién **eres tú**?
   —Me llamo Ismael Figueroa García y **soy** estudiante de universidad.
   —Ismael, ¿cómo **eres**?
   —**Soy** inteligente, romántico y responsable.

Remember to watch for the words in **red.** Check the translation at the bottom of the page only if you need to.

1. *"Who are you and what are you like?" "I'm Ángela Suárez Del Pino. I'm optimistic and tolerant."*
2. *"Who are you?" "My name is Ismael Figueroa García, and I'm a university (college) student." "Ismael, what are you like?" "I'm intelligent, romantic, and responsible."*

Use the following verb forms to describe yourself or another person.

ser (*to be*):* Formas singulares		
(yo)	soy	I am
(tú)	eres	you (*familiar*) are
(usted)	es	you (*formal*) are
(él, ella)	es	he/she is

a verb / **un verbo** = a word that describes an action or a state of being

Conversación

A. ¿Cómo es usted? Indique todas las palabras apropiadas (*appropriate words*).

Yo soy…

_____ diligente	_____ elegante	_____ importante
_____ idealista	_____ pesimista	_____ independiente
_____ impaciente	_____ materialista	_____ estudiante
_____ extravagante	_____ normal	_____ diferente
_____ prudente	_____ profesor	_____ profesora
_____ valiente	_____ ¿ ?	_____ ¿ ?

B. ¿Quién es… ? With a classmate, take turns asking and answering questions, following the model.

MODELO: eficiente ⟶
—¿Quién es eficiente?
—El profesor / La profesora de español es eficiente. (Yo soy eficiente.)

1. arrogante
2. egoísta
3. emocional
4. rebelde
5. independiente
6. liberal
7. materialista
8. paciente
9. realista

C. Descripciones

Paso 1. Form complete sentences, using **no** when necessary.

El presidente de esta (*this*) nación (no) es…

1. pesimista
2. importante
3. inteligente
4. flexible
5. tolerante

Paso 2. Now compare your descriptions with those of two classmates to see if they match. You can ask: **En tu opinión, ¿cómo es el presidente?**

You will learn more about **ser** *in* **Gramática 6 (Cap. 3).**

¿Cómo es usted? (Part 1)

Suggestions

- The communicative focus of this section is on simple descriptions using cognate adjectives and the singular forms of *ser* (plus singular subject pronouns). This is enough material for most true beginning students to master at one time. However, if your class can handle more material, you may wish to present the entire conjugation of *ser*, as well as the plural subject pronouns. If your class has students who already know some basic Spanish, including the plural forms of *ser* and the subject pronouns, you may wish to recognize their knowledge and let them know that the whole class will study this material in upcoming chapters.
- Active vocabulary (in addition to the singular forms of *ser*): *¿quién?*
- The rest of *ser* is presented in *Gram. 6* (*Cap. 3*). Subject pronouns are presented in their entirety in *Gram. 3* (*Cap. 2*), and more details about their use are given in *Gram. 8* (*Cap. 2*).
- Introduce the forms of *ser* in brief sentences using the adjectives just presented in the *Nota*.
- Make sure students connect the *eres/es* forms with familiar/formal concepts already discussed for greetings.

Con. Note

Students have not yet learned adjective/noun agreement. The text's activities avoid having students produce sentences that require gender agreement by using adjectives and nouns that are the same for masculine and feminine. Gender is taught in *Gram. 1* (*Cap. 2*) and *Gram. 5* (*Cap. 3*).

Con. C: Suggestion

Call students' attention to the placement of *no* before the verb. Negation will be formally presented in *Gram. 3* (*Cap. 2*).

Con. C: Note

Active vocabulary: *no*

Optional

See optional activity, IM.

NATIONAL STANDARDS: Communities

Poll students to see who has heard of the following famous Hispanics: *Penélope Cruz, Javier Bardem, Gael García Bernal, Pedro Almodóvar, Pau Gasol, Rafael Nadal*, and *Albert Pujols*. Ask students to give the names of other famous Hispanics they know.

¡Aquí se habla español!

Notes

- *Las Islas Canarias* and *las Islas Baleares* are shaded but not labeled on the map on page 11 because they are part of Spain. Belize and Andorra are *not* Spanish speaking. This is not visible on this map.
- Definite articles are not used with place names on maps in the Spanish-speaking world. Exception: El Salvador, where the article is part of the name.
- Top nine world languages based on the number of native speakers (source: www.ethnologue.com, 2009)

  Chinese (Mandarin) 845 million
  Spanish 329 million
  English 328 million
  Arabic 221 million
  Hindi 182 million
  Bengali 181 million
  Portuguese 178 million
  Russian 144 million
  Japanese 122 million
  Malay Indonesian 176 million
  French 129 million
  German 128 million

- Because of the wide geographical area in which Spanish is spoken (North America, South America, Europe, Africa, Asia), the impact of Spanish on a global level is huge.

Suggestion

Have students give examples of uses of Spanish in this country: place and street names, restaurants, advertising, music, friends of Hispanic descent, television programs about Hispanics or with Hispanic characters, and so on. Explain the derivations of any terms students mention, if you know them.

Comprensión

1. How many people in the world speak Spanish? (329 million)
2. How many people speak Spanish in the U.S.? (50.5 million)
3. Is Spanish exactly the same the world over? (no)
4. On what cultures are Spanish-speaking countries in the Americas based? (European, indigenous, African)

Follow-up

- Use the place names on this map to continue pronunciation practice. Write the names of the countries on the board as students say them, then use the list as a basis for choral repetition drill.
- Have students discuss, research, and make pie charts that illustrate the ethnic make-up of their community.

¡Aquí se habla español!

If you sometimes have the feeling that Spanish is everywhere, that's because it's true, and it may become even more so during your lifetime. Here are some interesting facts.

- Spanish is spoken as a first or second language by about 450 million people. This makes Spanish the second most widely spoken language in the world. (Chinese is the most widely spoken.) Some Spanish speakers also speak an indigenous language, like **náhuatl** in Mexico, **mapuche** in Chile, or **catalán** in Spain.
- Spanish is an official language of twenty-one countries.
- Over 40 million people in the United States speak Spanish, making it the fourth largest Spanish-speaking country in the world.
- Spanish is the official language of Puerto Rico, an **Estado Libre** (*Free State*) associated with the United States.
- Spanish is present in Equatorial Guinea (where it is an official language) and in the Philippines as a heritage from the not so distant past when they were colonies of Spain.
- Spanish is second only to English in terms of the number of people studying it worldwide.

La Misión Basílica San Diego de Alcalá, cerca de San Diego, California

Knowing a second language has many personal and professional advantages. If you live in a country like the United States, there is no need to explain to you why it is a good thing to study Spanish. The language and its culture are part of the country's historical and cultural past. And, from an economic standpoint, Spanish speakers provide a huge market of consumers of all kinds of goods and services, including the entertainment industry and the world of art.

Spanish is also a great asset for traveling for business or pleasure, within this country or abroad. Like all languages spoken by a large number of people, modern Spanish varies from region to region. The Spanish of Madrid is different from that spoken in Mexico City, Buenos Aires, or Los Angeles. Although these differences are most noticeable in pronunciation ("accent"), they are also found in vocabulary and special expressions used in different areas of the world. But the majority of structures and vocabulary are common to the many varieties of Spanish.

Knowing Spanish also opens the door to a fascinating culture. Actually, *cultures*, plural, would be more accurate. Spanish was the language of one of the most impressive intersections of culture and civilization the world has ever known, when a small group of Spaniards landed on an island in the Caribbean over 500 years ago. No two of the Spanish-speaking

Comparing Origins of U.S. Hispanic Population
Total Hispanic Population
2010 Estimate*
50.5 Million

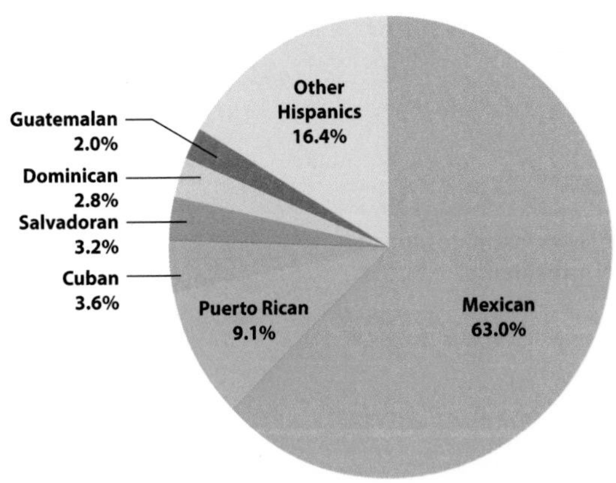

* Source: 2010 U.S. Census

NATIONAL STANDARDS: Communities

- Not all people of Hispanic origin have Spanish surnames, and many people with Spanish surnames do not consider themselves of Hispanic origin.
- The term *chicano,* although not as popular today as it was in the 1970s and early 1980s, is still used by many Mexican-Americans to refer to themselves and to the literature, art, and dialect of their community. Students should be aware of different terms and expect individual preferences from people in the Mexican-American community.

American countries that arose from that fusion of European and indigenous cultures (including those of Africans, brought to work as slaves) are alike. They offer a rich and diverse cultural panorama, one that you will learn about in every chapter of *Puntos de partida*.

So . . . welcome to the Spanish-speaking world! Actually, you know, you are already in it.

The United States is generally expressed as **los Estados Unidos** *in Spanish. The phrase is abbreviated in a number of ways:* **E.U., EE. UU.** *(the double vowels indicate plurality),* ***EEUU*** *(without the periods),* **USA,** *and* **U.S.A.** *(the latter pronounced as one word).* **U.S.A.** *is not recommended usage.* **Los Estados Unidos de América (E.U.A.)** *is also used. The abbreviation* ***EEUU*** *will be used in* Puntos de partida.

Mundo interactivo

You've been selected to work as an intern at a Spanish-language news station, HispanaVisión! Your guide, Laura Sánchez Tejada, will direct you to complete a series of tasks throughout the *Puntos* program. You should now be prepared to work with Laura to complete Scenario 1, Activity 1 in Connect Spanish (**www.connectspanish.com**).

Note

The following are the ten states in the United States with the highest Hispanic population according to the U.S. Census Bureau (2006).

STATE	TOTAL NUMBER OF HISPANICS	% OF STATE POPULATION
California	13,074,155	35.9%
Texas	8,385,118	35.7%
Florida	3,642,989	20.1%
New York	3,139,590	16.3%
Illinois	1,888,439	14.7%
Arizona	1,803,377	29.2%
New Jersey	1,364,699	15.6%
Colorado	934,410	19.7%
New Mexico	860,687	44.0%
Nevada	610,051	24.4%

Heritage Speakers

- Anime a los estudiantes hispanohablantes de la clase a que les pregunten a sus parientes y conocidos de origen hispánico los nombres con los cuales se refieren a sí mismos por su país de origen, nombres tales como *tica* o *boricua.* Luego invítelos a compartir esta información con sus compañeros de clase.
- Los hispanohablantes de este país usan palabras adaptadas del inglés en el habla cotidiana. Muchas veces los hispanohablantes de países latinoamericanos o de España no conocen estas palabras, lo cual puede impedir la comprensión. Algunas de estas palabras son *elevador* en vez de *ascensor, aplicación* en vez de *solicitud, bonche* en vez de *montón, grados* en vez de *notas, lonche* en vez de *almuerzo,* entre otras.

NATIONAL STANDARDS: Cultures

Every two weeks a language dies. Linguists estimate that, given the current rate of language extinction, more than half of the 7,000 languages spoken on Earth will disappear within the next 100 years. Many of these languages only exist orally, with no written form, and some have yet to be recorded. When the last living speakers of a language die, they take with them a wealth of knowledge about their culture, their history, and the environment in which they have lived.

Resources: Transparency 5

Los números del 0 al 30; *Hay*

Suggestions

- Adapt model sentences to your classroom.
- Practice the numbers 0–10: count forward; count by twos in evens and odds; count backwards from 10–0.
- Practice the numbers 11–20: evens 0–20.
- Practice the numbers 21–30: odds 0–30.
- Count from 0 to 30 by threes; by fives; by tens.
- Point out the written accents on 16, 21 (shortened masculine form), 22, 23, 26; final *-e* of *veinte* and final *-a* of *treinta*.
- Write numbers on the board and identify them (sometimes incorrectly). Students indicate their comprehension with *sí* or *no*. Encourage them to correct your "mistakes."
- Say these pairs of numbers; have students repeat the larger one: *dos / doce; once / uno; treinta / veinte; tres / trece; cuatro / catorce; quince / cinco; diez / once.*
- Emphasize that *hay* means both *there is* and *there are.*
- Model the question form: *¿Hay ______?* with rising intonation.

Note

In this edition of *Puntos de partida,* vocabulary that becomes active in paradigm sentences (other than material that is otherwise called out for active use, such as the numbers and *hay* in this section) will be noted in these annotations. The word *pero* becomes active in the second example on page 13.

Reciclado: Using magazine or newspaper ads or photos, ask *¿Hay +* number*?* questions with previous cognate vocabulary.

SEGUNDA° PARTE

°Second

Los números del 0 al 30; *Hay*

a noun / **un sustantivo** = a word that denotes a person, place, thing, or idea

Hay un profesor.
Hay tres estudiantes.

En un salón de clase, en Los Ángeles, California

Los números del 0 al 30

0	cero				
1	uno	11	once	21	veintiuno
2	dos	12	doce	22	veintidós
3	tres	13	trece	23	veintitrés
4	cuatro	14	catorce	24	veinticuatro
5	cinco	15	quince	25	veinticinco
6	seis	16	dieciséis*	26	veintiséis
7	siete	17	diecisiete	27	veintisiete
8	ocho	18	dieciocho	28	veintiocho
9	nueve	19	diecinueve	29	veintinueve
10	diez	20	veinte	30	treinta

¡OJO!

uno, dos,... veinti**uno,** veintidós,...
but
un señor, veinti**ún** señores
una señora, veinti**una** señoras

Nota comunicativa

El género (*gender*) y los números

The number *one* has several forms in Spanish. **Uno** is the form used in counting. The forms **un** and **una** are used before *nouns* (**los sustantivos**). How will you know which one to use? It depends on the *gender* (**el género**) of the noun.

All nouns are either masculine or feminine in Spanish. For example, the noun **señor** is masculine (*m.*) in gender, and the noun **señora** is feminine (*f.*). (Even nouns that are not sex-linked have gender.) To express *one* with these nouns, say **un señor** and **una señora.** The number **veintiuno** has similar forms before nouns: **veintiún señores, veintiuna señoras.** Just get used to using **un** and **una** with nouns now. You'll learn more about gender and number in **Capítulo 2.**

The numbers 16 to 19 and 21 to 29 can be written as one word (**dieciséis... veintiuno...**) *or as three words* (**diez y seis... veinte y uno...**).

Culture

If students go to a restaurant or café in Latin America or Spain, their bill may look very different from those in this country. Handwritten numbers can be quite different. For example, the number 1 is usually written as an inverted check mark (1), and can easily be mistaken for the number 7. The 7, however, is usually written with a slash across the middle (7̶). The number 8 is frequently written starting with the lower loop.

Hay

The word **hay** expresses both *there is* and *there are* in Spanish. It can be made negative (**no hay**) and can also be used to ask a question: **¿Hay... ?** (*Is there . . . ? Are there . . . ?*)

—¿Cuántos estudiantes **hay** en la clase?	*"How many students are there in the class?"*
—(**Hay**) Treinta.	*"(There are) Thirty."*
Hay un teatro en esta universidad, pero **no hay** museo.	*There's a theatre at this university, but there isn't a museum.*

hay = there is / there are

Práctica

A. Una canción infantil. (*A children's song.*) This is a popular song for children from all over the Spanish-speaking world. Complete it with the missing numbers. It's basic math!

Dos y dos son _cuatro_, y ocho _dieciséis_,
cuatro y dos son _seis_, y ocho _veinticuatro_,
Seis y dos son _ocho_, y _ocho_ treinta y dos…

B. Los números. Practique los números, según (*according to*) el modelo.

MODELO: 1 señor → Hay **un** señor.

1. 4 señoras	**6.** 1 clase (*f.*)	**11.** 28 naciones
2. 12 pianos	**7.** 21 ideas (*f.*)	**12.** 5 guitarras
3. 1 café (*m.*)	**8.** 11 personas	**13.** 1 león (*m.*)
4. 21 cafés (*m.*)	**9.** 15 estudiantes	**14.** 30 señores
5. 14 días	**10.** 13 teléfonos	**15.** 20 oficinas

C. Problemas de matemáticas. Express the following simple mathematical equations in Spanish. Note: + (**y**), − (**menos**), = (**son**).

MODELOS: $2 + 2 = 4$ → Dos y dos son cuatro.
$4 - 2 = 2$ → Cuatro menos dos son dos.

1. $2 + 4 = 6$	**8.** $15 - 2 = 13$	**15.** $8 - 7 = 1$
2. $8 + 17 = 25$	**9.** $9 - 9 = 0$	**16.** $13 - 9 = 4$
3. $11 + 1 = 12$	**10.** $13 - 8 = 5$	**17.** $2 + 3 + 10 = 15$
4. $3 + 18 = 21$	**11.** $14 + 12 = 26$	**18.** $28 - 6 = 22$
5. $9 + 6 = 15$	**12.** $23 - 13 = 10$	**19.** $30 - 17 = 13$
6. $5 + 4 = 9$	**13.** $1 + 4 = 5$	**20.** $28 - 5 = 23$
7. $1 + 13 = 14$	**14.** $1 + 3 - 1 = 3$	**21.** $19 - 7 = 12$

Conversación

Intercambios (*Exchanges*)

1. ¿Cuántos (*How many*) estudiantes hay en la clase de español? ¿Cuántos estudiantes hay en clase hoy (*today*)? ¿Hay tres profesores o un profesor / una profesora?
2. ¿Cuántos días hay en una semana (*week*)? ¿Hay seis? **(No, no hay...)** ¿Cuántos días hay en un fin de semana (*weekend*)? ¿Cuántos días hay en el mes (*month*) de febrero? ¿en el mes de junio? ¿Cuántos meses hay en un año (*year*)?
3. En una universidad, hay muchos edificios (*many buildings*). En esta (*this*) universidad, ¿hay una cafetería? **(Sí, hay... / No, no hay...)** ¿un teatro? ¿un laboratorio de lenguas (*languages*)? ¿un bar? ¿una clínica? ¿un hospital? ¿un museo? ¿muchos estudiantes? ¿muchos profesores?

Prác. A: Notes

- The last line given of the song uses the number 32, which is beyond the scope of the material presented in this section. However, students should be able to figure it out easily.
- The final line of the song has been omitted. In various parts of the Spanish-speaking world, the song has different endings, some with religious connotations. Here are three of them.

Ánimas benditas, me arrodillo yo.
(Holy souls, I kneel.)
Ánimas benditas, no les temo yo.
(Holy souls, I'm not afraid.)
Y diez que le sumo, son cuarenta y dos.
(When I add 10, it comes to 42.)

Prác. B: Suggestion

Have students read aloud, practicing pronunciation.

Prác. B: Variation

Use this or a similar activity for in-class dictation. See "Teaching Techniques: Dictation," IM.

Prác. C: Variations

- Do as a pair activity in which one partner reads the equation and the other says the answer.
- Write additional problems on large flash cards. Have students read the problems aloud and give answers.
- Teach *¿Cuántos son?* Give additional problems orally.

Prác. C: Follow-up

- *Un problema para Einstein:* $10 - 5 + 7 - 4 + 12 - 15 + 9 - 11 + 17 - 14 + 16 = ?$ (Answer: 22)
- Explain that × = *por.* Have students read and solve these equations orally.

1. $2 \times 2 = ?$	**5.** $4 \times 4 = ?$
2. $2 \times 6 = ?$	**6.** $11 \times 0 = ?$
3. $18 \times 1 = ?$	**7.** $3 \times 8 = ?$
4. $3 \times 7 = ?$	**8.** $2 \times 15 = ?$

Con. Notes

- Students may answer in complete sentences.
- Point out that a double *no* (*No, no…*) is used in complete sentences that express negative answers.
- In this edition of *Puntos de partida,* vocabulary that becomes active in exercises and activities will be noted in these annotations. The word *hoy* becomes active in *Con. 1.*

Heritage Speakers

- Recuérdeles a los estudiantes hispanohablantes de la clase que la forma *hay* es impersonal y que no cambia: *Hay un hombre; Hay dos libros.* Recuérdeles que lo mismo ocurre en los tiempos pasados: cuando expresan *there was/were, había y hubo* no cambian cuando van delante de un sustantivo plural: *Había muchos libros; Hubo varios problemas.*
- Pregúnteles a los estudiantes hispanohablantes de la clase qué canciones infantiles aprendieron de niños y anímelos a cantar alguna.

Los gustos y preferencias (Part 1)

Suggestions

- The focus of this section is on informal (*te gusta*) versus formal (*le gusta*) usage to express *you like*. If your class does well with this material, you may also wish to introduce *le gusta* = *he/she likes*. You should certainly use *le gusta* in your input: *A Jorge le gusta…*
- Encourage students to learn all of the *gustar* phrases as set expressions. There is no need to explain the *gustar* construction at this time; activities will not require students to produce *gustan* on their own.
- Students should relate *te/le gusta* to the informal/formal concept discussed in *Cap. 1: Primera parte.*
- Contrast the indefinite articles practiced earlier and the definite articles practiced here, but do not require mastery of the concept at this time.
- Active vocabulary: *también*

Note

Introduce *gustar* + infinitive to expand the communicative use of *gustar* phrases, as well as to introduce the concept of the infinitive, which is formally presented in *Gram. 3* (*Cap. 2*).

Preliminary Exercise

Ask the following questions. *¿Qué te/le gusta más* (new word), *el fútbol o el fútbol americano? ¿el tenis o el voleibol?* You might also ask: *¿Qué le gusta a* (name of classmate)*?* Do not emphasize or expect students to produce the *a* + *name phrase.*

Prác. A: Notes

- Students may be confused by the narrative point of view in the exercise. They are not asked to answer the questions, only to tell which pronoun they associate with each item.
- Active vocabulary.

Culture

In *Gram. 22* (*Cap. 8*) students will learn to use the Spanish verb *gustar*. You may wish to tell them that it can have romantic connotations when used in the first and second person singular forms (*yo* and *tú*).

¿Te gusto? Do you like me? / Are you attracted to me?

Appropriate substitutes are *encantarle, agradarle*, or *caerle bien*.

Los gustos° y preferencias (Part 1)*

Los… *Likes*

¡OJO!

En español, **fútbol** = *soccer* y **fútbol americano** = *football.*

—¿**Te gusta** el fútbol?
—Sí, ¡**me gusta** mucho!
—Y **a usted**, señor, ¿también **le gusta** el fútbol?
—No, **no me gusta** el fútbol, pero sí **me gusta** el fútbol americano.

El equipo (*team*) nacional español de fútbol, campeón de la Copa del Mundo (*World Cup*) en 2010 (dos mil diez)

Use these patterns with the verb **gustar** to express likes and dislikes.

I like ______.	Me **gusta** ______.
I don't like ______.	**No** me **gusta** ______.
You (don't) like ______.	**(No)** Te **gusta** ______. (*familiar*) **(No)** Le **gusta** ______. (*formal*)
Do you like?	¿Te **gusta** ______? (*familiar*) ¿(A usted) Le **gusta** ______? (*formal*)

an infinitive / **un infinitivo** = a verb form that indicates action or state of being without referring to a specific person or time

In the following activities you will use **el** to mean *the* with masculine nouns and **la** with feminine nouns. Don't try to memorize which words are masculine or feminine. Just get used to using **el** and **la** with nouns.

You will also use Spanish verbs in the infinitive form, which always ends in **-r.** Here are some examples: **estudiar** = *to study*, **comer** = *to eat*. You will be able to guess the meaning of other infinitives from context (the surrounding words).

Práctica

A. ¿Yo, tú o usted? Indicate which pronoun you associate with each question or statement.

1. ¿Te gusta la pizza? tú
2. ¿Le gusta la Coca-Cola? usted
3. Me gusta mucho el chocolate. yo

B. Versión bilingüe. Match the ideas.

1. __c__ —¿Te gusta esquiar? —No, no me gusta.
2. __a__ —¿Le gusta esquiar? —Sí, me gusta.
3. __b__ —Me gusta esquiar. —¿Sí? A mí no me gusta.

a. "Do you (*formal*) like to ski?" "Yes, I like to."
b. "I like to ski." "Yeah? I don't like to."
c. "Do you (*familiar*) like to ski?" "No, I don't like to."

"Do you like soccer?" "Yes, I like it a lot!" "And (what about) you, sir, do you also like soccer?" "No, I don't like soccer, but I do like football."

You will learn more about* **gustar *in* **Gramática 22 (Capítulo 8).**

Conversación

A. Los gustos y preferencias

Paso 1. Make a list of six things you like and six things you don't like, following the model. You may choose items from the **Vocabulario útil** box.

MODELO: Me gusta **la clase de español.** No me gusta **la clase de matemáticas.**

Vocabulario útil

Vocabulario útil is not active; that is, you don't need to focus on learning it. But it will help you do this activity.

el actor _____, **la actriz** _____
el café, el té, la limonada, la Coca-Cola
el/la cantante (singer) _____ (**¡OJO!** The word **cantante** is used for both men *and* women.)
el cine (*movies*), **el teatro, la ópera, el arte abstracto, el fútbol**
la música moderna, la música clásica, el ***rap,*** **la música** ***country***
la pizza, la pasta, la comida (*food*) **mexicana, la comida de la cafetería**

1. Me gusta _____. No me gusta _____.
2. _____
3. _____
4. _____
5. _____
6. _____

Paso 2. Now ask a classmate if he or she shares your likes and dislikes.

MODELO: ESTUDIANTE 1: ¿Te gusta la clase de español?
ESTUDIANTE 2: Sí, me gusta (la clase de español).
ESTUDIANTE 1: ¿Y la clase de matemáticas?
ESTUDIANTE 2: Sí, también me gusta (la clase de matemáticas).

B. Más gustos y preferencias

Paso 1. Here are some useful verbs and nouns to talk about what you like. For each item, combine an infinitive (shaded) with a noun to form a sentence that is true for you. Can you use context to guess the meaning of verbs you don't know?

MODELO: Me gusta _____. → Me gusta **estudiar inglés.**

1.	beber	café chocolate limonada té
2.	comer	enchiladas ensalada hamburguesas pasta pizza
3.	estudiar	computación (*computer science*) español historia matemáticas
4.	hablar	con mis amigos (*with my friends*) español por teléfono (*on the phone*)
5.	jugar	al basquetbol al béisbol al fútbol al fútbol americano al tenis
6.	tocar	la guitarra el piano el violín

Paso 2. Ask a classmate about his or her likes, using your own preferences as a guide.

MODELO: ¿Te gusta **comer enchiladas**?

Paso 3. Now ask your professor if he or she likes certain things. **¡OJO!** Remember to address your professor in a formal manner if that is his or her preference.

MODELO: ¿Le gusta **jugar al tenis**?

Vocabulario útil

Notes

- The *Vocabulario útil* boxes occur throughout *Puntos de partida* when additional vocabulary is needed to complete an activity.
- Emphasize that students need not memorize this vocabulary. It is provided to help them complete a specific activity in the text.
- When *Vocabulario útil* features appear, model new vocabulary for students in the context of brief sentences, if possible, before letting them continue the activity.
- In Latin America, rap is sometimes called *el cotorreo* (*cotorrear* means to talk without saying anything interesting) or *la música* rap.

Con. A: Extension

Use other names of currently famous people and cognates for sports and games: *el béisbol, el voleibol, el basquetbol, hacer jogging, jugar al bingo, practicar deportes,* and so on.

Con. B: Follow-up

Paso 2. Have students expand each interview to three sentences by adding rejoinders like *a mí* and *también: A mí me gusta tocar el violín también.*

NATIONAL STANDARDS: Communication

Have students interview their classmates, asking them about their *gustos y preferencias*. Provide students with sample questions.

¿Te gusta estudiar español?
¿Te gusta la comida italiana?
¿Te gusta jugar al basquetbol?

Once students complete their interviews, follow up with questions that have students share information: *¿A quién le gusta la comida italiana?* (Teach the meaning of *¿a quién?*)

¿Qué hora es?

Reciclado: Review the numbers 1–30 before beginning this section.

Suggestions

- Use a clock made from a paper plate to introduce telling time, and follow the step-by-step progression of the explanation in the text.
- Remind students that *Es la una* but *Son las dos* (*las tres,* and so on).
- Point out that *son* is the plural form of *es*.
- In Mexico and some parts of Central America, one frequently hears *¿Qué horas son?*
- Practice telling time with the most basic forms before presenting the *Nota comunicativa*.

Nota comunicativa

Suggestions

- Model expressions with various times shown on your clock.
- Point out that *de la mañana* is used until lunch and *de la tarde* until the evening meal. Make sure students associate this information with the greetings *buenos días* and *buenas tardes/noches.*
- Emphasize the difference between *Es/Son* vs. *A la(s)*.
- Ask *¿A qué hora es la clase de español?* After the students respond, repeat the answer, adding *en punto.* Repeat the question for a number of shared experiences: *la sesión de laboratorio, la clase de historia,* and so on.
- Students will learn the expressions *por la mañana/tarde/noche* in *Cap. 2.* If you wish, you can introduce and explain them at this point (as well as the alternative expressions *en la mañana/tarde/noche*), stressing that they are used with conjugated verbs, in contrast to *de la mañana/ tarde/noche,* which are used with specific hours of the day. Contrast *estudio por/en la tarde* (general time frame) with *estudio a las dos de la tarde todos los días* (specific time).
- As in English, digital clocks have influenced the way some Spanish speakers tell time. Using the traditional system, Spanish speakers say: *Son las nueve menos veinte.* However, with the advent of digital readouts, it is not uncommon to hear: *Son las ocho (y) cuarenta (minutos).* The traditional method for telling time is generally preferred. However, you may wish to introduce *cuarenta* and *cincuenta* to practice telling time in the new pattern.

¿Qué hora es?

Es **la una.**

Son **las dos.**

Son **las cinco.**

¿Qué hora es? is used to ask *What time is it?* In telling time, one says ***Es* la una** but ***Son* las dos (las tres, las cuatro,** and so on).

Es la una y { cuarto. / quince.

Son las dos y { media. / treinta.

Son las cinco y diez.

Son las ocho y veinticinco.

Note that from the hour to the half-hour, Spanish, like English, expresses time by adding minutes or a portion of an hour to the hour.

Son las dos menos { cuarto. / quince.

Son las ocho menos diez.

Son las once menos veinte.

From the half-hour to the hour, Spanish usually expresses time by subtracting minutes or a part of an hour from the *next* hour.

¡OJO!

Es la... / Son las... = to tell time

A la... / A las... = to tell *at* what time something happens

Nota **comunicativa**

Cómo expresar la hora

de la mañana	A.M., in the morning
de la tarde	P.M., in the afternoon (and early evening)
de la noche	P.M., in the evening
en punto	exactly, on the dot, sharp
¿a qué hora... ?	(at) what time . . . ?
a la una (las dos,...)	at 1:00 (2:00, . . .)
Son las cuatro **de la tarde en punto.**	It's exactly 4:00 P.M.
—¿**A qué hora** es la clase de español?	"What time is Spanish class (at)?"
—Es **a las** once **de la mañana.**	"It's at 11:00 A.M."

Culture

Time is often listed in 24-hour style for Spanish publications such as TV guides and transportation schedules.

12:01 A.M.	= 00:01	4:15 P.M.	= 16:15
8:00 A.M.	= 08:00	7:05 P.M.	= 19:05
12:00 Noon	= 12:00	10:20 P.M.	= 22:20
1:30 P.M.	= 13:30	11:10 P.M.	= 23:10

Heritage Speakers

Pregúnteles a los estudiantes hispanohablantes de la clase si ellos mismos o personas que conocen dicen *¿Qué horas son?* en vez de *¿Qué hora es?* Esta forma se oye en su casa.

Resources: Transparency 6

Práctica

A. ¡Atención! Listen as your instructor says a time of day. Find the clock face that corresponds to the time you heard and say its number in Spanish.

1.

2.

3.

4.

5.

6.

7.

B. ¿Qué hora es? Express the time in full sentences in Spanish.

1. 1:00 P.M.
2. 6:00 P.M.
3. 11:00 A.M.
4. 1:30
5. 3:15
6. 6:45
7. 4:15
8. 11:45 exactly
9. 9:10 on the dot
10. 9:50 sharp

Conversación

A. Entrevista

Paso 1. Ask a classmate at what time the following events or activities take place. He or she will answer according to the cue.

MODELO: la clase de español (10:00 A.M.) ⟶
ESTUDIANTE 1: ¿A qué hora es la clase de español?
ESTUDIANTE 2: A las diez de la mañana… ¡en punto!

1. la clase de francés (1:45 P.M.)
2. la sesión de laboratorio (3:10 P.M.)
3. la excursión (8:45 A.M.)
4. el concierto (7:30 P.M.)
5. la clase de física (11:50 A.M.)
6. la fiesta (10:00 P.M.)

Paso 2. Now ask at what time your partner likes to perform these activities. He or she will provide the necessary information.

MODELO: cenar (*to have dinner*) ⟶
ESTUDIANTE 1: ¿A qué hora te gusta cenar?
ESTUDIANTE 2: Me gusta cenar a las ocho de la noche.

1. almorzar (*to have lunch*)
2. mirar (*to watch*) la television
3. ir (*to go*) al (*to the*) gimnasio
4. ir al cine
5. estudiar
6. ir a una fiesta

B. Una situación en la calle (*street*)**.** Complete el diálogo con un compañero / una compañera.

SR. ROLDÁN: Buenos días, Sra. Valdés. ¿Cómo ____está____?
SRA. VALDÉS: Muy bien. ¿____Y usted____, Sr. Roldán?
SR. ROLDÁN: ____(Muy) Bien____. Perdón, ¿qué hora ____es____?
SRA. VALDÉS: ____Son____ las ____seis y media____ (*6:30*), señor.
SR. ROLDÁN: ____Muchas____ gracias, señora.

Mundo interactivo

You should now be prepared to work with Scenario 1, Activity 2 in Connect Spanish (**www.connectspanish.com**).

Prác. A: Suggestion

You might present the items in this order: *Son las nueve y media de la mañana.* **(6)** *Son las dos de la tarde.* **(2)** *Son las doce menos veinte de la noche.* **(1)** *Son las cinco y cuarto de la noche (mañana).* **(5)** *Son las diez y veintidós de la noche.* **(3)** *Son las dos y dieciocho de la tarde.* **(4)** *Es la una y cinco de la noche (mañana).* **(7)**

Prác. A: Follow-up

Have students respond *sí* or *no* to the following statements. Vary the time as needed for your students. This is an opportunity to review the infinitives from *Con. B* (p. 15). Pantomime as needed to convey meanings.

1. *Son las once de la noche. Es hora de estudiar.*
2. *Son las siete de la mañana. Es hora de hablar español.*
3. *Son las ocho de la mañana. Es hora de beber café en la cafetería.*
4. *Son las seis y media de la tarde. Es hora de comer en un restaurante elegante.*

Prác. B: Suggestions

- Ask students at what time they like to . . . *tocar (un instrumento musical), comer, estudiar (español), practicar deportes,* and so on.
- Introduce the interrogative *¿cuándo?*
- Emphasize that students must include the phrase *a la(s): Me gusta (comer) a las (doce en punto).*

Con. A: Variation

Expand the exchange in *Paso 2* with *a mí* and *también: A mí me gusta estudiar español a las ocho de la noche también.*

Con. A: Follow-up

Put the following evening television schedule on the board. Read incomplete sentences and have students respond with *a la(s)… : Hay un programa cómico (romántico, dramático, de animales, de música, para toda la familia, interesante) a* ______.

7:00—*Los Simpson*
7:30—*El Zoológico de Barcelona*
8:00—*¡Festival de música!*
8:30—*Dibujos animados*
9:00—*Survivor*
10:00—*Cine Club: Historia de amor*

You may want to challenge students more by using 24-hour times as is common in the Spanish-speaking world: 7:00 = 19:00 hours; 7:30 = 19:30; 8:00 = 20:00, and so on.

Heritage Speakers

En algunos dialectos, *almorzar* significa *comer a media mañana* y corresponde a la expresión *to have brunch* en inglés.

Con. B: Suggestions

- Have students repeat the dialogue with different times of day: 10:00 A.M., 4:30 P.M., and so on.
- Have several pairs of students present brief dialogues to the class. Encourage the others to listen to the skits. Ask brief comprehension questions based on them.

Pronunciación

Note

Point out the different pronunciations of the English vowel *a: far, fat, fate, fail, sofa;* also point out the silent letter *e: make, mate, crate.*

Preliminary Exercises

- Pronounce these words in random order and have students tell whether each word is *español* or *inglés.*

Eng.	Sp.	Eng.	Sp.
me	*mi*	may	*me*
Fay	*fe*	no	*no*
ace	*es*	Sue	*su*
cone	*con*	lay	*le*
tea	*ti*	two	*tú*
low	*lo*	say	*se*
dose	*dos*	day	*de*
sea	*si*	Kay	*que*

- Write the following two columns on the board. Read aloud one word at a time. Students will decide if the word you read was from column A or B. You may wish to translate unfamiliar words for the students.

	A	B
1.	*mesas*	*meses*
2.	*señoras*	*señores*
3.	*calor*	*color*
4.	*emite*	*imite*
5.	*pelar*	*polar*
6.	*legar*	*lugar*

- **Trabalenguas.** Here is a popular nonsense rhyme, the Spanish version of "Eeny, meeny, miney, moe." (Note: The person who corresponds to **fue** is "it.")

  Pin, marín
  de don Pingüé
  cúcara, mácara
  títere, fue.

- Here are two more rhymes for pronunciation practice.

  Borriquito como tú,
  Que no sabe ni la u.
  Borriquito como tú,
  Yo sé más que tú.

  A, e, i, o, u,
  El burro sabe más que tú.

Prác. A: Extension

Present the last names in the following sentences; have students practice the phrases and then complete sentences. Emphasize clear diction and the use of mouth muscles.

a: Hasta mañana, señora Santana.
e: De nada, señora Pérez.
i: ¿Es usted tímida, señorita Muñoz?
o: Con permiso, señor Ortega.
u: ¿Y usted, señora Cruz?

Pronunciación: Las vocales:° *a, e, i, o, u*

°*vowels*

There is a very close relationship between the way Spanish is written and the way it is pronounced. This makes it relatively easy to learn the basics of Spanish spelling and pronunciation.

Many Spanish sounds, however, do not have an exact equivalent in English, so you can't always trust English to be your guide to Spanish pronunciation. Even words that are spelled the same in both languages are usually pronounced quite differently.

English vowels can have many different pronunciations or may be silent. Spanish vowels are always pronounced, and they are almost always pronounced in the same way. They are always short and tense. They are never drawn out with a *u* or *i* glide as in English: **lo** ≠ *low;* **de** ≠ *day.*

¡OJO!

The *uh* sound or schwa (which is how most unstressed vowels are pronounced in English: c**a**nal, wait**e**d, at**o**m) does not exist in Spanish.

a: pronounced like the *a* in *father,* but short and tense
e: pronounced like the *e* in *they,* but without the *i* glide
i: pronounced like the *i* in *machine,* but short and tense*
o: pronounced like the *o* in *home,* but without the *u* glide
u: pronounced like the *u* in *rule,* but short and tense

Práctica

A. Palabras (*Words*). Repeat the following words after your instructor.

1. hasta tal nada mañana natural normal fascinante
2. me qué Pérez Elena rebelde excelente elegante
3. sí señorita permiso terrible imposible tímido Ibiza
4. yo con como noches profesor señor generoso
5. uno usted tú mucho Perú Lupe Úrsula

B. Las naciones

Paso 1. Here is part of a rental car ad in Spanish. Say aloud the names of the countries where you can find this company's offices. Can you recognize all of the countries?

Paso 2. Find the following information in the ad.

1. How many cars does the agency have available? 40.000
2. How many offices does the agency have? 1.000
3. What Spanish word expresses the English word *immediately*? inmediatamente

Ansa International
RENT A CAR
Si necesita un coche para su trabajo o placer, nosotros tenemos el adecuado para Vd.
Con una flota de 40.000 coches y 1.000 oficinas, estamos a su servicio en los siguientes países:
ALEMANIA
ARABIA SAUDITA
ARGENTINA
AUSTRIA
BELGICA
BRASIL
CHIPRE
DINAMARCA
ESPAÑA
FINLANDIA
FRANCIA
GRAN BRETAÑA
GRECIA
HOLANDA
IRLANDA
ISLANDIA
ITALIA
JAMAICA
LUXEMBURGO
MALASIA
MARRUECOS
MARTINICA
PARAGUAY
PORTUGAL
SUECIA
SUIZA
URUGUAY
U.S.A.
En la mayoría de los casos, podemos confirmar su reserva inmediatamente.
Cuando esto no sea posible, su reserva le será confirmada en un plazo máximo de 48 horas.

*The word **y** [and] is also pronounced like the letter **i**.

Prác. B: Note

Vd. (in the ad) is a less common abbreviation for *usted.* The more common abbreviation is *Ud.,* which students will learn in *Cap. 2.*

Prác. B: Suggestions

- Model the names of the countries, followed by choral and individual repetitions.
- Have students identify other cognates in the ad.
- Allow students to answer *Paso 2* items 1 and 2 in English.

TELEPUNTOS

SALU2

Mundo interactivo

You've been selected to work as an intern at a Spanish-language news station, HispanaVisión! Laura Sánchez Tejada will direct you to complete a series of tasks for the *Salu2* program. Work with Laura on Scenario 1, Activities 1 and 2 in Connect Spanish (**www.connectspanish.com**).

El presentador Víctor Gutiérrez es de California, de origen mexicano. La presentadora Ana García Blanco es de Panamá, pero ahora vive (*she now lives*) en Los Ángeles. La reportera es Laura Sánchez Tejada. Es de México.

Antes de mirar° — Antes… *Before watching*

What is a morning news and talk television show usually like? Check all of the phrases that apply.

- ☐ un poco (*a little*) cómico
- ☐ un poco serio
- ☐ informativo
- ☐ muy dramático
- ☐ para (*for*) una audiencia diversa
- ☐ solo para las personas mayores (*only for older people*)

PROGRAMA 1: ¡Salu2 desde° Los Ángeles! — *from*

You will not understand every word of *Salu2*, the morning television show that you are about to see, but you will easily be able to get the gist of the show and understand most of the greetings.

Reading part of the script before watching each segment of *Salu2* will help you understand more of the show.

These words and phrases (given in the order in which they appear in the show) will help you understand more when you watch this episode.

Fragmento del guion° — *script*

VÍCTOR: Muchas gracias, Laura. La presencia del español en la ciudad de Los Ángeles es impresionante, ¿no crees,[a] Ana?

ANA: Absolutamente. Y personas de todo tipo hablan español, no solo los hispanos. Bueno, es hora de decir[b] adiós por hoy. Espero que les haya gustado nuestro primer programa.[c] Nos vemos muy pronto.

VÍCTOR: Desde el estudio de *Salu2* en la ciudad de Los Ángeles, California, les mandamos[d] saludos a todos los telespectadores y esperamos verlos en nuestro próximo programa.[e] ¡Hasta entonces![f]

[a]¿no… *don't you think* [b]es… *it's time to say* [c]Espero… *I hope you liked our first program.* [d]les… *we send* [e]esperamos… *we hope to see you at our next program* [f]¡Hasta… *Until then!*

Vocabulario de este° programa — *this*

hoy les presentamos	today we're introducing… to all of you
un nombre	a name
los hispanohablantes	Spanish-speakers
antiguo	former
la ciudad	the city
el país	the country, nation
vamos a hablar/ escuchar	we're going to talk/listen to
cuarenta y ocho	forty-eight
les saludo	I'm greeting all of you
la playa	the beach
disculpa	pardon me
¿de dónde vienes?	**¿de dónde eres?**
(yo) vengo de	**(yo) soy de**

If you scan **Después de mirar** *before* watching the show, you will understand more of what is in the program.

Después de mirar° — Después… *After watching*

¿Está claro? ¿Cierto o falso? Corrija (*Correct*) las oraciones falsas.

	CIERTO	FALSO
1. *Salu2* es un programa matinal (*morning*) de televisión.	☑	☐
2. Es un programa informativo para un público hispanohablante diverso.	☑	☐
3. El estudio está en San Francisco.	☐	☑
4. Hay tres presentadores (*anchors*) y una reportera.	☐	☑
5. Pocas (*Few*) personas hablan español en Los Ángeles.	☐	☑

Producción personal

Filme los saludos de dos o tres personas en español.

TelePuntos

Notes

- Pages 19–21 are optional. You may cover some, all, or none of this material in class, or assign it to students—as a group or individually—for homework or extra credit. Page 22 (*En resumen: En este capítulo*) is a summary of all of the chapter's active material.
- Starting in *Capítulo 2, TelePuntos* will be a two-page spread, with more supporting materials than are offered in this chapter.

Suggestions

- It is important to give students a general orientation to the *Salu2* program (in English or in Spanish, depending on your preference).
- If you are using the video in class, show it once, ask brief comprehension questions, then show it again.
- Even if you plan to ask students to watch the video in your campus media center or on their own, it is a good idea to show the first program in class to get them started and teach them good viewing habits. It is especially important to stress that students should watch the shows as many times as they want or need to in order to complete the *Después de mirar* activities.
- You may wish to tell students to scan *Después de mirar* before viewing a given episode.
- See the IM for more suggestions and activities.

Fragmento del guion

Note

The word *guion* is used here and throughout the *Puntos* program without an accent, according to the new *RAE* guidelines.

Después de mirar

Answers

3. *Falso: El estudio está en Los Ángeles.* **4.** *Falso: Hay dos presentadores y una reportera.* **5.** *Falso: Muchas personas hablan español en Los Ángeles.*

Producción personal

Notes

- This section, which is included in every chapter, provides a short video assignment for students. All assignments are independent of each other, as it is assumed that most instructors will not assign this feature in every chapter.
- See the IM for additional suggestions for this chapter's assignment as well as for general guidelines and suggestions for video assignments.

A leer

Notes

- In addition to discussing aspects of the geography of the Spanish-speaking world, this reading also mentions the two primary Portuguese-speaking countries of the world, *el Brasil* and *Portugal*, to further students' knowledge of these countries and languages, which have historical links to Spanish.
- The geographical features cited in the reading are intended as examples or highlights only. There are of course jungles in countries other than *Venezuela*, *Colombia*, *el Ecuador*, and *el Perú*, volcanoes in areas other than *México*, *la América Central*, and *la cordillera de los Andes*, and so on. You should feel free to expand the information given in the reading.

Suggestions

- Before students begin the reading, review the definite and indefinite articles (for recognition) with them. Emphasize *un* → *el* and *una* → *la*. Present the plural definite articles (*los*, *las*).
- Point out that students should guess the underlined words from context, and discuss the first such word (*cordillera*) with them.
- Have students point out or underline words in the text that they recognize as cognates.
- Point out other morphological endings that students can recognize very easily.

  -ción = -tion
  acción, legalización
  -gión = -gion
  religión, region
  -tad = -ty
  facultad, libertad
  -dad = -ty
  universidad, ciudad
  -tud = -tude
  multitud, longitud
  -mente = -ly
  rápidamente, constantemente
  -ista = -ist
  artista, dentista, oculista
  -able = -able/-ible
  responsable, considerable
- Have students bring images from magazines, books, and the Internet that illustrate different aspects of Hispanic geography. You might assign specific topics to students or groups, and have them give brief oral presentations based on their findings.

A LEER°

A... *Let's read*

Estrategia

Guessing Meaning from Context

There are a number of easily guessable cognates in the following reading about the geography of the Hispanic world. You should also be able to guess the meaning of the underlined words—all geographical features—from context (the words around them). Remember to read the photo captions as well. And, before you start to read, scan the reading's headings, to get a sense for overall content.

La geografía del mundo° hispano

°*world*

Introducción

La geografía del mundo hispano es muy variada. ¡Hay de todo[a]!

En América

La cordillera de los Andes, Chile

En México y la América Central hay muchos volcanes activos. También hay volcanes en la cordillera de los Andes, que cruza[b] Sudamérica en el oeste del continente. En la Argentina y el Uruguay hay vastas pampas. En partes de Venezuela, Colombia, el Ecuador y el Perú hay regiones tropicales de selvas densas. En el Perú está[c] el inmenso río Amazonas (que cruza también el Brasil, donde se habla portugués). El enorme lago Titicaca está en una meseta entre[d] Bolivia y el Perú.

En el Caribe

Una playa de Puerto Rico

Cuba, Puerto Rico y la República Dominicana son tres islas situadas en el mar Caribe. Las playas del Caribe y de la Península de Yucatán son[e] populares entre[f] los turistas de todo[g] el mundo.

[a]de... *a bit of everything* [b]que... *that crosses* [c]*is* [d]*between* [e]*are* [f]*among* [g]*all around*

- Ask students to give examples of geographical features from the Hispanic world that are not found in the reading. Accept answers in English, and give the Spanish equivalents if you know them.

NATIONAL STANDARDS: Cultures

Students may associate *el Amazonas* with *el Brasil*, but the river in fact starts in *el Perú*, at the confluence of the *Ucayali* and *Marañón* rivers. About half of the Amazon's 6,280 kilometers are in *el Brasil*, the rest in *el Perú*. *El Amazonas* is considered one of the world's most important rivers, not only because of the water it carries to the Atlantic Ocean but because of the size of its basin (*la cuenca amazónica*).

En la Península Ibérica y África

Una meseta de La Mancha, España

España comparte[h] la Península Ibérica con Portugal (donde también se habla portugués). España tiene una geografía muy variada. En el norte están los Pirineos, la cordillera que separa España del resto de Europa. El país[i] está rodeado de[j] una costa magnífica. La Guinea Ecuatorial está en la costa oeste del continente de África y en varias islas.

[h]*shares* [i]*country* [j]rodeado... *surrounded by*

¿Y las ciudades[k]?

Es importante mencionar las ciudades del mundo hispano. Hay ciudades fascinantes de una gran diversidad histórica y cultural: Madrid, España; San Juan, Puerto Rico; México, D.F. (Distrito Federal); Antigua, Guatemala; Cusco, Perú; Buenos Aires, Argentina; y muchas más.[l]

[k]cities [l]muchas... *many more*

La ciudad de Montevideo, Uruguay

Comprensión

Ejemplos (*Examples*). Give examples of similar geographical features found in this country or close to it. Then give examples from the Spanish-speaking world.

MODELO: un río → *the Mississippi*, el río Orinoco

1. un lago
2. una cordillera
3. un río
4. una isla
5. una playa
6. una costa
7. un mar
8. un volcán
9. una península

Possible answers: 1. Lake Tahoe, *el lago Titicaca* **2.** the Rocky Mountains, (*la cordillera de*) *los Andes* **3.** the Missouri, *el río Amazonas* **4.** Manhattan, la isla de *Puerto Rico* **5.** Miami Beach, *la playa de la península de Yucatán* **6.** the Pacific Northwest, *la costa de España* **7.** the Mediterranean, *el mar Caribe* **8.** Mt. Shasta, *los volcanes de los Andes* **9.** the Gaspe Peninsula, *la península de Yucatán*

Comprensión

Note

This activity asks students to demonstrate their understanding of the words underlined in the reading and of other words from the reading.

Suggestion

Have students do this activity in pairs. Then go through the items, asking students to give their examples orally.

Follow-up

Remind students of the meanings of *¿Dónde?* and *¿Qué?* (*Where?* and *What?*), then ask questions to practice new vocabulary from this reading passage. For example:

¿Dónde hay pampas?
¿Dónde hay volcanes?
¿Qué forman España y Portugal?
¿Qué son Cuba, Puerto Rico y la República Dominicana? ¿Dónde están?

Optional Follow-up

Have students write short sentences with the following words, based on information in *A leer* or on their own knowledge of world geography. Offer the following models as a guide.

MODELOS: *una ciudad → Buenos Aires es una ciudad de la Argentina.*
un lago → En el Canadá hay muchos lagos.

1. *una ciudad*
2. *una capital*
3. *un lago*
4. *un volcán*
5. *una playa*
6. *una isla*
7. *una nación*
8. *una península*
9. *un río*
10. *un mar*

NATIONAL STANDARDS: Comparisons

Have students compare the geographical diversity of the Spanish-speaking world with the geography of this country. How many features can they match? Which ones are related? (For example, the Andes, the Rockies, and the Pacific Ring of Fire.)

En resumen: En este capítulo

Vocabulario

Notes

- Students are *not* expected to know every word they have used in *Cap. 1*. Only active vocabulary is listed here.
- In subsequent chapters of *Puntos de partida,* end-of-chapter vocabulary lists will be completely bilingual in most cases. In this list, however, many words and expressions are given in Spanish only to help students get used to dealing directly with Spanish without translation, because many students are already familiar with some basic Spanish vocabulary (even if they have not studied Spanish formally), and because the equivalents of all non-translated words are easy to find in the preceding pages of the short *Cap. 1*.

Suggestions

- If you have not already done so, use the material from the last few pages of the book to familiarize students with frequently used classroom commands and other useful phrases.
- You should stress the importance of learning the words in the group titles (e.g., *saludos*). If students learn those words, it will be easier for you to keep your classes (and quizzes and exams!) in Spanish as much as possible.
- You may wish to stress the importance of students' learning *Las palabras interrogativas* and *Palabras adicionales*. "Connector" words like *pero, también,* and so on will help students express themselves more easily.
- Subsequent chapters all have a review section, called *Un poco de todo*. To review much of this chapter's content, put this chart on the board and ask students to complete it.

FORMAL	INFORMAL
usted	______
______	eres
______	¿Cómo te llamas?
¿Cómo está?	______
______	¿De dónde eres?
¿Le gusta?	______

Vocabulario personal

Suggestions

- Call students' attention to the *Vocabulario personal* box when you preview the book's chapter structure.
- When you prepare students for a chapter quiz or exam, it is a good idea to ask them to jot down in the *Vocabulario personal* box any additional vocabulary that you want them to know.

Heritage Speakers

Anime a los estudiantes hispanohablantes de la clase a presentar diálogos en el salón de clase, usando los saludos y otras expresiones de cortesía.

EN RESUMEN En este capítulo

LearnSmart

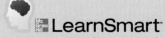

Visit **www.connectspanish.com** to practice the vocabulary and grammar points covered in this chapter.

Vocabulario

Although you have used and heard many words in this first chapter of *Puntos de partida*, the following words are the ones considered to be active vocabulary. Be sure that you know all of them, including the meaning of the group titles, before beginning **Capítulo 2.**

Saludos y expresiones de cortesía

Buenos días. Buenas tardes. Buenas noches.
Muy buenas.
¡Hola! ¿Qué tal? ¿Cómo está? ¿Cómo estás?
Muy bien. Regular. Bien.
¿Y tú? ¿Y usted?
Adiós. Hasta mañana. Hasta luego. Nos vemos.

¿Cómo te llamas? ¿Cómo se llama usted?
Me llamo ______.

¿De dónde eres (tú)? ¿De dónde es (usted)?
(Yo) Soy de ______.

señor (Sr.), señora (Sra.), señorita (Srta.)
profesor, profesora

Gracias. Muchas gracias.
De nada. No hay de qué.
Por favor. Perdón. (Con) Permiso.
Mucho gusto. Igualmente. Encantado/a.

el saludo	greeting

¿Cómo es usted?

ser: soy, eres, es

All forms of infinitives highlighted in red can be found in Appendix 5.

Los números del 0 al 30

cero	**diez**	**veinte**
uno	**once**	**treinta**
dos	**doce**	
tres	**trece**	
cuatro	**catorce**	
cinco	**quince**	
seis	**dieciséis**	
siete	**diecisiete**	
ocho	**dieciocho**	
nueve	**diecinueve**	

Los gustos y preferencias

¿Te gusta ______? ¿(A usted) Le gusta ______?
(Sí,) Me gusta ______. (No,) No me gusta ______.

los gustos	likes

¿Qué hora es?

es la... , son las...
y/menos cuarto (quince)
y media (treinta)
en punto
de la mañana (tarde, noche)
¿a qué hora... ?, a la(s)...

Las palabras interrogatives

¿cómo?	how?; what?
¿dónde?	where?
¿qué?	what?
¿quién?	Who?

Palabras adicionales

sí/no	yes/no
hay	there is/are
no hay	there is not / are not
¿hay?	is there / are there?
hoy/mañana	today/tomorrow
y/o	and/or
a	to; at (*with time*)
de	of; from
en	in; on; at
pero	but
también	also
la palabra	word

Vocabulario personal

Use this space for other words and phrases you learn in this chapter.

Español	**Inglés**

An Introduction to the Rest of…

Puntos de partida

Puntos de partida

Each chapter of the rest of this textbook has a chapter theme and follows a consistent organization. In addition, every chapter focuses on one or more countries of the Spanish-speaking world.

The opening pages of the chapter: Here you will begin to learn about the country or countries of focus as well as see an overview of the chapter's vocabulary and grammar content in **En este capítulo.**

Vocabulario: Preparación: This section presents vocabulary related to each chapter's theme.

Pronunciación: Found in **Capítulos 2–4,** this section presents important aspects of Spanish pronunciation and orthography.

Gramática: This section presents grammar points in context and offers many opportunities for you to practice Spanish, alone and with a partner or group. In a subsection of **Gramática** called **Un poco de todo** (*A bit of everything*), you will practice all of the grammar points from the chapter plus review important grammar topics from previous chapters.

TelePuntos: Here you can watch a video to learn more about what's happening in the Spanish-speaking world, as well as about the hosts of ***Salu2* (Saludos),** a Spanish-language news program from the Los Angeles area that you learned about in **Capítulo 1.**

A leer (*Let's read*)**:** In this reading section, you will learn more about the chapter's country of focus (**Lectura cultural**) and also read authentic materials from the Spanish-speaking world (**Del mundo hispano**), including literature.

A escuchar (*Let's listen*)**:** On this page you will practice authentic listening tasks and learn about Hispanic music.

A escribir (*Let's write*)**:** Here you will practice real-world writing tasks in Spanish.

En resumen: En este capítulo: This section shows you vocabulary and grammar you need to know from each chapter.

Notes

- The following sections are new to this edition of *Puntos de partida: TelePuntos*, *A leer* (replacing *Lectura*), *A escuchar*, and *A escribir* (replacing *Redacción*).
- Remember that vocabulary that becomes active in exercises and activities will be noted in these annotations.

Suggestion

It is a good idea to take class time to "walk" students through *Cap. 2*, to be sure that they understand the consistent structure of the rest of the chapters of the text. All ancillary materials (those for students and those for instructors) will be coordinated with the major headings of this repeating chapter structure.

Multimedia: The Internet

Spanish Internet sites are a wonderful resource for any class, and suggestions in the Instructor's Edition will often propose that you ask students to do an Internet search for information. Specific sites are provided on occasion, but Internet sites are often unstable, even those maintained by governments and universities, and information obtained on the Internet is not always reliable. For this reason, it is better to show students how to do good Internet searches in Spanish. Direct them to Spanish-language search engines (*Google en espanol* is a good one), and suggest that they take advantage of library resources on their campus to learn how to do proper Internet searches and identify reputable sites.

Chapter Opening Photo and Chapter Theme

In this repeating section of this Instructor's Edition, you will find questions in Spanish that will allow you to discuss the photo and introduce the chapter's theme. When you use them in this chapter, be aware of the needs of true beginning students; use gestures, pantomime, and write key words on the board. Be content with *sí/no* answers in many cases.

Chapter Theme–Related Questions

- *¿Es Ud. un(a) estudiante de tiempo* (new word) *completo? ¿de tiempo parcial?*
- *¿Es Ud. un estudiante típico / una estudiante típica?*
- (Name of your university), *¿es grande o pequeña* (new words)*? ¿urbana o rural?*
- *¿Hay residencias* (new word) *para los estudiantes? ¿Cómo se llaman?*
- *¿Cómo se llama la biblioteca más grande* (new words)*?*
- *¿Estudia Ud. matemáticas/literatura/historia/sicología/sociología/biología?*

Reciclado

Use vocabulary and grammar from the previous chapter to discuss the photo. Emphasize cognate adjectives and *ser* to describe the people in this photo.

Reciclado: Encourage students to generate cognate adjectives by asking:

- *¿Cómo son los estudiantes de* ______ (name of university)*?*
- *¿Son inteligentes? ¿elegantes? ¿idealistas? ¿interesantes? ¿pesimistas? ¿responsables? ¿serios? ¿extrovertidos?*

You can also call on individual students to provide additional adjectives describing the students at your university.

Los Estados Unidos de América

Datos esenciales

The Instructor's Edition will provide basic information about each chapter's country of focus on this chapter opening spread. Additional information (such as geographical features, historical timelines, holidays, and so on) can be found in the IM. There is also additional information about the country of focus in *A leer: Lectura cultural* and *A escuchar* (in both the student text and the Instructor's Edition).

Nombre oficial: *Estados Unidos de América*
Lema: *«In God We Trust»*
Capital: *Washington, D.C.*

2 En la universidad

En un salón de clase universitario

- Are there many Hispanic students at your college or university? What about Hispanic professors?
- What languages are taught on your campus? Which is the most popular?
- Is there a foreign language requirement on your campus? Are there requirements for math or science?

McGraw Hill connect SPANISH

www.connectspanish.com

Resources

For Students

- Connect Spanish (**www.connectspanish.com**), which contains all content from the following resources, as well as the *Mundo interactivo scenarios,* the LearnSmart adaptive learning system, and more!
- **Physical Resources:** Workbook / Laboratory Manual, Laboratory Audio Program, DVD

For Instructors

- Connect Spanish (**www.connectspanish.com**), which contains access to all student sections of Connect Spanish, as well as helpful time-saving tools and resources such as an integrated gradebook, Instructor's Manual, Testing Program, digital transparencies, Audioscript, Videoscript, and more!

Los Estados Unidos de América

310 (trescientos diez) millones de habitantes

- En los Estados Unidos hay más de 50 (cincuenta) millones de personas de origen hispano.
- Es el cuarto (*fourth*) país del mundo por (*country of the world in*) número de hispanohablantes.
- En todo el territorio estadounidense, especialmente en el suroeste, hay lugares (*places*) con nombres (*names*) en español.

En este capítulo

CONTENT / **CONTENIDO**	OBJECTIVES / **OBJETIVOS**
Classroom vocabulary 26, academic subjects 28	To talk about your academic environment and what you are studying
Diphthongs and linking 31	To learn more about Spanish pronunciation
Singular and plural nouns, gender, and articles 32, 35	To name people, places, things, and ideas
Verbs that end in **-ar**, subject pronouns 38	To express actions
Questions 30, 45	To form questions in several ways
Los Estados Unidos de América 52	To learn about the important Hispanic presence in the United States

Ciudades principales: *Nueva York, Los Ángeles, Chicago, Houston, Phoenix, Filadelfia, San Antonio, San Diego, Dallas*

Lengua oficial: *No hay lengua oficial, aunque el inglés es la lengua de hecho.*

Población hispana total, según país de origen: *61% de México, 12% de Puerto Rico, 4% de Cuba, 23% del resto de los países*

Jefe de estado actual: *el Presidente Barack Obama, demócrata, desde 2009*

Forma de gobierno: *República democrática*

Moneda: *el dólar estadounidense*

Religión: *51% protestantes, 24% católicos, 13% otras religiones, 12% sin religión*

Point out

Remind students that the 1500s and 1600s were a time of intense Spanish exploration in many parts of what is now the continental United States, long before the arrival of the Pilgrims and before American independence in 1776 (at which time over half of what is now the United States was controlled by Spain). Additional facts to discuss include:
1. 1700–1776 = the founding of Spanish missions in Arizona and California;
2. 1846–1848 = the war with Mexico that ended with the treaty of Guadalupe Hidalgo (1848), in which large parts of what is now the American South and Southwest were ceded to the United States by the Mexican government;
3. 1898 = the Spanish American war, a result of which was that Puerto Rico became a U.S. territory.

Suggestions

- Discuss U.S. Hispanics who have been in the news in the last few years. Examples from the recent past include: *Bill Richardson, gobernador del estado de Nuevo México; Antonio Villaraigosa, alcalde de Los Ángeles; Sonia Sotomayor, primera hispana en la Corte Suprema.*
- See additional suggestions in the IM.

Multimedia

The *Instructor's Manual* (IM) provides suggestions for using the multimedia materials in the classroom.

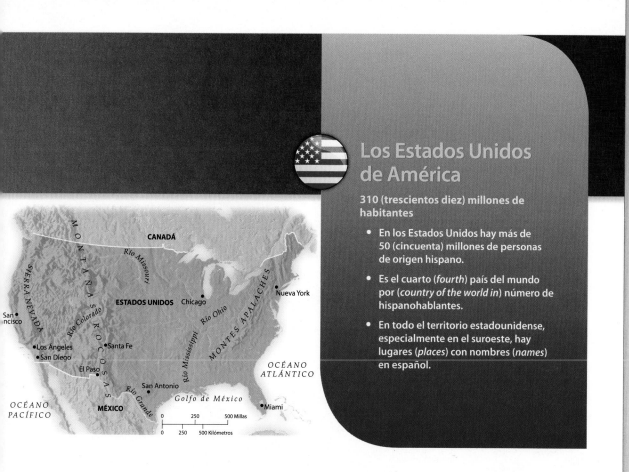

Vocabulario: Preparación
En el salón de clase
Notes

- See the model for vocabulary presentation and other material in the *Cap. 2 Vocabulario: Preparación* section of "Chapter-by-Chapter Supplementary Materials" in the IM.
- This first vocabulary list is relatively short. For true beginners, it will be appropriately challenging.
- Optional vocabulary: *el borrador, la carpeta, el cartel* (*el afiche, el póster*), *el estadio, el gimnasio, el laboratorio* (*de lenguas*), *las luces, la pizarra, el pupitre, el reloj, el sacapuntas, la tiza* (*el clarión, el yeso*).

Suggestions

- Hold up objects or photographs, or point to class members; model pronunciation while students listen. Use both definite and indefinite articles. Students will learn the concept of gender later. For now, they should only listen to the words.
- Pronounce seven or eight vocabulary words from this section. Encourage students to identify the "class" of the word, that is, whether it responds to *¿Dónde?, ¿Qué?,* or *¿Quién?*
- Identify and, at times, misidentify several objects or persons (point to them, show pictures, and so on). Have students respond *sí/no* or *correcto/incorrecto.*
- Indicate objects or persons and offer a choice: *¿Qué es esto, una mesa o una silla?* Have students answer in Spanish.
- Point out the differentiation between *el salón de clase* (= classroom) and *la clase* (= a group of students; an academic course or class).
- Emphasize the difference between *librería* and *biblioteca.*
- **Pronunciación:** See Pronunciation Notes, IM.
- Check students' comprehension by asking questions such as these (*¿Cierto o falso?*).
  1. *Una librería es un lugar. No es una persona.* (*cierto*)
  2. *La residencia es para los profesores.* (*falso*)
  3. *Un consejero es una persona. No es un animal.* (*cierto*)

VOCABULARIO Preparación

En el salón de clase

¿DÓNDE? **Lugares en la universidad**

la biblioteca	the library
la cafetería	the cafeteria
el edificio	the building
la librería	the bookstore
la oficina	the office
la residencia	the dormitory
el salón de clase	the classroom

¿QUIÉN? **Personas**

el bibliotecario	the (male) librarian
la bibliotecaria	the (female) librarian
el compañero (de clase)	the (male) classmate
la compañera (de clase)	the (female) classmate
el compañero de cuarto	the (male) roommate
la compañera de cuarto	the (female) roommate
el consejero	the (male) advisor
la consejera	the (female) advisor
el hombre	the man
la mujer	the woman
el secretario	the (male) secretary
la secretaria	the (female) secretary

¿QUÉ? **Objetos**

la computadora (portátil)	(laptop) computer
el dinero	money
el pizarrón (blanco)	(white) board
el teléfono (celular)	(cellular) telephone

Culture

In most Hispanic countries, there is no equivalent of an academic or guidance counselor like those in this country.

Multimedia: Audio

Students can listen to and practice this chapter's vocabulary in Connect Spanish: **www.connectspanish.com.**

Resources: Transparency 7

Classroom Scene

Conversación

A. Identificaciones. ¿Es hombre o mujer?

MODELO: ¿El profesor? ⟶ Es hombre.

1. ¿La consejera? Es mujer.
2. ¿La estudiante? Es mujer.
3. ¿El secretario? Es hombre.
4. ¿El estudiante? Es hombre.
5. ¿La bibliotecaria? Es mujer.
6. ¿El compañero de cuarto? Es hombre.

B. ¿Dónde están (*are they*)**?** Tell where these people are and identify the numbered people and things.

MODELO: El dibujo 1: **Están** en el salón de clase.
1 ⟶ la profesora, 2 ⟶ la estudiante,...

Así se dice

el bolígrafo = la pluma, el birome, el esfero
la calculadora = la máquina de calcular
la computadora = el computador (*Latin America*), el ordenador (*Spain*)
la computadora portátil = el portátil (*Latin America, Spain*)
el escritorio = el mesabanco
el pizarrón = el encerado, la pizarra, el tablero
el salón de clase = el aula, la sala (de clase)

In general, use **el profesor / la profesora** to refer to a college teacher, or **el doctor / la doctora**, as appropriate. However, there are many institutional and national differences in usage. Ask your instructor what title to use to address or refer to him or her.

Young people often shorten some words. Can you guess what **el boli** and **la profe** mean?

1.

2.

3.

Con. B: Answers: Drawing 1. *Están en el salón de clase.* **1.** *la profesora* **2.** *la estudiante* **3.** *el papel* **4.** *la ventana* **5.** *la mesa* **6.** *el lápiz* **7.** *la computadora portátil* **8.** la *calculadora* **9.** *el pizarrón (blanco)* **Drawing 2.** *Están en la biblioteca.* **1.** *el estudiante* **2.** *la estudiante* **3.** *el bibliotecario* **4.** *el diccionario* **5.** *el libro* **6.** *el cuaderno* **7.** *el escritorio* **8.** *la silla* **9.** *el (teléfono) celular* **Drawing 3.** *Están en la librería.* **1.** *la estudiante* **2.** *el lápiz* **3.** *el cuaderno* **4.** *el bolígrafo* **5.** *la mochila* **6.** *el dinero*

Bright Idea

Note

Bright Idea annotations have been provided by users of *Puntos de partida*. Look for these ideas in every chapter.

Suggestion

Present the concept of false cognates, then present the following false cognates related to this chapter's theme vocabulary: *la carpeta, la librería* (active here), *el colegio, la materia* (active, p. 28), *el idioma, las notas, la residencia* (active here).

Then discuss with students the fact that there is no direct equivalent in Spanish for English *college* or *community college. Secondary education* is called *el colegio, la preparatoria* (*la prepa*), or *la* (*educación*) *secundaria.* The concepts of *college* or *university* are generally expressed by *la universidad.*

Con. A: Follow-up

Have students give male counterparts of *la profesora, la secretaria, la estudiante, la consejera, la compañera de cuarto.* Then have them give the female counterparts of *el profesor, el consejero, el compañero de cuarto.*

Con. B: Suggestions

- Emphasize the use of *están* for giving location. Point out that it is the plural form (*they are*, as in the activity's title) and tell students that they will learn more about the verb *estar* later on in this chapter.
- Give statements about the drawings. Have students tell whether statements are true or false. Here are some samples for drawing 1.
  1. *Hay un consejero en el salón de clase.* (*falso*)
  2. *Hay 20 estudiantes en la clase.* (*falso*)
  3. *Hay una profesora.* (*cierto*)

Con. B: Variations

- Present *el ⟶ un, la ⟶ una* before doing this variation. Then have students identify persons and objects, using short sentences: *Hay un profesor / una profesora. Hay un(a)...*
- Have students tell where individual objects and persons are, using short complete sentences: *La estudiante está en la biblioteca.*

Heritage Speakers

- Anime a los hispanohablantes a nombrar otros objetos en el salón de clase, por ejemplo: *el reloj de pared, la luz,* etcétera.
- Pídales que expliquen en inglés la diferencia entre *dormitorio* (=*habitación*) y *residencia estudiantil* (=*dorm*).
- La palabra *bolígrafo* se usa mayormente en España. Anime a los hispanohablentes a indicar cómo se dice *bolígrafo* en su casa o en el país de donde su familia (*la pluma, el birome, el lapicero*).

Resources: Transparency 8

Nota cultural

Note

All *Notas culturales* are in Spanish in this edition of *Puntos de partida*. In early chapters, they are in list or graph form, becoming more developed narratives as students' ability to read Spanish increases. All *Notas culturales* end with a personal or "thought" question for students to answer. Comprehension questions appear in the Instructor's Edition.

Suggestion

Have students talk about the oldest universities in this country. Which ones are they? Where are they located? Compare the locations of these universities to the ones mentioned in the *Nota*. What was important about the cities? What do they have in common? Are they still significant social and/or economic centers?

Notes

- The very first university in the western hemisphere was *la Universidad de Santo Domingo*, founded in 1538 in what is now the Dominican Republic. Contrast that date with the ones given in the next point.
- Here are some of the oldest universities of the United States and Canada: Harvard University (1636), College of William and Mary (1693), Université Laval (1663).

Comprensión

1. *De las universidades que funcionan todavía, ¿cuál es la más antigua?* (*la Universidad de Salamanca*)
2. *Nombra* (new word) *tres países hispanohablantes con universidades muy antiguas.* (*España, el Perú, la Argentina, Bolivia, Guatemala, Cuba*)

Las materias

Suggestions

- Model the names of academic subjects. Have students raise their hand each time they hear the name of a subject that they are taking.
- Point out the many cognates that end in *-ía* and *-ción*.
- **Pronunciación:** See Pronunciation Notes, IM.
- Have students generate as many words as possible that they associate with the following: *las ciencias, la sicología, la biblioteca, la administración de empresas.*
- Offer optional vocabulary: *la antropología, la biología, la contabilidad* (accounting), *la geografía, la geología, la ingeniería, el mercadeo, el periodismo.*

Resources: Transparency 9

Nota **cultural**

Las universidades en el mundo° hispano — *world*

Las universidades más antiguas[a] del mundo hispano que funcionan todavía[b] son las siguientes.[c]

En España

- la Universidad de Salamanca, Salamanca (1220 = mil doscientos veinte)

En la América Latina

- la Universidad de San Marcos, ahora[d] la Universidad Nacional Mayor de San Marcos, Lima, Perú (1551 = mil quinientos cincuenta y uno)
- la Universidad de Córdoba, ahora la Universidad Nacional de Córdoba, Argentina (1621 = mil seiscientos veintiuno)
- la Universidad San Francisco Xavier de Chuquisaca, Sucre, Bolivia (1624 = mil seiscientos veinticuatro)
- la Universidad de San Carlos de Guatemala, Antigua, Guatemala (1676 = mil seiscientos setenta y seis)
- la Universidad de San Antonio Abad, ahora la Universidad Nacional de San Antonio Abad del Cusco, Perú (1692 = mil seiscientos noventa y dos)

El *campus* de la Universidad de San Marcos, en Lima, Perú

- la Universidad de San Jerónimo, ahora la Universidad de La Habana, Cuba (1728 = mil setecientos veintiocho)

¿Cuál es la universidad más antigua de su país[e]?

[a]más... *oldest* [b]que... *that are still in existence* [c]las... *the following* [d]*now* [e]su... *your country*

Las materias° — Las... *Subject areas*

The names for most of these subject areas are cognates. See if you can recognize their meaning without looking at the English equivalent. You should learn in particular the names of subject areas that are of interest to you.

la administración de empresas	business administration
las comunicaciones	communications
la economía	economics
el español	Spanish
la filosofía	philosophy
la literatura	literature
las matemáticas	mathematics
la sociología	sociology

Así se dice

la administración de empresas = el comercio, los negocios (*U.S.*)
la computación = la informática (*Spain*)
el español = el castellano (*Spain, Latin America*)

las ciencias	sciences
naturales	natural
políticas	political
sociales	social
las humanidades	humanities
las lenguas (extranjeras)	(foreign) languages

NATIONAL STANDARDS: Connections

Provide information students may need to complete *Con. A* on p. 29.

- James D. Watson (1928–) and Francis Crick (1916–2004): Co-creators of the double helix molecular model of DNA, along with Maurice Wilkins
- Sigmund Freud (1856–1939): Austrian author and father of psychoanalysis
- B.F. Skinner (1904–1990): American psychologist and founder of the school of psychology known as Behaviorism
- Socrates (470 B.C.–399 B.C.): A celebrated Greek philosopher born in Athens, Greece

(Cont.)

Conversación

A. Asociaciones. ¿Qué materia(s) asocia usted con (*with*) las siguientes (*following*) personas y cosas (*things*)?

1. Watson and Crick las ciencias naturales
2. el doctor Sigmund Freud, el profesor B.F. Skinner la sicología
3. CNN, NBC, ESPN las comunicaciones
4. Sócrates, Aristóteles la filosofía
5. Gabriel García Márquez, J.K. Rowling la literatura
6. Frida Kahlo, Pablo Picasso el arte
7. Microsoft, IBM la computación
8. la civilización azteca, la Guerra (*War*) Civil americana la historia

B. ¿Qué estudia usted? Create sentences about your academic interests by using one word or phrase from each column. Can you guess the meaning of the phrases in the left-hand column? If you need help, they are translated at the bottom of the page*.

1. (No) Estudio _____. 2. (No) Deseo estudiar _____. 3. (No) Necesito estudiar _____. 4. (No) Me gusta estudiar _____.	+	español, francés, inglés arte, filosofía, literatura, música ciencias políticas, historia antropología, sicología, sociología biología, física, química matemáticas, computación ¿ ?

Con. A: Extension
Hold up various books that students have at their desks and have them identify by the titles the subjects for which they use the books. Then have students identify the classes for which they might need the following books: *Aristóteles, La revolución de los zares, La familia, Cómo usar el telescopio, Los microbios.*

Vocabulario útil

la contabilidad	accounting
la ingeniería	engineering
el mercadeo	marketing
el periodismo	journalism

These boxes will help you review content you already know on which new material is based.

¿Recuerda usted?°

°¿Recuerda... *Do you remember?*

In **Capítulo 1,** you used a number of interrogative words to get information: **¿cómo?, ¿dónde?, ¿qué?,** and **¿quién?** What do those words mean in the following sentences?

1. ¿Cómo estás? How?
2. ¿Cómo es usted? What?
3. ¿De dónde eres? Where?
4. ¿Qué hora es? What?
5. ¿Quién es la consejera? Who?

As you listen to your instructor say questions with those words, you will notice that, in Spanish, the voice falls at the end of questions that begin with interrogative words.

¿Qué hora es? ¿Cómo es usted?

You will learn more about interrogatives in the **Nota comunicativa** on the next page and in **Gramática 4** in this chapter.

an interrogative word / **una palabra interrogativa** = a word used to ask a question about specific information (*who?, where?,* and so on)

*1. *I'm studying* (*I'm not studying*) **2.** *I want to study* (*I don't want to study*) **3.** *I need to study* (*I don't need to study*) **4.** *I like to study* (*I don't like to study*)

Con. A: Variation
Have students work in pairs. One student names a textbook or topic in English and the other gives subject matter in Spanish. Model the activity and emphasize use of the definite article with name of subject if you wish.

Con. A: Note
Active vocabulary: *con*

Con. B: Suggestion
Model names of academic subjects before asking for student responses. Encourage students to listen to their classmates. Check for comprehension: *Tim, ¿qué estudia Emily?*

Con. B: Variation
Invite students to play the role of *consejero/a* and advise incoming freshmen on what to study, depending on their majors. Follow these models: *Usted necesita estudiar _____. Usted necesita tomar _____ créditos de _____.*

Con. B: Reciclado and Preview
This activity recycles the *me gusta* + noun construction from *Cap. 1.* It also previews the concept of the first person singular present tense verb ending (*-o*) as well as how to make conjugated verbs negative.

¿Recuerda usted?
Note
This is the first *¿Recuerda usted?* feature of *Puntos de partida.* Its purpose is to review content on which new content is based. Answers to the brief exercises in these sections are available at **www.connectspanish.com**.

Reciclado
Review all questions with interrogative words from *Cap. 1,* stressing falling intonation.

Heritage Speakers
Anime a los hispanohablantes a hablar de una persona famosa del país de origen de su familia o que nombren a algunos hispanos famosos de este país.

- Aristotle (384 B.C.–322 B.C.): Greek philosopher and student of Plato, who was a student of Socrates
- Gabriel García Márquez (1927–): Colombian author of *Cien años de soledad* (*100 Years of Solitude*) and winner of the Nobel Prize in Literature (1982)
- J. K. Rowling (1965–): Born in Chepstow, Gwent, England, author of the *Harry Potter* series
- Frida Kahlo (1907–1954): Mexican surrealist artist who was married to Diego Rivera
- Pablo Picasso (1881–1973): Famous Spanish painter born in Malaga, Spain

Nota comunicativa

Note

Remember that all material in *Nota comunicativa* boxes is active unless otherwise indicated.

Suggestions

- Have students tell what interrogative words they associate with the following information. Then have them ask the questions that would result in these answers.
    1. *¡A las tres en punto!*
    2. *De Nicaragua.*
    3. *Soy profesor.*
    4. *Muy bien, gracias.*
    5. *¡Es muy arrogante!*
    6. *Hay 5 millones (de habitantes).*
    7. *Dos pesos.*
    8. *(La capital) Es Caracas.*
    9. *Es un instrumento musical.*
    10. *Son las once.*
- Be sure to emphasize falling intonation in questions with interrogative words.

Notes

- Although they are presented here, the interrogatives *¿cuántos?/¿cuántas?* are not emphasized in this text until adjective agreement is presented in *Gram. 6* (*Cap. 2*). Until then, students will always be guided as to which form to use (as in *Con. C*).
- Plural forms of most interrogatives are presented in *Cap. 9*.

Con. C: Suggestions

- Call students' attention to the words and letters in boldface type. They mark the use of different persons, and students should be able to relate them to phrases that they learned in *Cap. 1: me llamo, te llamas, me gusta, te gusta.* Also, students' attention to the possessives *mi* and *tu*, which are not yet active material but which students should be able to relate to *me* and *te*. It is not necessary to explain all of the grammar that is used in this activity; for now, students just need to notice the features that this "conversation" requires.
- Ask students to take notes on what their partner says in *Paso 2*, so that you can do the suggested follow-up activity and/or *Redacción*.

Con. C: Follow-up

- Put the following third person words and phrases on the board: *Estudia... Su materia favorita / profesor favorito / profesora favorita... Le gusta...*
- Model the conversation with one student, then model telling the class what he/she said, using the preceding words.
- Ask several students to share what they learned from their partner with the whole class.

Nota **comunicativa**

Las palabras interrogativas

Use **¿qué?** to mean *what?* when you are asking for a definition or an explanation. Use **¿cuál?** to mean *what?* in all other circumstances. You will learn more about using these words in **Gramática 22 (Capítulo 9).**

¿Qué es un hospital?	**¿Cuál** es la capital de Colombia?
¿Qué es esto (*this*)?	**¿Cuál** es tu materia favorita?

Guess the meaning of the following interrogatives from the context in which they appear.

1. —**¿Cuándo** es la clase? —Es mañana, a las nueve.
2. —**¿Cuánto** cuesta (*costs*) el cuaderno? —Dos dólares.
3. —**¿Cuántos** estudiantes hay en la clase? —Hay quince.
4. —**¿Cuántas** naciones hay en Centroamérica? —Hay siete.

Remember to drop your voice at the end of a question that begins with a Spanish interrogative word, the opposite of what happens in English, where the voice usually rises at the end of such questions. This feature of Spanish may cause you to "hear" a Spanish question as a statement at first, but you'll get used to it. Compare these questions.

¿Qué es un tren?	*What's a train?*
¿Cuándo es el programa?	*When is the program?*

You will use many of the preceding interrogative words in **Conversación C.**

C. Intercambios (*Exchanges*)

¿Dónde le gusta estudiar a usted?

Paso 1. Answer the following questions. Pay attention to the words and endings in bold—you have seen most of them before and should be able to guess what they mean.

1. —¿Qué **estudias** este (*this*) semestre/trimestre?
   —**Estudio** ______________________.
2. —¿Cuál es **tu** (*your*) materia favorita?
   —**Mi** materia favorita es el/la ______________________.
3. —¿Quién es **tu** profesor favorito o profesora favorita?
   —**Mi** profesor favorito / profesora favorita es ______________________. Es el profesor / la profesora de ______________ (materia).
4. —¿Cuántas horas **estudias** por día (*per day*)?
   —**Estudio** ______________ horas por día.
5. —¿Dónde **estudias**?
   —**Estudio** en ______________ (la residencia, la biblioteca, mi cuarto, la cafetería...).
6. —¿**Te gusta** estudiar por (*in*) la mañana, por la tarde o por la noche (*at night*)?
   —**Me gusta** estudiar por ______________________.

Estrategia

Use **el** or **la** with a title when talking about a person, as in item 3.

el profesor Arana
la señora Castellano
el doctor Brook

Paso 2. Now practice the conversation in **Paso 1** with a classmate. Use **¿Y tú?** to ask about your partner.

MODELO: **ESTUDIANTE 1:** ¿Qué **estudias** este semestre/trimestre?
ESTUDIANTE 2: **Estudio** matemáticas, historia, literatura y español. ¿Y tú?
ESTUDIANTE 1: **Yo estudio** español, biología, física y arte.

Mundo interactivo

You should now be prepared to work with Scenario 1, Activity 3 in Connect Spanish (**www.connectspanish.com**).

PRONUNCIACIÓN

Diphthongs and Linking

¿Recuerda usted?

Review what you already know about the pronunciation of Spanish vowels by saying the following names and nicknames aloud.

1. Ana **2.** Pepe **3.** Pili **4.** Momo **5.** Lulú

Two successive weak vowels **(i, u)** or a combination of a strong vowel **(a, e, o)** and a weak vowel **(i, u)** are pronounced as a single syllable in Spanish, forming a *diphthong* **(un diptongo): L*ui*s, s*ie*te, c*ua*derno.**

When words are combined to form phrases, clauses, and sentences, they are linked together in pronunciation. In spoken Spanish, it is often difficult to hear the word boundaries—that is, where one word ends and another begins.

a diphthong / **un diptongo** = a combination of two vowel sounds in one syllable

Práctica

A. Vocales. Más práctica con las vocales.

1. hablar	regular	reservar	compañera
2. trece	clase	papel	general
3. pizarrón	oficina	bolígrafo	libro
4. hombre	profesor	dólares	los
5. universidad	gusto	lugar	mujer

B. Diptongos. Practique las siguientes (*following*) palabras.

1. historia	secretaria	gracias	estudiante	materia
2. bien	Oviedo	siete	ciencias	diez
3. secretario	biblioteca	adiós	diccionario	Antonio
4. cuaderno	Eduardo	el Ecuador	Guatemala	Managua
5. bueno	nueve	luego	pueblo	Venezuela

C. Frases y oraciones (*sentences*)**.** Practice saying each phrase or sentence as if it were one long word, pronounced without a pause.

1. el papel y el lápiz
2. la profesora y la estudiante
3. las ciencias y las matemáticas
4. la historia y la sicología
5. la secretaria y el profesor
6. el inglés y el español
7. la clase en la biblioteca
8. el libro en la librería
9. Es la una y media.
10. Hay siete estudiantes en la oficina.
11. No estoy muy bien.
12. No hay consejero aquí (*here*).

Prác. C: Suggestion
Before students attempt to pronounce the phrases, do the activity as a dictation, and emphasize the linking effect.

Prác. C: Extension
13. *Hay siete edificios en la universidad.*
14. *Estudio historia y comercio.*
15. *Deseo estudiar computación y matemáticas.*
16. *Necesito un diccionario y una mochila.*

Con. C: Redacción

- *Redacción* activities appear at least twice per chapter, at least once in *Vocabulario: Preparación* and at least once in *Gramática.* These activities can be assigned when they occur or later on in your coverage of the chapter. They should be adapted to fit your classes, including specifications for length and other details.
- Begin this first brief writing assignment by following steps 1 and 2 in *Con. C.*
- Based on the notes taken during their "conversation," ask students to write 6 sentences about their partner. Students should use their partner's name in the first sentence.
- Collect the writing assignment and read some of the best and/or most interesting ones to the class without identifying the student described. Ask the class to guess the name of the student.

Pronunciación

Notes

- Hint for remembering weak vowels: *u* and *i* are weak.
- Tell students that the letter *y* is pronounced like the vowel *i* when standing alone (*y* means *and*) or when ending a word (*¡ay!, hay*).

Preliminary Exercise

Pronounce these English and Spanish words in random order. Have students identify each as *español* or *inglés.*

ENGLISH	SPANISH
Ray	*rey*
lay	*ley*
eye	*hay*
soy	*soy*

Prác. A: Suggestion

Reciclado: Review the pronunciation of single vowel sounds before beginning the activity.

Prác. A: Note

Point out that *hombre* should not be pronounced as *hambre*; *dólares* should not sound like *dolores.*

Prác. B: Follow-up

Have students sound out the vowels and diphthongs first; then add consonant sounds.

1. *la civilización india*
2. *los negocios internacionales*
3. *una bibliotecaria italiana*
4. *una especialidad fascinante*
5. *los tiempos verbales*

Heritage Speakers

Escriba la siguiente canción en el pizarrón para que los estudiantes la copien. Pídales que graben las voces de personas hispanohablantes a quienes ellos conocen mientras aquellas lean la canción. Luego toque las grabaciones en el salón de clase para que los estudiantes oigan la variedad de acentos.

¡Al Uruguay, guay!
Yo no voy, voy
porque temo naufragar.
Mándeme a París
si es que le da igual.

¿Recuerda usted?

Note the occasional insertion of brief exercises based on English grammar into the *¿Recuerda usted?* boxes, grammar explanation, and Instructor's Edition annotations.

Gramática 1

Singular Nouns: Gender and Articles

Notes

- The presentation device in *Gramática en acción* (*GEA*) introduces material that appears in both *Gram. 1* and *2*. Follow suggestions for using presentation devices (collectively referred to as *GEA's*) in the IM.
- Emphasize with students that the grammar point of focus will appear in red text in the presentation device or minidialogue in *GEA*. The grammar point of focus is *not* highlighted in *Comprensión* activities.
- Remind students that the English equivalent of most presentation devices is provided at the foot of the page, as is also the case with minidialogues.
- Point out to students that the second name (*María*) of the writer of the list is common for Hispanic males, especially in combination with the first name *José*.

Follow-up

1. *¿Qué estudia José María?* (español y cálculo)
2. *¿Cómo se llama la novela famosa de la lista?* (Don Quijote)
3. *¿Cuántos cuadernos hay en la lista?* (1)
4. *¿Cuántos libros de texto hay en la lista?* (4)
5. *¿Cuántos cuadernos en línea hay en la lista?* (1)

GRAMÁTICA

¿Recuerda usted?

As you know, in English and in Spanish, a noun is the name of a person, place, thing, or idea. You have been using nouns since the beginning of *Puntos de partida*. Remember that **el** and **la** mean *the* before nouns. If you can change the Spanish words for *the* to *one* in the following phrases, you already know some of the material in **Gramática 1.**

1. el libro un **2.** la mesa una **3.** el profesor un **4.** la estudiante una

1 Naming People, Places, Things, and Ideas (Part 1)

Singular Nouns: Gender and Articles*

Grammar Tutorial 1
connect SPANISH
www.connectspanish.com

Gramática en acción: La lista de José María

Note the use of **red** in **Gramática en acción** to indicate examples of the grammar point of focus.

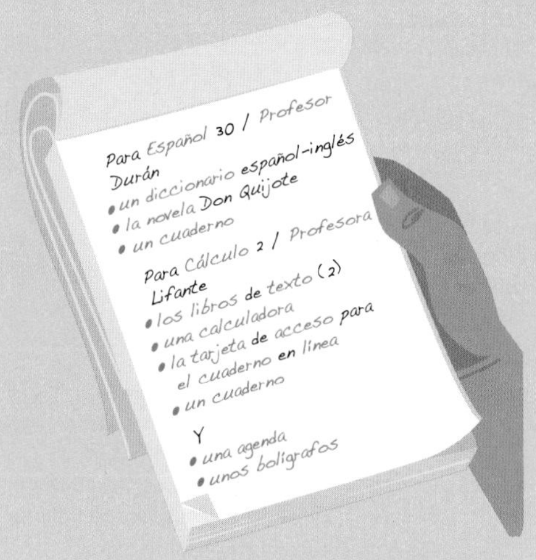

Para Español 30 / Profesor Durán
• un diccionario español-inglés
• la novela Don Quijote
• un cuaderno
Para Cálculo 2 / Profesora Lifante
• los libros de texto (2)
• una calculadora
• la tarjeta de acceso para el cuaderno en línea
• un cuaderno
Y
• una agenda
• unos bolígrafos

Comprensión

	CIERTO	FALSO
1. La profesora de matemáticas es la profesora Durán.	☐	☑
2. El cuaderno es para (*for*) la clase de literatura.	☑	☐
3. La agenda es para la clase de matemáticas.	☐	☑

You use nouns to name people, places, things, and ideas. In Spanish, all *nouns* (**los sustantivos**) have either masculine or feminine *gender* (**el género**). This is a purely grammatical feature; it does not mean that Spanish speakers perceive things or ideas as having male or female attributes.

Since the gender of all nouns must be memorized, it is best to learn the definite article along with the noun; that is, learn **el lápiz** rather than just **lápiz.** The definite article is given with nouns in vocabulary lists in this book.

José María's list *For Spanish 30 / Professor Durán • a Spanish-English dictionary • the novel* Don Quijote *• a notebook. For Calculus 2 / Professor Lifante • the textbooks (2) • a calculator • the access card for the online workbook • a notebook. And • a calendar/datebook • a few ballpoint pens*

**The grammar sections of* Puntos de partida *are numbered consecutively throughout the book. If you need to review a particular grammar point, the index will refer you to its page number.*

NATIONAL STANDARDS: Comparisons

Like Spanish, many other languages have the concept of gender. For example, French, Italian, and Portuguese have both masculine and feminine nouns. In German, nouns can be masculine, feminine, or neuter. English has gender as well (masculine, feminine, and neuter), but it is not as obvious. Have students identify the gender of the subjects in the following sentences using the underlined possessive adjectives as a guide.

The boy has <u>his</u> book.
The girl has <u>her</u> homework.
The committee has <u>its</u> meeting in October.

Nouns / **Los sustantivos**				
	Masculine / **Masculino**		Feminine / **Femenino**	
Definite Articles / **Los artículos definidos**	el **hombre** el **libro**	the man the book	la **mujer** la **mesa**	the woman the table
Indefinite Articles / **Los artículos indefinidos**	un **hombre** un **libro**	a man a book	una **mujer** una **mesa**	a woman a table

an article / **un artículo** = a determiner that sets off a noun
a definite article / **un artículo definido** = an article that indicates a specific noun (*the*)
an indefinite article / **un artículo indefinido** = an article that indicates an unspecified noun (*a, an*)

Note the two-column format of grammar explanations. Explanations are on the left, examples are on the right, and red highlighting will help you see what's important.

Gender / El género

1. **Masculine Nouns**
Nouns that refer to male beings and most other nouns that end in **-o** are *masculine* (**masculino**) in gender.
sustantivos masculinos — **hombre, libro**

2. **Feminine Nouns**
Nouns that refer to female beings and most other nouns that end in **-a, -ión, -tad,** and **-dad** are *feminine* (**femenino**) in gender.
sustantivos femeninos — **mujer, mesa, nación, libertad, universidad**

3. **Other Endings**
Nouns that have other endings and that do not refer to either male or female beings may be masculine or feminine. The gender of these words must be memorized.
el lápiz, el papel, el salón de clase
la clase, la noche, la tarde

4. **Spelling Changes**
Many nouns that refer to people indicate gender . . .
- by changing the last vowel — **el compañero → la compañera**; **el bibliotecario → la bibliotecaria**

OR

- by adding **-a** to the last consonant of the masculine form to make it feminine — **un profesor → una profesora**

5. **Articles and *e* → *a***
Many other nouns that refer to people have a single form for both masculine and feminine genders. Gender is indicated by an article.
However, a few such nouns that end in **-e** also have a feminine form that ends in **-a.**

Masculino	Femenino
el **estudiante**	la **estudiante**
el **dentista**	la **dentista**
el **presidente**	la **presidenta**
el **cliente**	la **clienta**
el **dependiente** (*clerk*)	la **dependienta**

¡OJO!

A common exception to the normal rules of gender is the word **el día,** which is masculine in gender. Many words ending in **-ma** are also masculine: **el problema, el programa, el sistema,** and so on.

Gender

Notes

- Emphasize to students that the grammar explanations are presented in a two-column format, with the explanation on the left and examples on the right.
- This presentation of gender and the rules that govern it in Spanish includes just the basics. If you wish to give students more information, you should expand the presentation to meet their needs. Additional material might include: *-pa* and *-ta* words (*m.*, see below), *-e* (mostly *m.*), *-z* (mostly *f.*), and so on.
- Explain that the "matching" between the article and the noun is called *la concordancia* (agreement).
- An alternative to the *-ión* rule (most are feminine) is to tell students that words ending in *-xión*, *-ción*, and *-sión* are always feminine, which covers the common exceptions to the *-ión* rule (*el camión, el avión*).

Emphasis 4: Suggestion

Call students' attention to *la persona* (active vocabulary in this chapter). Tell them that *la persona* is used whether the person talked about is male or female: *Ernesto es una buena persona.*

Emphasis 5: Suggestion

- Emphasize that like *estudiante,* some words refer to both men and women: *turista, artista* (in addition to the examples given). The feminine of the word *poeta* is traditionally *poetisa,* but is often replaced today by *la poeta.*

Optional

- Optional *-ma* word: *el tema.*
- You may also wish to introduce *-pa* and *-ta* words, which are also masculine: *el mapa, el cometa, el planeta.* Like the *-ma* words, they are of Greek origin.

Notes

- Active vocabulary: *el/la cliente/a, el/la dependiente/a, el día*
- The words *noche* and *tarde* (active in *Cap. 1*) are noted in point 3.

Heritage Speakers

- Pídales a los hispanohablantes que le den otros sustantivos que no cambian al referirse a hombres o mujeres, como *turista* o *artista.*
- Pregúnteles cuál forma usan: *la cliente* o *la client**a**, la presidente* o *la president**a**, la dependiente* o *la dependient**a**.*
- Señáleles que en algunos países hispanohablantes se dice *la presidente* o *la jefe* en vez de *la presidenta* o *la jefa. La presidenta* también puede significar *la esposa del presidente.*

Articles

Emphasis 2: Suggestions

- Explain that the words *un/una* can mean *one*, *a*, or *an*.
- Remind students that in English, too, the context in which we find a word can determine our understanding of it. Have students consider how they know what the word *will* means in the examples *Will you do this?*, *Will and I went to the park*, and *The lawyer wrote the will.*

Emphasis 2: Note

Plural forms of the definite and indefinite articles are presented in *Gram. 2* of this chapter.

Preliminary Exercises

- As a gender quiz, give students these words and have them tell whether each is *femenina* or *masculina*.

1. *teléfono*	**6.** *hombre*
2. *mujer*	**7.** *estudiante*
3. *noche*	**8.** *día*
4. *programa*	**9.** *compañero*
5. *comedia*	**10.** *libertad*

- Have students try the *Autoprueba* before they begin the *Práctica* section.

Prác. A: Note

Active vocabulary: *ahora*

Prác. A: Follow-up

Have students give the feminine or masculine counterparts for the following words (ask for articles with answers).

1. *el hombre*
2. *la compañera*
3. *el secretario*
4. *un cliente*
5. *una presidenta*
6. *un turista*

Prác. A, Paso 1: Extension

13. *fiesta*	**17.** *pizarrón*
14. *clase*	**18.** *cuarto*
15. *puerta*	**19.** *lengua*
16. *amigo*	**20.** *teléfono*

Prác. B: Variation

Vary *Paso 1* of this activity by using the following model to form the sentences: *estudiante/librería* → *El estudiante está en la librería.*

Articles / **Los artículos**

1. Definite Articles

In English, there is only one *definite article* (**el artículo definido**): *the*. In Spanish, there are two definite articles for singular nouns, one masculine (**el**) and one feminine (**la**).

Artículo definido: *the*
m. sing. → **el**
f. sing. → **la**

2. Indefinite Articles

In English, the singular *indefinite article* (**el artículo indefinido**) is *a* or *an*. In Spanish, the indefinite article, like the definite article, must agree with the gender of the noun: **un** for masculine nouns, **una** for feminine nouns. **Un** and **una** can mean *one* or *a/an*, depending on context.

Artículo indefinido: *a, an*
m. sing. → **un**
f. sing. → **una**

¡OJO!
Only the *indefinite* article (never the definite article) is used directly after the word **hay: Hay un** libro / **unos** cuadernos en la mesa.

Gender Summary

MASCULINO	FEMENINO
el, un	**la, una**
-o	-a
-ma	-ión
	-dad, -tad

Autoprueba

Give the correct definite article: **el** or **la.**

1. ____ libro	4. ____ escritorio
2. ____ mujer	5. ____ libertad
3. ____ oficina	6. ____ acción

Answers: **1.** *el* **2.** *la* **3.** *la* **4.** *el* **5.** *la* **6.** *la*

Brief **Autopruebas** (*Self-tests*) appear at the end of grammar explanations. Take them to see if you understand the basics of the grammar point.

Práctica

A. Los artículos

Paso 1. Dé (*Give*) el artículo definido apropiado **(el, la).**

1. escritorio el	**4.** mochila la	**7.** universidad la	**10.** nación la
2. biblioteca la	**5.** hombre el	**8.** dinero el	**11.** bibliotecario el
3. bolígrafo el	**6.** diccionario el	**9.** mujer la	**12.** calculadora la

Paso 2. Ahora (*Now*) dé el artículo indefinido apropiado (**un, una**).

1. día un	**3.** problema un	**5.** clase una	**7.** condición una
2. mañana una	**4.** lápiz un	**6.** papel un	**8.** programa un

B. Escenas de la universidad

Paso 1. Haga una oración (*Form a sentence*) con las palabras indicadas.

MODELO: estudiante / librería → Hay un estudiante en la librería.

1. consejero / oficina	**6.** bolígrafo / silla
2. profesora / salón de clase	**7.** palabra / papel
3. lápiz / mesa	**8.** oficina / residencia
4. cuaderno / escritorio	**9.** compañero / biblioteca
5. libro / mochila	**10.** diccionario / librería

Paso 2. Now create new sentences by changing one of the words in each item in **Paso 1.** Try to come up with as many variations as possible.

MODELOS: Hay un estudiante en la residencia. Hay una profesora en la librería.

Prác. B: Answers: Paso 1.
1. *Hay un consejero en la oficina.* **2.** *Hay una profesora en el salón de clase.* **3.** *Hay un lápiz en la mesa.* **4.** *Hay un cuaderno en el escritorio.* **5.** *Hay un libro en la mochila.* **6.** *Hay un bolígrafo en la silla.* **7.** *Hay una palabra en el papel.* **8.** *Hay una oficina en la residencia.* **9.** *Hay un compañero en la biblioteca.* **10.** *Hay un diccionario en la librería.*

NATIONAL STANDARDS: Communication

Have students give the male or female counterparts, as needed.

1. *Pablo Ortiz es consejero. ¿Y Paula Delibes?*
2. *Camilo es estudiante. ¿Y Conchita?*
3. *Carmen Leal es profesora. ¿Y Carlos Ortega?*
4. *Juan Luis es dependiente. ¿Y Juanita?*
5. *Josefina es una compañera de Luz. ¿Y José?*

Heritage Speakers

Pregúnteles a los hispanohablantes si usan la forma masculina o femenina de las siguientes palabras: *el/la sartén, el/la mar, el/la azúcar, el/la Internet, el/la radio.* ¿Hay estudiantes que usen las dos formas?

Conversación

A. Definiciones. En parejas (*pairs*), definan las siguientes palabras en español, según (*according to*) el modelo.

MODELO: biblioteca / ¿ ? ⟶ **ESTUDIANTE 1:** ¿Qué es una biblioteca?
ESTUDIANTE 2: Es un edificio.

Categorías: edificio, materia, objeto, persona

1. cliente / ¿ ?
2. bolígrafo / ¿ ?
3. residencia / ¿ ?
4. dependienta / ¿ ?
5. hotel (*m.*) / ¿ ?
6. computadora / ¿ ?
7. computación / ¿ ?
8. inglés / ¿ ?
9. ¿ ?

B. Nuestra (*Our*) **universidad.** En parejas, hagan oraciones (*form sentences*) sobre su (*about your*) universidad.

MODELOS: mi consejero/a ⟶ El profesor Márquez es mi consejero.
cafetería ⟶ Hay una cafetería. Se llama (*It's called*) Foster Hall.

1. mi consejero/a
2. mi profesor(a) de ____ (materia)
3. edificio de ____ (materia)
4. biblioteca principal
5. cafetería
6. edificio de clases

Estrategia

Remember to use the article **el** or **la** to name someone who has a title: **el profesor Márquez.**

2 Naming People, Places, Things, and Ideas (Part 2)

Nouns and Articles: Plural Forms

Grammar Tutorial 2
connect SPANISH
www.connectspanish.com

Gramática en acción: Un anuncio

Cursos de Idiomas en el Extranjero[a]
Financiación SIN INTERESES en 3, 6 ó 12 meses
Cursos para jóvenes de 7 a 17 años
Cursos para adultos a partir de 18 años
Cursos en Universidades: Idioma general y/o técnico
Minimasters en Universidades
USA, Inglaterra e Irlanda
Programa residencial en Sevilla y/o Madrid con inglés
Preparación para TOEFL, GMAT, SAT, GRE, USMLE
Cursos de idiomas en Madrid
Instituto ProLengua ofrece pagar su curso aplazado en 3, 6 ó 12 meses
INSTITUTO PROLENGUA
Infórmate
902-253 797

[a]en... *abroad*

You don't have to understand all of the words in this ad (**anuncio**) to get its general meaning.

Comprensión

1. How many nouns (including proper nouns) can you find in the ad? Can you guess the meaning of most of them? approx. 20
2. Some of the nouns in the ad are plural. Can you tell how to make nouns plural in Spanish? add *-s* or *-es*
3. Look for the Spanish equivalent of these words: *adults, preparation, program, courses.* adultos, preparación, programa, cursos
4. The word **idioma** is a false cognate; it never means *idiom*. What do you think it means? language

Con. A: Suggestions

- Point out to students that the Spanish word *materia* can mean *material* (what something is made of) as well as subject matter (*biología, historia,* and so on).
- Use places and persons from your campus and city as cues.

Con. A: Extension

10. *librería* **11.** *historia* **12.** *cuaderno* **13.** *libro* **14.** *dinero* **15.** *compañera de clase* **16.** *física* **17.** *manual* (*m.*) *de laboratorio* **18.** *laboratorio de lenguas* **19.** *profesor/profesora* (name)

Con. B: Reciclado and Preview

- Note the re-entry of *hay* and *se llama* (with a slightly different meaning: *is called*) from *Cap 1.*
- Encourage the use of *hay* with plural nouns (to preview *Gram. 2*) in sentences such as: *En nuestra universidad hay ____ edificios.*

Con. B: Suggestions

- Emphasize the use of articles with titles (*el profesor X, la profesora Y*).
- Introduce *está* and encourage students to form sentences with it: *El departamento de español está en el edificio Fisk.*

Con. B: Optional

Asociaciones. Students name people and things that they associate with the following places.

1. *la biblioteca*
2. *la librería*
3. *una oficina*
4. *una residencia*
5. *la capital de esta nación*
6. *la universidad*

Gramática 2

Nouns and Articles: Plural Forms

Reciclado: Review the *GEA* that precedes *Gram. 1* before presenting the material in this section.

Suggestions

- Have students form small groups to translate the main points of the ad.
- Have students read the ad aloud to practice pronunciation of vowels.

Heritage Speakers

- Anime a los hispanohablantes a ayudar a sus compañeros monolingües a comprender el anuncio.
- Invite a un hispanohablante a leer el anuncio en voz alta para que la clase oiga la pronunciación de las vocales.

NATIONAL STANDARDS: Connections

The TOEFL, GMAT, SAT, GRE, and USMLE are standardized tests commonly used in the United States. TOEFL = Test of English as a Foreign Languages; GMAT = Graduate Management Admission Test; SAT = Scholastic Aptitude Test; GRE = Graduate Record Examination; USMLE = United States. Medical Licensing Examination.

Emphasis 1: Suggestion

Point out that the stress does not shift when plurals are formed. Word stress and accentuation will not be formally presented until *Caps. 3* and *4*, so you may wish to discuss addition/deletion of accent marks in plurals now.

Emphasis 3: Suggestion

Emphasize that even if a group includes only one male but many females, the masculine plural form is used. If the feminine plural is used, it excludes any male membership in the group: *los estudiantes* refers to males or females; *las estudiantes* includes only females.

Note

Active vocabulary: *el/la amigo/a, el/la extranjero*

Preliminary Exercises

- Have students listen to the following words and tell whether they are singular or plural.
  1. *el diccionario*
  2. *la librería*
  3. *los papeles*
  4. *el lápiz*
  5. *unos bolígrafos*
  6. *las clases*
  7. *una profesora*
  8. *las universidades*
- Remind students to try the *Autoprueba* before they begin the *Práctica* section.

Prác. A: Follow-up

Have students give the plural of the following.

1. *Juana, una estudiante; Juana y Elena…*
2. *Ramón, un extranjero; Ramón y Ricardo…*
3. *Ramón, un extranjero; Ramón y Raquel…*
4. *David, un amigo; David y Cecilia…*
5. *David, un amigo; David y Roberto…*

Prác. B: Extension

Have students provide examples of certain nouns (some plural, some singular). Use names in the class or at the university (the name of the instructor, the names of two or three students together, the name of the president, the names of professors, and so on).

	Singular	Plural	
Nouns Ending in a Vowel	el **libro** la **mesa** un **libro** una **mesa**	los **libros** las **mesas** unos **libros** unas **mesas**	the books the tables some books some tables
Nouns Ending in a Consonant	la **universidad** un **papel**	las **universidades** unos **papeles**	the universities some papers

1. **Plural Endings**
   Spanish nouns that end in a vowel form plurals by adding **-s.** Nouns that end in a consonant add **-es.** Nouns that end in the consonant **-z** change the **-z** to **-c** before adding **-es: lápiz ⟶ lápices.**

   Sustantivos plurales
   vowel + **-s**
   consonant + **-es**
   -z ⟶ -ces

2. **Plural of Articles**
   The definite and indefinite articles also have plural forms: **el ⟶ los, la ⟶ las, un ⟶ unos, una ⟶ unas. Unos** and **unas** mean *some, several,* or *a few.*

   Artículos plurales
   el ⟶ los **un ⟶ unos**
   la ⟶ las **una ⟶ unas**

3. **Groups of People**
   In Spanish, the masculine plural form of a noun is used to refer to a group that includes both males and females.

   los amigos = *the friends* (all male or both male and female)
   las amigas = *the friends* (only female)
   unos extranjeros = *some foreigners* (all male or both male and female)
   unas extranjeras = *some foreign women*

Plural Forms Summary

el ⟶ los **un ⟶ unos**
la ⟶ las **una ⟶ unas**

vowel + **-s**
consonant + **-es**
-z ⟶ -ces

Autoprueba

Match the noun with the correct article.

1. libros	a. el
2. hombre	b. las
3. librería	c. los
4. profesoras	d. una

Answers: **1.** c **2.** a **3.** d **4.** b

Práctica

A. Singular ⟶ plural. Dé (*Give*) la forma plural.

1. la mesa
2. el papel
3. el amigo
4. la oficina
5. un cuaderno
6. un lápiz
7. una universidad
8. un bolígrafo
9. un teléfono

B. Plural ⟶ singular. Dé la forma singular.

1. los profesores
2. las computadoras
3. las bibliotecarias
4. los estudiantes
5. unos hombres
6. unas tardes
7. unas residencias
8. unas sillas
9. unos escritorios

Prác. A: Answers: 1. *las mesas* **2.** *los papeles* **3.** *los amigos* **4.** *las oficinas* **5.** *unos cuadernos* **6.** *unos lápices* **7.** *unas universidades* **8.** *unos bolígrafos* **9.** *unos teléfonos*

Prác. B: Answers: 1. *el profesor* **2.** *la computadora* **3.** *la bibliotecaria* **4.** *el estudiante* **5.** *un hombre* **6.** *una tarde* **7.** *una residencia* **8.** *una silla* **9.** *un escritorio*

NATIONAL STANDARDS: Comparisons

Point out that Spanish, like English, has nouns that are used mainly or only in the plural. Many of these are the same in English and Spanish. Here are several examples.

binoculars	*los prismáticos, los gemelos*
eyeglasses	*los anteojos, los lentes*
pants	*los pantalones*
scissors	*las tijeras*

Ask students if they can think of additional English examples.

Conversación

A. Identificaciones. Nombre (*Name*) las personas, los objetos y los lugares.

MODELOS: Hay ____ en ____. ⟶ Hay **unos estudiantes** en **el salón de clase.**
Hay **un profesor** en **el laboratorio.**

1.

2.

Vocabulario útil

el experimento
el laboratorio
la planta

B. ¡Ojo alerta!*

Paso 1. ¿Cuáles son las semejanzas (*similarities*) y las diferencias entre (*between*) los dos cuartos? Hay por lo menos (*at least*) seis diferencias.

MODELOS: En el dibujo A, hay ____.
En el dibujo B, hay solo (*only*) ____.
En el escritorio del dibujo A, hay ____.
En el escritorio del dibujo B, hay ____.

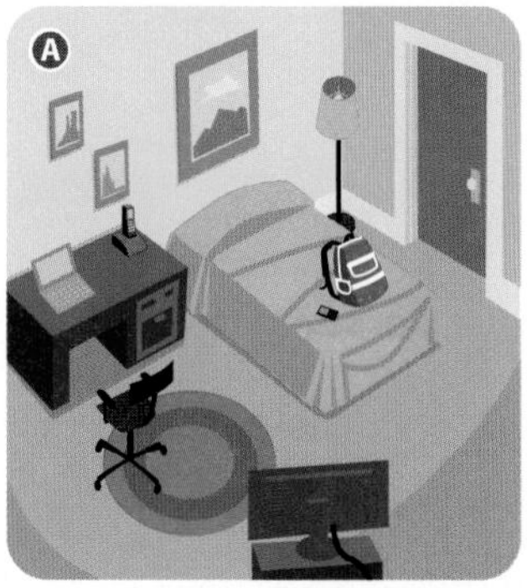

Vocabulario útil

la cama bed
la lámpara
el monitor
la televisión

Con. B: Answers: 1. two doors in B versus one in A **2.** a TV in A versus none in B **3.** two lamps in B versus one in A **4.** stand alone computer monitor in B versus none in A **5.** two phones in A versus one in B **6.** backpack in A versus none in B

Paso 2. Ahora indique qué hay en su propio (*your own*) cuarto. Use palabras del **Paso 1.**

MODELO: En mi cuarto hay ______. En mi escritorio hay ______.

*In Spanish, activities like this one are often called **¡Ojo alerta!** = *Eagle Eye!*

Con. A: Suggestions

- Encourage students to speak further about people, places, things, and ideas by asking questions such as: *¿Quién es? (¿Quiénes son?) ¿Qué es? ¿Cuántos/as ____ hay? ¿Dónde está(n)?*
- Introduce *muchos/as*.

Reciclado: Review numbers and questions by asking questions such as: *¿Cuántos/as estudiantes / mesas / sillas / libros hay en el salón de clase?* Remind students to use *hay* in their answers.

Con. B: Notes

- In recent usage, *la televisión* is increasingly heard instead of *el televisor*. Both terms will be used in this text, with *la televisión* preferred (as a closer cognate) in early chapters.
- Active vocabulary: *solo*
- Note the adverb *solo* no longer needs an accent, according to the *RAE*.

Con. B: Extension

Ask questions and pantomime keywords to elicit chapter vocabulary, for example, *¿Qué hay en nuestro* (pantomime) *salón de clase?*

Reciclado: Have students form pairs to review cognates presented in the explanations and activities in *Cap. 1* and scan the realia and drawings in that chapter and in *Cap. 2.* Then invite them to give as many nouns as they can that fit into the following categories.

1. *lugares de la universidad*
2. *objetos en una librería*
3. *personas en una librería*
4. *problemas de los estudiantes*

Con. B: Follow-up

As a whole-class activity, ask students what things they associate with certain places, for example: *¿Qué hay en una oficina típica de la universidad? ¿Qué hay en un salón de clase que no hay en una oficina? ¿y en la biblioteca?*

Redacción: Assign *Paso 2* of *Con. B* for homework as a written assignment. Prepare students for this activity by encouraging them to name all of the objects that they know how to express in Spanish so far. Provide additional vocabulary: *el estéreo, el* iPod, *el PDA, la televisión.*

Resources: Transparencies 10, 11

NATIONAL STANDARDS: Comparisons

The formation of plural nouns in Spanish is quite easy and predictable in comparison to English. Note that some English nouns ending in *-f* or *-fe* change to *-ves* in the plural (*wife ⟶ wives; calf ⟶ calves*). Others undergo a vowel change such as *fireman ⟶ firemen, foot ⟶ feet; goose ⟶ geese.* Some nouns ending in *-o* take *-s* in the plural while others take *-es* (*memo ⟶ memos; potato ⟶ potatoes*). There are still other nouns that do not change at all in the plural: *deer, fish,* and *sheep.* Pluralization of nouns in English is further complicated by the sheer number of borrowings from other languages.

¿Recuerda usted?

Note

This brief exercise serves as an advance organizer to heighten students' awareness of verbs as a part of speech. This will work particularly well if you have covered *Con. B* (p. 29) in class. A similar brief exercise on the subject of a sentence is in the suggestions for the first part of *Gram. 3* below.

Gramática 3

Subject Pronouns (Part 1); Present Tense of *-ar* Verbs; Negation

Note

The *GEA* introduces material that will appear in *Gram. 3*. You may prefer to focus on subject pronouns alone before introducing the *GEA*. Continue to use the guidelines for presentation devices in the IM.

Suggestions

- Remind students about the function of red text in *GEA*.
- If you covered *Con. B* (*Las materias*, p. 29) in the *Vocabulario: Preparación* section, students should have an awareness of the first person singular ending (-o). Elicit discussion of other endings that appear in *GEA* and link them (by writing on board) with subject pronouns.
- Take each verb form in *GEA* and turn it into questions about yourself, then about students. For example: *Yo no trabajo en la biblioteca. Trabajo en mi oficina… y en el salón de clase. ¿Trabaja usted en la biblioteca?*
- Have students indicate subjects.
  1. Olga is going to write a message.
  2. The car ran off the road.
  3. Are we there yet?
  4. Love conquers all.
  5. I've had it!
- Read through the *GEA* with students, asking them to pick out the subject and subject pronouns.
- Active vocabulary: *por teléfono*

Follow-up

Ask students if these statements are *cierto* or *falso* for them.

1. *Usted trabaja en la librería.*
2. *Usted estudia en la residencia.*
3. *Hoy hay examen en la clase de español.*
4. *Usted habla por teléfono en la biblioteca.*
5. *En la residencia es posible hablar por teléfono.*

¿Recuerda usted?

These sentences contain Spanish verbs that you have already used. Pick them out.

1. Soy estudiante en la Universidad de ______.
2. Este (*This*) semestre/trimestre, estudio español.
3. En el futuro, deseo estudiar francés.

If you selected **estudiar** in addition to three other words, you did very well! You will learn more about Spanish verbs and how they are used in **Gramática 3.**

3 Expressing Actions

Subject Pronouns (Part 1): Present Tense of -ar Verbs; Negation

Grammar Tutorial 3
connect SPANISH
www.connectspanish.com

Gramática en acción: Una escena en la biblioteca

- Dos estudiantes trabajan hoy en esta sección de la biblioteca.
- Yo no trabajo en la biblioteca.
- Hoy Manuel y yo estudiamos para un examen de historia.
- Un profesor habla por teléfono con un amigo.
- ¿Habla Ud. por teléfono en la biblioteca? No se permite, ¿verdad?

Comprensión

En la escena…

1. ¿cuántos estudiantes trabajan? dos
2. ¿cuántos estudiantes estudian? dos
3. ¿quién habla? una estudiante
4. ¿quién habla por teléfono? el profesor

Subject Pronouns / Los pronombres personales

a subject / **un sujeto** = the person or thing that performs the action in a sentence

a pronoun / **un pronombre** = a word that takes the place of a noun or represents a person

Singular		Plural	
yo	I	**nosotros / nosotras**	we
tú	you (*fam.*)	**vosotros / vosotras**	you (*fam. Sp.*)
usted (Ud.)*	you (*form.*)	**ustedes (Uds.)***	you (*form.*)
él	he	**ellos**	they (*m., m. + f.*)
ella	she	**ellas**	they (*f.*)

A scene at the library • *Two students are working in this section of the library today.* • *I don't work at the library.* • *Today Manuel and I are studying for a history test.* • *A professor is talking to a friend on the phone.* • *Do you talk on the phone in the library? It's not allowed, is it?*

*__Usted__ *and* __ustedes__ *are frequently abbreviated in writing as* __Ud.__ *or* __Vd.__, *and* __Uds.__ *or* __Vds.__, *respectively.*

NATIONAL STANDARDS: Comparisons

Point out that students have learned that there are four different ways to say *you* in Spanish: *tú/vosotros* and *usted/ustedes*. Although in English there is only one gramatically acceptable way to convey the second person, several dialectal forms have evolved in order to differentiate between singular and plural *you*. In casual speech, it is not uncommon to hear expressions such as *you all, y'all, you(s) guys, and you 'ens*. Although these forms are not considered to be gramatically correct, one often hears them in conversations.

1. **Subject Pronouns**
The person that performs the action in a sentence is expressed by *subject pronouns* (**los pronombres personales**).

In Spanish, many subject pronouns have masculine and feminine forms. The masculine plural form is used to refer to a group of males as well as to a group of males and females.

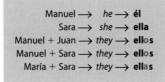

Manuel → *he* → **él**
Sara → *she* → **ella**
Manuel + Juan → *they* → **ellos**
Manuel + Sara → *they* → **ellos**
María + Sara → *they* → **ellas**

2. **Pronouns for** *you*
Spanish has different words for *you*. In general, **tú** is used to refer to a close friend or a family member, while **usted** is used with people with whom the speaker has a more formal or distant relationship. The situations in which **tú** and **usted** are used also vary among different countries and regions.

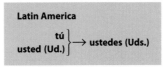

tú → close friend, family member
usted (Ud.) → formal or distant relationship

3. **Plural of** *you*
In Latin American Spanish, the plural for both **usted** and **tú** is **ustedes.** In Spain, however, **vosotros/vosotras** is the plural of **tú,** while **ustedes** is used as the plural of **usted** exclusively.

Latin America

tú, **usted (Ud.)** → **ustedes (Uds.)**

Spain

tú → **vosotros/vosotras**
usted (Ud.) → **ustedes (Uds.)**

4. **Omitting Subject Pronouns**
Subject pronouns are not used as frequently in Spanish as they are in English, and they may usually be omitted. You will learn more about the uses of Spanish subject pronouns in **Gramática 8 (Capítulo 3).**

Present Tense of -ar Verbs / El tiempo presente de los verbos *-ar*

1. **Infinitives**
As you know, the *infinitive* (**el infinitivo**) of a verb indicates the action or state of being, with no reference to who or what performs the action or when it is done (present, past, or future). Infinitives in English are indicated by *to: to* speak, *to* eat, *to* live. In Spanish, all infinitives end in **-ar, -er,** or **-ir.**

-ar:	**hablar**	to speak
-er:	**comer**	to eat
-ir:	**vivir**	to live

an infinitive / **un infinitivo** = a verb form that indicates action or state of being without reference to person, tense, or number
a tense / **un tiempo** = the quality of a verb form that indicates time: present, past, or future

Subject Pronouns

Emphasis 1: Suggestion

Point out that there is no Spanish equivalent for *it* as a subject.

Emphasis 2: Note

Point out to students that people in some countries (among them, Argentina, Uruguay, and Costa Rica) use *vos* instead of *tú*, sometimes with different verb forms: *vos sos, vos hablás, vos vivís.* These forms will not be presented formally in *Puntos de partida.*

Emphasis 2: Suggestion

Reciclado: As you introduce *tú* and *Ud.*, review what students already know about formal and informal usages by asking them to pose these questions to you or to another student, as appropriate.

1. *¿Cómo está?*
2. *¿Cómo estás?*
3. *¿De dónde es Ud.?*
4. *¿De dónde eres?*
5. *¿Cómo se llama Ud.?*
6. *¿Cómo te llamas?*

Emphasis 3: Note

Vosotros will not be actively practiced in activities and exercises of the *Puntos de partida* student text.

Preliminary Exercises

Have students answer the following questions.

- What subject pronoun would you use in English to speak *about* the following persons?
  1. yourself (I)
  2. two men (they)
  3. a female child (she)
  4. yourself (male) and your sister (we)
  5. yourself (female) and your mother (we)
  6. your uncle (he)
- What subject pronoun would you use in Spanish to speak *to* the following persons?
  1. *una profesora* (*Ud.*)
  2. *unos consejeros* (*Uds.*)
  3. *un estudiante* (*tú*)
  4. *unas amigas* (*Uds.*)
  5. *tu mamá* (*tú*)
  6. *un dependiente* (*Ud.*)
- What subject pronoun would you *substitute* in Spanish for each of the following persons?
  1. *su amiga Eva* (*ella*)
  2. *Luis* (*él*)
  3. *Fausto y yo* (male) (*nosotros*)
  4. *Ud.* (female) *y Cecilia* (*Uds.*)
  5. *Ud.* (male) *y Cecilia* (*Uds.*)
  6. *Vicente y David* (*ellos*)
  7. *la señora Álvarez y Ud.* (*Uds.*)

Culture

Emphasize the difference between *tú* and *Ud.*, explaining that the nature of the relationship between two people determines the form they will use. Point out that the contexts for *tú* and *Ud.* are very different throughout the Spanish-speaking world, and they vary from country to country, and from one generation to another. In some countries (for example: Spain, Puerto Rico, and Cuba) people are much more liberal in the use of *tú* than others (for example: Colombia, Honduras, or Costa Rica).

Present Tense of *-ar* Verbs

Suggestions

- Model the pronunciation of each infinitive several times. Then use the *yo* form of each in a brief, simple sentence about yourself, repeating several times and pantomiming if necessary.
- Have students generate all forms of one verb, after you give the subject pronouns.
- Transform a base sentence into a simple *Ud.* question directed to a student, coaching him or her to answer using the *yo* form. Example: *bailar* ⟶ *Me gusta bailar. Bailo muy bien. Y Ud., ¿baila bien?*
- Ask students: *¿Cómo se dice* I/we dance, I/we sing, I/we buy . . . *?*
- Emphasize *tocar* (music), and those infinitives that include prepositions in their meaning: *buscar, escuchar, pagar*.
- Offer the following optional verbs: *caminar, fumar, mirar* (*la televisión*).

Notes

- Students are introduced to the verb *desear* in this chapter. *Querer,* which is introduced in *Gram. 10* (*Cap. 4*), is more common, but using *desear* (a regular *-ar* verb) now allows students to communicate their wants and desires.
- Note the addition of *mandar un mensaje / to text* to the active vocabulary of *Cap. 2.* The text will use *mandar* primarily in that context until the introduction of indirect object pronouns in *Cap. 8*.

Emphasis 6: Suggestion

Explain the use of present tense questions to indicate near-future actions: *¿Hablas con Juan mañana?* (Will you speak to Juan tomorrow?)

Negation

Suggestion

Point out that the second *no* = the English *not*.

Preliminary Exercises

- Explain the purpose of a rapid response drill. Have students give the corresponding forms.

  yo: *bailar, estudiar, tocar, escuchar*
  tú: *buscar, hablar, pagar, tomar*
  Ud./él/ella: *cantar, necesitar, regresar, enseñar*
  nosotros/as: *comprar, pagar, estudiar, escuchar*
  vosotros/as: *desear, regresar, cantar, bailar*
  Uds./ellos/ellas: *practicar, tomar, desear, mandar*

2. Conjugating Verbs

To *conjugate* (**conjugar**) a verb means to give the various forms of the verb with their corresponding subjects: *I speak, you speak, she speaks,* and so on. All regular Spanish verbs are conjugated by adding *personal endings* (**las terminaciones personales**) that reflect the subject doing the action. These are added to the *stem* (**la raíz** or **el radical**), which is the infinitive minus the infinitive ending.

Infinitive / **Infinitivo**		Stem / **Raíz**
hablar	⟶	**habl-**
comer	⟶	**com-**
vivir	⟶	**viv-**

3. Present Tense Endings

The right-hand column shows the personal endings that are added to the stem of all regular **-ar** verbs to form the *present tense* (**el presente**).

las terminaciones -*ar* del tiempo presente
-o, -as, -a, -amos, -áis, -an

hablar (*to speak; to talk*): **habl-**					
Singular			**Plural**		
(yo)	**hablo**	I speak	(nosotros) (nosotras)	**hablamos**	we speak
(tú)	**hablas**	you speak	(vosotros) (vosotros)	**habláis**	you speak
(Ud.) **(él)** **(ella)**	**habla**	you speak he speaks she speaks	(Uds.) (ellos) (ellas)	**hablan**	you speak they (*m., m. + f.*) speak they (*f.*) speak

4. Important *-ar* Verbs

Here are some **-ar** verbs used in this chapter.

Los verbos *-ar*	
bailar	to dance
buscar	to look for
cantar	to sing
comprar	to buy
desear	to want
enseñar	to teach
escuchar	to listen (to)
estudiar	to study
hablar	to speak; to talk
mandar un mensaje	to (send a) text
necesitar	to need
pagar	to pay (for)
practicar	to practice
regresar	to return (*to a place*)
tocar	to play (*a musical instrument*)
tomar	to take; to drink
trabajar	to work

¡OJO!

Note that in Spanish the meaning of the English word *for* is included in the verbs **buscar** (*to look for*) and **pagar** (*to pay for*); *to* is included in **escuchar** (*to listen to*).

Heritage Speakers

- Pídales a los hispanohablantes que expliquen la diferencia entre *regresar, volver* y *devolver*. También explique que para expresar *to return a phone call* es preferible decir *devolver una llamada* o *volver a llamar,* no *llamar atrás*.
- Anime a los hispanohablantes a formar parejas con estudiantes monolingües para que hagan y contesten preguntas entre sí con estos verbos. Por ejemplo: *¿A qué hora regresas de la universidad?* ⟶ *Regreso a las seis.*

5. **Conjugated Verb** + *Infinitive*
As in English, when two Spanish verbs are used in sequence and there is no change of subject, the second verb is usually in the infinitive form.

Necesito mandar un mensaje.
I need to send a text (message).

Me gusta bailar.
I like to dance.

6. **Tense**
In both English and Spanish, conjugated verb forms also indicate the *time* or *tense* (**el tiempo**) of the action: *I speak* (present), *I spoke* (past).

Some English equivalents of the present tense forms of Spanish verbs are shown at the right.

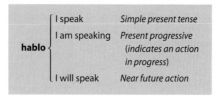

hablo	I speak	*Simple present tense*
	I am speaking	*Present progressive (indicates an action in progress)*
	I will speak	*Near future action*

¡OJO!

The exact English equivalent of a Spanish verb form depends on the context in which the verb appears. In the following sentence, the word **mañana** indicates a future action, so **hablo** means *I will:* **Hablo con Juan mañana.**

Negation / La negación

In Spanish the word **no** is placed before the conjugated verb to make a negative sentence.

subject + **no** + *verb*

El estudiante **no habla** español.
The student doesn't speak Spanish.

No, **no necesito** dinero.
No, I don't need money.

Práctica

A. Asociaciones. ¿Qué verbos asocia Ud. con las siguientes ideas? Dé infinitivos.

1. español
2. mucho (*a lot of*) dinero
3. en la librería
4. en el salón de clase
5. un coche (*car*)
6. a la residencia
7. Coca-Cola o café (*coffee*)
8. la música

B. ¡Anticipemos! Mis compañeros y yo

Paso 1. ¿Sí o no? Cambie (*Change*) las oraciones falsas.

MODELO: Toco el piano → Sí, toco el piano.
(No, no toco el piano. Toco la guitarra.)

1. Necesito más (*more*) dinero.
2. Trabajo en la biblioteca.
3. Canto en un coro (*choir*) de la universidad.
4. Tomamos ocho clases cada (*every*) semestre/trimestre.
5. Bailamos salsa en el salón de clase.
6. Deseamos hablar español correctamente.
7. El profesor / La profesora enseña italiano.
8. El profesor / La profesora habla muy bien el alemán (*German*).

Paso 2. En parejas (*pairs*), hagan y contesten preguntas (*ask and answer questions*) basadas en el **Paso 1.**

MODELO: Toco el piano. →
ESTUDIANTE 1: ¿Tocas el piano?
ESTUDIANTE 2: Sí, **toco** el piano. (No, no **toco** el piano.)

Autoprueba

Give the present tense endings for **pagar.**

1. yo pag____
2. tú pag____
3. ella pag____
4. nosotros pag____
5. ellos pag____

Answers: **1.** pago **2.** pagas **3.** paga **4.** pagamos **5.** pagan

¡Anticipemos! means *Let's look ahead!* These activities allow you to use new grammar but without having to come up with the forms on your own. As you do these activities, think about the grammar point you are practicing (**-ar** verbs, in this case) and how it is used in the activity.

NATIONAL STANDARDS: Cultures

Salsa is a dance typically associated with Hispanics, but it is now part of mainstream culture in this country. It originated in Cuba and later spread to Puerto Rico, then to the rest of Latin America. The dance is still essentially Cuban, with deep Afro-Cuban beats and the musical influence of *son, guaguancó,* and *rumba*. As you might imagine, the name *salsa* comes from the Spanish word for *sauce,* which connotes a spicy flavor in Western Hemisphere Spanish.

- Have students give the subject pronouns for *enseño, cantamos, estudian, paga, trabajan, desean, buscas, compra, habláis, regresas, bailan, tomo, escucha, necesitamos, toco, mandan.*
- Explain the purpose of the pattern practice (see "Teaching Techniques: Drills" in the IM), and tell students how you want them to do it.

En la clase de español

1. *Ud. estudia mucho.* (*nosotros, yo, ellos, Juan, tú, vosotras*)
2. *Sara necesita un diccionario.* (*yo, Carlos y tú, tú, nosotras, Ada, vosotros*)

En una fiesta en la residencia

1. *Clara toma Coca-Cola.* (*tú, Ud., él, Uds., Elena y yo, vosotras*)
2. *Tú cantas y bailas.* (*nosotros, los amigos, Uds., Eva y Diego, yo, vosotros*)

Prác. A: Notes

- This activity focuses exclusively on the *meaning* of the new *-ar* infinitives.
- Active vocabulary: *el café, mucho.*

Prác. A: Suggestion

Reverse the activity. Do the items in the student text, then ask students to close their books. Give an infinitive and ask students for associated words and phrases. They need not be items from *Prác. A.*

Prác. A: Possible answers

1. *hablar* **2.** *pagar* **3.** *comprar* **4.** *escuchar, estudiar, hablar* **5.** *comprar* **6.** *regresar* **7.** *tomar* **8.** *escuchar*

Prác. A: Extension

9. *en una fiesta* (*bailar, cantar, escuchar, tomar*) **10.** *el béisbol o el golf* (*practicar*) **11.** *un piano o una flauta* (*practicar, tocar*) **12.** *en un restaurante* (*pagar, tomar, trabajar*)

Prác. B: Notes

- See the IM for a discussion of input activities such as this one.
- Point out to students that, generally, the subject pronoun is not used before the verb in a sentence except for clarity or emphasis. The conjugated verb informs the listener as to the identity of the subject.
- Active vocabulary: *más, el italiano, el alemán*

Prác. B: Suggestions

- **Paso 2.** Encourage students to create their own questions.
- Ask students to find the conjugated verb in each sentence, then give the infinitive.

Prác. C: Notes

- Use item 3 to practice *vosotros,* if you wish. *Vosotros* forms are not explicitly practiced in the student text.
- This activity gives students very focused practice with the most basic concepts of subject pronouns and subject/verb agreement with *-ar* verbs. No context has been provided because the purpose of the activity is to focus on grammar concepts. Enough is happening linguistically in these sentences (from the standpoint of the true beginning student) to make context unnecessary.
- Active vocabulary: *con frecuencia, el francés, la matrícula*

Prác. D: Notes

- The majority of the items in comprehension activities of this kind are inferential; that is, students need to apply their knowledge of the paragraph to the individual items in order to decide if an item is *cierto* or *falso*.
- Active vocabulary: *el apartamento, regresar a casa*

Prác. D: Suggestion

Have students explain their answers in simple sentences, for example:

1. *Falso. Marcos está en el apartamento con los estudiantes.* Students might disagree about and discuss items of this kind. For example, another student might say: *¡Sí! Hay profesores en las fiestas de los estudiantes,* and so on.

Prác. D: Follow-up

Do orally or as dictation.

Cambie por el plural.

1. *Él no desea tomar cerveza.*
2. *Ud. baila muy bien.*
3. *¿Compro el lápiz mañana?*
4. *Hablas con la dependienta.*
5. *¿Hay solo una extranjera en la clase?*

Cambie por el singular.

6. *Ellas no buscan el dinero.*
7. *¿Enseñan Uds. solo dos clases de español?*
8. *Necesitamos unos libros de texto.*
9. *Las mujeres estudian sicología.*
10. *¿Pagan Uds. solo 30 pesos?*

Con. A: Notes

- This kind of activity is called a sentence builder. Each subject and verb can be used with more than one item from the right-hand column; many sentences are possible. The use of *no* is optional. (See the IM for more information.) Emphasize that forms of *desear* and *necesitar* must be followed by an infinitive. Also emphasize that verbs of motion, like *regresar*, are followed by *a*.
- Active vocabulary: *en casa, muy, tarde, temprano*

Prác. C: Answers
Paso 1. 1. *Ellas no desean estudiar francés.* **2.** *Uds. bailan muy bien el tango.* **3.** *¿Mandan Uds. muchos mensajes?* **4.** *Escuchamos la radio con frecuencia.*
Paso 2. 1. *Ella no busca el dinero.* **2.** *El/La estudiante no necesita seis clases.* **3.** *Pago mucho dinero de matrícula.* **4.** *¿Compra Ud. / Compras tú muchos libros?*

C. Una o más personas

Paso 1. Cambie por (*Change to*) un sujeto plural.

MODELOS: Él no desea tomar café. ⟶
Ellos no **desean** tomar café.
Yo no deseo tomar café. ⟶
Nosotros no **deseamos** tomar café.

1. Ella no desea estudiar francés (*French*).
2. Ud. baila muy bien el tango.
3. ¿Mandas muchos (*a lot of*) mensajes?
4. Escucho la radio con frecuencia.

Paso 2. Ahora cambie por un sujeto singular. En los números 2 y 4 hay más de una opción.

1. Ellas no buscan el dinero.
2. Los estudiantes no necesitan seis clases.
3. Pagamos mucho dinero de matrícula (*tuition*).
4. ¿Compran Uds. muchos libros?

D. En una fiesta. The following paragraphs describe a party. First scan the paragraphs to get a general sense of their meaning. Then complete the paragraphs with the correct form of the numbered infinitives.

¿A Ud. le gustan las fiestas?

Esta noche[a] hay una fiesta en el apartamento de Marcos y Julio. Todos[b] los estudiantes (cantar[1]) y (bailar[2]). Una persona (tocar[3]) la guitarra y otras personas (escuchar[4]) la música.

Jaime (buscar[5]) una Coca-Cola. Marta (hablar[6]) con un amigo. María José (desear[7]) enseñarles a todos[c] un baile[d] de Colombia. Todas las estudiantes desean (bailar[8]) salsa con el estudiante mexicano —¡él (bailar[9]) muy bien!

La fiesta es estupenda, pero todos (necesitar[10]) regresar a casa[e] o a su[f] cuarto temprano.[g] ¡Hay clases mañana!

[a]Esta... *Tonight* [b]*All* [c]enseñarles... *to teach everyone* [d]*dance* [e]a... *home* [f]*their* [g]*early*

Prác. D: Answers
1. *cantan* **2.** *bailan* **3.** *toca* **4.** *escuchan* **5.** *busca* **6.** *habla* **7.** *desea* **8.** *bailar* **9.** *baila* **10.** *necesitan*

Comprensión

	CIERTO	FALSO
1. Marcos es profesor de español.	☐	☑
2. A Jaime le gusta el café.	☐	☑
3. María José es de Colombia.	☑	☐
4. Los estudiantes desean bailar.	☑	☐

Conversación

A. Oraciones lógicas. Form at least eight complete logical sentences by using one word or phrase from each column. The words and phrases may be used more than once, in many combinations. Be sure to use the correct form of the verbs. Make any of the sentences negative, if you wish.

MODELO: Yo no estudio francés.

yo tú (un[a] estudiante) nosotros (los miembros de esta clase) los estudiantes de aquí el extranjero un secretario una profesora de español una dependienta	+	(no) { buscar comprar enseñar estudiar hablar mandar pagar regresar tocar tomar trabajar	+	la guitarra, el piano, el violín el edificio de ciencias en la cafetería, en la universidad, en casa en una oficina, en una librería a casa muy tarde (*very late*)/temprano (*early*) a la biblioteca a las dos muchos/pocos mensajes francés, alemán, italiano, inglés bien el español los libros de texto con un cheque libros y cuadernos en la librería
	+	(no) { desear necesitar	+	tomar una clase de computación hablar bien el español estudiar más comprar una calculadora, una mochila pagar la matrícula en septiembre

¡OJO!

Remember that the verb form that follows **desear** or **necesitar** is the infinitive, just as in English.

Nota comunicativa

Cómo expresar las partes del día

You can use the preposition **por** to mean *in* or *during* when expressing the part of the day in which something happens.

Estudio **por** la mañana y trabajo **por** la tarde. **Por** la noche, estoy en casa.
I study in the morning and I work in the afternoon. At night I'm at home.

¡OJO!

Remember that **de la mañana (tarde, noche)** are used when a specific hour of the day is mentioned. Also, remember to use **a la una / a las dos (tres…)** to express a specific time of day.

Generalmente estudio en casa **por** la mañana.

Hoy estudio con Javier en la biblioteca **a las** diez **de** la mañana.

B. Intercambios (*Exchanges*)

Paso 1. Use los siguientes verbos y frases para crear (*create*) cinco preguntas (*questions*) interesantes.

MODELO: ¿**Cantas** bien?

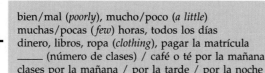

1. cantar o bailar **2.** estudiar o trabajar **3.** necesitar **4.** tomar **5.** tomar	+	bien/mal (*poorly*), mucho/poco (*a little*) muchas/pocas (*few*) horas, todos los días dinero, libros, ropa (*clothing*), pagar la matrícula _____ (número de clases) / café o té por la mañana clases por la mañana / por la tarde / por la noche

Paso 2. En parejas, túrnense (*take turns*) para hacer y contestar (*answer*) sus (*your*) preguntas del **Paso 1.**

MODELO: ESTUDIANTE 1: ¿Cantas bien?
ESTUDIANTE 2: Sí, **canto** bien. (No, **canto** mal.)

Nota comunicativa

Suggestion

Point out that the Spanish prepositions do not translate exactly as students might expect: *at night* = *por la noche* or *de la noche*. In these phrases the preposition *a* is not used.

Con B: Note

Active vocabulary: *mal, poco* ([a] little)

Con. B: Follow-up

Ask a sample question of several individual students, then have them report answers to others, for example: *Juan, ¿Ana estudia mucho o poco?* → *Ana estudia mucho.*

Con. B: Variation

Say the following statements. If students believe you, they respond with *Es cierto*. If they think you are lying, they say *Es falso*.

1. *Hablo español, inglés y francés.*
2. *Bailo muy bien.*
3. *No regreso a casa hoy.*
4. *Por la noche, enseño a estudiantes extranjeros.*
5. *Toco la guitarra.*

Encourage students to make up original statements of their own to say to the class.

Redacción

As homework, ask students to write out the answers that their partner gave to the *Intercambios* questions. Model sample answers when you make this assignment, to stress the use of *él/ella* forms. Collect the homework and use the assignment as the basis for in-class discussion, based on the information in the answers.

If you do not do *Con. B* as an interactive activity, assign it as written homework, with students creating sentences based on their own lives.

Con. B: Optional

The *Intercambios* activities in the first chapters of *Puntos de partida* are relatively structured, allowing little room for students to get in over their heads or encounter linguistic difficulties. If you prefer a more controlled format for partner/pair activities, use the items given in *Intercambios* as the basis for questions (written on the board) for students to use to interview each other. For example, based on item 1 in the student text: *¿Cantas bien?, ¿Bailas mucho?*, and so on.

Optional (Full-class discussion)

1. *¿Estudia Ud. mucho o poco? ¿Dónde estudia? ¿en casa, en la residencia, en la biblioteca? ¿Cuándo le gusta estudiar, por la mañana, por la tarde o por la noche?*
2. *¿Toca un instrumento musical? ¿Cuál es?* (Offer cognates: *el piano, la guitarra, el violín*)
3. *¿Trabaja? ¿Dónde? ¿Cuántas horas al día? ¿Trabaja todos los días de la semana?*
4. *¿Qué necesita pagar este semestre/trimestre? ¿libros de texto? ¿diccionarios? ¿la matrícula?*

(Cont. at left.)

Nota comunicativa

Suggestions

- Emphasize the irregular *yo* form and the accents on other forms.
- Emphasize the use of *estar* for (1) condition or state of health, (2) location. Students have used *estar* to express both concepts since *Cap. 1*.
- At this time, avoid explaining differences between *ser* and *estar*. If students ask, just tell them more than one verb expresses *to be* in Spanish.

Preliminary Exercises

Have students use the cues to form sentences.

- *¿Cómo están Uds.?*
  1. *yo / muy bien*
  2. *tú / bien*
  3. *el profesor (la profesora) / muy bien*
  4. *nosotros / mal*
  5. *Julio / mal también*
  6. *Uds. / bien*
- *¿Dónde están las siguientes ciudades?*
  1. *Amarillo, Los Ángeles, San Agustín, Toledo, Santa Fe, Reno*
  2. *Managua, Guadalajara, Buenos Aires, La Habana, Quito, La Paz, Bogotá*

Con. C: Note

Emphasize the use of the definite article with titles when talking about persons, as in *El Sr. Ramírez habla español*. Contrast this with *Buenos días, Sr. Ramírez*. No article is used when speaking directly to a person.

Con. C: Variation

Bring illustrations to class. Using *¿quién(es)?*, ask questions based on them, for example, *¿Quién busca el libro?*, and so on. Students respond with the name of the person only.

Resources: Transparency 12

Nota **comunicativa**

El verbo *estar*

Estar is a Spanish **-ar** verb that means *to be*. You have already used forms of it to ask how others are feeling or to tell where things are located. Here is the complete present tense conjugation of **estar.** Note that the **yo** form is irregular. The other forms take regular **-ar** endings, and some have an accent to maintain the stress pattern.

yo	**estoy**	nosotros/as	**estamos**
tú	**estás**	vosotros/as	**estáis**
Ud., él, ella	**está**	Uds., ellos, ellas	**están**

You will learn the uses of the verb **estar,** along with those of **ser** (a second Spanish verb that means *to be*) gradually, over the next several chapters. Review what you already know by answering these questions.

1. ¿Cómo está Ud. en este momento (*right now*)?
2. ¿Cómo están sus (*your*) compañeros? (Mis compañeros…)
3. ¿Dónde está Ud. en este momento?

You will use **estar** in **Conversación C.**

C. ¿Dónde están? Tell where these people are and what they are doing.

MODELO: FOTO 1: La Sra. Martínez ____. →
La Sr. Martínez **está en una oficina. Trabaja por la tarde. Necesita…**

Estrategia

Remember to use the definite article with titles when you are talking *about* a person: **el señor Santana, la profesora Aguilar,** and so on.

Vocabulario útil

hablar por teléfono	**tomar apuntes** to take notes
mandar un mensaje	**usar una computadora**
preparar la lección	
pronunciar las palabras	

1. La Sra. Martínez ____.
   Trabaja por ____.
   Necesita ____.
   Busca ____.

2. Estas (*These*) personas ____.
   El profesor ____.
   Una estudiante ____.
   Un estudiante ____.

Heritage Speakers

En algunos dialectos del español, especialmente en los del sur de los Estados Unidos y California, algunos hispanohablantes dicen *tomar notas* por *tomar apuntes*. La palabra *nota* en español significa *calificación* y equivale a la palabra *grade* en inglés. También hay algunas personas que usan la palabra *grado* en vez de *calificación*. Para decir *grade* en español, se recomienda usar *nota* o *calificación* en vez de *grado*.

4 Getting Information (Part 1)

Asking Yes/No Questions

Grammar Tutorial 4
connect SPANISH
www.connectspanish.com

Gramática en acción: La matriculación

PENÉLOPE: ... y ahora necesito una clase más por la mañana. ¿Hay sitio en la clase de Sociología 2?
JAVIER: A ver... No, no hay.
PENÉLOPE: ¿Hay un curso de historia o de matemáticas?
JAVIER: Solo por la noche. ¿Deseas tomar una clase por la noche?
PENÉLOPE: ¡Ay, chico, es imposible! Trabajo por la noche.
JAVIER: Pues... ¿qué tal la clase de Literatura latinoamericana?
PENÉLOPE: ¡Perfecto! ¡Me gustan mucho las novelas de Isabel Allende y la poesía de Pablo Neruda! ¿Cuándo es la clase?

Comprensión

1. ¿Necesita Penélope dos clases más? no, una
2. ¿Hay sitio en Sociología 2? no
3. ¿Cuál es el problema con los cursos de historia y matemáticas? Son por la noche y Penélope trabaja.
4. ¿Qué curso recomienda Javier por fin? Literatura latinoamericana

You have been asking questions since the beginning of *Puntos de partida*, and you learned more about asking questions in **Nota comunicativa (Vocabulario: Preparación).** This section will help you review all that you know about this topic as well as learn another way to ask questions in Spanish.

1. **Types of Questions**
   There are two kinds of questions (**preguntas**) in English and in Spanish.
   - *Information questions* ask for information, for facts. They typically begin with *interrogative words* (**las palabras interrogativas**). You have already learned a number of them.

Preguntas informativas

—¿**Qué** lengua habla Ud.?
—Hablo español.

¡OJO!

Remember that intonation drops at the end of an information question in Spanish, whereas it rises in English.

   - *Yes/No questions* can be answered by a simple **sí** or **no.**

Preguntas sí/no

—¿Habla Ud. francés?
—No.

Registration *PENÉLOPE: . . . and now I need one more class in the morning. Is there room in Sociology 2? JAVIER: Let's see . . . No, there isn't (room). PENÉLOPE: Is there a history or a math course? JAVIER: Only at night. Do you want to take a night class? PENÉLOPE: Come on, that's impossible! I work at night. JAVIER: Well . . . what about the Latin American Literature class? PENÉLOPE: Perfect! I love Isabel Allende's novels and Pablo Neruda's poetry. When's the class?*

Gramática 4

Asking Yes/No Questions

Note

No *¿Recuerda Ud.?* section precedes this grammar point, since that material was presented earlier in this chapter.

Follow-up

- Encourage students to react (*sí* or *no*) to the desirability of taking the following courses at the following times: *el inglés por la mañana / por la noche; el cálculo por la mañana / por la tarde; la sicología por la tarde / por la mañana; las ciencias por la noche.*
- After you have presented the grammar, return to the *GEA* and ask students to analyze the questions in the dialogue and in the comprehension questions. They should be able to identify all of them by type.
- Point out to students the colloquial use of *¿qué tal... ?* to ask *what about... ?*

Gram. 2: Note

Active vocabulary: *aquí, todos los días*

Heritage Speakers

En los Estados Unidos, algunos hispanohablantes dicen *registrar/registración* por *matricularse/matrícula.* Fuera de los Estados Unidos, la palabra *registrar* significa *el acto de inscribir en una oficina un documento público*, por ejemplo, *registrar un nacimiento.* Para decir *to register / sign up for a class* en español, se recomienda usar *matricularse.*

NATIONAL STANDARDS: Cultures

- Isabel Allende (1942–): Chilean journalist and creative writer (especially of historical fiction) who now resides in the United States.
- Pablo Neruda (1914–1973): Chilean poet and politician who won the Nobel Prize for Literature in 1971

Inversion: Suggestions

- Point out that English also puts a verb form in front of the subject when forming *yes/no* questions: *You work here?* ⟶ *Do you work here?*
- You may wish to point out to students that the position of the subject in inversion questions can vary greatly and that the meaning of the question can vary slightly depending on where the inverted subject is placed. Long subjects in particular are placed at the end of a question: *¿Baila con Guillermo la estudiante alemana?* However, it is not necessary to go into great detail about this. Exercises and activities will be very clear so that students don't get into linguistic difficulties.

Preliminary Exercise

Have students listen to and identify the following as statements or questions.

1. *¿Regresa Ud. mañana?*
2. *Pepe necesita un bolígrafo.*
3. *¿Hablamos bien?*
4. *¿Bailas con Carmen?*
5. *Uds. estudian mucho.*
6. *¿Desean tocar el piano?*
7. *¿Alicia toca el violín?*
8. *Tomas una clase de comunicaciones.*
9. *Uds. compran cuadernos en la librería.*
10. *¿El profesor solo habla español en clase?*

Prác. B: Suggestion

Point out that the answer and the question do not need to contain identical information. For example: [Question] *¿Es Ud. turista?* [Answer] *Sí, soy de los Estados Unidos.* See how many different questions students can invent.

Prác. B: Note

Active vocabulary: *un poco*

Prác. B: Extension

7. *Sí, regreso a casa a las diez.*
8. *No, no canto bien.*
9. *Sí, hablo mucho por teléfono.*
10. *Sí, bailo en las fiestas.*

2. Forming Yes/No Questions

There are two ways to form this kind of question.

- Rising intonation: The simplest way is to make your voice rise at the end of a statement. Doing so makes the statement into a question.
- Inversion: Another way to form yes/no questions is to invert (transpose) the order of the subject and verb, in addition to making your voice rise at the end of the question. You can also put the subject all the way at the end of the question.

STATEMENT: Ud. trabaja aquí todos los días.
You work here every day.

QUESTION: ¿Ud. trabaja aquí todos los días?
Do you work here every day?

STATEMENT: **Ud.** trabaja aquí todos los días.

QUESTIOÇN: ¿Trabaja **Ud.** aquí todos los días?

STATEMENT: **María** manda muchos mensajes.

QUESTION: ¿Manda muchos mensajes **María**?

Autoprueba

Give the English equivalent for these yes/no questions.

1. ¿Habla Ud. inglés?
2. ¿Necesitan Uds. otra clase?
3. ¿Tomas biología?
4. ¿Trabajo mañana?

Answers: **1.** *Do you speak English?* **2.** *Do you (pl.) need another class?* **3.** *Are you taking (a) biology (class)?* **4.** *Do (Will) I work tomorrow?*

Práctica

A. Opciones

Paso 1. Ask the following yes/no questions, being sure to make your voice rise at the end of each one.

1. ¿Alicia toca el violín?
2. ¿Uds. compran mochilas en la librería?
3. ¿Ud. habla español en clase?
4. ¿Miguel René y Silvia estudian por la tarde?
5. ¿Muchos estudiantes mandan mensajes?

Paso 2. Now change the order of subject and verb to ask the questions in another way.

MODELO: **1.** ¿Alicia toca el violín? ⟶ ¿Toca **Alicia** el violín?

When you do item 1, ask the question in a way that is different from that given in the model.

B. Una conversación entre (*between*) **Diego y Lupe.** Diego and Lupe recently met each other. While having coffee, Lupe asks Diego some questions to find out more about him. Ask Lupe's questions that led to Diego's answers.

MODELO: Sí, estudio antropología. ⟶ ¿**Estudias** antropología?

1. Sí, soy estadounidense (*from the United States*).
2. Sí, estudio con frecuencia.
3. No, no toco el piano. Toco la guitarra clásica.
4. No, no deseo trabajar más horas.
5. No, no hablo francés, pero hablo italiano un poco.
6. No, no soy reservado. ¡Soy muy extrovertido!

NATIONAL STANDARDS: Comparisons

Many people believe that intonation is a reflection of a speaker's emotions, but the use of intonation in languages is conventionalized. When a speaker uses the wrong intonation in a second language, the message may be unclear or distorted.

Heritage Speakers

Anime a los hispanohablantes que lean algunas preguntas y repuestas y pídales a los angloparlantes que imiten la entonación.

Conversación

A. Intercambios: Sus (*Your*) **actividades**

Paso 1. Use the following cues as a guide to form questions that you will ask a classmate. You may ask other questions as well. Write the questions on a sheet of paper. **¡OJO!** Use the **tú** form of the verbs.

MODELO: escuchar música por la mañana →
¿**Escuchas** música por la mañana?

1. estudiar en la biblioteca por la noche
2. practicar español con un amigo o amiga
3. tomar un poco de (*a little bit of*) café por la mañana
4. bailar mucho en las fiestas
5. tocar un instrumento musical
6. regresar a casa muy tarde/temprano
7. comprar los libros en la librería de la universidad
8. hablar mucho por teléfono
9. trabajar los fines de semana (*weekends*)
10. usar (*to use*) un diccionario bilingüe

Paso 2. Now use the questions to get information from your partner. Jot down his or her answers for use in **Paso 3.**

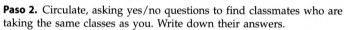

MODELO: **ESTUDIANTE 1:** ¿Escuchas música por la mañana?
ESTUDIANTE 2: Sí, (No, no) **escucho** música por la mañana.

Paso 3. With the information you gathered in **Paso 2,** report your partner's answers to the class. (You will use the **él/ella** form of the verbs when reporting.)

MODELO: Jenny no **escucha** música por la mañana.

B. ¿Qué clases tomas?

Paso 1. Make a list in Spanish of the classes you are taking. Ask your instructor or use a dictionary to find the names of classes you don't know how to say in Spanish. If you ask your instructor, remember to ask in Spanish: **¿Cómo se dice ____ en español?**

Paso 2. Circulate, asking yes/no questions to find classmates who are taking the same classes as you. Write down their answers.

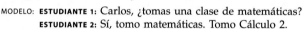

MODELO: **ESTUDIANTE 1:** Carlos, ¿tomas una clase de matemáticas?
ESTUDIANTE 2: Sí, tomo matemáticas. Tomo Cálculo 2.

Paso 3. Report back the information you have learned to the whole class.

MODELO: Carlos y yo tomamos matemáticas. Jennie y yo… Solo yo tomo geología.

Mundo interactivo

You should now be prepared to work with Scenario 1, Activity 4 in Connect Spanish (**www.connectspanish.com**).

Con. A: Note

Active vocabulary: *un poco de*

Con. A: Variation

For *Paso 2,* invite students to interview you to practice *Ud.* forms.

Con. A: Follow-up

- **Redacción:** Have students use either cues in *Paso 1* or the information they gathered in *Paso 2* to write a short paragraph either about themselves (*yo*) or about their partner (third person).
- For *Paso 3,* ask students: *¿Cuántas personas en la clase… bailan mucho (poco) en las fiestas / practican español con un compañero (una compañera)? ¿Quién baila mucho? ¿Quién no toma café? ¿Qué le gusta tomar por la mañana?* As much as possible, use words like *poco* vs. *mucho, pocos/as* vs. *muchos/as,* and *solo/a.*

Con. B: Note

Note the focused practice with *tú* forms in *Paso 2* and with *nosotros* forms in *Paso 3.*

Con. B: Suggestions

- Be sure that all students have written down the names of their courses before beginning to circulate around the room. Tell individual students to write the names of any courses you have to provide for them in the *Vocabulario personal* box in the *En resumen* section of this chapter.
- Encourage quick exchanges and suggest that students not ask any one student more than two questions in a row. Once students learn the rules of such circulation activities, they will perform them quickly. Be prepared for some confusion the first time you try one in class.

NATIONAL STANDARDS: Communication

In activities like the ones included in the *Conversación* section, students are asking real questions about real information. Note in *Con. A* that students are told to write the questions on a piece of paper. You may instead provide the questions in the form of a handout.

Heritage Speakers

Pregúnteles a los hispanohablantes si prefieren decir *tomar un curso* o *hacer un curso.* La expresión *tomar un curso* se usa en muchos países latinoamericanos, mientras que esta expresión suena extraña en España, donde prefieren decir *hacer* o *coger un curso.* No importa la expresión que se use, las dos expresiones se entienden perfectamente bien.

Un poco de todo

A: Suggestions

- **Pronunciación:** Present the pronunciation of *orquesta*. It is very similar to English *orchestra*, but the spelling is quite different.
- Have students describe the following persons by telling what they do and, if possible, where they do it.
  1. *un secretario*
  2. *una profesora*
  3. *un estudiante*
  4. *una dependienta*
  5. *un bibliotecario*

A: Redacción

Have students take notes on their partner's answers in *Paso 2*, then write a short description of their partner's activities. Read some of the best and/or most interesting paragraphs to the class, without identifying the student, and ask the class to guess who is described.

B: Suggestions

- Explain that this type of exercise is called a "cloze" passage. Explain its purpose (see the "Drills" section of the "Teaching Techniques" chapter in the IM).
- It is a good idea to work through this first cloze passage in class to help students understand how the activity works.
- In particular, help students understand item 16. When the subject pronoun is given in italics, it is not necessary actually to use it to complete the sentences; it is there only as a clue for students, especially in situations in which the subjects are alternating.

B: Note

The following grammar topics are included in *Lengua y cultura:* lexical items, *hay*, gender and number of nouns, articles, *-ar* verbs, modal verb + infinitive.

B: Pronunciación

Use the *Lengua y cultura* passage as an opportunity to present and practice the pronunciation of the letter *x*, similar to /j/ (as in *Texas* and *mexicoamericanos*).

B: Follow-up

Encourage students to work in groups of three to form as many questions as they can based on the information in the paragraph. Two students will write the questions, the third will answer them.

Un poco de todo

A. Intercambios: En la universidad

Paso 1. Tell what you and others do at the following university locations. Give as many actions as you can think of for each place.

MODELO: en el salón de clase → En el salón de clase la profesora enseña español y los estudiantes hablamos (hablan) español.

1. en el salón de clase
2. en la librería
3. en la biblioteca
4. en la oficina del consejero

Paso 2. Now form questions about things that typically happen at a university. Use the options given with the infinitives or provide your own options. Then use your questions to interview one of your classmates. You will answer his or her questions.

MODELO: comprar / libros →
¿Compras libros en la librería del *campus*? ¿Qué compras en la librería?

1. estudiar en la biblioteca / todos los días / los fines de semana
2. trabajar en el *campus* / buscar trabajo
3. tocar en la orquesta de la universidad / la guitarra en casa
4. tomar / seis clases este semestre / trimestre

B. Lengua y cultura: Dos universidades fabulosas... y diferentes. Complete the following description of two well-known universities. Give the correct form of the verbs in parentheses, as suggested by context. When the subject pronoun is in *italics*, don't use it in the sentence. When two possibilities are given in parentheses, select the correct word.

La Colección Latinoamericana Benson, una colección comprensiva de libros, documentos, revistas (*magazines*) y periódicos (*newspapers*) relacionados con (*related to*) Latinoamérica

Act. B, Select Answers: **7.** *toman* **12.** *practican* **13.** *participan* **15.** *pagan* **16.** *Desea*

¿Busca Ud. la universidad perfecta? (Hay/Es[1]) dos (universidad/universidades[2]) muy famosas en los Estados Unidos. La primera[a] es (el/la[3]) Universidad de Texas, en Austin. ¡Es (un/una[4]) universidad muy grande[b]! Hay veinticuatro grupos sociales para estudiantes hispanos y una (librería/biblioteca[5]) con una colección latinoamericana fantástica, la Colección Latinoamericana Benson. (Los/Las[6]) materias más populares en la UT son: administración de empresas, ingeniería, humanidades y comunicaciones. Muchos estudiantes (tomar[7]) cursos en (el/la[8]) Instituto de Estudios Latinoamericanos y en (el/la[9]) Centro para Estudios Mexicoamericanos.

Stanford, en (el/la[10]) estado de California, es una universidad menos grande.[c] Tiene[d] una residencia para estudiantes de español, la Casa Zapata. Allí,[e] (los/las[11]) estudiantes (practicar[12]) español y (participar[13]) en celebraciones hispanas. Las materias más populares en Stanford son:[f] biología, economía, inglés y ciencias políticas. (El/La[14]) problema en Stanford es que los estudiantes (pagar[15]) mucho por[g] la matrícula.

¿Prefiere Ud. la UT o Stanford? ¿(*Ud.*: Desear[16]) (estudia/estudiar[17]) en California o en Texas?

[a]La... *The first one* [b]*big* [c]menos... *smaller* [d]*It has* [e]*There* [f]*are* [g]*for*

Heritage Speakers

Anime a los hispanohablantes a formar parejas con estudiantes monolingües para que hagan y contesten preguntas entre sí con estos verbos. Por ejemplo: E1: *¿Fumas tú en casa?* E2: *No, yo no fumo. ¿Tomas tú refrescos en las fiestas?* E1: *Sí, tomo muchos refrescos en las fiestas, especialmente cuando bailo mucho.*

Resources: Desenlace

In the *Cap. 2* segment of "Chapter-by-Chapter Supplementary Materials" in the IM, you will find a chapter-culminating activity. You can use this activity to consolidate and review the vocabulary and grammar skills students have acquired.

Resources: Transparency 13

Comprensión. The following statements are false. Correct them.

1. En la Universidad de Texas hay dos grupos sociales para estudiantes hispanos. Hay 24.
2. En el Instituto de Estudios Latinoamericanos hay pocos (*few*) estudiantes. Hay muchos estudiantes.
3. La Universidad de Stanford está en Texas. Está en California.
4. La Casa Zapata es una biblioteca importante. Es una residencia para estudiantes.

C. ¿Qué pasa (*What's happening*) **en la fiesta?**

Paso 1. En parejas, describan la escena.

MODELO: En la fiesta, Pilar y Ana bailan. Nora…

Vocabulario útil

descansar to rest
escuchar
fumar to smoke
hablar
mirar to watch
  una película a movie
  la tele TV
tocar
  la batería drum set
  la guitarra
  el piano
tomar
  refrescos soft drinks

Paso 2. Ahora comparen la escena con las fiestas en su (*your*) universidad. Usen **nosotros.**

MODELO: En las fiestas, mis amigos y yo **bailamos.**

En su° comunidad

°*your*

All Spanish-speaking countries use the word **universidad** to refer to colleges or universities, big or small, public or private. But there is a lot of variation in the words that Spanish speakers use for *elementary school*, *middle school*, and *high school*. There is also great variation in how the following words and phrases are expressed: (*academic*) *grade* (and what symbols are used to give grades), *to pass*, *to fail*.

PREGUNTAS POSIBLES

- Ask someone who was raised in a Hispanic country what language is used in his or her country to express different levels of schooling and the grading system.
- Ask the person to describe his or her educational experience in the country of origin.
- If relevant, ask for a comparison with the educational system in this country.

NATIONAL STANDARDS: Communities

En su comunidad, which occurs at the end of every *Un poco de todo* section, is new to this edition of *Puntos de partida*. These activities are experiential in nature. They ask students to explore the Spanish-speaking community on their campus or in their area, thus encouraging students to use Spanish outside the classroom.

Bright Idea

B: Suggestion

Have students indicate what they felt was most important when they were looking for a university.

¿los profesores?
¿la fama de la universidad?
¿las «fraternidades»?
¿los grupos sociales?

Then ask: *¿Existe una universidad perfecta?*

C: Preliminary Exercise

Have students respond *lógico* or *ilógico*.

1. *Cuando estoy en el cine, fumo.*
2. *Descanso generalmente por la mañana.*
3. *Los estudiantes tocan la batería en mis clases.*
4. *Siempre hay música cuando Uds. estudian.*
5. *Uds. miran películas en el laboratorio de lenguas.*

En su comunidad

Notes

- *En su comunidad* is a new feature of this edition of *Puntos de partida*. These activities require students to find a Spanish speaker in their community and get information from them.
- Students might also complete these activities by doing research on-line.
- An additional option is to have students work with the same native informant for the whole semester/quarter or academic year.

Suggestions

- Establish clear guidelines for the selection of the native informant. For example: Can students talk to instructors or TAs in your department? Or do you prefer that they find someone off-campus?
- Ask students to get the following basic information: the informant's country of origin, how long he or she has lived in this country, and if the informant visits his or her country of origin frequently.
- Regardless of how you have students do this assignment, be certain to make class time available for students to share with the whole class what they have learned. Be clear about whether or not students will simply report orally or whether you expect them to turn something in.
- See additional suggestions in the IM.

TelePuntos

Note

Pages 50–55 are optional. You may cover some, all, or none of this material in class, or assign it to students—as a group or individually—for homework or extra credit. Pages 56–57 (*En resumen: En este capítulo*) are a summary of all of the chapter's active material.

Suggestions

- If you are using the video in class, show it once, ask brief comprehension questions, then show it again.
- Even if you plan to ask students to watch the video in your campus media center or on their own, it is a good idea to show the second program in class to get them started and teach them good viewing habits. It is especially important to stress the need to watch the shows as many times as they want or need to in order to complete the *Después de mirar* activities.

Antes de mirar

Suggestions

- Emphasize the phrase en *el extranjero* and also tell students to listen for the adjective *extranjeros.*
- The concept of *major* is often expressed as *concentración* in Spanish. (The word *especialización* is used to express *major* in the text, but it is not used in this video program.) In many Hispanic countries, university studies are also referred to as *la carrera,* a term that expresses both *university major* as well as *career.* This may be because, traditionally, in the Hispanic world, one studies to have a career, much more so than in this country, which has a tradition of liberal arts education, not preparation for a specific career.

Programa 2

Notes

- All of the language in *Programa 2* is scripted language, and it is more challenging than that of *Programa 1.* However, students should be able to grasp the general ideas presented in the show.
- Some past tense verbs are used in this show, but most of them are previewed for students in *Fragmento del guion.*
- Emphasize to students that the more carefully they study the preliminary activities (*Antes de mirar, Vocabulario de este programa, Fragmento del guion*), the more they will understand when viewing the episode. Scanning *Después de mirar* before viewing is also an excellent strategy.

TELEPUNTOS

SALU2

La Universidad de Guanajuato, México, fundada en 1744 (mil setecientos cuarenta y cuatro)

Antes de mirar°

°Antes… *Before watching*

El Programa 2 está relacionado con la universidad. Antes de mirar, conteste las siguientes preguntas.

1. ¿Cuál es su concentración (*your major*)? (Mi concentración…)
2. ¿Desea Ud. estudiar español en otro país (*country*)? ¿En cuál (*which one*)?
3. ¿Estudian muchos estudiantes de su (*your*) universidad en el extranjero (*abroad*)?

PROGRAMA 2: ¡Qué bacán!°

°¡Qué… *How great!*

You will not understand every word of this episode. But if you pay close attention to the images and listen for recognizable cognates and vocabulary that you already know, you will be able to get the gist of the show's content.

Remember that these words and phrases (given in the order in which they appear in the show) will help you understand more when you watch this episode.

Vocabulario de este° programa

°*this*

la vida	life	**vamos**	let's go
el/la periodista	reporter, journalist	**está a cuatro horas de**	is four hours away from
pasé	I spent	**caminan**	(they) walk
vamos a ver	we're going to see	**el orfanato**	orphanage
la ciudad	city	**es divertido**	it's fun
los barrios	neighborhoods	**yo debo**	I should
atrae (atraer)	it attracts (to attract)	**que tengan un buen día**	have a good day
aprenden (aprender)	they learn (to learn)		
como decimos	as we say		

Remember that reading part of the script before watching each segment of *Salu2* will help you understand more of the show.

Fragmento del guion°

°*script*

VÍCTOR: Pero, Ana, el tema[a] de la universidad no es interesante solo para los universitarios. También lo es[b] para los padres,[c] que con frecuencia pagan la universidad, ¿no?

ANA: Es cierto. La universidad es bien cara.[d] A propósito,[e] Víctor, ¿qué carrera estudiaste[f] en la universidad?

VÍCTOR: ¿Mi *major*? ¿Mi concentración? Tengo una doble concentración en inglés y sociología de UCLA, la Universidad de California, en Los Ángeles. Y después estudié para una maestría[g] en medios de comunicación, en UCLA también. ¿Y cuál fue[h] tu concentración?

ANA: Mi concentración, o mi carrera, como se dice en mi país, es comunicación social. Y yo soy de la Ciudad de Panamá y estudié[i] en la Universidad de Panamá.

[a]*topic* [b]También… *It is also (interesting)* [c]*parents* [d]bien… *very expensive* [e]A… *By the way* [f]¿qué… *in preparation for what career did you study?* [g]después… *then I did a Master's* [h]*was* [i]*I studied*

Ana y Víctor, los presentadores de *Salu2*

Mundo interactivo

Continue your work as an intern at HispanaVisión with Laura Sánchez Tejada, the roving reporter of *Salu2*, as you complete Scenario 1, Activities 3 and 4 in Connect Spanish (**www.connectspanish.com**).

Al mirar°

Al... *While you watch*

Mientras (*While*) mira el programa, indique los temas que aparecen (*appear*) en el programa. **¡OJO!** No todos los temas de la lista aparecen.

1. ☑ los estudios universitarios de los presentadores
2. ☐ los estudios universitarios de Laura, la reportera
3. ☑ el costo de estudiar en la universidad
4. ☑ universidades en el extranjero

El Centro de Idiomas, una de las modernas instalaciones de la Universidad del Pacífico

Después de mirar°

Después... *After watching*

A. ¿Está claro? ¿Cierto o falso? Corrija (*Correct*) las oraciones falsas.

	CIERTO	FALSO
1. Víctor estudió (*studied*) arquitectura en la universidad.	☐	☑
2. Ana estudió un semestre en la Argentina.	☐	☑
3. La Universidad del Pacífico está en Lima, Perú.	☑	☐
4. Los estudiantes extranjeros pueden ser (*can be*) voluntarios en Guanajuato, México.	☑	☐
5. La Universidad de Guanajuato tiene (*has*) un estupendo Centro de Idiomas (*Languages*).	☐	☑

B. Un poco más. Conteste las siguientes preguntas.

1. ¿Qué tipo de institución es la Universidad del Pacífico, privada o pública?
2. ¿Por qué es un buen lugar para estudiar la Universidad del Pacífico? (Tiene [*It has*]...)
3. ¿Qué actividades hacen (*do*) los estudiantes en la Universidad de Guanajuato?

C. Y ahora, Uds. En grupos, hablen de (*talk about*) su deseo o intención de estudiar en el extranjero.

MODELO: ESTUDIANTE 1: ¿Te gustaría (*Would you like*) estudiar en el extranjero?
ESTUDIANTE 2: No, no deseo estudiar en el extranjero.
ESTUDIANTE 3: Me gustaría (*I'd like*) estudiar en el extranjero, en (país).

Sobre° el programa

About

Víctor es de origen mexicano por ambos lados[a] de su[b] familia: su padre[c] es mexicoamericano de primera[d] generación y su madre es mexicoamericana de tercera[e] generación.

Víctor prefiere identificarse como chicano. «Chicano/a» es una palabra originalmente peyorativa[f] que fue reivindicada[g] de manera positiva durante el movimiento de los derechos civiles[h] en los años 60.[i] Hoy, en muchas universidades estadounidenses hay departamentos de estudios chicanos.

[a]por... *on both sides* [b]*his* [c]*father* [d]*first* [e]*third* [f]*negative* [g]que... *that was reclaimed* [h]derechos... *Civil Rights* [i]en... *in the 60s*

Remember that if you scan all of the activities in **Después de mirar** *before* watching the show, you will understand more of what is in the program.

Act. A, Answers: 1. *Falso: Víctor estudió inglés, sociología y comunicación.* **2.** *Falso: Víctor estudió un semestre en la Argentina.* **5.** *Falso: La Universidad del Pacífico tiene un estupendo Centro de Idiomas.*

Act. B, Answers: 1. *Es una universidad privada.* **2.** Possible answers: *Tiene un Centro de Idiomas. Está en el centro de Lima.* **3.** Possible answers: *Caminan en la ciudad. Hay teatros, museos y plazas. Practican el rápel. Trabajan en un orfanato.*

Producción personal

Filme una entrevista (*interview*) con dos o tres estudiantes sobre las materias que estudian y su (*their*) concentración universitaria.

Al mirar

Suggestion

Ask students to read the items before they start to watch. Since it is a short list, students should be able to keep the items in mind while watching (and should not need to look away from the screen to check off options).

Después de mirar

B: Optional

- Show the segment again and ask students to identify adjectives that express *fabulous, amazing: fantástico, impresionante, estupendo, increíble, bacán, padre, chévere, excelente, padrísimo.*
- Ask students if they remember which countries these expressions are associated with: *bacán* (*Perú*), *padre/padrísimo* (*México*), *chévere* (*Panamá*); also, most Caribbean countries, although that is not mentioned in the program).

C: Follow-up

- Ask students at which of the two universities profiled in the program they would prefer to study.
- As a whole class discussion, expand the conversation to discuss how long students want to study abroad: *¿Cuánto tiempo desean pasar en otro país? ¿un año académico, un semestre/trimestre, un verano?* (Write options on the board, as all of these words are new vocabulary.)

Sobre el programa

Optional: Comprensión

1. *¿De dónde es la familia de Víctor?* (*de México*) **2.** *¿Cuál es la identificación étnica de Víctor?* (*chicano*) **3.** *¿Dónde hay departamentos de estudios chicanos?* (*en las universidades de los Estados Unidos [estadounidenses]*)

Producción personal

Note

See the IM for additional suggestions for this chapter's assignment as well as for general guidelines and suggestions for video assignments.

A leer

Notes

A leer replaces *Lectura* sections from previous editions of *Puntos de partida*. The left-hand page includes author-written readings, primarily about the country of focus. The right-hand page offers authentic readings of various kinds, related to the chapter theme.

Lectura cultural

Notes

- This page of *A leer* offers two kinds of readings: **1.** information about the chapter's theme as it relates to the country of focus (always the first reading on the page, the one that is untitled, with a large initial letter) plus information about the theme in the rest of the Spanish-speaking world (*En otros países hispanos*); **2.** additional short items about the country of focus, varying in nature from chapter to chapter.
- For more information about the country of focus, see the chapter's opening pages and the IM.
- See the IM for some aspects of Spanish language usage in the U.S.

Lectura cultural

Notes

- *Quisqueya* is the *taíno* name for the island of *Española*, shared by *Haití* and *la República Dominicana.*
- *La Raza* is an expression very connected to Chicanos and the Chicano movement. It means *The Race*, and it comes from José de Vasconcelos' notion of a "cosmic race." Vasconcelos, a 20th century Mexican thinker, sees Latin Americans as a mestizo race, destined to a great future.

Exploración lingüística

Ask students to find the following in the reading. Some of these words are glossed and some are not.

- *Un sinónimo de estudiante. ¡OJO! Esta palabra tiene un falso cognado en inglés.* (*alumno/a*)
- *Un adjetivo relacionado con la palabra estudiante.* (*estudiantil*)
- *Las palabras en español que significan* reason *and* ambiance. (*razón, ambiente*)

En otros países hispanos

Note

Some of the most important Hispanic universities include: *la Universidad Nacional de México* (*UNAM*), *la Universidad de Chile, la Universidad de Córdoba* (*Argentina*), *la Universidad Complutense de Madrid* (*España*).

Tres símbolos...

Suggestion

Ask students to do an Internet search for Hispanic murals in the U.S. You may wish to suggest that students explore Judith Baca's website: www.judybaca.com.

A LEER°

A... *Let's read*

Lectura cultural

Los Estados Unidos

Un treinta y cinco por ciento de los latinos estadounidenses que[a] terminan la secundaria[b] continúan con los estudios universitarios. Algunos[c] estudian cerca de[d] casa, tal vez viviendo[e] con su familia por razones económicas o culturales. Otros estudian en universidades más distantes. En un ambiente[f] universitario es común encontrar[g] organizaciones latinas que apoyan[h] a los alumnos.[i] Estas organizaciones pueden estar dedicadas[j] a un grupo específico de latinos, como **Fuerza Quisqueyana** (dominicanos) o **Raza** (chicanos), o pueden ser para todos los latinos, como **Latinos Unidos.** Las organizaciones latinas coordinan eventos sociales y académicos —un baile con música salsa y merengue o una charla[k] con un escritor[l] latino. En algunas universidades hasta[m] hay una **Casa Latina,** donde los miembros de la organización viven juntos.[n]

¿Es Ud. miembro de algunas organizaciones estudiantiles? ¿De cuáles?

[a]*who* [b]*high school* [c]*Some* [d]cerca... *close to* [e]tal... *possibly living* [f]*environment* [g]*to find* [h]que... *that support* [i]*students* [j]pueden... *can be devoted* [k]*talk* [l]*writer* [m]*even* [n]viven... *live together*

En otros países° hispanos

°*countries*

- **En todo el mundo[a] hispanohablante** Hay universidades nacionales que son gratuitas[b] o muy económicas en comparación con las universidades privadas. Las universidades nacionales son con frecuencia las más prestigiosas y antiguas[c] del país.
- **En el Ecuador** Hay dos ciclos escolares: uno para la región de la Sierra, de octubre a junio, y el otro para la costa, de abril a enero.[d] La diferencia existe para evitar que haya escuela en los meses de lluvia,[e] porque[f] hay peligro de inundaciones.[g]

[a]*world* [b]que... *that are free* [c]las... *oldest* [d]*January* [e]para... *to avoid having school in the months of the rainy season* [f]*because* [g]peligro... *danger of flooding*

Tres símbolos latinos en los Estados Unidos

- **Los Departamentos de Estudios Latinos** Estos[a] demuestran que la presencia de la población latina estadounidense es cada vez mayor[b] en el mundo académico.
- **La bodega** Es todo un supermercado en una tienda pequeña[c] y toda una institución latina en el barrio.[d]

La memoria de nuestra tierra (*our land*), **parte de un mural de Judith Baca**

- **Los murales y el arte urbano** La tradición muralista mexicana con motivos[e] indigenistas está muy presente en las comunidades latinas de los Estados Unidos.

[a]*These* [b]cada... *increasingly greater* [c]tienda... *small shop* [d]*Hispanic neighborhood*

[e]*themes, elements*

Una cita°

°*quote*

"We would like you to know
we are not all brown.
Genetic history has made
some of us blue eyed as any
German immigrant
and as black as a descendant
of an African slave.
We never claimed to be
a homogeneous race."

Ana Castillo, autora chicana, del poema «We would like you to know»

COMPRENSIÓN

1. ¿Qué porcentaje de latinos estadounidenses estudia en la universidad? 35%
2. ¿Por qué viven con su familia algunos estudiantes universitarios latinos? por razones económicas o culturales
3. Si un estudiante no es dominicano o latino de origen, ¿cuál de las organizaciones latinas que (*that*) se mencionan en el texto es la mejor (*best*) para él? Latinos Unidos

Del mundo hispano°

Del... *From the Hispanic world*

Antes de leer°

Antes... *Before reading*

What is a good way for an adult to learn English? If in school (**una escuela**), what kind of school? With how many other learners in class? How many hours a day or a week?

Lectura: Un anuncio° de Inglés USA

Lectura... *Reading: An ad*

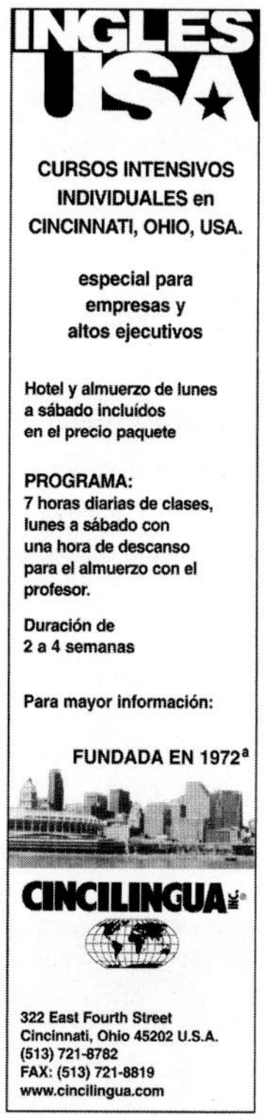

INGLES USA
CURSOS INTENSIVOS INDIVIDUALES en CINCINNATI, OHIO, USA.
especial para empresas y altos ejecutivos
Hotel y almuerzo de lunes a sábado incluídos en el precio paquete
PROGRAMA:
7 horas diarias de clases, lunes a sábado con una hora de descanso para el almuerzo con el profesor.
Duración de 2 a 4 semanas
Para mayor información:
FUNDADA EN 1972[a]
CINCILINGUA
322 East Fourth Street
Cincinnati, Ohio 45202 U.S.A.
(513) 721-8782
FAX: (513) 721-8819
www.cincilingua.com

[a]mil novecientos setenta y dos

Comprensión

A. Traducciones (*Translations*)**.** Empareje (*Match*) las frases en español del anuncio con sus equivalentes en inglés.

1. __c__ para empresas y altos ejecutivos
2. __e__ lunes a sábado
3. __a__ una hora de descanso
4. __f__ el almuerzo
5. __d__ semanas
6. __b__ mayor

a. *an hour-long break*
b. *more*
c. *for businesses and corporate executives*
d. *weeks*
e. *Monday through Saturday*
f. *lunch*

B. En el anuncio. Busque (*Look for*) la siguiente información en el anuncio. Si no está (*If it doesn't appear*), conteste (*answer*) **No hay información.**

1. ¿Cómo se llama la escuela? Cincilingua
2. ¿Dónde está la escuela? Cincinnati, OH, USA
3. ¿Cuántos estudiantes hay en una clase? 1, cursos individuales
4. ¿Cómo son (*are*) los profesores de la escuela? No hay información.
5. ¿Qué tipo de estudiantes hay en la escuela? ejecutivos
6. ¿De dónde son los estudiantes? No hay información.
7. ¿Cuántas horas de clase hay al (*per*) día? 7

Una cita

Notes

- Ana Castillo (Chicago, IL, 1953–): Chicana feminist writer; author of many acclaimed works, including *The Mixquiahuala Letters, So Far from God,* and *Peel my Love like an Onion.* More information is available at www.anacastillo.com
- This quote speaks to the frequent assumption that all Hispanics are alike (the same assumption often made about other ethnic or interest groups as well).

Del mundo hispano

Notes

- This page of the *A leer* section offers authentic readings from the Spanish-speaking world.
- The readings are realia-based in the first half of the text, with realia, newspaper excerpts, and so on, from a variety of countries. These readings are coordinated with the chapter theme but not with the country of focus.
- The second half of the text offers unabridged literary selections.
- All sections are supported by pre- and post-reading activities, as well as by a variety of discussion, writing, and Internet activities.
- See the IM for optional follow-up, writing, and Internet activities.

Antes de leer

Suggestion

Do this activity the day before assigning the reading, with students working in pairs or groups. Ask pairs/groups to share their answers with the whole class.

Estrategia: Scanning

Have students scan the text for words they think they understand and words they don't or can't figure out. Then tell students to find out how right they were by doing *Comp. A,* which provides translations for a number of words and phrases.

Comp. B: Suggestion

Ask students how they might obtain the answers that are not given in the ad (questions 4 and 6). Assign finding that information as homework.

A escuchar

Notes

- Although the development of listening skills has been integrated into *Puntos de partida* since its first edition, there has never been a section devoted to that skill in the student text. *A escuchar* provides that focus.
- The majority of the *A escuchar* page develops an authentic listening task, with pre- and post-listening activities. The listening passage is available to students in a variety of formats, so they can listen to it on their own. However, if you prefer, you can focus on listening by playing the CD in class or by reading the audioscript aloud. Either is quite feasible, as the listening passages are relatively short.
- Instructors familiar with the *Música de...* feature of the previous edition can find that information in the IM as *¡Más música!* In addition, the *Ritmos y sonidos* CD (songs from the Spanish-speaking world that accompanied the Eighth Edition) can still be used with this edition of the text.
- See the IM for the audioscript and more information about traditional music in the U.S.

Antes de escuchar

Suggestions

- This is a brainstorming activity to activate prior knowledge about the content of the listening passage. In subsequent chapters, questions will be in Spanish.
- Have students work in pairs or groups, then have them share information with the class.

Escuche

Notes

- In this chapter, students can listen to an ad for summer courses at an international university.
- If listening is assigned as homework, ask students to listen to the passage twice.

¡Música!

Notes

- Gloria Estefan (1957–) is perhaps the most popular Latin crossover artist in the U.S. She began her career in the 1980s with the Miami Sound Machine. She is one of the 100 best-selling singers worldwide.
- For more information about accessing the playlist at the iTunes store, go to the *Puntos de partida* iMix section on Connect Spanish (**www.connectspanish.com**).
- For helpful tips on using songs in the classroom, see the IM.

A ESCUCHAR°

A... *Let's listen*

Antes de escuchar°

Antes... *Before listening*

Have you ever taken a summer course or courses? Why do you or other people take them? How many weeks do summer courses last, in your experience?

Vocabulario para escuchar

el anuncio	ad
el verano	summer
mayo	May
la semana	week
julio	July
agosto	August

Escuche°

Listen

Un anuncio para los cursos de verano de la Universidad Internacional

A university advertises its summer courses on the radio.

Listen according to the instructions from your professor.

Después de escuchar°

Después... *After listening*

A. Información básica. Indique las respuestas (*answers*) apropiadas.

1. El periodo de matrícula es en...
   _X_ mayo ___ junio ___ julio ___ agosto
2. Hay cursos de...
   ___ 2 semanas _X_ 4 semanas _X_ 8 semanas ___ 10 semanas
3. Con seguridad (*For sure*) hay cursos de... según (*according to*) el anuncio.
   _X_ sociología ___ arte _X_ matemáticas ___ literatura
4. Por Internet se ofrecen (*are offered*) cursos de...
   ___ alemán ___ filosofía _X_ italiano _X_ portugués

B. Más información. Dé (*Give*) la siguiente información, según el anuncio.

1. El nombre de la Residencia García Lorca
2. La dirección de la página web www.universidadinternacional.es
3. El número de teléfono de contacto 902-923-1314

Go to the iMix section in Connect Spanish (**www.connectspanish.com**) to access the iTunes playlist "*Puntos9*," where you can purchase "Esta fiesta no va a acabar" by Gloria Estefan.

¡Música!

La cantante cubanoamericana Gloria Estefan es muy famosa en todo el mundo.[a]

Gloria y su esposo,[b] el productor Emilio Estefan, son sin duda[c] los latinos más influyentes en el panorama musical de los Estados Unidos.

La canción[d] «Esta fiesta no va a acabar[e]» es del álbum *90 millas*.[f]

[a]todo... *the whole world* [b]su... *her husband* [c]sin... *without a doubt* [d]*song* [e]no... *will never end* [f]*miles*

Gloria Estefan, en Los Ángeles, California

A ESCRIBIR°

A… *Let's write*

El tema

Este° semestre/trimestre en la universidad *This*

Preparar

Paso 1. Fill out the chart with your personal information.

Me llamo
Mi especialización (*major*) es
Clases que (*that*) tomo este semestre/trimestre:
Mi clase favorita es
Trabajo en

¿Qué clases toma Ud. este semestre?

Paso 2. Now interview a classmate to fill out the following chart with his/her information.

You can ask most of the questions, but here are two that you will need.

¿Cuál es **tu** especialización?

¿Cuál es **tu** clase favorita?

Se llama
Su (*His/Her*) especialización es
Clases que toma este semestre/trimestre:
Su (*His/Her*) clase favorita es
Trabaja en

Redactar° *Writing*

Combine the information from the two charts in **Preparar** to write the first draft of your essay. Before you begin to write, organize your information into two lists: what you and your classmate have in common and what you don't.

Vocabulario útil

además	besides
pero	but
también	also, too

Editar

Review your essay to check for:

- word spelling and accent marks
- gender and number agreement between articles and nouns
- verb conjugation
- use of subject pronouns only when they are needed

Now prepare the final draft of your essay.

A escribir

Notes

- *A escribir* replaces *Redacción* sections from previous editions of *Puntos de partida.*
- Distinct from *Redacción*, which was tied to or based on the *Lectura* in *Un paso más, A escribir* sections are independent of the chapter's readings, although they are based on the chapter's theme.

Suggestions

- Suggested length for this writing assignment: approximately 80 words
- Suggested structure (3 paragraphs)
  - **P. 1.** About the student writer (first person)
  - **P. 2.** About the interviewee (third person)
  - **P. 3.** Brief conclusion, stating major similarity or difference

Redactar, Editar

Suggestions

- Tell students to avoid translating their ideas from English to Spanish. Instead, they should write directly in Spanish, using primarily the grammar and vocabulary they know and/or have seen used in the text.
- Emphasize that subject pronouns are not used in Spanish every time there is a conjugated verb. That topic is not treated in depth until *Cap. 3* of *Puntos de partida*, so you need to touch on it lightly here.
- Encourage students to look up a few new words in a dictionary or in the end-of-text Spanish-English Vocabulary in the text. It is recommended that you practice with them, to show them how to get all the information possible from a dictionary entry. That said, do not encourage students to use the dictionary frequently when writing their essays. As suggested in the first bullet point, it is best for them to stick to what they know.

En resumen: En este capítulo
Vocabulario

Notes

- While the *Vocabulario* section may seem long to you, note that it contains a number of close or exact cognates, making mastery of it a less daunting task than it might seem at first glance.
- Note (and tell students) that *Vocabulario* relists a number of words that were active in *Cap. 1: el día* (*1 = Buenos días*), *por la mañana/tarde/noche* (*1 = de la mañana/tarde/noche*), and so on. (See Word Families below.)
- In addition, words like *estudiar, hablar,* and *tocar* were used in *Cap. 1* but were not made active there.
- A number of words in this and subsequent *Vocabulario* sections are double listed, that is, used both as a section title (e.g., *Los lugares*) and listed as a separate vocabulary item, unless they are easily recognizable cognates. While this feature of the *Vocabulario* section lengthens the lists, it also makes them more user-friendly for students.
- The following non-cognate vocabulary items were used in direction lines in *Cap. 2* and will be used in subsequent chapters without glossing, but they are not considered to be "active" until they are listed in *Vocabulario: dé, haga una oración / hagan oraciones, intercambios, parejas, preguntas, siguientes.*

Word Families

This feature of *Puntos de partida* lists active vocabulary words for a given chapter that are related to each other (*En este capítulo*) or to previously learned vocabulary (*Entre capítulos*), that is, word or phrase families. ***¡OJO!*** notes words that are false or otherwise potentially confusing matches. You may wish to share these lists with students, as it will make learning some new vocabulary more efficient and help students relate new material to old.

En este capítulo

- *a casa, en casa*
- *la biblioteca, el/la bibliotecario/a*
- *el café, la cafetería*
- *la computación, la computadora*
- *con, con frecuencia*
- *el cuarto, el/la compañero/a de cuarto*
- *estudiar, el/la estudiante*
- *las lenguas extranjeras, el/la extranjero/a*
- *la librería, el libro (de texto)*
- *poco, un poco de*

Entre capítulos

- *a casa = a* (1)
- *con, con frecuencia = con permiso* (1)
- *el día, todos los días = buenos días* (1)
- *en casa = en* (1), *en punto* (1)
- *muy = muy bien* (1), *muy buenas* (1)
- *por la mañana/tarde/noche = de la mañana/tarde/noche* (1)

¡OJO!

- *mucho* (*adv.*) ≠ *muchas* (*adj.*) *gracias* (1), *mucho* (*adj.*) *gusto* (1)
- *tarde* (*adv.*) ≠ *buenas tardes* (*n.*) (1)

EN RESUMEN En este capítulo

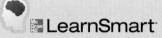

LearnSmart™
Visit **www.connectspanish.com** to practice the vocabulary and grammar points covered in this chapter.

Gramática en breve

1. Singular nouns: Gender and Articles

Noun Endings

Masculine: **-o**
Feminine: **-a, -ión, -dad, -tad**
Masculine or feminine: **-e**

2. Nouns and Articles: Plural Forms

Plural Endings

-o ⟶ **-os**
-a ⟶ **-as**
-e ⟶ **-es**
consonant + **-es**

	Definite Articles	Indefinite Articles
Masculine	**el** ⟶ **los**	**un** ⟶ **unos**
Feminine	**la** ⟶ **las**	**una** ⟶ **unas**

3. Subject Pronouns; Present Tense of *-ar* Verbs; Negation

Subject Pronouns

yo, tú, Ud., él, ella, nosotros/as, vosotros/as, Uds., ellos/as

Regular -ar *Verb Endings*

-o, -as, -a, -amos, -áis, -an

4. Asking Yes/No Questions

- Rising intonation
- Inversion of word order: *subject + verb ⟶ verb + subject*

Vocabulario

¡OJO!

Infinitives listed in colored text in **Vocabulario** lists are conjugated in their entirety (all tenses and moods) in Appendix 5. Be sure that you know the meaning of the group headings in addition to the meaning of the words in each group. (If the word or words in a group heading are not close cognates, their meaning will be given elsewhere in the **Vocabulario** section. If you are not sure of the meaning of a word, you can always look it up in the end-of-book Spanish-English Vocabulary.)

Los verbos

bailar	to dance
buscar	to look for
cantar	to sing
comprar	to buy
desear	to want
enseñar	to teach
escuchar	to listen (to)
estar (estoy, estás, . . .)	to be
estudiar	to study
hablar	to speak; to talk
hablar por teléfono	to talk on the phone
mandar un mensaje	to (send a) text
necesitar	to need
pagar	to pay (for)
practicar	to practice
regresar	to return (*to a place*)
regresar a casa	to go home
tocar	to play (*a musical instrument*)
tomar	to take; to drink
trabajar	to work

Los lugares

el apartamento	apartment
la biblioteca	library
la cafetería	cafeteria
el cuarto	room
el edificio	building
la fiesta	party
la librería	bookstore
el lugar	place
la oficina	office
la residencia	dormitory
el salón de clase	classroom
la universidad	university

Las personas

el/la amigo/a	friend
el/la bibliotecario/a	librarian
el/la cliente/a	client
el/la compañero/a (de clase)	classmate
el/la compañero/a de cuarto	roommate
el/la consejero/a	advisor
el/la dependiente/a	clerk
el/la estudiante	student
el/la extranjero/a	foreigner
el hombre	man
la mujer	woman
el/la secretario/a	secretary

Repaso: el/la profesor(a)

Repaso (*Review*) indicates vocabulary listed as active in this chapter that you learned in previous chapters.

56 ■ cincuenta y seis

Capítulo 2 En la universidad

Los objetos

el bolígrafo	pen
la calculadora	calculator
la computadora	computer
la computadora portátil	laptop (computer)
el cuaderno	notebook
el diccionario	dictionary
el dinero	money
el escritorio	desk
el lápiz (*pl.* **lápices**)	pencil
el libro (de texto)	(text)book
la mesa	table
la mochila	backpack
el papel	paper
el pizarrón (blanco)	(white)board
la puerta	door
la silla	chair
el teléfono (celular)	(cell) phone
la ventana	window

Las materias

la administración de empresas	business administration
la ciencia	science
la computación	computer science
la física	physics
la materia	subject area
la química	chemistry
la sicología	psychology

Cognado(s) lists vocabulary whose meaning you should be able to recognize because the words are close cognates of English.

Cognados: el arte, las ciencias naturales/políticas/sociales, las comunicaciones, la economía, la filosofía, la historia, las humanidades, la literatura, las matemáticas, la sociología

Las lenguas (extranjeras)

el alemán	German
el español	Spanish
el francés	French
el inglés	English
el italiano	Italian
la lengua (extranjera)	(foreign) language

Otros sustantivos

el café	coffee
la clase	class (*of students*); class, course (*academic*)
el día	day
la matrícula	tuition

Las palabras interrogativas

¿cuál?	what?; which?
¿cuándo?	when?
¿cuánto?	how much?
¿cuántos/as?	how many?

Repaso: ¿cómo?, ¿dónde?, ¿qué?, ¿quién?

¿Cuándo?

ahora	now
con frecuencia	frequently
el fin de semana	weekend
por la mañana/tarde	in the morning/afternoon
por la noche	at night, in the evening
tarde/temprano	late/early
todos los días	every day

Los pronombres personales

yo, tú, usted (Ud.), él/ella, nosotros/nosotras, vosotros/vosotras, ustedes (Uds.), ellos/ellas

Palabras adicionales

aquí	here
con	with
en casa	at home
mal	poorly
más	more
mucho	much; a lot
muy	very
poco	(a) little
un poco (de)	a little bit (of)
solo	only

Repaso: no

Vocabulario personal

Remember to use this space for other words and phrases you learn in this chapter.

Español	Inglés

- Have students use the adverbs from *¿Cuándo?* and the verbs from *Los verbos* to make a chart that plots when and how often they do some things.
- Have students indicate whether or not they have the following things.

cuaderno	*mochila*
lápiz	*papel*
calculadora	*bolígrafo*
diccionario	*dinero*
computadora (portátil)	*teléfono celular*

Bright Idea

Give students tips on how best to learn vocabulary. Here are some suggestions.

- **Flash cards:** Have students write the Spanish word on one side and the English translation(s) on the other. Tell students to keep the cards in a box and keep adding to it, chapter by chapter.
- **Tri-fold lists:** Have students write the Spanish word in the far left column and the English translation(s) in the far right column. To study, they fold the sheet to see only English or only Spanish.
- **Cover-up:** Have students cover up one column of the text's bilingual vocabulary lists and work their way down through the words.
- **Word associations:** Words in the text's end-of-chapter vocabulary are grouped by theme. Call students' attention to this feature and tell them to look back to previous chapters to find related vocabulary groups. The *Repaso* feature of the text will help them to do this.

Remind students not to be discouraged. Increasing one's vocabulary in any language takes time and patience. In later chapters, have students compare what they know now to what they knew when they first started studying Spanish.

Suggestions

- Have students create word puzzles that they can exchange and solve.
- Have students play charades, using nouns from the list. For example, for *profesor,* the student stands and pantomimes teaching the class.
- Have students draw pictures on the board depicting the vocabulary and have their classmates describe what is happening in Spanish.
- Have students guess who is talking based on the following context clues.
  1. *Trabajo en la escuela. Hablo con muchos estudiantes sobre los cursos que toman y sobre sus planes para sus estudios en la universidad.* (*consejero/a*)
  2. *Soy de Colombia, pero ahora estoy aquí en los Estados Unidos.* (*estranjero/a*)
  3. *Enseño español y matemáticas en la universidad y hay muchos estudiantes en mis clases.* (*profesor[a]*)
  4. *Trabajo en JCPenney y hablo con muchos clientes todos los días.* (*dependiente/a*)

Chapter Opening Photo and Chapter Theme

Chapter Photo Questions

For the third question, students will probably mention *Cinco de Mayo*. You may wish to take this opportunity to clarify that this is *not* Mexican Independence Day but rather a Mexican pride/heritage holiday celebrated primarily in this country and in Puebla, Mexico, where Mexican troops won a victory over the French on May 5, 1862. Mexican Independence Day is celebrated on September 16.

Chapter Theme–Related Questions

- *¿Es grande su familia? ¿pequeña?* (new words)
- *¿Trabaja mucho su papá? ¿y su mamá?*
- *¿Trabajan sus abuelos* (new word) *o están jubilados* (*retirados*)*?*
- *¿Su familia está en* _____ (name of the state where your college or university is)?
- *¿Es Ud. casado/a* (new word)*? ¿Tiene hijos* (new words)*?*

NATIONAL STANDARDS

Connections

The next 5 chapters of *Puntos de partida* will focus on the country of *México* (*Cap. 3*) and the Spanish-speaking countries of Central America: *Guatemala* and *Honduras* (*Cap. 4*), *El Salvador* and *Nicaragua* (*Cap. 5*), *Costa Rica* (*Cap. 6*), *Panamá* (*Cap. 7*). These countries are united geographically as well as by cultural elements, especially their indigenous heritage (Aztec, Maya, Zapotec, among others). In addition, the area has strong ties to the U.S. because of the large number of Mexicans, Central Americans, and people descended from them who live here.

3 La familia

Una familia mexicana, en una celebración especial

- Do you have a large family?
- How does your family celebrate holidays and special occasions? Do family members of several generations gather together often?
- Do you know any holidays that are specific to Mexicans? What other holidays do you think many Mexicans celebrate?

Mc Graw Hill connect | SPANISH

www.connectspanish.com

Resources

For Students

- Connect Spanish (**www.connectspanish.com**), which contains all content from the following resources, as well as the *Mundo interactivo* scenarios, the LearnSmart adaptive learning system, and more!
- **Physical Resources:** Workbook / Laboratory Manual, Laboratory Audio Program, DVD

For Instructors

- Connect Spanish (**www.connectspanish.com**), which contains access to all student sections of Connect Spanish, as well as helpful time-saving tools and resources such as an integrated gradebook, Instructor's Manual, Testing Program, digital transparencies, Audioscript, Videoscript, and more!

México

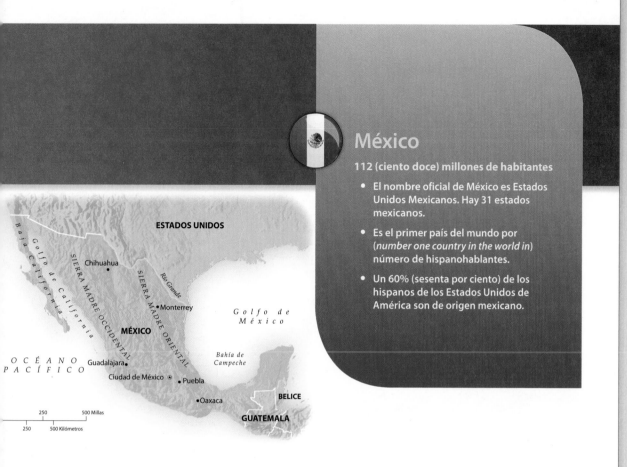

112 (ciento doce) millones de habitantes

- El nombre oficial de México es Estados Unidos Mexicanos. Hay 31 estados mexicanos.
- Es el primer país del mundo por (*number one country in the world in*) número de hispanohablantes.
- Un 60% (sesenta por ciento) de los hispanos de los Estados Unidos de América son de origen mexicano.

En este capítulo

CONTENT / **CONTENIDO**	OBJECTIVES / **OBJETIVOS**
Family vocabulary 60, Adjectives 64	To talk about the members of your family and tell what they are like
Numbers 31–100 62	To count in Spanish
Adjective endings 66	To describe people, places, things, and ideas
The verb **ser** 72	To express *to be* in many contexts
Possessive adjectives 77	To express possession (what someone has)
Verbs that end in **-er** and **-ir**, subject pronouns 80	To express actions
México 90	To learn about Mexico and Mexican culture

Multimedia

The *Instructor's Manual* (IM) provides suggestions for using the multimedia materials in the classroom.

México

Note

Active vocabulary: The words *el país* and *el mundo* become active in this section. They have been glossed consistently in this context since the beginning of *Puntos de partida*. They will not be glossed within this chapter. The is the only instance in the text of vocabulary that becomes active in a chapter opening page.

Datos esenciales

The Instructor's Edition will provide basic information about each chapter's country of focus on this chapter opening spread. Additional information (such as geographical features, historical timelines, holidays, and so on) can be found in the IM. There is also additional information about the country of focus in *A leer: Lectura cultural* and *A escuchar* (in both the student text and the Instructor's Edition).

Nombre oficial: *Estados Unidos Mexicanos*
Capital: *Ciudad de México = México, Distrito Federal, o simplemente el Distrito Federal o el D.F.*
Ciudades principales: *Guadalajara, Monterrey, Puebla, León, Tijuana*
Lenguas oficiales: *el español y aproximadamente 62 idiomas indígenas*
Composición étnica: *60% mestizos, 30% indígenas, 9% europeos, 1% otros*
Jefe de estado actual: *el Presidente Felipe de Jesús Calderón Hinojosa, desde 2006*
Forma de gobierno: *República democrática*
Moneda: *el peso mexicano*
Religión: *77% católicos, 6% protestantes, 0.3% otros, 14% sin especificar, 3% sin religión*

Suggestions

- Point out to students that the name *México* comes from *los mexicas*, the original name of *los aztecas*. *Los mexicas* were the founders of *Tenochtitlán*, which was one of the largest cities in the world in the 16th century. Mexico City is built on its remains.
- The oldest of the Mexican indigenous civilizations is the Olmec (*los olmecas*), the creators of the famous colossal heads in Mexico.
- See the IM for more suggestions.

Heritage Speakers

Si tiene en su clase estudiantes mexicanos o mexicoamericanos que han ido al D.F., anímelos a hacer una presentación en la que hablen de las experiencias que tuvieron allí.

NATIONAL STANDARDS: Cultures

Mexicans rarely refer to Mexico City as *la Ciudad de México*. Rather, they prefer to call it by the initials for *el Distrito Federal, el D.F.* By some estimates, the population of the Mexico City metropolitan area is over 20 million.

Resources: Transparency 23

Vocabulario
Preparación
La familia y los parientes

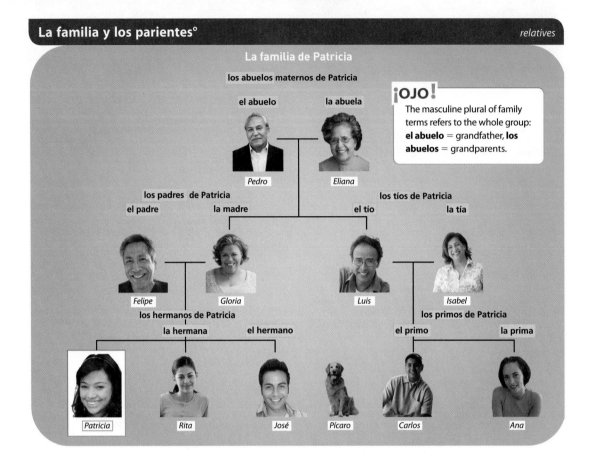

Notes

- See the model for vocabulary presentation and other material in the *Cap. 3 Vocabulario: Preparación* section of "Chapter-by-Chapter Supplementary Materials" in the IM.
- Point out that *parientes* is a false cognate.
- Point out that *esposo* is a cognate, but that *prima* is a false cognate, a word that, although it sounds much like the word in English, does not have a similar meaning.
- Emphasize the use of the masculine plural form—*el abuelo y la abuela* becomes *los abuelos,* and so on.

Suggestions

- Have students give the feminine equivalents of *el padre, el abuelo,* and so on; then give the masculine equivalents of *la tía, la esposa,* and so on.
- Have students identify relationships.
  1. *Es el hijo de mis tíos.* (*mi primo*)
  2. *Es la esposa de mi hermano.* (*mi cuñada*)
  3. *Es la madre de mi padre.* (*mi abuela*)
  4. *Es el hijo de mi madre.* (*mi hermano / yo*)
  5. *Es la hija de mi hermana.* (*mi sobrina*)
- Point out that many terms of endearment (*los términos de cariño/afecto*) are used among Hispanic family members. *Los padres a los hijos: mi hijo* (*m'ijo*), *mi hija* (*m'ija*); *nene/a; cielo* (lit., heaven); *corazón* (lit., heart); *mi vida* (lit., my life); *mi amor* (lit., my love). *Los hijos a los padres: papá, papi, papito, papaíto; mamá, mami, mamita, mamaíta* (See also *Así se dice.*)
- Point out that diminutives are commonly used as terms of endearment: *abuelo → abuelito; hija → hijita; Juan → Juanito; Elena → Elenita.* Use diminutives freely, as appropriate, as you speak Spanish in class.

Pronunciación: See Pronunciation Notes, IM.

Multimedia: Audio

Students can listen to and practice this chapter's vocabulary in Connect Spanish: **www.connectspanish.com**.

Resources: Transparency 24

VOCABULARIO Preparación

La familia y los parientes°

relatives

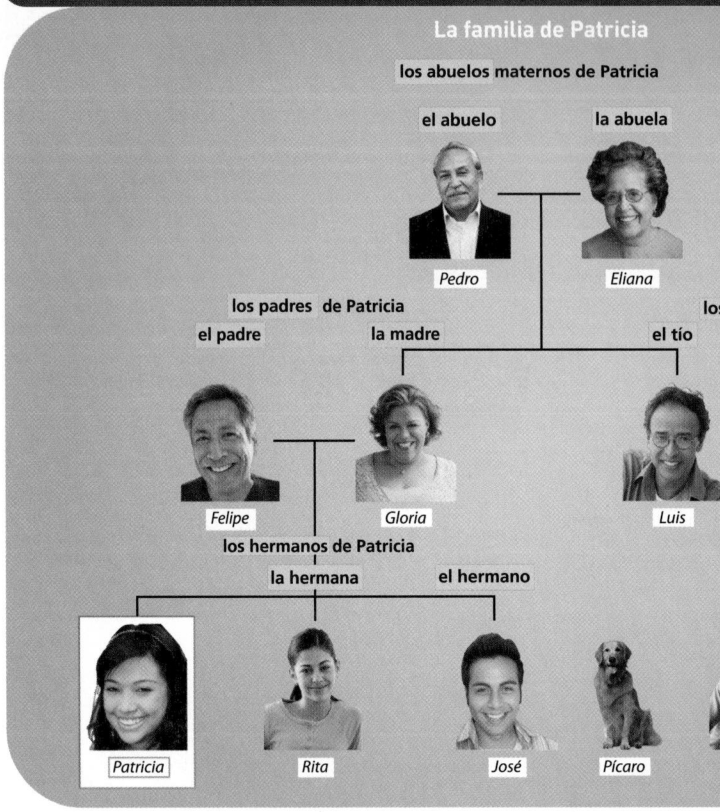

¡OJO!

The masculine plural of family terms refers to the whole group: **el abuelo** = grandfather, **los abuelos** = grandparents.

la madre (mamá)	mother (mom)
el padre (papá)	father (dad)
los padres	parents
la hija	daughter
el hijo	son
los hijos	children
la esposa	wife
el esposo	husband
la nieta	granddaughter
el nieto	grandson
la sobrina	niece
el sobrino	nephew

Las mascotas° — *Las… Pets*

el gato	cat
el pájaro	bird
el perro	dog

Formas del verbo tener° *to have*

tengo	I have
tienes	you (*fam.*) have
tiene	you (*form.*) have, he/she has

Remember that the complete conjugation of infinitives in red is given in Appendix 5.

Heritage Speakers

- El concepto de la familia entre los hispanos no solamente incluye a la familia nuclear sino también a la familia extendida. Cuando llega un nuevo miembro a la familia, como el marido de una hermana, el concepto de la familia crece para incluir a consuegros, cuñados, los concuños o concuñados, etcétera.
- Pregúnteles a los hispanohablantes qué términos de cariño se usan en su familia.

Vocabulario útil

Learn as many of the following terms for additional family relationships as you need to describe your own family as completely as possible. Write the terms you learn in **Vocabulario personal** (page 95).

el padrastro / la madrastra	stepfather / stepmother
el hijastro / la hijastra	stepson / stepdaughter
el hermanastro / la hermanastra	stepbrother / stepsister
el medio hermano / la media hermana	half-brother / half-sister
el suegro / la suegra	father-in-law / mother-in-law
el yerno / la nuera	son-in-law / daughter-in-law
el cuñado / la cuñada	brother-in-law / sister-in-law
...(ya) murió	. . . has (already) died

Así se dice

The terms **mamá/mami** and **papá/papi** are used to speak *to* one's parents.

Many Spanish speakers use the terms **abuelito/tata** and **abuelita/nana** to speak *to* their grandparents.

Conversación

A. ¿Cierto o falso? Look at the drawings of the family that appear on page 60. Decide whether each of the following statements is true (**cierto**) or false (**falso**) according to the drawings. Correct the false statements.

	CIERTO	FALSO	
1. José es el hermano de Ana.	☐	☑	Es el hermano de Patricia.
2. Eliana es la abuela de Patricia.	☑	☐	
3. Ana es la sobrina de Felipe y Gloria.	☑	☐	
4. Patricia y José son primos.	☐	☑	Son hermanos.
5. Gloria es la tía de José.	☐	☑	Es la madre de José.
6. Carlos es el sobrino de Isabel.	☐	☑	Es el hijo de Isabel.
7. Pedro es el padre de Luis y Gloria.	☑	☐	
8. Isabel y Gloria son las esposas de Luis y Felipe, respectivamente.	☑	☐	

B. ¿Quién es?

Paso 1. Complete las siguientes oraciones lógicamente.

1. La madre de mi (*my*) padre es mi abuela.
2. El hijo de mi tío es mi primo.
3. La hermana de mi padre es mi tía.
4. El esposo de mi abuela es mi abuelo.

Paso 2. Ahora defina la relación de estas (*these*) personas, según (*according to*) el modelo de las oraciones del **Paso 1.**

MODELOS: El ____ de mi ____ es mi ____.
La ____ de mi ____ es mi ____.

1. prima **2.** sobrino **3.** tío **4.** abuelo

C. Intercambios. Find out as much as you can about the family of a classmate, using the following dialogue as a guide.

MODELO: **E1:*** ¿Cuántos hermanos tienes?
E2: Bueno (*Well*), tengo seis hermanos y una hermana.
E1: ¿Y cuántos primos?
E2: ¡Uf! Tengo un montón (*bunch*). Más de (*than*) veinte.

Vocabulario útil

¿cuántos? (*with male relatives*)
¿cuántas? (*with female relatives*)

*From this point on in the text, ESTUDIANTE 1 *and* ESTUDIANTE 2 *will be abbreviated as* E1 *and* E2, *respectively.*

Así se dice

Notes

- The use of family terms varies from country to country, and it also varies according to social class and to the formality or informality of the communicative situation. You may wish to give students more information than that provided here and in the student text.
- Stress that the terms *mami/papi* and *nana/tata* would rarely be used by an adult to talk *about* his or her relatives. They are used primarily in direct address.
- It is possible to use *abuelito/abuelita* to talk about one's grandparents, but only in a very informal situation or in an intimate setting. Similarly, the active vocabulary terms *mamá* and *papá* can be used to speak about one's parents, but usually in an informal or intimate setting.
- Here is vocabulary for referring to same-sex parents: *las familias reconstituidas, los matrimonios entre personas del mismo sexo, unión civil, pareja de hecho.*

Reciclado: Have your students describe what particular family members like or do not like. Accept yes/no answers.

¿A su padre le gusta mirar la televisión?
¿A su madre le gusta bailar?

Con. A: Suggestions

- Introduce your own or a fictitious family with a family tree on the board or on an overhead transparency. Start with the recognizable cognates *padre* (*papá*) and *madre* (*mamá*); do two family members at a time, assigning names and defining relationships as you go along; students just listen during this phase.
- After several generations are on the board, go back to check comprehension, asking questions with alternatives: *¿Quién es él, mi abuelo o mi padre?*
- Ask students if they have a brother, grandmother, and so on. You may also introduce related vocabulary such as: *soltero/a, casado/a, la familia nuclear,* and *la familia extendida.*
- To follow up, have students use your presentation as a guide when presenting their own family members to the class.

Con. A: Note

Active vocabulary: *según*

Con. B: Suggestions

- Do as listening comprehension activity, with students providing completions.
- Have students identify the members of each group: *los hijos → el hijo y la hija.*
  1. *los abuelos* **2.** *los padres* **3.** *los hermanos* **4.** *los nietos* **5.** *los tíos* **6.** *los sobrinos*

Con. C: Suggestion

Model dialogue with several students before allowing class to work in pairs. Model options for a small family.

Los números del 31 al 100

Reciclado

- Review numbers 1–30 with counting drills, math games, and telling time.
- Remind students of the *-e* ending in *veinte* vs. the *-a* in *treinta, cuarenta, cincuenta,* and so on.

Note

The list of numbers includes the *cien* form only, as students will not need *ciento* to do the activities in this chapter. *Ciento* is introduced in *Cap. 4*.

Suggestions

- Ask *¿Cómo se dice* thirty-one? ¿thirty-two? Students produce numbers 31–39.
- Model 40, 50, . . . 100.
- Have class count in unison (40–49, 50–59). Then have students count in round robin (60–69, 70–79). Finally, have volunteers count (80–100). Count from 1 to 100 by 10s and 5s. Have volunteers count in reverse.
- Set up a bingo (*lotería*) game in which students fill out cards with numbers from 1–100 using digits and without repeating numbers. Call out numbers in Spanish. The winner (across, down, or diagonal) declares *¡Lotería!* and must read back winning numbers in Spanish.
- Emphasize that, from 31 on, numbers must be written as three words (except the multiples of 10).
- Write on the board: *un hombre, cuarenta y un hombres; una mesa, sesenta y una mesas.* Point out similarities and emphasize ending of *un* and *una* for plural.
- You may wish to tell students that *ciento* is used for numbers greater than 100: *ciento uno, ciento dos,* and so on.
- Dictate cognate nouns and numbers with several students working at the board: *100 estéreos, 76 trombones, 65 saxofones, 92 guitarras, 56 pianos,* and so on.
- Write the following series on the board and have volunteers read and complete them aloud:
  1. *1, 4, 7, 10, ¿ . . . ?*
  2. *0, 1, 10, 2, 3, 32, ¿ . . . ?*
  3. *10, 15, 13, 18, 16, 21, ¿ . . . ?*
  4. *2, 4, 3, 9, 4, 16, 5, 25, 6, ¿ . . . ?*
- You may wish to introduce the alternative form of telling time (*la una* [*y*] *cuarenta, las dos* [*y*] *cincuenta y cinco*. . .) if you have not already done so.

Note

Active vocabulary: *la casa*

Los números del 31 al 100

Continúe las secuencias:

- treinta y uno, treinta y dos…
- ochenta y cuatro, ochenta y cinco…

31	treinta y uno	**40**	cuarenta
32	treinta y dos	**50**	cincuenta
33	treinta y tres	**60**	sesenta
34	treinta y cuatro	**70**	setenta
35	treinta y cinco	**80**	ochenta
36	treinta y seis	**90**	noventa
37	treinta y siete	**100**	cien
38	treinta y ocho		
39	treinta y nueve		

Felipe
Eliana
cincuenta y cinco años
Isabel
setenta y ocho años
Luis
Gloria
treinta y nueve años
Pedro
cuarenta y cinco años
cuarenta y siete años
Patricia
ochenta y cinco años
«El abuelito Pedro tiene 85 años.»
«La abuelita Eliana tiene 78 años.»

Beginning with 31, Spanish numbers are *not* written in a combined form. **Treinta y uno,* cuarenta y dos, sesenta y tres,** and so on, must be three separate words.

Cien is used before nouns and in counting.

cien casas	*a (one) hundred houses*
noventa y ocho, noventa y nueve, **cien**	*ninety-eight, ninety-nine, one hundred*

MARCELA CAROLINA
& ALBERTO ANDRÉS
EN COMPAÑÍA DE SUS PADRES
LILIA MERCEDES
BADILLO VDA[a] DE MARINO
ALBERTO BARROSO OSORIO
URSULA CABARCAS
DE BARROSO
PARTICIPAN[b]
LA CEREMONIA RELIGIOSA
QUE SE CELEBRARÁ[c]
EN LA
IGLESIA ERMITA[d]
DEL CABRERO
CARTAGENA DE INDIAS
25 DE DICIEMBRE DE 2010, 9 PM.
RECEPCION
CASA DE RAFAEL NUÑEZ
BARRIO EL CABRERO
CALLE REAL No 41 - 89

[a]viuda (*widow*) [b]*will take part in* [c]se… *will be celebrated* [d]iglesia… *hermitage church*

Conversación

A. Más problemas de matemáticas. Recuerde (*Remember*): + **y,** − **menos,** = **son.**

1. 30 + 50 = 80 **2.** 45 + 45 = 90 **3.** 32 + 58 = 90 **4.** 77 + 23 = 100 **5.** 100 − 40 = 60

Nota cultural

El sistema hispano de apellidos° *°last names*

En los países hispanos las personas llevan sistemáticamente dos apellidos oficiales. Típicamente, el primer[a] apellido es el del[b] padre y el segundo,[c] el de la madre.

PADRE	MADRE
Antonio **Lázaro** Ochoa	Marina **Aguirre** Salmero

HIJOS

Marta **Lázaro Aguirre**
Jacobo **Lázaro Aguirre**

Según el sistema hispano, ¿cómo se llamaría Ud.?[d]

[a]*first* [b]el… *that of the* [c]*second* [d]¿cómo… *what would your name be?*

*Remember that when **uno** is part of a compound number (**treinta y uno,** and so on), it becomes **un** before a masculine noun and **una** before a feminine noun: **setenta y un hombres; cincuenta y una mesas.**

NATIONAL STANDARDS: Connections

Have students look up telephone books for different Spanish-speaking cities online. Some phone books allow you to look at multiple listings, and others will search specific names and last names. In some cases, searches of last names require the two last names.

Heritage Speakers

Pregúnteles a los hispanohablantes qué apellidos tienen. Si son estudiantes de la segunda o tercera generación, ¿siguen usando este sistema?

Resources: Transparencias 25, 26

B. Los números de teléfono

Paso 1. Here is part of a page from a Mexican telephone book. What do you know about the names?

Paso 2. With a classmate, practice giving telephone numbers at random from the list. Your partner will listen and identify the person. **¡OJO!** In many Hispanic countries phone numbers are said differently than in this country. Follow the model.

MODELO: 415 0046 (4-15-00-46) →

E1: Es el *cuatro-quince-cero-cero-cuarenta y seis.*

E2: Es el número de *A. Lázaro Aguirre.*

Paso 3. Now give your classmate your phone number and get his or hers.

MODELO: Mi número es el…

LAZARO AGUIRRE, A. –Schez Pacheco, 17	415 0046
LAZCANO DEL MORAL, A. –E. Larreta, 14	215 8194
LAZCANO DEL MORAL, A. –Ibiza, 8	274 6868
LEAL ANTON, J. –Pozo, 8	222 3894
LIEBANA RODRIGUEZ, A. Guadarrama, 10	463 2593
LOPEZ BARTOLOME, J. –Palma, 69	232 2027
LOPEZ CABRA, J. –E. Solana, 118	407 5086
LOPEZ CABRA, J. –L. Van, 5	776 4602
LOPEZ GONZALEZ, J. A. –Ibiza, 27	409 2552
LOPEZ GUTIERREZ, G. –S. Cameros, 7 ...	478 8494
LOPEZ LOPEZ, J. –Alamedilla, 21	227 3570
LOPEZ MARIN, V. –Illescas, 53	218 6630
LOPEZ MARIN, V. –N. Rey, 7	463 6873
LOPEZ MARIN, V. –Valmojado, 289	717 2823
LOPEZ NUÑEZ, J. –Pl. Pinazo, s/n	796 0035
LOPEZ NUÑEZ, J. –Rocafort, Bl. 321	796 5387
LOPEZ RODRIGUEZ, C. –Pl. Jesús, 7	429 3278
LOPEZ RODRIGUEZ, J. –Pl. Angel, 15	239 4323
LOPEZ RODRIGUEZ, M. E. B. Murillo, 104	233 4239
LOPEZ TRAPERO, A. –Cam. Ingenieros, 1 .	462 5392
LOPEZ VAZQUEZ, J. –A. Torrejón, 17	433 4646
LOPEZ VEGA, J. –M. Santa Ana, 5	231 2131
LORENTE VILLARREAL, G. –Gandía, 7 ...	252 2758
LORENZO MARTINEZ, A. –Moscareta, 5 .	479 6282
LORENZO MARTINEZ, A. –P. Laborde, 21	778 2800
LORENZO MARTINEZ, A. Av. S. Diego, 116	477 1040
LOSADA MIRON, M. –Padilla, 31	276 9373
LOSADA MIRON, M. –Padilla, 31	431 7461
LOZANO GUILLEN, E. Juan H. Mendoza, 5	250 3884
LOZANO PIERA, F. J. –Pingüino, 8	466 3205
LUDEÑA FLORES, G. –Lope Rueda, 56 ...	273 3735
LUENGO CHAMORRO, J. Gral Ricardos, 99	471 4906
LUQUE CASTILLO, J. –Pto Arlaban, 121 ..	478 5253
LUQUE CASTILLO, L. –Cardeñosa, 15	477 6644

Nota **comunicativa**

Cómo expresar la edad:° *tener… años*

°*age*

NORA: ¿Cuántos **años tienes**, abuela?

ABUELA: Setenta y ocho. ¿Y cuántos **años tienes tú**?

NORA: Yo **tengo** ocho.

In Spanish, age is expressed with the phrase **tener… años** (literally, *to have . . . years*).

C. Hablemos (*Let's talk*) **de la edad** (*age*)

Paso 1. Complete las siguientes oraciones.

1. Yo tengo ____ años.
2. La persona mayor (*oldest*) de mi familia es **mi** ____. Tiene ____ años.
3. La persona más joven (*youngest*) de mi familia es **mi** ____. Tiene ____ años.
4. En mi opinión, una persona es vieja (*old*) cuando tiene ____ años.
5. La edad ideal para casarse (*for getting married*) es a los ____ años.
6. La edad ideal para tener hijos es a los ____ años.

Paso 2. Ahora haga (*form*) preguntas basadas en las oraciones del **Paso 1** y haga (*conduct*) una encuesta (*poll*) entre (*with*) un mínimo de seis compañeros de clase.

MODELO: **2.** ¿Quién es la persona mayor de **tu** familia? ¿Cuántos años tiene?

Paso 3. Finalmente, presente sus (*your*) resultados a la clase.

Estrategia

Cambie (*Change*) la palabra **mi (en negrilla)** para formar las preguntas, según el modelo: **mi → tu**

Nota cultural

Notes

- Argentina is an exception to the two-surname system. There, most people use only the father's last name.
- The children of single mothers use both of the mother's last names.
- Many countries allow children to use the mother's last name first, then the father's.
- Married women traditionally take the husband's first last name as their second name. Using the names in the *Nota cultural*, if *Marta Lázaro Aguirre* were to marry *José Calderón Pacheco*, she would become *Marta Lázaro de Calderón*. However, the tradition of taking the husband's name is less the norm than it used to be, just as in this country.
- In Spain, women rarely take their husbands' names.
- It is not uncommon for Hispanics in this country to keep both last names by using hyphenation (*Calderón-Lázaro*) as many Americans and Canadians have done in recent years.
- *Una iglesia ermita* is a church complex that also has permanent housing for monks or nuns, who live there in solitude (but not necessarily cloistered) for the purposes of study, prayer and meditation, and isolation from the secular world.

Comprensión

1. *¿Cuántos apellidos oficiales tienen los hispanos?* (*dos*)
2. *El primer apellido, ¿es el de la madre?* (*Es el del padre.*)
3. *¿Tienen los hijos y las hijas de un matrimonio distintos apellidos?* (*no*)

Con. B: Variation

Do *Paso 2* as a dictation, with several students working at the board.

Nota comunicativa

Suggestions

- Introduce singular forms of *tener*. (Review them if you introduced them in the context of the family tree.)
- Model the age dialogue with several students, asking about the ages of some of their relatives.
- Present an alternate question about age: *¿Qué edad tiene(s)?*

Con. C: Note

The use of the possessive pronouns *mi* and *tu* is previewed in this activity.

NATIONAL STANDARDS: Communication

Have students ask six classmates how old they are and how old their grandparents are. Students share information by answering questions that you ask to determine the following information.

1. *la persona mayor* (new)
2. *la persona que tiene el abuelo mayor*
3. *la persona que tiene la abuela mayor*

Resources: Transparency 27

Los adjetivos

Note

The purpose of this section is to introduce the *meaning* of the adjectives, not the concept of adjective agreement. However, it is quite possible to use this material to introduce agreement, since the basics of the system (*-o* vs. *-a*) are given in the student text. The concept of adjective agreement is formally presented in *Gram. 5* in this chapter.

Suggestions

- Present adjectives in pairs or semantic groups (as organized in the presentation), using magazine images, names of famous people, and people in class.
- Suggestions for negative adjectives: *feo* (Frankenstein, *una gorila*); *gordo* (*un elefante*, Jack Black), *malo* (Dennis the Menace, Darth Vader), *tonto* (*Adam Sandler*, Steve Martin).
- Do several pairs; then check comprehension, offering students alternatives: *¿Es guapo o feo Darth Vader?*
- Point out that *bajo/a* refers to height and *corto/a* to length. Also, explain that *joven* is used with people, *nuevo/a* with things, and that *guapo/a* refers to males and females whereas *bonito/a* usually only refers to females and things.
- Explain that the adjectives *simpático/ antipático* refer to one's likeableness, not to a person's inherent kindness or goodness.
- Have students provide antonyms: *¿Cuál es el antónimo de rico?* → *pobre; ¿bajo?* → *alto;* and so on.
- Describe famous people or people in class using adjectives, sometimes incorrectly. Students respond *sí* or *no.*
- Optional: Introduce the words *soltero* (used with *ser*) and *casado* (used with *estar* as an adjective; *ser casado* = to be a married person).
- Optional: Provide additional vocabulary for physical description: *pelo rizado/lacio, pelirrojo, calvo, pelón.*

Pronunciación: See Pronunciation Notes, IM.

Con. B: Reciclado

Have students review cognates from *Cap. 1* before beginning the activity.

Redacción: Ask students to write a paragraph that describes their family. They should include at least:

- name and relation of six family members that they are close to
- age of some family members
- description of favorite two relatives (3 adj. each)

(Cont.)

Los adjetivos

guapo	handsome; good-looking
bonito	pretty
feo	ugly
grande	large, big
pequeño	small
simpático	nice, likeable
antipático	unpleasant
corto	short (*in length*)
largo	long
bueno	good
malo	bad
listo	smart; clever
tonto	silly, foolish
trabajador	hardworking
perezoso	lazy
rico	rich
pobre	poor
delgado	thin, slender
gordo	fat

To describe a masculine singular noun, use **alto, bajo,** and so on; use **alta, baja,** and so on for feminine singular nouns.

Conversación

A. Descripciones

Paso 1. En parejas, describan estas (*these*) imágenes opuestas (*opposite*).

MODELO:  Un _____ es _____ y el otro es _____.

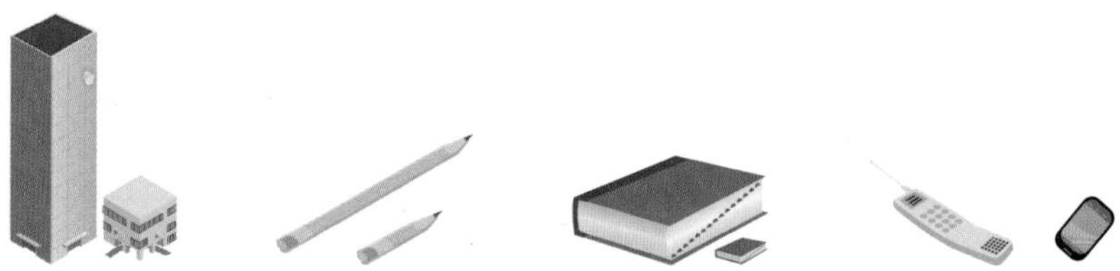

1. **2.** **3.** **4.**

Paso 2. Ahora describan a estas personas e ideas.

MODELO: fumar (*to smoke*) → Fumar es malo. No es bueno.

1. bailar
2. Einstein
3. Bill Gates
4. trabajar por siete dólares la hora
5. Adam Sandler
6. Frankenstein
7. el presidente

NATIONAL STANDARDS: Comparisons

In the United States and Canada, to indicate height using a hand gesture, we extend our arm with the palm of the hand facing the floor. In several Latin American countries, this same gesture is used to indicate the height of animals. To indicate the height of humans, Latin Americans generally extend the arm out, turning the hand vertically, with the palm facing outward.

Resources: Transparencies 28, 29

B. ¿Cómo es? Describe a famous male personality, using as many adjectives as possible so that your classmates can guess who the person is. Use cognate adjectives that you have seen in **Capítulos 1** and **2.**

MODELO: Es un hombre importante; controla una compañía de *software* muy importante. Es muy trabajador y muy rico. ⟶ Bill Gates

Mundo interactivo

You should now be prepared to work with Scenario 2, Activity 1 in Connect Spanish (**www.connectspanish.com**).

PRONUNCIACIÓN

Stress and Written Accent Marks (Part 1)

Some Spanish words have *written accent marks* over one of the vowels. That mark is called **el acento (ortográfico).** It means that the syllable containing the accented vowel is stressed when the word is pronounced, as in the word **bolígrafo (bo-LÍ-gra-fo),** for example.

Although all Spanish words of more than one syllable have a stressed vowel, most words do not have a written accent mark. Most words have the spoken stress exactly where native speakers of Spanish would predict it. These two simple rules tell you which syllable is accented when there is no written accent on the word.

1. Words ending in a vowel, **-n,** or **-s** = **las palabras llanas**

Las palabras llanas have the word stress on the *second-to-last syllable* (**la penúltima sílaba**). When they end in a vowel, **-n,** or **-s,** they don't need a written stress mark. This is the largest group of Spanish words; it includes most nouns and adjectives as well as their plurals, most verb forms, and so on. Here are some examples.

me-sa me-xi-ca-no e-xa-men gra-cias e-res

2. Words ending in consonants other than **-n** or **-s** = **las palabras agudas**

Las palabras agudas have the word stress on the *last syllable* (**la última sílaba**). When they end in consonants other than **-n** or **-s** (typically **-d, -l,** and **-r**), they don't need a written stress mark. This group includes all infinitives and many common words that end in **-dad, -or,** and **-al.**
Here are some examples.

us-ted es-pa-ñol pro-fe-sor es-tar doc-tor

¡OJO!

You will learn about words that have a written accent mark in **Capítulo 4.**

Práctica

A. Tipos de palabras: ¿Llanas o agudas? None of these words needs a written accent mark. Categorize each one as **llana** or **aguda,** then pronounce the word.

1. can-tan llana	**5.** me-sa llana	**9.** se-ñor aguda
2. ar-te llana	**6.** es-pa-ñol aguda	**10.** na-tu-ral aguda
3. cla-se llana	**7.** a-mi-gos llana	**11.** com-pu-ta-do-ra llana
4. mu-jer aguda	**8.** us-ted aguda	**12.** bai-las llana

Estrategia

Llana: ends in a vowel, **-n,** or **-s** = stress on the second-to-last syllable

Aguda: ends in a consonant other than **-n** or **-s** = stress on the last syllable

B. Vocales. Indicate the stressed vowel in the following words.

1. mo-chi-la	**4.** i-gual-men-te	**7.** li-be-ral
2. me-nos	**5.** E-cua-dor	**8.** hu-ma-ni-dad
3. re-gu-lar	**6.** e-le-gan-te	

Provide the adjectives *materno/a* and *paterno/a,* and also introduce the phrases *es soltero/a* and *está casado/a.*

You may wish to postpone this assignment until you have covered *Gram. 5* (Adjective Agreement) or you can use the assignment to preview agreement. Tell students to use *-a* adjectives with female relatives and *-o* adjectives with males.

Pronunciación

Notes

- Stress and accent marks are continued in *Cap. 4.*
- If you emphasize correct spelling and pronunciation on graded material, cover these sections on written accents carefully. Once you have introduced "Stress and Written Accent Marks (Part 2) (*Cap. 4*)," you can practice using accents through short dictations.

Preliminary Exercises

- Read these words and ask whether the stress is on the last (*última*) syllable or on the next-to-last (*penúltima*) syllable. Ask students to raise their hands when the stress is on the last syllable.

  hable, hablé *espere, esperé*
  doblo, dobló *pasó, paso*
  bajé, baje *pasé, pase*

- Ask whether stress is on the next-to-last or the third-from-last (*antepenúltima*) syllable. Have students raise their hands if the stress is on the penultimate syllable.

  como, cómico *político, polo*
  pero, período *cinco, simpático*

Suggestions

- You may wish to point out that a diphthong constitutes one syllable and follows the normal rules of accentuation. Emphasize that *a, e, o* in combination with each other cannot form a diphthong in Spanish. Any such combination remains as two different syllables.
- Dictate the following words, then have students decide: *¿Diptongo o no? Mao, Luis, Hawai, Leo, Bea, sierra, caos, poeta, ciencias, lengua.*
- Teach students to divide words into syllables to practice syllable structure in Spanish. This will help them recognize patterned prefixes and suffixes as well as write stress marks accurately.

Heritage Speakers

Pídales a los hispanohablantes que lean una serie de palabras, modelando la pronunciación para los angloparlantes. Déles palabras agudas (*papel, popular, regatear*), llanas (*biblioteca, consejero, profesora*) y esdrújulas (*música, América, bolígrafo*). Después pídales a los angloparlantes que imiten la pronunciación de las palabras.

Gramática 5
Adjectives: Gender, Number, and Position

Suggestions

- Before starting the *Gramática* section in this chapter, remind students about the repeating features of this part of the text: the use of colored text to help them focus on the grammar topic in minidialogues or presentation devices, the two-column set-up of the grammar explanations, the *Autoprueba*, and the purpose of *¡Anticipemos!* activities.
- Point out that *poema* is masculine in Spanish. Remind students about the words they learned in *Cap. 1* that end in *-a* but that are masculine: *el problema, el día,* and so on.
- Read both versions of the poem. Point out that there is only one English equivalent given. Have students note the differences between the two versions and who is described in each.
- Point out that the meaning of the adjective *amable* is not closely related to *amar* (*to love*). It means *kind*; never *lovely* or *loving*.

Notes

- Students have been working with adjectives since *Cap. 1*. For this reason, no additional focus on adjectives as a part of speech is provided in the student text. You may wish to provide the following exercise if your students need more practice with the concept of adjectives. Ask students to pick out the adjectives in the following sentences.
  1. Paula is a good friend.
  2. I am loyal and trustworthy.
  3. *Jorge es un amigo bueno.*
  4. *Tú no eres perezosa; eres muy trabajadora.*
- Active vocabulary: *amable, fiel*

Follow-up

Ask questions about the couple in the photo. Accept yes/no answers when appropriate.

¿Quiénes son?
¿Dónde están?
¿De dónde son?
¿Son hermanos (*amigos, estudiantes,* and so on)*?*
¿Qué hacen (new)*?*
¿Cómo son?
¿Son _____ (cue students with adjectives)*?*
¿Les gusta hablar (*bailar, estudiar,* and so on)*?*

GRAMÁTICA

Grammar Tutorial 5
connect SPANISH
www.connectspanish.com

5 Describing
Adjectives: Gender, Number, and Position

Gramática en acción: Un poema sencillo

Amigo
Fiel
Amable
Simpático
¡Lo admiro!

Amiga
Fiel
Amable
Simpática
¡La admiro!

¿Y Ud.?

According to their form, which of the following adjectives can be used to describe each person? Which can refer to you?

Marta: / Mario: { fiel amable simpática simpático

Adjectives (**Los adjetivos**) are words used to talk about nouns or pronouns. Adjectives may describe or tell how many there are.

You have been using adjectives to describe people since **Capítulo 1.** In this section, you will learn more about describing the people and things around you.

an adjective / **un adjetivo** = a word used to describe a noun or a pronoun

large *desk*	***few*** *desks*
tall *woman*	***several*** *women*

Adjectives with **ser** / **Los adjetivos con *ser***

In Spanish, forms of **ser** are used with adjectives that describe basic, inherent qualities or characteristics of the nouns or pronouns they modify. **Ser** establishes the "norm," that is, what is considered basic reality: *snow is cold, water is wet.*

Tú **eres amable.**
You're kind. (*You're a kind person.*)

El diccionario **es grande.**
The dictionary is big.

Mi hermana **es trabajadora.**
My sister is hardworking.

A simple poem *Friend Loyal Kind Nice I admire him/her!*

NATIONAL STANDARDS: Comparisons

In this chapter students will learn that the majority of adjectives in Spanish are placed after the noun. In English, however, descriptive adjectives precede the noun. When using more than one adjective, English has strict rules with regard to adjective placement in pre-noun position. Placement of these adjectives depends on the type of information that is communicated. For example, adjectives of opinion are placed before those of size, followed by age, shape, color, origin, and then material. English speakers will naturally say. "The big old red brick house." Usually, however, no more than three adjectives are used before a noun.

Forms of Adjectives / **Las formas de los adjetivos**

agreement / **la concordancia** = when one word "agrees," or must be coordinated, with an aspect of another (for example, *he* + *speaks* but *you* + *speak*)

Spanish adjectives agree in gender and number with the noun or pronoun they modify. Each adjective has more than one form.

1. Adjectives Ending in *-o*

Adjectives that end in **-o (alto)** have four forms, showing gender and number.

Adjetivos con 4 formas		
	Masculino	**Femenino**
Singular	amigo alto	amiga alta
Plural	amigos altos	amigas altas

2. Adjectives Ending in *-e* or a Consonant

Adjectives that end in **-e (amable)** or in most consonants (**fiel**) have only two forms, a singular and a plural form. The plural of adjectives is formed in the same way as that of nouns, by adding **-s** or **-es.**

[Práctica A–D]

Notes in brackets let you know you are now ready to do the indicated activities, in this case, **Práctica A–D** on pages 69–70.

Adjetivos con 2 formas		
	Masculino	**Femenino**
Singular	amigo amable amigo fiel	amiga amable amiga fiel
Plural	amigos amables amigos fieles	amigas amables amigas fieles

3. Adjectives Ending in *-dor*

Like adjectives that end in **-o,** these adjectives also have four forms.

Adjetivos con 4 formas		
	Masculino	**Femenino**
Singular	amigo trabajador	amiga trabajadora
Plural	amigos trabajadores	amigas trabajadoras

4. Nationality Adjectives

Most adjectives of nationality have four forms.

¡OJO!

Nationality adjectives ending in **-e** generally have only two forms: **estadounidense(s)** (from the United States), **canadiense(s).**

	Masculino	**Femenino**
Singular	el doctor mexicano español	la doctora mexicana española
Plural	los doctores mexicanos españoles	las doctoras mexicanas españolas

5. Names of Languages

The names of many languages—which are masculine in gender—are the same as the masculine singular form of the corresponding adjective of nationality.

[Práctica E]

Lengua	**Adjetivo**
el inglés	inglés, inglesa, ingleses, inglesas
el francés	francés, francesa, franceses, francesas
el italiano	italiano/a/os/as
el alemán	alemán, alemana/es/as

¡OJO!

Note that in Spanish the names of languages and adjectives of nationality are not capitalized, but the names of countries are: **el español, española,** but **España.**

Bright Idea

Suggestion

Have students write their own *poemas sencillos* in class, using the one presented as a model (p. 66). Suggest possible topics: *mi perro / madre / compañero/a de cuarto / novio/a* (new), and so on.

Adjectives with *ser*

Suggestion

Bring or have students bring magazine clippings of famous people. Have students identify and describe them.

Forms of Adjectives

Notes

- Gender agreement with adjectives may have been used by students since *Cap. 1.* Your handling of this grammar section will depend on how much you have stressed agreement so far.
- Active vocabulary: *alemán/alemana, español(a), estadounidense, inglés/inglesa, mexicano/a*

Suggestions

- Emphasize the concept of agreement.
- Point out that adjectives must agree with the gender of the noun they modify grammatically: *Pepe es una persona muy simpática.*
- Tell students that adjectives that end in *-ón, -án* and *-ín* also have four forms (like *-dor* adjectives).
- Remind students that adjectives must also agree with the noun they modify in number.

  Mi profesor es inteligente. / Mis profesores son inteligentes.
- Point out that adjectives of nationality can also be used as nouns: *el español* = the Spaniard, *los ingleses* = the English people, and so on.

Note

Many adjectives of nationality are presented in grammar points 4 and 5. Additional adjectives of nationality are included in the *Nota comunicativa*, p. 70. Be prepared to provide adjectives to describe the nationality of the students in your class and encourage students to write these adjective in *Vocabulario personal.*

NATIONAL STANDARDS: Comparisons

Explain to students that the concept of gender is marked in many languages in adjective and noun forms, and, in some languages such as Arabic, even in verb forms. In English the gender of people and some animals is distinguished lexically [boy/girl, bull/cow, waiter/waitress), but descriptive adjectives do not vary (tall boy, tall girl; brown bull, brown cow; nice waiter, nice waitress). And although English does not assign grammatical gender to objects or concepts, some traditionally have gender associations: Mother Earth, Mother Nature, Father Time, Father Sun. Ask students if they can think of additional items or concepts that they consider masculine or feminine (cars, ships, countries, cities, death).

Position of Adjectives

Emphasis 4: Suggestions

Ask students the following questions.

- *¿Cómo se dice en inglés… una ciudad grande / una gran ciudad; un estado grande / un gran estado?*
- *¿Cómo se dice en español…* a large university / a great university; a large book / a great book?

Notes

- In *Puntos de partida*, students will learn that some adjectives (*buen/buena, mal/mala, gran,* and demonstrative adjectives) appear in the pre-noun position. They do not learn, however, that adjectives may come before the noun when they provide gratuitous or subjective information: *la elegante princesa, la blanca nieve, la sangrienta guerra.*
- Active vocabulary: *la ciudad, el coche, este/a, esto, otro/a*

Forms of *this/these*

Note

Forms of *este* are not actively practiced in this section, but are included for recognition only, so that they may be used freely in direction lines and in reading passages. The complete set of demonstratives is introduced in *Gram. 9 (Cap. 4)*.

Suggestion

Remind students to try the *Autoprueba*.

Preliminary Exercise

Ask students specific questions about their university.

¿Cómo son los profesores de su universidad?
¿Son buenas las residencias?
¿Es deliciosa la comida de la cafetería?
¿Son baratos los libros de la librería?
¿Hay muchas actividades sociales?

Position of Adjectives / **La posición de los adjetivos**

As you have probably noticed, adjectives do not always precede the noun in Spanish as they do in English. Note the following rules for adjective placement.

1. Adjectives of Quantity
Like numbers, adjectives of quantity *precede* the noun, as do the interrogatives **¿cuánto/a?** and **¿cuántos/as?**

Hay **muchas sillas** y **dos escritorios.**
There are many chairs and two desks.

¿Cuánto dinero necesitas?
How much money do you need?

¡OJO!
Otro/a by itself means *another* or *other.* The indefinite article is never used with **otro/a.**

Busco **otro coche.**
I'm looking for another car.

2. Adjectives of Quality
Adjectives that describe the qualities of a noun and distinguish it from others generally *follow* the noun. Adjectives of nationality are included in this category.

un **perro listo**
un **dependiente trabajador**
una **mujer delgada** y **morena**
un **profesor español**

3. *Bueno* and *malo*
The adjectives **bueno** and **malo** may *precede or follow* the noun they modify. When they precede a masculine singular noun, they shorten to **buen** and **mal,** respectively.

un **buen perro** / un **perro bueno**
una **buena perra** / una **perra buena**
un **mal día** / un **día malo**
una **mala noche** / una **noche mala**

4. *Grande*
The adjective **grande** may also *precede or follow* the noun. When it precedes a singular noun—masculine or feminine—it shortens to **gran** and means *great* or *impressive.* When it follows the noun, it means *large* or *big.*

[Conversación]

Nueva York es una **ciudad grande.**
New York is a large city.

Nueva York es una **gran ciudad.**
New York is a great (impressive) city.

Forms of *this/these* / **Formas de *este/estos***

1. *This/These*
The demonstrative adjective *this/these* has four forms in Spanish.* Learn to recognize them when you see them.

este hijo	this son
esta hija	this daughter
estos hijos	these sons
estas hijas	these daughters

2. Esto
You have already seen the neuter demonstrative **esto.** It refers to something that is as yet unidentified.

¿Qué es **esto**?
What is this?

You will learn all forms of the Spanish demonstrative adjectives (this, that, these, those) in **Gramática 9 (Cap. 4).**

NATIONAL STANDARDS: Communication

Note that in some Hispanic countries, the word *perrita* is preferred when speaking about female dogs. For some native speakers, the term *perra* has negative connotations.

Adjective Agreement Summary

SINGULAR ENDINGS	PLURAL ENDINGS
-o, -a	**-os, -as**
-e	**-es**
-[consonant]	-[consonant] + **-es**

Autoprueba

Give the correct adjective endings.

1. una casa viej_____
2. los tíos español_____
3. un primo alt_____
4. un sobrino guap_____
5. las hermanas rubi_____
6. buen_____ amigos

Answers: **1.** *vieja* **2.** *españoles* **3.** *alto* **4.** *guapo* **5.** *rubias* **6.** *buenos*

Remember that the purpose of **¡Anticipemos!** is to show you a new grammar point in context before you begin to use it actively in conversation. Here, pay special attention to the endings on adjectives. Most of them are plural. Can you tell why the adjective **fácil** (*easy*) in items 5 and 6 is not plural?

Práctica

A. ¡Anticipemos! Hablando (*Speaking*) **de la universidad.** Tell what you think about aspects of your university by telling whether you agree (**Estoy de acuerdo.**) or disagree (**No estoy de acuerdo.**) with the statements. If you don't have an opinion, say **No tengo opinión.**

1. Hay suficientes actividades sociales.
2. Los estudiantes son dedicados.
3. Las residencias son buenas.
4. Hay suficientes gimnasios.
5. Es fácil aparcar el coche.
6. Es fácil llegar (*to get*) a la universidad en autobús.
7. Hay suficientes zonas verdes (*green*).
8. Los restaurantes, cafeterías y cafés son buenos.
9. Los precios de la librería son bajos.
10. Los bibliotecarios son amables.

B. Descripciones

Paso 1. Haga (*Form*) oraciones con los siguientes adjetivos para describirse (*to describe yourself*). **¡OJO!** Use la forma apropiada del adjetivo.

Soy…
No soy…

1. alto	**6.** fiel	**11.** dedicado
2. trabajadora	**7.** simpático	**12.** social
3. estadounidense	**8.** europeo	**13.** estudiosa
4. rico	**9.** moreno	**14.** listo
5. rubia	**10.** hispana (latina)*	**15.** gordo

Paso 2. Ahora haga oraciones para describir a su (*your*) padre/madre, a su esposo/a o a su mejor amigo/a (*best friend*).

MODELOS: Mi mejor amiga es moren**a**, simpátic**a** y pobre.
Mi esposo es alt**o**, trabaja**dor** y muy dedicad**o**.

__Hispano/a__ is a general term used by most Hispanics to refer to themselves. The term __latino/a__ is often used by Hispanics born in this country.

Prác. A: Reciclado

Note the recycling of university vocabulary from *Cap. 2.* You may wish to make up additional items to review that material.

Prác. A: Notes

- Active vocabulary: *hispano/a, llegar,* (*no*) *estoy de acuerdo*
- Pay special attention to items 5 and 6, in which the adjective (*fácil*) is singular because it is in an impersonal expression. Students should be able to grasp this concept easily, as it parallels English usage. It is also useful to point out the use of the infinitive (*aparcar, llegar*) in this structure. Calling students' attention to impersonal expressions will be helpful to them when they begin to work with the subjunctive.

Prác. A: Suggestion

Have students locate the adjectives in each sentence and tell which noun(s) they modify.

Prác. B: Suggestion

- Follow up *Paso 1* by asking students to use antonym adjectives. The same can be done with *Paso 2.*

Prác. C: Preliminary Exercise

Have students describe the following things. Cue students with questions and adjectives.

1. *¿Su familia?* → *(No) Es una familia grande.* (*interesante, importante, amable, intelectual*)
2. *¿Los perros?* → *(No) Son valientes.* (*fiel, impaciente, inteligente, importante*)
3. *¿Su universidad?* → *(No) Es nueva.* (*viejo, grande, pequeño, bueno, famoso, malo*)

Prác. C: Suggestion

Have students correct the form of the adjectives when inappropriate forms are provided.

Prác. D: Note

Active vocabulary: *por eso*

Prác. D: Follow-up

- Have students respond *cierto* or *falso*.
    1. *A Diego no le gusta estudiar.* (*falso*)
    2. *Diego es de Sudamérica.* (*falso*)
    3. *Le gustan los deportes* (new). (*cierto*)
    4. *No habla español porque es norteamericano.* (*falso*)
- Have students not only change *Diego* to *Dolores* but also change the text when possible to describe her as being the opposite of Diego. Then, change the subject of the paragraph to *Diego y Dolores.* **¡OJO!** Help students make changes they do not yet know how to make, e.g., *es* ⟶ *son*, *le gustan* ⟶ *les gustan*, and *tiene* ⟶ *tienen*.

Nota comunicativa

Suggestions

- Model the pronunciation of the nationalities before students begin *Prác. E, Paso 1*.
- **Pronunciation:** This list of nationality adjectives provides a good opportunity to focus on the pronunciation of the following letters and letter combinations: *c* + vowels (hard and soft *c*), *ch*, the letter *ñ*, *gu* + vowels.
  c: *costarricense, guatemalteco/a, nicaragüense, colombiano/a, ecuatoriano/a, coreano/a*
  ch: *chileno/a, chino/a*
  ñ: *hondureño/a, panameño/a, salvadoreño/a, brasileño/a*
  gu: *guatemalteco/a, nicaragüense, paraguayo/a, uruguayo/a*

Note

The plural of words like *israelí* and *pakistaní* can be formed in two ways: + *-s* or + *-es*. The plural with *-es* is used here. This rule is not considered active material in *Puntos de partida*.

C. La familia de Carlos. Estos son los parientes de Carlos (página 60). Complete las oraciones con los adjetivos apropiados según su forma.

1. **El tío Felipe** es ____. (trabajador / alto / nueva / gran / amable)
2. **Los abuelos** son ____. (rubio / antipático / inteligentes / viejos / religiosos / sinceras)
3. **Mi tía Gloria,** la madre de Patricia, es ____. (rubio / elegante / sentimental / buenas / gordas / simpática)
4. **Mis primos** son ____. (trabajadores / morenos / lógica / bajas / mala)

Prác. D, Answers: *una buena, lista, trabajadora, profesora, morena, guapa, atlética*

D. ¡Dolores es igual! Cambie (*Exchange*) **Diego** por **Dolores.**

Diego es un buen estudiante. Es listo y trabajador y estudia mucho. Es estadounidense de origen mexicano, y por eso[a] habla español. Desea ser profesor de antropología. Diego es moreno, guapo y atlético. Le gustan las fiestas grandes y tiene buenos amigos en la universidad. Tiene parientes estadounidenses y mexicanos. Diego tiene 20 años.

[a]por... *for that reason*

Nota **comunicativa**

Otras nacionalidades

You learned many nationality adjectives on page 67. Here are some more. If you don't find the adjective(s) you need to describe yourself and your family, ask your instructor. Write the adjectives you need in **Vocabulario personal** (page 91).

Centroamérica		Sudamérica		Europa y Asia	
costarricense	nicaragüense	argentino/a	ecuatoriano/a	chino/a	japonés, japonesa
guatemalteco/a	panameño/a	boliviano/a	paraguayo/a	coreano/a	pakistaní (*pl.* pakistaníes)
hondureño/a	salvadoreño/a	brasileño/a	peruano/a	indio/a	palestino/a
		chileno/a	uruguayo/a	israelí (*pl.* israelíes)	ruso/a
		colombiano/a	venezolano/a	iraní (*pl.* iraníes)	tailandés, tailandesa
				iraquí (*pl.* iraquíes)	vietnamita

E. ¿Cuál es su (*their*) **nacionalidad?**

Paso 1. Diga (*Tell*) la nacionalidad de las siguientes (*following*) personas.

1. Monique es de Francia; es francesa.
2. Piero y Andri son del Uruguay; son uruguayos.
3. Indira y su (*her*) hermana son de la India; son indias.
4. Ronaldo y Ronaldinho son del Brasil; son brasileños.
5. Saji es un hombre del Japón; es japonés.
6. La familia Musharraf es de Pakistán; son (*they are*) pakistaníes.
7. Paul es de Liverpool; es inglés.
8. Samuel y su (*his*) hermana son de Guatemala; son guatemaltecos.
9. Sonia es de Buenos Aires; es argentina.
10. Ramón y José son de Bogotá; son colombianos.
11. Jimena es de San José, Costa Rica; es costarricense.
12. Bill y Susan son de California; son estadounidenses.

NATIONAL STANDARDS: Communication

- Have students interview each other to determine at least three adjectives that best describe the interviewees. Have them report their findings about their classmates.
- Name famous people (imagine that they are all alive). Have students tell what language they speak and what their nationality is or where they are from. Examples: *Pablo Picasso* (*español*), *Napoleón* (*francés*), *Antonio Banderas* (*español*), *Beethoven* (*alemán*), *Enrique Iglesias* (*español*), *Marc Anthony* (*estadounidense*), *Pancho Villa* (*mexicano*), *Juan y Eva Perón* (*argentinos*).

Paso 2. En parejas, hagan oraciones con las nacionalidades hispanas, según el modelo. Busquen (*Look for*) los nombres de las naciones hispanas en el mapa de la página 11.

MODELO: **E1:** ¿Una mujer de Costa Rica?
E2: Es **costarricense.** ¿Y un hombre?
E1: Es **costarricense.** ¿Una mujer de El Salvador?
E2: Es...

Conversación

A. Asociaciones. En grupos, hablen (*talk*) de las personas o cosas (*things*) que (*that*) asocian con las siguientes frases. Expresen acuerdo (*agreement*) o desacuerdo (*disagreement*) con **(No) Estoy de acuerdo.**

MODELO: un gran hombre ⟶
E1: Creo que (*I believe that*) **el presidente** es un gran hombre.
E2: No estoy de acuerdo.

1. un mal restaurante
2. un buen programa de televisión
3. una gran mujer, un gran hombre
4. un buen libro (¿una novela?), un libro horrible
5. un buen coche

B. Descripciones. En parejas, describan a su (*your*) familia, haciendo (*forming*) oraciones completas con estas palabras, con cualquier (*any*) otro adjetivo que conozcan (*that you may know*) y con los adjetivos de nacionalidad. **¡OJO!** Cuidado (*Be careful*) con la forma de los adjetivos.

MODELO: Mi familia no es grande. Es pequeña. Mi padre tiene 50 años. Es pakistaní de nacimiento (*by birth*).

mi familia mi padre/madre mi esposo/a mi ¿ ? (otro pariente) mi perro/gato	+	(no) es	+	agresivo, amable, animado (*lively*), antipático, bueno, cariñoso (*affectionate*), comprensivo (*understanding*), difícil (*difficult*), famoso, grande, (im)paciente, importante, inteligente, interesante, malo, nuevo, pequeño, sensible (*sensitive*), sentimental, serio, simpático, tolerante, travieso (*mischievous*), viejo
	+	tiene... años		

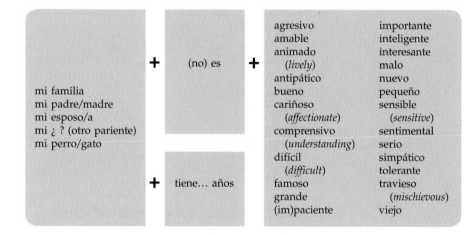

Heritage Speakers

Anime a los hispanoparlantes a describir a los miembros de su familia usando los adjetivos que conocen.

Prác. E: Suggestions

- Create additional items based on the *Paso 1* model to use other nationality adjectives. Here is a list of country names, for your reference: *la China, la Corea del Sur/Norte, la India, Israel, el Japón, Pakistán, Tailandia, Vietnam.*
- Take students to the maps inside the back cover and review the pronunciation of the names of Spanish-speaking countries before asking students to begin *Paso 2.*

Con. A: Suggestion

Reenter or introduce expressions such as *¿Ah, sí?, ¿De veras?, No, hombre,* and so on, and encourage students to use them in their reactions.

Con. A: Note

Active vocabulary: *que*

Con. B: Suggestions

- Provide additional adjectives: *amistoso* (friendly), *atrevido* (daring), *chistoso* (amusing), *encantador* (delightful), *sentimental,* and so on.
- Emphasize that students should follow the lead of the first column, using only singular nouns (to avoid agreement issues with possessive adjectives, which have not yet been introduced).
- Ask students to take notes on what their partners say about their families, in preparation for *Redacción.*

Con. B: Note

Active vocabulary: *inteligente*

Con. B: Redacción

If you had students take notes while doing *Con. B* in pairs, ask them to write a brief (50–60 word) summary of what their partner said about his/her family. Provide the vocabulary word *su* = *his/her* and model several sentences using it.

Con. B: Optional

Ask students, working in pairs, to ask each other questions about their families. They should take notes, then create a family tree based on the answers. Review *tengo, ¿tienes?,* and *¿cuántos/as?* before beginning this activity. Introduce *¿Cómo se llama?* and *¿Cómo se llaman?* Encourage students to stick to basic questions: how many? what are his/her/their names? After creating the family tree for their partner, students should share it with him/her, asking *¿Es correcto?* You may wish to collect the family trees to use as the basis for additional activities for your class.

Gramática 6

Present Tense of *ser*; Summary of Uses (Part 2)

Reciclado: Before teaching the conjugation of *ser*, review subject pronouns. Review the differences between *tú* and *Ud*. Have students tell you the difference between *nosotros/as* and *vosotros/as*. Ask where *vosotros* is used most.

Notes

- Students have used forms of *estar* in *¿Cómo está(s)?* and for telling location. There is no need to go into more detail about *ser* and *estar* at this time.
- Explain that *Pancho* is a nickname for *Francisco*.
- Active vocabulary: *médico/a*

Suggestion

Ask the following questions about the *GEA*.

¿Qué es Pancho?
¿Es estudiante o profesor?
¿De dónde es?
¿Quién es Lola?
¿Cómo es Lola?
¿Y cómo es Pancho?

Variation

Have students practice the sentences in small groups, using information about themselves (Pancho's introduction) and about an important person in their lives (Lola's introduction).

Reciclado

- Review *ser* for telling time (from *Cap. 1*). Telling time is not explicitly listed or reviewed in this section. You may wish to add it to your presentation or discussion.
- Most uses of *ser* in this section are a review of material formally presented or used in *Cap. 1*. Other uses of *ser* will appear in the later chapters: in *Cap. 4*, to tell what something is made of; in *Gram. 16* (*Cap. 6*) in contrast with *estar*; in *Cap. 9*, to mean *to take place*.

¿Recuerda Ud.?

Before beginning **Gramática 6,** review the forms and uses of **ser** that you know already by answering these questions.

1. ¿Es Ud. estudiante o profesor(a)? Soy estudiante.
2. ¿Cómo es Ud.? ¿Es una persona sentimental? ¿inteligente? ¿paciente? ¿elegante? Soy...
3. ¿Qué hora es? ¿A qué hora es la clase de español? Es la / Son las... Es a la(s)...
4. ¿Qué es un hospital? ¿Es una persona? ¿un objeto? ¿un edificio? Es un edificio.

6 Expressing *to be*

Present Tense of *ser;* Summary of Uses (Part 2)

Grammar Tutorial 6
connect SPANISH
www.connectspanish.com

Gramática en acción: Presentaciones

—¡Hola! Me llamo Francisco Durán, pero todos me llaman Pancho.

- Soy profesor de la universidad.
- Soy alto y moreno.
- Soy de Guanajuato, México.

—¿Y Lola Benítez, mi esposa?

- Es _____ (profesión). médica
- Es _____ y _____ (descripción). bonita, muy inteligente
- Es de _____ (origen). Mérida, México

ser (*to be*)			
(yo)	soy	(nosotros/as)	somos
(tú)	eres	(vosotros/as)	sois
(Ud.) (él) (ella)	es	(Uds.) (ellos) (ellas)	son

As you know, there are two Spanish verbs that mean *to be:* **ser** and **estar.** They are not interchangeable; the meaning that the speaker wishes to convey determines their use. In this chapter, you will review the uses of **ser** that you already know and learn some new ones. Remember to use **estar** to express location and to ask how someone is feeling. You will learn more about the uses of **estar** in **Gramática 15–16 (Cap. 6).**

Some basic functions of **ser** are presented on the following pages. You have used or seen all of them already in this and previous chapters.

Introductions *Hello! My name is Francisco Durán, but everyone calls me Pancho. • I'm a university professor. • I'm tall and brunet. • I'm from Guanajuato, Mexico. And Lola Benítez, my wife? • She's _____. • She's _____ and _____. • She's from _____.*

NATIONAL STANDARDS: Comparisons

Explain to students that in many languages, the most commonly used verbs such as *to be, to have,* and *to go* are often irregular. English and Spanish are no exception. Point out to students that *ser* will be irregular in many verb tenses, and ask students to name the forms of *to be* (I am, you are, he is, . . . ; I was, you were, he was, . . .). They will note that *to be* is also irregular in many tenses in English.

Identification / La identificación

To *identify* people (including their profession) and things

[Práctica A]

¡OJO!

Note that the indefinite article is not used after **ser** before unmodified (undescribed) nouns of profession: **Ella es profesora.** *but* **Ella es una buena profesora.**

Yo **soy estudiante.**
Alicia y yo **somos hermanas.**
La doctora Ramos **es profesora.**
Esto **es un libro.**

Description / La descripción

To *describe* people and things*

Soy sentimental.
I'm sentimental (a sentimental person).

El coche **es muy viejo.**
The car is very old.

Origin / El origen

With **de,** to express *origin*

[Práctica B–C]

Somos de los Estados Unidos, pero nuestros padres **son de la Argentina.** ¿**De dónde es** Ud.?
We're from the United States, but our parents are from Argentina. Where are you from?

Generalizations / Las generalizaciones

To express *generalizations* (with **es** + *adjective*)

¡OJO!

Note that **es** + *adjective* is followed by an infinitive in this context, just like in English.

[Conversación B]

Es necesario estudiar. Por eso no **es posible** mirar la televisión todos los días.
It's necessary to study. For that reason (That's why) it's not possible to watch television every day.

Here are two basic functions of **ser** that you have not yet practiced.

Possession / Las posesiones

With **de,** to express *possession*

¡OJO!

Note that there is no **'s** in Spanish.

[Práctica D]

—Este **es** el perro **de Carla.** ¿De quién son las gatas?
—**Son** las gatas **de Jorge.**
"This is Carla's dog. Whose are those (female) cats?"
"They're Jorge's cats."

Destination / El destino

With **para,** to tell for whom or what something *is intended*

[Conversación A]

¿Romeo y Julieta? **Es para** la clase de inglés.
Romeo and Juliet? It's for English class.

—¿**Para** quién **son** los regalos?
—(**Son**) **Para** mi nieto.
"Who are the presents for?"
"(They're) For my grandson."

You practiced this language function of* **ser *in* **Gramática 5** *in this chapter.*

Summary of Uses

Note

Students have not explicitly practiced *Possession* or *Destination.*

Possession

Note

The contraction of *de* + *el* is presented in *Nota comunicativa*, p. 74.

Suggestions

- Practice possessive phrases to emphasize that there is no *'s* in Spanish: *Es el libro de Anita. Son los lápices de la profesora.*
- Point out the difference between *el* (article) and *él* (subject pronoun). Emphasize that *de* does not contract with *él* nor with the *El* in *El Salvador.*
- Remind students to try the *Autoprueba.*

Note

Active vocabulary: *¿de quién?, mirar (la television), necesario/a, posible, para, el regalo, todo/a*

Reciclado: Review classroom vocabulary and practice *ser* + noun. Hold up or point to classroom objects, asking *¿Qué es esto?* Elicit plural forms by holding up two books, pencils, and so on.

Preliminary Exercises

Do a chain drill: *Ana es estudiante. yo → Yo soy estudiante. (Mario y Juan, Uds., Lilia y yo, tú, vosotros, Teresa)*

NATIONAL STANDARDS: Communication

Point out different things you can express with the verb *ser:* who someone/something is, whom something is for, and so on.

Prác. A: Suggestions

- Do as listening activity. Have students assume that you are Gloria or Felipe. Adjust items 1, 2, and 6 as needed.
- Ask personalized questions based on statements: *¿Tiene Ud. esposo/a? ¿Tiene abuelos/as? ¿Cuántos? ¿Tiene primos? ¿De quién es sobrino? ¿Es Ud. tío/a?* and so on.

Prác. A: Note

Active vocabulary: *si*

Prác. A: Optional

Do the following as an optional listening activity, adapting the details as needed to reflect reality. Since these are true/false items, they are not tied per se to the specific person who is in the White House. Ask students to correct false statements.

¿Cierto o falso?

1. *El presidente y su familia son estadounidenses.*
2. *El presidente es esposo.*
3. *La familia del presidente es pequeña.*
4. *La esposa del presidente es una persona mayor* (new word).
5. *Los hijos del presidente son jóvenes.*
6. *El presidente es médico.*
7. *El presidente y su esposa son personas interesantes.*
8. *El presidente y el vicepresidente dicen* (new): *«Somos republicanos».*

Prác. B: Suggestion

Model the pronunciation of names and countries before beginning this activity.

Prác. B: Note

Active vocabulary: *el estado*

Prác. B: Extension

- Review the names of languages (*alemán, español, francés, inglés, italiano*) and introduce *chino, portugués,* and *tailandés.* Have students expand by telling people's nationality and what language they speak. Remind students that the names of languages are not capitalized in written Spanish.
- Name real or fictitious people from the countries listed, asking *¿De dónde es ____?*
- Imagine that you are a friend of persons listed in *Prác. B.* Tell where both of you are from: *John y yo somos de ____. Hablamos ____.*

Nota comunicativa

Note

The contraction *al* is presented in *Gram. 11* (*Cap. 4*).

Autoprueba

Give the correct forms of **ser.**

1. yo ____	**3.** tú ____	**5.** Inés y yo ____
2. Ud. ____	**4.** Pedro ____	**6.** ellos ____

Answers: **1.** soy **2.** es **3.** eres **4.** es **5.** somos **6.** son

Práctica

A. ¡Anticipemos! Los parientes de Gloria. Mire (*Look at*) el dibujo (*drawing*) de la familia de Gloria en la página 60. Indique si (*if*) las siguientes oraciones son ciertas o falsas para Gloria.

1. Felipe y yo somos hermanos. F
2. Pedro es mi esposo. F
3. Pedro y Eliana son mis (*my*) padres. C
4. Carlos es mi sobrino. C
5. Mi hermano es el esposo de Isabel. C
6. El padre de Felipe no es abuelo todavía (*yet*). F
7. Mi familia no es muy grande. C

B. Nacionalidades

Paso 1. ¿De dónde son, según los nombres, apellidos y ciudades?

MODELO: João Gonçalves, Lisboa ⟶
João Gonçalves **es de** Portugal.

1. John Doe, Nueva York
2. Karl Lotze, Berlín
3. Graziana Lazzarino, Roma
4. Mongkut, Bangkok
5. María Gómez, San Salvador
6. Claudette Moreau, París
7. Timothy Windsor, Londres
8. Hai Chow, Beijing

Paso 2. Ahora, dé su (*your*) información personal. ¿De dónde es Ud.? ¿De este estado / esta provincia? ¿de una metrópoli? ¿de un área rural? ¿Es Ud. de una ciudad de nombre hispano? ¿Es de otro país?

Naciones

Alemania
China
El Salvador
los Estados Unidos
Francia
Inglaterra
Italia
Portugal
Tailandia

C. Personas extranjeras

Paso 1. ¿Quiénes son, de dónde son y dónde trabajan ahora?

MODELO: **Teresa:** actriz / de Madrid / en Cleveland ⟶
Teresa **es** actriz. **Es** de Madrid. **Ahora trabaja** en Cleveland.

1. **Carlos Miguel:** médico / de Cuba / en Milwaukee
2. **Pilar:** profesora / de Barcelona / en Miami
3. **Mariela:** dependienta / de Buenos Aires / en Nueva York
4. **Juan:** dentista* / de Lima / en Los Ángeles

Paso 2. Ahora hable sobre (*talk about*) un amigo o pariente, según el modelo del **Paso 1.**

Estrategia

There are verbs missing (indicated by /) from these phrases. Form complete sentences by supplying them, as in the model.

Prác. C, Paso 1: Answers: **1.** *Carlos Miguel es médico. Es de Cuba. Ahora trabaja en Milwaukee.* **2.** *Pilar es profesora. Es de Barcelona. Ahora trabaja en Miami.* **3.** *Mariela es dependienta. Es de Buenos Aires. Ahora trabaja en Nueva York.* **4.** *Juan es dentista. Es de Lima. Ahora trabaja en Los Ángeles.*

Nota comunicativa

La contracción del

The masculine singular article **el** contracts with the preposition **de** to form **del.** No other article contracts with **de.**

de + el ⟶ del

Es la casa **del** abuelito. Es la casa **de la** abuelita.

You will use the *contraction* (**la contracción**) **del** in **Práctica D.**

*A number of professions end in **-ista** in both masculine and feminine forms. The article indicates gender: **el/la dentista, el/la artista,** and so on.*

D. Usemos (*Let's use*) **la lógica.** ¿De quién son estas cosas (*things*), de la rica actriz Jennifer Sánchez o de Martín Osborne, el estudiante (pobre, naturalmente)? En parejas, hagan y contesten preguntas. Las respuestas pueden (*can*) variar.

MODELO: la mochila →
E1: ¿De quién es la mochila?
E2: Es la mochila **del** estudiante.

1. la casa grande
2. la computadora
3. la limosina
4. los libros de texto
5. el Óscar
6. los exámenes
7. los ex esposos
8. el teléfono celular
9. los mensajes

Estrategia

Use **son** with plural items: **¿De quién son los... ? Son...**

E. ¡Somos como una familia! Complete el párrafo con las formas correctas de **ser.**

Me llamo Antonia y __soy__ 1 de Chicago. (Yo) __Soy__ 2 estudiante de ingeniería en la Universidad de Illinois. Mis amigos __son__ 3 de todas partes[a] y muchos de ellos __son__ 4 hispanos. Mi familia __es__ 5 de origen mexicano y aunque nunca he vivido[b] en México, hablo bastante bien[c] el español. Me gusta hablar español con mi amigo Javier. Javier __es__ 6 de Costa Rica y estudia ingeniería también. Javier y yo __somos__ 7 los asistentes del profesor Thomas; por eso pasamos mucho tiempo juntos.[d] Javier __es__ 8 muy guapo y simpático, pero nosotros solo __somos__ 9 buenos amigos. Javier __es__ 10 el novio[e] de mi mejor[f] amiga.

[a]*places* [b]aunque... *although I have never lived* [c]bastante... *rather well* [d]pasamos... *we spend a lot of time together* [e]*boyfriend* [f]*best*

Comprensión

	CIERTO	FALSO
1. Antonia es una persona muy sociable.	☑	☐
2. Es de México.	☐	☑
3. Antonia y Javier son novios.	☐	☑

Conversación

Nota comunicativa

Cómo dar° explicaciones — °*to give*

In conversation, it is often necessary to explain a decision or tell why something is so. Here are some simple words and phrases for offering explanations.

porque because

—¿Por qué necesitamos una televisión nueva?
—Pues... **para** mirar el partido de fútbol... ¡Es la Copa Mundial!

—¿Por qué trabajas tanto?
—¡**Porque** necesitamos dinero!

para + *inf.* in order to (*do something*)

"Why do we need a new TV set?"
"Well . . . (in order) to watch the soccer game . . . It's the World Cup!"

"Why do you work so much?"
"Because we need money!"

¡OJO!

Note the differences between **porque** (one word, no accent) and the interrogative **¿por qué?** (two words, accent on **qué**), which means *why?*

Prác. B: Follow-up

¿Es Ud. del norte de los Estados Unidos / del Canadá? ¿del oeste? ¿del este? ¿del sur?

Prác. C: Follow-up

Have students create sentences about famous Hispanics. Put information on the board in columns to help students form sentences or ask cue questions.

¿De dónde es ______?
Personas: Laura Esquivel, Alex Rodríguez, Lee Treviño, Salvador Dalí, Julio Iglesias, Edward James Olmos, José Lima, Antonio Banderas, Jennifer Lopez, Penélope Cruz, Benicio del Toro
Categorías: atleta, pintor, cantante, escritor (new), *actor*
Naciones: la Argentina, España, los Estados Unidos, México, la República Dominicana

Prác. D: Suggestion

Have students give simple explanations using *porque* (new), *por eso.*

Prác. D: Answers

1. *Es la casa grande de la actriz.*
2. *Es la computadora del estudiante / de la actriz.*
3. *Es la limosina de la actriz.*
4. *Son los libros de texto del estudiante.*
5. *Es el Óscar de la actriz.*
6. *Son los exámenes del estudiante.*
7. *Son los ex esposos de la actriz.*
8. *Es el teléfono celular de la actriz / del estudiante.*
9. *Son los mensajes de la actriz / del estudiante.*

Prác. E: Redacción

Have students write/narrate brief descriptions about themselves based on this paragraph.

Nota comunicativa

Reciclado: The expression *por eso* became active in *Gram. 5* in this chapter. You may wish to use it here because of its conceptual similarity to *porque* and *para.*

NATIONAL STANDARDS: Communication

The activation and practice of words like *por eso, porque, para,* and so on, will help students communicate more smoothly. In *Puntos de partida,* these words are introduced as early as possible to enhance students' communicative abilities.

Con. A: Suggestions

- For *Paso 1,* provide several additional models with simple explanations, using *porque, para,* and *por eso.*
- For *Paso 2,* after students have completed the interviews, have them report their findings back to the class. As a group, review numbers by discussing how much each gift might cost, providing additional numbers as needed, e.g.: *ciento cincuenta, doscientos.* Introduce words such as *caro/a* and *barato/a.*

Bright Idea

Suggestion

Ask the class as a whole questions like the following. Have them explain why using *porque.*

¿Quién necesita una televisión nueva / un coche nuevo / más dinero? ¿Por qué?

Con. A: Follow-up

¿Qué regalos son buenos/malos para las madres? ¿Y para los padres? ¿Qué les regala Ud. a sus hermanos? ¿a sus hijos?

Con. B: Suggestions

- Have students guess the meaning of *fumar cigarrillos* from context.
- Present phrases such as *¿Ah sí?, ¡No me digas!, ¿De veras?, No, hombre,* and so on, for students to use to respond to answers given by others.

Prác. B: Note

Active vocabulary: *mucho/a*

Con. B: Follow-up

- Have students present information about themselves, their families, and where they are from. Remind them not to overuse *yo: Yo soy Phillip. Soy de Garfield Heights. Tengo tres hermanos y una hermana. Mis abuelos son de Rusia.*
- Have students present the information about themselves in a brief composition, which you correct before they present it to the class.

Redacción: Ask students to describe a typical family gathering at home. They should address the following questions.

¿A qué hora llegan todos?
¿Quién(es) llega(n) tarde? ¿Quién(es) no llega(n)?
¿Qué toman Uds.?
¿Es posible bailar? ¿cantar? ¿hablar con los parientes?
¿Es necesario ser amable con todos?
¿A qué hora termina la fiesta?

A. El regalo ideal

Paso 1. Look at Diego's list of gifts and what his family members like. With a partner, decide who receives each gift and why. The first one is done for you.

MODELO: **1.** la novela de J. K. Rowling →
E1: ¿Para quién es la novela de J. K. Rowling?
E2: Es para la prima.
E1: ¿Por qué?
E2: Porque lee (*she reads*) novelas.

LOS REGALOS DE DIEGO

2. __f__ la calculadora
3. __d__ los libros de literatura clásica
4. __b__ los CDs de Bach
5. __a__ la televisión
6. __c__ el teléfono celular
7. __e__ el dinero

LOS MIEMBROS DE LA FAMILIA DE DIEGO

a. el padre: Mira las noticias (*news*).
b. los abuelos: Escuchan mucho la música clásica.
c. la madre: Habla por teléfono mucho.
d. el hermano: Lee historias viejas.
e. la hermana: Necesita pagar la matrícula.
f. el primo: Estudia matemáticas.
g. la prima: Lee novelas.

Vocabulario útil

el coche
el radio
la ropa clothing

Paso 2. With a partner, exchange ideas about good gifts for members of your family and also about good gifts for you.

MODELO: Para mi mamá, deseo comprar ropa, porque ella necesita ropa nueva. Yo necesito ropa nueva también.

B. ¿Qué opina Ud.? Exprese opiniones originales, afirmativas o negativas, con estas palabras.

MODELO: En mi opinión, es importante hablar español en la clase de español.

(no) es importante (no) es muy práctico (no) es necesario (no) es absurdo (no) es fascinante (no) es una lata (*pain, drag*) (no) es posible	+	mirar la televisión todos los días hablar español en la clase tener muchas (*many*) mascotas llegar a clase puntualmente tomar café en el salón de clase hablar con los animales / las plantas tomar mucho café y fumar cigarrillos trabajar dieciocho horas al día tener muchos hermanos ser amable con todos los miembros de la familia estar mucho tiempo (*a lot of time*) con la familia

¿Recuerda Ud.? Answers: **1.** *la casa de Juan* **2.** *el abuelo de Jorge y Estela* **3.** *la sobrina del hombre* **4.** *el libro del estudiante / de la estudiante*

¿Recuerda Ud.?

You have already learned one way to express possession in Spanish: **de** + *noun.* Express these ideas in Spanish.

1. Juan's house
2. Jorge and Estela's grandfather
3. the man's niece
4. the student's book

You will learn another way to express possession in **Gramática 7.**

¿Recuerda Ud.?

Note

Possession with *de* was, of course, just presented in *Gram. 6.* The purpose of *¿Recuerda Ud.?* in this context is to make the use of *de* (versus English *'s*) even more salient, plus offer additional focused practice with *de* + *el* → *del.*

7 Expressing Possession

Unstressed Possessive Adjectives (Part 1)*

Grammar Tutorial 7
connect SPANISH
www.connectspanish.com

Gramática en acción: Invitación y posesión

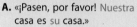

A. «¡Pasen, por favor! Nuestra casa es su casa.»

B. «¡No son tus juguetes! ¡Son mis juguetes!»

Comprensión

1. En el dibujo A, ¿de quién es la casa?
2. ¿Quiénes visitan la casa?
3. En el dibujo B, ¿de quién son los juguetes?
4. ¿Quién desea jugar (*to play*) con los juguetes?

Possessive adjectives (**Los adjetivos posesivos**) are words that tell *to whom* or *to what* something belongs: *my* (book), *his* (sweater). You have already seen and used several possessive adjectives in Spanish. Here is the complete set.

Possessive Adjectives / Los adjetivos posesivos

my	mi **hijo / hija** mis **hijos / hijas**	our	nuestro **hijo** nuestros **hijos**	nuestra **hija** nuestras **hijas**
your (*fam.*)	tu **hijo / hija** tus **hijos / hijas**	your (*fam.*)	vuestro **hijo** vuestros **hijos**	vuestra **hija** vuestras **hijas**
your, his, her, its	su **hijo / hija** sus **hijos / hijas**	your, their	su **hijo / hija** sus **hijos / hijas**	

a possessive adjective / **un adjetivo posesivo** = an adjective that expresses who owns or has something

1. Agreement with Person or Thing Possessed

In Spanish, the ending of a possessive adjective agrees in form with the person or thing possessed, not with the owner or possessor. Note that these possessive adjectives are placed before the noun.

Son {**mis** / **tus** / **sus**} hermanos.

The possessive adjectives **mi(s), tu(s),** and **su(s)** show agreement in number only. **Nuestro/a/os/as** and **vuestro/a/os/as,** like all adjectives that end in **-o,** show agreement in both number and gender.

Es {**nuestra** / **vuestra** / **su**} familia.

Invitation and Ownership ***A.*** *"Come in, please! Our house is your house."* ***B.*** *"They're not your toys! They're my toys!"*

Another kind of possessive is called the* stressed possessive adjective. *It can be used as a noun. You will learn more about using stressed possessive adjectives in* **Capítulo 17.

Gramática 7

Unstressed Possessive Adjectives (Part 1)

Suggestions

- With Drawing A, introduce other typical Spanish expressions of welcome or inviting someone to feel at home as a guest: *Mi casa es tu/su casa. Esta es tu/su casa. Está(s) en su/tu casa. Están en su casa.* Some students will know many of these already.
- With Drawing B, you may wish to discuss the stressed possessives, as the boy might also have said: *¡Son míos!* Stressed possessives are presented as a *Nota comunicativa* in Cap. 17, p. 501. Some instructors like to present them at the same time as the unstressed forms.
- Remind students that *mi(s), tu(s),* and *su(s)* have been widely used in the text up to this point, with *su(s)* always glossed.
- Point out the formal vs. informal in *su* and *tu.*
- Remind students that *'s* does not exist in Spanish. To express possession, the preposition *de* is used.

  el libro de Juan
  la chaqueta de Susana
- Have students identify the possessive forms that are the same for two different grammatical persons (*Ud.* and *él/ella,* and so on). Point out that the ambiguity of *su(s)* (*su hijo* = your/his/her/their son) can be clarified using *el hijo de él/ella,* and so on.
- Remind students that *nuestro* and *vuestro,* like most *-o* adjectives, have four forms: *nuestro, nuestra, nuestros, nuestras; vuestro, vuestra, vuestros, vuestras.*
- Emphasize that possessive adjectives must agree with the noun they modify, that the choice between *mi/mis, tu/tus, su/sus,* and so on depends on the number of the following noun, not on the number of the possessor(s).

Reciclado: Have students describe people they know using adjectives from this chapter and *Cap. 1.* (*Mis tíos son ricos.*)

Resources: Transparency 30

Emphasis 2: Suggestion

Provide model sentences until students are comfortable with this concept. Note that *Prác. B* practices the meanings of *su(s)* in a very focused way.

Emphasis 3: Suggestion

Before presenting this point, it may help students to see this chart as a reminder about usage.

LATIN AMERICA
tú → *Uds.*
Ud. → *Uds.*

SPAIN
tú → *vosotros/as*
Ud. → *Uds.*

Preliminary Exercises

- Remind students to try the *Autoprueba.*
- Have students give the following forms orally.
  1. *Dé la forma singular: nuestras abuelas, sus universidades, tus amigos, vuestros consejeros.*
  2. *Dé la forma plural: nuestro profesor, nuestra clase, vuestro compañero, vuestra actividad, tu televisión, su perro.*
- Have students relate possessives to their respective subject pronouns: *mi* → *yo* (*sus, tus, mi, nuestras, vuestros, su, tu*)

Prác. B: Notes

- The purpose of this exercise is to allow students to explore the meanings of *su(s)* in a focused way.
- Note that it is impossible to assign a specific meaning to item *a* in each set, as there is no context to "fix" the meaning of *su* or *sus*.
- You may wish to tell students that they are asked to give the *likely* meanings. It is possible that someone in the class will note that, in reality, even the meaning of all of the other sentences is uncertain without a full context.

Prác. B: Follow-up

¿Cómo se dice en español?

1. his house, her house, your (*form.*) house, their house → *su casa*
2. his houses, her houses, your (*form.*) houses, their houses → *sus casas*

Prác. C: Note

The focus of this activity is purely on possessive forms. The directions explicitly call students' attention to the mechanical aspects of the practice. The activity also deals on a superficial level with the concepts of direct and indirect address.

2. *Su(s)*
The word **su(s)** has several equivalents in English: *your* (sing.), *his, her, its, your* (pl.), and *their.* Usually its meaning is clear in context. When the meaning is not clear, the construction **de** + *pronoun* is used to indicate possession.

su hijo = el hijo **de**	Ud., Uds. él/ella ellos/ellas
sus hijos = los hijos **de**	Ud., Uds. él/ella ellos/ellas

3. *Su(s)* versus *vuestro/a/os/as*
The forms **vuestro/a/os/as** are the possessives that correspond to the subject pronoun **vosotros.** They are only used in Spain.

Latin America

Uds. → **su, sus**

Spain

vosotros → **vuestro/a/os/as**
Uds. → **su, sus**

Autoprueba

Give the correct possessive adjective.

1. la casa de nosotros = _____ casa
2. los perros de Juan = _____ perros
3. las clases de Luisa = _____ clases

Answers: **1.** *nuestra* **2.** *sus* **3.** *sus*

Práctica

A. Las posesiones. Indique los sustantivos correctos para cada (*each*) adjetivo posesivo según su forma.

1. **su:** problema primos dinero tías escritorios familia
2. **tus:** perro idea hijos profesoras abuelo examen
3. **mi:** ventana médicos cuarto coche abuela gatos
4. **sus:** animales oficina nietas padre hermana abuelo
5. **nuestras:** guitarra libros materias lápiz sobrinas tía
6. **nuestros:** gustos consejero parientes puertas clases residencia

B. ¿Qué significan *su* y *sus*? Tell what the words **su** and **sus** mean in the following sentences. **¡OJO!** You may not be able to answer in all cases!

1. su hijo
- **a.** ¿Dónde está su hijo? ¿ ?
- **b.** ¿Dónde están Elena y su hijo? her
- **c.** ¿Dónde están Pablo y su hijo? his
- **d.** Señor, ¿dónde está su hijo? your
- **e.** María y Ramón, ¿dónde está su hijo? your
- **f.** Señores, ¿dónde están sus hijos? your
- **g.** ¿Dónde están Pablo y Elena y su hijo? their

2. sus hijos
- **a.** ¿Dónde están sus hijos? ¿ ?
- **b.** ¿Dónde están Elena y sus hijos? her
- **c.** ¿Dónde están Pablo y sus hijos? his
- **d.** Señor, ¿dónde están sus hijos? your
- **e.** María y Ramón, ¿dónde están sus hijos? your
- **f.** Señores, ¿dónde están sus hijos? your
- **g.** ¿Dónde están Pablo y Elena y sus hijos? their

C. La familia de Maribel

Paso 1. Change the following sentences, spoken by Maribel, to reflect a plural noun. The noun is indicated in magenta. Note that the possessive adjective itself does not change; only its form changes.

MODELO: «Mi hermano es alto.» → «**Mis** hermanos son altos.»

1. «Mi hermana es lista.» «Mis hermanas son listas.»
2. «Mi primo está en California.» «Mis primos están en California.»
3. «Mi tío habla español.» «Mis tíos hablan español.»
4. «Mi abuela mira mucho la tele (televisión).» «Mis abuelas miran mucho la tele.»

Prác. C: Extension

5. *«Mi tía trabaja mucho.»*
6. *«Mi amiga baila el tango.»*
7. *«Mi sobrino es inteligente.»*
8. *«Mi padre está en casa.»*

Paso 2. Now restate the sentences in **Paso 1** to quote what Maribel said. The possessive adjective itself will change from first person (**mi**) to third person singular (**su**).

MODELO: «Mi hermano es alto.» ⟶ **Su** hermano es alto.

Paso 3. Now restate the sentences in **Paso 1** to make them express what Maribel and her brother Julio would say about their family. The possessive adjective itself will change from first person singular (**mi**) to first person plural (**nuestro**).

MODELO: «Mi hermano es alto.» ⟶ **Nuestro** hermano es alto.

D. David y su familia

Paso 1. Complete las oraciones según el modelo y, según el dibujo.

MODELO: familia / pequeño ⟶
Su familia **es** pequeñ**a**.

1. hijo / guapo Su hijo es guapo.
2. perro / feo Su perro es feo.
3. hija / rubio Su hija es rubia.
4. padre / viejito Su padre es viejito.
5. esposa / bonito Su esposa es bonita.

Paso 2. Imagine que Ud. es David y modifique (*change*) las respuestas (*answers*).

MODELO: familia / pequeño ⟶
Mi familia es pequeñ**a**.

Paso 3. Imagine que Ud. es la esposa de David. Hable por (*Speak for*) Ud. y por su esposo. Modifique solo las respuestas del 1 al 3.

MODELO: familia / pequeño ⟶
Nuestra familia es pequeñ**a**.

Conversación

A. ¿Sí o no? Are the following things or people in your classroom right now? In these items, **su** = *your* (**de Ud.**).

MODELOS: ¿su libro? ⟶ Sí, **mi** libro está en mi mochila. (No, **mi** libro está en casa.)
¿los amigos de Uds.? ⟶ No, **nuestros** amigos no están en el salón de clase. Están en la cafetería.

1. ¿su computadora portátil? mi…
2. ¿los libros de Uds.? nuestros…
3. ¿el profesor / la profesora de Uds.? nuestro/a…
4. ¿la computadora del profesor / de la profesora de Uds.? nuestra…
5. ¿los teléfonos celulares de Uds.? nuestros…
6. ¿su silla? mi…
7. ¿sus padres? / ¿su esposo/a? mis padres / mi esposo/a…
8. ¿la mochila de otro estudiante? su…
9. ¿su dinero? (la cartera = *wallet*) mi…

Prác. C: Answers
Paso 2. 1. *Su hermana…* **2.** *Su primo…* **3.** *Su tío…* **4.** *Su abuela…*
Paso 3. 1. *Nuestra hermana…* **2.** *Nuestro primo…* **3.** *Nuestro tío…* **4.** *Nuestra abuela…*

Estrategia

You must provide a possessive adjective for the noun, then a verb, as in the model. Then be sure that the adjective agrees with the noun!

Prác. D, Paso 2, Answers:
1. *Mi hijo es guapo.* **2.** *Mi perro es feo.* **3.** *Mi hija es rubia.* **4.** *Mi padre es viejito.* **5.** *Mi esposa es bonita.*

Prác. D, Paso 3, Answers:
1. *Nuestro hijo es guapo.*
2. *Nuestro perro es feo.*
3. *Nuestra hija es rubia.*

Estrategia

Remember to use forms of **estar** to express location.

Prác. C: Optional

Paso 4. Ask students to change the *Paso 1* sentences to use *nuestro* forms and also make the sentences plural *«Mi hermano es alto.» ⟶ «Nuestros hermanos son altos.»*

Prác. D: Follow-up

Ask students to create 4 sentences about their family (following the approximate model of the items in *Prác. C*) that begin with *Mi(s)…* and 4 that begin with *Nuestro/a/os/as…* For the latter items, students should indicate who is speaking: *Hablamos mi hermano Juan y yo. Hablamos mi esposo y yo.*

Prác. D: Variation

Have students work in pairs to think of famous families, like presidents' families or those from TV programs, and to describe each member to the rest of the class until their classmates guess them correctly.

Con. A: Reciclado

Note the recycling of *Cap. 2* vocabulary and *estar* in this activity.

Con. A: Emphasis

Emphasize the use of *estar* for location in the model. Encourage students to use *estar* in their sentences.

Resources: Transparency 31

Con. B: Follow-up

Ask students to complete the following statements.

1. *Mi perro/gato…*
2. *Mis padres/abuelos…*
3. *Profesor(a), su casa/coche…*
4. *En nuestro salón de clase…*

Con. B: Suggestion

Remind students to use *tu* forms with classmates. Students will need to use *su* forms, however, to report information to the class about someone else (his/her/their).

Con. B: Optional

Asociaciones: Working in groups, students create as many associations as they can with the following phrases. All students in the group must agree with the associations. Review phrases for agreement and disagreement before beginning the activity. Then, for each item, have a few groups share back their associations.

MODELO: *nuestra clase de español* → *Nuestra clase de español es grande. En nuestra clase de español hay 20 hombres y 15 mujeres.*

1. *nuestra clase de español*
2. *nuestra universidad/librería*
3. *nuestra ciudad / nuestro estado*
4. *nuestra cafetería*
5. *nuestro equipo* (new) *de fútbol*

¿Recuerda Ud.?

Suggestion

Have students conjugate the following verbs chorally.

bailar	*desear*
buscar	*enseñar*
cantar	*pagar*

Gramática 8
Present Tense of *-er* and *-ir* Verbs; Subject Pronouns (Part 2)

Notes

- The *GEA* starts out and ends with *-ar* verbs.
- Active vocabulary: *la carta*

Suggestions

- Call students' attention to the verb endings. Ask: What's the difference between *llama* and *estudia*, for example, and *vive* and *come*?
- Ask students to use Samuel's questions (*¿Y Ud.?*) to interview each other.
- Read Samuel's description sentence by sentence. Ask students whether each sentence is true or false for them. Students correct each false sentence to make it true for them, using *-o*.

Multimedia: Internet

Have students look up the website for *la Universidad Nacional Autónoma de México.* You might assign specific topics to different students or groups, e.g., campus information, classes offered. Then have a class discussion comparing *UNAM* to your university or other universities in the United States and Canada.

B. Intercambios. Take turns asking and answering questions about your families. Talk about what family members are like, their ages, some things they do, and so on. Use the model as a guide. Take notes on what your partner says. Then report the information to the class.

MODELO: tu abuela →
E1: Mi abuela es alta. ¿Y tu abuela? ¿Es alta?
E2: Bueno, no. Mi abuela es baja.
E1: ¿Cuántos años tiene?…

1. tu familia en general
2. tus padres
3. tus abuelos
4. tus hermanos/hijos
5. tu esposo/a / compañero/a de cuarto/casa

¿Recuerda Ud.?: Answers
1. *nosotros/as* 2. *tú* 3. *vosotros/as* 4. *Uds., ellos/as* 5. *yo* 6. *Ud., él, ella*

¿Recuerda Ud.?

The personal endings used with **-ar** verbs share some characteristics with **-er** and **-ir** verbs, which you will learn in **Gramática 8.** Review the present tense endings of **-ar** verbs by telling which subject pronoun(s) you associate with each of these endings.

1. -amos 2. -as 3. -áis 4. -an 5. -o 6. -a

8 Expressing Actions
Present Tense of -er and -ir Verbs; Subject Pronouns (Part 2)

Grammar Tutorial 8
connect SPANISH
www.connectspanish.com

Gramática en acción: Un estudiante típico

- Se llama Samuel Flores Toledo.
- Estudia en la UNAM (Universidad Nacional Autónoma de México).
- Vive con su familia en la Ciudad de México, el D.F. (Distrito Federal).
- Come pizza y tacos con frecuencia.
- Bebe café por la mañana.
- Recibe muchos e-mails y cartas de sus primos del Canadá.
- Lee y escribe mucho para su especialización.
- Aprende inglés porque desea visitar a su familia en Ontario.

Samuel Flores Toledo

¿Y Ud.? Conteste estas preguntas de Samuel. Use formas verbales que terminan en **-o** (= **yo**).

1. ¿Dónde vives tú?
2. ¿Comes muchos tacos?
3. ¿Recibes muchos e-mails?
4. ¿Lees y escribes mucho para tu especialización? ¿O no tienes especialización todavía (*yet*)?

A typical student • *His name is Samuel Flores Toledo.* • *He studies at UNAM (the National Autonomous University of Mexico).* • *He lives with his family in Mexico City,* **el D.F.** *(Federal District).* • *He frequently eats pizza and tacos.* • *He drinks coffee in the morning.* • *He gets a lot of e-mails and letters from his cousins in Canada.* • *He reads and writes a lot for his major.* • *He's learning English because he wants to visit his family in Ontario.*

Present Tense of **-er/-ir** Verbs / **El tiempo presente de los verbos *-er/-ir***

1. Present Tense Endings

The present tense of **-er** and **-ir** verbs is formed by adding personal endings to the stem of the verb (the infinitive minus its **-er/-ir** ending). The personal endings for **-er** and **-ir** verbs are the same except for the first and second person plural.

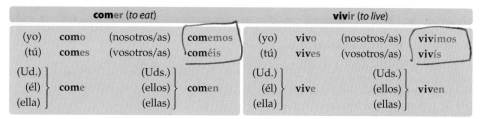

comer (*to eat*)				**vivir** (*to live*)			
(yo)	**como**	(nosotros/as)	**comemos**	(yo)	**vivo**	(nosotros/as)	**vivimos**
(tú)	**comes**	(vosotros/as)	**coméis**	(tú)	**vives**	(vosotros/as)	**vivís**
(Ud.) (él) (ella)	**come**	(Uds.) (ellos) (ellas)	**comen**	(Ud.) (él) (ella)	**vive**	(Uds.) (ellos) (ellas)	**viven**

Las terminaciones **-er/-ir** del tiempo presente			
-er		**-ir**	
-o	-emos	-o	-imos
-es	-éis	-es	-ís
-e	-en	-e	-en

2. Important *-er/-ir* Verbs

These are the frequently used **-er** and **-ir** verbs you will find in this chapter.

-er verbs		**-ir** verbs	
aprender	to learn	**abrir**	to open
aprender + a + *inf.*	to learn how to (*do something*)	**asistir (a)**	to attend, go to (*a class, function*)
beber	to drink	**escribir**	to write
comer	to eat	**recibir**	to receive
comprender	to understand	**vivir**	to live
creer (en)	to think; to believe (in)		
deber + *inf.*	should, must, ought to (*do something*)		
leer	to read		
vender	to sell		

- **Deber,** like **desear** and **necesitar,** is followed by an infinitive.

  Debes leer tus e-mails todos los días.
  You should read your e-mails on a daily basis.

- **Aprender** + **a** + *infinitive* means *to learn how to* (*do something*).

  Muchos niños **aprenden a hablar** español con sus abuelos.
  Many children learn to speak Spanish with their grandparents.

Present Tense of *-er* and *-ir* Verbs

Suggestions

- Introduce *comer* as a model *-er* verb. Talk through the conjugation, using forms in complete sentences and questions, but writing only the verb forms on the board.
- Emphasize that the only two endings that differ between *-er* and *-ir* verbs are *nosotros* (*comemos / vivimos*) and *vosotros* (*coméis / vivís*). All other endings are exactly alike.
- Point out that only the *vosotros* forms have an accent mark.
- Point out that many Spanish speakers say *el correo electrónico* instead of *el e-mail / los e-mails.*

Reciclado

- Review subject pronouns and have students indicate the difference between *tú/vosotros* and *Ud./Uds.*
- Have students recite chorally regular *-ar* verb endings.

Suggestions

- Introduce the meaning of *leer* and use forms in questions to students, writing only the verb forms on the board.
- Follow the same procedure with *escribir* and *vivir.*
- You may want to point out the emphatic phrases: *I do eat . . .* → *yo sí como…*
- Point out that *asistir* is a false cognate.
- Point out that *deber* + inf. is preferred to *necesitar* + inf.

Note

Active vocabulary: *el/la niño/a*

Heritage Speakers

Anime a los hispanohablantes a formar parejas con estudiantes monolingües para que se hagan y contesten preguntas entre sí con estos verbos. Por ejemplo: *¿A qué hora asistes a la clase de español?* → *Asisto a la clase de español a las ocho de la mañana.*

Resources: Transparency 32

NATIONAL STANDARDS: Communication

In Spanish, the verb *tutear* means to speak to someone using the familiar *tú* form. Generally, *tú* is used as the familiar form and *Ud.* is used to show respect. As mentioned previously, the form *vos* is similar to *tú* and is used in several Central American countries, in addition to Argentina and Uruguay. The use of *tú, vos,* or *Ud.* depends on a variety of factors: age, social status, or socioeconomic status. For example, professors, teachers, and parents use *tú* with young adults and children. Nevertheless, an abrupt change from *tú* or *vos* to *Ud.* can indicate a change of tone in a conversation. In Bogota, Colombia, the use of *tú* is very limited. It is used mainly by parents, grandparents, and couples.

Uses of Subject Pronouns

Note

Emphasize that the omission of the subject pronouns is the norm in Spanish: *Bebemos café por la mañana.*

Suggestions

- Emphasize the content of *¡OJO!* to your students.
- Tell them that the text can be their guide to the use or non-use of subject pronouns. Point out that some subject pronouns appear in parentheses in exercises or activities (example: *Prác. D,* p. 84). In such cases, the pronouns are included only as an aid to students, to make sure that they can do the item easily; the parenthetical pronoun would *not* be needed or used by a native speaker of Spanish in that context.

Preliminary Exercises

- Have students give the corresponding forms.

dictado

yo: *aprender, vender, comprender, escribir*
tú: *comer, leer, beber, vivir*
Ud./él/ella: *beber, creer, abrir, recibir*
nosotros: *comprender, deber, asistir, vivir*
vosotros: *deber, vender, aprender, abrir*
Uds./ellos/ellas: *creer, leer, comer, escribir*

- Do a transformation activity:

Ud./tú → yo.
¿Come Ud.? → Sí, como.
¿Comen Uds.? → Sí, comemos.

- Have students give new sentences based on cues.

En la sala de clase

1. *Yo asisto a clase todos los días.* (*tú, nosotros, Ud., todos los estudiantes, Carlos, vosotros*)
2. *Aprendes español en clase, ¿verdad?* (*nosotros, yo, Ud., la estudiante francesa, Uds., vosotros*)

En una fiesta de Navidad (new)

1. *Todos comen y beben.* (*yo, los tíos, tú, Uds., la prima y yo, Ud., vosotras*)
2. *Los niños abren regalos.* (*papá, tú, nosotras, los hijos de Juan, Alicia, los nietos, vosotros*)

Prác. A: Notes

- This activity focuses exclusively on the meaning of the new *-er* and *-ir* infinitives.
- Active vocabulary: *el regalo, la revista*

3. English Equivalents of the Present Tense
Remember that the Spanish present tense has a number of present tense equivalents in English. It can also be used to express future meaning.

como = *I eat, I am eating, I will eat*

Uses of Subject Pronouns / **Los usos de los pronombres personales**

In English, a verb must have an expressed subject (a noun or pronoun): ***the train*** *arrives,* ***she*** *says.* In Spanish, however, as you have probably noticed, an expressed subject is not required. Verbs are accompanied by a subject pronoun only for clarification, emphasis, or contrast.

- *Clarification:* When the context does not make the subject clear, the subject pronoun is expressed. This happens most frequently with third person singular and plural verb forms.

Ud. / él / ella vende
Uds. / ellos / ellas venden

- *Emphasis:* Subject pronouns are used in Spanish to emphasize the subject when in English you would stress it with your voice.

—¿Quién debe pagar? *"Who should pay?"*
—¡Tú debes pagar! *"**You** should pay!"*

- *Contrast:* Contrast is a special case of emphasis. Subject pronouns are used to contrast the actions of two individuals or groups.

Ellos leen mucho; nosotros leemos poco.
They *read a lot;* ***we*** *read little.*

¡OJO!
Avoid using subject pronouns in Spanish when they are not necessary. The overuse of subject pronouns sounds overbearing to native speakers of Spanish.

¿Cuántas personas viven en el D.F.? Busque (*Look up*) el número de habitantes de la ciudad en el Internet.

Autoprueba

Give the correct verb forms.

1. Elena (comer) _____
2. yo (beber) _____
3. nosotros (leer) _____
4. José (escribir) _____
5. Uds. (vivir) _____
6. tú (abrir) _____

Answers: **1.** *come* **2.** *bebo* **3.** *leemos* **4.** *escribe* **5.** *viven* **6.** *abres*

Práctica

A. Asociaciones. ¿Qué verbos asocia Ud. con las siguientes ideas? Dé infinitivos.

1. un libro o una revista (*magazine*) leer
2. una composición, un ensayo (*essay*) o una carta escribir
3. un café o una Coca-Cola beber
4. en la cafetería comer
5. las materias aprender
6. la opinión de un pariente creer
7. una librería o un supermercado vender
8. una puerta o una ventana abrir
9. clases y conciertos asistir a
10. en la residencia o en una casa vivir
11. estudiar más deber
12. regalos abrir

B. En la clase de español

Paso 1. ¡Anticipemos! ¿Cierto o falso para su clase? Corrija (*Correct*) las oraciones falsas.

MODELO: Bebemos café en el salón de clase. ⟶ Cierto. (Falso. No bebemos café en el salón de clase. Bebemos café en casa.)

	CIERTO	FALSO
1. Debemos estudiar más esta materia.	☐	☐
2. Leemos los capítulos completos de *Puntos de partida.*	☐	☐
3. Todos comprendemos bien el español de nuestro profesor / nuestra profesora.	☐	☐
4. Asistimos a esta clase todos los días.	☐	☐
5. Abrimos los libros con frecuencia en esta clase.	☐	☐
6. En esta clase escribimos mucho.	☐	☐
7. En esta clase aprendemos a hablar y comprender español.	☐	☐
8. Vendemos nuestros libros al final del año.	☐	☐

Prác. B, Paso 1: Extension

9. *Recibo muchos paquetes de mi familia.*

10. *Como en casa/_____* (dining facility) *por la noche.*

11. *Vivo con mi familia este semestre/trimestre.*

12. *Mi profesor(a) cree que yo debo asistir a clase con más frecuencia.*

13. *Debo aprender a leer más rápido.*

Paso 2. Now turn to the person next to you and rephrase each sentence, using **tú** forms of the verbs. Your partner will indicate whether the sentences are true for him or her.

MODELO: Bebemos café en el salón de clase. ⟶

E1: **Bebes** café en el salón de clase, ¿verdad (*right*)?

E2: Sí, bebo café en el salón de clase. (No, no bebo café en el salón de clase. Bebo café en la cafetería.)

Prác. B, Paso 2: Follow-up: Ask students about their partner's answers; they will use third person singular verbs.

C. Diego habla de su padre. Complete el siguiente párrafo con la forma correcta de los verbos entre paréntesis.

Mi padre (vender[1]) coches y trabaja mucho. Mis hermanos y yo (aprender[2]) mucho de papá. Según mi padre, los jóvenes (deber[3]) (asistir[4]) a clase todos los días, porque es su obligación. Papá también (creer[5]) que no es necesario mirar la televisión por la noche. Es más interesante (leer[6]) el periódico,[a] una revista o un buen libro. Por eso nosotros (leer[7]) o (escribir[8]) por la noche y no miramos la televisión. Yo admiro a mi papá y (creer[9]) que él (comprender[10]) la importancia de la educación.

[a]*newspaper*

Prác. C, Answers: 1. *vende* **2.** *aprendemos* **3.** *deben/debemos* **4.** *asistir* **5.** *cree* **6.** *leer* **7.** *leemos* **8.** *escribimos* **9.** *creo* **10.** *comprende*

Comprensión. ¿Cierto o falso? Corrija (*Correct*) las oraciones falsas.

	CIERTO	FALSO
1. Diego y sus hermanos venden coches.	☐	☑
2. Diego mira mucho la televisión.	☐	☑
3. El padre de Diego lee mucho.	☑	☐

Comprensión, Answers: 1. *Falso: El padre vende coches.* **2.** *Falso: Diego no mira mucho la televisión.*

Heritage Speakers

Anime a los hispanohablantes a hablar del pariente que más admiran (padre, madre, tío, abuela). Pídales que expliquen a qué se dedica esa persona, cuáles son sus pasatiempos y por qué lo/la admiran.

Prác. A: Suggestions

- Reverse the activity. Read through the suggestions in the student text, then ask students to close their books. Give an *-er* or *-ir* infinitive and ask students for associated words and phrases. They need not be items from *Prác. A.*
- After you are sure that students have a good command of the meanings of the infinitives, ask them to interview you based on the cues in *Prác. A.* This will provide focused practice with *Ud.* forms if that is the form of address that you ask students to use when speaking to you.

Prác. B: Preliminary Exercises

- Before beginning *Paso 2,* have students respond *sí* or *no* to the following sentences.
  1. *Los estudiantes de esta clase deben…*

     comer durante la clase / asistir a clase todos los días / ir al laboratorio de lenguas con frecuencia aprender muchas cosas nuevas todos los días
  2. *El profesor* (*La profesora*) *de español cree en…*

     hablar español en clase / explicar toda la gramática / dar (new) *exámenes con frecuencia / llevar sombrero para enseñar*
- ¡Estos estudiantes son fantásticos!

  Have students give sentences starting with *Debemos…* to show how good they are.

Prác. B: Note

All of the items use *nosotros* forms to show the contrast between *-er* and *-ir* verbs in those forms.

Prác. B: Suggestion

Ask students to find the conjugated verb in each sentence, then give the infinitive.

Prác. C: Suggestions

- Model the pronunciation of each infinitive in the paragraph. Use the *yo* form of each in a brief simple sentence about yourself, then in *Ud.* and *Uds.* questions to students.
- Have students scan the paragraph for meaning before attempting to do the items. After the individual items are done, have a volunteer read the entire paragraph.

Prác. C: Note

Active vocabulary: *el periódico*

Prác. D: Answers

3. *Mis padres celebran su aniversario de boda.*
4. *Las mujeres de la familia y unos hombres preparan la comida.*
5. *Mis tíos beben café y miran la tele.*
6. *Mis primas pequeñas leen revistas para niños.*
7. *Mi hermano debe estudiar pero lee las noticias del fútbol de México en el Internet.*
8. *No comprende todo porque su español no es perfecto.*
9. *Creo que mi mamá y mis tías son cocineras excelentes.*
10. *Deseo ser un buen cocinero también.*

Prác. D: Follow-up

1. *¿Qué hay en casa del narrador hoy?*
2. *¿Qué es una tamalada?*
3. *¿Qué aniversario celebran los padres del narrador?*
4. *¿Quiénes preparan la comida?*
5. *¿Quién lee en el Internet?*
6. *¿Quién lee revistas?*
7. *¿Quién bebe cerveza y mira la tele?*
8. *¿A qué hora es la comida?*
9. *¿Quiénes son cocineras excelentes?*
10. *¿Quién desea ser un buen cocinero?*

Prác. D: Reciclado

Use this activity as a springboard to review interrogative words from *Cap. 2.* Give students an interrogative word for which they provide a full question.

Nota comunicativa

Note

Have students use *casi nunca* and *nunca* at the beginning of a sentence only, to avoid the double negative. Students will learn the double negative in *Gram. 19* (*Cap. 7*).

Reciclado: *Todos los días* and *con frecuencia* were presented in *Cap. 2.*

Multimedia: Internet

Have students search the Internet for more information about Carmen Lomas Garza.

Culture

- Many Hispanic families spend Saturdays and/or Sundays together as a family, often for an outing to a park, plaza, or local tourist destination. Families also gather frequently in homes of extended family members, in restaurants, and in parks. The day may simply be spent at home together, as in *Prác. D.* Ask students what some of the weekend routines and traditions of their families are. Do they spend the time together as a family?

Tamalada (*Making Tamales*), por (*by*) Carmen Lomas Garza (estadounidense)

D. Este domingo (*Sunday*)**, tamalada.** Form complete sentences based on the words given, in the order given. Add words when necessary and make adjectives agree with nouns. Conjugate the infinitives. Don't use the subject pronouns in parentheses. The first two sentences are done for you as models.

Una tamalada consiste en hacer (*making*) y comer tamales, una comida (*food*) típica de México y Centroamérica. Hay ocasiones en que hacer tamales es una fiesta familiar. Este domingo es un día especial para la familia de la pintura. Habla Luis.

MODELOS: **1.** hay / tamalada hoy / por / tarde ⟶ Hay **una** tamalada hoy por **la** tarde.

2. todo / familia / asistir / tamalada en / nuestra casa ⟶ Tod**a la** familia asist**e a la** tamalada en nuestra casa.

3. mi / padres / celebrar / su aniversario de boda (*wedding*)
4. la / mujeres / de la familia / y / un / hombres / preparar la comida (*meal*)
5. mi / tíos / beber / café / y / mirar la tele
6. mi / primas / pequeño / leer / revistas para niños
7. mi hermano / deber estudiar / pero / leer / noticias (*news*) del fútbol de México / en el Internet
8. (él) no / comprender todo / porque / su español / no / ser perfecto
9. (yo) creer que / mi / mamá / y / tías / ser cocineras (*cooks*) / excelentes
10. (yo) desear ser / uno / bueno / cocinero también

Conversación

Nota **comunicativa**

Cómo expresar la frecuencia de las acciones

OFTEN AT THE END OF OR WITHIN A SENTENCE	OFTEN AT THE BEGINNING OF A SENTENCE
a veces at times	**casi nunca** almost never
con frecuencia frequently	**nunca** never
siempre always	
todos los días every day	
una vez a la semana once a week	

Hablo con mis amigos **todos los días.** Hablo con mis padres **una vez a la semana. Casi nunca** hablo con mis abuelos. Y **nunca** hablo con mis tíos que viven en Italia.

- Carmen Lomas Garza is a Chicana artist who was born in Kingsville, Texas, near Corpus Christi. She started painting when she was 13 years old. She currently lives in San Francisco, California, where she continues to paint today. Her paintings depict fond memories of her childhood and her daily life with family and the community, as well as memorable joyous events. You may wish to bring a copy of Carmen Lomas Garza's book *Family Pictures* (*Cuadros de familia*) (Children's Book Press, 2005) and have students describe the activities of family members.

A. ¿Con qué frecuencia?

Paso 1. How frequently do you do the following things? Indicate the frequency of each activity with one of the indicated phrases, then say each sentence aloud. Remember to put **casi nunca** and **nunca** at the beginning of the sentence.

todos los días **con frecuencia** **a veces** **casi nunca** **nunca**

MODELOS: **Casi nunca** asisto al laboratorio de computadoras.
Asisto al laboratorio **a veces.**

1. Recibo e-mails y cartas.
2. Escribo poemas.
3. Leo novelas románticas.
4. Como en una pizzería.
5. Recibo y leo revistas.
6. Aprendo palabras nuevas en español.
7. Asisto a todas las clases.
8. Compro regalos para los amigos.
9. Vendo los libros al final del semestre/trimestre.

Paso 2. Now compare your answers with those of a classmate. Then answer the following questions. **¡OJO! los/las dos** = *both (of us)*; **ninguno/a** = *neither*.

	YO	MI COMPAÑERO/A	LOS/LAS DOS	NINGUNO/A
1. ¿Quién es muy estudioso/a?	☐	☐	☐	☐
2. ¿Quién come mucha pizza?	☐	☐	☐	☐
3. ¿Quién compra muchas cosas?	☐	☐	☐	☐
4. ¿Quién es muy romántico/a?	☐	☐	☐	☐
5. ¿Quién recibe muchos e-mails?	☐	☐	☐	☐
6. ¿Quién escribe mucho?	☐	☐	☐	☐
7. ¿Quién lee mucho?	☐	☐	☐	☐

B. Intercambios. Use the following cues to interview a classmate. Include expressions of frequency when appropriate.

MODELO: leer + novelas de horror ⟶ Carmen, ¿lees novelas de horror?

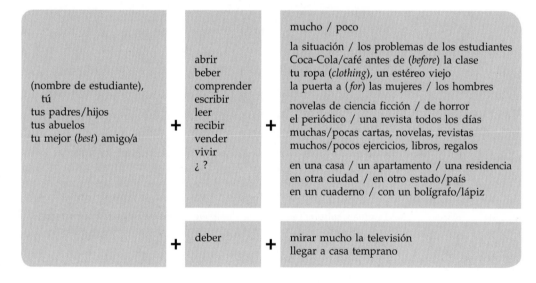

(nombre de estudiante), tú tus padres/hijos tus abuelos tu mejor (*best*) amigo/a	+	abrir beber comprender escribir leer recibir vender vivir ¿ ?	+	mucho / poco la situación / los problemas de los estudiantes Coca-Cola/café antes de (*before*) la clase tu ropa (*clothing*), un estéreo viejo la puerta a (*for*) las mujeres / los hombres novelas de ciencia ficción / de horror el periódico / una revista todos los días muchas/pocas cartas, novelas, revistas muchos/pocos ejercicios, libros, regalos en una casa / un apartamento / una residencia en otra ciudad / en otro estado/país en un cuaderno / con un bolígrafo/lápiz
	+	deber	+	mirar mucho la televisión llegar a casa temprano

Mundo interactivo

You should now be prepared to work with Scenario 2, Activity 2 in Connect Spanish (**www.connectspanish.com**).

Con. A: Extension

Have students add three original items before doing *Paso 2*.

Con. A: Follow-up

- Have students interview their partner to obtain more specific information about the items in *Paso 2*. Examples: *¿Cuál es tu pizzería favorita? ¿Qué recibes por correo* (new), *cartas o revistas?* and so on. Remind students to use *tu(s)* in this activity.
- Have students prepare a brief *informe oral* about their partner or about the similarities and differences between themselves and their partner, using all the information they have learned about him or her.

Con. B: Suggestion

Have students use the cues to interview you.

Redacción: Ask students to take notes during their *entrevistas,* then write up the information they have learned in the form of a brief paragraph about their partner and his/her family and friends. Collect the paragraphs and use the information in them as the basis for a *¿cierto o falso?* listening comprehension activity, adjusting the information as needed to create *falso* items.

Heritage Speakers

Anime a los hispanohablantes a hablar de su rutina diaria y que digan con qué frecuencia hacen las cosas que hacen.

Un poco de todo

A: Suggestions

- To practice the Hispanic two-surnames system, follow A with an activity in which students assign last names to everyone. Give them the grandfather's name: *Fernando Suárez Maldonado.* Then let them invent other names, starting with the grandmother, who would be *Laura ______ de Suárez,* and so on.
- Follow up the student text activity by asking students to invent other family members, at least 5, and place them in the family tree. You might have students work in pairs or groups, then compare several expanded trees as a whole class.

A: Answers

2. *El (Mi) nuevo nieto es de los Estados Unidos.*
3. *El padre del (de mi) nieto es mi hijo.*
4. *El abuelo es mi esposo, pero ya murió.*
5. *Una de las tías del nieto es médica.*
6. *Otra tía es una artista famosa.*
7. *La madre del niño es estadounidense.*
8. *La hermana del niño se llama Laura, como yo.*

Redacción: After the family tree in A is completed, ask students to write at least one sentence describing each family member in the tree. Students should not repeat information that is already in the items in A.

NATIONAL STANDARDS

Cultures

The artist, Frida Kahlo (1907–1954), was an influential Mexican painter who was married to the famous muralist Diego Rivera (1886–1957). Her work was constantly self-referential. She portrayed herself in a wide variety of contexts and outfits that speak of her difficult life and her connection to her culture: her relationship with her husband, her physical suffering due to a horrible accident in her youth that left her in constant pain, and her love for her cultural roots.

NATIONAL STANDARDS

Communities

The art of Frida Kahlo and Diego Rivera is internationally famous. Both spent a few years living and painting in the U.S. Ask students to research their lives to find out when they were in this country, what they did here, and where there are still works by either of them.

Un poco de todo

A. Un árbol genealógico. When you flesh them out by adding words, conjugating infinitives, and making adjectives agree with nouns, the following sentences will create the description of a family in which there is a new grandchild. The first sentence is done for you as a model. Use the names in parentheses and the information in all of the sentences, including the model, to fill out the family tree. Then answer the questions in **Comprensión.**

MODELO: **1.** yo / ser / Laura / y / ser / mexicano →
Yo **soy** Laura y **soy** mexican**a**.

2. nuevo / nieto / ser de / Estados Unidos (Fernando)
3. padre / de / nieto / ser / mi hijo (Juan)
4. abuelo / ser / mi esposo / pero / ya murió (*has already passed away*) (Fernando)
5. uno / de las tías / de / nieto / ser / médica (Pilar)
6. otro / tía / ser / artista / famoso (Julia)
7. madre / de / niño / ser estadounidense (Paula)
8. hermana / de / niño / se llama, Laura como yo

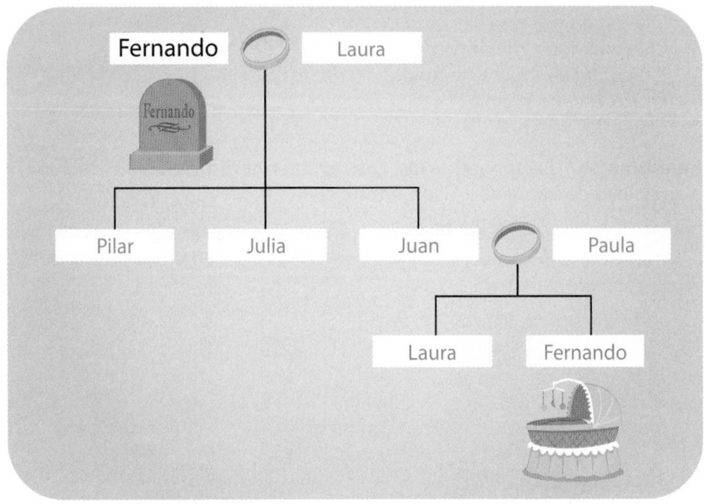

Comprensión. Conteste estas preguntas, según la descripción de la familia.

1. ¿De dónde es la familia paterna? Es de México.
2. ¿Dónde vive la familia del nuevo nieto? Vive en los Estados Unidos.
3. ¿Cómo se llama el abuelo de la familia? El abuelo se llama Fernando.

Act. B: Answers: **1.** *grandes* **2.** *grandes* **3.** *es* **4.** *muchos* **5.** *trabajan* **6.** *viven* **7.** *creen* **8.** *principal* **9.** *están* **10.** *familiares* **11.** *varias* **12.** *muchas*

B. Lengua y cultura: Las familias. Complete the following paragraphs about families. Give the correct form of the words in parentheses, as suggested by context.

¿Existe la familia hispana típica? La idea de que las familias hispanas son muy (grande[1]) es un estereotipo del pasado,[a] especialmente en las (grande[2]) ciudades. Ahora, la norma (ser[3]) una familia con dos o tres hijos. Es difícil tener (mucho[4]) hijos cuando el padre y la madre

[a]*past*

Resources: Transparency 33

Heritage Speakers

Anime a los hispanohablantes a crear un árbol genealógico parecido al que aparece en esta página. Invítelos a dar una breve descripción de los miembros de su familia.

(trabajar[5]) fuera de la casa,[b] y cuando los abuelos o tías no (vivir[6]) en casa para cuidar[c] a los niños. A pesar de[d] la reducción en el número de hijos, los hispanos (creer[7]) que la familia es su institución (principal[8]). Muchos hispanos mantienen[e] relaciones con parientes que (estar[9]) en otro país y muchos les mandan[f] dinero y regalos para ayudarlos.[g] En las reuniones (familiar[10]) también es frecuente incluir a parientes de (vario[11]) generaciones.

En su opinión, ¿hay (mucho[12]) diferencias entre su familia y las familias hispanas que conoce[h]?

[b]fuera... *outside the home* [c]cuidar... *care for* [d]A... *In spite of* [e]*keep up, maintain* [f]*send to them* [g]*help them* [h]*you know*

Comprensión. ¿Cierto o falso? Corrija (*Correct*) las oraciones falsas. En las grandes ciudades, la norma es familias pequeñas.

1. Todas las familias hispanas son grandes. Falso.
2. Por lo general (*Generally*), las familias urbanas son pequeñas. Cierto.
3. Para los hispanos, la familia es una institución social fundamental. Cierto.

Frida y Diego Rivera (1931), por Frida Kahlo: ¿Una familia hispana típica?

C. Una fiesta. There is a Spanish saying, "**Una fiesta se hace** (*is made*) **con tres personas: una canta, otra baila y la otra toca.**" Working in groups of four, use this saying as a model to tell what the following things are "made of." Use as many **-ar, -er,** and **-ir** verbs as you can, as well as the irregular verbs **ser** and **estar,** the forms of **tener** that you know (**tengo, tienes, tiene**), and the verb form **hay.**

MODELO: una clase → Una clase se hace con un profesor o una profesora. Esta persona enseña la clase. También hay unos estudiantes. Desean aprender la materia y estudian mucho. Leen su libro de texto y escriben informes (*papers*). También hay un salón de clase, un pizarrón...

¿Cómo se hace... ?

1. una clase de español
2. una fiesta en esta universidad
3. una universidad
4. una familia

En su comunidad

Entreviste a (*Interview*) una persona hispana de su universidad o ciudad sobre (*about*) su familia.

PREGUNTAS POSIBLES

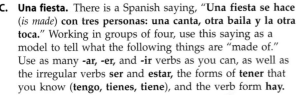

- ¿Tiene esta persona una familia grande o pequeña? ¿Cuáles son los miembros de la familia?
- ¿Cuál es el país de origen de los abuelos de la persona? ¿Viven solos (*alone*) o con un pariente?
- ¿Los parientes se reúnen (*get together*) con frecuencia? ¿En qué ocasiones?

Resources: Desenlace

In the *Cap. 3* segment of "Chapter-by-Chapter Supplementary Materials" in the IM, you will find a chapter-culminating activity. You can use this activity to consolidate and review the vocabulary and grammar skills students have acquired.

B: Note

The following grammar topics are included in *Lengua y cultura:* adjective agreement, *-ar/-er/-ir* verbs, *ser.*

B: Suggestion

Have students work in small groups to rewrite the paragraph in such a way that it describes the "typical" view of U.S. or Canadian families. Compare the paragraphs of the different groups. In what ways are they similar? How are they different? Can students explain what accounts for their differences and similarities?

C: Suggestions

- Before beginning this activity, review with students the vocabulary groups they have learned so far: classroom words, academic subjects, family names, numbers 0–100, adjectives. Suggest that they scan the *En resumen: Vocabulario* lists of *Caps. 1–2.*
- Have different pairs or groups work on different descriptions rather than doing all four items. Collect the descriptions from each group and correct them. During the next class period, return the descriptions to their authors and have students read them aloud. Vote on the best/most creative description.

En su comunidad

Notes

- Remember that it is possible for students to complete this activity by doing research on-line.
- Remember also that an additional option is to have students work with the same native informant for the whole semester/quarter or academic year.

Suggestions

- Remind students to get the following basic information: the informant's country of origin, how long he or she has lived in this country, and if the informant visits his or her country of origin frequently.
- See the IM for more suggestions.

TelePuntos

Note

Pages 88–93 are optional. You may cover some, all, or none of this material in class, or assign it to students—as a group or individually—for homework or extra credit. Pages 94–95 (*En resumen: En este capítulo*) are a summary of all of the chapter's active material.

Suggestions

- If you are using the video in class, show it once, ask brief comprehension questions, then show it again.
- Even if you plan to ask students to watch the video in your campus media center or on their own, it is a good idea to continue to stress the need to watch the shows as many times as they want or need to in order to complete the *Después de mirar* activities.

Antes de mirar

Suggestion

Give the following definitions, orally or in writing, and ask students to match them with the four types of families given in the text.

Es una familia con…

- *solo un padre o solo una madre* (*monoparental*)
- *padres que son homosexuales* (*con ambos padres del mismo sexo*)
- *un padre y una madre divorciados y casados con otras personas* (*reconstituida*)
- *una madre y un padre casados* (*tradicional*)

Programa 3

Notes

- Most of the language of *Programa 3* will be reasonably accessible to students. However, the interview with José Lorca will at times be challenging due to his natural hesitations and the occasional lack of clarity. See *Fragmento del guion* and the IM for additional comments on this language usage.
- Emphasize to students that the more carefully they study the preliminary activities (*Antes de mirar, Vocabulario de este programa*, and *Fragmento del guion*), the more they will understand when viewing the episode. Scanning *Después de mirar* before viewing is also an excellent strategy.

TELEPUNTOS SALU2

Una familia mexicana que extraña (*misses*) a sus parientes mexicanos: Minerva (a la derecha [*on the right*]), Araceli y sus hijos

Antes de mirar°

Antes… *Before watching*

Indique los distintos tipos de familias que Ud. conoce (*are familiar with*) personalmente.

- ☐ familia tradicional (padre y madre casados [*married*] y que viven juntos [*together*])
- ☐ familia monoparental
- ☐ familia reconstituida (uno de los padres o ambos [*both*], divorciados y casados con [*married to*] otra persona)
- ☐ familia con ambos padres del mismo (*same*) sexo

PROGRAMA 3: Padres modernos

You will not understand every word of this episode. Remember that if you pay close attention to the images and listen for recognizable cognates and vocabulary that you already know, you will be able to get the gist of the show's content.

Vocabulario de este programa

disfrutar	enjoy	**dos mil cinco**	2005	**cumplió 15 años**	turned 15
enfermo/a	sick	**no es nada extraño**	isn't unusual at all	**fue**	she went; it was
cansado/a	tired	**único/a**	unique; only	**la quinceañera**	fifteenth birthday celebration
cuidar a/de	to take care of	**una vida mejor**	a better life		
los padrinos	godparents	**mil novecientos noventa y nueve**	1999		
el padrino	godfather			**ver**	to see
la madrina	godmother	**han crecido juntos**	they've grown up together	**¿te acuerdas de… ?**	do you remember . . . ?
el/la ahijado/a	godson/goddaughter				
hace (10, 30,… años)	(10, 30, . . . years) ago	**dejar atrás**	to leave behind		
		hubo	there was		

Fragmento del guion°

script

LAURA: En este parque barcelonés, hablamos con José Lorca y su familia. José nos explica quién se preocupa[a] del cuidado[b] de sus hijos, especialmente de la pequeña.

JOSÉ: Normalmente nos lo repartimos.[c] Su madre, unos días, un día sí, un día no. Y yo un día sí, un día no. Porque nuestro trabajo nos lo permite.[d]

LAURA: Gracias a su flexibilidad laboral,[e] José y su esposa alternan los días en que cuidan a su hija pequeña desde por la mañana hasta la noche. Así[f] la niña no pasa tiempo sola[g] en casa.

JOSÉ: Nos repartimos las faenas[h]… . Las faenas de casa nos las repartimos… también… El día que se queda uno[i]… pues… desde que se levanta[j]… les prepara el desayuno.[k] Los… a ella la ayuda[l]… a prepararse un poco para ir al colegio.[m]

[a]se… *is concerned* [b]*care* [c]nos… *we share it* [d]nuestro… *our work allows us to do that* [e]*work* [f]*In that way* [g]*alone* [h]*chores* [i]El… *The day that one (of us) stays home* [j]desde… *from when he or she gets up* [k]les… *he or she prepares breakfast* [l]a… *he or she helps her [the daughter]* [m]ir… *go to school*

José Lorca, un padre español con su hjia, en Barcelona, la segunda (*second*) ciudad más grande de España

Mundo interactivo

Continue your work as an intern at HispanaVisión with Laura Sánchez Tejada, the roving reporter of *Salu2*, as you complete Scenario 2, Activities 1 and 2 in Connect Spanish (**www.connectspanish.com**).

Al mirar°

°Al... *While you watch*

Mientra (*While*) mira el programa, indique las familias que se mencionan específicamente en este programa. **¡OJO!** En el programa no se menciona la familia de cada (*each*) persona de la lista.

La familia de...

1. ☑ Víctor	**3.** ☐ Laura	**5.** ☑ Minerva
2. ☑ Ana	**4.** ☑ José Lorca	**6.** ☑ Araceli

Después de mirar°

°Después... *After watching*

A. ¿Está claro? ¿Cierto o falso? Corrija las oraciones falsas.

	CIERTO	FALSO
1. Víctor está casado.	☑	☐
2. Ana tiene una hija.	☐	☑
3. José es un padre barcelonés que tiene una hija pequeña.	☑	☐
4. Minerva y su hija no tienen familia en California.	☐	☑

B. Un poco más. Conteste las siguientes preguntas.

1. ¿Quién cuida a la hija enferma de Víctor hoy?
2. ¿Quién es padrino o madrina, Víctor o Ana?
3. En casa de José, ¿quién hace (*does*) las faenas de casa?
4. ¿El año pasado (*Last year*), ¿qué tipo de celebración hubo en México en la familia de Minerva y Araceli?

C. Y ahora, Uds. En grupos, hablen de (*talk about*) la familia. ¿Es importante la familia extendida en su caso? ¿Qué parientes incluye? ¿Incluye a padrinos y ahijados? ¿a parientes que viven en otro país? ¿Cómo es su familia? ¿Es tradicional? ¿patriarcal? ¿matriarcal?

Sarita, la hija adoptada de Víctor y su esposa

Sobre° el programa

°*About*

Sara Gutiérrez Rojo es la hija de Víctor y su esposa, Marina Rojo. Sara es adoptada. Su llegada[a] a la familia fue[b] un acontecimiento[c] muy celebrado por todos. Sara es guatemalteca de nacimiento;[d] tiene 5 años y es una niña extrovertida y simpática. Víctor y Marina tienen una sorpresa para Sarita: en unos meses[e] —si todo va bien[f]— Sarita va a tener[g] un hermanito o una hermanita,[h] también de Guatemala.

[a]*arrival* [b]*was* [c]*event* [d]de... *by birth* [e]*months* [f]si... *if all goes well* [g]va... *is going to have* [h]hermanito... *little brother or little sister*

Producción personal

Filme una o dos entrevistas (*interviews*) con personas que hablan de sus familias.

Act. A, Answers: 2. *Falso: Tiene una ahijada.* **4.** *Falso: La hermana de Minerva, Araceli, vive en California.*

Act. B, Answers: 1. *la abuela de Sarita (la madre de Víctor)* **2.** *Ana es madrina.* **3.** *Los dos esposos hacen las faenas de casa.* **4.** *la quinceañera de una sobrina de Minerva y Araceli*

Fragmento del guion

Note

All of José Lorca's natural language is given to students in this section so that they can read through it, then understand it when they see it. It is a good idea to work through the *Fragmento* with students ahead of time to point out characteristics of natural language such as hesitations and fragmentation. You may also wish to explore with students the following feature of Spanish (reflected in the glosses on the *Fragmento*) that contrasts with English: Spanish does not really specify the sex of the spouse who stays home (*se levanta, prepara, ayuda*); the subject is *uno,* masculine, but understood as generic (neither masculine nor feminine) in this context. To get the same meaning in English, *he* or *she* must be expressed as a subject.

Al mirar

Suggestion

Ask students to read the items before they start to watch. Since it is a short list, students should be able to keep the items in mind while watching (and should not need to look away from the screen to check off options).

Después de mirar

A: Suggestion

Explain that having a special celebration for a girl's fifteenth birthday is a tradition observed all over Latin America. It's called *la quinceañera*. You may wish to refer to pages 267 and 275 in *Cap. 9*.

C: Follow-up

- Ask students if there are people in their family that they miss: *¿A quién extraña? ¿Dónde están esas personas?*
- After students have discussed these topics on their own, have a whole-class discussion about these types of families. Survey the class to see which type of family is most common.

Sobre el programa

Optional: Comprensión

¿Cierto o falso? Corrija las oraciones falsas.

1. *Sarita es la hija biológica de Víctor y Ana.* (*Falso: Es una hija adoptada.*)
2. *Sarita tiene hermanos.* (*Falso: Va tener un hermanito o una hermanita en unos meses.*)
3. *Sarita es de Guatemala.* (*Cierto*)
4. *Sarita es una niña tímida.* (*Falso: Es una niña extrovertida.*)

Producción personal

Note

See the IM for additional suggestions for this chapter's assignment as well as for general guidelines and suggestions for video assignments.

Lectura cultural

Notes

- Remember that this page of *A leer* offers two kinds of readings: **1.** information about the chapter's theme as it relates to the country of focus (always the first reading on the page, the one that is untitled, with a large initial letter) plus information about the theme in the rest of the Spanish-speaking world (*En otros países*); **2.** additional short items about the country of focus, varying in nature from chapter to chapter.
- The Instructor's Edition on this page offers some additional information on the country of focus. For more information about the country of focus, see the chapter's opening pages and the IM.
- See the IM for some expressions used in Mexico.

Note

Photo: The Day of the Dead is celebrated on November 2 in Mexico and in some other (but not all) Spanish-speaking countries. Many observers of the tradition create an altar in their homes with a photo of the deceased and some of his/her favorite possessions and food. Family members visit the cemetery during the evening and decorate the tomb with flowers (especially marigolds, *las maravillas*) and candles. The custom is a positive one, not morbid at all. The Day of the Dead festivities in Oaxaca are especially well-known.

Exploración lingüística

Ask students to find the following in the reading. Some of these words are glossed and some are not.

- *un sustantivo opuesto a ventaja* (*desventaja*)
- *una palabra que es un adjetivo y un sustantivo* (*joven*)
- *un adjetivo opuesto a dependiente* (*autosuficiente*)

Tres símbolos mexicanos

Suggestions

- Bring in a photo of the Mexican flag (or an actual flag). Ask students if the flag of this country awakens deep feelings in the citizenry.
- Present *la Virgen de Guadalupe*, an omnipresent symbol of the matriarchal Mexican culture, even for nonbelievers. There is a *Lengua y cultura* feature about *la Virgen* in *Cap. 9*, p. 282.
- Ask students to do an Internet search for indigenous cultures in Mexico, especially *los aztecas, los mayas, los olmecas*, or *los zapotecas*. Much well illustrated information is available in English and in Spanish, on academic as well as non-academic sites.

Una importante figura histórica

Suggestion

Be sure that all students in the class understand what is meant by *Sor* (= Sister [in a religious order]).

A LEER

Lectura cultural

México

Por tradición,[a] las familias en México son muy unidas. Esto tiene muchas ventajas[b] en el desarrollo[c] de los niños y los adolescentes, que sienten el apoyo[d] de sus padres, hermanos y parientes cercanos.[e] Es raro oír hablar[f] de las desventajas[g] de la extrema unión familiar. Sin embargo,[h] en México muchos creen que esta gran unión resulta, a veces, en que los jóvenes pierdan[i] parte de su identidad individual, ya que permanecen bajo[j] la protección de sus padres hasta que[k] son adultos. No es extraño[l] que la vida responsable y la autosuficiencia de un joven se pospongan[m] hasta el momento en que contrae matrimonio.[n]

¿Cómo se comparan las familias de este país con las familias de México?

[a]Por… *Traditionally* [b]*advantages* [c]*development* [d]sienten… *feel the support* [e]*close* [f]oír… *to hear talk* [g]*disadvantages* [h]Sin… *However* [i]*lose* [j]ya… *since they remain under* [k]hasta… *until* [l]*unusual* [m]se… *are postponed* [n]en… *when he or she gets married*

En otros países hispanos

- **En todo el mundo hispanohablante** Es impresionante cómo los hispanos de todos los países coinciden en cuanto a[a] la importancia de la familia. También es típico en todo el mundo hispano que los hijos se independicen tarde.
- **En Chile** «Estar casados[b] a la chilena» = vivir juntos[c] en pareja.[d]
- **En la Argentina y España** En los dos países el matrimonio entre personas del mismo[e] sexo es legal.

[a]en… *with regards to* [b]*married* [c]*together* [d]en… *out of wedlock* [e]*same*

Tres símbolos mexicanos

- **La bandera y el himno[a] nacional** Es increíble el respeto y la emoción que estos emblemas inspiran en los mexicanos.
- **La tortilla de maíz[b]** Es el alimento[c] esencial de los mexicanos desde[d] 1500 A.C. (mil quinientos antes de Cristo).
- **Los centros arqueológicos** Hay muchos por todo el país, pero los más importantes son las ruinas mayas de Chichén Itzá (cerca de[e] Cancún), el complejo[f] de Teotihuacán (cerca del D.F.) y las ruinas zapotecas (cerca de Oaxaca).

[a]La… *The flag and anthem* [b]*corn* [c]*food* [d]*since* [e]cerca… *close to* [f]*building complex*

Una familia mexicana que visita el cementerio para celebrar el Día de los Muertos (*Dead*), San Pedro Tlahuac, México

Una importante figura histórica

Sor[a] Juana Inés de la Cruz: Poeta del siglo[b] XVII, publicó su obra en vida.[c] Es una de los grandes poetas de la lengua española y una mujer muy ilustrada.[d] Escribió[e] lo siguiente sobre sus estudios: «Yo no estudio para saber[f] más, sino[g] para ignorar[h] menos».

[a]*Sister* [b]*century* [c]publicó… *she published her work during her lifetime* [d]*learned* [e]*She wrote* [f]para… *so that I know* [g]*but rather* [h]para… *so that I am ignorant of*

COMPRENSIÓN

1. ¿Por qué la familia mexicana tiene normalmente una influencia muy buena en los hijos? Tienen el apoyo de toda su familia.
2. ¿Por qué puede tener (*can it have*) una mala influencia? A veces los jóvenes pierden parte de su identidad individual.
3. ¿La familia mexicana es única en el mundo hispano? No.

Del mundo hispano

Antes de leer° — Antes… *Before reading*

Match the sentences with the numbers given in **Números útiles.** If you don't know, guess! All numbers will be used. **¡OJO!** In Spanish, decimals are marked with a comma: 3.4 = **3,4 (tres coma cuatro).**

Números útiles: 1,32; 1,65; 2; 2,06; 2,2; 3; 4; 5; 6; 8; 40

1. 40: número de semanas de un embarazo (*pregnancy*) normal
2. 2: número de bebés, si son mellizos o gemelos (*twins*)
3. 8: número de bebés, si son octillizos
4. 6: número de bebés, si son sextillizos
5. 5: número de bebés, si son quintillizos
6. 3: número de bebés, si son trillizos
7. 2,2: número de libras (*pounds*) en 1 kilogramo
8. 1,65: promedio (*average number*) de hijos por mujer en Puerto Rico
9. 1,32: promedio de hijos por mujer en España
10. 2,06: promedio de hijos por mujer en los Estados Unidos

Lectura: Un parto° excepcional en Puerto Rico

°*birth*

SEXTILLIZOS EN PUERTO RICO

Emilio Figueroa observa el 27 de diciembre en Puerto Rico, a uno de sus hijos, luego que[a] su esposa, Máxima Pérez, 33, quien se sometió[b] a un tratamiento de fertilidad, dio a luz[c] a sextillizos mediante una cesárea. Los bebés nacieron[d] tras[e] 29 semanas de embarazo y pesaron[f] entre 800 y 1.000 gramos. Es la primera vez[g] que en el país se produce un parto de seis criaturas. EFE

[a]luego… *after* [b]se… *went through* [c]dio… *gave birth* [d]*were born* [e]*after* [f]*they weighed* [g]la… *the first time*

Comprensión

A. Resumen de la noticia (*Summary of the news item*). Para resumir la información de la noticia, complete las oraciones con las palabras apropiadas.

esposo fertilidad isla padres seis sextillizos

Noticias de la isla[1] de Puerto Rico:

La Sra. Máxima Pérez y su esposo,[2] el Sr. Emilio Figueroa, son ahora los padres[3] de seis[4] hijos, gracias a un tratamiento de fertilidad.[5] No hay otro caso de sextillizos[6] en la historia de Puerto Rico.

B. En el texto. Encuentre (*Find*) las siguientes ideas y palabras en la noticia.

1. *birth* parto
2. *babies* (*2 words*) bebés, criaturas
3. *through a C-section* mediante una cesárea
4. *fertility treatment* tratamiento de fertilidad

Del mundo hispano

Notes

- This page of the *A leer* section offers authentic readings from the Spanish-speaking world.
- The readings are realia-based in the first half of the text, with realia, newspaper excerpts, and so on, from a variety of countries. These readings are coordinated with the chapter theme but not with the country of focus.
- The second half of the text offers unabridged literary selections.
- All sections are supported by pre- and post-reading activities, as well as by a variety of discussion, writing, and Internet activities.
- See the IM for optional follow-up, writing, and Internet activities.

Antes de leer

Notes

- The word *sixtillizos* is also used instead of *sextillizos*.
- Source: *CIA World Factbook, 2010,* www.cia.gov/library/publications/the-world-factbook/

Suggestion

Do this activity the day before assigning the reading, with students working in pairs or groups. Ask pairs/groups to share their answers.

Lectura

Note

EFE = a permissions annotation (like AP, Associated Press)

Estrategia

Using Context to Read

A number of words and expressions will surely be new for students in this reading. This problem is compounded by the fact that the first sentence is almost four lines long and that it consists of seven word or number groups separated by commas. This style of writing is not uncommon in Spanish. Help students by reminding them that the main ideas are apparent in the photograph and the title. Tell them that there are two subjects, *Emilio* and *su esposa,* and ask them to find the main verb for each.

Comprensión:

Suggestion

After doing *Comp. A* and *B*, ask some additional comprehension questions.

1. *¿Cómo se llama el padre?* (*Emilio Figueroa*)
2. *¿Cómo se llama la madre?* (*Máxima Pérez*)
3. *¿Cuántos hijos tienen estos señores?* (*6*)
4. *¿De cuántas semanas fue el embarazo?* (*29*)
5. *¿Por qué tienen sextillizos?* (*tratamiento de fertilidad*)
6. *¿Hay muchos casos de sextillizos en Puerto Rico?* (*No, es el primer caso.*)

A escuchar
Notes
- Although the development of listening skills has been integrated into *Puntos de partida* since its first edition, there has never been a section devoted to that skill in the student text. *A escuchar* provides that focus.
- The majority of the *A escuchar* page develops an authentic listening task, with pre- and post-listening activities. The listening passage is available to students in a variety of formats (see the Preface), so they can listen to it on their own. However, if you prefer, you can focus on listening by playing the CD in class or by reading the Audioscript aloud. Either is quite feasible, as the listening passages are relatively short.
- In addition, each page also focuses on the contemporary music of the Spanish-speaking world, in *¡Música!*, which offers information about songs that students can download at iTunes.
- Instructors familiar with the *Música de…* feature of the previous edition can find that information in the IM as *¡Más música!* In addition, the *Ritmos y sonidos* CD (songs from the Spanish-speaking world that accompanied the Eighth Edition) can still be used with this edition of the text.
- See the IM for the Audioscript and more information about music in Mexico.

Escuche
Notes
- In this chapter, students can listen to the description of a Mexican-American family.
- If listening is assigned as homework, ask students to listen to the passage at least twice.

Después de escuchar
A: Suggestion
Tell students not to worry if they don't get each name correctly the first time they listen. The main thing is to identify the family members as they are being described. The layout of the family tree will help them.

B: Follow-up
In pairs, have students compare Lucía's family to their own.

MODELO: *La familia de Lucía es originaria de México, pero mi familia es de Italia.*

A ESCUCHAR

Vocabulario para escuchar

la escuela	school
la cuñada	sister-in-law
travieso/a	troublemaker
las mellizas	twins
juntas	together
los padrinos	godparents

Antes de escuchar
¿Tiene Ud. hermanos casados (*married*)? ¿Tiene buenas relaciones con sus cuñados (*in-laws*)? ¿Tiene padrinos (*godparents*) o es padrino o madrina de un niño?

Escuche°
°*Listen*

La familia de Lucía

Una persona describe la familia de Lucía Jiménez Flores. Escuche según las indicaciones de su profesor(a).

Después de escuchar°
°Después… *After listening*

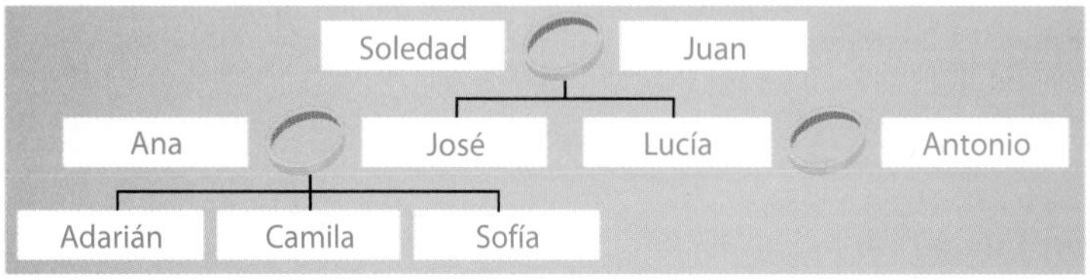

A. El árbol genealógico de la familia. Complete el árbol genealógico con los nombres de los miembros de la familia.

B. ¿Quién es quién? Complete las oraciones.

1. La cuñada de Lucía se llama ___Ana___.
2. El cuñado de José se llama ___Antonio___.
3. Lucía tiene tres ___sobrinos___.
4. La abuela de Camila tiene ___70___ años.
5. El nombre del padre de Lucía es ___Juan___.
6. La familia de Lucía es de ___Oaxaca___ (ciudad).
7. En México, Lucía tiene muchos ___parientes___.

¡Música!
La cantante[a] de música pop Julieta Venegas nació[b] en California, pero se crió[c] en Tijuana, México. Además de[d] cantar, toca varios instrumentos musicales (guitarra, acordeón y teclados[e]). Su canción «Bien o mal» es del álbum *Otra cosa*.[f]

[a]*singer* [b]*was born* [c]se… *grew up* [d]Además… *Besides* [e]*keyboards* [f]*thing*

Go to the iMix section in Connect Spanish (**www.connectspanish.com**) to access the iTunes playlist "*Puntos9*," where you can purchase "Bien o mal" by Julieta Venegas.

Julieta Venegas, en Houston, Texas

¡Música!
Notes
- Julieta Venegas (1970–) is a pop rock singer and the winner of various Grammy and MTV awards. She is very well known in the Spanish-speaking world.
- For helpful tips on using songs in the classroom, see the IM.

Resources: Transparency 34

A ESCRIBIR°

A… *Let's write*

El tema

Mi familia

Preparar

Dibuje (*Draw*) un árbol genealógico de su familia, similar a los que ha visto (*those that you've seen*) en este capítulo. Incluya (*Include*) un mínimo de 10 miembros de su familia con:

- el nombre de cada (*each*) persona y su edad (*age*)
- su origen o nacionalidad
- una característica interesante y particular (*unique*) de cada persona

Redactar°

Writing

Escriba (*Write*) un ensayo (*essay*) sobre (*about*) su familia, combinando toda la información de **Preparar.**

Empiece (*Start*) el ensayo con una frase descriptiva sobre su familia.

MODELOS: Mi familia es una familia típica americana.
Mi familia no es una de las familias típicas de este país.
Creo que mi familia es muy interesante.

Luego (*Then*) escriba unas oraciones sobre cada miembro de su familia.

MODELO: Mi padre se llama John. Tiene 63 años. Es estadounidense y es muy trabajador.

Concluya (*Conclude*) el ensayo con una explicación sobre su familia. Por ejemplo: ¿Es una familia típica? ¿unida? ¿Por qué sí o por qué no?

Editar

Revise (*Review*) el ensayo para comprobar (*to check*):

- la ortografía (*spelling*) y los acentos
- la posición y la concordancia (*agreement*) de los adjetivos descriptivos y los adjetivos posesivos
- la variedad del vocabulario
- la conjugación de los verbos

Finalmente, prepare su versión final para entregarla (*hand it in*).

A escribir

Notes

- *A escribir* replaces *Redacción* sections from previous editions of *Puntos de partida.*
- Distinct from *Redacción*, which was tied to or based on the *Lectura* in *Un paso más, A escribir* sections are independent of the chapter's readings, although they are based on the chapter's theme.

Preparar

Suggestions

- Tell students to review the chapter vocabulary and the *Nota comunicativa* on *tener… años.*
- Suggest that students provide 2–3 adjectives for each family member.
- Encourage students to look up new adjectives in a dictionary. It is a good idea to practice with them to show them how to get all the information possible from a dictionary entry.

Redactar

Suggestions

- Suggested length for this writing assignment: approximately 90 words
- Suggested structure (2 paragraphs)

  P. 1 Description of family members, beginning with a general comment about the family

  P. 2 Short conclusion expressing opinon about the family
- Tell students to avoid translating their ideas from English to Spanish. Instead, they should write directly in Spanish, using primarily the grammar and vocabulary they know and/or have seen used in the text.
- Remind students to start the essay with a descriptive opening sentence and to conclude the essay with a summary of any type.

En resumen: En este capítulo Vocabulario

Note

The following vocabulary items were used in direction lines in *Cap. 3* and will be used in subsequent chapters without glossing, but they are not considered to be active until they are listed in *Vocabulario: complete, corrija, el dibujo, mire, modifique, la respuesta, sobre.*

Word Families

En este capítulo

- *el estado, estadounidense*
- *este/a, esto*
- *porque, que*

Entre capítulos

- *a veces = a* (1)
- *alemán/alemana = el alemán* (2)
- *bueno… , bueno/a = buenos días* (1), *buenas tardes/noches* (1), *muy buenas* (1)
- *la casa, casado/a = a casa* (2), *en casa* (2)
- *¿de quién? = ¿quién?* (1), *de* (1)
- *del = de* (1)
- *español(a) = el español* (2)
- *inglés/inglesa = el inglés* (2)
- *mucho/a = muchas gracias* (1)
- *necesario/a = necesitar* (2)
- *los números 30–90 = los números 3–9* (1)
- *nuestro/a = nosotros/as* (2)
- *¿por qué? = ¿qué?* (1), *no hay de qué* (1), *¿qué tal?* (1)
- *todo/a = todos los días* (2)
- *trabajador(a) = trabajar* (2)
- *tu(s) = tú* (2)
- *vuestro/a = vosotros/as* (2)

¡OJO!

- *el perro ≠ pero* (1)
- *si ≠ sí* (1)

Suggestions

- **La familia y los parientes: ¿Quién es?** Have students identify the family member based on the following definitions.
  1. *Es el hermano de mi madre.* (*mi tío*)
  2. *Son los hijos de mi tío.* (*mis primos*)
  3. *Es la hija de mi hermana.* (*mi sobrina*)
  4. *Es el papá de mi mamá.* (*mi abuelo*)
- **Los verbos:** Practice verb conjugations chorally with students using the verbs from the vocabulary list. Have them give you some infinitives of other verbs they have learned so far and have them conjugate those verbs as well.

EN RESUMEN En este capítulo

LearnSmart

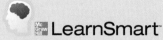

Visit **www.connectspanish.com** to practice the vocabulary and grammar points covered in this chapter.

Gramática en breve

5. Adjectives: Gender, Number, and Position

Adjective Endings

Singular	Plural
-o	**-os**
-a	**-as**
-e	**-es**
-[consonant]	-[consonant] + **-es**

6. Present Tense of *ser;* Summary of Uses

ser: soy, eres, es, somos, sois, son

Uses of **ser:** identification, description, origin, generalizations, possession, destination

de + el ⟶ del

7. Unstressed Possessive Adjectives

yo ⟶ mi(s)	**nosotros ⟶ nuestro/a(s)**
tú ⟶ tu(s)	**vosotros ⟶ vuestro/a(s)**
Ud., él, ella ⟶ su(s)	**Uds., ellos, ellas ⟶ su(s)**

8. Present Tense of *-er* and *-ir* Verbs; Subject Pronouns

Regular -er Verb Endings

-o, -es, -e, -emos, -éis, -en

Regular -ir Verb Endings

-o, -es, -e, -imos, -ís, -en

When to use subject pronouns: for clarification, emphasis, and contrast

Vocabulario

Los verbos

abrir	to open
aprender	to learn
aprender a + *inf.*	to learn how to (*do something*)
asistir (a)	to attend, go to (*a class, function*)
beber	to drink
comer	to eat
comprender	to understand
creer (en)	to think; to believe (in)
deber + *inf.*	should, must, ought to (*do something*)
escribir	to write
leer	to read
llegar	to arrive
mirar	to look at, watch
mirar la tele(visión)	to watch television
recibir	to receive
ser **(soy, eres,…)**	to be
vender	to sell
vivir	to live

La familia y los parientes

el/la abuelo/a	grandfather/grandmother
los abuelos	grandparents
el/la esposo/a	husband/wife
el/la hermano/a	brother/sister
los hermanos	siblings
el/la hijo/a	son/daughter
los hijos	children
la madre (mamá)	mother (mom)
el/la nieto/a	grandson/granddaughter
el/la niño/a	small child; boy/girl
el padre (papá)	father (dad)
los padres	parents
el pariente	relative
el/la primo/a	cousin
los primos	cousins
el/la sobrino/a	nephew/niece
el/la tío/a	uncle/aunt
los tíos	aunts and uncles

Las mascotas

el gato	cat
la mascota	pet
el pájaro	bird
el perro	dog

Otros sustantivos

la carta	letter
la casa	house, home
la ciudad	city
el coche	car
el estado	state
el/la médico/a	(medical) doctor
el mundo	world
el país	country
el periódico	newspaper
el regalo	present, gift
la revista	magazine

Los adjetivos

alto/a	tall
amable	kind; nice
antipático/a	unpleasant

bajo/a	short (*in height*)
bonito/a	pretty
buen, bueno/a	good
corto/a	short (*in length*)
delgado/a	thin, slender
este/a	this
estos/as	these
feo/a	ugly
fiel	faithful
gordo/a	fat
gran, grande	large, big; great
guapo/a	handsome; good-looking
joven	young
largo/a	long
listo/a	smart; clever
mal, malo/a	bad
moreno/a	brunet(te)
mucho/a	a lot (of)
muchos/as	many
nuevo/a	new
otro/a	other, another
pequeño/a	small
perezoso/a	lazy
pobre	poor
rico/a	rich
rubio/a	blond(e)
simpático/a	nice, likeable
todo/a	all; every
tonto/a	silly, foolish
trabajador(a)	hardworking
viejo/a	old

Cognados: hispano/a, inteligente, necesario/a, posible

Los adjetivos de nacionalidad

alemán/alemana	German
español(a)	Spanish
estadounidense	U.S.
inglés/inglesa	English
mexicano/a	Mexican

Los adjetivos posesivos

mi(s)	my
tu(s)	your (*fam. sing.*)
nuestro/a(s)	our
vuestro/a(s)	your (*fam. pl. Sp.*)
su(s)	his, hers, its, your (*form. sing.*); their, your (*form. pl.*)

Los números del 31 al 100

treinta, cuarenta, cincuenta, sesenta, setenta, ochenta, noventa, cien

¿Con qué frecuencia… ?

a veces	sometimes, at times
casi	almost
casi nunca	almost never
nunca	never
siempre	always
una vez a la semana	once a week

Repaso: con frecuencia, todos los días

Palabras adicionales

¿de quién?	whose?
del	of the, from the
estar de acuerdo / no estar de acuerdo	to agree / to disagree
esto	this (*neuter*)
para	(intended) for; in order to
por eso	for that reason
¿por qué?	why?
porque	because
que	that, which; who
según	according to
si	if
tener… años (tengo, tienes, tiene)	to be . . . years old

Repaso: ¿de dónde es Ud.?

Vocabulario personal

Remember to use this space for other words and phrases you learn in this chapter.

Español	Inglés

- Have students list adjectives that they associate with different nationalities. Encourage them to discuss whether or not these associations are stereotypical.
- To practice possessive adjectives, ask students questions about their family and possessions: *¿Tiene coche su padre? ¿Cuántos años tiene su coche? ¿Cuántos teléfonos hay en su casa? ¿en la casa de sus padres?,* and so on.
- Have students make and exchange word puzzles.
- Play *El ahorcado* (Hangman), using family words and adjectives.
- Have students group the adjectives in different ways (opposites, negative/positive).

Reciclado: Remind students that *asistir* is a false cognate. *To assist* in Spanish is *atender*, *ayudar*, or *servir*.

Heritage Speakers

En México, la palabra *huevón* se usa como sinónimo de *perezoso,* aunque se considera una grosería en muchos países latinoamericanos. Aunque se oye la palabra *huevón* en la conversación común y corriente de algunas personas, se recomienda el uso de *perezoso*.

Chapter Opening Photo and Chapter Theme

Chapter Theme–Related Questions

- *¿Le gustan los colores de los tejidos* (new word) *de Guatemala y Honduras? ¿Tiene algo hecho* (new word) *de esos tejidos? ¿Un bolso* (new word), *una mochila, una camisa* (new word)*?*
- *¿Compra mucha ropa* (new word) *o poca ropa? ¿Qué compra más, pantalones, camisetas, camisas, suéteres o zapatos* (new words)*?*
- *¿Dónde le gusta comprar ropa? ¿En el centro comercial porque hay muchas tiendas diferentes? ¿En los almacenes* (new word) *grandes como Sears? ¿O en tiendas* (new word) *pequeñas? ¿en tiendas étnicas?*
- *¿Compra mucho por el Internet? ¿Qué compra? ¿libros, música, ropa, comida, objetos electrónicos? ¿Compra cosas para Ud. o regalos* (new word) *para otras personas?*
- *¿Hay mercados* (new word) *donde Ud. vive? ¿Mercados con productos comestibles locales? ¿mercados de ropa nueva o de segunda mano* (new word)*? ¿Le gusta ir de compras* (new words) *a los mercados?*

Reciclado

Use vocabulary and grammar from previous chapters to discuss the photo. Emphasize adjectives and adjective agreement with this photo, as well as *-ar* verbs.

Point out

- Students from large urban centers may be familiar with the word *mercado.* Have students describe *mercados* they have seen or tell what they think a *mercado* would be like. Ask them where a *mercado* might be located, how it would be set up, what products vendors might sell, and so on.
- If students are not familiar with *mercado,* define the word. Also ask them to guess the meaning of *centro comercial.* You might have someone take notes of students' ideas and revisit them after completing this chapter.

Heritage Speakers

Pregúnteles a los hispanohablantes si usan el Internet para comprar cosas de países hispánicos. ¿Cuál es su sitio Web hispano favorito?

4 De compras°

°De... *Shopping*

En un mercado (*market*), en Tecpán, Guatemala

- Have you ever seen these kinds of textiles? Where?
- Where can you buy clothing in your area?
- What clothing items do you buy most frequently?

Connect SPANISH

www.connectspanish.com

Resources

For Students

- Connect Spanish (**www.connectspanish.com**), which contains all content from the following resources, as well as the *Mundo interactivo scenarios,* the LearnSmart adaptive learning system, and more!
- **Physical Resources:** Workbook / Laboratory Manual, Laboratory Audio Program, DVD

For Instructors

- Connect Spanish (**www.connectspanish.com**), which contains access to all student sections of Connect Spanish, as well as helpful time-saving tools and resources such as an integrated gradebook, Instructor's Manual, Testing Program, digital transparencies, Audioscript, Videoscript, and more!

Guatemala

13,5 (trece y medio) millones de habitantes

Honduras

8 millones de habitantes

- Guatemala es el centro de la civilización maya. También hay población maya en Honduras, México, El Salvador y Belice.
- Honduras tiene una población afroindígena muy grande: los garífunas, que viven a lo largo del (*along the*) Golfo de Honduras, de Belice a Nicaragua.

En este capítulo

CONTENT / **CONTENIDO**	OBJECTIVES / **OBJETIVOS**
Clothing 98, Colors 101	To talk about clothing items and shopping
Numbers 100 and up 103	To count in Spanish
Demonstratives (*this, that,* and so on) 107	To point out things at different distances
The Verbs **tener, venir, poder, preferir, querer** 111	To express actions
The Verb **ir** and **ir** + **a** + *infinitive* 116	To express *to go* and to talk about future actions
Guatemala and **Honduras 122**	To learn about two Central American countries that have large indigenous populations

97

Guatemala y Honduras

Datos esenciales

The Instructor's Edition will provide basic information about each chapter's country of focus on this chapter opening spread. Additional information can be found in the IM. There is also additional information about the country of focus in *A leer: Lectura cultural.*

GUATEMALA

Nombre oficial: *República de Guatemala*
Lema: *«El país de la eterna primavera»*
Capital: *la Ciudad de Guatemala*
Ciudades principales: *Antigua, Escuintla, Quezaltenango, Mixco*
Lenguas: *El español es la lengua oficial aunque existen 21 grupos etnolingüísticos que todavía conservan sus idiomas, entre ellos el maya-quiché, el garífuna y el xinca.*
Composición étnica: *mestizos (llamados* ladinos *en Guatemala) y europeos: 60%; indígenas de diversas etnias mayas 40%, siendo la etnia más numerosa la maya quiché (9%)*
Jefe de estado: *el Presidente Álvaro Colom Caballeros, desde 2008*
Forma de gobierno: *República presidencialista*
Moneda: *el quetzal*
Religión: *mayoría católica, seguida de un alto y creciente número de protestantes, especialmente evangélicos*

HONDURAS

Nombre oficial: *República de Honduras*
Lema: *«Libre, soberana e independiente»*
Capital: *Tegucigalpa («Tegus», de manera no oficial)*
Ciudades principales: *San Pedro Sula, La Ceiba*
Lengua oficial: *el español*
Composición étnica: *mestizos 90%, indígenas mayas 6%, negros garífunas 2%, blancos 2%*
Jefe de estado: *el Presidente Porfirio Lobo, desde 2010*
Forma de gobierno: *República presidencialista*
Moneda: *el lempira (nombre de un cacique indígena que luchó contra los españoles)*
Religión: *mayoría católica, seguida de un alto y creciente número de protestantes, especialmente evangélicos*

Resources: Transparency 35

NATIONAL STANDARDS: Cultures

There are twenty-three Mayan languages spoken in Guatemala. Many indigenous ethnic groups speak Spanish as a second language, although they prefer to speak their native Mayan language. Guatemala was one of the first countries of Central America officially to recognize Mayan languages by passing the "Law on National Languages," which enabled indigenous groups to carry out official business in their native tongue.

Multimedia

The *Instructor's Manual* (IM) provides suggestions for using the multimedia materials in the classroom.

Vocabulario Preparación
De compras: La ropa
Notes

- See the model for vocabulary presentation and other material in the *Cap. 4 Vocabulario: Preparación* section of "Chapter-by-Chapter Supplementary Materials" in the IM.
- In many Hispanic countries, store hours in the morning are similar to those in the United States and Canada; however, some shops close in the early afternoon until 4 P.M. and generally reopen until 8 or 9 P.M. Many stores are closed on Sundays and holidays.
- Note the change from *la bolsa* to *el bolso* in this edition of *Puntos de partida*. We believe that this term is more widely used to express *purse* in the Spanish-speaking world.
- Make sure that students note that the word for clothes, *la ropa*, is always singular in Spanish, although it is always plural in English.

Suggestions

- Present basic color vocabulary first.
- Clothing vocabulary is presented here in *Cap. 4* before the introduction of reflexive pronouns (*Cap. 5*). For this reason, the verb *ponerse* is not used, especially in sentences such as: *Me pongo pantalones para ir a clase. Llevar* and *usar* are used instead.
- Model the pronunciation of clothing, pointing out items in the classroom or in photos. Stop after every three or four items to go back and review, indicating the item and asking students: *¿Es una blusa o una camisa?, ¿Es una camisa o un suéter?,* and so on.
- Emphasize the use of *los pantalones cortos*, not *los cortos*.
- Offer additional clothing vocabulary: *el anillo, el collar, el pañuelo, los pendientes/aretes, la pulsera / el brazalete.*
- Offer additional vocabulary for describing clothing: *a la medida, de gamuza/nilón/poliéster, de tacón alto.*
- Offer additional shopping vocabulary: *¿cuánto es?, el mostrador, la vitrina.*
- Make statements about what students are wearing and have them respond *sí* or *no.*

  Roberto lleva un abrigo. → *No, Roberto lleva una chaqueta.*

  To follow up, have students invent similar sentences.

VOCABULARIO Preparación

De compras: La ropa°

°De… *Shopping: Clothing*

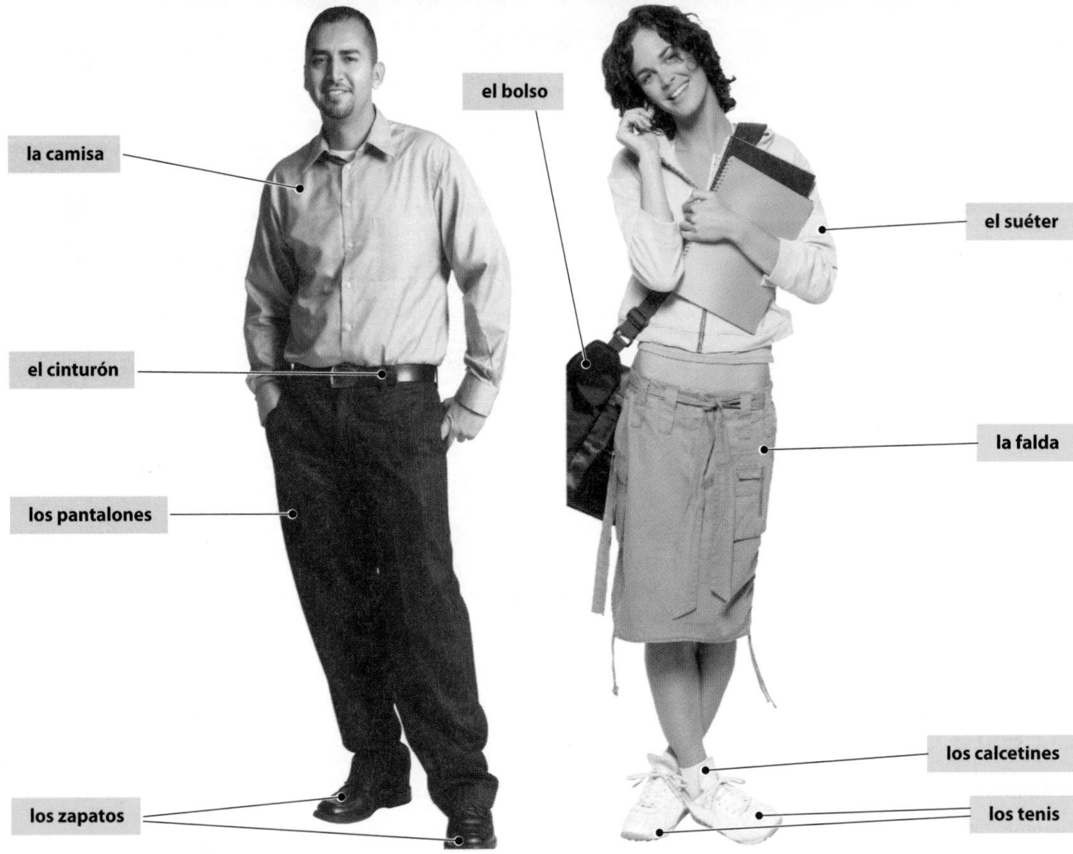

Los verbos

comprar	to buy
llevar	to wear; to carry; to take
regatear	to haggle, bargain
usar	to wear; to use
vender	to sell
venden de todo	they sell (have) everything

Los lugares

el almacén	department store
el centro	downtown
el centro comercial	shopping mall
el mercado	market(place)
la plaza	plaza
la tienda	shop, store

¿Cuánto cuesta(n)?

la ganga	bargain
el precio	price
el precio fijo	fixed (set) price
las rebajas	sales, reductions
barato/a	inexpensive
caro/a	expensive
cómodo/a	comfortable

Culture

In some Spanish-speaking countries, *vaqueros* is used for *jeans*. In Mexico, jeans are often called *pantalones de mezclilla*. Some Spanish speakers use the singular *el pantalón* to talk about pants. *Billetera* is used for a man's wallet. *Cartera*, on the other hand, is often used for a woman's purse. Some native speakers say *a cuadros/lunares/rayas* rather than *de*.

Resources: Transparency 36

Otras palabras y expresiones útiles

el abrigo	coat
la blusa	blouse
la camiseta	T-shirt
la cartera	wallet; handbag
la chaqueta	jacket
la corbata	tie
la gorra	baseball cap
el impermeable	raincoat
las medias	stockings
la ropa interior	underwear
las sandalias	sandals
el sombrero	hat
el traje	suit
el traje de baño	bathing suit
el vestido	dress
de cuadros (lunares, rayas)	plaid (polka-dot, striped)
es de (algodón, cuero, lana, oro, plata, seda)*	it is made of (cotton, leather, wool, gold, silver, silk)
Es de última moda. / **Está de moda.**	It's trendy (hot).

Así se dice

el almacén = los grandes almacenes (*Spain*)
el bolso = la bolsa (*Mexico*)
la camiseta = la polera (*Argentina*), el polo (*Peru*)
la cartera = la billetera (*Argentina, El Salvador*); *coin purse* = el monedero
la falda = la pollera (*Argentina, Uruguay*)
los *jeans* = los mahones (*Puerto Rico, Dominican Republic*), los vaqueros (*Spain*)
el suéter = el jersey (*Spain*), el pulóver (*Argentina*)

De moda is often expressed as **en onda** (*Mexico*) or **en voga.**

To talk about sales, you can say **hay rebajas** or say that something **está de/en rebaja** or **está en liquidación/venta.**

Conversación

A. La ropa

Paso 1. ¿Qué ropa llevan estas personas?

Personas: el chico (*guy*), la chica (*girl*), el hombre, la mujer

1.

2.

3.

Paso 2. De estas personas, ¿quién trabaja hoy? ¿Quién no trabaja en este momento? ¿Quién va a (*is going to*) una fiesta?

*Note another use of **ser** + **de:** to tell what material something is made of.

Con. A, Answers: 1. *El hombre lleva un traje, una camisa, una corbata y zapatos.* **2.** *La mujer lleva un vestido y zapatos.* **3.** *El chico lleva una camisa, unos jeans, un suéter y tenis. La chica lleva una sudadera, una blusa, pantalones y zapatos.*

- Discuss the concept of *mercado* vs. *tienda.* Point out the existence of large department stores and malls as well as small shops and open-air markets.

Pronunciación: See Pronunciation Notes, IM.

Así se dice

Explain to students that clothing vocabulary varies widely across the Spanish-speaking world. Stress the need to adapt to local usages and to use question strategies to find out what usage is in a given travel destination: *¿Cómo se llama esto?, ¿Qué es esto?*

Preliminary Exercises

- Have students give the words defined.
  1. *el antónimo de vender*
  2. *una tienda grande*
  3. *la cantidad de dinero que es necesario pagar*
  4. *un sinónimo de* llevar
  5. *la parte céntrica de una ciudad*
  6. *un grupo de tiendas grandes y pequeñas*
  7. *el antónimo de* vender muy poco
  8. *el antónimo de* pagar el precio indicado
  9. *el antónimo de* caro
  10. *el antónimo de* estilos de los años setenta
- Point out a new use of *ser: ser + de.*
- **Reciclado:** Write the following phrases on the board: *de metal, de papel, de plástico, de madera* (demonstrate). Point to classroom objects and have students tell what they are made of: *¿De qué es esto* (point to a chair or another wooden object)*?* → *De madera.*
  1. *el dinero*
  2. *el lápiz*
  3. *el libro*
  4. *el cuaderno*
  5. *el bolígrafo*
  6. *la mesa*
  7. *la foto*

Con. A: Reciclado

Have students give the people names and review the use of definite articles with titles: *el señor González,...*

Con. A: Note

Active vocabulary: *el/la chico/a*

Resources: Transparency 37

Multimedia: Audio

Students can listen to and practice this chapter's vocabulary in Connect Spanish: **www.connectspanish.com.**

Heritage Speakers

Pídales a los hispanohablantes que describan la ropa que llevan hoy mismo.

Con. B: Notes

- The word *boutique* (*f.*) is pronounced in Spanish pretty much as it is in French; but most speakers will say an -*s* sound at the end of the plural form.
- Call students' attention to the use of *materia* in item 8 and tell them that the word can mean both *academic subject* and *material* (of which something is made) in Spanish, depending on the context.

Con. B: Follow-up

Have students answer the following questions.

1. *¿Dónde compra Ud. la ropa generalmente, en una tienda o en un almacén?*
2. *En esta ciudad, ¿hay tiendas o mercados donde regateen los clientes? ¿donde haya buenas rebajas?*
3. *¿Lleva Ud. _______ hoy?*
4. *¿Necesita Ud. comprar ropa nueva? ¿Qué necesita comprar? ¿Qué tipo de ropa compra con más frecuencia?*
5. *Imagine que Ud. es un profesor muy formal / un estudiante típico / el presidente / un artista famoso de Hollywood. ¿Qué lleva hoy?*
6. *Por lo general, ¿le gusta llevar ropa elegante o ropa vieja?*

Con. C: Follow-up

Survey the class for some items to determine what the most popular answers are.

Redacción: Have students work in pairs to convert the items in *Con. C* into questions to use to interview each other. Ask them to take notes. Then have students describe the clothing preferences of their partner in a brief paragraph.

Con. C: Optional

Have students give the appropriate clothing (*la ropa apropiada*) for:

¿para los yuppies?
¿los cantantes country-western?
¿los líderes militares?
¿los detectives?
¿los personajes (new) *bíblicos?*

Nota comunicativa

Note

Point out that there are many tag questions in English, e.g., *won't you?, doesn't he?, will they?*, and so on. Spanish tag questions are invariable, that is, they don't change regardless of the number or gender of the subject.

Con. D: Note

Active vocabulary: *sobre*

B. Asociaciones. Complete las siguientes oraciones lógicamente con palabras de **De compras: La ropa.**

1. Un almacén es una tienda grande, con muchos departamentos.
2. No es posible regatear cuando hay precios fijos.
3. En la librería, venden de todo: textos y otros libros, cuadernos, lápices,…
4. Hay grandes rebajas en las tiendas al final de la temporada (*season*), en las cuales (*in which*) todo es muy barato.
5. Siempre hay *boutiques* en los centros comerciales.
6. El centro de una ciudad es la parte céntrica.
7. Esta ropa no es para hombres: ___________.
8. Esta ropa es para hombres y mujeres: ___________.
9. La ropa de ___________ (material) es muy elegante.

Estrategia

The preposition **para** followed by an infinitive can be used to express *in order to.*

Para ir al centro, me gusta llevar pantalones, una camiseta y sandalias.
(In order) To go downtown, I like to wear pants, a T-shirt, and sandals.

C. El estilo personal. Complete las siguientes oraciones lógicamente para hablar de sus preferencias con relación a la ropa.

1. Para ir a la universidad, llevo _____.
2. Para ir a las fiestas con los amigos, llevo _____.
3. Para pasar un día en la playa (*beach*), me gusta llevar _____.
4. Para estar en casa todo el día, me gusta llevar _____.
5. Nunca uso _____.
6. No puedo vivir sin (*I can't live without*) _____ y _____.

Nota comunicativa

Preguntas coletilla (*tag*)

Tag phrases can change statements into questions.

Aquí venden de todo, { **¿no?** / **¿verdad?** }	*They sell everything here, right? (don't they?)*
No necesito impermeable hoy, **¿verdad?**	*I don't need a raincoat today, do I?*

¿Verdad? is found after affirmative or negative statements; **¿no?** is usually found after affirmative statements only.

¡OJO!

The inverted question mark comes immediately before the tag question, not at the beginning of the statement.

D. Intercambios. Usen las coletillas **¿no?** y **¿verdad?** para intercambiar (*exchange*) información de sus hábitos y preferencias sobre (*about*) las compras.

MODELO: Hay un buen centro comercial cerca de (*close to*) tu casa. →
E1: Hay un buen centro comercial cerca de tu casa, ¿no? (¿verdad?)
E2: Sí, hay un centro comercial muy grande a cinco millas (*five miles away*) de mi casa. (No, no hay un buen centro comercial cerca de mi casa.)

1. Hay un buen centro comercial cerca de tu casa.
2. Te gusta la ropa deportiva (*sports*) más que la ropa elegante.
3. Tienes muchos zapatos.
4. Te gusta llevar ropa de moda.
5. No compras en las tiendas de ropa usada (*used*).
6. Compras muchas cosas (*things*) por el Internet.
7. No hay muchos mercados en esta ciudad.

NATIONAL STANDARDS: Comparisons

Have students search the Internet for department stores in Latin America and Spain and write one or two paragraphs describing the clothes and fashions these sites advertise, including the predominant colors, styles, and fabrics. Have them convert prices in the local currency into dollars. Some department stores with online sites are: *Eclipse* (Nicaragua), *El Palacio de Hierro* (Mexico), *Sanborns* (Mexico), *El Corte Inglés* (Spain), *Almacenes París* (Chile), *Beco* (Venezuela). There are also many exclusively online stores.

Los colores: ¿De qué color es?

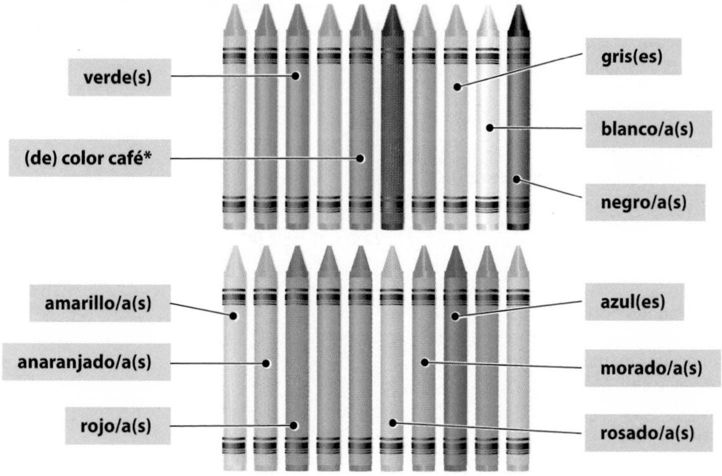

¡OJO!

The names of colors are masculine, like the word **color: el rojo, el azul,** and so on. Note that three colors (**azul, gris, verde**) have only one singular form for masculine and feminine: **el traje azul, la camisa azul.**

Conversación

A. Muchos colores. ¿Cuántos colores hay en este cuadro (*painting*) de Erwin Guillermo? ¿Cuáles son?

***El cortejo* (*Courting*), por Erwin Guillermo (1951–, Guatemala)**

Así se dice

anaranjado = naranja
(de) color café = marrón, pardo
morado = (de) color violeta, púrpura, purpúreo
rosado = (de) color rosa, rosa

Note that some Spanish speakers use **marrón** for objects and **pardo** for animals. Hair and eye color are usually expressed with **castaño.**

*The expression **(de) color café** is invariable:* **el sombrero (de) color café, la falda (de) color café, los pantalones (de) color café.**

Con. D: Preliminary Exercise

Have students respond *sí* or *no.*

1. *Ud. trabaja en la biblioteca, ¿no?*
2. *Ud. siempre llega tarde a clase, ¿verdad?*
3. *Ud. lleva* jeans *hoy, ¿no?*
4. *Ud. toma café por la mañana, ¿verdad?*
5. *Uds. llegan a la universidad a las seis de la mañana, ¿no?*

Con. D: Suggestion

As with previous *Intercambios* activities, you can easily convert the items in this activity into cues (written on the board or on an overhead transparency) that students can use to form questions in a more active way.

Los colores

Suggestions

- Model words and phrases using clothing students are wearing. Verify student comprehension periodically with *¿sí o no?* questions.
- **Reciclado:** Emphasize gender and number agreement for colors. Emphasize that gender is invariable for *azul, verde,* and *gris.*
- Offer these optional color words: *beige* (pronounced like in English), *celeste* (sky blue), *kaki, claro, oscuro.*
- Use nominalized forms as you review colors, for example, *La camisa de Janet es roja. ¿Y la de Susie?*
- Have students tell what colors they associate with the following: *¿Qué color asocia con… ? el mar Caribe, una cebra, un parque, una banana, el café, una rosa, un gato, esta universidad, un tigre, un teléfono*

Pronunciación: See Pronunciation Notes, IM.

Con. A: Note

Note that students are asked to give the names of colors, not to name what is seen in the art or make colors agree.

NATIONAL STANDARDS: Connections

Erwin Guillermo lives and works in Guatemala City. His style, representative of contemporary Guatemalan art, is expressionist, figurative, and symbolic. His works feature themes such as traditions, politics, festivities, and popular icons. Often, as in the piece shown, he depicts the human figure in a very stylized, sensual way, within a context of very colorful tropical fruits and animals.

Resources: Transparency 38

Nota cultural

Note

Fashion by Hispanic designers both inside and outside this country is becoming more famous. The Hispanic designers Carolina Herrera (originally from Venezuela) and Narciso Rodríguez (an American of Cuban origin) are fashion icons.

Suggestions

- Ask students who have traveled to a Hispanic country to talk about what they noticed in terms of clothing.
- Assign students to do an Internet search for two traditional items of clothing from a country of their (or your) choice. Students should mention the names of the items and their clothing equivalent (pants, shirt, and so on).

Comprensión: ¿Cierto o falso?

1. *Los estudiantes hispanos llevan ropa muy diferente de la ropa que llevan los estudiantes de este país.* (falso)
2. *Las profesionales hispanas llevan ropa femenina.* (cierto)
3. *La ropa tradicional no varía de región a región en el mundo hispano.* (falso)

Con. B: Note

Students are asked to give the names of colors, not complete sentences in which the colors agree with the nouns.

Con. C: Note

Point out that the adjective *alerta* is used to modify both masculine and feminine nouns.

Con. C: Expansion

Have students describe the differences between these department stores: JCPenney, Saks Fifth Avenue, Macy's, and WalMart.

Resources: Transparency 39

Nota **cultural**

La ropa en el mundo hispano

Para los jóvenes
No hay grandes diferencias entre[a] la ropa juvenil[b] de los Estados Unidos y el Canadá y la[c] del mundo hispanohablante.

Para los adultos y los profesionales
En general, a los hispanos les gusta llevar ropa bonita y elegante. Además,[d] las mujeres profesionales tienen otras opciones en lugar del traje de chaqueta[e] que generalmente usan las mujeres en los Estados Unidos, y llevan ropa claramente más femenina.

La ropa tradicional
La ropa tradicional en el mundo hispano es muy diversa, porque hay muchos países y regiones diferentes. Algunas prendas[f] son ahora conocidas[g] en todo el mundo:

- la guayabera[h] (Caribe)
- el poncho (los Andes)
- el traje de flamenca (España)

En los países de cultura maya
En estos países hay tejidos muy bellos y coloridos,[i] que varían según la región y que forman parte de la ropa habitual de las mujeres indígenas. Una prenda distintiva es el huipil, una especie de blusa, que varía de región a región.

Una mujer guatemalteca que hace tejidos (*is weaving*)

¿Hay ropa tradicional en este país?

[a]*between* [b]*worn by young people* [c]*that* [d]*In addition* [e]*en... instead of the suits* [f]*articles of clothing* [g]*known* [h]*elegant short-sleeved shirt worn outside the pants* [i]*tejidos... beautiful and colorful textiles*

Con. B: Possible Answers:
1. *verde* 2. *negro* 3. *azul* 4. *gris* 5. *rojo* 6. *rojo, blanco y azul* 7. *amarillo y color café* 8. *blanco y negro* 9. *amarillo* 10. *anaranjado* 11. *gris* 12. Answers will vary.

Vocabulario útil

multicolor	
un par de	a pair of

Con. C: Answers
1. suit and tie in Drawing A, jacket and sweater in Drawing B 2. polka-dot dress in A, green dress in B. 3. pink shirt vs. orange shirt 4. red sweater vs. striped sweater 5. *100 pesos* vs. *40 dólares* 6. shoes vs. tie 7. name of store (*Rodríguez* vs. *Rodrigo*) 8. black purse vs. red purse

B. Asociaciones. ¿Qué colores asocia Ud. con… ?

1. el dinero
2. la una de la mañana
3. una mañana bonita
4. una mañana fea
5. el demonio
6. este país
7. una jirafa
8. un pingüino
9. un limón
10. una naranja
11. un elefante
12. las flores (*flowers*)

C. ¡Ojo alerta! ¿Escaparates (*Window displays*) **idénticos?** These window displays are almost alike . . . but not quite! Can you find at least nine differences between them?

MODELO: En el dibujo A hay ____, pero en el dibujo B hay ____.

A

B

NATIONAL STANDARDS: Connections

Have students research clothing associated with different areas of the Hispanic world (e.g., *sarapes* in Mexico, bowler and other kinds of hats in Bolivia). Remind them to note the materials used and suggest reasons for using these particular ones (e.g., wool in the Andes for warmth and because it is an available resource).

Culture

In the Caribbean and other warm parts of Latin America, it is common for men to wear an article of clothing called *una guayabera*. It's an elegant short-sleeved shirt, often embroidered or with pleats, which is worn outside the pants (not tucked in). It is ideal for warm, humid climates and can be worn in formal or informal situations.

D. ¿De qué color es?

Paso 1. Tell the color of things in your classroom, especially the clothing your classmates are wearing.

MODELO: El bolígrafo de Anita es amarillo. Un libro de Anita es azul…

Paso 2. Now describe what someone in the class is wearing, without revealing his or her name. Can your classmates guess whom you are describing?

MODELO: E1: Lleva botas negras, una camiseta blanca y *jeans*.
E2: Es Anne.

Los números a partir del 100°

°a… *from 100 on*

Continúe las secuencias:

- noventa y nueve, cien, ciento uno…
- mil, dos mil…
- un millón, dos millones…

100	cien, ciento	**700**	setecientos/as
101	ciento uno/una	**800**	ochocientos/as
200	doscientos/as	**900**	novecientos/as
300	trescientos/as	**1.000**	mil
400	cuatrocientos/as	**2.000**	dos mil
500	quinientos/as	**1.000.000**	un millón
600	seiscientos/as	**2.000.000**	dos millones

¡Doscientos quince dólares!
$215

- **Cien** is used in counting and when referring to exactly one hundred of something. **Ciento** is used to express the numbers 101 through 199: …noventa y nueve, **cien, ciento** uno, **ciento** dos…
- **Cien** is used before numbers greater than 100: **cien mil, cien millones.**
- When counting, the masculine form of words containing **cientos** is used: **…doscientos uno, doscientos dos…**
- To talk about the quantity of something, words containing **cientos** take the gender of the noun they quantify: **doscientos veintiún dólares, quinientas ocho sillas.**
- **Mil** means *one thousand* or *a thousand*. It does not have a plural form in counting, but **millón** does. When followed directly by a noun, **millón** (**dos millones,** and so on) must be followed by **de.**

mil gracias	
3.000 habitantes	tres mil habitantes
14.000.000 **de** habitantes	catorce millones **de** habitantes

¡OJO!

In many parts of the Spanish-speaking world, a period in numerals is used where English uses a comma, and a comma is used to indicate the decimal where English uses a period.
\$1.500 \$1.000.000 \$10,45 65,9%

- Note how years are expressed in Spanish.

1899	mil ochocientos noventa y nueve
2008	dos mil ocho

Los números a partir del 100

Suggestions

- **Reciclado:** Review numbers from 0–100. Point out the relationship between *dos → doscientos, tres → trescientos,* and so on.
- Model pronunciation of hundreds forms. Give addition and subtraction problems using hundreds (some incorrect) and have students respond *sí* or *no.* When *no,* have them give the correct answer.
- Emphasize the following:
  1. 500, 700, 900 have irregular forms.
  2. *Un* is not used with *mil* (1000).
  3. The hundreds must agree in gender; use *-cientas* before feminine nouns.
  4. There is no *y* in *ciento uno,* and so on.
  5. A period usually marks the thousands in Spanish, instead of a comma as in English.
  6. No period is used in expressing the year. This usage corresponds to English usage.
  7. Only the word *millón* (*millones*) is followed by *de.* Compare: *cuatro millones de habitantes* versus *cuatro millones doscientos habitantes.*
- Write complex numbers on the board for students to read aloud, e.g., 154, 672.
- Have students count by thousands (*mil, dos mil,…*) and then by millions (*un millón, dos millones,…*) to emphasize the singular *mil* and plural *millones.*
- Point out that *millón* (singular) has an accent mark but *millones* does not.
- Have students say the following in Spanish:
  1. 500 men, 500 women, 700 male professors
  2. 1,000 books, 2,000 friends, 3,000 universities
  3. a million dollars; 3 million Americans; 7 million euros
- Students will get further practice in saying the years in *Cap. 6.* Introduce this skill here by saying the current year in Spanish, and writing it on the board as you speak. Say a few more years, writing at the same time.

Pronunciación: See Pronunciation Notes, IM.

NATIONAL STANDARDS: Comparisons

In this chapter, students learn that numbers are written differently in the Spanish-speaking world. The decimal point is used for a comma and vice-versa. If you are working on a computer spreadsheet in a Spanish-speaking country, you will quickly notice that the default setting for numbers is the opposite. This can be remedied easily by changing the default settings on the computer to the decimal point/comma protocol of your choice.

Resources: Transparency 40

Con. A: Preliminary Exercises

- Dictate the following numbers in Spanish as students write them in digit form.
  1. *100, 50, 60*
  2. *400, 600, 800*
  3. *2.000, 1.000.000, 50.000*
  4. *150, 500, 1.500*
  5. *660, 960, 760*
- Write these numbers on the board and model them. Then have students say them.
  1. *2, 12, 20, 200*
  2. *3, 13, 30, 300*
  3. *4, 14, 40, 400*

Con. A: Optional

Tabla de conversión

1 libra = 453 gramos

Note

To convert kilograms to pounds, use the following formula: *kilogram* × *2.2* = *lbs.*

Con. A: Suggestions

- Ask students the following questions.
  1. *Las palabras* peso, pesado *y* pesar *están relacionadas. ¿Qué significan?*
  2. *¿Cuál es el animal más pesado? ¿el menos pesado? ¿Cuánto pesa cada uno?*
  3. *Busque las palabras en español para* terrestrial *y* mammal.
  4. *¿Cuánto pesan los animales en libras* (new)*?*
- For *Paso 2,* model the question: *¿Cuánto pesa un gato/perro?*

Con. B: Suggestions

- Introduce the names of the currencies of Guatemala (*el quetzal*) and Honduras (*el lempira*). Emphasize the pronunciation of the letter *z* in Spanish (like *s* in most countries).
- Check the current exchange rate. At the time of publication, it was approximately: *1 dólar estadounidense = 8 quetzales, 20 lempiras.*
- Working in pairs, ask students to calculate the prices *quetzales* and *lempiras*. Give them a time limit and give a prize to the pair of students who gets the most items correct within the time limit.
- Here are the answers, based on the preceding exchange rates.

Quetzales: **1.** *800* **2.** *1.200* **3.** *9.600* **4.** *1.800* **5.** *3.200* **6.** *2.640* **7.** *600.000* **8.** *16.000.000* **9.** *126.400.000*

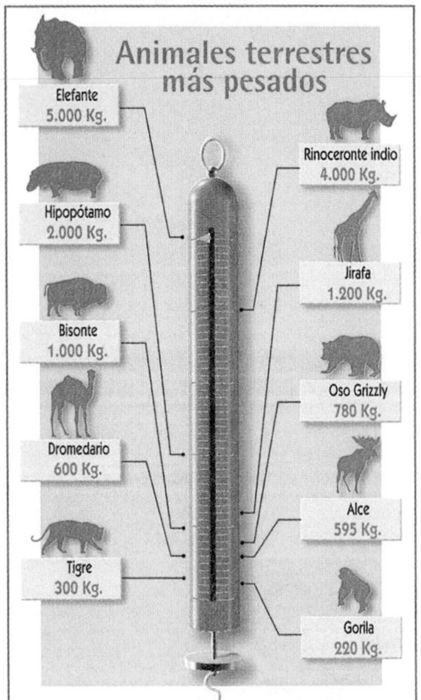

De los animales terrestres, el elefante, con sus 5.000 kilos de peso medio entre todas sus especies, es sin duda el mamífero más pesado. El hipopótamo y el rinoceronte son los siguientes en la lista, y el hombre, ni aparece.

1 kilo = 2,2 libras

Conversación

A. ¿Cuánto pesan? (*How much do they weigh?*)

Paso 1. Estos son los animales terrestres más grandes. ¿Cuánto pesan en kilos? **¡OJO!** Use el artículo masculino para todos los nombres, menos para (*except for*) **jirafa.**

MODELO: El elefante pesa cinco mil kilos.

Paso 2. Pregúntele (*Ask*) a un compañero o compañera cuánto pesan aproximadamente en libras los siguientes animales y objetos.

1. un perro/gato
2. su mochila con los libros
3. un coche
4. su libro de español
5. el animal más grande del mundo

B. ¿Cuánto cuestan? Exprese los siguientes precios en dólares en español.

1. unos *jeans* de moda: $100
2. unos tenis tipo NBA: $150
3. un anillo (*ring*) de diamantes: $1.200
4. unos aretes (*earrings*) de oro: $225
5. una tela (*fabric*) de artesanía local de excelente calidad: $400
6. un cinturón de cuero de un diseñador (*designer*) famoso: $330
7. un coche europeo: $75.000
8. una casa grande en una zona residencial muy exclusiva: $2.000.000
9. un edificio de apartamentos: $15.800.000

C. Más o menos

Paso 1. With a classmate, determine how much the following items probably cost, using **¿Cuánto cuesta(n)... ?** Keep track of the prices that you decide on. Follow the model.

MODELO: una chaqueta de cuero →
E1: ¿Cuánto cuesta una chaqueta de cuero?
E2: Cuesta doscientos dólares.

1. una calculadora pequeña
2. un coche nuevo/usado
3. una computadora portátil Mac o IBM
4. un reloj Timex / de oro
5. unos tenis (**¡OJO! cuestan**)
6. una casa en esta ciudad
7. un teléfono celular
8. un iPod

Paso 2. Now compare the prices you selected with those of others in the class. What is the most expensive thing on the list? **(¿Cuál es el objeto más caro** [*most expensive*]**?)** What is the least expensive? **(¿Cuál es el más barato?)**

Mundo interactivo

You should now be prepared to work with, Scenario 2, Activity 3 in Connect Spanish (**www.connectspanish.com**).

Lempiras: **1.** *2.000* **2.** *3.000* **3.** *24.000* **4.** *4.500* **5.** *8.000* **6.** *6.600* **7.** *1.500.000* **8.** *40.000.000* **9.** *316.000.000*

Multimedia: Internet

Have students look up currency conversion websites to convert from one currency to another.

Resources: Transparency 41

PRONUNCIACIÓN

Stress and Written Accent Marks (Part 2)

¿Recuerda Ud.?

In the **Pronunciación** section of **Capítulo 3**, you learned that most Spanish words do not need a written accent mark because their pronunciation is completely predictable. Review the two basic rules of Spanish word stress by looking at the examples and completing the rules. The stressed syllable is underlined.

- Examples: **<u>li</u>bro, <u>me</u>sa, e<u>xa</u>men, i<u>ma</u>gen, <u>e</u>res, <u>gra</u>cias**

  A word that ends in a ___vowel___, ___n___, or ___s___ is stressed on the next-to-last syllable.

- Examples: **bai<u>lar</u>, us<u>ted</u>, pa<u>pel</u>, es<u>toy</u>**

  A word that ends in ___a consonant other than *n* or *s*___ is stressed on the last syllable.

The written accent mark is used in the following situations.

- A written accent mark is needed when a word does not follow the two basic rules reviewed in **¿Recuerda Ud.?**
- Look at the words in this group.

ta-bú	a-le-mán	in-glés
ca-fé	na-ción	es-tás

The preceding words end in a vowel, **-n,** or **-s,** so one would predict that they would be stressed on the *second-to-last syllable* (**la penúltima sílaba**). But the written accent mark shows that they are in fact accented on the *last syllable* (**la última sílaba**).

- Now look at the words in this group.

lá-piz dó-lar ál-bum á-gil dó-cil

The preceding words end in a consonant (other than **-n** or **-s**), so one would predict that they would be stressed on the last syllable. But the written accent mark shows that they are in fact accented on the next-to-last syllable.

- All words that are stressed on the *third-to-last syllable* (**la antepenúltima sílaba**) must have a written accent mark, regardless of which letter they end in. These are called **palabras esdrújulas.**

bo-lí-gra-fo ma-trí-cu-la ma-te-má-ti-cas

Con. B: Variation

Play a *¿más o menos?* guessing game. Think or have students think of a number for others to guess. After each guess, the leader tells whether the number is *más* or *menos. 650: ¿500? → más, ¿700? → menos, ¿600? → más, ¿650? → ¡Eso es!* (new)

Con. C: Suggestion

- Many students will not know the price of the suggested items. Encourage students to guess.
- Do *Paso 2* as a whole-class feedback activity. First, agree on the most logical price for each item, then have students answer.

Bright Idea
Con. C: Follow-up

Tell students they have $500 or $1,000 (or ?) to spend on themselves. Have them tell what they would buy.

Pronunciación

Reciclado: Review information from *Cap. 3.* Write *bailar* and its present tense paradigm on the board. Use it for the following.

- Have students separate the forms into syllables.
- Encourage them to read syllables aloud slowly.
- Ask them whether *-ai-* (*bailar*) is a diphthong or not.
- Have them identify the stressed syllables.
- Ask why words do or do not require accent marks.

Note

Students are not accustomed to separating syllables in English. Syllable division in English is not as necessary as it is in Spanish. Also, English syllables are not as obvious as Spanish syllables.

Suggestions

- Some students will grasp the basic concepts easily; others will struggle with the rules. Rather than just stating rules, the *¿Recuerda Ud.?* section and the first two bullet points attempt to show students how to think through the concepts. Our experience has shown that this is ultimately more useful to students than rote rule memorization.
- It may be helpful to some students to restate the first two bullets of the explanation as follows: Words that end in a vowel, *-n,* or *-s* that are stressed on the last syllable will have a written accent mark. Words that

(*Cont.*)

Heritage Speakers

- Anime a los hispanohablantes a modelar la pronunciación de las palabras que se usan en esta sección para practicar la colocación de los acentos escritos. Invite a los angloparlantes a imitar su pronunciación, repitiendo las palabras que oyen.
- Invite a los hispanohablantes a que lean en voz alta los nombres de los animales del anuncio de la página 104 y que la clase los repita.

end in a consonant other than *-n* or *-s* that are stressed on the last syllable will have a written accent mark.

- Regardless of how your students react to this material, you need to establish a policy for your classroom with regard to grading. Is credit taken off for missing accent marks? For misplaced accents?
- Point out that accent marks are added or deleted to preserve the original stress pattern when words are made plural.

  Accent deleted: *nación* → *naciones; francés* → *franceses*
  Accent added: *joven* → *jóvenes; examen* → *exámenes*

Preliminary Exercises

- Write pairs of words on the board that vary only in stress. Read one word of each pair of words aloud at random. Students decide which word you said.

hable	*hablé*	*espere*	*esperé*
doblo	*dobló*	*paso*	*pasó*
baje	*bajé*	*pase*	*pasé*
bajo	*bajó*	*papa*	*papá*

- Read these words aloud and have students identify the stressed syllable.

  ¿Última o penúltima?
  esta *español* *inglés*
  está *Pérez* *chimpancé*
  ¿Penúltima o antepenúltima?
  política *Italia* *teléfono*
  delgado *estados* *Toledo*
  simpático
  ¿Última, penúltima o antepenúltima?
  busco *clásico* *clasifico*
  buscó *lógico* *clasificó*
  típico

- ***¿Diptongo o no?***
  María *estudia* *aéreo*
  baila *patio* *geografía*
  día *tío*

Prác. A: Follow-up

- Give students a *dictado* that includes sentences such as:
  1. *José es rico.*
  2. *Ramón es romántico.*
  3. *El Sr. Gómez es simpático.*
  4. *David es perezoso y antipático.*
  5. *Joaquín es alto y guapo.*
  6. *El Sr. Pérez es bajo y viejo.*
- Have several students write the dictation on the board while the rest of the class works at their seats. Correct errors on the board, paying special attention to accents and why they are needed or not needed.

- When two consecutive vowels do not form a diphthong (see **Pronunciación, Cap. 2**), the vowel that receives the spoken stress will usually have a written accent mark. This pattern is very frequent in words that end in **-ía.**

  Ma-rí-a po-li-cí-a as-tro-no-mí-a
  dí-a bio-lo-gí-a

¡OJO!
Contrast the pronunciation of those words with the following words in which the vowels **i** and **a** *do* form a diphthong: **Patricia, Francia, infancia, distancia.**

- Some one-syllable words have accents to distinguish them from other words that are pronounced the same but have different meanings. This type of accent does not follow the general rules of accentuation; it is called the *diacritic accent* (**el acento diacrítico**).

  él (*he*)/el (*the*)
  sí (*yes*)/si (*if*)
  tú (*you*)/tu (*your*)
  mí (*me*)/mi (*my*)

- Interrogative and exclamatory words have a written accent on the stressed vowel. For example:

  ¿quién?
  ¿dónde?
  ¡Qué ganga! (*What a bargain!*)

Práctica

A. Sílabas. The following words have been separated into syllables for you. Read them aloud, paying careful attention to where the spoken stress should fall. Don't worry about the meaning of words you haven't heard before. The rules you have learned will help you pronounce them correctly.

1. a-quí	pa-pá	a-diós	bus-qué
2. prác-ti-co	mur-cié-la-go	te-lé-fo-no	ar-chi-pié-la-go
3. Ji-mé-nez	Ro-drí-guez	Pé-rez	Gó-mez
4. si-co-lo-gí-a	so-cio-lo-gí-a	sa-bi-du-rí-a	e-ner-gí-a
5. his-to-ria	te-ra-pia	Pre-to-ria	me-mo-ria

B. Reglas (*Rules*)**.** Indicate the stressed vowel of each word in the following list. Give the rule that determines the stress of each word.

① written accent
② ends in consonant ≠ *-n, -s*
③ ends in vowel, *-n, -s*

1. exámenes ①	**9.** están ①
2. lápiz ①	**10.** hombre ③
3. necesitar ②	**11.** peso ③
4. perezoso ③	**12.** mujer ②
5. actitud ②	**13.** plástico ①
6. acciones ③	**14.** María ①
7. dólares ①	**15.** Rodríguez ①
8. francés ①	**16.** Patricia ③

NATIONAL STANDARDS: Comparisons

Like Spanish, other Romance languages have written accent marks or diacriticals. French, for example, has five different accent marks: an acute accent (´), a grave accent (`), the circumflex (ˆ), the cedille (ç), and the trema or dieresis (¨). In addition to the acute, grave, and cedille diacriticals, Portuguese has a tilde (˜), which nasalizes the vowels.

GRAMÁTICA

¿Recuerda Ud.?

You learned the four forms of the demonstrative adjective **este** in **Gramática 5 (Cap. 3).** Review them now by completing these phrases.

1. est_os_ pantalones **2.** est_a_ falda **3.** est_as_ blusas **4.** est_e_ abrigo

9 Pointing Out People and Things

Demonstrative Adjectives (Part 2) and Pronouns

Grammar Tutorial 9
connect SPANISH
www.connectspanish.com

Gramática en acción: Suéteres a buenos precios

Susana busca un suéter en el mercado con su amigo Jorge.

SUSANA: ¿Cuánto cuesta este suéter?

VENDEDOR: Bueno, ese que Ud. tiene en la mano cuesta 800 quetzales. Este aquí cuesta 700 quetzales.

SUSANA: ¡Qué caros!

VENDEDOR: Es que todos son de pura lana. Mire aquellos suéteres de rayas sobre aquella mesa. Solo cuestan 300 quetzales. Son acrílicos.

SUSANA: Muchas gracias.

Comprensión

¿Quién habla, Susana, su amigo Jorge o el vendedor?

1. «Estos suéteres de rayas son bonitos. Y solo cuestan 300 quetzales.» Jorge
2. «Los suéteres en aquella mesa no son de pura lana.» el vendedor
3. «Compro este suéter. Me gusta la ropa de lana.» Susana
4. «Estos suéteres acrílicos son más baratos que aquellos de lana.» Jorge

Demonstrative Adjectives / Los adjetivos demostrativos

	Singular			Plural		Adverbs / **Los adverbios**
this	**este abrigo**	**esta gorra**	these	**estos abrigos**	**estas gorras**	**aquí** = here
that	**ese abrigo**	**esa gorra**	those	**esos abrigos**	**esas gorras**	**allí** = there
	aquel abrigo	**aquella gorra**		**aquellos abrigos**	**aquellas gorras**	**allá** = way over there

¡OJO! Note that the final **-e** in the singular forms **este** and **ese** changes to an **-o-** in the plural: **estos, esos.**

Sweaters at good prices *Susana is looking for a sweater in the market with her friend Jorge. SUSANA: How much is this sweater? SALESMAN: Well, that one that you have in your hand costs 800 quetzales. This one here costs 700 quetzales. SUSANA: (They're) So expensive! SALESMAN: It's because they're all pure wool. Take a look at those striped sweaters on that table (over there). They only cost 300 quetzales. They're acrylic. SUSANA: Thanks a lot.*

Resources: Transparency 42

Gramática 9 Demonstrative Adjectives (Part 2) and Pronouns

Notes

- In order to appreciate the use of demonstrative pronouns in the dialogue, students need to look carefully at the scene as well as pay attention to the content of the dialogue, especially the references to the material the sweaters are made of.
- Be sure that students understand that *el vendedor* = *salesman.*

Suggestions

- Have students act out the *GEA* and try to define the highlighted words before checking the translation below.
- Ask students to explain the difference between a demonstrative adjective and demonstrative pronoun. Give them these examples in English, then ask them to provide others.

  This car is John's. vs. *This* (*one*) is John's.

  That cat is white. vs. *That* (*one*) is white.

Bright Idea

Suggestion

Have three students stand in three distinct areas of the room, perhaps placing one student just outside the classroom door. Stand at one end with one student. Then as you indicate the student closest to you, say, *"Este/a estudiante aquí se llama* [name of student]." Then point to the student who is farther away, but not farthest away, from you and say, *"Ese/a estudiante allí se llama* [name of student]." Finally point to the student who is farthest away and say *"Aquel* [*Aquella*] *estudiante allá se llama* [name of the student]."

Follow-up

Give students the following information:

En los países hispanos no es extraño ver a vendedores en la calle. Algunos vendedores están siempre en el mismo lugar. Otros son ambulantes. ¿Es esto normal en su país? ¿En qué casos? (large cities, university centers, Girl Scouts, and so on)

Notes

- Some Spanish speakers still prefer to use accents on demonstrative pronouns: *este coche y ése, aquella casa y ésta.* However, as explained in the footnote, it is correct in modern Spanish, per the *Real Academia Española,* to omit the accent on these forms when context makes the meaning clear and no ambiguity is possible. Students will not be exposed to these accented forms in *Puntos de partida,* unless they appear in a piece of realia that is reproduced as originally published. You may wish to make students aware of these accented forms.
- The use of adverbs of place varies from dialect to dialect in Spanish. Many Spanish speakers observe the following distinctions, which correspond neatly to the three sets of demonstrative adjectives.

  este = aquí, acá
  ese = allí, ahí
  aquel = allá

  If those distinctions are valid for your dialect, stress that concept in your explanation.

Suggestions

- Hold up a book and say *este libro.* Place the book near a student and say *ese libro.* Place the book far from both yourself and the student and say *aquel libro.*
- Emphasize that the masculine singular forms do not end in *-o.*
- Point out that distance may be physical (*aquella casa que está lejos*) or temporal (*en aquella época*). Also remind students that distance is relative to the speaker and also depends on the context.
- **Reciclado:** In order to practice demonstrative adjectives, use real objects in the classroom: *este lápiz, ese pizarrón, estos cuadernos.* You may also bring or have students bring in photographs or magazine clippings of buildings, houses, or city scenes to use in small group activities or to display in the classroom. Students can then describe the scenes.

  Esta casa es bonita.
  Esta ciudad es moderna.
  Estos edificios son enormes.

Optional

Introduce the adverbs and prepositions of place *cerca / cerca de* and *lejos / lejos de* as well as the comparative forms *más cerca de* and *más lejos de* and use them in sentences, along with *aquí/allí/allá,* asking students to fill in the blanks with the appropriate demonstratives.

Resources: Transparency 43

1. **Agreement**
   Demonstrative adjectives are used to indicate a specific noun or nouns. In Spanish, **los adjetivos demostrativos** precede the nouns they modify. They also agree in number and gender with the nouns.

a demonstrative adjective / **un adjetivo demostrativo** = an adjective used to indicate a particular person, place, thing, or idea

an adverb / **un adverbio** = a word (such as *very* and *quickly*) that modifies a verb, adjective, or another adverb

2. **Using *este* and *ese***
   When two people are speaking, the forms of **este** (*this/these*) are used to refer to nouns that are close to the speaker in space or in time. The forms of **ese** (*that/those*) refer to nouns that are close to the person spoken *to.* When the point of view in the conversation changes, the use of **este** and **ese** may change as well, just like in English: what is *this*/**este** for one person becomes *that*/**ese** for the other. When the noun is distant from both speakers, **ese** is used in Spanish.

3. **Using *ese* and *aquel***
   There are two ways to say *that/those* in Spanish. The forms of **ese** refer to nouns that are not close to the speaker(s), as you just learned. The forms of **aquel** refer to nouns that are even farther away from the speaker(s).

   In the preceding chart, the words **aquí, allí,** and **allá** are associated with the forms of **este, ese,** and **aquel,** respectively. However, it is not obligatory to use these words with the demonstrative adjectives.

¿Esos pantalones?
No, aquellos allá.

Este niño es mi hijo. **Ese** joven allí es mi hijo también. Y **aquel** señor allá es mi esposo.
This boy is my son. That young man there is also my son. And that man way over there is my husband.

Demonstrative Pronouns / Los pronombres demostrativos

1. **Demonstrative Pronouns**
   In English, the *demonstrative pronouns* are the demonstrative adjective + *one(s),* as in the examples to the right. In Spanish, **los pronombres demostrativos** are the same as demonstrative adjectives, except that the noun is not used and there is no direct equivalent for English *one(s).**

2. **Agreement**
   In Spanish, demonstrative pronouns agree in gender and number with the noun they are replacing: **ese libro, en la mesa ⟶ ese, en la mesa.**

   [Práctica A]

—¿Te gusta **aquella** casa allá?
—¿Cuál?
—**Aquella,** la de las ventanas grandes.
—¡Ah, **aquella!** Sí, me gusta mucho. Mucho más que **esta** . . .

"Do you like ***that*** *house way over there?"*
"Which one?"
"That one, *the one with the big windows."*
"Oh, ***that one!*** *Yes, I like it a lot. A lot more than* ***this one*** *. . . "*

*Some Spanish speakers still prefer to use accents on these forms: **este coche y ése, aquella casa y ésta.** *However, it is correct in modern Spanish, according to the* **Real Academia Española** *in Spain, to omit the accent on these forms when context makes the meaning clear and no ambiguity is possible. To learn more about these forms, consult Appendix 2.*

3. **Neuter Demonstratives**
Use the neuter demonstratives **esto, eso,** and **aquello** to refer to as yet unidentified objects or to a whole idea, concept, or situation.
[Práctica B–C]

¿Qué es **esto**?
What is this?

Eso es todo.
That's it. That's all.
¡**Aquello** es terrible!
That's terrible!

¡OJO!

Esto es una mochila. (to identify in general)
This is a backpack.

Esta es mi mochila. (to identify one out of a group)
This (one) is my backpack.

Autoprueba

Match each word with the corresponding meaning in English.

1. _____ estas
2. _____ aquellos
3. _____ ese
4. _____ esas
5. _____ este

a. *that*
b. *those (over there)*
c. *these*
d. *this*
e. *those*

Answers: 1. c 2. b 3. a 4. e 5. d

Práctica

A. Cambios (*Changes*)

Paso 1. Cambie (*Change*) las formas de **este** por **ese** y añada (*add*) **también,** según el modelo.

MODELO: Este abrigo es muy grande. →
Ese abrigo **también** es muy grande.

1. Esta falda es muy pequeña.
2. Este diccionario es muy largo.
3. Este libro es muy bueno.
4. Esta corbata es muy fea.

Paso 2. Ahora cambie **este** por **aquel** y añada **allá.**

MODELO: Este abrigo es muy grande. →
Aquel abrigo **allá también** es muy grande.

Paso 3. Finalmente, cambie las oraciones del singular al plural.

MODELO: Este abrigo es muy grande. →
Est**os** abrig**os son** muy grande**s**.

B. Situaciones. Empareje (*Match*) cada (*each*) situación de la columna A con un comentario de la columna B.

A

1. __c__ Aquí hay un regalo para Ud.
2. __d__ Ocurre un accidente de coche.
3. __b__ No hay clases mañana.
4. __a, d__ La matrícula cuesta más este semestre/trimestre.
5. __b__ Ud. tiene A en su examen de español.

B

a. ¡Eso es un desastre!
b. ¡Eso es magnífico!
c. ¿Qué es esto?
d. ¡Eso es terrible!

Prác. A: Answers
Paso 1. **1.** *Esa falda también es muy pequeña.* **2.** *Ese diccionario también es muy largo.* **3.** *Ese libro también es muy bueno.* **4.** *Esa corbata también es muy fea.*

Paso 2. **1.** *Aquella falda allá también es muy pequeña.* **2.** *Aquel diccionario allá también es muy largo.* **3.** *Aquel libro allá también es muy bueno.* **4.** *Aquella corbata allá también es muy fea.*

Paso 3. **1.** *Estas faldas son muy grandes.* **2.** *Estos diccionarios son muy largos.* **3.** *Estos libros son muy buenos.* **4.** *Estas corbatas son muy feas.*

Preliminary Exercises

Have students respond to the following requests.

1. *Dé el plural de* (point to or hold up objects): *este lápiz, este libro, este bolígrafo, esta mesa, este bolso, esta carta.*
2. *Dé el singular de* (point to or hold up objects): *estos libros, estos bolígrafos,* and so on.
3. *Dé el plural de* (point to articles of clothing worn by students): *ese zapato, ese traje, ese abrigo, esa chaqueta, esa falda, esa camisa,* and so on.

Expand to practice with other objects and articles of clothing in the classroom.

Prác. A: Follow-up

Have students point out things in class using the demonstratives. Students must repeat the appropriate form of demonstrative to double-check comprehension, e.g., *Esa ventana es grande.* → *¿Esta/Esa/Aquella ventana?* → *Sí, esa.*

Prác. A: Reciclado

Ask personalized questions regarding items in the classroom. Use possessive pronouns as well as demonstratives. Have students respond with the correct statements: *¿Es ese mi lápiz, _____?* → *No, este es el lápiz de _____. ¿Son estos libros de los estudiantes de filosofía?* → *No, son nuestros libros.* Emphasize the *de* + *noun* in case of ambiguity.

Prác. B: Note

Active vocabulary: *el examen*

Prác. B: Variation

Have students provide similar cues to other students, who then react appropriately.

NATIONAL STANDARDS: Communication

Point out to students that interjections are an integral part of everyday language. As in English, Spanish interjections evolve and go into and out of fashion with different generations, and they generally vary from country to country. Students should already be familiar with the interjection *¡Ojo!* For *Práctica B,* students might enjoy using some interjections with the responses. List some of the following for them.

¡Ah! ¡Huy! ¡Oh! ¡Ay! (pain)
¡Vaya! ¡Ajá! ¡Qué bien! (admiration or approval)
¡Ay, no! ¡Caramba! ¡Pero… hombre! (irritation)
¡Anda! ¡No me digas! ¡Vaya! (surprise)
¡Oiga! ¡Oigan! ¡Oye! ¡Qué va! ¡Qué barbaridad! (disapproval)
¡Ánimo! ¡Sus! ¡Ándale! ¡Venga! (encouragement)
¡Hurra! ¡Viva! ¡Arriba! ¡Bravo! (enthusiasm)

Prác. C: Suggestion

Make sure that students understand that the mannequin in the red sweater is closest to the salesman and the client.

Con.: Follow-up

Working with the whole class, have students follow the same models to describe people and objects in their classroom. Model using demonstratives by describing things that are close to you, somewhat farther away, and very far away. Ask a student at the back of the class to describe the same objects.

Con.: Optional

- Ask the following questions.
  1. *¿Qué va a hacer Ud. esta noche? ¿y este fin de semana?*
  2. *¿Cómo es esta universidad? ¿Cómo es esta clase? Y este libro, ¿cómo es?*
  3. *¿Cómo es esta ciudad? ¿y este estado / esta provincia?*
  4. *¿Cómo se llama el decano* (new) *de esta facultad? ¿el rector* (new) *de esta universidad? ¿el presidente / primer ministro de este país?*
  5. *¿Cuántos estados / Cuántas provincias hay en este país?*
  6. *¿Tiene Ud. muchos exámenes esta semana? ¿Tiene que estudiar mucho esta noche?*
- Have students work in pairs to create descriptions according to the following model.

  MODELO: E1: *Es de madera.*
  E2: *Es esta mesa.*
- Have students work in pairs to decide what things or persons in the classroom correspond to the following phrases. If the phrase does not apply, they should say *No hay nada.*

  MODELO: *aquella mochila negra →*
  Aquella mochila negra es de Joe.
  1. *aquella mochila negra*
  2. *esa mesa*
  3. *esta cama*
  4. *este libro*
  5. *aquellos libros de español*
  6. *aquella calculadora*
  7. *esta profesora*
  8. *esas compañeras de clase*

Reciclado: Have students bring in photos of their family and describe them to the class, using demonstratives, as needed. Other students should ask questions about the people in the photos. The same activity can be done with magazine photos (ads or photos of famous people).

C. En una tienda

Paso 1. Complete el siguiente diálogo con los demostrativos apropiados. Asuma (*Take*) el punto de vista (*point of view*) del vendedor y el cliente.

VENDEDOR: ¿Qué suéter le gusta? ¿ Este [1] rojo que está aquí?

CLIENTE: No, el rojo no.

VENDEDOR: ¿ Ese [2] suéter amarillo?

CLIENTE: No, tampoco[a] el amarillo. ¡Me gusta aquel[3] anaranjado de allá!

[a]No… *No, not [the yellow one] either*

Paso 2. Ahora empareje (*match*) el color de los pantalones con el demostrativo apropiado, según la distancia.

1. b los pantalones negros
2. a los pantalones azules
3. c los pantalones color kaki

a. estos
b. esos
c. aquellos

Conversación

En la alcoba (*bedroom*) **de Ernesto.** Working with a partner, imagine that you are the person depicted in the drawing, who is looking into Ernesto's bedroom. Some objects and items of clothing are close to you, some are a bit farther away, and some are at the other end of the room. Describe them as accurately as you can, using the appropriate demonstrative adjectives and all of the vocabulary you have learned so far.

MODELOS: Ese gato es blanco y aquel gato es negro.
Este libro es verde.

Vocabulario útil

la cama	bed
el estante	book shelf
la mesita	nightstand

Resources: Transparencias 44, 45

¿Recuerda Ud.?

You began using the singular forms of the verb **tener** in **Capítulo 3.** Review them by completing the following verb forms.

1. tú t_ie_nes **2.** yo te_ng_o **3.** Julio t_ie_ne

You will learn about similar patterns in **Gramática 10.**

10 Expressing Actions and States

Tener, venir, poder, preferir, querer; Some Idioms with tener

Grammar Tutorial 10
connect SPANISH
www.connectspanish.com

Gramática en acción: Un mensaje telefónico

Hola, Jorge. Soy Jaqui. Esta tarde tengo que comprar un regalo para Miguel y no quiero ir sola. ¿Vienes conmigo? Podemos encontrarnos en ese centro comercial que está cerca de tu casa. O si prefieres, puedo pasar por ti antes. ¡Llámame!

Comprensión

Ahora vuelva a contar (*retell*) el mensaje de Jaqui. Estas formas verbales son como **tiene**.

1. Jaqui tien_e_ que comprar un regalo.
2. Quier_e_ ir de compras con Jorge.
3. Pued_e_ encontrarse con Jorge en el centro comercial.
4. O si Jorge prefier_e_, Jaqui pued_e_ pasar por la casa de él.

Tener, venir, poder, preferir, querer

Remember that infinitives in red are conjugated in their entirety in Appendix 5.

tener (*to have*)		**venir** (*to come*)		**poder** (*to be able, can*)		**preferir** (*to prefer*)		**querer** (*to want*)	
tengo	tenemos	vengo	venimos	puedo	podemos	prefiero	preferimos	quiero	queremos
tienes	tenéis	vienes	venís	puedes	podéis	prefieres	preferís	quieres	queréis
tiene	tienen	viene	vienen	puede	pueden	prefiere	prefieren	quiere	quieren

A phone message *Hello, Jorge. It's Jaqui. This afternoon I have to buy a gift for Miguel, and I don't want to go alone. Will you come with me? We can meet at that shopping center that's near your house. Or if you prefer, I can come by for you ahead of time. Call me!*

Gramática 10

Tener, venir, poder, preferir, querer; Some Idioms with *tener*

Notes

- These 5 verbs are grouped together for a variety of reasons. Two of them share an irregularity in the first person singular (*tengo, vengo*). All of them show the stem-changing pattern that students will learn about in *Gram. 13* (*Cap. 5*), so this section is a preview of that concept. Finally, three of them (*poder, preferir, querer*) are modal verbs (like *deber, desear, necesitar*) that are often followed by an infinitive. Introducing these additional modal verbs allows students immediately to expand their ability to communicate.
- No subject pronouns are included with this verb chart, so that singular and plural forms could be shown side to side in order to emphasize the "boot" shape of the paradigms. You may wish to ask students to tell you which subject pronouns correspond to the forms.

Follow-up

Ask students to create the message that Jorge will leave on Jaqui's phone.

Optional

Use the following nursery rhyme to review the forms of *tener* and also to introduce the concept of related verb forms: *tener* and *mantener.*

Canción infantil
Tengo, tengo, tengo,
tú no tienes nada.
Tengo tres ovejas
en una cabaña.
Una me da leche,
otra me da lana
y otra me mantiene
toda la semana.

Suggestion

Point out the similarities and differences among stem-changing verbs: some *yo* forms have a *-g-*; the *nosotros* and *vosotros* forms have the same stem as the infinitive; the stem becomes a diphthong (*e* → *ie* and *o* → *ue*) when stressed (with the exception of *tengo* and *vengo*).

Reciclado: Ask questions about students' color preferences: *Para la ropa, ¿prefiere el azul o el negro? ¿el verde o el amarillo?* and so on. *Para un coche, ¿prefiere el blanco o el negro? ¿los colores oscuros* (write on board) *o claros?* and so on.

Bright Idea

Suggestion

Point out to students that a helpful way to remember which forms have a stem change is to remember the "boot" shape shown in the paradigms. Forms inside the boot show a stem change; those outside do not. There are two exceptions in chart: *yo* forms of *tener* and *venir.* They are not included in the "boot" but do have an irregularity.

Some Idioms with *tener*

Suggestions

- **Reciclado:** Start by reminding students about a *tener* idiom that they already know: *tener… años.* Ask questions about age, using as many numbers from 30–100 as possible.
- Point out that there is generally no word-to-word correspondence of idioms between the two languages.
- Using complete sentences, model the idioms with information about yourself.
- Give students these optional phrases: *mucha prisa, mucho miedo, mucho sueño.*
- Point out that *tener que* is used much more frequently than *necesitar* in Spanish. *Necesitar* is generally reserved for an actual physical or ethical need, for example: *Necesito comprar unos zapatos de tenis nuevos.* (Mine have a big hole in them.) *Necesitamos mejorar la situación del consumo de energía en este país.* (It's a pressing need.)

Notes

- The idiomatic expression *tener miedo* is often used with *de* when it is followed by a verb form and with *a* (with an indirect object pronoun) when it is followed by a noun: *Tengo miedo de que me muerda el perro.* vs. *Les tengo miedo a los perros.* Both structures are beyond students' linguistic control at this point in the text.
- Students will learn *tener calor/frío* in *Cap. 6* with weather and *tener hambre/sed* in *Cap. 7* with foods.

The five verbs shown on the preceding page share a number of characteristics.

- The **yo** forms of **tener** and **venir** are irregular.
- In other forms of **tener** and **venir,** and in **preferir** and **querer,** when the stem vowel **e** is stressed, it becomes **ie.**
- Similarly, the stem vowel **o** in **poder** becomes **ue** when stressed.
- The verbs **poder, preferir,** and **querer** can be followed by an infinitive, in the same way as **deber, desear,** and **necesitar.** Verbs like these are called *stem-changing verbs.* You will learn more verbs of this type in **Gramática 13 (Cap. 5).**

tener: yo **tengo,** tú **tienes** (e → ie)…
venir: yo **vengo,** tú **vienes** (e → ie)…
preferir, querer: (e → ie)
poder: (o → ue)

In vocabulary lists, these changes are shown in parenthesis after the infinitive: **poder (puedo).**

¿**Puedes correr** muy rápido?
Can you run very fast?

¿Qué **quieres/prefieres hacer** hoy?
What do you want/prefer to do today?

¡OJO!
The **nosotros** and **vosotros** forms of these verbs do not have changes in the stem vowel because it is not stressed.

¡OJO!
You will learn to use the verb hacer (*to do or to make*) in **Gramática 12 (Cap. 5).** Learn to recognize it in questions and direction lines.

Some Idioms with **tener** / **Algunos modismos con *tener***

1. **Conditions or States**
   Many ideas expressed in English with the verb *to be* are expressed in Spanish with *idioms* (**los modismos**) that use **tener.** Idioms are often different from one language to another. For example, in English, *to pull Mary's leg* usually means *to tease her*, not *to grab her leg and pull it.* In Spanish, *to pull Mary's leg* is **tomarle el pelo a Mary** (lit., *to take hold of Mary's hair*).
   You already know one **tener** idiom: **tener… años.** Here are some more **tener** idioms. They all describe a condition or state.

an idiom / **un modismo** = an expression whose meaning cannot be inferred from the literal meaning of the words that form it

tener **sueño**

tener **prisa**

tener **razón**

no tener **razón**

tener **miedo (de)**

Heritage Speakers

Pregúnteles a los hispanohablantes si se les ocurren otras expresiones con *tener*, como *tener ánimo, tener cuidado, tener paciencia, tener fama* y *tener suerte.*

Resources: Transparency 46

2. ***Tener* Idioms** + *Infinitive*
Other **tener** idioms include the following:

tener ganas de + *infinitive* = to feel like (*doing something*)
tener que + *infinitive* = to have to (*do something*)

¡OJO!

Note that the English equivalent of the infinitive in expressions with **tener ganas** is expressed with *-ing*, not with the infinitive as in Spanish.

Tengo ganas de comer.
I feel like eating.

¿No **tiene** Ud. **que leer** este capítulo?
Don't you have to read this chapter?

Autoprueba

Give the missing letters in each verb.

1. p____des	**4.** t____nemos
2. pr____fiere	**5.** qu____ro
3. ve____o	**6.** t____nen

Answers: **1.** p**ue**des **2.** pr**e**fiere **3.** ve**ng**o **4.** t**e**nemos **5.** qu**ie**ro **6.** t**ie**nen

---

Práctica

A. ¡Sara tiene mucha tarea (*homework*)**!**

Paso 1. Haga (*Form*) oraciones completas con las palabras indicadas. Añada (*Add*) palabras si es necesario.

MODELO: Sara / tener un examen / mañana ⟶
Sara **tiene** un examen mañana.

1. por eso / (ella) tener que estudiar / mucho hoy
2. (ella) venir a universidad / todos los días
3. hoy / trabajar / hasta nueve de noche
4. preferir estudiar / en la biblioteca
5. querer leer más / pero / no poder
6. por eso / regresar a casa
7. tener / ganas de leer más
8. pero unos amigos / venir / a mirar televisión
9. Sara / decidir / mirar la televisión con ellos

Paso 2. Now retell the same sequence of events, first as if they had happened to you, using **yo** as the subject of all but item 8, then as if they had happened to you and your roommate, using **nosotros/as.**

B. Situaciones. Match each statement with the appropriate response.

SITUACIONES

1. __c__ El niño es muy joven.
2. __b__ En esa casa, hay un perro grande y furioso.
3. __a__ Son las tres de la mañana.
4. __f__ Pablito dice (*says*): «Dos y dos son… seis».
5. __d__ Ahora Pablito dice: «Buenos Aires es la capital de la Argentina».
6. __g__ Tenemos que estar en el centro a las tres y ya son (*it's already*) las tres menos cuarto.
7. __e__ Los exámenes de la clase de español son muy fáciles (*easy*).

RESPUESTAS

a. Tengo mucho sueño.
b. Yo tengo miedo del perro.
c. Solo tiene dos años.
d. Tiene razón.
e. Por eso no tengo que estudiar mucho.
f. No tiene razón.
g. Por eso tenemos mucha prisa.

Prác. A: Answers
Paso 1. 1. *Por eso tiene que estudiar mucho hoy.* **2.** *Viene a la universidad todos los días.* **3.** *Hoy trabaja hasta las nueve de la noche.* **4.** *Prefiere estudiar en la biblioteca.* **5.** *Quiere leer más, pero no puede.* **6.** *Por eso regresa a casa.* **7.** *Tiene ganas de leer más.* **8.** *Pero unos amigos vienen a mirar la televisión.* **9.** *Sara decide mirar la televisión con ellos.*

Paso 2. 1. *tengo* **2.** *Vengo* **3.** *trabajo* **4.** *Prefiero* **5.** *Quiero* **6.** *regreso* **7.** *Tengo* **9.** *Decido*

1. *tenemos* **2.** *Venimos* **3.** *trabajamos* **4.** *Preferimos* **5.** *Queremos* **6.** *regresamos* **7.** *Tenemos* **9.** *Decidimos*

Preliminary Exercises

- Have students imagine that it is exam week and the following situations take place. Have them give new sentences based on the cues.
  1. *Sara tiene muchos exámenes. (Pepe, nosotros, Alicia y Carlos, yo, tú, vosotras)*
  2. *Ramón viene a la biblioteca todas las noches. Prefiere estudiar allí. (yo, los estudiantes, tú, Uds., nosotras, vosotros)*
  3. *Silvia quiere estudiar más, pero no puede. (yo, ella, nosotros, todos, tú, vosotros)*
- Have students answer these questions based on the cues.
  1. *¿Qué tiene Ud. que hacer esta noche?* ⟶ *Tengo que llegar a casa temprano. (asistir a una clase a las siete, aprender una palabra en español, estudiar el Capítulo 4, leer toda la noche, hablar con un amigo, ¿ … ?)*
  2. *Pero, ¿qué tiene ganas de hacer?* ⟶ *Tengo ganas de bailar. (abrir una botella de vino, mirar la televisión, comer en un buen restaurante, ¡no estudiar más!, ¿ … ?)*

Prác. A: Suggestion

Remind students how to do these kinds of exercises: conjugate verbs, make adjectives agree with nouns, add words if necessary, do not use subjects in parentheses.

Prác. B: Preliminary Exercises

- Dictate the following sentences.
  1. *Tienen prisa y miedo.*
  2. *Tiene toda la razón.*
  3. *No tienen ganas de estudiar.*
  4. *Tenemos que trabajar.*
- Have students give expressions they associate with the following.
  1. *el cliente*
  2. *los tres cochinitos* (draw a pig face or tail on the board)
  3. *el lobo* (draw a wolf face on the board)
  4. *el conejo blanco de Alicia* (draw rabbit ears on the board)

Con. A: Suggestion

Coach students to help them invent a situation for or a story about the drawing. Caution them to stay within the limits of the language they know. Offer brief model sentences: *Isabel no estudia mucho.*

Con. A: Follow-up

Ask the following questions.

¿Es Ud. como Isabel?
¿Qué problemas tienen en común Isabel y Ud.?
¿Cómo es su cuarto?
¿Vive Ud. solo/a?

Nota comunicativa

Follow-up

- Ask: *¿Cuál es el antónimo de mucho/a(s)?*
- Have students give sentences using *poco/a(s).*

Heritage Speakers

En algunos dialectos del español del suroeste de los Estados Unidos, se oye decir *muncho* por *mucho.* Aunque *muncho* es parte del habla cotidiana en esos dialectos, *mucho* es la forma más aceptada en todos los dialectos.

Conversación

A. Los estereotipos. Draw some conclusions about Isabel based on this scene. Think about things that she has, needs to or has to do or buy, likes, and so on. When you have finished, compare your predictions with those of a classmate. Did you reach the same conclusions?

MODELO: Isabel tiene cuatro gatos. Tiene que…

Vocabulario útil

la guitarra
el juguete toy
los muebles furniture
el sofá

estar en malas condiciones to be in bad shape
hablar por teléfono
tener alergia a to be allergic to

Nota comunicativa

Mucho y poco

In this chapter, you learned that words like **aquí, allí,** and **allá** are *adverbs* (**los adverbios**), words that modify a verb (*run* ***quickly***), an adjective (***very*** *smart*), or another adverb (***very*** *quickly*). One very common Spanish adjective that you have used frequently is **muy** (*very*).

In the first chapters of *Puntos de partida*, you have used the words **mucho** and **poco** as both adjectives and adverbs. In English and in Spanish, adverbs are invariable in form. Spanish adjectives, however, agree in gender and number with the words they modify, as you know.

ADVERBIOS:	**mucho**	Rosa estudia **mucho.**	*Rosa studies a lot.*
	poco	Julio come **poco.**	*Julio doesn't eat much.*
ADJETIVOS:	**mucho/a**	Rosa tiene **mucha** ropa.	*Rosa has a lot of clothes.*
		Tiene **muchos** zapatos.	*She has a lot of shoes.*
	poco/a	Julio come **poca** pasta.	*Julio doesn't eat much pasta.*
		Come **pocos** postres.	*He eats few desserts.*

Many adverbs are used in **Conversación B** and **C** on the following page.

NATIONAL STANDARDS: Cultures

Remind students that a word they learned for pet is *mascota* (*Cap. 2*). Point out that, as in this country, cats, dogs, and birds are popular pets in the Spanish-speaking world. A pet with ancient origins is the Chihuahua. There are many legends about the ancestors of the present-day Chihuahua, a breed of dog discovered in Mexico about 100 years ago. Its true origins are still a mystery, but we do know that it was a popular pet and a religious necessity among the ancient Toltec and Aztec tribes. Archaeologists have found remains of this breed in human graves in Mexico and in some parts of the United States. Mexicans favor the jet black Chihuahua with tan markings or the black and white spotted Chihuahua. In this country, people prefer the solid colors.

Resources: Transparency 47

B. Circunstancias personales

Paso 1. Choose a partner, but before working with him or her, try to predict the choices he or she will make in each of the following cases.

MODELO: Tiene muchos / pocos libros. →
Mi compañero tiene pocos libros.

1. Estudia mucho / poco este semestre/trimestre.
2. Tiene mucho / poco dinero. Es muy rico/a / pobre.
3. Viene en coche / en autobús / a pie (*on foot*) a la universidad todos los días.
4. Prefiere estudiar en la biblioteca / casa / la residencia.
5. Quiere comprar un abrigo de cuero / una sudadera con el logotipo (*logo*) de la universidad.
6. Puede correr (*run*) una milla en menos / más de (*than*) cinco minutos.
7. Tiene muchas ganas de estudiar / bailar esta noche.
8. Tiene mucha / poca ropa.
9. Su color favorito es el verde / rojo / amarillo.
10. Prefiere usar botas / zapatos / sandalias.

Paso 2. Now, using tag questions, ask your partner questions to find out if you guessed correctly in **Paso 1.**

MODELO: **E1:** Tienes muchos libros, ¿verdad?
E2: Sí, tengo muchos libros. (No, tengo pocos libros.)

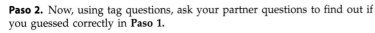

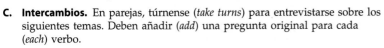

C. Intercambios. En parejas, túrnense (*take turns*) para entrevistarse sobre los siguientes temas. Deben añadir (*add*) una pregunta original para cada (*each*) verbo.

VERBO INICIAL	OPCIONES
preferir	¿los gatos o los perros? ¿mirar una película (*movie*) en casa o en el cine (*movie theater*)? ¿la ropa elegante o la ropa cómoda? ¿ ?
tener	¿mucho dinero o muchas deudas (*debts*)? ¿una familia grande o pequeña? ¿sueño en clase con frecuencia? ¿ ?
venir	¿a clase tarde o temprano? ¿de una familia anglosajona, hispana o de otro origen? ¿a clase todos los días? ¿ ?
(¿qué?) querer	¿comprar esta semana? ¿ser en el futuro (profesión)? ¿mirar en la tele esta noche? ¿ ?
poder	¿hablar una lengua extranjera? ¿vivir sin (*without*) dinero? ¿escribir poesías? ¿ ?

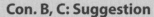

Con. B, C: Suggestion

Before allowing students to start each activity, ask them to pick out the obvious adverbs in each item, primarily adverbs of time: *mucho/poco, muy, todos los días, con frecuencia, tarde, temprano, todos los días, esta semana,* and *esta noche.* If you wish, you can also explore the concept of adverbial phrases like *en coche, en autobús*, and so on.

Con. B: Suggestions

- Have students work in groups to compare notes. Then assign different areas of the board where all groups can write a short list of their conclusions. Compare all of the lists. Emphasize note taking.
- After students have used the items to ask each other questions, ask them to do the same activity but focusing on you. In *Paso 1*, they will predict your choices. In *Paso 2*, they will ask you questions. (For items 1 and 4, suggest that students substitute the verb *trabajar*.) As you answer each question, take the opportunity to expand on your answer and engage students in follow-up questions.

Con. C: Suggestion

If you do both *Con. B* and *C* on the same day, ask students to change seats to work with a different partner. If students tend to sit next to / work with the same partner, it may be a good idea to ask them to change seats on a somewhat regular basis.

Con. C: Follow-up

Have selected students report back information they have learned. You may wish to help them organize their presentations.

Gramática 11

Ir; The Contraction *al; Ir + a + Infinitive*

Notes

- *Ir* and *venir* are used somewhat differently than their English equivalents. *Venir* means *to come to* (*where the speaker is*). *Ir* refers to going to some place other than where the speaker is. The speaker of *¿Vienes a mi casa?* is at his/her house when asking the question. Otherwise, he/she would ask *¿Vas a mi casa?*
- *¡Ya voy!* means *I'm coming,* not *I'm going.*

Pronunciación

- Use this grammar section to focus on the pronunciation of word-initial letter *v* (pronounced like *b* in most dialects of Spanish): *voy, vas, va, vamos, vais, van.*
- **Reciclado:** Link this focus to the sounds of the letter *b* in clothing words and colors (*Vocabulario: Preparación* in this chapter): *las botas, la blusa, el bolso, el abrigo, la corbata, el sombrero, el traje de baño, el impermeable; blanco.* Have students listen to the different pronunciation of *b* in *bolso* vs. *el bolso* or *un bolso.*

Suggestion

Call students' attention to the use of *¿adónde?* in the *GEA* and example. This word becomes active here.

Follow-up

Ask students:

¿Qué voy a hacer yo mañana / esta tarde / noche?

Then give them sentences about things you may or may not do.

Voy a bailar en una fiesta esta noche.

Students guess if your sentences are true (*Es verdad*) or false (*No es cierto*).

Suggestions

- Point out the difference between *el* (article) and *él* (subject pronoun). Remind students that *de + él* and *a + él* do not contract.
- Point out that *de + El* and *a + El* do not contract when *El* is part of a proper noun: *Vamos* a *El Salvador. Es un artículo* de *El País.*

11 Expressing Destination and Future Actions

Ir; The Contraction al; Ir + a + *Infinitive*

Grammar Tutorial 11
connect SPANISH
www.connectspanish.com

Gramática en acción: ¿Adónde vas?

El Mercado Central, Ciudad de Guatemala

Rosa y Casandra son compañeras de casa.

CASANDRA: ¿Adónde vas?
ROSA: Voy al Mercado Central.
CASANDRA: ¿Qué vas a hacer allá?
ROSA: Voy a comprar unos regalos para mi familia en Nueva Jersey.
CASANDRA: ¿Vas a viajar a los Estados Unidos pronto?
ROSA: Sí, en quince días.

Comprensión

¿Cierto o falso? Corrija las oraciones falsas.

	CIERTO	FALSO
1. Rosa va a estudiar. Va al Mercado Central.	☐	☑
2. Rosa va a comprar regalos.	☑	☐
3. Casandra va a los Estados Unidos. Rosa va a los Estados Unidos.	☐	☑

The Verb ir / El verbo *ir*

ir (*to go*)			
(yo)	voy	(nosotros/as)	vamos
(tú)	vas	(vosotros/as)	vais
(Ud., él, ella)	va	(Uds., ellos/as)	van

Ir is the irregular Spanish verb used to express *to go.*

Rosa **va** al centro.
Rosa is going downtown.
¿Adónde **vas** tú?
Where are you going?

The first person plural of **ir, vamos** (*we go, are going, do go*), is also used to express *let's go.*

Vamos a clase ahora mismo.
Let's go to class right now.

The Contraction al / La contracción *al*

As you can see in the preceding examples, the verb **ir** is often followed by the preposition **a** to indicate where someone is going (to).

When **a** is followed by **el,** it contracts to **al,** just as **de** + **el** ⟶ **del (Capítulo 3). Al** and **del** are the only *contractions* (**las contracciones**) in Spanish.

a + el ⟶ al

Voy **al** centro comercial.
I'm going to the mall.

Vamos a la tienda.
We're going to the store.

Where are you going? *Rosa and Casandra are housemates.* CASANDRA: *Where are you going?* ROSA: *I'm going to the Central Market.* CASANDRA: *What are you going to do there?* ROSA: *I'm going to buy some presents for my family in New Jersey.* CASANDRA: *Are you going to travel to the United States soon?* ROSA: *Yes, in two weeks.*

Heritage Speakers

Los hispanohablantes tienden a usar la expresión *ir a + infinitivo* en vez del futuro. Por ejemplo, es más común oír *va a llamar* en vez de *llamará.* Pregúnteles a los hispanohablantes en qué situaciones usan el futuro en vez de *ir a + infinitivo.*

NATIONAL STANDARDS: Communication

In English, when someone calls or summons you, it is not uncommon to answer by saying. "I'm coming." In Spanish, however, the verb of choice is *ir.* To say "I'm coming," in Spanish, speakers say *"Ya voy"* or *"Voy en seguida."* In Mexico, speakers might say *"¡Ahorita voy!"*

Ir + a + *Infinitive*

Ir + **a** + *infinitive* is used to describe actions or events in the near future.

Van a venir a la fiesta esta noche.
They're going to come to the party tonight.

> **¡OJO!**
> This structure is like **aprender** + **a** + *infinitive*, which you learned in **Gramática 8 (Cap. 3).**

Using ir to Talk About the Future / El uso de *ir* para hablar del futuro

You can use the verb **ir** + **a** + *infinitive* to talk about the near future in Spanish.

> **¡OJO!**
> This use of **a** is different from the use of **a** to indicate where someone is going. Some Spanish verbs when they are followed by an infinitive simply take **a** (like **aprender** + **a** + *infinitive* [**Gramática 8, Cap. 3**]) or another preposition or another word (like **tener que** + *infinitive*).

Van a venir a la fiesta esta noche.
They're going to come to the party tonight.

Voy a comer en un restaurante en el centro.
I'm going to eat at a downtown restaurant.

but

Voy al centro para comer.
I'm going downtown to eat.

Práctica

A. ¿Adónde van de compras? Haga oraciones completas, usando (*using*) **ir.** ¡OJO! **a** + **el** ⟶ **al.**

MODELO: Marta / el centro ⟶ Marta **va al** centro.

1. tú y yo / la *boutique* Regalitos
2. Francisco / el almacén Goya
3. Juan y Raúl / el centro comercial
4. (tú) / el Mercado Central
5. Ud. / la tienda Gómez
6. yo / ¿ ?

B. Mañana

Paso 1. Use las siguientes frases para expresar lo que (*what*) Ud. va a hacer o no hacer mañana.

MODELO: estudiar ⟶ Mañana **no voy a** estudiar.

1. ir a un centro comercial
2. comer en la cafetería de la universidad
3. estudiar en la biblioteca
4. escribir e-mails
5. venir a la clase de español
6. poder hacer toda mi tarea (*homework*)
7. bailar en una discoteca

Paso 2. Ahora use las frases del **Paso 1** para entrevistar a un compañero o compañera.

MODELO: estudiar ⟶ ¿**Vas a** estudiar mañana?

Autoprueba

Give the subject pronouns for these forms of **ir.**

1. va
2. vamos
3. voy
4. van
5. vas

Answers: **1.** Ud., él, ella **2.** nosotros/as **3.** yo **4.** Uds., ellos/as **5.** tú

Conversación

A. ¿Adónde va Ud. si... ? ¿Cuántas oraciones puede hacer?

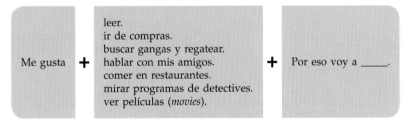

Me gusta	+	leer. ir de compras. buscar gangas y regatear. hablar con mis amigos. comer en restaurantes. mirar programas de detectives. ver películas (*movies*).	+	Por eso voy a _____.

Vocabulario útil

el cine movie theater
el mercadillo flea market

Using *ir* to Talk About the Future

Point out that this usage is similar to English: *I'm going **to** Spain* vs. *I'm going **to** see you.* English, of course, does not add an additional proposition (second example sentence), but it can add an additional word: *I'm looking **forward** to seeing you.*

Preliminary Exercise

Have students give the Spanish equivalents.

1. I'm going to the market.
2. He's going to the bookstore.
3. My mother is going downtown.
4. You're going to read.
5. We're going to be sleepy.
6. Tom and you are going to eat.

Prác. A: Notes

- Students will learn more about verbs like this in *Cap. 13*. For now, they should just learn phrases like *ir + a + inf., aprender + a + inf.* and *tener + que + inf.* as they are presented.
- Active vocabulary: *ir de compras*

Prác. A: Answers

1. *Tú y yo vamos a la boutique Regalitos.* **2.** *Francisco va al almacén Goya.* **3.** *Juan y Raúl van al centro comercial.* **4.** *Vas al Mercado Central.* **5.** *Ud. va a la tienda Gómez.* **6.** Answers will vary.

Prác. A: Optional

Give students the following cues that describe a trip to a mall, using the *ir + a + infinitive* structure. Ask them to work through the cues using various subjects: *yo, nosotros, Rigoberto y Cecilia, Ud.* Before doing the exercise with *ir + a + infinitive*, it is a good idea to work through the items in the simple present tense, as presented.

1. *llegar al centro a las once*
2. *comer un sándwich*
3. *comprar unos chocolates*
4. *buscar una camiseta y una sudadera*
5. *mirar una película*
6. *regresar a casa a las cinco*

Prác. B: Extension

Ask students to use the cues to interview you. Alternatively, ask a student to join you at the front of the room and have other students ask the two of you questions (using *Uds.* or *vosotros/as* forms). Your student partner will answer for both of you. He/She may need to ask you a question as well in order to formulate the correct answer.

Con. A: Suggestion

Do the activity as a conversational exchange between you and the students, or have students work in pairs to ask and answer questions. *¿Adónde vas si te gusta... ?* ⟶ *Voy a...*

Con. B: Emphasis

Before allowing students to begin the activity, model several questions with *¿adónde?* For example: *Si vas a ir de compras, ¿adónde vas? Si vas a leer una novela, ¿adónde vas?*

Con. B: Suggestion

- Have students add their own preference to the questions. The answers can be reported back, with students using the *nosotros* form whenever possible.
- **Reciclado:** Use the cues in *Con. B* to discuss the activities of members of students' families: *Mañana, ¿va a ir de compras su padre? ⟶ Mi padre no va a ir de compras mañana.*

Con. B: Follow-up

- Ask the following questions.
  ¿Cuál es su actividad favorita? ¿y su escritor favorito (escritora favorita)? ¿Cuántas horas mira la televisión por semana?
- Discuss students' answers as a whole-class activity.
  Las actividades de los números pares (2, 4, 6,…) son mentales. Las de los números impares son físicas. ¿Cómo es su compañero/a? ¿Es activo/a físicamente? ¿O prefiere las actividades mentales?

Un poco de todo

A: Note

This activity focuses on modal verbs and on the *verb + preposition + infinitive* construction.

Reciclado: Add other modal verbs and *verb + preposition + infinitive* verbs that students have already learned to use: *desear, necesitar, deber, aprender a.*

A: Suggestion

Have students make two or three statements about themselves, using verbs from the second column.

B: Note

The following grammar topics are included in *Lengua y cultura:* gender, adjective agreement, demonstratives, preposition + *infinitive*, *-er* verbs, *ir* (+ *a* + *infinitive*), *poder* and *tener*, *tener* idioms.

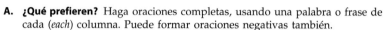

Mundo interactivo

You should now be prepared to work with Scenario 2, Activity 4 in Connect Spanish (**www.connectspanish.com**).

B. Intercambios. En parejas, túrnense (*take turns*) para hacer y contestar preguntas sobre sus planes para el fin de semana. Aquí hay unas actividades posibles. Traten de obtener (*Try to get*) mucha información. **¡OJO! ¿adónde?** = *where to?*

MODELO: ir de compras ⟶ ¿**Vas a ir** de compras **este fin de semana**? ¿Adónde vas a ir? ¿Por qué vas a ese centro comercial? ¿Qué vas a comprar?

1. ir de compras
2. leer una novela
3. asistir a un concierto
4. estudiar para un examen
5. ir a una fiesta
6. escribir una carta
7. ir a bailar
8. escribir un ensayo (*essay*)
9. practicar un deporte (*sport*)
10. mirar mucho la televisión

Estrategia

Remember that all of the phrases in the middle column are followed by the infinitive. You must conjugate only the verbs in the middle column.

Un poco de todo

A. ¿Qué prefieren? Haga oraciones completas, usando una palabra o frase de cada (*each*) columna. Puede formar oraciones negativas también.

yo mi mejor (*best*) amigo/a mi esposo/a mis padres/hijos nuestro profesor / nuestra profesora mi familia tú y yo	+	(no) { ir a poder preferir querer tener ganas de tener que	+	estudiar en la biblioteca visitar mi universidad ir de compras al centro comprar cuando hay rebajas escribir un informe (*report*) para la clase de ¿ ? ir al cine (*movies*) llevar ropa cómoda leer novelas de ciencia ficción / terror / ¿ ?

B. Lengua y cultura: Pero, ¿no se puede* (*can't one*) **regatear?** Complete the following paragraphs about shopping. Give the correct form of the words in parentheses, as suggested by context. When two possibilities are given in parentheses, select the correct word.

Una zapatería, en Quetzaltenago, Guatemala

¿A Ud. le gusta ir de compras? En (los/las[1]) ciudades hispanas, hay una (grande[2]) variedad de tiendas para (ir[3]) de compras. Hay almacenes, centros comerciales y *boutiques* (elegante[4]), como en (este[5]) país, en donde los precios son siempre (fijo[6]).

También hay tiendas que (vender[7]) un solo[a] producto. Por ejemplo,[b] en una zapatería solo hay zapatos. En español el sufijo **-ería** se usa[c] para (formar[8]) el nombre de la tienda. ¿Dónde (creer[9]) Ud. que venden papel y (otro[10]) artículos de escritorio? ¿A qué tienda (ir[11]) a ir Ud. a comprar fruta?

Finalmente, vamos (a/de[12]) mencionar los mercados porque hay muchos en el mundo hispano. En (este[13]) mercados hay (pequeño[14]) tiendas permanentes o temporales[d]

[a]*single* [b]Por… *For example* [c]se… *is used* [d]*temporary*

B: Answers: 1. *las* **2.** *gran* **3.** *ir* **4.** *elegantes* **5.** *este* **6.** *fijos* **7.** *venden* **8.** *formar* **9.** *cree* **10.** *otros* **11.** *va* **12.** *a* **13.** *estos* **14.** *pequeñas*

Note that placing the word* **se *before a verb changes its meaning slightly:* **puede** = *he/she/you can;* **se puede** = *one can. You will learn how to use this structure in* **Capítulo 8.**

Resources: Desenlace

In the *Cap. 4* segment of "Chapter-by-Chapter Supplementary Materials" in the IM, you will find a chapter-culminating activity. You can use this activity to consolidate and review the vocabulary and grammar skills students have acquired.

donde Ud. (poder[15]) encontrar[e] desde comida[f] típica hasta artesanías[g] locales o ropa interior. Allí los compradores[h] (regatear[16]) los precios, porque el primer[i] precio casi siempre (ir[17]) a ser muy alto.

[e]*find* [f]*food* [g]*arts and crafts* [h]*shoppers, buyers* [i]*first*

15. *puede* **16.** *regatean* **17.** *va*

Comprensión. Complete las oraciones.

1. En las ciudades hispanas hay *boutiques*, tiendas, almacenes, centros comerciales y mercados.
2. El nombre de muchas tiendas especializadas en un tipo de producto termina en -ería.
3. Una tienda de zapatos se llama una zapatería.
4. Si a Ud. le gusta practicar español y regatear, debe ir a un mercado.

C. Encuesta (*Poll*)

Paso 1. Entreviste a (*Interview*) un mínimo de seis compañeros de clase para saber la siguiente información. Apunte (*Write down*) sus respuestas.

- un aspecto de la moda actual (*current*) que tiene ganas de tener o llevar
- algo (*something*) dictado por la moda que cree que es absurda

Vocabulario útil

un agujero (*hole*) **en la nariz** (*nose*) / **la lengua** (*tongue*)
unos aretes de oro
unos *jeans* de Ralph Lauren o Narciso Rodríguez
llevar faldas muy, muy cortas
llevar la gorra de atrás para adelante (*backwards*)
llevar los pantalones muy bajos (*low*)
los tatuajes

Paso 2. Organice los resultados de su encuesta para presentarlos al resto de la clase. **¡OJO! nadie** = *no one.*

MODELO: Seis estudiantes quieren tener tatuajes. Nadie quiere comprar aretes de oro. Tres estudiantes creen que es bueno llevar faldas muy, muy cortas. Uno/a cree…

En su comunidad

Entreviste a (*Interview*) una persona hispana de su universidad o ciudad para informarse de (*find out about*) sus preferencias con respecto a las compras y la moda.

PREGUNTAS POSIBLES

- ¿Cuáles son las tiendas favoritas de esta persona para comprar comida (*food*)? ¿para comprar ropa?
- ¿Hay mercados en su país de origen? ¿Qué venden en los mercados? ¿Se puede regatear allí?
- En su opinión, ¿dónde hay más preocupación por la ropa, en este país o en su país de origen?

B: Follow-up

- Have students give the names of stores. Write the first example on the board.

  La tienda donde se venden zapatos se llama… → una zapatería
  fruta → frutería
  carne (new) → *carnicería*
  papel → papelería
  pan (new) → *panadería*
  perfume → perfumería
  ¿y animales? **¡OJO!** → *tienda de animales*

- Have students write similar paragraphs, comparing shopping experiences in different towns and cities, or in different kinds of stores and shopping areas.

C: Suggestions

- Brainstorm additional ideas about current fashions to add to the *Vocabulario útil* list and help students express them in Spanish.
- Model various ways of asking the interview questions before students start to circulate.
- Allow students 5 minutes to survey their classmates.
- Have students work in pairs to create their own options for item 1. Encourage them to be creative and funny! As a follow-up, have students share some of their options and answers: *¿Qué prefieres (tener)? Prefiero (tener) ____ a ____. No quiero tener ninguno/a.* Students then elaborate on their answers.

C: Extension

Have the class discuss their opinions about the following.

1. *las personas que solo llevan ropa de colores oscuros*
2. *las personas que llevan* jeans *rotos en las rodillas* (new)
3. *la ropa de los diseñadores famosos que vemos* (new) *en las revistas como* Elle, Vogue, *etcétera*
4. *la ropa que llevan los artistas que van a la ceremonia del Óscar*
5. *los padres que escogen* (new) *la ropa de sus hijos*

C: Redaccion

Ask students to write up their own responses to the interview questions and to summarize the responses of the six students they interviewed. They should finish this written assignment by saying whether they are in general agreement or disagreement with their interviewees.

En su comunidad

Suggestions

- Remind students to get the following basic information: the informant's country of origin, how long he or she has lived in this country, and if the informant visits his or her country of origin frequently.
- Given students' limited control of Spanish at this point, you may prefer that they do this cultural interview in English. If the interview is done in English, ask students to include other questions related to shopping and fashion.
- Regardless of how you have students do this assignment, be certain to make class time available for students to share with the whole class what they have learned. Be clear about whether or not students will simply report orally or whether you expect them to turn something in.

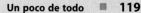

TelePuntos

Note

Pages 120–125 are optional. You may cover some, all, or none of this material in class, or assign it to students—as a group or individually—for homework or extra credit. Pages 126–127 (*En resumen: En este capítulo*) are a summary of all of the chapter's active material.

Suggestions

- If you are using the video in class, show it once, ask brief comprehension questions, then show it again.
- Whether you plan to ask students to watch the video in your campus media center or on their own, it is a good idea to continue to stress the need to watch the shows as many times as they want or need to in order to complete the *Después de mirar* activities.

Antes de mirar

Suggestions

- Point out that *alta costura* is a direct translation of the French *haute couture*.
- After students have completed this activity, conduct an informal poll (asking students to raise their hands) to determine the clothing options preferred by class members.

Fragmento del guion

Suggestion

Make sure that students recognize the words *ícon / icónico* as cognates. You may wish to discuss the concept of icons as symbols of aspects of culture. Ask students to name icons from the music world, the political arena, and so on.

Al mirar

Suggestion

Most of the *Palabras útiles* list is taken from the program, so going over these adjectives before students start to watch will enhance comprehension.

TELEPUNTOS

¿Un cambio de imagen (*change of image*) para Víctor?

Antes de mirar

¿Qué tipo de ropa prefiere Ud., por lo general? Indique su estilo personal con una de las opciones.

- ☐ ropa de alta costura (*high fashion*), de marcas (*labels*) famosas
- ☐ ropa informal pero atractiva, como camisetas con diseños (*designs*) interesantes y *jeans* de moda
- ☐ ropa de estilos variados —a veces elegante, a veces informal— pero siempre de las mejores (*best*) marcas
- ☐ ropa cómoda, barata y práctica: La moda no es importante para Ud.

Programa 4: Suggestions

- Most of the grammatical structures of *Programa 4* will be reasonably accessible to students. However, there is unfamiliar vocabulary in the show. Be sure that students have at least read through *Vocabulario de este programa* as well as the captions that accompany the video stills; doing so will prepare them for what they will hear in the program.
- Emphasize to students that the more carefully they study the preliminary activities (*Antes de mirar, Vocabulario de este programa, Fragmento del guion*), the more they will understand. Scanning *Después de mirar* before viewing is also an excellent strategy.

PROGRAMA 4: ¡Moda, moda, moda!

En este programa, Laura entrevista a tres diseñadores (*designers*) de ropa. ¿Cómo son sus diseños?

Vocabulario de este programa

te ves	you look	**vestido/a**	dressed
no creas	don't get the idea	**la calle más antigua**	the oldest street
suave	nice, mild	**único/a**	unique
Cristóbal Colon	Christopher Columbus	**la lucha**	fight
llegó	arrived	**sobresalir**	to excel
propio/a	own	**un poquito sucio, con sangre**	a little dirty, with blood
costura y diseño	sewing and design	**ha peleado**	he has fought
juvenil	youthful, young	**la gente**	people
la venta	sales	**vivo/a**	alive, vibrant

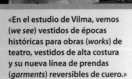

«En el estudio de Vilma, vemos (*we see*) vestidos de épocas históricas para obras (*works*) de teatro, vestidos de alta costura y su nueva línea de prendas (*garments*) reversibles de cuero.»

Fragmento del guion

LAURA: Ahora estamos en Icónica, donde el viejo San Juan[a] se hace[b] global con los diseños de camisetas. Hablamos con el dueño,[c] Javier Claudio.

JAVIER: Yo creo que en Puerto Rico por la condición del Caribe, que es un clima tropical y es caluroso,[d] pues los jóvenes universitarios mayormente[e] andan[f] siempre en T-shirts y mahones,[g] quizás[h] andan también en pantalones cortos y tenis. De hecho, eso fue lo que me llevó a mí a hacer[i] la marca Icónica.

LAURA: Javier nos habla del concepto de sus diseños.

JAVIER: Pues Icónica, como dice[j] el nombre, son íconos de la cultura popular, son cosas que nos representan como cultura global, no necesariamente de Puerto Rico, pero como cultura global.

[a]el… *old San Juan (original historic center of San Juan, where many restaurants and shops are located today)* [b]se… *becomes* [c]*owner* [d]*hot* [e]*mainly* [f]*go around* [g]*jeans* [h]*maybe* [i]De… *Actually, that's what inspired me to create* [j]*says*

Mundo interactivo

Continue your work as an intern at HispanaVisión with Laura Sánchez Tejada, the roving reporter of *Salu2*, as you complete Scenario 2, Activities 3 and 4 in Connect Spanish (**www.connectspanish.com**).

Al mirar

Escoja (*Choose*) uno o dos adjetivos para describir el estilo personal de las siguientes personas.

Palabras útiles: a la moda, bonito/a, cómodo/a, de alta costura, elegante, histórico/a, icónico/a, (in)formal, juvenil, moderno/a, relajado/a, serio/a, simbólico/a, único/a

1. Víctor cómodo
2. Ana elegante
3. Laura informal
4. Vilma Martínez de alta costura
5. Javier Claudio icónico
6. Christian Vidaurrázaga simbólico

El diseño de una camiseta de Dimex: Un campeón (*champion*) de lucha libre (*wrestling*) en la batalla de la vida (*battle of life*)

Después de mirar

A. ¿Está claro? Las siguientes oraciones son falsas. Corríjalas. (*Correct them.*)

1. En Puerto Rico solo hay ropa de los Estados Unidos.
2. El estilo de los diseños de Ropaje es obviamente juvenil y moderno.
3. Las camisetas de Icónica solo se pueden comprar por (*can be bought on*) el Internet.
4. Los diseños de Dimex están inspirados en la cultura popular global.
5. Ana se identifica culturalmente con los diseños de Dimex.

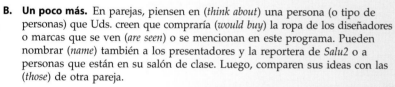

B. Un poco más. En parejas, piensen en (*think about*) una persona (o tipo de personas) que Uds. creen que compraría (*would buy*) la ropa de los diseñadores o marcas que se ven (*are seen*) o se mencionan en este programa. Pueden nombrar (*name*) también a los presentadores y la reportera de *Salu2* o a personas que están en su salón de clase. Luego, comparen sus ideas con las (*those*) de otra pareja.

MODELO: Ropajes ⟶ un director de teatro o cine (*movies*)

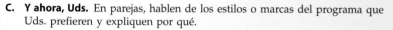

1. Ropajes
2. Dimex
3. Icónica
4. Zara, Mango, Carolina Herrera, Óscar de la Renta, Narciso Rodríguez

C. Y ahora, Uds. En parejas, hablen de los estilos o marcas del programa que Uds. prefieren y expliquen por qué.

Sobre el programa

Ana García-Blanco, la presentadora, y Laura, la reportera, tienen estilos de vestir muy diferentes. El estilo de Laura es juvenil e[a] informal. Casi nunca lleva falda y usa colores vivos. El estilo de Ana, en cambio,[b] es más clásico y femenino: faldas, collares[c] y pañuelos,[d] y prefiere los colores típicos de la ropa de las mujeres profesionales.

Cuando era[e] estudiante, Ana trabajó[f] como modelo fotográfica para una cadena[g] de grandes almacenes de su país, Panamá. Esto tal vez[h] explica por qué siempre está vestida a la moda.

[a]y [b]en… *on the other hand* [c]*necklaces* [d]*scarves* [e]*she was* [f]*worked* [g]*chain* [h]tal… *perhaps*

Act. A: Answers: 1. *En Puerto Rico hay diseñadores puertorriqueños.* **2.** *Son de estilo elegante y serio.* **3.** *Las camisetas también se pueden comprar en Puerto Rico.* **4.** *Están inspirados en la cultura popular mexicana y chicana.* **5.** *Víctor se identifica con Dimex.*

Sobre el programa: Comprensión (Optional)

Entre Ana y Laura,

1. *¿quién tiene el estilo de vestir más profesional? (Ana)*
2. *¿quién prefiere los colores vivos? (Laura)*
3. *¿quién fue modelo en su país? (Ana)*

Follow-up

Ask students in which shops from the show they think that Ana and Laura would shop for clothes.

Producción personal

Filme una o dos entrevistas (*interviews*) con personas que hablan de su estilo de vestir y de sus tiendas de ropa favoritas.

Después de mirar

B: Suggestions

- To get students started, you may wish to provide a list of possible people or categories in addition to the one given in the model: *un actor / una actriz, un angelino / una angelina, un chicano / una chicana, un diseñador / una diseñadora, un(a) estudiante universitario/a, un(a) inmigrante, un(a) joven de 15 años, un latino / una latina, un luchador, un mexicano / una mexicana, un puertorriqueño / una puertorriqueña, un(a) turista.* Most of these terms appear in the program. In addition, remind students to think about people in your class and other people in the show.
- Students may struggle with item 4 unless they have personal knowledge of these brands and designers, which are mentioned but not profiled in the program. Before assigning this activity, ask students what they know about them or assign the brands and designers as an Internet research project. Alternatively, you can present the following general information (being careful to explain unfamiliar vocabulary).

Zara *(www.Zara.com) es una compañía española transnacional. Tiene muchas tiendas en todas las ciudades más grandes de los Estados Unidos.*

Mango *(MNG) (www.mango.com) es otra compañía española transnacional con sede en Barcelona. En los Estados Unidos es conocido como MNG by Mango y está en las tiendas de JCPenney.*

Carolina Herrera *(carolinaherrera.com) es una diseñadora venezolana, cuya compañía tiene su sede en Nueva York. Sus diseños son internacionalmente famosos. La lista de mujeres famosas que han llevado su ropa incluye a Renée Zellweger, Jacqueline Kennedy Onassis y Shakira.*

Óscar de la Renta *(www.oscardelarenta.com) es un diseñador nacido en la República Dominicana; ahora es ciudadano estadounidense. Mucha gente famosa lleva sus diseños.*

Narciso Rodríguez *(narcisorodriguez.com) es un diseñador cubanoamericano de New Jersey. Muchas actrices llevan sus diseños, y también Michelle Obama.*

C: Suggestion

After students have discussed this topic in pairs, conduct an informal poll to see what styles or labels students have mentioned. Ask students to defend their choices.

Producción personal

Note

See the IM for additional suggestions for this chapter's assignment as well as for general guidelines and suggestions for video assignments.

Lectura cultural
Notes

- The Instructor's Edition on this page offers some additional information on the country of focus. For more information about the country of focus, see the chapter's opening pages and the IM.
- See the IM for some expressions used in Guatemala and Honduras.
- Ceramic products from the Lenca culture are another sought-after purchase in Honduras.

Exploración lingüística

Ask students to find the following in the reading. Some of these words are glossed and some are not.

- *una palabra relacionada con el verbo regatear* (*el regateo*)
- *unos sustantivos relacionados con los verbos comprar y vender* (*compradores, vendedores*)
- *unas palabras relacionadas con el turismo* (*turistas, turístico*)

En otros países hispanos
Suggestions

- Once they learn about bargaining, students tend to think that it can be done anywhere. You may wish to stress the fact (as mentioned in the reading) that one does not bargain in city stores and malls. In fact, shopping customs in Hispanic countries are not that much different from those of this country.
- Update the economic situation of Cuba, as needed.

Tres símbolos guatemaltecos y hondureños
Suggestions

- The ***Popol Vuh*** is a collection of narratives that relates to the history and beliefs of the Mayas. Our knowledge of it is based on the manuscript of a Spanish priest who transcribed it in the very early 18th century. Early chapters narrate the creation of the world from the Maya perspective, which has many similarities to the creation as described in Genesis in the Hebrew Scriptures.
- You may wish to tell students about the Maya city of *Copán*, in Honduras. It was an important center for astronomy and art, as well as trade. Like other Maya cities, *Copán* was mysteriously abandoned at the height of its power, around 800 A.D. When the media talk about the mysterious disappearance of the Maya, they are referencing a historical event. The Maya people are very much present in modern day Central America.

Una cita
Suggestion

The Quiché Maya are the largest of the Maya ethnic groups. For the Maya, as is true for most indigenous American peoples, their relationship to the land is the basis of their cultural values and religious beliefs.

A LEER

Lectura cultural
Guatemala y Honduras

En Guatemala y Honduras hay mercados donde se puede comprar artículos de artesanía[a] a buen precio. Son famosos los mercados guatemaltecos de las ciudades de Guatemala, Antigua, Chichicastenango y Quezaltenango. En estos mercados existe la costumbre[b] del «regateo»: el comprador[c] de un artículo debe negociar el precio con el vendedor.[d] Los vendedores invitan a los compradores a regatear y con frecuencia se escucha decir:[e] « …pero tiene rebaja, ofrezca un precio[f]».

¿Hay mercados de artesanías en la zona donde Ud. vive?

Entre toda la hermosa[g] artesanía guatemalteca es necesario mencionar los tejidos[h] de tradición maya, famosos por su colorido y belleza.[i] En Honduras, además de[j] las artesanías tradicionales, hay varios artículos codiciados por[k] los turistas: el café, el ron,[l] la vainilla, la cerámica y los puros.[m]

[a]*arts and crafts* [b]*custom* [c]*buyer, customer* [d]*seller* [e]se… *one hears people say* [f]pero… *but a discount is possible, make an offer* [g]bonita [h]*weavings* [i]*beauty* [j]además… *besides* [k]codiciados… *coveted by* [l]*rum* [m]puros… *cigars*

En otros países hispanos

- **En todo el mundo hispanohablante** Por supuesto[a] se puede encontrar[b] todo tipo de tiendas y centros comerciales (llamados[c] «el *Mall*» en algunos[d] países), generalmente en las ciudades grandes. En muchos de estos negocios,[e] no es aceptable regatear, aunque[f] en los mercados centrales y artesanales, regatear es común. Allí se puede comprar todo tipo de productos comestibles,[g] cosméticos, ropa y artículos para la casa. Algunos mercados son muy turísticos, pero la mayoría son para la gente[h] local.
- **En Cuba** En este país las compras se hacen[i] en familia. Debido a que[j] el libre[k] comercio no existe en la Isla, los viajes para hacer compras[l] son bien limitados. Pero es posible que esto cambie[m] en el futuro.

[a]Por… *Of course* [b]*find* [c]*called* [d]*some* [e]*businesses* [f]*although* [g]*edible* [h]*people* [i]se… *are done* [j]Debido… *Since* [k]*free* [l]los… *shopping trips* [m]*will change*

El Oakland Mall, en la Ciudad de Guatemala, Guatemala

Tres símbolos guatemaltecos y hondureños

- **El *Popol Vuh*** La cultura maya es el sustrato fundamental de Guatemala y Honduras. El *Popol Vuh* es el libro sagrado[a] de los mayas, escrito en el siglo XVI.[b] Es la historia de la creación del mundo, según las creencias[c] mayas.
- **Los tamales y las tortillas de maíz** Estos son alimentos muy básicos y tradicionales. Se dice[d] que en Guatemala un plato de comida[e] sin tortillas de maíz, no es comida.
- **Los productos agrícolas** Honduras es el mayor[f] productor de café en Centroamérica, y el tercero[g] en Latinoamérica. Las bananas son otro producto muy importante de este país.

[a]*sacred* [b]escrito… *written in the 16th century* [c]*beliefs* [d]Se… *It is said* [e]*food* [f]*largest* [g]*third*

Una cita° *quote*

«Jaquin ka retzelaj ri uwachulew, kuretzelaj ri ub'aqil.»
«Aquel que se hace[a] enemigo de la tierra,[b] se hace enemigo de sí mismo.[c]»

Proverbio maya-quiché

[a]Aquel… *He who becomes* [b]*earth, land* [c]sí… *himself*

COMPRENSIÓN

1. ¿En qué lugares hay mercados de artesanías en Guatemala?
2. ¿Qué cosas compran muchos turistas en Honduras?
3. ¿Qué opciones tiene la persona que quiere ir de compras en el mundo hispanohablante?

Comprensión: Answers: 1. *Hay mercados artesanales en las ciudades de Guatemala, Antigua, Panajachel y Quetzaltenango.* **2.** *el café, el ron, la vainilla, la cerámica y los puros* **3.** *Hay tiendas, centros comerciales y mercados centrales y artesanales.*

Del mundo hispano

Antes de leer

Conteste las siguientes preguntas.

1. ¿Qué significa para Ud. la frase «ropa activa»? ¿Cuándo debe uno llevar ropa activa?
2. ¿En qué ocasiones es buena idea usar ropa activa en una ciudad grande?
3. Para Ud., ¿es importante que la ropa tenga (*have*) las siguientes cualidades? Explique por qué sí o por qué no.
    - Repele los mosquitos.
    - Sirve para proveer (*provide*) protección solar.
    - Es impermeable.
    - Neutraliza malos olores (*odors*).

Algo[a] más que ropa

por Gregori Dolz

Desde[b] las calles[c] de Manhattan a las colinas nevadas[d] de Aspen, Exofficio proporciona[e] a sus clientes algo más que ropa activa. Parte de sus beneficios ayudan a[f] causas medioambientales[g] como la Conservation Alliance o World Concern, que auxilian[h] a comunidades necesitadas[i] de todo el mundo. Además,[j] sus prendas[k] proporcionan protección contra los insectos, contra el sol[l] y el agua, contra los olores corporales[m] y muchas otras inconveniencias.

» www.exofficio.com

[a]*Something* [b]*From* [c]*streets* [d]*colinas… snowy hills* [e]*offers* [f]*ayudan… help* [g]*environmental* [h]*help* [i]*needy* [j]*In addition* [k]*ropa* [l]*sun* [m]*bodily*

Lectura: Algo más que ropa

Comprensión

A. Un resumen del artículo

Las tres oraciones del artículo «Algo más que ropa» describen tres de las características de la compañía Exofficio y de la ropa que vende. Empareje (*Match*) las tres oraciones del artículo con los siguientes resúmenes.

NÚMERO DE ORACIÓN	RESÚMENES
2	**a.** La compañía dona (*donates*) parte de sus ganancias (*earnings*) a organizaciones conservacionistas y humanitarias.
3	**b.** La ropa de Exofficio protege (*protects*) contra diversos inconvenientes.
1	**c.** Uno puede usar la ropa de Exofficio en muchos lugares diferentes.

B. Ud. y Exofficio

Indique la importancia que tienen para Ud. las siguientes características de Exofficio y la ropa que produce. Luego explique su respuesta.

	MUY IMPORTANTE	IMPORTANTE	POCO IMPORTANTE	NADA IMPORTANTE
1. La compañía dona parte de sus ganancias a varias causas.	□	□	□	□
2. Es ropa protectora.	□	□	□	□
3. Es «ropa activa» que uno puede usar en muchas situaciones.	□	□	□	□

Antes de leer

Suggestion

Have students discuss these questions in pairs or small groups, then ask them to share their answers with the whole class. You may wish to write key terms on the board that might help students express their answers. Ask students to list places (specific or general) in which protection from insects, sun, rain, bad odors, and so on, would be important.

Lectura

Note

Exofficio is a U.S.-based company, with headquarters in the state of Washington. As the article indicates, one of its most important corporate values is a concern for humanitarian issues on a global level.

Estrategia

Finding Key Words

Each of the three sentences in the article describes a principal characteristic of Exofficio's clothing and of the company itself. Ask students to underline the key words to help them find the main point of each sentence.

Comprensión

A: Suggestion

Ask students whether the order of the sentences in the article reflects how they would prioritize these characteristics.

B. Suggestions

- Give students another way to refer to levels of importance: *(no) me importa mucho/poco, no me importa nada.*
- Do as a full-class brainstorming activity. Have students think about their answers and write down their explanations. Then ask volunteers to share their answers and explanations with the whole class. Try to generate discussion and/or debate about the most interesting or surprising explanations.

A escuchar

Notes

- In this chapter, students can listen to a conversation about a shopping trip.
- The text suggests that students listen to the passage as many times as they need to in order to do the *Después de escuchar* activities. If that is not what you want students to do, give them alternate instructions.
- *Zara* is a Spanish clothing franchise, with stylish and affordable clothing for all. There are *Zara* stores in Mexico, D.F., as well as in several major U.S. cities, like New York, Chicago, and so on.
- See the IM for the Audioscript and more information about music in Guatemala and Honduras.

Después de escuchar

B: Suggestions

- Ask students if they know other ways to say the missing parts in the dialogue. They have learned *¿Qué tal?* and they know another alternative to *quedar* that appears in the dialogue (*nos vemos*).
- Ask students to role-play the call, giving them leeway to improvise. Ask them to focus on the point of the call: to invite a friend to do something together and make a specific plan to meet.

¡Música!

Notes

- Ricardo Arjona (1964–) is very popular in many Spanish-speaking countries. He was also a notable basketball player who played with the Guatemalan national team.
- For helpful tips on using songs in the classroom, see the IM.

A ESCUCHAR

Antes de escuchar

¿Espera Ud. (*Do you wait for*) las rebajas para ir de compras? ¿Para comprar qué tipo de cosas (*things*) busca Ud. rebajas? ¿para comprar ropa? ¿objetos electrónicos?

Escuche

Una llamada telefónica para ir de compras a las rebajas

Unas amigas, Lidia y Cristina, hablan de sus planes para ir de compras. Escuche según las indicaciones de su profesor(a).

Vocabulario para escuchar

la llamada	(telephone) call	**empiezan**	they start
¿Qué onda?	What's up? (*Mexico*)	**¡Qué padre!**	Great! (*Mexico*)
conmigo	with me		

Después de escuchar

A. ¿Cierto o falso? Las siguientes oraciones son falsas. Corríjalas (*Correct them*).

	CIERTO	FALSO
1. Las rebajas empiezan hoy. Empiezan mañana.	☐	☑
2. Cristina tiene clases mañana por la mañana. No tiene clases mañana.	☐	☑
3. Lidia no tiene clases mañana. Tiene clase de literatura.	☐	☑
4. Cristina y Lidia van a encontrarse en la universidad. Van a encontrarse en el centro comercial.	☐	☑
5. Lidia no tiene hermanos. Juana es su hermana.	☐	☑

B. Intercambios. Invente la parte que falta (*is missing*) de los intercambios, usando expresiones del diálogo.

1. —___¿Bueno?___

—Hola, soy yo.

2. —___¿Qué onda?___

—Muy bien. ¿Y tú?

3. —___¿Nos vemos a las 7 en Zara?___

—Perfecto. En Zara, a las 7.

¡Música!

Ricardo Arjona es un cantante internacional y el más famoso de Guatemala. También toca la guitarra y el piano. Ha ganado[a] dos premios Grammy.

La canción «Cómo duele»[b] es del álbum *5to Piso*.[c]

[a]Ha... *He has won* [b]«Cómo... *"It hurts so much"* [c]5to... *5th Floor*

Go to the iMix section in Connect Puntos (**www.connectspanish.com**) to access the iTunes playlist *"Puntos9,"* where you can purchase "Cómo duele" by Ricardo Arjona.

Ricardo Arjona, en Coral Gables, Florida

A ESCRIBIR

El tema

El estilo del campus: Información para los nuevos estudiantes universitarios

Preparar

Paso 1. Haga una lista de la ropa que Ud. necesita para vivir en la universidad. ¿Qué ropa necesita un estudiante para las siguientes ocasiones?

- ir a clase y a la biblioteca
- salir (*to go out*) con amigos
- asistir a eventos en el *campus,* como conciertos o fiestas
- comer en la cafetería
- relajarse (*to relax*) en la residencia o en casa

Paso 2. En general, ¿cree Ud. que los estudiantes necesitan mucha ropa? ¿Qué tipo de ropa es común en su *campus*? ¿Ropa elegante o informal? ¿Hay varios estilos?

Redactar

Imagine que Ud. forma parte del *Freshman Student Orientation Committee* y es responsable de la sección sobre el estilo de ropa en el *campus* para el sitio Web de su universidad. Escriba un ensayo, combinando (*combining*) toda la información de **Preparar.** Sus ideas del **Paso 2** van a ser útiles para el enfoque (*focus*) general del ensayo y para la introducción. Concluya (*Conclude*) el ensayo con una observación general, personal, sobre cómo se visten (*dress*) los estudiantes en su universidad.

Editar

Revise (*Review*) el ensayo para comprobar (*to check*):

- la ortografía y los acentos
- la posición y la concordancia (*agreement*) de los adjetivos descriptivos y los adjetivos posesivos
- la variedad del vocabulario
- la conjugación de los verbos

Finalmente, prepare su versión final para entregarla (*hand it in*).

Preparar

Suggestion

Have students interview each other to gain information and to brainstorm.

Redactar

Suggestions

- Tell students to avoid translating their ideas from English to Spanish. Instead, they should write directly in Spanish, using primarily the grammar and vocabulary they know and/or have seen used in the text.
- Remind students to start the essay with a descriptive opening sentence and to conclude the essay with a summary of any type.
- Suggested length for this writing assignment: approximately 100 words
- Suggested structure (2 paragraphs)

  P. 1. Description of wardrobe, mixing general information (third person plural) with the personal (first person)

  P. 2. Conclusion focusing on campus style

En resumen: En este capítulo

Vocabulario

Reciclado: Review numbers from 0–100 again, then do a quick exercise with numbers from 100–900. Give students a number cue and ask them to give you the corresponding hundreds number: *dos* ⟶ *doscientos,* and so on.

Note

The following vocabulary items were used in direction lines in *Cap. 3* and will be used in subsequent chapters without glossing, but they are not considered to be active until they are listed in *Vocabulario: cambie* (*Ud.*), *empareje, haga, hacer, túrnense.*

Word Families

En este capítulo

- *allá, allí*
- *aquel, aquello*
- *la camisa, la camiseta*
- *ese, eso*

Entre capítulos

- *¿adónde?* = *¿dónde?* (1)
- *al* = *a* (1)
- *allá, allí* = *aquí* (2)
- *de* + noun phrases = *de* (1)
- *la materia* (material) = *la materia* (subject matter) (2)
- *¿no?* = *no* (2)
- *poco/a* (*adj.*) = *poco* (*adv.*) (2)
- *preferir* = *la preferencia* (1)
- *tener* idioms = *tener… años* (3)

¡OJO!

- *la cartera* ≠ *la carta* (3)

Suggestions

- Bring or have students bring magazine clippings with images of people wearing a variety of clothes and colors. Hold up one image and allow students 20 seconds to look at it. Then put it away and have them jot down in Spanish as many things about the picture as they can remember. You might place a volunteer at the board to write his or her version, and use that as a starting point for students to recall what they saw.
- Give students 5 minutes to write a short paragraph that uses as many words from the vocabulary as possible. Find out who used the most words. Have volunteers read their paragraphs.

EN RESUMEN En este capítulo

LearnSmart

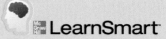

Visit **www.connectspanish.com** to practice the vocabulary and grammar points covered in this chapter.

Gramática en breve

9. Demonstrative Adjectives and Pronouns

this ⟶ *these*	*that/those*	*that/those* (*over there*)
este ⟶ **estos**	**ese** ⟶ **esos**	**aquel** ⟶ **aquellos**
esta ⟶ **estas**	**esa** ⟶ **esas**	**aquella** ⟶ **aquellas**
neuter: **esto**	neuter: **eso**	neuter: **aquello**

10. *Tener, venir, poder, preferir, querer;* Some Idioms with *tener*

tener: tengo, tienes, tiene, tenemos, tenéis, tienen
venir: vengo, vienes, viene, venimos, venís, vienen
poder: puedo, puedes, puede, podemos, podéis, pueden
preferir: prefiero, prefieres, prefiere, preferimos, preferís, prefieren
querer: quiero, quieres, quiere, queremos, queréis, quieren

Idioms with **tener:**

tener miedo de / prisa / razón / sueño
no tener razón
tener ganas de + *inf.* **/ que** + *inf.*

11. *Ir;* The Contraction *al; Ir* + *a* + *Infinitive*

ir: voy, vas, va, vamos, vais, van
a + el ⟶ al

Vocabulario

Remember that changes like **e** ⟶ **ie** and **o** ⟶ **ue** will be shown like this in vocabulary lists.

Los verbos

ir (voy, vas,…)	to go
ir a + *infinitive*	to be going to (*do something*)
poder (puedo)	to be able, can
preferir (prefiero)	to prefer
querer (quiero)	to want
tener (tengo, tienes,…)	to have
venir (vengo, vienes,…)	to come

La ropa

llevar	to wear; to carry; to take
usar	to wear; to use
el abrigo	coat
los aretes	earrings
la blusa	blouse
el bolso	purse
las botas	boots
los calcetines	socks
la camisa	shirt
la camiseta	T-shirt
la cartera	wallet; handbag
las chanclas	flip-flops
la chaqueta	jacket
el cinturón	belt
la corbata	tie
la falda	skirt
la gorra	baseball cap
el impermeable	raincoat
los *jeans*	blue jeans
las medias	stockings
los pantalones	pants
los pantalones cortos	shorts
el reloj	watch
la ropa	clothing
la ropa interior	underwear
las sandalias	sandals
el sombrero	hat
la sudadera	sweatshirt
el suéter	sweater
los tenis	tennis shoes
el traje	suit
el traje de baño	swimsuit
el vestido	dress
los zapatos	shoes

De compras

ir (voy, vas…) de compras	to go shopping
regatear	to haggle, bargain

Repaso: comprar, vender

la ganga	bargain
el precio (fijo)	(fixed, set) price
las rebajas	sales, reductions
¿cuánto cuesta(n)?	how much does it (do they) cost?
de todo	everything
Es de última moda. / **Está de moda.**	It's trendy (hot).

Heritage Speakers

Es muy probable que los hispanohablantes usen otras palabras para hablar de la ropa. Por ejemplo, en algunos países hispanohablantes se dice los *calzoncillos* en vez de *la ropa interior.* Pregúnteles a los hispanohablantes si han oído las siguientes palabras y pídales que den sinónimos de algunas de las palabras de la lista de vocabulario.

la chamarra = *la chaqueta*
los vaqueros = *los jeans*
la bañera, el bañador = *el traje de baño*
la cartera, la bolsa = *el bolso*
la correa = *el cinturón*
la billetera = *la cartera*
los pendientes, los aros = *los aretes*
el púlover/pulóver, el jersey = *el suéter*

Los materiales

de...	
cuadros	plaid
lunares	polka-dot
rayas	striped
es de...	it is made of . . .
algodón (*m.*)	cotton
cuero	leather
lana	wool
oro	gold
plata	silver
seda	silk
el material	material

Los lugares

el almacén	department store
el centro	downtown
el centro comercial	shopping mall
el mercado	market(place)
la tienda	shop, store

Cognado: la plaza

Los colores

amarillo/a	yellow
anaranjado/a	orange
azul	blue
blanco/a	white
(de) color café	brown
gris	gray
morado/a	purple
negro/a	black
rojo/a	red
rosado/a	pink
verde	green

Otros sustantivos

el/la chico/a	guy/girl
el examen	exam, test

Los adjetivos

barato/a	inexpensive
caro/a	expensive
cómodo/a	comfortable
poco/a	little, few

Repaso: mucho/a

Los números a partir del 100

ciento, ciento uno, ciento dos... ciento noventa y nueve, doscientos/as, trescientos/as, cuatrocientos/as, quinientos/as, seiscientos/as, setecientos/as, ochocientos/as, novecientos/as, mil, un millón (de)

Repaso: cien

Las formas demostrativas

aquel, aquella, aquellos/as	that, those ([way] over there)
ese/a, esos/as	that, those
eso, aquello (neuter)	that, that ([way] over there)

Repaso: este/a, esto (neuter)**, estos/as**

Palabras adicionales

¿adónde?	where (to)?
al	to the
allá	(way) over there
allí	there
sobre	about
tener...	
ganas de + *inf.*	to feel like (*doing something*)
miedo (de)	to be afraid (of)
prisa	to be in a hurry
que + *inf.*	to have to (*do something*)
razón	to be right
sueño	to be sleepy
no tener razón	to be wrong
vamos	let's go
¿no? ¿verdad?	right, don't they (you, and so on)?

Repaso: aquí, mucho (*adv.*), **poco** (*adv.*), **tener... años**

Vocabulario personal

Suggestions

- Have a "number bee" competition. Give the contestants increasingly complicated numbers in digit form, and have them say the number in Spanish. Continue until you have one number bee champion.
- Use the *tener* expressions to ask absurd questions. Have students respond with corrections.

  —*¿Tienes miedo de los zapatos?*
  —*No, pero tengo miedo de hablar en público.*

- Remind students about the new verb system for *Puntos de partida*, Ninth Edition: infinitives that are all in color can be found in the verb charts in Appendix 5, stem changes are highlighted with color, and so on.

Chapter Opening Photo and Chapter Theme

Chapter Theme-Related Questions

Draw a house on the board as you mention various rooms.

- *¿Vive Ud. en el centro? ¿en una zona comercial o residencial? ¿en el campus?*
- *¿Vive Ud. en una casa, en un apartamento o en una residencia estudiantil?*

Note: In these questions, the word *casa* is used in a generic sense to mean *housing*.

- *¿Cómo es su casa? ¿Es grande o pequeña? ¿cómoda o incómoda? ¿Es una casa elegante o tradicional? ¿Cuántos cuartos tiene? ¿Y cuántos cuartos de baño?*
- *¿Qué partes de la casa son más importantes para Ud.? ¿Su alcoba? ¿la cocina? ¿el cuarto de baño?* (all new)

Reciclado: Use vocabulary and grammar from previous chapters to discuss the photo. Emphasize adjectives and adjective agreement with this photo, as well as demonstratives and all verbs learned so far.

Heritage Speakers

Pregúnteles a los hispanohablantes si viven en una casa de arquitectura de estilo tradicional latinoamericano. Si alguien contesta que sí, pídale que describa su casa.

5 En casa

Una casa de la ciudad de San Juan del Sur, Nicaragua

- What kinds of housing would you expect to find in a typical Central American town of 100,000 people?
- What is housing like in your area? What types of housing are available? What are the advantages and disadvantages of each?
- What do you think the house in the photo is like inside? Do you think that this home has a garden or patio?

Connect | SPANISH

www.connectspanish.com

Resources

For Students

- Connect Spanish (**www.connectspanish.com**), which contains all content from the following resources, as well as the *Mundo interactivo* scenarios, the LearnSmart adaptive learning system, and more!
- **Physical Resources:** Workbook / Laboratory Manual, Laboratory Audio Program, DVD

For Instructors

- Connect Spanish (**www.connectspanish.com**), which contains access to all student sections of Connect Spanish, as well as helpful time-saving tools and resources such as an integrated gradebook, Instructor's Manual, Testing Program, digital transparencies, Audioscript, Videoscript, and more!

El Salvador

6 millones de habitantes

- El Salvador es el país más pequeño de Centroamérica, pero tiene la densidad de población más alta de la América continental.

Nicaragua

6 millones de habitantes

- Nicaragua tiene diecisiete volcanes y dos lagos inmensos.

En este capítulo

CONTENT / **CONTENIDO**	OBJECTIVES / **OBJETIVOS**
Parts of a House and Furniture 130	To talk about where you live
Days of the Week 132, Prepositions of Time 134	To talk about your routine
The Verbs **hacer, oír, poner, salir, traer, ver** 136, Present Tense of Stem-changing Verbs 142	To express actions
Reflexives 147	To express reflexive actions (*self/selves*) and to talk about your daily routine
El Salvador and Nicaragua 156	To learn about two Central American countries that are rich in natural diversity

El Salvador y Nicaragua

Datos esenciales

The Instructor's Edition will provide basic information about each chapter's country of focus on this chapter opening spread. Additional information (such as geographical features, historical timelines, holidays, and so on) can be found in the IM. There is also additional information about the country of focus in *A leer: Lectura cultural* and *A escuchar* (in both the student text and the Instructor's Edition).

EL SALVADOR

Nombre oficial: *República de El Salvador*
Lema: *«Dios, Unión, Libertad»*
Capital: *San Salvador*
Ciudades importantes: *Santa Ana, San Miguel*
Lengua oficial: *el español*
Composición étnica: *90% mestizos, 9% blancos, 1% indígenas*
Jefe de estado actual: *el Presidente Mauricio Funes, desde 2009*
Forma de gobierno: *República democrática*
Moneda: *el dólar estadounidense*
Religión: *57% católicos, 21% protestantes, 17% sin religión, 5% otras religiones*

NICARAGUA

Nombre oficial: *República de Nicaragua*
Lema: *«En Dios confiamos»*
Capital: *Managua, cuyo nombre viene de Mana-ahuacl, que en nahuatl quiere decir rodeado de agua*
Ciudades importantes: *León, Granada*
Composición étnica: *69% mestizos y blancos, 17% negros, 9% indígenas, 5% otros*
Jefe de estado actual: *el Presidente Daniel Ortega, desde 2007*
Forma de gobierno: *República democrática*
Moneda: *el córdoba*
Religión: *59% católicos, 22% evangélicos, 16% sin religión, 3% otras religiones*

Point out

- El Salvador is the only Central American country that does not have a coastline on the Atlantic.
- The Nacaraguan priest, poet, and author *Ernesto Cardenal* is a major poet known not only in Nicaragua but in the Spanish-speaking world. A Christian-Marxist, *Cardenal* is known as a spokesperson for justice and self-determination in Latin America.
- See the IM for more suggestions.

Multimedia

Instructor's Manual (IM) provides suggestions for using the multimedia materials in the classroom.

Resources: Transparency 48

Vocabulario Preparación

Note

See the model for vocabulary presentation and other material in the *Cap. 5 Vocabulario: Preparación* section of "Chapter-by-Chapter Supplementary Materials" in the IM.

Los muebles, los cuartos y otras partes de la casa (Part 1)

Notes

- Additional vocabulary related to the house and to personal belongings is presented in *Caps. 10* (domestic chores) and *13* (housing). There is too much such vocabulary to present in one chapter, of course. The presentation of these lexical items over a number of chapters presents natural opportunities for review/reentry of this vocabulary, which will be noted in the Instructor's Edition and developed in the student text, as appropriate.
- Note that the word *televisión* is used by most Spanish speakers to express both the medium and the machine; *el televisor* is less frequently used, and it will not be used in *Puntos de partida*. However, a distinction is still made by many Spanish speakers between *el radio* (the machine or *el aparato*) and *la radio* (the medium), a distinction that will be used.
- Point out the difference between *el estudio* (office in a home) and *la oficina* (general business office). *El consultorio* is often used to refer to a doctor or dentist's office.

Suggestions

- Offer optional vocabulary, such as *el balcón, la cama de matrimonio / sencilla, la entrada, el inodoro, la terraza.*
- Point out that *la habitación* (introduced in *Así se dice*) is also used to refer to rooms in general. Other synonyms for *alcoba* include *cuarto, dormitorio, pieza,* and *recámara.*
- Optional vocabulary: Introduce prepositions of place (*Cap. 6*).
- Have students tell the words they associate with the following (*¿Qué palabras asocia Ud. con… ?*): *el coche, los* picnics *o las barbacoas, la ropa, nadar* (pantomime), *estudiar, una cena elegante, las mascotas, los libros*
- Have students tell whether each of the following associations is *lógico* or *ilógico.*

VOCABULARIO Preparación

Los muebles,° los cuartos y otras partes de la casa (Part 1*)

°Los… *Furniture*

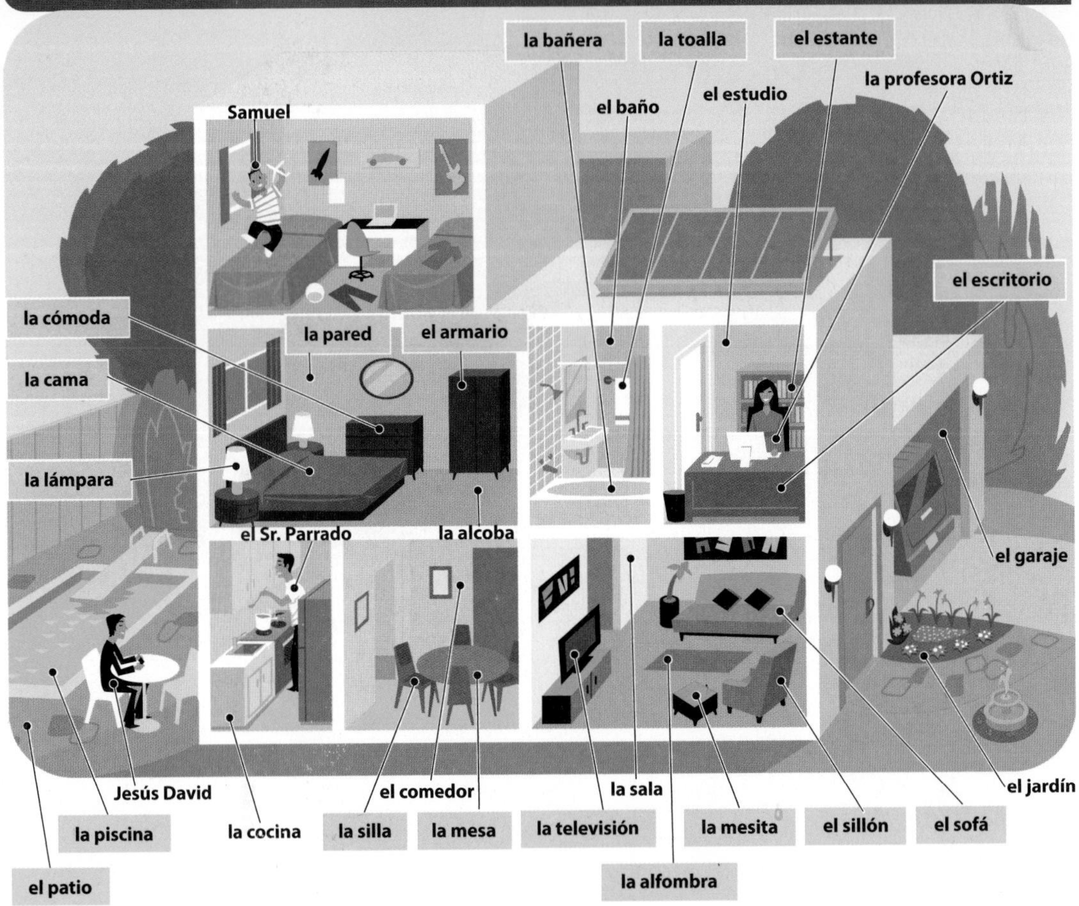

Así se dice

el armario = el ropero
la bañera = la tina
el estudio = el despacho (*Sp.*)
el lavabo = la pileta (*L.A.*)
la piscina = la alberca (*Mex.*), la pileta (*Arg.*)
la sala = el living
la televisión = el televisor

There is great variation in the ways in which Spanish-speakers refer to the bedroom. It is called **la habitación** (also a synonym for any room of a house) by many native speakers, **el dormitorio** by Argentines, and **la recámara** by Mexicans.

This is the first group of words you will learn for talking about where you live and the things found in your house or apartment. You will learn additional vocabulary for those topics in* **Capítulos 10 *and* **12.**

Multimedia: Audio

Students can listen to and practice this chapter's vocabulary in Connect Spanish: **www.connectspanish.com.**

Heritage Speakers

- Explique a la clase que en algunos países hispánicos se usa la palabra *tina* en vez de *bañera*. Pregúnteles a los hispanohablantes cuál de las dos palabras usan, o si usan otra. ¿Qué otros nombres saben o usan para las partes de la casa?
- Anime a los hispanohablantes a describir su casa o apartamento, indicando por ejemplo cuántas plantas tiene, si hay jardín, cuántas habitaciones hay, etcétera.

Resources: Transparency 49

Conversación

A. Asociaciones. ¿Qué cuarto(s) o lugar de la casa asocia Ud. con estas actividades? **¡OJO! se** + *verb* = *one* + *verb.*

1. Es donde se trabaja en la computadora. el estudio
2. Es donde se come con toda la familia. el comedor
3. La parte de la casa para el coche. el garaje
4. Allí se nada (*one swims*). la piscina
5. Allí se duerme (*one sleeps*). la alcoba
6. Es donde se prepara la comida (*food*). la cocina

B. Asociaciones

Paso 1. En parejas, hagan y contesten preguntas para hacer una lista de los muebles o partes de la casa que Uds. asocian con las siguientes actividades.

1. estudiar para un examen
2. dormir la siesta (*to take a nap*) por la tarde
3. pasar (*to spend*) una noche en casa con la familia
4. celebrar con una comida (*meal*) especial
5. lavar (*to wash*) el perro
6. hablar de temas (*topics*) serios con los amigos (padres, esposo/a, hijos)

Paso 2. Ahora comparen sus respuestas con las (*those*) del resto de la clase. ¿Tienen todos las mismas costumbres (*same customs*)?

C. ¿Qué hay en esta casa? En parejas, digan (*say*) los nombres de las partes de esta casa y lo que (*what*) hay en cada cuarto.

MODELO: 7 →
E1: El número 7 es el patio.
E2: ¿Qué hay en el patio? ¿Hay piscina?
E1: No, solo hay plantas.

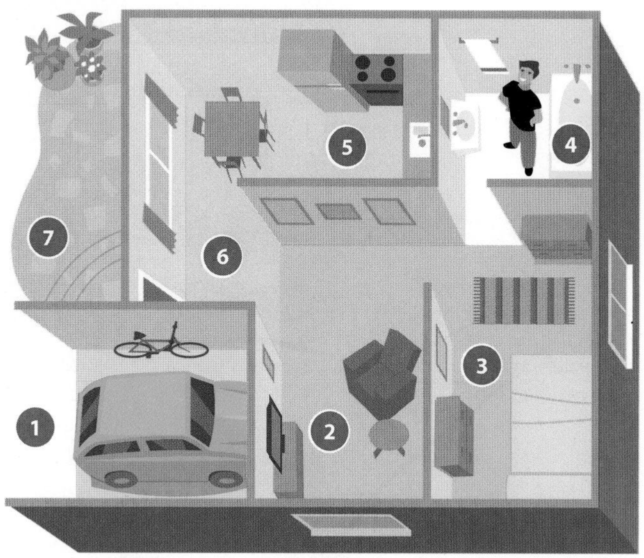

D. Diseño (*Design*) **o decoración**

Paso 1. En parejas, dibujen (*draw*) el plano de un apartamento o casa con al menos (*at least*) dos alcobas y un baño. Luego (*Then*) amueblen (*furnish*) el apartamento o casa con los muebles necesarios. (Si prefieren, pueden dibujar su propio [*own*] cuarto o un cuarto ideal.)

Paso 2. Ahora describan su apartamento o casa a otra pareja de compañeros. Ellos deben dibujar el plano de la casa que Uds. describen sin (*without*) mirar el dibujo de Uds.

1. *los platos y la cocina*
2. *el sofá y la piscina*
3. *el garaje y el coche*
4. *la alcoba y el armario*
5. *la cama y el comedor*
6. *el lavabo y el escritorio*

- Use the vocabulary presentation drawing on p. 130 as the basis for *¿cierto o falso?* statements. For example: *La profesora Ortiz está en la cocina.* (*falso*)
- Have students draw a simple sketch of their bedroom, then describe it to a partner, who tries to draw it based on what he/she hears. Introduce the phrases: *a la derecha, a la izquierda.*
- Ask students the following questions: *¿Tiene Ud. un cuarto o mueble favorito en su casa o apartamento? ¿Cuál es? ¿Por qué lo prefiere?*

Reciclado: Review clothing vocabulary by having students tell what rooms or furniture they associate with the following words: *¿Qué palabras asocia Ud. con… ? la ropa, el traje de baño, la ropa interior, el abrigo, las chanclas*

Pronunciación: See Pronunciation Notes, IM.

Con. B: Note

Active vocabulary: *siguiente*

Con. C: Note

Active vocabulary: *lo que*

Con. C: Redacción

Have students draw the basic floorplan and furniture in their home or their dorm. Then ask them to describe in writing where they live, indicating what they like to do in the different areas. Read some of the best compositions to the class without identifying the writers and ask students to guess who wrote each one.

Con. D: Note

Active vocabulary: *luego, sin*

Con. D: Suggestions

- Allow only a short period for the creation of the drawings in *Paso 1*. Circulate among student pairs to make sure that they are on task and are speaking in Spanish.
- Before starting *Paso 2*, model several descriptive phrases: *Nuestra casa tiene ______ alcobas, ______ baños… En la sala hay un sofá. A la derecha del sofá hay una mesita y una lámpara.*
- Circulate all of the original drawings and allow the class to pick the best designed house.

Resources: Transparency 50

Transparency 32 includes additional vocabulary you may want to present to your students.

Nota cultural

Notes

- Rural estates are often called *haciendas* in Spanish America. The names for them vary widely in Spain: *un cortijo* (*Andalucía*), *un caserío* (Basque region), *una masía* (*Cataluña*), and so on.
- *Patios* (more like courtyards than the typical patio in this country) and *jardines* are a highly valued part of the traditional Hispanic home, although they are not very common in urban areas. They vary in style depending on the area and type of housing.
- In Latin America, many cities have very old (16th century) houses next to modern, contemporary buildings, all sharing the same space.
- Describe some Hispanic houses or house styles you know.
- Ask students who have traveled to a Hispanic country to talk about what they noticed in terms of housing.
- Assign an Internet search for traditional houses from a country of students' (or your) choice.

Comprensión

1. *¿Cómo se dice* home *en español?* (*casa, hogar*)
2. *¿Qué factores influyen en el estilo de las casas de un país? (el uso, la zona, el clima, las tradiciones, el factor económico)*
3. *¿Dónde vive la mayoría de las personas en las ciudades? (en apartamentos)*

¿Qué día es hoy?

Suggestions

- Model the pronunciation of the words in the list.
- Give the day of the week and have students say the next day.
- Have students make associations: *¿Qué día de la semana asocia Ud. con… ? (las fiestas, la religión, el laboratorio de lenguas, la clase de español,* Modern Family *[el programa de la tele], el fin de semana, las elecciones)*
- Emphasize that days of the week are not capitalized in Spanish and that *lunes* is the first day of the week on Hispanic calendars.
- **Optional Vocabulary:** *de hoy en ocho días* = a *week from today*
- Have students respond *sí* or *no.*
  1. *Hoy es* ______.
  2. *Mañana es* ______.
  3. *Ayer fue* ______.
  4. *Pasado mañana es* ______.
  5. *Anteayer fue* ______.

Nota cultural

Las casas en el mundo hispano

La palabra **casa** se usa de manera genérica en español para significar hogar,[a] como en estos ejemplos.

ir/regresar a casa	to go/return home
estar en casa	to be at home
Estás en tu casa.	Welcome. (*Lit.* You're in your home.)

Hay una gran variedad de tipos de casas en el mundo hispano y no se puede decir que haya[b] «una casa típica». Las construcciones dependen del[c] uso, de la zona (rural o urbana), del clima y de las tradiciones históricas y culturales. Y, por supuesto,[d] del factor económico. En las ciudades, la mayoría de las personas no vive en casas sino[e] en apartamentos. Otras palabras para apartamento son **piso** (España) y **departamento** (México, Argentina).

[a]*home* [b]decir… *say that there is* [c]*on the* [d]por… *of course* [e]*but rather*

El Museo Casa Natal de Rubén Darío, en Ciudad Darío, Nicaragua

¿Y su familia? ¿Vive en una casa o en un apartamento? ¿Es común en su ciudad o estado vivir en una casa?

¿Qué día es hoy?

¡OJO!

Do not use **en** with days of the week in Spanish. Use **el** (for singular) or **los** (to generalize), as appropriate.

1. Javier asiste a clase el lunes a las ocho.

2. Javier mira la televisión el martes.

3. Javier va al gimnasio el miércoles.

4. Javier trabaja cuatro horas el jueves.

5. El viernes va al mercado con unos amigos.

6. El fin de semana juega al basquetbol con sus amigos.

NATIONAL STANDARDS: Cultures

Just as the physical aspects of housing vary widely from culture to culture all over the world, so does the sense of "home" and privacy. Hispanics often have a very generous sense of hospitality, and they will offer guests food in abundance, even if the guests have not been invited for a meal. Nevertheless, the Hispanic home is a much more private place than it is for people in this country. See the brief reading about this topic in *Lectura cultural* in this chapter.

Resources: Transparency 51

Hoy es viernes (domingo,...).	Today is Friday (Sunday, . . .).
Mañana es sábado (lunes,...).	Tomorrow is Saturday (Monday, . . .).
Ayer fue martes (miércoles,...).	Yesterday was Tuesday (Wednesday, . . .).
el fin de semana	the weekend
pasado mañana	the day after tomorrow
anteayer	the day before yesterday
el próximo jueves (viernes,...) / **el jueves (viernes,...) que viene**	next Thursday (Friday, . . .)
la semana que viene / **la próxima semana**	next week

- In Spanish-speaking countries, the week usually starts with **lunes.**
- The days of the week are not capitalized in Spanish.
- Except for **el sábado / los sábados** and **el domingo / los domingos,** all the days of the week use the same form for the plural as they do for the singular: **el lunes / los lunes.**

Nota **comunicativa**

Cómo expresar *on* con los días de la semana

The definite article (singular or plural) is used to express **on** with the days of the week in Spanish.

Esta semana, tengo que ir al mercado **el** lunes.
This week, I have to go to the market on Monday.

Por lo general voy al gimnasio **los** domingos.
I generally go to the gym on Sundays.

As in the preceding examples, use **el** before a day of the week to refer to a specific day (**el lunes** = *on Monday*), and **los** to refer to that day of the week in general (**los lunes** = *on Mondays*).

Conversación

A. La semana

Paso 1. Complete las oraciones.

1. Hoy es ________. Mañana es ________.
2. Ayer fue ________ y anteayer fue ________.
3. Si hoy es sábado, mañana es domingo. Ayer fue viernes.
4. Si ayer fue domingo, hoy es lunes y mañana es martes.
5. Hay clase de español los ________, ________ y ________.
6. No tengo clases los ________ ni (*nor*) los ________.
7. Mi próximo examen de ________ es este ________.
8. Trabajo los ________ por la mañana/tarde/noche.
9. Los ________ por la tarde nunca estudio en la biblioteca.
10. Casi todos los ________ salgo (*I go out*) con mis amigos.

Paso 2. En parejas, intercambien (*exchange*) la información de los números 6–10. Luego digan (*tell*) a la clase las actividades que tienen en común.

Pronunciación: See Pronunciation Notes, IM.

Nota comunicativa

- Emphasize that *on Monday* is *el lunes,* and *on Mondays, los lunes.*
- Have students respond *sí* or *no.*
  1. *No tenemos clase el miércoles.*
  2. *Los lunes siempre tenemos examen.*
  3. *En esta universidad, hay clases los sábados.*
  4. *Los domingos es bueno estudiar mucho.*

Con. A: Note

Stress the use in items 2–4 of *ayer* and *anteayer* (item 2).

Con. A: Reciclado

Remind students of meaning of *de la mañana* (*tarde, noche*) in contrast with *por la mañana* (*tarde, noche*).

Con. A: Follow-up

Dictate the following sentences. Have students respond *sí* or *no* to each.

1. *Los viernes por la tarde hay muy pocas personas en la biblioteca, ¿verdad?*
2. *Por lo general, los lunes son días fenomenales, ¿no?*
3. *Los días del fin de semana son martes y miércoles, ¿no?*
4. *Muchas personas no tienen que trabajar los sábados, ¿verdad?*

NATIONAL STANDARDS: Comparisons

Generalizations about housing in the Hispanic world are particularly difficult to make. Features of Hispanic housing in some parts of the world that seem different to some residents of this country include the presence of a room for a servant and the relatively plain exterior of many Hispanic homes, especially compared with their well-decorated interior. Some Hispanics note the following about the housing in this country: the reliance on air conditioning (compared with fresh air ventilation/cooling), and the lawn and extensive landscaping, especially in suburban areas.

NATIONAL STANDARDS

Communication

Have students work in pairs to describe and compare their weekly schedules with their partner's.

Con. B: Reciclado

Note the review of all modal expressions that students have learned to date, plus *ir a*. Emphasize the use of the infinitive following those expressions. Put on the board a list of all verbs students know, plus cognate verbs, and encourage them to use as many verbs as they can in full sentences with the days of the week and the modal expressions.

Con. B: Note

Active vocabulary: *cada, el cine, descansar, por lo general*

Con. B: Redacción

Ask students to write up their list of activities as a composition. Read some of the best compositions to the class without identifying the writers and ask students to guess who wrote each one.

¿Cuándo?: Las preposiciones (Part 1)

Suggestions

- This is the first of two vocabulary sections on prepositions. The second, on spatial relationships, is in *Cap. 6.*
- Model the pronunciation of the prepositions.
- Emphasize the use of *de* with *antes de* and *después de* but not with *durante* or *hasta.*
- Tell students that *antes de* and *después de* can be followed by a noun or an infinitive.
- Review the concept of adverbs and contrast the use of the preposition *después de* with the adverb *después*. Examples: *Estudio después de comer. Estudio y después como.* There are several "sequencing" activities with adverbs later on in this chapter.
- Ask the following questions.
  1. *¿Qué día viene después del miércoles: jueves o domingo? ¿Qué día viene antes del martes: miércoles o viernes?*
  2. *¿Hasta qué hora mira Ud. la televisión los lunes? ¿y los viernes? ¿Hasta cuándo prefiere estudiar cuando tiene un examen?*

Reciclado: The concept of the infinitive following prepositions was seen in *Cap. 4: para* + infinitive, *ir a* + infinitive.

B. Mi semana. Expresse una actividad para cada (*each*) día de la semana, según el modelo.

MODELOS: **El lunes** tengo que ir al gimnasio.
Por lo general (Generalmente) voy al gimnasio **los lunes.**
Voy a ir al gimnasio **el lunes.**

Estrategia

Remember to use an infinitive after **ir a** if you want to use a verb. To express a place after **ir a,** remember to form the contraction **al** if necessary. The infinitive is used after all of the other verbs in the middle column.

lunes martes miércoles jueves viernes sábado domingo	+	ir a + *place* ir a + *inf.* deber desear necesitar poder preferir tener ganas de tener que	+	el bar la biblioteca el centro el cine (*movies*) el gimnasio el museo el parque ¿ ? descansar (*to rest*) en cama hasta muy tarde jugar (*to play*) al (tenis, golf, voleibol, basquetbol) ¿ ?

¿Cuándo? • Las preposiciones (Part 1)*

1. Antes de la fiesta, Rosa prepara la ensalada.

2. Durante la fiesta, Rosa baila.

3. Después de la fiesta, Rosa limpia la sala.

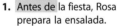

a preposition / **una preposición** = a word or phrase that specifies the relationship of one word to another

The prepositions (as well as the words that they link) are indicated in the first two sentences. Can you pick out the prepositions in the last two?

1. The book is *on* the table.
2. The homework is *for* tomorrow.
3. Los sábados descanso en cama hasta muy tarde.
4. Voy a estar con la familia de mi esposo este fin de semana.

You will learn prepositions that express spatial relationships in the **Vocabulario: Preparación** *section of* **Capítulo 6.**

Resources: Transparency 52

Some common Spanish prepositions you have already used include **a, con, de, en, hasta** (*until*, as in **hasta mañana**), **para,** and **por** (*in, during*, as in **por la mañana**).

¡OJO!

As you know, the infinitive is the only verb form that can follow a preposition.

¿Adónde vas **después de** estudiar?
Where are you going after studying (after you study)?

Conversación

A. ¿Cuándo?

Paso 1. Complete las siguientes oraciones lógicamente. Puede usar sustantivos, infinitivos, días de la semana, etcétera.

1. Por lo general, prefiero estudiar antes de / después de mirar la tele.
2. Siempre tengo mucho sueño durante la clase de ____.
3. Voy a la clase de español antes de / después de ____ la clase de ____.
4. Los ____ (día o días), estoy en la universidad hasta ____ (hora).
5. No puedo ir a fiestas durante la semana. Voy los ____ (día o días).
6. Tengo que estudiar en esta universidad hasta el año ____, para poder graduarme.

Paso 2. Ahora entreviste a (*interview*) un compañero o compañera, usando (*using*) las oraciones del **Paso 1.**

MODELOS: ¿Prefieres estudiar antes de mirar la tele?
¿Prefieres estudiar antes o después de mirar la tele?
¿Cuándo prefieres estudiar, antes o después de mirar la tele?

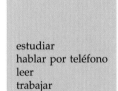

B. Intercambios. En parejas, túrnense para entrevistarse. Hagan sus preguntas, usando una palabra o frases de cada columna.

estudiar hablar por teléfono leer trabajar ¿ ?	+	antes de después de durante hasta	+	tu programa favorito de televisión las clases las conferencias (*lectures*) de ____ los viernes por la noche, los domingos por la mañana... estudiar, mirar la tele,... las tres de la mañana, medianoche (*midnight*), muy tarde,... ¿ ?

Mundo interactivo
You should now be prepared to work with Scenario 3, Activity 1 in Connect Spanish (**www.connectspanish.com**).

Con. B: Reciclado

Review telling time. Write the following times on the board.

9:15 A.M.	7:45 P.M.
1:10 P.M.	3:30 A.M.

Then ask students: *¿Cómo se dice… ?* As students interview each other in *Con. B*, encourage them to ask partners for specific times of day when they provide answers.

Con. B: Follow-up

Use the information in this activity to create a descriptive table of students' habits. Have students try to characterize themselves as a class (*¿trabajadores? ¿estudiosos?*).

Redacción: Ask students to interview the same person in *Paso 2* of *Con. A* and in *Con. B*. They should take notes about the information they learn, then write up what they found out about their partner in the form of a short composition.

Pronunciación

Notes

- Beginning in this chapter, the sounds of Spanish consonants are systematically presented and practiced in the Workbook / Laboratory Manual. For example, the letter *b* and *v* are presented in *Cap. 5* of that ancillary.
- In our experience, the acquisition of native-like pronunciation is a process that occurs over time for most students, so be patient with your students' pronunciation, especially with details like *b* versus *v* (not observed by all native Spanish speakers in this country, for example), the nasalization of the *-ión* ending, and so on.
- The more native or native-sounding Spanish your students hear, the better their pronunciation will be. This point in the text provides a good opportunity for you to stress the use of the various audio-related features of the *Puntos* program.

Heritage Speakers

Explique que algunos hispanohablantes, especialmente los puertorriqueños, pronuncian la *v* en algunas palabras en español como la *v* del inglés. Este fenómeno se debe mayormente al deseo de diferenciar entre los grafemas *b* y *v*. Pídales a varios hispanohablantes que pronuncien la *v* para que sus compañeros oigan cómo la pronuncian.

Gramática 12

¿Recuerda Ud.?

Given the high frequency of use of *tengo* in the beginning chapters of *Puntos de partida,* students should be quite comfortable with this irregularity

Hacer, oír, poner, salir, traer, ver

Note

Drawing 2: If you have not yet introduced *¿cómo?* for asking for clarification or for repetition, take advantage of this opportunity to do so. Some native speakers will also say *¿qué?* in this context, but that usage is not accepted by all Spanish speakers and can sound harsh to some. In Mexico, *¿mande?* is commonly used when asking for clarification.

Follow-up

- Ask students to make statements about their own lives following the model of the sentences in *GEA.*
- Expand the *Comprensión* questions, as follows.
  1. *Haga una lista de todos los objetos que Rigoberto puede tener en la mochila. ¡Un premio* (new) *para la lista correcta más larga!*
  2. *¿Qué dice Rigoberto cuando no oye bien en clase?*
  3. *¿Cuál es el programa favorito de Rigoberto?* (Note: The answer requires real-world information. It is a good idea for you to check the TV listings for the current season before asking this question.)
  4. *¿Quién es Elena?* (Introduce *novia* but ask for other information about her as well: *una estudiante,* ethnic background, and so on.)

Reciclado: Have students restate the *GEA* statements by incorporating the specific times seen in the drawings.

Note

Subject pronouns are not included with this verb chart. You may wish to ask students to identify them.

GRAMÁTICA

¿Recuerda Ud.?

Most of the verbs presented in **Gramática 12** share a first person singular irregularity with two verbs that you learned in **Capítulo 4.** Review what you know about those two verbs by completing their first person forms.

(yo) ven__g__o (yo) ten__g__o

12 Expressing Actions

Hacer, oír, poner, salir, traer, ver

Grammar Tutorial 12
connect SPANISH
www.connectspanish.com

Gramática en acción: Aspectos de la vida de Rigoberto

1. Traigo muchos libros al salón de clase.

2. No oigo bien. Por eso hago muchas preguntas en clase.

3. Pongo la tele y veo mi programa favorito.

4. Salgo con Elena los fines de semana.

Comprensión

1. ¿Qué trae Rigoberto al salón de clase? ¿Qué tiene en la mochila?
2. ¿Por qué hace muchas preguntas en clase? ¿Ve bien? ¿Oye bien?
3. ¿A qué hora pone la tele? ¿Por qué prefiere mirar la tele a esa hora?
4. ¿Con quién sale? ¿Es una relación nueva o vieja?

hacer (*to do; to make*)		**oír** (*to hear*)		**poner** (*to put; to place*)		**salir** (*to leave; to go out*)		**traer** (*to bring*)		**ver** (*to see*)	
hago	hacemos	oigo	oímos	pongo	ponemos	salgo	salimos	traigo	traemos	veo	vemos
haces	hacéis	oyes	oís	pones	ponéis	sales	salís	traes	traéis	ves	veis
hace	hacen	oye	oyen	pone	ponen	sale	salen	trae	traen	ve	ven

Aspects of Rigoberto's life ***1.*** *I bring a lot of books to class.* ***2.*** *I don't hear well. That's why I ask a lot of questions in class.* ***3.*** *I turn on the TV and watch my favorite program.* ***4.*** *I go out with Elena on weekends.*

Heritage Speakers

Anime a los hispanohablantes a hablar de las diferencias entre las generaciones en los países de habla española. ¿Son parecidas a las diferencias generacionales que existen en este país?

Resources: Transparency 53

1. *hacer*

Hacer expresses English *to do* or *to make*. It is also used in a number of common idioms, which are illustrated in the examples at the right.

hacer ejercicio
hacer ejercicios
hacer un viaje
hacer una pregunta

Note that the phrase **hacer ejercicio** is used to express physical exercise; an exception is **hacer ejercicios aeróbicos.** An exercise for an academic class is expressed with **ejercicio** (singular or plural).

¿Por qué no **haces** la tarea?
Why aren't you doing the homework?

Hace ejercicio en el gimnasio, pero **hace ejercicios aeróbicos** en casa.
She exercises in the gym but does aerobics at home.

Alicia **hace los ejercicios** en el cuaderno.
Alicia does the exercises in the notebook.

Quieren **hacer un viaje** al Perú.
They want to take a trip to Peru.

Los niños siempre **hacen muchas preguntas.**
Children always ask a lot of questions.

---

2. *oír*

Oír means *to hear*. The command forms of **oír** are used to attract someone's attention in the same way that English uses *Listen!* or *Hey!*

oye (tú) **oiga** (Ud.) **oigan** (Uds.)

¡OJO!

oír = to hear
escuchar = to listen to
Some native speakers of Spanish use **oír** to mean *to listen to* things like music or the news. But **escuchar** can never mean *to hear.*

Oye, Juan, ¿vas a la fiesta?
Hey, Juan, are you going to the party?

¡Oigan! ¡Silencio, por favor!
Listen! Silence, please!

No **oigo** bien a la profesora.
I can't hear the professor well.

Oímos/Escuchamos música en clase.
We listen to music in class.

No **oigo** bien por el ruido.
I can't hear well because of the noise.

---

3. *poner*

Poner means *to put* or *to place*. Many Spanish speakers use **poner** with appliances to express *to turn on*.

Voy a **poner** la televisión.
I'm going to turn on the TV.

Siempre **pongo** leche y mucho azúcar en el café.
I always put milk and a lot of sugar in my coffee.

---

4. *salir*

Salir means *to leave* or *to go out*. Note in the example at the right how different prepositions are used with it to express different meanings.

salir de + *place*
salir con + *person*
salir para + *destination*

Here's another useful expression: **salir bien/mal,** which means *to turn/come out well/poorly, to do well/poorly.*

Salgo con el hermano de Cecilia.
I'm going out with / dating Cecilia's brother.

Salimos para la sierra pasado mañana.
We're leaving for the mountains the day after tomorrow.

Todo va a **salir bien.**
Everything is going to turn out OK (well).

No quiero **salir mal** en esta clase.
I don't want to do poorly in this class.

Salen de la clase ahora.
They're leaving class now.

Suggestions

- Point out that *hacer, oír, poner, salir,* and *traer* have the irregular *yo* form with a *-g-*.
- You might point out that *hacer,* like *to do* in English, is a "busy" verb, (has many meanings) but that it does not function as a helping verb in questions and negative expressions and for emphasis. Contrast the following sentences, in which the meaning of English *do* is contained in the verbs *oír* and *ver*.

  ¿Oyes eso?
  Do you hear that?
  No veo a Pablo, pero sí veo a su hermano.
  I don't see Pablo but I *do* see his brother.
- Emphasize the spelling change for the second and third person of *oír:* *i* → *y.*

Note

Active vocabulary: *el ruido, la tarea*

Heritage Speakers

Hay muchos hispanohablantes que usan *encender, conectar* o *prender* para expresar *to turn on*. Pregúnteles a los hispanohablantes cómo expresan las siguientes ideas en español.

to turn on . . .
. . . the lights
. . . the television
. . . the oven
. . . the car
. . . the water

Resources: Transparency 54

Suggestions

- Point out that *traer* is an antonym of *llevar.* As with *ir* vs. *venir* (see note in *Gram. 11*), *traer* implies that the speaker is in the place to which something would be brought.
- Remind students that *mirar* is used without a preposition to express *at.*
- Review the *mirar/buscar* contrast if your students are struggling with those two verbs.
- Use the verbs in sentences about yourself, following up with questions about the students.

  Veo las noticias en la televisión antes de clase. ¿Ud. ve la televisión en la mañana?

- Students may complain about the need to sort out the meanings of related verbs in Spanish. It may be useful to give them some examples of English verbs that are equally challenging to non-native speakers of English, especially *to do* and *to make*, which are related but not interchangeable by any means. One *does exercises* but *makes the bed*, *does the dishes* but *makes a pie*, *does one's duty*, but *makes amends*, and so on.

Note

Active vocabulary: *una película*

Preliminary Exercises

- Have students give the corresponding *yo* form to the following *Ud.* forms.

hace	*oye*
trae	*sale*
pone	*ve*

- Have students give the corresponding subject pronouns.

hago	*oímos*
hacemos	*salen*
hacen	*sales*
pongo	*salgo*
pone	*traéis*
pones	*traemos*
oye	*traigo*
oyes	*traes*

Prác. A: Suggestion

Ask students to find the main verb in each sentence and give its infinitive.

5. *traer*

Traer means *to bring.*

¿Por qué no **traes** ese radio a la cocina?
Why don't you bring that radio to the kitchen?

> **¡OJO!**
> **la televisión** (set, medium), but **el radio** (set), **la radio** (medium)

6. *ver*

Ver means *to see.* It can also mean *to watch* as in watching television or a movie, which is also expressed with the verb **mirar.**

No **veo** bien sin mis lentes.
I don't see well without my glasses.

Los niños **ven/miran** una película.
The kids are watching a movie.

> **¡OJO!**
> **Mirar** never expresses *to see* (except with movies). It only means *to watch, look at.*

Autoprueba

Give the correct present tense **yo** forms for these verbs.

1. hacer	**4.** oír
2. ver	**5.** traer
3. poner	**6.** salir

Answers: **1.** *hago* **2.** *veo* **3.** *pongo* **4.** *oigo* **5.** *traigo* **6.** *salgo*

Práctica

A. Cosas rutinarias

Paso 1. ¡Anticipemos! ¿Cierto o falso?

	CIERTO	FALSO
1. Hago ejercicio en el gimnasio con frecuencia.	☐	☐
2. Veo a mis amigos los viernes por la tarde.	☐	☐
3. Nunca salgo con mis primos.	☐	☐
4. Siempre hago los ejercicios para la clase de español.	☐	☐
5. Salgo para la universidad a las ocho de la mañana.	☐	☐
6. Nunca pongo la ropa en la cómoda o en el armario.	☐	☐
7. Siempre traigo todos los libros necesarios a clase.	☐	☐
8. Siempre oigo la radio durante el camino (*on the way*) a la universidad.	☐	☐

Paso 2. Now rephrase each sentence in **Paso 1** as a question and interview a classmate. Use the **tú** form of the verb.

MODELO: Hago ejercicio en el gimnasio con frecuencia. →
¿Haces ejercicio en el gimnasio con frecuencia?

B. Lógicamente

Paso 1. Complete las siguientes oraciones con la forma apropiada de **hacer, oír, poner, salir, traer** o **ver.** Use **no** cuando es necesario para que (*so that*) las oraciones sean (*will be*) apropiadas para Ud.

MODELO: Los estudiantes de esta clase ________ mucha tarea. →
Los estudiantes de esta clase **hacemos/hacen** mucha tarea.

1. (Yo) Pongo/Veo la tele por la noche.
2. Siempre (tú) sales los sábados por la noche con tus amigos.
3. (Nosotros) Traemos el libro de texto de español a clase.
4. Muchas personas no hacen ejercicio.
5. Los hispanos oyen/ponen mucho la radio.
6. Yo pongo azúcar (*sugar*) en mi café.
7. Mi mejor (*best*) amigo va a hacer un viaje a Nicaragua en diciembre.
8. En general, (yo) salgo bien en los exámenes.
9. Me gusta ver películas extranjeras.

Paso 2. Use las respuestas del **Paso 1** para hacerle preguntas a un compañero o compañera. ¿Está siempre de acuerdo con Ud. su compañero/a?

MODELO: Los estudiantes de esta clase **hacemos** mucha tarea. →
¿**Crees que** los estudiantes de esta clase hacemos mucha tarea?

C. Del periódico. Lea el anuncio (*ad*) de un periódico de Venezuela y conteste las preguntas.

1. ¿Cómo se expresan en inglés las primeras dos líneas del anuncio?
2. Encuentre (*Find*) los cognados y las palabras en inglés en el anuncio.
3. ¿Qué tipo de proyectos hace este grupo?
4. ¿Por qué es «intenso» el grupo?

Prác. C: Possible Answers: **1.** You bring the idea . . . We'll do the rest! **2.** Answers will vary. **3.** *proyectos editoriales* **4.** Answers will vary.

Prác. C: Notes

- This piece of realia is from *El Nacional*, a newspaper from Venezuela. While it is not related to the chapter's theme, its use of the verb *poner* and of subject pronouns for emphasis makes it quite useful.
- Note that the meanings of *poner* in this context (*contribute, do,* or *bring*) are not those given in the text's explanation of *poner*. This provides an opportunity to discuss with students the fluidity of language and how they must be open to meanings that are not, strictly speaking, the meanings they have been taught in this text.

Prác. C: Suggestion

If time permits, help students find and express in Spanish the website address of this company and its various e-mail addresses. If you haven't already, give students the following expressions: .com = *punto com;* @ = *arroba.*

Prác. C: Follow-up

Ask students to give their personal e-mail address, that of the university's website, and any other e-mail address that are important to them. Point out that @ = *arroba* and .com = *punto com.*

Con. A: Follow-up

Have students give the Spanish equivalents for the following sentences.

1. I'm going to turn on the TV. I want to turn on the radio.
2. She's going out with her boyfriend (*novio*). He wants to go out with Margarita.
3. She's leaving for Rome tomorrow. I'm leaving for Bogotá on Friday.
4. We have to take a trip. They should ask a question.

Con. A: Reciclado

Have students review clothing vocabulary. Write on the board:

La ropa. Voy a hacer un viaje y en la maleta (new) *voy a poner…*

Divide the class in small groups and have them take turns adding an item to the list of clothing they will pack. Each student must name all the items previously mentioned by others before adding his or her own.

Con. B: Suggestion

Handle one or all three parts of *Con. B* as a whole-class interview activity, with students circulating around the room, asking each group of questions of one student, then moving on to another student with the next group of questions. Ask students to take notes on the answers their interviewees give. Encourage students to ask questions of you as well, reminding them to use *Ud.* questions if that is the form of address that you ask them to use with you. After the interview portion of the activity is completed, ask students to share with the whole class one interesting answer or fact about their interviewee per group of questions.

Con. B: Note

Active vocabulary: *la cosa*

Conversación

A. Consecuencias lógicas. En parejas, indiquen acciones lógicas o consecuencias relacionadas con cada situación. No se limiten a usar los verbos de esta sección del libro. ¡Sean (*Be*) creativos y audaces (*daring*)!

El Lago de Nicaragua, el segundo lago de Latinoamérica por extensión (*size*), con el volcán Maderas al fondo (*in the background*)

Vocabulario útil

gritar (*to shout*) **«¡silencio!»**
hacer una cita to make an appointment
los vecinos neighbors

1. Me gusta esquiar en las montañas. Por eso…
2. Todos los días usamos este libro en la clase de español. Por eso…
3. Mis hijos / compañeros de cuarto hacen mucho ruido en la sala. Por eso…
4. La televisión no funciona. Por eso…
5. Hay mucho ruido en la clase. Por eso…
6. Estoy en la biblioteca y ¡no puedo estudiar más! Por eso…
7. Queremos bailar y necesitamos música. Por eso…
8. No comprendo la lección. Por eso…
9. Me gusta hacer ecoturismo y hablar español. Por eso…

B. Intercambios

Paso 1. En parejas, hagan y contesten las siguientes preguntas.

EN CASA

1. ¿Qué pones en el armario? ¿y en la cómoda? ¿en el cajón (*drawer*) del escritorio?
2. ¿Pones la televisión con frecuencia cuando estás en casa? ¿Qué programa(s) ves todos los días? ¿Qué programa muy popular no ves nunca? (Nunca veo…) ¿Cuál es el canal de televisión que más miras? ¿Por qué te gusta tanto (*so much*)?
3. ¿Pones el radio con frecuencia? ¿Prefieres oír las noticias (*news*) por radio o verlas (*to see them*) en la televisión? ¿Cuál es la estación de radio que más escuchas? ¿Por qué te gusta tanto?

Heritage Speakers

En algunos países hispanos se usa la palabra *clóset* o *placard* en vez de *armario*. Pregúnteles a los hispanohablantes cuál de las tres palabras usan o si usan otra. ¿Hay alguien que use la palabra *ropero*?

MIS ACTIVIDADES

4. ¿Qué haces los _____ (día) por la noche? ¿Cuándo sales con los amigos? ¿Adónde van cuando salen juntos (*together*)?
5. ¿Te gusta hacer ejercicio? ¿Haces ejercicios aeróbicos? ¿Dónde haces ejercicio?

PARA LAS CLASES

6. Generalmente, ¿qué traes a clase todos los días? ¿Crees que traes más cosas (*things*) que tus compañeros o menos? ¿Sales a veces para la clase sin tu libro de texto? ¿sin dinero? ¿Qué trae tu profesor(a) de español a clase?
7. ¿A qué hora sales para las clases los lunes? ¿A qué hora sales de clase los viernes?
8. ¿Cuándo haces la tarea? ¿Por la mañana? ¿Dónde haces la tarea? ¿En casa? ¿Haces la tarea mientras (*while*) ves la televisión? ¿mientras oyes música?
9. ¿Siempre sales bien en los exámenes? ¿En qué clase no sales bien? ¿Qué haces si sales mal en un examen?

Paso 2. Ahora digan a la clase dos o tres cosas que Uds. tienen en común.

MODELO: Jim y yo nunca ponemos la ropa en el armario. Hacemos ejercicio todos los días: Jim hace ejercicios aeróbicos y yo voy al gimnasio. Los dos vemos el programa *House* los lunes por la noche; es nuestro programa favorito.

¿Recuerda Ud.?

The change in the stem vowels of **preferir, querer,** and **poder** follows the same pattern as that of the verbs presented in **Gramática 10.** Review the forms of **preferir, querer,** and **poder** now.

poder: o ⟶ ¿ ?

p*ue*do	**podemos**
p*ue*des	**podéis**
p*ue*de	**p*ue*den**

preferir: e ⟶ ¿ ?

pref*ie*ro	**preferimos**
pref*ie*res	**preferís**
pref*ie*re	**pref*ie*ren**

querer: e ⟶ ¿ ?

qu*ie*ro	**queremos**
qu*ie*res	**queréis**
qu*ie*re	**qu*ie*ren**

If you could complete those verb forms correctly, you already know most of the important information in **Gramática 13.**

¿Recuerda Ud.?

Review *poder, preferir,* and *querer,* pointing out the diphthongization of the stem vowel in stressed positions, but not in the *nosotros* and *vosotros* forms.

Gramática 13

Present Tense of Stem-changing Verbs (Part 2)

Suggestions

- Even though students have not seen the infinitives on which the verbs used in the *GEA* are based, they should be able to generate the *yo* forms. Before doing *¿Y Ud.?*, you may wish to ask students to match the conjugated verb forms with the infinitives.
- Stem-changing verbs are frequently referred to as "shoe verbs" or "boot verbs" to help students remember which forms change and which ones do not. The term "boot" is used in this section.

Note

Active vocabulary: *la bebida*

Follow-up

- Personalize the *¿Y Ud.?* questions by asking follow-up questions of students about their activities not only at parties but in general.
- As a whole-class activity, talk about what makes a successful party and how this party is different, according to the following model: *En una fiesta exitosa hay… En esta fiesta (no) hay…*

13 Expressing Actions

Present Tense of Stem-changing Verbs (Part 2)

Grammar Tutorial 13 connect SPANISH www.connectspanish.com

Gramática en acción: ¿Una fiesta exitosa?

- Aurora duerme en el sofá.
- Samuel juega a las cartas… a solas.
- Ernesto sirve las bebidas. Kevin pide una Coca-Cola.
- Noemí sale y vuelve con más amigas.
- ¿Es una fiesta exitosa? ¿Qué piensa Ud.? ¿Por qué?

¿Y Ud.? ¿Qué hace en las fiestas?

1. ¿Duerme Ud. en el sofá?
2. ¿Juega a las cartas?
3. ¿Sirve las bebidas?
4. ¿Pide Coca-Cola?
5. ¿Sale y vuelve con más amigos?

e → ie: pensar (*to think*)		**o → ue: volver** (*to return*)		**e → i: pedir** (*to ask for; to order*)	
pienso	pensamos	vuelvo	volvemos	pido	pedimos
piensas	pensáis	vuelves	volvéis	pides	pedís
piensa	piensan	vuelve	vuelven	pide	piden

1. **Stem-changing Verbs**
   You have already used three *stem-changing verbs* **(los verbos que cambian el radical): poder, preferir,** and **querer.** And you also know two other verbs that are similar (**tener** and **venir**), but whose first person singular forms are irregular.

A successful party? *Aurora is sleeping on the couch. • Samuel is playing cards . . . alone. • Ernesto is serving beverages. Kevin asks for a Coke. • Noemí leaves and comes back with more friends. • Is it a successful party? What do you think? Why?*

Heritage Speakers

- En México y en algunos dialectos del español del suroeste de los Estados Unidos, el verbo *almorzar* significa *desayunar.* Pregúnteles a los hispanohablantes qué nombres dicen para las comidas del día.
- En algunos dialectos del español del suroeste de los Estados Unidos, se dice *volver (para) atrás* o *regresar* por *devolver.* Explique la diferencia entre *volver, devolver* y *regresar.*

Resources: Transparency 55

2. Stem Vowel Changes
In these verbs, the stem vowels **e** and **o** become **ie** and **ue**, respectively, in stressed syllables. There is also another group in which the stem vowel **e** becomes **i**. The stem-changing pattern of all three groups is shown at the right. The stem vowels are stressed (and so they change) in all present tense forms except **nosotros** and **vosotros.** All three groups follow this regular pattern, which looks like a boot.

Las vocales que cambian en el radical

e → ie	-ie-	-e-
	-ie-	-e-
	-ie-	-ie-
o → ue	-ue-	-e-
	-ue-	-e-
	-ue-	-ue-
e → i	-i-	-e-
	-i-	-e-
	-i-	-i-

¡OJO!
Nosotros and **vosotros** forms *do not* have a stem vowel change.

3. Important Stem-changing Verbs
Some stem-changing verbs practiced in this chapter include the following.

e → ie

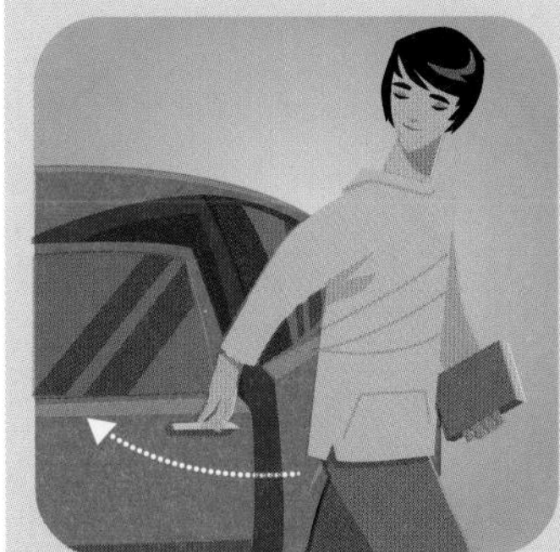

cerrar (cierro)
(*to close*)

empezar (empiezo)	to begin, start
entender (entiendo)	to understand
pensar (pienso)	to think
perder (pierdo)	to lose; to miss (*an event*)

o (u) → ue

dormir (duermo)
(*to sleep*)

almorzar (almuerzo)	to have lunch
jugar* (juego)	to play (*a game, sport*)
volver (vuelvo)	to return (*to a place*)

e → i

servir (sirvo) (para)
(*to serve; to be used* [*for*])

pedir (pido)	to ask for; to order

As you learned with **poder, preferir,** and **querer,** stem-changing verbs will be indicated in vocabulary lists with the **yo** form in parentheses, as shown here.

*__Jugar__ *is the only* **u → ue** *stem-changing verb in Spanish.* **Jugar** *is usually followed by* **al** *when used with the name of a sport:* **Juego al tenis.** *Some Spanish speakers, however, omit the* **al.**

Resources: Transparency 56

Emphasis 1: Suggestion

Write one of the verb paradigms on the board and draw a boot around the stem-changing verbs to help illustrate the pattern.

Emphasis 3: Suggestions

- True beginning students will sometimes want all of these verbs to be conjugated for them in the text. To do so would only increase students' reliance on the text rather than help them to recognize and apply patterns. To alleviate students' anxiety, stress that all of these verbs follow the same pattern that students have already learned with *poder, preferir,* and *querer,* and, if necessary, conjugate each infinitive with them so that they grasp the pattern clearly. The only new information here is the third class of stem-changing verbs (*e → i*) and the eleven new verbs listed here.
- Model infinitives you have not yet presented, creating a brief conversational exchange with each.
- Emphasize the spelling differences between *perder* and *pedir.*
- Model verbs with infinitives to emphasize the use of prepositions with some and not with others: *empezar a* + infinitive; *volver a* + infinitive; *pensar* + infinitive.
- Model sentences with *servir para: El lápiz sirve para escribir; El libro sirve para leer;* and so on.
- Tell students that *volver* means *to return* (*to a place*) and *devolver* means *to return* (*something*). *Devolver* will become active in *Cap. 17.*
- With students, turn to the end-of-chapter vocabulary section (pp. 160–161) for this chapter and show them how stem-change verbs are indicated (with the first person singular form). Do the same for the end-of-book vocabulary (Vocabularies, p. V-1).
- You may wish to introduce additional stem-changing verbs in this section. Be aware, however, that an additional list of new verbs (used with reflexive pronouns) will be introduced in *Gram. 14* in this chapter, so the "new verb load" of this chapter is already high.
- Optional verbs: *o → ue: devolver, encontrar, recordar; e → i: decir, mentir, repetir*

Emphasis 4, 5: Reciclado
Note the reentry of modal verbs from previous chapters.

Emphasis 5: Optional
The expression *pensar de* is used in Spanish to indicates one's opinion of someone or something: *¿Qué piensas de esta situación?*

Preliminary Exercises

- Have students give the correct form of each verb for the subject given.

yo:	*cerrar*	*almorzar*
	empezar	*pedir*
	entender	
tú:	*pensar*	*jugar*
	preferir	*dormir*
Ud./él/ella:	*perder*	*volver*
	empezar	*servir*
nosotros:	*empezar*	*jugar*
	preferir	*volver*
vosotros:	*pensar*	*dormir*
	cerrar	*servir*
	entender	
Uds./ellos/ ellas:	*preferir*	*jugar*
	almorzar	*pedir*

- Have students give new sentences based on the subject cues.
  1. *Sara y Anita almuerzan en el patio.*
     Ud. — *tú*
     nuestros hijos — *yo*
     nosotros — *vosotros*
  2. *Felipe pide un café.*
     yo — *Lisa*
     nosotros — *tú*
     ellos — *vosotros*
  3. *Yo prefiero descansar en la sala.*
     Sergio — *ellas*
     nosotros — *tú*
     Ana — *vosotras*
  4. *Yo pierdo muchas cosas.*
     ellos — *tú*
     yo — *los niños*
     Fernando — *vosotros*
  5. *Los González vuelven el sábado.*
     yo — *Manuel*
     nosotras — *tú*
     mis primas — *vosotros*

Prác. A: Note

Active vocabulary: *la llave*

Prác. A: Reciclado

- Ask students to think about all of the verbs they have learned so far as associations for the cues in this activity.
- Give students the following verb cues and ask them to name a stem-changing verb that they associate with it: *abrir, comer, leer, creer, descansar, terminar* (new), *tener razón, salir, aprender, comprender, buscar, regresar.*
- Give students the following place names and ask them to name a stem-changing verb that they associate with it: *la cafetería, la alcoba, el comedor, la residencia, el parque, el salón de clase, el garaje.*
- Use *servir* to review classroom vocabulary: *¿Para qué sirve el lápiz?* → *Sirve para escribir.* Other objects that can be used in this pattern: *el pizarrón blanco, la computadora, el libro, el cuaderno, el bolígrafo.*

4. *Verb + **a** + Infinitive*
Like **aprender** and **ir,** the stem-changing verbs **empezar** and **volver** are followed by **a** before an infinitive. The meaning of **empezar** does not change in this structure, but **volver a** + *infinitive* expresses *to do (something) again.*

Uds. **empiezan a hablar** muy bien el español.
You're starting to speak Spanish very well.

¿Cuándo **vuelves a jugar** al tenis?
When are you going to play tennis again?

5. *Conjugated Verb + Infinitive*
Like other verbs you already know (**desear, necesitar, deber,...**), **pensar** can be followed directly by an infinitive. In that case, it expresses *to intend, plan.*

The phrase **pensar en** can be used to express *to think about.*

¿Cuándo **piensas** almorzar?
When do you plan to eat lunch?

—¿**En** qué **piensas**?
—**Pienso en** las cosas que tengo que hacer el domingo.
"What are you thinking about?"
"I'm thinking about the things I have to do on Sunday."

6. Present Tense Equivalents
Remember that the Spanish present tense has a number of present tense equivalents in English. It can also be used to express future meaning.

cierro = *I close, I am closing, I will close*

Stem-Change Summary

empezar (empiezo)
jugar (juego)
volver (vuelvo)
pedir (pido)

Autoprueba

Complete the verb forms with the correct letters.

1. ent_____ndemos
2. d_____rmo
3. c_____rras
4. j_____gan
5. s_____rve
6. alm_____rzo

Answers: **1.** *entendemos* **2.** *duermo* **3.** *cierras* **4.** *juegan* **5.** *sirve* **6.** *almuerzo*

Práctica

A. Asociaciones

Paso 1. Dé por lo menos un infinitivo que asocia con las siguientes ideas y cosas.

1. una bebida servir
2. una lección entender
3. la casa volver (a)
4. una cama dormir
5. una hamburguesa almorzar, pedir
6. el tenis jugar
7. una opinión pensar
8. una puerta cerrar
9. las llaves (*keys*) perder

Paso 2. Explique para qué sirven las siguientes cosas.

MODELO: las cartas → **Sirven para** jugar.

1. las llaves Sirven para abrir una puerta.
2. un diccionario Sirve para entender.
3. una bandeja (*tray*) Sirve para servir.
4. un menú Sirve para pedir.

B. ¡Anticipemos!

Paso 1. ¿Cierto o falso? Si la declaración es cierta, diga en qué lugar de la casa o de la universidad Ud. hace las siguientes cosas.

1. Duermo la siesta casi todos los días.
2. Cierro la puerta para dormir la siesta.
3. Almuerzo solo/a (*alone*) con frecuencia.
4. Juego a las cartas con mis padres (mis hijos, mi esposo/a).
5. Por la mañana, pienso en las cosas que tengo que hacer.
6. Con frecuencia pido una pizza para almorzar.
7. Pierdo mis llaves con frecuencia.
8. Vuelvo a leer la lección de español antes de la clase.
9. Hay mucho que no entiendo en la clase de matemáticas.

Paso 2. En parejas, túrnense para entrevistarse, usando las declaraciones del **Paso 1.**

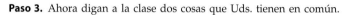

MODELO: ¿**Duermes** la siesta casi todos los días?

Paso 3. Ahora digan a la clase dos cosas que Uds. tienen en común.

MODELO: Nosotras dormimos la siesta casi todos los días. Dormimos en un sofá en una sala del centro estudiantil.

C. Una tarde típica en casa. ¿Cuáles son las actividades de todos? Haga oraciones completas, usando una palabra o frase de cada columna.

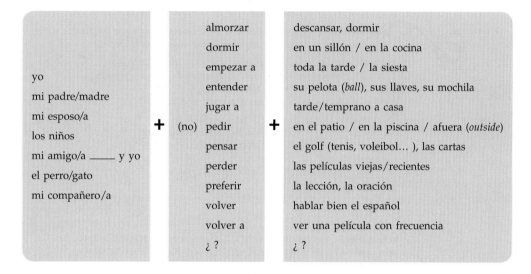

yo	+	(no) almorzar	+	descansar, dormir
mi padre/madre		dormir		en un sillón / en la cocina
mi esposo/a		empezar a		toda la tarde / la siesta
los niños		entender		su pelota (*ball*), sus llaves, su mochila
mi amigo/a _____ y yo		jugar a		tarde/temprano a casa
el perro/gato		pedir		en el patio / en la piscina / afuera (*outside*)
mi compañero/a		pensar		el golf (tenis, voleibol...), las cartas
		perder		las películas viejas/recientes
		preferir		la lección, la oración
		volver		hablar bien el español
		volver a		ver una película con frecuencia
		¿ ?		¿ ?

Prác. B: Suggestion

Ask students to find the main verb and give the infinitive in each sentence. Pay particular attention to the stem vowel in each case.

Prác. B: Note

Active vocabulary: *dormir la siesta, solo/a*

Prác. C: Optional

Use *pensar* + inf. and *volver/empezar a* + inf. in conversational exchanges with students.

1. *¿Dónde piensa Ud. almorzar mañana? ¿Dónde no vuelve a almorzar nunca?*
2. *¿Qué película / conjunto musical* (new) *piensa ver este fin de semana? ¿Qué película / conjunto musical no vuelve a ver nunca?*
3. *En esta clase, ¿quién empieza a hablar más / hablar muy bien el español?*

Prác. C: Reciclado

Use the activity to review the words for family members.

NATIONAL STANDARDS: Cultures

A *siesta* is a short nap taken in the early afternoon, often after the midday meal. The word *siesta* comes from the Latin *sexta,* the sixth hour, counting from dawn to the midday hour. Although *siestas* are a tradition in Latin America and in Spain, the custom is not as common as it used to be.

Con. A: Suggestions

- Assign *Paso 1* as homework and do *Paso 2* in class the following day.
- Create your own agenda and share it with the class before starting *Paso 2*. Be sure to include a number of things you want to do but would not normally do. Allow students time to edit their own agendas before continuing.

Con. A: Follow-up

Students report the actions they have in common: *Jim y yo pensamos dormir una siesta el domingo por la tarde.*

Redacción: Use either *Paso 1* or *Paso 2* or both as the basis for a writing assignment. Give students models for the use of modal verbs in their compositions: *El lunes por la mañana voy a _____. Por la tarde pienso _____. Por la noche tengo que _____.*

Con. A: Optional

In pairs students think of an action with 5–6 of the stem-changing verbs they know that they think could be done by the instructor: *La profesora sirve (va a servir) la comida el domingo.* You say whether you will do the activity described and extend the conversation, as appropriate: *No sirvo la comida el domingo, pero sí sirvo la comida el sábado. En esta clase, ¿quién va a servir la comida esta semana? ¿Cuándo?*

¿Recuerda Ud.?

Suggestion

Review the *llamarse* phrases students already know by identifying yourself, asking students to turn to each other and ask each other's name, and asking third person questions such as: *¿Cómo se llama el presidente / primer ministro? ¿el rector / la rectora de la universidad?* Stress the third person form (with *se*), which is the one students will have used the least.

Emphasis

Stress that, if students could do the brief *¿Recuerda Ud.?* exercise, they already know half of the grammar that is presented in *Gram. 14*

Conversación

A. Una semana ideal... ¡y posible!

Paso 1. ¿Qué va a hacer Ud. la semana que viene? Organice la próxima semana en la siguiente agenda. Escriba frases con el infinitivo, por ejemplo: **ver la televisión.** Incluya actividades que tiene que hacer, pero también algunas (*some*) que tiene ganas de hacer.

Estrategia

e → ie
o → ue
e → i

	por la mañana	por la tarde	por la noche
lunes			
martes			
miércoles			
jueves			
viernes			
sábado			
domingo			

Paso 2. En parejas, hablen de su horario (*schedule*) para esta semana, basándose (*based on*) en la agenda del **Paso 1.**

MODELO: ver la televisíon →
E1: ¿Qué **piensas** hacer el domingo por la tarde?
E2: **Pienso** ver la televisión. Y tú, ¿qué haces el domingo?
E1: El domingo **juego** al tenis con mi amigo Alex.

B. Intercambios. En parejas, túrnense para hacer y contestar preguntas sobre los temas (*topics*) siguientes con las frases sugeridas (*suggested*).

MODELOS: almorzar (¿dónde? ¿con quién? ¿a qué hora?) →
Por lo general, ¿dónde **almuerzas** de lunes a viernes?
¿Con quién **vas a almorzar** hoy?
¿A qué hora **piensas almorzar** el domingo?

Estrategia

generalizations: present tense
future: **ir** + **a** + *inf.*
definite plans: **pensar** + *inf.*

1. almorzar (¿dónde? ¿con quién? ¿a qué hora?)
2. perder (¿qué? ¿dónde? ¿con frecuencia? ¿siempre?)
3. dormir (¿cuántas horas? ¿mucho o poco? ¿siestas frecuentes o infrecuentes? ¿largas o cortas?)
4. jugar (¿juegos de mesa [*board games*]? ¿cuáles? ¿con quién? ¿dónde?)

¿Recuerda Ud.?

In **Capítulo 1,** you learned how to ask what someone's name is and express your own name by using phrases with the verb **llamar.** Show what you remember by completing the following phrases.

1. (yo) _me_ llamo **2.** (tú) _te_ llamas **3.** Ud. _se_ llama

The words with which you completed those phrases are part of a pronoun system that you will learn about in **Gramática 14.**

14 Expressing *-self/-selves*

Reflexive Pronouns (Part 1)*

Grammar Tutorial 14
connect SPANISH
www.connectspanish.com

Gramática en acción: La rutina diaria de Andrés

La rutina de Andrés empieza a las siete y media.

1.

2.

3.

4.

(1) Me despierto a las siete y media y me levanto en seguida. Primero, (2) me ducho y luego (3) me cepillo los dientes. (4) Me peino, (5) me pongo la bata y (6) voy al cuarto a vestirme. Por fin, (7) salgo para la universidad. No tomo nada antes de salir porque, por lo general, ¡tengo prisa!

5.

6.

7.

¿Y Ud.? ¿Cómo es su rutina diaria?

1. Yo me levanto a las _____.
2. Me ducho por la mañana/noche.
3. Me visto en el baño / mi cuarto.
4. Me peino antes de / después de vestirme.
5. Antes de salir para las clases, tomo / no tomo el desayuno.

Reflexive Pronouns / Los pronombres reflexivos

bañarse (*to take a bath*)

(yo)	**me baño**	I take a bath	(nosotros)	**nos bañamos**	we take baths
(tú)	**te bañas**	you take a bath	(vosotros)	**os bañáis**	you take baths
(Ud.)	**se baña**	you take a bath	(Uds.)	**se bañan**	you take baths
(él)	**se baña**	he takes a bath	(ellos)	**se bañan**	they take baths
(ella)	**se baña**	she takes a bath	(ellas)	**se bañan**	they take baths

Andrés's daily routine *Andrés's routine begins at seven-thirty. (1) I wake up at seven-thirty and I get up right away. First, (2) I take a shower and then (3) I brush my teeth. (4) I comb my hair, (5) I put on my robe, and (6) I go to my room to get dressed. Finally, (7) I leave for the university. I don't eat or drink anything before leaving because I'm generally in a hurry!*

You will learn more about using reflexive pronouns to express* each other *in* **Gramática 32 (Cap. 11).

Gramática 14
Reflexive Pronouns (Part 1)

Suggestions

- Point out the sequencing adverbs in *GEA*: *primero, luego, por fin*. There is follow-up with this material in the *Nota comunicativa* on page 150.
- Read the descriptions of the drawings, out of order, and ask students to identify the appropriate drawing by number.
- Put the descriptions, out of order, on the board or on an overhead transparency, and ask students to put them in order.

Note

Active vocabulary: *en seguida, por fin, primero, la rutina diaria*

Follow-up

Have students respond *cierto* or *falso* based on their own situations.

1. *Me despierto temprano.*
2. *Me levanto a las seis.*
3. *El sábado me levanto a las siete.*
4. *Prefiero bañarme por la mañana.*
5. *Me gusta acostarme a las diez.*
6. *El sábado me acuesto a las doce.*

Resources: Transparency 57

Reflexive Pronouns

Suggestion

Contrast *I bathe the kids* with *I bathe* (*myself*) (*I take a bath*). In the first sentence, the subject and object are different; in the second they are the same person (the object pronoun reflects the subject).

Emphasis 1: Suggestion

Refer students to *Gram. 2* and to the vocabulary list to see the *-se* at the end of reflexive verbs.

Emphasis 2: Suggestions

- Contrast *vestirse* (no need to specify the item of clothing) vs. *ponerse* and *quitarse* + clothing (i.e., used with specific items of clothing). Native speakers would not generally say *me pongo la ropa; vestirse* is used instead. However, *quitarse la ropa* is commonly used; the use of *desvestirse* is less frequent.
- **Optional:** Parts of the body for use with *lavarse: la cara, las manos, el pelo*. (Body parts are presented in the *Vocabulario: Preparación* sections of *Caps. 11* and *14*.)
- Model verbs from the chart in a conversational setting, saying sentences about yourself and following up with questions to students.

  Generalmente me acuesto a las once. Y Ud., ¿a qué hora se acuesta?
- Rapid response drill. Ask students short, yes/no questions, using all of the verbs in the chart.

  ¿Se baña? ⟶ *Sí, me baño.*
  ¿Se bañan? ⟶ *Sí, nos bañamos.*

Note

Many native speakers say *lavarse los dientes* instead of *cepillarse los dientes*. (Stress the use of the definite article with *dientes*.)

Emphasis 4: Suggestions

- Emphasize the change in meaning of some verbs: *dormir* (to sleep) vs. *dormirse* (to fall asleep); *poner* (to put, place) vs. *ponerse* (to put on).
- Point out that other verbs can change meaning in the reflexive. Write the following examples on the board:

nonreflexive	meaning	reflexive	meaning
caer (not active)	to fall	*caerse* (not active)	to fall down
comer	to eat	*comerse*	to eat (*something*) up
decidir	to decide	*decidirse*	to make up one's mind
ir	to go	*irse*	to go away

(cont.) ⟶

1. Reflexive Pronouns

The pronoun **se** at the end of an infinitive indicates that the verb is used reflexively. The *reflexive pronoun* (**el pronombre reflexivo**) in Spanish reflects the subject doing something to or for himself, herself, or itself. When the verb is conjugated, the reflexive pronoun that corresponds to the subject must be used.

Los pronombres reflexivos

me	myself	nos	ourselves
te	yourself (*fam., sing.*)	os	yourselves (*fam. pl. Sp.*)
se	himself, herself, itself; yourself (*form. sing.*)	se	themselves; yourselves (*form. pl.*)

bañarse = to take a bath (to bathe oneself)
me baño = I take a bath (bathe myself)
te bañas = you take a bath (bathe yourself)

¡OJO!

Many English verbs that describe parts of one's daily routine—to get up, to take a bath, and so on—are expressed in Spanish with a reflexive construction.

2. Important Reflexive Verbs

Here are some reflexive verbs you will find useful as you talk about daily routines.

¡OJO!

Notice that some of these reflexive verbs also have stem changes: **e ⟶ ie, o ⟶ ue, e ⟶ i.**

despertarse (me despierto) | **ducharse** | **afeitarse** | **vestirse (me visto)** | **sentarse (me siento)**

Note the **-se** on the end of these infinitives. This is how reflexive verbs will be shown in vocabulary lists.

acostarse (me acuesto)	to go to bed	**ducharse**	to take a shower
afeitarse	to shave	**levantarse**	to get up (out of bed); to stand up
bañarse	to take a bath	**llamarse**	to be called
cepillarse los dientes	to brush one's teeth	**peinarse**	to brush/comb one's hair
despertarse (me despierto)	to wake up	**ponerse (me pongo)**	to put on (*an article of clothing*)
divertirse (me divierto)	to have a good time, enjoy oneself	**quitarse**	to take off (*an article of clothing*)
		sentarse (me siento)	to sit down
dormirse (me duermo)	to fall asleep	**vestirse (me visto)**	to get dressed

Heritage Speakers

Pídales a los hispanohablantes que escriban una breve composición en la que describan un día típico de su vida.

Resources: Transparency 58

3. **Placement of Reflexive Pronouns**
Reflexive pronouns are placed before a conjugated verb. In a negative sentence, they are placed between the word **no** and the conjugated verb: **No *se* bañan.**

When a conjugated verb is followed by an infinitive, the pronouns may either precede the conjugated verb or be attached to the infinitive.

Me levanto temprano todos los días.
I get up early every day.
No me levanto temprano todos los días.
I do not get up early every day.

Me tengo que levantar temprano.
Tengo que **levantarme** temprano.
I have to get up early.

Debo **acostarme** más temprano.
Me debo acostar más temprano.
I should go to bed earlier.

4. **Nonreflexive Use of Verbs**
All of these verbs can also be used nonreflexively, often with a different meaning. Some examples of this appear at right.

dormir = to sleep	**dormirse** = to fall asleep
poner = to put, place	**ponerse** = to put on

¡OJO!
After **ponerse** and **quitarse,** the definite article, not the possessive as in English, is used with articles of clothing.

Se pone el abrigo.
He's putting on his coat.

Se quitan el sombrero.
They're taking off their hats.

¡OJO!
The reflexive pronoun must be repeated with each verb in a series of verbs.

Me levanto a las siete, **me ducho** y **me visto** antes de peinar**me.**

Mi esposo **se baña,** yo **me ducho** y los dos **nos peinamos** antes de las seis.

Reflexive Pronoun Summary

yo	→	me
tú	→	te
Ud., él, ella	→	se
nosotros/as	→	nos
vosotros/as	→	os
Uds., ellos, ellas	→	se

Autoprueba

Match each reflexive pronoun with the correct verb form.

1. se ____	a. bañas
2. nos ____	b. afeitamos
3. te ____	c. acuesto
4. me ____	d. levanta

Answers: **1.** d **2.** b **3.** a **4.** c

Práctica

A. Asociaciones. Dé todas las palabras que pueda (*you can*) asociar con los siguientes infinitivos. Piense (*Think*) en grupos de palabras que Ud. ya conoce (*you already know*): los cuartos de una casa, los muebles, la ropa, otros verbos, los adverbios, etcétera.

1. llamarse	**3.** bañarse	**5.** vestirse	**7.** divertirse
2. levantarse	**4.** sentarse	**6.** despertarse	**8.** acostarse

Prác. A: Possible Answers: **1.** *el nombre* **2.** *tarde* **3.** *el cuarto de baño, la toalla* **4.** *la silla* **5.** *los pantalones cortos* **6.** *la cama* **7.** *jugar* **8.** *la alcoba*

Bright Idea

Suggestion

Point out that, after the verbs *ponerse* and *quitarse,* the definite article and the singular form of clothing are used in Spanish, whereas English frequently uses a possessive adjective and the plural. Compare the following.

The children take off their hats.
Los niños se quitan el sombrero.

The children put on their coats.
Los niños se ponen el abrigo.

In some cases, where each individual has two of any given object, the plural form is used in Spanish.

Se ponen los zapatos / los guantes (new) */ los calcetines.*

Preliminary Exercises

- Have students give the subject pronoun that corresponds to each reflexive pronoun.

  te me nos os

  Ask what subject pronouns correspond to the reflexive pronoun *se.*
- Have students give the *yo* form of the following verbs.

  bañarse, ponerse, levantarse, despertarse, ducharse, dormirse, vestirse, acostarse
- Read the following sentences and have students tell whether they are reflexive or not.
  1. *María se despierta a las ocho de la mañana.*
  2. *María acuesta a los niños a las nueve de la noche.*
  3. *Se quita la ropa.*
  4. *Baña a los niños.*
  5. *María se sienta.*
  6. *Sienta a los niños.*
  7. *Levanta a los niños a las siete.*
  8. *Todos se divierten.*

Prác. A: Reciclado

Note the cue to students to use previously learned vocabulary. When you are doing activities of this type, suggest to students that they use the end-of-chapter vocabulary lists of preceding chapters for reference.

Prác. A: Suggestions

- Make this activity a contest with a prize for the student who comes up with the longest correct list in the time period. Try giving students only 3 minutes total to come up with their lists.
- Do the activity in reverse, as has generally been done with activities of this type (which practice only the meaning of new infinitives, not their conjugation). Possible cue items: *la cama, el lavabo, comer, los amigos, descansar, por la mañana, la ropa, el cuarto de baño, el pelo* (new), *la barba* (new)

Prác. B: Suggestion

Ask students to find the main verb in each sentence and give the infinitive. Pay particular attention to the need to use *-se* with the infinitive.

Prác. B: Variation

Have students correct the sentences to express what they actually do.

Prác. C: Extension

Have students use the cues to create sentences about their friend(s), boy/girlfriend, father/mother, spouse, grandchildren, and so on. Continue the activity for as long as it is interesting to students. To start off this activity, create an interesting example from your own circle, using an unusual person: a small child, a pet, an elderly relative, and so on.

Nota comunicativa

Active vocabulary: *después, finalmente* (others already active)

B. ¡Anticipemos! Su rutina diaria

Paso 1. ¿Hace Ud. lo mismo (*the same thing*) todos los días? Indique los días que hace las siguientes cosas.

	LOS LUNES	LOS SÁBADOS
1. Me levanto antes de las ocho.	☐	☐
2. Siempre me baño o me ducho.	☐	☐
3. Siempre me afeito.	☐	☐
4. Me pongo un traje / una falda.	☐	☐
5. Me quito los zapatos después de llegar a casa.	☐	☐
6. Me acuesto antes de las once de la noche.	☐	☐

Paso 2. ¿Es diferente su rutina los sábados? ¿Qué día prefiere? ¿Por qué?

Nota **comunicativa**

Cómo expresar una secuencia de acciones

The following adverbs and expressions will help you indicate the sequence of actions or events.

primero	first	**finalmente**	finally
después	then, later	**por fin**	finally
en seguida	immediately		
luego	then, afterward, next		

Primero, me ducho y me visto. **Luego,** tomo un café y leo el periódico. **Después,** me cepillo los dientes. **Finalmente,** salgo para el trabajo.

C. Mi rutina diaria

Paso 1. ¿Qué acostumbra Ud. hacer en un día típico? Use las siguientes frases para describir su rutina diaria. Añada (*Add*) otras ideas si quiere. Use las palabras de la **Nota comunicativa** en sus oraciones.

MODELO: despertarse a (hora) → Me despierto a las siete y me levanto **en seguida. Luego** me ducho. Me visto en la alcoba y **después** voy a la cocina para tomar café. **Finalmente** salgo…

1. despertarse a (hora)
2. levantarse a (hora)
3. (no) ducharse/bañarse por la mañana
4. vestirse antes/después de tomar algo
5. ir a la universidad y asistir a (número) clases
6. almorzar a (hora) y sentarse en (lugar) para estudiar
7. volver a (lugar) a (hora)
8. comer con (otra persona / otras personas o solo/a)
9. acostarse tarde/temprano
10. dormirse a (hora)

Paso 2. Use las oraciones del **Paso 1** para indicar lo que Ud. va a hacer mañana. Añada información si puede.

MODELO: despertarse a (hora) → Primero, **voy a despertarme (me voy a despertar)** a las diez. ¡Es sábado! Pienso… Debo… pero no voy a hacerlo (*do it*).

D. Un día típico

Paso 1. Complete las siguientes oraciones lógicamente para describir su rutina diaria. Use el pronombre reflexivo cuando sea necesario. **¡OJO!** Use el infinitivo después de las preposiciones.

1. Me levanto después de ____.
2. Primero (yo) ____ y luego ____.
3. Me visto antes de / después de ____.
4. Luego me siento a la mesa para ____.
5. Me gusta estudiar antes de ____ o después de ____.
6. Por la noche me divierto y luego ____.
7. Me acuesto antes de / después de ____ y finalmente ____.

Paso 2. Con las oraciones del **Paso 1,** describa los hábitos de su esposo/a, su compañero/a de cuarto/casa, sus hijos…

Conversación

A. Hábitos. Indique en qué cuarto o parte de la casa Ud. hace cada actividad. Debe indicar también los muebles y otros objetos que usa.

MODELO: estudiar →
Por lo general, estudio en la alcoba. Uso el escritorio, una silla, los libros y la computadora.

1. estudiar
2. dormir la siesta
3. quitarse los zapatos
4. bañarse o ducharse
5. despertarse
6. tomar el desayuno
7. sentarse a almorzar
8. vestirse
9. divertirse
10. acostarse

B. Intercambios: Su rutina

Paso 1. En parejas, túrnense para entrevistarse. Hagan preguntas, usando las ideas de las tres columnas y otras de su imaginación. Usen una palabra o frase de cada columna y traten de (*try to*) explicar sus acciones.

MODELO: E1: ¿A qué hora te acuestas?
E2: Siempre me acuesto muy tarde porque trabajo hasta las once de la noche en un restaurante. Luego tengo que estudiar un poco.

¿a qué hora? ¿con quién? ¿cuándo? ¿dónde? ¿durante ____? ¿hasta qué hora?	+	acostarse afeitarse cepillarse los dientes despertarse dormirse ducharse/bañarse levantarse peinarse sentarse vestirse/ponerse ____ volver	+	los días de la semana los fines de semana los lunes (martes…) todos los días tarde/temprano solo/a

Paso 2. Ahora digan a la clase un detalle (*detail*) interesante, raro o indiscreto de la vida (*life*) de su compañero/a.

MODELO: Sebastián se duerme a la una todas las noches con su perro y con sus dos gatos. ¡Debe tener una cama muy grande!

Mundo interactivo

You should now be prepared to work with Scenario 3, Activity 2 in Connect Spanish (**www.connectspanish.com**).

Prác. D: Note

Emphasize the use of the preposition + infinitive.

Prác. D: Suggestion

Have students make up routines for some typical characters: *los estudiantes típicos de esta universidad, su compañero/a de cuarto,* and so on.

Con. A: Suggestions

- Have students work in pairs or trios to elaborate on their answers and ask for extra information.
- Remind students to use the appropriate reflexive pronouns with infinitives, e.g., *Tengo que levantarme, Queremos divertirnos,* and so on.
- Emphasize that when two verbs appear in sequence, the reflexive object pronouns can be placed before the conjugated verb or come after and be attached to the infinitive. Students will learn more about object pronoun placement in *Caps. 7, 8,* and *9.*

Con. B: Reciclado

Note the review of interrogative words as well as the reentry of days of the week (from this chapter).

Con. A, Con. B

Redacción

Assign *Con. A, Con. B*, or both, as a writing assignment (for homework). The day the assignment is due, put students into pairs or groups to compare and discuss their assignments. Ask them to look for commonalities, then report them to the class.

Variation

Ask individual students to do only a few of the cue items from each activity.

Un poco de todo

A: Notes

- Point out that *atender* means *to assist* or *to help out*. As students know, *asistir* means *to attend* (*go to* [an event, a class]).
- Point out that, for many Spanish speakers, *ordenar* means *to put something in order;* it does not mean *to order* something at a restaurant. *Pedir* or *tomar* is used in that context.

A: Extension

Have students retell the story in the third person singular (*ella*).

Un poco de todo

A. Un día normal. Ángela es dependienta en una tienda de ropa para jóvenes en El Paso. ¿Cómo es un día normal de trabajo para ella? Complete la narración con los verbos apropiados, según los dibujos. **¡OJO!** Algunos verbos se usan más de una vez (*more than once*).

1.

2.

3.

4.

5.

6.

Vocabulario útil

almorzar (almuerzo)
cerrar (cierro)
comer
dormir (duermo)
empezar (empiezo)
hablar
ir
pedir (pido)
ser
volver (vuelvo)

1. Llego a la tienda a las diez menos diez de la mañana con mis compañeras de trabajo. Primero (yo) ___empiezo___ mi trabajo, ordenando (*putting in order*) la ropa. La ropa de la tienda ___es___ muy bonita.
2. A las diez abren la tienda y los clientes ___empiezan___ a llegar.
3. Mis compañeras no ___hablan___ español. Por eso yo siempre atiendo a los clientes hispanos.
4. (Yo) ___Almuerzo___ a las doce y media con mi amiga Susie, que trabaja en una zapatería. Generalmente (nosotras) ___comemos___ en la pizzería San Marcos y casi siempre ___pedimos___ pizza.
5. Luego, (yo) ___vuelvo___ a la tienda y ___vuelvo___ a trabajar. Nunca ___duermo___ la siesta.
6. Por fin, la supervisora ___cierra___ la tienda a las seis en punto. Luego yo ___vuelvo/voy___ a casa.

B. Lengua y cultura: Una tradición extendida —El Día de la Cruz (*Cross*). Complete the following paragraphs about a special holiday. Give the correct form of the words in parentheses, as suggested by context. When two possibilities are given in parentheses, select the correct word.

Heritage Speakers

Invite a los hispanohablantes a inventar diálogos basados en los dibujos para presentar a la clase. Luego, los otros estudiantes pueden hacerles preguntas sobre los diálogos.

Resources: Transparency 59

Nicaragua y El Salvador tienen tradiciones que reflejan su mezcla[a] étnica y cultural. Una de estas tradiciones es la fiesta (del / de la[1]) Día de la Cruz, una fiesta religiosa que se celebra (el/la[2]) 3 de mayo en El Salvador, en Nicaragua y en otros países hispanohablantes, incluyendo España. ¿(Por qué / Porque[3]) es una tradición tan[b] extendida la celebración del Día de la Cruz? Porque todos son países en donde muchas personas (pero no todas) observan las (tradición[4]) católicas.

En algunos[c] pueblos y (ciudad[5]) hay procesiones[d] que (salir[6]) por los barrios.[e] Muchas familias salvadoreñas (poner[7]) una cruz en su patio. Las (cruz[8]) están adornadas con mucha fruta y con fruta y flores[f] (con/de[9]) papel. Las personas (vestirse[10]) con ropa especial y (celebrar[11]) el día con comidas y bebidas típicas, con (su[12]) familia y con sus amigos.

En El Salvador la celebración del 3 de mayo (unir[g13]) el culto a la cruz de los cristianos con el culto a la tierra[h] de los indígenas. En el mes de mayo se cosecha[i] la fruta y también (empezar[14]) las lluvias.[j] (Por/Para[15]) eso es un (bueno[16]) momento para dar gracias[k] a la tierra. Además,[l] los campesinos (pedir[17]) una buena cosecha para el año entrante,[m] según la tradición indígena. Esto es solo *un* ejemplo de cómo la influencia indígena y la española se unen en las tradiciones latinoamericanas.

[a]reflejan... *show their mixture* [b]*so* [c]*some* [d]*religious parades, processions* [e]por... *out from (individual) neighborhoods* [f]*flowers* [g]*to join, unite* [h]*earth* [i]se... *is harvested* [j]*rains* [k]dar... *to thank* [l]*Besides* [m]*coming*

El Día de la Cruz en Panchimalco, El Salvador

Comprensión. ¿Cierto o falso? Corrija las oraciones falsas.

	CIERTO	FALSO
1. Nicaragua y El Salvador tienen mucho en común.	☑	☐
2. El Día de la Cruz es una celebración política. Es una celebración religiosa.	☐	☑
3. No hay comidas y bebidas especiales para el Día de la Cruz. Hay comidas y bebidas típicas.	☐	☑
4. En la celebración del Día de la Cruz, se unen las tradiciones cristianas con las indígenas.	☑	☐

En su comunidad

Entreviste a (*Interview*) una persona hispana de su universidad o ciudad sobre las viviendas (*housing*) de su país de origen.

PREGUNTAS POSIBLES

- ¿En qué tipo de vivienda vive la mayoría de las personas en su país de origen?
- ¿Hay un tipo o estilo de casa «típico»? ¿Cómo es?
- ¿Dónde vive su familia?

B: Note

The following grammar topics are included in *Lengua y cultura:* gender, pluralization of nouns (including *z* → *c* and *-ión* → *iones*), adjective agreement, possessives, uses of *de* (contractions, + noun), *-ar/-er/-ir* verbs, reflexives, stem-changing verbs, the irregular verbs *poner/salir*, lexical items (*porque* vs. *¿por qué?, por eso*).

B: Answers

1. *del* **2.** *el* **3.** *Por qué* **4.** *tradiciones* **5.** *ciudades* **6.** *salen* **7.** *ponen* **8.** *cruces* **9.** *de* **10.** *se visten* **11.** *celebran* **12.** *su* **13.** *une* **14.** *empiezan* **15.** *Por* **16.** *buen* **17.** *piden*

En su comunidad

Suggestions

- Remind students to get the following basic information: the informant's country of origin, how long he or she has lived in this country, and if the informant visits his or her country of origin frequently.
- Given students' limited control of Spanish at this point, you may prefer that they do this cultural interview in English. If the interview is done in English, ask students to include other questions related to housing.
- Regardless of how you have students do this assignment, be certain to make class time available for students to share with the whole class what they have learned. Be clear about whether or not students will simply report orally or whether you expect them to turn something in.

Resources: Desenlace

In the *Cap. 5* section of "Chapter-by-Chapter Supplementary Materials" in the IM, you will find a chapter-culminating activity. You can use this activity to consolidate and review the vocabulary and grammar skills students have acquired.

TELEPUNTOS

SALU2

«Bueno, mientras (*while*) asisto a la universidad vivo con mis padres. Lo mejor (*The best part*) de vivir con mis padres es la convivencia (*living together*) con ellos y lo peor (*the worst thing*) es que tengo que acatar sus reglas (*follow their rules*).»

Antes de mirar

¿Dónde vive Ud. ahora, mientras asiste a la universidad? ¿En una residencia universitaria? ¿en un apartamento compartido (*shared*) con otros estudiantes? ¿con su familia? ¿Dónde vive la mayoría de los estudiantes de su universidad?

PROGRAMA 5: Vivir con la familia

Este programa trata de (*deals with*) los lugares (*places*) donde viven los estudiantes universitarios hispanos mientras (*while*) estudian. Y una señora mexicana habla de por qué quiere rentar un cuarto de su casa a un estudiante extranjero.

Vocabulario de este programa

les vuelven a dar la bienvenida	welcome you again	**así lo hice yo**	that's what I did
enfocarse en	to focus on	**¿dónde viviste?**	where did you live?
en efecto	that's right	**güero/a**	blonde (*Mex.*)
hay que sumar	one must add	**la comida**	food
la colonia	neighborhood (*Mex.*)	**libre de**	free from
el apoyo	support	**acomodar**	to provide a home (for)
quejarse (de)	to complain (about)	**despedirse (me despido)**	to say good-bye
parecer	to seem		

Fragmento del guion

LORENA: Estoy ofreciendo un cuarto a un estudiante extranjero porque mi hija se va a casar.[a] Entonces...[b] no quiero quedarme sola.[c] Y quiero que una persona tenga[d] la oportunidad de venir y de disfrutar[e] un poco la vida[f] en familia que tenemos aquí en mi país.

LAURA: ¿Por qué es bueno vivir con esta familia?

LORENA: Bueno, aquí en casa va a tener todas las comodidades como si estuviera en su propia casa.[g] Porque a mí me gusta tener ordenado el cuarto, entonces no va a haber necesidad de que él vaya a pagar lavandería,[h] aquí mismo lo podemos hacer. Va a comer comida casera[i] muy rica. Y aparte[j] va a tener compañía todo el tiempo...

LAURA: La hija que se va a casar se llama Lorena, como su mamá. Lorena es la actual[k] habitante del cuarto.

LA HIJA DE LORENA: Bueno, este es mi cuarto. Es el cuarto que vamos a rentar para un estudiante extranjero. Este... es muy cómodo,[l] debido a que tiene mucha luz.[m] Cuentas con[n] tu televisión propia, Internet y, obviamente, teléfono. Aparte, es muy espacioso. Y seguro, se la va a pasar muy bien.[ñ]

[a]se... *is going to get married* [b]*Then* [c]quedarme... *to be left alone* [d]quiero... *I want a person to have* [e]*enjoy* [f]*life* [g]comodidades... *comforts as if he were in his own home* [h]no... *there will be no need for him to pay for laundry* [i]comida... *home-cooked food* [j]*besides* [k]*current* [l]*comfortable* [m]debido... *due to the fact that it has a lot of light* [n]Cuentas... Tienes [ñ]seguro... *for sure, he is going to have a great time*

«Bueno, los estudiantes aquí en México viven con sus padres por lo regular hasta que terminan de estudiar una carrera. Y hasta que no se casan ellos salen del hogar. (*And they don't leave home until they marry.*)»

TelePuntos

Note

Pages 154–159 are optional. You may cover some, all, or none of this material in class, or assign it to students—as a group or individually—for homework or extra credit. Pages 160–161 (*En resumen: En este capítulo*) are a summary of all of the chapter's active material.

Suggestions

- If you are using the video in class, show it once, ask brief comprehension questions, then show it again.
- Even if you plan to ask students to watch the video in your campus media center or on their own, it is a good idea to continue to stress the need to watch the shows as many times as they want or need to in order to complete the *Después de mirar* activities.

Antes de mirar

Suggestions

- After students have answered these questions on their own, start a whole-class discussion about living arrangements on your campus and how they might vary at different types of colleges and universities. If there are foreign students in your class, ask them what is typical in their countries.
- Ask students to discuss what they think the most typical living arrangement might be for students in Spanish-speaking countries.

Programa 5

Notes

- This is the first *Salu2* program in which past tenses are widely used. Past tense forms as well as a few subjunctive forms are previewed (in *Vocabulario de este programa, Al mirar,* and *Fragmento del guion*). It is important to stress to students that they will continue to hear unfamiliar verb forms in all of the programs. One strategy for coping with this is to listen for the root verb and "infer" the meaning. For example, when Laura says *Tuve la oportunidad de hablar con...*, it is a safe bet in the context that she is saying *I had the chance to talk with...*
- Point out that the students interviewed for this show use most of the typical words or sounds that Spanish speakers use to "buy time" while they mentally organize their thoughts before speaking: *bueno, OK, este,* and so on. These expressions are highly dialectical, and speakers of the same dialect are very likely to recognize each other through the use of these expressions.
- The language of the *El Sol y la Luna* dorm residents is typical of second generation Hispanic students. While the overall "flow" of their language is excellent, if you listen carefully to what they say, you will note a number of usages that you would probably correct (in writing, certainly, if not in speech). It is unlikely that, in *Capítulo 5,* your beginning students will notice any of them (and the brief exposure to them will not interfere with the language acquisition process).

Mundo interactivo

Continue your work as an intern at HispanaVisión with Laura Sánchez Tejada, the roving reporter of *Salu2*, as you complete Scenario 3, Activities 1 and 2 in Connect Spanish (**www.connectspanish.com**).

Al mirar

Empareje (*Match*) las siguientes citas (*quotes*) con estas personas: **Lorena, un estudiante de México, Víctor, Ana, una estudiante de El Sol y la Luna.**

1. «Lo mejor son las facilidades (*conveniences*) que tengo,… Y lo peor son las reglas (*rules*)… »
2. «En cambio, en los países hispanos, la mayoría de los estudiantes no deja su hogar (*don't leave home*) para ir a la universidad.»
3. «El primer semestre viví (*I lived*) con mi familia, porque era (*it was*) mucho más barato. Pero después me independicé (*I struck out on my own*)… »
4. «Ya aprendieron (*they learned*) mucho… Se envuelven (*They get involved*) en todo lo que hacemos.»
5. «Es una costumbre (*custom*) que se tiene (*we have*) de que el hijo viva (*lives*) con los padres hasta esa época.»

«Yo vivo aquí en el… la residencia el Sol (*Sun*) y la Luna (*Moon*) porque… quería (*I wanted*) estar rodeada de gente (*surrounded by people*) que hablara (*spoke*) mi… el mismo idioma (*same language*) que yo… que tuviera (*had*)… algunas de las costumbres y tradiciones que yo también tengo. Y… lo hice para que pudiera (*I did it so that I could*) acostumbrarme a la vida en la universidad… »

Después de mirar

A. ¿Está claro? ¿Cierto o falso? Corrija las oraciones falsas.

	CIERTO	FALSO
1. La mayoría de los estudiantes mexicanos entrevistados (*interviewed*) vive con su familia.	☑	☐
2. Víctor cree que, para los estudiantes universitarios, vivir con su propia (*own*) familia es una cosa buena.	☐	☑
3. Solo estudiantes hispanas viven en la residencia El Sol y la Luna.	☐	☑
4. Un estudiante extranjero vive ya (*already*) en casa de Lorena.	☐	☑

B. Un poco más. Conteste las siguientes preguntas.

1. Según los estudiantes mexicanos entrevistados, ¿qué es lo mejor de vivir con la familia? ¿Y lo peor?
2. ¿Dónde vivió (*lived*) Víctor de (*as a*) estudiante? ¿Y Ana?
3. ¿Cómo es la casa de Lorena? Y el cuarto que va a rentar, ¿cómo es?
4. ¿En qué están de acuerdo Ana y Víctor al final del programa?

C. Y ahora, Uds. En grupos, expresen sus opiniones sobre la idea de vivir con la familia mientras uno asiste a la universidad. Expliquen su respuesta.

Act. A, Answers: 2. *Falso: Cree que no es una cosa buena.* **3.** *Falso: Dos estudiantes no son hispanas.* **4.** *Falso: Lorena espera tener a un estudiante en su casa en el futuro.*

Act. B, Answers: 1. *Lo mejor: es muy céntrico, no tener que trabajar, el apoyo, las facilidades, la convivencia. Lo peor: el tráfico, las reglas de los padres.* **2.** *Primero vivió con su familia y luego con unos compañeros. Ana vivió con su familia.* **3.** *Tiene muchas comodidades (televisión propia, Internet, teléfono). El cuarto está ordenado. Es muy cómodo y espacioso. Tiene mucha luz.* **4.** *En que los exámenes son una constante en todos los países.*

Sobre el programa

El hogar de Ana y el[a] de Víctor representan diferentes maneras de vivir. El apartamento donde vive Ana en Los Ángeles está en una comunidad donde hay muchos profesionales de treinta y tantos[b] años. Son apartamentos diseñados[c] para personas solteras o parejas[d] sin hijos. Por eso los apartamentos tienen solo una o dos alcobas. Las cocinas son pequeñas. Víctor, en cambio,[e] vive en una casa en zona residencial en las afueras[f] de Los Ángeles, donde hay casas cómodas para familias con niños. Su casa tiene cuatro alcobas, una cocina amplia y un jardín pequeño con su propia[g] piscina.

[a]*that* [b]*treinta… thirty-something* [c]*designed* [d]*couples* [e]*en… on the other hand* [f]*outskirts, suburbs* [g]*own*

Producción personal

Filme una o dos entrevistas con estudiantes de su universidad que hablan del lugar donde viven mientras asisten a la universidad.

We suggest that you focus on the motivational aspect of the interviews, especially if you have Heritage Speakers in your classes. Their command of the past subjunctive is exemplary!

- Emphasize to students that the more carefully they study the preliminary activities (*Antes de mirar, Vocabulario de este programa,* and *Fragmento del guion*), the more they will understand when viewing the episode. Scanning *Después de mirar* before viewing is also an excellent strategy.

Fragmento del guion

Note

Comprehension of *Programa 5* is especially dependent on students' having read this *Fragmento* before viewing, due to the use of indicative past tense verb forms as well as of subjunctive forms (present and past). Take the opportunity to point out the subjunctive forms (three of them in this short excerpt) and to call attention to the greater frequency of use of the subjunctive in Spanish as compared with English.

Al mirar

Answers

1. *un estudiante de México* **2.** *Ana* **3.** *Víctor* **4.** *una estudiante de El Sol y la Luna* **5.** *Lorena*

Después de mirar

A: Suggestion

If you are showing the video in class, replay the segment with student interviews, and ask students to tally the answers as they watch. This will help students answer question 1.

C: Follow-up

- Ask students if they are surprised by the Mexican students' responses: *¿Les sorprenden las respuestas de los jóvenes mexicanos?*
- If you find your students are either put off or puzzled by the Mexican students' responses and attitudes, consider acting as a devil's advocate (*el abogado / la abogada del diablo*) to stimulate discussion. For example, you might suggest that Mexicans and other Hispanics remain more closely connected to their families than in this country because they do not leave home in their late teens in order to go to college.

Producción personal

Note

See the IM for additional suggestions for this chapter's assignment as well as for general guidelines and suggestions for video assignments.

Sobre el programa

Optional: Comprensión

1. *Hay muchas familias en la comunidad donde vive Ana.* (*Falso: Hay muchos profesionales.*)
2. *La cocina del apartamento de Ana es pequeña.* (*Cierto*)
3. *Víctor vive en el centro de Los Ángeles.* (*Falso: Vive en las afueras.*)

A leer

Note

The Instructor's Edition on this page offers some additional information on the countries of focus. For more information about the countries of focus, see the chapter's opening pages and the IM.

Lectura cultural

Notes

- The contrast between rich and poor in Spanish-speaking countries shows up strongly in housing (as is the case the world over). Students' impressions of housing in these countries may be particularly stereotypical. Take the opportunity to discuss this topic explicitly, and remind students about the extreme poverty that exists in parts of this country.
- Zoning or the lack of it is something that people from this country notice when traveling abroad, and one frequently sees quite expensive homes right next to poor ones. Discuss this with students, and link it to your college or university's area.
- If you have traveled to or lived in Spanish-speaking countries, show students photos of the homes in which you have lived. Discuss your experience with privacy in Hispanic homes.
- See the IM for some expressions used in El Salvador and Nicaragua.

Point out

Bajareque (also *bahareque* and *bareque*) is an indigenous building technique that is characteristic of all of Central and South America, including the Caribbean. The word itself comes from the *taíno* language of the people who inhabited the Spanish-speaking Caribbean islands. Because *bajareque* homes are simple and made with local and natural elements, they are often the homes in which the poor live today.

Exploración lingüística

Ask students to find the following in the reading. Some of these words are glossed and some are not.

- *conectores de ideas* (*como, desde… hasta, sin embargo, por ejemplo*)
- *palabras que equivalen a* casa *en el sentido hispano de* lugar para vivir (*vivienda, hogar*)

A LEER

Lectura cultural

El Salvador y Nicaragua

Como en todo el mundo, la vivienda[a] en El Salvador y Nicaragua puede variar mucho, desde lujosas[b] mansiones para las personas ricas hasta casas muy pobres y humildes[c] que tienen un solo cuarto para toda una familia. En las ciudades principales hay viviendas modernas comparables a las que[d] se ven en otros países.

En las ciudades de León y Granada, en Nicaragua, hay hermosas[e] casas de la época colonial. Estas casas cuentan con[f] muchos cuartos y tienen techos de tejas,[g] un jardín en medio de la casa y un patio trasero.[h]

¿Cómo son las viviendas en el lugar donde Ud. vive? ¿De qué tipos son?

[a]*housing* [b]desde… *from luxurious* [c]*humble, simple* [d]las… *those that* [e]*beautiful* [f]cuentan… tienen [g]techos… *tiled roofs* [h]*out back*

Una casa de barajeque, en Nicaragua

En otros países hispanos

- **En todo el mundo hispanohablante** Los hispanos en general tiene un concepto muy generoso de la hospitalidad y sienten[a] mucha satisfacción al ofrecer algo[b] de comer y beber a sus invitados.[c] Sin embargo,[d] hay algo típico en la hospitalidad de los hispanos: su hogar[e] suele ser[f] un lugar mucho más privado que el estadounidense. Los invitados hispanos comprenden y respetan este sentido[g] de privacidad. Por ejemplo, es una falta[h] de respeto abrir el refrigerador en la casa de un amigo sin su permiso, aun[i] cuando se trate de[j] la casa de un amigo íntimo.
- **En Centroamérica y Sudamérica** Las casas tradicionales de origen indígena son de bajareque, un tipo de construcción que consiste en paredes de palos[k] sostenidos por barro y cañas.[l]

[a]*they feel* [b]al… *when they offer something* [c]*guests (in their home)* [d]Sin… *Nevertheless* [e]*home* [f]suele… *is usually* [g]*sense* [h]*lack* [i]*even* [j]se… *it involves* [k]*sticks or logs* [l]sostenidos… *held up by mud and reeds*

Tres símbolos salvadoreños y nicaragüenses

- **El volcán Izalco** Este volcán salvadoreño es todo un símbolo del país. Recibe el nombre de «El Faro[a] del Pacífic». Nicaragua y El Salvador son países volcánicos que están dentro del llamado[b] Arco[c] Volcánico Centroamericano. En Nicaragua solamente[d] hay diecisiete volcanes.

[a]*Lighthouse* [b]dentro… *inside the so-called* [c]*Arch* [d]*alone*

- **El lago de Nicaragua** Este es uno de los lagos más grandes del mundo. En él hay volcanes, islas y… ¡más de 400 islotes[e]!
- **La marimba** Este instrumento musical caracteriza la música de Centroamérica, sobre todo la de estos dos países.

[e]*small islands*

Una cita° *quote*

«Para cambiar[a] un sistema opresivo, solo se requiere de[b] la existencia de un hombre con un mínimo de dignidad.»

Augusto César Sandino (1895–1934), líder revolucionario nicaragüense

[a]*change* [b]se… se necesita

COMPRENSIÓN

1. ¿En qué son similares las viviendas en El Salvador y Nicaragua a las (*those*) del resto del mundo? Hay mansiones y viviendas pobres.
2. En general, ¿cómo es la hospitalidad de los hispanos? generosa pero formal
3. ¿Qué es una casa de bajareque? una casa tradicional hecha de palos, barro y cañas

Del mundo hispano

Antes de leer

¿Cómo es su casa? Piense (*Think*) en la casa de su familia o en el lugar donde vive ahora y dé la siguiente información.

1. Nº (Número) de alcobas y de baños
2. Área en pies cuadrados (*square feet*), aproximadamente
3. ¿Tiene cocina? ¿patio? ¿jardín? ¿garaje? (¿Para cuántos coches?)
4. ¿Está en una comunidad privada con portón (*gate*) y guardia?
5. ¿Qué otras comodidades (*facilities*) tiene? (piscina, gimnasio, etcétera)

Vocabulario útil

la recámara = la alcoba
la vivienda place to live (*house or apartment*)
m² = abreviatura de *metros cuadrados* (*square*)

Lectura: Anuncios de bienes raícesº

Anuncios… *Real estate ads*

RESIDENCIAL
Santa Fe
$1'450,000
3rec, 3baños, 2plantas
109m2C, 126m2T
Cocina integral[a] amplia, closet, cuarto de servicio,[b] cochera 2 autos, jardín exterior, patio interior, acabados de primera[c]
Tel. 11372885
ID. 52*131133

RESIDENCIAL SANTA MARGARITA 3rec, 2,5baños, 2plantas, 106m2C, 100m2T, $850M Casa en coto privado,[d] seguro, portón eléctrico, estancia cocina integral, patio, estacionamiento 2 autos, trámite de crédito gratuito[e] 04433 11770400, 39442933

TUZANIA
Zapopan
3 Recs, 1 Baño, 1 planta, 89mts construcción, 89mts terreno, Bonita Casa
$449.000 Tel. 3629 6555

CULTURA Inmobiliaria
PROVIDENCIA
www.culturainmobilaria.com.mx
Departamento en Torre Ontario, planta baja, 232m2 terreno, 238m2 const., 2 niveles, 3 recámaras, 3,5 baños, jardín común, cochera 2 autos, seguridad 24hrs $4.200.000
37002053 • 15683392

Bugambilias
4 recámaras con vestidor y baño, Star TV, gimnasio, terraza, cocheras, en coto, 480m2C, 404m2T
$5.300.000
04433 12451107
04433 12862475

[a]cocina… *kitchen with built-in cabinets and kitchen appliances* [b]cuarto… *servant quarters* [c]acabados… *first-class finishing touches* [d]coto… *private gated community* [e]trámite… *free credit check*

Comprensión

A. Características de las viviendas mexicanas. Para cada vivienda, busque la siguiente información: número de recámaras y baños, tamaño (*size*) de la construcción y del terreno, número de espacios para coches, precio, otros atractivos.

B. Estas viviendas. Conteste las siguientes preguntas.

1. ¿Cuál es la vivienda más grande (*biggest*)? ¿más pequeña? ¿más cara?
2. En los anuncios, hay dos maneras de expresar «garaje». ¿Cuáles son?
3. ¿Cuántos dígitos tienen los números de teléfono en esta ciudad?
4. ¿Cuál es la vivienda más apropiada para las siguientes personas: una familia con 3 hijos, una pareja sin hijos, Ud. solo/a? Explique su respuesta.

Del mundo hispano

Note

See the IM for optional follow-up, writing, and Internet activities.

Antes de leer: Suggestion

Have students do this individually, then compare their answers in groups.

Antes de leer

Answers

Número de recámaras y baños: *Res. Santa Fe = 3 y 3, Res. Santa Margarita = 3 y 2,5, Tuzania = 3 y 1, Cultura inmobilaria = 3 y 3, Bugambilias = 4 y 4*

Tamaño de la construcción y del terreno: *Res. Santa Fe = 109m²C y 126m²T, Res. Santa Margarita = 106m²C y 100m²T, Tuzania = 89m²C y 89m²T, Cultura inmobilaria = 238m²C y 232m²T, Bugambilias = 480m²C y 404m²T*

Número de espacios para coches: *Res. Santa Fe = 2, Res. Santa Margarita = 2, Tuzania = (No dice.), Cultura inmobilaria = 2, Bugambilias = (No dice.)*

Precio (en pesos mexicanos): *Res. Santa Fe = 1,45 millones, Res. Santa Margarita = 850 mil, Tuzania = 449 mil, Cultura inmobilaria = 4,2 millones, Bugambilias = 5,3 millones*

Otros atractivos:

- *Res. Santa Fe: 2 plantas, cocina integral, closet, cuarto de servicio, jardín exterior, patio interior, acabados de primera*
- *Res. Santa Margarita: 2 plantas, coto privado, seguro, portón eléctrico, cocina integral, patio, trámite de crédito gratuito*
- *Tuzania: 1 planta, bonita casa, en Zapopan*
- *Cultura inmobilaria: departamento en una torre, 2 niveles, jardín común, seguridad*
- *Bugambilias: Star TV, gimnasio, terraza, en coto*

Comprensión

B: Suggestions

Some of these questions ask for comparisons, a structure that is not introduced until *Cap. 6*. Students need only understand them at this point (and the first one is glossed). Allow them to answer these questions with single words; i.e., do not require them to produce complete sentences with the comparative construction.

Resources: Transparency 60

Antes de escuchar: Suggestion

You should also ask students to think of the necessary things that are typically shared with other students in an apartment. This will prepare them to focus on this aspect of the listening passage.

Escuche

Notes

- In this chapter, students can listen to a conversation about furnishing an apartment.
- The text suggests that students listen to the passage as many times as they need to in order to do the *Después de escuchar* activities. If that is not what you want students to do, give them alternate instructions.
- See the IM for the Audioscript and more information about music in El Salvador and Nicaragua.

Suggestion

Ask students to concentrate on the list of things mentioned for each room the first time they listen. They can pay more attention to details the second time they listen.

Después de escuchar

A: Answers

Alcoba de Víctor: *cama doble, escritorio, silla, cómoda, estantes, televisor pequeño*
Alcoba de Enrique: *cama, escritorio, silla, mesita, lámpara, estantes*
Sala comedor: *sofá cama, dos plantas, dos sillones, lámpara, plasma*

B: Answers

1. *Víctor = una lámpara, Ernesto = una cómoda* **2.** *el baño* **3.** *una mesa y 4 sillas* **4.** *2*

B: Follow-up

Ask students to tell what they need for their living quarters. Be prepared to help them with vocabulary. Note: In the vocabulary and grammar sections of *Cap. 5*, students have already been asked to describe where they live. If you feel that it is not too repetitive, it would be appropriate to ask them to do that now as well.

¡Música!

Note

- Carlos Wiltshire is the real name of *Carlos de Nicaragua.* He has lived in many parts of the world, including the U.S. He currently lives in France.
- For helpful tips on using songs in the classroom, see the IM.

A ESCUCHAR

Antes de escuchar

¿Qué es más usual entre los estudiantes universitarios: alquilar (*to rent*) un apartamento amueblado o uno sin amueblar (*furnished or unfurnished*)? ¿Tiene Ud. muchos muebles propios (*of your own*) donde Ud. vive? En su cuarto, casa o apartamento, ¿qué cosas son de Ud.?

Vocabulario para escuchar

amueblar	to furnish
ya	already
la plasma	flat-screen TV

Escuche

Una conversación para amueblar un nuevo apartamento

Enrique y Víctor hablan de los muebles que necesitan. Escuche según las indicaciones de su profesor(a).

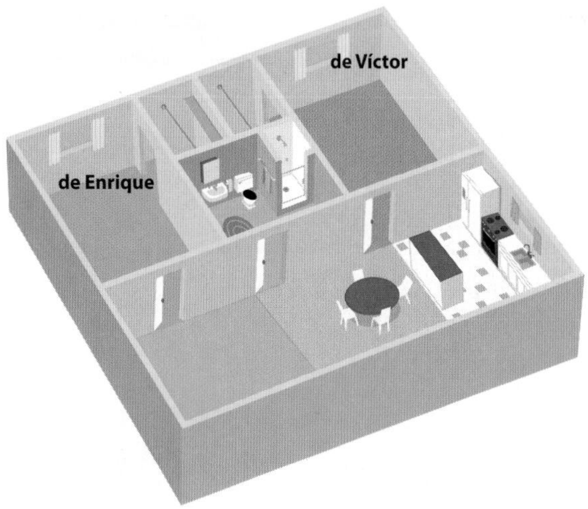

Después de escuchar

A. ¿Qué necesitan? Enrique y Víctor acaban de alquilar (*have just rented*) un apartamento que tiene muy pocos muebles, pero no importa porque ellos tienen varias cosas. Dibuje o escriba en el plano del apartamento el nombre de los muebles y cosas que ellos ya tienen para cada cuarto.

B. Más detalles. Conteste las siguientes preguntas.

1. ¿Qué cosas tienen que comprar Víctor y Enrique para sus alcobas?
2. ¿Qué parte de la casa no mencionan en la conversación?
3. ¿Qué muebles no necesitan comprar para la sala comedor?
4. ¿Cuántos televisores tienen entre los dos?

¡Música!

La música de Carlos de Nicaragua es una fusión de reggae con otras influencias latinas, especialmente de la salsa y el rock. Canta con su grupo Familia.

La canción «Suena[a] el reggae» es del álbum *Militante.*

[a] *Is playing*

Carlos de Nicaragua, en Dublin, Irlanda

Go to the iMix section in Connect Spanish (**www.connectspanish.com**) to access the iTunes playlist *"Puntos9,"* where you can purchase "Suena el reggae" by Carlos de Nicaragua.

Resources: Transparency 61

A ESCRIBIR

El tema

Una semana típica para estudiantes universitarios

Preparar

En una hoja de papel aparte, complete una tabla como la siguiente con información sobre 5 o 6 actividades que Ud. hace de lunes a viernes y durante el fin de semana en una semana típica. Luego entreviste a (*interview*) dos compañeros de clase sobre sus actividades y complete la tabla con su respectiva información.

	l m m j v	s d
Ud.		
compañero/a A		
compañero/a B		

Redactar

Escriba un ensayo sobre la semana típica de los estudiantes de esta universidad, combinando (*combining*) toda la información de **Preparar.** Asegúrese (*Be sure*) de que tiene un párrafo introductorio, con una idea central para el ensayo, y un párrafo de cierre (*closing*).

Editar

Revise el ensayo para comprobar:

- la ortografía y los acentos
- la posición y la concordancia (*agreement*) de los adjetivos descriptivos y adjetivos posesivos
- la variedad del vocabulario
- la conjugación de los verbos

Finalmente, prepare su versión final para entregarla.

Preparar

Suggestions

- Ask students to think about what is considered "typical" of students in general and of students from their college or university. Examples: Do most students study a substantial number of hours a week? Do they also work? Do they live with their families or with other students in university housing?
- Suggest that students include some basic chores typical of college students.
- Suggest that students include some time prepositions from the chapter's vocabulary.
- Before they start their interviews, tell students to review *las palabras interrogativas* (*Nota comunicativa,* p. 30) and the formation of yes/no questions (pp. 45–46). Ask them to prepare a series of 5 questions to help them get the information they need for their essay.

Redactar

Suggestions

- Suggested length for this writing assignment: approximately 100 words
- Suggested structure (3 paragraphs)

P. 1. Introduction: State whether there is a "typical" week for students or not.
P. 2. Examples from the student writer (first person) and interviewees (third person singular or plural)
P. 3. Short conclusion defending the idea presented in the introduction

Editar

Follow-up

Have a whole-class discussion about the following topic: What does a person's schedule say about that person's personality or lifestyle?

En resumen
En este capítulo
Vocabulario

Suggestions

- Introduce the concept of diminutives (*mesa* → *mesita*) and augmentatives (*silla* → *sillón*).
- Have students play Hangman (*El ahorcado*) using different groups of words.
- Play password with the house vocabulary. The cues may not include the target word or any form of it. You can divide the class into two teams, and while one member takes a turn giving a one-word cue, the other team members try to guess the word.

Note

The following vocabulary items were used in direction lines in *Cap. 5* and will be used in subsequent chapters without glossing, but they are not considered to be active until they are listed in *Vocabulario*: *diga(n)* (*Ud[s].*), *entreviste a, usando.*

Word Families

En este capítulo

- *ayer, anteayer*
- *bañarse, la bañera, el baño*
- *después* (adv.), *después de* (prep.)
- *dormir, dormirse*
- *poner, ponerse*

Entre capítulos

- *la bebida = beber* (3)
- *el comedor = comer* (3)
- *diario/a = el día* (2)
- *el estudio = estudiar* (2)
- *hasta = hasta luego* (1)
- *llamarse = me llamo, te llamas, se llama* (1)
- *lo que = que* (3)
- *la mesita = la mesa* (2)
- *la sala = el salón (de clase)* (2)
- *la semana que viene = el fin de semana* (2)
- *el sillón = la silla* (2)
- *vestirse = el vestido* (4)

¡OJO!

- *la cómoda ≠ cómodo/a* (4)
- *los platos ≠ la plata* (4)
- *primero* (adv.) *≠ el primo* (3)
- *salir ≠ la sala*
- *solo/a ≠ solo* (2)

EN RESUMEN En este capítulo

LearnSmart™

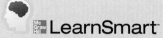

Visit **www.connectspanish.com** to practice the vocabulary and grammar points covered in this chapter.

Gramática en breve

12. Present Tense of *hacer, oír, poner, salir, traer, ver*

hacer: hago, haces, hace, hacemos, hacéis, hacen
oír: oigo, oyes, oye, oímos, oís, oyen
poner: pongo, pones, pone, ponemos, ponéis, ponen
salir: salgo, sales, sale, salimos, salís, salen
traer: traigo, traes, trae, traemos, traéis, traen
ver: veo, ves, ve, vemos, veis, ven

13. Present Tense of Stem-changing Verbs

Stem-changing Patterns

e → ie		o → ue		e → i	
-ie-	-e-	-ue-	-o-	-i-	-e-
-ie-	-e-	-ue-	-o-	-i-	-e-
-ie-	-ie-	-ue-	-ue-	-i-	-i-

14. Reflexive Pronouns

yo	→ **me**	**nosotros/as**	→ **nos**
tú	→ **te**	**vosotros/as**	→ **os**
Ud./él/ella	→ **se**	**Uds./ellos/ellas**	→ **se**

Vocabulario

Los verbos

almorzar (almuerzo)	to have lunch
cerrar (cierro)	to close
descansar	to rest
dormir (duermo)	to sleep
dormir la siesta	to take a nap
empezar (empiezo)	to begin, start
empezar a + *inf.*	to begin to (*do something*)
entender (entiendo)	to understand
hacer	to do; to make
hacer ejercicio	to exercise
hacer un viaje	to take a trip
hacer una pregunta	to ask a question
jugar (juego) (a, al)	to play (*a game, sport*)
oír (oigo, oyes,...)	to hear; to listen to (*music, the radio*)
pedir (pido)	to ask for; to order
pensar (pienso) (en)	to think (about)
pensar + *inf.*	to intend, plan to (*do something*)
perder (pierdo)	to lose; to miss (*an event*)
poner (pongo)	to put; to place; to turn on (*an appliance*)
salir (salgo) (de)	to leave (*a place*)
salir bien/mal	to turn/come out well/badly; to do well/poorly
salir con	to go out with, date
salir para	to leave for (*a place*)
servir (sirvo)	to serve
servir para	to be used for
traer (traigo)	to bring
ver (veo)	to see
volver (vuelvo)	to return (*to a place*)
volver a + *inf.*	to (*do something*) again

Los verbos reflexivos

acostarse (me acuesto)	to go to bed
afeitarse	to shave
bañarse	to take a bath
cepillarse los dientes	to brush one's teeth
despertarse (me despierto)	to wake up
divertirse (me divierto)	to have a good time, enjoy oneself
dormirse (me duermo)	to fall asleep
ducharse	to take a shower
levantarse	to get up (out of bed); to stand up
llamarse	to be called
peinarse	to brush/comb one's hair
ponerse (me pongo)	to put on (*an article of clothing*)
quitarse	to take off (*an article of clothing*)
sentarse (me siento)	to sit down
vestirse (me visto)	to get dressed

Los cuartos y otras partes de una casa

la alcoba	bedroom
el baño	bathroom
la cocina	kitchen
el comedor	dining room
el estudio	office (*in a home*)
el jardín	garden
la pared	wall
el patio	patio; yard
la piscina	swimming pool
la sala	living room

Cognado: el garaje

Repaso: la casa, el cuarto

Los muebles y otras cosas de una casa

la alfombra	rug
el armario	armoire, free-standing closet
la bañera	bathtub
la cama	bed
la cómoda	bureau; dresser
el estante	bookshelf
la lámpara	lamp
el lavabo	(bathroom) sink
la mesita	end table
el mueble	piece of furniture
el plato	dish; plate
el sillón	armchair
la toalla	towel

Cognado: el sofá

Repaso: el escritorio, la mesa, la silla, la televisión

Otros sustantivos

la bebida	drink
el cine	movies; movie theater
la cosa	thing
el diente	tooth
el ejercicio	exercise
la llave	key
la película	movie
la pregunta	question
el ruido	noise
la rutina	routine
la tarea	homework
el viaje	trip

Los adjetivos

cada *inv.**	each, every
diario/a	daily
siguiente	following
solo/a	alone

Las preposiciones

antes de	before
después de	after
durante	during
sin	without

Repaso: a, con, de, en, hasta, para, por (*in, during*)

¿Qué día es hoy?

los días de la semana
lunes, martes, miércoles, jueves, viernes, sábado, domingo

anteayer	the day before yesterday
ayer fue (miércoles...)	yesterday was (Wednesday . . .)
el lunes (martes...)	on Monday (Tuesday . . .)
los lunes (los martes...)	on Mondays (Tuesdays . . .)
pasado mañana	the day after tomorrow
el próximo (martes...)	next (Tuesday . . .)
la próxima semana	next week
la semana (el lunes...) que viene	next week (Monday . . .)

Repaso: el día, el fin de semana, hoy, mañana

Palabras adicionales

después *adv.*	afterwards
en seguida	immediately
finalmente	finally
lo que	what, that which
luego	then, afterward, next
por fin	finally
por lo general	generally
primero	first

Vocabulario personal

*The abbreviation inv. means invariable (in form). The adjective **cada** is used with masculine and feminine nouns (**cada libro, cada mesa**), and since its meaning (each) is singular, it is never used with plural nouns.*

Suggestions

- Write the following on the board.

  Ayer fue ______.
  Hoy es ______. ______ voy a ______.
  Pero antes, tengo que ______.
  Después voy a ______.
  Por lo general, ______ todos los ______.

  Have students complete these sentences in writing, using vocabulary to fill the blanks. Then ask them to share and correct them with a partner. Have several students read their sentences aloud.
- Have students write a paragraph about an activity that they perform routinely. Ask them to use as many of the new prepositions as possible and to:

1. tell when they perform this activity,
2. where they perform it, and
3. what steps they take and in what order.

Chapter Opening Photo and Chapter Theme

Chapter Theme–Related Questions

- *¿Cómo es el clima en su país o estado? ¿Muy variado o poco variado? ¿Es extremo, es decir, hace mucho calor y mucho frío?*
- *¿Hay cuatro estaciones (primavera, verano, otoño e invierno)? ¿O hay solo dos?*
- *¿Cuál es su estación favorita? ¿Por qué?*
- *¿Qué clima prefiere para sus vacaciones?*

Reciclado: Review clothing and parts of the house. Ask questions that relate weather to those topics.

1. *¿Qué ropa deben llevar las personas en este clima?*
2. *¿Qué llevan Uds. cuando hace calor? ¿Y cuando hace frío?*
3. *¿Dónde prefiere Ud. estar (en su casa) cuando hace frío? ¿Y cuando hace calor?*

Culture

Although the weather can be hot around the equator and in many Latin American countries, not all Hispanic countries have tropical climates. Temperatures are closely related to altitude—the higher the altitude, the cooler the climate. The great mountain chains found in Latin America make for a varied climate throughout the continent. Both Argentina and Chile have territory in Antarctica (*la Antártida*).

6 Las estaciones y el tiempo°

°Las... *Seasons and the weather*

El bosque tropical lluvioso (*tropical rain forest*) **de Costa Rica**

- What kind of climate would you expect to find in Costa Rica?
- What do you like to do when the weather is good?
- What's the climate like where you live?

Connect Spanish

www.connectspanish.com

Resources

For Students

- Connect Spanish (**www.connectspanish.com**), which contains all content from the following resources, as well as the *Mundo interactivo* scenarios, the LearnSmart adaptive learning system, and more!
- **Physical Resources:** Workbook / Laboratory Manual, Laboratory Audio Program, DVD

For Instructors

- Connect Spanish (**www.connectspanish.com**), which contains access to all student sections of Connect Spanish, as well as helpful time-saving tools and resources such as an integrated gradebook, Instructor's Manual, Testing Program, digital transparencies, Audioscript, Videoscript, and more!

Costa Rica

4,5 (y medio) millones de habitantes

- La Constitución de Costa Rica prohíbe la organización de fuerzas armadas (*armies*).
- El ecoturismo es fundamental para la economía de Costa Rica y para preservar sus bosques (*forests*) y selvas (*jungles*), que cubren (*cover*) un 30% (por ciento) de su territorio.

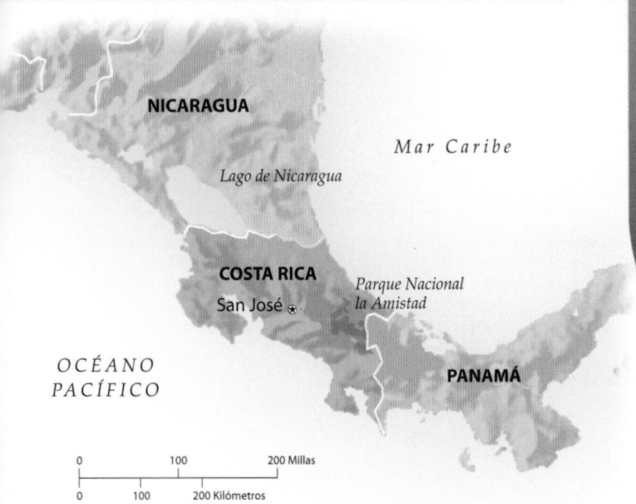

En este capítulo

CONTENT / **CONTENIDO**	OBJECTIVES / **OBJETIVOS**
The Weather 164, Months and Seasons 166	To talk about the weather and the yearly calendar
Prepositions of Place 168	To locate things in relation to other things
Present Progressive (*-ing*) 170	To express actions that are happening right now
Ser versus **estar** 175	To summarize everything you know about two Spanish verbs that express *to be*
Comparisons 182	To compare people, things, and actions
Costa Rica 192	To learn about a Central American country that has a long and peaceful democratic history

Costa Rica

Datos esenciales

The Instructor's Edition will provide basic information about each chapter's country of focus on this chapter opening spread. Additional information (such as geographical features, historical timelines, holidays, and so on) can be found in the IM. There is also additional information about the country of focus in *A leer: Lectura cultural* and *A escuchar* (in both the student text and the Instructor's Edition).

Nombre oficial: *República de Costa Rica*
Lema: *«¡Vivan el trabajo y la paz!»*
Capital: *San José*
Otras ciudades: *Cartago, San Isidro, Puerto Limón*
Composición étnica: *94% mestizos y blancos, 3% negros, 1% indígenas, 1% chinos, 1% otros*
Jefe de estado actual: *la Presidenta Laura Chinchilla Miranda, desde 2010*
Forma de gobierno: *Democracia presidencialista*
Moneda: *el colón costarricense, pero el dólar estadounidense circula libremente*
Religión: *76% católicos, 14% evangélicos, 7% otras religiones, 3% sin religión*

Point out

- Costa Rica was not developed as a Spanish colony to the same extent that other Central American countries were, for a number of reasons. Costa Rica was geographically distant from Guatemala, the seat of the Spanish government, and it did not have extensive mineral resources, nor the abundant indigenous work force to develop those that did exist. As a result, the few settlers that arrived turned to agriculture.
- The United Fruit Company influenced politics in the Caribbean and Central America (including Costa Rica) for decades, beginning in the late 1800s and early 1900s.

Suggestion

Have students list their ideas about Costa Rica, including information on geography, politics, economy, culture, music, and cuisine. When you finish the chapter, return to the lists and ask students what ideas they would change and/or add. The success of this activity will depend not only on the content about Costa Rica presented in the text but also on the extent to which you have time to supplement that content with your own knowledge and experiences and also with information given in this Instructor's Edition and the IM.

Multimedia

The *Instructor's Manual* (IM) provides suggestions for using multimedia materials in the classroom.

Resources: Transparency 62

Vocabulario: Preparación
¿Qué tiempo hace hoy?
Suggestions

- See the model for vocabulary presentation and other material in "Teaching Techniques" for the *Cap. 6 Vocabulario: Preparación* section of "Chapter-by-Chapter Supplementary Materials" in the IM.
- **Reciclado:** Model weather expressions. As you present each, have students tell you what kind of clothing is worn for that weather.
- **Pronunciación:** See Pronunciation Notes, IM.
- Optional vocabulary: *hay* (*mucha*) *niebla/neblina, hay* (*mucha*) *humedad, lloviznar, truenos y relámpagos, el aumento de la temperatura global, derretirse, el hielo, la nieve, el glaciar.*
- Point out that *el tiempo* means both weather and time. *El tiempo* should not be confused with *la hora.*
- Point out that one does not begin a sentence about the weather by saying *El tiempo...* but rather *Hace...* This is difficult for students, since frequent English equivalents are *The weather is...* or *It is...*
- Contrast *hacer, tener,* and *estar.* Discuss the differences among the following expressions: *hace frío/calor* for weather, *tener frío/calor* for people, *estar frío/caliente* to indicate the condition of things.

Bright Ideas

- To help students learn weather expressions, organize them (on board) by main word in the expressions: *hace..., hay..., está...*
- Introduce same weather phenomena by drawing a simple map of this country on board, including major cities with recognizable weather patterns, then talking about weather in those cities.

Con. A: Possible Answers

1. *Hace calor.* **2.** *Hace fresco.* **3.** *Hace frío.* **4.** *Llueve.* **5.** *Nieva.*

Con. A: Follow-up

Ask the following questions.

1. *¿En dónde prefiere Ud. vivir, donde hace calor o donde hace fresco?*
2. *¿Le gusta vivir donde llueve mucho? ¿donde nieva mucho?*
3. *Describa la diferencia entre el clima de Michigan y el de Texas.*

VOCABULARIO Preparación

¿Qué tiempo hace hoy?°

°¿Qué... *What's the weather like today?*

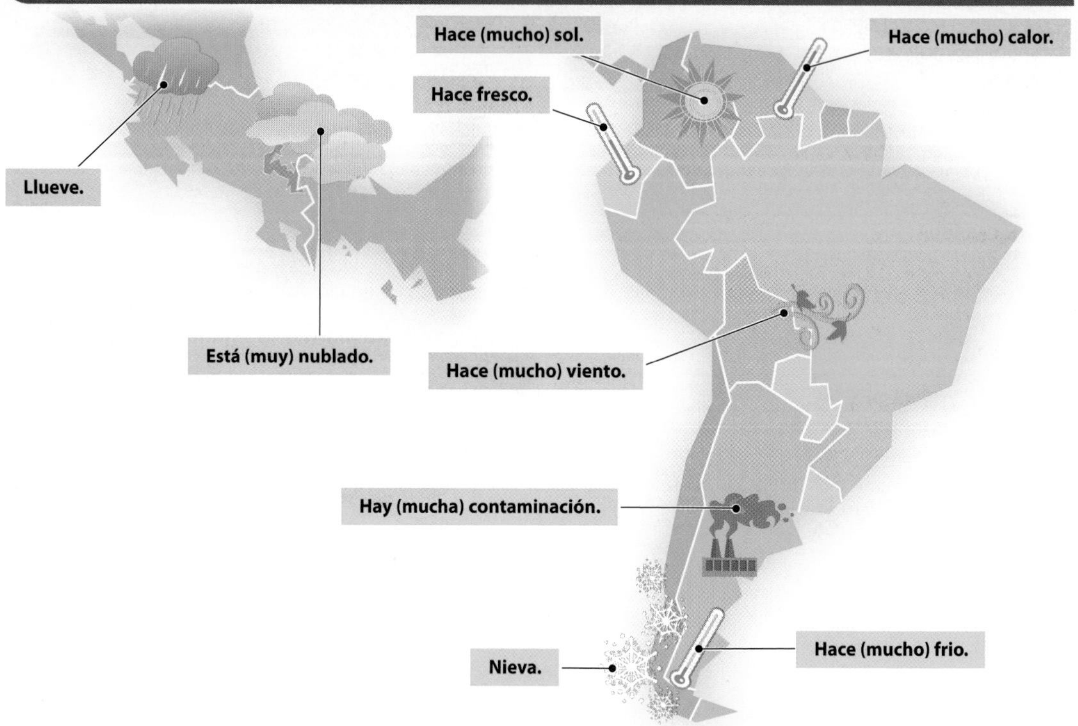

Hace (mucho) sol.
Hace (mucho) calor.
Hace fresco.
Llueve.
Está (muy) nublado.
Hace (mucho) viento.
Hay (mucha) contaminación.
Nieva.
Hace (mucho) frío.

In Spanish, many weather conditions are expressed with the verb form **hace,** and there is no literal English equivalent for it. The adjective **mucho** is used with the nouns **frío, calor, viento,** and **sol** to express *very.*

Hace (muy) buen/mal tiempo.	It's (very) good/bad weather. *It's (very) nice/bad out.*

Pronunciation hint: Remember that, in most parts of the Spanish-speaking world, **ll** is pronounced exactly like **y: llueve.** Also remember that the letter **h** is silent in Spanish.

Así se dice

Here are some other weather expressions that you might hear. However, it's best to stick with the standard phrases presented in **¿Qué tiempo hace hoy?**

Está nublado. = Está nubloso.
Nieva. = Está nevoso.
Llueve. = Está lluvioso.
Hace sol. = Está soleado.

Conversación

A. El tiempo y la ropa. Diga qué tiempo hace, según la ropa de cada persona.

MODELO: Todos llevan traje de baño y chanclas. →
Hace calor. (Hace buen tiempo.)

1. María lleva pantalones cortos y una camiseta.
2. Juan lleva suéter, pero no lleva chaqueta.
3. Roberto lleva sudadera y chaqueta.
4. Ramón lleva impermeable y botas y también tiene paraguas (*umbrella*).
5. Todos llevan abrigo, botas y sombrero.

Multimedia: Internet

Have students search for a weather site in Spanish and bring a printout from it to class. Have students identify the weather expressions they are learning and others they may recognize, e.g., *temperatura.*

Resources: Transparency 63

B. El clima en el mundo

Paso 1. ¿Qué clima o condición asocia Ud. con las siguientes ciudades?

1. Seattle, Washington
2. Los Ángeles, California
3. San Juan, Puerto Rico
4. Buffalo, Nueva York
5. las Islas Hawai
6. Chicago, Illinois

Paso 2. ¿Qué clima o condición asocia Ud. con los siguientes lugares?

1. un desierto
2. una playa (*beach*)
3. una montaña muy, muy alta
4. una ciudad grande
5. la Antártida
6. una zona tropical
7. una zona templada
8. Londres

C. El tiempo y las actividades. Haga oraciones completas, indicando una actividad apropiada para cada situación. Es necesario conjugar los verbos a la derecha (*right*).

cuando hace buen/mal tiempo cuando hace calor cuando hace frío cuando hay mucha contaminación cuando llueve cuando nieva	+	(no)	+	jugar al basquetbol/voleibol con mis amigos almorzar afuera (*outside*) / en el parque divertirse en el parque / la playa con mis amigos salir de casa volver a casa trabajar o estudiar quedarse (*to stay*) en casa

Nota **comunicativa**

Otras expresiones con *tener*

Several other conditions are expressed in Spanish with **tener** idioms—not with *to be*, as in English.

tener (mucho) calor	to be (very) warm, hot
tener (mucho) frío	to be (very) cold

These expressions are used to describe people or animals only. *To be comfortable*—neither hot nor cold—is expressed with **estar bien.**

D. ¿Tienen frío o calor? ¿Están bien? En parejas, describan el tiempo que hace en cada dibujo. También deben indicar cómo están las personas. Si Uds. creen que no tienen ni (*neither*) frío ni (*or*) calor, pueden decir (*say*): **«Está(n) bien».**

1. **2.** **3.** **4.** **5.** **6.**

Con. B: Possible Answers
Paso 1. **1.** *Llueve. Hace fresco.* **2.** *Hace calor. Hace sol. Hay contaminación.* **3.** *Hace calor. Hace sol.* **4.** *Hace frío. Nieva.* **5.** *Hace calor. Hace sol.* **6.** *Hace frío. Hay mucho viento.*

Paso 2. **1.** *Hace calor. Hace sol. No llueve mucho.* **2.** *Hace calor. Hace sol. Llueve.* **3.** *Hace mucho frío. Nieva. Hay mucho viento.* **4.** *Hay mucha contaminación.* **5.** *Hace mucho frío. Hay mucho viento.* **6.** *Hace mucho sol. Hace calor. Llueve mucho.* **7.** *Hace fresco.* **8.** *Está nublado a veces.*

Con. D: Answers: **1.** *Hace frío. Tienen frío.* **2.** *Hace mucho sol y calor. Tiene calor.* **3.** *Hay mucho viento. Tiene frío.* **4.** *Llueve. Tiene frío.* **5.** *Hay mucha contaminación.* **6.** *Hace fresco. Están bien.*

Con. B: Suggestions

- Do *Paso 1* as a full-class activity, to model how *Paso 2* might be done.
- Have students do *Paso 2* in pairs or groups, then share information.

Con. B: Note

Active vocabulary: *el clima, la playa, afuera, quedarse*

Con. B: Follow-up

Ask students the following questions. Use this opportunity to discuss students' stereotypical view of the climate in Spanish-speaking countries. Many students will think it is always hot.

1. *¿Llueve mucho en Inglaterra? ¿en el desierto del Sahara?*
2. *¿Nieva mucho en El Salvador? ¿en Minnesota?*
3. *¿Hace mucho frío en Siberia? ¿en el Ecuador?*
4. *¿Hace mucho sol en la Florida? ¿en la Argentina?*
5. *¿Hace calor en Panamá? ¿en Alaska?*

Con. C: Suggestions

- Ask if the following activities are typical on campus in bad weather.
  1. *Cuando hace frío, los estudiantes juegan al basquetbol en el gimnasio.*
  2. *Cuando nieva, pasan la tarde en la residencia estudiantil.*
  3. *Cuando nieva, hacen muñecos de nieve* (new).
  4. *Cuando llueve, no salen de la residencia.*
- Ask: *Cuando hace calor…*
  1. *¿bebe Ud. agua, refrescos* (new)*, o un jugo de fruta?*
  2. *¿prefiere estar en casa o afuera?*
  3. *¿prefiere estar en el parque o en la playa?*
  4. *¿juega al tenis (al…) o duerme?*

Nota comunicativa

Suggestions

- With *tener* + noun expressions, *very* is expressed with *mucho/a: tener mucho frío/calor; tener muchas ganas.*
- Point out that *tener* means *to feel* in these idioms.
- Point out that *to have a cold* in Spanish is *tener un resfriado (catarro/gripe).*

Con. D: Preliminary Exercise

Ask students the following questions before beginning the activity.

1. *¿Qué tiempo hace hoy?*
2. *Imagine que hoy es un día fatal. ¿Qué tiempo hace hoy?*
3. *Hoy es un día estupendo. ¿Qué tiempo hace hoy?*

Heritage Speakers

Aunque a veces se oye la palabra *polución* en algunos dialectos del español que se habla en este país, la palabra *contaminación* es la preferida.

Resources: Transparency 64

Con. D: Note

Active vocabulary: *estar bien*

Los meses y las estaciones del año

Suggestions

- Model months of the year, linking them to seasons: *Los meses de otoño son septiembre, octubre y noviembre, ¿verdad?* and so on. Then ask students what the weather is like in each season: *En muchas partes de este país hace frío en enero, ¿cierto o falso?* and so on.
- Remind students that months are not capitalized in Spanish.
- Note the introduction of the abbreviation for *primero* (*1°*). An alternative abbreviation is 1^{ero}.
- Optional for expressing the first day of the month: *el uno de* ______.

Así se dice

Ask students what they prefer

¿Prefiere Ud…?

1. *¿los días cortos del invierno o los días largos del verano?*
2. *¿el tiempo del otoño o el de la primavera?*
3. *¿las actividades de verano o las de invierno?*

Reciclado: Review numbers and years with the following questions.

¿En qué año estamos?
¿En qué año nació Ud. (new)*?*
¿En qué año nació su padre (*madre, abuela,…*)*?*
¿En qué año piensa graduarse?

Review the days of the week and use of *el* with the days.

Pronunciación: See Pronunciation Notes, IM.

Preliminary Exercise

Use a calendar page for the current month to practice dates: *¿Qué día de la semana es el* (5) *de* (*mes*)*?*

Optional: Present the following month-related *refranes*.

- *Febrerillo loco, marzo ventoso y abril lluvioso, hacen a mayo florido y her- moso.*
- *Julio normal, seca el manantial* (spring waters [new]).
- *A primeros de noviembre, tu fuego* (new) *enciende.*
- *En septiembre, cosecha* (new) *y no siembres.*

Con. A: Note

Thirty days hath September, / April, June, and November. / All the rest have thirty-one, / Except February alone, / Which has twenty-eight in fine, / And each leap year twenty-nine.

Los meses y las estaciones° del año

°*seasons*

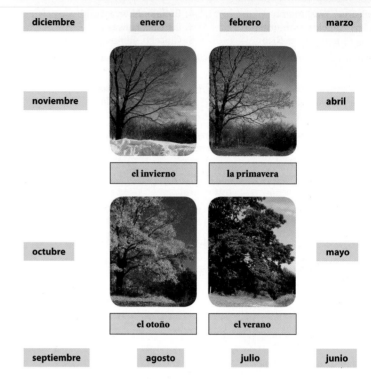

diciembre | enero | febrero | marzo

noviembre

abril

el invierno | la primavera

octubre

mayo

el otoño | el verano

septiembre | agosto | julio | junio

Así se dice

Other ways to ask what day it is include:

¿En qué fecha estamos?
¿Qué día es hoy?
¿A cuántos estamos?

In the last sentence, **cuántos** is masculine because it refers to **días** (*m.*).

¿Cuál es la fecha de hoy? **¿Qué fecha es hoy?**	What's today's date?
(Hoy) Es el primero de abril.	(Today is) It's the first of April.
(Hoy) Es el cinco de febrero.	(Today is) It's the fifth of February.

- The ordinal number **primero (1°)** is used to express the first day of the month. Cardinal numbers (**dos, tres,** and so on) are used for other days.
- The definite article **el** is used before the date. However, when the day of the week is expressed, **el** is omitted: **Hoy es jueves, 3 de octubre.**
- As you know, **mil** is used to express the year (**el año**) after 999.

1950 mil novecientos cincuenta   2011 dos mil once

Conversación

Con. A: Answers: 1. *Treinta* **2.** *septiembre* **3.** *uno*

A. Un poema. Complete el siguiente poema sobre los meses del año. ¿Cuál es el equivalente del poema en inglés?

_____[1] (número) días tiene noviembre,
con abril, junio y _____.[2]
De veintiocho solo hay uno,
Y los demás,[a] treinta y _____.[3]

[a]los… *the rest*

Heritage Speakers

Pregúnteles a los hispanohablantes qué días festivos celebran. Pídales que describan las celebraciones.

Multimedia: Internet

Have students who are interested look for the Colombian newspaper *El tiempo* on the Internet to find their horoscope in Spanish.

Resources: Transparency 65

B. Las fechas

Paso 1. Exprese estas fechas en español. ¿En qué estación caen (*do they fall*)?

MODELO: February 15 ⟶ Es el quince de febrero. Cae (*It falls*) en invierno.

1. March 7
2. August 24
3. December 1
4. June 5
5. September 19, 1997
6. May 30, 1842
7. January 31, 1660
8. July 4, 1776

Paso 2. ¿Cuándo se celebran?* ¿Y en qué día de la semana caen este año?

1. el Día del Año Nuevo
2. el Día de los Enamorados (de San Valentín)
3. la Navidad (*Christmas*)
4. el Día de los Inocentes (*Fools*), en los Estados Unidos
5. su cumpleaños (*birthday*)
6. el cumpleaños de su novio/a (*boyfriend/girlfriend*), esposo/a, mejor (*best*) amigo/a,...

Nota **cultural**

El clima en el mundo hispano

El mundo hispanohablante es inmenso. Se extiende en las Américas desde los Estados Unidos hasta la Tierra del Fuego, en la Argentina. Por eso, el clima de los países hispanohablantes es muy variado.

- No todos los países tienen cuatro estaciones. Hay países, como Costa Rica y otros países centroamericanos y sudamericanos, que solo tienen dos: una estación seca[a] y otra húmeda, con mucha lluvia. Esto es normal en los países de la zona tropical.
- El Niño es un fenómeno meteorológico muy importante que afecta directamente a varios países hispanos. Está caracterizado por temperaturas más calientes de lo normal[b] en la zona ecuatorial del océano Pacífico. El fenómeno se llama El Niño porque se presenta típicamente alrededor de[c] Navidad, época en que nace el Niño Jesús.[d] El fenómeno opuesto[e] a El Niño es La Niña, que trae temperaturas excepcionalmente frías.

[a]*dry* [b]más... *warmer than normal* [c]alrededor... *around* [d]nace... *Baby Jesus is born (Christian faiths)* [e]*opposite*

La costa del Perú, donde se descubrió (*was discovered*) el fenómeno de El Niño en el siglo (*century*) XIX

¿Cómo es el clima de su estado o país? ¿Están las estaciones bien diferenciadas?

C. Entrevista

Paso 1. En parejas, túrnense para entrevistarse sobre los siguientes temas. Deben obtener detalles interesantes y personales de su compañero/a.

MODELO: la fecha de su cumpleaños ⟶
¿Cuál es la fecha de tu cumpleaños? ¿Qué tiempo hace, generalmente, ese día? ¿Cómo celebras tu cumpleaños?

1. la fecha de su cumpleaños
2. su signo del horóscopo
3. su estación favorita
4. una estación que no le gusta

Paso 2. Digan a la clase lo que Uds. tienen en común.

MODELO: Nosotras tenemos el cumpleaños en abril. La fecha de María es el 16 y mi fecha es el 18. Nuestro signo es Aries. Las dos (*Both of us*) preferimos la primavera. ¿Por qué? Porque nuestro cumpleaños es en primavera y es una estación muy bonita.

Los signos del horóscopo

Aries	Libra
Tauro	Escorpión
Géminis	Sagitario
Cáncer	Capricornio
Leo	Acuario
Virgo	Piscis

Note that the word* **se *before a verb changes the verb's meaning slightly.* **¿Cuándo se celebran?** = *When are they celebrated? You will see this construction throughout* Puntos de partida.

Con. B: Notes

- The verb *caer* is presented in this context only, and it is not made active.
- Friday the 13th is considered to be a day of bad luck in this country. In Spanish-speaking countries, however, bad luck may fall on *martes trece.*
- Active vocabulary: *celebrar, el cumpleaños, el/la novio/a*

Con. B: Extension

- Ask students what holidays they associate with the following.
  1. *desfiles* (new)
  2. *tomar/beber champán*
  3. *mandar tarjetas, chocolates, flores*
  4. *barbacoas y picnics en el parque, fuegos artificiales* (new)
  5. *bromas* (new)
  6. *un árbol decorado, regalos*
- Write important years on board and have students say them in Spanish. Then match years and events.

1.	1492	a.	*la Declaración de la Independencia* (**2**)
2.	1776	b.	*el asesinato de John F. Kennedy* (**5**)
3.	1945	c.	*Cristóbal Colón llega a América* (**1**)
4.	2001	d.	*la bomba atómica* (**3**)
5.	1963	e.	*una película famosa* (**4**)
6.	1984	f.	*la novela de George Orwell* (**6**)

Con. C: Redacción

Assign *Con. C* for written homework. Collect the responses and correct them. Write one about yourself. Then hand out the paragraphs in class but not to their authors. Ask students to read the paragraph they have aloud. The class will try to guess who wrote each paragraph.

Nota cultural

Suggestions

- Ask students who have traveled to a Hispanic country to talk about the weather they experienced there.
- Ask students to do an Internet search for the specific weather pattern of a country of their (or your) choice.

Comprensión

1. *¿Qué países tienen solo dos estaciones?* (*los países de la zona tropical*)
2. *¿En qué se diferencian las dos estaciones?* (*Una es seca; la otra es húmeda.*)
3. *¿Qué tipo de fenómeno es El Niño?* (*un fenómeno meteorológico*)
4. *¿Con qué mes se asocia la llegada de este fenómeno?* (*diciembre*)
5. *¿Cuál es el fenómeno opuesto a El Niño?* (*La Niña*)

NATIONAL STANDARDS: Comparisons

Point out that the seasons in the southern hemisphere are the opposite of those in the U.S. and Canada. Have students associate seasons there, for example, *la primavera = agosto, septiembre, octubre*. Have students talk about how the difference in seasons in this country and South America may affect the dates that are important to them (holidays, birthdays, anniversaries). Would they, in this country, celebrate those dates differently if they fell in a different season? Also, have them calculate when the school year begins and ends in the southern hemisphere. Some schools list their calendars on the Internet.

¿Dónde está?: Las preposiciones (Part 2)

Reciclado: Review the concept of prepositions (*Cap. 5*) and the prepositions of time (*Cap. 5*) with questions about days of the week and months of the year: (*Julio*) *viene antes de* (*diciembre*), *¿verdad?* Be sure to include a number of false statements.

Suggestions

- Have students locate their country, city, or university using these prepositions. Write model sentences on the board.

  España está en la Península Ibérica al lado de Portugal. Está al sur de Francia y al norte de África.
- Optional vocabulary: *arriba de, enfrente de, sobre*.
- Point out that *enfrente de* frequently means *facing*, not always *in front of*.
- Optional concept: Contrast prepositions of place (location) with adverbs: *cerca, lejos, arriba, abajo, delante, detrás*.
- Remind students: *en* = in, at, on; *a* = to (direction and movement).

Bright Idea

Suggestion

Teach students the following rhyme with hand signals.

Izquierda, derecha, delante, detrás,
cerca, lejos y algo más,
abajo, arriba, debajo, encima,
y ahora señores, se acaba la rima.

Heritage Speakers

- Invite a los hispanohablantes a explicar la diferencia entre *delante de* y *enfrente de*. Pídales que den ejemplos de cada expresión.
- En algunos dialectos del español, especialmente en el Distrito Federal (méx.), de vez en cuando se oye *cercas* en vez de *cerca*, la forma preferida.

¿Dónde está? • Las preposiciones (Part 2)

Pablito está a la derecha de Teresa.

Teresa está entre Carmen y Pablito.

El libro está encima de la mesa.

La mochila está debajo de la mesa.

cerca de	close to	**delante de**	in front of
lejos de	far from	**detrás de**	behind
debajo de	below	**a la derecha de**	to the right of
encima de	on top of	**a la izquierda de**	to the left of
al lado de	alongside of	**al norte/sur/ este/oeste de**	to the north/south/ east/west of
entre	between, among		

Nota comunicativa

Los pronombres preposicionales

In Spanish, the pronouns that are objects of prepositions are identical in form to the subject pronouns, except for **mí** and **ti.**

Julio está **delante de mí.**	*Julio is in front of me.*
María está **detrás de ti.**	*María is behind you.*
Me siento **a la izquierda de ella.**	*I sit on her left.*

Mí and **ti** combine with the preposition **con** to form **conmigo** (*with me*) and **contigo** (*with you*), respectively.

—¿Vienes **conmigo**?	*"Are you coming with me?"*
—Sí, voy **contigo.**	*"Yes, I'll go with you."*

¡OJO!

Note that **mí** has a written accent, but **ti** does not. This is to distinguish the object of a preposition (**mí**) from the possessive adjective (**mi**).

NATIONAL STANDARDS: Comparisons

The origin of the word *izquierda* has been the focus of much debate by linguists. The Latin word for left (*sinister, sinistra, sinistrum*) was not adopted in Spanish due to the negative context that was associated with *sinister*. Despite the existence of a Latinate word for *left*, the Basque word for *left, izquierda*, was adopted instead.

Resources: Transparency 66

Conversación

A. ¿Quién o qué? Escoja a (*Choose*) una persona o un objeto en el salón de clase. Luego, sin nombrarlo/la (*without naming him/her/it*), use las preposiciones de lugar para explicar dónde está. La clase va a adivinar (*guess*) qué persona, objeto o mueble es.

MODELO: Está a la derecha de Paul ahora, pero generalmente se sienta detrás de mí. Siempre llega a clase con Paul. ¿Quién es?

B. ¿De qué país se habla?

Paso 1. Escuche (*Listen to*) la descripción de un país de Sudamérica que da (*gives*) su profesor(a). ¿Puede Ud. decir (*tell*) cuál es ese país?

Paso 2. Ahora describa un país de Sudamérica. Sus compañeros de clase van a decir cuál es. Siga (*Follow*) el modelo, usando todas las frases que sean (*are*) apropiadas.

MODELO: Este país está al norte/sur/este/oeste de _____. También está cerca de _____. Pero está lejos de _____. Está entre _____ y _____. Su capital es _____. ¿Cómo se llama?

C. Intercambios. Find out as much information as you can about the location of each others' hometown or state, or country of origin. You should also tell what the weather is like, and ask if the other person would like to go there with you.

MODELO: E1: ¿De dónde eres?
E2: Soy de Tylertown.
E1: ¿Dónde está Tylertown?
E2: Está cerca de…

Mundo interactivo

You should now be prepared to work with Scenario 3, Activity 3 in Connect Spanish (**www.connectspanish.com**).

Con. A: Suggestion

Have students work in pairs to complete this activity.

Con. A: Reciclado

Note the review of classroom furniture and other objects in this activity.

Con. A: Variations

Play Ten Questions. Think of a person or object in the classroom. Students are allowed ten yes/no questions to locate and identify the person or object, e.g., *¿Está lejos de la puerta?* Follow up with students thinking of the object or person.

Reciclado: Continue to review classroom objects by making statements about your classroom that incorporate prepositions of location: *La mesa está detrás de Uds., ¿verdad?* Review furniture with prepositions by returning to the drawing on page 168 and making similar statements.

Con. B: Suggestions

- Model for **Paso 1:** *Este país está al sur de los Estados Unidos. También está cerca de Panamá. Pero está lejos de la Argentina. ¿Cómo se llama?*
- Have students give information about the location of their hometown or state/province, or about your country of origen, as well as about the weather there.

  MODELO: *Soy de Sevilla. Está en el sur de España, cerca de África. En verano hace mucho calor, pero nunca hace mucho frío. Llueve en otoño, en invierno y parte de la primavera, pero por lo general no llueve mucho. Casi nunca llueve en verano.*
- Have students close their books. Give the name of Central and South American countries at random and ask students to give the capital. Reverse the procedure (give the capital and ask students for the country). Add *España / Madrid* (not shown in the text's maps) to the questions.

Con. B: Note

Active vocabulary: *la capital*

Pronunciación: See the Laboratory Manual for presentation and practice of the letters *r* and *rr*.

Multimedia: Internet

Have students search the Internet for more information about Central and South America's geography, climate, people, economy, transportation, and military. You might assign different countries and have students give brief oral presentations about the geography and climate of their assigned country.

Resources: Transparencies 67, 68

Gramática 15
Present Progressive: *Estar + -ndo*

Follow-up

After covering the *GEA*, ask students the following question.

¿Cuáles son algunas de las actividades que Ud. puede hacer pero que no está haciendo en este momento?

Coach students, based on activities they mentioned in the previous class discussion (*¿Y Uds.?*).

Carlos, ¿estás mirando la televisión en este momento?

Uses of the Progressive

Suggestions

- Use the visual in the *GEA* to teach the concept of the progressive; students should be able to produce progressive forms by following the models given.
- Emphasize that the Spanish progressive is used only for describing actions actually in progress (p. 171). Ask which of the following sentences would be expressed with progressive forms in Spanish.
  1. They are reading the newspaper now.
  2. Mary is typing all her homework this year.
  3. I'm speaking English right now.
  4. We're going to San Francisco next summer.
- As all instructors know, it is very tempting to students to use the present progressive in Spanish in situations where English would use it, in questions such as: *What courses are you taking this semester?* or *What novel are you reading these days?* Strictly speaking, many Spanish speakers would not use the Spanish progressive in such questions, and they would *never* use it in a question about the future, such as *Where are you going tomorrow?* or in a statement about the future, such as *I'm doing my homework after class.*
- Many but not all native speakers of Spanish *will* use the progressive in sentences like example 2. Instructors should decide what is acceptable usage for their classroom.

Note

Active vocabulary: *ahora mismo*

GRAMÁTICA

15 *¿Qué están haciendo?*
Present Progressive: **Estar + -ndo**

Grammar Tutorial 15
connect SPANISH
www.connectspanish.com

Gramática en acción: ¿Qué está haciendo Elisa?

Elisa es periodista. Por eso escribe y habla mucho por teléfono en su trabajo. Pero ahora mismo no está trabajando. Está descansando en casa. Está oyendo música, leyendo una novela y tomando un café.

¿Y Uds.?

En el salón de clase, ¿quién está haciendo las siguientes cosas en este momento? **¡OJO! nadie** = *nobody.*

1. _____ está hablando en su teléfono celular.
2. _____ está leyendo un periódico.
3. _____ está tomando un café.
4. _____ está mandando mensajes.
5. _____ está escuchando su iPod.

The Progressive / El progresivo

estoy **estás** **está** **estamos** **estáis** **están**	**tomando** **escribiendo** **abriendo**	I am you (*fam.*) are he, she, it, you (*form.*) are we are you (*pl. fam.*) are they, you (*pl. form.*) are	drinking writing opening

Uses of the Progressive / Los usos del progresivo

1. **The Progressive**
   Spanish and English form the *progressive* (**el progresivo**) in similar ways, as you can see in the preceding chart, but the use of the progressive is not the same in both languages.

the progressive / **el progresivo** = a verb form that expresses continuing or developing action

What's Elisa doing? *Elisa is a journalist. That's why she writes and talks a lot on the phone in her job. But she's not working right now. She's resting at home. She's listening to music, reading a novel, and having a cup of coffee.*

2. **Uses of the Progressive**
English uses the present progressive to tell what *is happening right now* (sentence 1 to the right). It also uses the present progressive to tell what *is happening over a period of time* (sentence 2) and what *is going to happen* (sentence 3).

However, in Spanish, the present progressive is used only to express an action that *is happening right now* (sentence 1). To express actions that are happening over a period of time, Spanish uses the simple present tense (sentence 2). To express actions that are going to happen, Spanish uses the simple present tense or **ir** + **a** + *infinitive* (sentence 3), but never the progressive.

1. *Ramón is eating right* now.
Ramón **está comiendo** ahora mismo.
2. *Adelaida is studying chemistry this semester.*
Adelaida **estudia** química este semestre.
3. *We're buying the house tomorrow.*
Compramos (Vamos a comprar) la casa mañana.

Forming of the Present Progressive / La formación del presente progresivo

1. **Spanish Present Progressive**
The Spanish *present progressive* (**el presente progresivo**) is formed with **estar** plus the *present participle* (**el gerundio**).

The present participle is formed by adding **-ando** to the stem of **-ar** verbs and **-iendo** to the stem of **-er** and **-ir** verbs.*

The present participle never varies; it always ends in **-o.**

a present participle / **un gerundio** = the verb form that ends in *-ing* in English

estar + *present participle*

tomar	⟶ **tomando**	taking; drinking
comprender	⟶ **comprendiendo**	understanding
abrir	⟶ **abriendo**	opening

¡OJO!
Unaccented **i** represents the sound [y] in the participle ending **-iendo: comiendo, viviendo.** Unaccented **i** between two vowels becomes the letter **y.**

leer: le + iendo ⟶ leyendo
oír: o + iendo ⟶ oyendo

2. **Present Participle of *-ir* Stem-changing Verbs**
-Ir stem-changing verbs also have a stem change in the present participle. In these verbs, the stem vowel **e** changes to **i** and the stem vowel **o** changes to **u.** Sometimes that change is the same as in the present tense (e.g., **pedir**) and sometimes it is different (e.g., **preferir** and **dormir**).

In vocabulary lists from this point on in *Puntos de partida,* this stem change will be shown in parentheses after the first person singular form of the verb. The verbs you have learned so far that show this change are: **divertirse, dormir(se), pedir, preferir, servir,** and **vestirse.**

preferir (prefiero) (i) ⟶ prefiriendo
pedir (pido) (i) ⟶ pidiendo
dormir (duermo) (u) ⟶ durmiendo

Note that (**duermo**) shows you the present tense stem change for **dormir: o ⟶ ue.** The (**u**) shows you the change in the present participle of **dormir: o ⟶ u (durmiendo).**

3. **Position of Reflexive Pronouns**
Refexive pronouns can be attached to a present participle or precede the conjugated form of **estar.** Note the accent on the present participle when pronouns are attached.

Pablo **se está** bañando.
Pablo está **bañándose.** } *Pablo is taking a bath.*

*__Ir, poder,__ and **venir** have irregular present participles: **yendo, pudiendo, viniendo.** These three verbs, however, are seldom used in the progressive.*

Emphasis 1: Note

Be aware of the possibility of confusion between the English term *gerund* and the Spanish *gerundio*. In English, the *gerund* is an *-ing* form used as a noun (as in ***Swimming** is good exercise*). The *-ing* form used in the phrase *I am **swimming*** is the *present participle* (= *el gerundio* in Spanish). There is no need to explain this distinction to your class, but students well versed in English grammar may notice it. As you know, *el gerundio* is never used as a noun in Spanish.

Emphasis 2: Suggestions

- Lead students through the conjugation of the *-ir* stem-changing verbs that they have learned so far (listed in this grammar point) so that they clearly see how these verbs work. While *pedir* and *servir* will seem easy, since their present participle change is identical to that of the present tense, the other verbs will be more challenging.
- Tell students to turn to the end-book vocabulary and ask them to look up some of these verbs, so that they clearly see the system in action and understand it.

Emphasis 3: Suggestion

Ask students to explain to you why there is no accent mark on *bañando* but there is one on *bañándose*. Remind them about *palabras llanas* and *palabras esdrújulas.*

Preliminary Exercise

Have students give new sentences based on the cues.

1. *—Todos los amigos de Ud. están en una fiesta. Ud. quiere asistir también. ¿Por qué?*
—Todos están bailando. (*tomar, cantar, comer, abrir botellas de champán, hablar mucho*)

   Point out that *todos* means *everyone* and is used with a plural verb.
2. *—Pero Ud. no puede ir. ¿Por qué no puede?*
—Estoy estudiando. (*trabajar, escribir los ejercicios, leer el periódico, mirar un programa muy interesante, aprender el vocabulario nuevo*)

Heritage Speakers

Los tiempos progresivos también pueden formarse combinando el gerundio con los verbos *andar, continuar, ir, seguir* y *venir* (véase los ejemplos). Invite a los hispanohablantes a dar algunos ejemplos de estas construcciones. ¿Se puede usar el verbo *estar* en las mismas construcciones?

Carlos anda buscando su abrigo.
Estos días vamos entendiéndolo mejor.
Sigue lloviendo.
Lorena siempre viene quejándose de algo.

Prac. A: Note

Active vocabulary: *el mediodía, mismo/a, la respuesta*

Prác. A: Suggestion

Ask students to give the infinitive for each present participle.

Prác. A: Variations

- Do *Paso 1* as a partner/pair activity, then have students share their results with the whole class in *Paso 2: A las ocho de la mañana los sábados, yo estoy durmiendo pero María está haciendo ejercicio.*
- Have students select someone with whom they spend time to talk about (*amigo/a, compañero/a de cuarto, esposo/a*). They should do the items in this activity using *nosotros*.

Prác. B: Notes

- The purpose of this exercise is explicitly to contrast routine activities with what is currently happening—the only use of the Spanish present progressive.
- Active vocabulary: *pasar*

Prác. B: Answers

1. *está pasando* **2.** *están tomando* **3.** *está jugando* **4.** *están cenando*

Prác. B: Follow-up

- Ask additional questions related to each scenario.
  1. *¿De qué están hablando? ¿De los parientes en Costa Rica? ¿de los parientes en este país?*
  2. *¿De qué están hablando? ¿De las clases de Lola? ¿de sus amigos?*
  3. *¿A qué están jugando? ¿A las cartas? ¿Dónde están jugando? ¿En el patio?*
  4. *¿Dónde están comiendo? ¿En el comedor? ¿Quiénes están comiendo en casa hoy?*
- Ask students the following personal questions.
  1. *¿Está Ud. hablando español ahora? ¿cantando? ¿tomando Coca-Cola? ¿escribiendo?*
  2. *¿Están Uds. bailando ahora? ¿regresando a casa? ¿regateando? ¿leyendo? ¿hablando con el profesor / la profesora?*

Autoprueba

Form the correct present participle.

a. -ando **b.** -iendo **c.** -yendo

1. pid_____
2. bañ_____
3. hac_____
4. le_____
5. durm_____
6. estudi_____

Now tell which of the following sentences is expressed by the Spanish present progressive.

1. I'm texting right now.
2. I'm leaving for Costa Rica tomorrow.
3. I'm exercising a lot this term.

Answers: **1.** b **2.** a **3.** b **4.** c **5.** b **6.** a; *Only sentence 1.*

Práctica

A. ¡Anticipemos! Un sábado típico

Paso 1. Imagine que es un sábado típico para Ud. Indique lo que Ud. está haciendo a las horas indicadas. En algunos (*some*) casos hay más de una respuesta posible.

A las ocho de la mañana…	SÍ	NO
1. estoy durmiendo.	☐	☐
2. estoy duchándome.	☐	☐
3. estoy haciendo ejercicio.	☐	☐
4. estoy trabajando.	☐	☐
5. estoy _____.	☐	☐

Al mediodía (*noon*)…	SÍ	NO
1. estoy almorzando.	☐	☐
2. estoy estudiando.	☐	☐
3. estoy tomando un café.	☐	☐
4. estoy viendo una película.	☐	☐
5. estoy _____.	☐	☐

A las diez de la noche…	SÍ	NO
1. estoy preparándome para salir.	☐	☐
2. estoy bailando en una fiesta.	☐	☐
3. estoy trabajando.	☐	☐
4. estoy hablando por teléfono.	☐	☐
5. estoy _____.	☐	☐

Paso 2. Ahora, en parejas, túrnense para determinar si hacen las mismas (*same*) cosas a la misma hora.

MODELO: **E1:** A las ocho de la mañana los sábados, ¿estás durmiendo?
E2: No, a esa hora estoy trabajando.

B. La familia de Lola. Hoy no es un día como todos los días para la familia de Lola, porque su tío de Costa Rica está de visita. Complete las siguientes oraciones para expresar lo que está pasando (*happening*).

MODELO: Casi siempre, Lola almuerza con su hija. Hoy Lola… (almorzar con su tío en un restaurante) ⟶
Hoy Lola **está almorzando** con su tío en un restaurante.

1. Generalmente, Lola pasa la mañana en la universidad. Hoy Lola… (pasar el día con su tío Ricardo)
2. Casi siempre, Lola va a casa después de sus clases. Hoy Lola y su tío… (tomar un café en casa)
3. De lunes a viernes, Marta, la hija de Lola, va a la escuela (*school*) por la tarde. Pero esta tarde ella… (jugar con Ricardo)
4. Generalmente, la familia cena (*has dinner*) a las nueve. Esta noche todos… (cenar a las diez)

Heritage Speakers

Los tiempos progresivos se usan para expresar acciones en curso, sean del presente o del pasado. El verbo *estar* puede conjugarse en cualquier tiempo verbal (*estoy/estaba/estuve/estaré/estaría comiendo*), pero el presente progresivo y el imperfecto progresivo ocurren con mayor frecuencia.

Invite a los hispanohablantes a explicar la diferencia entre *Están viendo las noticias* y *Estarán viendo las noticias.*

Multimedia: Internet

Have students search the Internet for information and pictures of Costa Rica. You might assign specific topics and have students give brief oral presentations based on their findings.

C. En casa con la familia Duarte

Paso 1. Describa lo que pasa en cada dibujo, explicando quién está haciendo la acción —el padre, la madre, la hija, los gemelos (*twins*), el perro— y a qué hora. Use los verbos de la lista u otros verbos, si desea. Puede hacer más de (*than*) una oración para cada dibujo, si quiere. **¡OJO!** Hay verbos reflexivos en las listas.

MODELO: salir de la ducha (*shower*) ⟶ El padre **está saliendo** de la ducha a las seis de la mañana.

Por la mañana: A las seis de la mañana

1. 2. 3. 4.

Verbos

dormir todavía (*still*)
leer el periódico
levantarse
salir de la ducha
tomar un café

Más tarde: A las ocho de la mañana

5. 6. 7. 8.

Verbos

desayunar
leer sus e-mails
pensar en el examen que tiene hoy
salir para la universidad
trabajar en la oficina
vestirse

Por la tarde: A las seis y media de la tarde

9. 10. 11. 12.

Verbos

hacer la tarea
jugar
leer su libro de texto
preparar la cena (*dinner*)
quitarse la ropa

Paso 2. Ahora explique qué hacen Ud. y otros miembros de su familia o sus compañeros de cuarto/casa a la misma hora que ve en los dibujos.

Prác. C: Notes

- Call students' attention to the culturally appropriate use of *tarde* (*Por la tarde: a las seis y media de la tarde*) in the third set of drawings.
- Active vocabulary: *todavía*

Prác. C: Possible Answers

1. *La hija está levantándose* (*se está levantando*). **2.** *El padre está saliendo de la ducha.* **3.** *La madre está leyendo el periódico y tomando un café.* **4.** *Los gemelos están durmiendo todavía. El perro está durmiendo también.* **5.** *La madre se está vistiendo* (*está vistiéndose*). **6.** *El padre está trabajando en la oficina y leyendo sus e-mails.* **7.** *Los gemelos están desayunando. El perro está desayunando también.* **8.** *La hija está saliendo para la universidad.* **9.** *La madre se está quitando* (*está quitándose*) *la ropa.* **10.** *La hija está leyendo su libro de texto y haciendo la tarea.* **11.** *Los gemelos están jugando con el perro.* **12.** *El padre está preparando la cena.*

Prác. C: Follow-up

Ask students the following personal questions.

Generalmente, ¿qué está haciendo Ud. / su familia a las 6 de la mañana?
¿a las 8 de la mañana?
¿a las 7:30 de la tarde?
¿a las 9:30 de la noche?
¿al mediodía?
¿a la medianoche (new)*?*

Reciclado

- Note the review of daily routine verbs as well as the review of the contrast between *por/de la mañana* (*tarde, noche*).
- Remind students that, with reflexive verbs, the article is used instead of the possessive adjective with body parts and personal possessions.

  María se quita ***el*** *sombrero /* ***los*** *zapatos /* ***los*** *guantes.*

Resources: Transparency 69

Con.: Notes

- This activity shows how the present participle functions with other verbs, just as in the English sentence *Do you spend more time reading or watching TV?* Present participles can also function as nouns in English, but not in Spanish; only the infinitive functions as a noun in Spanish
- subject: I like **reading.** = *Me gusta **leer.***
- object of a preposition: I insist on **traveling** today. = *Insisto en **viajar** hoy.*

Students do not have to know these linguistic facts, yet they certainly can profit from knowing this information. For now, remind students that Spanish cannot use a present participle after a preposition, only an infinitive.

Active vocabulary: *la medianoche*

Con.: Suggestion

Have students work in pairs and then report comparisons to the class.

Fred pasa más tiempo leyendo y yo paso más tiempo mirando la tele.
Fred y yo pasamos más tiempo leyendo.

Conversación

Nota comunicativa

El gerundio con otros verbos

As in English, the Spanish present participle **(el gerundio)** can be used with verbs other than **estar.** The following verbs are commonly used with the present participle.

• **pasar tiempo** + *present participle*	*to spend time* (doing something)
¿**Pasas** mucho tiempo **viendo** la televisión?	*Do you spend a lot of time watching television?*
• **seguir (sigo) (i) / continuar (continúo)*** + *present participle*	*to continue* (doing something)
Sigue lloviendo en Nueva York.	*It continues to rain in New York.*
• **divertirse (me divierto) (i)** + *present participle*	*to enjoy* (doing something)
¿Te **diviertes** mucho **tocando** el piano?	*Do you have a good time playing the piano?*

Remember that the letter in parentheses indicates the change in the present participle of the verb, which in this case would be **siguiendo.**

Intercambios

Paso 1. En parejas, túrnense para entrevistarse sobre los siguientes temas. Deben obtener detalles interesantes y personales de su compañero/a.

MODELOS: ¿Pasas mucho tiempo mirando la tele? ¿Cuántas horas al (*per*) día? ¿Qué programas te gusta mirar? ¿Cómo te diviertes más, bailando o tocando un instrumento musical?

		infinitivo ⟶ gerundio
continuar/seguir divertirse estar pasar más tiempo pasar mucho/poco tiempo	+	bailar hasta la medianoche (*midnight*) estudiar hablar español después de la clase leer ¿ ? mandar mensajes mirar la tele oír música ser amigo/a de tu mejor (*best*) amigo/a de la escuela primaria trabajar (en ¿ ?) ¿ ?

Paso 2. Digan a la clase lo que Uds. tienen en común.

*Note the present tense conjugation of **continuar,** which has an accent on the **u** when it is stressed:* **continúo, continúas, continúa, continuamos, continuáis, continúan.**

¿Recuerda Ud.?

You have been using forms of **ser** and **estar** since **Capítulo 1.** The following section will help you consolidate everything you know so far about these two verbs, both of which express *to be* in Spanish. You will learn a bit more about them as well.

Before you begin **Gramática 16,** think in particular about the following questions: **¿Cómo está Ud.? ¿Cómo es Ud.?** What do these questions tell you about the difference between **ser** and **estar**?

está = health or how someone is feeling
es = what someone is like

16 *¿Ser o estar?*

Summary of the Uses of **ser** and **estar**

Grammar Tutorial 16
connect SPANISH
www.connectspanish.com

Gramática en acción: Una conversación a larga distancia

Aquí hay un lado de la conversación entre una esposa que está en un viaje de negocios y su esposo, que está en casa. Habla el esposo.

Aló. [...] ¿Cómo estás, querida? [...] ¿Dónde estás ahora? [...] ¿Qué hora es allí? [...] ¡Huy!, es muy tarde. Y el hotel, ¿cómo es? [...] Oye, ¿qué estás haciendo ahora? [...] Ay, lo siento. Estás muy ocupada. ¿Con quién tienes cita mañana? [...] ¿Quién es el dueño de la compañía? [...] Ah, él es de Costa Rica, ¿verdad? [...] Bueno, ¿qué tiempo hace allí? [...] Muy bien. Hasta luego, ¿eh? [...] Adiós.

Comprensión

Complete las oraciones con **es** o **está.**

1. El esposo ___está___ en casa.
2. La esposa ___es___ una mujer de negocios.
3. La esposa ___está___ en un viaje de negocios.
4. ¿Cómo ___es___ el hotel? No lo sabemos. (*We don't know.*)
5. ___Es___ muy tarde donde está la esposa.
6. La esposa ___está___ trabajando ahora.
7. El dueño de la compañía ___es___ de Costa Rica.

A long-distance conversation *Here is one side of a conversation between a wife who is on a business trip and her husband, who is at home. The husband is speaking. Hello . . . How are you, dear? . . . Where are you now? . . . What time is it there? . . . Boy, it's very late. And how's the hotel? . . . Hey, what are you doing now? . . . Gosh, I'm sorry. You're very busy. Who do you have an appointment with tomorrow? . . . Who's the owner of the company? . . . Ah, he's from Costa Rica, isn't he? . . . Well, what's the weather like there? . . . Very well. See you later, OK? . . . Good-bye.*

Gramática 16
Summary of the Uses of *ser* and *estar*

Follow-up

Ask the following questions to check comprehension of the *GEA*.

1. *¿Quiénes son las dos personas?*
2. *¿Dónde están?*
3. *¿Qué están haciendo en este momento?*
4. *¿Es una situación normal? ¿Es agradable para los esposos?*

Note

Active vocabulary: *querido/a*

Suggestions

- Review the uses of *ser* and *estar.*
- Have students give additional examples of each use listed, where possible.
- Have students explain why *ser* and *estar* are used each time in the *GEA* and in *Comprensíon.*
- Assume the identity of a famous person (actor, artist, singer, athlete, and so on). Have students ask you yes/no questions to determine your identity. They may ask about your place of origin, your personality traits, your nationality, your profession, and so on. Model questions to get them started.
  1. *¿Es Ud. hombre?* (*mujer/niño/animal*)
  2. *¿Es Ud. una persona mayor?* (*joven/guapo/rubio/moreno*)
  3. *¿Es de los Estados Unidos?* (*del Canadá / de México*)
  4. *¿Es casado?* (*soltero/viudo*) (all new)
  5. *¿Está en* (*lugar*) *hoy?*
  6. *¿Está muy ocupado viviendo su vida estos días?* (*contento*)
  7. *¿Está en* (*programa de televisión / película*)*?*

NATIONAL STANDARDS: Comparisons

Point out the use of different expressions to answer the telephone in Spanish: *aló* in many Latin American countries, *bueno* in Mexico, and *diga* or *dígame* in Spain. To ask who is calling in order to pass the message, Spanish speakers generally ask *¿De parte de quién?* (Different ways to answer the phone in different countries are presented in the IM.)

Suggestions

- Have students identify which verb would be used with the following.

  para decir (new) *la hora*
  con el gerundio
  para identificar a una persona
  para expresar las posesiones
  para expresar el lugar
  para decir la fecha
  para decir la nacionalidad
  para identificar la profesión de una persona
  para indicar de qué materia es algo (new)
  para expresar el destino de algo
- Review *estar* for location, then read the following places aloud and have students tell where they are.
  1. *Madrid, Barcelona, Toledo, Segovia*
  2. *Bolivia, Colombia, el Paraguay, el Brasil*
  3. *Acapulco, Cancún, Puerto Vallarta*
  4. *Costa Rica, Guatemala, Nicaragua, Panamá*
  5. *Amarillo* (*Texas*), *Toledo* (*Ohio*), *Santa Cruz* (*California*), *San Agustín* (*la Florida*)

Note

Active vocabulary: *está bien*

Optional: Present the use of *ser* to tell the location of an event. You might compare these sentences: *¿Dónde es el examen?, ¿Dónde está el examen?* The English equivalent (*Where's the exam?*) is ambiguous in meaning; it could mean *where is the exam taking place?* or *where is the actual exam form?*

Ser and *estar* with Adjectives

Emphasis 1: Suggestion

Point out that *ser* + *adjective* represents the norm; *estar* + *adjective* represents a change from the norm.

Emphasis 1: Note

Active vocabulary: *cariñoso/a*

Reciclado

- In *Cap. 1*, students learned that *ser* is used to express time. Review the use of *ser* with time expressions (not explicitly practiced in student text exercises and activities in this section).
- Review adjective-noun placement with students.
- Have students provide the four forms for adjectives ending in *-o* and in *-dor*.
- Have students explain the forms for adjectives of nationality such as *francés, inglés, portugués,* and *irlandés.*

Summary of the Uses of ser / **Resumen de los usos de *ser***	
• To *identify* people (including their profession) and things	Ella es **doctora.** Tikal es **una ciudad maya.**
• To express *nationality;* with **de** to express *origin*	Son **cubanos.** Son **de** La Habana.
• With **de** to tell of what *material* something is made	Este bolígrafo es **de plástico.**
• With **de** to express *possession*	Es **de** Carlota.
• With **para** to tell *for whom something is intended*	El regalo es **para** Sara.
• To tell *time* and give the date	Son **las once.** Es **la una y media.** Hoy es **martes,** tres de octubre.
• With *adjectives* that describe *basic, inherent characteristics*	Ramona es **inteligente.**
• To form many *generalizations* (only **es**)	Es **necesario** llegar temprano. Es **importante** estudiar.

Summary of the Uses of estar / **Resumen de los usos de *estar***	
• To tell *location*	El libro está **en la mesa.**
• To describe *health*	Estoy muy **bien,** gracias.
• With *adjectives* that describe *conditions*	Estoy muy **ocupada.**
• In a number of *fixed expressions*	**(No)** Estoy **de acuerdo.** Está **bien.** (*It's fine, OK.*)
• With *present participles* to form the *progressive tense*	Estoy **estudiando** ahora mismo.

Ser and **estar** with Adjectives / ***Ser* y *estar* con adjetivos**

1. *Ser* = Fundamental Characteristics

Ser is used with adjectives that describe the fundamental qualities (**las características fundamentales**) of a person, place, or thing.

Esa mesa es muy **baja.**
That table is very short.

Sus calcetines son **morados.**
His socks are purple.

Este sillón es **cómodo.**
This armchair is comfortable.

Sus padres son **cariñosos.**
Their parents are affectionate people.

2. *Estar* = Conditions

Estar is used with adjectives to express conditions or observations that are true at a given moment but that do not describe inherent qualities of the noun. The adjectives at right are generally used with **estar.**

Temporary Conditions / **Las condiciones temporales**			
abierto/a	open	**limpio/a**	clean
aburrido/a	bored	**loco/a**	crazy
alegre	happy	**molesto/a**	annoyed
cansado/a	tired	**nervioso/a**	nervous
cerrado/a	closed	**ocupado/a**	busy
congelado/a	frozen; very cold	**ordenado/a**	neat
contento/a	content, happy	**preocupado/a**	worried
desordenado/a	messy	**seguro/a**	sure, certain
enfermo/a	sick	**sucio/a**	dirty
furioso/a	furious, angry	**triste**	sad

3. *Ser* or *estar*?

Many adjectives can be used with either **ser** or **estar,** depending on what the speaker intends to communicate. In general, when *to be* implies *looks, feels,* or *appears,* **estar** is used. Compare the pairs of sample sentences.

Daniel **es guapo.**
Daniel is handsome. (*He is a handsome person.*)
Daniel **está** muy guapo esta noche.
Daniel looks very nice (*handsome*) *tonight.*

—¿Cómo **es** Amalia?
—**Es simpática.**
"What is Amalia like (*as a person*)*?"*
"She's nice."

—¿Cómo **está** Amalia?
—**Está enferma** todavía.
"How is Amalia (*feeling*)*?"*
"She's still sick."

Autoprueba

¿**Ser** o **estar**?

	SER	ESTAR
1. to describe a health condition	☐	☐
2. to tell time	☐	☐
3. to describe inherent characteristics	☐	☐
4. to tell where a thing or person is located	☐	☐
5. to tell someone's profession	☐	☐
6. to say who something belongs to	☐	☐
7. to tell where someone is from	☐	☐
8. to describe a temporary condition	☐	☐
9. to make a generalization	☐	☐
10. to tell what something is intended for	☐	☐

Answers: **1.** *estar* **2.** *ser* **3.** *ser* **4.** *estar* **5.** *ser* **6.** *ser* **7.** *ser* **8.** *estar* **9.** *ser* (*es*) **10.** *ser*

Emphasis 2: Suggestions

- Point out that *estar* is used to express an unexpected quality.

  ¡Qué fría está el agua!

  To express what is expected, *ser* is used.

  El agua es fría. (The speaker expects the water to be cold and water is cold in its natural state (unless it is heated by something).
- Offer the following additional vocabulary: *de buen humor, de mal humor, despistado/a, enojado/a, enfadado/a, roto/a.*

Emphasis 3: Suggestion

Emphasize that to express how something looks, tastes, feels, or appears, *estar* is used. Contrast pairs of sentences and meanings found in this section.

Emphasis 3: Notes

- Point out that *Daniel está muy guapo esta noche* does not imply that he is by nature ugly, but rather comments on his appearance at a given point in time (he is especially handsome) or expresses the surprise of the speaker at how handsome he is tonight.
- As you know, many of the adjectives listed in *Gram. 2* change meaning when used with *ser* vs. *estar: aburrido* (*boring* vs. *bored*), *cansado* (*tiresome* vs. *tired*), and so on. This is not considered active material in *Puntos de partida.*
- Active vocabulary: *esta noche*

Preliminary Exercises

- Have students tell whether *ser* or *estar* is required for the following sentences.
  1. She is a very pretty woman.
  2. María is very pretty tonight.
  3. I'm nervous because of the test.
  4. We are in class now.
  5. These students are from Canada.
  6. It's 2:00.
  7. This is my mom.
- Have students form sentences based on the cues. For example,

  ¿El vestido? (*muy elegante*) ⟶
  El vestido es muy elegante.

  1. *¿John?* (*norteamericano*)
  2. *¿Mi escritorio?* (*desordenado*)
  3. *¿Los Hernández* (The Hernández family)*?* (*ocupados*)
  4. *¿Yo?* (*muy bien*)
  5. *¿Su abuelo?* (*muy viejo*)
  6. *¿El problema?* (*difícil*)
  7. *¿María?* (*de acuerdo con nosotros*)
  8. *¿Mis hijos?* (*simpáticos y buenos*)
  9. *¿La tienda?* (*abierta ahora*)

Prác. A, B, C: Suggestion

Have students justify the use of *ser* or *estar* in each case.

Prác. A: Suggestion

Ask students to work in pairs and redo *Prác. A,* changing *La computadora…* to *Las computadoras…*

Prác. A: Note

Active vocabulary: *fácil*

Prác. B: Suggestions

- After students have completed the items on their own, have them work in pairs to ask and answer questions based on the items.
- Then ask students to tell the class two things they have in common and two things they don't. Provide a model.

Prác. C: Possible Answers

1. *Son nuestros primos de San José.* **2.** *Son de Costa Rica.* **3.** *Son simpáticos.* **4.** *Están contentos en este momento.* **5.** *Están cansados por el viaje.* **6.** *Están aquí por un mes.* **7.** Answers will vary.

Prác. C: Follow-ups

- Think (or have students think) of an object or a person without saying who or what it is. Have students ask questions to guess.

  ¿Dónde está?
  ¿Cómo es?
  ¿De qué color es?
  ¿De dónde es?
- Have students bring in magazine photos of families and/or their own family photos and describe the family in the photo, using *ser* and *estar*. Alternatively, they can ask the class questions about the photos.
- Have students choose an object or person and create their own *ser/estar* sentences about it.
  1. *la (sala de) clase*
  2. *el profesor / la profesora*
  3. *los estudiantes de la clase* (students use *nosotros*)

Práctica

A. Un regalo estupendo. Use **es** o **está** para describir el siguiente regalo que los padres de su compañero/a de cuarto acaban de comprarle (*have just bought for him*).

La computadora…

1. _está_ en la mesa del comedor.
2. _es_ un regalo de cumpleaños.
3. _es_ para mi compañero de cuarto.
4. _es_ de la tienda Computec.
5. _está_ en una caja (*box*) verde.
6. _es_ de los padres de mi compañero.
7. _es_ un regalo muy caro, pero estupendo.
8. _es_ de metal y plástico gris.
9. _es_ una IBM, el último (*latest*) modelo.
10. _es_ muy fácil (*easy*) de usar.

B. Descripciones. Haga oraciones con **soy** o **estoy.** Corrija las ideas incorrectas.

Yo (no)…

1. _soy_ estadounidense.
2. _soy_ de Nevada.
3. _soy_ estudiante de primer año en la universidad. (2nd = segundo, 3rd = tercer, 4th = cuarto)
4. _estoy_ muy cansado/a hoy.
5. _estoy_ bien en este momento.
6. _estoy_ de acuerdo con las ideas del presidente / primer ministro.
7. _estoy_ estudiando química en este momento.
8. _soy_ muy inteligente.

Nota **comunicativa**

El uso de adjetivos + *por*

Por often expresses *because of* or *about,* especially with adjectives such as **contento/a, furioso/a, nervioso/a,** and **preocupado/a.**

Amalia está preocupada **por** los exámenes finales.
Amalia is worried about her final exams.

The word **por** is used in this way in **Prácticas C** and **D.**

C. ¿Quiénes son? En parejas, hagan oraciones con **ser** o **estar,** inventando detalles para describir a las personas y cosas que se ven en la foto.

1. ¿quiénes?
2. ¿de qué país?
3. simpáticos/antipáticos / ¿ ?
4. en este momento, contentos/tristes / ¿ ?
5. molestos/cansados por el viaje / ¿ ?
6. aquí por un mes / una semana / ¿ ?
7. ¿ ?

Nuestros primos de San José

Multimedia: Internet

Ask students to check the website for *La Nación* (www.nacion.com) and bring to class at least two headlines they find.

D. Publicidad. Complete el siguiente anuncio (*ad*) con la forma apropiada de **ser** o **estar,** según el contexto.

Costa Rica… belleza[a] natural

¿(*Tú:* Eres [1]) de una gran ciudad? ¿(*Tú:* Eres [2]) una persona aventurera? ¿(Es [3]) la naturaleza una gran atracción en tu vida[b]? ¿(Estás [4]) preocupado/a por los cambios[c] en el clima global? Entonces,[d] Costa Rica (es [5]) el país para ti. Imagina: (estás [6]) en un lugar cerca del mar[e] en donde hay increíbles especies de animales y plantas: iguanas, caimanes, tortugas, orquídeas, heliconias…

(*Nosotros:* Somos [7]) los expertos en turismo natural en Costa Rica. Todos nuestros guías[f] (son [8]) costarricenses de nacimiento,[g] pero (*ellos:* están [9]) contentos de conocer[h] a personas de todo el mundo y hacer nuevos amigos. Con sus conocimientos,[i] con su gran paciencia, con su español, (*ellos:* son [10]) como profesores… pero sus clases (son [11]) mucho más interesantes que las clases académicas… ¡y menos difíciles!

No (es [12]) necesario viajar[j] a Costa Rica en una estación específica. (Es [13]) bueno viajar a Costa Rica en cualquier[k] mes del año.

¡Ven![l] ¡Costa Rica (está [14]) esperándote[m]!

[a]*beauty* [b]*life* [c]*changes* [d]*Then* [e]*ocean* [f]*guides* [g]de… *by birth* [h]de… *to meet* [i]*knowledge* [j]*to travel* [k]*any* [l]*Come (to visit)!* [m]*waiting for you*

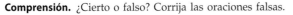

Una heliconia

Comprensión. ¿Cierto o falso? Corrija las oraciones falsas.

	CIERTO	FALSO	
1. En Costa Rica, la naturaleza tiene mucha importancia para el turismo.	☑	☐	
2. El turista no va a ver animales exóticos en Costa Rica.	☐	☑	El turista puede ver iguanas, caimanes y más.
3. El turista puede aprender español allí.	☑	☐	
4. En Costa Rica, no todas las estaciones son apropiadas para el turismo. Es bueno viajar a Costa Rica en cualquier mes.	☐	☑	

E. Una conversación a large distancia

Paso 1. En parejas, vuelvan a leer (*re-read*) lo que el esposo le dice (*says*) a su esposa, que está en un viaje de negocios (columna A). Luego, emparejen sus palabras con las frases de la columna B, que son las respuestas de la esposa.

A

1. d Aló.
2. i ¿Cómo estás, querida?
3. h ¿Dónde estás ahora?
4. c ¿Qué hora es allí?
5. a ¡Huy!, es muy tarde. Y el hotel, ¿cómo es?
6. f Oye, ¿qué estás haciendo ahora?
7. k Ay, lo siento. Estás muy ocupada. ¿Con quién tienes cita mañana?
8. e ¿Quién es el dueño de la compañía?
9. b Ah, él es de Costa Rica, ¿verdad?
10. j Bueno, ¿qué tiempo hace allí?
11. g Muy bien. Hasta luego, ¿eh?
12. Adiós.

B

a. muy moderno / me gusta mucho
b. sí / pero / vivir en Nueva York ahora
c. las once de la noche
d. hola, querido / ¿qué tal?
e. el Sr. Cortina
f. tener que trabajar todavía
g. sí / hasta pronto
h. en Nueva York
i. un poco cansada / pero / bien
j. buen tiempo / pero / un poco nublado
k. con un señor de Computec

Paso 2. Ahora inventen la conversación completa entre los esposos. Primero, hagan oraciones completas, usando **ser, estar** o **hacer** cuando no hay otro verbo, con las frases de la columna B. Luego lean la conversación, haciendo los papeles (*roles*) de los dos esposos.

Prác. D: Suggestion

Follow the previous suggestions for handling contextual paragraph activities.

- Remind students that when a subject pronoun is given in italics in this type of exercise, there is no need to use it explicitly. It is there as a clue for students.
- Have students create a similar ad for the area where your university is located. You will need to supply appropriate vocabulary for local sites of interest.

Prác. D: Note

Active vocabulary: *difícil*

Prác. D: Follow-up

Ask students the following questions to check comprehension and to personalize.

1. *¿Hay mucha belleza natural en Costa Rica? (sí)*
2. *¿Qué flores hay en Costa Rica? ¿Qué animales hay? (orquídeas, heliconias; iguanas, caimanes, tortugas)*
3. *¿Es Ud. una persona aventurera? ¿una persona que tiene mucho interés en la naturaleza? ¿una persona que se preocupa mucho por el clima global?*
4. *¿Piensa Ud. viajar a Costa Rica algún* (new) *día?*

Prác. E: Suggestion

Have several students read their dialogues aloud to the whole class.

Prác. F: Note

The purpose of *Paso 1* is to give students practice with the "new" adjectives presented in the preceding section. No *ser* vs. *estar* decisions are called for.

Prác. F: Suggestion

Have students do the entire exercise working in pairs or in groups, adding details to make the description more complete. Ask pairs or groups to turn in their descriptions of the house and give a prize for the best (= most detailed and most correct) description.

Prác. F: Follow-up

- Have students talk about inherent traits of the house and its inhabitants by making sentences with *ser: La casa es grande.*
- Have students imagine what the following people are doing at 6:30 in the afternoon.
  1. *Ud., su profesor(a)*
  2. *dos compañeros de clase*
  3. *sus padres (hijos, esposo/a)*
  4. *el presidente / primer ministro y su esposa*

F. Una tarde terrible

Paso 1. Hoy es un día desastroso para la familia Castañeda. Ud. va a describir su casa en el **Paso 2.** Para prepararse, repase (*review*) primero unos adjetivos, cambiando (*exchanging*) las palabras rosadas por antónimos en las siguientes oraciones.

1. No hace buen tiempo; hace mal tiempo.
2. El bebé no está bien; está mal/enfermo.
3. El gato no está limpio; está sucio.
4. El esposo no está tranquilo; está preocupado/nervioso por el bebé.
5. El garaje no está cerrado; está abierto.
6. Los niños no están ocupados; están preocupados, porque tienen miedo.
7. La esposa no está contenta; está nerviosa/preocupada por el tiempo.
8. El baño no está ordenado; está desordenado.

Estrategia

lo que están haciendo = el presente progresivo
el estado de ánimo = el presente simple
lo que usualmente hacen = el presente simple

Paso 2. Ahora use los adjetivos del **Paso 1** y otros que Ud. conozca (*you know*) para expresar lo que *están haciendo* todos los miembros de la familia *en este momento*. Póngales (*Give*) nombres a todos y exprese el estado de ánimo de ellos (*their feelings*) o sus deseos. ¡Use su imaginación! Si puede, diga también lo que *usualmente hacen* estas personas a esta hora.

Vocabulario útil

la cena	dinner	**ladrar**	to bark
cenar	to have dinner	**llorar**	to cry
cocinar	to cook	**los truenos y relámpagos**	thunder and lightning
conducir (conduzco)*	to drive		

*Only the first person singular of the verb **conducir** is irregular, as noted. The other forms of the present tense are regular: **conduces, conduce...***

Heritage Speakers

En Latinoamérica, es más común usar el verbo *manejar* o *guiar* en vez de *conducir,* pero en España se dice *conducir.* Pregúnteles a los hispanohablantes qué término prefieren usar.

Resources: Transparency 70

Conversación

A. Ana y Estela. Conteste las preguntas para describir el siguiente dibujo de un cuarto de dos estudiantes. **¡OJO!** Invente otros detalles necesarios.

Vocabulario útil

el cajón drawer
el cartel poster
la foto

1. ¿Quiénes son las dos compañeras de cuarto?
2. ¿Dónde estudian? ¿Qué estudian?
3. ¿De dónde son?
4. ¿Cómo son?
5. ¿Dónde están en este momento?
6. ¿Qué hay en el cuarto?
7. ¿Cómo está el cuarto?
8. ¿Son ordenadas las dos o desordenadas?

B. Intercambios. ¿Cómo están Uds. en estas situaciones? En parejas, túrnense para hacer y contestar preguntas, según el model.

MODELO: cuando / tener mucha tarea →
E1: ¿Cómo estás cuando **tienes** mucha tarea?
E2: Estoy cansado y estresado, como ahora. ¿Y tú?
E3: Yo también.

1. cuando / tener mucha tarea / una tarea fácil/difícil
2. cuando / no tener trabajo académico
3. cuando / sacar (*to get*) A/D en un examen
4. en verano/invierno
5. cuando llueve/nieva
6. los lunes por la mañana / los domingos por la tarde / los…
7. después de una fiesta / un examen
8. durante la clase de
9. ¿ ?

Vocabulario útil

agobiado/a overwhelmed
desahogado/a relieved
enérgico/a
estresado/a

Con. A: Suggestion

Have students prepare descriptions of famous people, using a minimum of 5 sentences. Then have volunteers present their descriptions to the class. For example:

Cameron Díaz → Es actriz. Es muy guapa. Es rubia. Tiene muchos novios.

Con. A: Extension

Bring or have students bring magazine ads and clippings to class. Have students describe what they see and invent background stories. Use questions similar to those in *Con. A* to get students going.

Con. B: Notes

- The purpose of this activity is to give students focused practice with *estar* + adjectives that describe states in relatively simple sentences, in contrast to adjectives that are used with *ser*.
- Many Spanish speakers prefer to use *sentirse* in sentences of this kind. You may wish to introduce *sentirse* (*me siento*) as an option before doing the activity if you are uncomfortable with the use of *estar* in these sentences.
- *Sentirse* and other verbs for expressing emotions are presented in *Cap. 9*.

Con. B: Extension

10. *cuando una persona / hablar y hablar y hablar*
11. *cuando / estar con la familia*
12. *cuando / estar de vacaciones*
13. *cuando / no funcionar el coche*
14. *cuando ir / al dentista*

Con. B: Variation

Have students complete sentences, telling what they are usually doing if they are (adjective).

1. *Estoy preocupado/a cuando* ______.
2. *Estoy aburrido/a cuando* ______.
3. *Estoy furioso/a cuando* ______.
4. *Estoy de buen/mal humor cuando* ______.

Resources: Transparency 71

Gramática 17
Comparisons

Note

Active vocabulary: *sin embargo*

Suggestion

After students have read the *GEA* and completed *¿Y Ud.?*, take them through the lines one by one, asking them how to express *as big as, as many as,* and so on. Write the Spanish comparatives on the board as students answer, adding the part of speech compared and putting their answers in a coherent order. You will have a chart that looks something like this.

tan + ***adjetivo*** + *como*
tanto/a + ***sustantivo*** + *como*
más/menos + ***sustantivo*** + *que*
más/menos + ***adjetivo*** + *que*

Point out to students that all that students need to learn in this section are these structures to compare adjectives and nouns, and similar structures to compare actions.

Reciclado: Review prepositions of location by discussing the location of *Buenos Aires* and *San José* (see maps located at the back of the textbook).

Follow-up

Have students compare their university with another.

¿Cuál es más grande? ¿Es tan cara su universidad como ______ (la otra)?
Los estudiantes de esta universidad, ¿estudian tanto como los estudiantes de la otra (universidad)?

Bright Idea

Follow-up

Have students compare their city with New York, Chicago, Toronto, or Montreal.

¿Cuál es más grande/pequeña?
¿Cuál tiene edificios más altos?
¿Cuál es más bonita?
¿Cuál es más/menos cosmopolita?

Heritage Speakers

Pídales a los hispanohablantes que busquen información sobre la historia de San José o de Buenos Aires en la biblioteca y en el Internet. Anímelos a escribir varios párrafos acerca de la ciudad que escojan.

17 Describing
Comparisons

Grammar Tutorial 17
connect SPANISH
www.connectspanish.com

Gramática en acción: Buenos Aires y San José

El centro de Buenos Aires, Argentina

El centro de San José, Costa Rica

- Buenos Aires es más grande que San José.
- Tiene más edificios altos que San José.
- Generalmente, en Buenos Aires no hace tanto calor como en San José.

Pero…

- San José es menos antigua que Buenos Aires.
- No tiene tantos habitantes como Buenos Aires.
- Sin embargo, los costarricenses son tan simpáticos como los argentinos.

¿Y Ud.?

1. Mi ciudad/pueblo…
   - es / no es tan grande como Chicago.
   - es más/menos cosmopolita que Quebec.
2. Me gusta ______ (nombre de mi ciudad/pueblo)…
   - más que ______ (nombre de otra ciudad).
   - menos que ______ (nombre de otra ciudad).
   - tanto como ______ (nombre de otra ciudad).

In English *comparisons* (**las comparaciones**) are formed in a variety of ways. Equal comparisons are expressed with the word *as*. Unequal comparisons are expressed with the adverbs *more* or *less,* or by adding *-er* to the end of the adjective.

as cold ***as***
as many ***as***

more intelligent,
less important,
tall***er***, smart***er***

a comparative / **un comparativo** = a form of or structure with nouns, adjectives, and adverbs used to compare nouns, qualities, or actions

Buenos Aires and San José *Buenos Aires is bigger than San José. • It has more tall buildings than San José. • It is not as hot in Buenos Aires as it is in San José, generally. But… San José is newer (lit., less ancient) than Buenos Aires. • It doesn't have as many inhabitants as Buenos Aires. • Nevertheless, Costa Ricans are as nice as Argentines.*

NATIONAL STANDARDS: Culture

San José, founded in 1738, became capital of Costa Rica in 1823. Its current population is around 400,000, but that of the whole metropolitan area is well over 2 million. The city offers various attractive museums and parks. The city's official web site is www.msj.go.cr.

Buenos Aires was founded twice. The first time was in 1539, but it was subsequently destroyed by indigenous people; the second, permanent founding date is 1580. The city's name comes from the original name of the settlement, *Nuestra Señora del Buen Aire*. With close to 13 million inhabitants, Buenos Aires ranks tenth in the

(Cont.)

Comparatives / **Los comparativos**					
Inequality / **La desigualdad**				Equality / **La igualdad**	
más... que **más que**	more . . . than more than	**menos... que** **menos que**	less . . . than less than	**tan... como** **tanto/a/os/as... como** **tanto como**	as . . . as as much/many as as much as

Inequality / **La desigualdad**

1. Comparing Adjectives, Adverbs, and Verbs

Para describir:

more/less + adjective } *+ than*
adjective + -er

más/menos + *adjective* + **que**

Juan es **más alto que** Elena.
Juan is taller than Elena (is).

Elena es **menos alta que** Juan.
Elena is shorter than Juan (is).

Para describir cómo se hace una acción:

more/less + adverb } *+ than*
adverb + -er

más/menos + *adverb* + **que**

Juan corre **más rápido que** Elena.
Juan runs faster (more quickly) than Elena (does).

Elena corre **menos rápido que** Juan.
Elena runs slower (less quickly) than Juan (does).

¡OJO!

While the repetition of the verb is optional in English, as shown in the examples, the second verb is *never* repeated in Spanish.

Para expresar la frecuencia o intensidad de una acción:

verb + more/less than

verb + **más/menos que**

Juan **corre más que** Elena.
Juan runs more than Elena (does).

Elena **corre menos que** Juan.
Elena runs less than Juan (does).

2. Comparing Nouns

Para comparar la cantidad:

more/less (fewer) + noun + than

más/menos + *noun* + **que**

Rigoberto tiene **más coches que** Carmen.
Rigoberto has more cars than Carmen (does).

Carmen tiene **menos coches que** Rigoberto.
Carmen has fewer cars than Rigoberto (does).

3. *More/Less than + number*

¡OJO!

The preposition **de** is used instead of **que** when the comparison is followed by a number.

Para expresar una cantidad:

more/less (fewer) than + number + noun

más/menos de + *number* + *noun*

Juan tiene **más de dos** lápices.
Juan has more than two pencils.

Elena tiene **menos de dos** lápices.
Elena has less than two pencils.

Inequality

Emphasis 1, 2: Note

The examples are presented in this order: adjective, adverb, verb, noun.

Suggestions

- Provide additional examples for each part of speech, especially if you wish to emphasize that aspect of the presentation.
- **Optional:** Present the high frequency expression *más o menos:* (1) In response to inquiries about how one is: *Estoy más o menos (bien).* (2) To express "approximately": *Carolina tiene cuatro años, más o menos.*
- **Optional:** Introduce the exception to the *más/menos de* + number rule. *Que* can be used after a negative: *No tengo más que un hijo.*

world in size according to the population of its metropolitan area, and it is the third largest city in Latin America, after Mexico City and Sao Paulo. It is one the greatest cultural centers of the Americas, with many museums, theaters, restaurants, and so on. The city's official website is www.buenosaires.gov.ar.

Resources: Transparencies 72–74

Equality

Note

The examples are presented in this order: adjective, adverb, verb, noun.

Suggestion

Provide additional examples for each part of speech, especially if you wish to emphasize that aspect of the presentation.

Equality / La igualdad

1. Comparing Adjectives, Adverbs, and Verbs

¡OJO!
Remember that the second verb, optional in English, is *never* repeated in Spanish.

> **Para describir:**
> *as + adjective + as*
> **tan** + *adjective* + **como**

Patricia es **tan alta como** Ernesto. También es **tan delgada como** él.
Patricia is as tall as Ernesto (is). She's also as thin as he (is).

> **Para describir cómo se hace una acción:**
> *as + adverb + as*
> **tan** + *adverb* + **como**

Patricia juega al tenis **tan bien como** Juan. También juega **tan agresivamente como** él.
Patricia plays tennis as well as Juan (does). She also plays as aggressively as he (does).

> **Para expresar la frecuencia o intensidad de una acción:**
> *verb + as much as*
> *verb* + **tanto como**

Patricia **juega** al tenis **tanto como** Juan. También **gana tanto como** él.
Patricia plays tennis as much as Juan (does). She also wins as much (often) as he (does).

2. Comparing Nouns

¡OJO!
Like all adjectives, **tanto** must agree in gender and number with the noun it modifies: **tanto dinero, tanta prisa, tantos abrigos, tantas hermanas.**

> **Para comparar la cantidad:**
> *as much/many + noun + as*
> **tanto/a/os/as** + *noun* + **como**

Ernesto tiene **tantos trofeos como** Patricia. También tiene **tantas raquetas de tenis como** ella.
Ernesto has as many trophies as Patricia (does). He also has as many tennis rackets as she (does).

Patricia y Ernesto tienen **tantas hermanas como** hermanos.
Patricia and Ernesto each have as many sisters as (they have) brothers.

Resources: Transparencias 75–79

Irregular Forms / **Las formas irregulares**

- **bueno/a/os/as** *adj.* ⟶ **mejor, mejores** — Estos coches son **buenos,** pero esos son **mejores.** *These cars are good, but those are better.*
- **bien** *adv.* ⟶ **mejor** — Yo hablo español **bien,** pero mi amigo Dennis lo habla **mejor.** *I speak Spanish well, but my friend Dennis speaks it better.*
- **malo/a/os/as** *adj.* ⟶ **peor, peores** — La nueva película de este director es **mala,** pero su primera es **peor.** *This director's new movie is bad, but his first one is worse.*
- **mal** *adv.* ⟶ **peor** — La profesora canta **mal,** pero yo canto **peor.** *The professor sings badly, but I sing worse.*
- **viejo/a/os/as** ⟶ **mayor, mayores** — La abuela es **viejita,** pero el abuelo es **mayor** que ella. *Grandmother is old, but grandfather is older than she (is).*
- **joven, jóvenes** ⟶ **menor, menores** — Delia es **joven,** pero su esposo es todavía **menor** que ella. *Delia is young, but her husband is even younger than she (is).*

Comparison Summary

más… que	menos… que	tan… como
más que	menos que	tanto/a/os/as… como tanto como

Práctica

A. Alfredo y Gloria. Compare lo que tienen Alfredo y Gloria, según los modelos.

+ ⟶ **más**   – ⟶ **menos**   = ⟶ **la misma** (*same*) **cantidad**

MODELO: Alfredo: + bicicletas ⟶ Alfredo tiene **más** bicicletas **que** Gloria.

1. Alfredo: – camisetas
2. Gloria: + sudaderas
3. Alfredo: = canciones (*songs*) en su iPod
4. Gloria: = clases
5. Alfredo: = amigos
6. Gloria: + amigos de habla española

MODELO: Gloria: + alcobas ⟶ El apartamento de Gloria tiene **más** alcobas **que** el apartamento de Alfredo.

7. Alfredo: – cuartos en total
8. Gloria: = baños
9. Alfredo: = camas
10. Gloria: = estantes

MODELO: Alfredo: = estudiar ⟶ Alfredo estudia **tanto como** Gloria.

11. Gloria: = hacer ejercicio
12. Alfredo: + salir con los amigos
13. Gloria: – dormir
14. Alfredo: = mirar su Facebook

Autoprueba

Match each word with the corresponding comparative word.

a. como   **b.** que

1. más + ____
2. tantos + ____
3. peor + ____
4. tan + ____
5. menos + ____
6. tanta + ____

Answers: **1.** *b* **2.** *a* **3.** *b* **4.** *a* **5.** *b* **6.** *a*

Irregular Forms

Suggestions

- Emphasize the four forms of *bueno/malo* (gender and number agreement) in contrast with the two forms of *mejor* and *peor* (just number agreement).
- Explain that *más grande* and *más pequeño* compare size. *Mayor* and *menor* generally refer to age.

Preliminary Exercises

- Have students name someone who meets the following criteria.

  Dé el nombre de alguien…

  1. *tan guapo como Enrique Iglesias.*
  2. *tan bonita como Penélope Cruz.*
  3. *tan rico como Bill Gates.*
  4. *tan inteligente como Einstein.*
  5. *tan fiel como Romeo y Julieta.*

- Have students tell if they have the following.

  ¿Tiene Ud…

  1. *tanto dinero como Bill Gates?*
  2. *tantos años como su profesor(a) de español?*
  3. *tantas clases como su compañero/a de cuarto (esposo/a)?*
  4. *tantos problemas como su mejor amigo/a?*
  5. *tantos tíos como tías?*

Reciclado: Request specific information from two or more students in order to model comparisons. Compare one student's information with that of another, then ask students to compare their own information with that of one of their classmates. Possible topics: number of classes they are taking, number of credit hours, what time they get up (go to bed), how many hours they sleep, how old they are, number of family members, number of hours per week they work (study, play a sport, listen to music), how many pairs of shoes (sweatshirts, T-shirts) they have, number of rooms (television sets, sofas) in their house or apartment.

Prác. A: Suggestions

- Do as a partner activity.
- If you are doing this as a whole-class activity, encourage students to form both *más* and *menos* comparisons with appropriate items.

Resources: Transparency 80

Prác. A: Answers

1. *Alfredo tiene menos camisetas que Gloria* **2.** *Gloria tiene más sudaderas que Alfredo.* **3.** *Alfredo tiene tantas canciones en su iPod como Gloria.* **4.** *Gloria tiene tantas clases como Alfredo.* **5.** *Alfredo tiene tantos amigos como Gloria.* **6.** *Gloria tiene más amigas de habla española que Alfredo.* **7.** *El apartamento de Alfredo tiene menos cuartos en total que el apartamento de Gloria.* **8.** *El apartamento de Gloria tiene tantos baños como el apartamento de Alfredo.* **9.** *El apartamento de Alfredo tiene tantos camas como el apartamento de Gloria.* **10.** *El apartamento de Gloria tiene tantos estantes como el apartamento de Alfredo.* **11.** *Gloria hace tanto ejercicio como Alfredo.* **12.** *Alfredo sale con los amigos más que Gloria.* **13.** *Gloria duerme menos que Alfredo.* **14.** *Alfredo mira su Facebook tanto como Gloria.*

B. Opiniones. Modifique las siguientes declaraciones para expresar su opinión personal. Si Ud. está de acuerdo con la declaración, diga: **«Estoy de acuerdo».**

MODELO: El cine es tan interesante como la televisión →
Para mí, el cine es **más** interesante **que** la televisión.

1. El fútbol es tan divertido (*entertaining*) como el fútbol americano.
2. La clase de historia es más interesante que la clase de español.
3. En esta universidad, las artes son tan importantes como los deportes (*sports*).
4. El español es tan difícil como el inglés.
5. Me divierto tanto con mis amigos como con mis padres.
6. Los niños duermen menos que los adultos.
7. Los profesores trabajan más que los estudiantes.
8. Aquí llueve más en primavera que en invierno.

C. Más opiniones

Paso 1. Compare las siguientes personas y cosas para expresar su opinión sobre ellas. Puede añadir (*add*) más palabras si quiere.

MODELO: el basquetbol y el golf:
interesante, rápido, fácil de aprender →
El basquetbol es **menos** interesante **que** el golf.

1. Meryl Streep y Cameron Díaz:
joven, bonito, tener premios Óscar, actriz
2. Ud. y sus padres (hijos):
joven, conservador, tener experiencia, desordenado
3. un Prius y un Cadillac:
grande, barato, gastar (*to use*) gasolina, elegante
4. los perros y los gatos:
independiente, inteligente, cariñoso, activo
5. Orlando Bloom y Tom Cruise:
joven, guapo, serio, actor
6. Texas y Delaware:
grande, habitantes, petróleo, lejos de California

Paso 2. En parejas, comparen sus opiniones. Traten de (*Try to*) explicar sus razones.

MODELO: el basquetbol y el golf:
interesante, rápido →
E1: El basquetbol es **menos** interesante **que** el golf.
E2: No estoy de acuerdo. El basquetbol es **más** interesante **que** el golf porque es **más** rápido.

Conversación

A. Comparaciones. Complete las siguientes oraciones según su opinion personal.

1. En mi familia, yo soy mayor que ____ y menor que ____.
2. En esta clase, ____ estudia tanto como yo.
3. En esta universidad, los estudiantes ____ más que ____.
4. ____ es más guapo que Juanes.
5. ____ es más guapa que Shakira.
6. ____ tiene tanto talento como Carlos Santana.

Prác. B: Suggestions

- Have students create their own sentences about their university and have others tell whether they agree or not. Those that disagree should change the sentence so that it is true for them.

  Nuestra universidad es tan buena como la Universidad de Texas. →
  No, nuestra universidad es mejor que la Universidad de Texas.

- *¿Cómo se dice?* Ask students how the following are said in Spanish.
  1. I enjoy myself more/less than my roommate.
  2. I work as much as she does.
  3. She watches TV as much as all of us.
  4. We eat more/less than she does.

Prác. B: Extension

9. *Los exámenes de matemáticas son más fáciles que los exámenes de español.*
10. *El dinero es tan importante como la salud* (new).
11. *Los amigos son tan importantes como la familia.*
12. *En esta universidad, los estudios son menos importantes que los deportes.*
13. *En mi vida, los estudios son más importantes que los deportes.*
14. *Necesito más el dinero que la amistad* (new).

NATIONAL STANDARDS

Communities

- **Juanes** (Medellín, Colombia, 1972–) is the stage name of Juan Esteban Aristizábal Vásquez. He started his career in a heavy metal band and had his first solo album in 2000. He has won one Grammy and seventeen Latin Grammys. He has defended a number of political and social causes, notably the use of Spanish, and so far he has refused to sing and record in English. Official website: www.juanes.net.
- **Shakira** (Barranquilla, Colombia, 1977–) is the stage name of Shakira Isabel Mebarak Ripoll. Her family is of Lebanese and Spanish origin. She recorded her first album when she was only 13 years old. She is a UNICEF Goodwill Ambassador and an active philanthropist. Official website: www.shakira.com.
- **Carlos Santana** was born July 20, 1947, in Autlán, Mexico. His band, Santana, is one of the most influential bands in rock music. In 1969 Santana performed at Woodstock, reaching new audiences outside the Mission district of San Francisco. Santana's combination of rock and Latin music was completely new, powerful, and riveting. His comeback CD *Supernatural* won several Grammy awards, bringing his total to ten Grammys and three Latin Grammys. Official website: www.santana.com.

Conversación

A. La familia de Lucía y Miguel

Paso 1. En parejas, miren la foto e identifiquen a los miembros de la familia de Lucía. Piensen en la edad (*age*) de cada persona.

MODELO: Sancho es mayor que sus hermanos.

Paso 2. Comparen a cada miembro de la familia con otra persona.

MODELO: Amalia es menor que Sancho pero es más alta que él.

Paso 3. Ahora comparen a los miembros de su propia (*own*) familia. Haga por lo menos cinco declaraciones.

MODELOS: **E1:** Mi hermana Mary es mayor que yo, pero yo soy más alto que ella.
E2: Mi abuela es mayor que mi abuelo, pero ella es más activa que él.

Lucía, con su esposo, sus padres y sus hijos.

B. La rutina diaria... en invierno y en verano

Paso 1. ¿Es diferente nuestra rutina diaria en cada estación? Complete las siguientes oraciones sobre su rutina.

	EN INVIERNO	EN VERANO
1. me levanto a ____ (hora)	________	________
2. almuerzo en ____	________	________
3. me divierto con mis amigos / mi familia en ____	________	________
4. estudio ____ horas todos los días	________	________
5. estoy / me quedo en ____ (lugar) por la noche	________	________
6. me acuesto a ____	________	________

Vocabulario útil

el gimnasio
el parque
afuera outside

Paso 2. En parejas, comparen sus actividades de invierno con las de verano.

MODELO: **E1:** En invierno, ¿te levantas más temprano que en verano?
E2: No, en invierno, me levanto tan temprano como en verano. (No, en invierno, me levanto a la misma hora que en verano.)

Paso 3. Ahora digan a la clase una o dos cosas que Uds. tienen en común.

MODELO: Nosotros nos levantamos más tarde en verano que en invierno. En verano no hay clases y, por lo general, nos acostamos más tarde.

Mundo interactivo

You should now be prepared to work with Scenario 3, Activity 4 in Connect Spanish (**www.connectspanish.com**).

Con. A: Reciclado

Have students bring a picture of their family to class and introduce and compare members as in *Con. A*.

Con. B: Follow-up

Have students use the items as a guide to ask a partner about the same information. As follow-up homework, have students write a comparison of their activities with their partner's.

Redacción: Ask students to take notes as they work on *Pasos 2* and *3*. After they have completed these *pasos* in class, assign a summary for homework. Ask students to compare not only the activities they have discussed in the *pasos* but also to make inferences about their own and their partner's personality traits. Tell students that their summaries should include at least one comparison of equality, one of inequality, one involving verbs, and one involving adjectives.

Optional

Working in pairs, have students ask each other questions about how many times a week they do the following. Then ask them to compare their activities to those of their partner.

MODELO: **E1:** *¿Cuántas veces a la semana vas al gimnasio?*
E2: *Tres veces.*
E1: *Yo voy cinco veces. Voy al gimnasio más que tú.*

1. *ir al gimnasio*
2. *estudiar en la biblioteca*
3. *ir al cine*
4. *ir a un bar*

Heritage Speakers

Invite a los hispanohablantes que han vivido en un país latinoamericano a escribir unos párrafos comparando y contrastando su rutina diaria en este país con la que tenían en el país latinoamericano donde vivían. ¿Es diferente su rutina diaria ahora?

Un poco de todo

A: Suggestion

Encourage students to be creative and to use verbs and phrases other than those on the list.

B: Preliminary Exercise

Describe the weather typical of three to four areas of this country, and have students guess which areas you are talking about. Ask them what role an area's climate plays in the image of that place.

En el verano, casi siempre hay mucha humedad (es muy húmedo) y llueve casi todas las tardes. También hay tormentas tropicales y huracanes. (Louisiana or Florida)

B: Note

The following grammar topics are included in *Lengua y cultura:* gender, adjective agreement, adjective vs. adverb, apocopation of adjectives, demonstratives, use of prepositions, *-ar* verbs, irregular verbs (*hacer, ir, salir*), stem-changing verbs (*poder, nevar*), *ser* vs. *estar.*

B: Follow-up

Ask students the following questions to personalize the information.

¿Le gustaría (new) *pasar la Navidad en Sudamérica? ¿Por qué?*
¿Qué asocia Ud. con la Navidad?
¿Qué hace durante las vacaciones de diciembre?

Un poco de todo

A. ¿Qué están haciendo?

Paso 1. Diga qué están haciendo las siguientes personas, usando una palabra o frase de cada columna y la forma progresiva. Si Ud. no sabe (*know*) qué están haciendo esas personas, ¡use su imaginación!

MODELO: (Yo) Estoy escribiendo la tarea.

- yo
- mi mejor amigo/a
- mis padres
- mi equipo (*team*) deportivo favorito
- el rector / la rectora (*president*) de la universidad
- el/la líder (*leader*) de este país
- el profesor / la profesora de español
- _____ (un compañero / una compañera que está ausente hoy)

+

- descansar
- dormir(se)
- escribir
- hacer
- jugar (al)
- leer
- practicar
- trabajar
- viajar (*to travel*)
- ¿ ?

+

- fútbol/basquetbol
- un libro / una novela
- a los estudiantes / a sus consejeros
- la tarea
- un informe
- ejercicio físico
- ¿ ?

Paso 2. Ahora complete las siguientes oraciones con un gerundio.

MODELO: Me divierto más _____. → Me divierto más **jugando al fútbol.**

1. Me divierto más _____.
2. Mi mejor amigo/a se divierte más _____.
3. Sigo _____ mucho, aunque (*although*) no es bueno.
4. Mi mejor amigo/a continúa _____, aunque no me gusta.

B. Lengua y cultura: Dos hemisferios. Complete the following paragraphs with the correct forms of the words in parentheses, as suggested by context. When two possibilities are given in parentheses, select the correct word.

B: Answers: 1. *muchas* **2.** *es* **3.** *es* **4.** *salgo* **5.** *llevar* **6.** *los* **7.** *puede* **8.** *a* **9.** *cortos* **10.** *durante* **11.** *hace* **12.** *nieva* **13.** *gran* **14.** *mucho* **15.** *ese* **16.** *toman* **17.** *va* **18.** *hacer* **19.** *es* **20.** *llevan*

Es diciembre en Buenos Aires. ¿Qué tiempo hace?

¿Sabe Ud.[a] algo de las diferencias entre los hemisferios del norte y del sur? Hay (mucho[1]) diferencias entre el clima del hemisferio norte y el del hemisferio sur. Cuando (ser/estar[2]) invierno en este país, por ejemplo, (ser/estar[3]) verano en la Argentina, en Bolivia, en Chile… Cuando yo (salir[4]) para la universidad en enero, con frecuencia tengo que (llevar[5]) abrigo y botas. En (los/las[6]) países del hemisferio sur, un estudiante (poder[7]) asistir (a/de[8]) un concierto en febrero llevando solo pantalones (corto[9]), camiseta y sandalias. En muchas partes de este país, (antes de / durante[10]) las vacaciones de diciembre, casi siempre (hacer[11]) frío y a veces (nevar[12]). En (grande[13]) parte de Sudamérica, al otro lado del ecuador, hace calor y (muy/mucho[14]) sol durante (ese[15]) mes. A veces en los periódicos, hay fotos de personas que (tomar[16]) el sol y nadan[b] en las playas sudamericanas en enero.

Tengo un amigo que (ir[17]) a (hacer/tomar[18]) un viaje a Buenos Aires. Él me dice[c] que allí la Navidad[d] (ser/estar[19]) una fiesta de verano y que todos (llevar[20]) ropa como la que[e] llevamos nosotros en julio. Parece[f] increíble, ¿verdad?

[a]¿Sabe… *Do you know* [b]*are swimming* [c]Él… *He tells me* [d]*Christmas* [e]la… *that which* [f]*It seems*

Resources: Desenlace

In the *Cap. 6* section of "Chapter-by-Chapter Supplementary Materials" in the IM, you will find a chapter-culminating activity. You can use this activity to consolidate and review the vocabulary and grammar skills students have acquired.

Comprensión. ¿Probable o improbable?

	PROBABLE	IMPROBABLE
1. Los estudiantes argentinos van a la playa en julio.	☐	☑
2. Muchas personas sudamericanas hacen viajes de vacaciones en enero.	☑	☐
3. En Santiago (Chile) hace frío en diciembre.	☐	☑

C. Expresiones

Paso 1. Las comparaciones se usan mucho en refranes y expresiones populares e idiomáticas. En parejas, lean las siguientes expresiones. ¿Tienen equivalentes en inglés?

1. pesar (*to weigh*) menos que un mosquito
2. ser más pesado (*overbearing, boring*) que el matrimonio
3. ser más bueno que el pan (*bread*)
4. ser más largo que un día sin pan
5. estar más claro que el agua (*water*)
6. ser más alto que un pino (*pine tree*)
7. ser tan rápido como un chisme (*rumor*)

Paso 2. Ahora, en parejas, inventen por lo menos cuatro expresiones que se parecen a (*resemble*) las del **Paso 1.** Pueden cambiar la terminación de las expresiones del **Paso 1** (pesar menos que… ¿ ?) o crear expresiones originales (ser tan divertido como… , ser más larga que una semana sin…).

Al crear (*When you are creating*) las expresiones, piensen en cosas y cualidades que, en la cultura de este país, son generalmente positivas o negativas. En las expresiones del **Paso 1,** por ejemplo, se usa la palabra **pan** dos veces (*times*). ¿Cómo se presenta el pan en la cultura hispana en estas expresiones, como una cosa muy positiva o negativa?

En su comunidad

Entreviste a (*Interview*) una persona hispana de su universidad o ciudad sobre el clima de su país de origen y los horarios (*schedules*) de clases durante el año.

PREGUNTAS POSIBLES

- ¿Hay en su país cuatro estaciones o solo dos?
- ¿Coinciden con las estaciones del lugar donde Ud. vive ahora?
- ¿Cómo es el clima en cada estación?
- ¿En qué mes empiezan las clases en las escuelas? ¿Y en qué mes terminan?
- ¿Es igual para los ciclos de la universidad?

Bright Idea

B: Comprensión: Extension

4. *Los estudiantes chilenos llevan abrigo en enero.* (*improbable*)
5. *Los argentinos se ponen guantes* (new) *en julio.* (*probable*)
6. *Muchos sudamericanos toman el sol en la playa en agosto.* (*improbable*)

Reciclado: To review *ser, estar*, and *tener* phrases used in this chapter, have students ask and answer questions about the figures in Transparency 45.

C: Redacción: Assign *Paso 2* as a written assignment, to be handed in by pairs of students. Create a list of the most creative expressions and share them with the class. Have students vote on the best expression in each of the 7 categories. Highlight cultural comparisons that emerge in the expressions.

En su comunidad

Suggestions

- Remind students to get the following basic information: the informant's country of origin, how long he or she has lived in this country, and if the informant visits his or her country of origin frequently.
- This activity could also be assigned as an online research project on a country of the student's choice or assigned by you.
- See the IM for additional suggestions and guidelines.

TELEPUNTOS

SALU2

El monumento a la Mitad del Mundo (*Middle of the World*): «Aquí, turistas ecuatorianos y de todos los países vienen a poner un pie (*foot*) en cada (*each*) hemisferio».

Antes de mirar

Conteste las siguientes preguntas sobre el clima y la geografía.

1. ¿En qué hemisferio están los Estados Unidos, en el hemisferio norte o el hemisferio sur? ¿Al norte de qué trópico están los Estados Unidos, al norte del Trópico de Cáncer o del Trópico de Capricornio? Norte; Cáncer
2. ¿Cuáles son dos de los países latinoamericanos que atraviesa (*crosses*) la línea del ecuador (*equator*)? Colombia, el Ecuador (el Brasil también)
3. ¿Qué tipo de clima asocia Ud. con una zona tropical? Hace mucho calor. Llueve mucho.

PROGRAMA 6: En la Mitad del Mundo

Este programa presenta aspectos del clima y la artesanía (*traditional crafts*) del Ecuador.

Vocabulario de este programa

disfrutar	to enjoy	**la banda**	strip
la nieve	snow	**atravesar (atravieso)**	to cross
la temporada	season	**rodear**	to surround
la lluvia	rain	**contrarrestar**	to counteract
seco/a	dry	**lluvioso/a**	rainy
mejor te quedas	you'd better stay	**la bufanda**	scarf
me gustaría	I would like	**la lana**	wool
infatigable	tireless	**era muy duro**	it was very hard

Fragmento del guion

LAURA: La lengua materna de José es el quechua, la lengua que hablaban[a] los incas y que hoy siguen hablando muchas personas desde Ecuador hasta Chile. José nos enseñó[b] cómo él mismo[c] hace los tintes[d] para la lana que usa en los tejidos de su taller.[e] Estos tintes son completamente naturales y los colores son increíbles. Vemos cómo un insecto tan pequeño, la cochinilla, produce un intenso color rojo.

JOSÉ: Si es que le guardo[f] un año o dos años mejor todavía más fuerte[g]... y bueno un poco de ácido natural... llegó [a ser] un poquito claro.[h]

LAURA: José Cotocachi no ha cambiado[i] su arte para la venta[j] masiva como otros artesanos de Otavalo. Él nos explicó[k] cómo ha cambiado[l] el mercado de Otavalo y los negocios.

JOSÉ: Porque antes, antes era[m] solo el sábado, la feria. Eso era feria auténtica, ¿no? Bueno, todos los artesanos trabajábamos[n] hasta... de lunes a viernes... sábado a las cuatro de la mañana ya salíamos[ñ] a vender. Ahora ya no es así.[o]

[a]*used to speak* [b]nos... *showed us* [c]él... *he himself* [d]*dyes* [e]tejidos... *fabrics of his shop* [f]Si... *If I keep it* [g]todavía... *even stronger* [h]llegó... *it got lighter* [i]no... *hasn't changed* [j]*sale* [k]Él... *He explained to us* [l]ha... *has changed* [m]antes... *before it was* [n]*used to work* [ñ]*we were already going out* [o]ya... *it's no longer like that*

El Sr. José Cotocachi, maestro tejedor (*master weaver*) de tercera (*third*) generación que mantiene (*maintains*) la tradición textil de su familia

TelePuntos

Note

Pages 190–195 are optional. You may cover some, all, or none of this material in class, or assign it to students—as a group or individually—for homework or extra credit. Pages 196–197 (*En resumen: En este capítulo*) are a summary of all of the chapter's active material.

Suggestions

- If you are using the video in class, show it once, ask brief comprehension questions, then show it again.
- Even if you plan to ask students to watch the video in your campus media center or on their own, it is a good idea to continue to stress the need to watch the shows as many times as they want or need to in order to complete the *Después de mirar* activities.

Antes de mirar

Note

The equator also crosses several countries in Africa (including *la República de Guinea Ecuatorial,* where Spanish is spoken as an official language) and some Atlantic and Pacific islands.

Programa 6

Note

This program will be easily accessible to students.

Suggestions

- Emphasize word families from the show that are related to the text's active weather vocabulary: ***llueve*** = *la lluvia, lluvioso/a;* ***nieva*** = *la nieve.*
- Tell students that the highest capital city in the world is *La Paz* (*Bolivia*).
- Emphasize to students that the more carefully they study the preliminary activities (*Antes de mirar, Vocabulario de este programa,* and *Fragmento del guion*), the more they will understand. Scanning *Después de mirar* before viewing is also an excellent strategy.

Fragmento del guion

Notes

- As noted in the program, José Cotocachi is a native speaker of Quechua. Since Spanish is a second language for him, his Spanish is not completely native. An example of this is shown in the script fragment: "*Llegó [a ser] un poquito claro,*" meaning that a natural acid lightens the original color. Students are not likely to notice this aspect of José's speech.
- Many indigenous languages are spoken in Latin America, some by thousands and even millions of people. (Some of the more widely spoken indigenous languages are *maya, náhuatl, aymará,* and *mapuche.*). Many speakers of these languages are completely bilingual in their native language and Spanish. In fact, those who go to school for a number of years will become literate in Spanish (which is typically the language used in schools) and not in their indigenous tongue. In recent years, Latin American governments have become more concerned with the issue of indigenous rights and the importance of maintaining indigenous languages, but there is a lot more to do in order to ensure that those languages are kept alive for future generations.

Mundo interactivo

Continue your work as an intern at HispanaVisión with Laura Sánchez Tejada, the roving reporter of *Salu2,* as you complete Scenario 3, Activities 3 and 4 in Connect Spanish (**www.connectspanish.com**).

Al mirar

Mientras mira el programa, indique las condiciones meteorológicas que se ven en este programa en la columna de la izquierda y la ropa que lleva la gente (*people*) en la columna de la derecha.

CONDICIONES METEOROLÓGICAS	ROPA
☐ cielos sin nubes (*cloudless skies*)	☑ gente con ropa de verano
☑ cielos con muchas nubes	☑ gente con ropa abrigada (*warm*)
☑ lluvia	☑ gente con ropa para protegerse de la lluvia

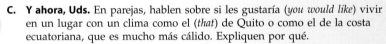

«Quito está en el corazón (*heart*) de los Andes ecuatorianos, a casi 3.000 metros de altura (*high*) y es la segunda (*second*) entre las capitales más elevadas del mundo.»

Después de mirar

A. ¿Está claro? Las siguientes oraciones son falsas. Corríjalas (*Correct them*).

1. A Ana no le gusta la nieve.
2. El clima de Panamá es muy diferente del clima del Ecuador.
3. La Mitad del Mundo es una ciudad del Ecuador.
4. En los países tropicales hay dos temporadas, una cálida (*hot*) y otra fría.
5. En Quito no llueve mucho.
6. Otavalo es una ciudad ecuatoriana donde hay muchas fábricas (*factories*).
7. Otavalo está en la costa del Ecuador.

B. Un poco más. Conteste las siguientes preguntas.

1. ¿Es muy cálido el clima en todas las zonas tropicales del mundo? Dé un ejemplo.
2. ¿Qué factor geográfico afecta el clima del Ecuador?
3. Además del (*Besides*) español, ¿qué otra lengua se habla en el Ecuador y en otros países andinos?
4. ¿Qué prendas (*items*) textiles producen los otavaleños?
5. ¿Qué pasa en una feria?

C. Y ahora, Uds. En parejas, hablen sobre si les gustaría (*you would like*) vivir en un lugar con un clima como el (*that*) de Quito o como el de la costa ecuatoriana, que es mucho más cálido. Expliquen por qué.

MODELO: Me gustaría vivir en un lugar con un clima similar al (*to that*) de Quito porque me gusta la lluvia…

Act. A, Answers: 1. *A Ana le gusta la nieve; no le gusta el frío.* **2.** *El clima de Panamá es similar al de muchas partes del Ecuador.* **3.** *La Mitad del Mundo es un monumento.* **4.** *Hay dos temporadas, una lluviosa y otra seca.* **5.** *Llueve mucho: 8 meses al año.* **6.** *Es una ciudad donde hay una feria de artesanía.* **7.** *Está en los Andes.*

Act. B, Answers: 1. *No. El clima no es muy cálido en Quito.* **2.** *los Andes* **3.** *el quechua* **4.** *ponchos, bufandas y alfombras* **5.** *Hay personas que venden y compran artesanía.*

Sobre el programa

Víctor tiene un hermano mayor que se llama Miguel. No está casado,[a] pero vive con su novia desde hace[b] cinco años. Víctor y Miguel están muy unidos y su relación es como la[c] de dos mejores amigos, aunque[d] no viven en el mismo lugar. Miguel es meteorólogo y trabaja para la NASA, en la Florida. Le encanta[e] su trabajo pero no le gusta que la gente le pida[f] el pronóstico del tiempo[g] constantemente. Su frase favorita sobre el clima es: «No siempre llueve al gusto de todos[h]».

[a]*married* [b]vive… *he has been living with his girlfriend for* [c]*that* [d]*although* [e]Le… *He really likes* [f]que… *for people to ask him for* [g]pronóstico… *weather forecast* [h]a… *to everyone's liking*

Producción personal

Filme el pronóstico del tiempo sobre los próximos tres días.

Al mirar

Suggestions

- Ask students to describe each location (*Quito, Otavalo*) in the show, based on their answers.
- Take the opportunity to review clothing vocabulary.

Después de mirar

A: Optional Follow-up

Use the information in the program to talk about the weather in Costa Rica (the chapter's country of focus). Based on Ana's comments about Panama as well on other information in the segment, what kind of weather should students expect in Costa Rica? You may wish to have students do an Internet search on this topic.

B: Suggestions

- Encourage students to expand on their answers with information they know that is not in the program.
- The biggest surprise about weather for some students is to realize that "tropical" may not necessarily mean "hot." You can expand on this topic by asking: *¿Por qué creen Uds. que es tan* (so) *diferente la temperatura en la costa del Ecuador a la temperatura de Quito?* (*el efecto de la altitud y del océano*)
- You can introduce the subjunctive with: *¿Qué les sorprende del clima de Ecuador? ¿Les sorprende que no haga mucho calor en Quito? ¿Les sorprende que en la zona ecuatorial no haga mucho calor?*

C: Suggestion

After students have discussed this topic in pairs, have each pair share their opinions with the whole class. Keep a tally of answers.

Sobre el programa

Suggestion

Explain that Miguel's phrase is *un refrán* (a saying). Have students discuss its meaning, and try to translate it to English.

Optional: Comprensión

1. *¿Quién es Miguel? ¿Cuál es su apellido?* (*el hermano mayor de Víctor, Gutiérrez*)
2. *¿Cómo es la relación entre Víctor y Miguel?* (*muy unida, de mejores amigos*)
3. *¿Cuál es su profesión? ¿Le gusta?* (*meteorólogo, le gusta mucho*)
4. *¿Qué no le gusta?* (*que la gente le pida el pronóstico del tiempo constantemente*)
5. *¿Qué significa su frase favorita?* (*lit.,* "It doesn't always rain to everyone's liking.")

Producción personal

Note

See the IM for additional suggestions for this chapter's assignment as well as for general guidelines and suggestions for video assignments.

Lectura cultural

Notes

- The Instructor's Edition on this page offers some additional information on the country of focus. For more information about the country of focus, see the chapter's opening pages and the IM.
- See the IM for some expressions used in Costa Rica.

First Reading: Notes

- Costa Rica is home to many species of migratory animals, who spend part of the year in the country's parks and natural preserves.
- The very small and much photographed red-eyed tree frog is one of the most famous Costa Rican species.

Exploración lingüística

Ask students to find the following in the reading. Some of these words are glossed and some are not.

- *un adjetivo que se relaciona con «lluvia»* (*lluviosa*)
- *todos los adjetivos que se relacionan con el clima y la geografía* (*muchos*)
- *la palabra que significa* majority (*mayoría*)

Tres símbolos costarricenses

Notes

- Costa Rica currently has a parliamentary democracy and an advanced social welfare system.
- *Las carretas* were used to transport coffee beans to market in the 19th century.

Un concepto importante

Notes

- More than one-quarter of Costa Rica has been set aside as a natural preserve.
- *El Parque Nacional Arenal* is one of the most popular tourist attractions in Costa Rica. It includes *el Volcán Arenal,* which has erupted a number of times since 1968.

A LEER

Lectura cultural

Costa Rica

Se puede decir[a] que el clima de Costa Rica es tropical. Esto significa que propiamente[b] no tiene una estación de invierno. Lo que sí tiene son dos temporadas:[c] una seca[d] y otra lluviosa.[e] En la mayor parte del país, esta última[f] ocurre entre mayo y noviembre. En las zonas más lluviosas del país, las lluvias son muy copiosas[g] y llegan a ocasionar muchas inundaciones.[h]

Sin embargo, el clima de Costa Rica es muy diverso. Esto llama mucho la atención de los turistas, ya que[i] en pocas horas se puede pasar de un clima lluvioso en las montañas a uno caluroso[j] en la playa.

¿Es muy variado el clima en el estado / la provincia donde Ud. vive? ¿Cómo es?

[a]*say* [b]*really* [c]*seasons* [d]*dry* [e]*rainy* [f]*last one (i.e., last season)* [g]*heavy* [h]llegan… *they cause a lot of floods* [i]ya… *since* [j]uno… *a warm one (i.e., warm climate)*

Una carreta de Sarchí, Costa Rica

En otros países hispanos

- **En todo el mundo hispanohablante** Hay muchos tipos de climas en el mundo hispanohablante. Solo hay que pensar en que se habla español desde la Antártida, que comprende territorio chileno y argentino, hasta los Estados Unidos y el Canadá, en otras palabras, en los hemisferios sur y norte. Y no olvidemos[a] a España (en Europa) y la Guinea Ecuatorial (en África).
- **En Chile** En este país se encuentra[b] el desierto de Atacama, el más seco del mundo.
- **En España** La diversidad climática y geográfica de este país europeo es espectacular para su tamaño.[c] La zona más caliente de Europa (el área de Córdoba y Sevilla) coexiste con una de las cordilleras[d] más altas del continente (la Sierra Nevada). Hasta hay una zona desértica (en Almería).

[a]no… *let's not forget* [b]se… *is found* [c]*size* [d]*mountain ranges*

Tres símbolos costarricenses

- **La paz** Esta es la cualidad que más caracteriza al país. Hay una expresión que lo ilustra: «Donde haya un costarricense, habrá paz».[a]

[a]Donde… *Wherever there is a Costa Rican, there will be peace*

- **La democracia** Este concepto va unido al anterior.[b] Costa Rica se caracteriza por tener una de las democracias más estables de todo el mundo.
- **La carreta** Es un medio de transporte tradicional y ahora es considerada un símbolo de la patria.[c]

[b]va… *goes with the last one* [c]*nation (in the patriotic sense)*

Un concepto importante

Costa Rica tiene una importante industria ecoturística que, al mismo tiempo que preserva su biodiversidad, la explota.[a] Es un modelo que debe ser imitado por otros países.

[a]la… *exploits it*

COMPRENSIÓN

1. ¿Por qué no tiene el clima costarricense cuatro estaciones? porque es tropical
2. ¿Cuáles son los meses secos en Costa Rica? entre diciembre y abril
3. ¿Dónde hace un frío glacial en el mundo hispanohablante? en la Antártida

Del mundo hispano

Antes de leer

Conteste las siguientes preguntas.

1. ¿Cree Ud. que es posible usar los calendarios de años anteriores (*previous*) a este año?
2. Mire el calendario que aparece en esta lectura. ¿Qué día de la semana se representa con la X? ¿Por qué cree que se usa la X?
3. ¿Cuál es el primer día de la semana en los calendarios de los países hispanos?

Vocabulario útil

guardar	to save, keep
promover	to promote, encourage
el reciclaje	recycling

Lectura: ¿Se pueden usar calendarios de otros años?

CURIOSIDADES ¿Se pueden usar calendarios de otros años?

ENERO

L	M	X	J	V	S	D
			1	2	3	4
5	6	7	8	9	10	11
12	13	14	15	16	17	18
19	20	21	22	23	24	25
26	27	28	29	30	31	

FEBRERO

L	M	X	J	V	S	D
						1
2	3	4	5	6	7	8
9	10	11	12	13	14	15
16	17	18	19	20	21	22
23	24	25	26	27	28	

MARZO

L	M	X	J	V	S	D
						1
2	3	4	5	6	7	8
9	10	11	12	13	14	15
16	17	18	19	20	21	22
23/30	24/31	25	26	27	28	29

ABRIL

L	M	X	J	V	S	D
		1	2	3	4	5
6	7	8	9	10	11	12
13	14	15	16	17	19	20
21	22	23	24	25	26	27
28	29	30				

MAYO

L	M	X	J	V	S	D
				1	2	3
4	5	6	7	8	9	10
11	12	13	14	15	16	17
18	19	20	21	22	23	24
25	26	27	28	29	30	31

JUNIO

L	M	X	J	V	S	D
1	2	3	4	5	6	7
8	9	10	11	12	13	14
15	16	17	18	19	20	21
22	23	24	25	26	27	28
29	30					

JULIO

L	M	X	J	V	S	D
		1	2	3	4	5
6	7	8	9	10	11	12
13	14	15	16	17	18	19
20	21	22	23	24	25	26
27	28	29	30	31		

AGOSTO

L	M	X	J	V	S	D
					1	2
3	4	5	6	7	8	9
10	11	12	13	14	15	16
17	18	19	20	21	22	23
24/31	25	26	27	28	29	30

SEPTIEMBRE

L	M	X	J	V	S	D
	1	2	3	4	5	6
7	8	9	10	11	12	13
14	15	16	17	18	19	20
21	22	23	24	25	26	27
28	29	30				

REPETIMOS CADA 28 AÑOS

¿Alguien[a] guarda el calendario de hace 28 años? Si la respuesta es afirmativa, es el momento de sacarlo,[b] ya que[c] coincide día por día con el de este año 2010. Esa ha sido[d] la curiosa iniciativa que la asociación ecologista más importante de Italia, Legambiente, ha puesto en marcha[e] para promover el reciclaje. Resulta que, cada 28 anos, los calendarios se repiten, siendo iguales en todas sus fechas. La explicación es que cada año solo puede comenzar en un día de la semana, por lo que existirían[f] 7 calendarios posibles... si no existieran años bisiestos.[g] Según los cálculos, al repetirse los años bisiestos cada 4 años, y los normales cada 7, el ciclo dura 28 años.

Y la próxima... ¿Cuándo nació la corbata?

[a]*Someone* [b]*take it out* [c]ya... *since* [d]ha... *has been* [e]ha... *has put in motion* [f]por... *in which case, there would be* [g]años... *leap years*

Comprensión

A. Según el texto. Conteste las siguientes preguntas.

1. ¿Cómo se llaman los años de 366 días? bisiestos
2. ¿Con qué frecuencia se repiten los calendarios? cada 28 años
3. ¿Qué es Legambiente? una asociación ecologista italiana
4. ¿Qué acción recomienda Legambiente? el reciclaje de los calendarios viejos

B. Comentario. ¿Cree Ud. que es buena idea seguir la recomendación de Legambiente? ¿Es algo práctico y fácil de hacer? Explique sus razones.

Del mundo hispano

Note

See the IM for optional follow-up, writing, and Internet activities.

Antes de leer

Suggestions

- Point out that this type of question/answer text is fairly common as an element of some Hispanic newspapers and magazines; questions of general interest are posed and answers are offered.
- *X* stands in for *miércoles*, since the day starts with the same letter as *martes*. Not all Hispanic calendars use this convention.
- Ask students what's done in English-language calendars to avoid repeating the *T* of *Tuesday* and *Thursday*. (Answer: Sometimes *Th* is used for *Thursday*, sometimes an *R* or an *H* is used.)
- Ask what students do with their calendars at the end of each year. Do they save them to reuse them? Do they ever save and use the photos in decorative calendars as posters?

Estrategia: Using the Organization of a Text

Since the title of this reading is a question, the answer will be found in the text. Students can scan the text for the answer, then look for the additional information offered. (Examples: Why use old calendars? Why do calendars repeat? Why do we have to wait more than just 7 years for calendars to repeat?)

Antes de escuchar

Suggestions

- For this listening passage, it is important that students review the *Vocabulario útil* as well as the additional information given in *Después de escuchar A* before they start to listen.
- You may wish to present the following information about temperatures to students. Celsius (°C) is used in Hispanic countries. Fahrenheit (°F) is used in the United States. Canada primarily uses Celsius, although Fahrenheit is sometimes used. Give students the following conversion formulas.

  °F to °C: Subtract 32, multiply by 5, divide by 9

  °C to °F: Multiply by 9, divide by 5, add 32

Escuche

Notes

- In this chapter, students can listen to a weather report for the country of Argentina.
- The text suggests that students listen to the passage as many times as they need to in order to do the *Después de escuchar* activities. If that is not what you want students to do, give them alternate instructions.
- See the IM for the Audioscript and more information about music in Costa Rica.

Después de escuchar

A: Answers

Jujuy y Salta: *20 / 5 lluvia;* ***Mendoza:*** *21 / 3 sol, lluvia;* ***Córdoba:*** *18 / 5 sol;* ***Buenos Aires:*** *16 / 6 sol, lluvia, granizo;* ***Pampa:*** *20 / 7 sol;* ***Bariloche:*** *9 / –2 nieve;* ***Río Gallegos:*** *2 / 5 nieve*

B: Answers

1. *mal tiempo, lluvia y nieve* **2.** *final del invierno, principio de la primavera (primaveral)*

B: Follow-up

Have the students compare the Argentine forecast to a typical late winter / early spring forecast for the area they are from in this country.

¡Música!

Suggestion

- Another interesting Costa Rican band is *Malpaís.* Their music mixes folk music with other Latin influences.
- For helpful tips on using songs in the classroom, see the IM.

A ESCUCHAR

Vocabulario para escuchar

despejado	clear, no clouds
los grados	degrees
soleado	sunny
la franja	coastal area
el granizo	hail
la borrasca	storm
la bajada	dip, lowering
bajo	below

Antes de escuchar

¿Mira Ud. el pronóstico (*report*) del tiempo todos los días? ¿Lo ve (*Do you see it*) en la tele o en el Internet o lo oye (*do you hear it*) en la radio? ¿Le gustan los pronósticos con muchos detalles o solo quiere saber (*know*) la información básica, como la temperatura máxima y mínima y si se espera sol o lluvia?

Escuche

El pronóstico del tiempo

¿Qué tiempo va a hacer este fin de semana en la Argentina? Escuche según las indicaciones de su profesor(a).

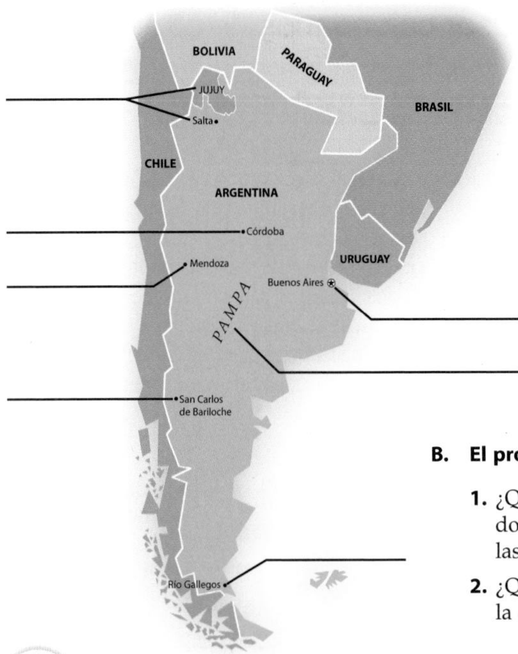

Después de escuchar

A. Temperaturas y condiciones atmosféricas. Complete los espacios en blanco (*blanks*) en el mapa con las temperaturas máximas y mínimas. También dibuje (*draw*) el símbolo correspondiente a las condiciones atmosféricas que se mencionan.

Se espera nieve.  Se espera lluvia. 

Se espera granizo.  Se espera sol. 

B. El pronóstico en general. Conteste las siguientes preguntas.

1. ¿Qué tiempo va a hacer el domingo en la mayoría de las regiones argentinas?
2. ¿Qué estación es hoy en la Argentina?

Go to the iMix section in Connect Spanish (**www.connectspanish.com**) to access the iTunes playlist *"Puntos9,"* where you can purchase "No me diga" by Evolución.

¡Música!

Evolución es un grupo de San José que empezó[a] haciendo rock alternativo. Ahora hace música con influencias más variadas y melódicas. Su canción «No me diga»[b] es del álbum *Amor artificial*.

[a]*started* [b]*No... "Don't tell me"*

Evolución, en concierto

Resources: Transparencias 81, 82

A ESCRIBIR

El tema

Las estaciones y el tiempo

Preparar

Paso 1. Piense en la estación del año que Ud. prefiere. ¿Por qué prefiere esa estación? ¿Con qué la asocia (*do you associate it*)? ¿Cuál es la estación del año que menos le gusta? ¿Por qué? Complete el cuadro con su información.

Paso 2. Entreviste a dos compañeros de clase sobre la estación del año que más les gusta y la que (*that which*) menos les gusta. También debe preguntarles por qué. Luego complete el cuadro con su respectivo información.

nombre	estación preferida	estación que menos le gusta	¿por qué?
yo			
compañero/a 1			
compañero/a 2			

Redactar

Escriba un ensayo comparativo, combinando toda la información de **Preparar.** Asegúrese (*Be sure*) de que tiene una idea que desarrollar (*to develop*).

MODELOS: No todos estamos de acuerdo sobre nuestra estación preferida.
Todas las estaciones del año tienen su encanto (*charm*).

No se olvide de (*Don't forget to*) incluir un párrafo de cierre (*closing paragraph*) que señale la idea más interesante de su ensayo.

Editar

Revise el ensayo para comprobar (*to check*):

- la ortografía y los acentos
- la posición y la concordancia de los adjetivos descriptivos
- los usos de **ser** y **estar**
- la variedad del vocabulario
- la conjugación de los verbos

Finalmente, prepare su versión final para entregarla.

Preparar

Suggestions

- Have students review the form of *gustar* that they learned in *Cap. 1.*
- Help students find an idea to frame this essay. Additional ideas: There is not one season that is everyone's favorite. One season is most popular among young people. Activities for every season.

Redactar

Suggestions

- Suggested length for this writing assignment: approximately 100 words
- Suggested structure (3 paragraphs)
  - **P.1.** Presentation of the main idea of the essay
  - **P.2.** Examples from the student writer (first person) and interviewees (third person, singular and plural)
  - **P.3.** Short paragraph defending the idea presented in the introduction

Editar: Follow-up

What can a preference for a given season say about a person's personality?

En resumen: En este capítulo

Vocabulario

Suggestions

- Divide the class into two teams. Call out the name of a month and have representatives from each team take turns mentioning a word or phrase related to that month. Other members of the team can offer suggestions if their representative falters. When all related terms have been suggested, call out another month.
- Play charades in Spanish, using nouns, adjectives, and comparisons from the *Vocabulario* list.

Note

The following vocabulary item was used in direction lines in *Cap. 6* and will be used in subsequent chapters without glossing, but it is not considered to be active until it is listed in *Vocabulario: el detalle.*

Word Families

En este capítulo

- *conmigo, contigo*
- *en, entre*
- *fácil, difícil*
- *hace calor, tener calor*
- *hace frío, tener frío*
- *mí, conmigo*
- *mismo/a, ahora mismo*
- *ordenado/a, desordenado/a*
- *tan... como, tanto... como*
- *ti, contigo*
- *tiempo* (weather; time)

Entre capítulos

- *abierto/a* = *abrir* (3)
- *ahora mismo* = *ahora* (2)
- *al lado de* = *al* (4)
- *cansado/a* = *descansar* (5)
- *cerrado/a* = *cerrar* (5)
- *entre* = *en* (1)
- *esta noche* = *este* (2), *buenas noches* (1)
- *estar bien* = *estar* (2)
- *más… que* = *más* (2)
- *medianoche, mediodía* = *y media* (1)
- *menos… que* = *menos cuarto/quince* (1)
- *mí* = *mi* (4)
- *pasar* = *pasado mañana* (3)
- *el primero de* = *primero* (adv.) (5)
- *querido/a* = *querer* (4)
- *sin embargo* = *sin* (5)
- *ti* = *tú* (2), *tu* (4)

¡OJO!

- *llover* ≠ *llevar* (2)
- *el mes* ≠ *la mesa* (2)
- *la primavera* ≠ *primero* (5), *el primero de* (6)

EN RESUMEN En este capítulo

LearnSmart

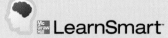

Visit **www.connectspanish.com** to practice the vocabulary and grammar points covered in this chapter.

Gramática en breve

15. Present Progressive

estar + -ndo
-ar ⟶ -ando
-er/-ir ⟶ -iendo

Unaccented **-i- ⟶ -y- (leyendo)**

-ir Stem-changing Verbs:
e ⟶ i (pidiendo)
o ⟶ u (durmiendo)

16. Summary of the Uses of *ser* and *estar*

ser	estar
inherent qualities, characteristics	mental, physical, health conditions
identification (including profession)	location
nationality, origin	present progressive
possession	
time and date	
generalizations	

Idioms with **tener** (expressing *to be*)

tener (mucho) calor, (mucho) frío

17. Comparisons

Comparisons of Inequality	Comparisons of Equality
más/menos… que	**tan… como**
más/menos que	**tanto/a/os/as… como**
más/menos de + *número*	
mejor/peor que	
mayor/menor que	

Vocabulario

Los verbos

celebrar	to celebrate
continuar (continúo)	to continue
pasar	to spend (*time*); to happen
quedarse	to stay, remain (*in a place*)
seguir (sigo) (i)	to continue
Repaso: divertirse (me divierto) (i)	

Remember that the parenthetical letter gives you the stem change for the present participle.

¿Qué tiempo hace?

el clima	climate
el tiempo	weather; time
está (muy) nublado	it's (very) cloudy, overcast
hace…	it's . . .
(muy) buen/mal tiempo	(very) good/bad weather (very) nice out
(mucho) calor	(very) hot
fresco	cool
(mucho) frío	(very) cold
(mucho) sol	(very) sunny
(mucho) viento	(very) windy
hay (mucha) contaminación	there's (lots of) pollution
llover: llueve	to rain (it's raining)
nevar: nieva	to snow (it's snowing)

Los meses del año

el año	year
la fecha	date (*calendar*)
el mes	month
¿Cual es la fecha de hoy? ¿Qué fecha es hoy?	What's today's date?
el primero de	the first of (*month*)

enero	**julio**
febrero	**agosto**
marzo	**septiembre**
abril	**octubre**
mayo	**noviembre**
junio	**diciembre**

Las estaciones del año

la estación	season
la primavera	spring
el verano	summer
el otoño	fall, autumn
el invierno	winter

Los lugares

la capital	capital city
la playa	beach

Otros sustantivos

el cumpleaños	birthday
la medianoche	midnight
el mediodía	noon
el/la novio/a	boyfriend/girlfriend
la respuesta	answer

Los adjetivos

abierto/a	open
aburrido/a	bored
alegre	happy
cansado/a	tired
cariñoso/a	affectionate
cerrado/a	closed
congelado/a	frozen; very cold
contento/a	content, happy
desordenado/a	messy
difícil	hard, difficult
enfermo/a	sick
fácil	easy
furioso/a	furious, angry
limpio/a	clean
loco/a	crazy
mismo/a	same
molesto/a	annoyed
nervioso/a	nervous
ocupado/a	busy
ordenado/a	neat
preocupado/a	worried
querido/a	dear
seguro/a	sure, certain
sucio/a	dirty
triste	sad

Las comparaciones

más/menos de + *number*	more/less than + *number*
más/menos... que	more/less (-er) . . . than
tan... como	as . . . as
tanto como	as much as
tanto/a(s)... como	as much/many . . . as
mayor	older
mejor	better; best
menor	younger
peor	worse

Las preposiciones

a la derecha de	to the right of
a la izquierda de	to the left of
al lado de	alongside of
cerca de	close to
debajo de	below
delante de	in front of
detrás de	behind
encima de	on top of
entre	between, among
lejos de	far from

Los puntos cardinales

el norte, el sur, el este, el oeste

Palabras adicionales

afuera	outdoors
ahora mismo	right now
conmigo	with me
contigo	with you (*fam.*)
esta noche	tonight
está bien	it's fine, OK
estar bien	to be comfortable (*temperature*)
mí (*obj. of prep.*)	me
por	about; because of
sin embargo	nevertheless
tener (mucho) calor	to be (very) warm, hot
tener (mucho) frío	to be (very) cold
ti (*obj. of prep.*)	you (*fam.*)
todavía	still

Vocabulario personal

Suggestions

- Using a map or a globe, have students compare geographical locations. Prompt them with questions.

  ¿Qué ciudad está más al norte, Nueva York o Quito?

  Have students answer in full sentences.
- Place a common classroom item in different places in the classroom (behind the door, underneath a desk, and so on) and have students describe its location.

Chapter Opening Photo and Chapter Theme

Note (photo)

Students were introduced to the *-ería* suffix in *Un poco de todo: B. Lengua y cultura* (*Cap. 4*). Ask them to see if they notice the missing accent mark on *Frutería*. The word *LÁGRIMA* is also missing its accent mark, but accents are often optional on capital letters.

Chapter Theme–Related Questions

1. *¿Qué comidas hispanas le gustan?*
2. *¿Cree que la comida hispana es más picante* (new) *que la estadounidense o la canadiense? ¿menos picante?*
3. *¿Qué es una tortilla? (Puede contestar en inglés, si prefiere.) ¿Conoce otro tipo de tortilla? ¿Hay algo como la tortilla en la comida de este país?*
4. *Si Ud. come carne, ¿hay partes del animal que no come nunca? ¿los sesos* (new)*? ¿la sangre* (new)*? ¿los intestinos?*
5. *¿A qué hora cena? ¿Cuándo come la comida más fuerte del día?*
6. *¿Prefiere comer en casa o en un restaurante?*
7. *Si vive en una residencia estudiantil, ¿le gusta la comida que sirven allí?*

Reciclado: Review nationality adjectives in the context of foods that students may know from Spanish-speaking countries and from countries all over the world.

7 ¡A comer!°

°¡A... *Let's eat!*

Una frutería, en la Ciudad de Panamá, Panamá

- ¿Qué tipo de comida espera Ud. encontrar (*to find*) en Panamá?
- ¿Hay restaurantes de cocina (*cuisine*) hispana en su ciudad? ¿Come Ud. allí con frecuencia? ¿Cuál es su comida o plato favorito de origen hispano?
- Por lo general, ¿qué comida (*meal*) del día le gusta más: el desayuno (*breakfast*), el almuerzo o la cena?

connect SPANISH

www.connectspanish.com

Resources

For Students

- Connect Spanish (**www.connectspanish.com**), which contains all content from the following resources, as well as the *Mundo interactivo* scenarios, the LearnSmart adaptive learning system, and more!
- **Physical Resources:** Workbook / Laboratory Manual, Laboratory Audio Program, DVD

For Instructors

- Connect Spanish (**www.connectspanish.com**), which contains access to all student sections of Connect Spanish, as well as helpful time-saving tools and resources such as an integrated gradebook, Instructor's Manual, Testing Program, digital transparencies, Audioscript, Videoscript, and more!

Panamá

3,5 (y medio) millones de habitantes

- El Canal de Panamá fue originalmente una idea de los españoles del siglo (*century*) XVI, pero su construcción no comenzó (*didn't begin*) hasta 1904. Se abrió al comercio en 1914.
- El arroz con pollo (*chicken with rice*) es uno de los platos panameños más típicos. Los tamales y los frijoles también son parte de la comida en Panamá, pero no son exactamente como los mexicanos.

En este capítulo

Panamá

Datos esenciales

The Instructor's Edition will provide basic information about each chapter's country of focus on this chapter opening spread. Additional information (such as geographical features, historical timelines, holidays, and so on) can be found in the IM. There is also additional information about the country of focus in *A leer: Lectura cultural* and *A escuchar* (in both the student text and the Instructor's Edition).

Nombre oficial: *República de Panamá*
Lema: *«Pro Mundi Beneficio» (Por el beneficio del mundo [latín])*
Capital: *la Ciudad de Panamá*
Composición étnica: *70% mestizos, 14% negros y mulatos (mezcla de sangre africana y europea), 10% blancos, 6% indígenas*
Lengua oficial: *el español (muchos panameños son bilingües en español e inglés)*
Jefe de estado actual: *el Presidente Ricardo Martinelli, desde 2009*
Forma de gobierno: *República presidencialista*
Moneda: *el balboa y el dólar estadounidense*
Religión: *85% católicos, 15% protestantes*

Point Out

- In recent history, the Panama Canal was conceived and initiated in 1881 by a Frenchman, Ferdinand-Marie de Lesseps, who was the developer of the Suez Canal. De Lesseps was forced to leave the Panama Canal uncompleted because of malaria and yellow "fever" epidemics. After modifying the design, the U.S. completed the project in 1914.
- The Panama Canal was operated by the U.S. until 1999.
- Students may be aware of the history of *el General Manuel Noriega*, who ousted the Panamanian president in 1985 and became acting head of the government. *Noriega* was brought to trial in the U.S. for drug-related and other illegal activities and convicted in 1992.

Suggestion

Have students list their ideas about Panama, including information on geography, politics, economy, culture, music, and cuisine. When you finish the chapter, return to the lists and ask students what ideas they would change and/or add. The success of this activity will depend not only on the content about Panama

← (Cont.)

presented in the text but also on the extent to which you have time to supplement that content with your own knowledge and experiences and also with information given in this Instructor's Edition and the IM.

Multimedia

The IM provides suggestions for using multimedia materials in the classroom.

Resources: Transparency 83

Vocabulario: Preparación
La comida

Note

See the model for vocabulary presentation and other material in the *Cap. 7 Vocabulario: Preparación* section of "Chapter-by-Chapter Supplementary Materials" in the IM.

Suggestions

- This is the minimum vocabulary students need to communicate about food. Encourage them to ask how to say foods that are not listed in the text. If you are not a native speaker of Spanish, bring a dictionary to class while working on this chapter.
- Remind students about the *Vocabulario personal* box on the end-of-chapter vocabulary page.
- Use magazine pictures of food items large enough to see easily. As you say each new target vocabulary item, write it on the board. Present foods a few at a time by food groups, check comprehension, present another group, check, and so on.
- Work with half of the vocabulary one day (up to and including *Otras verduras*) and the other half on the second day.
- Optional vocabulary: *el cubierto* (*el tenedor, la cuchara, el cuchillo, la servilleta, el vaso, la copa, la taza*)
- You may want to tell students that the gender of *azúcar* is grammatically ambiguous and is therefore variable. It is more frequently masculine, but it is often modified by a feminine adjective: *No vamos a tener* **el azúcar necesaria.**

Pronunciación: See Pronunciation Notes, IM.

VOCABULARIO Preparación

La comida y las comidas°

La... *Food and meals*

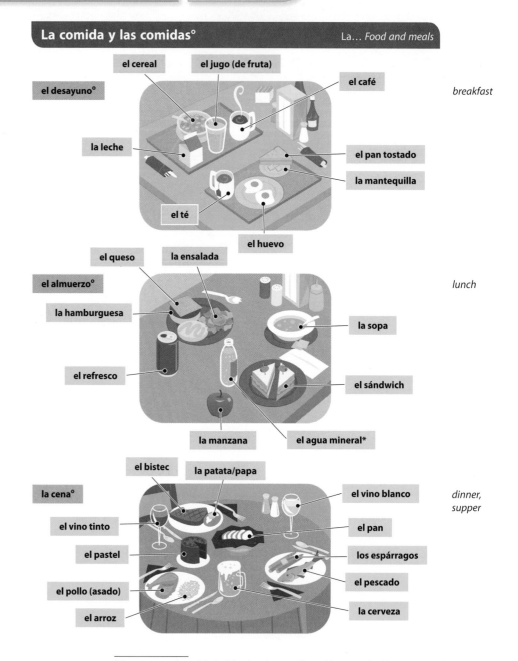

el desayuno° — *breakfast*

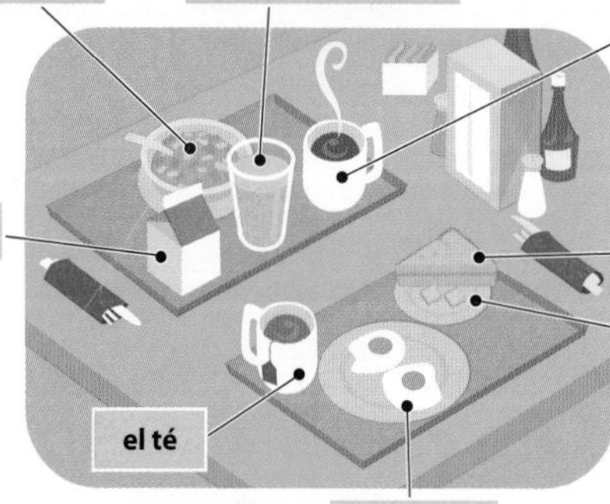

el almuerzo° — *lunch*

la cena° — *dinner, supper*

*The noun **agua** (water) is feminine, but the masculine articles are used with it in the singular: **el agua.** Adjectives that modify it are feminine: **el agua fría.** This occurs with all feminine nouns that begin with a stressed **a** sound, for example, **el/un ama de casa** (homemaker).

Heritage Speakers

- En muchos países latinoamericanos, las compras se pueden hacer en supermercados modernos o en mercados al aire libre. Pídales a los hispanohablantes que comparen y contrasten los mercados de los dos tipos.
- En algunos dialectos del español la palabra *almorzar* significa *comer a media mañana* y es parecida a la expresión en inglés *to have brunch.*

Resources: Transparency 84

Otras frutas

la banana	banana
la naranja	orange
el tomate	tomato

Otras verduras

las arvejas	green peas
los champiñones	mushrooms
los frijoles	beans
la lechuga	lettuce
la zanahoria	carrot

Otras carnes

la barbacoa	barbeque
la chuleta (de cerdo)	(pork) chop
el jamón	ham
el pavo	turkey
la salchicha	sausage; hot dog

Otros pescados y mariscos

el atún	tuna
los camarones	shrimp
la langosta	lobster
el salmón	salmon

Otros postres

los dulces	sweets; candy
el flan	(baked) custard
la galleta	cookie
el helado	ice cream

Otras comidas

el aceite	oil
el azúcar	sugar
la pimienta	pepper
la sal	salt
el yogur	yogurt

Los verbos

desayunar	to have (eat) breakfast
almorzar (almuerzo)	to have (eat) lunch
cenar	to have (eat) dinner, supper
cocinar	to cook

Así se dice

In **La comida y las comidas,** you learned two words for *potato:* **la papa** (*L.A.*) and **la patata** (*Sp.*). There is great variety in the words used to refer to foods in the Spanish-speaking world. The following are only a few of the most common ones.

las arvejas = los guisantes (*Sp.*)
los camarones = las gambas (*Sp.*)
el jugo = el zumo (*Sp.*)
el refresco = la gaseosa, la soda (**¡OJO!** = *soda water* in some areas)

There are many ways to express **la tienda de comestibles** (*grocery store*): **la abacería, el almacén** (which you have learned means *department store* in most areas), **la bodega** (popular in the Caribbean), **la pulpería** (*C.A., S.A.*), **la trucha** (*C.A.*).

Nota **comunicativa**

Más vocabulario para hablar de la comida

tener (mucha) hambre/sed	to be (very) hungry/thirsty
merendar (meriendo)	to snack
la merienda	snack
los comestibles	groceries, foodstuff
el plato	dish (*food prepared in a particular way*)
el plato principal	main course
caliente	hot (*in temperature, not taste*)
frito	fried
picante	hot, spicy
rico/a	tasty, savory; rich (*in the caloric sense*)

La merienda (typically a late afternoon snack) is a traditional custom in those countries where the dinner hour is quite late, such as Spain, for example, where people may have dinner at 10:00 or 11:00 P.M. or even later. **La merienda** tides people over until the late evening meal.

Reciclado

- Ask students which foods they associate with the seasons of the year.
- Review the names of the colors and have students tell what foods or drinks they associate with these colors. If you do this on the first day of vocabulary presentation, allow students to have their books open.
- Recycle place names. Have students tell what foods or drinks they associate with the following places.

Francia	*Centroamérica*
Inglaterra	*Colombia*
México	*San Francisco*
China	*Quebec*

- Have students give *tener* expressions for the following:
  1. *Si una persona quiere dormir,…*
  2. *Tim tiene un examen a las nueve, pero ya son las nueve menos diez y todavía está en casa.*
  3. *La temperatura está a 32 grados Fahrenheit y Ud. solo lleva camiseta.*
  4. *Es la una de la mañana y Ud. camina* (new) *solo/a por un lugar peligroso* (new) *de la ciudad.*

Así se dice

The variation in food words across the Hispanic world is too extensive to be covered in an introductory text. *Puntos de partida* makes one variation active (*la papa / la patata*), to introduce the concept of variation and then presents just a few of the most common ones in *Así se dice.*

Nota comunicativa

Reciclado

- Note the reentry of *tener* idioms as well as the introduction of known vocabulary with new meanings. Reenter the use of *¿cómo se dice… ?* to find out what something is called.
- Emphasize the fact that Spanish speakers, by and large, do not have difficulty communicating with Spanish speakers from other parts of the world, but that lexical variations are very common.
- Optional: *rico/a = delicioso/a, gustoso/a, sabroso/a.*

Heritage Speakers

Algunos mexicanos y mexicoamericanos dicen «guajolote» (palabra de origen náhuatl) en vez de «pavo.» Pregúnteles a los hispanohablantes qué palabras diferentes usan para referirse a la comida.

NATIONAL STANDARDS: Comparisons

Discuss the variety of words for names of food in the Spanish-speaking world. For example:

papas (L.A.) vs. *patatas* (Sp.)
banana (L.A.) vs. *plátano* (Sp.) vs. *guineo* (P.R.)
frijoles (L.A.) vs. *judías* (Sp.)
camarones (L.A.) vs. *gambas* (Sp.)
arvejas (L.A.) vs. *guisantes* (Sp.)
tortilla (flat corn meal or flour pancake, L.A.) vs. *tortilla* (potato and onion omelet, Sp.)
sándwich (with *pan de molde,* like the U.S. loaf) vs. *bocadillo* (with *pan de barra,* like French bread)

Con. A: Suggestions

- Remind students that *tomar* also means *to drink* and is synonymous with *beber*.
- Point out to students that an American-style breakfast (with eggs, meat, and so on) is not usual in all parts of the Spanish-speaking world. In Spain, breakfasts are lighter, with *café con leche* and toast. Mexican and Central American breakfasts have become quite similar to those in this country, with many kinds of meat and eggs available, along with refried beans, fruit, and pastries.

Con. A: Note

Active vocabulary: *ligero/a*

Con. A: Follow-up

Have students give alternative menus for the types of meals listed.

Nota cultural

Suggestions

- Ask students to list all of the cognates they can find in the *Nota cultural*. It should be easily comprehensible without the use of a dictionary.
- Point out that, like *la comida*, which means *food*, *meal*, and the *main meal* of the day, depending on the context, the word *la cocina* means both *kitchen* and *cuisine* (and in Spain and some Latin American countries it also means *stove*).
- Ask students who have traveled to a Hispanic country to talk about the food they ate there.

Comprensión

1. *¿Por qué no se puede hablar de «una cocina hispana»? (Hay una gran variedad que cambia de región a región.)*
2. *¿Qué ingredientes se utilizan por toda Latinoamérica? (el maíz, las papas, los frijoles, los tomates, los aguacates, el arroz)*
3. *¿Qué productos son de origen americano? (el maíz, las papas, los frijoles, los tomates, los aguacates)*
4. *¿Qué influencias culinarias están presentes en todos los países latinoamericanos? (la española y la indígena)*
5. *¿Qué influencia culinaria es importante en la cocina argentina? ¿Y en la peruana? (la italiana, la china)*

Notes

- The potato, first cultivated in the Andes mountains of Peru and Bolivia, was a staple in the Incan diet. Spanish conquistador *Pedro Cieza de León* wrote the first recorded information about potatoes in 1553 in his journal, *La crónica del Perú*. Imported to Europe, the potato from South America had a lasting effect on European cuisine and especially on Irish history via the Irish Potato Famine.
- The first domesticated tomato is believed to have been a little yellow fruit similar to the cherry tomato, grown by the Aztecs in Central America. The word *tomato* comes from the Aztec word *tomatl*. The tomato is essential to today's European cuisine, especially that of Italy.

Conversación

A. ¿Qué quiere tomar? Empareje las descripciones con las comidas.

DESCRIPCIONES

1. __c__ una sopa fría, langosta, espárragos, ensalada de lechuga y tomate, vino blanco y, para terminar, un pastel
2. __d__ jugo de fruta, huevos con jamón, pan tostado y café
3. __e__ un vaso (*glass*) de leche y unas galletas
4. __a__ pollo asado, arroz, arvejas, agua mineral y, para terminar, una manzana
5. __b__ una hamburguesa con patatas fritas, un refresco y un helado

COMIDAS

a. un menú ligero (*light*) para una dieta
b. una comida rápida
c. una cena elegante
d. un desayuno estilo norteamericano
e. una merienda

B. Definiciones

Paso 1. Dé las palabras definidas.

1. un plato de lechuga y tomate la ensalada
2. una bebida alcohólica blanca o roja el vino
3. una verdura anaranjada la zanahoria
4. una carne típica para una barbacoa en este país el cerdo, la salchicha, el pollo, el bistec
5. la comida favorita de los ratones (*mice*) el queso
6. una verdura que se come frita con las hamburguesas la patata/papa
7. una fruta roja o verde la manzana

Paso 2. Ahora, en parejas, túrnense para crear (*create*) definiciones de comidas y bebidas, según el modelo del **Paso 1.** Una persona da (*gives*) la definición y la otra da la palabra correspondiente.

Nota **cultural**

La comida del mundo hispano

No se puede hablar de una sola comida hispana, porque en el mundo hispanohablante hay una gran variedad culinaria. La comida cambia de país a país, dependiendo de los productos locales y de influencias nativas y externas. Sin embargo, sí hay productos de origen americano que se utilizan[a] en prácticamente todas las cocinas latinoamericanas:

- el maíz, las papas, los frijoles, los tomates, los aguacates[b]

El arroz es también fundamental, pero es de origen asiático. Fue introducido en América por[c] los españoles.

Una de las influencias básicas en la cocina[d] de todos los países latinoamericanos es la cocina española. Se combina con la tradición culinaria indígena de cada región y, en algunos[e] países, también con la tradición culinaria africana, gracias a la influencia de los esclavos[f] que fueron traídos[g] a América. Otros grupos de inmigrantes también dejaron claramente su huella[h] en la cocina de algunos países, como es el caso de los italianos en la Argentina y de los chinos en el Perú.

[a]*se... are used* [b]*avocados* [c]*by* [d]*cuisine* [e]*some* [f]*slaves* [g]fueron... *were brought* [h]dejaron... *left a clear imprint*

El maíz, uno de los ingredientes básicos de casi todos los países latinoamericanos, en Lima, Perú

¿Cuáles son los ingredientes básicos de la cocina de su familia o su país?

C. Consejos (*Advice*) **a la hora de comer.** ¿Qué debe comer o beber su compañero o compañera en las siguientes situaciones? Déle consejos, según el modelo.

MODELO: Tengo mucha/poca hambre (sed). ⟶
E1: Tengo mucha hambre.
E2: Debes comer un bistec con papas fritas.

1. Tengo mucha/poca hambre (sed).
2. Tengo hambre a las cuatro de la mañana, después de una fiesta.
3. Estoy a dieta.
4. Estoy de vacaciones en Maine (Texas, California, la Florida,...).
5. Es hora de merendar. Estoy en (casa, la universidad).
6. Soy un vegetariano estricto / una vegetariana estricta.

D. Las preferencias gastronómicas

Paso 1. Complete las siguientes oraciones para describir lo que Ud. come y no come.

1. Por la mañana siempre como ________.
2. En el desayuno me gusta comer ________.
3. Para cenar, prefiero comer ________.
4. Nunca como ________ y nunca bebo ________.
5. No me gusta comer ________, pero lo/la como (*I eat it*) en casa de mis padres/hijos/abuelos.

Paso 2. Haga una lista de los tres tipos de cocinas (*cuisines*) que Ud. prefiere.

Paso 3. Entre todos, comparen las listas. ¿Cuáles son los platos, lugares para comer y cocinas favoritos de la clase? ¿Cuáles son los ingredientes más necesarios para cocinar sus platos favoritos?

¿Qué sabe Ud. y a quién conoce?

As you know, two Spanish verbs express *to be:* **ser** and **estar.** They are not interchangeable, and their use depends on the meaning the speaker wishes to express. Similarly, two Spanish verbs express *to know:* **saber** and **conocer. Conocer** is frequently used with the word **a** when referring to a person (as in the phrase **¿a quién conoce?** from the title of this section).

¡OJO! Note the **a** before the phrase **una persona.** You will learn about this **a** in **Gramática 18** in this chapter. For now, always use it when you see it in the text.

saber = to know (*facts or information*); to know how to (*do something*)

sé	sabemos
sabes	sabéis
sabe	saben

conocer = to know (*a person*); to meet (*a person*); to be acquainted, familiar with (*a place or thing*)

conozco	conocemos
conoces	conocéis
conoce	conocen

Con. C: Note

Active vocabulary: *el consejo, estar a dieta*

Con. C: Follow-up

Ask questions about foods.

1. *¿Cuál tiene más cafeína, el café o el té? ¿Cuál prefiere Ud.? ¿Lo* (new) *toma por la mañana o por la noche?*
2. *¿Come Ud. carne? ¿Qué tipo de carne prefiere: el bistec, la hamburguesa, el jamón o las chuletas de cerdo? ¿Le gusta comer sándwiches?*
3. *¿Come Ud. muchas ensaladas? ¿Come la ensalada antes del plato principal o después?*
4. *En su opinión, ¿qué comida es más picante, la comida india o la comida mexicana? ¿la china o la tailandesa? ¿Cuál es más popular en este país?*

Con. D: Note

Active vocabulary: *cocina* (= cuisine)

Redacción: Assign *Con. D* as written homework. Collect the responses and use them in class in the following ways.

- Read selected responses aloud (correcting errors) and ask students to guess who wrote them.
- Tally the responses and put the information on the board (or an overhead). Have a class discussion based on the class responses.

¿Qué sabe Ud. y a quién conoce?

Saber and *conocer*

Reciclado: Note that *saber* and *conocer* are linked here to the concept of two Spanish verbs that express one English verb, which students know from the *ser* vs. *estar* contrast.

Suggestions

- Call students attention to the irregular *yo* forms in the charts and model their pronunciation.
- Call attention to the use of the personal *a*. Ask students what makes the sentence that has the personal *a* different from others.
- Ask the following questions to practice usage.
  1. *¿Qué restaurantes conoce Ud. muy bien?*
  2. *¿Cómo es la comida allí?*
  3. *¿Come Ud. allí con frecuencia?*
  4. *¿Cuántos platos sabe Ud. preparar?*
  5. *¿Cuál es su plato favorito?*
  6. *¿Conoce Ud. a un dueño de un restaurante?*
  7. *¿Conoce Ud. a un chef famoso?*

NATIONAL STANDARDS: Comparisons

Have students imagine that they are going to plan which foods to prepare to celebrate international week. Have different pairs or groups research on the Internet or in the library typical dishes from different Spanish-speaking countries. Then have them present their findings to the rest of the class. Invite them to describe in Spanish some of the ingredients they will need. After the presentations, discuss the differences and similarities between foods from different places.

Resources: Transparency 85

Notes

- The uses of *saber* and *conocer* are not always exact. There are gray areas (knowing a language, history, or poetry, for example), where only context and the speaker's meaning determine whether *saber* or *conocer* is appropriate.
- There is a tendency for students to confuse *poder* with *saber* (= *to be able to* [*do something*]) because of the English word *can*. Point out that, in general terms, *poder* means to have the physical ability to do something, whereas *saber* means to have knowledge or to know something intellectually. Provide sentences like the following to contrast this usage and ask students to tell you what they mean: *¿Sabe Ud. bailar? / ¿Puede Ud. bailar con esos zapatos? ¿Sabe Ud. cocinar? / ¿Puede Ud. cocinar esta noche?*
- Active vocabulary: *la dirección, la letra, el nombre*

Preliminary Exercises

- Have students state the following ideas in Spanish.
  1. I know the truth.
  2. She knows the President.
  3. They know how to dance.
  4. Do you know New York? (Are you familiar with it?)
  5. We don't know the answer.
  6. Everyone wants to meet the new student.
- Ask students which verb (*saber* or *conocer*) they associate with the following concepts.
  1. *un número de teléfono*
  2. *su mejor amigo/a*
  3. *una dirección de e-mail*
  4. *México*
  5. *tocar el piano*
  6. *un bibliotecario*
  7. *la letra de su canción favorita*
  8. *hacer ejercicios aeróbicos*

Con. A: Suggestions

- Ask students to explain the use of *saber* or *conocer* in each item.
- Expand each item with follow-up questions. If students say that they do know certain information, ask them to provide it (or at least start to provide it).

Con. A: Note

Active vocabulary: *contestar*

Conversación

A. ¡Anticipemos!

Paso 1. ¿Cierto o falso? Diga si las siguientes declaraciones son ciertas o falsas para Ud. Corrija las declaraciones falsas.

	CIERTO	FALSO
1. Sé la dirección de e-mail de mi profesor(a) de español.	☐	☐
2. Sé los nombres de las capitales de todos los países latinoamericanos.	☐	☐
3. Sé la letra del himno nacional de este país.	☐	☐
4. Sé tocar un instrumento musical.	☐	☐
5. Conozco al padre / a la madre de mi mejor amigo/a.	☐	☐
6. Conozco a un actor famoso / una actriz famosa.	☐	☐
7. Conozco Panamá.	☐	☐
8. Conozco un restaurante panameño.	☐	☐

Paso 2. Ahora, en parejas, túrnense para hacer y contestar preguntas basadas en las oraciones del **Paso 1.**

MODELO: **E1:** ¿**Sabes** la dirección de e-mail del profesor / de la profesora?
E2: No, no lo sé. ¿Y tú?
E1: Yo sí. / Yo tampoco. (*Me either.*)

Estrategia

Use the word **lo** (*it*) when expressing *I know* (**Lo sé**) and *I don't know* (**No lo sé.**) in Spanish when you are referring to knowing a specific piece of information that has just been mentioned, as in the model (**lo** = the e-mail address).

B. Los usos de *saber* y *conocer*

Paso 1. Llene (*Fill in*) los espacios en blanco con la forma apropiada de **saber.** Luego dé su equivalente en inglés.

—¿(Tú) __Sabes__ [1] la dirección de un restaurante panameño?

—¡Cómo no![a] Hay uno en la calle[b] Park. El chef, Felipe, (__sabe__ [2]) hacer unos platos muy originales.

—¿(Tú) __Sabes__ [3] a qué hora abren los sábados?

—No (yo) __sé__ [4] exactamente. ¿Por qué no llamamos al restaurante?

[a]¡Cómo... *Of course!* [b]*street*

Paso 2. Ahora llene los espacios en blanco con la forma apropiada de **conocer.** Luego dé su equivalente en inglés.

—¿(Tú) __Conoces__ [1] ese restaurante panameño que está en la calle Park?

—Sí, y también (yo) __conozco__ [2] al chef, Felipe.

—¿Ah sí? Yo quiero __conocer__ [3] a Felipe. Es muy famoso.

C. ¿Dónde cenamos?

Lola y Manolo quieren salir a cenar. Complete su diálogo con la forma apropiada de **saber** o **conocer.**

LOLA: ¿(Tú) __Sabes__ [1] adónde quieres ir a cenar?

MANOLO: No __sé__.[2] ¿Y tú?

LOLA: No, pero hay un restaurante nuevo en la calle Betis. Creo que se llama Guadalquivir. ¿__Conoces__ [3] el restaurante?

MANOLO: No, pero (yo) __sé__ [4] que tiene mucha fama. Es el restaurante favorito de Pepa. Ella __conoce__ [5] al dueño.[a]

LOLA: ¿(Tú) __Sabes__ [6] qué tipo de comida tienen?

MANOLO: No, pero podemos llamar a Pepa. ¿(Tú) __Sabes__ [7] su teléfono?

LOLA: Está en mi teléfono celular. Llámala[b] y pregúntale[c] si ella __sabe__ [8] si aceptan reservaciones o no.

MANOLO: De acuerdo.

[a]*owner* [b]*Call her* [c]*ask her*

Comprensión

1. ¿Saben Lola y Manolo dónde quieren cenar?
2. ¿Conocen el nuevo restaurante?
3. ¿Saben qué tipo de comida se sirve allí?
4. ¿Saben el número de teléfono de Maripepa?
5. ¿Conocen al dueño del restaurante?

D. ¿Sabe Ud. mentir (*to lie*) **bien?**

Paso 1. Escriba dos oraciones con **saber** sobre algunas (*some*) cosas que sabe hacer y dos con **conocer** sobre personas interesantes que conoce. Algunas oraciones deben ser falsas. **¡OJO!** No se olvide de (Don't forget) usar la **a** con **conocer.**

Paso 2. En grupos de tres, túrnense para presentar sus oraciones. Los compañeros que escuchan deben adivinar (*guess*) cuáles son las oraciones falsas.

E. Encuesta (*Poll*) **sobre los talentos especiales de la clase**

Paso 1. Haga una lista de tres cosas interesantes que Ud. sabe hacer bien. Use infinitivos, según el modelo.

MODELO: tocar el acordeón, hacer paella, esquiar

Paso 2. Ahora haga una encuesta entre por lo menos (*at least*) siete compañeros de clase para ver si los talentos de Ud. son únicos o comunes en su clase. Si sus compañeros tienen un talento que Ud. también tiene, deben firmar (*sign*) en el espacio indicado.

MODELO: tocar el acordeón → ¿**Sabes** tocar el acordeón? Si **sabes, firma** aquí.

Talento 1: ________	Talento 2: ________	Talento 3: ________

F. Intercambios

1. ¿Qué restaurantes conoces en esta ciudad? ¿Cuál es tu restaurante favorito? ¿Por qué es tu favorito? ¿Es buena la comida allí? ¿Qué tipo de comida sirven? ¿Te gusta el ambiente (*atmosphere*)? ¿Comes allí con frecuencia? ¿Llamas para hacer reservaciones?
2. ¿Qué platos sabes hacer? ¿Tacos? ¿enchiladas? ¿pollo frito? ¿hamburguesas? ¿Te gusta cocinar? ¿Cocinas con frecuencia? ¿Qué ingredientes usas con más frecuencia? ¿Tienes una receta (*recipe*) favorita?

Mundo interactivo

You should now be prepared to work with Scenario 4, Activity 1 in Connect Spanish (**www.connectspanish.com**).

Con. B: Follow-up

Ask students the following questions.

Paso 1

1. *¿Sabe el número de teléfono de su profesor(a) de español?*
2. *¿Sabe hacer algún* (new) *plato de comida hispana?*

Paso 2

1. *¿Conoce a un jugador* (new) *de fútbol americano de esta universidad?*
2. *¿Conoce al presidente / a la presidenta (al rector / a la rectora) de esta universidad?*

Con. B: Note

Active vocabulary: *el/la dueño/a*

Con. C: Answers

Remember that students are not yet familiar with direct object pronouns. Their answers to these questions may be repetitive. Encourage the use of *lo* when appropriate.

1. *No, no saben dónde quieren cenar. (No, no lo saben.)* **2.** *No, no conocen el nuevo restaurante. (No, no lo conocen.)* **3.** *No, no lo saben.* **4.** *Sí, saben su teléfono.* **5.** *No, no lo conocen. Maripepa conoce al dueño.*

Con. D: Follow-up

Ask students to report back to the whole class the most interesting information that they learned.

Con. E: Follow-up

Discuss the results. *¿Qué sabe hacer más gente* (new)*? ¿A cuántas personas conoce Ud. que (hacen…)?*

Con. E: Redacción

Ask students to summarize the results of their poll by comparing what they know how to do with the answers of their classmates. Model the use of *Nadie…* at the beginning of a sentence.

Con. F: Suggestion

Assign the questions as written homework. In class, ask students to read and discuss their answers in pairs or in small groups.

Con. F: Note

Active vocabulary: *la receta*

Pronunciación: See the Laboratory Manual for presentation and practice with the letters *d* and *t*.

Gramática 18
Direct Objects: The Personal *a*

Note

Since the concept of the personal *a* was introduced informally in the preceding *Vocabulario: Preparación* section, you can refresh students' memories about the concept by asking them to tell you the difference between the following sentences.

Conozco ***a*** *Penélope.*
Conozco el restaurante ***de*** *Penélope.*

Extension

5. *el agua: La tomo todos los días. La tomo de vez en cuando. Nunca la tomo.*
   ¡OJO! The direct object for *el agua* is *la* because it is a feminine noun.
6. *el jamón: Lo como todos los días…*

Heritage Speakers

- Fíjese que algunos hispanohablantes no usan la *a* personal en el habla cotidiana. Su uso ocurre mayormente cuando hay confusión entre el complemento directo e indirecto. Compare las siguientes oraciones.

  Le presento mi esposa al embajador.
  Le presento el embajador a mi esposa.

  Pregúnteles a los hispanohablantes si tienden a usarla o no, y en qué contextos.
- Note que la *a* personal no se usa con complementos directos cuando estos se refieren a personas indefinidas o cuya existencia se desconoce. Invite a los hispanohablantes a explicar la diferencia entre las siguientes oraciones.

  Carlos ***busca*** *un consejero que lo pued****a*** *ayudar.*
  Carlos ***conoce*** *a un consejero que lo pued****e*** *ayudar.*

  Sin embargo, los pronombres *alguien, nadie, alguno* y *ninguno* siempre requieren el uso de la *a* personal.

The Personal *a*

Suggestions

- Introduce third person direct object pronouns first. Put a number of objects on the desk (*un libro, una flor, un coche* [toy car]) and model sentences with a noun-to-pronoun transformation: *Miro el libro.* → *Lo miro.*
- Follow a similar sequence with feminine singular nouns, then plural masculine and feminine nouns.

GRAMÁTICA

Grammar Tutorial 18
connect SPANISH
www.connectspanish.com

18 Expressing *what* or *who(m)*

Direct Objects: The Personal **a;** Direct Object Pronouns

Gramática en acción: De compras en el supermercado

¿Y Ud.?

Indique cuáles de estas declaraciones expresan lo que Ud. hace.

1. **la fruta**
   - La como todos los días. Por eso tengo que comprarla con frecuencia.
   - La como de vez en cuando (*once in a while*). Por eso no la compro a menudo (*often*).
   - Nunca la como. No necesito comprarla.
2. **el pollo**
   - Lo como todos los días. Por eso tengo que comprarlo con frecuencia.
   - Lo como de vez en cuando. Por eso no lo compro a menudo.
   - Nunca lo como. No necesito comprarlo.
3. **los refrescos**
   - Los bebo todos los días. Por eso tengo que comprarlos con frecuencia.
   - Los bebo de vez en cuando. Por eso no los compro a menudo.
   - Nunca los bebo. No necesito comprarlos.
4. **las bananas**
   - Las como todos los días. Por eso tengo que comprarlas con frecuencia.
   - Las como de vez en cuando. Por eso no las compro a menudo.
   - Nunca las como. No necesito comprarlas.

NATIONAL STANDARDS: Comparisons

In many Hispanic countries, families can purchase fresh (unpasteurized) milk on a daily basis from street vendors or from local shops. This milk has to be boiled in order to make it safe for consumption. During the boiling process, a thick cream separates from the milk and rises to the top. This cream, called *nata de leche*, is frequently used when making desserts. Are there any places where one can buy fresh milk in your area?

The Personal a / La *a* personal

> *the direct object* / **el complemento directo** = the noun or pronoun that receives the action of the verb

1. Direct Objects

In English and in Spanish, the *direct object* (**el complemento directo**) of a sentence answers the question *what?* or *who(m)?* in relation to the subject and verb.

SUBJECT (S)	VERB (V)	DIRECT OBJECT (DO)
Ana	is preparing	**dinner.**
They	can't hear	**the waiter.**

What is Ana preparing? ⟶ **dinner**
Who(*m*) can't they hear? ⟶ **the waiter**

Indicate the subjects, verbs, and direct objects in the following sentences.

1. *I don't see Betty and Mary here.*
2. *We don't have any money.*
3. No veo a Betty y María aquí.
4. No tenemos dinero.
5. Julio va a poner la sopa en la mesa.
6. ¿Necesitas el libro y un bolígrafo?

2. The Personal *a*

In Spanish, the word **a** immediately precedes the direct object of a sentence when the direct object refers to a specific person or persons or a pet. This **a,** called the personal **a (la *a* personal),** has no equivalent in English.*

The personal **a** is not used when the direct object is a nonspecific person or an unknown person.

Vamos a visitar **a nuestros abuelos.**
We're going to visit our grandparents.
but
Vamos a visitar **la casa de nuestros abuelos.**
We're going to visit our grandparents' house.

Necesitan **a sus padres.**
They need their parents.
but
Necesitan **el coche de sus padres.**
They need their parents' car.

Conozco **a un buen chef.**
I know a great chef.
but
Necesito **un buen chef para una fiesta.**
I need a great chef for a party.

¡OJO!
The personal **a** is used before the interrogative words **¿quién?** and **¿quiénes?** when they function as direct objects.

¿A quién llamas? ¿**al** camarero?
Who(m) are you calling? The waiter?

¡OJO!
The English verbs *to listen **to** / look **at** / wait **for*** are all followed by prepositional phrases (a *preposition* + *noun* or *pronoun*). However, the Spanish equivalents of those verbs (which are **escuchar, mirar,** and **esperar**) are not followed by prepositions. They *are* followed by the personal **a** before a specific person or pet. Compare these pairs of sentences.

Miro el menú. *I'm looking at the menu.*
Miro **al** niño. *I'm looking at the boy.*

Escucho la radio. *I'm listening to the radio.*
Escucho **al** niño. *I'm listening to the boy.*

Espero el autobús. *I'm waiting for the bus.*
Espero **al** niño. *I'm waiting for the boy.*

3. Other Uses of *a*

Don't confuse the personal **a** with other uses of the word **a** that you have learned so far.

- **a** = the preposition *to*
- **a** = used after some verbs before an infinitive

[Práctica A]

Voy **a** la universidad.
En esta clase **aprendemos a** hablar español.
Vamos a salir mañana.

*The personal **a** is not generally used with **tener (Tenemos cuatro hijos.)** or **hay (Hay tres niños en la sala.).**

- After presenting third person object pronouns with visuals, expand their use to include the meaning of *you.* Have students stand up as appropriate.

  Yo lo/la veo (a Ud., Roberto, and so on)
  ¿Ud. me ve (a mí)? ⟶ Sí, professor(a), lo/la veo.
- Point out that, like the subject pronoun *ellos,* the direct object pronoun *los* can refer to either a masculine group or a combination of masculine and feminine nouns.
- Point out that like direct object nouns, direct object pronouns answer the question *what?* or *who(m)?* after the verb.
- Point out that many verbs commonly used with reflexive pronouns can also be used with direct object nouns and pronouns when the action of the verb is directed at someone other than the subject of the sentence. The meaning of the verb will change slightly. Provide the following examples.

  *Generalmente me despierto a las ocho. La radio **me** despierta.*
  *En un restaurante, el camarero **nos** sienta.*

Emphasis 1: Suggestions

- Illustrate the concept of direct objects by tapping someone on the shoulder, tossing an eraser to a student, breaking a piece of chalk. Ask: Who/What is first affected by the action? ⟶ person, eraser, chalk.
- Point out that the direct object answers the question *what?* or *who(m)?* after the verb.
- Use the brief exercise in the right-hand column to emphasize the lack of explicit subject pronouns in items 3, 4, and 6.

Emphasis 1: Notes

- In English, the distinction between *who* (subject) and *whom* (direct object) is no longer salient for all native speakers. It is especially irrelevant to many of today's students. For this reason, we include both options (*who* and *whom*) to refer to the direct object of a sentence. Students who know the difference between *who* and *whom* will already understand the concept of the direct object.
- Emphasize that pets are often treated like people and take a personal *a: Veo un perro allí* but *Veo a Bear, mi perro, allí.*
- Note the introduction of the concept of an unspecified person. Not only will this help students use the personal *a* correctly, but it will also prepare them for the use/non-use of the subjunctive in sentences such as: *Busco un profesor que sepa…*

Emphasis 2: Note

Active vocabulary: *esperar, el menú*

Direct Object Pronouns

Preliminary Exercises

Use the following chain drill to practice the use of the *a* personal. Then have students match the questions to the answers.

1. —*¿A quién ve? ¿Qué ve?*
   —*Veo el libro.* (*el profesor, el pizzarón, los estudiantes, la mesa, mi amigo/a, la puerta*)
2. —*¿A quién busca? ¿Qué busca?*
   —*Busco a mi amigo José.* (*mi libro, Felipe, el amigo de Tomás, el profesor, un cuaderno*)

Emphasis 1: Suggestions

- Stress the position of the object pronoun.
- Use the following question to practice new words. Write a model answer on the board.

  —*Ud. hace un pastel. ¿Necesita las siguientes cosas? los huevos, la leche, el azúcar, el chocolate, la vainilla, la sal, la harina* (new)…

  Students respond:

  Claro que (no) *lo/la necesito.*
- Ask students to rephrase the second line of the first two pairs of examples without the direct object pronoun. (*¿Necesitas las zanahorias ahora mismo?, No conozco a Diego.*) Call their attention to the repetition of the direct object nouns.
- Introduce the concept of transitive verbs (those that must always have a direct object, such as want, need, and so on).
- Personalize the use of the object pronouns by asking questions that involve the students.

  —*¿Quién me mira? ¿*[student] *me mira?* →
  —*Sí,* [student] *lo/la mira.*
  —*¿Quién nos mira* [the student stands with the instructor]*?*
  ¿[student] *nos mira?* →
  —*Sí,* [student] *los/las mira.*

Emphasis 1: Reciclado

Review clothing vocabulary. Have students answer the following questions using direct object pronouns. Write a model answer on the board.

—*Ud. hace la maleta* (You are packing) *para un viaje a Acapulco. ¿Necesita las siguientes cosas?*
el traje de baño
las sandalias
las gafas (new) *de sol*
el libro de español
el libro de sicología
los pantalones cortos
las camisetas
la crema bronceadora
el reloj
—*Claro que* [no] *lo/la/los/las necesito.*

Emphasis 2: Suggestion

Be sure that students understand what is meant by the "main" verb in this explanation. Ask them to pick out the main verb in the examples.

Direct Object Pronouns / **Los pronombres del complemento directo**

me	me	**nos**	us
te	you (*fam. sing.*)	**os**	you (*fam. pl.*)
lo*	you (*form. sing.*), him, it (*m.*)	**los**	you (*form. pl.*), them (*m., m. + f.*)
la	you (*form. sing.*), her, it (*f.*)	**las**	you (*form. pl.*), them (*f.*)

1. Direct Object Pronouns

Like direct object nouns, *direct object pronouns* (**los pronombres del complemento directo**) are the first recipient of the action of the verb. They serve to avoid the unnecessary repetition of a noun that has already been mentioned, as in the first two examples to the right.

Note that direct object pronouns are placed before a conjugated verb and after the word **no** when it appears. Third person direct object pronouns are used only when the direct object noun has already been mentioned.

[Práctica B–C]

—¿Dónde están **las zanahorias**?
—¿**Las** necesitas ahora mismo?
"Where are the carrots?"
"Do you need them right now?"

—¿Conoces a **Diego**?
—No, no **lo** conozco.
"Do you know Diego?"
"No, I don't know him."

—¿Quién **te** llama más por teléfono?
—Mi mamá **me** llama más.
"Who calls you the most?
"My mother calls me the most."

2. With Infinitives or Present Participles

The direct object pronouns can precede the main verb or follow (and be attached to):

- an infinitive
- a present participle

[Práctica D–F]

Las tengo que leer. / Tengo que **leerlas.** — *I have to read them.*

Lo estoy comiendo. / Estoy **comiéndolo.** — *I am eating it.*

3. Multiple Meanings of *lo/la/los/las*

Note that the direct object pronouns **lo/la/los/las** have different meanings depending on the context.

No **lo** veo por la niebla.
I don't see { *it* / *him* / *you* (*form.*) } *because of the fog.*

4. The Pronoun *lo*

Note that the direct object pronoun **lo** can refer to actions, situations, or ideas in general. When used in this way, **lo** expresses English *it* or *that.*

Lo comprende muy bien.
He understands it (*that*) *very well.*

No **lo** creo.
I don't believe it (*that*).

Lo sé.
I know (*it*).

Summary of Direct Object Pronouns

yo → **me**	nosotros/as → **nos**
tú → **te**	vosotros/as → **vos**
Ud., él → **lo**	Uds., ellos → **los**
Ud., ella → **la**	Uds., ellas → **las**

Autoprueba

Give the direct object pronouns that correspond to these nouns.

1. ______ la lechuga
2. ______ los tomates
3. ______ el pan
4. ______ las zanahorias
5. ______ todo

Answers: **1.** *la* **2.** *los* **3.** *lo* **4.** *las* **5.** *lo*

*In Spain and in some other parts of the Spanish-speaking world, **le** is frequently used instead of **lo** for the direct object pronoun him. This usage, called **el leísmo,** will not be followed in Puntos de partida.

Práctica

A. *¿A personal o no?* Complete las siguientes oraciones. **¡OJO!** Use la **a** personal cuando sea (*whenever it is*) necesario. Recuerde: **a** + **el** ⟶ **al.**

Busco…	Miro…
1. el presidente. al	**7.** la televisión.
2. una clase de historia.	**8.** mis niños en el parque. a
3. mi amiga. a	**9.** películas en español.
4. la clase de matemáticas.	**10.** el profesor / la profesora en clase. al / a la
5. un trabajo (*job*).	**11.** _____ el pizarrón blanco en clase.
6. mi perro Sultán. a	**12.** _____ las noticias (*news*) todas las noches.

B. Correspondencias. Empareje los nombres y los pronombres personales con sus correspondientes pronombres del complemento directo. Hay más de una correspondencia posible en algunos (*some*) casos.

PRONOMBRES	NOMBRES Y PRONOMBRES PERSONALES	
1. _c, g_ los	**a.** Ana	**e.** Jorge
2. _a, h_ la	**b.** tú	**f.** Elena y Rosa
3. _b_ te	**c.** Pedro y Carolina	**g.** Uds.
4. _e, h_ lo	**d.** María y yo	**h.** Ud.
5. _f, g_ las		
6. _d_ nos		

C. ¿Qué comen los vegetarianos?

Paso 1. Aquí hay una lista de diferentes comidas. ¿Cree Ud. que las come un vegetariano? Conteste según los modelos.

MODELOS: el bistec ⟶ No **lo** come.
la banana ⟶ **La** come.

1. las patatas	**5.** las zanahorias	**9.** los champiñones
2. el arroz	**6.** las manzanas	**10.** los frijoles
3. las chuletas de cerdo	**7.** los camarones	**11.** la ensalada
4. los huevos	**8.** el pan	**12.** los dulces

Paso 2. Si hay estudiantes vegetarianos en la clase, pídales que verifiquen (*ask them to verify*) las respuestas de Ud.

Prác. C: Answers: 1. *Las come.* **2.** *Lo come.* **3.** *No las come.* **4.** *Los come.* **5.** *Las come.* **6.** *Las come.* **7.** *No los come.* **8.** *Lo come.* **9.** *Los come.* **10.** *Los come.* **11.** *La come.* **12.** *Los come*

D. La cena de Lola y Manolo.

Paso 1. La siguiente descripción de la cena de Lola y Manolo es muy repetitiva. Combine las oraciones, cambiando los sustantivos de complemento directo rosados por (*with*) pronombres.

MODELO: El camarero (*waiter*) trae un menú. Lola lee el menú. ⟶
El camarero trae un menú y Lola **lo** lee.

1. El camarero trae una botella de vino tinto. Pone la botella en la mesa.
2. El camarero trae las copas (*glasses*) de vino. Pone las copas delante de Lola y Manolo.
3. Lola quiere la especialidad de la casa. Va a pedir la especialidad de la casa.
4. Manolo prefiere el pescado fresco (*fresh*). Pide el pescado fresco.
5. Lola quiere una ensalada también. Por eso pide una ensalada.
6. El camarero trae la comida. Sirve la comida.
7. «¿La cuenta (*bill*)? El dueño está preparando la cuenta para Uds.»
8. Manolo quiere pagar con tarjeta (*card*) de crédito. Pero no trae su tarjeta.
9. Por fin, Lola toma la cuenta. Paga la cuenta.

Paso 2. Las siguientes oraciones describen la cena de Lola y Manolo. Diga en español a qué se refieren los pronombres indicados. Luego diga quién hace cada acción.

1. Las pone en la mesa.	**3. La** sirve.	**5. La** paga.
2. Lo pide.	**4.** No **la** trae.	

Prác. D: Answers
Paso 1. 1. *… y la pone…* **2.** *… y las pone…* **3.** *… y la va a pedir (va a pedirla).* **4.** *… y lo pide.* **5.** *… y por eso la pide.* **6.** *… y la sirve.* **7.** *… y la pide.* **8.** *… la está preparando (está preparándola) para Uds.* **9.** *Pero no la trae.* **10.** *… y la paga.*

Paso 2. 1. *las copas: el camarero* **2.** *el pescado fresco: Manolo* **3.** *la comida: el camarero* **4.** *la tarjeta de crédito: Manolo* **5.** *la cuenta: Lola*

Reciclado: Ask the following questions to practice the use of *saber* and *conocer* with object pronouns.

1. *¿Sabe Ud. mi nombre?* ⟶ *Sí, lo sé.*
   ¿los nombres de todos los estudiantes de la clase?
   ¿la fecha de hoy?
   ¿la fecha de mi cumpleaños?
   ¿las formas del verbo saber*?*
   ¿todo el vocabulario nuevo?
2. *¿Conoce Ud. a* [student in class]*?*
   ¿Conoce Ud. personalmente a Dakota Fanning?
   ¿a Justin Bieber?
   ¿a mis padres?
   ¿al novio / a la novia de [student in class]*?*

Prác. A: Follow-up

- Have students say the following sentences in Spanish.
  1. I'm looking at the TV (at María).
  2. *We're listening to the radio (to the professor).*
  3. She's looking for her pen (for her brother).
  4. They're waiting for their car (for the doctor).
- Emphasize the contrast between Spanish (direct object, with the a personal in some cases) and English (prepositional phrase in the translation of these sentences) by asking students to translate them to Spanish.

Prác. C: Variation

Have students answer the question: *¿Qué comen los niños pequeños?* Use the same list and add.

13. *la leche*	**15.** *el chocolate*
14. *los purés*	**16.** *el vino*

Prác. C: Follow-up

Follow up with these questions.

¿Come Ud. las siguientes comidas cuando está a dieta?
¿los helados? ⟶ *No, no los como.*
¿la ensalada?
¿los pasteles?
¿las papas fritas?
¿el pollo?
¿la pizza?
¿el queso?
¿el pan?

Prác. D: Note

Active vocabulary: *el/la camarero/a, la cuenta, fresco/a, la tarjeta de crédito*

Prác. D: Follow-up

Continue to check comprehension with the following questions.

1. *La ensalada, ¿la pide Lola?*
2. *Y el pescado, ¿lo pide Lola también?*
3. *¿Quién pide la especialidad de la casa?*
4. *Y la tarjeta de crédito, ¿la tiene Manolo?*
5. *Y la cuenta, ¿quién la paga?*

Prác. E: Notes

- This activity makes salient the use of direct object pronouns with human direct objects. The use of *lo/la/los/las* corresponding to *Ud./Uds.* may be especially difficult for students.
- Active vocabulary: *ayudar, invitar, llamar*

Prác. E: Suggestions

- Make sure that students understand that *lo/la/los/las* are the equivalents of *Ud./Uds.* and that they must match in gender with the persons referred to.
- Have students translate each item to English to emphasize the meaning of the direct object pronouns, which students tend to read as subject pronouns.

Nota comunicativa

Suggestion

Do a series of actions, then state in Spanish what you have just done; e.g., write your name on the board, then erase it, turn the lights off or on, open and close a book, sit down, stand up, and so on.

Note

Remind students that they have already learned the *preposition* + *inf.* structure.

Prác. F: Preliminary Exercise

Have students answer questions using *acabar de.*

¿Quiere comer? → Acabo de comer.

1. *ver la televisión*
2. *leer*
3. *ir al centro*
4. *desayunar*
5. *almorzar*
6. *cenar*

Prác. F: Suggestion

Point out that the questions in this exercise are typical of one way to ask someone to do something (*interrogative* + *present tense*). Depending on the speaker's tone, they can sound somewhat forceful, just like in English.

Prác. F: Reciclado

Have students tell what they have just done before leaving these places.

¿Qué acaba de hacer Ud. cuando sale de…

1. *un mercado?*
2. *una discoteca?*
3. *un restaurante?*
4. *una librería?*
5. *el laboratorio de química?*
6. *una clase de literatura inglesa?*
7. *un café?*

E. Minidiálogos. Complete los siguientes minidiálogos con los pronombres del complemento directo que faltan (*are missing*).

1. —¿Me quieres (*do you love*)?
   —¡Te quiero muchísimo!
2. —No tenemos ni un (*not even one*) dólar. ¿Nos invitas a un café?
   —No los/las puedo invitar porque yo no tengo dinero tampoco (*either*).
3. —Buenas noches, señor. ¿Lo atienden ya (*Is someone already helping you*)?
   —No, todavía no, gracias.
   — Perdón. Entonces (*Then*) voy a atenderlo yo. ¿Qué desea?
4. —¡Mi hija nunca me llama por teléfono!
   —¡Tu hija solo tiene 19 años! Seguro que te llama si necesita dinero.
5. —¿Cuándo van a visitarlos a Uds. sus primos panameños?
   —Nos van a visitar este verano.
6. —Buenos días, señora. ¿En qué puedo ayudarla (*to help*)?
   —Buenos días. Busco una blusa negra de mi talla (*size*).

Nota **comunicativa**

Cómo expresar una acción muy reciente: *acabar* + *infinitivo*

To talk about what you have *just* done, use the phrase **acabar** + **de** + *infinitive.*

Acabo de almorzar con Beto.	*I just had lunch with Beto.*
Acabas de celebrar tu cumpleaños, ¿verdad?	*You just celebrated your birthday, didn't you?*

Note that the infinitive follows **de.** Remember that the infinitive is the only verb form that can follow a preposition in Spanish.

F. ¡Acabo de hacerlo! Imagine that a friend is pressuring you to do the following things. With a classmate, tell him or her that you just did each one, using either of the forms in the model.

MODELO: E1: ¿Por qué no haces la ensalada? →
E2: Acabo de hacer**la.** (**La** acabo de hacer.)

1. ¿Por qué no preparas las chuletas para la fiesta?
2. ¿Vas a comprar la fruta hoy?
3. ¿Por qué no pagas los cafés?
4. ¿Vas a cocinar la comida para la cena?
5. ¿Puedes pedir la cuenta?
6. ¿Quieres ayudarme?

Prác. F: Variation

Have students work in groups of two or three to make suggestions to each other. Students should respond to suggestions by saying they have just done it.

¿Quiere Ud. comer? → No, acabo de comer.
¿Quiere Ud. mirar la televisión? → No, acabo de mirarla.

Conversación

A. ¡Ayuda! (*Help!*)

Paso 1. Todos necesitamos ayuda alguna vez (*at some point*), ¿no? ¿Quién los ayuda a Uds. en los siguientes casos?

MODELO: con las cuentas → **Mis padres me** ayudan con las cuentas.

1. con las cuentas
2. con la tarea
3. con la matrícula
4. con el horario de clases
5. resolver los problemas personales
6. pagar las deudas (*debts*)
7. estudiar para los exámenes
8. con el español

Paso 2. Ahora, en parejas, túrnense para hacer y contestar preguntas basadas en el **Paso 1.**

MODELO: con las cuentas →
E1: ¿Quién **te** ayuda con las cuentas?
E2: Generalmente, **mis padres me** ayudan un poco. A veces también **me** ayudan **mis abuelos.**

B. Una encuesta sobre la comida. Hágales (*Ask*) preguntas a sus compañeros de clase para saber si consumen las comidas o bebidas indicadas y con qué frecuencia. Deben explicar por qué toman o comen cierta cosa o no.

MODELO: la carne → E1: ¿Comes carne?
E2: No, no **la** como casi nunca porque tiene mucho colesterol.

Vocabulario útil

la cafeína
las calorías
el colesterol
la grasa fat
estar **a dieta**
ser **alérgico/a a**
ser **bueno/a para la salud** (health)
me pone(n) nervioso/a it/they make me nervous
me sienta(n) mal it/they don't agree with me
lo/la/los/las detesto

1. la carne
2. los mariscos
3. el yogur
4. la pizza
5. las hamburguesas
6. el pollo
7. el café
8. los dulces
9. las bebidas alcohólicas
10. el atún
11. los espárragos
12. el hígado (*liver*)

¿Recuerda Ud.?

You have been using a few words that express indefinite and negative qualities since the first chapter of this text. Review what you already know about the content of **Gramática 19** by giving the English equivalent of the following words.

1. siempre _always_ 2. nunca _never_ 3. también _also_

Estrategia

Use the word **nadie** before the object pronoun and verb to express that *no one* does something. For example, in item 1: **Nadie me ayuda con las cuentas.**

Vocabulario útil

ayudar + **a** + *inf.* to help to (*do something*)

Con. A: Suggestions

- Model for students the use of *ayudar* + *a* + *inf.* before beginning the activity.
- Model the use of *nadie*, which (along with other indefinite and negative words) will be introduced in the next grammar section.

Con. A: Notes

- Additional items:
  9. *preparar la cena*
  10. *cuando tiene problemas con el coche*
- Active vocabulary: *la ayuda*

Con. B: Suggestions

- Model the use of singular and plural options with *me pone(n) nervioso/a* and *me sienta(n) mal.*
- **Optional:** Introduce *me da(n) asco.* However, be aware that *me* functions as an indirect object in this expression, which may be confusing to students at this point.
- Use the following questions to start class discussion.
  1. *¿Quién lo/la invita a cenar con frecuencia? ¿Y a ir al cine? ¿a tomar un café? ¿a salir por la noche? ¿a bailar? ¿A quién quiere invitar a cenar?*
  2. *¿Quién lo/la busca cuando necesita ayuda con el español? ¿Y cuando necesita hablar de un problema personal? ¿cuando necesita dinero?*

Gramática 19
Indefinite and Negative Words

Suggestions

- Act out models for using indefinite and negative words. To show comprehension, have students produce sentences that describe the situations you are setting up. Hints: place one book on one desk, several on another, and none on a third to show *some books* vs. *one book* vs. *no book* (something vs. nothing) or point to a chair where no one is sitting, and so on.
- Alternatively, use the drawing in *Prác. A* on p. 214 as a vehicle for introducing these words.
- Ask students to translate each of the example sentences in this box and in those on the next page, to make sure that they understand the meaning of the negative words and also to call their attention to the double negative, which is explained on the next page.

Note

Active vocabulary: *preparar*

Follow-up

- In *¿Y Ud.?*, students do not need to use the *parecerse a* structure of the last question in their response. Model answers that use vocabulary and structures that they know.

  Mi refrigerador es/está…
  En mi refrigerador hay…
- Ask the following additional questions to personalize information and to check comprehension of the presentation.
  1. *¿Qué hay en el refrigerador A? ¿en el B?* (Suggestion: Help students with vocabulary items if you have not used vocabulary for condiments.)
  2. *¿Qué no hay?* (Suggestion: Guide students to use the double negative with categories of food: mariscos, verduras, and so on.)
  3. *¿A Ud. le gusta comprar los comestibles?*
  4. *En su casa o apartamento, ¿quién compra la comida?* (Suggestion: Prompt students to answer using a direct object pronoun: *Yo la compro.*)

19 Expressing Negation
Indefinite and Negative Words

Grammar Tutorial 19
connect SPANISH
www.connectspanish.com

Gramática en acción: ¿Un refrigerador típico?

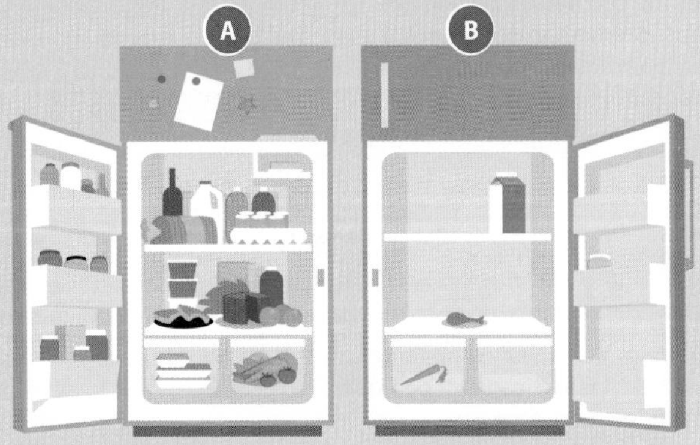

Empareje las siguientes respuestas con el refrigerador A o el B.

1. ¿Hay algo bueno de comer en este refrigerador?
   ___A___ Sí, hay algo.
   ___B___ No, no hay nada.
2. ¿Hay fruta y pan?
   ___A___ Sí, hay fruta y pan.
   ___B___ No, no hay fruta. Tampoco hay pan.
3. ¿Hay chuletas de cerdo?
   ___B___ No, no hay ninguna chuleta.
   ___A___ Sí, hay algunas chuletas.
4. En esta casa, ¿alguien compra comida con frecuencia?
   ___B___ No, nadie la compra.
   ___A___ Sí, alguien la compra.

¿Y Ud.?

¿Cuál de los dos refrigeradores se parece (*resembles*) más al refrigerador de su casa o apartamento? ¿Cuál se parece más al típico refrigerador de los estudiantes? ¿de una familia con hijos? ¿de jóvenes profesionales?

Indefinite and Negative Words / **Las palabras indefinidas y negativas**

You have been using many indefinite and negative words since the first chapters of *Puntos de partida.*

los adverbios indefinidos y negativos		
siempre	always	Siempre estudio en casa. Estudio en casa siempre.
nunca, jamás	never	Nunca estudio en la biblioteca. No estudio nunca en la biblioteca.
también	also	Yo también sé preparar una paella. Yo sé preparar una paella también.
tampoco	neither, not either	Tampoco sé preparar una paella. Yo no sé preparar una paella tampoco.

A typical refrigerator? **1.** *Is there something good to eat in this refrigerator? Yes, there is something. No, there is nothing.* **2.** *Is there (some) fruit and bread? Yes, there is (some) fruit and bread. No, there is no fruit. There isn't any bread either.* **3.** *Are there pork chops? No, there aren't any chops.* (*Lit., No, there is no chop.*) *Yes, there are some chops.* **4.** *In this house, does anyone buy food frequently? No, no one buys it. Yes, someone buys it.*

Heritage Speakers

En algunos dialectos del español del suroeste de los Estados Unidos, a veces se oye decir *nadien* o *naidien* por *nadie.* Estas formas se usan en el habla popular de algunos grupos, pero la forma *nadie* es la preferida. Pregúnteles a los hispanohablantes si han oído este vocablo alguna vez o si ellos mismos lo usan entre amigos.

Resources: Transparency 86

Los sustantivos indefinidos y negativos		
alguien **nadie**	someone, anyone no one, nobody, not anybody	Conozco **a** alguien en esa fiesta. No conozco **a** nadie en esa fiesta.
algo **nada**	something, anything nothing, not anything	Sé algo de la cocina panameña. No sé nada de la cocina panameña.

Pronunciation hint: Pronounce the **d** in **nada** and **nadie** as a fricative, that is, like the *th* sound in *the*: **[na-đa]**, **[na-đie]**.

Los adjetivos indefinidos y negativos		
algún, alguna, algunos/as **ningún, ninguna**	some, any no, not any	**algún** tomate, **algunas** chuletas **ningún** tomate, **ninguna** chuleta

¡OJO!

Note how **alguno** and **ninguno** shorten (**algún, ningún**) before masculine singular nouns. You've seen something similar with **uno (⟶ un), bueno (⟶ buen),** and **grande (⟶ gran).**

algún / ningún problema
alguna / ninguna cosa
algunos problemas
algunas cosas

The Double Negative / **La negativa doble**

When a negative word comes after the main verb, Spanish requires that another negative word—usually **no**—be placed before the verb. When a negative word precedes the verb, **no** is not used.

no + *verb* + *negative word*
negative word + *verb*

¿**No estudia nadie**? ¿**Nadie estudia**?	*Isn't anyone studying?*
No estás en clase **nunca**. **Nunca estás** en clase.	*You're never in class.*
No quieren cenar aquí **tampoco**. **Tampoco quieren** cenar aquí.	*They don't want to have dinner here either.*

The Adjectives **algún** and **ningún** / **Los adjetivos *algún* y *ningún***

Algún (**Alguna/os/as**) and **ningún** (**ninguna**) are adjectives. Unlike **nadie** and **nada** (nouns) or **nunca, jamás,** and **tampoco** (adverbs), **algún** and **ningún** must agree with the noun they modify. **Ningún** (**Ninguna**) is rarely used in the plural.

—¿Hay **algunos recados** para mí hoy?
—Lo siento, pero hoy no hay **ningún recado** para Ud.
"Are there any messages for me today?"
"I'm sorry, but there are no messages for you today."
("There is not a single message for you today.")

Autoprueba

Give the corresponding negative word.

1. siempre
2. también
3. alguien
4. alguna
5. algo

Answers: **1.** *nunca* **2.** *tampoco* **3.** *nadie* **4.** *ninguna* **5.** *nada*

Los sustantivos indefinidos y negativos

Suggestions

- Emphasize the use of the personal *a* with *alguien* and *nadie* when they are direct objects.
- Point out that the use of *nadie* after the verb is somewhat more frequent than its use before it.

The Adjectives *algún* and *ningún*

Note

This explanation does not include the use of *alguno* and *ninguno* after the noun. You should introduce that material if you wish.

Suggestions

- Emphasize that the plural forms *ningunos/as* are rarely used. As in the example, indefinite questions with plural *algunos/as* frequently require singular *ningún/ninguna* in the negative answers. The exceptions would be nouns usually used in plural in Spanish, e.g., *pantalones, medias, vacaciones,* and so on. In these cases, many native speakers simply avoid the double negative:

  Hace años que no tomo vacaciones.
- Offer optional vocabulary: *o… o…* and *ni… ni…*

Heritage Speakers

En algunos dialectos del español, se oye decir *nunca jamás* para expresar *never again o never ever*. Pregúnteles a los hispanohablantes si han oído esta expresión alguna vez o si ellos mismos la usan de vez en cuando. ¿Conocen la expresión *por siempre jamás*?

Bright Idea

Suggestion

Remind students (in *Prác. A* and *B*) that the personal *a* is omitted after *hay* and (in most cases) after forms of the verb *tener*.

Hay muchos estudiantes.
Tengo muchos estudiantes.
Veo a muchos estudiantes.

Prác. A: Suggestion

Use items from *Prác. A* as an inductive activity to present and practice the double negative.

Prác. A: Follow-up

Students, working in small groups, create at least four additional true/false sentences based on the drawing. There are many additional details in the drawing that are not included in the exercise: the animals, the telephone, the patio, and so on. Have groups read their sentences to their classmates, who must say *cierto* or *falso* and correct the false statements. Give a prize to the group that comes up with the most innovative statements.

Prác. B: Preliminary Exercise

Say the following words and have students respond with the corresponding opposite.

algo
alguien
algún
nada
nadie
ningún
nunca
siempre
también
tampoco

Prác. B: Reciclado

Recycle words about houses and rooms. Ask students about things that they do or do not have in their rooms or houses.

¿Tiene baño privado?

Also ask questions about their routines.

¿Come con frecuencia en la cocina?
¿Cocina todos los días?

Prác. A: Answers: 1. *Hay alguien en el baño.* **2.** *Nadie está haciendo la cena en la cocina. (No está haciendo la cena en la cocina nadie.)* **6.** *No hay ningún plato en la mesa del comedor.* **7.** *Hay algunos niños en la casa.*

Prác. B: Answers: 1. *No hay nada interesante en el menú.* **2.** *No tienen ningún plato típico.* **3.** *El profesor no cena allí tampoco.* **4.** *Mis amigos nunca almuerzan allí. (Mis amigos no almuerzan allí nunca.)* **5.** *No preparan ningún menú especial para grupos grandes.* **6.** *Nunca hacen platos nuevos. (No hacen platos nuevos nunca.)* **7.** *Y tampoco sirven paella, mi plato favorito. (Y no sirven tampoco paella, mi plato favorito.)*

Estrategia

Remember that **ninguno** is always used in the singular and that it shortens to **ningún** before a masculine, singular noun.

Prác. C: Possible Answers Paso 1. 1. *… no hay ninguna actividad interesante…* **2.** *Nunca me divierto… (No me divierto nunca…)* **3.** *No hay ningún político bueno…* **4.** *Ningún profesor (Ninguno de mis profesores) de este año es simpático.* **5.** *Ninguna comida de la cafetería me gusta. (No me gusta ninguna comida…)*

Práctica

A. ¡Anticipemos! ¿Qué pasa esta noche en casa? Indique si las siguientes oraciones son ciertas o falsas. Corrija las oraciones falsas.

	CIERTO	FALSO
1. No hay nadie en el baño.	☐	☑
2. En la cocina, alguien está haciendo la cena.	☐	☑
3. No hay ninguna persona en el patio.	☑	☐
4. Hay algo en la mesa del comedor.	☑	☐
5. Algunos amigos se están divirtiendo en la sala.	☑	☐
6. Hay algunos platos en la mesa del comedor.	☐	☑
7. No hay ningún niño en la casa.	☐	☑

B. ¡Por eso no come nadie allí! Exprese negativamente, usando la negativa doble.

MODELO: Hay alguien en el restaurante. ⟶ **No** hay **nadie** en el restaurante.

1. Hay algo interesante en el menú.
2. Tienen algunos platos típicos.
3. El profesor cena allí también.
4. Mis amigos siempre almuerzan allí.
5. Preparan un menú especial para grupos grandes.
6. Siempre hacen platos nuevos.
7. Y también sirven paella, mi plato favorito.

C. Todo lo contrario

Paso 1. Cambie las siguientes declaraciones para que sean (*so that they are*) completamente negativas. Luego indique si las oraciones son ciertas o falsas para Ud. Corrija o explique las oraciones falsas.

MODELO: Hay algunas personas antipáticas en mi familia. ⟶
No hay **ninguna persona antipática** en mi familia. No es cierto. Mi tío Marc es muy antipático. (Es cierto. Todos mis parientes son muy simpáticos.)

1. Esta semana hay actividades interesantes en la universidad.
2. Siempre me divierto tomando café con mis amigos.
3. Hay algunos políticos buenos hoy día.
4. Todos mis profesores de este año son simpáticos.
5. Me gusta toda la comida de la cafetería.

Resources: Transparency 87

Paso 2. Ahora invente preguntas para las siguientes respuestas. **¡OJO!** Hay más de una respuesta posible en algunos casos.

MODELO: No, no hay nada interesante en la tele. →
¿Hay algo interesante en la tele (esta noche)?

1. No, no hay ningún programa interesante esta noche.
2. No, no hay ningún estudiante de Nicaragua.
3. No, esta semana no pasan (*they're not showing*) ninguna buena película aquí.
4. No, nunca ceno en la universidad.
5. No, tampoco estudio en la biblioteca.

Conversación

A. Intercambios. En parejas, túrnense para entrevistarse sobre los siguientes temas. Deben obtener detalles interesantes y personales de su compañero/a.

MODELO: E1: ¿Tienes alguna buena excusa para no ir al gimnasio esta semana?
E2: No, no tengo ninguna buena excusa esta semana. (Sí, tengo una buena excusa. ¡No tengo tiempo!)

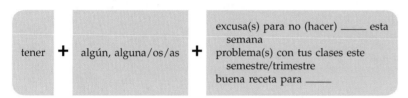

tener	+	algún, alguna/os/as	+	excusa(s) para no (hacer) ____ esta semana problema(s) con tus clases este semestre/trimestre buena receta para ____

B. Lo que come el profesor / la profesora

Paso 1. En parejas, escriban cuatro oraciones sobre los hábitos de su profesor(a) de español con respecto a la comida. Usen palabras negativas e indefinidas.

MODELO: La profesora nunca come mariscos.

Paso 2. En parejas, háganle preguntas a su profesor(a) para confirmar sus opiniones. ¿Quiénes conocen mejor a su profesor(a)?

MODELO: La profesora nunca come mariscos. →
Profesora, ¿Ud. come mariscos con frecuencia?

¿Recuerda Ud.?

Review what you already know about irregular first person present tense forms by giving the **yo** form of the following infinitives. You will need to know this information in **Gramática 20.**

1. salir salgo
2. tener tengo
3. conocer conozco
4. pedir pido
5. hacer hago
6. dormir duermo
7. perder pierdo
8. traer traigo

Prác. C: Answers
Paso 2. 1. *¿Hay algunos programas interesantes… ?* **2.** *¿Hay algunos estudiantes de Nicaragua… ?* **3.** *¿Pasan algunas buenas películas… ?* **4.** *¿Siempre / Con frecuencia cenas… ?* **5.** *¿También estudias… ?*

Prác. C: Follow-up

Expand each item by asking related questions of students, varying the information in the items as much as possible.

Con. A: Optional

Elicit negative expressions naturally by asking one or more sets of these questions.

1. *¿Vamos a vivir en la luna* (new) *algún día? ¿Vamos a viajar* (new) *a otros planetas? ¿Vamos a vivir allí algún día? ¿Vamos a establecer contacto con seres* (new) *de otros planetas algún día?*
2. *¿Algunos de los estudiantes de esta universidad son de países extranjeros? ¿De dónde son? ¿Algunos de sus amigos son de habla española? ¿De dónde son?*
3. *En esta clase, ¿quién…*
   siempre tiene algunas buenas ideas?
   tiene algunos amigos españoles?
   siempre lo entiende todo?
   nunca contesta ninguna pregunta?
   va a ser muy rico algún día?
   nunca tiene tiempo para divertirse?
   nunca mira la televisión?
   no practica ningún deporte?
   siempre invita a los otros a comer?
4. *¿Hay algo más importante que el dinero? ¿que la amistad? ¿que el amor?*
5. *En la clase, ¿hay alguien más inteligente que el profesor / la profesora? ¿más estudioso/a que Ud.? ¿más rico/a que Ud.?*
6. *La perfección es una meta* (new) *imposible, ¿verdad? ¿Hay alguna clase perfecta en esta universidad? ¿Hay alguna residencia perfecta? ¿una familia perfecta? ¿Tiene Ud. alguna idea de lo que es el compañero perfecto / la compañera perfecta? ¿un plan perfecto para esta noche?*

Gramática 20
Commands (Part 1): Formal Commands

Suggestion

Help students formulate recipes for simple foods, such as a salad or a sandwich.

Note

Commands are strong forms, even when they are formal. They show power or control on the part of the person who says them. Encourage students to use *por favor* whenever possible to soften their requests, particularly until they learn more polite forms. Also make them aware of the importance of tone: a command uttered with a soft tone will not sound like a command but rather communicate a request.

Formal Command Forms

Emphasis: First Verb Chart

Note that this chart includes examples of all variations of formal commands: regular verbs, a stem-changing verb, and an irregular verb (based on the *yo* form).

Emphasis 1,2: Suggestions

- Help students understand what is meant by the formal command forms using the "opposite" vowel.

  -ar → *-e*
  -er/-ir → *-a*

- Present the regular command forms.
- Use the following rapid response drill.

  ¿Cuál es el mandato formal (Ud.) de ______?
  cierro
  pienso
  vuelvo
  duermo
  sirvo
  pido

Heritage Speakers

Pídales a los hispanohablantes que le expliquen al resto de la clase las diferencias entre la comida auténtica de Latinoamérica y España, y la comida latinoamericana y española que se consume en este país.

Resources: Transparency 88

20 Influencing Others
Commands (Part 1): Formal Commands

Grammar Tutorial 20
connect SPANISH
www.connectspanish.com

Gramática en acción: Receta para guacamole

El guacamole

Ingredientes:
1 aguacate[a]
1 diente de ajo,[b] prensado[c]
1 tomate
jugo de un limón
sal
un poco de cilantro fresco[d]

Cómo se prepara
Corte el aguacate y el tomate en trozos[e] pequeños. Añada el jugo del limón, el ajo, el cilantro y la sal a su gusto. Mezcle bien todos los ingredientes y sírvalo con tortillas de maíz[f] fritas.

[a]*avocado* [b]*diente... clove of garlic* [c]*crushed* [d]*fresh* [e]*pieces* [f]*corn*

En español, los mandatos se usan con frecuencia en las recetas. Estos verbos se usan en forma de mandato en esta receta. ¿Puede encontrarlos?

añadir	to add
cortar	to cut
mezclar	to mix
servir (sirvo) (i)	

¿Y Ud.? ¿Le gusta el guacamole? ¿Lo hace con frecuencia? ¿Con qué lo sirve?

Formal Command Forms / Los mandatos formales

In *Puntos de partida* you have seen formal commands in the direction lines of activities since the beginning of the text: **haga, complete, conteste,** and so on.

Commands (imperatives) are verb forms used to tell someone to do something. In Spanish, *formal commands* (**los mandatos formales**) are used with people whom you address as **Ud.** or **Uds.*** Here are some of the basic forms.

a command or *imperative* / **un mandato** = a verb form used to tell someone to do something

	hablar	comer	escribir	volver	poner
Ud.	hable	coma	escriba	vuelva	ponga
Uds.	hablen	coman	escriban	vuelvan	pongan
English	*speak*	*eat*	*write*	*come back*	*put, place*

1. Regular Verbs

Most formal command forms can be derived from the **yo** form of the present tense.

Note that the "opposite" vowel is used:

-ar → e
-er/-ir → a

***-ar:* -o → -e, -en**		***-er/-ir:* -o → -a, -an**	
hablo →	hable hablen	como →	coma coman
		escribo →	escriba escriban

2. Stem-changing Verbs

Formal commands for stem-changing verbs will show the stem change, since the stem vowel is stressed. Base the command on the **yo** form to get the stem change right.

pensar (pienso) → **piense** Ud.
volver (vuelvo) → **vuelva** Ud.
pedir (pido) → **pida** Ud.

*You will learn how to form informal (**tú**) commands in **Gramática 36 (Cap. 13).**

Multimedia: Internet

Have students imagine that they have won a cooking contest for the best homemade recipe. The prize is a trip for four to Spain to eat in the best restaurants, and the contest organizers have asked the winners to find five Spanish restaurants on the Internet. Have students work in small groups to search for restaurants in Spain on the Internet. You might assign a specific city to each group. Have the groups list the restaurants they find, the type of food served there (some menus are available online), price range, and so on, and present their findings to the class.

3. **Verbs Ending in *-car, -gar, -zar***
These verbs have a spelling change to preserve the **-c-**, **-g-**, and **-z-** sounds.

c ⟶ qu	**buscar: busque** Ud.
g ⟶ gu	**pagar: pague** Ud.
z ⟶ c	**empezar: empiece** Ud.

¡OJO!

From this chapter on, these three spelling changes for verbs in formal commands will be indicated in parentheses in vocabulary lists. If these three verbs were active in this chapter, they would be listed in the end-of-chapter vocabulary list as follows: **buscar (qu), pagar (gu), empezar (empiezo) (c).**

4. **Verbs with Irregular Present Tense *yo* Forms**
These verbs reflect the irregularity in the **Ud./Uds.** commands.

conocer: **conozco**	⟶ **conozca** Ud.
decir* (*to say, tell*): **digo**	⟶ **diga** Ud.
hacer: **hago**	⟶ **haga** Ud.
oír: **oigo**	⟶ **oiga** Ud.
salir: **salgo**	⟶ **salga** Ud.
tener: **tengo**	⟶ **tenga** Ud.
traer: **traigo**	⟶ **traiga** Ud.
venir: **vengo**	⟶ **venga** Ud.
ver: **veo**	⟶ **vea** Ud.

5. **Irregular Formal Commands**
A few verbs have irregular **Ud./Uds.** command forms.

dar* (*to give*)	⟶ **dé** Ud., *but* **den** Uds.
estar	⟶ **esté** Ud.
ir	⟶ **vaya** Ud.
saber	⟶ **sepa** Ud.
ser	⟶ **sea** Ud.

Position of Pronouns / El lugar de los pronombres

1. **Pronouns with Affirmative Commands**
Direct object pronouns and reflexive pronouns must *follow* affirmative commands and be attached to them. In order to maintain the original stress of the verb form, an accent mark is added to the stressed vowel if the original command has two or more syllables.

una palabra:	*mandato + pronombre*
Pídalo Ud.	*Order it.*
Siéntese, por favor.	*Sit down, please.*

2. **Pronouns with Negative Commands**
Direct object and reflexive pronouns must *precede* the verb form in negative commands.

tres palabras:	**no** + *pronombre* + *mandato*
No lo pida Ud.	*Don't order it.*
No se siente.	*Don't sit down.*

¡OJO!

Now that you know how to form formal commands, be sure to use them carefully when speaking to native speakers of Spanish. Commands are strong forms in any language. It is wise to soften formal commands with **por favor** and by using a polite tone, just as you would in English.

*__Decir__ *and* __dar__ *are used primarily with indirect objects. Both of these verbs and indirect object pronouns will be formally introduced in* **Gramática 21 (Cap. 8)**.

Emphasis 3: Suggestions

Present commands with spelling changes, including these verbs (which are all the *-car/-gar/-zar* verbs students have learned to date).

-car: *buscar, practicar, tocar*
-gar: *jugar, llegar*
-zar: *almorzar, empezar*

Emphasis 4: Suggestion

First, review verbs with irregular *yo* forms. Next, give students the *Ud.* command form and have students give the infinitive, then give students the infinitive and have them respond with the *Ud.* command form.

Emphasis 5: Suggestion

Point out that there are only five irregular commands. The accent is needed on *dé* (but not on *den*) to distinguish it from the preposition *de*. Remind students that *esté* and *estén* both require accents.

Position of Pronouns

Suggestion

Stress the use of written accents in command forms with attached direct object and reflexive pronouns.

Preliminary Exercises

- Have students give the singular formal command of the following verbs.

ir	*ser*
comer	*volver*
bailar	*levantarse*
estar	

- Have students give the plural formal command of the following verbs.

saber	*jugar*
conocer	*dormir*
tener	*acostarse*
esperar	

- Ask students the following questions.

¿Dónde se pone el pronombre de complemento directo ***lo,*** *delante de estos verbos o detrás?*

no coma	*no compren*
mire	*no paguen*
estudie	*haga*

Heritage Speakers

En algunos dialectos del español que se hablan tanto en los países de habla española como en los Estados Unidos, a veces se oye decir *siéntesen, acuéstesen* o *vístasen* para la tercera persona plural (*Uds.*). Aunque haya personas que usen estas formas en el habla popular, las formas preferidas son *siéntense, acuéstense* y *vístanse.*

Prác. A: Suggestion

Ask students to identify each command and give the corresponding infinitive form.

Prác. A: Extension

Have students change the commands to singular forms.

Reciclado: Create lists of verb phrases (using primarily verbs that students already know) that describe a sequence of activities in a particular context: the first day of school, one's daily routine, giving a dinner party at one's home, and so on. Students will use the lists to create a sequence of *Ud.* (or *Uds.*) commands. Have students work on this activity in pairs or groups, and suggest that they add infinitives to the sequence whenever possible. Give a prize to the pair or group that is able to create the longest accurate list of commands.

Example: *Una cena en casa para celebrar algo importante*

1. *hacer la lista de los invitados*
2. *llamar a los amigos para invitarlos*
3. *ir a la tienda a comprar los comestibles*
4. *preparar algunos platos especiales*
5. *poner* (new) *la mesa*
6. *ponerse ropa elegante*
7. *abrir la puerta cuando lleguen los invitados*
8. *servir una cena muy elegante*
9. *comer y beber mucho*
10. *divertirse mucho con sus amigos*
11. *decir* (new) *«buenas noches» a todos*
12. *limpiar* (new) *el comedor y la cocina*
13. *acostarse muy tarde*
14. *dormir toda la mañana el día siguiente*

Prác. C: Note

The verbs on which commands should be based are indicated in magenta in addition to being numbered.

Summary of Formal Commands

-ar ⟶ -e(n)
-er/-ir ⟶ -a(n)
Affirmative: *command* + *pronoun* (1 word)
Negative: no + *pronoun* + *command* (3 words)

Autoprueba

Complete the **Ud.** commands with the correct endings.

1. sirv_____	**3.** estudi_____	**5.** le_____
2. com_____	**4.** duerm_____	**6.** prepar_____

Answers: **1.** *sirva* **2.** *coma* **3.** *estudie* **4.** *duerma* **5.** *lea* **6.** *prepare*

Práctica

A. ¡Anticipemos! Mandatos típicos en el salón de clase

Paso 1. Indique los mandatos que Ud. oye en la clase de español. Si hay algo que Ud. nunca oye, diga: **«Este nunca lo oigo.»**

1. Traigan los libros a clase.
2. Cierren los libros.
3. Siéntense en círculo.
4. Lleguen a tiempo.
5. No se duerman en clase.
6. Repitan más alto (*louder*).
7. Hagan esta actividad como tarea.
8. ¡No hablen en inglés!

Paso 2. Ahora, en parejas, inventen tres mandatos que les gustaría darle (*you would like to give*) a su profesor(a) de español o a otro profesor.

Prác. B: Answers: 1. *Lleguen Uds. a tiempo.* **2.** *Lean Uds. la lección.* **3.** *Escriban Uds. una composición.* **4.** *Abran Uds. los libros.* **5.** *Vuelvan Uds. a clase mañana.* **6.** *Traigan Uds. los libros a clase.* **7.** *Estudien Uds. los nuevos verbos.*

B. Profesor(a) por un día. Imagine que Ud. es el profesor o la profesora hoy. ¿Qué mandatos va a darles (*will you give*) a sus estudiantes?

MODELOS: hablar español ⟶ **Hablen** Uds. español.
hablar inglés ⟶ **No hablen** Uds. inglés.

1. llegar a tiempo
2. leer la lección
3. escribir una composición
4. abrir los libros
5. volver a clase mañana
6. traer los libros a clase
7. estudiar los nuevos verbos
8. ¿ ?

C. ¡Pobre Sr. Casiano!

Paso 1. El Sr. Casiano no se siente (*feel*) bien. Lea la descripción que él da de las cosas que hace.

Trabajo[1] muchísimo[a] —¡me gusta trabajar! En la oficina, soy[2] impaciente y critico[3b] bastante[c] a los otros. En mi vida personal, a veces soy[4] un poco impulsivo. Fumo[5d] bastante y también bebo[6] cerveza y otras bebidas alcohólicas, a veces sin moderación... Almuerzo[7] y ceno[8] fuerte,[e] y desayuno[9] poco. Por la noche, con frecuencia salgo[10] con los amigos —me gusta ir a las discotecas— y vuelvo[11] tarde a casa.

[a] *a great deal* [b] critico ⟶ criticar [c] *a good deal* [d] Fumo ⟶ fumar (*to smoke*) [e] *a lot*

Prác. C: Answers
Paso 2. 3. *no critique a los otros.* **4.** *no sea impulsivo.* **5.** *no fume.* **6.** *no beba cerveza y otras bebidas alcohólicas.* **7.** *no almuerce fuerte.* **8.** *no cene fuerte.* **9.** *no desayune poco.* **10.** *no salga con los amigos por la noche.* **11.** *no vuelva tarde a casa.*

Comprensión. ¿Cierto o falso?

	CIERTO	FALSO
1. El Sr. Casiano es una persona muy simpática.	☐	☑
2. Tiene algunos hábitos malos.	☑	☐
3. Por la noche, siempre está en casa.	☐	☑

Paso 2. ¿Qué *no* debe hacer el Sr. Casiano? Aconséjelo (*Advise him*) y dígale (*tell him*) lo que no debe hacer. Use los verbos rosados o cualquier (*any*) otro, según los modelos.

MODELOS: **1.** Trabajo ⟶ Sr. Casiano, **no trabaje** tanto.
2. soy ⟶ Sr. Casiano, **no sea** tan impaciente.

D. Estrategias para adelgazar (*lose weight*). ¿Qué debe o no debe comer y beber una persona que quiere adelgazar? En parejas, imaginen una conversación entre esa persona y su médico.

MODELOS: ensalada ⟶ E1: ¿Ensalada? E2: Cómala. postres ⟶ E1: ¿Postres? E2: No **los** coma.

1. bebidas alcohólicas No las beba.
2. verduras Cómalas.
3. pan No lo coma.
4. dulces No los comas.
5. leche entera (*whole*) No la beba.
6. hamburguesas con queso No las coma.
7. frutas frescas Cómalas.
8. refrescos dietéticos Bébalos.
9. pollo Cómalo.
10. carne No la coma.
11. pizza No la coma.
12. jugo de fruta No lo beba.

Prác. E: Extension: 8. *despertarse más temprano* 9. *vestirse mejor* 10. *ayudar en las tareas domésticas*

Prác. E: Variation: Have students give advice (Uds. commands) to their roommates.

E. ¡Qué desastre! Imagine los mandatos que un padre o una madre les daría (*would give*) a sus hijos adolescentes. ¿Le resultan (*Do they sound*) familiares a Ud. estos mandatos?

MODELO: no acostarse muy tarde ⟶ ¡**No se acuesten** muy tarde!

1. levantarse más temprano
2. bañarse todos los días
3. quitarse esa ropa sucia
4. ponerse ropa limpia
5. no divertirse todas las noches con los amigos
6. ir más a la biblioteca y estudiar más
7. ¿ ?

Prác. E: Answers: 1. *¡Levántense más temprano!* 2. *¡Báñense todos los días!* 3. *¡Quítense esa ropa sucia!* 4. *¡Pónganse ropa limpia!* 5. *¡No se diviertan todas las noches con los amigos!* 6. *¡Vayan más a la biblioteca y estudien más!*

Conversación

A. Consejos sobre los buenos modales (*good manners*) **en la mesa**

Paso 1. Use las siguientes ideas para dar consejos en forma de mandatos formales sobre cómo se debe comer en una ocasión formal. **¡OJO!** Algunos consejos son normas de los buenos modales en los países hispanos y *no* coinciden con los modales que se practican en este país. ¿Puede decir cuáles son los modales hispanos?

1. poner las dos manos en la mesa ponga; modal hispano
2. no poner los codos (*elbows*) en la mesa ponga
3. para cortar, agarrar (*to hold*) el tenedor con la mano izquierda y el cuchillo con la derecha agarre
4. cortar solo el pedazo (*piece*) de comida que puede poner en la boca corte
5. no cambiar (*to change*) de mano el tenedor para llevar la comida a la boca cambie; modal hispano
6. no eructar (*to burp*) en público eructe

Paso 2. Ahora, en grupos, inventen por lo menos (*at least*) cuatro consejos más.

Vocabulario útil

la boca llena	one's mouth full
la cuchara	spoon
el cuchillo	knife
la mano	hand
la servilleta	napkin
el tenedor	fork
masticar (qu)	to chew
servirse (me sirvo) (i) a uno mismo	to help one's self
despacio	slowly

Con. A: Note
While most South American and Spanish native speakers practice these table manners, not all Spanish speakers do.

Con. A, Paso 2: Suggestion
After students have created their commands, have them take turns giving commands to the class (or to a few individuals in the class), who will follow them.

B. ¿Chefs? Demuéstreles (*Show*) a sus compañeros de clase su talento culinario. Escriba una receta para un plato delicioso, usando las dos recetas de este capítulo (páginas 216 y 225) como modelo.

Con. B: Suggestions
- Not all students will be capable of—or even interested in—doing this activity. You may wish to assign it for extra credit.
- Provide a list of useful vocabulary, including measurements.

Redacción: Assign *Con. B* as written homework (perhaps as extra credit, as already suggested). If a fair number of students do the activity, correct their recipes and ask them to rewrite them. Then give *El libro de cocina de la clase de español* to the whole class.

Prác. D: Reciclado

- Have students give the negative command for each of these affirmative commands.
  1. *Cómprelo.*
  2. *Estúdielas.*
  3. *Mírelo.*
  4. *Llámeme.*
  5. *Apréndalo.*
  6. *Escríbame.*
- Have students give the affirmative command for each of these negative commands.
  1. *No lo coma.*
  2. *No lo lea.*
  3. *No lo haga.*
  4. *No lo sirva.*
  5. *No lo traiga.*

Prác. D: Follow-up

Give students the following situation and have them provide appropriate commands.

Luisa y Carlos están en el primer grado (new) *y es el primer día de escuela. La maestra les explica las reglas de conducta, especialmente las cosas prohibidas. ¿Qué mandatos les da?*

Offer students the following suggestions.

no comer en el salón de clase
no hablar cuando habla la maestra
no pegar (new) *a los amiguitos*
no traer animales a clase
no escribir en las paredes
no llegar tarde

¿Qué otros mandatos, afirmativos o negativos, recuerdan Uds. de la escuela primaria?

Prác. E: Preliminary Exercises

- Have students give the negative command for each of the following affirmative commands.
  1. *Acuéstense.*
  2. *Aféitense.*
  3. *Lávense.*
  4. *Siéntense.*
- Have students give the affirmative command for each of the following negative commands.
  1. *No se bañen.*
  2. *No se levanten.*
  3. *No se quiten los zapatos.*
  4. *No se pongan la chaqueta.*

Resources: Transparency 89

Un poco de todo

A: Answers

Paso 2. 1. *¡No vayan a comer allí!* **2.** *¡Coman muchas tapas!* **3.** *¡Almuercen y cenen aquí!* **4.** *¡Vengan y conozcan nuestra comida!* **5.** *¡Pídanlos!* **6.** *¡Siéntense donde quieran!*

A: Follow-up

¿Probable o improbable?

1. *Los dueños son de China.* (*improbable*)
2. *Es uno de los restaurantes más baratos de la ciudad.* (*improbable*)
3. *Algunos de los chefs son hispanos.* (*probable*)
4. *Los dueños del restaurante de la Avenida de la Constitución son parientes de estos dueños.* (*improbable*)

B: Note

The following grammar topics are included in *Lengua y cultura*: adjective agreement, demonstratives, *seguir* + *present participle*, affirmative and negative words, *-ar/-er/-ir* verbs, irregular verbs (*tener, ser, estar, saber, conocer*), stem-changing verbs (*seguir, preferir, perder, pedir*), formal commands, *ser* vs. *estar*, *saber* vs. *conocer*.

B: Photo

The rice in Panamanian *arroz con pollo* is somewhat orange in color because it is made with a sauce made with tomatoes or carrots and often *achiote* (seeds of the *achiote* shrub). The name for this American condiment ends in *-ote*, which indicates the word's Nahuatl origin. Unlike many Caribbeans and Central Americans, *los panameños* eat red or pinto beans (*los porotos*) more frequently than black beans.

B: Suggestion

Ask students the following questions.

1. *¿Prefiere Ud. cenar en casa o en la cafetería estudiantil?*
2. *¿Hay días en que no almuerza/cena? ¿Por qué?*
3. *¿Prefiere Ud. una hamburguesa o un bistec?*
4. *¿Qué/Dónde come Ud. cuando tiene mucha prisa / mucho dinero / poco dinero?*
5. *¿Qué bebida prefiere por la mañana/noche?*
6. *¿Qué le gusta comer como merienda?*

Mundo interactivo

You should now be prepared to work with Scenario 4, Activity 2 in Connect Spanish (**www.connectspanish.com**).

Un poco de todo

A. El Restaurante *Mundo latino*

Paso 1. Los dueños de un restaurante que ofrece comida panhispana hablan de su restaurante. Complete sus declaraciones con las palabras más lógicas.

1. «Siempre / Algunas veces ofrecemos comida de la mejor calidad.»
2. «A nuestro restaurante vienen personas de algunos / todos los países hispanohablantes y salen contentos.»
3. «En este estado nadie / alguien sabe más que nosotros de la comida panhispana.»
4. «Siempre / Nunca improvisamos: nuestras recetas son el resultado de mucha investigación (*research*), muchos viajes y de comer mucha comida rica elaborada (*created*) por familias y chefs hispanos.»

Paso 2. Ahora complete las siguientes recomendaciones de los dueños del **Restaurante Mundo latino.** Dé para cada una los mandatos formales apropiados y lógicos, en plural. Siga el modelo.

MODELO: «Nuestro ceviche es excelente.»
(pedir + *pronombre de complemento directo*) ⟶ **¡Pídanlo!**

1. «El restaurante de la Avenida de la Constitución es el peor (*the worst*) de todos los restaurantes de la ciudad.» (no ir a comer allí)
2. «Nuestras tapas son tan deliciosas que no es suficiente comer una.» (comer muchas tapas)
3. «En nuestro restaurante se puede almorzar y cenar.» (almorzar y cenar aquí)
4. «Aquí se puede degustar (*taste*) comida deliciosa de todos los países hispanos.» (venir y conocer nuestra comida)
5. «Tenemos platos vegetarianos, como la tortilla española y los frijoles panameños.» (pedir + *pronombre de complemento directo*)
6. «Como en un bar español, aquí se puede comer en una mesa o en la barra (*bar*).» (sentarse donde quieran ([*wherever you like*])

B. Lengua y cultura: La cocina panameña. Complete the following paragraphs with the correct form of the words in parentheses, as suggested by context. When two possibilities are given in parentheses, select the correct word. **¡OJO!** As you conjugate the verbs in this activity, note that you will make formal commands with some infinitives.

El arroz con pollo, un típico plato panameño

NATIONAL STANDARDS: Comparisons

Use Activity B as a springboard for a discussion about differences in cuisine among Spanish-speaking countries. Have students research different countries and areas, and have the class create a culinary map that shows traditional dishes from different countries. Remind students that some areas do have similar or the same dishes; for example, *moros y cristianos* (black beans and rice) is prepared in several Caribbean countries, including Puerto Rico, Cuba, and Colombia. Encourage them to find other similarities (*ceviche, sancocho*, and so on).

¿Creen Uds. que la comida panameña es similar a la[a] de México y que los tacos y las tortillas (ser/estar[1]) parte de la comida típica de los panameños? Si creen eso, entonces[b] no (*Uds.:* saber/conocer[2]) (algo/nada[3]) de la comida de (este[4]) nación. (*Uds.:* Seguir[5]) (leer[6]), porque van a aprender mucho.

La influencia (extranjero[7]) en la comida de la cosmopolita Ciudad de Panamá es muy visible. Hay (mucho[8]) restaurantes que (servir[9]) comida italiana, china, (francés[10]), etcétera.

Sin embargo, los panameños no (perder[11]) su identidad nacional, y frecuentemente (preferir[12]) la comida tradicional. En la cocina panameña hay muchos platos de mariscos y pescados, entre ellos **el ceviche.** Las personas vegetarianas no (tener[13]) problema (también/tampoco[14]) porque hay una variedad de platos (preparado[15]) con arroz y verduras. El arroz es un ingrediente importante en la comida de Panamá. Si Ud. desea (saber/conocer[16]) cuál es el plato nacional de Panamá, los panameños (contestar[17]): «el arroz con pollo.» (*Ud.:* Pedirlo[18]). Le va a gustar.

[a]*to that* [b]*then*

Comprensión. Conteste las siguientes preguntas.

1. ¿Cómo se sabe que la Ciudad de Panamá es cosmopolita?
2. ¿Cuál es el plato que representa mejor la cocina panameña?
3. ¿Qué ingredientes son comunes en la comida de Panamá?

C. Publicidad. Como se ve en este anuncio de un periódico argentino, en español (como en inglés) los mandatos se usan con frecuencia en los anuncios y en la publicidad en general. En parejas, creen (*create*) un anuncio publicitario para un lugar de su universidad o de su ciudad, como un restaurante, un estadio, un cine, etcétera. El humor es siempre apreciado por sus compañeros.

"Argentina crece[a] leyendo"
Plan Nacional de Lectura
en las Bibliotecas Populares
Muy cerca de su casa hay una biblioteca popular.
Acérquese,[b] visítela, conózcala.
CONABIP
Secretaría de Cultura
PRESIDENCIA DE LA NACION
Argentina

[a]*grows* [b]acercarse = *to approach, draw near*

En su comunidad

Entreviste a una persona hispana de su universidad o ciudad sobre la cocina y la comida de su país.

PREGUNTAS POSIBLES

- ¿Cuáles son los ingredientes más importantes?
- ¿Puede encontrar estos ingredientes en los supermercados de aquí?
- ¿Cuál es la comida principal del día? ¿Comen un desayuno fuerte (*heavy*)?
- ¿Cuáles son algunos de los platos típicos?
- ¿Hay muchos restaurantes especializados en la comida de su país en este estado? ¿Cuál es su favorito?

Act. B: Answers: 1. *son* **2.** *saben* **3.** *nada* **4.** *esta* **5.** *Sigan* **6.** *leyendo* **7.** *extranjera* **8.** *muchos* **9.** *sirven* **10.** *francesa* **11.** *pierden* **12.** *prefieren* **13.** *tienen* **14.** *tampoco* **15.** *preparados* **16.** *saber* **17.** *contestan* **18.** *Pídalo.*

Comprensión: 1. *Hay muchos restaurantes que sirven comida extranjera.* **2.** *el arroz con pollo* **3.** *mariscos, pescados, el arroz y las verduras*

B: Optional

Have students imagine that a foreigner in this country asks them about certain foods and where he/she can find them in your area. Have students give as much information as possible.

1. *una tortilla española*
2. *una langosta*
3. *una hamburguesa*
4. *unas chuletas*
5. *pizza*
6. *arándanos* (blueberries)

C: Suggestions

- Read through the ad as a whole-class activity before assigning this activity. Make sure that students understand the sense of "*Argentina crece leyendo.*"
- Handle Activity C as a group activity.
- Working as a whole class, brainstorm locations about which students could create ads, in addition to those suggested in the text. Then create lists of infinitives associated with each location.

En su comunidad

Suggestions

- Remind students to get the following basic information: the informant's country of origin, how long he or she has lived in this country, and if the informant visits his or her country of origin frequently.
- This activity could also be assigned as an online research project on a country of the student's choice or assigned by you.
- See the IM for additional suggestions and guidelines.

Resources: Desenlace

In the *Cap. 7* segment of "Chapter-by-Chapter Supplementary Materials" in the IM, you will find a chapter-culminating activity. You can use this activity to consolidate and review the vocabulary and grammar skills students have acquired.

TelePuntos

Note

Pages 222–227 are optional. You may cover some, all, or none of this material in class, or assign it to students—as a group or individually—for homework or extra credit. Pages 228–229 (*En resumen: En este capítulo*) are a summary of all of the chapter's active material.

Suggestions

- If you are using the video in class, show it once, ask brief comprehension questions, then show it again.
- Even if you plan to ask students to watch the video in your campus media center or on their own, it is a good idea to continue to stress the need to watch the shows as many times as they want or need to in order to complete the *Después de mirar* activities.

Antes de mirar

Suggestions

- Use this activity to discuss the culinary diversity of the Hispanic world. You may wish to stress how certain Hispanic cuisines (such as Mexican cuisine) and specific dishes (such as *tacos, tortillas, salsa picante, chiles,* and so on) have become mainstream in this country.
- The types of Hispanic food available in this country vary from region to region. Focus on what is available in your area.
- If you did not already assign it, ask students to read this chapter's *Nota cultural* on page 202 before viewing this segment.

Programa 7

Note

This program will be easily accessible to students, since the narration is well supported by visuals of the foods mentioned.

Suggestion

Emphasize to students that the more carefully they study the preliminary activities (*Antes de mirar, Vocabulario de este programa,* and *Fragmento del guion*), the more they will understand. Scanning *Después de mirar* before viewing is also an excellent strategy.

Fragmento del guion

Suggestions

- Ask students to scan the *Fragmento* and tell which part of the program it comes from. What key words and expressions were most useful to students in determining their answer?
- Ask students what the purpose is of the presenters inviting viewers to join them for lunch. Is this type of ending common in TV programs of this kind?

TELEPUNTOS

Un sándwich cubano en el restaurante The Art of Freedom Café, en la Calle Ocho de Miami. Va a estar bien sabroso (*so delicious*), ¿no?

Antes de mirar

¿Hay restaurantes que ofrezcan (*offer*) comida hispana donde Ud. vive? ¿En qué tipo de comida se especializan? ¿Tiene Ud. alguna comida hispana favorita? ¿Usa Ud. (o su familia) algún ingrediente típico de la comida de algún país hispanohablante en su cocina?

PROGRAMA 7: ¡Qué rico!°

°¡Qué... *How delicious!*

En este programa hay reportajes sobre la comida de varios países hispanohablantes. Los presentadores también hablan de la comida y hacen planes para almorzar.

Vocabulario de este programa

el cafecito	(little cup of) coffee	**el castellano**	**el español**
fuerte	strong	**la herencia**	heritage
viví	I lived	**nos dejó**	left to us
la calle	street	**el chorizo**	sausage
no sabía	I didn't know	**la carne picada**	ground meat
la sartén	frying pan	**la cebolla**	onion
la playa	beach	**el puerco**	**el cerdo**
la tapa	"small plate," appetizer	**el vendedor ambulante**	street vendor
espeso/a	thick		
me ha abierto el apetito	has whet my apetite		

Fragmento del guion

VÍCTOR: Después de mirar este reportaje, me muero de hambre.[a] ¿Vamos a almorzar después del programa?
ANA: ¡OK! ¿Qué te apetece comer?[b]
VÍCTOR: No sé... Es difícil elegir[c] con tantas opciones de comida hispana aquí en Los Ángeles. Aquí podemos encontrar casi todo lo que se ve en el programa de hoy.
ANA: Pues yo tengo ganas de comer unas pupusas[d] salvadoreñas.
VÍCTOR: Mmm. ¡Buena idea! Pero antes vamos a cerrar el programa.
ANA: Nos despedimos[e] por hoy y les recordamos[f] que en el próximo programa vamos a mostrar los mejores videos filmados por telespectadores sobre sus viajes más memorables. ¡No se lo pierdan![g]
VÍCTOR: Pues nos volvemos a ver en *Salu2* en un programa dedicado a los viajes. Y ahora, ¡a comer! ¿Nos acompañan?[h]

[a]me... *I'm starving* (lit., *I'm dying of hunger*) [b]¿Qué... *What do you feel like eating?* [c]*to choose* [d]*thick corn tortilla filled with various ingredients* [e]Nos... *We say good-bye* [f]les... *we remind you* [g]¡No... *Don't miss it!* [h]¿Nos... *Want to join us?*

«Sin duda (*Undoubtedly*), los tacos son la comida callejera (*street*) por excelencia. Los hay de muchos tipos: al pastor, de carne, de pescado, etcétera. En efecto, cualquier alimento sabroso envuelto (*any tasty food wrapped*) en tortillas de esta manera puede llamarse taco.»

Mundo interactivo

Continue your work as an intern at HispanaVisión with Laura Sánchez Tejada, the roving reporter of *Salu2,* as you complete Scenario 4, Activities 1 and 2 in Connect Spanish (**www.connectspanish.com**).

Al mirar

Mientras mira el programa, escriba el nombre de todas las comidas e ingredientes del programa que le gustaría (*you would like*) probar. Antes de empezar, estudie el **Vocabulario de este programa** y todos los titulares (*photo captions*) para familiarizarse con los nombres de las comidas e ingredientes que van a aparecer en el programa.

¿Qué parte del programa *Salu2* se ve en esta foto?

Después de mirar

A. ¿Está claro? Empareje (*Match*) las siguientes comidas con su lugar de origen.

COMIDAS	LUGARES DE ORIGEN
1. _e_ la paella	a. la Argentina
2. _c_ la «medianoche» (*midnight*)	b. América
3. _a_ el choripán	c. Cuba
4. _b_ el chocolate	d. El Salvador
5. _f_ el taco	e. España
6. _d_ la pupusa	f. México
	g. Europa

B. Un poco más. Conteste las siguientes preguntas.

1. ¿Qué comidas típicas de España se mencionan en el programa?
2. ¿Qué es el choripán? ¿Cuál es el origen de su nombre?
3. ¿Cuál es la comida callejera por excelencia en México?
4. ¿Cuáles son dos de los ingredientes originarios de (*from*) América, esenciales en la comida internacional?
5. ¿Cómo se siente (*feels*) Víctor al final del programa? ¿Por qué se siente así (*that way*)?

Act. B, Answers: 1. *la paella, el jamón serrano, los churros con chocolate* **2.** *Es un tipo de hot dog. El nombre viene de las palabras chorizo y pan.* **3.** *los tacos* **4.** *el chocolate y el tomate* **5.** *Víctor tiene mucha hambre. Porque hablan mucho de comida en el programa.*

C. Y ahora, Uds. En parejas, clasifiquen como **comidas rápidas** o **comidas para un día especial** las comidas que se presentan en el programa. Luego, para acompañar cada comida, nombren otra comida y una bebida.

Sobre el programa

A Ana le encanta[a] la buena comida. Pero no solo le gusta comer sino que[b] cocina muy bien. Esto le viene de[c] familia.

En Panamá, sus abuelos paternos tenían[d] un restaurante especializado en comida criolla[e] y española. (Los padres de su abuelo eran[f] españoles.) Ahora un primo de Ana es el dueño[g] y el restaurante se considera[h] uno de los mejores de la Ciudad de Panamá. Por el lado materno,[i] tanto la madre como la abuela de Ana[j] son magníficas cocineras.

Cuando puede, Ana hace la comida con su madre para las fiestas familiares. A su familia le gustan mucho los platos panameños tradicionales, pero últimamente[k] Ana les ha preparado[l] platos de la tradición culinaria de todo el mundo hispano. A todos les gusta especialmente la paella.

[a]le… le gusta [b]sino… *but also* [c]le… *comes down to her from her* [d]*had* [e]Creole (*mixture of indigenous and Spanish traditions*) [f]*were* [g]*owner* [h]se… *is considered* [i]Por… *On her mother's side* [j]tanto… *both Ana's mother and grandmother* [k]*lately* [l]les… *has prepared for them*

Producción personal

Filme un segmento para *Salu2* que presente al menos dos platos o dos ingredientes tradicionales de una cocina nacional o regional.

Al mirar

Suggestion

Go over the list of foods in *Después de mirar A* in order to preview additional food items before students watch the segment.

Después de mirar

A: Suggestions

- Ask students if they know other dishes or ingredients from each country represented in the activity.
- Ask students which of the foods featured in the program they would most like to eat or try.

B: Point out

- *Churros* are found all over Latin America, and increasingly in this country as well. They can be found frozen in many supermarkets that carry Hispanic food.
- *El jamón serrano* is made from the meat of *el cerdo ibérico,* a type of pig raised in Spain and fed with the acorns of *la encina* (Spanish oak tree).
- *Los nopalitos* are the pads of the prickly pear cactus (*el nopal*) cut up in bite-sized pieces. Its fruit, also edible, is called *la tuna.* It is sweet and juicy, full of tiny seeds, and has many thorns in its thick peel.

C: Follow-up

After students have worked in pairs, have them report their answers to the whole class. Compare and discuss answers.

Sobre el programa

Optional: Comprensión

¿Cierto o falso? Corrija las oraciones falsas.

1. *A Ana no le gusta cocinar.* (*Falso: Le gusta mucho cocinar y cocina bien.*)
2. *Sus abuelos tenían un restaurante en Panamá.* (*Cierto*)
3. *Ana es la dueña de un restaurante en Panamá.* (*Falso: El primo de Ana es el dueño.*)
4. *A la familia de Ana solo le gusta la comida panameña.* (*Falso: Le gusta la comida de otros países hispanos también.*)

Producción personal

Note

See the IM for additional suggestions for this chapter's assignment as well as for general guidelines and suggestions for video assignments.

Lecturaural

Notes

- The Instructor's Edition on this page offers some additional information on the country of focus. For more information about the country of focus, see the chapter's opening pages and the IM.
- See the IM for some expressions used in Panamá.

First Reading: Suggestions

- Ask students if there is any dish similar to *empanadas* in their culture.
- Ask students if any have tried any of the dishes mentioned in the readings. Those who have can explain what the dishes are like.
- In groups, students can make a list of the different Hispanic dishes and cuisines they have tasted. Have students share their experiences with the class.
- Have students research and prepare short presentations on different nacional cuisines.

Exploración lingüística

Ask students to find the following in the reading. Some of these words are glossed and some are not.

1. *La palabra que corresponde a* fritters *en español (frituras)*
2. *Los verbos que no están en el presente (En todo el mundo hispanohablante: llegó, fueron, inventaron, habían heredado)*
3. *Un adjetivo que significa «en todas partes» (En los Estados Unidos: omnipresente)*

Tres símbolos panameños

Notes

- Vasco de Balboa explored the Isthmus of Panama in 1513 and founded the first settlements on the north coast. He discovered that the distance from the Atlantic Ocean to the Pacific was short. The Canal would not be started until the late 19th century.
- Boats going through the Canal pass through two artificial lakes and three sets of locks and canals.

Una figura importante

Suggestions

- Ask some students to research Moscoso's life and present their findings to the class.
- Discuss the importante of having women in such high positions and how this relates to the stereotype of *machismo* often associated with Hispanic countries.

A LEER

Lectura cultural

Panamá

El arroz con pollo al estilo panameño es uno de los platos más típicos de Panamá. Otro plato típico es el sancocho, una sopa que también es parte de la cocina de otros países caribeños y que lleva algún tipo de carne, verduras y legumbres.[a] Y es necesario mencionar también las frituras, es decir,[b] la comida frita. Hay gran variedad de frituras: la yuca frita, las carimañolas (unas bolas de masa[c] de yuca con carne dentro[d]), los patacones (rebanadas[e] de plátano frito), las empanadas[f] al estilo panameño, etcétera.

¿Cuáles son los platos más populares de su estado o región?

De beber, se debe probar[g] las chichas, que son refrescos naturales de frutas panameñas, como el coco, la guanábana y el maracuyá.[h]

[a]*beans* [b]es… *that is* [c]bolas… *balls of dough* [d]*inside* [e]*slices* [f]*see* **En otros países** [g]*try* [h]coco… *coconut, soursop, and passion fruit*

Unas ricas (*delicious*) empanadas

En otros países hispanos

- **En todo el mundo hispanohablante** Las empanadas son probablemente la constante culinaria más notable de todos los países hispanohablantes. Consisten en una masa de pan[a] rellena[b] de algo dulce o salado.[c] Pueden ser pequeñas e individuales o grandes para ser compartidas.[d] La idea llegó[e] a América con los españoles. Pero los españoles no fueron los que inventaron[f] las empanadas, sino que ellos las habían heredado de[g] los árabes. ¡Una larga y deliciosa tradición!
- **En los Estados Unidos** La comida latina es omnipresente en los Estados Unidos hoy día. La cocina mexicana es muy popular, como también lo es su variante Tex-Mex, genuinamente estadounidense. Prácticamente todas las otras cocinas hispanas están bien representadas en este país en la actualidad:[h] las empanadas (de cualquier[i] país), las pupusas[j] salvadoreñas, la tortilla[k] española (con patatas y cebollas[l]), el arroz con gandules[m] puertorriqueño, el dulce de leche[n] (que se consume en casi todos los países latinoamericanos), etcétera.

[a]masa… *bread dough* [b]*filled* [c]*salty* [d]*shared* [e]*arrived* [f]no… *weren't the ones who invented* [g]sino… *but rather, they were inherited from* [h]en… *currently* [i]*any* [j]*corn* masa *stuffed with cheese, refried beans, or meat, then fried like a tortilla* [k]*omelet* [l]*onions* [m]*pigeon peas* [n]dulce… *caramel*

Tres símbolos panameños

- **El Canal de Panamá** Es una de las grandes obras[a] de ingeniería del mundo. Tiene cuarenta y ocho millas de canales y esclusas[b] que unen el Atlántico con el Pacífico.
- **La bandera[c] panameña** Es muy distintiva: tiene los colores rojo, blanco y azul y estrellas,[d] como muchas otras, pero su disposición es única.
- **La pollera y el montuno** Estos son los trajes típicos panameños para la mujer y el hombre, respectivamente.

[a]*works* [b]*locks* [c]*flag* [d]*stars*

Una figura importante

En el año 2000, Mireya Moscoso fue la primera mujer elegida[a] presidenta en Panamá. Puso[b] a otras mujeres en varios de los altos cargos[c] en su gabinete.[d]

[a]*elected* [b]*She put* [c]*positions* [d]*cabinet*

COMPRENSIÓN

1. ¿Qué son las frituras panameñas? la comida frita
2. ¿Qué es la chicha? un refresco natural de frutas
3. ¿Qué comida es muy típica de todo el mundo hispano? la empanada

Del mundo hispano

Antes de leer

En algunos aspectos, la siguiente receta es diferente de las (*those*) que normalmente se usan para preparar una lasaña. ¿En qué es diferente esta receta de otras?

Lectura: Receta para lasaña de tortillas

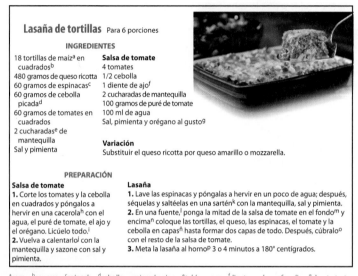

Lasaña de tortillas Para 6 porciones

INGREDIENTES

18 tortillas de maíz[a] en cuadrados[b]
480 gramos de queso ricotta
60 gramos de espinacas[c]
60 gramos de cebolla picada[d]
60 gramos de tomates en cuadrados
2 cucharadas[e] de mantequilla
Sal y pimienta

Salsa de tomate
4 tomates
1/2 cebolla
1 diente de ajo[f]
2 cucharadas de mantequilla
100 gramos de puré de tomate
100 ml de agua
Sal, pimienta y orégano al gusto[g]

Variación
Substituir el queso ricotta por queso amarillo o mozzarella.

PREPARACIÓN

Salsa de tomate

1. Corte los tomates y la cebolla en cuadrados y póngalos a hervir en una cacerola[h] con el agua, el puré de tomate, el ajo y el orégano. Licúelo todo.[i]
2. Vuelva a calentarlo[j] con la mantequilla y sazone con sal y pimienta.

Lasaña

1. Lave las espinacas y póngalas a hervir en un poco de agua; después, séquelas y saltéelas en una sartén[k] con la mantequilla, sal y pimienta.
2. En una fuente,[l] ponga la mitad de la salsa de tomate en el fondo[m] y encima[n] coloque las tortillas, el queso, las espinacas, el tomate y la cebolla en capas[ñ] hasta formar dos capas de todo. Después, cúbralo[o] con el resto de la salsa de tomate.
3. Meta la lasaña al horno[p] 3 o 4 minutos a 180° centígrados.

[a]*corn* [b]*squares* [c]*spinach* [d]cebolla… *minced onion* [e]*tablespoons* [f]diente… *clove of garlic* [g]al… *to taste* [h]póngalos… *boil them in a pot* [i]*Blend it.* [j]Vuelva… *Reheat it* [k]séquelas… *dry them* (*the spinach leaves*) *and sauté them in a frying pan* [l]*serving dish* [m]*bottom* [n]*on top* [ñ]*layers* [o]*cover it* [p]*oven*

Lectura: Lasaña de tortillas

Comprensión

A. Los mandados de la receta. Todos los verbos para preparar esta receta son mandatos formales. Empareje los siguientes mandatos con su traducción en inglés, según el contexto de la receta.

MANDATOS		TRADUCCIONES	
1. _d_ corte	4. _c_ coloque	a. *put* (*into*)	d. *cut*
2. _e_ sazone	5. _a_ meta	b. *wash*	e. *season*
3. _b_ lave		c. *place, arrange*	

B. Paso por (*by*) **paso.** Ponga en orden cronológico (de 1 a 4) los siguientes pasos para la lasaña, según la receta.

_4_ Cocinar la lasaña en el horno.
_2_ Hervir las espinacas y luego cocinarlas en una sartén.
_1_ Preparar la salsa de tomate.
_3_ Poner en una fuente, en capas, todos los ingredientes preparados para formar la lasaña.

Del mundo hispano

Note

See the IM for optional follow-up, writing, and Internet activities.

Antes de leer

Suggestion

Have students work on this activity in pairs. Follow up with full class discussion, making a list of the differences on the board.

Answers

Answers will vary but most groups will come up with two: the use of corn tortillas instead of pasta and the measurements in the metric system.

Follow-up

Ask students what the measurements in the recipe mean and if they know their equivalents in measurements used in this country. Ask them to research this topic for the next class meeting.

The following information may be useful: In the United States, ingredients are not usually specified by weight, but rather by volume. Therefore ounces (*onzas*) are used rather than grams (*gramos*), and cups (*tazas*) or fluid ounce measures rather than liters/milliliters (*litros/mililitros*). A recipe in this country will call for half a small onion or one bunch of spinach instead of 60 grams of either. Weight measurements are typically used only when the ingredient is purchased in a container (as with ricotta or tomato puree) or frozen. Conversions for this recipe: *100 gramos* ≈ 3.5 ounces; *100 milliliters* ≈ .42 cups or 3.4 fluid ounces; *60 grams* ≈ half a small onion, one small tomato, 1/8 lb. frozen spinach; *180 grados centígrados* ≈ 350 degrees Fahrenheit.

Estrategia: Predicting Content

Recipes should be a familiar text type for most students. The titles and subtitles (which divide the recipe into two main parts) will help students understand the text. Before asking students to do the reading, you may wish to ask them to tell you (in English) what steps and what verbs would typically be found in a recipe. Students who are experienced cooks might be able to do that specifically for lasagna. Then, after students have done the reading, compare their predictions with what is found in the actual text.

Comprensión

A: Suggestions

- Remind students to find the context for these verbs in the recipe if they need it to understand the verb's meaning. Only verbs that are easily guessable are included; most verbs that students do not know yet are glossed in the reading.
- Alternatively, you could list the commands from the exercise on the board, then ask students to give the infinitive of each. An additional activity for this exercise would be to make a chart on the board with these infinitives, then have students give the *Ud.* command form for each one.

B: Follow-up

Ask students, working in pairs, to tell which steps of the recipe's two parts correspond to each of the steps in this activity.

A escuchar

Notes

- In this chapter students can listen to a couple order a meal in an upscale restaurant.
- The text suggests that students listen to the passage as many times as they need to in order to do the *Después de escuchar* activities. If that is not what you want students to do, give them alternate instructions.
- See the IM for the Audioscript and more information about music in Panama.

Después de escuchar

A: Follow-up

En su opinión, ¿tienen hambre los señores Robles? Dé unos ejemplos para apoyar (support) *su respuesta.*

B: Follow-up

Ask students to write a brief restaurant review in Spanish about the food (quality, quantity, description) and service (if they wish) at one of their favorite restaurants on or near campus. Their critique will be posted for the students on your class's web site. The goal of the review is to help people not familiar with the restaurant decide if it is the place for them.

¡Música!

Notes

- Rubén Blades (1948–), an influential salsa singer and songwriter, is well respected the world over. His work often explores social problems with compelling lyrics. With a doctorate in law from Harvard University, Blades has political aspirations. He ran (unsuccessfully) for the presidency of Panama, and later was Minister of Tourism for five years.
- *"Pedro Navaja"* is a song inspired by the English-language song "Mac the Knife." It tells the story of the end of a criminal's life with a dark humorous twist. The musical coda at the end of this song (*«La vida te da sorpresas, sorpresas te da la vida, ¡Ay Dios!»*) is sung all over the Hispanic world.
- For helpful tips on using songs in the classroom, see the IM.

A ESCUCHAR

Antes de escuchar

¿Sale con frecuencia a comer en restaurantes? ¿Tiene algún restaurante favorito? ¿En qué se especializa?

Escuche

En un restaurante

Los señores Robles piden la cena. Escuche según las indicaciones de su profesor(a).

Vocabulario para escuchar

la carta	menu	**mixto/a**	mixed (with **paella** = having both meat and seafood)
entrantes	starters, first courses	**cómo no**	of course
el segundo plato	main course		

Después de escuchar

A. ¿Qué desean? Los señores Robles cenan esta noche en un restaurante elegante. ¿Qué piden?

1. El Sr. Robles:
   Entrante ensalada de la casa, sin cebolla   Segundo plato paella
2. La Sra. Robles:
   Entrante sopa de mariscos
   Segundo plato arroz con pollo
3. De beber:
   vino de la casa, argentino

B. Más detalles. Conteste las siguientes preguntas.

1. ¿Qué platos tienen fama en este restaurante? la paella y el arroz con pollo
2. ¿Cuándo van a pedir el postre los Sres. Robles? después de comer los platos principales, con el café

¡Música!

Rubén Blades es uno de los cantautores[a] de salsa más conocidos[b] en todo el mundo. Y la canción «Pedro Navaja[c]» es probablemente la más famosa de su álbum *Siembra,*[d] un álbum que se considera uno de los más importantes en toda la historia salsera.[e]

[a]*singer-songwriters* [b]*known, famous* [c]*Knife* [d]*Sowing time* [e]de salsa

Go to the iMix section in Connect Spanish (**www.connectspanish.com**) to access the iTunes playlist *"Puntos9,"* where you can purchase "Pedro Navaja" by Rubén Blades.

El cantautor panameño Rubén Blades, en Miami, Florida

A ESCRIBIR

El tema

La comida en las cafeterías de esta universidad

Preparar

Paso 1. Piense en la comida que hay en las cafeterías de esta universidad.

- ¿Ofrecen una selección variada, como comidas vegetarianas, comidas bajas en calorías, etcétera?
- ¿Cuáles son los platos más populares?
- En general, ¿es rica la comida? ¿Es cara o barata?
- ¿Hay alguna cafetería mejor que las otras?

Elija un posible tema central y haga una lista de 4 o 5 preguntas relacionadas con ese tema.

Paso 2. Use las preguntas del **Paso 1** para entrevistar a un mínimo de dos compañeros de clase. En este ensayo, Ud. va a contrastar las opiniones de ellos con las suyas (*yours*).

Redactar

Desarrolle (*Develop*) su ensayo usando toda la información de **Preparar.** Preste atención al tono. ¿Es serio, divertido, satírico? También determine si va a dirigirse (*address*) directamente a sus lectores (*readers*) o no. Si se dirige directamente a ellos, ¿va a usar la forma familar de **tú** o la formal de **Ud.**?

Editar

Revise (*Review*) el ensayo para comprobar (*to check*):

- la ortografía y los acentos
- la organización de las ideas
- la consistencia del tono
- el uso de los pronombres (evitar [*avoid*] el uso excesivo de pronombres personales; evitar la repetición innecesaria de los sustantivos con el uso de los pronombres de complemento directo)

Finalmente, prepare su versión final para entregarla.

Preparar

Suggestions

- Ask students to review indefinite and negative words (*Gram. 19*).
- Remind students to use *todo/a* to express English phrases with *all: todo el mundo* (new), *todos los días, todos los platos de la cafetería,* and so on.

Redactar

Suggestions

- Suggested length for this writing assignment: approximately 100 words
- Suggested structure: 2 paragraphs
  - **P. 1.** Description of the cafeteria offerings on campus and of students' eating preferences and habits, mixing general information (third person plural) with personal (first person singular)
  - **P. 2.** Conclusion focusing on the campus cafeteria food. The tone of the essay will determine the content of this paragraph.

Editar

Follow-up

What do people's food preferences say about them? What do the campus's eating options say about the campus?

En resumen: En este capítulo

Vocabulario

Suggestions

- Have students respond *cierto* or *falso*.
  1. *El bistec es carne de cerdo.*
  2. *El bistec es más caro que la hamburguesa.*
  3. *Los sándwiches de jamón son populares.*
- Ask students: *¿Cuál es correcto?*
  1. *En Nebraska, ¿sirven más el bistec o los mariscos frescos?*
  2. *¿Cuál es más barata, la hamburguesa o la langosta?*
  3. *¿Se usa* Shake 'n' Bake *con los mariscos o con el pollo?*
- Have students work in small groups to write up a menu for tonight's meal. To compare the menus, have a member of each group read their menu. The class should vote on the most appealing menu.
- Remind students that *saber* and *conocer* are irregular in the *yo* form: *conozco, sé.*
- Ask students to give words or phrases that they associate with *saber* and *conocer.* When an appropriate word or phrase is given, ask another student to make a complete sentence or question with it.
- Have students complete the following sentences in as many ways as possible.
  1. *Los niños beben* ______ *por la mañana. Los adultos beben* ______ *por la mañana.*
  2. *Puedo comer* ______ *en McDonald's.*
  3. *Para el desayuno se bebe* ______. *Con la cena se bebe* ______.
  4. *Los conejos* (new) *comen* ______.
  5. *Un almuerzo sencillo* (new) *incluye* ______.
  6. *La merienda de un niño incluye* ______. *La merienda de un adulto incluye* ______.
  7. *Generalmente se come* ______ *para el desayuno.*
  8. *Los Oreos son un tipo de* ______. (Note: los o-RE-os en español.)
  9. *Una cena elegante consiste en* ______. *Una cena sencilla consiste en* ______.
  10. *Una persona vegetariana come* ______. *Una persona omnívora come* ______.

EN RESUMEN En este capítulo

LearnSmart
Visit **www.connectspanish.com** to practice the vocabulary and grammar points covered in this chapter.

Gramática en breve

18. Direct Object Pronouns

me, te, lo/la, nos, os, los/las

19. Indefinite and Negative Words

algo	**nada**
alguien	**nadie**
algún (alguna/os/as)	**ningún (ninguna)**
siempre	**nunca, jamás**
también	**tampoco**

no + *verb* + *negative word*

negative word + *verb*

20. Formal Commands

-ar ⟶ **-e(n)**
-er/-ir ⟶ **-a(n)**

Affirmative: *command* + *pronoun* (1 word)
Negative: no + *pronoun* + *command* (3 words)

Vocabulario

Los verbos

acabar de + *inf.*	to have just (*done something*)
ayudar	to help
conocer (conozco)	to know, be acquainted, familiar with; to meet
contestar	to answer
esperar	to wait (for); to expect
invitar	to invite
llamar	to call
saber (sé)	to know
saber + *inf.*	to know how to (*do something*)

La comida

cenar	to have/eat dinner, supper
cocinar	to cook
desayunar	to have/eat breakfast
merendar (meriendo)	to have a snack
preparar	to prepare

Repaso: almorzar (almuerzo) (c)

Remember that this letter indicates the spelling change that happens in the formal commands of verbs that end in **-car, -gar,** or **-zar.**

el aceite	oil
el arroz	rice
las arvejas	green peas
el atún	tuna
el azúcar	sugar
el bistec	steak
los camarones	shrimp
la carne	meat
los champiñones	mushrooms
la chuleta (de cerdo)	(pork) chop
la comida	food
los dulces	sweets; candy
los espárragos	asparagus
el flan	(baked) custard
los frijoles	beans
la galleta	cookie
el helado	ice cream
el huevo	egg
el jamón	ham
la langosta	lobster
la lechuga	lettuce
la mantequilla	butter
la manzana	apple
los mariscos	shellfish
la naranja	orange
el pan	bread
el pan tostado	toast
la papa (frita)	(French fried) potato
el pastel	cake; pie
la patata (frita)	(French fried) potato
el pavo	turkey
el pescado	fish
la pimienta	pepper
el pollo (asado)	(roast) chicken
el postre	dessert
el queso	cheese
la sal	salt
la salchicha	sausage; hot dog
la sopa	soup
las verduras	vegetables
la zanahoria	carrot

Cognados: la banana, la barbacoa, el cereal, la ensalada, la fruta, la hamburguesa, el salmón, el sándwich, el tomate, el yogur

Las bebidas

el agua (mineral)	(mineral) water
la cerveza	beer
el jugo (de fruta)	(fruit) juice
la leche	milk

Así se dice

The following information will be useful if you choose to explore the topic of variation in food words with your students. The list contains both words that are introduced in the text as well as optional vocabulary: ***la banana*** = *el banano, el guineo, el plátano;* ***la barbacoa*** = *el asado, la parrillada;* ***el bistec*** = *el biftec, el bisté;* ***el bróculi*** = *el brócoli;* ***el cerdo*** = *el cochino, el chancho, el guarro, el marrano, el puerco* (Note: *la carne de cerdo* is a relatively generalized term.); ***los champiñones*** = *los hongos, las setas* (Sp.); ***la chuleta*** = *la costilla;* ***la dona*** = *el buñuelo* (Sp.); ***las espinacas*** = *la espinaca;* ***las fresas*** = *las frutillas* (Arg., Uru.); ***los frijoles*** = *los porotos* (Arg., Uru.); ***las habichuelas*** = *las judías verdes* (Sp.), *los ejotes* (Mex.), *las chauchas* (Mex.); ***la naranja*** = *la china;* ***el pastel*** = *el queque, la torta;* ***la piña*** = *el ananá;* ***el sándwich*** = *el emparedado, el bocadillo* (Sp.), *la torta* (Mex.)

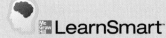

el refresco	soft drink
el vino (blanco, tinto)	(white, red) wine

Cognado: el té

Repaso: la bebida, el café

Las comidas

el almuerzo	lunch
la cena	dinner, supper
la comida	meal
el desayuno	breakfast
la merienda	snack

En un restaurante

el/la camarero/a	waiter/waitress
la cuenta	check, bill
el plato	dish; course
el plato principal	main course

Cognado: el menú

Repaso: los platos (*dishes*)

Otros sustantivos

la ayuda	help
la cocina	cuisine
los comestibles	groceries, foodstuff
el consejo	(piece of) advice
la dirección	address
el/la dueño/a	owner
la letra	(*song*) lyrics
el mandato	command
el nombre	name
la receta	recipe
la tarjeta de crédito	credit card

Los adjetivos

asado/a	roast(ed)
caliente	hot (*temperature*)
fresco/a	fresh
frito/a	fried
ligero/a	light, not heavy
picante	hot, spicy
rico/a	tasty, savory; rich
tostado/a	toasted

Las palabras indefinidas y negativas

algo	something, anything
alguien	someone, anyone
algún (alguna/os/as)	some, any
jamás	never
nada	nothing, not anything
nadie	no one, nobody, not anybody
ningún (ninguna)	no, not any
tampoco	neither, not either

Repaso: nunca, siempre, también

Palabras adicionales

estar a dieta	to be on a diet
tener (mucha) hambre	to be (very) hungry
tener (mucha) sed	to be (very) thirsty

Vocabulario personal

Note

The following vocabulary item was used in direction lines in *Cap. 7* and will be used in subsequent chapters without glossing, but it is not considered to be "active" until it is listed in *Vocabulario: llene* (*Ud*). (From this point on in the text, the *Ud.* command form for a verb will be listed in this way only if the corresponding infinitive is not yet active.)

Word Families

En este capítulo

- *algún/alguna, alguien*
- *la ayuda, ayudar*
- *la cena, cenar*
- *la cocina* (cuisine), *cocinar*
- *el desayuno, desayunar*
- *la fruta, el jugo de fruta*
- *la merienda, merendar*
- *nada, nadie*
- *el refresco, fresco/a*

Entre capítulos

- *el almuerzo* = *almorzar* (5)
- *caliente* = *hace/tener calor* (6)
- *la cocina* (cuisine), *cocinar* = *la cocina* (room) (5)
- *la comida, los comestibles* = *comer* (3), *el comedor* (5)
- *el consejo* = *el/la consejero/a* (2)
- *fresco/a, el refresco* = *hace fresco* (6)
- *la naranja* = *anaranjado/a* (4)
- *el pescado* = *el pez* (3)
- *el plato* (dish, plate) = *los platos* (dishes, plates) (5)
- *preguntar* = *hacer una pregunta* (5)
- *rico/a* (with food) = *rico/a* (3)
- *el vino blanco* = *blanco* (4)

¡OJO!

- *los camarones* ≠ *el camarero*
- *el hambre* ≠ *el hombre* (2)
- *el jugo* ≠ *jugar* (5)
- *la leche* ≠ *la lechuga*
- *la papa* ≠ *papá* (3)
- *el plato* ≠ *la plata* (4)
- *la sed* ≠ *la seda* (4)
- *el té* ≠ *te* (direct object pronoun)

Suggestion

Have students write brief reviews of restaurants based on recent visits. Encourage them to use negative and indefinite words.

Chapter Opening Photo and Chapter Theme

Chapter Theme-Related Questions

Para las vacaciones, ¿le gusta…

1. *viajar lejos de aquí?*
2. *hacer* camping *en las montañas?*
3. *ir a una ciudad histórica con muchos lugares de importancia cultural?*
4. *ir a una playa bonita?*
5. *viajar en autobús por todo el país?*

Follow-up

¿Adónde fue (new) *en sus vacaciones más recientes? ¿Fue a las montañas? ¿a la playa? ¿a otro país? ¿a otro estado?*

¿Fue en autobús/coche/tren/avión? ¿Por cuánto tiempo?

¿Dónde va a pasar sus próximas vacaciones?

Elicit *sí/no* answers, as students have not learned preterite forms. Pantomime and use drawings for unfamiliar vocabulary as necessary for communication.

Reciclado: Review clothing vocabulary by asking students what they would pack for a vacation in various locations.

Multimedia

The IM provides suggestions for using multimedia materials in the classroom.

8 De viaje°

De… *On a trip, Traveling*

En la zona colonial de Santo Domingo, República Dominicana

- ¿Dónde le gusta pasar las vacaciones? ¿En la playa? ¿en las montañas? ¿en una ciudad o en un nuevo país?
- Cuando está en la playa, ¿le gusta nadar? ¿tomar el sol? ¿hacer *surfing* u otros deportes?
- ¿Qué es lo peor (*the worst part*) de salir de viaje: hacer la maleta, el viaje mismo (*itself*) o regresar?

connect | SPANISH

www.connectspanish.com

Resources

For Students

- Connect Spanish (**www.connectspanish.com**), which contains all content from the following resources, as well as the *Mundo interactivo* scenarios, the LearnSmart adaptive learning system, and more!
- **Physical Resources:** Workbook / Laboratory Manual, Laboratory Audio Program, DVD

For Instructors

- Connect Spanish (**www.connectspanish.com**), which contains access to all student sections of Connect Spanish, as well as helpful time-saving tools and resources such as an integrated gradebook, Instructor's Manual, Testing Program, digital transparencies, Audioscript, Videoscript, and more!

La República Dominicana

10 millones de habitantes

- La República Dominicana comparte (*shares*) la isla de La Española (*Hispaniola*, en inglés) con el país de Haití.
- La ciudad de Santo Domingo, capital del país, fue fundada (*founded*) por el hermano de Cristóbal Colón en 1496. Es la más antigua (*oldest*) de todas las ciudades fundadas por los europeos en América.

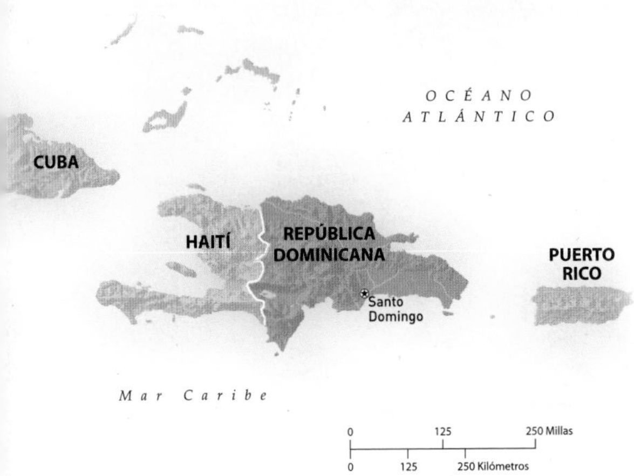

En este capítulo

CONTENT / **CONTENIDO**	OBJECTIVES / **OBJETIVOS**
Traveling 232, Vacations 234	To talk about travel to places you would like to visit and to those you do
Indirect Object Pronouns 238	To express *to* and *for who*(*m*)
Gustar 243	To express likes and dislikes
The Preterite 248	To start talking about the past
La República Dominicana 258	To learn about a Caribbean island nation that loves **merengue,** beaches, and baseball

La República Dominicana

Datos esenciales

The Instructor's Edition will provide basic information about each chapter's country of focus on this chapter opening spread. Additional information (such as geographical features, historical timelines, holidays, and so on) can be found in the IM. There is also additional information about the country of focus in *A leer: Lectura cultural* and *A escuchar* (in both the student text and the Instructor's Edition).

Nombre oficial: *República Dominicana*
Lema: *«Dios, Patria y Libertad»*
Capital: *Santo Domingo*
Otras ciudades importantes: *La Vega, Santiago*
Composición étnica: *73% mulatos, 16% blancos, 11% negros*
Lengua oficial: *el español*
Jefe de estado actual: *el Presidente Leonel Fernández Reyna, desde 2004 (y también 1996–2000)*
Forma de gobierno: *Democracia representativa*
Moneda: *el peso dominicano, con el símbolo RD$*
Religión: *95% católicos, 5% otros*

Point Out

- Spain gave the other half of Hispaniola to France in 1697. For that reason, the language and culture of Haiti are quite different from those of the Dominincan Republic.
- The Dominican Republic is also known as *la República del Béisbol*, since it produces more major league baseball players than any country except the United States.

Suggestion

Have students tell what they know about the Dominican Republic, including information on geography, politics, economy, culture, music, and cuisine. When you finish the chapter, return to the lists and ask students what ideas they would change and/or add. The success of this activity will depend not only on the content about the Dominican Republic presented in the text but also on the extent to which you have time to supplement that content with your own knowledge and experiences and also with information given in this Instructor's Edition and the IM.

Resources: Transparency 90

NATIONAL STANDARDS: Connections

The next four chapters of *Puntos de partida* will focus on countries (other than Mexico and the Central American countries) that are in or border on the Caribbean Sea. This includes the island countries of the Dominican Republic (*Cap. 8*), Cuba (*Cap. 9*), and Puerto Rico (*Cap. 10*), as well as the South American country of Venezuela (*Cap. 11*). These countries are united by cultural elements, especially the indigenous heritage of African slaves, who were brought to the Americas to work on plantations and in the mines. The area has strong ties to the United States because of the large number of Dominicans, Cubans, and Puerto Ricans, and their descendants, who live in the country. Puerto Rico's ties are very strong: it is a commonwealth territory of the United States and its people enjoy the benefits of U.S. citizenship and federal programs.

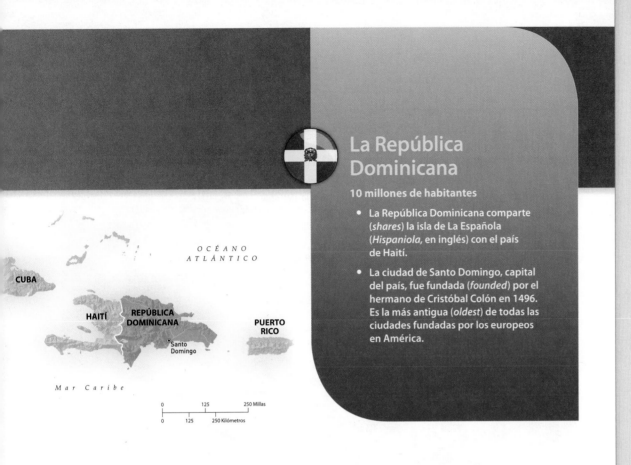

Vocabulario: Preparación

De viaje

Note

See the model for vocabulary presentation and other material in the *Cap. 8 Vocabulario: Preparación* section of "Chapter-by-Chapter Supplementary Materials" in the IM.

Suggestions

- Model each word, then ask questions to contextualize it.
  1. ***El aeropuerto:*** *¿Qué tipo de transporte hay allí? ¿Hay un aeropuerto en esta ciudad? ¿Y en su ciudad de origen?*
  2. ***La asistenta de vuelo:*** *¿Dónde trabaja? ¿Qué hace?*
  3. ***El vuelo:*** *Generalmente, ¿tienen letras o números los vuelos? ¿Adónde van muchos vuelos diarios que salen del aeropuerto de _____ (ciudad)?*
  4. ***El boleto:*** *¿Qué tipos de boletos hay?*
  5. ***La tarjeta de embarque:*** *¿Cuándo es necesario tenerla?*
- Point out the meanings of the verbs *bajar* and *subir*: *bajar* = to go down vs. *bajarse de* = to get out of (a vehicle) and *subir* = to go up vs. *subir a* = to get in/on (a vehicle).
- Point out to students that, for many Spanish speakers, the use of *volar* is somewhat different in Spanish and in English. In some dialects, *volar* is something that birds and planes do; people must *volar en avión*. Examples: *Me gusta volar en avión. Voy a volar en avión a Sudamérica este verano.*
- Have students name items and activities they associate with the following. *¿Qué asocia Ud. con… un avión, una asistente de vuelo, el equipaje, la sala de espera?*
- Use the impersonal *se* in input or questions to prepare students for the *Nota comunicativa* of this section. For example: *¿Dónde se compran boletos de avión?*
- Read the following sentences as a *dictado* or as listening comprehension. In either case, have students correct false statements.
  1. *Si hay una demora, el avión llega temprano.* (*F*)
  2. *Los pasajeros hacen las maletas después de hacer un viaje.* (*F*)
  3. *El avión está atrasado; no tenemos que esperarlo.* (*F*)
  4. *Hay muchas personas en la sala de espera; no hay ningún asiento desocupado.* (*C*)
  5. *El asistente de vuelo nos sirve la comida durante el vuelo.* (*C*)

Pronunciación: See Pronunciation Notes, IM.

Resources: Transparency 91

VOCABULARIO Preparación

De viaje

Los medios de transporte

la cabina	cabin (*on a ship*)
el crucero	cruise (ship)
la estación	station
de autobuses	bus station
de trenes	train station
el puerto	port
la sala de espera	waiting room
la sala de fumar/fumadores	smoking area
el vuelo	flight
ir **en…**	to go/travel by . . .
autobús	bus
avión	plane
barco	boat, ship
tren	train

El viaje

el asiento	seat
el billete (*Sp.*) / **el boleto** (*L.A.*)	ticket
de ida	one-way ticket
de ida y vuelta	round-trip ticket
el billete/boleto electrónico	e-ticket
la demora	delay
la llegada	arrival
el pasaje	fare, price (*of a transportation ticket*)
el pasaporte	passport
la puerta de embarque	boarding gate
la salida	departure
la tarjeta de embarque	boarding pass

anunciar	to announce
bajarse (de)	to get down (from); to get off (of) (*a vehicle*)
estar atrasado/a	to be late
facturar el equipaje	to check baggage
guardar (un puesto)	to save (a place [*in line*])
hacer cola	to stand in line
hacer escalas/paradas	to make stops
hacer la(s) maleta(s)	to pack one's suitcase(s)
hacer un viaje	to take a trip
ir al extranjero	to go abroad
pasar por	to go / pass through
la aduana	customs
el control de seguridad	security (check)
quejarse (de)	to complain (about)
salir/llegar (gu) a tiempo	to depart/arrive on time
subir (a)	to go up; to get on (*a vehicle*)
viajar	to travel
volar (vuelo) en avión	to fly, go by plane

Conversación

A. Hablando de medios de transporte. ¿Con qué medio de transporte relaciona Ud. las siguientes personas y cosas? Hay más de una respuesta posible en algunos casos.

1. un crucero
2. un(a) asistente de vuelo
3. un puerto
4. una estación
5. una cabina
6. una agencia de viajes
7. un asiento
8. un(a) piloto
9. un capitán / una capitana
10. la llegada

B. Un viaje al extranjero

Paso 1. Use los números del 1 al 9 para organizar un viaje de manera lógica.

a. _7_ subir al avión cuando se anuncia el vuelo
b. _4_ pasar por el control de seguridad
c. _3_ hacer cola para obtener la tarjeta de embarque y facturar el equipaje
d. _2_ pedir un taxi y llegar al aeropuerto
e. _6_ oír el anuncio de la salida del vuelo
f. _1_ hacer la maleta y poner el pasaporte en el bolso
g. _5_ esperar en la puerta de embarque mandando mensajes
h. _8_ sentarse en el asiento junto a la ventanilla (*window*)
i. _9_ llegar al aeropuerto de destino (*destination*) y pasar por el control de inmigración y la aduana

Paso 2. Ahora narre la secuencia en primera persona (**yo**).

C. Definiciones

Paso 1. Dé las palabras definidas.

1. Es necesario pasar por este control al llegar a otro país. el control de seguridad, la aduana, la inmigración
2. Es la cosa que se compra antes de hacer un viaje. el billete/boleto
3. Es el antónimo de **subir a.** bajarse de
4. Se va allí cuando se hace un viaje en avión. el aeropuerto
5. Se va allí cuando se hace un viaje en tren. la estación de trenes
6. Es la persona que nos ayuda durante un vuelo. el/la asistente de vuelo

Paso 2. Ahora prepare dos definiciones para leer a toda la clase. Use frases como las del **Paso 1** (**Es la cosa que... Se va allí... Es el antónimo de...**) y las siguientes: **el sinónimo de... , el lugar donde... , es cuando...** Sus compañeros van a dar (*give*) la palabra que Ud. define.

Con. A: Possible Answers: **1.** *el barco* **2.** *el avión* **3.** *el barco* **4.** *el tren, el autobús* **5.** *el barco, el tren, el avión* **6.** *el avión, el tren, el barco, el coche* **7.** *el tren, el avión, el autobús* **8.** *el avión* **9.** *el barco* **10.** *el avión, el tren, el barco, el autobús*

Con. B: Answers: *Paso 2:* **1.** *Hago… y pongo* **2.** *Pido… y llego* **3.** *Hago…* **4.** *Paso…* **5.** *Espero…* **6.** *Oigo…* **7.** *Subo…* **8.** *Me siento…* **9.** *Llego… y paso…*

Así se dice

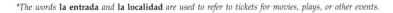

El autobús is expressed in a variety of ways in different parts of the Spanish-speaking world. Here are a few of the most common ones.

el camión (*Mex.*)
el bus (*C.A.*)
la guagua (*Cuba, P.R.*)
el colectivo (*Arg.*)

Here are some other common travel-related variations.

la maleta = la valija (*Arg.*), la petaca (*Mex.*)

El boleto is generally understood to express ticket* throughout the Spanish-speaking world. The word **el tiquete** is heard in Mexico and Central America, as well as in this country, and **el billete** is used in Spain.

*The words **la entrada** and **la localidad** are used to refer to tickets for movies, plays, or other events.

Con. A: Suggestions

- Ask students to name places they have been to via each of the means of transportation named in the chapter.
- Ask students to give the advantages and disadvantages of each means of transportation.

Con. B: Suggestions

- Have students read all of the items before starting this activity.
- After the class has agreed on a sequence of events, go through the items one by one and add sequencing or time-related phrases to flesh out the description. For example: *número 1: Son las cinco de la mañana. Estoy atrasado/a. Por eso salgo para el aeropuerto en taxi.*

Con. B: Note

Active vocabulary: *la ventanilla*

Con. B: Follow-up

Reciclado: Have students imagine they are traveling with friends and need to give them commands for each circumstance represented in the activity. MODELO: **f:** *Hagan la maleta.*, and so on.

Con. B: Optional

¿Qué va a hacer Ud. en estas situaciones?

1. *Ud. tiene poco dinero. Si tiene que viajar, ¿qué clase de pasaje va a comprar?*
2. *Ud. tiene mucho miedo de volar en avión, pero tiene que ir desde Nueva York a Madrid. ¿Qué alternativa tiene?*
3. *Ud. viaja en tren y no puede cargar* (new) *las maletas. ¿Qué hace?*

Con. C: Extension

7. *un barco grande que hace viajes de 5 días o de varias semanas* (*el crucero*)
8. *el lugar donde tenemos que tener el pasaporte* (*la inmigración*)

Heritage Speakers

- Anime a los hispanohablantes a hablar de sus vacaciones favoritas.

  ¿Adónde fue?
  ¿Cómo fue? ¿En avión, coche, tren?
  ¿Cuánto tiempo estuvo de vacaciones?
- Pídales a los hispanohablantes que escriban una composición breve usando las oraciones de *Con. B.* Pueden añadir otros detalles también.

Con. D: Suggestion

Do this as a whole-class activity or as a whole-class composition, with you writing sentences on the board.

De vacaciones

Notes

- Expressions using the word *vacaciones* are potentially confusing to students. We suggest that you stress in particular the need to use the plural (*vacaciones*) in contrast to the singular word used in English. You will need to make your own decision about how accurately you will require students to use these expressions. Note that the Spanish verbs correspond directly to their English equivalents.
- Additional care is needed with the use of *el océano* and *el mar*. The former refers to actual bodies of water, the latter is what most Spanish speakers would use to express traveling on the ocean (*viajar por mar*) or swimming (*nadar en el mar*).

Suggestions

Reciclado: Have students tell what the weather would be like and what clothing they would pack for the following vacations: *hacer un crucero por el Caribe, hacer* camping *en las montañas en verano, esquiar en las montañas en invierno, pasar una semana en un hotel en una playa tropical, pasar un fin de semana en un hotel de Nueva York en marzo.*

- Model vocabulary in sentences about yourself and in communicative exchanges with the students.

  Mi familia va de vacaciones todos los años. Nos gusta hacer camping *en la playa. ¿Le gusta a Ud. hacer* camping*? ¿Prefiere ir a la playa o a las montañas? ¿Sabe Ud. levantar una tienda de campaña? ¿Qué le gusta hacer cuando está de vacaciones?* And so on.

- Have volunteers compare this family's choices with a typical vacation they take with their family.

  Esta familia va de vacaciones en camioneta. Mi familia prefiere viajar en avión.

- Offer additional vocabulary words to help students talk about their own vacations: *bucear, esquiar, hacer* surfing, *el lago, montar en tabla de vela, el río, el saco de dormir.*

D. En el aeropuerto. En parejas, nombren (*name*) o describan las cosas y acciones representadas en este dibujo.

De vacaciones°

°De... *On vacation*

el *camping*	campground
el mar	sea
el océano	ocean
estar de vacaciones	to be on vacation
hacer *camping*	to go camping
ir de vacaciones a...	to (go on) vacation to/in . . .
pasar las vacaciones en...	to spend one's vacation in . . .
salir de vacaciones	to leave on vacation
tomar unas vacaciones	to take a vacation

NATIONAL STANDARDS: Communication

Words for vehicles vary from country to country. *El coche* is the most common term for car in Spain, while *el carro* is more common in most of Latin America. For some Spanish speakers, *la camioneta* means a van, station wagon, or pickup truck. For some speakers, *el camión* refers to a large commercial truck, but for others it is a pickup truck or bus.

Resources: Transparencias 92, 93

Así se dice

la camioneta = la ranchera, la rubia, el coche rural, el coche familiar, el monovolumen (*Sp.*)

el *camping* = el campamento

hacer *camping* = acampar

sacar fotos = tomar fotos

la tienda de campaña = la tienda de acampar, la carpa, la casa de campaña

Conversación

A. ¿Qué hace Ud.? Diga si las siguientes declaraciones son ciertas o falsas para Ud. Corrija las declaraciones falsas.

	CIERTO	FALSO
1. Cuando estoy de vacaciones, tomo el sol.	☐	☐
2. Prefiero ir de vacaciones a las montañas.	☐	☐
3. Duermo muy bien en una tienda de campaña.	☐	☐
4. Saco muchas fotos cuando estoy de vacaciones.	☐	☐
5. Es fácil ir a playas bonitas desde (*from*) aquí.	☐	☐

Nota **cultural**

Los nuevos tipos de turismo en el mundo hispano

Los turistas de hoy no son fáciles de complacer.[a] Por eso hay nuevas industrias para satisfacer su interés en la ecología, la agricultura o la aventura: el ecoturismo, el agroturismo y el aventurismo. Los países hispanos ofrecen diversas oportunidades para disfrutar de[b] estas nuevas formas de hacer turismo.

El ecoturismo consiste en viajar a lugares no explotados por el ser humano.[c] Los lugares del mundo hispano que ofrecen amplias oportunidades para el ecoturismo son las selvas tropicales de Centroamérica y la Amazonia, especialmente en Costa Rica y el Ecuador. Las Islas Galápagos y la Patagonia (en el sur de la Argentina y Chile) también son destinos[d] populares entre los ecoturistas.

El agroturismo indica viajes a lugares rurales donde el turista se queda en casas rurales renovadas, a veces visitando más de una casa o zona durante su viaje. Algunas excursiones son informativas o educativas, con visitas a granjas y campos de cultivo.[e] Otras son simplemente parte de un programa para renovar casas y pueblos rurales. España ofrece varias oportunidades al agroturista por todo el país. La isla Chiloé de Chile también tiene una organización agroturística.

El aventurista, o sea[f] el turista que busca viajes emocionantes, a veces peligrosos,[g] también tiene amplias oportunidades en los países hispanos. En los Andes, la Patagonia y las montañas de España, puede practicar alpinismo, ciclismo de montaña, navegación en rápidos, esquí y *snowboard* extremos.

[a]*please* [b]disfrutar... *enjoying* [c]por... *by humans* [d]*destinations* [e]granjas... *farms and croplands* [f]o... *or in other words* [g]*dangerous*

Un grupo de estudiantes en una excursión ecoturística en la selva (*jungle*) amazónica, Perú

¿Practica Ud. alguno de estos tipos de turismo? ¿Dónde lo hace?

Con. A: Suggestion

After students have completed the activity, working silently at their seats, use the items as conversation starters. Do each item yourself, saying whether it is *cierto/falso* for you and expanding the item conversationally. Example: *número 1: Cuando estoy de vacaciones, tomo el sol. Falso. Cuando estoy de vacaciones, no tomo el sol. No es bueno tomar el sol porque puede causar cáncer de la piel* (new). *¿Cuántos de Uds. sí toman el sol cuando están de vacaciones?...*

Nota cultural

Suggestions

- Describe some of the places in the Hispanic world you have been to or know well. Then ask students the names of the places they have visited.
- Ask students which places mentioned in the *Nota cultural* they would like to visit and why.
- Ask students for the meaning of these words: *alpinismo, ciclismo de montaña, navegación en rápidos.*
- Ask students to list all the words they know or can find in the *Nota cultural* with the same root as *turismo.*

Comprensión

1. *¿Qué es el ecoturismo?* (*viajar a lugares no explotados por el ser humano*)
2. *¿Cuál es la diferencia entre el agroturismo y el ecoturismo?* (*El agroturismo indica viajes a lugares rurales.*)
3. *¿Cuáles son algunos de los deportes emocionantes que se mencionan?* (*el alpinismo, el ciclismo de montaña, la navegación en rápidos, el esquí y el* snowboard *extremos*)

NATIONAL STANDARDS: Culture

The Galapagos Islands are located some 650 miles off the western coast of South America. This remote group of volcanic islands remains much as it was a couple of million years ago. Over millenia, animal and plant life from the Americas reached the islands and gradually evolved into new species, many of which are found nowhere else on the planet.

Heritage Speakers

Invite a los hispanohablantes a compartir unos comentarios sobre algún lugar hispano interesante que conozcan.

Con. B: Suggestions

- Point out the three preterite forms of *ser* and *ir*, which are the same, needed for this activity: *yo fui, tú fuiste,* (*las vacaciones*) *fueron*. (The preterite of *ser* and *ir* is presented in *Gram. 23*, in this chapter.)
- Note that students are asked to give infinitives for *Paso 1*, item 10, since they do not learn to form the preterite until *Gram. 23.*
- This activity can be assigned as homework. In addition to completing the paragraphs, ask students to be ready to ask at least 5 questions to get additional information from their classmates.
- Before students interview each other in *Paso 2*, ask them to provide some of the questions they prepared. Write them on the board. Be ready to provide additional questions, such as the following: *¿Por cuántos días vas de vacaciones? ¿Te gusta ir a ese lugar? ¿Por qué? ¿En qué lugar pasaste tus vacaciones más memorables? ¿Por qué fuiste a ese lugar? ¿Con quién fuiste? ¿Fueron unas vacaciones caras o baratas? ¿Por cuántos días fuiste?*
- If you would like students to report what they learned about their classmates' vacations, present *fue* (*he/she went; it was*). Students have already learned *fue* = *was* in the context of dates: *Ayer fue…*

Redacción: Ask students to hand in their completed paragraphs (*Con. B*). You can also ask for a summary of what their partner told them. If you do so, be sure to introduce *fue*.

Nota comunicativa

Notes

- The passive *se* has been presented for passive recognition and used frequently in listening comprehension activities and reading passages.
- This *Nota* does not emphasize the difference between the personal *you/they* that refers to specific persons vs. the impersonal *you/they*, which is nonspecific. If it is a goal of your course for students to master that difference, you will want to explain this point in more detail.

Suggestion

Have students state the following ideas in Spanish.

1. You study a lot here. (*Se estudia mucho aquí.*)
2. You don't talk in the library. (*No se habla en la biblioteca.*)
3. You wear a suit in the office. (*Se lleva traje en la oficina.*)
4. You bargain at the market. (*Se regatea en el mercado.*)

B. Intercambios

Paso 1. Complete el siguiente párrafo sobre sus vacaciones típicas y sus vacaciones más memorables.

En mis vacaciones típicas, voy a ____[1] en ____[2] (*medio de transporte*) en el mes de ____.[3] Voy con ____[4] (*personas*) y esto es lo que hago: ____.[5]

En mis vacaciones más memorables, fui[a] a____[6] en ____[7] en el mes de ____.[8] Fui con ____.[9] Las vacaciones fueron[b] memorables porque hice[c] las siguientes actividades: ____[10] (*infinitivos*).

[a]*I went* [b]*were* [c]*I did*

Paso 2. Ahora, en parejas, túrnense para hacer y contestar preguntas basadas en las ideas del **Paso 1.** Obtengan (*Get*) mucha información de su compañero/a.

MODELOS: ¿Adónde vas para tus vacaciones, generalmente? ¿Hay un lugar que siempre visitas para las vacaciones? ¿Vas allí todos los años? ¿Por qué vas allí? Y para tus vacaciones más memorables, ¿a qué lugar fuiste?

Estrategia

you went = **(tú) fuiste**

Nota **comunicativa**

Otros usos de la palabra *se*

It is likely that you have often seen and heard the phrase shown in the photo that accompanies this box: **Se habla español.** (*Spanish is spoken* [*here*]). Here are some additional examples of this use of **se** with Spanish verbs. Note how the meaning of the verb changes slightly.

Se venden billetes aquí.	*Tickets are sold here.*
Aquí no **se fuma.**	*You don't* (*One doesn't*) *smoke here. Smoking is forbidden here.*

Be alert to this use of **se** when you see it because it will occur with some frequency in readings and in direction lines in *Puntos de partida*. The activities in this text will not require you to use this grammar point on your own, however.

Nueva York

C. ¿Dónde se hace esto? Indique el lugar (o los lugares) donde se hacen las siguientes actividades.

MODELO: Se come. ⟶ Se come en un restaurante, en casa, en la cafetería…

1. Se factura el equipaje y se anuncian los vuelos.
2. Se hacen las maletas.
3. Se compran los boletos.
4. Se espera en la sala de espera.
5. Se pide una bebida.
6. Se mira una película.
7. Se nada y se toma el sol.

D. De viaje. Conteste las siguientes preguntas.

1. ¿Qué lengua se habla en Francia? ¿en el Brasil? ¿en el Perú? ¿en este país?
2. ¿Cuáles son las diferentes maneras de viajar? Se viaja en…

E. La publicidad

Paso 1. Lea con cuidado (*carefully*) este anuncio de una aerolínea latinoamericana.

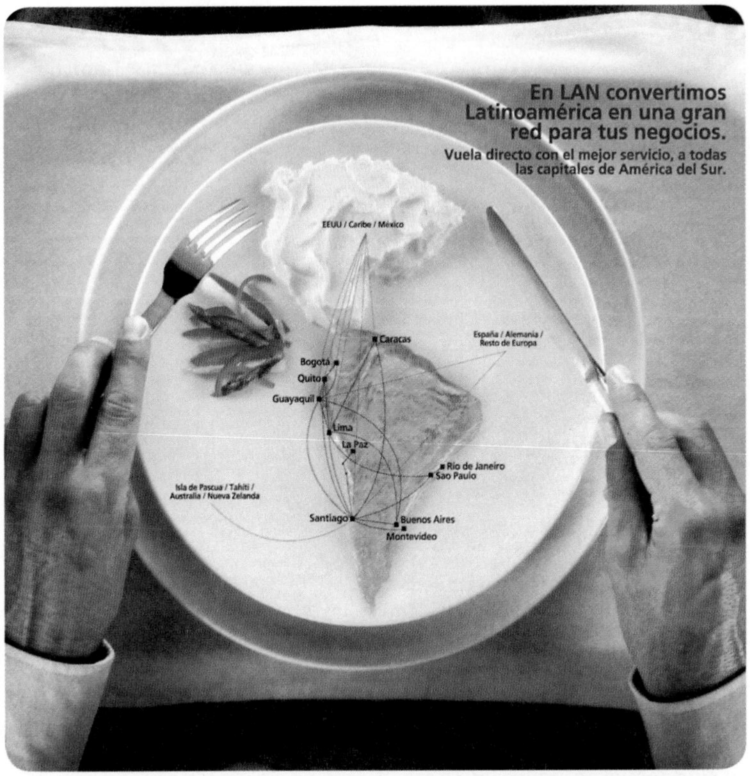

Paso 2. Ahora, en parejas, contesten las siguientes preguntas. ¡Piensen como expertos en *marketing*!

1. ¿Cómo se llama la aerolínea?
2. ¿A qué tipo de persona va dirigido (*directed*) el anuncio?
3. ¿Por qué se usa un plato con comida en el anuncio?
4. ¿Qué se ve en el plato? ¿Qué representa?
5. ¿En qué tipo de publicación creen Uds. que se encuentra (*is found*) este anuncio?

¿Recuerda Ud.?

In **Gramática 18 (Cap. 6),** you learned how to use direct object pronouns to avoid repetition. Can you identify the direct object pronouns in the following exchange? To what or to who(m) do these pronouns refer?

ROBERTO: ¿Tienes los boletos?
ANA: No, no los tengo, pero mi agente de viajes ya los tiene listos (*ready*). los = los boletos
ROBERTO: Si quieres, te acompaño a la agencia. te = a ti (Ana)
ANA: Encantada. Casi nunca te veo. te = a ti (Roberto)

Mundo interactivo

You should now be prepared to work with Scenario 4, Activity 3 in Connect Spanish (**www.connectspanish.com**).

Vocabulario útil

el continente
los negocios businesses
la red network

Con. C: Suggestion

To get students started, put a short list of place names on the board: *en el aeropuerto, en casa, en el avión, en la playa.*

Con. C: Extension

8. *Se hacen las camas.*
9. *No se fuma.*
10. *Se hace cola.*

Con. C: Reciclado

Encourage students to give as many answers as possible for each item. Note that most place names introduced so far in the text can be used in answers.

Con. C: Optional

- *¿Cierto o falso?* Ask students to correct false statements.
  1. *Se habla español en el Brasil.*
  2. *En México se comen tacos.*
  3. *En Chile se puede esquiar en junio.*
  4. *En España a veces se cena a las once de la noche.*
  5. *La paella se hace con lechuga.*
  6. *En la Argentina se dice* (new) *«chau».*
  7. *Se habla español en Miami.*
- Have students make up similar items and present them to the class.
- Have students tell what is and is not done in certain places.

  ¿Qué se hace y no se hace… en la biblioteca? →
  En la biblioteca, se estudia, pero no se habla.
  1. *¿en una clase de idiomas?*
  2. *¿en un mercado al aire libre?*
  3. *¿en un avión?*
  4. *¿en una discoteca?*
  5. *¿en una tienda de ropa?*
  6. *¿en una fiesta?*
  7. *¿en la cafetería?*
  8. *¿en caso de emergencia?*

Con. E: Suggestion

Ask students to name the countries of which some of the cities depicted in the ad are capitals.

Con. E: Redacción

Assign *Con. E* as an individual writing assignment. Add the preceding *Suggestion* to the assignment.

Pronunciación: See the Laboratory Manual for presentation and practice of the letters *g, gu,* and *j.*

Gramática 21
Indirect Object Pronouns; *Dar* and *decir*

Notes

- Direct object pronouns were presented in *Gram. 18* (*Cap. 6*).
- Active vocabulary: *el pasillo*

Suggestions

- Ask students to identify the people in the drawings. Provide vocabulary if students cannot provide it. Drawing 1: *el agente de la aerolínea, el pasajero* (*el hombre de negocios*). Drawing 2: *el agente de seguridad, la pasajera* (*la mujer de negocios*).
- After students have completed the dialogues, ask them to continue each conversation.

Follow-up

Ask the following question to introduce the concept of indirect objects.

¿Qué palabras en cada oración indican las personas afectadas por las acciones de los verbos?

Emphasize the meaning of the indirect object pronouns.

me = to me
le = to him/her/you (form. sing.)
les = to them/you (form. pl.)

GRAMÁTICA

21 Expressing *to* who(m) or for who(m)
Indirect Object Pronouns; **Dar** and **decir**

Grammar Tutorial 21
connect SPANISH
www.connectspanish.com

Gramática en acción: En el aeropuerto

En el mostrador
—¿Me puede dar un asiento de ventanilla, por favor?
—Lo siento, pero ya no hay. Pero sí puedo asignarle un asiento de pasillo.

En el control de seguridad
—¿Me enseña la tarjeta de embarque, por favor?
—¿Le enseño también el pasaporte?

Comprensión

¿Dónde se oye, en el mostrador o en el control de seguridad?

1. «¿Puede enseñarme (*show me*) lo que hay en su bolso?» control de seguridad
2. «No me gusta sentarme en el asiento de en medio (*middle*).» mostrador
3. «En un momento le doy la nueva tarjeta de embarque.» mostrador
4. «¿Me enseña el pasaporte, por favor?» control de seguridad / mostrador

the indirect object / **el complemento indirecto** = the noun or pronoun that indicates *to who(m)* or *for who(m)* an action is performed

Indirect Object Pronouns / **Los pronombres de complemento indirecto**

me	to/for me	nos	to/for us
te	to/for you (*fam. sing.*)	os	to/for you (*fam. pl.*)
le	to/for you (*form. sing.*), him, her, it	les	to/for you (*form. pl.*), them

¡OJO!
Note that indirect object pronouns have the same form as direct object pronouns, except in the third person: **le, les.**

At the airport *At the counter: "Could you please give me a window seat?" "I'm sorry, but there aren't any more (available). But I* ***can*** *give you an aisle seat." At the security check: "Could you please show me your boarding pass?" "Should I show you my passport too?"*

Resources: Transparency 94

1. **Indirect Objects**
   Indirect object nouns and pronouns are the second recipient of the action of the verb. They usually answer the question *to who(m)?* or *for who(m)?* in relation to the verb. The word *to* is frequently omitted in English.

	INDIRECT	DIRECT	
Ana is preparing	**them**	dinner.	
I'll give	**her**	the gift	tomorrow.

For whom is Ana preparing dinner? → **(for) them**
To who(m) am I giving the gift? → **(to) her**

Indicate the direct and indirect objects in the following sentences.

1. *He'll give me the car tomorrow.*
2. *Please tell me the answer now.*
3. Me va a dar el coche mañana.
4. Dígame la respuesta ahora, por favor.
5. El profesor nos va a hacer algunas preguntas.
6. ¿No me compras una revista ahora?

2. **Placement of Indirect Object Pronouns**
   Like direct object pronouns, *indirect object pronouns* (**los pronombres de complemento indirecto**) can precede the main (conjugated) verb or follow (and be attached to):
   - an infinitive
   - a present participle

No, no te **presto** el coche.
No, I won't lend you the car.

Voy a **guardarte** el asiento.
Te **voy** a guardar el asiento.
I'll save your seat for you.

Le **estoy** escribiendo una carta a Marisol.
Estoy **escribiéndole** una carta a Marisol.
I'm writing Marisol a letter.

3. **With Commands**
   As with direct object pronouns, indirect object pronouns are attached to the affirmative command form and precede the negative command form.

Sírvanos un café, por favor.
Serve us some coffee, please.

No me **dé** su número de teléfono ahora.
Don't give me your phone number now.

4. **Multiple Meanings of *le(s)***
   Le and **les** can have several different meanings. When context does not make the meaning clear, the meaning is clarified with a prepositional phrase: **a** + *pronoun object of a preposition.*

Voy a **mandarle** un telegrama. = meaning of **le** unclear unless clarified

Voy a mandarle un telegrama **a Ud.**
…**a él.**
…**a ella.**
I'm going to send you/him/her a telegram.

5. **Redundancy in Third Person**
   It is common for a Spanish sentence that has a third person noun indirect object to have not only the **a** + *noun phrase* but also an apparently repetitive **le** or **les.** The pronoun (**le** or **les**) usually precedes the **a** + *noun phrase* in the sentence.

Vamos a **contarle** el secreto **a Juan.**
Let's tell Juan the secret.
(Lit., *Let's tell **to him** the secret **to Juan**. him = Juan*)

¿Les guardo los asientos **a Jorge y Marta?**
Shall I save the seats for Jorge and Marta?
(Lit., *Shall I **for them** save the seats **for Jorge and Marta?** them = Jorge and Marta*)

Heritage Speakers

Note que en español se usa la preposición *a* con los pronombres de complemento directo mientras que en inglés se usa *from.* Anime a los hispanohablantes a explicar la diferencia entre los siguientes pares de oraciones.

Le robaron los dulces a Roberto.
Le robaron los dulces de Roberto.

Teresa le envió la carta a Fernando.
Teresa le envió la carta de Fernando.

Indirect Object Pronouns

Suggestion

Point out that indirect object pronouns have the same form as direct object pronouns except in the third person singular and plural: *le* and *les.* Gender is not reflected in any of the indirect object pronouns.

Emphasis 1: Suggestion

Illustrate the concept of the indirect object by suggesting that a student has asked you to get another student's attention for him/her. Tap the student: I tapped John for Tom. Ask: Who is directly affected? Students should answer: John, the direct object. Ask: Who was indirectly affected (second recipient of the action)? Students should answer: Tom, the indirect object.

Bright Idea

Suggestion

Have students use these two questions to identify and distinguish direct and indirect objects.

To identify the direct object, they should ask: *verb* what/who?

To identify the indirect object they should ask: *verb* to/for what/who(m)?

I bought them the cheapest tickets. →
I bought what? (direct object = tickets)
I bought for who(m)? (indirect object = them)

Emphasis 1: Note

Direct and indirect object pronouns are not used together until *Gram. 26* (*Cap. 9*).

Emphasis 4: Note

The use of the seemingly redundant *le(s)* with *a* + *pronoun* is normal, not the exception. In general, the *le(s)* is obligatory and *a* + *pronoun* is optional, even if it conveys more information than *le(s).*

Emphasis 5: Note

The redundancy (the use of *both* the indirect object pronoun and the *a* + *noun phrase*) in the third person is a feature of very correct Spanish, but it is a usage that is not observed 100% of the time by all native speakers. It may not be realistic to expect first-year students to master this point in spontaneous conversation, but it is included here because students will see and hear this usage in this text and in authentic materials. Remember, of course, that this redundancy (*pronoun* + *a* + *noun phrase*) is obligatory with *gustar* (*Gram. 22,* next section).

Emphasis 6: Suggestions

- Offer this additional verb to practice indirect objects: *permitir.*
- Additional optional material related to indirect objects: *pedir prestado, tenerle miedo a.*
- Point out that the indirect object for verbs of separation, such as *comprar* and *quitar,* is expressed with *a* in Spanish, whereas in English *from,* not *to* or *for,* is used.

  Le quito el bolígrafo al niño. (from the child)

  Le compra un periódico al vendedor. (from the salesperson)

  Native English speakers have a tendency to say *del niño* and *del vendedor* instead of the correct Spanish construction.
- *Gustar* and verbs like it also use indirect object pronouns. *Gustar* is presented in the next grammar section in this chapter, along with other verbs like *gustar* (*Nota comunicativa*). Additional verbs of this type are introduced in some *Vocabulario: Preparación* sections, as needed, always with a footnote that explains their use.

Dar and *decir*

Note

The introduction of *dar* and *decir* has been delayed so that they could be used naturally with indirect object pronouns.

Suggestions

- Point out the irregular *yo* form of *dar.* Also, emphasize the forms of *decir:* the *-g-* in the first person singular (*yo*) and the *e* ⟶ *i* stem-changing pattern.
- Model the differences between *dar* vs. *regalar* and *decir* vs. *hablar* (*charlar*).

Prác.: Preliminary Exercises

- Use the following chain drill to practice indirect object pronouns.
  1. *Les escribo tarjetas postales a mis padres.* (*a ti, a Ud., a Andrés, a Uds., a Alicia, a vosotros*)
  2. *Ahora le compro un regalo a Jorge.* (*a Sergio, a ti, a Eva, a Uds., a Martín y Rosa, a vosotros*)
  3. *El conductor le dice la hora de la llegada.* (*a mí, a ellos, a ti, a nosotros, a Uds.*)
  4. *Juan le da el billete, ¿verdad?* (*a ti, a nosotros, a mí, a Uds., a ellas*)
- Act out the following question/answer series with students.

6. Verbs Often Used with Indirect Objects
Here are some verbs frequently used with indirect objects. Be sure you know their meaning before starting the activities in the **Práctica** section.

contar (cuento)	to tell, narrate	**pedir (pido) (i)**	to ask for
entregar (gu)	to hand in	**preguntar**	to ask (*a question*)
escribir	to write	**prestar**	to lend
explicar (qu)	to explain	**prometer**	to promise
hablar	to speak	**recomendar (recomiendo)**	to recommend
mandar	to send	**regalar**	to give (*as a gift*)
mostrar (muestro)	to show	**servir (sirvo) (i)**	to serve
ofrecer (ofrezco)	to offer		

Dar and decir

Juan les dice a sus padres que necesita dinero.

dar (*to give*)		decir (*to say; to tell*)	
doy	damos	digo	decimos
das	dais	dices	decís
da	dan	dice	dicen

Su padre le da un cheque.

1. *Dar/Decir* + Indirect Objects
The verbs **dar** and **decir** are almost always used with indirect object pronouns in Spanish.

¿Cuándo **me das** el dinero?
When will you give me the money?

¿Por qué no **le dice** Ud. la verdad, señor?
Why don't you tell him/her the truth, sir?

¡OJO!
In Spanish there are two verbs for *to give:* **dar** (*to give in general*) and **regalar** (*to give as a gift*). Also, do not confuse **decir** (*to say* or *to tell*) with **hablar** (*to speak*) or **contar** (*to tell, narrate*).

2. Formal Commands of *dar* and *decir*
Dar and **decir** also have irregular formal command forms. There is a written accent on **dé** to distinguish it from the preposition **de.**

Mandatos formales
dar ⟶ dé, den
decir ⟶ diga, digan

Summary of Indirect Object Pronouns

a mí ⟶ **me**	a nosotros/as ⟶ **nos**
a ti ⟶ **te**	a vosotros/as ⟶ **vos**
a Ud., él, ella ⟶ **le**	a Uds., ellos, ellas ⟶ **les**

Autoprueba

Complete the sentences with the correct indirect object pronoun.

1. Tus abuelos _____ dan el coche a ti, Carolina, no a tu hermano.
2. Los Sres. Gómez _____ mandan este mensaje, señor.
3. No _____ dé las galletas a los niños, por favor.
4. ¿_____ pasas el pan? Está muy lejos de mí.
5. Profesora, no podemos terminar el examen si no _____ da más tiempo.

Answers: **1.** te **2.** le **3.** les **4.** Me **5.** nos

Heritage Speakers

Pídale a un(a) hispanohablante que explique la diferencia entre *pedir* y *preguntar,* y que dé ejemplos.

Resources: Transparency 95

Práctica

A. Asociaciones. ¿Qué verbos asocia Ud. con los siguientes objetos y situaciones?

1. un coche, el dinero
2. la comida en un restaurante
3. las fotos
4. hacer algo por (*for*) alguien
5. la gramática, un profesor
6. la tarea, un informe (*report, paper*)
7. algo de comer o beber
8. algo para un cumpleaños
9. un restaurante, una película, un libro
10. flores (*flowers*), un e-mail
11. un secreto, un chiste (*joke*)

B. ¡Anticipemos!

Paso 1. Indique si las siguientes declaraciones son ciertas o falsas para Ud.

	CIERTO	FALSO
1. Todos los años le mando una tarjeta de cumpleaños a mi abuelo/a.	☐	☐
2. El Día de la Madre le regalo flores a mi madre.	☐	☐
3. Todos los días les escribo e-mails a mis padres (hijos).	☐	☐
4. Siempre les entrego la tarea a los profesores a tiempo.	☐	☐
5. Mis amigos me dan dinero para mi cumpleaños.	☐	☐
6. Un buen amigo me presta su coche cuando lo necesito.	☐	☐
7. Los profesores nos cuentan chistes en clase con frecuencia.	☐	☐
8. El profesor / La profesora de español nos da mucha tarea.	☐	☐

Paso 2. Ahora, en parejas, túrnense para entrevistarse, usando las declaraciones del **Paso 1** como modelo. Deben corregir los detalles incorrectos.

MODELO: **E1:** ¿Tus amigos **te** dan dinero para tu cumpleaños?
E2: ¡No! Mis abuelos **me** dan dinero. (Nadie **me** da dinero.)

C. De vuelta (*Returning*) **a la República Dominicana**

Paso 1. Algunos amigos dominicanos necesitan ayuda para arreglar (*arrange*) su vuelta a casa. Explíqueles cómo Ud. los puede ayudar, usando las siguientes palabras.

MODELO: imprimir (*to print*) el boleto electrónico → **Les** imprimo el boleto electrónico.

1. llamar un taxi
2. bajar (*to carry down*) las maletas de su habitación
3. guardar (*to keep an eye on*) el equipaje
4. guardar un puesto en la cola
5. comprar una revista
6. por fin dar un abrazo (*hug*)

Paso 2. Ahora describa las acciones, pero desde el punto de vista (*point of view*) de sus amigos.

MODELO: imprimir el boleto electrónico → **Nos** imprimes el boleto electrónico.

Prác. A: Possible Answers: **1.** *prestar, dar* **2.** *servir, pedir* **3.** *mostrar, mandar* **4.** *prometer, ofrecer* **5.** *explicar* **6.** *entregar, preguntar* **7.** *pedir* **8.** *regalar* **9.** *recomendar* **10.** *mandar* **11.** *decir, contar*

Estrategia

Be sure to change the indirect object pronouns when you form the questions.

me → **te**
nos → **les** or **nos**

Prác. C: Answers
Paso 1. **1.** *Les llamo…* **2.** *Les bajo…* **3.** *Les guardo…* **4.** *Les guardo…* **5.** *Les compro…* **6.** *Por fin les doy…*
Paso 2. **1.** *Nos llamas…* **2.** *Nos bajas…* **3.** *Nos guardas…* **4.** *Nos guardas…* **5.** *Nos compras…* **6.** *Por fin nos das…*

¿Ud. me da el libro?
¿Ud. nos da el dinero (student standing with you)?
¿Uds. me dicen siempre la verdad? ¿la hora? ¿Me dan las respuestas correctas?
¿Les digo yo siempre la fecha de los exámenes? ¿Les digo cuál es la tarea para mañana? ¿cosas interesantes sobre la cultura hispana?

- Have students answer the following questions.

  En la clase de español, ¿quién le… a Ud.?
  explicar la gramática
  hacer preguntas
  dar exámenes
  prestar un papel
  dar las respuestas durante un examen

  Encourage students to answer in complete sentences. Model the first answer.

  La profesora me explica la gramática.

  As students answer, avoid overt correction; instead, repeat all answers, including corrections when necessary.

- Have students pass around a small object (ball, toy, book, pen). As they do it, have them provide a sentence about what they did or about what they are about to do. Their sentences should include both direct and indirect objects.

  Voy a darle la pelota a Jim. / Le doy la pelota a Jim.

  Other useful verbs that you might write on the board are *tirar* (new), *pasar, llevar.*

Prác. A: Notes

- Remember that activities of this kind give students practice with new verbs (in this case, the verbs on page 240) before students are asked to use the verbs actively in activities. There is, of course, more than one possible association for each category.
- Active vocabulary: *el chiste, la flor, por* (for)

Prác. B: Suggestion

Ask students to identify the indirect object pronoun in each sentence and tell to whom it refers, with an *a* + *pronoun* or *noun phrase*. In some cases, the *a* phrase is in the sentence.

Prác. C: Suggestion

Ask students to indicate the direct and indirect objects (nouns or pronouns) in each item.

Prác. C: Follow-up

Ask students what things others do for them when they are about to travel. If they can't think of anything, ask them to use the phrases in *Prác. C.*

Prác. D: Follow-up

Follow up the activity with these questions.

1. *¿A quién le manda Ud. flores? ¿Quién le manda flores a Ud.?*
2. *¿A quién le escribe Ud. cartas? ¿Qué tipo de cartas escribe Ud.? ¿Cartas políticas? ¿amistosas? ¿de amor? ¿Quién le escribe cartas a Ud.?*
3. *¿Les va a comprar algo a sus padres/hijos este año? ¿a su mejor amigo/a? ¿a su profesor(a)?*

Prác. E: Follow-up

Ask questions about the story and have students answer as if they were *Benjamín*.

Reciclado: Have students define the following persons by telling what they do for others.

1. *los profesores*
2. *los consejeros*
3. *los bibliotecarios*
4. *los padres*
5. *un dependiente en una tienda de ropa*
6. *una camarera en un restaurante*
7. *un(a) asistente de vuelo*
8. *un maletero*

Con.: Suggestions

- Ask some questions based on the cues before assigning the activity to pairs.

  ¿A quién le da Ud. consejos?
  ¿De quién acepta consejos?
  ¿A quién le pide Ud. ayuda con el español?
  ¿A quién le da ayuda?, and so on.
- Have students report to the class at least two interesting things they learned about their partner.

Vocabulario útil

dar
decir
ofrecer (ofrezco)
prestar
regalar
servir (sirvo) (i)

Prác. D: Possible Answers: **1.** *le da/ofrece/regala* **2.** *le da* **3.** *le da/ofrece/regala* **4.** *les ofrece* **5.** *les prestan* **6.** *les sirven/ofrecen* **7.** *les digo*

D. ¿Qué hacen estas personas? Complete las siguientes oraciones lógicamente con un verbo y un pronombre de complemento indirecto.

MODELO: El vicepresidente *le ofrece* consejos al presidente.

1. Romeo _____ flores a Julieta.
2. Snoopy _____ besos (*kisses*) a Lucy… ¡Y a ella no le gusta!
3. Eva _____ una manzana a Adán.
4. El Doctor Phil _____ consejos a sus televidentes.
5. Los bancos _____ dinero a las personas que quieren comprar una casa.
6. Los asistentes de vuelo _____ bebidas a los pasajeros.
7. Yo siempre _____ la verdad a todos.

E. En un restaurante. Explíquele al pequeño Benjamín, que solo tiene 4 años, lo que se hace en un restaurante. Llene los espacios en blanco con pronombres de complemento indirecto.

Primero el camarero *nos*[1] ofrece una mesa desocupada.[a] Luego tú *le*[2] pides el menú al camarero. También *le*[3] haces preguntas sobre los platos y las especialidades de la casa y *le*[4] dices lo que quieres comer. El camarero *nos*[5] trae la comida. Por fin tu papá *le*[6] pide la cuenta al camarero. Si tú quieres pagar, *le*[7] pides dinero a tu papá y *le*[8] das el dinero al camarero.

[a]*vacant*

Conversación

Intercambios. En parejas, túrnense para entrevistarse sobre los siguientes temas. Traten de (*Try to*) continuar la conversación.

hacer buenos regalos →

MODELO: **E1:** **¿Quién te** hace buenos regalos?
E2: Mis padres siempre me hacen buenos regalos.
E1: **¿Qué te** regalan, por ejemplo?
E2: Bueno, me regalan dinero, CDs, muebles para mi apartamento…

1. hacer buenos regalos / regalar cosas feas
2. decir la verdad / mentiras (*lies*)
3. contar secretos / los secretos de otras personas
4. hacer favores / recomendaciones / la cena
5. escribir e-mails / poemas de amor / tarjetas postales cuando están de vacaciones
6. mostrar las fotos de sus vacaciones / las notas (*grades*) de sus exámenes
7. servir la comida / bebidas
8. pedir/dar ayuda / consejos
9. prestar dinero / ropa / su coche
10. prometer cosas que luego no hace
11. recomendar películas / restaurantes / clases en la universidad
12. ¿ ?

¿Recuerda Ud.?

In **Capítulo 1** you started to use forms of **gustar** to express your likes and dislikes. Review what you know by answering the following questions. Then, changing their form as needed, interview your instructor.

1. ¿Te gusta el café (el vino, el té…)?
2. ¿Te gusta jugar al béisbol (al golf, al voleibol, al…)?
3. ¿Te gusta viajar en avión (fumar, viajar en tren…)?
4. ¿Qué te gusta más, estudiar o ir a fiestas (trabajar o descansar, cocinar o comer)?

1–4: *(No) Me gusta…* *¿Le gusta…*

22 Expressing Likes and Dislikes

Gustar (Part 2)

Grammar Tutorial 22
connect SPANISH
www.connectspanish.com

Gramática en acción: Las vacaciones chilenas

Según el anuncio, a muchos chilenos les gusta viajar a otros países. Lea el anuncio y luego indique si las oraciones son ciertas o falsas.

1. A los chilenos les gusta viajar solo en este hemisferio.
2. A los chilenos les gustan mucho las playas.
3. Solo les gusta viajar a los países de habla española.

MEDIO MILLÓN DE CHILENOS
DE VACACIONES 2010 AL EXTRANJERO
Y USTED... NO SE QUEDE SIN VIAJAR
¡ RESERVE AHORA MISMO !
El próximo verano '10, con el bajo valor del dólar, muchas personas desearán viajar, los cupos disponibles se agotarán rapidamente. ¡Asegure sus vacaciones! Elija ahora cualquiera de nuestros fantásticos programas.
MIAMI - ORLANDO - BAHAMAS - MÉXICO - CANCÚN
ACAPULCO - IXTAPA - COSTA RICA - RÍO - SALVADOR
PLAYA TAMBOR - PUNTA CANA - LA HABANA
VARADERO - GUATEMALA - SUDÁFRICA
Infórmese sobre nuestro SÚPER CRÉDITO PREFERENCIAL
Economy Tour
Santa Magdalena 94, Providencia
2334429 - 2331774 - 2314252
2328294 - 2318608 - 2334862
Fax: 2334428

¿Y a Ud.?

¿Le gusta viajar? ¿Le gustan los viajes en avión? ¿Cuál de estos lugares le gustaría (*would you like*) visitar?

Using **gustar** / **Los usos de *gustar***

Spanish	English Phrasing	Literal Equivalent
Me gusta la playa.	*I like the beach.*	The beach is pleasing to me.
No le gustan sus cursos.	*He doesn't like his courses.*	His courses are not pleasing to him.
Nos gusta esquiar.	*We like to ski.*	Skiing is pleasing to us.

You have been using the verb **gustar** since the beginning of *Puntos de partida* to express likes and dislikes. However, **gustar** does not literally mean *to like*, but rather *to be pleasing*.

Me gusta viajar.
Traveling is pleasing to me. (I like to travel.)

Me gustan los viajes de aventura.
Adventure trips are pleasing to me. (I like adventurous trips.)

Gramática 22

Gustar (Part 2)

Note

Students have been using the *gustar* construction since *Cap. 1.*

Follow-up

After discussing the ad, ask the following questions.

1. *A las personas de este país, ¿les gusta ir a la playa? ¿Qué playas les gusta visitar? ¿Les gusta viajar en avión?*
2. *Y a Ud., ¿le gustan más las playas o las montañas? ¿Adónde le gustaría viajar este verano?*

Constructions with *gustar*

Notes

- Spanish constructions with *gustar* are similar to some English ones.

  The very idea disgusts me.
  Snakes frighten me.
  Books bore me.
  This movie sickens me.

- Note the use of *is pleasing to…* in the literal translation of the model sentences, to link English usage to the Spanish indirect object pronoun.

Heritage Speakers

En español, el verbo *gustar* puede tener connotaciones románticas cuando se usa en las formas de primera y segunda persona singular: *gusto, gustas.*

—*¿Te gusto?* (Do you like me? / Am I attractive to you?)
—*Sí, me gustas mucho.* (Yes, I like you. / Yes, you are attractive to me.)

Resources: Transparency 96

Emphasis 1: Suggestions

- Talk through the three examples in this section. Emphasize the singular subject (*asiento*), the plural subject (*asientos*), and the infinitive subject (also singular).
- Remind students to use the definite article when referring to something in general.

  *I like tacos. = Me gustan **los** tacos.*
- Emphasize that *no* in the *gustar* construction is placed just before the indirect object pronoun.
- Point out that in Spanish there is no need to use equivalents of the English pronouns *it* or *them* to identify the thing or things liked.

  I like it. = Me gusta.
  I don't like them. = No me gustan.
- Introduce verbs that are similar to *gustar.*

  encantar *interesar*
  faltar *parecer*
  importar *quedar*

Emphasis 2: Suggestion

Talk through the two sets of examples in this section. In the first sentence, emphasize the singular person (*el niño*) but the plural subject (*aviones*) and a resultant plural verb (*gustan*). In contrast, the second sentence has several people (*Raquel, Arturo*) but a singular subject (*viajar*) and a resultant singular verb (*gusta*). While some students will grasp the use of *gustar* intuitively, others may need the analysis/contrast.

Emphasis 2: Note

Active vocabulary: *juntos/as*

Emphasis 3: Suggestions

- In the *Clarification* examples, contrast the use of *le* in each of the example sentences. In the first set, *le* = *Ud.*; in the second, *le* = *él.*
- Optional: Present other exceptions to the *mí/ti* rule: *según tú y yo, entre tú y yo.*

Would Like / Wouldn't Like

Note

Gustaría will be used only with infinitives until all forms of the conditional are presented (*Cap. 18*).

1. *Gustar* + Indirect Object Pronouns

Gustar is always used with an indirect object pronoun: Someone or something is pleasing *to* someone else. The verb must agree with the subject of the sentence—that is, the person or thing that is pleasing.

(**no**) *indirect object pronoun* + **gusta(n)** + *subject*

Me gusta **este asiento** de pasillo.
This aisle seat is pleasing to me. (I like this aisle seat.)

No **me** gustan **los asientos** de ventanilla.
Window seats are not pleasing to me. (I don't like window seats.)

Me gusta mucho **volar** en avión.
Flying is really pleasing to me. (I really like to fly.)

Me gusta nadar y **tomar** el sol.
I like to swim and sunbathe.

¡OJO!
An infinitive is a singular subject in Spanish. **Gusta** is used even if there are two or more infinitive subjects.

2. Redundancy of Indirect Object

When the person pleased is stated as a noun or a proper name, the indirect object pronoun must be used *in addition to* the phrase **a** + *noun/name.*

a + *noun / name* + (**no**) *indirect object pronoun* + **gusta(n)** + *subject*
(no) *indirect object pronoun* + **gusta(n)** + *subject* + **a** + *noun / name*

Al niño no **le** gustan los aviones.
No **le** gustan los aviones **al niño.**
The child doesn't like airplanes.

A Raquel y a Arturo les gusta viajar juntos.
Les gusta viajar juntos **a Raquel y Arturo.**
Raquel and Arturo like to travel while on vacation.

¡OJO!
Remember: The indirect object pronoun *must* be used with **gustar** even when the prepositional phrase **a** + *noun* or *pronoun* is used.

3. Clarification or Emphasis

A phrase with **a** + *pronoun* is often used for clarification or emphasis. The prepositional phrase can appear before the indirect object pronoun or after the verb.

CLARIFICATION
¿**Le** gusta **a Ud.** viajar? ¿**A Ud. le** gusta viajar?
Do you like to travel?

¿**Le** gusta **a él** viajar? ¿**A él le** gusta viajar?
Does he like to travel?

EMPHASIS
A mí me gusta viajar en avión, pero **a mi esposo le** gusta viajar en coche. Y **a ti,** ¿en qué **te** gusta viajar?
I like to travel by plane, but my husband likes to travel by car. How do you like to travel?

¡OJO!
Remember that **mí** (accent) and **ti** (no accent) are used as the object of most prepositions, except **conmigo** and **contigo.** Subject pronouns (**Ud., él, ella,…**) are used as the object of all prepositions for all other persons.

[Práctica A]

Would Like / Wouldn't Like = Gustaría

What one *would* or *would not* like to do is expressed with the form **gustaría*** + *infinitive* and the appropriate indirect objects.

[Práctica B]

A mí me gustaría viajar a Colombia.
I would like to travel to Colombia.

Nos gustaría hacer *camping* este verano.
We would like to go camping this summer.

*This is one of the forms of the conditional of **gustar.** You will study all of the forms of the conditional in **Gramática 50 (Cap. 18).**

Práctica

A. Los gustos y preferencias

Paso 1. Exprese sus gustos con oraciones completas.

MODELOS: ¿el café? ⟶ (No) **Me gusta** el café.
¿los pasteles? ⟶ (No) **Me gustan** los pasteles.

1. ¿el vino? (No) Me gusta…
2. ¿los niños pequeños? (No) Me gustan…
3. ¿el merengue? (tipo de música dominicana) (No) Me gusta…
4. ¿volar en avión? (No) Me gusta…
5. ¿el invierno? (No) Me gusta…
6. ¿hacer cola? (No) Me gusta…
7. ¿el chocolate? (No) Me gusta…
8. ¿las películas de terror? (No) Me gustan…
9. ¿las clases que empiezan a las ocho de la mañana? (No) Me gustan…
10. ¿cocinar? (No) Me gusta…
11. ¿la gramática? (No) Me gusta…
12. ¿sus clases este semestre/trimestre? (No) Me gustan…
13. ¿los vuelos con muchas escalas? (No) Me gustan…
14. Marc Anthony (No) Me gusta…

Paso 2. Ahora, en parejas, túrnense para entrevistarse sobre las ideas del **Paso 1.** Luego digan a la clase dos cosas que Uds. tienen en común.

MODELO: E1: **A mí** no me gusta el café.
E2: **A mí tampoco.** ⟶
E1: (*a la clase*): A mí no me gusta el café y a Miguel tampoco (le gusta).

Vocabulario útil

A mí también.	So do I.	**Pues a mí, sí.**	Well, I do.
A mí tampoco.	I don't either. / Neither do I.	**Pues a mí, no.**	Well, I don't.

B. Las vacaciones de los Soto

Paso 1. Haga oraciones completas para describir lo que les gusta hacer a los miembros de la familia Soto. Luego diga lo que les gustaría hacer en sus vacaciones.

MODELO: padre / nadar: ir a la playa ⟶
Al padre **le gusta** nadar. **Le gustaría** ir a la playa.

1. padres / el mar: ir a la playa
2. hermanos pequeños / nadar: también ir a la playa
3. hermano, Ernesto / hacer *camping:* ir a las montañas
4. abuelos / descansar: quedarse en casa
5. madre / la tranquilidad: visitar un pueblecito (*small town*) en la costa
6. hermana, Elena / discotecas: pasar las vacaciones en una ciudad grande

Paso 2. Conteste las siguientes preguntas.

1. ¿A quién le gustaría ir a Nueva York? a Elena
2. ¿A quién le gustaría viajar a Acapulco? al padre, a los hermanos pequeños
3. ¿Quién no quiere salir de casa? los abuelos
4. ¿A quién le gustaría ir a la República Dominicana? a la madre
5. ¿Quién quiere ir a Colorado? Ernesto

Autoprueba

Complete each verb with **-a** or **-an.**

1. Me gust____ las playas de México.
2. Les gust____ esquiar en las montañas.
3. No nos gust____ viajar con mi padre.
4. ¿Te gust____ este restaurante?
5. A Julio le gust____ mucho las fotos de mi viaje.

Answers: **1.** *gustan* **2.** *gusta* **3.** *gusta* **4.** *gusta* **5.** *gustan*

Prác. A: Extension
Paso 1.
15. *¿el béisbol?* ([No] *Me gusta…*) **16.** *¿el fútbol?* ([No] *Me gusta…*)

Paso 2. Have students add to the list in *Paso 1* two or three things that they like or dislike.

Prác. B: Answers
Paso 1.
1. *A los padres les gusta el mar. Les gustaría ir a la playa.*
2. *A los hermanos pequeños les gusta nadar. También les gustaría ir a la playa.*
3. *Al hermano, Ernesto, le gusta hacer camping. Le gustaría ir a las montañas.*
4. *A los abuelos les gusta descansar. Les gustaría quedarse en casa.*
5. *A la madre le gusta la tranquilidad. Le gustaría visitar un pueblecito en la costa.*
6. *A la hermana, Elena, le gustan las discotecas. Le gustaría pasar las vacaciones en una ciudad grande.*

Prác. B: Extension
Paso 1.
7. *ti / (no) / los sitios que prefiere la familia Soto: visitar a la familia*
8. *el perro / (no) / quedarse en casa: ir con la familia*
9. *la tía Ramona / las visitas de la familia: recibirlos en su casa*

Paso 2.
6. *¿Quién quiere recibir a la familia en su casa? (la tía Ramona)*

Preliminary Exercises

- To make sure the *gustar* construction is clearly understood, have students give the Spanish for the following sentences, then have them give literal equivalents in English of the Spanish construction, e.g.:

  I like the car. ⟶ *Me gusta el coche.* ⟶ The car is pleasing to me.

  1. We/He/You/I like(s) the car.
  2. I/We/She/They like(s) to read.
  3. She likes the soup/chicken/coffee.
  4. He likes tomatoes / tacos / movies / to go to the movies. (**¡OJO!** Use the definite articles.)

- Have students give the Spanish equivalents of these sentences to stress the redundancy of the indirect object pronoun and noun.

  1. My father likes to travel.
  2. My mother likes trains.
  3. The boys like the beach.
  4. María likes to swim.

Prác. A: Suggestions

Paso 1. Emphasize the use of the definite article in Spanish to talk about things in general (compared to the lack of the article in English) by asking students to translate a few sentences.

Me gusta el café. ⟶ I like coffee.
Me gusta el vino. ⟶ I like wine.

Paso 2. Model exchanges of several kinds for students.

—Me gusta el café.
—A mí también.
—Pues a mí, no.

—No me gusta el café.
—A mí tampoco.
—Pues a mí, sí.

Prác. B: Note

These sentences require the redundant use of the indirect object pronoun and noun.

NATIONAL STANDARDS: Comparison

Expand on *Prác. A*, item 14. Have students brain-storm the names of at least 30 top pop music artists and list them on the board. How many of the artists are Hispanic? [Some other Hispanic pop stars include Jennifer Lopez, Christina Aguilera, Gloria Estefan, Shakira, and Santana.) Have a volunteer stand at the board and tally how many students like each artist (*¿A quién le gusta la música de... ?*), then compare how well the Hispanic artists fare against the other artists. Have students consider how U.S. and Canadian pop music has influenced Hispanic pop stars and how Hispanic music has influenced U.S. and Canadian pop stars.

Con. B: Suggestions

- Do the activity as a whole-class discussion or whole-class composition, with you or a student writing sentences on the board. Use the activity as a vehicle for review of major structures presented so far: verbs of all classes, possessives, pronouns, and so on.
- Supplement this activity with magazine photos of famous or unknown people.

Reciclado: Help students get going (and keep them within the limits of what they know how to express) by providing them with a list of topics that they can discuss: age, family members, living situation, favorite clothing, things they like or don't like to do, food they like to eat, and so on.

Con. B: Optional

Reciclado: Review previously learned vocabulary groups by asking questions with *gustar: las materias, la comida, el tiempo, las estaciones, las actividades.*

Conversación

A. ¿Conoce bien a... ?

Paso 1. Piense en su profesor(a) de español. En su opinión, ¿le gustan a él/ella las siguientes cosas o no?

	SÍ, LE GUSTA(N).	NO, NO LE GUSTA(N).
1. la música clásica	☐	☐
2. el color negro	☐	☐
3. las canciones (*songs*) de los años 80	☐	☐
4. viajar en coche	☐	☐
5. la comida mexicana	☐	☐
6. dar clases por la mañana	☐	☐
7. estudiar otras lenguas	☐	☐
8. el arte surrealista	☐	☐
9. las películas trágicas	☐	☐
10. ¿ ?	☐	☐

Paso 2. Ahora entreviste a su profesor(a) para saber si le gustan las cosas del **Paso 1** o no.

MODELOS: ¿A Ud. le gusta la música clásica?
A Ud. le gusta la música clásica, ¿verdad?

Paso 3. Ahora entreviste a un compañero o compañera sobre las mismas cosas.

MODELO: **E1:** ¿Te gusta la música clásica?
E2: Sí. ¿Y a ti?

B. Perfil personal. En parejas, inventen con detalles las preferencias de las siguientes personas.

Vocabulario útil

la música *rap, hip hop*

jugar (juego) (gu) a los videojuegos
patinar en monopatín to skateboard

1. Toño

2. los Sres. Sánchez

3. Memo

NATIONAL STANDARDS: Culture

Latinos have played an important role in the development of hip hop music and rap. In Mexico, hip hop began with the success of *Caló* in the early 90s. In the mid 90s, Latino rap groups such as *Cypress Hill* hit the charts in the United States, while Mexican rap groups such as *Control Machete* became exceedingly popular in the Hispanic world.

Resources: Transparency 97

Nota **comunicativa**

Otros verbos que expresan los gustos y preferencias

Here are some ways to express intense likes and dislikes

- **mucho / muchísimo, (para) nada**

Me gusta mucho/muchísimo.	*I like it a lot / a whole lot.*
No me gusta (para) nada.	*I don't like it at all.*

- **encantar** (*like* **gustar**), **interesar** (*like* **gustar**)

Me encantan las películas extranjeras.	*I love foreign films.*
Me interesa aprender otras lenguas.	*I'm interested in learning other languages.*

Verbs that are used like **gustar** will be noted in vocabulary lists with the parenthetical note (*like* **gustar**).

- **odiar**

Unlike **encantar** and **interesar,** which are used like **gustar, odiar** is conjugated like regular **-ar** verbs. It is a transitive verb, that is, a verb that can take a direct object.

Odio los champiñones.	*I hate mushrooms.*
Mi madre **odia** viajar sola.	*My mother hates traveling alone.*

Use as many of the preceding verbs and expressions as you can in the following activity.

C. Intercambios. En parejas, túrnense para describir lo que les gusta y lo que odian cuando están en las siguientes situaciones. Inventen los detalles necesarios.

MODELO: en la playa ⟶ Cuando estoy en la playa, me gusta mucho nadar en el mar, pero no me gusta el sol ni me gusta la arena (*sand*). Por eso no me gusta pasar todo el día en la playa. Prefiero nadar en una piscina.

Situaciones

en un autobús	**en el salón de clase**
en un avión	**en el coche**
en la biblioteca	**en una discoteca**
en una cafetería	**en una fiesta**
en casa con mis amigos	**en un parque**
en casa con mis padres/hijos	**en la playa**
en un centro comercial	**en un tren**

¿Recuerda Ud.?

You have already learned one of the irregular past tense verb forms that is presented in **Gramática 23.** Review it now by telling what day yesterday was: **Ayer...** fue...

Nota comunicativa

Notes

- Emphasize that *odiar* is not used like *gustar:* (*Yo*) *Odio el café.* / (*A mí*) *Me gusta el café.*
- Remind students that they can also use *preferir* to express what they like to do.
- Optional vocabulary: *en absoluto, chocar, detestar, motestar.*

Suggestion

Ask students to make lists of their favorite and least favorite things and categorize them as:

Cosas que odio
Cosas que no me gustan
Cosas que me interesan
Cosas que me gustan mucho
Cosas que me encantan

Then ask them to compare their lists with those of a partner.

A mí me encanta la música rock, pero Juan la odia.

Con. C: Reciclado

- Note the recycling of places for which students have already learned large groups of lexical items.
- Get students started with this activity by brainstorming vocabulary related to several of the places.

Con. C: Suggestions

- Limit the number of situations students discuss to 3–5, allowing them to choose those they prefer.
- Ask pairs to share information they have learned about their partner with the class.
- Use *me molesta*(*n*) instead of *odio.*

Con. C: Follow-up

Reciclado: Have students describe the likes and dislikes of various family members on different topics. In addition to *gustar,* encourage students to use *encantar, interesar, molestar, odiar,* and *preferir.*

23 Talking About the Past (Part 1)

Preterite of Regular Verbs and of **dar, hacer, ir,** and **ser**

Grammar Tutorial 23
connect SPANISH
www.connectspanish.com

Gramática en acción: Un viaje a la República Dominicana

Elisa es reportera. Hace poco, fue a la República Dominicana para escribir un artículo sobre la isla de La Española. Habla Elisa.

- Hice el viaje en avión.
- El vuelo fue largo porque el avión hizo escala en Miami.
- Pasé una semana entera en la Isla.
- Visité muchos sitios de interés turístico e histórico.
- Comí mucha comida típica del Caribe.
- Tomé el sol, nadé en el mar y escribí muchas tarjetas postales.
- ¡Lo pasé muy bien!

Comprensión

¿Cierto o falso? Corrija las oraciones falsas.

Comprensión: Answers
1. *Fue para escribir un artículo.*
3. *Visitó muchos sitios de interés turístico e histórico.*
4. *Lo pasó muy bien.*

	CIERTO	FALSO
1. Elisa fue a la República Dominicana para pasar sus vacaciones.	☐	☑
2. El avión hizo escala en los Estados Unidos.	☑	☐
3. Elisa no visitó ningún lugar importante de la isla.	☐	☑
4. No lo pasó bien en la playa.	☐	☑

So far, you have almost always talked in the present tense. In this section, you will use forms of the preterite, one of the past tenses in Spanish. To talk about the past in Spanish, there are two *simple tenses* (tenses formed without an auxiliary or "helping" verb): the *preterite* and the *imperfect*. In this chapter, you will learn the regular forms of the preterite and those of four irregular verbs: **dar, hacer, ir,** and **ser.** Then in **Capítulos 9, 10,** and **11,** you will learn more about both tenses.

Preterite: Regular Verbs / **El pretérito: Los verbos regulares**

***-ar* Verbs**	
hablar	
hablé	I spoke (did speak)
hablaste	you spoke
habló	you/he/she spoke
hablamos	we spoke
hablasteis	you spoke
hablaron	you/they spoke

***-er/-ir* Verbs**			
comer		**vivir**	
comí	I ate (did eat)	**viví**	I lived (did live)
comiste	you ate	**viviste**	you lived
comió	you/he/she ate	**vivió**	you/he/she lived
comimos	we ate	**vivimos**	we lived
comisteis	you ate	**vivisteis**	you lived
comieron	you/they ate	**vivieron**	you/they lived

A trip to the Dominican Republic *Elisa is a reporter. A little while ago, she went to the Dominican Republic to write an article about the island of Hispaniola. Here's Elisa. • I made the trip by plane. • The flight was long because the plane made a stop in Miami. • I spent a whole week on the Island. • I visited a lot of interesting tourist and historical sites. • I ate a lot of typical Caribbean food. • I sunbathed, swam in the ocean, and wrote a lot of postcards. • I had a really good time!*

Gramática 23

Preterite of Regular Verbs and of *dar, hacer, ir,* and *ser* (Part 1)

Suggestions

- Emphasize that the narration talks about a past event.
- Model the narration for students.
- Ask students what the verbs *pasé, visité, tomé,* and *nadé* have in common (they are all *-ar* verbs, this is the first person preterite ending).
- Ask students to guess what the first person preterite ending is for *-er* and *-ir* verbs (*comí, escribí*).
- Ask students to look for two forms of *hacer* in the preterite (*hice, hizo*). Discuss why there is a *-c-* in *hice* but a *-z-* in *hizo.*
- Ask students to find the two uses of *fue* (one in *Comprensión*) and ask them what it means in each context.

Reciclado: Follow up the narration by having students respond to the following questions, using direct object pronouns.

Elisa Velasco, ¿visitó lugares interesantes en la República Dominicana?
¿Entrevistó (write on board) *a muchas personas?*
¿Comió comida típica?
¿Visitó las playas puertorriqueñas?
¿Hizo el viaje en avión?
¿Pasó una semana en la República Dominicana?
¿Tomó el sol en las playas?

Preterite of Regular Verbs

Note

There will be explicit opportunities to practice the preterite and the imperfect in *Cap. 9–11. Hace* (= *ago*) is presented in *Cap. 14.* In addition, this topic is carefully recycled throughout the rest of the text's chapters.

Heritage Speakers

Anime a un(a) hispanohablante a leer en voz alta lo que dice Elisa.

1. **Uses of the Preterite**
   The *preterite* (**el pretérito**) has several equivalents in English. For example, **hablé** can mean *I spoke* or *I did speak.* The preterite is used to report finished, completed actions or states of being in the past. If the action or state of being is viewed as completed—no matter how long it lasted or took to complete—it will be expressed with the preterite.

   Pasé dos meses en el Caribe.
   I spent two months in the Caribbean.

   El verano pasado **hicimos** *camping* en Puerto Rico.
   Last summer we went camping in Puerto Rico.

2. ***Nosotros* forms**
   Note that the **nosotros** forms of regular preterites for **-ar** and **-ir** verbs are the same as the present tense forms. Context usually helps determine meaning.

   Ayer **hablamos** del viaje con nuestros amigos. Hoy **hablamos** con el agente de viajes a las dos de la tarde.
   Yesterday we spoke about the trip with our friends. Today we're speaking with the travel agent at 2:00 P.M.

3. **Accent Marks**
   Note the accent marks on the first and third person singular of the preterite tense. These accent marks are dropped in the conjugation of **ver: vi, vio.**

   bailé, bailó
   bebí, bebió
   asistí, asistió

   but

   vi, vio

4. **Verbs ending in *-car*, *-gar*, and *-zar***
   These verbs show a spelling change in the first person singular (**yo**) of the preterite. (This is the same change you have already learned to make in formal commands, **Gramática 20 [Cap. 7]).**

-car → qu	**busqué**	**buscamos**
buscar	**buscaste**	**buscasteis**
	buscó	**buscaron**
-gar → gu	**pagué**	**pagamos**
pagar	**pagaste**	**pagasteis**
	pagó	**pagaron**
-zar → c	**empecé**	**empezamos**
empezar	**empezaste**	**empezasteis**
	empezó	**empezaron**

5. **Unstressed *-i-***
   An unstressed **-i-** between two vowels becomes **-y-**. Also, note the accent on the **í** in the **tú, nosotros,** and **vosotros** forms.

creer		**leer**	
creí	creímos	leí	leímos
creíste	creísteis	leíste	leísteis
creyó	creyeron	leyó	leyeron

6. ***-ar* and *-er* Stem-changing Verbs**
   Stem-changing verbs that end in **-ar** and **-er** are completely regular in the preterite. However, the preterite of **-ir** stem-changing verbs is not regular. You will learn the preterite of those verbs in **Gramática 25 (Cap. 9).**

   despertar (despierto): desperté, despertaste,...
   volver (vuelvo): volví, volviste,...

Heritage Speakers

En algunos dialectos del español, hay una tendencia a añadir una *-s* al final de la segunda persona del singular (*tú*) del pretérito, por ejemplo, *hablaste → hablastes, comiste → comistes, viviste → vivistes.* Aunque se oyen estas formas, es preferible no añadir la *-s* al final.

En algunos dialectos del español, a veces se oye decir *vide, vidiste, vido, ...,* en vez de *vi, viste, vio...* Aunque se oyen estas formas, las que se presentan aquí son las preferidas.

Suggestions

- Model the pronunciation of regular forms, emphasizing the stress on *yo* and *Ud.* forms.
- Point out that the *nosotros* preterite forms of *-ar* and *-ir* verbs are identical to present tense forms. Context will clarify the meaning.
- Use *llamar, aprender,* and *recibir* in brief conversational exchanges with students, first in a sentence about yourself, then asking *Ud./Uds.* questions of the students.
- Point out the importance of word stress to distinguish some verbal forms, such as *hablo* (I speak) vs. *habló* (he/she/you spoke); *hable* (speak, *Ud.* command) vs. *hablé* (I spoke).
- Say the following word pairs and have students identify the preterite form: *hable, hablé; hablo, habló; bailé, baile; busqué, busque; estudio, estudió; tomó, tomo.*
- Say the following verbs and have students give the corresponding subject pronoun.

  Singular forms:

pregunté	*bajó*	*ayudaste*
fumé	*llamé*	*anunció*
mandaste	*bebió*	*aprendí*
comiste	*contesté*	*ayudó*

  Plural forms:

escuchamos	*terminaron*	*mirasteis*
estudiamos	*bailaron*	*regresaron*
pagamos	*bebieron*	*comimos*
aprendisteis		

- Say the following verbs and have students tell whether each could be present, past, or both.

miró	*mandé*	*escuché*
escucha	*escribimos*	*fumaste*
bebió	*ayudamos*	*vive*
volvió	*creo*	*empiezan*
leyó	*pagáis*	*buscaste*

- Say the following verbs and have students tell whether each is a command or a form of the preterite.

estudie	*estudié*	*fume*
fumen	*ayudé*	*busque*
leyó	*hablé*	*pagué*
lleve	*decidí*	

- Point out that no written accent is needed for the *yo* and *Ud.* forms of *ver* because they are single syllables: *vi, vio.* Other single-syllable forms also will not require an accent (*dar, ir, ser*).
- Write some formal commands using *-gar, -car,* and *-zar* verbs on the board (*toque, llegue, empiece*) to emphasize that these are the same spelling changes they use in the preterite.

Irregular Preterite Forms

Suggestions

- Present additional sentences using the preterite of *ser* and *ir* to show that context clarifies the meaning.
- Remind students that single-syllable forms such as the *yo* and *Ud.* forms of *dar, ver,* and *ir* do not require an accent: *di, dio; vi, vio; fui, fue.*

Preliminary Exercises

- Use the following rapid-response drill before beginning the activities.

  Ud. → *yo*
  Uds. → *nosotros.*

  MODELO: *¿Llamó?* → *Sí, llamé,*

¿Estudió?	*¿Trabajó?*
¿Habló?	*¿Escuchó?*
¿Terminó?	*¿Mandó?*
¿Bajó?	*¿Cantó?*
¿Bailó?	*¿Comió?*
¿Bebió?	*¿Abrió?*
¿Asistió?	*¿Escribió?*
¿Preguntaron?	*¿Nadaron?*
¿Bajaron?	*¿Mandaron?*
¿Escucharon?	*¿Miraron?*
¿Bebieron?	*¿Comieron?*
¿Comprendieron?	*¿Vivieron?*
¿Recibieron?	

- Use the following chain drill before beginning the activities.
  1. *Pepe estudió hasta muy tarde.* (*yo, Uds. tú, Graciela, nosotros, vosotros*)
  2. *Tú escribiste todos los ejercicios.* (*Rodrigo, yo, nosotras, ellas, Uds., vosotros*)
  3. *Julio fue al laboratorio.* (*yo, Paula, tú, nosotros, Estela y Clara, vosotras*)
  4. *Ana hizo los experimentos.* (*yo, nosotros, Uds., tú, Adolfo*)

Prác. A: Suggestions

- In *Paso 1*, ask students to find the preterite verb form in each sentence and give its infinitive.
- Review the use of *también/tampoco* before beginning *Paso 2*. Emphasize the use of *tampoco* to agree with a negative: *Yo tampoco.*

Irregular Forms / **Las formas irregulares**

1. ***Dar***

   The preterite endings for **dar** are the same as those used for regular **-er/-ir** verbs, except that the accent marks are dropped.

dar	
di	**d**imos
diste	**d**isteis
dio	**d**ieron

2. ***Hacer***

   All forms of **hacer** are irregular in the preterite, especially the third person singular, **hizo,** which is spelled with a **z** rather than a **c** to keep the [s] sound of the infinitive.

hacer	
hice	**h**icimos
hiciste	**h**icisteis
hizo	**h**icieron

3. ***Ir* and *ser***

   These verbs have identical forms in the preterite. Context will make the meaning clear. In addition, forms of **ir** are often followed by **a** (as in the first example), so they are easy to spot in the preterite.

ir/ser	
fui	fuimos
fuiste	fuisteis
fue	fueron

Fui a la playa el verano pasado.
I went to the beach last summer.

Fui agente de viajes.
I was a travel agent.

Autoprueba

Give the correct preterite forms.

1. (nosotros) buscar
2. (mi papá) volver
3. (yo) despertarme
4. (Ud.) ver
5. (ellas) leer
6. (tú) ser

Answers: **1.** bus**ca**mos **2.** volvió **3.** me desperté **4.** vio **5.** leyeron **6.** fuiste

Práctica

A. ¡Anticipemos!

Paso 1. ¿Es esto lo que Ud. hizo el verano pasado? Lea las siguientes declaraciones y conteste **sí** o **no,** según su experiencia.

El verano pasado…

	SÍ	NO
1. tomé clases en la universidad.	☐	☐
2. asistí a un concierto.	☐	☐
3. trabajé mucho.	☐	☐
4. hice *camping* con algunos amigos / mi familia.	☐	☐
5. pasé todo el tiempo con mis padres / mis hijos / mi esposo/a.	☐	☐
6. me quedé en este pueblo / esta ciudad.	☐	☐
7. fui a una playa.	☐	☐
8. hice un viaje a otro país.	☐	☐
9. fui a muchas fiestas.	☐	☐
10. no hice nada especial.	☐	☐

Paso 2. Ahora, en parejas, túrnense para entrevistarse sobre las ideas del **Paso 1.** Luego digan a la clase dos cosas que Uds. tienen en común.

MODELO: tomé clases en la universidad. →
E1: El verano pasado, ¿**tomaste** alguna clase en la universidad?
E2: No, ¿y tú?
E1: Yo tampoco. →

Nosotros no **tomamos** ninguna clase el verano pasado.

B. El viernes por la tarde

Paso 1. Los siguientes dibujos representan lo que Julio hizo el viernes por la tarde. Empareje las acciones con los dibujos.

ACCIONES

- 10 **a.** regresar a casa muy tarde
- 1 **b.** volver a casa después de trabajar
- 9 **c.** ir a un café a tomar algo y conversar mucho
- 2 **d.** llamar a su amigo Rigoberto y los dos decidir ir al cine juntos
- 8 **e.** no gustarles nada la película
- 4 **f.** cenar rápidamente
- 3 **g.** ducharse y afeitarse
- 7 **h.** entrar en la Sala 6 y sentarse
- 5 **i.** ir al cine en autobús
- 6 **j.** encontrarse (*to meet up*) en el cine y luego hacer cola para comprar las entradas (*tickets*)

1. 2. 3. 4. 5. 6. 7. 8. 9. 10.

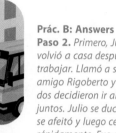

Paso 2. Ahora use las frases para narrar una secuencia de acciones. **¡OJO!** En algunas oraciones **Julio** es el sujeto; en otras, el sujeto es plural = **ellos (Julio y Rigoberto).**

Comprensión. ¿Cierto, falso o no lo dice?

	CIERTO	FALSO	NO LO DICE
1. El amigo de Julio se llama Rigoberto.	☑	☐	☐
2. Son compañeros de clase.	☐	☐	☑
3. A los dos amigos les interesa el cine.	☑	☐	☐
4. Vieron una película extranjera.	☐	☐	☑
5. Odiaron la película.	☑	☐	☐
6. Comieron algo en el café.	☐	☐	☑
7. Julio regresó a casa en autobús.	☐	☐	☑

Prác. B: Answers

Paso 2. *Primero, Julio volvió a casa después de trabajar. Llamó a su amigo Rigoberto y los dos decidieron ir al cine juntos. Julio se duchó y se afeitó y luego cenó rápidamente. Fue al cine en autobús. Los dos amigos se encontraron en el cine y luego hicieron cola para comprar las entradas. Entraron en la Sala 6 y se sentaron. No les gustó nada la película. Después, fueron a un café a tomar algo y conversaron mucho. Finalmente, Julio regresó a casa muy tarde.*

Estrategia

Use words like **primero, luego, después, finalmente,** and so on, to make your narrative flow smoothly.

Prác. B: Note

This is one of several narration sequences that appears in this text. Use the drawing to give input with the preterite and the imperfect (even though students have not yet learned the imperfect). After introducing the imperfect (*Cap. 10*) and then the contrasts between imperfect and preterite (*Cap. 11*), come back to this drawing and exploit its narrative potential.

Prác. B: Variation

Have students tell the story from Julio's point of view, which will involve primarily first person singular (*yo*) and plural (*nosotros*) forms.

Prác. B: Suggestion

Read the following paragraph out loud. Then give students infinitive cues, phrase by phrase, and ask them to retell the story in writing.

Anoche Miguel volvió a casa a las siete. Hizo su comida y cenó rápidamente. Estudió para prepararse para un examen de filosofía hasta las ocho y después habló por teléfono con una compañera de clase. Y a las nueve en punto llegaron sus padres.

Give students the following false statements and ask them to correct them.

1. *Miguel regresó a casa a las once de la noche.*
2. *Estudió para un examen de matemáticas.*
3. *Habló por teléfono con su madre.*
4. *Sus padres llegaron a las diez en punto.*

NATIONAL STANDARDS: Communication

Have students work in small groups to invent stories of an imaginary vacation they took last summer. First, have them research Hispanic travel agencies or travel agencies that publish their information in Spanish on the Internet. Then, have them choose a destination in the Spanish-speaking world. Then, have them narrate the trip they took there. Remind them to use the *nosotros* form of the preterite and to address the following questions.

¿Adónde viajaron?
¿Dónde se quedaron?
¿Qué atracciones turísticas visitaron?

Resources: Transparency 98

Prác. C: Suggestions

- Call students' attention to the names that come before each set of items: *Teresa, Liliana, Teresa y Liliana*. They should begin the first item in each set with the name indicated. Students will use third person plural (*ellas*) forms for the third set. Remind students not to use subject pronouns, since the meaning is clear.
- After students complete the activity as written, go over the items again, asking additional questions about Teresa and Liliana's activities as well as personal questions about students.
- Have student repeat the activity but in the first person (*yo* for the first two sets, *nosotras* for the third set).
- Note the use of direct and indirect object pronouns in items 9, 12, and 16. Ask students to identify the type of object pronoun used in each item and what it refers to.

Redacción: As a homework assignment, ask students to write a composition that describes the activities of the three apartment mates. You may wish to review sequencing words and phrases such as *Primero…*, *Luego…*, *Después…*, *Finalmente…*, as well as other connectors like *por eso, porque, pero, y, o*, and so on.

Prác. D: Suggestions

- Remind students that subject pronouns in parentheses are not used. They are provided to help students stay on track in the activity.
- Have students read through the list before starting the activity.
- Read the sentences using the present tense, and have students write them as dictation, changing all the verbs to the preterite.
- After completing the activity as written, give the narrator a name and ask students to redo the activity in the third person.

Heritage Speakers

- Anime a un(a) hispanohablante a describir lo que hizo ayer.
- Pídales a los hispanohablantes que escriban una composición, usando las frases de *Prác. C*.

¿Quién es, Teresa o Liliana? ¿Cómo lo sabe?

C. El día de ayer de dos compañeras

Paso 1. Teresa y Liliana son compañeras de apartamento en la universidad. Hagan oraciones completas según el modelo para describir su día.

MODELO: 7:30 levantarse ⟶ Se levantó a las siete y media.

TERESA

1. 8:00 ducharse y desayunar Se duchó, desayunó
2. 9:00 salir de casa / ir a la universidad Salió, fue
3. 10:00 llegar a la biblioteca / estudiar toda la mañana Llegó, estudió
4. 12:00 almorzar con unos compañeros de la universidad Almorzó
5. 1:00 hacer experimentos en el laboratorio de química Hizo
6. 3:15 volver a casa Volvió

LILIANA

7. 9:45 despertarse, pero no levantarse pronto Se despertó, se levantó
8. 10:30 desayunar y empezar a hacer la tarea de matemáticas Desayunó, empezó
9. 12:30 terminarla y ver la tele La terminó, vio
10. 2:00 empezar a hacer un pastel para el cumpleaños de Miriam Empezó
11. 2:30 mandar unos e-mails. Mandó
12. 4:30 terminar la tarta / decorarla Terminó, la decoró

TERESA Y LILIANA

13. 5:00 ir al gimnasio cerca de su apartamento / allí hacer ejercicio por una hora Fueron, hicieron
14. 6:30 volver a casa / ducharse y hablar de la fiesta de Miriam Volvieron, se ducharon, hablaron
15. 7:00 ir a un restaurante para cenar con Miriam y otros amigos Fueron
16. 9:30 ir a casa de Miriam / cantarle «Cumpleaños feliz» / darle su regalo y comer el pastel Fueron, le cantaron, le dieron, comieron

Paso 2. Ahora describa el día de ayer de Ud., mencionando por lo menos diez acciones. ¿Hizo algo similar a lo que hicieron Teresa y Liliana?

MODELO: Como Teresa, yo también me duché y desayuné a las ocho.

D. Un semestre en la República Dominicana. Cuente la siguiente historia desde el punto de vista de la persona indicada, usando el pretérito de los verbos.

MODELO: (yo) viajar a la República Dominicana el año pasado ⟶ **Viajé** a la República Dominicana el año pasado.

1. (yo) pasar todo el semestre en Santo Domingo. Pasé
2. Mis padres pagarme el vuelo… me pagaron
3. …pero (yo) trabajar para ganar el dinero para la matrícula y los otros gastos (*expenses*). trabajé
4. vivir con una familia dominicana encantadora (*charming*). Viví
5. aprender mucho sobre la vida y la cultura dominicanas. Aprendí
6. visitar muchos sitios de interés turístico e histórico. Visité
7. Mis amigos escribirme con frecuencia. me escribieron
8. (yo) mandarles muchas tarjetas postales. Les mandé
9. También comprarles recuerdos (*souvenirs*) a todos. les compré
10. volver al Canadá a fines de agosto. Volví

NATIONAL STANDARDS: Connections

- Cristóbal Colón (c. 1451–May 20, 1506) was an Italian navigator, colonizer, and explorer whose voyages across the Atlantic Ocean led to the discovery of the American continents by Europeans.
- Dorothy Gale (*Dorotea*) is a fictional character and protagonist in the *Oz* novels, written in the early 1990s by the American author L. Frank Baum. The character was immortalized by Judy Garland in the 1939 film *The Wizard of Oz* (*El mago de Oz*).
- The Apollo 11 moon landing occurred on July 20, 1969, when astronauts Neil Armstrong and Buzz Aldrin landed the Lunar Module *Eagle* on the moon, then walked, collected samples, took photos, and deployed experiments on the lunar surface while Michael Collins remained in lunar orbit.

(Cont.)

Conversación

A. Humor viajero. Mire el dibujo y conteste las preguntas.

David Sebastián Ojeda, Pasaje Blanco 1662, Morón, prov. de Buenos Aires, tel. 4697-6858; artepiero@hotmail.com

¿El piloto o Superhombre? ¿Quién…

1. no vio el avión?
2. no vio a Superhombre?
3. sufrió un accidente?
4. juró (*swore*) algo?
5. no llegó a su destino?
6. fue al hospital?
7. hizo un informe (*report*) sobre el accidente?

B. Viajes famosos. En parejas, digan adónde llegaron o viajaron las siguientes personas y en qué medio de transporte viajaron. Luego traten de (*try to*) añadir por lo menos un detalle más: ropa especial, compañeros de viaje, etcétera.

1. Cristóbal Colón
2. Dorotea, en *El mago de Oz*
3. los astronautas de Apollo 11 en 1969
4. E.T.
5. Robinson Crusoe

Vocabulario útil

el camino road
el espantapájaros scarecrow
el extraterrestre
el hombre de lata tin man
la isla
el león
la luna
el náufrago castaway
la nave espacial
la órbita
la Tierra Earth
el tornado

Con. A: Suggestions

- Encourage students to use direct object pronouns in their responses.
- Return to this activity after students have learned the imperfect and, as a whole-class activity, tell a more complete story based on the cartoon.

Con. A: Optional

Guessing game: Ask students to think of one interesting activity that they did last week. Note: It must be one that they know how to express in Spanish, so that the rest of the class can guess it. Students should take turns being the one to think of an activity. Other students will ask yes/no questions using the preterite to try to guess the activity. Suggest that students ask questions based on the following interrogatives: *¿dónde?, ¿adónde?, ¿cuándo?, ¿con quién?* You should be the first one to model responses.

Con. B: Suggestions

- Brainstorm vocabulary that students already know before they begin this activity. For example: *Cristóbal Colón: el barco, el viaje, la Niña, la Pinta, la Santa María.*
- If students are unfamiliar with some of the names in this activity, give them information about them (see National Standards: Connections) or substitute current events with which they are familiar. Some examples are: recent trips made by the president or other world leaders, tours done by performing artists, and so on.

NATIONAL STANDARDS: (Cont.)

- *E.T.: The Extra-Terrestrial* is a 1982 American science fiction film by Steven Spielberg. It tells the story of a lonely boy, Elliott, who befriends a friendly extraterrestrial, called E.T., who is stranded on Earth.
- *Robinson Crusoe* is a 1719 novel by Daniel Defoe about a castaway who spends 28 years stranded on a remote island near Venezuela.

Con. C: Follow-up

- For the next class, have students write down:
  1. one or two unusual things they did in the past
  2. one or two unusual things they did *not* do

  Have students read their statements in class as others tell whether they think the statements are *cierto* or *falso.*
- Have students write questions about personal habits and life events they can then use to interview classmates. Write the following verbs on the board to give them ideas: *despertarse, regresar, pagar, enamorarse* (new), *sacar una nota* (new).
- Ask students the following questions about the people listed or other well-known people. Have them use their imagination and make up necessary details: *¿Qué hicieron estas personas ayer?* (*Lady Gaga, el presidente, Jon Stewart, Kristen Stewart, el profesor / la profesora*) Write the following actions on the board to support their responses: *dar un discurso* (new), *ensayar* (new), *cantar, enseñar, no hacer nada.*

Con. C: Optional

Paso 1. *Describa lo que hicieron las siguientes personas ayer, sin decir su nombre. Si no sabe los detalles, ¡invéntelos! Para los números 1 y 4, escoja a una persona fácil de reconocer. Dé también una descripción de lo que Ud. hizo ayer.*

1. *un actor famoso / una actriz famosa*
2. *un rey* (new) *o una reina* (new)
3. *un empleado / una empleada de la Casa Blanca*
4. *un(a) atleta profesional*
5. *un niño de dos años*
6. *Ud. o uno de sus compañeros de clase*

Paso 2. *Lea una o dos de sus descripciones sin decir quién es la persona. Sus compañeros de clase deben tratar de adivinar quién es.*

MODELO: E1: *Se levantó a las cinco de la mañana. Fue a su estudio. Habló con el director y Orlando Bloom antes de empezar. Luego se acostó y…*
E2: *Es un actor famoso. Es Johnny Depp.*

Con. C, Paso 1: Redacción: Assign as a writing assignment. Require that students list a minimum of 12 activities. Tell students that compositions that contain a number of time adverbs (p. 150) and time prepositions (pp. 134–135) used accurately will receive extra credit.

C. Intercambios

Paso 1. Escriba una lista de diez de las acciones que Ud. hizo ayer. Use los siguientes verbos y añada cuatro más de su preferencia. Haga oraciones completas.

MODELO: levantarse ⟶ Ayer **me levanté** a las seis de la mañana.

1. levantarse	6. ir
2. empezar	7. ¿ ?
3. leer	8. ¿ ?
4. dar	9. ¿ ?
5. hacer	10. ¿ ?

Paso 2. En parejas, túrnense para entrevistarse sobre las acciones de su lista del **Paso 1.**

MODELO: E1: Ayer **me levanté** a las seis de la mañana. ¿A qué hora **te levantaste tú**?
E2: **Me levanté** a las diez.

Paso 3. Ahora digan a la clase en qué acciones los dos coincidieron ayer.

Mundo interactivo

You should now be prepared to work with Scenario 4, Activity 4 in Connect Spanish (**www.connectspanish.com**).

Un poco de todo

A. Preguntas: La última (*last*) vez. Conteste las siguientes preguntas. Añada más detalles si puede.

MODELO: La última vez que Ud. fue a una fiesta, ¿le llevó un regalo al anfitrión / a la anfitriona (*host/hostess*)? ⟶
Sí, **le** llevé flores / una botella de vino. (No, no **le** llevé nada.)

La última vez que Ud.…

1. hizo un viaje, ¿le mandó una tarjeta postal a algún amigo o amiga?
2. tomó el autobús/metro, ¿le ofreció su asiento a una persona mayor?
3. vio a su profesor(a) de español en público, ¿le habló en español?
4. comió en un restaurante, ¿le recomendó algún plato a su compañero/a?
5. entró en un edificio, ¿le abrió la puerta a otra persona?
6. voló en avión, ¿le pidió algo a uno de los asistentes de vuelo?
7. le regaló algo a alguien, ¿le gustó el regalo a la persona?
8. le prometió a alguien hacer algo, ¿lo hizo?
9. se quejó de algo, ¿a quién habló?

B. Lengua y cultura: Mi abuela dominicana. Complete the following paragraphs with the correct form of the words in parentheses, as suggested by context. When two possibilities are given in parentheses, select the correct word. **¡OJO!** The verbs in the paragraphs will be present tense or preterite; the context will indicate which tense to use.

Act. B: Answers: 1. *hermana* **2.** *Fuimos* **3.** *-la* **4.** *dio* **5.** *Mi* **6.** *a* **7.** *va*

Ayer llegó de visita mi abuela Manuela. Ella vive en Santo Domingo, con mi tía Zaira, la (hermana/sobrina[1]) de mi mamá. (*Nosotros:* Ir[2]) a recibir (la/le[3]) al aeropuerto y nos (*ella:* dar[4]) un abrazo[a] muy fuerte. (Mi/Mí[5]) abuela va (a/de[6]) pasar dos meses con nosotros en Connecticut, y luego (ir[7]) a quedarse un mes con el tío Julián en Nueva Jersey. Así es la vida[b] de muchas abuelas con hijos en otro país.

[a]*hug* [b]Así… *Such is the life*

Un poco de todo

A: Suggestions

- Have students complete the activity in pairs, then report to the class at least two interesting things they learned about their partner.
- Have students invent their own questions using the format of these items. They can take turns asking each other questions.

A: Reciclado

Recycle family and food words. Have students say the following sentences in Spanish.

1. My father likes vegetables, but he doesn't like cheese.
2. My mother likes milk, but she doesn't like apple juice.
3. My grandparents like eggs, but they don't like meat.
4. I like everything (*todo*) but my siblings don't like anything!

A mi abuela le (gusta/gustaría[8]) tener a todos sus hijos y (nietos/sobrinos[9]) en Santo Domingo y siempre (ser/estar[10]) muy triste cuando (volver[11]) a la República Dominicana (antes de / después de[12]) visitarnos. Pero también (le/la[13]) gusta mucho la vida en los Estados Unidos. (*Ella:* Decir[14]) que aquí se vive muy bien y que las casas (ser/estar[15]) muy buenas. (El/La[16]) problema es que no le (gustan/gustarían[17]) los inviernos de (este / esto[18]) país. ¡Es lógico! A ella le (gusta/gustan[19]) las playas y las palmeras, porque es lo que (conoce/sabe[20]) bien.

Cuando mi abuela regresa a Santo Domingo, (les/los[21]) mandamos con ella muchos regalos a nuestros (padres/parientes[22]). Casi todos los años mi familia (viaje/viaja[23]) a la República Dominicana, porque mis padres (vivir[24]) allá hasta que (ir[25]) a estudiar a la Universidad de Massachusetts. ¡(A/–[26]) mí me encanta ir de vacaciones a la República Dominicana!

Una abuela con su hija y su nieta

Comprensión. Conteste las siguientes preguntas.

1. ¿Quién habla en la narración? ¿Se sabe si es hombre o mujer? un nieto o una nieta de Manuela
2. ¿Dónde vive la tía Zaira? en Santo Domingo
3. ¿Qué le gusta de la vida en los Estados Unidos a la abuela? Se vive bien y las casas son buenas.
4. ¿Qué no le gusta? los inviernos
5. ¿Cuándo emigraron a los Estados Unidos los padres del narrador / de la narradora? cuando fueron a estudiar a la universidad

8. *gustaría* **9.** *nietos* **10.** *está* **11.** *vuelve* **12.** *después de* **13.** *le* **14.** *Dice* **15.** *son* **16.** *El* **17.** *gustan* **18.** *este* **19.** *gustan* **20.** *conoce* **21.** *les* **22.** *parientes* **23.** *viaja* **24.** *vivieron* **25.** *fueron* **26.** *A*

C. Intercambios

Paso 1. En parejas, túrnense para entrevistarse sobre su último (*last*) viaje. Deben obtener información relacionada con las siguientes preguntas.

1. ¿cuándo?
2. ¿adónde?
3. ¿en qué medio de transporte?
4. ¿cuántos días?
5. ¿con quién?

Paso 2. Ahora digan a la clase los detalles esenciales del viaje de su compañero/a.

MODELO: Susie fue a Puerto Rico el verano pasado. Hizo el viaje en avión. Se quedó en Puerto Rico una semana. Viajó con su novio y su familia.

En su comunidad

Entreviste a una persona hispana de su universidad o ciudad sobre sus últimas (*last*) vacaciones y los lugares más populares de su país para ir de vacaciones.

PREGUNTAS POSIBLES

- ¿Cuándo fue de vacaciones a su país la última vez? ¿Con quién fue? ¿Cuánto tiempo pasó allá? ¿Se quedó en casa de su familia o en un hotel? ¿Con cuánta frecuencia va de vacaciones a su país?
- ¿Cuáles son los lugares de vacaciones más famosos de su país? ¿Los visitan solo los turistas extranjeros o los nacionales también? ¿Cuál es su lugar favorito? ¿Por qué?

B: Notes

- The following grammar topics are included in *Lengua y cultura:* gender, demonstratives, possessives, use of prepositions, direct and indirect object pronouns, object of preposition pronouns, lexical items (time prepositions, family), *-ar/-er* verbs, irregular verbs (*ir, decir, ser, estar, saber, conocer*), stem-changing verbs (*volver*), preterite tense, *ser* vs. *estar, saber* vs. *conocer,* use of *gustar.*
- The narrative contains an example of the use of the personal *a* with *tener* (*tener a todos sus hijos y nietos*): *to have someone in a place.* You may wish to point this out to students, as they have learned not to use the personal *a* with *tener.*

B: Suggestion

Ask if any students (not just Hispanic students) have immigrant parents. Ask when their parents came to this country and if their grandparents visit them here or vice versa.

1. *¿Alguien tiene padres que nacieran en otro país?*
2. *¿Cuándo llegaron sus padres a este país?*
3. *¿Tiene muchos parientes en el país de origen de sus padres?*
4. *¿Vienen sus parientes a visitarlo/la con frecuencia?*
5. *¿Con cuánta frecuencia viaja Ud. a ______ para visitar a sus parientes?*
6. *¿Cuándo fue la última* (new) *vez que hizo el viaje?*

Ask these questions in the form of an interview of a student who has immigrant parents, or give the questions to students and allow them to conduct the interview.

En su comunidad

Suggestions

- Remind students to get the following basic information: the informant's country of origin, how long he or she has lived in this country, and if the informant visits his or her country of origin frequently.
- This activity could also be assigned as an online research project on a country of the student's choice or assigned by you.
- See the IM for additional suggestions and guidelines.

Resources: Desenlace

In the *Cap. 8* segment of "Chapter-by-Chapter Supplementary Materials" in the IM, you will find a chapter-culminating activity. You can use this activity to consolidate and review the vocabulary and grammar skills students have acquired.

TELEPUNTOS Salu2

Un arcoíris (*rainbow*) en las Cataratas (*Falls*) del Iguazú: «La caída (*plunging*) de agua desde una altura de ochenta metros es simplemente indescriptible… Hay que estar allí para oír el rugido (*roar*) de las cataratas, sentir (*to feel*) el vapor del agua… »

Antes de mirar

¿Cuál es su destino (*destination*) turístico favorito en este país para las vacaciones de verano? ¿y para las vacaciones de primavera? ¿Tiene su familia un lugar favorito para las vacaciones de familia? Si Ud. tiene hijos, ¿tienen ellos un destino favorito? ¿Qué lugar del mundo hispano le gustaría visitar a Ud.?

PROGRAMA 8: ¡De viaje!

En este programa, se puede ver los mejores de los más de 200 videos de destinos turísticos que los telespectadores de *Salu2* mandaron al programa. ¡La elección (*choice*) fue difícil!

Vocabulario de este programa

el ambiente	ambiance, atmosphere	**bajar por cuerda**	to descend by rope
enterrado/a	buried	**el recorrido**	tour
el puesto	stall, stand	**el mirador**	viewing stand
la gente	people	**los caminos**	flows
la selva	jungle	**el fuego**	fire
la especie	species	**la piedra**	stone
el concursante	contestant	**el depredador**	predator
nacer	to be born	**el ser humano**	human being
hace + *time*	*time* + ago	**la criatura**	**el animal**
la copa	(tree) top		

Fragmento del guion

ANSELMO BINOTTI: De Cusco nos fuimos al Valle Sagrado[a] de los Incas para visitar un santuario de llamas. Estuvimos con personas de esta comunidad mientras hacían tejidos[b] tradicionales. Es un arte que ha pasado[c] de generación en generación y un gran ejemplo de la hermosa[d] artesanía peruana. Pero lo mejor del viaje fue Machu Picchu, considerada una de las siete maravillas[e] del mundo actual.[f] Llegamos allí en tren, en un viaje espectacular por los Andes. Machu Picchu es un lugar rodeado de[g] misterio. Permaneció oculto[h] cientos de años, hasta que un explorador lo descubrió en 1911. Nadie sabe si este lugar fue un fuerte[i] militar o un santuario o una ciudad habitada. […] La última[j] noche estuvimos en el nuevo Parque de las Fuentes[k] para ver un espectáculo[l] de agua, luz[m] y sonido, muy bonito. En resumen, un viaje inolvidable.[n] ¡Les recomiendo mucho que no dejen de visitar[ñ] Perú!

[a]Valle… *Sacred Valley* [b]hacían… *they made weavings* [c]ha… *has passed* [d]*beautiful* [e]*wonders* [f]*modern* [g]rodeado… *surrounded by* [h]Permaneció… *It remained hidden* [i]*fort* [j]*last* [k]*Fountains* [l]*show* [m]*light* [n]*unforgettable* [ñ]no… *don't miss out on visiting*

«Primero estuvimos (*we were*) varios días en Cusco, la antigua (*ancient*) capital del Imperio inca. Está a más de 3.000 metros de altitud, y esta altitud puede provocar malestar (*discomfort*) físico. ¡Pero el malestar no es nada comparado a la belleza (*beauty*) de la ciudad!»

TelePuntos

Note

Pages 256–261 are optional. You may cover some, all, or none of this material in class, or assign it to students—as a group or individually—for homework or extra credit. Pages 262–263 (*En resumen: En este capítulo*) are a summary of all of the chapter's active material.

Suggestions

- If you are using the video in class, show it once, ask brief comprehension questions, then show it again.
- Even if you plan to ask students to watch the video in your campus media center or on their own, it is a good idea to continue to stress the need to watch the shows as many times as they want or need to in order to complete the *Después de mirar* activities.

Antes de mirar

Suggestions

- After students have answered these questions, have them share their answers with the whole class and tally the answers. Is there any consensus about favorite places in this country? Is there any consensus about favorite places in the Spanish-speaking world that students would like to visit?
- Locate on a map some of the places in the Spanish-speaking world that students would like to visit. Ask if anyone in the class has visited any of them.

Programa 8

Notes

- This program will be easily accessible to students because its organizing concept can be grasped easily. However, much of the narration is done in the preterite, a tense that students have just learned, so that will be a challenge. As an advance organizer, you may wish to ask students what tense they think the *Salu2* viewers will use as they narrate their videos.
- In addition, the narration contains a lot of vocabulary that, while guessable if students were to encounter it in reading mode, will be difficult for students to "catch" the first time they watch the show. For this reason, it is a good idea to go over *Vocabulario de este programa* in class, even if you do not regularly do so.
- Emphasize to students that the more carefully they study the preliminary activities (*Antes de mirar, Vocabulario de este programa,* and *Fragmento del guion*), the more they will understand. Scanning *Después de mirar* before viewing is also an excellent strategy.

Mundo interactivo

Continue your work as an intern at HispanaVisión with Laura Sánchez Tejada, the roving reporter of *Salu2*, as you complete Scenario 4, Activities 3 and 4 in Connect Spanish (**www.connectspanish.com**).

Al mirar

Al mirar, Answers: *LUGARES: unas cataratas, una ciudad antigua, una ciudad moderna, unas montañas, un parque tropical, una playa, unas ruinas arqueológicas, un volcán*

Mientras mira el programa, indique los lugares, animales y aves (*birds*) que se ven.

LUGARES

- ☐ un aeropuerto
- ☐ un casino
- ☐ unas cataratas
- ☐ una ciudad antigua
- ☐ una ciudad moderna
- ☐ un desierto
- ☐ unas montañas
- ☐ un palacio
- ☐ un parque tropical
- ☐ una playa
- ☐ unas ruinas arqueológicas
- ☐ un volcán

ANIMALES Y AVES

- ☐ un elefante
- ☐ flamencos
- ☐ iguanas
- ☐ leones marinos
- ☐ una llama
- ☐ mariposas (*butterflies*)
- ☐ monos (*monkeys*)
- ☐ pelícanos
- ☐ pingüinos
- ☐ píqueros de patas azules (*blue-footed boobies*)
- ☐ pizotes (*coatis*)
- ☐ un tigre
- ☐ tortugas
- ☐ un tucán

ANIMALES Y AVES: flamencos, iguanas, leones marinos, una llama, mariposas, monos, pelícanos, pingüinos, píqueros de patas azules, pizotes costarricenses, tortugas, un tucán

Después de mirar

A. ¿Está claro? Empareje las siguientes descripciones con el destino turístico apropiado.

DESCRIPCIONES

1. __c__ Se puede bajar en tirolesa, hacer un recorrido en moto todo terreno y montar a caballo (*ride horseback*).
2. __g__ No se sabe exactamente qué función tuvo (*it had*) en su época.
3. __b__ Tienen una altura de 80 metros.
4. __d__ Es uno de los más altos de Centroamérica.
5. __e__ Allí hay pingüinos y tortugas.
6. __a__ Eva Perón está enterrada allí, en el Cementerio de La Recoleta.
7. __f__ Está a más de 3.000 metros.

DESTINOS TURÍSTICOS

- **a.** Buenos Aires
- **b.** las Cataratas del Iguazú
- **c.** la Reserva de Monteverde
- **d.** el Volcán Arenal
- **e.** las Islas Galápagos
- **f.** Cusco
- **g.** Machu Picchu

Una turista que baja en tirolesa (*zip line*) en la Reserva de Monteverde en Costa Rica: «Es súper emocionante (*exciting*) subir hasta las ramas (*branches*) de los árboles y tirarse (*jump out*)».

B. Un poco más. Conteste las siguientes preguntas.

1. ¿Quién filmó los videos que se ven en este programa?
2. ¿Por qué se ven estos videos en el programa de hoy?
3. ¿Por qué fue Ana a Costa Rica?
4. ¿Por qué fue Ana a las Galápagos?
5. ¿Cuál de los cuatro países que se ven en este programa conoce Víctor?

Act. B, Answers: 1. *Cuatro telespectadores de* Salu2 *filmaron los videos.* **2.** *Porque son los videos favoritos de los presentadores de* Salu2. **3.** *Fue allí de vacaciones con su hermano y la novia de él.* **4.** *Para hacer un documental.* **5.** *la Argentina.*

C. Y ahora, Uds. En grupos de tres o cuatro, indiquen cuál, en su opinión, es el mejor destino turístico de los cuatro. Expliquen por qué.

Sobre el programa

A Laura le encanta viajar; esa probablemente fue la razón principal por la que[a] estudió comunicación y por la que es la reportera de *Salu2*. Hace un año, conoció a un productor de *Salu2* en México. Este productor pensó que Laura sería[b] una reportera perfecta, porque es joven y mexicana, como gran parte de los telespectadores del programa. El productor le ofreció el trabajo a Laura y ella aceptó sin pensárselo dos veces.[c]

[a]por... *why* [b]*would be* [c]sin... *instantly, without thinking*

Producción personal

Haga un foto montaje con voz en off (*voiceover*) sobre (*about*) un destino turístico. Puede ser su destino favorito o un lugar que le gustaría visitar algún día.

Fragmento del guion

Suggestions

- After students have read the excerpt, ask them to underline all of the preterite tense verbs that occur in it.
- Focus students' attention on *estuvimos* in the second sentence, and ask what the infinitive of the verb is and what tense they think it is in.

Al mirar

Suggestion

Be sure that students have read the lists before watching the episode. Because there are two long checklists, you may wish to suggest that they not check off their responses while watching, but rather after the episode is over or during a second viewing.

Después de mirar

C: Suggestions

- Remind students to use *gustar* and verbs like *gustar* in this activity.
- After students have made their decisions in groups, poll the class to find out which destination got the most votes.

Sobre el programa

Suggestion

Ask students to share their speculations about Laura's *razón personal* for loving San Francisco.

Optional: Comprensión

1. *¿Qué carrera estudió Laura?*
2. *¿Por qué es una reportera perfecta para el programa* Salu2?
3. *¿Dónde conoció a un productor de* Salu2?
4. *¿Pensó Laura mucho antes de aceptar el puesto de reportera?*

Producción personal

Note

See the IM for additional suggestions for this chapter's assignment as well as for general guidelines and suggestions for video assignments.

Lectura cultural

Notes

- The Instructor's Edition on this page offers some additional information on the country of focus. For more information about the country of focus, see the chapter's opening pages and the IM.
- See the IM for some expressions used in the Dominican Republic.

First Reading: Notes

- Santo Domingo is the oldest city founded by Europeans in the Western Hemisphere.
- Additional tourist spots in the Dominican Republic include *Samaná, La Romana, Puerto Plata,* and *Barahona.*
- More Dominicans now live in the New York area than in Santo Domingo.
- UNESCO's list of nearly 1000 World Cultural Heritage sites serves to highlight cultural and natural places of outstanding value to the world.

Suggestion

- Ask student to name places in the U.S. that have Hispanic history. Some notable examples are the Sarasota area and St. Augustine, in Florida; the Alamo and San Antonio, in Texas; and the California missions.
- Ask students to do an Internet search to find out why the following places and others were named in Spanish: *Colorado, Las Cruces, El Paso, Los Ángeles, San Francisco, Boca Ratón,* and so on.

Exploración lingüística

Ask students to find the following in the reading. Some of these words are glossed and some are not.

1. *Vocabulario relacionado con el turismo (sector, lugares de interés, visitante, destinos turísticos, motor, turistas)*
2. *Palabras que significan o que están relacionadas con el concepto de* beautiful (*bellas, hermosas, maravillosas, fabulosas*)

Tres símbolos dominicanos

Notes

- *El güiro* is a hollow gourd whose surface is intricately carved; it is rubbed with a stick to produce a sound. This instrument, with varying names, is used all over the Caribbean and in other Hispanic countries.
- *El casabe* was prepared by the indigenous people of other nearby Caribbean countries as well. *La yuca* is called la *mandioca* in some countries.

A LEER

Lectura cultural

La República Dominicana

El turismo es el sector económico más importante de la República Dominicana. La biodiversidad de sus bosques,[a] sus parques nacionales, sus ríos, lagos, playas, ciudades y zonas rurales, hacen de la República Dominicana un país que ofrece lugares de interés para cualquier[b] visitante. Uno de los destinos[c] turísticos más populares es Punta Cana, al este del país. Allí se puede disfrutar[d] de un clima tropical y de bellas[e] playas de arena[f] blanca y fina. Santo Domingo, la capital del país, tiene una hermosa zona colonial con museos, casas antiguas y otros monumentos históricos. En 1990, fue reconocida[g] como Patrimonio Cultural de la Humanidad[h] por la UNESCO.

¿Cuáles son las atracciones turísticas más populares de su estado/provincia?

[a]*forests* [b]*any* [c]*destinations* [d]*enjoy* [e]*beautiful* [f]*sand* [g]*recognized* [h]Patrimonio... *World Cultural Heritage site*

En la zona colonial de Santo Domingo

En otros países hispanos

- **En todo el mundo hispanohablante** En muchos países hispanos, y no solo en los países tropicales, hay playas maravillosas.[a] Por ejemplo, el Uruguay, la Argentina y Chile tienen costas fabulosas sin estar en el trópico.
- **En España** La industria del turismo es un importante motor[b] de la economía española. España es el cuarto[c] país del mundo receptor de turistas extranjeros, después de China, Francia y los Estados Unidos.
- **En los Estados Unidos** Probablemente nunca se le ha ocurrido[d] a Ud. hacer turismo en los Estados Unidos para saber de la historia del mundo hispano. Gran parte del actual[e] territorio estadounidense fue antes territorio español. Así que podría[f] visitar lugares históricos en la Florida, Texas, California, etcétera, para tener idea de la presencia histórica de la cultura hispana sin salir de este país.

[a]*wonderful* [b]*engine* [c]*fourth* [d]nunca... *it's never occurred to you* [e]*present-day* [f]*you could*

Tres símbolos dominicanos

- **El güiro** Este es un instrumento de origen africano que se usa en la música dominicana.
- **El casabe** Es un tipo de tortilla que se hace con la yuca.[a] Es un alimento[b] básico de la cocina dominicana. También era[c] uno de los alimentos de los taínos, los indígenas de la isla.
- **El colmado** Así se llama la tienda del barrio[d] en donde se vende de todo, desde comida preparada hasta herramientas.[e] Pero lo más importante es que es un lugar de encuentro[f] para la gente[g] del barrio.

[a]*manioc, cassava root* [b]*food* [c]*it was* [d]*neighborhood* [e]*tools* [f]lugar... *meeting point* [g]*people*

Una figura importante del período colonial

Fray Bartolomé de Las Casas (1484–1566) nació[a] en España, pero vivió muchos años en la isla de La Española. Trabajó toda su vida por crear leyes[b] para proteger[c] a los indígenas, no solo de La Española sino[d] también de todas las colonias españolas de la época.

[a]*was born* [b]por... *to create laws* [c]*protect* [d]*but*

COMPRENSIÓN

1. ¿Cuáles son dos lugares turísticos importantes en la República Dominicana? Punta Cana, Santo Domingo
2. ¿Qué país hispanohablante está muy alto en la lista de países receptores de turistas? España
3. ¿Por qué se puede decir que en los Estados Unidos es muy importante la presencia histórica de los países hispanos? Porque gran parte del actual territorio estadounidense fue antes territorio español.

- Neighborhood general stores similar to *el colmado* are traditional in most Hispanic countries.

Una figura importante...

Notes

- Fray Bartolomé de las Casas is the earliest and best known activist for the rights of the indigenous people, at a time when the existence of slavery as an institution was not questioned by most people.
- *Fray,* which in English is *friar,* refers to a male member of a religious community that is supported by donations or other charitable support.

(Cont.)

Del mundo hispano

Antes de leer

En un crucero, ¿qué condiciones son importantes para Ud.?
Para mí es importante…

- ☐ que el servicio sea (*be*) excelente.
- ☐ que el precio sea económico.
- ☐ que la comida sea deliciosa.
- ☐ que haga (*it make*) paradas en muchos puertos.
- ☐ que las bebidas sean gratis
- ☐ ¿ ?

Lectura: Un anuncio para un crucero

Comprensión

A. Los mejores cruceros. Estas oraciones resumen los ocho puntos del anuncio. Ordénelas del 1 al 8, según el anuncio. **¡OJO!** Una de las oraciones del resumen es extra.

- **a.** __5__ El precio es bueno y garantizado.
- **b.** __3__ Las personas que quieren beber más (o menos) pueden comprar ofertas especiales.
- **c.** __1__ El español es la lengua del crucero.
- **d.** __8__ Se visitan muchos destinos (*destinations*) en comparación con otras compañías.
- **e.** __6__ La calidad del servicio es excelente.
- **f.** ____ Hay piscinas y gimnasios a bordo.
- **g.** __2__ La comida es muy buena.
- **h.** __7__ No tiene que usar dinero en efectivo (*cash*) durante el viaje.
- **i.** __4__ Hay salidas de muchos puertos.

B. Estudio de marketing. ¿A qué tipo de turistas se dirige (*is aimed*) este anuncio de Iberocruceros? Estudie el contenido de los ocho puntos y también el uso de **tú, Ud.** o **Uds.** para imaginar a la persona que se interesa en este tipo de crucero.

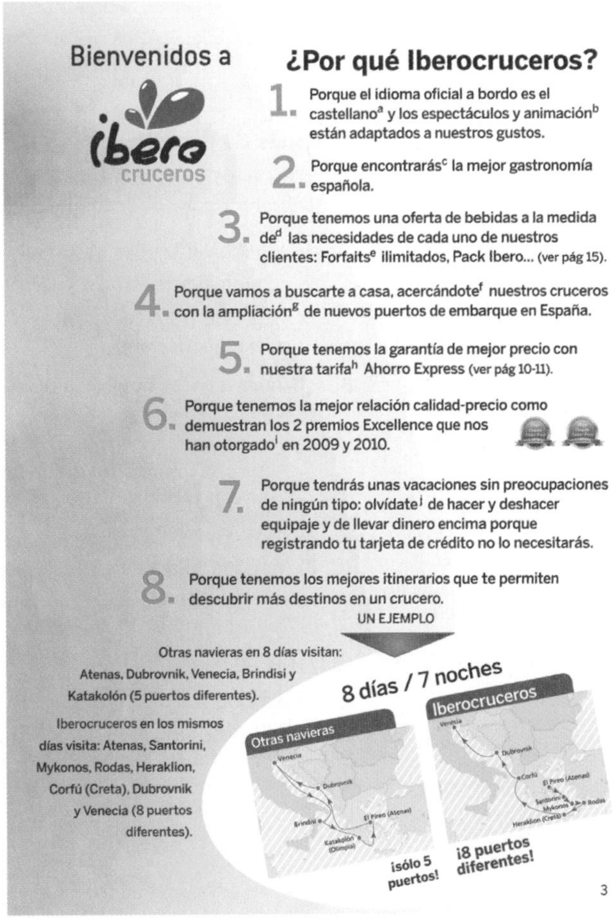
Bienvenidos a
ibero cruceros
¿Por qué Iberocruceros?
1. Porque el idioma oficial a bordo es el castellano[a] y los espectáculos y animación[b] están adaptados a nuestros gustos.
2. Porque encontrarás[c] la mejor gastronomía española.
3. Porque tenemos una oferta de bebidas a la medida de[d] las necesidades de cada uno de nuestros clientes: Forfaits[e] ilimitados, Pack Ibero… (ver pág 15).
4. Porque vamos a buscarte a casa, acercándote[f] nuestros cruceros con la ampliación[g] de nuevos puertos de embarque en España.
5. Porque tenemos la garantía de mejor precio con nuestra tarifa[h] Ahorro Express (ver pág 10-11).
6. Porque tenemos la mejor relación calidad-precio como demuestran los 2 premios Excellence que nos han otorgado[i] en 2009 y 2010.
7. Porque tendrás unas vacaciones sin preocupaciones de ningún tipo: olvídate[j] de hacer y deshacer equipaje y de llevar dinero encima porque registrando tu tarjeta de crédito no lo necesitarás.
8. Porque tenemos los mejores itinerarios que te permiten descubrir más destinos en un crucero.
UN EJEMPLO
Otras navieras en 8 días visitan: Atenas, Dubrovnik, Venecia, Brindisi y Katakolón (5 puertos diferentes).
Iberocruceros en los mismos días visita: Atenas, Santorini, Mykonos, Rodas, Heraklion, Corfú (Creta), Dubrovnik y Venecia (8 puertos diferentes).
8 días / 7 noches
Otras navieras
Iberocruceros
¡sólo 5 puertos!
¡8 puertos diferentes!
3

[a]español [b]actividades [c]*you will find* [d]a… *geared to* [e]*Passes* [f]*bringing closer to you* [g]*expansion* [h]*fare* [i]han… *they've given* [j]*forget*

Del mundo hispano

Note

See the IM for optional follow-up, writing, and Internet activities.

Antes de leer

Suggestions

- Tell students that the verb form used in the options (*sea[n]*, *haga*) is the subjunctive. If you introduced it in *Cap. 7*, students should recognize it. If you didn't, take the opportunity to talk about it briefly. However, since the forms are glossed, students should not have difficulty with the items.
- For the blank option, ask students, working in pairs, to come up with other desirable features of a cruise.

Estrategia: Scanning and Getting Clues from Format

Ask students to scan the ad to get a sense of its format. Then ask them to pick out the key words about each of the advantages the ad cites. This will help students complete the *Comprensión* activity more efficiently.

Comprensión

A: Suggestions

- If you did not assign this as homework, students can work on it in groups or pairs.
- After checking the items, discussion can center around the most and least attractive aspects of this company's offering. For example: Is it good to go with a company whose crew speaks your language? Why? What are the advantages of individualized drink packages (*Forfaits*)?

B: Suggestions

- Assign this activity in pairs or groups.
- Suggest to students that they first determine the mode of address (*tú*; not *Ud.*, which would be more formal, or *Uds.*, which would imply couples or families). Ask them to come up with potential characteristics point by point, then see what kind of person is described. For example, the first point implies that Iberocruceros travelers are Hispanic and that they probably don't speak English.

Una figura importante (Cont.)

- Two early Dominican freedom fighters from the first half of the 16th century are Enriquillo, a native *taíno* leader, and Sebastián Lemba, an African slave.
- The Mirabal sisters (Patria, Minerva, and María Teresa) are 20th century heroines who actively opposed the brutal Trujillo rule. They were assassinated on November 25, 1960, a date that has been chosen as *el Día Internacional de la No Violencia Contra la Mujer,* in their honor.

A escuchar
Antes de escuchar
Suggestion

Do this activity as a whole-class brainstorming activity. Students will most likely come up with all of the activities mentioned in the dialogue.

Escuche
Notes

- In this chapter students can listen to two friends discuss what they did yesterday and make plans for today. It is a good idea for students to take notes on the conversation. Tell them to write the names *Arturo* and *David* on a piece of paper and keep track of the details that are mentioned by each.
- See the IM for the Audioscript and more information about music in the Dominican Republic.

Después de escuchar
A: Follow-up

Ask students to return to the lists they made in *Antes de escuchar* to see how many of the activities they came up with were mentioned.

B: Follow-up

Ask students to predict what the four friends will do at the beach today.

¡Música!
Notes

- Juan Luis Guerra has won numerous awards, including Grammys and Latin Grammys. He is an accomplished musician, formally trained at the Berklee College of Music. He has collaborated with top artists from all over the world.
- See information in the IM about *el merengue* and *la bachata*.
- For helpful tips on using songs in the classroom, see the IM.

A ESCUCHAR

Antes de escuchar

Por lo general, ¿qué hace Ud. en su tiempo libre (*free time*)? ¿Qué actividades le gusta hacer cuando va a la playa? ¿y cuando va al centro de su ciudad?

Escuche

Las actividades de ayer y de hoy

Arturo y David hablan de lo que hicieron ayer y lo que van a hacer hoy. Escuche según las indicaciones de su profesor(a).

Vocabulario para escuchar

¡No me digas que… !	Don't tell me that . . . !	**¿De veras?**	Really?
apagado	turned off	**corriendo**	running (that is, in a hurry)

Después de escuchar

A. ¿Qué pasó ayer? Conteste las siguientes preguntas según la conversación telefónica para decir lo que hicieron ayer unos amigos dominicanos.

1. ¿Qué hicieron David y Paula?
2. ¿Qué hicieron Arturo y Cristina?
3. ¿Cuál de los cuatros amigos hizo la actividad más relajada (*relaxing*)?

B. ¿Qué va a pasar hoy? ¿Cierto o falso? Corrija las oraciones falsas.

	CIERTO	FALSO
1. Arturo y Cristina no quieren salir con David y Paula. Sí quieren salir con ellos.	☐	☑
2. Hace viento hoy.	☑	☐
3. Van a la playa en coche. Van en camioneta.	☐	☑
4. No van a llevar nada de comer. Van a llevar sándwiches y fruta.	☐	☑

Go to the iMix section in Connect Spanish (**www.connectspanish.com**) to access the iTunes playlist *"Puntos9,"* where you can purchase "Ojalá que llueva café" by Juan Luis Guerra.

¡Música!

Juan Luis Guerra (1957–) es uno de los cantantes dominicanos con mayor proyección[a] internacional. Se especializa en bachata y merengue, dos tipos de música dominicana. Su canción «Ojalá que[b] llueva café», del álbum del mismo[c] nombre, es famosa en todo el mundo.

[a]*fame, reach* [b]Ojalá… *I hope that* [c]*same*

Juan Luis Guerra, en Las Vegas, Nevada

A ESCRIBIR

El tema

Unas vacaciones memorables

¿Prefiere Ud. para sus vacaciones la playa? ¿las montañas? ¿las ciudades grandes? (En la Playa Cabarete, República Dominicana)

Preparar

Piense en las vacaciones más memorables de su vida. ¿Son memorables porque fueron buenas o porque fueron un desastre?

Paso 1. Haga una lista cronológica de todos los eventos y actividades que ocurrieron durante esas vacaciones.

Paso 2. Haga una lista de las cosas que más le gustaron y de las cosas que no le gustaron. ¿Por qué cree que esas vacaciones son memorables? Piense en la razón principal y explique cuál es.

Redactar

Desarrolle (*Develop*) el ensayo usando toda la información de **Preparar.** Antes de empezar, piense en el tono de su ensayo. ¿Es alegre, cómico, íntimo? El tono debe estar presente desde el principio del ensayo.

Editar

Revise el ensayo para comprobar (*to check*):

- la ortografía y los acentos (**¡OJO!** con las formas del pretérito)
- la organización de las ideas (una clara secuencia de acciones y buenas transiciones)
- la consistencia del tono
- el uso de los pronombres (evitar [*avoid*] el uso excesivo de pronombres personales; evitar la repetición innecesaria de los sustantivos con el uso de los pronombres de complemento directo)

Finalmente, prepare su versión final para entregarla.

A escribir

Note

The *A escribir* section in *Cap. 9* is very similar to the one in this chapter, with the difference of the topic (vacations vs. a special celebration). You may wish to treat the composition in this chapter as a trial run for the one in the next chapter, by doing peer-editing, or making general comments for improvement for the whole class to implement in the next chapter's composition.

Preparar

Suggestions

- **Paso 1.** Remind students to use the preterite to create the list of events.
- **Paso 2.** Since students do not yet know the imperfect, tell them to focus on the events themselves that they liked and didn't like, not on the underlying circumstances, reasons, or feelings.

Redactar

Suggestions

- Advise students to find a tone compatible with their memory. For instance, an ironic tone matches a vacation with some mishap that was not too serious (such as suitcases that got lost); a more intimate tone works better for a vacation with a special someone.
- Suggested length for this writing assignment: approximately 100 words
- Suggested structure: 2 paragraphs

  P. 1. Development of the list of activities that occurred during the vacation

  P. 2. Exploration of the things that the student liked or did not like about the vacation

Editar

Follow-up

Ask students to summarize what happened on their memorable vacation and what they liked best about it in a few sentences. Have students share their experiences with the class and have the class vote on the most memorable vacation.

En resumen: En este capítulo

Vocabulario

Suggestions

- Ask students the following questions.
  1. *¿Quién sirve la comida en el avión, el piloto o el asistente de vuelo?*
  2. *Si una persona toma el vuelo número 60, ¿viaja en tren o en avión?*
  3. *¿Hay camareros en los autobuses?*
- *¿Cierto o falso?*
  1. *Los pasajeros sirven las bebidas.*
  2. *Los asistentes de vuelo compran su propio* (new) *boleto para el viaje.*
  3. *El piloto lleva uniforme.*
  4. *Los pasajeros llevan uniforme.*
  5. *Hay un vuelo en tren de Philadelphia a Boston.*
  6. *Si Ud. no tiene mucho tiempo, debe comprar un boleto en avión.*
- Point out the parenthetical spelling changes noted for *entregar, explicar, ofrecer,* and *sacar.* Ask students to tell you what they represent.

Word Families

En este capítulo

- *el autobús, la estación de autobuses*
- *el avión, volar en avión, el vuelo, el/la asistente de vuelo*
- *de vacaciones, estar de vacaciones, ir de vacaciones, pasar las vacaciones, salir de vacaciones*
- *de viaje, viajar*
- *fumar, la sala de fumar*
- *gustar, me gustaría*
- *la maleta, hacer las maletas, el maletero*
- *el pasaje, el pasajero*
- *la puerta de embarque, la tarjeta de embarque*
- *el tren, la estación de trenes*

Entre capítulos

- *el asiento* = *sentarse* (5)
- *bajarse* = *bajo/a* (3), *debajo de* (6)
- *de viaje* and related travel words = *hacer un viaje* (5)
- *encantar* = *encantado/a* (1)
- *gustar, me gustaría* = *me/te/le gusta* (1), *mucho gusto* (1), *los gustos* (1)
- *ida* = *ir* (4)
- *Ir al extranjero* = *extranjero/a* (2)
- *la llegada* = *llegar* (2)
- *el mar* = *los mariscos* (7)
- *muchísimo* = *mucho* (2)
- *el pasaporte, pasar por el control de la seguridad* = *pasar* (6)
- *la puerta de embarque* = *la puerta* (2)
- *preguntar* = *la pregunta* (5)
- *regalar* = *el regalo* (3)

EN RESUMEN En este capítulo

Gramática en breve

21. Indirect Object Pronouns; *Dar* and *decir*

me, te, le, nos, os, les

dar: doy, das, da, damos, dais, dan
decir: digo, dices, dice, decimos, decís, dicen

22. *Gustar*

(no) *indirect object pronoun* + **gusta** + *singular subject*
(no) *indirect object pronoun* + **gustan** + *plural subject*

Would like: **gustaría(n)**

23. Preterite of Regular Verbs and of *dar, hacer, ir,* and *ser*

-ar Verbs: **-é, -aste, -ó, -amos, -asteis, -aron**
-er/-ir Verbs: **-í, -iste, -ió, -imos, -steis, -ieron**

dar: di diste, dio, dimos, disteis, dieron
hacer: hice, hiciste, hizo, hicimos, hicisteis, hicieron
ir/ser: fui, fuiste, fue, fuimos, fuisteis, fueron

Vocabulario

Los verbos

contar (cuento)	to tell, narrate
dar (doy)	to give
decir (digo)	to say; to tell
encantar (*like* **gustar**)	to like very much, love
entregar (gu)	to hand in
explicar (qu)	to explain
gustar	to be pleasing
interesar (*like* **gustar**)	to interest (*someone*)
mostrar (muestro)	to show
odiar	to hate
ofrecer (ofrezco)	to offer
preguntar	to ask (*a question*)
prestar	to lend
prometer	to promise
recomendar (recomiendo)	to recommend
regalar	to give (*as a gift*)

Repaso: escribir, hablar, mandar, pedir (pido) (i), servir (sirvo) (i)

De viaje

de viaje	on a trip, traveling
la aduana	customs (*at a border*)
el aeropuerto	airport
el asiento	seat
el/la asistente de vuelo	flight attendant
el autobús	bus
el avión	airplane
el barco	boat, ship
el billete (*Sp.*) / **el boleto** (*L.A.*)	ticket
de ida	one-way ticket
de ida y vuelta	round-trip ticket
electrónico	e-ticket
la cabina	cabin (*on a ship*)
la cola	line (*of people*)
el control de seguridad	security (check)
el crucero	cruise (ship)
la demora	delay
el equipaje	baggage, luggage
la escala	stop
la estación	station
de autobuses	bus station
de trenes	train station
la llegada	arrival
la maleta	suitcase
el maletero	porter
el medio de transporte	means of transportation
la parada	stop
el pasaje	fare, price (*of a transportation ticket*)
el/la pasajero/a	passenger
el pasaporte	passport
el pasillo	aisle
el/la piloto	pilot
la puerta de embarque	boarding gate
el puerto	port
el puesto	place (*in line*)
la sala de espera	waiting room
la sala de fumar/fumadores	smoking area
la salida	departure
la tarjeta (postal)	(post)card
la tarjeta de embarque	boarding pass
el tren	train
la ventanilla	small window (*on a plane*)
el vuelo	flight

Repaso: el viaje

Heritage Speakers

Hay varias maneras de expresar *flight attendant* según el dialecto del español que se hable. Algunos sinónimos de *el/la asistente de vuelo* son *la azafata, el/la auxiliar de vuelo, el/la aeromozo/a* y *el/la cabinero/a.* En algunos dialectos de Chile se dice *hostess.* Pregúnteles a los hispanohablantes cómo se dice *el/la asistente de vuelo* en su dialecto. ¿Hay alguien en la clase que use la palabra *sobrecargo* para expresar *flight attendant*?

anunciar	to announce
bajarse (de)	to get down (from); to get off (of) (*a vehicle*)
facturar el equipaje	to check baggage
fumar	to smoke
guardar (un puesto)	to save (a place [*in line*])
hacer cola	to stand in line
hacer escalas/paradas	to make stops
hacer la(s) maleta(s)	to pack one's suitcase(s)
ir al extranjero	to go abroad
ir en...	to go/travel by . . .
autobús	bus
avión	plane
barco	boat, ship
tren	train
pasar por el control de seguridad / la aduana	to go/pass through security (check) / customs
quejarse (de)	to complain (about)
subir (a)	to go up; to get on (*a vehicle*)
viajar	to travel
volar (vuelo) en avión	to fly, go by plane

Repaso: hacer un viaje, llegar (gu), salir

De vacaciones

de vacaciones	on vacation
la camioneta	station wagon; van
el *camping*	campground
la foto(grafía)	photo(graph)
el mar	sea
la montaña	mountain
el océano	ocean
la tienda (de campaña)	tent

Repaso: la playa, el sol

estar de vacaciones	to be on vacation
hacer *camping*	to go camping
ir de vacaciones a...	to go on vacation to/in . . .
nadar	to swim
pasar las vacaciones en...	to spend one's vacation in . . .
sacar (qu) fotos	to take photos
salir de vacaciones	to leave on vacation
tomar el sol	to sunbathe
tomar unas vacaciones	to take a vacation

Otros sustantivos

el chiste	joke
la flor	flower

Los adjetivos

atrasado/a (*with* **estar**)	late
juntos/as	together

Palabras adicionales

a tiempo	on time
me gustaría (mucho)...	I would (really) like . . .
muchísimo	an awful lot
(para) nada	at all
por	through; for

Vocabulario personal

- *la sala de espera* = *esperar* (7)
- *la sala de espera, la sala de fumar* = *la sala* (5)
- *la salida* = *salir* (5)
- *la tarjeta postal, la tarjeta de embarque* = *la tarjeta de crédito* (7)
- *tomar el sol* = *hace sol* (6), *tomar* (2)
- *la ventanilla* = *la ventana* (2)
- *vuelta* = *volver* (5)

¡OJO!

- *el/la asistente* ≠ *asistir* (3)
- *el medio* ≠ *las medias* (4)
- *nadar* ≠ *nada* (7)
- *el puerto* ≠ *la puerta* (2)
- *la tienda (de campaña)* ≠ *la tienda* (4)

Suggestion

Show students an image of a scene that includes vocabulary items. Put the image away and have students write as many sentences as possible describing the scene. They should use words from *Vocabulario*. Have students read or write their sentences on the board in order to compare descriptions.

Chapter Opening Photo and Chapter Theme

Chapter Theme–Related Questions

Suggestions

- Ask students the following questions to introduce the chapter topic.
  1. *¿Pasa Ud. los días festivos con su familia, con sus amigos o solo/a?*
  2. *¿Cuál es su día festivo favorito? ¿Cuál es el día festivo que menos le gusta?*
  3. *¿Hace Ud. algo especial el día de su cumpleaños? ¿Qué hace?*
  4. *¿Se celebra en su casa algún día festivo de otro país? ¿Cuál es? ¿Cómo se celebra?*
  5. *¿Conoce Ud. alguna fiesta de otra cultura? ¿Qué le gusta de esa fiesta? ¿En qué se parece* (new) *a las fiestas que Ud. celebra?*
- Give students the names of holidays that they would like to describe or discuss.
- Ask students: *¿Recuerda en qué año celebró su mejor cumpleaños? ¿y el peor?*

Reciclado: Review the months of the year by asking in what month various holidays are celebrated in this country. The names of many holidays or special days are cognates. Examples: *el Día de la Madre, el Día del Padre, el Día de San Valentín, el Día de la Independencia.*

9 Los días festivos°

°Los… *Holidays*

Una mujer vestida con traje tradicional durante una celebración cubana

- En este país, ¿hay más días festivos de carácter religioso o de carácter civil? ¿Cuáles son los días festivos más importantes para Ud. y su familia?
- ¿Cree Ud. que las grandes celebraciones nacionales en los países hispanohablantes son motivados por fiestas religiosas o por fiestas civiles?
- En su familia, ¿es muy importante celebrar los cumpleaños? ¿Los celebran con grandes comidas familiares? ¿Cuál fue el último cumpleaños que celebraron?

connect SPANISH

www.connectspanish.com

Resources

For Students

- Connect Spanish (**www.connectspanish.com**), which contains all content from the following resources, as well as the *Mundo interactivo* scenarios, the LearnSmart adaptive learning system, and more!
- **Physical Resources:** Workbook / Laboratory Manual, Laboratory Audio Program, DVD

For Instructors

- Connect Spanish (**www.connectspanish.com**), which contains access to all student sections of Connect Spanish, as well as helpful time-saving tools and resources such as an integrated gradebook, Instructor's Manual, Testing Program, digital transparencies, Audioscript, Videoscript, and more!

Cuba

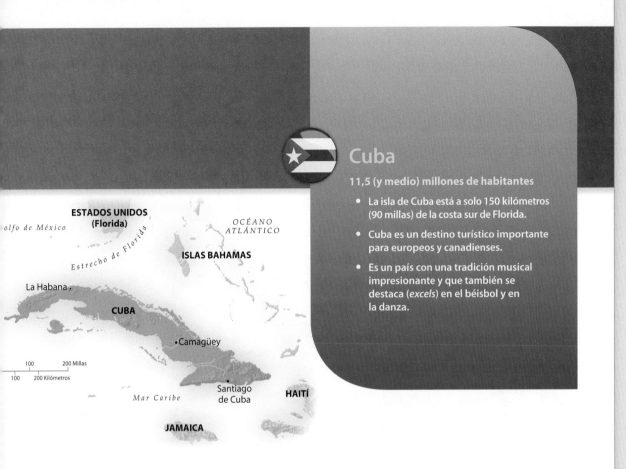

11,5 (y medio) millones de habitantes

- La isla de Cuba está a solo 150 kilómetros (90 millas) de la costa sur de Florida.
- Cuba es un destino turístico importante para europeos y canadienses.
- Es un país con una tradición musical impresionante y que también se destaca (*excels*) en el béisbol y en la danza.

En este capítulo

Cuba

Datos esenciales

Nombre oficial: *República de Cuba*
Lema: *«Patria y libertad»*
Capital: *La Habana*
Otras ciudades: *Santiago, Camagüey, Holguín, Matanzas*
Composición étnica: *65% blancos, 25% mulatos, 10% negros*
Jefe de estado actual: *Raúl Castro Ruiz, desde 2008*
Forma de gobierno: *Estado socialista o democracia popular*
Lengua oficial: *el español*
Moneda: *el peso cubano*
Religión: *mayoría católica; presencia de otras religiones, en particular, de la santería (un rito de origen africano). Durante el régimen de Fidel Castro (hermano de Raúl), había restricciones en cuanto a las prácticas religiosas. Ahora hay una actitud más flexible a este respecto.*

Point Out

- Cuba gained its independence from Spain during the Spanish-American War of 1898.
- Fidel Castro and Ernesto "Che" Guevara were the leaders of the socialist revolution that overturned the rule of Cuban dictator Fulgencio Batista in 1959.
- One result of the revolution was the emigration of many Cubans to the United States (and other countries). Many of them established themselves in the south Florida area, where many second- and third-generation Cuban Americans live now.
- The United States does not maintain diplomatic relations with Cuba, and travel to the island is prohibited to U.S. citizens. In addition, the United States imposed a commercial, financial, and economic embargo against Cuba in 1960, which has since been strengthened and is still in effect.

Suggestion

Have students list their ideas about Cuba, including information on geography, politics, economy, culture, music, and cuisine. When you finish the chapter, return to the lists and ask students what ideas they would change and/or add. The success of this activity will depend not only on the content about Cuba presented in the text but also on the extent to which you have time to supplement that content with your own knowledge and experiences and also with information given in this Instructor's Edition and the IM.

Heritage Speakers

Pídales a los hispanohablantes que comenten alguna costumbre hispana típica de un día festivo. Pregúnteles si su familia celebra días festivos que no celebran los anglosajones. ¿Cuáles son y en qué se diferencian de los días festivos que celebran sus amigos anglosajones?

Multimedia

The IM provides suggestions for using multimedia materials in the classroom.

Resources: Transparency 99

Vocabulario: Preparación
Una fiesta de cumpleaños para Javier

Notes

- See the model for vocabulary presentation and other material in the *Cap. 9 Vocabulario: Preparación* section of "Chapter-by-Chapter Supplementary Materials" in the IM.
- Much of the vocabulary in this section is review. The vocabulary load is purposefully light, since the vocabulary in the next section (*Las emociones…*) is challenging and the grammar sections in the chapter are typically perceived by students to be challenging. Note that some additional vocabulary is made active in *Vocabulario útil* (p. 267).

Suggestions

- Model vocabulary in short sentences and questions, e.g.: *Cuando hago una fiesta en mi casa, siempre sirvo botanas/tapas y refrescos. ¿Qué botanas le gustan a Ud.? ¿Hay fiestas en las que Ud. se divierta más? ¿En cuáles?*
- Ask: *De tus amigos, ¿quién…*
  1. *falta a clase con frecuencia?*
  2. *nunca falta a clase?*
  3. *nunca se divierte?*
  4. *siempre lo pasa bien?*
- Emphasize the use of *dar* and *hacer* to express *to give/have a party*. Students' tendency will be to say *tener una fiesta,* which does not express the act of throwing a party but rather the idea of having someone throw one for you.
- Emphasize the different ways to express *to have a good time: divertirse, pasarlo bien.* Some heritage speakers will say *tener un buen tiempo.* Stress saying that *tener un buen tiempo* does not communicate the concept clearly to most native speakers of Spanish.
- Emphasize *ser en* = to take place, vs. *estar en* = to be in a place (location).
- There are many versions of the "Happy Birthday to You" song in Spanish. (One version is: *"¡Cumpleaños feliz! Te deseamos a ti que los cumplas en tu día, que los cumplas feliz."*) Present the version you are familiar with and encourage students to sing it to a classmate who is having a birthday soon or who has just had one.

Pronunciación: See Pronunciation Notes, IM.

VOCABULARIO **Preparación**

Una fiesta de cumpleaños para Javier

Para comer y beber

las botanas (*Mex.*) / **las tapas**	appetizers

Otros sustantivos

el anfitrión / la anfitriona	host (*of an event*)
el día festivo	holiday
el/la invitado/a	guest

Los verbos

celebrar	to celebrate
cumplir años	to have a birthday
darle una fiesta (a alguien)	to give (*someone*) party
faltar (a)	to be absent (from), not attend
gastar	to spend (*money*)
hacerle una fiesta (a alguien)	to have a party (for someone)
invitar	to invite
pasarlo bien/mal	to have a good/bad time
regalar	to give (*as a gift*)
reunirse (me reúno) con*	to get together (with)
ser + en + *place*	to be, occur in/at (*a place*)
¿Dónde es la fiesta?	Where is the party (at)?

Repaso: divertirse (me divierto) (i)

Palabras adicionales

¡Felicitaciones!	Congratulations!
gracias por + *noun*	thanks for + *noun*
Gracias por el regalo.	Thanks for the present.
gracias por + *inf.*	thanks for + *verb* (*-ing*)
Gracias por invitarme.	Thanks for inviting me.

¡OJO!
Remember that a preposition is followed by an infinitive in Spanish.

*Note the accent that occurs on **-u-** in forms of **reunirse** when the syllable is stressed: **me reúno, te reúnes, se reúne, nos reunimos, os reunís, se reúnen.** This pattern is like that of stem-changing verbs (that is, the stem vowel changes when it is stressed.)*

Culture

Holidays vary widely from one country to another in the Hispanic world, sometimes even from region to region. Here are some popular Hispanic holidays.

- ***La Misa de Aguinaldo*** (Christmas bonus) is celebrated in Mexico, San Salvador, and in some states in the United States with a high percentage of Mexicans. This holiday is celebrated during the *novena* (nine days before Christmas Eve).

Resources: Transparency 100

Vocabulario útil

Los días festivos hispanos

¡OJO!
Only the highlighted items in this list are active vocabulary.

Durante una «parranda» (*big party*), en el pueblo de Remedios, Cuba

el Día de los Reyes Magos	Day of the Magi (Three Kings) / Epiphany (Jan. 6)	**el Janucá**	Hanukkah
la Pascua	Easter	**la Nochebuena**	Christmas Eve
la Pascua judía	Passover	**la Navidad**	Christmas
la Semana Santa	Holy Week	**la Nochevieja**	New Year's Eve
el Día de la Raza	Columbus Day / Hispanic Awareness Day in some parts of the U.S. (Oct. 12)	**el día del santo**	saint's day (*the saint for whom one is named*)
el Día de los Muertos	Day of the Dead (Nov. 2)	**la quinceañera**	*young woman's fifteenth birthday party*

Los días festivos en los Estados Unidos y el Canadá: el Día de San Patricio, el Cinco de Mayo, el Día del Canadá, el Cuatro de Julio, el Día de Acción de Gracias

Así se dice

hacer una fiesta = hacer un juerga (*Sp.*), armar (un) bochinche (*Cuba*)
la quinceañera = la fiesta de quince años
el pastel = la torta, la tarta, el queque (*L.A.*)

la Pascua = la Pascua Florida
el Día de los Muertos = el Día de los Difuntos
la Navidad = las Pascuas

The figure of **Santa Claus** is a familiar one in Hispanic countries. That is what he is called in Mexico and Puerto Rico. In other parts of the Spanish-speaking world, he is more often called **Papá Noel.**

Conversación

A. Una fiesta de cumpleaños para Javier. Conteste las siguientes preguntas sobre el dibujo de la página 266.

1. ¿Qué tipo de fiesta es? ¿Dónde es la fiesta?
2. ¿Quiénes son los anfitriones de la fiesta? ¿Quién es el invitado de honor?
3. ¿Qué hay de comer y de beber? ¿Qué hacen los invitados?
4. ¿Qué le dan los invitados a Javier, además de (*besides*) regalos?
5. ¿Quién falta a la fiesta? ¿Quién lo invita por teléfono?
6. ¿Qué le van a decir todos a Javier cuando corta el pastel?
7. ¿Qué cree Ud. que Javier les va a decir a Carmen y Pedro después de la fiesta?

B. Asociaciones. ¿Qué palabras asocia Ud. con las siguientes ideas? Dé por lo menos dos palabras asociadas con cada idea.

1. un cumpleaños
2. una fiesta
3. los fuegos artificiales (*fireworks*)
4. un árbol (*tree*)
5. los regalos
6. una comida grande

Con. A: Possible Answers: **1.** *Es una fiesta de cumpleaños. Es en casa de Carmen y Pedro.* **2.** *Carmen y Pedro son los anfitriones. Javier es el invitado de honor.* **3.** *Hay botanas/tapas, un pastel de cumpleaños, refrescos, vino y champán. Los invitados hablan, comen y bailan. Se divierten mucho.* **4.** *Los invitados le dan tarjetas.* **5.** *Jorge falta a la fiesta. Lo invita por teléfono Maricela.* **6.** *Todos le van a decir: «¡Felicitaciones!»* **7.** *Les va a decir: «Gracias por la fiesta».*

Con. B: Possible Answers: **1.** *cumplir años, un pastel, una fiesta, unas velas* **2.** *un cumpleaños, el anfitrión, los invitados, ser en* **3.** *el Día de la Independencia, una barbacoa* **4.** *la Navidad, los regalos, el Papá Noel* **5.** *la Navidad, el Papá Noel, un día festivo, un cumpleaños* **6.** *la Navidad, el Día de Acción de Gracias, la Pascua (judía)*

Vocabulario útil

Note

Photo: Upon the arrival of socialism in Cuba, *Nochebuena* and other Christmas celebrations were substituted by *"Las parrandas,"* during which revelers enjoy fireworks and parades until the wee hours of the morning.

Suggestions

- Emphasize to students that only the yellow-highlighted words are in the end-of-chapter *Vocabulario*. Provide vocabulary for important holidays that students need and that are not listed here.
- Use a calendar and present the holidays month-by-month. Explain holidays of importance to Hispanics. If you know when your saint's day is, point it out and explain its relevance.
- Optional vocabulary: *el Día de la Madre* (*de las Madres*), *el Día del Padre* (*de los Padres*), */ el Día de San Valentín, el Viernes Santo, judío/a, musulmán/musulmana.*
- Not all students will be familiar with or understand the significance of religious holidays associated with the Catholic tradition, many of which are listed here because of their importance in Hispanic cultures. You may wish to discuss those holidays briefly.
- Point out that there are variations of names for some holidays. *La Nochebuena* is often written as *la Noche Buena*, and *la Nochevieja* as *la Noche Vieja*. Although *Navidad* is the word for *Christmas*, you can express *Merry Christmas* as *¡Felices Pascuas!* or *¡Feliz Navidad! Pascua* is used in the singular and plural, and the expression *Felices Pascuas* can express *Happy Holidays* in a sense that includes other religious holidays. Point out the difference between the U.S. secular holiday Halloween and the religious holiday *el Día de los Muertos* (November 2). Tell students that *el Cinco de Mayo* is celebrated primarily in this country, and that is it *not* Mexican Independence Day.

Reciclado: Review months and seasons by asking questions such as: *¿Qué día festivo se celebra en febrero? ¿en octubre? ¿en invierno?*

Redacción: Ask students to write a paragraph describing *Una fiesta de cumpleaños para Javier,* following the lead of the questions in *Con. A* and adding additional details.

Con. B: Note

Active vocabulary: *el árbol*

Culture (*continued*)

- ***La Gritería*** is a celebration that occurs in Nicaragua and Colombia on December 7th, the day the Roman Catholic Church recognizes as the eve of the Immaculate Conception of the Virgin Mary, who was the mother of Christ. The word *gritería* refers to the shouting from door to door of *¿Qué causa tanta alegría? ¡La Concepción de María!*
- ***El Velorio*** (Gathering) ***de Reyes*** is a tradition among rural people of the west coast of Puerto Rico. It is usually sponsored by a family that wishes to thank the Magi for a special blessing they have received. An altar is set up in the home on the night of the 5th of January and decorated with flowers and three boughs. Neighbors visit and a trained singer makes up impromptu *décimas* (very formal poems).

Con. C: Note

Active vocabulary: *por lo menos*

Con. C: Extension

6. *el día en que se celebra el nacimiento* (new) *de Jesús* (*la Navidad*)
7. *la noche en que se celebra el fin del año* (*la Nochevieja*)
8. *la semana antes de la Pascua* (*la Semana Santa*)

Con. D: Follow-up

Paso 2

Have students describe the holidays in brief paragraphs. Then have them read their paragraphs to the class without identifying the holiday.

Redacción: Assign *Paso 3* of *Con. D* as a written homework assignment. Read selected paragraphs aloud in class, omitting the name of the invented holiday. Ask the class to guess the new holiday and also who wrote the paragraph.

Nota cultural

Suggestion

Not all Hispanics are Christians, and not all countries celebrate the same things in the same way. Moreover, Hispanics in this country may have lost or adapted some of their traditions.

Comprensión

1. *¿Cuáles son las fiestas religiosas mencionadas?* (*la Nochebuena, el Día de los Reyes Magos*)
2. *En España, ¿quién(es) les trae(n) regalos de Navidad a los niños?* (*los Reyes Magos*)
3. *¿Qué fiesta marca una transición en la vida de las muchachas?* (*la quinceañera*)

Las emociones y los estados afectivos

Suggestions

- Optional vocabulary: *enojado/a, llegar a ser, hacerse, acordarse de.*
- *To become* can also be expressed with reflexive forms: *alegrarse, enojarse, enrojecerse, entristecerse,* and so on.
- Contrast the following: *olvidar, olvidarse de, recordar.*

Vocabulario útil

el fin end
el nacimiento birth

Con. C: Possible Answers
1. *las botanas/tapas* 2. *el Día de los Muertos* 3. *la quinceañera* 4. *¡Felicitaciones!* 5. *la Pascua judía, el Janucá*

C. Definiciones

Paso 1. Dé las palabras definidas.

1. Algo de comer o beber que se sirve en las fiestas.
2. El día en que, por tradición, algunas personas visitan los cementerios.
3. La fiesta de una muchacha que cumple 15 años.
4. Lo que se le dice a un amigo que celebra algo.
5. Una fiesta de los judíos (*Jewish people*) que dura 8 días.

Paso 2. Ahora cree (*create*) por lo menos (*at least*) dos definiciones como las del **Paso 1.** La clase va a adivinar (*guess*) la palabra definida.

Nota cultural

Los días festivos importantes del mundo hispano

Algunas fiestas se celebran en casi todos los países hispanos.

- **La Nochebuena** En esta fiesta los hispanos cristianos siguen principalmente sus tradiciones religiosas. Celebran la víspera[a] de la Navidad con una gran cena. Muchas familias van a la Misa del Gallo,[b] un servicio religioso que se celebra a medianoche. En algunos países, los niños reciben la visita de Papá Noel, quien les deja regalos.
- **La Nochevieja** Es una ocasión para grandes celebraciones, tanto entre familia como en lugares públicos. En España y otros países algunos siguen la tradición de comer una uva[c] por cada una de las doce campanadas[d] de medianoche.
- **El Día de los Reyes Magos** En España y otros países, se celebra el 6 de enero como el día de los Reyes Magos. Ellos son los encargados[e] de traer regalos. Muchos niños ponen sus zapatos en la ventana o balcón antes de acostarse la noche del 5 de enero. Los Reyes llegan en camellos durante la noche y llenan los zapatos con regalos y dulces.
- **El Día de la Independencia** Todos los países latinoamericanos celebran el día de la declaración de su independencia de España. Por ejemplo, Cuba celebra su independencia el 10 de octubre; México, el 16 de septiembre; Bolivia, el 6 de agosto; el Paraguay, el 15 de mayo y El Salvador, el 15 de septiembre.

Unos bailarines (*dancers*) durante las celebraciones del Día de los Reyes Magos, en La Habana, Cuba

- **La quinceañera** Esta fiesta, celebrada en muchos países latinoamericanos y en este país, celebra la llegada de las niñas a los 15 años, es decir, su transición de niña a mujer. La familia y los amigos de la joven le dan una gran fiesta, en la que[f] ella se viste de largo.[g] A veces se celebra una misa especial, pero siempre hay una cena y una fiesta con música para bailar.

¿Cuáles de estas fiestas se celebran en su familia? Si no se celebra ninguna de ellas, ¿cuáles son las fiestas familiares de más importancia para Ud.?

[a]eve [b]Misa... *Midnight Mass* [c]grape [d]bell strokes [e]los... *in charge* [f]la... *which* [g]se... *dresses up (in a gown)*

D. Hablando de fiestas

Paso 1. ¿Cuáles de estas fiestas le gustan a Ud.? ¿Cuáles no le gustan? Explique por qué. Compare sus respuestas con las (*those*) de sus compañeros de clase. ¿Tienen los mismos gustos?

MODELO: el Cuatro de Julio → Me gusta mucho el Cuatro de Julio porque vemos fuegos artificiales en el parque y...

1. el Cuatro de Julio
2. el Día de Acción de Gracias
3. la Nochevieja
4. la Navidad

Paso 2. Ahora piense en su fiesta favorita. Puede ser una de la lista del **Paso 1** o una del **Vocabulario útil** de la página 267. Piense en cómo celebra Ud. esa fiesta, para explicárselo (*explain it*) luego a la clase. Debe pensar en lo siguiente.

- los preparativos que Ud. hace de antemano (*beforehand*)
- la ropa especial que lleva
- las comidas o bebidas especiales que compra o hace

Vocabulario útil

el árbol	tree
la corona	wreath
el desfile	parade
la fiesta del barrio	neighborhood (block) party
los fuegos artificiales	fireworks
el globo	balloon

NATIONAL STANDARDS: Comparisons

- *La quinceañera* is not celebrated in Spain.
- In more traditional Mexican families, the girl celebrating her *quinceañera* is serenaded by a *mariachi* band in front of her house the night before her 15th birthday. The next day, the girl has a party at her house. The men and boys take turns dancing with the girl. The first dance is traditionally a waltz that she dances with her father.

(Cont.)

- el lugar donde se celebra
- los adornos especiales que hay o que Ud. pone

Paso 3. ¿Hay algún día festivo que debe existir, según Uds., pero que no existe? En grupos, inventen por lo menos dos días festivos: **el Día de...** Presenten sus días festivos originales a la clase y explíquenles a sus compañeros cómo se deben celebrar.

Las emociones y los estados afectivos°

estados... *emotional states*

reír(se)* ([me] río) (i) (de) | **sonreír(se)* ([me] sonrío) (i)** | **llorar** | **enojarse (con)** | **enfermarse**

discutir (con/sobre)	to argue (with/about)	**sentirse (me siento) (i)**	to feel (*an emotion*)
olvidar(se) (de)	to forget (about)	**ponerse** + *adj.*	to become, get + *adj.*
portarse bien/mal	to (mis)behave	**alegre, contento/a, feliz** (*pl.* **felices**) (*happy*), **rojo/a, triste...**	
quejarse (de)	to complain (about)		
recordar (recuerdo)	to remember		

Conversación

A. ¿Cuándo... ?

Paso 1. ¿En qué ocasiones o situaciones es posible sentir las siguientes emociones o tener estas reacciones? En parejas, completen las oraciones, según su experiencia.

MODELOS: Me quejo en (*lugar*) / cuando... (*acción*) →
E1: Me quejo en **el aeropuerto** cuando **hago cola.**
E2: Yo también, y también me quejo en **una tienda** cuando **un dependiente no me atiende.**

1. Me quejo en / cuando...
2. Me río mucho en / cuando...
3. Sonrío en / cuando...
4. Lloro en / cuando...
5. Mis padres/hijos se enojan en / cuando... (Mi esposo/a / novio/a se enoja en / cuando...)
6. Los niños se portan bien/mal en / cuando...
7. Las mascotas se portan bien/mal en / cuando...
8. Nos enfermamos en / cuando...

Paso 2. Ahora comparen sus respuestas con las (*those*) del resto de la clase. ¿En qué son similares o diferentes las respuestas de todos?

The verbs* **reír (*to laugh*) *and* **sonreír** (*to smile*) *are* **e → i** *stem-changing verbs. Due to the double vowels, accents are required on all present tense forms of these verbs, but not on their present participles:* **(son)río, (son)ríes, (son)ríe, (son)reímos, (son)reís, (son)ríen,** *but:* **(son)riendo.**

Con.: Follow-up

Ask Students:

1. *¿Se ríe Ud. con frecuencia? ¿fácilmente? ¿Sonríe fácilmente? ¿Sonríe cuando está nervioso/a? ¿Cuándo no debemos sonreír?*
2. *¿Cuál fue la última vez en que Ud. se sintió muy feliz? ¿Qué pasó ese día?*
3. *¿Llora Ud. mucho? ¿Quiénes lloran más, los niños o los adultos? ¿las mujeres o los hombres? Cuando alguien llora, ¿qué indica?*
4. *¿Se enoja Ud. fácilmente? ¿Discute con frecuencia con alguien?*
5. *¿Cuándo se pone Ud. nervioso/a? ¿Durante un examen? ¿cuando habla español? ¿durante una entrevista?*
6. *¿Tiene Ud. hoy todas las cosas necesarias para la clase? ¿Se olvidó de traer algo? ¿Se olvidó alguna vez de tener un examen?*
7. *¿Recuerda Ud. fácilmente los nombres? ¿los números? ¿los números de teléfono? ¿el vocabulario nuevo?*

Heritage Speakers

Pídales a los hispanohablantes que describan la manera en que su familia celebra las fiestas tradicionales de su país de origen. Pregúnteles, por ejemplo, cómo celebran la Nochebuena, qué caracteriza el Día de los Reyes Magos, adónde van con sus parientes el Día de los Muertos. Si la fiesta se suele celebrar de un modo parecido al de este país (como, por ejemplo, la Navidad), pregúnteles qué opinan con respecto a las diferencias que hay en la celebración de esta fiesta entre una cultura y la otra. Pregúnteles, por ejemplo: *¿Opinan Uds. que la Navidad se celebra con más religiosidad entre los hispanos? ¿En cuál de las celebraciones tiene más influencia el comercio? ¿Qué hacen los latinoamericanos el Domingo de Pascua? ¿Se celebra la Fiesta de las Luces de la misma manera en su país?*

NATIONAL STANDARDS: (Cont.)

- In Puerto Rico, the elaborate celebration, called a *debut,* is often a matter of social or economic standing. For a middle- or upper-class teenager it's held in a hall and several hundred friends and relatives may attend.
- Have students compare the *quinceañera* celebration with the concept of the "sweet sixteen" birthday.

Resources: Transparency 101

Nota comunicativa

Suggestions

- Emphasize the change in stress and written accent in *fácil* ⟶ *facilísimo* and *difícil* ⟶ *dificilísimo*.
- Emphasize and model the spelling changes: *c* ⟶ *qu*, *g* ⟶ *gu*, *z* ⟶ *c*. Ask students where they have seen these changes before (preterite, formal commands).
- Some Spanish speakers also use *re-*, *requete-*, and *super-* to add the idea of extremely (very, exceptionally) to the quality, e.g., *rebueno, requetebueno, superbueno.*

Optional

1. *¿Es Ud. perezosísimo/a?*
2. *¿Hay una persona riquísima en su familia? ¿Quién es? ¿Hay una persona altísima? ¿interesantísima? ¿simpatiquísima?*

Bright Idea

Suggestion

Give students sentences with *muy, muy* and have them reword the sentences using *-ísimo* endings. For example: *Lupe está muy, muy contenta porque va a una fiesta de Nochevieja.* ⟶ *Lupe está contentísima porque va a una fiesta de Nochevieja.*

Con. B: Suggestion

Call students' attention to *avergonzado/a* (in *Vocabulario útil*) and model its pronunciation. Then tell students that the word *embarazado/a* (which they tend to try to use to mean *embarrassed*) is a false cognate.

Con. B: Note

Active vocabulary: *avergonzado/a*

Con. B: Extension

9. *Es su cumpleaños. Nadie le regaló nada.*
10. *En un examen de química, Ud. no puede recordar una fórmula.*
11. *Un amigo tiene un problema muy grave.*
12. *Ud. le pide a alguien que no fume, pero la persona sigue fumando.*

Con. C: Suggestions

- You can tally the responses quickly by counting the number of students in the class, then asking for a show of hands for *cierto*. Subtract that number from the total number of students to get the *falso* responses.
- Have students write down a description of a negative aspect of a holiday, for them in particular or for others.

Nota **comunicativa**

Cómo enfatizar: *-ísimo/a*

To emphasize the quality described by an adjective or an adverb, add **-ísimo/a/os/as** to an adjective and **-ísimo** to an adverb. This change adds the idea *extremely* or *very, very* to the quality expressed. You have already used one emphatic adverb: **Me gusta muchísimo.**

Estas tapas son **dificilísimas** de preparar. — *These appetizers are very, very hard to prepare.*

- If the word ends in a consonant, **-ísimo** is added to the singular form: **difícil** ⟶ **dificilísimo** (and any accents on the word stem are dropped).
- If the word ends in a vowel, the final vowel is dropped before adding **-ísimo: rápido** ⟶ **rapidísimo** (and any accents on the word stem are dropped).
- Spelling changes occur when the final consonant is **c, g,** or **z: riquísimo, larguísimo, felicísimo.**

Vocabulario útil

avergonzado/a embarrassed
de buen/mal humor
contento/a
feliz/triste
furioso/a
impaciente
nervioso/a
serio/a

B. Reacciones. ¿Cómo se pone Ud. en estas situaciones? Use los adjetivos y verbos que Ud. sabe y también algunas formas enfáticas (**-ísimo/a**). ¿Cuántas emociones puede Ud. describir?

MODELO: Llueve todo el día. ⟶ Me pongo **triste/tristísimo.**

1. Llueve el día de su cumpleaños.
2. Es Navidad. Alguien le hace un regalo carísimo.
3. Ud. quiere bañarse. No hay agua caliente.
4. Ud. está solo/a en casa una noche y oye un ruido.
5. Ud. da una fiesta en su casa o apartamento. Todos están muy serios.
6. Hoy hay un examen importante. Ud. no estudió nada anoche.
7. Ud. cuenta un chiste pero nadie se ríe.
8. Ud. acaba de terminar un examen difícil. Cree que lo hizo muy mal.

C. Opiniones

Paso 1. ¿Son ciertas o falsas para Ud. las siguientes declaraciones?

EN LAS FIESTAS DE FAMILIA	CIERTO	FALSO
1. Las fiestas de familia me gustan muchísimo.	☐	☐
2. Un pariente siempre se queja de algo.	☐	☐
3. Uno de mis parientes me hace preguntas indiscretas.	☐	☐
4. Alguien siempre bebe/come demasiado (*too much*).	☐	☐
LOS DÍAS FESTIVOS EN GENERAL		
5. La Navidad / La Fiesta de las Luces es solo una excusa para gastar dinero.	☐	☐
6. Se empieza a celebrar la Navidad con demasiada anticipación (*too early*).	☐	☐
7. Las vacaciones de primavera son demasiado breves.	☐	☐
8. Solo las personas que practican una religión deben tener vacaciones en los días festivos religiosos.	☐	☐

Mundo interactivo

You should now be prepared to work with Scenario 5, Activity 1 in Connect Spanish (**www.connectspanish.com**).

Paso 2. Su profesor(a) los va a ayudar a resumir las respuestas de toda la clase. Analícenlas. ¿Están todos de acuerdo con los resultados?

¿Recuerda Ud.?

You have already learned the irregular preterite stem and endings for the verb **hacer.** All of the verbs presented in **Gramática 24** have irregular stems and they all use the same preterite endings as **hacer.** Review those endings by completing the following forms.

1. yo: hic_e_ **2.** nosotros: hic_imos_ **3.** Ud.: hiz_o_ **4.** ellos: hic_ieron_

NATIONAL STANDARDS: Comparisons

Some important Hispanic holidays are not generally celebrated in the United States or Canada. One example is *el Día de los Reyes Magos* (*6 de enero*). Other important holidays are historical dates or local fairs celebrated by a specific country, area, or town. For example, Mexicans commemorate *el Cinco de Mayo*, and in Pamplona, Spain, *la fiesta de San Fermín* is celebrated in July. These holidays are well-known in the United States and Canada. Some holidays that are celebrated in the United States and Canada are also celebrated in the Spanish-speaking world but on different dates, for example, *el Día del Padre* and *el Día de la Madre.*

GRAMÁTICA

24 Talking About the Past (Part 2)

Irregular Preterites

Grammar Tutorial 24
connect | SPANISH
www.connectspanish.com

Gramática en acción: Una fiesta de fin de año

Esto es lo que pasó en una fiesta de fin de año en casa de Sofía y Paco. Mire con atención los verbos en rojo. Son formas del pretérito de unos verbos que son irregulares en el pretérito. ¿Puede Ud. dar el infinitivo de esos verbos y contestar las preguntas?

1. ¿Quién estuvo hablando por teléfono?
2. ¿Quién dio la fiesta?
3. ¿Quién no pudo ir a la fiesta?
4. ¿Quién puso su copa sobre la televisión?
5. ¿Quién hizo mucho ruido?
6. ¿Quién no quiso beber más?
7. ¿Quién tuvo que irse temprano?

¿Y Ud.?

1. ¿Estuvo Ud. alguna vez en una fiesta como esta? (Estuve...)
2. ¿Tuvo que irse temprano de la fiesta? (Tuve...) ¿O se quedó hasta medianoche? (Me quedé...)
3. ¿Recuerda qué ropa se puso para la fiesta? (Me puse...)

Irregular Forms / **Las formas irregulares**

1. **Additional Irregular Forms**
You have already learned the irregular preterite forms of **dar, hacer, ir,** and **ser.** The verbs to the right are also irregular in the preterite. They have an irregular stem (shown in red). The first and third person singular endings are the only irregular endings (in contrast to the stressed endings of the regular preterite forms). The verb **estar** is conjugated for you. The other verbs listed are conjugated like **estar.**

estar	
estuve	estuvimos
estuviste	estuvisteis
estuvo	estuvieron

¡OJO! There are no accents on -e and -o.

estar:	estuv-
poder:	pud-
poner:	pus-
querer:	quis-
saber:	sup-
tener:	tuv-
venir:	vin-

Las terminaciones irregulares	
-e	-imos
-iste	-isteis
-o	-ieron

The descriptions should be anonymous. Have students hand in their ideas. Redistribute the descriptions to other students, and have them write responses to the negative aspect of the holiday in the form of advice or recommendations for having a better time or improving the situation. Return the complaint and the advice to the original author of the negative description. Alternatively, read the negative descriptions to the class, and have students give advice orally.

Pronunciación: See the Laboratory Manual for presentation and practice of the letters *c* and *qu*.

Gramática 24
Irregular Preterites

GEA: Suggestions

- Before asking the questions provided, ask questions in the present tense about the details of the drawing, following the order of the questions in the text. Example: **1.** *¿Quién habla (está hablando) por teléfono? ¿Por qué no está Jorge en la fiesta?* Transition into the *GEA* questions by telling students: *Ahora vamos a hablar de la misma fiesta, pero en el pasado.*
- Note that the 8 questions in the text can be answered by using the highlighted verb form. For the *¿Y Ud.?* questions, students will need to use *yo* forms (given in parentheses).

GEA: Note

Active vocabulary: *el fin de año*

GEA: Answers

1. *estar: Marina estuvo hablando por teléfono.*
2. *dar: Sofía y Paco dieron la fiesta.*
3. *poder: Jorge no pudo ir a la fiesta.*
4. *poner: Ernesto puso su copa de champán sobre la televisión.*
5. *hacer: Sultán hizo mucho ruido.*
6. *querer: Patricia no quiso beber más.*
7. *tener: Esteban (La familia) tuvo que irse temprano.*

Suggestions

- Review stress patterns. Point out that the first and third person singular of irregular forms have no accent on the *-e* or *-o*. Students should not confuse these with the present indicative *él/ella/Ud.* or *yo* forms, respectively.
- Emphasize and model verbs that change meaning in the preterite.

Heritage Speakers

Algunos hispanohablantes dicen *dijieron* y *trajieron* en vez de *dijeron* y *trajeron*. Otros verbos parecidos incluyen: *atraer, bendecir, contraer, distraer, introducir, producir, reducir, traducir*. Sin embargo, las formas aceptadas en el uso formal terminan en *-eron* en vez de *-ieron*.

Resources: Transparency 102

Bright Idea

Suggestion

Have students brainstorm ways to organize the verbs with regard to their preterite forms or offer the following groups.

-u-: *tener, poner, estar, saber, poder*
-i-: *hacer, venir, querer*
-j-: *decir, -ucir* verbs, *traer*

Emphasis 3: Suggestion

Emphasize that *hubo* expresses both *there was* and *there were*. Some students may be tempted to incorrectly use *hubieron*.

Changes in Meaning

Suggestion

Point out that not all native speakers observe the change in meaning rules, especially those born in this country.

Note

Active vocabulary: *ya*

Preliminary Exercises

- Have students give the infinitive for these *yo* forms: *quise, puse, estuve, dije, vine, traje.*
- Have students give the subject pronoun for these forms: *vino, supe, dijo, tuviste, estuvo, puse, pudo, trajiste, quise.*
- Have students give the preterite.

  yo: *estar, poder, poner*
  tú: *querer, saber, tener*
  Ud.: *decir, traer, estar*
  nosotros: *poder, poner, saber*
  Uds.: *tener, decir, traer*

- Use the following chain drill to practice the preterite forms.

  ¿Qué pasó en la fiesta del Día del Año Nuevo?

  1. *Todos estuvieron unas horas en casa de Mario.* (*yo, Raúl, Uds., tú, nosotros, vosotras*)
  2. *Muchos trajeron comida y bebidas.* (*Ud., nosotros, tú, Rosalba, Uds., vosotros*)
  3. *Todos dijeron que la fiesta estuvo estupenda.* (*tú, Anita, Uds., yo, ellas, vosotros*)

- Have students tell if the following forms are present indicative or preterite.

dice	*dije*	*decimos*
está	*estamos*	*estuvimos*
puede	*podemos*	*pudimos*
puse	*ponemos*	*pusimos*
tuve	*tenemos*	*traigo*
trajo	*traemos*	*trajimos*
vinimos	*venimos*	*vinieron*

- Ask students:
  1. *¿Tuvo Ud. una entrevista ayer? ¿un examen? ¿una cita con el dentista?*
  2. *¿Estuvo Ud. en España el verano pasado? ¿en México? ¿en la Florida?*
  3. *¿Es verdad que Ud. se puso rojo/a ayer? ¿Por qué razón?*
  4. *¿Quién no pudo dormir bien anoche? ¿Le ocurre esto con frecuencia?*
  5. *¿Quién dijo una mentira* (new) *ayer? ¿A quién se la dijo?*
  6. *¿Quién vino temprano hoy a clase? ¿Quién no vino a clase ayer?*

2. Preterite of *decir* and *traer*

The irregular preterite stems of these two verbs end in **-j-**. They use the same endings as the verbs on page 271, except that the **-i-** of the third person plural is omitted: **dijeron, trajeron.**

decir: dij- } **-e, -iste, -o, -imos, -isteis,** -eron
traer: traj- }

3. Preterite of *hay: Hubo*

Hay comes from the infinitive **haber.** Its preterite form is **hubo** = *there was/were.*

Hubo un accidente ayer en el centro.
There was an accident yesterday downtown.

Hubo muchos regalos debajo del árbol.
There were a lot of presents under the tree.

Changes in Meaning / Cambios de significado

Several of the following Spanish verbs have an English equivalent in the preterite tense that is different from that of the infinitive.

Infinitive	Present Tense	Preterite Meaning
saber =	to know (*facts, information*)	to find out, learn
	Ya lo **sé.** *I already know it.*	Lo **supe** ayer. *I found it out (learned it) yesterday.*
conocer =	to know, be familiar with (*people, places*)	to meet (*for the first time*)
	Ya la **conozco.** *I already know her.*	La **conocí** ayer. *I met her yesterday.*
querer =	to want	to try
	Quiero hacerlo hoy. *I want to do it today.*	**Quise** hacerlo ayer. *I tried to do it yesterday.*
no querer =	not to want	to refuse
	No quiero hacerlo hoy. *I don't want to do it today.*	**No quise** hacerlo anteayer. *I refused to do it the day before yesterday.*
poder =	to be able to (*do something*)	to succeed (*in doing something*)
	Puedo leerlo *I can (am able to) read it.*	**Pude** leerlo ayer. *I could (and did) read it yesterday.*
no poder =	not to be able, capable (*of doing something*)	to fail (*to do something*)
	No puedo leerlo. *I can't (am not able to) read it.*	**No pude** leerlo anteayer. *I couldn't (did not) read it the day before yesterday.*

Autoprueba

Give the correct irregular preterite forms.

1. (yo) saber
2. (ellos) tener
3. (tú) venir
4. (él) poner
5. (nosotros) querer
6. (Ud.) poder
7. (ellos) decir
8. hay

Answers: 1. *supe* 2. *tuvieron* 3. *viniste* 4. *puso* 5. *quisimos* 6. *pudo* 7. *dijeron* 8. *hubo*

Práctica

A. En una fiesta. ¿Cómo se dice en inglés?

1. No pude abrir la botella de champán.
2. Supe que se murió (*died*) el abuelo de un amigo.
3. Conocí al primo cubano de una amiga.
4. No quise hablar con Jorge. Él es muy descortés con todos.

Prác. A: Answers: 1. I could not (failed to) open the bottle of champagne. **2.** I found out that the grandfather of a friend died. **3.** I met the Cuban cousin of a friend. **4.** I refused to speak with Jorge. He's very rude to everyone.

B. ¡Anticipemos! La última Nochevieja

Paso 1. Piense Ud. en lo que hizo la Nochevieja del año pasado. ¿Es cierto o falso que Ud. hizo las siguientes cosas?

	CIERTO	FALSO
1. Fui a una fiesta en casa de un amigo / una amiga.	☐	☐
2. Di una fiesta en mi casa.	☐	☐
3. No estuve con mis amigos, sino (*but rather*) con la familia.	☐	☐
4. Quise ir a una fiesta, pero no pude.	☐	☐
5. Les dije «¡Feliz Año Nuevo!» a muchas personas.	☐	☐
6. Conocí a algunas personas interesantes.	☐	☐
7. Tuve que hacer la comida para una fiesta.	☐	☐
8. Me puse ropa elegante esa noche.	☐	☐
9. Pude quedarme despierto/a (*awake*) hasta medianoche.	☐	☐
10. No quise bailar. Me sentía (*I felt*) mal.	☐	☐

Paso 2. Ahora, en parejas, comparen sus respuestas. Si es posible, digan a la clase dos acciones en que coincidieron.

C. Una Nochebuena en Santiago de Cuba

Paso 1. Complete la siguiente narración sobre la celebración de la Nochebuena de una familia cubana de la ciudad de Santiago, al sur de la isla de Cuba. Habla Manuel, el padre de la familia. Use el pretérito de los verbos.

El año pasado mi esposa y yo celebramos la Nochebuena en casa con toda la familia. (Estar[1]) con nosotros mi primo Andrés, de la Florida, quien (quedarse[2]) con nosotros toda la semana. (Venir[3]) mis padres, mis suegros,[a] hermanos y cuñados[b] con sus hijos. También (*nosotros:* invitar[4]) a nuestros vecinos[c] de toda la vida,[d] los Benjumea. Pero ellos no (poder[5]) asistir porque (irse[6]) a La Habana para estar con su hija, que (tener[7]) un niño en noviembre.

Mi esposa (preparar[8]) lechón asado, moros y cristianos, yuca y tostones.[e] ¡Qué sabroso todo! Mi cuñado (traer[9]) turrón[f] español y cava.[g] A las 10:30, mi hermana (decir[10]) que era[h] hora de ir a la Misa del Gallo[i] y (llevar[11]) a los abuelos a la iglesia.[j] Los demás[k] no (querer[12]) ir y seguimos armando bochinche hasta que (volver[13]) los otros. Todo (ir[14]) bien chévere.[l] Como regalo de Navidad, mi primo Andrés me (dar[15]) un álbum con fotos y cartas de mis parientes en la Florida y Nueva Jersey. Yo (ponerse[16]) tan emocionado[m] que (llorar[18]).

El lechón (*suckling pig*) con moros (= frijoles) y cristianos (= arroz)

[a]*in-laws* [b]*brothers- and sisters-in-law* [c]*neighbors* [d]de... *long-time (lit., of one's whole life)* [e]*fried plantains* [f]*sweet Christmas candy* [g]*Spanish champagne* [h]*it was* [i]Misa... *Midnight Mass* [j]*church* [k]Los... *The others* [l]*great* [m]*touched, emotional*

Comprensión

1. ¿Qué tuvo de especial la Nochebuena del año pasado para Manuel?
2. ¿Por qué no pudieron asistir los Benjumea?
3. ¿Quiénes fueron a la Misa del Gallo?
4. ¿Qué comieron y bebieron todos?

Paso 2. Ahora complete las siguientes oraciones basadas en lo que pasó en la celebración de la pasada Navidad, Pascua judía u (*or*) otra fiesta de importancia para su familia. Conjugue los verbos en el pretérito, añadiendo el sujeto y otra información apropiada.

(Continúa.)

Prác. C: Answers: 1. *Estuvo* **2.** *se quedó* **3.** *Vinieron* **4.** *invitamos* **5.** *pudieron* **6.** *se fueron* **7.** *tuvo* **8.** *preparó* **9.** *trajo* **10.** *dijo* **11.** *llevó* **12.** *quisieron (quisimos)* **13.** *volvieron* **14.** *fue* **15.** *dio* **16.** *me puse* **18.** *lloré*

Estrategia

Not all of the verbs in this story are irregular in the preterite. As you conjugate each infinitive, first ask yourself if its preterite is regular or irregular.

Comprensión, Answers: **1.** *Estuvieron en la celebración muchos parientes.* **2.** *Porque se fueron a La Habana para estar con su hija.* **3.** *La hermana de Manuel y los abuelos fueron a la Misa del Gallo.* **4.** *Comieron lechón asado, moros y cristianos, yuca y tostones. Bebieron cava.*

Prác. A: Note

Translation exercises are rarely suggested or included in *Puntos de partida,* but they are useful at times. This brief translation activity focuses students' attention on the meanings of these verbs in the preterite.

Prác. B: Suggestion

Ask students to find the preterite verb form(s) in each sentence and give the infinitive.

Prác. C: Suggestions

- Emphasize that there is a mixture of verbs in this activity. All verbs are in the third person singular or plural, except for the last two. Review the endings for regular and irregular verbs for those persons before students start the activity.
- Have students retell the story from the point of view of someone else in the family, *la hermana de Manuel*, for example.

Prác. C: Notes

- In the Hispanic world, *la Nochebuena* can be a fun celebration, more of a party than the quieter U.S. and Canadian versions. It is common to invite neighbors and friends.
- All of the foods mentioned are typical of Cuba and the entire Caribbean region. Be sure that students read the photo caption, as some of them are explained there.
- *El turrón* is of Spanish origin, but it is enjoyed throughout Latin America as well. It is made with almonds and honey, and there are two kinds: one, hard and crunchy (*el turrón duro*), the other soft and creamy (*el turrón blando o de Jijona*).
- *La Misa del Gallo* is explained in *Nota cultural* (p. 268), and the idiomatic expression *armar (un) bochinche* is in *Así se dice* (p. 267).

Prác. C: Follow-up

Ask your Christian students how their *Nochebuena* compares to the celebration described in this activity. Ask non-Christians to compare *la Nochebuena* to a traditional holiday comparable to it in their culture.

Prác. C: Variation

Have students use the activity as a guide for describing their own Christmas (or other holiday) celebrations (orally or in writing).

Prác. D: Suggestion

Before forming sentences, have students match the information. Help them with information they do not know.

Prác. D: Note

Active vocabulary: *el hecho*

Prác. D: Answers

- *En 1957 los rusos pusieron un satélite en el espacio por primera vez.*
- *En 1969 los estadounidenses pusieron a un hombre en la luna*
- *Adán y Eva supieron el significado de un árbol especial.*
- *George Washington estuvo en Valley Forge con sus soldados.*
- *Los europeos trajeron el caballo al Nuevo Mundo.*
- *Los aztecas conocieron a Hernán Cortés en Tenochtitlán.*
- *Stanley conoció a Livingston en África.*

Con. A: Suggestions

- In the model for *Paso 2,* point out the use of *los/las dos + plural verb* to indicate plurality of subject to express either *we* or *they*. Explain that *Los dos **fuimos** = We both went* vs. *Los dos **fueron** = They both went.* In the first example (as in the model), *los dos* takes the place of *nosotros/as.*
- Invite students to use the same questions to interview you. Ask them to use the *Ud.* form, especially if they normally address you as *tú.*

Con. B: Suggestion

In *Paso 2,* have the other students ask the reporter questions to get as much additional information as they can.

Con. B: Note

Active vocabulary: *el detalle*

MODELO: (celebrar) ____ (*fiesta*) en ____ (*lugar*) →
Mi familia celebró la Navidad en **casa de mis abuelos.**

1. (celebrar) ____ (*fiesta*) en ____ (*lugar*)
2. (asistir), pero (no poder)
3. (ir) ____ (*servicio religioso*) antes/después de la comida
4. (comer) ____ (*platos*) y (beber) ____ (*bebidas*)
5. (ponerse) muy emocionado/a porque ____
6. (dar + *pronombre de complemento indirecto*) un regalo a ____ (*otra persona*)

D. Hechos (*Events*) históricos. Describan Uds. algunos hechos históricos, usando una palabra o frase de cada columna. Use el pretérito de los verbos. Su profesor(a) los puede ayudar con los datos (*information*) que no saben.

en 1957 los rusos en 1969 los estadounidenses Adán y Eva George Washington los europeos los aztecas Stanley	+	conocer estar poner saber traer	+	en Valley Forge con sus soldados a un hombre en la luna (*moon*) un satélite en el espacio por primera vez el significado (*meaning*) de un árbol especial a Livingston en África el caballo (*horse*) al Nuevo Mundo a Hernán Cortés en Tenochtitlán

Conversación

A. Intercambios

Paso 1. Forme preguntas en el pretérito con los siguientes verbos. En el **Paso 2,** Ud. va a usar las preguntas para entrevistar a un compañero o compañera de clase.

MODELO: conocer → ¿Cuándo **conociste** a tu mejor amigo/a?

1. conocer	3. estar	5. hacer
2. saber	4. tener	6. dar

Paso 2. En parejas, túrnense para hacer y contestar sus preguntas. Luego digan a la clase algo que los/las dos tienen en común.

MODELO: conocer → Los dos **conocimos** a nuestros mejores amigos en la escuela secundaria.

B. La última fiesta que Ud. dio

Paso 1. Haga una lista de todos los detalles (*details*) que Ud. recuerda de la última fiesta que organizó. Puede ser una fiesta que Ud. organizó solo/a o con su familia o con un grupo de amigos. Haga por lo menos ocho oraciones completas para describir la fiesta y use cinco de los siguientes verbos: **conocer, dar, estar, invitar, organizar, poder, saber, ser, venir.**

MODELO: Di una fiesta para el cumpleaños de mi mejor amigo.
Mi amigo Clark y yo organizamos la fiesta…

Paso 2. Ahora, entreviste a un compañero o compañera sobre la última fiesta que organizó él o ella. Haga preguntas con las palabras interrogativas: (**¿Cúando?, ¿Dónde?, ¿Quién?, ¿Con quién?, ¿Qué?,** y **¿Por qué?**) y el pretérito.

MODELOS: ¿Cuándo dieron la fiesta?
¿Qué sirvieron de comer y beber?

Luego digan a la clase dos detalles interesantes sobre las fiestas que Uds. organizaron.

Culture

- ***Hernán Cortés*** (1485–1547): Spanish explorer and conqueror of the Aztec Empire, Cortés was born in Medellín, Extremadura. He studied law at the University of Salamanca but cut short his university career in 1501 and decided to try his fortune in the Americas. Head of the Spanish forces, he entered the Aztec capital in 1519.
- ***The Aztecs and Tenochtitlán:*** The Aztecs built a great empire and developed a complex social, political, and religious structure. Their capital, *Tenochtitlán*, in central Mexico, was possibly the largest city in the world at the time of the Spanish conquest.

(Cont.)

¿Recuerda Ud.?

You learned in **Gramática 15 (Cap. 6)** to make a change in the **-ndo** form of **-ir** stem-changing verbs. That same change occurs in some forms of the preterite of those verbs. Review the change in the preterite by completing the following forms.

1. pedir: p_i_diendo **2.** dormir: d_u_rmiendo

You will learn about this change in preterite in **Grámatica 25.**

Grammar Tutorial 25
connect SPANISH
www.connectspanish.com

25 Talking About the Past (Part 3)
Preterite of Stem-changing Verbs

Gramática en acción: Una fiesta de quinceañera

Escoja las respuestas más lógicas para describir la fiesta de quinceañera de Lupe Carrasco. Al leer (*While you are reading*), mire con atención los verbos en rojo. Son formas del pretérito de verbos que cambian el radical. ¿Puede Ud. dar el infinitivo de esos verbos?

1. Para su fiesta, Lupe se vistió con…
   - ☑ un vestido blanco muy elegante.
   - ☐ una camiseta y *bluejeans*.
2. Mientras Lupe cortaba[a] el pastel de cumpleaños, la madre de ella…
   - ☑ empezó a llorar.
   - ☐ se rio mucho.
3. Lupe pidió un deseo[b] al cortar[c] el pastel. Ella…
   - ☐ les dijo a todos qué fue lo que pidió.
   - ☑ prefirió guardarlo en secreto.
4. En la fiesta sirvieron…
   - ☑ champán y refrescos.
   - ☐ solo té y café.
5. Todos los invitados…
   - ☑ se divirtieron mucho.
   - ☐ se quejaron.
6. A las tres de la mañana, el último invitado
   - ☑ se despidió.[d]
   - ☐ se sonrió.

Otra costumbre de quinceañera común en Cuba: Ir por la ciudad en coche, como los recien casados (*newlyweds*) en este país

¿Y Ud.?

1. ¿Recuerda Ud. qué hizo cuando cumplió 15 años?
2. ¿Qué regalos pidió? (Pedí…)
3. ¿Qué sirvieron en la fiesta? (Sirvieron…)
4. ¿Se divirtió? (Me divertí…)
5. ¿Cómo se sintió ese día? (Me sentí…)

[a]Mientras… *As she was cutting* [b]*wish* [c]al… *as she cut* [d]se… *said good-bye*

Gramática 25
Preterite of Stem-changing Verbs

GEA: Suggestions

- After completing the *GEA,* go back to item 1 and ask students to give you the infinitive and present tense form that corresponds to *se vistió.* Write them on the board. Do the same for at least one *-ir* stem-changing verb from items 2–5, writing the forms on the board.
- Ask students what happens to *-ir* stem-changing verbs in the third person preterite ($e \rightarrow i$) and if they remember that change from any other verb form (= the present participle).
- Ask the *¿Y Ud.?* questions, making sure that students use the suggested *yo* forms if necessary in their answers.
- Ask students what happens to *-ir* stem-changing verbs in the first person preterite (no change).
- Ask additional questions about the party, asking students to invent the details: *¿A qué hora llegaron los invitados? ¿A qué hora se fueron? ¿Con quién bailó Lupe?* And so on.

GEA: Note

Active vocabulary: *despedirse*

Heritage Speakers

Anime a los hispanohablantes a describir una quinceañera a la que hayan asistido. ¿Conocen a la muchacha quinceañera? ¿Quién es? ¿Cuántas personas asistieron? ¿Qué comieron? ¿Qué hicieron? ¿Se divirtieron?

Culture (Cont.)

- ***Dr. David Livingston*** (1813–1873): This Scottish explorer and medical missionary in today's Botswana, Africa, discovered Victoria Falls. While searching for the source of the Nile River, he disappeared.
- ***Sir Henry Morton Stanley*** (1841–1904): A British journalist and explorer, Stanley was sent to Africa in 1871 by the New York *Herald* to find David Livingston. He succeeded.

Emphasis 1: Note

Only the preterite / present participle stem change is highlighted in the verbs on this page, not the present tense stem change (which would usually also be highlighted).

Emphasis 1: Suggestions

- Emphasize and model a few *-ar* and *-er* stem-changing verbs that do not have stem changes in the preterite (as they do in the present indicative).
  1. **(ue):** *contar, recordar, encontrar, jugar, volver, llover* (third person singular only)
  2. **(ie):** *empezar, recomendar, cerrar, despertarse, nevar* (third person singular only)
- Have students give the third person singular and plural preterite of the *-ar* and *-er* stem-changing verbs.

Emphasis 2: Suggestion

Remind students that the stem change indicated in word lists—(*i*), (*u*)—occurs in the third person singular and plural of the preterite and in the *-ndo* forms. These changes only occur in *-ir* verbs. Model these verbs.

dormir: *durmió, durmieron, durmiendo*
preferir: *prefirió, prefirieron, prefiriendo*
repetir: *repitió, repitieron, repitiendo*

Emphasis 3: Suggestion

The only new verbs in this section are: *conseguir, despedirse* (introduced in *GEA*), *morir(se), sugerir.* The second meaning of *seguir* = *to follow* is also new.

Preliminary Exercises

- Have students give the third person singular and plural preterite.
  1. **(ue, u):** *dormir, morir, dormirse*
  2. **(i, i):** *pedir, repetir, despedir*
  3. **(ie, i):** *preferir, sentir, sentirse, divertirse, sugerir*
- Have students do the following chain drill to practice the preterite.

  Todos pasaron un día fatal ayer.
  1. *Dormimos muy mal anoche.* (*yo, todos, Irma, tú, Ud., vosotros*)
  2. *No recordaste traer los ejercicios.* (*Raúl, nosotros, Ud., ellos, vosotros*)
  3. *Raúl perdió las llaves del coche.* (*tú, Horacio y Estela, yo, Ud., vosotras*)
  4. *Pedimos mariscos.* (*yo, Jacinto, tú, Uds., vosotros*)
  5. *Todos se rieron mucho de Nati.* (*nosotros, Esteban, yo, Uds., vosotras*)

1. Preterite of *-ar* and *-er* Stem-changing Verbs

In **Gramática 23** (**Cap.** 8) you learned that **-ar** and **-er** stem-changing verbs have no stem change in the preterite (or in the present participle).

El pretérito de los verbos en *-ar/-er*

recordar (recuerdo)		perder (pierdo)	
recordé	recordamos	perdí	perdimos
recordaste	recordasteis	perdiste	perdisteis
recordó	recordaron	perdió	perdieron
recordando		perdiendo	

2. Preterite of *-ir* Stem-changing Verbs

-Ir stem-changing verbs *do* have a stem change in the preterite, but only in the third person singular and plural, where the stem vowels **e** and **o** change to **i** and **u,** respectively. This is the same change that occurs in the present participle of **-ir** stem-changing verbs.

e ⟶ i
o ⟶ u

El pretérito de los verbos en *-ir*

pedir (pido) (i)		dormir (duermo) (u)	
pedí	pedimos	dormí	dormimos
pediste	pedisteis	dormiste	dormisteis
pidió	pidieron	durmió	durmieron
pidiendo		durmiendo	

Remember that this change is indicated in parentheses after the infinitive in vocabulary lists. Now you know that it indicates *two* different changes: one in the present participle and one in the third persons singular and plural of the preterite.

3. Important *-ir* Stem-changing Verbs

You already know or have seen many of these verbs. The reflexive meaning, if different from the nonreflexive meaning, is in parentheses.

despedirse (me despido) (i) (de)

conseguir (consigo) (i)	to get, obtain	**seguir (sigo) (i)**	to continue; to follow
conseguir + *inf.*	to succeed in (*doing something*)	**sentirse (me siento) (i)**	to feel (*an emotion*)
		servir (sirvo) (i)	to serve
despedir(se) ([me] despido) (i) (de)	to say good-bye (to)	**sonreír(se) ([me] sonrío) (i)**	to smile
divertir(se) ([me] divierto) (i)	to entertain (to have a good time)	**sugerir (sugiero) (i)**	to suggest
dormir(se) ([me] duermo) (u)	to sleep (to fall asleep)	**vestir(se) ([me] visto) (i)**	to dress (to get dressed)
morir(se) ([me] muero) (u)	to die		
pedir (pido) (i)	to ask for; to order		
preferir (prefiero) (i)	to prefer		
reír(se) ([me] río) (i) (de)	to laugh (at)		

¡OJO!

Note these irregularities:
ri-ió ⟶ rio; ri-ieron ⟶ rieron
son-ri-ió ⟶ sonrió;
son-ri-ieron ⟶ sonrieron

Summary of the Preterite of Stem-changing Verbs

-ar / -er = no change
-ir = change in the third persons singular and plural

e ⟶ i
o ⟶ u

Autoprueba

Complete the verbs with preterite stems.

1. nos div_____rtimos
2. se d_____rmieron
3. tú s_____rviste
4. se v_____stió
5. yo sug_____rí
6. Uds. p_____dieron

Answers: **1.** *divertimos* **2.** *durmieron* **3.** *serviste* **4.** *vistió* **5.** *sugerí* **6.** *pidieron*

Resources: Transparency 103

Culture

- ***Cinderella:*** Cinderella (*la Cenicienta*) is the heroine of a European folktale, the theme of which appears in numerous stories worldwide. More than 500 versions of the story have been found in Europe alone. Its essential

(Cont.)

Práctica

A. ¡Anticipemos! ¿Quién lo hizo? ¿Ocurrieron algunas de estas cosas en clase la semana pasada? Conteste con el nombre de las personas que lo hicieron. Si nadie lo hizo, conteste con **Nadie...**

1. _____ se vistió con ropa muy elegante.
2. _____ se vistió con ropa extravagante.
3. _____ se durmió en clase.
4. _____ le pidió al profesor / a la profesora más tarea.
5. _____ se sintió muy contento/a.
6. _____ se divirtió muchísimo. Se rio y sonrió mucho.
7. _____ no sonrió para nada.
8. _____ sugirió tener la clase afuera.
9. _____ prefirió no contestar ninguna pregunta.

B. Historias breves. Cuente las siguientes historias breves en el pretérito. Luego continúelas, si puede.

1. **En un restaurante:** Juan (sentarse) a la mesa. Cuando (llegar) el camarero, le (pedir) una cerveza. El camarero no (recordar) lo que Juan (pedir) y le (servir) una Coca-Cola. Juan no (querer) beber la Coca-Cola. Le (decir) al camarero: «Perdón, señor. Le (*yo:* pedir) una cerveza». El camarero le (contestar): «_____».
2. **Un día típico:** Rosa (acostarse) temprano y (dormirse) en seguida. (Dormir) bien y (despertarse) temprano. (Vestirse) y (salir) para la universidad. En el autobús (ver) a su amigo José y los dos (sonreír) pero no (hablarse). A las nueve _____.
3. **Anoche:** Yo (vestirse), (ir) a una fiesta, (divertirse) mucho y (volver) tarde a casa. Mi compañero de cuarto (decidir) quedarse en casa y (ver) la televisión toda la noche. No (divertirse), (perder) una fiesta excelente y después lo (sentir) mucho. Yo _____.

C. Las historias que todos conocemos

Paso 1. Empareje los personajes (*characters*) de la columna de la izquierda con las acciones de la columna de la derecha para crear oraciones en el pretérito basadas en unos cuentos o historias muy famosos. ¿Puede adivinar (*guess*) quiénes son Caperucita Roja, la Cenicienta y Blancanieves?

PERSONAJES

- Caperucita Roja
- el lobo (*wolf*)
- el Príncipe
- la Cenicienta
- las hermanastras de la Cenicienta
- Blancanieves
- los siete enanos (*dwarves*)
- Romeo
- Julieta

ACCIONES

- conocer a una mujer misteriosa en un baile
- divertirse bailando con un joven muy guapo
- dormirse después de comer una manzana
- morirse por el amor de su novia
- perderse en el bosque (*forest*)
- perder un zapato muy bonito
- ponerse un vestido muy bonito
- encontrar (*to find*) un zapato de cristal (*glass*)
- preferir salir con un joven de una familia rival
- sentirse preocupados por su amiga
- vestirse de (*as a*) vieja
- no conseguir ponerse el zapato de cristal
- seguir viviendo con su madre

El Príncipe conoció...
La Cenicienta se divirtió...
Blancanieves se durmió...
Romeo se murió...
Caperucita Roja se perdió...
La Cenicienta perdió...
La Cenicienta se puso...
El Príncipe encontró...
Julieta prefirió...
Los siete enanos se sintieron...
El lobo se vistió...
Las hermanastras de la Cenicienta no consiguieron...
Las hermanastras de la Cenicienta siguieron...

Paso 2. Ahora, en parejas, inventen dos acciones más en el pretérito para cada historia, pero sin incluir el nombre del personaje. La clase va a adivinar a qué personaje, cuento o historia se refieren sus oraciones.

MODELO: Una mujer **quiso** ponerse el zapato de cristal, pero no **pudo** ponérselo. → la hermanastra de la Cenicienta

Prác. B: Answers: 1. *se sentó, llegó, pidió, recordó, pidió, sirvió, quiso, dijo, pedí, contestó,* (answers will vary) **2.** *se acostó, se durmió, Durmió, se despertó, Se vistió, salió, vio, sonrieron, se hablaron,* (answers will vary) **3.** *me vestí, fui, me divertí, volví, decidió, vio, se divirtió, perdió, sintió,* (answers will vary)

Prác. B: Follow-up: Ask the following questions after completing the activity. **1.** *¿Dónde almorzó Ud. ayer? ¿Qué pidió? ¿Quién se lo sirvió? ¿Quién pagó la cuenta?* **2.** *¿A qué hora se acostó Ud. anoche? ¿Durmió bien? ¿Se sintió descansado/a cuando se despertó? ¿Cómo se vistió esta mañana, con ropa elegante o informal?* **3.** *¿Qué película o programa de televisión le pareció más divertido el año pasado? ¿Se rio Ud. mucho cuando lo/la vio? ¿Les gustó también a sus amigos?*

- Practice just the meaning of the *-ir* stem-changing verbs listed on this page with the following *Asociaciones* activities.
- **Reciclado: Asociaciones:** Ask students to give the infinitives they associate with the following phrases.
  1. *ponerse ropa*
  2. *pensar que una cosa es mejor que otra*
  3. *continuar*
  4. *pasarlo muy bien*
  5. *reaccionar a algo cómico (dos respuestas)*
  6. *darle comida o una bebida a alguien*
  7. *estar mucho tiempo en cama*
  8. *hablar con el camarero en un restaurante*
- **Asociaciones:** Ask students to give phrases that they associate with the following infinitives. Suggested answers are provided.
  1. *despedirse (adiós, buenas noches, salir...)*
  2. *morirse (ser viejo/a, enfermarse, un accidente...)*
  3. *sugerir (una idea, un consejo, el consejero...)*

Prác. A: Suggestion

Ask students to find the preterite verb form(s) in each sentence and give the infinitive.

Prác. B: Suggestion

Have students read through each sequence first before beginning the activity.

Prác. B: Note

The reciprocal reflexive is used in the last item in *Un día típico* (*hablarse*). Most students should be able to guess the meaning from context.

Prác. C: Suggestion

Before students start to work in pairs, ask them to look at the groups of characters in the left-hand column and guess their English equivalents.

Prác. C: Note

Active vocabulary: *adivinar, encontrar*

Culture (Cont.)

features include a youngest daughter who is mistreated by her jealous stepmother and elder stepsisters or a cruel father, and the intervention of a supernatural helper on her behalf. A prince falls in love with her and marries her. One of the oldest known literary renderings of the theme is a Chinese version that dates from the 9th century A.D.

- ***Romeo and Juliet:*** This tragedy by William Shakespeare was probably written in 1595. It is the story of two feuding noble families (the Capulets and the Montagues) whose children meet and fall in love.

Con. A: Suggestion

Before or after students have interviewed each other, ask them to use the same questions to interview you. Tell them to change the *tú* forms of the questions to *Ud.* forms to practice the irregular preterite forms presented in this section.

Con. A: Extension

8. *Anoche, ¿te despediste de alguien a las tres de la mañana? ¿De quién?*
9. *¿Te reíste alguna vez cuando oíste la noticia* (new) *de algo trágico?*
10. *¿Qué no recordaste a tiempo la semana pasada?*

Redacción: Assign *Con. B* as written homework. Turn one (or more) of the paragraphs into a fill-in-the-blank activity (changing the verbs into infinitives) and do it with the whole class. Ask students to guess who is the author of the paragraph.

Optional

For homework have each student write six trivia questions on 3 × 5 index cards. The questions should be in the preterite, with answers on the back. In class divide the students into groups of two to four to form an even number of teams (four teams, six teams, eight teams). Each team gets together to select the ten best questions and to correct the Spanish. The teams should write the selected questions individually, without answers, on 3 × 5 cards. Have pairs of teams compete against each other by taking turns asking and responding to questions. Members from each team take turns selecting a card from the opposing team and answering the question.

Conversación

A. Una entrevista indiscreta

Paso 1. Lea las siguientes preguntas y escriba una respuesta para cada una. **¡OJO!** Tres de sus respuestas deben ser falsas.

1. ¿A qué hora te dormiste anoche?
2. ¿Perdiste mucho dinero alguna vez?
3. ¿Con qué programa de televisión te divertiste mucho en los días o meses pasados… pero te avergüenzas de (*you're ashamed to*) admitirlo?
4. ¿Te vestiste de animal alguna vez? ¿En qué ocasión?
5. ¿Seguiste haciendo algo después de que tu padre/madre (compañero/a, esposo/a) te dijo que no lo hicieras (*not to do it*)?
6. ¿Pediste una bebida alcohólica antes de tener 21 años?
7. ¿Qué cosa o tarea no conseguiste terminar el mes pasado?

Paso 2. En parejas, usen las preguntas del **Paso 1** para entrevistarse. Traten de (*Try to*) adivinar las respuestas falsas de su compañero/a. ¿Conoce bien a su compañero/a?

Paso 3. Ahora presenten a la clase por lo menos una de las respuestas interesantes de su compañero/a. La clase va a adivinar si la respuesta es cierta o falsa.

MODELO:
E1: Julie, ¿a qué hora te dormiste anoche?
E2: Me dormí a las tres de la mañana.
E1: (*a la clase*): Julie se durmió a las tres de la mañana anoche.
CLASE: No es cierto.
E1: Tienen razón. No es cierto. Me dormí a las once.

Vocabulario útil

la bruja witch
el disfraz costume
el esqueleto
la máscara
el monstruo

B. Una fiesta de Halloween

Paso 1. Use las siguientes preguntas como guía para hablar con toda la clase de una fiesta inolvidable de Halloween.

1. ¿De qué se vistió?
2. ¿Cómo se sintió cuando se vio con el disfraz?
3. ¿Fue de casa en casa pidiendo dulces?
4. ¿Qué les dijo a los vecinos (*neighbors*)?
5. ¿Qué le dieron los vecinos?
6. ¿Se rieron los vecinos cuando lo/la vieron?
7. ¿Consiguió muchos dulces?
8. ¿También fue a una fiesta?
9. ¿Qué sirvieron en la fiesta?
10. ¿Se divirtió mucho?

Paso 2. De todos los miembros de la clase, ¿quién describió el disfraz más cómico? ¿el más espantoso (*frightening*)? ¿el más original? ¿el más bonito? ¿Hubo algún incidente divertido? ¿Qué pasó?

NATIONAL STANDARDS: Comparisons

- Halloween is not generally celebrated in Hispanic countries. Instead, the first of November (All Saints' Day) and the second of November (All Souls' Day) are celebrated as religious and family holidays.
- *El Día de los Muertos* (the Day of the Dead) is celebrated on November 2, especially in Mexico and some Central American countries. The celebration may be traced to the festivities held during the Aztec month of *Miccailhuitontli,* ritually presided over by the goddess

(Cont.)

26 Avoiding Repetition

Expressing Direct and Indirect Object Pronouns Together

Grammar Tutorial 26
connect SPANISH
www.connectspanish.com

Gramática en acción: Berta habla de la fiesta de Anita

Empareje las oraciones con los dibujos correspondientes. Luego trate de (*try to*) adivinar lo que significan las palabras en rojo en cada oración.

1. __B__ «Me encantó el CD que Anita puso en la fiesta. Por eso ella me lo prestó para oírlo en casa.»
2. __C__ «Sergio sacó muchas fotos durante la fiesta. Luego nos las mostró en su computadora portátil.»
3. __A__ «Hice un pastel y se lo di a Anita para la fiesta.»

Comprensión

¿Cierto o falso? Corrija las oraciones falsas.

	CIERTO	FALSO
1. ¿El pastel? Berta se lo dio a Anita.	☑	☐
2. ¿El CD? Sergio se lo prestó a Berta. Anita se lo prestó a Berta.	☐	☑
3. ¿Las fotos? Anita se las mostró a todos. Sergio se las mostró a todos.	☐	☑

complemento indirecto	complemento directo
me +	lo/la/los/las
te +	lo/la/los/las
(le →) se +	lo/la/los/las

complemento indirecto	complemento directo
nos +	lo/la/los/las
os +	lo/la/los/las
(les) → se +	lo/la/los/las

Order of Pronouns / La secuencia de los pronombres

1. *Indirect Object Pronoun* + *Direct Object Pronoun*
When a sentence has both a direct and an indirect object pronoun, the indirect (**I**) precedes the direct (**D**): **ID**. This is the *opposite* of the order of these pronoun in English. No other word can come between the two Spanish pronouns.

¿El almuerzo? **Te lo** hago ahora mismo.
Lunch? I'll get it ready for you right now.

¿El trofeo? No **nos lo** dieron.
The trophy? They didn't give it to us.

Gramática 26

Expressing Direct and Indirect Object Pronouns Together

Suggestions

- Because this grammar point is not given a lot of emphasis in *Puntos de partida*, no *¿Recuerda Ud.?* activity is provided for it. You may wish to review direct and indirect object pronouns before beginning the grammar section. Give students sentences such as the following and ask them to tell you whether the sentences contain direct and/or indirect objects (nouns or pronouns).
  1. *Julio tiene un perro, pero nunca le da de comer.*
  2. *Sara siempre les escribe cartas en español a sus padres.*
  3. *Guárdenme un puesto en la cola, por favor.*
  4. *¿Qué me dices? ¡No lo creo!*
- You may wish to treat this grammar point as a topic for passive recognition or, at best, partial control. Activities will always provide a structure that will help students be successful when doing them, but it is probably not realistic to expect students to use these pronouns accurately in spontaneous speech.
- After students have completed the matching activity, ask them to give you the sense (not necessarily an exact translation) of each sentence. Then ask what the pronouns *lo* (1 and 2) and *las* (3) refer to. Do the same with the items in *Comprensión*.

Resources: Transparency 104

NATIONAL STANDARDS: (Cont.)

Mictecacihuatl (Lady of the Dead), and dedicated to children and the dead. Today, families celebrate *el Día de los Muertos* by visiting the graves of their close relatives. In the cemetery, family members spruce up the gravesite, decorate it with flowers, set up and enjoy a picnic, and interact socially with other families gathered there. Families remember the departed by telling stories about them. *El Día de los Muertos* is an important social ritual that recognizes the natural cycle of life and death.

Emphasis 2: Suggestion

Remind students that most verbs require an accent mark after object pronouns are attached to the end of infinitives, commands, and gerunds.

Le(s) → *se*

Emphasis 1: Suggestions

- Emphasize and model the change of *le(s)* → *se* before *lo/la/los/las.*
- In sentences with both direct and indirect third person object pronouns, students should focus only on the gender of the direct object pronoun, since indirect object pronouns will always be *se.*
- To emphasize written accents on affirmative commands with pronouns, give the following dictation.

démelo *pídaselo*
cómpramelo *dénselo*
tómenselo

Emphasis 1: Note

This grammar explanation does not treat structures like *se le ve, se le nota,* and so on, which will sound much like the *se lo* pronoun construction to students. Explore this topic with your students if you feel it to be appropriate.

Bright Idea

Suggestion

Have students note clothing and things that classmates have, then have them ask to borrow some things.

MODELO: *Juan, ¿me prestas la chaqueta? →*
Sí, te la presto. / No, no te la presto.

Preliminary Exercises

- Ask students which of the following sentences could refer to *el dinero* (*sí* or *no*).
  1. *¿Me lo prestas?*
  2. *Voy a dársela.*
  3. *Te lo mando mañana.*
- Ask students which of the following sentences could refer to *las recomendaciones* (*sí* or *no*).
  1. *Te los doy, si quieres.*
  2. *¿Cuándo se las pediste?*
  3. *Sí, quiero que me las traiga ahora.*

2. Position of Pronouns

The position of double object pronouns with respect to the verb is the same as that of single object pronouns.

- before a conjugated verb (as in the examples in 1)
- after an infinitive or present participle or before the conjugated verb that precedes it
- before a negative formal command and after an affirmative one

¿El CD? Acaban de **dármelo.** (**Me lo** acaban de dar.)
¿Los pronombres de complemento? Estoy **explicándotelos** ahora. (**Te los** estoy explicando ahora.)
¿La comida? No **me la** traiga ahora. Ah, sí… Por favor, **tráigamela.**

¡OJO!

Remember to add an accent mark when two pronouns are added to the end of an infinitive, present participle, or affirmative command.

Le(s) → se

1. Use of *se*

When both the indirect and the direct object pronouns begin with the letter **l**, the indirect object pronoun *always* changes to **se.** The direct object pronoun does not change. The change of **le** → **se** always happens in the Spanish equivalents of third person expressions such as these: *it to him/her/them, them to him/her/them.*

Only four third-person pronoun combinations are possible in Spanish: **se lo, se la, se los, se las.**

- se = represents the indirect object pronoun (**le** or **les**)
- **lo/la/los/las** = direct object pronouns (no change)

Les dimos el auto. (les lo) → **Se lo** dimos.	*We gave them the car.* *We gave it to them.*
Le escribí la carta ayer. (le la) → **Se la** escribí ayer.	*I wrote her the letter yesterday.* *I wrote it to her yesterday.*
Le regaló esos zapatos. (le los) → **Se los** regaló.	*He gave him those shoes.* *He gave them to him.*
Les mandamos las invitaciones. (le las) → **Se las** mandamos.	*We sent them the invitations.* *We sent them to them.*

2. Clarifying *se*

Since **se** can stand for **le** (*to/for you* [sing.], *him, her*) or **les** (*to/for you* [pl.], *them*), it is often necessary to clarify its meaning by using **a** plus the pronoun object of prepositions.

¿La carta? Voy a escribírsela. (meaning of **se** unclear unless clarified)

¿La carta? Voy a escribírsela **a Ud.** / **a Uds.**
a él / **a ellos.**
a ella / **a ellas.**

The letter? I'm going to write it to you (sing.) / you (pl.).
to him / to them (m. or m. and f.).
to her / to them (f.).

Summary of Indirect and Direct Object Pronouns

INDIRECT	DIRECT
me/te/nos/os **le(s)** → se	+ **lo/la/los/las**

Autoprueba

Match each sentence with the correct double object pronouns.

1. Le dieron el libro. → ______ ______ dieron.
2. Les sirvieron la paella. → ______ ______ sirvieron.
3. Le di las direcciones. → ______ ______ di.
4. Les trajo los boletos. → ______ ______ trajo.

a. Se las
b. Se los
c. Se lo
d. Se la

Answers: 1. c 2. d 3. a 4. b

Práctica

A. ¡Anticipemos! Oraciones que se oyen en casa. ¿A qué objetos se refieren las siguientes oraciones? Identifique también el pronombre de complemento indirecto en cada oración.

	ORACIONES	OBJETOS
b; me	1. «¿Me **la** pasas? Gracias.»	a. unas fotos
e; me, Me	2. «Tengo muchas ganas de comprárme**los** todos. Me encanta esa música.»	b. la ensalada
a; se, Les	3. «¿Por qué no se **las** mandas a los abuelos? Les van a gustar muchísimo.»	c. unos billetes de avión para Guadalajara
c; te	4. «Tengo que reservárte**los** hoy mismo, porque mañana se vence (*expires*) la oferta especial de Aeroméxico.»	d. la fiesta
d; se, le	5. «Yo se **la** di a Lupe para su cumpleaños. Antonio y Diego le hicieron un pastel.»	e. los CDs de Luis Miguel

B. En la mesa. Imagine que Ud. acaba de comer, pero todavía tiene hambre. Pida más comida, según el modelo. Fíjese en (*Note*) el uso del tiempo presente para pedir algo de manera informal.

MODELO: ensalada → ¿Hay más **ensalada**? ¿Me **la** pasas, por favor?

1. pan Me lo...
2. tortillas Me las...
3. tomates Me los...
4. fruta Me la...
5. vino Me lo...
6. jamón Me lo...

C. En el aeropuerto. Cambie los sustantivos por pronombres para evitar (*avoid*) la repetición.

MODELO: ¿La maleta? Van a prestarme la maleta mañana. →
Van a prestár**mela** (**Me la** van a prestar) mañana.

1. ¿La hora de la salida? Acaban de decirnos la hora de la salida.
2. ¿El horario (*schedule*)? Sí, léame el horario, por favor.
3. ¿Los boletos? No, no tiene que darle los boletos aquí.
4. ¿El equipaje? ¡Claro que le guardo el equipaje!
5. ¿Los boletos? Ya te compré los boletos.
6. ¿El puesto? No te preocupes. Te puedo guardar el puesto.
7. ¿La clase turística? Sí, les recomiendo la clase turística, señores.
8. ¿La cena? La asistente de vuelo nos va a servir la cena en el avión.

Conversación

A. ¿Quién le regaló eso?

Paso 1. Haga una lista de los cinco mejores regalos que Ud. ha recibido (*have received*) en su vida (*life*). Si no sabe cómo expresar algo, pregúnteselo a su profesor(a).

Paso 2. Ahora déle a un compañero o una compañera su lista. Él/Ella le va a preguntar: **¿Quién te regaló ____?** Use pronombres en su respuesta. **¡OJO!** Fíjese en (*Note*) estas formas en plural **(ellos): regalaron, dieron, mandaron.**

MODELO: E1: ¿Quién te regaló **los aretes de oro**?
E2: Mis padres **me los** regalaron.

Paso 3. Ahora describa a la clase por lo menos uno de los regalos interesantes que recibió su compañero/a.

MODELO: Cintia recibió **unos aretes de oro** como regalo. **Se los** regalaron sus padres.

B. ¿Quién le dio qué a quién?

Paso 1. En parejas, hagan y contesten preguntas para determinar quién regaló cada objeto y a quién se lo regaló. Sigan el modelo.

Prác. B: Variation: Have students work in pairs. One student says just the question with the object pronouns (e.g., *¿me la pasas, por favor?*) and the other must give the food item(s) to which the question might refer.

Prác. C: Answers: 1. *Acaban de decírnosla.* (*Nos la acaban de decir.*) **2.** *Sí, léamelo, por favor.* **3.** *No, no tiene que dárselos aquí.* (*No, no se los tiene que dar aquí.*) **4.** *¡Claro que se lo guardo!* **5.** *Ya te los compré.* **6.** *Te lo puedo guardar.* (*Puedo guardártelo.*) **7.** *Sí, se la recomiendo, señores.* **8.** *La asistente de vuelo nos la va a servir en el avión.* (*La asistente de vuelo va a servírnosla en el avión.*)

Mundo interactivo
You should now be prepared to work with Scenario 5, Activity 2 in Connect Spanish (**www.connectspanish.com**).

Prác. A: Notes

- Students do not need to produce the double object pronouns in this activity. As with previous *¡Anticipemos!* activities, the purpose here is for students to see and understand the grammar structure in a natural context. No production of the structure is required here.
- Getting the correct answers depends not only on matching the gender of the direct object pronoun to the objects but also on meaning.

Prác. B: Reciclado

Note the review of food vocabulary.

Prác. B: Suggestions

- Point out to students that, as shown in this activity, the use of the simple present tense in a question is the easiest way to ask someone to do something, and it does not sound as harsh as a command form.
- Have students use the emphatic *a mí* phrase in their responses.

Prác. C: Reciclado

Note the review of travel vocabulary.

Con. A: Suggestion

Start the activity by assigning pairs to practice giving definitions. Have students explain what the gifts were (without naming them) while classmates try to guess the correct item. The name of the object can be given in English. The important task is to practice circumlocution.

Redacción: As a composition assignment, ask students to describe the history of their favorite gift (or their partner's): who gave it to them, why, when, and so on.

Optional Exercises

- Have students toss a ball or toy (or any other small object). Have each student give a command or a sentence about what the recipient should do with the object once he/she gets it. Write the following verbs on the board.

  tirar (new) *dar*
  pasar *llevar*
  traer

  Model the following sentences to set up the activity:

  Désela a la profesora.
  Tíresela a Manuel.
  Tráigamela.
- Tell students that you are supposed to throw a party this evening but that you have the following problems. Have them give you advice to help you out, e.g.:

No hay refrescos en casa. → *No se preocupe. Yo se los compro.*

1. *No hay leche en casa.*
2. *No tengo suficiente champán para la fiesta.*
3. *Me olvidé de mandar las invitaciones para la fiesta de cumpleaños.*
4. *No recordé hacer un pastel.*

NATIONAL STANDARDS: Cultures

Luis Miguel Gallego Basteri (1970–), commonly known as Luis Miguel, is a Mexican singer famous for his pop music, *boleros*, *mariachis*, and romantic ballads. He is the winner of four Latin Grammy awards and five Grammys, winning his first Grammy when he was 15 years old. His fans frequently refer to him as *el Sol de México.*

Con. B: Suggestion

Have students guess the occasion for the gifts and also why the gift was given.

Un poco de todo

A: Optional

Provide these lists of verbs. Then have students use the verbs to describe what *Javier* did yesterday. Follow up by having students use verbs from these lists to describe what they did yesterday.

POR LA MAÑANA

despertarse a las siete
levantarse en seguida
ducharse
afeitarse
vestirse
peinarse
desayunar
tomar solo un café con leche
ir a la universidad
asistir a clases toda la mañana

POR LA TARDE

almorzar con unos amigos en la cafetería
divertirse hablando con ellos
despedirse de ellos
ir a la biblioteca
quedarse allí estudiando hasta las cuatro y media
volver a casa después
ayudarlo/la a su amigo a hacer la cena

POR LA NOCHE

cenar con Rosa
querer estudiar por una hora
no poder (*estudiar*)
mirar la televisión con sus amigos
darles las buenas noches (*a sus amigos*)
salir a reunirse con otros amigos en un bar
volver a casa a las dos de la mañana
quitarse la ropa
acostarse
leer un rato (new) *para poder dormirse*
dormirse por fin a las tres

Resources: Transparency 105

MODELO: E1: ¿Quién regaló **la computadora portátil**?
E2: Los Sres. Santana **la** regalaron.
E1: De acuerdo. ¿A quién **se la** regalaron?
E2: **Se la** regalaron a Jesús David.

OBJETOS

RECIPIENTES

Pilar — Raúl — los Sres. Santana — Jesús David

Paso 2. Ahora comparen sus respuestas con las (*those*) de otra pareja. ¿Están de acuerdo?

Un poco de todo

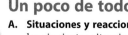

A. Situaciones y reacciones. En parejas, imaginen que Uds. se encontraron en las siguientes situaciones en el pasado. ¿Cómo se pusieron en esos momentos? ¿Qué sintieron? ¿Qué hicieron? Contesten individualmente y comparen sus respuestas.

MODELO: Su compañero/a de cuarto hizo mucho ruido cuando regresó a casa a las cuatro de la mañana. →
E1: Me enojé y no quise decirle nada.
E2: Pues yo me puse furiosísima, pero hablé con ella y me prometió no volver a hacerlo.

SITUACIONES

1. Su compañero/a de cuarto (esposo/a) hizo mucho ruido cuando regresó a casa a las cuatro de la mañana.
2. El profesor le dijo que no habría (*there would be no*) clase mañana.
3. Ud. rompió el reloj que era (*was*) regalo de su abuelo.
4. Su hermano perdió el CD que a Ud. más le gusta.
5. Su mejor amigo lo/la llamó a las seis de la mañana para cantarle «Feliz cumpleaños».
6. Ud. recibió un gran aumento de sueldo (*raise*), pero no hubo aumento para los otros empleados.

B. Lengua y cultura: La Virgen de Guadalupe, quince siglos (*centuries*) **de historia.** Complete the following paragraphs with the correct form of the words in parentheses, as suggested by context. When two possibilities are given in parentheses, select the correct word. Use the present tense or the preterite of the infinitives, according to context.

Multimedia: Internet (p. 283)

Have students search the Internet for images and websites related to the celebration of the *Virgen de Guadalupe* in Spain and Mexico. You might have groups develop visual and oral presentations about these festivals.

Culture (p. 283)

- Several rivers in the southern half of Spain start with the phrase *guada-*, which comes from the Arabic *oudel* meaning *river: el Guadalquivir, el Guadalete, el Guadalhorce,* and so on.

(Cont.)

En todos los países hispanohablantes, hay festividades religiosas que son días de fiesta nacionales. Un ejemplo es el día de Navidad, que se (celebrar[1]) en todo el mundo hispano. Otra de las celebraciones religiosas, que también (es/está[2]) una fiesta nacional en (mucho[3]) países, es el 12 de diciembre, día de la fiesta de la Virgen de Guadalupe, una imagen venerada[a] por todo el mundo católico pero especialmente en México.

La historia de esta imagen (venir[4]) desde[b] los árabes* a través de[c] España y del México colonial hasta nuestros días. «Guadalupe» es una palabra de origen árabe que significa «río oculto».[d] Ahora es (el/la[5]) nombre de una pequeña ciudad (español[6]) donde hay un monasterio famoso.

La historia de la Virgen de Guadalupe en España (empezar[7]) en el siglo VI.[e] El Papa[f] Gregorio tenía[g] una estatua de la Virgen y (se lo / se la[8]) regaló al Obispo[h] Leandro de Sevilla. Pero luego la estatua (desaparecer[9]) durante los siglos en que los árabes ocuparon la Península. Después de la expulsión de los árabes, un pastor[i] cristiano (le/la[10]) (encontrar[11]) cerca de la ciudad de Guadalupe. Por eso la estatua (tomar[12]) el nombre de la Virgen de Guadalupe.

En lo que hoy es México, la historia de la Virgen comienza muchos años después, en el siglo XVI. Un campesino[j] indígena, Juan Diego, se convirtió[k] al cristianismo. Un día (*él*: ver[13]) a la Virgen en un lugar llamado Tepeyac, un lugar sagrado[l] de los aztecas dedicado al culto[m] de la diosa[n] madre Tonantzín. Por un milagro,[ñ] la Virgen (dejar[o14]) su imagen impresa[p] en la tilma[q] de Juan Diego. Esta imagen (recibir[15]) el nombre de Virgen de Guadalupe porque Tepeyac (es/está[16]) cerca del pueblo mexicano de Guadalupe.

La imagen de la Virgen de Guadalupe mexicana (es/está[17]) muy diferente de la imagen de la Virgen española, pero las dos responden al arte predominante en (su[18]) respectivas épocas. La tilma de Juan Diego, con la imagen de la Virgen, todavía se puede (ver[19]) en la Basílica[r] de Nuestra Señora de Guadalupe, en la Ciudad de México.

[a]imagen... *image venerated, adored* [b]*from* [c]a... *through* [d]río... *hidden river* [e]el... *the sixth century* (el siglo seis) [f]*Pope* [g]*had* [h]*Bishop* [i]*shepherd* [j]*peasant* [k]se... *converted* [l]*sacred, holy* [m]*worship* [n]*goddess* [ñ]*miracle* [o]*to leave* [p]*imprinted* [q]*shawl* [r]*large church*

La tilma (*shawl*) de Juan Diego en la Basílica de Nuestra Señora (*Lady*) de Guadalupe, en la Ciudad de México

Act. B: Answers: 1. *celebra* **2.** *es* **3.** *muchos* **4.** *viene/vino* **5.** *el* **6.** *española* **7.** *empezó/empieza* **8.** *se la* **9.** *desapareció* **10.** *la* **11.** *encontró* **12.** *tomó* **13.** *vio* **14.** *dejó* **15.** *recibió* **16.** *está* **17.** *es* **18.** *sus* **19.** *ver*

Comprensión. ¿Cierto o falso? Corrija las oraciones falsas.

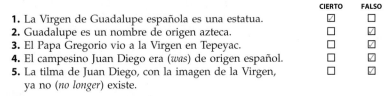

	CIERTO	FALSO
1. La Virgen de Guadalupe española es una estatua.	☑	☐
2. Guadalupe es un nombre de origen azteca.	☐	☑
3. El Papa Gregorio vio a la Virgen en Tepeyac.	☐	☑
4. El campesino Juan Diego era (*was*) de origen español.	☐	☑
5. La tilma de Juan Diego, con la imagen de la Virgen, ya no (*no longer*) existe.	☐	☑

Comprehensión, Answers: 2. *Es de origen árabe.* **3.** *Juan Diego vio a la Virgen en Tepeyac.* **4.** *Era un campesino indígena.* **5.** *La tilma de Juan Diego está en la Basílica de la Virgen de Guadalupe, en la Ciudad de México.*

En su comunidad

Entreviste a una persona hispana de su universidad o ciudad sobre las celebraciones tradicionales de su país y de su familia.

PREGUNTAS POSIBLES

- ¿Cuáles son los días festivos más importantes de su país? ¿Son celebraciones de origen civil o religioso? ¿Se celebran en familia o hay eventos en la ciudad con motivo de estos días festivos?
- ¿Cuáles son las celebraciones más importantes en su familia? ¿Y sus favoritas? ¿Por qué?
- ¿Cuál fue la última fiesta que Ud. celebró en su país? ¿Cómo y con quién la celebró?

**Los árabes (musulmanes) conquistaron la Península Ibérica en el año 711. Inmediatamente los cristianos iniciaron una guerra de reconquista* (war of reconquest) *que terminó en 1492, el mismo año en que Cristóbal Colón llegó a América.*

B: Suggestions

- After doing the activity, help students to construct an approximate timeline of events, with dates and centuries: *el siglo VI, 711, 1492, el siglo XVI, hoy día.* Be sure that they read the footnote.
- Emphasize with students the blending of cultures that is seen in this story: elements from Peninsular Spanish and indigenous American traditions.
- As you work with this activity, be aware that not all students will be familiar with the customs of the Catholic Church, so you should be prepared to explain briefly customs such as the veneration of statues, patron saints, church officials (the Pope, the Bishop), and so on.
- See also *Lectura cultural, Cap. 3*, for more information about *la Virgen de Guadalupe* in Mexico.

B: Notes

- The following grammar topics are included in *Lengua y cultura:* gender, possessive adjective, adjective agreement, direct and indirect object pronouns, double object pronouns, *-ar/-er/-ir* verbs, irregular verbs (*venir, ver*), stem-changing verbs (*empezar, encontrar, volver*), preterite tense, *ser* vs. *estar.*

En su comunidad

Suggestions

- Remind students to get the following basic information: the informant's country of origin, how long he or she has lived in this country, and if the informant visits his or her country of origin frequently.
- This activity could also be assigned as an online research project on a country of the student's choice or assigned by you.
- See the IM for additional suggestions and guidelines.

Resources: Desenlace

In the *Cap. 9* segment of "Chapter-by-Chapter Supplementary Materials" in the IM, you will find a chapter-culminating activity. You can use this activity to consolidate and review the vocabulary and grammar skills students have acquired.

Culture (Cont.)

- There is yet another Guadalupe statue in Spain: the *Virgen* is the patron saint of the island of La Gomera (one of the Canary Islands). According to legend, a statue of her was found by sailors who were on their way to America in the 16th century. Seeing lights from their ship, they stopped at the island and found the statue.

TelePuntos

Note

Pages 284–289 are optional. You may cover some, all, or none of this material in class, or assign it to students—as a group or individually—for homework or extra credit. Pages 290–291 (*En resumen: En este capítulo*) are a summary of all of the chapter's active material.

Suggestions

- Use this activity to review vocabulary related to holidays, as it is important to comprehension of this program. On the board, group holidays according to categories: *fiestas religiosas, fiestas históricas, fiestas en honor de alguien.*
- Ask students for religious holidays they may celebrate that are not observed by the majority of people in their country.
- Point out that the translation for Memorial Day in Spanish literally means the *Day of the Fallen in War.*

Programa 9

Notes

- This program will be easily accessible to students because its language is relatively simple. Some narration is done in the preterite, but students should be more comfortable with that tense in this chapter.
- Students may find that the images of *el Mes Morado* are strange or weird, depending on their religious background (or lack thereof). Encourage students to take notes on the elements of *el Mes Morado* tradition, in preparation for *Y ahora, Uds.*
- Emphasize to students that the more carefully they study the preliminary activities (*Antes de mirar, Vocabulario de este programa*, and *Fragmento del guion*), the more they will understand. Scanning *Después de mirar* before viewing is also an excellent strategy.

Vocabulario de este programa

Suggestions

- The terms *empanadas* and *pupusas* (from *Programa 7*) are not relisted here. You may wish to present them again.
- Bring up the issue of different *acepciones* (meanings) for one word by highlighting the two meanings of *manzana* (*apple* and *city block*). Similarly, *block* is a concept expressed in different ways in the Hispanic world.
- For the benefit of students who may now know much about Catholicism, you may wish to point out that it is a religion that not only allows visual representations but very much encourages them. Images related to Jesus' last day on earth (walking with the cross, being nailed to the cross, and so on) are very common in the Catholic tradition, and they are venerated by Catholics.

TELEPUNTOS

SALU2

SALU2

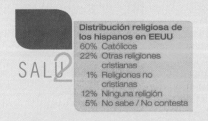

Distribución religiosa de los hispanos en EEUU

60%	Católicos
22%	Otras religiones cristianas
1%	Religiones no cristianas
12%	Ninguna religión
5%	No sabe / No contesta

El porcentaje (*percentage*) de católicos entre la población hispana es muy alto, pero otras religiones cristianas, especialmente los evangélicos, atraen a más y más personas cada año.

Antes de mirar

¿Es religioso o histórico el origen de la mayoría de los días festivos y celebraciones de su país? Dé algunos ejemplos. ¿Cuáles son las fiestas que más se celebran en su comunidad? ¿Se celebra la Navidad? ¿el Día de la Independencia? ¿el Día de los Caídos en la guerra (*Memorial Day*)? ¿O se celebran más otras fiestas?

PROGRAMA 9: De fiesta en fiesta

Este programa muestra dos fiestas que se celebran en diferentes lugares del mundo hispanohablante. Además (*In addition*), presenta datos estadísticos sobre la afiliación religiosa de los hispanos en los Estados Unidos.

Fragmento del guion

VÍCTOR: Y volviendo a los días de fiesta, Ana, ¿qué fiestas se celebran en tu país?

ANA: Pues, la verdad[a] es que tenemos muchos. Por ejemplo: el 28 de noviembre celebramos la independencia de España. Y el 3 de noviembre celebramos la separación con Colombia. Y, cómo no,[b] las grandes celebraciones religiosas, como la Navidad, la Semana Santa[c] y el Domingo de Pascua de Resurrección.[d] Me imagino que tu familia celebra estas fechas también, ¿no?

VÍCTOR: Pues la Nochebuena, la Navidad y la Pascua de Resurrección, sí. Pero la Semana Santa no es una celebración típica en los Estados Unidos, excepto por el Viernes Santo,[e] en que no hay clases en muchas escuelas.[f]

ANA: Y seguro que tampoco celebran el Mes Morado, una tradición netamente[g] peruana que nos va a mostrar en el siguiente reportaje nuestra buena reportera Laura Sánchez Tejada.

[a]*truth* [b]cómo… *of course* [c]Semana… *Holy Week* [d]Domingo… *Easter Sunday* [e]Viernes… *Good Friday* [f]*schools* [g]*100%*

Vocabulario de este programa

de nuevo	again
aunque	although
el/la seguidor(a)	follower
venerado/a	worshipped
Cristo crucificado	Christ on the Cross
la fe	faith, religion
el/la esclavo/a	slave
el muro	wall
el terremoto	earthquake
asolar	to devastate
rendir (rindo) (i) culto	to worship
el castellano	**el español**
platicar (qu)	to chat
la gente	people
sino	but rather
ha llegado a ser	has become
la manzana	block
el escenario	stage

Al mirar

Mientras mira el programa, indique todos los contextos en que aparecen números en este programa.

1. ☑ fechas y años
2. ☐ la edad (*age*) de una persona
3. ☑ siglos
4. ☑ porcentajes
5. ☑ cantidad de cosas
6. ☑ países donde se habla español
7. ☑ batallas (*battles*) mexicanas
8. ☑ cantidad de personas
9. ☐ población de una ciudad

La procesión del Señor de los Milagros (*Our Lord of the Miracles*) durante la celebración del Mes Morado: Una tradición de cinco siglos (*centuries*)

Mundo interactivo

Continue your work as an intern at HispanaVisión with Laura Sánchez Tejada, the roving reporter of *Salu2*, as you complete Scenario 5, Activities 1 and 2 in Connect Spanish (**www.connectspanish.com**).

Después de mirar

A. ¿Está claro? Empareje los números con conceptos del programa.

CONCEPTOS

1. __d__ año de una victoria mexicana contra los franceses
2. __e__ manzanas que ocupa Fiesta Broadway en Los Ángeles
3. __c__ escenarios para presentaciones artísticas en Fiesta Broadway
4. __b__ siglos que la tradición de venerar al Señor de los Milagros existe entre los peruanos
5. __f__ porcentaje de hispanos católicos en los Estados Unidos
6. __g__ países donde se habla español
7. __h__ porcentaje de hispanos cristianos no católicos en los Estados Unidos
8. __a__ fecha de la Independencia de Panamá
9. __i__ personas que asisten a Fiesta Broadway

NÚMEROS

a. 28 de noviembre
b. cerca de 5
c. 6
d. 1862
e. 24
f. 60 (aproximadamente)
g. 21
h. 22
i. 500.000

Fiesta Broadway, en Los Ángeles, California: Una celebración que conmemora la victoria mexicana contra las fuerzas invasoras francesas en Puebla el 5 de mayo de 1862

B. Un poco más. Conteste las siguientes preguntas.

1. ¿Cuál es la afiliación religiosa de un 12 por ciento de los hispanos en los Estados Unidos?
2. ¿Qué celebración religiosa es importante en Panamá, pero no en los Estados Unidos?
3. ¿En qué mes es el Mes Morado? ¿En qué ciudad peruana se celebra este mes?
4. ¿Qué grupo de hispanos en los Estados Unidos se identifica con la fiesta del Cinco de Mayo?
5. ¿Qué tiene de especial la Fiesta Broadway?

Act. B, Answers: 1. *ninguna religión* **2.** *la Semana Santa* **3.** *octubre, Lima* **4.** *los mexicanos* **5.** *Answers will vary.*

C. Y ahora, Uds. En grupos, hablen de la tradición del Mes Morado en Lima. ¿Hay alguna tradición similar en su ciudad, estado/provincia o país? ¿En qué consiste esta celebración y cuáles son sus características?

Sobre el programa

Este año, Víctor y su esposa Marina invitaron a Ana y a Laura a una fiesta en casa de ellos para celebrar el Cinco de Mayo con su familia. Era[a] la primera celebración del Cinco de Mayo a que asistía[b] Laura, ya que[c] en Nuevo León, su estado mexicano, no se celebra esta fiesta.

Por supuesto,[d] en la fiesta había[e] comida mexicana en abundancia. Ana llevó de postre un plato típico panameño, goyoría de plátano[f] verde y miel de caña.[g] Laura llevó una botella de tequila, porque cocinar no es su fuerte.[h]

[a]*It was* [b]*attended* [c]ya… *since* [d]Por… *Of course* [e]*there was* [f]goyoría… *a plantain-based dessert* [g]miel… *sugar cane molasses* [h]*forte, strength*

Producción personal

Filme una entrevista con una persona hispana no estadounidense de su universidad o comunidad. La persona que Ud. entrevista debe hablar de un día festivo de su país de origen que no se celebra en este país.

Fragmento del guion

Suggestions

- Before reading the *Fragmento,* make sure that students have read about *la Semana Santa* in the *A leer: Lectura cultural* section in this chapter.
- Again, for the benefit of students who may not be familiar with Catholicism, you may wish to share the following information: *El Viernes Santo* is the most solemn day of *la Semana Santa,* and it is one of the most important days of the Catholic liturgical year. It commemorates the day Jesus died on the cross. Its solemnity gives way to the celebration of *el Domingo de Pascua,* which commemorates the resurrection of Christ.

Al mirar

Suggestion

Go over the list with students before they watch the show to make sure that they understand all of the items. Suggest to students that they not look at the list while watching the program.

Después de mirar

B: Suggestions

- Ask students why the October celebration in Lima is called *el Mes Morado*. (Many participants wear purple during the celebration. Purple is the color that Nazarene nuns wear in Lima, and it has become the color of the festival as well.)
- Ask students if they understood the other name for *el Señor de los Milagros* (*el Cristo Moreno*) and ask why they think that name is also used.

C: Suggestions

- After students have discussed *el Mes Morado* in groups, have them share with the whole class the elements of the celebration that they remember.
- Ask if students are familiar with a similar celebration in this country. While such celebrations are not common, there are some in some areas.

Sobre el programa

Optional: Comprensión

¿Cierto o falso? Corrija las oraciones falsas.

1. *Para Víctor y su familia, celebrar el Cinco de Mayo es una tradición.* (*Cierto*)
2. *En el estado de Nuevo León, México, el Cinco de Mayo es una fiesta muy importante.* (*Falso: En Nuevo León no se celebra el Cinco de Mayo.*)
3. *Laura cocina muy bien.* (*Falso: Laura no cocina bien.*)
4. *Ana llevó una botella de tequila a la fiesta en casa de Víctor.* (*Falso: Laura llevó una botella de tequila. Ana llevó un postre panameño que ella cocinó.*)

Producción personal

Note

See the IM for additional suggestions for this chapter's assignment as well as for general guidelines and suggestions for video assignments.

Lectura cultural

Notes

- For more information about Cuba, see the chapter's opening pages and the IM.
- See the IM for some expressions used in Cuba.

First Reading: Notes

- Carlos Manuel de Céspedes (1819–1874) is a Cuban national hero. His *Declaración de Independencia* in 1868 started the Ten Years' War against Spain, the first Cuban attempt to gain independence. He was killed in action.
- *La Guerra de Independencia Cubana*, or *la Guerra del 95* (1895), is Cuba's last war against Spain. It started with the call for independence known as *el Grito de Baire*, and eventually became what is known in this country as the Spanish-American War of 1898, in which Spain ceded Cuba (as well as Puerto Rico and the Philippines) to the United States. This war effectively marks the end of the Spanish Empire. Cuba was a U.S. colony until 1902, when *la República de Cuba* was declared. Official U.S. intervention in the government of the island ended in 1909.
- The phrase *cambio político* refers, of course, to the Cuban Revolution and Castro's rise to power in 1959. Ask some students to research the topic online and do a mini presentation on this topic, mainly a timeline.

Exploración lingüística

Ask students to find the following in the reading. Some of these words are glossed and some are not.

1. *Palabras relacionadas con la historia (la independencia, nacional, el patriota, la libertad, el dominio, colonial, la guerra, el cambio político)*
2. *Una palabra en español que se relaciona con las palabras inglesas* dominate, dominant, domineering (*el dominio*)
3. *Dos conectores (palabras o expresiones que conectan las ideas en una párrafo) (en efecto, sin embargo)*

En otros países hispanos

Suggestion

Ask students what U.S. city also has a famous Carnival. (New Orleans)

A LEER

Lectura cultural

Cuba

En Cuba se conmemoran dos días muy importantes. El primero es el 10 de octubre, que se conoce como el Día de la Independencia Nacional. En este día el patriota cubano Carlos Manuel de Céspedes declaró libres a todos los esclavos.[a] También llamó a todos los cubanos a liberarse del dominio[b] colonial de España, marcando el inicio[c] de la primera guerra[d] de independencia de Cuba.

¿En qué son similares los días festivos cubanos y los (*those*) de este país? ¿En qué son diferentes?

El otro día festivo de mucha importancia para todos los cubanos es la Navidad. Como resultado del cambio[e] político de 1959 y durante muchos de los años bajo el régimen de Fidel Castro, no se les permitió a los cubanos celebrar la Navidad de manera oficial. Sin embargo, todo cambió[f] con la visita a Cuba del Papa[g] Juan Pablo II (Segundo) a Cuba en el año 1998. Desde entonces[h] los cubanos pueden asistir a la iglesia y celebrar este día tan importante con su familia y amigos.

[a]*slaves* [b]*control* [c]*beginning* [d]*war* [e]*change (that is, the regime of Fidel Castro)* [f]*changed* [g]*Pope (Head of the Catholic Church)* [h]Desde... *Since then*

En otros países hispanos

En todo el mundo hispanohablante Estas festividades se celebran en todas partes.

- **La Semana Santa** Así[a] se llama a la semana que va desde el Domingo de Ramos[b] hasta el Domingo de Pascua. En muchas ciudades hay procesiones[c] para conmemorar la pasión, muerte[d] y resurrección de Jesús. Coincide con el principio[e] de la primavera o el otoño, según el hemisferio, y es una semana en que se cierran los colegios[f] y universidades y muchas personas toman vacaciones.
- **El Carnaval** Esta fiesta precede al comienzo de la Cuaresma.[g] El Carnaval más famoso del mundo es el de Río de Janeiro (Brasil), pero hay Carnavales hispanos que también son famosos por la exuberancia de su música, bailes y colorido, como los Carnavales de Cádiz (España), Barranquilla (Colombia) y Santiago de Cuba (Cuba).
- **«El puente»** La palabra significa *bridge* en inglés. En el contexto de los días festivos, un puente es un fin de semana largo creado por un día festivo.

[a]*That's how* [b]el... *Palm Sunday* [c]*street processions* [d]la... *passion (that is, suffering), death* [e]*beginning* [f]*schools* [g]*Lent (period from Ash Wednesday to Good Friday)*

Un desfile (*parade*) de Carnaval, en Santiago de Cuba

Tres símbolos cubanos

- **La palmera** Este árbol se encuentra por todas partes de la Isla. Su dibujo también está en el escudo[a] nacional como símbolo del espíritu cubano: siempre alto y orgulloso.[b]
- **El mar** Cuba no se entiende sin el mar, que es parte esencial de su geografía e historia.
- **El tabaco** Se dice que Cuba produce el mejor tabaco del mundo.

[a]*shield, coat of arms* [b]alto... *high-spirited and proud*

Una importante figura histórica

José Martí (1853–1895) fue un pensador[a] y escritor[b] cubano. Inició y fue líder de la Segunda Guerra[c] de Independencia contra España. Se le considera el Apóstol[d] de la independencia cubana.

Yo soy un hombre sincero[e]
De donde crece[f] la palma,
Y antes de morirme quiero
Echar[g] mis versos del alma.[h]

de *Versos sencillos* (1891)

[a]*intellectual* [b]*writer* [c]Segunda... *Second War* [d]*Apostle (that is, founding voice)* [e]*simple* [f]*grows* [g]*Release, Cast* [h]*soul*

COMPRENSIÓN

1. ¿Cuáles son los días festivos más importantes de Cuba? el Día de la Independencia y la Navidad
2. ¿Desde cuándo se permite celebrar la Navidad sin restricciones otra vez en Cuba? desde 1998
3. ¿Cuáles son otros de los días festivos importantes del mundo hispano? la Semana Santa y el Carnaval

Tres símbolos cubanos

Notes

- Palms are also referenced in the opening lines to *Versos sencillos*, quoted in *Una figura...*
- Cuban cigars are famous the world over, and the culture of the cigar factories is also famous, especially for its emphasis on literacy (one person would read while others worked making cigars).

Del mundo hispano

Antes de leer

Es muy común hacer algunos propósitos (*resolutions*) cuando un año empieza. ¿Los hace Ud., generalmente? Haga una lista de cuatro propósitos que Ud. hizo en años pasados o tuvo la intención de hacer. Use infinitivos en su lista. ¿Los cumplió todos? (*Did you achieve all of them?*)

Lectura: Propósitos para el Año Nuevo

12 propósitos para el 2012

Complete la siguiente declaración:

Yo, ______________________ (nombre), me comprometo[a] a cumplir ________ (número) propósitos de esta lista en los próximos 365 días.

- Leer un libro cada dos meses.
- No excederte en tus horas de trabajo.
- Comer más sano.[b]
- Asistir a una muestra[c] de cine o de arte.
- Comprar la membresía[d] de un gimnasio.
- Tomar dos litros de agua diariamente.
- Ir a una ceremonia religiosa ajena a la tuya.[e]
- Regalar sin razón.[f]
- Desayunar bien.
- Ir a votar.
- Ir de excursión a un lugar remoto.
- Separar la basura en orgánica e inorgánica.

[a]me... *I promise* [b]más... *in a more healthy manner* [c]*exhibition* [d]*membership* [e]ajena... *different from mine* [f]sin... *for no reason*

Comprensión

Una vida mejor. Los propósitos que una persona hace para el año nuevo generalmente son con la intención de mejorar (*improving*) su vida (*life*) de alguna manera. Clasifique los (*those*) de esta lectura según su categoría y explique por qué puso cada propósito en la categoría que Ud. eligió (*chose*). (Algunos pueden ir en más de un grupo.)

1. Los que pueden mejorar la salud (*health*) física
2. Los que pueden mejorar la salud mental o espiritual
3. Los que pueden mejorar las relaciones con los otros y con el medio ambiente (*environment*)

Del mundo hispano

Note

See the IM for optional follow-up, writing, and Internet activities.

Antes de leer

Suggestions

- Tell students to use infinitives in their resolutions, as in the *Lectura.*
- Ask students to submit their New Year's resolutions anonymously. You can then read them to the whole class and/or write them on the board. Tell students to look ahead at the three categories in *Comprensión*, then classify the resolutions written by their classmates.
- Have students react to the anonymous resolutions by telling whether or not they would also commit to each resolution, and why or why not. This could also be done in written format and anonymously.

Estrategia: Guessing Meaning from Context

Most vocabulary in this reading will be accessible to students, but words or expressions that may not be and that are not glossed include *excederte* and *diariamente*. Ask students to guess from the context what these words mean, and help them with leading questions, e.g.: *¿Se parece esta palabra a otra palabra que Ud. sí sabe?*

Comprensión

Suggestion

Answers will vary. As you go over them in a whole-class format, ask students to justify orally why they have chosen the categories they have. For the *propósitos* that seem to you to belong in more than one category, or for those that have sparked differing opinions, ask for students' opinions and justifications.

Una importante figura histórica (p. 286)

Notes

- *Martí* was born in *La Habana*. He was exiled for 17 years because of his opposition to Spanish rule.
- He died in one of the first battles of the war for independence.
- The lines quoted are one of the most famous stanzas of *Versos sencillos*. They are probably known by most Spanish speakers the world over, and they also appear in the famous song "*Guantanamera.*"

Resources: Transparency 106

Antes de escuchar

Suggestion

You may wish to conduct this as a whole-class brainstorming activity.

Escuche

Notes

- In this chapter students can listen to a phone message left by a friend who attended a wedding for a friend who missed the event.
- If the listening is assigned as homework, ask students to listen to the passage at least twice.
- It is a good idea to prepare students for the difficulty of understanding this phone message, and phone messages in general. There is no negotiation of meaning, there are few natural pauses, and often the topic is unexpected. Students will understand more of the message if they read *Después de escuchar A* before listening to the message. Doing so will give them some basic information. Then ask them to read *Después de escuchar B* before listening the second time.
- See the IM for the Audioscript and more information about music in Cuba.

Después de escuchar

B: Follow-up

Ask students what seems usual and unusual about this wedding.

¡Música!

Notes

- *Celia Cruz* was also known as *la Guarachera de Cuba* and *la Reina Rumba*.
- She never returned to Cuba after leaving the island in 1960.
- Her famous signature cry (*¡Azúcar!*) represents her philosophy of life.
- "*La vida es un carnaval*" represents a very Latin way of seeing the world: although life is hard, one has to have a good time and enjoy oneself as much as possible.
- For helpful tips on using songs in the classroom, see the IM.

A ESCUCHAR

Antes de escuchar

¿Qué actividades generalmente se hacen en una boda (*wedding*)? Haga una lista de todas las actividades que pueda imaginar. Consulte el **Vocabulario para escuchar** al hacer (*while making*) su lista.

Vocabulario para escuchar

¡qué lástima!	what a shame!
los novios	bride and groom
cortar	to cut
ensuciarse la cara	to dirty each other's faces
tirar	to throw, toss
lo sintió mucho	was very sorry
el recuerdo	souvenir, party favor

Escuche

Un mensaje telefónico

Pilar dejó un mensaje en el teléfono de una amiga para contarle de una boda a la que asistió anoche. Escuche según las indicaciones de su rofesor(a).

Después de escuchar

A. ¿Quién hizo qué? Indique quién hizo qué, emparejando las acciones con las personas que las hicieron. Hay más de una opción en algunos casos.

	ACCIONES	PERSONAS
a, c, d, e	**1.** bailar	**a.** Estela
e	**2.** cortar el pastel y tirarlo	**b.** un conjunto (*group*) musical
c, d	**3.** llorar	**c.** Pilar
a	**4.** mandar un recuerdo	**d.** la mamá de Estela
b	**5.** tocar salsa	**e.** los novios
f	**6.** no ir a la boda	**f.** la amiga de Pilar y de Estela

Act. B, Answers: 1. *sí* **2.** *Osvaldo* **3.** *Tuvo una emergencia en el hospital.* **4.** *Cree que está durmiendo.* **5.** *Probablemente es médica.*

B. Más información. ¿Qué más se sabe o deduce Ud. del mensaje?

1. La amiga de Pilar, ¿es amiga de Estela también?
2. ¿Cómo se llama el novio?
3. ¿Por qué no fue la amiga de Pilar a la boda?
4. ¿Por qué cree Pilar que su amiga no contesta su llamada (*call*)?
5. ¿Cuál es la profesión de la amiga de Pilar?

Celia Cruz, durante los Premios (*Awards*) Grammy Latinos, en Hollywood, 2002

¡Música!

Celia Cruz (1925–2003) fue una de las artistas latinas más famosas y queridas en todo el mundo. Nació[a] y desarrolló[b] su carrera como cantante en Cuba, pero vivió gran parte de su vida[c] en los Estados Unidos.

[a]*She was born* [b]*developed* [c]*life*

Go to the iMix section in Connect Spanish (**www.connectspanish.com**) to access the iTunes playlist "*Puntos9*," where you can purchase "La vida es un carnaval" by Celia Cruz.

A ESCRIBIR

El tema

Una celebración memorable

Preparar

¿Cuál es la celebración más memorable de su vida (*life*)? ¿un baile de fin de curso (*prom night*)? ¿una boda (*wedding*)? ¿un cumpleaños? ¿una fiesta de Nochevieja? ¿el bautizo (*baptism*) de una hija o un hijo? ¿Qué es memorable de esa celebración?

Paso 1. Haga una lista cronológica de todos los eventos y actividades que ocurrieron antes y durante la celebración.

Paso 2. Haga una lista de las cosas que más le gustaron y de las que no le gustaron. Piense también en la razón principal por la que (*which*) esa celebración es tan memorable para Ud.

Redactar

Desarrolle (*Develop*) el ensayo usando toda la información de **Preparar.** No se olvide de expresar sus sentimientos. ¿Cómo se sintió durante la celebración misma (*itself*)? ¿Y después?

Editar

Revise el ensayo para comprobar (*to check*):

- la ortografía y los acentos (**¡OJO!** con las formas del pretérito)
- la organización de las ideas (una clara diferencia entre la narración de los eventos y los sentimientos de Ud.)
- la consistencia del tono
- el uso de los pronombres (evitar [*avoid*] el uso excesivo de pronombres personales; evitar la repetición innecesaria de los sustantivos con el uso de los pronombres de complemento directo e indirecto)

Finalmente, prepare su versión final para entregarla.

A escribir

Note

If you assigned the writing assignment in *Cap. 8*, which is on a very similar topic, ask students to review the corrections on that composition in order to avoid similar mistakes in this one.

Preparar

Suggestions

- **Paso 1.** Remind students to use the preterite for this list of events.
- **Paso 2.** Since students do not yet know the imperfect, tell them to focus on the events themselves that they liked and didn't like, not on the underlying circumstances, reasons, or feelings.

Redactar

Suggestions

- Suggested length for this writing assignment: approximately 125 words
- Suggested structure: 2 paragraphs

  P. 1. Narration of sequence of events and actions

  P. 2. Discussion of student's feelings at the event and a recap of why this celebration was so memorable for them

Editar

Follow-up

Ask students to summarize in a few sentences what happened at the memorable event and what they liked best about it. Have students share their experiences with the class and have the class vote on the most memorable one.

En resumen:
En este capítulo
Vocabulario

Word Families

En este capítulo

- *el día festivo, la fiesta*
- *feliz, ¡felicitaciones!*
- *-ísimo/a, -ísimo* (adv.)

Entre capítulos

- *cumplir años* = *el cumpleaños* (6)
- *el deseo* = *desear* (2)
- *el día festivo* = *el día* (2)
- *enfermarse* = *enfermo/a* (6)
- *el estado afectivo* = *el estado* (3)
- *festivo/a* = *la fiesta* (2)
- *el fin de año* = *el fin de semana* (2)
- *gracias por* = *gracias* (1)
- *el/la invitado/a* = *invitar* (7)
- *(la) medianoche* = *buenas noches* (1)
- *la Nochevieja* = *buenas noches* (1), *viejo/a* (3)
- *la Nochebuena* = *buenas noches* (1), *bueno/a* (3)
- *pasarlo bien/mal* = *pasar* (6)
- *el pastel de cumpleaños* = el cumpleaños (6), *el pastel* (7)
- *ponerse* + adj. = *poner(se)* (5)
- *la quinceañera* = *quince* (1)
- *ser en* = *ser* (1, 3)

¡OJO!

- conseguir ≠ seguir
- despedirse ≠ pedir
- sentirse ≠ sentarse

Suggestions

- Give a series of situations or problems and have students react quickly by expressing how they would feel. For example:

  un examen difícil → *Me pongo nervioso.*

  un chiste cómico → *Me río.*

- Play a game of word associations with words from the *Vocabulario*. Continue round-robin associations for at least ten turns for each word. For example, *botanas* → *sándwiches* → *fiestas* → *cumpleaños*, and so on.

EN RESUMEN En este capítulo

LearnSmart

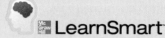

Visit **www.connectspanish.com** to practice the vocabulary and grammar points covered in this chapter.

Gramática en breve

24. Irregular Preterites

Irregular Preterite Endings

estuv-, pud-, pus-, quis-, sup-, tuv-, vin- + **-e, -iste, -o, -imos, -isteis, -ieron**

dij-, traj- + **-e, -iste, -o, -imos, -isteis, -eron**

hay: haber → **hubo** (*there was/were*)

25. Preterite of Stem-changing Verbs

Preterite Stem-changing Patterns

-ar/-er = no change

-ir = change in the third person singular and plural

e → **i**

o → **u**

26. Direct and Indirect Object Pronouns Together

Indirect	Direct
me/te/nos/os	+ **lo/la/los/las**
le(s) → **se**	

Vocabulario

Los verbos

adivinar	to guess
conseguir (*like* **seguir**)	to get, obtain
conseguir + *inf.*	to succeed in (*doing something*)
despedir(se) (*like* **pedir**) **(de)**	to say good-bye (to)
encontrar (encuentro)	to find
morir(se) ([me] muero) (u)	to die
sugerir (sugiero) (i)	to suggest

Repaso: dormir(se) ([me] duermo) (u), pedir (pido) (i), preferir (prefiero) (i), servir (sirvo) (i), vestir(se) ([me] visto) (i)

Los días festivos y las fiestas

el anfitrión, la anfitriona	host (*of an event*)
las botanas (*Mex.*)	appetizers
el champán	champagne
el día festivo	holiday
el/la invitado/a	guest
el pastel de cumpleaños	birthday cake
las tapas	appetizers
la vela	candle

Repaso: el cumpleaños, la fiesta, el pastel, el refresco, el regalo, la tarjeta

cumplir años	to have a birthday
dar una fiesta	to give a party
faltar (a)	to be absent (from), not attend
gastar	to spend (*money*)
hacer una fiesta	to have a party
pasarlo bien/mal	to have a good/bad time
reunirse (me reúno) (con)	to get together (with)
ser en + *place*	to take place in/at (*a place*)

Repaso: bailar, celebrar, divertirse (me divierto) (i), invitar, regalar

Las emociones y los estados afectivos

el estado afectivo	emotional state
discutir (con/sobre)	to argue (with/about)
enfermarse	to become sick
enojarse (con)	to get angry (with)
llorar	to cry
olvidar(se) (de)	to forget (about)
ponerse + *adj.*	to become, get + *adj.*
portarse bien/mal	to (mis)behave
recordar (recuerdo)	to remember
reír(se) ([me] río) (i) (de)	to laugh (about)
sentirse (me siento) (i)	to feel (*an emotion*)
sonreír(se) (*like* **reír**)	to smile

Repaso: quejarse (de)

Otros sustantivos

el árbol	tree
el detalle	detail
el fin de año	end of the year
el hecho	fact, event

Los adjetivos

avergonzado/a	embarrassed
feliz (*pl.* **felices)**	happy
festivo/a	festive, celebratory
-ísimo/a	very very

Algunos días festivos

la Navidad	Christmas
la Nochevieja	New Year's Eve
la Nochebuena	Christmas Eve
la Pascua	Easter
la quinceañera	young woman's fifteenth birthday party

Palabras adicionales

demasiado (*adv.*)	too; too much
¡Felicitaciones!	Congratulations!
gracias por + *noun* or *inf.*	thanks for
-ísimo (*adv.*)	very very
por lo menos	at least
ya	already

Repaso: muchísimo

Vocabulario personal

- Have students respond *probable* or *improbable*.
  1. *Ud. se siente triste cuando sus amigos se olvidan de su cumpleaños.*
  2. *Ud. se ríe cuando su novio/a sale con otra persona.*
  3. *El profesor se enoja cuando los estudiantes se portan bien.*
- Ask students:

  ¿En qué días festivos mandamos tarjetas?
  1. *la Navidad*
  2. *el Cuatro de Julio*
  3. *el Día de San Valentín*
  4. *el cumpleaños*

  ¿Qué colores asociamos con estos días festivos?
  5. *la Pascua*
  6. *la Navidad*
  7. *el Cuatro de Julio*
  8. *el Día de San Patricio*

Chapter Opening Photo and Chapter Theme

Chapter Theme–Related Questions

- Ask students the following questions to help introduce the chapter theme.
  1. *¿Qué opina Ud. de los deportes? ¿Cree Ud. que son divertidos? ¿Le aburren?*
  2. *¿Cuál es el deporte más popular en su país? ¿Lo juega Ud.? ¿Va a los partidos?*
  3. *¿Sabe Ud. esquiar? ¿Quién lo/la enseñó? ¿Se puede esquiar cerca de donde Ud. vive? ¿Cuáles son los mejores lugares para esquiar en este país?*
  4. *En su casa, apartamento o residencia, ¿quién hace los quehaceres domésticos, es decir, las tareas de la casa?*
  5. *En su opinión, ¿cuál es el aparato doméstico más útil?*
- Explain *tiempo libre* in Spanish: *el tiempo que tenemos para divertirnos y descansar.* Ask students for an English equivalent.
- If students do not know the name for a particular *aparato doméstico,* have them use gestures and circumlocution to communicate it, then give them the word in Spanish.

Reciclado: Review vacation vocabulary from *Cap. 8* as well as the various ways that students know to express likes and dislikes (*gustar* and *preferir,* as well as the verbs introduced in *Nota comunicativa,* p. 247). It is also a good idea to review verbs used with the present participle: *pasar tiempo* + *gerundio, divertirse* + *gerundio* (*Nota comunicativa,* p. 174).

10 El tiempo libre

Una bailarina de bomba y plena, en la plaza de Recreo, en Loíza, Puerto Rico

- ¿Qué le gusta a Ud. hacer en su tiempo libre? ¿Tiene que pasar a veces parte de su tiempo libre haciendo quehaceres domésticos (*household chores*)?
- ¿Es el baile una de sus diversiones preferidas? ¿Qué tipo de baile le gusta más? ¿Qué estilos de baile hispanos conoce Ud.?
- ¿Prefiere las actividades que se hacen al aire libre (*outdoors*)? ¿O prefiere las actividades sedentarias?

Mc Graw Hill connect™ SPANISH

www.connectspanish.com

Resources

For Students

- Connect Spanish (**www.connectspanish.com**), which contains all content from the following resources, as well as the *Mundo interactivo* scenarios, the LearnSmart adaptive learning system, and more!
- **Physical Resources:** Workbook / Laboratory Manual, Laboratory Audio Program, DVD

For Instructors

- Connect Spanish (**www.connectspanish.com**), which contains access to all student sections of Connect Spanish, as well as helpful time-saving tools and resources such as an integrated gradebook, Instructor's Manual, Testing Program, digital transparencies, Audioscript, Videoscript, and more!

Puerto Rico

4 millones de habitantes

- Puerto Rico es un Estado Libre Asociado a los Estados Unidos. Esto significa que Puerto Rico no es independiente, pero sí tiene autonomía interna. Los puertorriqueños son ciudadanos (*citizens*) estadounidenses.
- Los puertorriqueños tienen una gran conciencia (*awareness*) de su historia y de la importancia de su cultura. Se sienten muy orgullosos (*proud*) de su herencia indígena, africana e hispana.

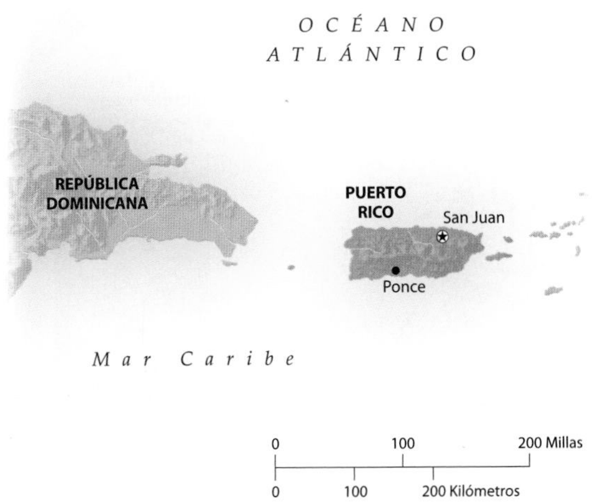

En este capítulo

CONTENT / **CONTENIDO**	OBJECTIVES / **OBJETIVOS**
Pastimes 294, Domestic Chores 296	To talk about what we do when we are not studying or working
The Imperfect 299	To talk about the past
Summary of Interrogative Words 305	To learn more about asking questions
Superlatives 307	To express the best or worst of a group
Puerto Rico 314	To learn about a Caribbean island nation that has a close relationship with the United States

Puerto Rico

Datos esenciales

The Instructor's Edition will provide basic information about each chapter's country of focus on this chapter opening spread. Additional information (such as geographical features, historical timelines, holidays, and so on) can be found in the IM. There is also additional information about the country of focus in *A leer: Lectura cultural* and *A escuchar* (in both the student text and the Instructor's Edition).

Nombre oficial: *Estado Libre Asociado de Puerto Rico (Los puertorriqueños le llaman Borinquen, nombre de raíces taínas.)*
Lema: *«Joannes est nomen eius» (Juan es su nombre [latín])*
Capital: *San Juan*
Otras ciudades: *Ponce*
Composición étnica: *76% blancos, 7% negros, 2% amerindios, 3% asiáticos, 4% mestizos, 8% otros*
Jefe de estado actual: *el Presidente Barack Obama, demócrata, desde 2009; el Gobernador Luis Fortuno, desde 2009*
Forma de gobierno: *república democrática*
Lenguas oficiales: *el español y el inglés*
Moneda: *el dólar estadounidense*
Religión: *85% católicos, 15% otros*

Point Out

- Since Puerto Ricans are U.S. citizens, they can vote in U.S. elections when they live in one of the 50 states, but they cannot vote in U.S. elections when they live on the island. That right is reserved for admitted states and the District of Columbia.
- There is a very fluid connection between the island (Puerto Rico) and the mainland (continental United States) for many Puerto Rican families, whose members often go back and forth on a regular basis. Puerto Rico is also a major vacation destination for non-Hispanic Americans, especially those who live on the East Coast.
- As is the case with many Caribbean countries, the sea is very influential in Puerto Rican life and culture.

Suggestion

Have students list their ideas about Puerto Rico, including information on geography, politics, economy, culture, music, and cuisine. When you finish the chapter, return to the lists and ask students what ideas they would change and/or add.

Multimedia

The IM provides suggestions for using multimedia materials in the classroom.

Resources: Transparency 107

Vocabulario: Preparación

Los pasatiempos, diversiones y aficiones

Note

See the model for vocabulary presentation and other material in the *Cap. 10 Vocabulario: Preparación* section of "Chapter-by-Chapter Supplementary Materials" in the IM.

Reciclado

- Note that, as usual, previously active vocabulary is relisted in this *Vocabulario: Preparación* section: *hacer* camping, *jugar* (*juego*) (*gu*), *nadar, sacar* (*qu*) *fotos, tomar el sol.*
- **Suggestion:** Ask students to name other leisure-time activities that they have learned to express in Spanish. Active vocabulary in that category includes the following: *asistir a, bailar, cantar, descansar, ir de compras / al centro comercial, tocar* (*un instrumento musical*), *leer, mirar la televisión.*

Suggestions

- Point out to students that *jugar* is followed by *a* + *article* + *activity*. With sports, this is generally *jugar al*. With other activities, the article will vary according to the activity (as in *jugar a las cartas*).
- Remind students that the parenthetical (*esquío*) indicates how *esquiar* is conjugated in the *yo* form of the present tense. Ask them to generate the rest of the present tense forms of *esquiar* and write them on the board, emphasizing the accent marks on *-i-* when it is stressed.
- Optional vocabulary: *hacer* snowboard/snowboarding or simply *hacer* snow.
- Have students name activities they associate with the following places.

  ¿Qué se hace en… ?

  1. *un estadio*
  2. *el campo* (new)
  3. *un gimnasio*
  4. *una piscina*
  5. *el cine*
  6. *un teatro*

Reciclado: Have students tell what sport or activity they associate with the following things.

¿Con qué deporte o actividad asocia Ud.… ?

el verano, el invierno, el otoño, la primavera, una cita (new) *especial, un día de lluvia*

VOCABULARIO **Preparación**

Los pasatiempos, diversiones y aficiones°

°Los… *Pastimes, fun activities, and hobbies*

montar a caballo

caminar

patinar en línea, el patinaje

esquiar (esquío), el esquí

jugar (juego) (gu) al ajedrez

correr

dar una caminata

ir a una discoteca

Los pasatiempos

los ratos libres	spare (free) time
dar/hacer una fiesta	to give a party
dar un paseo	to take a walk
hacer *camping*	to go camping
hacer planes para + *inf.*	to make plans to (*do something*)
hacer un *picnic*	to have a picnic
ir…	to go . . .
al cine	to the movies
a un bar	to a bar
al teatro / a un concierto	to the theater / to a concert
a ver una película	to see a movie
jugar (juego) (gu) a las cartas	to play cards
sacar (qu) fotos	to take pictures
tomar el sol	to sunbathe
visitar un museo	to visit a museum
aburrirse	to get bored
ser…	to be . . .
aburrido/a	boring
divertido/a	fun

Los deportes

el ciclismo	bicycling
el fútbol	soccer
el fútbol americano	football
hacer *surfing*	to surf
nadar	to swim
la natación	swimming
pasear en bicicleta	to ride a bicycle
patinar	to skate
patinar en línea	to rollerblade

Cognados: el basquetbol, el béisbol, el golf, el hockey, el tenis, el voleibol

el equipo	team
el jugador / la jugadora	player
el partido	game, match
entrenar	to practice, train
ganar	to win
jugar (juego) (gu) al + *sport*	to play (*a sport*)
perder (pierdo)	to lose
practicar (qu)	to participate (*in a sport*)
ser aficionado/a (a)	to be a fan (of)

Resources: Transparency 108

Conversación

Con. A, Paso 1: Extension: 6. *Es más interesante leer libros que ver la televisión.* **7.** *Me gusta oír la radio tanto como mirar la televisión.*

A. Sus pasatiempos favoritos

Paso 1. ¿Cierto o falso? Corrija las oraciones falsas, según su opinión.

	CIERTO	FALSO
1. Es más aburrido ver un partido en la tele que en el estadio.	☐	☐
2. Lo paso mejor con mi familia que con mis amigos.	☐	☐
3. Las actividades educativas me gustan más que las deportivas (*sporting*).	☐	☐
4. Odio el béisbol tanto como el fútbol.	☐	☐
5. Los estudiantes universitarios tienen tanto tiempo libre como los (*those*) de la escuela secundaria.	☐	☐

Paso 2. Ahora haga una lista de sus pasatiempos favoritos y de los que Ud. odia o no le interesan.

Paso 3. Compare su lista con la (*that*) de un compañero o compañera de clase con quien Ud. no habla con frecuencia. ¿Les gustan los mismos pasatiempos?

B. Definiciones

Paso 1. Dé las palabras definidas.

MODELO: entrar en un lugar para ver una película ⟶ ir al cine

1. un grupo de jugadores — el equipo
2. salir bien en una competencia; salir mal — ganar, perder
3. practicar un deporte intensamente — entrenar
4. asistir a todos los partidos de un equipo en particular — ser aficionado/a
5. un deporte que se practica en una piscina — la natación, nadar

Paso 2. Ahora defina las siguientes palabras, según el modelo del **Paso 1.**

1. un jugador
2. un partido
3. aburrirse
4. hacer un *picnic*
5. dar un paseo

Así se dice

el basquetbol = el baloncesto (*Sp.*)
hacer *camping* = hacer acampada, acampar
hacer *surfing* = hacer *surf* (*P.R.*), surfear
pasear en bicicleta = andar en bicicleta, montar en bicicleta
la película = el filme, el film
el voleibol = el vólibol, el volibol

Con. A, Pasos 2, 3: Suggestion: Tally the results of the whole class to determine what are the number 1, 2, and 3 pastimes in the most liked and least liked categories. Put students into discussion groups by sports liked and disliked. Ask the "sports liked" group to come up with the disadvantages of their sport and vice versa (the "sports disliked" group must come up with advantages). Have students share the results of their discussions.

Nota cultural

Los deportes más populares del mundo hispano

Dos deportes predominan en el panorama deportivo del mundo hispano: el fútbol y el béisbol.

- **El fútbol** Sin duda este es el rey[a] de los deportes en el mundo hispano, como en el resto del mundo. Ningún evento deportivo se compara en seguimiento[b] a la Copa Mundial de Fútbol. Se estima que unos 700 millones de telespectadores miraron el partido final de la Copa 2010, que ganó España. En todos los países hispanos, el fútbol se juega en cualquier calle,[c] plaza o espacio abierto y hay innumerables ligas[d] de todo tipo.
- **El béisbol** Un deporte inmensamente popular en los países de la costa caribeña es el béisbol. En las grandes ligas estadounidenses hay muchos jugadores de primer orden con apellidos hispanos, dos de ellos son Rodríguez y Pujols. Muchos de estos «peloteros[e]», como se les llama[f] en muchos países, vienen de las ligas de sus respectivos países de origen, como la República Dominicana, Venezuela y México.
- **El basquetbol, el tenis y el ciclismo** Estos deportes también tienen gran seguimiento en el mundo hispano.

[a]*king* [b]*following* [c]cualquier… *any street* [d]*leagues* [e]*ball-players* (la pelota = *ball*) [f]se… *they are called*

El basquetbol está creciendo[g] en cuanto al[h] número de espectadores y tiene dos grandes potencias[i] hispanas: España y la Argentina. Estos países obtuvieron la medalla[j] de plata y de bronce, respectivamente, en los Juegos Olímpicos de Pekín en 2008. En la NBA estadounidense hay varios jugadores hispanos, entre ellos el formidable español Pau Gasol, que juega en el equipo de los Lakers de Los Ángeles.

César Crespo (derecha), durante la Serie del Caribe, en el Estadio Roberto Clemente, Puerto Rico

¿Qué otros deportistas hispanos puede Ud. nombrar?

[g]*growing* [h]en… *as far as the* [i]*superpowers* [j]obtuvieron… *won the medal*

Optional: Provide additional vocabulary related to *Los pasatiempos, diversiones y aficiones: andar en patineta* (Mex.) / *monopatín* (Sp.), *el atletismo, carreras y saltos* (track), *ir de copas* (to go to the bars), *jugar al boliche / a los bolos, el patinaje, patinar sobre hielo, la película romántica / de amor, la película del oeste / de vaqueros, la película policíaca / de suspense*

Pronunciación: See Pronunciation Notes, IM.

Con. A: Reciclado

Note the review of comparative forms in this activity, in preparation for presentation of superlatives (*Gram. 29*) in this chapter.

Con. A: Note

Active vocabulary: *la escuela, deportivo/a*

Nota cultural

Suggestions

- Ask how many students like and play soccer. Then have those people explain to their classmates what makes soccer, in their opinion, a fun sport. Discuss as a class why soccer is less popular in this country than in Latin America and Europe.
- Outside of the Caribbean countries, *el beisbolista* is a more common term for baseball player.
- The passion for baseball is huge in Cuba, the Dominican Republic, Puerto Rico, and Venezuela. The sport also has a lot of fans in Mexico and other Central American countries. In fact, the interest is growing in Spain as well, as Latin American immigrants settle there and continue to practice their favorite sport.

Comprensión

1. *¿Qué deporte atrae más televidentes en el mundo? (el fútbol)*
2. *¿En qué países del mundo hispano es popular el béisbol? (en los países de la costa caribeña)*
3. *¿Qué otros deportes son importantes en el mundo hispano? (el basquetbol, el tenis, el ciclismo)*

Heritage Speakers

En algunos dialectos del español del suroeste de los Estados Unidos y del Caribe, se dice *jugar béisbol* en vez de *jugar al béisbol.* En el habla popular, con frecuencia se omite la contracción *al* después de *jugar.*

Multimedia: Internet

Many Hispanic soccer clubs have websites. Have students look for the International Football (Soccer) Hall of Fame Web page as well as for sites about world soccer. Have them look up information on world soccer and the World Cup using the Spanish words *Mundial de fútbol.* The sites they find will provide links to images, statistics, and general information about particular teams, players, and leagues.

Corrí en el SRC
Miré un partido de F.A.
~~Esta~~ Jugué al mini golf con mis hijos.

Con. C: Suggestions

Use the data from either *Paso 1* or *2* to have a class discussion about using one's time.

- Different ages: *¿En qué puede ser diferente el uso que hace de su tiempo una persona de 20 años y una persona de 35 años? ¿una persona de 20 años y una persona de 65 años?*
- Other variables: *¿En qué puede ser diferente el uso que, en general, hace de su tiempo un hombre y una mujer? ¿una persona con hijos o sin ellos? ¿una persona rica y una que, aunque no tiene mucho dinero, tampoco es pobre? ¿una persona casada* (new) *y una persona soltera* (new)*?*

Los quehaceres domésticos

Reciclado: Recycle house vocabulary with the following question.

¿Qué quehaceres domésticos asocia Ud. con la cocina? ¿el garaje? ¿la alcoba? ¿la sala? ¿el baño?

Suggestions

- Optional vocabulary: *el fregadero, lavar las ventanas, la licuadora, pintar las paredes, sacudir los muebles / quitar el polvo*
- Have students tell what words or expressions they associate with the following things.

¿el aire acondicionado?	*¿el refrigerador?*
¿la cafetera?	*¿cocinar?*
¿la estufa?	*¿limpiar la casa?*
¿la secadora?	*¿el congelador?*
	¿la tostadora?

Resources: Transparency 109

¿Cómo pasa Ud. su tiempo?	
Actividad	**Media[a] de tiempo diario (aproximadamente)**
Estudios	3 horas 50 minutos
Medios de comunicación	1 hora 45 minutos
Aficiones e informática[b]	1 hora 15 minutos
Vida social y diversión	1 hora 15 minutos
Hogar[c] y familia (tareas domésticas)	1 hora
Deportes y actividades al aire libre	30 minutos

[a]*Average* [b]*computers* [c]*Home*

(Basado en datos de 2009–2010 del Instituto Nacional de Estadística de España)

C. ¿Cómo pasa Ud. su tiempo?

Paso 1. Lea las actividades de los jóvenes españoles menores de 25 años de edad y haga una lista de actividades que se pueden incluir en cada categoría. Para la lista, use infinitivos (por ejemplo: **leer libros**). Luego, para cada categoría, indique si en un día típico Ud. pasa más o menos tiempo que los españoles en las mismas actividades.

MODELOS: Paso más tiempo en los estudios que los jóvenes españoles.
Paso menos tiempo haciendo tareas domésticas que los jóvenes españoles.

Paso 2. Ahora, en parejas, comparen sus listas y el tiempo que cada uno de Uds. pasa haciendo las actividades de las diferentes categorías.

Los quehaceres domésticos°

Los... *Household chores*

planchar la ropa

pasar la aspiradora

hacer **la cama**

poner **la mesa**

sacar (qu) la basura

lavar los platos

Algunos aparatos domésticos

la aspiradora	vacuum cleaner
la cafetera	coffeemaker
el congelador	freezer
la estufa	stove
el horno de microondas	microwave oven
la lavadora	washing machine
el lavaplatos	dishwasher
el refrigerador	refrigerator
la secadora	clothes dryer
la tostadora	toaster

Heritage Speakers

- Pídales a los hispanohablantes que compartan otras palabras o variaciones que usan para describir los aparatos y quehaceres domésticos.
- Pídales a los hispanohablantes que comparen la información del recorte en *Con. C* con su experiencia personal. Pregúnteles si creen que los jóvenes españoles son como los típicos jóvenes de otros países hispanos.

Más quehaceres domésticos

barrer el piso to sweep the floor
dejar (en) to leave behind (in [*a place*])
dejar sin hacer to leave (*something*) undone
lavar la ropa to wash clothes
limpiar (la casa) to clean (house)
quitar la mesa to clear the table

Así se dice

el congelador = la nevera
la estufa = la cocina
hacer la cama = tender la cama
lavar los platos = fregar los platos
el refrigerador = el frigorífico, la heladera, la refrigeradora, la nevera

Conversación

A. Los quehaceres domésticos. ¿En qué cuarto o parte de la casa se hacen las siguientes actividades? Hay más de una respuesta en muchos casos.

1. Se hace la cama en ____.
2. Se saca la basura de ____ y se pone en ____.
3. Uno se baña en ____ pero baña al perro en ____.
4. Se barre el piso del / de la ____.
5. Se pasa la aspiradora en ____.
6. Se lava y se seca la ropa en ____.
7. La ropa se plancha en ____.
8. Se usa la cafetera en ____.

B. Las marcas (*Brand names*). ¿Para qué se usan o para qué sirven los siguientes productos?

1. Mr. Coffee
2. Glad bags
3. Lysol
4. Tide
5. Saran wrap

C. Intercambios

Paso 1. En parejas, túrnense para hacer y contestar preguntas sobre cómo pasan Uds. el fin de semana. Basen sus preguntas en las siguientes ideas. Deben obtener detalles interesantes y personales de su compañero/a.

1. cuándo empieza el fin de semana (¿día? ¿hora?)
2. cómo se divierten
3. cuánta tarea hacen
4. cuánto duermen (¿por la noche? ¿la siesta?)
5. los quehaceres domésticos que tienen que hacer
6. cómo se sienten el domingo por la noche

Paso 2. Digan a la clase dos detalles interesantes sobre lo que hace su compañero/a.

Redacción: Ask students to write two short paragraphs based on the information they learned in *Paso 1* of *Con. C*.

- First paragraph: *Lo que es el fin de semana para mi compañero/a de clase: definición, cuándo empieza, actividades favoritas*
- Second paragraph: *Análisis de las actividades de mi compañero/a de clase*

In the second paragraph, students should give their opinion about their partner's weekend activities. Offer the following optional vocabulary: *muy/poco inclinado/a a los deportes, las actividades al aire libre, las actividades intelectuales, muy parrandero/a* (party-loving).

Con. A: Possible Answers: **1.** *la alcoba* **2.** *la cocina, el garaje* **3.** *el cuarto de baño, el patio/garaje* **4.** *comedor/cocina* **5.** *la sala* **6.** *el garaje* **7.** *la alcoba* **8.** *la cocina*

Con. B: Possible Answers: **1.** *Sirve para preparar el café.* **2.** *Se usan para poner y sacar la basura.* **3.** *Sirve para limpiar el cuarto de baño.* **4.** *Se usa para lavar la ropa.* **5.** *Sirve para poner la comida en el refrigerador.*

Con. C: Suggestions

- Point out to students that most of the items on the list of ideas are indirect questions that they will need to turn into direct questions to pose to their partner. Call students' attention to the accent marks on the interrogative words in indirect questions.
- Model question formation based on the ideas before asking students to start their interviews. Model the use of other basic questions, model the use of other questions to get more information.

Con. A: Suggestions

- Have students complete these sentences with the correct activity, based on the noun at the beginning of the sentence.
  1. *La secadora sirve para ____.*
  2. *La plancha sirve para ____.*
  3. *En la cocina se puede ____.*
  4. *La lavadora sirve para ____.*
- Ask students these questions.
  1. *¿Ud. hace la cama todos los días? Si tiene prisa por la mañana, ¿hace la cama o la deja sin hacer? Cuando visita la casa de su familia, ¿su mamá (abuela) le hace la cama?*
  2. *¿Cuándo limpia Ud. la casa, durante el fin de semana? ¿La limpia entera o solo una parte? ¿Alguien lo/la ayuda? ¿Siempre deja algo sin hacer?*
  3. *¿Qué prefiere Ud. hacer, planchar o pasar la aspiradora? ¿lavar la ropa o barrer el piso? ¿quitar la mesa o lavar los platos?...*
  4. *Yo odio* (fill in what you dislike). *¿Quién también odia ____?*

Reciclado: Recycle commands. Have students give commands to an imaginary robot in the following circumstances.

¿Qué mandatos le va a dar al robot en las siguientes circunstancias?

1. *Ud. tiene hambre.*
2. *La comida está hecha* (new) *y Ud. quiere sentarse a la mesa a comer.*
3. *La sala está muy oscura porque entra muy poca luz* (new).
4. *Ud. quiere que la casa esté bien arreglada* (new) *porque esta noche vienen algunos amigos muy importantes a visitarlos.*

NATIONAL STANDARDS: Communication

The ability to express meaning through circumlocution and gestures is an important part of speaking a second language. *Con. B* asks students to produce very simple circumlocutions (a skill that they began to practice as soon as they learned the phrase *servir para* in *Cap. 5*). For this activity, offer a more complex model than those suggested as answers. For example: *Lysol* → *Lysol es un producto líquido que se usa para limpiar los cuartos sucios, como los cuartos de baño, por ejemplo.* To follow up, give pairs of students cards with English words for which they do not know the Spanish equivalent. Their task is to explain the item to their partner, to see if the partner can guess the word. Some possible words: *pizza cutter, shoelace, body lotion, lightbulb, bookmark, cigarette lighter, rubber band, toothpick.* Students will not know all of the related words that they need, but they can gesture, mime, or point.

Nota comunicativa

Suggestions

- Model and review *Tengo que…*, *Necesito…*, *Debo…*, then introduce the expression *tocarle* to express the concept *to be someone's turn* or *responsibility to do something.* Point out that the structure for *tocar* is similar to the *gustar* construction.
- Ask students the following questions.
  1. *¿Qué tiene que hacer Ud. esta tarde? ¿y mañana? ¿Tiene que hacer alguna tarea? ¿Para qué clase?*
  2. *¿Cómo debe ser una persona para ser un buen amigo / una buena amiga* (*un buen padre / una buena madre, un buen estudiante / una buena estudiante*)*?*
  3. *¿Necesita ir al médico pronto? ¿al dentista? ¿a la oficina de matrícula? ¿a la oficina de su consejero/a?*
  4. *En su casa / apartamento, ¿a quién le toca barrer esta semana? ¿ir al supermercado? ¿lavar la ropa?*
  5. *Por lo general, en una familia típica ¿a quién le toca lavar la ropa, al esposo o a la esposa? ¿hacer la comida? ¿hacer una barbacoa? ¿arreglar el coche? ¿poner y quitar la mesa? ¿sacar la basura?*

NATIONAL STANDARDS

Cultures

Read the following information to the class, and use it as a springboard for discussing domestic services.

Las criadas: *Muchas familias hispanas de las clases acomodadas* (new) *tienen una criada que vive en casa. La criada, o «la muchacha del servicio», como la llaman en algunas partes, siempre tiene su propia alcoba y su propio baño. Ella cocina, cuida a* (new) *los niños, lava la ropa y ayuda a mantener la casa limpia. Muchas veces la criada parece otro miembro de la familia.*

Si Ud. visita una casa hispana que tiene una criada, recuerde que ella tiene mucho trabajo. No le cause trabajo extra. Si Ud. va a pasar una o varias noches en la casa, pregúntele a la señora de la casa qué le sugiere que le dé a la criada como agradecimiento (new) *antes de que Ud. se vaya. En algunas casas es costumbre dejarle una propina* (new)*; en otras, un regalito. A veces no se le deja nada, pero siempre hay que darle las gracias.*

Nota **comunicativa**

Cómo expresar la obligación

You already know several ways to express the obligation to do something.

Tengo que / **Necesito** / **Debo**	barrer el piso.	*I have to* / *I need to* / *I should*	*sweep the floor.*

Of the three, **tener que** + *infinitive* expresses the strongest sense of obligation.

The concept *to be someone's turn or responsibility* (to do something) is expressed in Spanish with the verb **tocar (qu)** plus an indirect object.

—**¿A quién le toca** lavar los platos esta noche? — *"Whose turn is it to wash the dishes tonight?"*

—**A mí me toca** solamente sacar la basura. Creo que **a papá le toca** lavar los platos. — *"I only have to take out the garbage. I think it's Dad's turn to wash the dishes."*

D. Sus hábitos domésticos

Paso 1. ¿Es Ud. una persona que tiene su casa limpia? Indique con qué frecuencia hace Ud. los siguientes quehaceres. Si vive en una residencia estudiantil, piense en lo que hace cuando vive con su familia.

Frecuencia

0 = nunca
1 = a veces
2 = frecuentemente
3 = todos los días

MODELO: ____ hacer la cama ⟶ __3__ hacer la cama: Hago la cama todos los días.

1. __3__ hacer la cama
2. __2__ poner la mesa
3. __1__ preparar la comida
4. __2__ lavar los platos
5. __1__ limpiar la casa
6. __2__ sacar la basura
7. __0__ pasar la aspiradora
8. __1__ limpiar la estufa
9. __3__ planchar la ropa
10. __1__ barrer el piso

Paso 2. Ahora, en parejas, túrnense para entrevistarse sobre sus hábitos domésticos, basándose en el formulario del **Paso 1.** De los dos, ¿quién se preocupa más por su hogar (*home*)? ¿por la limpieza (*cleanliness*)? ¿Quién mantiene (*keeps*) más limpia la casa?

MODELO: hacer la cama ⟶

E1: ¿Con qué frecuencia haces la cama? (¿A quién le toca hacer las camas en tu casa?)

E2: Nunca la hago. (Las hago a veces. En mi casa, le toca a mi madre hacer las camas.)

Paso 3. Con el mismo compañero / la misma compañera, hagan una lista de los quehaceres que les toca hacer esta semana. Luego comparen su lista con las (*those*) del resto de la clase.

Mundo interactivo

You should now be prepared to work with Scenario 5, Activity 3 in Connect Spanish (**www.connectspanish.com**).

GRAMÁTICA

¿Recuerda Ud.?

In **Capítulos 8** and **9,** you learned the forms and some uses of the preterite. Before you learn the other simple past tense (in **Gramática 27**), you might want to review the forms of the preterite in those chapters. The verbs in the following sentences are in the preterite. Can you identify any words in the sentences that emphasize the completed nature of the actions expressed by the verbs?

1. Esta mañana me levanté a las seis.
2. Ayer fui al cine con un amigo.
3. La semana pasada pinté las paredes de la cocina.

27 Talking About the Past (Part 4)

Descriptions and Habitual Actions in the Past: Imperfect of Regular and Irregular Verbs

Grammar Tutorial 27
connect SPANISH
www.connectspanish.com

Gramática en acción: Los indígenas taínos

Los indígenas taínos eran los habitantes originales de las Antillas Mayores, que son las islas de Puerto Rico, Cuba, Haití y la Republica Dominicana (que comparten la que antes fue la isla de La Española) y Jamaica. Allí vivían cuando los españoles llegaron al Caribe a finales del siglo XV. El pueblo taíno era pacífico y generoso y tenía una sociedad matrilineal. Llamaban a su jefe «cacique» y hablaban una lengua que nos ha dejado en el español palabras como *barbacoa, hamaca, canoa, tabaco* y *huracán.*

¿Y Ud.?

1. ¿Qué pueblos indígenas habitaban la zona donde Ud. vive antes de la llegada de los europeos?
2. ¿Qué otros pueblos indígenas vivían en este país antes del siglo XVI?
3. ¿Cómo era la sociedad de estos pueblos?
4. ¿Sabe Ud. qué significan en ingles las últimas palabras del párrafo?

The Taíno Indians *The Taíno Indians were the original inhabitants of the Greater Antilles, which are the islands of Puerto Rico, Cuba, Haiti, and the Dominican Republic (which share what was formerly the island of Hispaniola), and Jamaica. They were living there when the Spaniards arrived in the Caribbean at the end of the fifteenth century. The Taíno people were peaceful and generous, and they had a matrilineal society. They called their chief* cacique, *and they spoke a language that has left us words such as* barbacoa, hamaca, canoa, tabaco, *and* huracán *in Spanish.*

Gramática 27
Imperfect of Regular and Irregular Verbs

GEA: Suggestions

- Start out with a discussion of the geography of the Caribbean. (Students have been seeing maps relatively similar to this one since *Cap. 8.*)
- Introduce the new tense with the *GEA* topic: *Vamos a leer sobre el pueblo que vivía en Puerto Rico antes de la llegada de los españoles. Para hablar de esto, necesitamos un nuevo tiempo verbal, el imperfecto, que sirve para describir las cosas que ocurrieron en el pasado.*
- Explain that the name *Antillas* is the name given to the islands in the Caribbean, including *las Bahamas.* There are *Antillas Mayores* and *Antillas Menores,* according to the size of the islands.
- Explain that the *taínos* died out quite soon after the arrival of the Spanish; most had disappeared by 1493. However, although some other Caribbean people have *taíno* blood, Puerto Ricans feel a great sense of cultural connection with the *taínos.* This heritage is especially notable in their folklore.

Follow-up

Ask students the following questions to follow up the *GEA* introduction of "the way things used to be" use of the imperfect.

Cuando Ud. era pequeño/a…

1. *¿creía en Santa Claus?*
2. *¿iba a ceremonias religiosas con su familia?*
3. *¿jugaba a algún deporte con sus padres? ¿con sus hermanos?*
4. *¿siempre hacía sus quehaceres?*

Optional

To use the imperfect in a sports-related context (one of this chapter's themes), tell students about the game that the Aztecs used to play. *En las ciudades de los aztecas, en lo que hoy es México, había un campo como el de una cancha* (new) *de básquetbol. Allí se celebraban partidos que eran parte de una ceremonia. Los participantes jugaban con una pelota* (new) *de goma dura* (new), *que solo podían mover con las caderas* (new) *y las rodillas* (new). *Todavía no se sabe exactamente el significado del partido, pero se cree que algunos participantes morían al fin del partido.*

Multimedia: Internet

Have students search the Internet for more information on early civilizations in the Americas. Encourage them to look for images of the cities and for information about rituals and the famous Aztec calendar. You might assign specific topics and have students develop brief oral presentations based on their findings.

Resources: Transparency 110

Forms of the Imperfect

Suggestions

- Remind students that the imperfect is the second of two simple past tenses. This section presents and practices only the imperfect. *Gram. 30* in *Cap. 11* contrasts the two tenses, but some activities before that section will combine the two tenses in controlled situations.
- Use the regular imperfect forms of *trabajar, beber,* and *vivir* in conversational exchanges with students.
- Emphasize that *would* can imply both conditional and habitual actions in the past. Only the latter (habit) is expressed by the imperfect.
- Point out that there are no stem changes in the imperfect.
- Remind students that *hay* is invariable, meaning both *there is* and *there are*. Similarly, *había* is invariable = *there was/were.*
- Present and model the irregular forms of *ir, ser,* and *ver.*
- Point out that the *yo* form is identical to the *Ud./él/ella* form. Context will often make the meaning clear, but the subject pronouns are more frequently used with the imperfect forms in order to clarify the meaning.

You have already used the *preterite* (**el pretérito**) to express events in the past. The *imperfect* (**el imperfecto**) is the second simple past tense in Spanish. In contrast to the preterite, which is used when you view actions or states of being as begun or completed in the past, the imperfect is used when you view past actions or states of being as habitual or as "in progress." The imperfect is also used for describing the past.

Forms of the Imperfect / **Las formas del imperfecto**

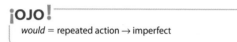

hablar		**comer**		**vivir**	
hablaba	hablábamos	comía	comíamos	vivía	vivíamos
hablabas	hablabais	comías	comíais	vivías	vivíais
hablaba	hablaban	comía	comían	vivía	vivían

1. English Equivalents

The imperfect has several English equivalents. The simple English equivalents (*I spoke, we ate, he lived*) can correspond to either the preterite or the imperfect.

You'll learn more about this in **Capítulo 11.**

yo hablaba = *I spoke, I was speaking, I used to speak, I would speak*
comíamos = *we ate, we were eating, we used to eat, we would eat*
él vivía = *he lived, he was living, he used to live, he would live*

¡OJO!
would = repeated action → imperfect

Comíamos allí todos los domingos.
We would eat there every Sunday.

Pronunciation Hints

- The **b** between vowels, such as in the imperfect ending **-aba,** is pronounced as a fricative [ƀ] sound.
- In **-er/-ir** imperfect forms, it is important not to pronounce the ending **-ía** as a diphthong, but to pronounce the **i** and the **a** in separate syllables. The accent mark over the **í** helps remind you of this.

Los verbos en *-ar*		**Los verbos en *-er/-ir***	
-aba	-ábamos	-ía	-íamos
-abas	-abais	-ías	-íais
-aba	-aban	-ía	-ían

2. Stem-changing Verbs and *hay*

Stem-changing verbs do not show a change in the imperfect.

almorzar (almuerzo) ⟶ almorzaba
perder (pierdo) ⟶ perdía
pedir (pido) (i) ⟶ pedía

The imperfect of **hay** is **había** (*there was, there were, there used to be*).

Había muchos estudiantes en el salón de clase.
There were a lot of students in the class.

3. Irregular Imperfect Forms

Only three verbs are irregular in the imperfect: **ir, ser,** and **ver.**

ir		**ser**		**ver**	
iba	íbamos	era	éramos	veía	veíamos
ibas	ibais	eras	erais	veías	veíais
iba	iban	era	eran	veía	veían

4. First and Third Person Forms

Note that the first and third person forms are identical for **-ar, -er,** and **-ir** verbs. When context does not make meaning clear, subject pronouns are used.

Los sábados **yo jugaba** al tenis y **él paseaba** en bicicleta.
On Saturdays I used to play tennis and he used to ride his bike.

Heritage Speakers

- En el habla popular, algunos hispanohablantes usan la forma plural de *haber* (*habían*) cuando el sustantivo que la sigue es plural. Por ejemplo, es común oír *Habían muchas personas* en vez de *Había muchas personas.* Sin embargo, la forma singular *había* es la forma aceptada para expresar *there was/were.*
- En algunos dialectos rurales del español, hay hispanohablantes que dicen *traíba* o *comiba* en vez de *traía* o *comía*, que son las formas aceptadas en el uso formal.

Uses of the Imperfect / **Los usos del imperfecto**

If you know when to use the imperfect, it will be easy to understand when the preterite is used. When talking about the past, the preterite *is* used when the imperfect *isn't*. That's an oversimplification, but at the same time it's a general rule of thumb that will help you out at first.

The imperfect has the following uses. Note that the first three are very clearly indicated by the English equivalents of the imperfect.

- To describe *repeated habitual actions* in the past

  used to + *verb*, would + *verb*

  Siempre nos quedábamos en aquel hotel.
  We always stayed (used to stay, would stay) at that hotel.

  Todos los veranos iban a la costa.
  Every summer they went (used to go, would go) to the coast.

- To describe an *action that was in progress* (when something else happened)

  was/were + *-ing*

  Ramón **pedía** la cena (cuando Cristina **llamó**).
  Ramón was ordering dinner (when Cristina called).

- To describe two *simultaneous past actions in progress*, with **mientras**

  was/were + *-ing*

  Tú **leías mientras** Juan **escribía** la carta.
  You were reading while Juan was writing the letter.

- To describe ongoing *physical, mental,* or *emotional states* in the past

  Estaban muy **distraídos.**
  They were very distracted.

  La **quería** muchísimo.
  He loved her a lot.

- To tell *time* in the past and to express *age* with **tener**

  Era la una. / **Eran las dos.**
  It was one o'clock. / It was two o'clock.

  Tenía 18 años.
  She was 18 years old.

¡OJO!
Just as in the present, the singular form of the verb **ser** is used with one o'clock, the plural form from two o'clock on.

Summary of the Uses of the Imperfect

used to, would
was/were + *-ing*
simultaneous actions (**mientras**)
physical, mental, and emotional states
time
age

¡OJO!
simple past = imperfect *or* preterite

Autoprueba

Give the correct imperfect ending for each verb.

1. yo habl_____
2. Uds. er_____
3. nosotros com_____
4. Pedro ib_____
5. tú ten_____

Answers: 1. *hablaba* 2. *eran* 3. *comíamos* 4. *iba* 5. *tenías*

Uses of the Imperfect

Suggestions

- Emphasize that preterite and imperfect are both past "tenses." Their use depends on which aspect of a past action the user focuses on (beginning/completion aspect or the ongoing/habitual aspect).
- Have students give the Spanish for some expressions: *I always used to stay . . . Every summer we used to go . . .*, and so on. Vary the subjects in your sentences.
- Emphasize the English cues associated with the imperfect: *used to, would* (habitual action), *every day, was/were ______-ing.*
- Point out: *mientras* indicates simultaneous actions.
- Point out that in the imperfect, unlike in the preterite, *saber, conocer, querer,* and *poder* retain the base meaning of their infinitives. See *Gram. 30* (*Cap. 11*) for more details.
- Contrast an action in progress and the past progressive. Reenter the contrast between the simple present tense and the present progressive.

Preliminary Exercises

- Use the following rapid response drill to practice the forms.

  Dé el imperfecto:
  yo: *escuchar, mirar, querer, asistir*
  tú: *pensar, visitar, tener, pedir*
  Ud./él/ella: *preguntar, comprar, enseñar, volver, abrir, servir*
  nosotros: *jugar, bailar, tomar, aprender, preferir, venir*
  Uds./ellos/ellas: *trabajar, ganar, creer, divertir, ser*

- Use these chain drills to practice the imperfect forms.

  En la escuela primaria…

  1. *Tina estudiaba y jugaba mucho.* (*yo, Uds., tú, nosotros, Julio, vosotros*)
  2. *Todos bebían leche y dormían la siesta.* (*Tina, tú, nosotros, Alicia, yo, vosotros*)

  ¿Qué hacían Uds. anoche a las doce?

  1. *Ceci veía un programa interesante.* (*tú, yo, Uds., Pablo, ellas, vosotros*)
  2. *Mis padres iban a acostarse.* (*tú, yo, nosotros, Ana, ellas, vosotros*)
  3. *Yo (no) estaba ______.* (*leer, mirar la televisión, escribir una carta, dormir, llorar, comer, ¿ ?*)

Práctica

A. ¡Anticipemos! Mi niñez (*childhood*)

Paso 1. ¿Es esto lo que Ud. hacía cuando tenía 10 años? Diga si las siguientes declaraciones son ciertas o falsas, según su experiencia de niño/a (*as a child*).

	CIERTO	FALSO
1. Cuando tenía 10 años, estaba en cuarto grado (*fourth grade*).	☐	☐
2. Todas las noches me acostaba a las nueve.	☐	☐
3. Los sábados me levantaba temprano para mirar los dibujos animados (*cartoons*).	☐	☐
4. Mis padres me pagaban por los quehaceres que hacía: cortar el césped (*cutting the grass*), lavar los platos…	☐	☐
5. Me gustaba ir con mi madre/padre al supermercado.	☐	☐
6. Le pegaba (*I used to hit*) a mi hermano/a.	☐	☐
7. Tocaba un instrumento musical en la orquesta de la escuela.	☐	☐
8. Mis héroes eran personajes (*characters*) de los dibujos animados.	☐	☐

Paso 2. Ahora corrija las declaraciones falsas, según su experiencia. Luego compare sus respuestas con las (*those*) del resto de la clase.

B. La vida a los 7 años

Paso 1. Haga oraciones sobre la vida de Tina, que vivía en Puerto Rico cuando tenía 7 años. Use el imperfecto de los verbos.

1. (vivir) en Bayamón, Puerto Rico Tina vivía
2. (asistir) a una escuela católica Asistía
3. (hablar) español todo el tiempo Hablaba
4. (aprender) inglés en la escuela Aprendía
5. (dibujar [*to draw*]) mucho en clase y (jugar) con sus compañeros Dibujaba, jugaba
6. (ir) a casa de sus abuelos después de la escuela y (ver) su programa favorito en la tele Iba, veía
7. sus padres: (llegar) por ella a las 7:30 y (llevarla) a casa llegaban, la llevaban

Paso 2. Ahora haga oraciones similares a las oraciones del **Paso 1** pero con información de su propia (*own*) vida a los 7 años.

MODELO: (vivir) en Bayamón, Puerto Rico. ⟶
Yo **vivía** en St. Louis, Missouri.

Nota **comunicativa**

El progresivo en el pasado

Sometimes you want to emphasize that an action was in progress in the past. To do so, you can use the past progressive. It is formed with the imperfect of **estar** plus the present participle (**-ndo**) of another verb.*

Estábamos cenando a las diez.
We were having dinner at ten.

¿No **estabas estudiando**?
Weren't you studying?

You will use the past progressive in this way in **Práctica C.**

*A progressive tense can also be formed with the preterite of **estar. Estuvimos cenando hasta las doce.** The use of the progressive with the preterite of **estar,** however, is relatively infrequent, and it will not be practiced in Puntos de partida.

Prác. A: Suggestion

Ask students to find the imperfect verb form(s) in each sentence and give the infinitive.

Prác. A: Note

Active vocabulary: *de niño/a, la niñez, pegar*

Prác. A: Extension

Have students add two to three original sentences about their childhood.

Prác. A: Follow-up

Poll students to see which descriptions were true for them.

Prác. B: Suggestions

- Make sure that students do not repeat the subject in all items of *Paso 1*. They should use *Tina* as the subject in the first item, but it is not necessary to specify the subject in items 2–6, since context clearly establishes who the sentences are about.
- Make sure that students note the change of subject in item 7.
- Ask students:

  ¿Qué cosas no hacía Ud. que Tina sí hacía? ¿Qué cosas no hacía Tina que Ud. sí hacía?

Prác. B: Extension

Have students describe *Tina* and her sister.

Describan a Tina y a su hermanita Mariana en aquel entonces (new).

Prác. B: Follow-up

Ask students the following questions after completing the activity.

De niño/a, ¿cómo era?

1. *¿Cantaba/Jugaba Ud. mucho en la primaria?*
2. *¿Bebía mucha leche/Coca-Cola? ¿Dormía la siesta? ¿De qué hora a qué hora?*
3. *¿Veía Ud. programas interesantes en la televisión cuando era niño/a? ¿Cuáles le gustaban más?*
4. *¿A qué hora se acostaba Ud. cuando tenía 3 (7, 12) años? ¿Le gustaba acostarse tan temprano/tarde? ¿Leía Ud. a veces en la cama?*

Heritage Speakers

Anime a un(a) hispanohablante a describir su primer día de escuela en este país. ¿Cómo fue ese día? ¿Hablaba inglés? ¿Cómo era la escuela? ¿Le gustaba su maestro/a? ¿Fue una experiencia positiva o negativa?

C. El trabajo de niñera (*baby-sitter*)

Paso 1. El trabajo de niñera puede ser muy pesado (*difficult*). ¿Qué estaba pasando cuando la niñera perdió por fin la paciencia? Describa todas las acciones que pueda, usando **estaba(n)** + *present participle* (**-ndo**).

MODELO: El bebé estaba llorando.

Vocabulario útil

el bebé	
el timbre	doorbell
discutir	to argue
gritar	to shout
ladrar	to bark
pelear	to fight
sonar (suena)*	to ring; to sound

Paso 2. De jóvenes, ¿trabajaban Uds. de niñeros/as? ¿Tenían que cuidar a sus hermanos menores? ¿a los niños de sus parientes? En parejas, túrnense para hablar de sus experiencias de trabajo cuando eran más jóvenes. Háganse preguntas para obtener mucha información. Si no trabajaron de niñeros/as, cuenten sus experiencias en otros trabajos o sus experiencias *con* un niñero o niñera.

Vocabulario útil

caerse	to fall down
cuidar	to take care of
sacar (qu)	to take something out

MODELO: E1: Cuando yo tenía 15 años, cuidaba a mi hermano menor.
E2: ¿Lo cuidabas todos los días? ¿Cuánto te pagaban tus padres? ¿Se portaba bien tu hermano menor? ¿Te daba mucho trabajo? ¿Qué cosas malas hacía siempre?

Conversación

A. Intercambios

Paso 1. En parejas, túrnense para entrevistarse sobre su adolescencia y los años de la escuela secundaria. Usen las siguientes categorías para organizar su conversación. Deben obtener detalles interesantes y personales de su compañero/a.

MODELO: gustar: molestar (*to annoy*) a alguien →
E1: Cuando tenías 15 años, ¿a quién te gustaba molestar?
E2: Me gustaba molestar a mi hermano menor. Él a veces tomaba mis cosas sin mi permiso.
E1: ¿Y ahora todavía te gusta molestarlo?
E2: La verdad es que sí. (*Actually, yes.*)

(Cont.)

*__Sonar__ *is a stem-changing verb. Remember that the stem of present participles does not change with* **-ar** *verbs* (**sonando**).

Optional

- Give students the following dictation but have them write the verbs in the imperfect tense.
  1. *Olga va a la universidad todos los días. Siempre asiste a sus clases. Hace muchas preguntas porque es inteligente. Sus profesores están contentos con ella.*
  2. *Yo trabajo en una oficina. Mi jefe* (new), *que se llama Ángel, nos hace trabajar mucho. Siempre almorzamos juntos en el mismo restaurante y a veces jugamos al basquetbol por la tarde.*
  3. *Vivo en Sacramento. Siempre llueve mucho en invierno y en primavera, pero me gusta mucho el clima. Además* (new), *las montañas están cerca y puedo esquiar.*
- Ask students the following questions.
  1. *El semestre/trimestre pasado, ¿venía Ud. a la universidad todos los días? ¿Asistía a todas sus clases? ¿Hacía muchas preguntas?*
  2. *En la secundaria, ¿trabajaba Ud. después de las clases? ¿los fines de semana? ¿durante las vacaciones? ¿Dónde? ¿Cómo se llamaba su jefe? ¿Cuántas horas trabajaba por semana?*
  3. *De niño/a, ¿dónde vivía Ud.? ¿Llovía mucho allí? ¿Le gustaba el clima?*

Con. C: Note

Active vocabulary: *de joven, el niñero / la niñera, pelear, pesado/a, sonar*

Con. C, Paso 1: Possible Answers

Los niños estaban peleando. El teléfono estaba sonando. Los padres estaban discutiendo. El radio estaba sonando. Alguien estaba sonando el timbre de la casa. El perro estaba ladrando y corriendo. El gato estaba corriendo.

Con. C: Suggestion

Let students talk in pairs for only a short period of time. Follow up *Paso 2* by asking several pairs of students to relate their experiences to the whole class. Ask questions to get more details, modeling the correct use of the preterite and the imperfect in your questions. Do not expect students to use those tenses accurately without guidance from you.

Resources: Transparency 111

Con. A: Suggestions

- Model one question for each category before asking students to start the activity.
- Give students additional vocabulary to allow them to talk about grade-school activities: *los dibujos animados, los dibujos cómicos, jugar a «indios y vaqueros».*

Con. A: Follow-up

Complete the sentences to model an answer, then elicit sentences from students with a follow-up question.

1. *En otra época* (new) *siempre me gustaba* ______. *No me gustaba nada* ______.
2. *Siempre veía* (*programa de televisión*), *pero ahora prefiero ver* ______.
3. *De niño/a, siempre leía* ______, *pero ahora leo* ______.

Con. B: Variation

Have students give statements about current times (habits, preferences, and so on). The class responds by contrasting that statement with a statement about the past (how things used to be). Suggest the following topics: *los precios, las computadoras, la sencillez/complejidad de la vida, la seguridad* (new) *personal, el impacto del gobierno* (new) *en la vida diaria, el uso de las drogas y bebidas alcohólicas, la música.*

Con. B: Suggestion

Have students write the following information in complete sentences. Help them with the names of professions and animals.

1. *De joven yo quería ser* ______ (*profesión*) *porque…*
2. *Cuando yo estaba en la escuela primaria, era* ______ (*adjetivo*). *Siempre…*
3. *En la escuela secundaria, el animal que me simbolizaba mejor era* ______, *porque…*

Collect the completed sentences, then read them aloud and have the class guess the identity of the writers.

Bright Idea
Con. B: Suggestion

Have students bring in photos of themselves to talk about how they were (*¿cómo eran?*) as well as what they liked to do (*¿qué les gustaba hacer?*). Then have them contrast what they are like and what they like to do now with how they were and what they liked then.

1. gustar: molestar a alguien, oír un tipo de música, vestirse con un estilo de ropa
2. preferir: programas de tele, películas, materias, comidas y bebidas
3. comer: a qué hora, dónde, con quién
4. leer: revistas, novelas
5. hacer: los fines de semana, después de las clases
6. discutir: con quién, sobre qué

Paso 2. Ahora digan a la clase dos cosas que Uds. tenían en común.

MODELO: A Frank y a mí nos gustaba oír música rock. Preferíamos ver películas de acción.

Con. B, Redacción: Following the model of sentences in *Con. B*, ask students to compare pastime and sports-related activities of today with those of their childhood and with those of their parents (or simply those at the beginning of the 20th century). By this point in the chapter, students should have vocabulary for discussing the sports in which they participate, which may not be active vocabulary in this chapter, but you may wish to ask if students need any help in that area. Provide some vocabulary suggestions for the parent or last century activities, to help students get going: *patinar, ir al parque con frecuencia, llevar a los niños al parque, pasear en barco.*

B. Los tiempos cambian (*change*). Las siguientes oraciones describen aspectos de la vida de hoy. En parejas, túrnense para describir cómo son las cosas ahora y cómo eran en otra época (*in another era*).

MODELO: E1: Ahora casi todos los bebés nacen (*are born*) en un hospital, pero antes…
E2: Antes casi todos los bebés **nacían** en casa.

AYER

HOY

1. Ahora muchas personas viven en una casa muy grande con un jardín pequeño.
2. Las personas se comunican electrónicamente.
3. Muchísimas mujeres trabajan fuera de casa.
4. Muchas personas van al cine y miran la televisión.
5. Ahora las mujeres —no solo los hombres— llevan pantalones.
6. Ahora hay enfermeros (*male nurses*) y maestros (*male teachers*) —no solo enfermeras y maestras.
7. Ahora tenemos coches pequeños que gastan (*use*) poca gasolina.
8. Ahora usamos más máquinas y por eso hacemos menos trabajo físico.
9. Ahora las familias son más pequeñas.
10. Muchas parejas viven juntas sin casarse (*getting married*).

¿Recuerda Ud.?

You have been using interrogative words since the beginning of *Puntos de partida*, so not much will be new for you in **Gramática 28.** Review what you already know by telling which interrogative word or phrase you associate with the following phrases.

1. un lugar — ¿dónde?
2. la hora — ¿cuándo?, ¿(a) qué (hora)?
3. una persona — ¿quién?
4. la manera de hacer algo — ¿cómo?
5. una selección — ¿cuál?
6. la razón (*reason*) por algo ¿por qué?
7. el lugar de origen de una persona ¿de dónde?
8. un destino (*destination*) ¿adónde?
9. una cantidad ¿cuánto/a/os/as?
10. ser el dueño (*owner*) de algo ¿de quién?

Resources: Transparency 112

28 Getting Information (Part 2)
Summary of Interrogative Words

Grammar Tutorial 28
connect | SPANISH
www.connectspanish.com

Gramática en acción: Un restaurante de Connecticut

El Boricua
RESTAURANTE • CLUB DE BAILE
32 GARVEY ST., NEW HAVEN, CT
Gran espacio para banquetes y celebraciones
Especialidad en comida puertorriqueña
Venga y deléitese con nuestros sabrosos platos
ABIERTO TODOS LOS DÍAS DESDE LAS 11:30 A.M. - 2:00 A.M.
VIERNES, 6 DE OCTUBRE
• LOS GRANDES SALSEROS DE CONNECTICUT •
ORQUESTA INTENSIDAD

1. ¿Cómo se llama el restaurante?
2. ¿En qué ciudad de Connecticut está?
3. ¿En qué tipo de cocina se especializa el restaurante?
4. ¿Qué grupo toca el viernes, 6 de octubre?

¿Y Ud.?

¿Cuántas preguntas más puede Ud. hacer sobre este restaurante, por lo que dice el anuncio?

Here are all of the interrogatives that you have learned so far. Only the information about using **¿qué?** and **¿cuál(es)?,** both of which express *what?* or *which?* in Spanish, is new.

¡OJO!
Remember that interrogative words always have an accent mark in Spanish, and that questions have two question marks: **¿ ?**

¿Cómo?	How?	**¿Dónde?**	Where?
¿Cuándo?	When?	**¿De dónde?**	From where?
¿A qué hora?	At what time?	**¿Adónde?**	Where (to)?
¿Qué?	What? Which?	**¿Cuánto/a?**	How much?
¿Cuál(es)?	What? Which one(s)?	**¿Cuántos/as?**	How many?
¿Por qué?	Why?	**¿Quién(es)?**	Who?
		¿De quién(es)?	Whose?

Uses of ¿qué? and ¿cuál? / Los usos de *¿qué?* y *¿cuál?*

1. ***¿Qué?*** + *verb* = **Definition or Explanation**
   Start a question with **¿qué?** when you are looking for a definition or an explanation.

   ¿Qué es esto? *What is this?*
   ¿Qué quieres? *What do you want?*
   ¿Qué tocas? *What (instrument) do you play?*

2. ***¿Qué?*** + *noun* = **Identification**
   The interrogative **¿qué?** can be directly followed by a noun. The question asks the listener to identify or specify information, often making a choice.

   ¿Qué deporte prefieres? *What (Which) sport do you prefer?*
   ¿Qué playa te gusta más? *What (Which) beach do you like most?*
   ¿Qué instrumento musical tocas? *What (Which) musical instrument do you play?*

Gramática 28 Summary of Interrogative Words

GEA: Suggestion

After reviewing the ad, have students work in pairs to make lists of questions (*¿Y Ud.?*), along with all possible answers. Then combine pairs of students into groups of four. One pair asks their questions, the other pair tries to answer quickly, with information from the ad.

Notes

- Students have actively used all of the interrogatives in this section. Treat this section as a summary, using it to emphasize variations of the interrogative forms, e.g., *¿dónde?* vs. *¿de dónde?* vs. *¿adónde?*
- There is much regional and dialectical variation in the use of *¿qué?* and *¿cuál(es)? Puntos de partida* presents *¿qué?* + *noun* as the default choice because it makes the topic easier for beginners, but *¿cuál(es)?* + *noun* is of course possible as well.
- Question asking has been heavily emphasized in the activities in previous chapters of *Puntos de partida,* and it will continue to be stressed in the rest of the text. For this reason, practice materials in this section are not extensive. Practice with the *¿qué?* vs. *¿cuál(es)?* choice is emphasized.
- Optional: Introduce high-frequency expressions with interrogatives: *¡Quién sabe! ¿Qué (le) vamos a hacer?, ¿Cómo quieres que te lo diga?,* and so on.

Suggestions

- Point out the plural forms of *¿cuál?* and *¿quién?* Point out the difference in meaning in English between *¿cuánto/a?* and *¿cuántos/as?*
- Point out that *¿cómo?* is used to request repetition or clarification in communicative exchanges. (In Mexico, people ask *¿Mande?*)
- An alternate explanation for *¿cuál(es)?* is to say that it is used where *¿qué?* isn't, that is, when there is no definition and when not followed by a noun.

Bright Idea

Suggestion

Point out the difference between *¿qué?* and *¿cuál?* by using contrastive sentences.

¿Qué es su hermano? (Es profesor.) ¿Cuál es su hermano? (Es el muchacho que lleva la camisa roja.)

Heritage Speakers

En algunos dialectos del español de Latinoamérica, se usa *¿cuál(es)?* antes de un sustantivo cuando la selección de objetos es limitada. Por ejemplo, *¿Cuál chaqueta te gusta más?* en vez de *¿Qué chaqueta te gusta más?*

Resources: Transparency 113

Preliminary Exercises

- Ask students whether the following questions would require *¿qué?* or *¿cuál?* in Spanish.
  1. What is an aardvark? (*¿Qué?*)
  2. What is the capital of Bolivia? (*¿Cuál?*)
  3. What are the colors of the U.S. flag? (*¿Cuáles?*)
  4. What's that? (*¿Qué?*)
- Ask students the following questions.
  1. *¿Cuál es la capital de ______?*
  2. *¿Cuál es su número de teléfono?*
  3. *¿Qué es esto?* (indicate an object or use a visual)
  4. *¿Qué es un elefante? ¿un restaurante? ¿una discoteca? ¿Qué son las sandalias?*

Prác. A: Suggestion

Ask students to explain their choice in each case.

Con. A: Suggestions

- Tell students that, if they prefer not to give out real information, such as their phone and social security numbers, they can invent the information for the purpose of the activity.
- Think of or have a student think of a famous person. Have the class try to identify the person by asking questions using interrogative words. Students may not repeat interrogative words during a single round of guessing.

Con. A: Follow-up

Ask students the following questions to summarize findings.

1. *¿Nacieron en la misma ciudad algunas personas de la clase?*
2. *¿En quiénes confían más Uds.?*
3. *¿Cuál es la tienda más popular entre los estudiantes de esta clase?*
4. *¿Quién tiene un examen pronto* (new)*?*

Con. B: Variation

Have students work in pairs to interview each other about how they generally spend their free time. Give them the following steps to prepare and conduct their interviews.

Paso 1. *En preparación para la entrevista, haga una lista de ocho a diez preguntas básicas que va a hacerle a su compañero/a. Estas preguntas van a servir de base para otras preguntas, según las respuestas de su compañero/a.*

Paso 2. *Haga la entrevista. Apunte* (new) *las respuestas de su compañero/a. Hágale todas las preguntas que pueda.*

Paso 3. *Ponga en orden los apuntes de la entrevista y comparta con la clase algunos de los datos que consiguió en su entrevista.*

3. *¿Cuál(es)?* + *verb* = Choice

A question with **¿cuál(es)?** also asks for a choice, but **¿cuál(es)?** is followed by a verb, not by a noun. Sometimes a phrase like **de los dos (tres,...)** makes the choice more explicit. Note that **¿cuál(es)?**, not **¿qué?**, expresses *which one(s)?*

¿**Cuál es** la clase más grande?
What (Which [one]) is the biggest class?

¿**Cuáles son** tus jugadores favoritos?
What (Which [ones]) are your favorite players?

¿**Cuál es** la capital del Uruguay?
What is the capital of Uruguay?

¿**Cuál es** tu (número de) teléfono?
What is your phone number?

> Compare these sentences:
>
> **¿Qué libro** quieres? = *which book?*
>
> **¿Cuál quieres?** = *which one?*
>
> **¿Cuál de los dos quieres?** = *which one (of the two)?*

Autoprueba

Match each word with the kind of information it asks for.

1. ¿Cuándo?	a. un lugar
2. ¿Dónde?	b. una selección
3. ¿Qué?	c. un número o una cantidad
4. ¿Cuánto?	d. una definición
5. ¿Cuál?	e. la hora
	f. una explicación

Answers: 1. e 2. a 3. d, f 4. c 5. b

Práctica

¿Qué o cuál(es)?

1. ¿<u>Qué</u> es esto? —Un lavaplatos.
2. ¿<u>Qué</u> son los Juegos Olímpicos? —Son un conjunto (*group*) de competiciones deportivas.
3. ¿<u>Cuál</u> es el quehacer que más odias? —Lavar los platos.
4. ¿<u>Qué</u> bicicleta vas a usar? —La de mi hermana.
5. ¿<u>Cuáles</u> son los cines más cómodos? —Los del centro.
6. ¿<u>Qué</u> DVD debo pedir? —El de la nueva película de Salma Hayek.
7. ¿<u>Qué</u> es una cafetera? —Es un aparato que se usa para hacer café.
8. En la foto, ¿<u>cuál</u> es tu padre? —Es el hombre a la izquierda del coche.

Conversación

A. Entrevista: Datos (*Information*) **personales**

Paso 1. Haga preguntas para averiguar (*find out*) la siguiente información de un compañero o una compañera. Es posible usar varias palabras interrogativas.

MODELO: su dirección → ¿Cuál es tu dirección? (¿Dónde vives?)

1. su (número de) teléfono
2. su dirección
3. su cumpleaños
4. la ciudad en que nació (*he/she was born*)
5. su número de seguro (*security*) social
6. la persona en que más confía (*he/she trusts*)
7. su tienda favorita
8. la fecha de su próximo examen

Paso 2. Ahora, en parejas, usen sus preguntas del **Paso 1** para entrevistarse.

B. Intercambios

Paso 1. En parejas, túrnense para entrevistarse sobre los siguientes temas. Empiecen las preguntas con **¿Qué... ?**

MODELO: estaciones del año →
¿Qué estación del año prefieres?

1. estilo de música
2. pasatiempos o deportes
3. programas de televisión
4. materias este semestre/trimestre
5. colores
6. tipos de comida

29 Expressing Extremes
Superlatives

Grammar Tutorial 29
connect SPANISH
www.connectspanish.com

Gramática en acción: ¡El número uno!

¿Está Ud. de acuerdo? Corrija las declaraciones falsas, según su opinión.

	CIERTO	FALSO
1. Jennifer López es la mujer de origen puertorriqueño más conocida del mundo.	☐	☐
2. Roberto Clemente es el mejor beisbolista hispano de todos los tiempos.	☐	☐
3. Benicio del Toro es el actor puertorriqueño más famoso del mundo.	☐	☐

¿Y Ud.?

Complete las siguientes declaraciones para expresar su opinión.

1. El cantante hispano o hispana más popular del momento es ____.
2. La mejor actriz (*actress*) del momento es ____.
3. En la actualidad la música popular más interesante es ____ (la música de ____, la música de estilo ____).

Paso 2. Ahora túrnense para entrevistarse sobre los mismos temas del **Paso 1** pero hablando de sus preferencias de niño/a y empezando las preguntas con **¿Cuál(es)… ?** Deben obtener detalles interesantes y personales de su compañero/a.

MODELO: estaciones del año →
E1: De niño/a, ¿cuál era tu estación favorita de todas?
E2: Prefería el invierno.
E1: ¿Por qué?
E2: Porque me gustaba jugar en la nieve.

¿Recuerda Ud.?: Answers: 1. *Trabajo tanto como tú/Ud.* 2. *Trabajo más/menos que tú/Ud.* 3. *Bill Gates tiene más dinero que yo.* 4. *Mi compañero/a de casa tiene menos cosas que yo.* 5. *Tengo tantos amigos como tú/Ud.* 6. *Mi computadora es peor/mejor que esta.*

¿Recuerda Ud.?

Before beginning **Gramática 29,** review comparisons, which were introduced in **Gramática 17 (Cap. 6).** How would you say the following in Spanish?

1. I work as much as you (*sing.*) do.
2. I work more/less than you (*sing.*) do.
3. Bill Gates has more money than I have.
4. My housemate has fewer things than I do.
5. I have as many friends as you (*sing.*) do.
6. My computer is worse/better than this one.

Number one! *Do you agree?* **1.** *Jennifer Lopez is the best known woman of Puerto Rican origin in the world.* **2.** *Roberto Clemente is the best Hispanic baseball player of all time.* **3.** *Benicio del Toro is the most famous Puerto Rican actor in the world.*

¿Recuerda Ud.?: Reciclado

Review the comparative forms and structures before presenting the superlatives.

¿Cómo se dice?

1. taller than John
2. bigger than an apple
3. better than Susie
4. easier than Spanish
5. older than my grandmother

Gramática 29 Superlatives

Suggestions

- Emphasize the importance of the definite article. Remind students to use *de*, not *en* (for the English *in*).
- Tell students that Roberto Clemente (1934–1972), who played for the Pittsburgh Pirates from 1954 to 1972, was the first Puerto Rican to play in the U.S. major leagues. He was also the first Hispanic to be elected to the Baseball Hall of Fame, in 1973.
- Ask students questions like the following:

  ¿Es Jennifer López más bonita que Britney Spears?
  ¿Toca ____ mejor que ____?
  ¿Es Marc Antony más joven que Jennifer López?

Follow-up

Reciclado: After reviewing *¡El número uno!*, have students give superlatives in other categories: *la comida, los quehaceres domésticos, las marcas* (new) *de ropa, las tiendas.*

Multimedia: Internet

Have students search the Internet for information on Hispanic musicians. Encourage them to look for music clips, as well as official websites for the artist or for his or her fan club.

Heritage Speakers

Pídales a los hispanohablantes que mencionen o describan la música española y latinoamericana que conozcan, como *el flamenco, el tango, la cumbia, la salsa* o *la música mariachi*. Pídales que traigan ejemplos de música grabada a la clase.

Culture

Ask students which Hispanic artists have contributed to the rise in popularity of a *latino* sound in pop music. Which artist of the two pictured here do they prefer and why?

The following Hispanic artists have also had a major impact on music in English-speaking countries: *Pablo Casals, Gloria Estefan, Celia Cruz, Julio Iglesias, Juanes, Enrique Iglesias, Ricky Martin, Shakira, Tito Puente, Carlos Santana, Jon Secada*, and others.

Preliminary Exercise

Complete the following ideas with relevant information, then have students respond to each statement with *cierto* or *falso*.

1. ______ *es la persona más alta/baja/joven de la clase.*
2. *Los perros/gatos son los animales más fieles/cariñosos.*
3. *El ______ es el mejor/peor coche del mundo.*
4. ______ *es el mejor periódico de esta ciudad.*
5. *Los exámenes de ______ son los más difíciles/fáciles (de todos).*
6. ______ *es el actor más guapo (de todos).*
7. ______ *es la actriz más guapa (de todas).*
8. *Uds. son los estudiantes más trabajadores/amables/perezosos/simpáticos de la universidad.*

Prác. A: Suggestion

Ask students to identify all elements of the superlative constructions.

Superlatives / **Los superlativos**

1. Forming the Superlative

To express the *most/best,* and so on, use comparative forms with the definite article.

¡OJO! *in/of* = **de**

the superlative / **el superlativo** = an adjective or adverb that expresses an extreme

el/la/los/las + *noun* + **más/menos** + *adjective* + **de**

El basquetbol es **el deporte más competitivo del** mundo.
Basketball is the most competitive sport in the world.

El hockey es **el deporte más peligroso de** todos.
Hockey is the most dangerous sport of all.

2. *Mejor* and *peor*

These superlatives tend to precede the noun.

el/la/los/las + **mejor(es)/peor(es)** + *noun* + **de**

Son **los mejores refrigeradores de** la tienda.
They're the best refrigerators in the store.

La verdad es que es **el peor jugador del** equipo.
The truth is that he's the worst player on the team.

Summary of Superlatives

el/la/los/las + *noun* + **más/menos** + *adjective* + **de**
el/la/los/las + **mejor(es)/peor(es)** + *noun* + **de**

Autoprueba

Unscramble the words to express a superlative idea. The first word of each sentence is given for you.

1. **Es...** ciudad más el grande la parque de
2. **Son...** clase los difíciles de niños la más
3. **Visité...** del los mundo museos mejores
4. **Vi...** peor año película la del

Answers: **1.** *Es el parque más grande de la ciudad.* **2.** *Son los niños más difíciles de la clase.* **3.** *Visité los mejores museos del mundo.* **4.** *Vi la peor película del año.*

Práctica

A. ¡Anticipemos! ¿Está Ud. de acuerdo o no?

Paso 1. Indique si Ud. está de acuerdo o no con las siguientes declaraciones.

	SÍ	NO
1. El peor mes del año es enero.	☐	☐
2. La persona más influyente (*influential*) del mundo es el presidente de los Estados Unidos.	☐	☐
3. El problema más serio del mundo es la deforestación de la región del Amazonas.	☐	☐
4. El día festivo más divertido del año es la Nochevieja.	☐	☐
5. El mejor lugar de este *campus* para estudiar es la biblioteca.	☐	☐
6. La especialización más difícil de esta universidad es la ingeniería.	☐	☐
7. El descubrimiento (*discovery*) científico más importante del siglo XX fue la relatividad.	☐	☐
8. La ciudad más contaminada de los Estados Unidos es Los Ángeles.	☐	☐

Paso 2. En parejas, comparen sus respuestas del **Paso 1.** Si están de acuerdo en que una declaración es falsa, inventen otra.

MODELO: **4.** No estamos de acuerdo. Creemos que el día festivo más divertido del año es el Cuatro de Julio.

B. Superlativos

Paso 1. Modifique las siguientes oraciones según el modelo.

MODELO: Es una estudiante muy trabajadora. (la clase) ⟶
Es **la** estudiante **más trabajadora de la clase.**

1. Es un día festivo muy divertido. (el año)
2. Es una clase muy interesante. (todas mis clases)
3. Es una persona muy inteligente. (todos mis amigos)
4. Es una ciudad muy grande. (los Estados Unidos / el Canadá)
5. Es un estado muy pequeño / una provincia muy pequeña. (el país)
6. Es un metro muy rápido. (el mundo)
7. Es una residencia muy ruidosa (*noisy*). (la universidad)
8. Es una montaña muy alta. (el mundo)

Paso 2. Ahora repita cada oración con información verdadera.

MODELO: **Carla** es la estudiante más trabajadora de la clase.

Prác. B, Paso 1: Answers: **1.** *Es el día festivo más divertido del año.* **2.** *Es la clase más interesante de todas mis clases.* **3.** *Es la persona más inteligente de todos mis amigos.* **4.** *Es la ciudad más grande de los Estados Unidos / del Canadá.* **5.** *Es el estado más pequeño / la provincia más pequeña del país.* **6.** *Es el metro más rápido del mundo.* **7.** *Es la residencia más ruidosa de la universidad.* **8.** *Es la montaña más alta del mundo.*

Conversación

Intercambios. En parejas, túrnense para expresar sus opiniones sobre las siguientes ideas. Luego compartan (*share*) sus opiniones con la clase. Si Ud. y su compañero/a no están de acuerdo, deben hablar de los desacuerdos con la clase.

MODELO: el mejor restaurante de la ciudad ⟶
E1: Yo creo que ____ (*nombre del restaurante*) es el peor restaurante de la ciudad.
E2: Pues, para mí, ese restaurante es **malísimo,** pero no es el peor.* En mi opinión, el peor restaurante de la ciudad es ____.
E1: (*a la clase*) Nosotros no estamos de acuerdo. Yo creo que ____ es el peor restaurante de la ciudad, pero mi compañero/a cree que el peor es ____.

1. el hombre más guapo o la mujer más guapa del mundo
2. la noticia más seria de esta semana
3. un libro interesantísimo y otro aburridísimo
4. el peor restaurante de la ciudad y el mejor
5. el cuarto más importante de la casa y el menos importante
6. un plato riquísimo y otro malísimo
7. un programa de televisión interesantísimo y otro pesadísimo
8. un lugar tranquilísimo, otro animadísimo y otro peligrosísimo
9. la canción más bonita del año y la más fea
10. la mejor película del año y la peor

Estrategia

Emphatic forms formed with **-ísimo/a** cannot be used in a superlative construction. You can use **-ísimo/a** adjectives in this activity, but as shown in the model.

Mundo interactivo

You should now be prepared to work with Scenario 5, Activity 4 in Connect Spanish (**www.connectspanish.com**).

Notice how an adjective can be used as a noun:* **el peor restaurante (*the worst restaurant*) ⟶ **el peor** (*the worst* [*one*]). *You can learn more about using adjectives in this way in* Appendix 2, Using Adjectives as Nouns.

Prác. B, Paso 2: Selected Answers

4. *Nueva York / Toronto*
5. *Rhode Island / Prince Edward Island*
6. *el metro de Guangzhou (China)*
8. *Everest*

Prác. B: Extension

9. *El Presidente Reagan fue un presidente viejo. (el país)*
10. *El Presidente Kennedy fue un presidente joven. (el país)*
11. *Rip Van Winkle fue un hombre perezoso. (el pueblo)*
12. *El chihuahua es un perro pequeño. (el mundo)*
13. *Es una residencia muy ruidosa. (la universidad)*

Prác. B: Suggestion

Have students imagine that *Rodolfo*, a big exaggerator, visits their house during the Christmas holidays. Have them invent things he might say:

¿Qué va a decir Rodolfo sobre los siguientes aspectos del día de Navidad en su casa?

1. *¿su árbol de Navidad? (grande, elegante)*
2. *¿los platos? (ricos, muchos)*
3. *¿sus hermanitos? (felices)*
4. *¿los regalos? (caros, bonitos, muchos)*

Con.: Notes

- This activity integrates the superlative and absolute superlative forms.
- The model also presents an example of nominalization, explained in the footnote. You may wish to make this structure active, using the material in Appendix 2.

Con.: Follow-up

Have students work in small groups to describe the following, using superlatives.

1. Alaska
2. Rhode Island
3. John F. Kennedy
4. *el monte Everest*
5. *el río Amazonas*
6. *esta universidad*
7. *la comida de la residencia / cafetería estudiantil*

Suggest additional items about people, places, and things on your campus that students like to discuss.

Un poco de todo

A: Note

This activity prepares students to use the preterite and imperfect to narrate events in the past.

Bright Idea

A: Reciclado

- Review the verb endings for the preterite. Have students provide conjugations chorally of the following verbs.

  bañarse
  acostarse
  salir
  comer
  dormir

- Review verbs with spelling changes in the preterite. Have students indicate where these changes occur in the verb paradigm (*yo* forms).

INFINITIVE	CHANGE	FORMS
-car	*c → qu*	*yo busqué, toqué*
-gar	*g → gu*	*yo llegué, pagué*
-zar	*z → c*	*yo almorcé, empecé*

A: Paso 2: Redacción

Assign as a writing activity. Since a great amount of scaffolding is provided for the activity, students should be able to do it easily and accurately. Encourage them to add details to flesh out the description. Tell them that by completing the activity they will start to learn how to use the preterite and the imperfect to narrate past events, the topic of *Gram. 30* (*Cap. 10*).

Un poco de todo

A. ¿Qué hizo Ricardo ayer?

Paso 1. Narre lo que Ricardo hizo ayer, usando como base los dibujos y las ideas debajo de ellos.

Estrategia

- La primera frase debajo del dibujo indica una acción. Por eso el verbo se conjuga en el **pretérito.**
- La segunda frase describe un aspecto de la situación en ese momento. Por eso el verbo se conjuga en el **imperfecto.**

A: Paso 1, Possible Answers: 1. *Se quedó en cama durmiendo. Tenía sueño.* **2.** *Se duchó y se vistió rápidamente. Tenía prisa.* **3.** *Llegó tarde a clase. La profesora explicaba el nuevo capítulo.* **4.** *Almorzó con unos amigos. Tenía muchísima hambre.* **5.** *Jugó un partido de basquetbol. Había mucha gente en el gimnasio.* **6.** *Regresó a casa y preparó la cena. Era temprano todavía.* **7.** *Alguien lo llamó por teléfono. Era su madre.* **8.** *Se acostó y se durmió inmediatamente. Estaba cansadísimo.*

MODELO: despertarse temprano / ser 6:30 →
Ricardo **se despertó** temprano. **Eran** las seis y media de la mañana.

1. quedarse en cama durmiendo / tener sueño

2. ducharse y vestirse rápidamente / tener prisa

3. llegar tarde a clase / la profesora: explicar el nuevo capítulo

4. almorzar con unos amigos / tener muchísima hambre

5. jugar un partido de basquetbol / haber mucha gente (*people*) en el gimnasio

6. regresar a casa y preparar la cena / ser temprano todavía (*yet*)

7. alguien: llamarlo por teléfono / ser su mamá

8. acostarse y dormirse inmediatamente / estar cansadísimo

Vocabulario útil

primero…
luego… y…
después… y…
finalmente (por fin)…

Paso 2. Ahora vuelva a narrar el día de Ricardo, añadiendo (*adding*) otros detalles y acciones y usando palabras de **Vocabulario útil.**

MODELO: despertarse temprano / ser 6:30 →
Primero, Ricardo se despertó temprano. Eran las seis y media de la mañana. **Por eso estaba cansado y no tenía ganas de levantarse.**

Resources: Transparency 114

B. Lengua y cultura: Un poco de la historia de Puerto Rico. Complete the following passage with the correct form of the words in parentheses, as suggested by context. When two possibilities are given in parentheses, select the correct word. **¡OJO!** Give the preterite form of the verbs marked *P:* and the imperfect of those marked *I:*.

B: Answers: **1.** *vivían* **2.** *llegó* **3.** *Se* **4.** *tenía* **5.** *recibió* **6.** *Por* **7.** *había* **8.** *razón* **9.** *desapareció* **10.** *la* **11.** *llevaron* **12.** *eran* **13.** *empezó* **14.** *había* **15.** *se independizaron* **16.** *perdió* **17.** *recibió* **18.** *fueron* **19.** *estadounidenses*

¿Qué sabe Ud. de la historia de Puerto Rico? Aquí tiene alguna información.

En la isla de Puerto Rico, como en todas las Antillas Mayores, (*I:* vivir[1]) los indígenas taínos. Cristóbal Colón (*P:* llegar[2]) a la Isla en 1493, en su segunda[a] expedición al Nuevo Mundo. (Se/Le[3]) dice que el jefe[b] de los taínos, que (I: tener[4]) el título de cacique, (*P:* recibir[5]) a Colón con un collar[c] de oro. (Por/Para[6]) eso Colón pensó que (*I:* haber[7]) mucho oro en la Isla, pero no tenía (razón/prisa[8]). De todas formas,[d] los españoles explotaron la Isla intensamente. En poco tiempo, la población taína prácticamente (*P:* desaparecer[e9]) debido a[f] tres factores: (el/la[10]) explotación física causada por labores intensas,[g] las rebeliones de los nativos y las enfermedades[h] que los españoles (*P:* llevar[11]) consigo,[i] que (*I:* ser[12]) nuevas para los taínos. La población africana, que los españoles llevaron a la Isla como esclavos,[j] (*P:* empezar[13]) a llegar en el siglo[k] XVI.

En el siglo XIX, por toda Latinoamérica, (*I:* haber[14]) guerras[l] contra España para obtener la independencia. Pero las Antillas no (*P:* independizarse[15]). En 1898 Puerto Rico se convirtió en[m] territorio de los Estados Unidos, después de que España (*P:* perder[16]) la guerra que en los Estados Unidos (*P:* recibir[17]) el nombre de «*the Spanish American War*» (la Guerra Hispanoamericana).

En 1917 los puertorriqueños (*P:* ser[18]) declarados ciudadanos[n] (estadounidense[19]) y, desde 1953, su país es un Estado Libre Asociado a los Estados Unidos de América. Esto significa que aunque[ñ] no es independiente, tiene plena[o] autonomía interna.

Estatua y fuente (*fountain*) de La India Taína, en Caguas, Puerto Rico

[a]*second* [b]*chief* [c]*necklace* [d]De… *In any case* [e]*to disappear* [f]debido… *due to* [g]labores… *hard labor* [h]*illnesses* [i]*with them* [j]*slaves* [k]*century* [l]*wars* [m]se… *became a* [n]*citizens* [ñ]*although* [o]*full*

Comprensión. Conteste las siguientes preguntas.

1. ¿De qué grupo de islas forma parte Puerto Rico? las Antillas Mayores
2. ¿Quiénes eran los habitantes originales de Puerto Rico? los taínos
3. ¿Cuándo llegaron los españoles a Puerto Rico por primera vez? en 1493
4. ¿Después del siglo XVI, qué otros grupos raciales había en la Isla? los europeos, los africanos
5. ¿Desde cuándo es Puerto Rico territorio de los Estados Unidos? desde 1898
6. ¿Cuál es la situación política actual de Puerto Rico? Es un Estado Libre Asociado a los Estados Unidos.

En su comunidad

Entreviste a una persona hispana de su universidad o ciudad sobre lo que hace en su tiempo libre.

PREGUNTAS POSIBLES

- ¿Practica algún deporte? ¿Es su deporte favorito uno de los deportes más populares de su cultura?
- ¿Cuáles son sus pasatiempos favoritos? ¿Cuáles eran sus pasatiempos favoritos cuando era niño/a?
- ¿Hace muchos quehaceres domésticos? ¿Cuáles son? ¿Cuáles son los quehaceres que más odia? ¿Qué tareas domésticas tenía que hacer cuando tenía 12 o 13 años?

En su comunidad, Suggestions

- Remind students to get the following basic information: the informant's country of origin, how long he or she has lived in this country, and if the informant visits his or her country of origin frequently.
- This activity could also be assigned as an online research project on a country of the student's choice or assigned by you.
- See the IM for additional suggestions and guidelines.

B: Note

The following grammar topics are included in *Lengua y cultura:* gender, adjective agreement, lexical items (*por eso, tener* idioms), *se* vs. *le*, preterite and imperfect forms.

B: Suggestion

In preparation for *Cap. 11*, where students will actively practice the choice between the preterite and the imperfect, ask students to tell why each tense is indicated in the context of the passage, not only for the verbs that they have to conjugate but also for the past tense verbs that are given in the passage.

En su comunidad

Optional

- Have students imagine that they are one of the following people and that they are telling about their weekend.

  el presidente / la presidenta de los Estados Unidos (el primer ministro / la primera ministra del Canadá)
  un actor / una actriz de cine o de televisión
  un personaje (new) *de televisión muy conocido*

  Write the following *Palabras útiles* on the board.

  grabar (to record; to film on video), *filmar una película, reunirse* (*con*)

- Students often complain about too much homework on the weekends. Survey the class to find out how much time they really spend with their books. Write the following chart on the board or transparency, and have students copy and complete it on sheets of paper.

	LIBROS	AMIGOS	ALMOHADA (PILLOW)
el viernes	______	______	______
el sábado	______	______	______
el domingo	______	______	______
TOTAL	______	______	______

To follow up, ask questions to find out how much they study on weekends. Also, use the information to answer the following questions. Is there a correlation between students' study habits and their majors?

1. *¿Quién es la persona más estudiosa de la clase?*
2. *¿Quién es la persona más parrandera* (new)*?*
3. *¿Quién es la persona más perezosa?*

Resources: Desenlace

In the *Cap. 10* segment of "Chapter-by-Chapter Supplementary Materials" in the IM, you will find a chapter-culminating activity. You can use this activity to consolidate and review the vocabulary and grammar skills students have acquired.

TelePuntos

Note

Pages 312–317 are optional. You may cover some, all, or none of this material in class, or assign it to students—as a group or individually—for homework or extra credit. Pages 318–319 (*En resumen: En este capítulo*) are a summary of all of the chapter's active material.

Suggestions

- If you are using the video in class, show it once, ask brief comprehension questions, then show it again.
- Even if you plan to ask students to watch the video in your campus media center or on their own, it is a good idea to continue to stress the need to watch the shows as many times as they want or need to in order to complete the *Después de mirar* activities.

Antes de mirar

Suggestions

- You may wish to have students do this activity in pairs or in small groups.
- After students have discussed the questions on their own, ask them to share their answers to the last question (whether they are fans of any professional team) with the whole class.

Programa 10

Notes

- This program will be easily accessible to students if they are sports fans. The narration mixes present, preterite, and imperfect tenses, and there is some use (previewed in the text) of present prefect forms. There is also a fair amount of unfamiliar vocabulary and vocabulary that, while somewhat familiar, may be hard for students to catch on first viewing.
- You may wish to call your students' attention to the variation in the pronunciation of sports terms like *béisbol* (*beisbol* for some speakers), *basquetbol* (*básquetbol*), etc.
- If your students are especially interested in sports or are sports savvy, you may wish to do *¿Está claro?* as a previewing activity. Some students might know all of the items except for item 7, which is specific to the program.
- Preview *mil millones = 1.000.000.000*, which is heard in the program. Its English equivalent is one billion. *Un billón* is a false cognate in Spanish, as it actually means *un millón de millones* (a trillion).

TELEPUNTOS

Víctor es aficionado a los Dodgers y los Lakers, y también le gustan el fútbol y la lucha libre (*wrestling*). ¿Y qué deporte le gusta a Ana?

Antes de mirar

¿Cuáles son los deportes más populares de los Estados Unidos? ¿Y de Latinoamérica y España? ¿Cuál es su deporte favorito? ¿Lo practica o solo lo mira jugar? ¿Le interesan los deportes de su universidad? ¿Es Ud. aficionado/a a algún equipo profesional? ¿De cuál?

PROGRAMA 10: Deportes que mueven masas

En este programa hay dos reportajes: uno sobre un museo dedicado al deporte en San Juan, Puerto Rico, y otro sobre un partido de fútbol local en México.

Vocabulario de este programa

veamos	let's see	**el lanzador**	pitcher
de hecho	in fact	**la Copa Mundial**	World Cup
la magnitud	size	**disputarse**	to fight it out
los comienzos	beginning	**la escuela**	school
a fines del siglo XIX	towards the end of the 19th century	**el asiento**	seat
la gente	people	**disfrutar**	to enjoy
la guerra	war	**¿han escuchado?**	have you heard?
el lugar de nacimiento	birthplace	**angloparlante**	English-speaking
de primer orden	first-rate	**sabio/a**	wise
el pelotero	**el beisbolista**	**la cita**	date; appointment
la liga	league	**que la pasen bien**	have a good time
		que gane su equipo	may your team win

Fragmento del guion

LAURA: El fin de la segregación entre blancos y negros en los equipos en la década de 1940, facilitó la entrada de beisbolistas de Puerto Rico en las Grandes Ligas. Es cuando llega el gran Roberto Clemente. En 1973, Clemente se convirtió[a] en el primer beisbolista hispano en el Salón[b] de la Fama. La *Major League Baseball* creó[c] el Premio[d] Roberto Clemente, que se otorga[e] anualmente al pelotero con mayor compromiso[f] social. En tiempos recientes, el básquetbol y el fútbol están ganando más y más aficionados en Puerto Rico, a costa[g] del béisbol. Algunos equipos locales no tienen tantos espectadores como tenían antes. Pero el béisbol sigue siendo el deporte rey[h] para los puertorriqueños. La pasión por el béisbol se trasmite de una generación a otra.

DIRECTOR DEL MUSEO: El béisbol… su fuerte de enseñanza[i] está en los voluntarios. Aunque[j] hay programas, hay ligas, hay campeonatos, hay organizaciones que aglutinan[k] los equipos, pero en sí las destrezas,[l] la enseñanza para el mejoramiento[m] del joven, en el béisbol recae[n] en los voluntarios. En los papás, que ya han practicado[ñ] el béisbol, algunos han sido[o] atletas. O los maestros[p] que les gusta practicar el béisbol…

[a]se… *became* [b]*Hall* [c]*created* [d]*Award* [e]se… *is awarded* [f]*commitment* [g]a… *at the expense* [h]*king* [i]fuerte… *teaching strength* [j]*Although* [k]*build* [l]*skills* [m]*improvement* [n]*falls* [ñ]han… *have practiced* [o]han… *have been* [p]*teachers*

«El Museo del Deporte de Puerto Rico es un lugar maravilloso (*wonderful*) para las personas de todas las edades (*ages*) y en especial para los aficionados al béisbol.»

- Present *la Guerra de 1898* and ask students what that war is called in English (the Spanish-American War).
- Emphasize to students that the more carefully they study the preliminary activities (*Antes de mirar, Vocabulario de este programa,* and *Fragmento del guion*), the more they will understand. Scanning *Después de mirar* before viewing is also an excellent strategy.

Mundo interactivo

Continue your work as an intern at HispanaVisión with Laura Sánchez Tejada, the roving reporter of *Salu2,* as you complete Scenario 5, Activities 3 and 4 in Connect Spanish (**www.connectspanish.com**).

Al mirar

Mientras mira el programa, indique las épocas (*periods of time*) y años que se mencionan con relación al béisbol.

1. ☑ 1942
2. ☑ 1898
3. ☐ a fines del siglo XX
4. ☑ 1973
5. ☑ la década de 1940

«Y muchos [mexicanos] se unen a una porra (*fan club*) para acompañar a su equipo hasta el campo de fútbol y defenderlo a gritos (*with shouts [of support]*).»

Después de mirar

A. ¿Está claro? Las siguientes oraciones son falsas. Corríjalas.

1. El deporte rey de Puerto Rico es el fútbol.
2. El deporte rey de México es el béisbol.
3. El Museo del Deporte en San Juan está dedicado al fútbol especialmente.
4. El Museo del Deporte no es un buen lugar para los niños chiquitos.
5. El primer pelotero puertorriqueño que jugó en las grandes ligas estadounidenses fue Roberto Clemente.
6. El Premio Roberto Clemente se otorga al mejor pelotero del año.
7. El papá de Ana dice que los comentaristas hispanos de fútbol gritan «¡Gol!» mejor que los comentaristas angloparlantes.

B. Un poco más. Conteste las siguientes preguntas.

1. ¿A qué dos equipos profesionales es aficionado Víctor? ¿Qué otros deportes le interesan?
2. Según Víctor, ¿qué actividad no es un deporte olímpico?
3. ¿En qué época y por qué circunstancia histórica se expandió el béisbol como deporte de masa en Puerto Rico?
4. ¿En qué década del siglo XX y por qué se abrieron las puertas de las grandes ligas estadounidenses a los peloteros puertorriqueños?
5. Según el director del Museo del Deporte, ¿quiénes son las personas más importantes en la transmisión del béisbol?
6. ¿Qué tipo de visitantes recibe el Museo del Deporte? ¿Qué grupos visitan el Museo?
7. ¿Cuántas personas en todo el mundo vieron el campeonato (*championship [game]*) de la Copa Mundial de 2010?

C. Y ahora, Uds. En grupos, escojan uno de los dos deportes de los reportajes del programa y hablen sobre la situación de este deporte en este país. ¿Es uno de los más populares en cuanto al (*in terms of the*) número de aficionados y espectadores que tiene? ¿en cuánto al número de personas que lo practican? ¿Dónde se practica? Comparen la situación de este deporte en este país con su situación en México o Puerto Rico.

Act. A, Answers: 1. *Es el béisbol.* **2.** *Es el fútbol.* **3.** *Está dedicado al béisbol especialmente.* **4.** *Es un buen lugar para los chiquitos.* **5.** *Fue Hiram Bithorn.* **6.** *El Premio Roberto Clemente se otorga al pelotero con mayor compromiso social.* **7.** *El papá de Víctor dice eso.*

Act. B, Answers: 1. *Es aficionado a los Dodgers y los Lakers. Le interesan también el fútbol, el golf, la lucha libre y el tenis.* **2.** *caminar de tienda en tienda en un centro comercial* **3.** *a fines del siglo XIX, cuando los Estados Unidos tomaron posesión de Puerto Rico después de la guerra contra España en 1898* **4.** *en los años 50, por ser el final de la segregación entre blancos y negros* **5.** *los voluntarios, como los padres y los maestros* **6.** *Recibe visitantes de todo tipo. Los chiquitos y las escuelas van al museo.* **7.** *más de mil millones de personas*

Sobre el programa

Como muchos niños de todo el mundo, Víctor quería ser futbolista. Aunque[a] le encantaba ver los partidos de los Dodgers, su verdadera pasión siempre ha sido[b] el fútbol, una pasión que le transmitió su padre. Víctor jugaba en los equipos escolares donde su papá era entrenador[c] voluntario. Después, jugó de defensa en el equipo de la universidad. ¿Y Ana? Pues, a pesar del chiste[d] de Víctor en este programa, Ana era una buena deportista en la escuela secundaria, donde tenía el mejor récord en la carrera[e] de los 1.000 metros.

[a]*Although* [b]*ha... has been* [c]*coach* [d]*joke* [e]*race*

Producción personal

Filme una entrevista con un(a) atleta hispanohablante de su universidad. Si no encuentra ninguno/a, entreviste un(a) atleta anglohablante (*English-speaking*) y use su voz en off (*voiceover*) para traducir al español lo que dice su entrevistado/a.

Al mirar

Suggestions

- This activity previews numbers and dates from the show, so that students won't be overwhelmed when they hear them. It is especially hard for true beginners to process large numbers that occur in the middle of a narration.
- Follow up by asking students if they remember the context for these years and times.

Después de mirar

A: Suggestion

As previously noted, this activity could also be done as a previewing activity.

C: Suggestions

- You may wish to run this activity as free-form discussion. Encourage active engagement by all group members. Present the concept of *una tertulia* = a friendly but opinionated (in a positive way) conversation about a topic.
- Ask students to try to address all of angles addressed in the program and to think of others.
- After students have talked about the questions in groups, have each group present its findings to the whole class. Alternatively, ask groups to write up a summary of their discussion and hand it in for a group grade.

Sobre el programa

Optional: Comprensión

1. *¿Cuál de los deportes es la pasión de Víctor?* (*el fútbol*)
2. *¿Jugaba a ese deporte?* (*sí, en los equipos escolares y en la universidad*)
3. *¿Qué deporte practicaba Ana en la escuela secundaria?* (*Corría.*)

Producción personal

Note

See the IM for additional suggestions for this chapter's assignment as well as for general guidelines and suggestions for video assignments.

Lectura cultural

Notes

- The Instructor's Edition on this page offers some additional information on the country of focus. For more information about the country of focus, see the chapter's opening pages and the IM.
- See the IM for some expressions used in Puerto Rico.

First Reading: Suggestion

The small and spectacularly beautiful island of Vieques is to the east of the main island; it is accessible by a one-hour ferry ride. It was the subject of much international attention because of its population's resistance to its use by the U.S. Navy for military maneuvers, bombing practice, and storage of military explosives. The U.S. Navy ceased using Vieques as a bombing range in May 2003.

Exploración lingüística

Ask students to find the following in the reading. Some of these words are glossed and some are not.

- *Una palabra relacionada con encantado/a* (*encanto*)
- *Una palabra relacionada con el calor* (*cálido*)
- *Las palabras relacionadas con la playa* (*aguas, deportes acuáticos, el* surfing, *la costa*)

En otros países hispanos

Note

Hacer la sobremesa is a very Hispanic tradition. The phrase is difficult to translate, but "to linger for after-meal conversation" is a good approximation. This custom connects two activities that Hispanics all over the world cherish: eating and talking with family and friends. *La sobremesa* happens not only in one's home but in restaurants as well, and customers are rarely pressured to pay and leave quickly after their meal.

Tres símbolos puertorriqueños

Notes

- *El Viejo San Juan* is within the walls that originally protected the city. It is a major tourist attraction today, with many shops and restaurants as well as art galleries.
- The construction of *El Morro* began in 1539, to protect the bay and the city of San Juan from attacks by sea. The city was never conquered.
- *Taíno* culture dates from the 13th century. The remains of pre-*taíno* cultures include ball courts and ceremonial plazas.

A LEER

Lectura cultural

Puerto Rico

Una de las actividades favoritas de los puertorriqueños es pasar su tiempo libre en la playa. Puerto Rico está rodeado de[a] aguas cálidas.[b] Por eso es posible disfrutar de[c] sus hermosas[d] playas tropicales en cualquier[e] época del año, ya sea[f] disfrutando de un día de playa con la familia o los amigos o practicando deportes acuáticos, como el *surfing*. Todas las playas tienen su encanto,[g] pero entre las más hermosas se encuentran las[h] de la costa oeste y noroeste (en Cabo Rojo, Rincón o Isabela), las de la costa este y sureste (Fajardo, Humacao o Yabucoa) y las de las islas de Vieques y Culebra.

¿Qué lugares de su ciudad o estado/provincia son muy populares para divertirse o para practicar deportes?

[a]rodeado... *surrounded by* [b]*warm* [c]disfrutar... *to enjoy* [d]bonitas [e]*any* [f]ya... *whether it be* [g]*charm* [h]*those*

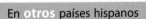

El Fuerte de San Felipe del Morro, que guardaba el puerto (*port*) de la bahía de San Juan, Puerto Rico

En otros países hispanos

- **En todo el mundo hispanohablante** El dominó y la sobremesa son pasatiempos muy populares en muchos países hispanos. El dominó es un juego muy fácil de aprender, pero el juego se complica muchísimo —y también se hace más interesante— jugando en parejas. La sobremesa es el tiempo que se pasa charlando[a] en la mesa después de la comida. No es nada extraño[b] que un grupo de parientes o amigos hispanos pase dos o tres horas sentados[c] a la mesa, primero comiendo, luego tomando café y charlando, hasta unir el almuerzo con la merienda.
- **En la Argentina** En este país sudamericano hay gran afición por el deporte del polo. La Argentina domina ese deporte en el panorama mundial.

[a]*chatting* [b]*strange* [c]*seated*

Tres símbolos puertorriqueños

- **El Viejo San Juan** Los puertorriqueños se sienten muy orgullosos[a] de su herencia cultural y de sus tradiciones, heredadas de los taínos, africanos y españoles. El Viejo San Juan representa la cultura y tradición españolas. Sus edificios coloniales, sus calles adoquinadas,[b] el Fuerte[c] San Felipe del Morro, la Catedral y otros edificios históricos representan la historia de la Isla como pueblo.[d]

[a]*proud* [b]*cobblestone* [c]*Fort* [d]*a people*

- **Los indígenas taínos** Los puertorriqueños recuerdan su pasado indígena, aunque[e] los indígenas taínos desaparecieron[f] poco después de la llegada de Cristóbal Colón a la Isla. Con frecuencia, los puertorriqueños se refieren a su isla como Borinquen, y a ellos mismos[g] como boricuas, que son palabras taínas.
- **El coquí** Es una pequeña rana[h] propia[i] de Puerto Rico. Su nombre es una imitación del sonido[j] de su canto:[k] «co-quí».

[e]*although* [f]*disappeared* [g]*themselves* [h]*frog* [i]*native* [j]*sound* [k]*croak, call*

Un lugar especial

Si quiere tener una experiencia natural espectacular, el lugar que debe visitar es la Reserva Natural de la Bahía Bioluminiscente Puerto de Mosquitos, en la Isla de Vieques. Por la noche se puede ver estelas[a] fosforecentes en el agua, causadas por la formación de altas concentraciones de dinoflagelados. Estos son microorganismos marinos que, al ser perturbados,[b] generan iridiscencia en el agua.

[a]*trails* [b]al... *when they are disturbed*

COMPRENSIÓN

1. ¿Cuál es el lugar principal de diversión para los puertorriqueños? la playa
2. ¿Cómo son las aguas de la costa puertorriqueña? cálidas
3. ¿Qué es la sobremesa? el tiempo que se pasa hablando en la mesa después de comer

Un lugar especial

Notes

- See the previous note on Vieques.
- Bioluminescence is a natural phenomenon that is observed at night, when the water seems to glow as it moves. This effect is produced by protozoans in the water. Very specific conditions make this phenomenon possible: shallow, warm waters and the presence of mangrove trees, the desintegration of whose roots produces a high concentration of bacteria in the water around them.
- There is another *bahía fosforescente/luminiscente* in Puerto Rico: *la Parguera*, which is on the southwestern side of the main island.

Del mundo hispano

Antes de leer

Cuando Ud. hace un largo viaje, de pasajero/a, ¿cómo pasa el tiempo? Piense en por lo menos cinco de las actividades que puede hacer mientras viaja.

Lectura: CyberViaje

Comprensión

A. Ideas principales. Las siguientes oraciones resumen las ideas de la lectura. Póngalas en el mismo orden (de 1 a 6) que se presentan en la lectura.

__4__ CyberViaje ofrece opciones de diversión durante el viaje.
__3__ Hay ocho opciones diferentes de CyberViaje.
__1__ CyberViaje es un servicio de una compañía de transporte de pasajeros.
__5__ Los profesionales que tienen que trabajar en la computadora mientras viajan tienen estas opciones.
__2__ Una compañía mexicana inventó la tecnología que usa CyberViaje.
__6__ Hay actividades para niños.

B. En contexto. Use el contexto de la lectura para imaginar qué significan las siguientes palabras y frases.

1. empresa
2. entretenimiento, pantalla
3. sencillo
4. los ojos
5. ya ni siquiera
6. los pequeños inquietos

GRUPO SENDA. CyberViaje

Con CyberViaje... viajar no será[a] igual

Grupo Senda, empresa líder de transporte de pasajeros, siempre a la vanguardia y comprometida[b] en brindar[c] una gran experiencia de viaje a sus clientes, presenta un nuevo servicio: **CyberViaje.**

¿Qué es CyberViaje? Es un centro personal de interacción y entretenimiento durante tu viaje, tan personalizado que frente a[d] cada asiento hay una pantalla touch screen [*funciona con solo tocar la pantalla*] con la que puedes seleccionar lo que más te guste. El innovador sistema tecnológico detrás de CyberViaje, llamado **VED,** fue desarrollado[e] por Videoturismo, una empresa orgullosamente[f] mexicana.

CyberViaje tiene tantas aplicaciones, y es muy sencillo de usar, desde que prendes[g] la pantalla te encuentras con todas estas opciones de entretenimiento: **Música • Películas • Documentales • Internet • Correo electrónico • Messenger • Videojuegos • Programas de Office.**

Las opciones están al alcance de tus dedos[h] y tú decides qué te gusta más: ¿Quieres cerrar los ojos y disfrutar de[i] la música? Solo tienes que escoger la opción en el menú de la pantalla y seleccionar el género qué más te agrade.[j] ¡O tal vez[k] prefieres ver una película! En CyberViaje vas a encontrar las mejores opciones en todos los géneros.

Si tu viaje es de negocios[l] y tienes que preparar un documento para tu reunión con los clientes, hacer una tabla de datos o elaborar una presentación, ya ni siquiera tienes que viajar con tu laptop, con CyberViaje puedes trabajar tus archivos[m] con el teclado[n] externo que se te proporciona[ñ] y cuando termines de trabajar lo grabas[o] en tu propia memoria USB.

Con CyberViaje también tienes una solución para los pequeños inquietos. Se acabó la época del «¿Falta mucho?[p]» o «¿Ya llegamos?[q]». Además de[r] tener buenas opciones de películas infantiles, pueden accesar divertidos videojuegos que los niños de todas las edades disfrutarán.

[a]no... *will not be* [b]*committed* [c]*offering* [d]frente... *in front of* [e]*developed* [f]*proudly* [g]desde... *as soon as you light up* [h]al... *within reach of your fingertips* [i]disfrutar... *enjoy* [j]te... *you like* [k]tal... *maybe* [l]*business* [m]*files* [n]*keyboard* [ñ]se... *is provided for you* [o]*you can record* [p]¿Falta... *How much longer is it?* [q]¿Ya... *Are we there yet?* [r]Además... *Besides*

B: Answers: 1. *company* **2.** *entertainment, screen* **3.** *simple* **4.** *eyes* **5.** *now you don't even* **6.** *restless little ones (i.e., children)*

Del mundo hispano

Note

See the IM for optional follow-up, writing, and Internet activities.

Antes de leer

Suggestion

Have students do this activity on their own, then share their answers with other students in a small group. Have groups share their lists with the whole class.

Estrategia

Finding the Main Ideas

This is a fairly long reading. The *Comprensión* activity offers a strategy for breaking down complicated texts: summarizing the main point of each paragraph or section in a few words or a sentence. In this way, the reader does not have to keep the entire text in mind as he/she works through it.

Antes de escuchar

Suggestion

You may wish to conduct this as a whole-class discussion, at least the part about the task that bothers students the most.

Escuche

Notes

- In this chapter students can listen to a conversation between housemates about the need to clean up the apartment and who is going to do what.
- If the listening is assigned as homework, ask students to listen to the passage at least twice.
- See the IM for the Audioscript and more information about music in Puerto Rico.

Después de escuchar

B: Follow-up

Ask students if they have (or have ever had) a housemate like Hilda.

¡Música!

Notes

- Marc Anthony was born in New York City of Puerto Rican parents. He has won two Grammys, three Latin Grammys, and numerous other awards and distinctions. He is considered the top selling *salsa* artist of all time. In addition to his music career, he has acted in several films. His official website is www.marcanthonyonline.com.
- For helpful tips on using songs in the classroom, see the IM.

A ESCUCHAR

Antes de escuchar

¿Qué quehaceres hace Ud. para mantener limpio su apartamento o alcoba? ¿Cuál de los quehaceres hace con más frecuencia? ¿Cuál le molesta más hacer?

Escuche

¡El apartamento es un desastre!

Algunos compañeros hablan de los quehaceres domésticos que tienen que hacer. Escuche según las indicaciones de su profesor(a).

Vocabulario para escuchar

verdadero	real	**no discutamos**	let's not argue
no te preocupes	don't worry	**yo me encargo de**	I'll take care of
arreglar	to tidy up	**¡muévete!**	move it!, get a move on!

Después de escuchar

A. ¿Quién lo va a hacer? Empareje cada tarea con la persona que la va a hacer.

TAREAS	PERSONAS
1. __c__ limpiar la cocina	a. Jorge
2. __a__ limpiar el baño	b. Hilda
3. __b__ pasar la aspiradora	c. Ana
4. __b__ sacar la basura	

B. Otros detalles. Conteste las siguientes preguntas según el diálogo.

1. ¿Por qué es urgente limpiar el apartamento? Porque los padres de Ana llegan mañana.
2. ¿Quién está dispuesto (*willing*) a ayudar? Jorge
3. ¿Quién no tiene muchas ganas de ayudar? Hilda

¡Música!

Marc Anthony, cuyo[a] nombre verdadero[b] es Marco Antonio Muñiz, es uno de los artistas hispanos más influyentes de los Estados Unidos. «Dímelo»,[c] cuya versión original en inglés «I Need to Know» fue un gran éxito,[d] es del álbum *Marc Anthony*.

[a]*whose* [b]*real* [c]*Tell (It to) Me* [d]*success*

Marc Anthony, en Miami, Florida

Go to the iMix section in Connect Spanish (**www.connectspanish.com**) to access the iTunes playlist "*Puntos9*," where you can purchase "Dímelo" by Marc Anthony.

A ESCRIBIR

El tema

Mi tiempo libre: Antes y ahora

Preparar

Paso 1. Piense en lo que Ud. hace en su tiempo libre en la actualidad. ¿Hace las actividades típicas de los estudiantes de su universidad? ¿Hay algún pasatiempo o actividad en su *campus* que lo distingue de los otros? ¿Practica Ud. uno de los deportes más populares? ¿Cómo se divierte los días de entresemana (*week days*)? ¿y durante el fin de semana?

Paso 2. Ahora piense en lo que hacía para divertirse en su tiempo libre cuando estaba en los últimos años de la escuela secundaria. ¿Era similar a lo que hace ahora? ¿Por qué era similar o no?

En el Bosque Nacional el Yunque, en Puerto Rico

Redactar

Escriba un ensayo en el que (*which*) compara el uso de su tiempo libre mientras asistía a la escuela secundaria y lo que hace en su tiempo libre ahora que asiste a la universidad. Indique también si Ud. era entonces (*back then*) uno de los estudiantes típicos de su escuela y si en la actualidad es uno de los estudiantes típicos de su universidad.

Editar

Revise el ensayo para comprobar (*to check*):

- la ortografía y los acentos (**¡OJO!** con las formas del imperfecto)
- la organización de las ideas (una clara diferencia entre lo que Ud. hace en la actualidad y lo que hacía mientras era estudiante de secundaria)
- la consistencia del tono
- el uso de los pronombres (evitar [*avoid*] el uso excesivo de pronombres personales; evitar la repetición innecesaria de los sustantivos con el uso de los pronombres de complemento directo e indirecto)

Finalmente, prepare su versión final para entregarla.

Preparar

Suggestions

- Point out that the present and the imperfect are the basic verb tenses for this writing assignment.
- Present a few useful words and phrases for contrasting time: *en esos años, en aquel entonces* (back then) vs. (*en*) *estos días* (nowadays), *en la actualidad / actualmente* (currently). Emphasize that the latter is a false cognate; actually = *en realidad / realmente.*

Redactar

Suggestions

- Suggested length for this writing assignment: approximately 120–140 words
- Suggested structure: 3 paragraphs
  - **P. 1.** First paragraph: How the student used to spend his or her free time (imperfect)
  - **P. 2.** Second paragraph: How the student spends his or her free time now (present)
  - **P. 3.** Third paragraph: Conclusion focusing on how lifestyle changes have changed the student's leisure activities, along with a comment about whether the changes are a good/welcome/necessary thing

Editar

Follow-up

Ask students to summarize the essence of their concluding paragraph and conduct a whole-class discussion about what they think about how their lives have changed.

En resumen: En este capítulo

Vocabulario

Reciclado: In addition to the vocabulary items that are explicitly listed as *Repaso*, note that the following vocabulary items are listed as active in a new context: *la cama, la casa, el cine, la mesa, los muebles, la pared, la película, los platos, la ropa, la ventana.*

Suggestions

- Bring or have students bring clippings that illustrate items and activities from the *Vocabulario*. Use these to review (have students describe, play word games, and so on).
- Have students respond *cierto* or *falso* to the following statements.
  1. *El béisbol requiere la participación de varias personas.*
  2. *El ejercicio es importante para la salud mental.*
  3. *Para una persona a quien le gusta estar entre mucha gente, la natación es el deporte favorito.*
- Have students answer the following questions.
  1. *¿Dónde se puede escuchar música, en un concierto o en un museo?*
  2. *¿Cuál es una actividad cultural, hacer camping o ir al teatro?*
  3. *¿Dónde se puede ver al actor favorito de uno, en un bar o en el cine?*
- Have students make single statements about something they used to do when they were younger (*de joven / de niño/a*). Have them make their statements in round-robin format, without repeating anything someone else has already said.
- Have students describe three to four activities that they think someone famous used to do as a child. They should not name the person they describe. The class should try to guess the identity.

EN RESUMEN En este capítulo

LearnSmart

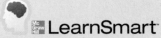

Visit **www.connectspanish.com** to practice the vocabulary and grammar points covered in this chapter.

Gramática en breve

26. The Imperfect

Regular* -ar *Endings
-aba, -abas, -aba, -ábamos, -abais, -aban

Regular* -er/-ir *Endings
-ía, -ías, -ía, -íamos, -íais, -ían

Verbs Irregular in the Imperfect
ir: iba, ibas, iba, íbamos, ibais, iban
ser: era, eras, era, éramos, erais, eran
ver: veía, veías, veía, veíamos, veíais, veían

27. Superlatives

el/la/los/las + *noun* + **más/menos** + *adjective* + **de**
el/la/los/las + **mejor(es)/peor(es)** + *noun* + **de**

28. Interrogative Words

¿qué? = definition, explanation
¿qué? = identification: + *noun* = *what/which . . . ?*
¿cuál(es)? = choice: + *verb* = *what/which (one) . . . ?*

Vocabulario

Los verbos

pegar (gu)	to hit
pelear	to fight
sonar (suena)	to ring; to sound
tocarle (qu) a uno	to be someone's turn

Repaso: deber, necesitar, tener que

Los pasatiempos, diversiones y aficiones

la afición	hobby
la diversión	fun activity
el pasatiempo	pastime
los ratos libres	spare (free) time
el tiempo libre	free time
aburrirse	to get bored
caminar	to walk
dar una caminata	to hike; to go for a hike
dar un paseo	to take a walk
hacer un *picnic*	to have a picnic
hacer planes (*m.*) **para** + *inf.*	to make plans to (*do something*)
ir...	to go . . .
a una discoteca / a un bar	to a disco / to a bar
al teatro / a un concierto	to the theater / to a concert
jugar (juego) (gu) al ajedrez / a las cartas	to play chess/cards
ser...	to be . . .
aburrido/a	boring
divertido/a	fun
visitar un museo	to visit a museum

Repaso: dar/hacer una fiesta, hacer *camping*, ir al cine / a ver una película, jugar (juego) (gu), sacar (qu) fotos, tomar el sol

Los deportes

el ciclismo	bicycling
correr	to run
el deporte	sport
esquiar (esquío)	to ski
el fútbol	soccer
el fútbol americano	football
hacer *surfing*	to surf
montar a caballo	to ride a horse
la natación	swimming
pasear en bicicleta	to ride a bicycle
el patinaje	skating
patinar	to skate
patinar en línea	to rollerblade

Cognados: el basquetbol, el béisbol, el esquí, el golf, el hockey, el tenis, el voleibol

Repaso: nadar

el equipo	team
el/la jugador(a)	player
el partido	game, match
entrenar	to practice, train
ganar	to win
ser aficionado/a (a)	to be a fan (of)

Repaso: jugar (juego) (gu) al + *sport*, **perder (pierdo), practicar (qu)**

Algunos aparatos domésticos

el aparato doméstico	home appliance
la aspiradora	vacuum cleaner
la cafetera	coffeemaker
el congelador	freezer
la estufa	stove
el horno de microondas	microwave oven
la lavadora	washing machine
el lavaplatos	dishwasher
el refrigerador	refrigerator
la secadora	clothes dryer
la tostadora	toaster

Los quehaceres domésticos

el quehacer doméstico	household chore
barrer (el piso)	to sweep (the floor)
dejar (en)	to leave behind (in [*a place*])
dejar sin hacer	to leave undone
hacer la cama	to make the bed
lavar	to wash
limpiar (la casa)	to clean (the house)
pasar la aspiradora	to vacuum
planchar	to iron
poner la mesa	to set the table
quitar la mesa	to clear the table
sacar (qu) la basura	to take out the trash

Repaso: la cama, la casa, la mesa, los platos, la ropa

Otros sustantivos

la escuela	school
el grado	grade, year (*in school*)
el/la niñero/a	baby-sitter
la niñez	childhood

Los adjetivos

deportivo/a	sporting, sports (*adj.*); sports-loving
doméstico/a	domestic, related to the home
libre	free, unoccupied
pesado/a	boring; difficult

Palabras adicionales

de/en la actualidad	currently, right now
de joven	as a youth
de niño/a	as a child
mientras	while

Repaso: ¿a qué hora?, ¿adónde?, ¿cómo?, ¿cuál(es)?, ¿cuándo?, ¿cuánto/a?, ¿cuántos/as?, ¿de dónde?, ¿de quién(es)?, ¿dónde?, ¿por qué?, ¿qué?, ¿quién(es)?

Vocabulario personal

Word Families

En este capítulo

- *la afición, aficionado/a*
- *caminar, la caminata*
- *el deporte, deportivo/a*
- *el esquí, esquiar*
- *lavar, la lavadora, el lavaplatos*
- *la niñez, el/la niñero, de niño/a*
- *pasear, el paseo*
- *el patinaje, patinar*

Entre capítulos

- *aburrirse* = *aburrido/a* (6)
- *la cafetería* = *el café* (2)
- *el congelador* = *congelado/a* (6)
- *la diversión, divertido/a* = *divertirse* (5)
- *hacer la cama* = *la cama* (5)
- *el jugador / la jugadora* = *jugar* (5)
- *lavar, la lavadora, el lavaplatos* = *el lavabo* (5)
- *el lavaplatos* = *el plato* (6)
- *limpiar* = *limpio/a* (6)
- *la natación* = *nadar* (8)
- *la niñez, el/la niñero/a, de niño/a* = *el/la niño* (3)
- *el pasatiempo* = *pasar* (6)
- *planchar la ropa* = *la ropa* (4)
- *poner/quitar la mesa* = *la mesa* (2)
- *quitar* = *quitarse* (5)
- *la tostadora* = *tostado/a* (7)

¡OJO!

- *el equipo* (team) ≠ el *equipaje*
- *pesado/a* ≠ *el pescado*

Heritage Speakers

En algunos dialectos del español que se habla en los Estados Unidos, a veces se usa la palabra *grado* en vez de *nota o calificación* por la influencia del inglés.

Chapter Opening Photo and Chapter Theme

Note: Hospital Universitario

The *Ciudad Universitaria* campus was inscribed as a World Heritage Site by UNESCO in 2000. This very modern campus was designed by the Venezuelan architect Carlos Raúl Villanueva and built in the middle of the 20th century.

Chapter Theme–Related Questions

- Have students discuss their ideas about exercise and health. Ask students the following personal questions.

  ¿Va a un gimnasio o hace deportes al aire libre?
  ¿Cuándo fue la última vez que hizo ejercicio?

- Have students respond *cierto* or *falso* to the following statements.
  1. *Yo no fumo. No bebo tampoco.*
  2. *Odio ir al dentista.*
  3. *No hago nada especial para mantener la salud.*
  4. *En este país, todos queremos estar delgados. Este énfasis exagerado no es bueno para la salud.*
  5. *En la cultura de este país se estima mucho la experiencia de las personas mayores.*
  6. *Los jóvenes universitarios no toman bebidas alcohólicas.*
  7. *Los adolescentes norteamericanos no fuman.*
  8. *Muchos estadounidenses van habitualmente al dentista.*
  9. *En este país son problemas sociales serios la anorexia y la bulimia.*

Reciclado: Review the preterite and the imperfect with health-related questions. Do not expect students to know which tense to use in all situations. Rather, they should be guided by the tense used in your questions.

11 La salud°

La... *Health*

El Hospital Clínico Universitario, en la Ciudad Universitaria, Caracas, Venezuela

- ¿Cómo es su salud en general? ¿Lleva Ud. una vida sana (*healthy*)?
- ¿Hace Ud. ejercicio con frecuencia? ¿Hizo Ud. ejercicio ayer?
- ¿Cuándo fue la última vez que Ud. fue al médico? ¿Fue por algo grave o era una visita rutinaria?

Connect SPANISH

www.connectspanish.com

Resources

For Students

- Connect Spanish (**www.connectspanish.com**), which contains all content from the following resources, as well as the *Mundo interactivo* scenarios, the LearnSmart adaptive learning system, and more!
- **Physical Resources:** Workbook / Laboratory Manual, Laboratory Audio Program, DVD

For Instructors

- Connect Spanish (**www.connectspanish.com**), which contains access to all student sections of Connect Spanish, as well as helpful time-saving tools and resources such as an integrated gradebook, Instructor's Manual, Testing Program, digital transparencies, Audioscript, Videoscript, and more!

Venezuela

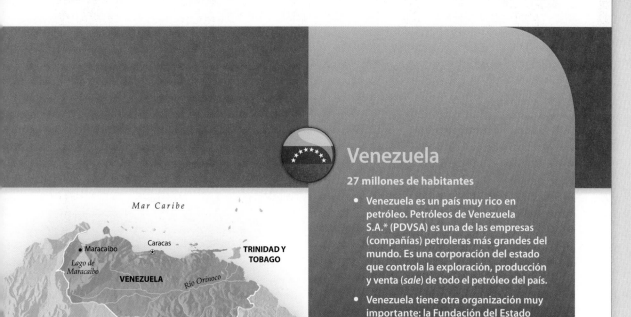

27 millones de habitantes

- Venezuela es un país muy rico en petróleo. Petróleos de Venezuela S.A.* (PDVSA) es una de las empresas (compañías) petroleras más grandes del mundo. Es una corporación del estado que controla la exploración, producción y venta (*sale*) de todo el petróleo del país.
- Venezuela tiene otra organización muy importante: la Fundación del Estado para el Sistema Nacional de las Orquestas Juveniles e Infantiles de Venezuela (FESNOJIV). Es una iniciativa que fomenta la instrucción musical «como instrumento de organización social y desarrollo (*development*) comunitario».

En este capítulo

CONTENT / **CONTENIDO**	OBJECTIVES / **OBJETIVOS**
Health and Well-being 322, Illnesses and Going to the Doctor 324	To talk about health and health-related topics
The Preterite and the Imperfect 327	How to use both of these tenses to talk about the past
Relative Pronouns 335	To connect ideas within a sentence
Reciprocal Actions 338	To express actions done to or for *each other*
Venezuela 344	To learn about a South American country that was home to Simón Bolívar, the George Washington of that continent

*S.A. = Sociedad Anónima (*Inc.*)

Venezuela

Datos esenciales

Nombre oficial: *República Bolivariana de Venezuela*
Lema: *«Dios y Federación»*
Capital: *Caracas*
Otras ciudades: *Maracaibo, Valencia, Barquisimeto*
Composición étnica: *67% mestizos, 21% blancos, 10% negros, 2% indígenas*
Jefe de estado actual: *Hugo Chávez*
Forma de gobierno: *República federal presidencialista*
Lengua oficial: *el español y más de 40 lenguas indígenas también*
Moneda: *el bolívar*
Religión: *96% nominalmente católicos, 2% protestantes, 2% otros*

Point Out

- The website for *la FESNOJIV* is www.fesnojiv.gob.ve/es/el-sistema.html
- Students can read more about Simón Bolívar in *Lectura cultural*, p. 344.
- Venezuela's biodiversity is truly amazing, and Venezuela is a member of *los Países Megadiversos Afines* (Like-Minded Megadiverse Countries), a group of eighteen nations that also includes Australia, Brazil, China, Colombia, Costa Rica, Ecuador, Mexico, Peru, and the United States.
- Columbus first sighted what is now Venezuela in 1498. He named the area *Venezuela* (little Venice) because the villages on Lake Maracaibo, built on pilings, reminded him of that Italian city.
- U.S.–Venezuelan relations have been delicate in recent years due to the presidency of Hugo Chávez.

Suggestion

Have students list their ideas about Venezuela, including information on geography, politics, economy, culture, music, and cuisine. When you finish the chapter, return to the lists and ask students what ideas they would change and/or add.

Multimedia: Internet

Have students search the Internet for health and fitness websites in Spanish. Suggest words, such as *salud,* for them to enter in their searches. They should be able to find several self-help resources for both adults and children. The information and advice on these pages can be used for communicative activities as students learn the health expressions in the chapter (doctor/patient or counselor/client situations).

NATIONAL STANDARDS: Connections

Ask students in Spanish how their diets have changed since they began their studies at the university. Younger students' diets tend to change radically once they leave home. Ask students if they eat more junk food than they did when they lived at home and whether or not they follow the recommended guidelines for proper nutrition. Discuss in Spanish what the guidelines are, perhaps drawing a chart on the board.

Resources: Transparency 115

Vocabulario: Preparación
La salud y el bienestar
Note
Users of previous editions of *Puntos de partida* will note the change from *las gafas* to *los anteojos/lentes*, terms that are more widely used in the Spanish-speaking world than *las gafas*.

Suggestions
- Optional vocabulary.

  LA CARA Y EL CUERPO: la barbilla, la cara, las cejas, la frente, la mejilla, el pecho, las pestañas

  ACTIVIDADES: hacer abdominales, hacer footing, *jugar a los bolos (al tenis, al ráquetbol), levantar pesas*
- Ask students the following questions to check comprehension and personalize.
  1. *¿Hace Ud. algún ejercicio físico? ¿Camina? ¿Corre? ¿Juega al ráquetbol? ¿No hace nada?*
  2. *En su opinión, ¿qué tipo de ejercicio es el mejor de todos? ¿Por qué?*
  3. *¿Lleva Ud. una vida sana? ¿Qué hace Ud. para cuidarse? ¿Come comidas sanas? ¿Duerme lo suficiente? ¿Practica algún deporte?*
- Point out that *sano/a* is a false cognate.

Reciclado: Take advantage of the discussion of health to review verbs for daily activities, with emphasis on what time students wake up, bedtime, resting, foods, drinking and smoking habits, exercise patterns, and so on.

Pronunciación: See Pronunciation Notes, IM.

VOCABULARIO **Preparación**

La salud y el bienestar°
La... *Health and well-being*

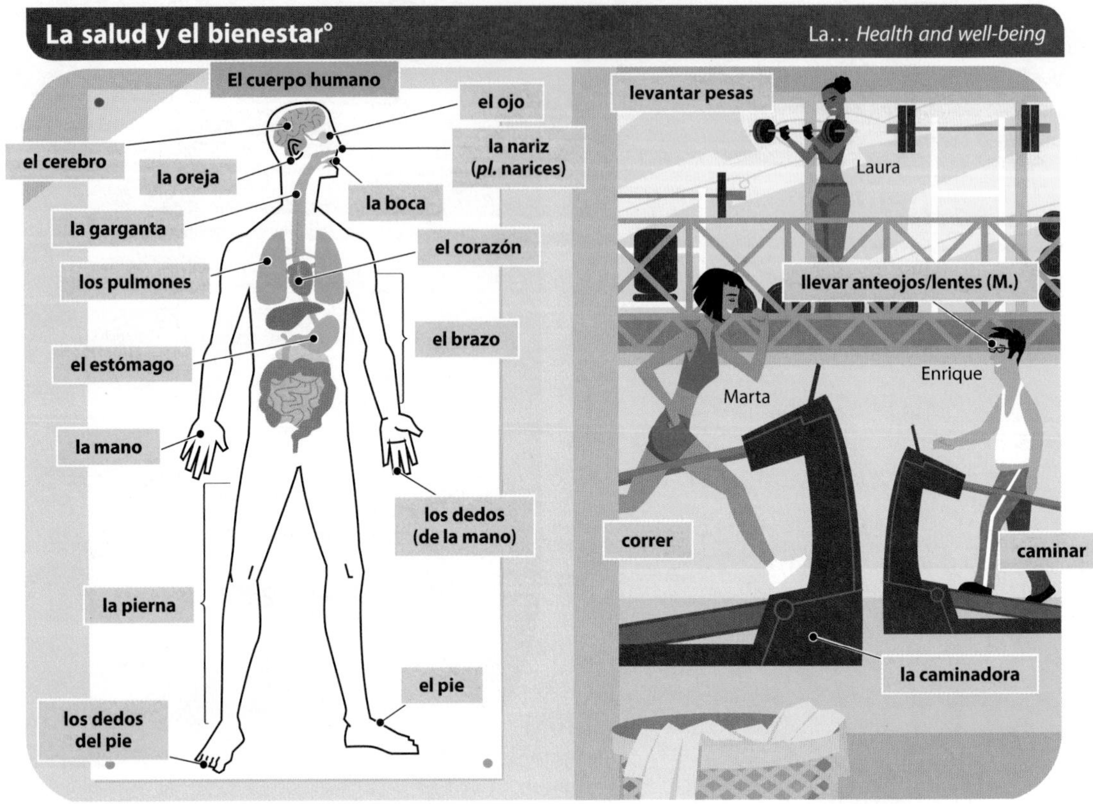

El cuerpo humano

la cabeza head
el oído inner ear

Para cuidar de la salud

comer comidas sanas to eat healthy food
cuidarse to take care of oneself
dejar de + *inf.* to stop (*doing something*)
dormir (duermo) (u) lo suficiente to get enough sleep
hacer ejercicio to exercise; to get exercise
hacer... to do . . .
ejercicios aeróbicos aerobics
(el método) Pilates Pilates
(el) yoga yoga
llevar lentes (*m.*) **de contacto** to wear contact lenses
llevar una vida sana/tranquila to lead a healthy/calm life
practicar (qu) deportes to practice, play sports
respirar to breathe

Así se dice

los anteojos, los lentes = las gafas (*Sp.*)
los lentes de contacto = las lentes de contacto (*Sp.*), las lentillas (*Sp.*)
la caminadora = la cinta de andar (*Sp.*), la cinta de correr, la cinta rodante, la trotadora (*P.R.*), la rueda de molino

Resources: Transparency 116

Conversación

A. Asociaciones

Paso 1. ¿Qué partes del cuerpo humano asocia Ud. con las siguientes palabras? **¡OJO!** A veces hay más de una respuesta posible.

1. un ataque
2. comer
3. cantar
4. los anteojos
5. pensar
6. la digestión
7. el amor (*love*)
8. fumar
9. la música
10. el perfume
11. caminar
12. una flor

Paso 2. ¿Qué palabras asocia Ud. con las siguientes partes del cuerpo?

1. los ojos
2. los dedos
3. la boca
4. el oído
5. el estómago
6. los pulmones

B. Hablando de la salud. ¿Qué significan, para Ud., las siguientes oraciones?

MODELOS: Se debe comer comidas sanas. →
Eso quiere decir (*means*) que es necesario comer muchas verduras, que…
También significa que no debemos comer muchos dulces o…

1. Se debe dormir lo suficiente todas las noches.
2. Hay que hacer ejercicio.
3. Es necesario llevar una vida tranquila.
4. En general, uno debe cuidarse mucho.
5. Es importante llevar una vida sana.

C. ¿Cómo vive Ud.? ¿Cómo vivía?

Paso 1. Diga si Ud. hace las siguientes cosas para mantener la salud y el bienestar.

	SÍ	NO
1. comer comidas sanas	☐	☐
2. no comer muchos dulces	☐	☐
3. caminar por lo menos dos millas por día	☐	☐
4. correr	☐	☐
5. hacer ejercicios aeróbicos	☐	☐
6. dormir por lo menos ocho horas por día	☐	☐
7. tomar bebidas alcohólicas en moderación	☐	☐
8. no tomar bebidas alcohólicas en absoluto (*at all*)	☐	☐
9. no fumar ni cigarrillos ni puros (*cigars*)	☐	☐
10. llevar ropa adecuada (abrigo, suéter, etcétera) cuando hace frío	☐	☐

Paso 2. ¿Lleva Ud. una vida sana? Haga una lista de las cosas buenas que Ud. hace por su salud. Puede usar frases del **Paso 1** pero debe añadir (*add*) otros hábitos suyos (*of yours*) también.

Paso 3. Ahora dígale a un compañero o a una compañera los hábitos saludables (*healthy*) de la lista que Ud. hizo en el **Paso 2.** Entre los dos, hagan una lista de hábitos originales y preséntenlos a la clase entera. ¿Qué pareja tiene los hábitos más saludables de la clase?

Con. A: Possible Answers
Paso 1. 1. *el corazón* **2.** *la boca, el estómago* **3.** *la boca, los pulmones* **4.** *los ojos* **5.** *el cerebro* **6.** *el estómago* **7.** *el corazón* **8.** *los pulmones, la boca, la nariz* **9.** *el oído* **10.** *la nariz* **11.** *las piernas* **12.** *la nariz*

Paso 2. 1. *ver* **2.** *tocar* **3.** *comer, hablar* **4.** *oír* **5.** *comer* **6.** *respirar*

Vocabulario útil

Eso quiere decir…
Esto significa que…
También…

Preliminary Exercise

Read the following statements and have students respond *cierto* or *falso*.

1. *Comemos con los pulmones.*
2. *Respiramos por la nariz.*
3. *La comida pasa por la boca y la garganta antes de llegar al estómago.*
4. *Los ojos se usan para ver.*
5. *Se come bien en las cafeterías de esta universidad.*
6. *Los estudiantes siempre se cuidan bien y duermen lo suficiente.*
7. *Alguien que lleva una vida sana fuma mucho y toma mucho café.*
8. *Las personas mayores no deben hacer ejercicio.*
9. *Los cigarrillos afectan principalmente los pulmones de la persona que los fuma.*
10. *Si una persona no ve bien, lo único que puede hacer es llevar anteojos.*

Con. B: Note

Active vocabulary: *eso quiere decir*

Con. B: Variation

Reciclado: Have students restate the items in the form of *Ud.* commands.

Con. C: Suggestion

Use these items to discuss the lifestyle of U.S./Canadian citizens and people in industrialized countries.

¿Llevamos una vida sana?

Con. C: Follow-up

Reciclado: Ask students to talk about what they used to do and didn't do as children to take care of their health, using the imperfect. Examples to get the discussion going: *comer muchos dulces, odiar comer frutas y verduras, pasar mucho tiempo jugando a los videojuegos.*

Con. C: Extensions

- Have students name and discuss other aspects of our preoccupation with health.
- Ask students the following question.

¿Hay personas que se preocupen demasiado por la salud? Describa a estas personas.

Bright Idea
Con. C: Expansion

Bring or have students bring images of famous people and tell how they grew up, where they grew up, and so on. Sports figures and popular singers will work well in this context. Tell students to follow the lead items in *Paso 1.* Note that students will use the imperfect.

Multimedia: Internet

Students can find diet and nutrition guidelines online that can serve as a springboard for the discussion of their food habits. *UNAM* includes a page on the subject at its website.

There are also pages online with health and fitness tests such as the longevity test. Encourage students to find such pages.

En el consultorio del médico

Suggestions

- *Preguntas*
  1. *¿Se necesita receta para comprar un jarabe para la tos? ¿para comprar pastillas para rebajar de peso* (new)*? ¿para comprar medicinas para diabéticos?*
  2. *¿Qué hace Ud. cuando le duele la cabeza/garganta?*
  3. *¿Se enferma Ud. con frecuencia? De niño/a, ¿se enfermaba Ud. fácilmente? ¿Cuántas veces al año se resfría Ud.? ¿Cuántas veces, más o menos* (do the hand gesture), *se resfrió Ud. el año pasado? ¿Qué puede hacer una persona para no resfriarse?*
  4. *¿Por qué nos piden los médicos que saquemos la lengua? ¿Qué significa cuando una persona le saca la lengua a otra persona que no es médico?*
- *¿Cierto o falso?*
  1. *Si la persona sentada a mi lado empieza a toser, me quedo donde estoy.*
  2. *Me pongo nervioso/a en el consultorio del médico.*
  3. *Cuando tengo que ir al médico porque estoy enfermo/a, me siento mejor antes de ver al médico en el consultorio.*
  4. *Cuando tengo un resfriado, nunca tomo pastillas ni jarabes ni antibióticos.*
  5. *Mente sana en cuerpo sano.*
  6. *Odio ir al dentista.*
  7. *Si no hago ejercicio todos los días, empiezo a sentirme nervioso/a.*
- Offer the following optional alternate expressions and vocabulary: *estar constipado/a* (Sp.) = *estar resfriado/a, operarse, ponerse enfermo/a* = *enfermarse la curita*
- Point out the difference between *ponerse enfermo/a* / *enfermarse* (to get/become sick) and *estar enfermo/a* (to be sick).
- Emphasize that the use of *doler* and *molestar* is similar to that of *gustar.*
- Point out that *la droga* is not a synonym for *la medicina.*

Heritage Speakers

La palabra *resfriado* tiene varios sinónimos, por ejemplo, *catarro* y *constipado. La gripe* o *la gripa* significa *influenza.* Pregúnteles a los hispanohablantes de la clase qué expresiones prefieren usar.

En el consultorio del médico°

En… *At the doctor's office*

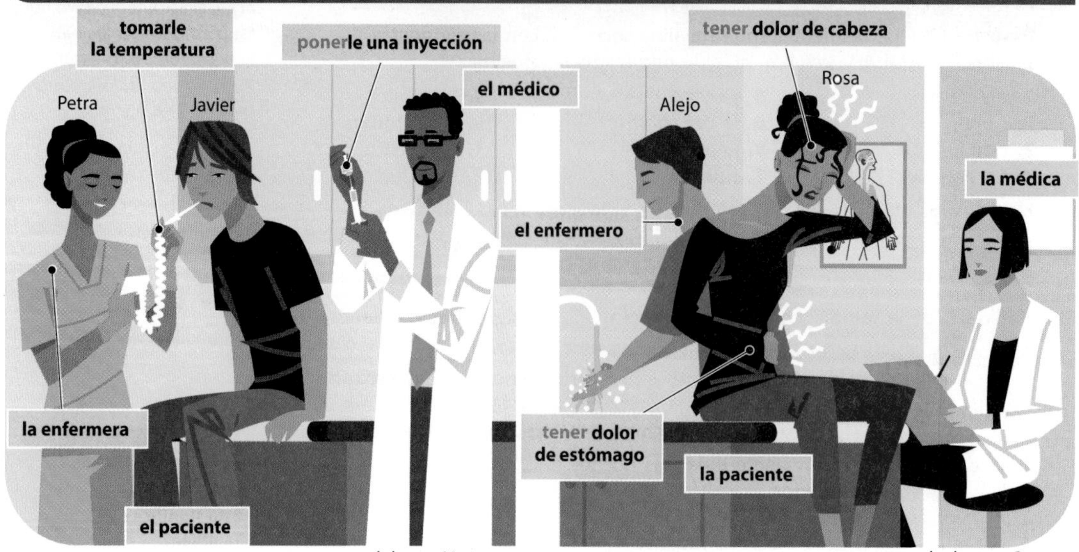

el antibiótico	antibiotic	**guardar cama**	to stay in bed
el dolor	pain, ache	**molestar***	to bother
el/la farmacéutico/a	pharmacist	**resfriarse (me resfrío)**	to get/catch a cold
la fiebre	fever	**sacar (qu)**	to extract
la gripe	flu	**sacar la lengua**	to stick out one's tongue
el jarabe	(cough) syrup	**sacarle un diente / una muela**	to extract (*someone's*) tooth/molar
la medicina	medicine	**sentirse (me siento) (i)**	to feel
la pastilla	pill	**tener dolor de cabeza/ estómago/muela**	to have a headache/ stomachache/toothache
la receta	prescription	**tener fiebre**	to have a fever
el resfriado	cold (*illness*)	**toser**	to cough
la tos	cough		
cansarse	to get tired	**mareado/a**	dizzy; nauseated
doler (duele)*	to hurt, ache	**resfriado/a**	congested, stuffed-up
enfermarse	to get sick		
estar sano/a	to be healthy		

En el consultorio, Notes:

- *To catch a cold* in some dialects of Spanish is *coger un resfriado (una gripa/gripe, un catarro).* In Spain speakers also use *constiparse* and *agarrarse un resfrío/resfriado.*
- *Estar constipado/a* means *to have one's nose clogged or stopped up.* It is a false cognate and does not mean *constipated* in English.
- Note the difference between *la inyección* = shot and *la vacuna* = vaccination. The former is active vocabulary.

Así se dice

el resfriado = el catarro, el resfrío
el consultorio = la consulta
la gripe = la gripa
ponerle una inyección = ponerle una vacuna

Use the term **el médico / la médica** to talk about doctors in general. However, when you use the doctor's name, you should use the title **doctor(a): el doctor Gómez, la doctora Velázquez.** (Remember that the definite article is used with titles when speaking about a person.) If you speak directly to a medical doctor, call him or her **Doctor** or **Doctora,** with or without the last name.

*The verbs **doler** and **molestar** are used like **gustar: Me duele la cabeza. Me molestan los ojos.***

NATIONAL STANDARDS: Comparisons

Unlike in this country, in some parts of Mexico and Latin America the term *doctor(a)* is frequently used as a general title of respect, regardless of whether or not the person is a medical doctor or if they have a doctorate from a university.

Resources: Transparency 117

Conversación

A. Estudio de palabras. Complete las siguientes oraciones con una palabra derivada de la palabra en letra rosada.

1. Si me resfrío, es cierto que tengo ____. un resfriado
2. La respiración ocurre cuando alguien ____. respira
3. Si me ____, estoy enfermo/a. Un(a) ____ me toma la temperatura. enfermo, enfermero/a
4. Cuando alguien tose, es porque tiene ____. tos
5. Si me duele el estómago, tengo ____ de estómago. dolor

B. Situaciones. Describa la situación de estas personas. Primero, indique dónde están y con quiénes están. Luego complete las oraciones que están debajo de cada foto.

1. Rosa está muy sana. Nunca le duele(n) ____. Nunca tiene ____. Siempre ____. Más tarde, ella va a ____.

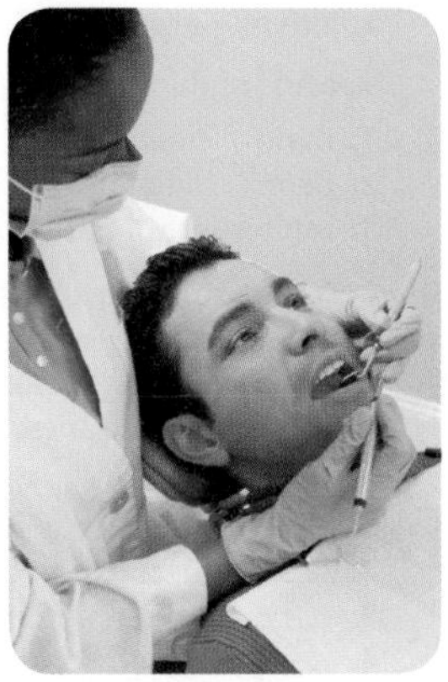

2. Martín tiene ____. Debe ____. El dentista va a ____. Después, Martín va a ____.

Nota **cultural**

El cuidado (*care*) **médico en el mundo hispano**

En el mundo hispano el cuidado médico puede ser muy variado. Depende principalmente del[a] nivel económico del país y después (como ocurre en este país) del nivel económico del individuo. Pero en todos los países hispanos hay excelentes médicos en todo tipo de especialidades, bien preparados[b] en las universidades de su país o en el extranjero. Es interesante notar los siguientes aspectos del cuidado médico en el mundo hispanohablante.

- **Los farmacéuticos y practicantes** Los hispanos consultan con frecuencia a estos profesionales cuando no pueden o no sienten la necesidad de acudir[c] a un médico. Por ejemplo, cuando uno tiene una enfermedad leve,[d] puede ir a la farmacia para pedir consejo sobre una medicina o conseguir un remedio, sin tener receta. Cuando se necesita un tratamiento simple, como ponerse una inyección, se puede llamar a un practicante, quien es más o menos como un enfermero.
- **Los remedios tradicionales o alternativos** Homeópatas, naturópatas, sanadores,[e] tiendas de botánica,[f]… Hay una importante tradición, de gran diversidad en el mundo hispanohablante, de consultar a personas que tienen conocimiento[g] de los remedios naturales o de curaciones basadas en la fe,[h] especialmente para las molestias y menores enfermedades más frecuentes.

A diferencia de las farmacias en este país, en las farmacias hispanas no se venden muchos productos para la higiene personal ni comestibles.

¿Con quién consulta Ud. cuando está enfermo/a?

[a]*on the* [b]*trained* [c]*go* [d]*minor, mild* [e]*healers* [f]*herbs*

[g]*knowledge* [h]*faith*

Con. A: Follow-up: Read these sentences and have students tell whether or not the statements are *cierto* or *falso* for them based on their last dental visit.

1. *Me examinó los dientes.*
2. *Me limpió los dientes. / Hizo una limpieza bucal.*
3. *Me puso una inyección.*
4. *Me sacó una muela.*
5. *Me empastó* (new) *un diente / una muela.*
6. *Me sacó unos rayos X.*
7. *Me hizo muchas preguntas.*
8. *Me preguntó si uso siempre hilo dental* (new).

Preliminary Exercise

Read the following definitions and have students give the word for each.

1. *Es un sinónimo de «ponerse enfermo».*
2. *Es un líquido que se toma contra la tos.*
3. *Esto se hace con un termómetro.*
4. *No se puede hacer esto sin los pulmones.*
5. *Es el papelito que nos da el médico cuando nos manda ir a la farmacia.*

Con. B: Note

Active vocabulary: *el/la dentista*

Nota cultural

Suggestions

- Explain that, like all of Western Europe, Spain has a socialized medical system of the "single payer" variety: taxes from employers as well as employees, depending on their ability to pay, contribute to it. Spanish health care is taken for granted by Spaniards, and it is a source of national pride as well as of occasional complaints.
- The use of common herbs and herbal teas (*infusiones*) to treat mild illnesses is widespread in the Hispanic world. Some very common infusions include *infusión/té de menta* (mint or peppermint), *de manzanilla* (chamomile), or *de tila* (linden tree leaves).
- Antibiotics are generally easily available in some Spanish-speaking countries without a prescription.
- *Los sanadores,* like traditional healers from many cultures, are alive and well in the modern Hispanic world. They may combine natural remedies, such as herbs, roots, and extracts, with the use of prayer and beliefs.

Comprensión

1. *Además de los médicos, ¿a quiénes consultan algunos hispanos sobre cuestiones de salud? (a farmacéuticos, practicantes, homeópatas, naturópatas y sanadores)*
2. *¿Qué es un practicante?* (*Es como un enfermero.*)
3. *¿Por qué consultan muchos hispanos con homeópatas, naturópatas y sanadores? (Tienen conocimiento de los remedios naturales o de las curaciones basadas en la fe.)*

NATIONAL STANDARDS: Comparisons

Unlike in this country, in many Spanish-speaking countries you do not need a prescription from a medical doctor in order to buy some drugs that would require a prescription here. It is not uncommon to see "patients" describing their symptoms to the *farmacéutico* who, in turn, prescribes the appropriate medication and dosage.

Nota comunicativa
Suggestions

- You may wish to point out that *lo* is an article, the neuter article, as compared with *el, la*, and so on, which are gender-linked articles.
- Point out that students have already learned one expression that involves nominalization with *lo: lo suficiente* (*dormir lo suficiente*).
- Have students express these phrases in Spanish: the important thing/part, the bad thing/part, the interesting thing/part. Model these expressions in communicative exchanges with students.

  ¿Qué es lo importante de hacer ejercicio?
  ¿Qué es lo malo de ir al consultorio de un médico?

Con. C: Preliminary Exercise

Have students nominalize the following adjectives with *lo*. Encourage them to use them in model sentences: *importante* ⟶ *lo importante* ⟶ *Lo importante en esta clase es practicar.*

1. *divertido*
2. *peor*
3. *interesante*
4. *curioso*
5. *necesario*
6. *bueno*

Con. C: Follow-up

- Using the same cues as in *Con. C*, ask students to talk about your university.
- Have students express their ideas about the more important things of life: *Lo más importante de la vida* (*no*) *es/son* ______. (*las clases, la libertad, las vacaciones, la salud, los amigos, la familia, ¿ ?*) Point out that *son* anticipates a plural noun.

Reciclado: Have students work in pairs to give each other good and bad news for each of the following situations.

MODELO:
en el restaurante ⟶ *Lo bueno es que la comida es excelente. Lo malo son los precios.*

1. *en la clase de español*
2. *en la oficina del profesor / de la profesora / en esta universidad*
3. *en el aeropuerto*
4. *en el consultorio del médico/dentista*
5. *en casa / durante un viaje*
6. *en el trabajo o durante una entrevista*

Nota **comunicativa**

Cómo expresar una cualidad general: *lo* + *adjetivo*

To describe the general qualities or characteristics of something, use **lo** with the masculine singular form of an adjective.

lo bueno/malo **lo más importante** **lo mejor/peor** **lo mismo**

This structure has a number of English equivalents, especially in colloquial speech.

lo bueno = the good thing/part/news, what's good

C. En el consultorio del médico o del dentista. En parejas, usen los siguientes adjetivos para describir una visita al médico o dentista, según el modelo.

MODELO: malo / bueno ⟶ **Lo malo** de ir al médico es la cuenta. **Lo bueno** es…

1. malo / bueno
2. peor / mejor
3. interesante / aburrido
4. curioso (*strange*) / especial
5. insoportable (*unbearable*)

D. Refranes sobre la salud. Empareje una frase de la columna A con otra de la columna B para formar algunos refranes muy comunes en el mundo hispano. En algunos casos lo/la puede ayudar la rima. Luego explique lo que significan los refranes. ¿Cuál es el equivalente en inglés?

COLUMNA A	COLUMNA B
1. __c__ La salud no se compra:	a. engorda (*fattens*).
2. __d__ Músculos de Sansón,	b. todos tenemos un poco.
3. __f__ Si quieres vivir sano,	c. no tiene precio.
4. __b__ De médico, poeta y loco,	d. y cerebro de mosquito.
5. __e__ Para enfermedad de años,	e. no hay medicina.
6. __g__ Ojos que no ven,	f. acuéstate y levántate temprano.
7. __a__ Lo que no mata (*doesn't kill*),	g. corazón que no siente.

¿Recuerda Ud.?

Since **Capítulo 8** you have been using first the preterite and then the imperfect in appropriate contexts. Indicate which tense you use to do each of the following.

	PRETERITE	IMPERFECT
1. to tell what you did yesterday	☑	☐
2. to tell what you used to do when you were in grade school	☐	☑
3. to explain the situation or condition that caused you to do something	☐	☑
4. to tell what someone did as the result of a situation	☑	☐
5. to talk about the way things used to be	☐	☑
6. to describe an action that was in progress	☐	☑

If you understand these uses of the preterite and the imperfect, the following summary of their uses in **Gramática 30** will be very easy for you.

Mundo interactivo

You should now be prepared to work with Scenario 6, Activity 1 in Connect Spanish (**www.connectspanish.com**).

Optional: Have students give *lo bueno/malo* or *lo mejor/peor* for the following situations.

1. *tener un resfriado*
2. *ir a una universidad cerca/lejos de la casa de uno*
3. *tener hijos cuando uno es joven* (*entre 18 y 25 años*) *o mayor* (*entre 50 y 60 años*)
4. *ser muy rico/a o muy pobre*
5. *ir al consultorio de un médico/dentista*

Con. D: Suggestion

Remind students to pay attention to rhyme when matching the items.

Pronunciación: See the Laboratory Manual for presentation and practice of the letters *s, z, ce,* and *ci.*

GRAMÁTICA

30 Narrating in the Past (Part 5)

Using the Preterite and the Imperfect

Grammar Tutorial 30
connect SPANISH
www.connectspanish.com

Gramática en acción: En el consultorio de la Dra. Méndez

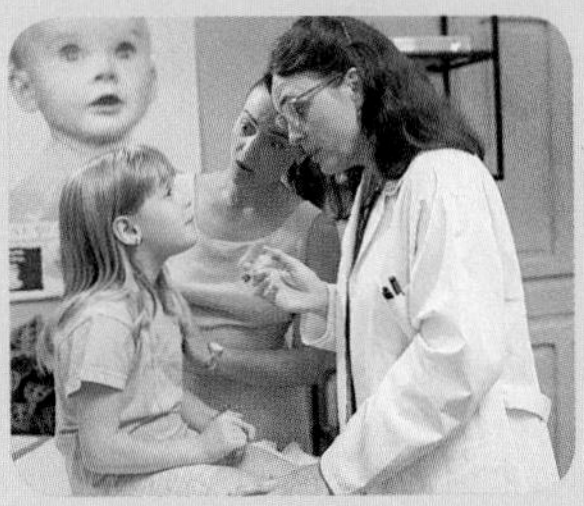

DRA. MÉNDEZ: ¿Cuándo empezó a sentirse mal su hija?
MADRE: Ayer por la tarde. Estaba resfriada, tosía mucho y se quejaba de que le dolían el cuerpo y la cabeza.
DRA. MÉNDEZ: ¿Y le notó algo de fiebre?
MADRE: Sí. Por la noche le tomé la temperatura y tenía treinta y nueve grados.*
DRA. MÉNDEZ: A ver… Abre la boca, por favor.

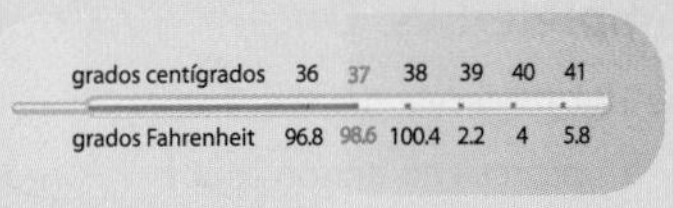

Comprensión

Locate all of the past tense verbs in the preceding dialogue that do the following.

1. indicate actions empezó, notó, tomé
2. indicate conditions or descriptions estaba, tosía, se quejaba, dolían, tenía

You have already learned and used the preterite (**Capítulos 8** and **9**) and imperfect tenses (**Capítulo 10**). In this chapter you will begin to use them together to talk about the past.

Keep this in mind: The preterite and the imperfect are both past tenses, and they are both used to talk about the same point in the past. They *differ* in the point of view (aspect) about the past that they each convey. This is the same as with English usage. When you decide to say *I ran, I used to run,* or *I was going to run,* you are making a decision about the aspect of the past action that you want to communicate.

Here are the main uses of the two tenses. You will learn about them on pages 328–329.

Pretérito	Imperfecto
• beginning/end of an action • completed action • series of completed actions • interrupting action • the action on the "stage"	• habitual/repeated action • ongoing action • background information • interrupted/ongoing action • the setting for the action

In Dr. Méndez's office *DR. MÉNDEZ: When did your daughter begin to feel ill? MOTHER: Yesterday afternoon. She was stuffed up, she was coughing a lot, and she was complaining that her body and head were hurting. DR. MÉNDEZ: And did you notice any fever? MOTHER: Yes. At night I took her temperature, and it was thirty-nine degrees. DR. MÉNDEZ: Let's see . . . Open your mouth, please.*

**Normal body temperature is 37 °C (98.6 °F).*

Gramática 30

Using the Preterite and the Imperfect

Note

This section contrasts the uses of the preterite and the imperfect and provides practice in deciding which tense to use. Students have been using these tenses in controlled activities in *Caps. 8–10.*

Follow-up

After reviewing the *GEA*, ask students the following questions to check comprehension.

¿Quién estaba enferma?
¿Qué síntomas tenía?

Bright Idea

Follow-up

On the board or a transparency, write a brief paragraph about a health incident. Have students note the verbs, then list them. Have students work on the board or transparency to put the verbs in categories (imperfect/preterite), then talk about the different reasons the verbs require preterite or imperfect.

Suggestions

- Emphasize the importance of the speaker's perspective. Many sentences are equally correct in either the imperfect or the preterite, but they will mean something different.
- Point out that every action or state can be seen as having three phases or aspects: a beginning, a middle, and an end. When the focus is on an action's beginning or ending, the preterite is used. When the focus is on the middle, or on the repetitive nature of an action, the imperfect is used.
- Offer students these examples.

  Two preterite actions occurring either sequentially or simultaneously in the past.

  Me puse los zapatos y me levanté.
  Elena se fue cuando yo entré.

  Two ongoing actions occurring simultaneously in the past.

  Hacía mi tarea mientras veía las noticias.

  One ongoing action in the past when another interrupts.

  Yo estudiaba cuando llegó Juan.

Resources: Transparency 118

Heritage Speakers

Pídales a los hispanohablantes que dramaticen una escena en el consultorio de un médico. ¿Qué enfermedad tendrá el paciente? ¿Es el paciente hipocondríaco?

Optional

Share the following formulas for converting Fahrenheit to Centigrade.

- *De F → C*
  $(Grados\ F - 32) \times 5 \div 9 = Grados\ C$
- *De C → F*
  $(Grados\ C \times 9 \div 5) + 32 = Grados\ F$

Beginning/End vs. Habitual

Note

The beginning of an action is usually expressed with the preterite: *Estuve en la oficina a las dos.* (I arrived at the office at two.) vs. *Estaba en la oficina a las dos.* (I was at the office at two. = I happened to be there, with no reference to arrival time.) An example of an exception is: *Isabel empezaba el ejercicio cuando su hermano entró.*

Series of Completed Actions vs. Background Details

Suggestions

- Model the difference in meaning of *pensó* (he thought, it occurred to him) and *pensaba* (he was of the opinion, planned/intended to). Use *creer* forms in a similar contrast.
- Offer students these additional examples.

  Carlos llamó al médico, hizo una cita para la una de la tarde y fue al consultorio. / Cuando se resfriaba, Carlos siempre llamaba al médico, hacía una cita e iba al consultorio.

Beginning/End vs. Habitual / **El comienzo/final o algo habitual**

Use the preterite to . . . /~~~~/

- tell about the beginning or the end of a past action

El sábado pasado, el partido de fútbol **empezó** a la una. **Terminó** a las cuatro. El entrenador **habló** a las cinco.

Last Saturday, the soccer game began at one. It ended at four. The coach spoke (began to speak) at five.

Use the imperfect to . . . ~~~~

- talk about the habitual nature of an action (something you always did)

Había un partido **todos los sábados.** Muchas personas **jugaban todas las semanas.**

There was a game every Saturday. Many people played every week.

Completed vs. Ongoing / **Completado o en progreso**

Use the preterite to . . . /

- express an action that is viewed as completed

El partido **duró** tres horas. **Ganaron** Los Lobos de Villalegre.

The game lasted three hours. The Lobos of Villalegre won.

Use the imperfect to . . . ~~~~/

- tell what was happening when another action took place

Yo no vi el final del partido. **Estaba** en la cocina cuando **terminó.**

I didn't see the end of the game. I was in the kitchen when it ended.

Use the imperfect to . . . ~~~~mientras~~~~
mientras~~~~, ~~~~

- tell about simultaneous events (with **mientras** = *while*)

Yo **estaba** en la cocina **mientras** todos **miraban** el partido.

I was in the kitchen while everyone was watching the game.

Mientras mi amigo **veía** el partido, **hablaba** con su novia.

While my friend was watching the game, he was talking with his girlfriend.

Series of Completed Actions vs. Background Details / **Una serie de acciones completadas o detalles de fondo**

Use the preterite to . . . ////

- express a series of completed actions

Durante el partido, los jugadores **corrieron, saltaron** y **gritaron.**

During the game, the players ran, jumped, and shouted.

Use the imperfect to . . . ~~~~

- give background details of many kinds: time, location, weather, mood, age, physical and mental characteristics

Todos los jugadores **eran** jóvenes; **tenían** 17 o 18 años. ¡Y todos **esperaban** ganar!

All the players were young; they were 17 or 18 years old. And all of them hoped to win!

Interrupting vs. Interrupted / **Interrumpiendo o interumpido**

The preterite and the imperfect frequently occur in the same sentence. In each of the sentences to the right, the imperfect tells what was happening when another action (or actions)—expressed with the preterite—broke the continuity of the ongoing activity.

Miguel **estudiaba** cuando **sonó** el teléfono.
Miguel was studying when the phone rang.

Cuando Angelina **abrió** la puerta y **entró** en la casa, los niños **estaban jugando** y **gritando.**
When Angelina opened the door and entered the house, the children were playing and shouting.

Action vs. the Setting / **La acción o el escenario**

The preterite and imperfect are also used together in the presentation of an event.

- The preterite narrates the actions. ///
- The imperfect sets the stage, describes the conditions that caused the action, or emphasizes the continuing nature of a particular action.

Era un día hermoso. **Hacía** mucho sol, pero no **hacía** mucho calor. Como no **tenía** que trabajar en la oficina, **salí** a comprar unas flores. Luego **me puse** camiseta y pantalones cortos y **decidí** trabajar todo el día en el jardín.
It was a beautiful day. It was very sunny, but it wasn't very hot. Since I didn't have to work at the office, I went out to buy some flowers. Then I put on a T-shirt and shorts and decided to work in the garden all day.

Changes in Meaning / **Los cambios de significado**

Remember that, when used in the preterite, **saber, conocer, querer,** and **poder** have English equivalents different from that of the infinitives. (See page 272.) In the imperfect, the English equivalents of these verbs do not differ from the infinitive meanings.

—Anoche **conocí** a Roberto.
—¿Anoche? Yo pensaba que ya lo **conocías.**

*"Last night **I met** Roberto."*
*"Last night? I thought **you** already **knew** him."*

Autoprueba

Indicate preterite (*P*) or imperfect (*I*).

1. background details
2. repeated actions
3. completed action(s)
4. habits
5. beginning of an action
6. ongoing or simultaneous actions

Answers: **1.** I **2.** I **3.** P **4.** I **5.** P **6.** I

Action vs. the Setting

Suggestions

- Tell students that the "backbone" of a story is always in the preterite, because a story is a series of actions. But stories would be "naked" without the descriptive elements provided by the imperfect.
- Read the following to continue a discussion of the preterite and imperfect in Spanish.

  Estos dos tiempos dan imágenes muy diferentes de una acción. Si Ud. dice, por ejemplo, «Cuando visité a mi tío, salí de casa a las seis de la mañana», yo entiendo que Ud. habla de solo una visita. En cambio, si Ud. dice: «Cuando visitaba a mi tío, salía de casa a las seis de la mañana», entiendo que iba a visitar a su tío con cierta frecuencia y que habla de algo rutinario que ocurría en todas sus visitas. Las dos oraciones son correctas gramaticalmente, pero solo Ud. puede saber cuál comunica la «verdad». Si Ud. dice, «Ayer por la tarde íbamos a la tienda», su oyente espera que Ud. siga hablando, que le cuente qué pasó mientras iban. Normalmente no lo va a interrumpir con un comentario. En cambio, si Ud. dice, «Ayer fuimos a la tienda por la tarde», su oyente puede interrumpirlo con una pregunta porque él va a creer que Ud. ya acabó una parte de su narración. Otra vez, las dos oraciones son «correctas». El uso del imperfecto o del pretérito depende totalmente de lo que Ud. quiere expresar.

Changes in Meaning

Suggestion

Model sentences with the preterite and the imperfect of *saber, conocer, poder,* and *querer* and have students explain the differences in meaning.

Heritage Speakers

Anime a los hispanohablantes a explicar la diferencia entre los siguientes pares de oraciones.

Juan me dijo que le dolía la cabeza. [indefinite period of time, perhaps continuing into present]
Juan me dijo que le dolió la cabeza. [a specific time period that is now over]

No sé cuánto costó. [implies someone made a purchase, but speaker does not know how much it cost that person]
No se cuánto costaba. [no purchase implied]

Preliminary Exercise

Read each sentence and have students tell if it would require preterite or imperfect in Spanish, and why.

1. She used to eat eggs every day.
2. I ate breakfast, brushed my teeth, and left for the university.
3. He was tall and blond.
4. She was playing the piano.
5. They began to sing.
6. Thomas was playing tennis while I was studying.
7. It was three o'clock.
8. The car was yellow and black.

Prác. A: Notes

- This activity helps students link conditions (imperfect) with actions (preterite) in logical sentence pairs. Even though students do not have to create the forms themselves, they are working with the preterite/imperfect contrast.
- Active vocabulary: *el chequeo, la cita, la sangre, la síntoma*

Prác. A: Suggestion

Ask students to say which tense (*pretérito* or *imperfecto*) they associate with each column.

Prác. A: Variation

This activity can be done in a question/answer format. Have students form the questions based on *ACCIONES*. Other students should answer beginning *CONDICIONES* with *Sí, porque…*

Nota comunicativa

Suggestions

- Model the cue words associated with the preterite and imperfect in exchanges with students. Discuss how the words relate to the concepts of the preterite and imperfect.
- Point out that *dos veces, tres veces,* and so on are associated with the preterite, not the imperfect, because they refer to completed past actions. Model and contrast these expressions with *todos los días,* e.g., *Fui al consultorio del médico tres veces este mes. Tenía un dolor de cabeza todos los días al levantarme.*
- Point out that some of the expressions most commonly associated with the preterite are useful for sequencing the actions in a story.

Práctica

A. ¡Anticipemos! En el consultorio. Las siguientes condiciones son razones para hacer una cita (*appointment*) con el médico o la médica. Empareje las condiciones o síntomas con las acciones que el médico / la médica hizo. Hay más de una respuesta posible en algunos casos.

CONDICIONES O SÍNTOMAS (Yo / A mí…)	ACCIONES (El médico / La médica…)
1. __c__ Tenía mucho frío y tiritaba (*I was shaking*).	**a.** Me hizo muchas preguntas.
2. __f__ Me dolía la garganta.	**b.** Me dio una receta.
3. __d, g__ Me dolía el pecho (*chest*).	**c.** Me tomó la temperatura.
4. __e__ Creía que estaba anémico/a.	**d.** Me auscultó (*listened to*) los pulmones y el corazón.
5. __a__ No sabía lo que tenía.	**e.** Me analizó la sangre (*blood*).
6. __b__ Necesitaba medicinas.	**f.** Me hizo sacar la lengua.
7. __a, c, d, f, g__ Solo necesitaba un chequeo (*check-up*) rutinario.	**g.** Me hizo toser.

Nota **comunicativa**

Algunas palabras y expresiones asociadas con el pretérito y el imperfecto

Certain words and expressions are frequently associated with the preterite, others with the imperfect.

Some words often associated with the preterite are:

ayer, anteayer, anoche (*last night*)
una vez, dos veces (*twice*)**…**
el año pasado, el lunes pasado…
de repente (*suddenly*)
en seguida

Some words often associated with the imperfect are:

todos los días, todos los lunes…
siempre, frecuentemente
mientras
de niño/a, de joven

Some English equivalents also associated with the imperfect are:

was ______*-ing, were* ______*-ing* (in English)
used to, would (when *would* implies *used to* in English)

As you continue to practice preterite and imperfect, these expressions can help you determine which tense to use. These words do not *automatically* cue either tense, however. The most important consideration is the meaning that you want to express.

Ayer cenamos temprano.	*Yesterday we had dinner early.*
Ayer cenábamos cuando Juan llamó.	*Yesterday we were having dinner when Juan called.*
Jugaba al fútbol **de niño.**	*He played soccer as a child.*
Empezó a jugar al fútbol **de niño.**	*He began to play soccer as a child.*

B. Pequeñas historias

Paso 1. Complete los siguientes párrafos con una de las palabras o frases de cada lista. Antes de empezar, mire la foto que acompaña cada párrafo para tener una idea general del tema de la historia.

1. nos quedamos
nos quedábamos
íbamos
nos gustó
nuestra familia decidió
vivíamos

Cuando éramos niños, Jorge y yo _____[1] en la Argentina. Siempre _____[2] a la playa, a Mar del Plata, para pasar la Navidad. Allí casi siempre _____[3] en el Hotel Fénix. Un año, _____[4] quedarse en otro hotel, el Continental. No _____[5] tanto como el Fénix y por eso, al año siguiente, _____[6] en el Fénix otra vez.

2. dio
era
estaba
examinó
llegó
puso
tomaba

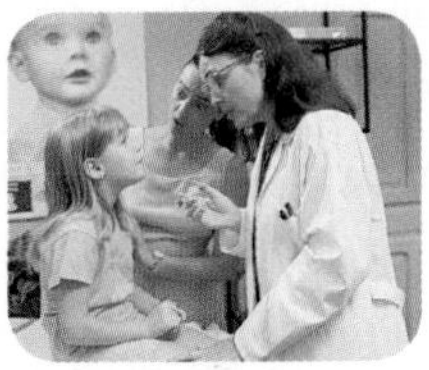

La niña tosió varias veces mientras la enfermera le _____[1] la temperatura. Por fin _____[2] la médica. Le _____[3] la garganta y le diagnóstico una infección. Luego le _____[4] una receta a la madre, que ahora _____[5] menos preocupada. Finalmente, la enfermera le _____[6] una inyección, porque _____[7] necesaria para todos los niños de su edad.

Paso 2. Ahora, para completar la última historia, debe elegir (*choose*) entre el pretérito y el imperfecto en cada caso. Antes de empezar, mire el dibujo que acompaña el párrafo.

Eran las once de la noche y yo (estaba / estuve[1]) leyendo un libro, cuando de repente se (apagaban / apagaron[a][2]) todas las luces[b] de la casa. (Ponía / Puse[3]) el libro en el suelo[c] y luego (usaba / usé[4]) mi celular para tener algo de luz. La verdad es que (tenía / tuve[5]) mucho miedo. Por eso, (salía / salí[6]) a la calle.[d] Entonces[e] (podía / pude[7]) ver que (había / hubo[8]) un apagón por todo el barrio.[f] La luz (volvía / volvió[9]) media hora después.

[a]apagar = *to go out* [b]*lights* [c]*floor* [d]*street* [e]*Then* [f]un… *a power outage in the whole neighborhood*

Prác. B: Suggestion

Ask students to explain why they choose preterite or imperfect.

Prác. B: Note

Active vocabulary: *examinar*

Prác. B: Answers

Paso 1. Párrafo 1. 1. *vivíamos* **2.** *íbamos* **3.** *nos quedábamos* **4.** *nuestra familia decidió* **5.** *nos gustó* **6.** *nos quedamos*

Párrafo 2. 1. *tomaba* **2.** *llegó* **3.** *examinó* **4.** *dio* **5.** *estaba* **6.** *puso* **7.** *era*

Paso 2. 1. *estaba* **2.** *apagaron* **3.** *Puse* **4.** *usé* **5.** *tenía* **6.** *salí* **7.** *pude* **8.** *había* **9.** *volvió*

Multimedia: Internet

Have students print out images from the Internet to bring to class. Working in groups of three to four students, each group writes an imaginary story about the image using the preterite and imperfect.

Prác. C: Notes

- This activity, like many in the text, is designed to help students develop a conceptual knowledge of the differences between the preterite and the imperfect. Students can also gain partial control of this topic in speaking. However, keep in mind that students will switch from past to present and even use infinitive forms in sustained production. This is natural at this level.
- In *Comprensión* item 4, note the use of preterite in this question. It is part of a sequence: action (*ver la película*) + reaction (*gustar*).

Prác. C: Suggestions

- Do as a whole-class narration with students taking turns to complete the story.
- After completing the story as written, ask students to retell the story in the first person from the point of view of Soledad or Rubén.
- Have students work in pairs to tell each other a story about themselves: the happiest / saddest / most embarrassing moment of their lives, how they met their best friend / spouse / boyfriend / girlfriend, and so on. Encourage students to ask their partner for details and to offer help if their partner needs it.

Prác. C: Answers

Comprensión: 1. *Rubén estudiaba.* **2.** *Le preguntó si quería ir al cine.* **3.** *Porque estaba un poco aburrido de estudiar.* **4.** *Sí, les gustó. Se sabe porque se rieron mucho.* **5.** *Porque hacía frío.* **6.** *Eran las dos de la mañana.* **7.** *Soledad se acostó y Rubén empezó a estudiar.*

Prác. D: Suggestions

- Have students read the entire paragraph to see where the story is going before making decisions about the preterite and imperfect. Remind students of the importance of the speaker's perspective.
- Point out that *rumba* = *fiesta* in Venezuela and Colombia.
- Ask students, working in pairs, to create four information questions that can be answered based on content in the paragraph. Then have pairs of students ask their questions of the whole class.
- Ask students if they have ever been to a party where the police showed up. On a volunteer basis, have them answer the question *¿Qué pasó?*

Una merienda típicamente española: churros (*fried dough rolled in sugar*) y chocolate

Prác. C: Answers: 1. *preguntó* **2.** *quería* **3.** *dijo* **4.** *se sentía* **5.** *salieron* **6.** *Vieron* **7.** *se rieron* **8.** *hacía* **9.** *entraron* **10.** *tomaron* **11.** *Eran* **12.** *regresaron* **13.** *se acostó* **14.** *estaba* **15.** *empezó*

Estrategia

Una pregunta *no* se contesta siempre con el mismo tiempo verbal de la pregunta. Por ejemplo, si es necesario explicar por qué ocurrió algo, se usa el imperfecto.

C. Rubén y Soledad. Primero lea el siguiente párrafo (sin conjugar los infinitivos) para tener una idea general de la historia y mire la foto. Luego complete el párrafo con la forma apropiada de los infinitivos, en el pretérito o en el imperfecto.

Rubén estaba estudiando cuando Soledad entró en el cuarto. Ella le (preguntar[1]) a Rubén si (querer[2]) ir al cine. Rubén le (decir[3]) que sí porque (sentirse[4]) un poco aburrido de estudiar. Los dos (salir[5]) en seguida para el cine. (Ver[6]) una película cómica y (reírse[7]) mucho. Luego, como (hacer[8]) frío, (entrar[9]) en su café favorito, El Gato Negro, y (tomar[10]) churros y chocolate. (Ser[11]) las dos de la mañana cuando por fin (regresar[12]) a casa. Soledad (acostarse[13]) en seguida porque (estar[14]) cansada, pero Rubén (empezar[15]) a estudiar otra vez.

Comprensión. Ahora conteste las siguientes preguntas, según el párrafo.

1. ¿Qué hacía Rubén cuando Soledad entró?
2. ¿Qué le preguntó Soledad a Rubén? (**Le preguntó si...**)
3. ¿Por qué le dijo Rubén que sí?
4. ¿Les gustó la película? ¿Cómo se sabe?
5. ¿Por qué tomaron churros y chocolate después de salir del cine?
6. ¿Qué hora era cuando regresaron a casa?
7. ¿Qué hicieron cuando llegaron a casa?

D. La fiesta de Roberto. Primero lea el siguiente párrafo (sin conjugar los infinitivos) para tener una idea general de la historia y mire la foto. Luego complete el párrafo con la forma apropiada de los infinitivos, en el pretérito, en el imperfecto o en el presente.

Prác. D: Answers: **1.** *hicimos* **2.** *era* **3.** *daba* **4.** *iban* **5.** *Había* **6.** *hablábamos* **7.** *bailábamos* **8.** *llamaron* **9.** *pareció/parecía* **10.** *hacíamos* **11.** *Llegaron* **12.** *dijeron* **13.** *era* **14.** *queríamos* **15.** *podíamos* **16.** *despedimos* **17.** *eran* **18.** *aprendió* **19.** *hace* **20.** *invita*

Comprensión: 1. *A Roberto sí le gustaban las fiestas.* **2.** *Sus fiestas siempre terminaban tarde.* **3.** *Una vez, sus vecinos se quejaron del ruido.* **4.** *Aquella noche, Roberto aprendió a invitar a sus vecinos a sus fiestas.*

Durante mi segundo año en la universidad, conocí a Roberto en una clase. Pronto nos (hacer[1]) muy buenos amigos. Roberto (ser[2]) una persona muy generosa que (dar[3]) una fiesta en su apartamento todos los viernes. Todos nuestros amigos (ir[4]). (Haber[5]) muchas bebidas y comida abundante, y todos (hablar[6]) y (bailar[7]) hasta muy tarde.

Una noche algunos de los vecinos[a] de Roberto (llamar[8]) a la policía porque les (parecer[b9]) que nosotros (hacer[10]) demasiado ruido. (Llegar[11]) dos policías al apartamento y le (decir[12]) a Roberto que la fiesta (ser[13]) demasiado ruidosa. Nosotros no (querer[14]) aguar la rumba,[c] pero ¿qué (poder[15]) hacer? Todos nos (despedir[16]) aunque[d] (ser[17]) solamente las once de la noche.

Aquella noche Roberto (aprender[18]) algo importantísimo. Ahora cuando (hacer[19]) una fiesta, siempre (invitar[20]) a sus vecinos.

[a]*neighbors* [b]*to seem* [c]*aguar... to spoil the party* [d]*although*

Comprensión. Las siguientes oraciones son falsas. Corríjalas.

1. A Roberto no le gustaban las fiestas.
2. Las fiestas de Roberto siempre terminaban temprano.
3. Los vecinos de Roberto nunca se quejaban del ruido de sus fiestas.
4. Roberto siempre invitaba a sus vecinos a sus fiestas.

Heritage Speakers

Recuerde a los hispanohablantes que *había* siempre se conjuga en la forma singular, no importa el número del sustantivo. Aunque hay hispanohablantes que dicen *Habían muchas bebidas…*, la forma preferida es *había* en el uso formal.

E. Lo mejor de estar enfermo

Paso 1. Haga oraciones completas conjugando los verbos en la forma correcta del pretérito o del imperfecto, según sea necesario (*as needed*).

1. Cuando yo (ser) niño, (pensar) que lo mejor de estar enfermo (ser) pasar el día en casa.
2. Lo peor (ser) que yo (resfriarse) con frecuencia durante las vacaciones.
3. Una vez (*yo:* ponerse) muy enfermo durante la Navidad.
4. Mi madre (llamar) al médico porque yo (tener) una fiebre muy alta.
5. El Dr. Matamoros (venir) a casa en seguida y (ponerme) una inyección de antibióticos porque yo (tener) una infección de la garganta.
6. Desgraciadamente (*Unfortunately*), mis padres (tener) que darme un baño de agua fría para bajarme la fiebre, y eso no (gustarme) para nada.
7. Tengo que decir que no (ser) la mejor Navidad de mi vida.
8. Mis primos (venir) a casa, pero yo (estar) demasiado enfermo para jugar.
9. ¡Pero esa Navidad mis abuelos (regalarme) mi primer Play Station!

Paso 2. Ahora vuelva a contar la historia desde el punto de vista (*point of view*) de la madre. Siga el modelo.

MODELO: Cuando **mi hijo era** niño, **él pensaba** que lo mejor…

Conversación

A. Una historia famosa

Paso 1. La siguiente historia está narrada en el presente. Póngala en el pasado, usando los verbos en el pretérito.

La niña abre[1] la puerta y entra[2] en la casa. Ve[3] tres sillas. Se sienta[4] en la primera silla, luego en la segunda, pero no le gusta[5] ninguna. Por eso se sienta[6] en la tercera. Ve[7] tres platos de comida en la mesa y decide[8] comer el más pequeño. Luego, va[9] a la alcoba para descansar un poco. Después de probar[a] las camas grandes, se acuesta[10] en la cama más pequeña y se queda[11] dormida.

[a]*trying*

Paso 2. ¿Reconoce Ud. la historia? Es el cuento de Ricitos de Oro y los tres osos (*bears*). Pero el cuento es un poco aburrido tal como está escrito (*as it is written*) en el **Paso 1.** Mejórelo (*Improve it*) con palabras de **Vocabulario útil** y dando detalles y descripciones (usando el imperfecto). También debe terminar el cuento: ¿Qué pasó al final?

MODELO: Había una vez una niña que **se llamaba** Ricitos de Oro. Un día la niña **fue…**

Vocabulario útil

Había una vez… + *imp.* Once upon a time there was…
Un día… + *pret.*

el bosque forest
la casita little house

huir to flee*

The present tense forms of* **huir *substitute a* **y** *for* **i** *in the stem-changing pattern* (**huyo, huyes…**). *The verb is regular in the imperfect, but adds a* **y** *(like* **leer** *and other verbs whose stem ends in a vowel) in the third person singular and plural of the preterite:* **huyó, huyeron.** *The present participle of* **huir** *is* **huyendo.**

Prác. E: Suggestions

- Review the function and position of object and reflexive pronouns in items 2, 3, 5, 6, and 9.
- Contrast the use of the preterite and impefect with *ser* in items 1 and 2 vs. item 7.
- Ask why the preterite is the correct answer in item 6 (had to and did).

Prác. E: Answers: 1. *era, pensaba, era* **2.** *era, me resfriaba* **3.** *me puse* **4.** *llamó, tenía* **5.** *vino, me puso, tenía* **6.** *tuvieron, me gustó* **7.** *fue* **8.** *vinieron, estaba* **9.** *me regalaron*

Con. A: Suggestion: Ask students, working in pairs, to create the beginning of at least two traditional stories or fables, using the traditional formula provided in *Vocabulario útil.* As students work, circulate among them to provide needed vocabulary, some of which may be quite specialized. When students have finished, ask 3–4 pairs of students to read their work; the rest of the class will try to guess the story.

Con. A, Paso 1: Answers: 1. *abrió* **2.** *entró* **3.** *Vio* **4.** *Se sentó* **5.** *gustó* **6.** *se sentó* **7.** *Vio* **8.** *decidió* **9.** *fue* **10.** *se acostó* **11.** *se quedó*

Prác. D: Extension

Have students interview classmates about the last party they attended. Provide students with a list of questions to guide them in their interviews. You can begin with these sample questions.

¿Cuándo fue la última vez que fuiste a una fiesta?
¿De quién era la fiesta?
¿Cuántas personas había en la fiesta?
¿Había muchas bebidas y comida abundante?

Once students finish their interviews, ask them what they found out about their classmates.

Prác. E: Note

Active vocabulary: *desgraciadamente*

Con. A, Paso 2: Suggestion

Point out that *Había una vez…* is followed by a noun with the imperfect in the second clause.

Con. A: Optional

- Ask students these questions about their first university class.
    1. *¿Cuál fue la primera clase que tuvo? ¿A qué hora era la clase y dónde era?*
    2. *¿Llegó a clase con alguien? ¿Ya tenía su libro de texto o lo compró después?*
    3. *¿Qué hizo Ud. después de entrar en la sala de clase? ¿Qué hacía el profesor o la profesora?*
    4. *¿A quién conoció Ud. aquel día? ¿Ya conocía a algunos estudiantes de la clase? ¿A quiénes conocía?*
    5. *¿Aprendió Ud. mucho durante la clase? ¿Ya sabía algo de esa materia?*
    6. *¿Le gustó el profesor o la profesora? Explique su respuesta. ¿Cómo era?*
    7. *¿Cómo se sentía Ud. durante la clase? ¿Nervioso/a? ¿aburrido/a? ¿cómodo/a?*
    8. *¿Les dio tarea el profesor o la profesora? ¿Pudo Ud. hacerla fácilmente?*
    9. *¿Cambió con el tiempo su primera impresión de la clase y del profesor o de la profesora o aún* (new) *tiene esa impresión? Explique su respuesta.*
- Have students write short paragraphs about their first day at the university (or a similar topic). Have them narrate their story in the past, using the preterite and the imperfect. Collect and choose the best two or three narrations, edit them, and develop activities based on them (on overhead transparencies or reproduced copies).

Resources: Transparency 119

Con. A: Redacción

Assign all of *Con. A* as written homework. In class, have a few students read just the ending that they have created for the story.

Con. B: Suggestion

Have students add three or more questions of their own to each list.

Con. B: Optional

Tell students to imagine that you are a detective who has to write a report about the theft of a rare book that disappeared from the university library yesterday. You need to know exactly where they were and what they were doing from ______ to ______ yesterday.

Con. C: Follow-up

After students have asked their questions in pairs, select two or three pairs of students with the best command of the language and have them perform their interviews in front of the class. Students in the class should use their own questions to ask for additional information after the pairs of students have finished their interview.

Con. C: Redacción

Assign *Paso 1* as written homework. Adjust the minimum number of sentences and use of the imperfect and preterite, as needed.

B. Intercambios

Paso 1. En parejas, hagan y contesten estas preguntas.

¿Cuántos años tenías cuando tus padres... ?

1. te dejaron cruzar la calle (*street*) solo/a
2. te permitieron ir de compras solo/a
3. te dejaron acostarte después de las nueve
4. te dejaron estar en casa sin niñero/a
5. te permitieron usar la estufa para cocinar
6. te dejaron ver una película para mayores de 17 años («*R*»)
7. te dejaron buscar tu primer trabajo
8. ¿ ?

Paso 2. Ahora haga preguntas basadas en las ideas de la siguiente lista para saber cuántos años tenía su compañero/a cuando hizo las cosas que se mencionaron.

MODELO: aprender a pasear en bicicleta →

¿**Cuántos años tenías** cuando **aprendiste** a pasear en bicicleta?

1. aprender a pasear en bicicleta
2. hacer su primer viaje en avión
3. tener su primera cita romántica
4. empezar a afeitarse / teñirse el pelo (*dye his/her hair*)
5. conseguir la licencia de manejar (*driver's license*)
6. abrir una cuenta (*account*) en el banco
7. dejar de crecer (*growing*)
8. ¿ ?

Paso 3. Ahora, en grupos de cuatro, comparen sus respuestas. ¿Son muy diferentes las respuestas que dieron? Entre todos, ¿quién tenía los padres más estrictos? ¿los menos estrictos?

C. Experiencias memorables

Paso 1. Haga preguntas sobre una de las siguientes experiencias. En el **Paso 2,** va a usar esas preguntas para entrevistar a uno de sus compañeros de clase. Haga por lo menos cinco preguntas, usando el pretérito o el imperfecto, según el contexto.

EXPERIENCIAS

la elección (*choice*) de universidad
el primer día de clases en la universidad
el primer trabajo
la primera cita
la última enfermedad

Paso 2. Ahora, en parejas, túrnense para hacerse preguntas sobre la experiencia del **Paso 1** que Uds. eligieron. No tiene que ser la misma experiencia.

Culture

Point out that many fairy tales told in English are also told throughout the Spanish-speaking world: *Caperucita Roja* (Little Red Riding Hood), *La Bella y la Bestia* (Beauty and the Beast), *Los tres cerditos* (The Three Little Pigs), among others.

Heritage Speakers

Al hacer *Con. B,* es muy probable que los hispanohablantes contesten las preguntas empleando el imperfecto del subjuntivo.

Cuando tenía 6 años, mis padres me dejaron que cruzara la calle solo.

Si es necesario, explíqueles a los anglohablantes que aprenderán ese tiempo verbal en el *Cap. 18.*

¿Recuerda Ud.?

Que is one of the most frequently used words in the Spanish language, and it has several meanings. Review what you already know about **que** by expressing the following sentences in English.

1. ¿Qué estudias? What are you studying?
2. Tengo que hacer la tarea. I have to do (my) homework.
3. No entiendo lo que Ud. me dice. I don't understand what you're telling me.
4. Creo que la fórmula es correcta. I think (that) the formula is correct.

In **Gramática 31,** you will learn more about **que** and other related terms that you have been using for a while: **quien** and **lo que.**

Grammar Tutorial 31
connect | SPANISH
www.connectspanish.com

31 Recognizing *que, quien(es), lo que*
Relative Pronouns

Gramática en acción: Tus médicos, tus mejores amigos

La Organización de Médicos Hispanohablantes: Siempre contigo

Tus médicos pueden ser tus mejores amigos.

- Son personas con quienes puedes hablar de TODO.
- Son personas que pueden ayudarte y explicarte TODO lo que tú necesitas saber de tu salud.
- Tienen consultorios que están CERCA de ti.
- Y además, ¡hablan ESPAÑOL!

¿Y Ud.?

Complete las oraciones con el nombre de una persona que Ud. conoce. Incluya la relación que tiene con Ud., por ejemplo: **mi madre.**

1. Una persona que tiene mi confianza total es _____.
2. Una persona con quien hablo si necesito ayuda, no importa en qué situación, es _____.
3. Una persona que sabe todo —o casi todo— lo que pasa en mi vida es _____.

Relative Pronouns / Los pronombres relativos

Relative pronouns (**Los pronombres relativos**) are words that connect ideas within one sentence. Most frequently they refer back to a noun or an idea that has already been mentioned. In both English and Spanish, these words make communication more efficient and fluid because they help to avoid unnecessary repetition while linking ideas.

a relative pronoun / **un pronombre relativo** = a pronoun that refers back to a noun or phrase already mentioned

Your doctors, your best friends *The Organization of Spanish-speaking Doctors: Always with you. Your doctors can be your best friends. • They're people with whom you can talk about ANYTHING. • They're people that can help you and explain (to you) EVERYTHING that you need to know about your health. • They have offices that are CLOSE to you. • And besides, they speak SPANISH!*

Gramática 31
Relative Pronouns
Notes

- Relative pronouns are introduced for recognition only. Activities will not emphasize productive use.
- The *que* that students will learn to recognize in subjunctive constructions is a relative conjunction, used to introduce dependent noun clauses (clauses that function as nouns).
- *Lo que* has been active since *Cap. 5,* primarily for use in direction lines.

Resources: Transparency 120

Emphasis 1: Suggestions

- You may wish to introduce the concept of dependent noun clauses introduced by *que*, which will help students when the subjunctive is introduced in *Cap. 12*.
- *Puntos de partida* does not introduce relative conjunctions such as *el que, el cual,* and so on. When they are used in the text's readings, they are glossed. You may wish to tell students about these conjunctions, as they will see them in authentic materials.
- Emphasize that *que* is the most frequently used of the three relative pronouns.

Emphasis 3: Note

The relative pronoun *que* introduces adjective clauses (clauses that modify nouns). The use of the subjunctive in such clauses is presented in *Cap. 16*. You may wish to point out here how these clauses modify the nouns *cita* and *médico*.

Emphasis 4: Note

Quien(es) can be used after a comma instead of *que* when referring to a person, but this usage is not obligatory and it is not that frequent, especially in colloquial Spanish: *El doctor Hernández,* ***que/quien*** *estudió en Guadalajara, es un médico excelente.*

Emphasis 5: Notes

- Emphasize that *lo que* is a neuter relative pronoun, and that it is *not* used to express direct questions (*¿Qué es esto? ¿Cuál es tu teléfono?*). *Lo que* is used to replace a concept, idea, or to refer to a situation in which there is no basis for assigning number or gender.
- When *lo que* refers to a plural noun, the verb is plural: *Lo que necesito son amigos.* This structure is not used in *Puntos de partida*.

NATIONAL STANDARDS:

Communication/Cultures

The relative pronouns that students have seen thus far all refer to antecedents found in the main clause. There are, however, other uses of relative pronouns in which there is no antecedent, and there are also other relative pronouns (*el que…*). These pronouns frequently appear in popular sayings or proverbs and correspond to *he who, the one who,* or *those who* in English. You may wish to write the Spanish sayings on the board and ask students to come up with their English equivalents, when there is one, or a good translation when the saying has no direct English equivalent.

Quien ríe el último, ríe mejor.	He who laughs last, laughs loudest.
Quien no se aventura, no cruza la mar.	Nothing ventured, nothing gained.
El que algo quiere, algo le cuesta.	There is no free lunch.
Quien espera, desespera.	A watched pot never boils.
El que no está en casa, no sabe lo que pasa.	When the cat's away, the mice will play.
Quien mal anda, mal acaba.	You get what's coming to you.
Quien ligero promete, despacio se arrepiente.	Promise in haste, repent at leisure.

I see a doctor. She is from Venezuela. → *I see a doctor* ***who*** *is from Venezuela.*

Veo a una médica. Es de Venezuela. → Veo a una médica **que** es de Venezuela.

Spanish has a rich and varied system of relative pronouns, but you will learn only three of them in this section.

1. Relative Pronouns
There are four principal *relative pronouns* in English: *that, which, who,* and *whom.* They are usually expressed in Spanish by the relative pronouns at the right, all of which you already know.

Los pronombres relativos
que = refers to things and people
quien(es) = refers only to people
lo que = refers to a situation

2. *Que/Quien(es)* vs. *¿qué?/¿quién(es)?*
The relative pronouns **que** and **quien(es)** sound like the interrogative words **¿qué?** and **¿quién(es)?**, but they are not the same. The relative pronouns link words within a sentence; the interrogative words ask questions (and they always have an accent mark to distinguish them from relative pronouns in writing). Can you give the English equivalent of the indicated words in the examples on the right?

—**¿Qué** es eso?
—Es una cosa **que** sirve para ver mejor.

—**¿Quién** es?
—Es el chico a **quien** conocí en el bus.

3. *que* = *that, which, who*
Que is by far the most frequently used relative pronoun in Spanish. It refers to people and things.

¡OJO!
Que cannot be used after a preposition to refer to people. See the next point (4).

Tuve **una cita** con el médico **que** duró una hora.
I had an appointment with the doctor ***that*** *lasted an hour.*

Es **un buen médico que** tiene mucha experiencia.
He's a good doctor ***who*** *has a lot of experience.*

4. *quien, quienes* = *who(m)*
Quien and **quienes** can refer only people. They are always used after a preposition.

La mujer con quien hablaba es mi médica.
The woman ***with whom*** *I was speaking is my doctor. (The woman I was speaking with is my doctor.)*

Las enfermeras a quienes les dimos las flores cuidaron a mi padre.
The nurses ***to whom*** *we gave the flowers took care of my dad. (The nurses we gave the flowers to took care of my dad.)*

5. *lo que* = *what, that which*
Lo que always refers to a whole situation or idea. It can refer to something that has been mentioned before or to something that will be referred to later in the sentence.

¡OJO!
If you can substitute *that which* for *what* in a sentence, use **lo que,** not **que.**

No entiendo **lo que dijo.**
I don't understand ***what*** *he said.*

Lo que necesito es **estudiar más.**
What (That which) *I need is to study more.*

Práctica

¿Que, quien(es) o lo que? Complete las oraciones en español con el pronombre relativo apropiado.

1. *That's what I'm going to do.* — Eso es <u>lo que</u> voy a hacer.
2. *That's what you did?* — ¿Eso es <u>lo que</u> hiciste?
3. *He's the doctor I trust the most.* — Es el médico en <u>quien</u> más confío.
4. *The doctors who worked in Latin America speak Spanish very well.* — Los médicos <u>que</u> trabajaron en Latinoamérica hablan español muy bien.
5. *The doctors I worked with in Latin America speak English very well.* — Los médicos con <u>quienes</u> trabajé en Latinoamérica hablan inglés muy bien.
6. *She's the nurse who saw me.* — Ella es la enfermera <u>que</u> me vio.

Autoprueba

Match each item with the corresponding relative pronoun.

1. ____ una cosa		a.	que
2. ____ un concepto		b.	quien
3. ____ a una persona		c.	quienes
4. ____ con dos amigos		d.	lo que
5. ____ una idea			

Answers: 1. a 2. d 3. b 4. c 5. d

Conversación

A. El estrés, la condición humana

Paso 1. Lea la siguiente tira cómica y conteste las preguntas.

[a]cansancio… *fatigue, restlessness, worry, nervousness, (emotional) imbalance, and anxiety*

1. Lo que quiere el padre de Libertad (la amiga de Mafalda) es <u>una receta para unas píldoras</u>.
2. Lo que tiene es <u>cansancio, intranquilidad, preocupación, nerviosismo, desequilibrio y ansiedad</u>.
3. Según el médico, lo que tiene su padre es <u>normalidad</u>.

Paso 2. En parejas, comparen lo que siente el padre de Libertad y lo que sienten Uds. a veces como estudiantes. ¿Es cierto que esos problemas son «comunes» durante ciertas épocas del año? ¿En cuáles?

B. En la preadolescencia

Paso 1. Complete las siguientes declaraciones con detalles de su vida personal.

Cuando yo tenía diez años más o menos…

1. lo que más me divertía era ____.
2. lo que más me molestaba era ____.
3. el personaje (*character*) de ficción que más me gustaba era ____.
4. la persona / las personas que yo más quería (*loved*) era(n) ____.
5. la persona / las personas con quien(es) yo quería estar era(n) ____.
6. el programa de televisión que yo veía siempre era ____.

Paso 2. Ahora, en parejas, comparen sus respuestas. Digan a la clase lo que Uds. tienen en común.

Prác.: Suggestion

You can use this exercise to contrast how relative pronouns work in English and in Spanish.

- Items 3 and 5: English can omit the relative pronoun; Spanish cannot.
- Item 5: Not only can English omit the relative pronoun (*that* or *whom*) but it allows the separation of the relative pronoun from its related word (*with*). In Spanish, a preposition can never be separated from its object.

Con. A: Note

Mafalda is a famous and popular comic strip by the Argentina cartoonist Joaquín Salvador Lavado, or *Quino,* his pen name. *Mafalda* is the main character of the comic strip. She is an approximately 6-year old girl who has strong political views of the world. Before students read this strip, you may wish to explain which of the girls is Mafalda (the brunette) and which is her friend Libertad.

Con. A: Follow-up

- Have students give advice to the following people using sentences like:

  La persona con quien debes hablar es… ; Lo que debes hacer es + inf.

  1. *Necesito descansar, y tengo tres días libres la semana que viene.*
  2. *Mi compañero/a de cuarto (esposo/a,…) no me ayuda en nada en el apartamento, y me molesta con su música por la noche.*
  3. *No sé qué clases debo tomar el semestre/trimestre que viene.*
- Ask students: *¿Qué critica la tira cómica?* Start a class discussion about life in modern industrialized society.

Con. B: Suggestions

- Model answers that use infinitives for items 1 and 2 before allowing students to start the activity.
- Ask students to ask you questions based on the items.
- Bring in articles from a Spanish-language newspaper or magazine and have students identify and analyze the use of relative pronouns.
- Have students respond not only with *lo que…* or *la persona con quien…* but also with formal commands.

Optional Activity

Lo que debes hacer es… *Imagine que Ud. está hablando con un amigo o una amiga que está en las siguientes situaciones. Déle consejos* (advice) *sobre lo que debe hacer o dígale con quién debe hablar. Siga el modelo.*

MODELOS: *Me duele la cabeza.* →
Lo que debes hacer es tomar dos aspirinas.
La persona con quien debes hablar es tu mamá. Ella va a saber lo que debes hacer.

1. *Tengo un resfriado horrible.*
2. *Necesito descansar, y tengo tres días libres la semana que viene.*
3. *Tengo ganas de comer comida china esta noche.*
4. *No sé qué clases debo tomar el semestre/trimestre que viene.*
5. *¡Tengo tantas presiones horribles en mi vida privada en este momento!*
6. *Vivo muy lejos de la universidad, y pierdo una hora en ir y venir todos los días.*

Gramática 32

Reciprocal Actions with Reflexive Pronouns

Suggestions

- Review the use of *nos, os,* and *se* in reflexive verbs from *Cap. 5*.
- Compare reflexive actions to reciprocal actions: *nos lavamos* vs. *nos queremos*. Point out the importance of context.
- Point out that reciprocal pronouns work as either direct or indirect object pronouns. In the sentences *Se quieren* (They love each other) and *Nos llamamos* (We call each other), the reciprocal pronouns are direct objects. In the sentences *Uds. se escribieron cartas* (You wrote each other letters) and *Nos compramos regalos* (We bought each other gifts), the reciprocal pronouns indicate indirect objects.
- Emphasize that not all verbs can be made reciprocal, as not all verbs can be reflexive: *caminar, correr…* Model some examples of intransitive verbs in exchanges with students.

  ¿Adónde se van Uds. después de la clase? vs. *¿Se ven Uds. después de la clase?*

  In the first example, *se van* is not a reciprocal (or a reflexive) construction; rather, *se* adds the meaning *away* or *off* to *ir*.

Emphasis 2: Reciclado

Optional: Ask students what body parts they associate with the following infinitives. Possible answers are given in parenthesis.

1. *abrazarse* (*los brazos*)
2. *besarse* (*la boca, los labios* [new]), *la cabeza*)
3. *quererse* (*el corazón, el cerebro*)
4. *saludarse* (*la mano*)
5. *pelearse* (*la mano, la boca, los brazos*)
6. *darse la mano* (*la mano, los brazos*)

¿Recuerda Ud.?

Before learning how to express reciprocal actions in **Gramática 32,** review the reflexive pronouns in **Gramática 14 (Cap. 5),** then provide the correct reflexive pronouns for the following sentences.

1. _Me_ levanté a las ocho y media.
2. Laura _se_ puso el vestido.
3. Mis amigos y yo _nos_ sentamos en un café.
4. ¿Prefieres duchar_te_ o bañar_te_?

Grammar Tutorial 32
connect SPANISH
www.connectspanish.com

32 Expressing *each other*

Reciprocal Actions with Reflexive Pronouns

Gramática en acción: La amistad

Los buenos amigos…

- se conocen bien.
- se respetan.
- se quieren.
- se recuerdan siempre.

En las culturas hispanas, cuando las buenas amigas se encuentran, se besan en la mejilla.

¿Y Ud.?

Cuando Ud. y sus amigos se encuentran, ¿cómo se saludan (*do you greet each other*)? ¿Se dan la mano? ¿Se besan?

Reciprocal Actions / Las acciones recíprocas

nos = each other (**nosotros/as**)	
os = each other (**vosotros/as**)	
se = each other (**Uds., ellos/as**)	

1. **Reciprocal Actions**
   Reciprocal actions (**Las acciones recíprocas**) are actions that involve two or more people doing something *to* or *for* each other. They are usually expressed in English with *each other* or *one another*. In Spanish, reciprocal actions are expressed with pronouns that are identical to the plural reflexive pronouns.

Nos queremos.	*We love each other.*
¿**Os** ayudáis?	*Do you help one another?*
Se miran con ternura.	*They're looking at each other tenderly.*

2. **Important Reciprocal Action Verbs**
   Verbs frequently used in this way include those at right, but any verb to whose meaning the phrase *each other* can be added can be used to express a reciprocal action: **hablarse, mirarse, pelearse,** and so on.

abrazarse (c)	to embrace
besarse	to kiss each other
darse la mano	to shake hands
encontrarse (se encuentran)	to meet (*someone somewhere*)
quererse	to love each other; to be fond of each other
saludarse	to greet each other

Friendship *Good friends . . . • know each other well. • respect each other. • are fond of each other. • always remember each other. In Hispanic cultures, when close women friends meet, they kiss each other on the cheek.*

NATIONAL STANDARDS: Cultures

Unlike majority culture customs in this country, it is common in Spanish-speaking countries and among Hispanics everywhere to give someone a peck on the cheek (*un beso*) or on both cheeks (*dos besos*) when greeting or saying good-bye, especially among close friends and family members. It does not necessarily indicate a romantic interest in the person. Depending on the local culture, kissing can occur between a man and a woman, a parent and a child, or two women. In Latin American cultures, two men do not usually give kisses on the cheek unless they are fathers and sons.

Práctica

A. ¡Anticipemos! Los buenos amigos. Indique las oraciones que describen lo que hacen Ud. y uno de sus mejores amigos para mantener su amistad (*friendship*).

1. ☐ Nos vemos con frecuencia.
2. ☐ Nos conocemos muy bien. No hay secretos entre nosotros.
3. ☐ Nos respetamos mucho.
4. ☐ Nos ayudamos cuando necesitamos ayuda.
5. ☐ Nos escribimos cuando estamos en lugares distantes.
6. ☐ Nos hablamos por teléfono con frecuencia.
7. ☐ Nos decimos la verdad siempre, lo bueno y lo malo.
8. ☐ Cuando no nos hablamos por mucho tiempo, comprendemos que es porque estamos muy ocupados.

B. ¿Qué pasa entre ellos? Describa las siguientes relaciones familiares o sociales, haciendo oraciones completas con una palabra o frase de cada columna.

MODELO: Los buenos amigos se conocen bien.

los buenos amigos los parientes los esposos los padres y los niños los amigos que no viven en la misma ciudad los profesores y los estudiantes los compañeros de cuarto/casa	+	(no)	+	visitarse con frecuencia quererse, respetarse ayudarse mutuamente (en los quehaceres domésticos, cuando tenemos problemas económicos o problemas personales) verse (todos los días, con frecuencia) llamarse por teléfono, escribirse mirarse (con cariño [*affection*]) necesitarse conocerse bien saludarse, darse la mano quejarse sinceramente

Autoprueba

Give the correct pronoun to express a reciprocal action.

1. ______ miramos
2. ______ pelearon
3. ______ veíais
4. ______ conocen
5. ______ llamaban
6. ______ saludamos

Answers: **1.** nos **2.** se **3.** os **4.** se **5.** se **6.** nos

Conversación

Intercambios

Paso 1. Haga por lo menos una pregunta con cada uno de los siguientes verbos. En el **Paso 2,** va a usar esas preguntas para entrevistar a uno de sus compañeros de clase sobre las relaciones personales de él/ella con su pareja (esposo/a o novio/a), sus amigos, sus padres y sus parientes.

MODELOS: saludarse dándose la mano →
¿Tus parientes y tú se saludan dándose la mano?
¿Tu pareja y tú se besan en público?

1. verse
2. escribirse
3. mantenerse en contacto
4. llamarse por teléfono
5. abrazarse
6. besarse
7. saludarse dándose la mano
8. pelearse

Paso 2. Ahora, en parejas, túrnense para hacerse las preguntas del **Paso 1.** Luego digan a la clase lo que tienen en común.

Mundo interactivo

You should now be prepared to work with Scenario 6, Activity 2 in Connect Spanish (**www.connectspanish.com**).

Preliminary Exercises

- Ask students how the following sentences are expressed in Spanish.
  1. We help each other. (you, they)
  2. We love each other. (you, they)
  3. We write to each other. (you, they)
- Have students restate the following sentences as reciprocal actions.
  1. *Estela me mira a mí. Yo miro a Estela.*
  2. *Eduardo habla con Pepita. Pepita habla con Eduardo.*
  3. *El padre necesita a su hijo. El hijo necesita a su padre.*
  4. *Tomás me conoce a mí. Yo conozco a Tomás.*
  5. *Tú le escribes a Luisa. Luisa te escribe a ti.*
  6. *La profesora escucha a los estudiantes. Los estudiantes escuchan a la profesora.*
  7. *Ud. quiere a su esposo. Su esposo la quiere también a Ud.*
  8. *Jorge le da la mano a Mario. Mario le da la mano a Jorge.*

Prác. A: Suggestion

Have students repeat items using *ellos* as the subject, then with *vosotros,* if you are using that form.

Prác. B: Follow-up

Ask students questions to personalize the construction.

1. *Ud. y sus amigos/as, ¿se llaman por teléfono? ¿Se ven frecuentemente? ¿Se ayudan? ¿Se escriben? ¿Se mandan regalos?*
2. *¿Con qué frecuencia se ven Ud. y su novio/a (esposo/a, mejor amigo/a)? ¿Cuánto tiempo hace que se conocen? ¿Se hacen regalos? ¿En qué ocasiones? ¿Se escriben? ¿Se telefonean? ¿Le gusta que se vean tanto (tan poco)?*
3. *¿Con qué frecuencia se ven Ud. y sus abuelos/primos? ¿Por qué se ven Uds. tan poco (tanto)? ¿Cómo se mantienen en contacto? En la sociedad norteamericana, ¿se ven los parientes con frecuencia? En su opinión, ¿es esto común entre los hispanos?*

Prác. B: Optional

Provide the following cues for students to construct a story about *La triste historia de amor de Orlando y Patricia.* Have students narrate the story in the preterite.

1. *verse en clase*
2. *mirarse*
3. *saludarse*
4. *empezar a llamarse por teléfono*
5. *escribirse durante las vacaciones*
6. *ayudarse cuando tienen problemas*
7. *casarse* (new)
8. *no llevarse bien* (new)
9. *separarse*
10. *divorciarse*

(← Cont.)

Heritage Speakers

Pídales a dos hispanohablantes que dramaticen algunas acciones recíprocas, como por ejemplo, *verse, saludarse,* y *hablarse por teléfono.* Los demás estudiantes explicarán las acciones: *Paco y Marta se saludan.*

Un poco de todo

A: Notes

- This retelling of the Little Red Riding Hood story is an authentic version from Spain. You and the students may be familiar with other versions of the story. Encourage students to provide additional details.
- *Había una vez, Había una vez y dos son tres,* and *Érase una vez* are traditional beginnings for tales. Some traditional endings include: *Y vivieron felices y comieron perdices* (new); *Y colorín, colorado, este cuento se ha acabado* (new), and *por siempre jamás.*

A: Optional

Now that students have at least conceptual control of the rules for using the preterite and imperfect, you may wish to return to any of the art-based narration sequences in previous chapters and ask students to do the exercises with those tenses.

A: Answers

1. *se llamaba* **2.** *eran* **3.** *los quería* **4.** *le dijo* **5.** *salió* **6.** *preguntó* **7.** *le contestó* **8.** *le dijo* **9.** *se fue* **10.** *llegó* **11.** *entró* **12.** *lo vio* **13.** *saltó* **14.** *corrió* **15.** *llegó* **16.** *Encontró* **17.** *estaba* **18.** *dijo* **19.** *le dijo* **20.** *se enteró* **21.** *avisó* **22.** *llegó* **23.** *Le disparó* **24.** *hizo* **25.** *se abrazaron* **26.** *le dieron*

A: Follow-up

Have students retell the story in their own words in Spanish.

A: Variation

Have students invent a new tale together in a round-robin format. The story can begin on one side of the room and "travel" from student to student. Each student says one sentence. Remind them to use the preterite and imperfect in the narration. Avoid direct correction. Repeat each sentence students say, rephrasing as necessary to correct errors.

Resources: Desenlace

In the *Cap. 11* segment of "Chapter-by-Chapter Supplementary Materials" in the IM, you will find a chapter-culminating activity. You can use this activity to consolidate and review the vocabulary and grammar skills students have acquired.

Un poco de todo

A. Caperucita Roja

Paso 1. Retell this familiar story, based on the drawings, sentences, and cues that accompany each drawing, using the imperfect or preterite of the verbs in parentheses. Using context, try to guess the meaning of words that are glossed with ¿ ?.

1. 

2. 

3. 

4. 

5. 

6. 

7. 

8. 

9. 

1. Había una vez[a] una niña que (llamarse[1]) Caperucita Roja. Todos los animales del bosque[b] (ser[2]) sus amigos y Caperucita Roja (quererlos[3]) mucho.
2. Un día su mamá (decirle[4]): —Lleva esta jarrita de miel[c] a casa de tu abuelita.
3. En el bosque, un lobo[d] (salir[5]) a hablar con la niña. Le (preguntar[6]): —¿Adónde vas, Caperucita? Esta (contestarle[7]): —Voy a casa de mi abuelita.
4. —Pues, si vas por este sendero,[e] vas a llegar antes, (decirle[8]) el malvado[f] lobo. Él (irse[9]) por otro camino más corto.
5. El lobo (llegar[10]) primero a la casa de la abuelita y (entrar[11]). Cuando la abuelita (verlo[12]), (saltar[g13]) de la cama y (correr[14]) a esconderse.[h]
6. Caperucita Roja (llegar[15]) por fin a la casa de la abuelita. (*Ella:* Encontrar[16]) a su «abuelita», que (estar[17]) en la cama. Le (decir[18]): —¡Qué dientes tan largos tienes! —¡Son para comerte mejor!— (decirle[19]) su «abuelita».
7. Una ardilla[i] del bosque (enterarse[j20]) del peligro y le (avisar[k21]) a un cazador.[l]
8. El cazador (llegar[22]) a la casa de la abuelita. (*Él:* Dispararle[m23]) al lobo y lo (hacer[24]) huir.[n]
9. Caperucita y su abuela (abrazarse[25]) felizmente y (darle[26]) las gracias al buen cazador.

[a]¿ ? [b]¿ ? [c]*jarrita... jar of honey* [d]¿ ? [e]*path* [f]¿ ? [g]*to jump* [h]*to hide* [i]¿ ? [j]*to find out* [k]*to warn* [l]¿ ? [m]*to shoot* [n]*to flee*

Paso 2. Hay varias versiones del cuento de Caperucita Roja. La que Ud. acaba de leer termina felizmente, pero otras no. Con otros dos compañeros, vuelva a contar la historia, empezando por el dibujo número 6. Inventen un diálogo más largo entre Caperucita y el lobo y cambien por completo el final del cuento.

Vocabulario útil

atacar (qu)	to attack	**matar**	to kill
comérselo/la	to eat something up		

Multimedia: Internet

Have students look for online versions of *Caperucita Roja* in Spanish. They can also find the following stories in Spanish on the Internet: *La Cenicienta, Peter Pan, Simbad el marinero, Los tres cerditos, Blancanieves, El flautista de Hamelín,* and *Merlín el mago.*

Resources: Transparency 121

B. Lengua y cultura: La leyenda del lago de Maracaibo. Complete the following legend with the correct form of the word in parentheses, as suggested by context. The verbs will be in the preterite or imperfect. When two possibilities are given in parentheses, select the correct word.

Había una vez[a] un cacique[b] indígena que se llamaba Zapara. Este[c] tenía una hija, Maruma, que (ser[1]) muy bonita. Al padre y a la hija (se / les[2]) (gustar[3]) pasar tiempo juntos y caminar por el bosque.[d]

Un día Zapara (comprender[4]) que su hija ya (ser[5]) una mujer y (se / le[6]) (decir[7]): «Debes escoger[e] esposo, pues ya tienes edad[f] para formar una familia. Pero (su / tu[8]) esposo debe ser guerrero,[g] como todos los hombres de nuestra familia».

Un día, mientras su padre (estar[9]) ausente, Maruma (salir[10]) sola a cazar[h] en el bosque. Estaba a punto de dispararle a un ciervo[i] cuando (un / —[11]) otro cazador[j] (matar[k12]) al animal. Maruma (ponerse[13]) muy enojada[l] pero el joven, (que / quien[14]) (ser[15]) guapo y simpático, dijo: «El ciervo es para (tú / ti[16]). Solo quiero conocerte. Me llamo Tamaré». A partir de ese día[m] los (joven[17]) (hacerse[n18]) amigos. Pronto se enamoraron.[ñ]

Desgraciadamente, el joven no era un buen guerrero y por eso el padre de Maruma (enojarse[19]) mucho cuando (saber[20]) que ella (querer[21]) casarse con él. Se enfadó tanto[o] que la naturaleza reaccionó y (haber[22]) grandes terremotos[p] e inundaciones:[q] las aguas cubrieron[r] las tierras del cacique Zapara y también a Maruma y Tamaré, formando así el lago de Maracaibo. Zapara se convirtió en una de sus pequeñas islas.

[a]Había… *Once upon a time there was* [b]*chief* [c]*He* [d]*forest* [e]*choose* [f]ya… *you're old enough* [g]*a warrior* [h]*hunt* [i]Estaba… *She was about to shoot a deer* [j]*hunter* [k]*to kill* [l]ponerse… *to become very angry* [m]A… *From that day on* [n]*to become* [ñ]se… *they fell in love* [o]Se… *He was so angry* [p]*earthquakes* [q]*floods* [r]*covered*

Un residente del lago de Maracaibo en su lancha (*boat*)

Comprensión. Conteste las siguientes preguntas.

1. ¿Quién era Zapara?
2. ¿Qué debía hacer su hija?
3. ¿De quién se enamoró (*fell in love*) Maruma?
4. ¿Por qué se enfadó Zapara?
5. ¿Cómo se formó el lago de Maracaibo?

En su comunidad

Entreviste a una persona hispana de su universidad o ciudad sobre el cuidado médico en su país de origen.

PREGUNTAS POSIBLES

- En su país de origen, ¿qué hace una persona cuando tiene una enfermedad que no es muy seria? ¿Va al médico? ¿Habla con el farmacéutico? ¿Va a alguna persona que cura con remedios naturales?
- ¿Qué alimentos se consideran muy sanos en su país? ¿Se usan algunos productos naturales? ¿Cuáles son? ¿Para qué sirven de remedio?
- ¿Cómo se dice *flu* en su país? ¿Y *cold*?

B: Answers: **1.** *era* **2.** *les* **3.** *gustaba* **4.** *comprendió* **5.** *era* **6.** *le* **7.** *dijo* **8.** *tu* **9.** *estaba* **10.** *salió* **11.** — **12.** *mató* **13.** *se puso* **14.** *que* **15.** *era* **16.** *ti* **17.** *jóvenes* **18.** *se hicieron* **19.** *se enojó* **20.** *supo* **21.** *quería* **22.** *hubo*

Comprensión, Answers: **1.** *un cacique indígena* **2.** *Debía escoger esposo* **3.** *de Tamaré, un cazador guapo y simpático* **4.** *Porque Tamaré no era un buen guerrero.* **5.** *Hubo grandes terremotos e inundaciones. Las aguas cubrieron las tierras del cacique y a los jóvenes.*

B: Suggestion

Review the contrastive uses of the preterite and imperfect before completing this activity.

¿El pretérito o el imperfecto? ¿Cuál se usa… ?
…para indicar el comienzo o el final de una acción?
…para hablar de una acción habitual en el pasado?
…para decir la hora?
…para expresar características mentales?

B: Note

The following grammar topics are included in *Lengua y cultura:* plural of nouns, possessive adjectives, *gustar,* object pronouns of all kinds, preterite and imperfect forms, use of the preterite vs. the imperfect, relative pronouns.

Redacción: Ask students to write a summary of either *Caperucita Roja* or *la leyenda del lago de Maracaibo* in 200 words, no more. Setting a word limit will force students to write the summary in their own words.

En su comunidad

Suggestions

- Remind students to get the following basic information: the informant's country of origin, how long he or she has lived in this country, and if the informant visits his or her country of origin frequently.
- This activity could also be assigned as an online research project on a country of the student's choice or assigned by you.
- See the IM for additional suggestions and guidelines.

NATIONAL STANDARDS: Communities

Ask students if they have participated in a student-exchange program or know of someone who has. Have them describe the experience, especially as it relates to a second language and/or cultural differences. Have students search the Internet for exchange programs with Spanish-speaking countries.

TELEPUNTOS

Antes de mirar

¿Tiene Ud. una farmacia favorita? ¿Qué cosas compra Ud. allí, además de (*besides*) medicinas? ¿Consulta Ud. a los farmacéuticos a veces? ¿Tiene algún remedio casero (*home*) para los catarros (*colds*)?

«La sávila (*aloe vera*) tiene veinte mil usos. Se usa para las quemadas (*burns*), se usa para el catarro, se usa para… broncear la piel (*tanning*)… Tenemos la tuna (*fruit of the prickly pear cactus*), que la usamos para los riñones (*kidneys*), se usa para el riñón, para la limpieza (*cleaning out* [*the system*]). Pero también se usa para el estómago… »

PROGRAMA 11: Remedios para todos

Este programa presenta reportajes sobre diferentes maneras de cuidar de la salud y curar enfermedades leves (*minor*) en el mundo hispano.

Vocabulario de este programa

acudir a	to go to	**la hoja**	leaf
proveer	to provide	**la miel**	honey
la cadena	chain, franchise	**el ataque de risa**	fit of laughter
de libre venta	**que se vende sin receta médica**	**constipado/a**	congested (*with a cold*)
la gente	people	**el empaste de mostaza**	mustard plaster
desde luego	of course	**la harina**	flour
ahorrar	to save (*time*)	**espeso/a**	thick
mezclarse	to become mixed	**el pecho**	chest
tuvo la amabilidad de concedernos	was nice enough to give us	**tapar**	to cover
pongo que la gente me soben los budas	I display Buda images for people to touch	**frotar**	to rub
		el ajo	garlic

Fragmento del guion

DOCTORA: Sin embargo,[a] pues nosotros los médicos estamos capacitados[b] para hacer otro tipo de cosas, como es hacer curaciones,[c] como es utilizar métodos anticonceptivos,[d] como es el hacer pequeñas cirugías.[e] Para esto hemos equipado[f] incluso nuestros consultorios con todo lo que la legislación de este país requiere para poder hacer también este tipo de procedimientos.[g]

LAURA: En México, como en Estados Unidos, no todas las personas tienen seguro[h] de salud. Por eso, es importante que la visita al médico y los medicamentos no cuesten mucho dinero.

DOCTORA: Porque con nosotros una consulta cuesta menos de tres dólares. Es decir, en pesos mexicanos cuesta treinta pesos. Entonces[i] esto es accesible[j] a la gran mayoría de los mexicanos. Igual… De igual forma,[k] los medicamentos que se venden en Farmacias Similares son medicamentos genéricos, que tienen hasta un setenta o un ochenta por ciento menos del valor[l] que lo que cuesta un medicamento en otras cadenas de farmacias. En México, si bien[m] es cierto que existe la seguridad social que protege a los trabajadores,[n] hay muchos millones de mexicanos que el gasto de salud[ñ] lo hacen de sus bolsas.[o] Se tiene pensado[p] que el ochenta por ciento del gasto en este país de salud sale de la bolsa de la gente.

[a]Sin… *However* [b]*trained* [c]*treatments* [d]métodos… *contraceptives* [e]*surgeries* [f]hemos… *we have equipped* [g]*procedures* [h]*insurance* [i]*Therefore* [j]*available, accessible* [k]De… *Similarly* [l]*value* [m]si… *although* [n]*workers* [ñ]el… *their health care costs, expenses* [o]lo… *they pay for them out of pocket* [p]Se… *It is believed*

«Actualmente (*Currently*) en México existen 4.029 Farmacias de Similares, que están distribuidas a lo largo y ancho de todo (*spread all over*) México. Estamos presentes en poblaciones (*towns*) de 5.000 habitantes hacia arriba (*and over*).»

TelePuntos

Note

Pages 342–347 are optional. You may cover some, all, or none of this material in class, or assign it to students—as a group or individually—for homework or extra credit. Pages 348–349 (*En resumen: En este capítulo*) are a summary of all of the chapter's active material.

Suggestions

- If you are using the video in class, show it once, ask brief comprehension questions, then show it again.
- Even if you plan to ask students to watch the video in your campus media center or on their own, it is a good idea to continue to stress the need to watch the shows as many times as they want or need to in order to complete the *Después de mirar* activities.

Antes de mirar

Suggestion

Ask students to share their home remedies with the class. It is likely that you will have to help with vocabulary.

Programa 11

Note

Students will easily get the gist of this program, but they may struggle with some of the details.

Suggestions

- Point out that at the beginning of the segment on *farmacias,* one of the business signs is in *catalán* (the language of Barcelona and its region, *Cataluña*): *farmàcia*. The grave accent (`) is used in *catalán,* as in French, but never in Spanish.
- The name of the Mexican pharmacy chain featured in the program is given both as *Farmacias de Similares* and *Farmacias Similares,* depending on the linguistic context in which the name appears. This distinction is beyond students' ability at this point; it is recommended that you accept both variations.
- Preview the concept of *botánicas* before students watch the program. *Las botánicas* can be quite picturesque, featuring traditional herbal remedies with plants as well as things used in *rituales* from Afro-Caribbean cultures and religions, such as *el vudú, la santería, el palo,* and so on. *Botánicas* are not homeopathy or naturopathology shops; those stores and specialists also exist in the Hispanic countries.
- Some students will not understand the cognate terms *rosario* and *incienso.* You may wish to explain them before showing the program.
- Emphasize to students that the more carefully they study the preliminary activities (*Antes de mirar, Vocabulario de este programa,* and *Fragmento del guion*), the more they will understand. Scanning *Después de mirar* before viewing is also an excellent strategy.

Mundo interactivo

Continue your work as an intern at HispanaVisión with Laura Sánchez Tejada, the roving reporter of *Salu2*, as you complete Scenario 6, Activities 1 and 2 in Connect Spanish (**www.connectspanish.com**).

Al mirar

Mientras mira el programa, indique todos los tratamientos que se mencionan en el programa.

1. ☑ remedios alternativos y naturales
2. ☑ pequeñas cirugías
3. ☑ tomar la tensión arterial
4. ☐ procedimientos que hacen los cirujanos
5. ☑ remedios caseros contra el catarro
6. ☐ procedimientos contra el cáncer
7. ☑ medicinas que se venden sin receta

En esta botánica (*herb store*) se venden velas (*candles*), imágenes, collares (*necklaces*), rosarios, incienso, agua florida (*aromatic essences*) y mucho más. ¡Hasta (*Even*) imágenes de Buda para la buena suerte (*luck*)!

Después de mirar

A. ¿Está claro? Complete las siguientes oraciones con información del programa.

1. A Víctor le duele la garganta porque tiene catarro (resfriado).
2. Hay Farmacias Similares en poblaciones mexicanas de más de 5.000 habitantes.
3. Una consulta médica en una de las Farmacias Similares cuesta treinta pesos, que son unos 3 dólares estadounidenses.
4. Millones de mexicanos pagan de sus bolsas por el cuidado de su salud.
5. Las botánicas son tiendas típicas de los países caribeños.
6. La sávila se usa, por ejemplo, para las quemadas y el catarro.
7. La tuna se usa para los riñones y para el estómago.

B. Un poco más. Conteste las siguientes preguntas.

1. ¿Qué le da Ana a Víctor para la garganta?
2. Según el programa, ¿por qué razones van los hispanos a una farmacia?
3. ¿Cómo son los precios en las Farmacias Similares?
4. ¿Por qué se llaman botánicas las tiendas como las (*those*) de la Sra. Santiago?
5. ¿En qué tipo de tratamientos se especializan las botánicas?
6. ¿Qué cosas se puede comprar en una botánica? ¿Para qué sirven?
7. ¿Qué remedio casero se ve en el programa? ¿En qué consiste?
8. ¿Qué remedio casero le recomienda Ana a Víctor?

C. Y ahora, Uds. En grupos, hablen de los remedios y productos que no necesitan receta médica que Uds. usan por razones de salud. ¿Qué tipo de remedios son? (¿farmacéuticos, herbales, homeopáticos,… ?) ¿Confían Uds. (*Do you trust*) en sus beneficios? ¿Les preocupan los posibles efectos secundarios?

Act. B, Answers: 1. *un té con limón y miel* **2.** *para comprar medicinas, consultar a un farmacéutico, pesar a su bebé, tomarse la presión arterial, pequeñas cirugías* **3.** *Son muy buenos, populares.* **4.** *El nombre está relacionado con las plantas.* **5.** *en tratamientos herbales* **6.** *Se puede comprar velas, agua florida, collares, imágenes,… Sirven para prácticas religiosas y prácticas relacionadas con la suerte.* **7.** *Es un remedio para el catarro. Consiste en hacer un empaste de mostaza.* **8.** *comer tres ajos con el jugo de dos limones*

Sobre el programa

El interés de Ana por las propiedades curativas de plantas muy comunes le viene de su madre y de sus abuelas, aunque[a] en el mundo hispano no es nada extraño[b] saber de estas cosas. ¿Quién no sabe que la menta[c] y la manzanilla[d] ayudan a la digestión? ¿O que la sávila es buena para las quemadas? Ana usa remedios herbales siempre que[e] puede para trastornos[f] leves. Otro remedio que le recomendó a Víctor para la tos del catarro es poner una cebolla cortada[g] en su mesita de noche a la hora de dormir. ¡Y Víctor dice que lo ayudó!

[a]*although* [b]*unusual* [c]*mint* [d]*chamomile* [e]*siempre… whenever* [f]*complaints* [g]*cebolla… cut onion*

Producción personal

Filme a una persona que hable de un remedio casero tradicional, similar a los que se ven en este programa.

Después de mirar

C: Suggestion

Limit the scope of students' conversation to one of the categories mentioned: *remedios farmacéuticos, herbales,* or *homeopáticos.*

Sobre el programa

Suggestions

- Extend the discussion by noting that common plants are traditional cures in *all* cultures, not just Hispanic ones. Although some are questionable, many provide beneficial remedies for a variety of ailments, with very few side effects.
- As is the case in all areas, the plants most frequently used in the Hispanic world for health (or other) issues vary from region to region, according to what it is available in the land.

Optional: Comprensión

Comprensión: Las siguientes oraciones son falsas. Corríjalas.

1. *La familia de Ana no tiene ningún interés en las plantas para curar enfermedades. (Su madre y sus abuelas tienen interés en las plantas curativas.)*
2. *La manzanilla ayuda a curar los catarros. (Ayuda a la digestión.)*
3. *Ana usa remedios herbales para enfermedades serias. (Los usa para enfermedades leves.)*
4. *Poner un ajo cortado en la mesita de noche es un remedio para la tos del catarro. (Poner una cebolla cortada es un remedio para la tos del catarro.)*

Producción personal

Note

See the IM for additional suggestions for this chapter's assignment as well as for general guidelines and suggestions for video assignments.

Lectura cultural

Notes

- The Instructor's Edition on this page offers some additional information on the country of focus. For more information about the country of focus, see the chapter's opening pages and the IM.
- See the IM for some expressions used in Venezuela.

First Reading: Suggestion

You may wish to engage students in a discussion about health care in this country. The United States has a combination of public and private systems of health care, while Canada's system is publicly funded. Although it is true that many people in Latin America do not have easy access to health care, the same is true in the United States.

Exploración lingüística

Ask students to find the following in the reading. Some of these words are glossed and some are not.

- *Palabras relacionadas con la salud (médico/a, sanitario/a, el cuidado, la visita, la hospitalización, la medicina)*
- *Lugares relacionados con la salud (dispensarios, clínicas, hospitales, el consultorio)*
- *El antónimo de afortunadamente (desgraciadamente)*

Tres símbolos venezolanos

Notes

- Soap operas are a staple of Spanish-language television, and they are not viewed with disdain, as they sometimes are in this country.
- It has been said that if a recording is successful in Venezuela, it will be a hit all over the Spanish-speaking world.
- *Las hallacas* are a culinary staple of Venezuelan Christmas and New Year's Eve celebrations. The white cornmeal dough is stuffed with seasoned meat, raisins, and olives, then wrapped in a plantain leaf and steamed or boiled.

Una figura histórica

Notes

- Bolívar was the leader of the independence movements of Venezuela, Colombia, Panamá, Peru, Bolivia, and Ecuador. He came from a wealthy family and was educated in Spain and other European countries before returning to Venezuela to spearhead the independence movement.

A LEER

Lectura cultural

Venezuela

En Venezuela hay un sistema de salud público y gratuito[a] que sirve, sobre todo,[b] a la gente[c] de la clase trabajadora que no puede pagar un seguro[d] médico privado. Existen dispensarios médicos, clínicas y hospitales que proveen de todo tipo de servicios relacionados con la salud a las personas que los necesitan.

También existe la posibilidad de tener atención médica privada a través de pólizas[e] de seguro, que se contratan generalmente a través del empleador.[f] Sin embargo, los venezolanos siempre tienen acceso al sistema público, que se paga con impuestos[g] obligatorios para la seguridad social. En general, el cuidado médico de familia, privado, es mucho más barato que en los Estados Unidos y no resulta muy caro ir al consultorio del doctor y pagar la visita sin tener un seguro. En cambio,[h] los servicios de emergencia y hospitalización son muy costosos[i] y para tenerlos es indispensable[j] un seguro médico.

¿Cómo compara Ud. el sistema de salud de este país con el (*that*) de Venezuela?

[a]*free* [b]sobre… *especially* [c]*people* [d]*insurance* [e]a… *through policies* [f]*employer* [g]*taxes* [h]En… *On the other hand* [i]*expensive* [j]*absolutely necessary*

En otros países hispanos

- **En Latinoamérica** Es muy diversa la manera en que cada país provee de asistencia sanitaria a sus habitantes: a través de[a] un sistema exclusivamente gubernamental[b] o por medio[c] de una combinación de sistemas públicos y privados. El acceso al cuidado médico también varía mucho de país a país. Hay países como la Argentina, Cuba y Costa Rica que proporcionan[d] acceso a todas la personas. Desgraciadamente, en otros países hay un considerable número de personas que no tienen acceso fácil a médicos y medicinas.
- **En España** España tiene un sistema nacional de seguridad social que cubre[e] el cuidado médico de todos sus ciudadanos. Este sistema, junto con[f] otros factores, contribuye a que los españoles tengan una de las esperanzas de vida[g] más largas del mundo.

[a]a… *via* [b]*government-run* [c]*means* [d]*provide* [e]*covers* [f]junto… *along with* [g]esperanzas… *life expectancies*

Un venezolano, que baila el limbo durante una fiesta, en Caracas

Tres símbolos venezolanos

- **Las mujeres** Muchos dicen que Venezuela es el país de las mujeres bellas.[a] Eso se debe probablemente a dos circunstancias. La primera es el hecho de que[b] las venezolanas han obtenido[c] el título de Miss Universo seis veces y el de Miss Mundo cinco veces. La segunda[d] es que en las últimas dos décadas del siglo[e] pasado Venezuela exportó telenovelas[f] de manera masiva a Latinoamérica, Europa y Asia.
- **«La rumba»** Al espíritu fiestero[g] de los venezolanos se le dice[h] «la rumba». Venezuela es el principal mercado de consumo de la música popular caribeña. Al venezolano le gusta organizar y celebrar fiestas en las cuales[i] siempre se baila salsa, merengue o cualquier otro ritmo caribeño, hasta el amanecer.[j]
- **La harina de maíz blanco**[k] El ingrediente básico con que se hacen dos de los platos típicos del país, las arepas (parecidas[l] a las tortillas) y las hallacas (empanadas venezolanas), es la harina de maíz blanco.

[a]bonitas [b]el… *the fact that* [c]han… *have won* [d]*second* [e]*century* [f]*soap operas* [g]*party-loving* [h]se… *(it) is called* [i]las… *which* [j]*dawn* [k]La… *White corn flour* [l]similares

Una figura histórica

Simón Bolívar (1783–1830) también se conoce como «El Libertador» de Sudamérica. Fue un militar y político venezolano, y sin duda la figura más notable de la independencia no solo de Venezuela sino[a] también de otros países sudamericanos.

[a]*but*

COMPRENSIÓN

1. ¿Qué sistema de salud usa con más frecuencia la clase trabajadora venezolana? el sistema público
2. ¿Cómo se paga el sistema público de salud en Venezuela? con impuestos obligatorios
3. ¿Los habitantes de qué país hispanohablante tienen una de las esperanzas de vida más largas del planeta? España

- Venezuela remained under Spanish rule until 1821, although it had declared itself a republic in 1811. For ten years it was part of *la Gran Colombia*, which also included Colombia and Ecuador.

Del mundo hispano

Antes de leer

Un epitafio es una breve inscripción que se pone en la tumba de una persona muerta (*deceased*). En su opinión, ¿cuáles de los siguientes temas son apropiados para un epitafio?

- ☐ datos biográficos
- ☐ descripción física
- ☐ aspectos de su profesión
- ☐ un símbolo de la persona
- ☐ sus gustos y preferencias
- ☐ aspectos de su personalidad
- ☐ la descripción de algunos de sus parientes
- ☐ su filosofía de la vida
- ☐ algo memorable que dijo una vez
- ☐ cómo murió

Lectura: «Epitafio», de Nicanor Parra

De estatura mediana,[a]
con una voz[b] ni delgada ni gruesa,[c]
hijo mayor de un profesor primario[d]
y de una modista de trastienda;[e]
flaco de nacimiento[f]
aunque[g] devoto de la buena mesa;[h]
de mejillas[i] escuálidas
Y de más bien[j] abundantes orejas;
con un rostro cuadrado[k]
en que los ojos se abren apenas[l]
y una nariz de boxeador mulato
baja a la boca de ídolo azteca
—todo esto bañado[m]
por una luz entre irónica y pérfida[n]—,
ni muy listo ni tonto de remate[ñ]
fui lo que fui: una mezcla[o]
de vinagre y de aceite de comer
¡un embutido[p] de ángel y bestia[q]!

[a]*average* [b]*voice* [c]*hearty* [d]de escuela primaria [e]modista... *backroom seamstress* [f]flaco... *thin since birth* [g]*although* [h]de... *to good food* [i]*cheeks* [j]más... *rather* [k]rostro... *square face* [l]*hardly* [m]*bathed* [n]*treacherous* [ñ]de... *hopelessly* [o]*mixture* [p]*sausage* [q]*beast*

Comprensión

A. En este epitafio. ¿Cuáles de los posibles temas para un epitafio que se mencionaron en **Antes de leer** aparecen en este poema? Busque en los versos (*lines*) del poema las palabras clave (*key*) que corresponden a cada tema.

B. Preguntas

Paso 1. ¿Cierto o falso? Busque en el poema las palabras específicas que justifiquen su respuesta.

	CIERTO	FALSO
1. Esta persona era alta. de estatura mediana	☐	☑
2. Sus padres eran médicos importantes. profesor primario y modista de trastienda	☐	☑
3. Esta persona era delgada. flaco de nacimiento	☑	☐
4. Tenía orejas grandes. abundantes orejas	☑	☐
5. Era inteligentísimo. ni listo ni tonto de remate	☐	☑
6. Su personalidad era contradictoria. de vinagre y aceite, ángel y bestia	☑	☐

Paso 2. ¿En qué verso del poema se revela que este epitafio es autobiográfico?
verso 16: fui lo que fui

Del mundo hispano

Note

See the IM for optional follow-up, writing, and Internet activities.

Antes de leer

Suggestions

- Tell students that *epitafio* is a cognate and, if possible, show some images of epitaphs (easily accessible through an Internet search for epitaph or *epitafio*). Be sure to screen them first.
- Answers to this activity will vary and, actually, depending on the context, all of them might be appropriate. You may want to ask students to justify why they would include the information they choose, that is why and in what situations it would be worth commemorating someone with these bits of information.

Estrategia: Making Sense Out of Long Sentences

Most epitaphs are very brief, one short sentence at most. This poem is composed of one sentence, but it is a long one, with many clauses. Advise students to match each line or group of lines with one of the categories of *Antes de leer* (similar to the advice provided in previous sections for summarizing the main point of each paragraph of a prose text). That will help them to grasp the "big picture" of the poem after they read: how it is organized and what it says. It will also make their answers to the *Comprensión* activities more specific.

Comprensión

A: Suggestion

Introduce the vocabulary needed to talk about a poem and poetry: *el/la poeta, el poema, el verso.*

A: Answers

Answers will vary but may include: *datos biográficos: 3–4; aspectos de su personalidad: 16–18; descripción física: 1–2, 5, 7–12; su filosofía de la vida: 16; sus inclinaciones: 6.*

Antes de escuchar

Suggestion

You may wish to conduct this as a whole-class discussion.

Escuche

Notes

- In this chapter students can listen to a radio interview with a representative from the Department of Public Health about the upcoming flu season.
- If the listening is assigned as homework, ask students to listen to the passage at least twice.
- See the IM for the Audioscript and more information about music in Venezuela.

B. Follow-up

- Use these questions to conduct a whole-class discussion.
    1. *En su opinión, ¿es importante vacunarse contra la gripe?*
    2. *¿Se vacuna Ud. contra la gripe regularmente?*
    3. *¿Le preocupan los posibles riesgos de una vacuna?*
    4. *¿Hay alguna persona de alto riesgo en su familia?*
- Ask students to create a poster ad for their university newspaper about the importance of getting a flu shot. The goal of the poster is to encourage students and faculty not familiar with the risks of the flu to get their shots and also to direct them to where they can get their immunizations.

¡Música!

Note

- D'León is also known as *el Sonero latino*. He sang for many years with a group called *Dimensión Latina*, with whom he recorded "*Llorarás*," the song included here and one of his most famous. D'León is an ambassador for Operation Smile, an international organization that helps children born with cleft palates and other face-disfiguring birth defects.
- For helpful tips on using songs in the classroom, see the IM.

Después de escuchar
A: Follow-up
Use these questions to conduct a whole class discussion.

1. *¿Quién de Uds. tuvo la gripe el año pasado?*
2. *¿Qué síntomas tuvo? ¿Estuvo enfermo/a muchos días?*
3. *¿Fue al médico o no fue necesario que fuera?*

B. Answers: 1. *todas las personas mayores de seis meses* **2.** *los niños de menos de 2 años, los adultos mayores de más de 65 años, las mujeres embarazadas, los trabajadores de salud y las personas que sufren enfermedades crónicas* **3.** *los bebés de menos de 6 meses*

Go to the iMix section in Connect Spanish (**www.connectspanish.com**) to access the iTunes playlist "*Puntos9*," where you can purchase "Llorarás" by Óscar d'León.

A ESCUCHAR

Antes de escuchar

¿Qué precauciones toma Ud. para no enfermarse? ¿Tuvo Ud. algún resfriado el año pasado? ¿alguna gripe? ¿Fue al médico con frecuencia durante el último año?

Escuche

Campaña de vacunación* contra la gripe: Información importante del Departamento de Salud sobre la gripe

*vaccination

Un representante del Departamento de Salud habla en la radio de la gripe y de la importancia de vacunarse contra ella. Escuche según las indicaciones de su profesor(a).

Vocabulario para escuchar

vacunarse	to get a shot	**la vacuna**	vaccination
la muerte	death	**de alto riesgo**	high-risk
contraer (*like* **traer**)	to get, contract (*an illness*)	**embarazadas**	pregnant
		peligrosa	dangerous

Después de escuchar

A. La gripe. Conteste las siguientes preguntas sobre esta enfermedad, según la información en el anuncio.

1. ¿Aproximadamente cuántas personas van al hospital cada año en los Estados Unidos a causa de la gripe? 220.000 personas
2. ¿Cuántas personas mueren anualmente en los Estados Unidos a causa de la gripe, aproximadamente? 55.000 personas
3. ¿Hay solo un tipo de virus de gripe? No, hay por lo menos tres: A, B y H1N1.

B. La vacuna. Conteste las siguientes preguntas sobre la campaña de vacunación.

1. ¿Quiénes deben vacunarse contra la gripe?
2. ¿Quiénes se consideran personas de alto riesgo?
3. ¿Quiénes no pueden recibir la vacuna?

¡Música!

Óscar d'León (1943–) es conocido[a] como «el Demonio de la salsa». Este cantante de Caracas lleva más de 40 años cantando. La canción «Llorarás[b]» es del álbum *El verdadero León*.

[a]*known* [b]*You'll cry*

Óscar d'Leon con su contrabajo, en Las Vegas, Nevada

A ESCRIBIR

El tema

Una enfermedad

Preparar

Piense en un caso específico de una enfermedad que Ud. tuvo alguna vez o la enfermedad que tuvo una persona a quien Ud. conoce bien. Conteste las siguientes preguntas sobre esa enfermedad.

1. ¿Era grave la enfermedad o leve (*minor*)? ¿Era una enfermedad crónica?

2. ¿Cuántos años tenía cuando tuvo esa enfermedad?

3. ¿Cómo se sentía Ud. (o la otra persona)? ¿Cuáles eran sus síntomas?

4. ¿Fue Ud. (o la otra persona) al médico? ¿Fue al hospital?

Ahora añada (*add*) algunos detalles más sobre la enfermedad.

Redactar

Usando las ideas de **Preparar,** escriba un ensayo en el que (*which*) narra la historia de una enfermedad. En esta narración va a usar el pretérito y el imperfecto. Asegúrese (*Make sure*) de que la secuencia de acciones esté clara y bien conectada; para esto se usa el pretérito. Use el imperfecto para añadir detalles descriptivos que hacen que la historia sea más comprensible (*understandable*) y vívida. No se olvide de la importancia del tono. El tono para narrar una enfermedad leve, típica de la niñez, tendrá que ser (*will have to be*) diferente del tono para narrar una enfermedad grave de adulto.

Editar

Revise el ensayo para comprobar (*to check*):

- la ortografía y los acentos
- la organización y la secuencia de las ideas (usando palabras y expresiones que marcan el paso del tiempo)
- la consistencia del tono
- el uso del pretérito y del imperfecto
- el uso de los pronombres

Finalmente, prepare su versión final para entregarla.

Preparar

Suggestions

- Ask students to review the uses of the preterite and the imperfect.
- Remind students to use the words and expressions presented in the *Nota comunicativa,* p. 330.
- Review with students the basic structure of a narrative essay. In a sense, a narrative essay is like story-telling. It needs a plot, a character or characters, a setting, some suspense, a climax, and an ending.
- Suggest that students use the following adverbs to help create smooth transitions between ideas in their narrative: *además, también, al principio, antes, después, entonces, luego, más tarde, primero, pronto, por fin, finalmente, al final,* and so on.

Redactar

Suggestions

- Suggested length for this writing assignment: approximately 150–200 words
- Suggested structure: 3 paragraphs

  P.1. The background information, as in: *It was a dark and stormy night . . .* (mostly imperfect)

  P.2. What actually happened (mostly preterite)

  P.3. The outcome of the illness and a conclusion to the essay

Editar

Follow-up

How do one's past experiences with life and death or the experiences of close friends and family affect them later in life?

En resumen: En este capítulo
Vocabulario

Suggestions

- Describe absurd creatures and have students draw them. For example, *Era una criatura inmensa. Tenía tres piernas y un brazo. En la cabeza tenía una oreja que llegaba a la frente…*
- Ask students the following questions.
  1. *¿Con qué parte del cuerpo se asocian estas cosas?*
     la comida | *las películas*
     la música | *el amor*
     el oxígeno | *el cálculo*
  2. *¿Se refiere a la médica o al paciente?*
     Examina los ojos.
     Tiene fiebre.
     Saca la lengua.
     Escribe recetas.
     Le duele la garganta.
     Recomienda un jarabe.
- Ask students the following questions.
  1. *Si una persona come hamburguesas y toma Coca-Cola con frecuencia, ¿come bien o come mal?*
  2. *Si se tiene que hacer ejercicios para mantener sano el corazón, ¿se debe caminar o correr para hacer ejercicio?*
  3. *Si se duerme siete horas y media cada noche, ¿se duerme lo suficiente o se necesita dormir más?*

Word Families

En este capítulo

- *darse la mano, la mano*
- *doler, el dolor*
- *el/la enfermero/a, la enfermedad*
- *el/la médico/a, la medicina*
- *resfriarse, resfriado/a, el resfriado*
- *la salud, saludarse*
- *toser, la tos*

Entre capítulos

- *anoche* = *buenas noches* (1)
- *el bienestar* = *bien* (2), *estar* (2)
- *la caminadora* = *caminar* (10)
- *cansarse* = *cansado/a* (6), *descansar* (5)
- *dejar de* = *dejar* (10)
- *dos veces* = *una vez* (2)
- *encontrarse* = *encontrar* (9)
- *el/la enfermero/a, la enfermedad* = *enfermo/a* (6)
- *examinar* = *el examen* (4)
- *guardar cama* = *guardar (un puesto)* (8), *la cama* (5)
- *hacer ejercicios aeróbicos* = *hacer ejercicio* (5)
- *la lengua* = *la lengua* (language) (2)
- *lo bueno* = *bueno/a* (3)
- *lo malo* = *malo/a* (3)
- *mareado/a* = *el mar* (8)
- *molestar* = *molesto/a* (6)
- *el oído* = *oír* (5)
- *pasado/a* = *pasar* (6)
- *quererse* = *querer* (4)
- *la salud, saludarse* = *el saludo* (1)

EN RESUMEN En este capítulo

LearnSmart
Visit **www.connectspanish.com** to practice the vocabulary and grammar points covered in this chapter.

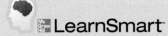

Gramática en breve

30. Using the Preterite and the Imperfect

Uses of the Preterite	Uses of the Imperfect
beginning/end of an action	habitual/repeated action
completed action	ongoing action
series of completed actions	background information
interrupting action	interrupted ongoing action
the action on the "stage"	the setting for the action

31. Relative Pronouns

que = refers to things and people
quien(es) = refers only to people
lo que = refers to a situation

32. Reciprocal Actions with Reflexive Pronouns

each other = **nos, os, se**

Vocabulario

Los verbos

abrazarse (c)	to embrace
besarse	to kiss each other
darse la mano	to shake hands
encontrarse (me encuentro) (con)	to meet (*someone somewhere*)
quererse	to love each other; to be fond of each other
saludarse	to greet each other

La salud y el bienestar

el bienestar	well-being
la caminadora	treadmill
la salud	health

Repaso: la comida

cansarse	to get tired
cuidarse	to take care of oneself
dejar de + *inf.*	to stop (*doing something*)
doler (duele) (*like* gustar)	to hurt, ache
examinar	to examine
guardar cama	to stay in bed
hacer…	to do…
ejercicios aeróbicos	aerobics
(el método) Pilates	Pilates
(el) yoga	yoga
levantar pesas	to lift weights
llevar una vida sana/tranquila	to lead a healthy/calm life
molestar (*like* gustar)	to bother
ponerle una inyección	to give (*someone*) a shot, injection
resfriarse (me resfrío)	to get/catch a cold
respirar	to breathe
sacar (qu)	to extract
sacar la lengua	to stick out one's tongue
sacarle un diente / una muela	to extract (*someone's*) tooth/molar
tener dolor de	to have a pain/ache in
tomarle la temperatura	to take someone's temperature
toser	to cough

Repaso: caminar, comer, correr, dormir (duermo) (u), enfermarse, hacer ejercicio, llevar (to wear), **pasear en bicicleta, practicar (qu), sentirse (me siento) (i)**

Algunas partes del cuerpo humano

la boca	mouth
el brazo	arm
la cabeza	head
el cerebro	brain
el corazón	heart
el cuerpo humano	human body
el dedo (de la mano)	finger
el dedo del pie	toe
el estómago	stomach
la garganta	throat
la lengua	tongue
la mano	hand
la muela	molar, back tooth
la nariz (*pl.* narices)	nose
el oído	inner ear
el ojo	eye
la oreja	(outer) ear
el pie	foot
la pierna	leg
los pulmones	lungs
la sangre	blood

Repaso: el diente

Las enfermedades y los tratamientos

los anteojos	glasses
el chequeo	check-up
el consultorio	(medical) office
el dolor (de)	pain, ache (in)
la enfermedad	illness, sickness
la fiebre	fever
la gripe	flu
el jarabe	(cough) syrup
los lentes	glasses
los lentes de contacto	contact lenses
la pastilla	pill
la receta	prescription
el resfriado	cold (*illness*)
el síntoma	symptom
la tos	cough
el tratamiento	treatment

Cognados: el antibiótico, la medicina, la temperatura

El personal médico

el/la enfermero/a	nurse
el/la farmacéutico/a	pharmacist

Cognado: el/la dentista, el/la paciente

Repaso: el/la médico/a

Otro sustantivo

la cita	date; appointment

Los adjetivos

mareado/a	dizzy; nauseated
pasado/a	past, last
resfriado/a	congested, stuffed up
sano/a	healthy
suficiente	enough
tranquilo/a	calm

Palabras adicionales

anoche	last night
de repente	suddenly
desgraciadamente	unfortunately
dos veces	twice
eso quiere decir…	that means . . .
frecuentemente	frequently
lo bueno	the good thing/news
lo malo	the bad thing/news
lo suficiente	enough

Repaso: anteayer, ayer, de joven, de niño/a, en seguida, lo que, mientras, que, quien(es), siempre, una vez

Vocabulario personal

En resumen En este capítulo ■ **349**

Chapter Opening Photo and Chapter Theme

Note

Call students' attention to the chapter title, which contains *la arroba* (@). In addition to being used in e-mail addresses, this symbol is sometimes used in informal writing to indicate both feminine and masculine forms. Thus, the title means *¡Conectados/as!* Ask students to explain the meaning of the chapter title, *Connected!* They will undoubtedly talk about being connected electronically to friends, acquaintances, and family. But there are other ways of being connected.

Chapter Theme–Related Questions Suggestion

Ask students the following questions to introduce the chapter topic.

1. *¿Hay plazas grandes y bonitas en su ciudad? ¿Qué se hace en ellas? ¿Qué personas pasan el tiempo allí?*
2. *En su ciudad, ¿dónde están las mejores zonas para vivir: en el centro o a las afueras? Para Ud., ¿qué condiciones debe tener una zona buena para vivir?*
3. *¿Dónde vive Ud.? ¿En una residencia estudiantil? ¿En un apartamento o en una casa?*
4. *¿Vive Ud. en el centro de la ciudad, en las afueras o en el campo?*
5. *¿Tienen computadora todos los estudiantes de su universidad? ¿Es requisito tener una? ¿Qué tipo de computadora tiene Ud.? ¿Es una portátil? ¿Cuándo la compró? ¿O se la regaló alguien?*
6. *¿Usa Ud. el Internet con frecuencia? ¿Cuáles son las páginas Web que visita con más frecuencia en el Internet?*
7. *¿Usa Ud. el Internet para hacer compras? ¿Qué compra Ud.? ¿discos compactos? ¿electrodomésticos? ¿ropa? ¿boletos de avión?*
8. *En su opinión, ¿cuál fue el invento más importante de los últimos cien años? ¿el carro? ¿el avión? ¿la computadora? ¿el Internet? ¿el teléfono? ¿otro?*
9. *¿Qué impacto tiene ese invento en la calidad de nuestra vida hoy día?*

Reciclado: Review the imperfect by asking students how they used to communicate with people when they were growing up. Review the preterite by asking how they communicated yesterday (number of e-mails, texts, phone calls, and so on).

12 ¡Conectad@s!°

°*Connected!*

Una de las varias placitas (*little plazas*) que hay en Cartagena, Colombia

- ¿Se siente Ud. identificado/a con la ciudad donde vive? ¿Y con el barrio (*neighborhood*) o la zona de la ciudad donde Ud. vive?
- ¿Cómo se mantiene en contacto con sus parientes y amigos que no viven cerca?
- ¿Puede Ud. imaginar su vida sin la tecnología? ¿Le gustaría depender menos de (*on*) la tecnología?

connect SPANISH

www.connectspanish.com

Resources

For Students

- Connect Spanish **(www.connectspanish.com)**, which contains all content from the following resources, as well as the *Mundo interactivo* scenarios, the LearnSmart adaptive learning system, and more!
- **Physical Resources:** Workbook / Laboratory Manual, Laboratory Audio Program, DVD

For Instructors

- Connect Spanish **(www.connectspanish.com)**, which contains access to all student sections of Connect Spanish, as well as helpful time-saving tools and resources such as an integrated gradebook, Instructor's Manual, Testing Program, digital transparencies, Audioscript, Videoscript, and more!

Colombia

44 millones de habitantes

- La diversidad natural de Colombia es magnífica. Este país comprende (*includes*) territorio caribeño, andino (*Andean*) y amazónico.
- Además (*In addition*), Colombia tiene muchísimos recursos naturales: petróleo, oro, platino y esmeraldas. Es uno de los principales productores y exportadores de café del mundo. También exporta flores.

En este capítulo

CONTENT / **CONTENIDO**	OBJECTIVES / **OBJETIVOS**
Housing and Neighborhoods 352	To talk about where we live
Technology 354	To talk about how we connect to the outside world
Informal Commands 357	To give directions and orders
The Subjunctive 362, Influence 368	To express subjective actions and states and to express influence in complex sentences
Colombia 376	To learn about the only South American country that has coasts on both on the Caribbean and the Pacific Oceans

Colombia

Datos esenciales

Nombre oficial: *República de Colombia*
Lema: *«Libertad y orden»*
Capital: *(Santa Fe de) Bogotá*
Otras ciudades: *Cali, Medellín, Barranquilla, Cartagena (de Indias)*
Composición étnica: *58% mestizos, 20% blancos, 14% mulatos, 4% negros, 3% afroamerindos, 1% indígenas*
Jefe de estado actual: *el Presidente Juan Manuel Santos Calderón*
Forma de gobierno: *República presidencialista*
Lengua oficial: *el español; también se hablan más de 60 lenguas indígenas*
Moneda: *el peso colombiano*
Religión: *90% católicos, 10% otros*

Point Out

- Colombia was named for Christopher Columbus.
- Colombia won its independence from Spain in 1819; *Simón Bolívar* was its first president.
- 12% of the world's coffee is produced in Colombia.

Suggestions

- Students may very well associate Colombia exclusively with drug trafficking and the violence associated with it, which has abated in recent years. You may wish to discuss this stereotype with them.
- Have students list their ideas about Colombia, including information on geography, politics, economy, music, and cuisine. When you finish the chapter, return to the lists and ask students what ideas they would change and/or add. The success of this activity will depend not only on the content about Colombia presented in the text but also on the extent to which you have time to supplement that content with your own knowledge and experiences and also with information given in this Instructor's Edition and the IM.

Multimedia

The IM provides suggestions for using multimedia materials in the classroom.

Resources: Transparency 122

NATIONAL STANDARDS: Connections

The Andes are an impressive geographical feature of South America, covering a large part of the continent. The next three chapters of *Puntos* will focus on the four countries that are most closely associated with the Andes: *Colombia* (*Cap. 12*), *Bolivia* and *Ecuador* (*Cap. 13*), and *Peru* (*Cap. 14*). (Note that Venezuela, Argentina, and Chile are also strongly associated with the Andean region, but they also have an additional identity, one with which we have chosen to associate them in this text: Venezuela with the Caribbean, Argentina and Chile with *el Cono Sur*.) In the Andean countries, the Andes are and have been throughout history both a theme and a shared symbol in music, art, literature, movies, and folklore. These countries have also been strongly influenced by their indigenous heritage, and the descendents of indigenous Andean civilizations are still a powerful force today, not only in culture but also in politics.

Vocabulario: Preparación
La ciudad y el barrio
Note
See the model for vocabulary presentation and other material in the *Cap. 12 Vocabulario: Preparación* section of "Chapter-by-Chapter Supplementary Materials" in the IM.

Reciclado: Review city place names from *Cap. 4: el centro (comercial), el mercado, la tienda,* and so on.

Suggestions
- Point out that streets and avenues in Spanish-speaking countries are often given the names of dates that recall political events (e.g., *Avenida 24 de Mayo* in Ecuador). In addition, you will find many more streets in the downtown areas named for military figures (*Avenida Mariscal Antonio de Sucre*) than you will find in this country.
- Emphasize the distinction between *la planta baja* and *el primer piso* (often referred to as the second floor by many English speakers). It may be helpful to ask students to think about tall office buildings and hotels, where the ground floor is often labeled as *G* in the elevator and the second floor as *1*, and so on, the same as in the Spanish system.
- Read the following definitions and have students give the words defined.
  1. *la persona que vive al lado* (*el/la vecino/a*)
  2. *el número y la calle donde Ud. vive* (*la dirección*)
  3. *la cantidad de dinero que Ud. paga cada mes por vivir en su apartamento* (*el alquiler*)
  4. *la parte principal de una ciudad, donde hay muchos edificios altos* (*el centro*)
  5. *el antónimo de centro* (*las afueras*)
  6. *la persona que alquila un apartamento* (*el/la inquilino/a*)
- Take a poll of students to see how many live in a house, in an apartment, in the dorm, or in a fraternity or sorority house. Keep track of the findings on the board. Discuss the results and have students compare the advantages and disadvantages of living in the different places: *¿Cuáles son las ventajas/desventajas de vivir… ?*
- Have students work in pairs to interview each other about where their girlfriend/boyfriend (husband/wife or best friend) lives.

VOCABULARIO Preparación

La ciudad y el barrio°
neighborhood

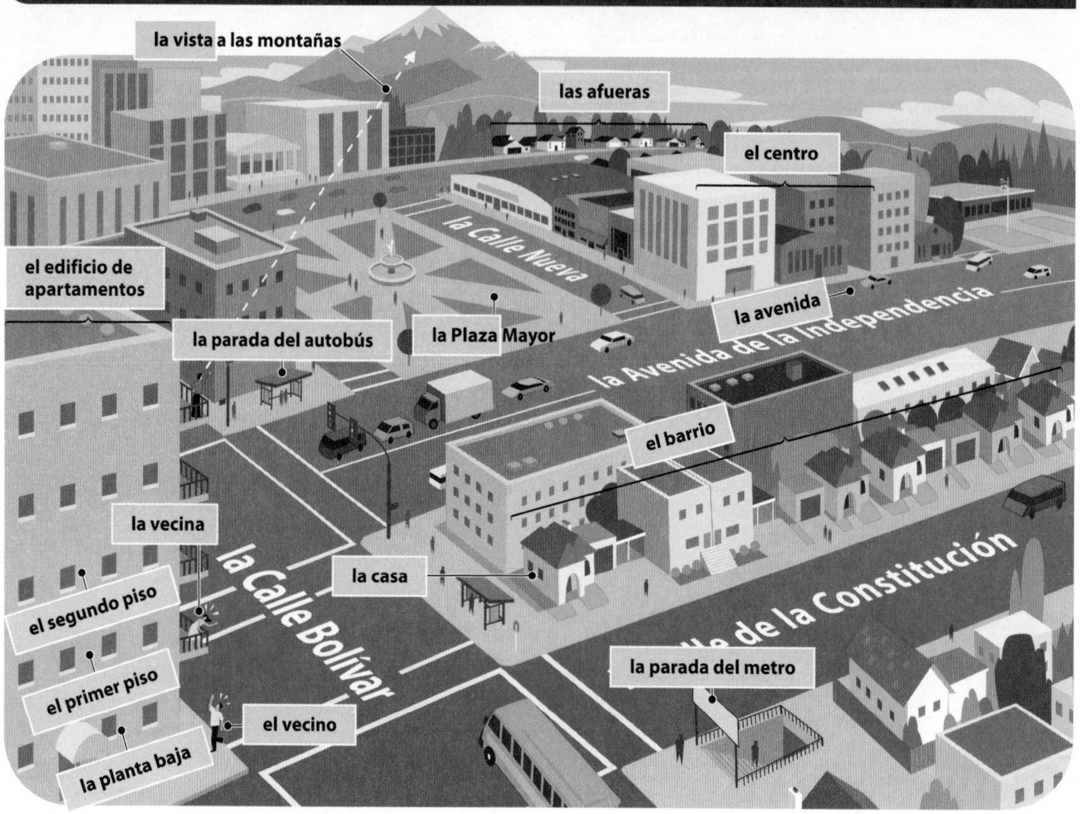

La vivienda	Housing
la residencia	residence
la residencia de ancianos	nursing home
la residencia (de estudiantes)	dormitory
el dueño / la dueña	owner; landlord, landlady
el inquilino / la inquilina	tenant; renter
el portero / la portera	building manager; doorman
el ascensor	elevator
el piso	floor (*of a building*)
el primer piso	first floor (*second story*)
el segundo piso	second floor (*third story*)
la planta baja	ground floor
la vista	view

La zona	
las afueras	outskirts; suburbs
la dirección	address
mudarse	to move (*residences*)

Los gastos*	Los… *Expenses*
alquilar	to rent
el alquiler	rent
la calefacción	heat
la electricidad	electricity
el gas	gas (*residential, not for cars*)

Resources: Transparency 123

Heritage Speakers
- Como se explica en *Así se dice*, hay varias maneras de decir *apartment* en español. Pregúnteles a los hispanohablantes de la clase cuál es la palabra que prefieren usar.
- Pídales a los hispanohablantes que escriban un breve ensayo sobre su vivienda ideal.

Así se dice

el apartamento = el departamento (*Mex., Arg.*), el piso (*Sp.*)
el ascensor = el elevador

El barrio is the word most generally used to express *neighborhood* in Spanish, although it is often said by Hispanics with more affection than its English counterpart. To talk about **mi barrio** is to talk about a place to which one is emotionally linked, not just the area where one lives. Many other words are used regionally and can depend on the kind of neighborhood. **La colonia** and **el fraccionamiento** are used in Mexico. Other common terms are **el vecindario** and **la zona residencial.**

¡OJO!

The word **suburbio** is a false cognate; it means *slum*. To indicate that you live in the suburbs, say **vivo en las afueras (de la ciudad).**

Conversación

A. Definiciones. Defina las siguientes palabras en español, según el modelo.

MODELO: la residencia de estudiantes →
Es un lugar donde viven muchos estudiantes. Por lo general está situada en el *campus* universitario.

1. el inquilino
2. el centro
3. el alquiler
4. el portero
5. la vecina
6. la dueña
7. la dirección
8. las afueras
9. el barrio
10. el ascensor
11. la avenida
12. la residencia de ancianos
13. la planta baja
14. la vista
15. la electricidad

Vocabulario útil

Es una persona que...
Es un lugar donde...
Es una cosa que...
Es lo que...

B. Buscamos un apartamento. Lea los siguientes avisos de venta (*sale ads*) de viviendas en Bogotá y conteste las preguntas. **¡OJO!** $ = el peso colombiano

1. ¿Qué tipo de vivienda se vende en cada anuncio? A: casa; B, C: apartamento
2. ¿Cuántas alcobas tiene cada vivienda? A: 4; B: 2; C: 2
3. ¿Cuál de las viviendas sería (*would be*) mejor para una familia con dos hijas adolescentes? ¿para una pareja de profesionales sin hijos y sin planes para tenerlos? ¿para una mujer profesional que ya tiene su primer trabajo, bien pagado (*well paying*)? familia: A; pareja de profesionales: C; mujer profesional: B

ZONA NORTE

Casa bien ubicada,[a] cerca de la Calle 170. Buenas rutas y cerca de colegios,[b] centros comerciales y supermercados. Zona de alta valorización.[c] 130 mts2.[d] Parqueadero privado con acceso directo a casa. 3 niveles;[e] 4 alcobas, 3 baños, sala-comedor, estudio y ático. $250.000.000 Celular: 3005566177

a.

BARRIO TEUSAQUILLO

Apartamento de 2 alcobas, 1 baño, cocina y sala-comedor. 3er[f] piso en edificio de 5 pisos con ascensor. Excelente ubicación cerca de bancos, supermercados, centros médicos y parque. $125.000.000 Celular: 3104488776 E-mail: micasa@gmail .com

b.

BARRIO PRADERA NORTE–TORRE[g] DE MADRID

2 habitaciones, dos baños, estudio, sala-comedor, pisos laminados, ascensor, garaje cubierto,[h] balcón. 100 mts2 4o[i] piso. Adicionales: piscina, gimnasio, sauna, cancha *squash*. $155.000.000 Tel. fijo[j] 6688775 Celular: 3169545650 E-mail: micasa@gmail.com

c.

[a]*situated, located* [b]*schools* [c]*de... high property values* [d]metros cuadrados (*square meters*) [e]*levels* [f]*tercer (third)* [g]*Tower* [h]*covered* [i]cuarto (*fourth*) [j]*Tel... Land line*

C. Mi situación de vivienda

Paso 1. Diga si las siguientes declaraciones son ciertas o falsas para Ud. Corrija las declaraciones falsas.

	CIERTO	FALSO
1. Mi familia vive en una casa de dos pisos.	☐	☐
2. Yo estoy de inquilino/a en la actualidad.	☐	☐
3. Vivo en un apartamento con otros estudiantes.	☐	☐

(Continúa.)

Con. A: Note

Active vocabulary: *el* campus

Con. A: Possible Answers

1. Es una persona que alquila un apartamento. 2. Es la parte central de una ciudad. 3. Es el dinero que le pagamos cada mes al dueño del apartamento donde vivimos. 4. Es la persona que cuida el edificio de apartamentos. 5. Es una persona que vive cerca de nosotros. 6. Es la persona que compró una vivienda. 7. Es la calle y el número de un lugar. 8. Es un lugar que no está cerca del centro de una ciudad. 9. Es la zona donde vivimos en una ciudad. 10. Es una cosa que nos sube o nos baja a los otros pisos de un edificio. 11. Es una calle grande. 12. Es donde viven las personas mayores. 13. Es el piso por donde se entra en un edificio. 14. Es lo que podemos ver desde nuestro apartamento. 15. Es un gasto que tenemos todos los meses.

Con. A: Variation

Play a Jeopardy game. Give or have students give a definition. The class (or teams) should respond with the corresponding question.

Es un lugar donde viven muchos estudiantes. → ¿Qué es una residencia?

Con. B: Notes

- *1 dólar estadounidense = 1.880 pesos colombianos; 1000 pesos colombianos = 0,5333 dólares estadounidenses, aproximadamente.* You may wish to provide a more up-to-date exchange rate.
- The symbol of the Colombian *peso*, $, is similar to that of the U.S. dollar.

Con. B: Follow-up

- *Paso 1.* Have students explain which ad appeals to them the most and why.
- *Paso 2.* Have students tally their answers on the board, then have a class discussion about the similarities and differences.

Con. C, Paso 1: Redacción

Assign as the basis for a composition. Set the extension and expectations clearly for students. For example:

- First paragraph: Where students live now
- Second paragraph: Where they would like to live in the future

Other possibilities: where they lived as children, where their parents lived, where they would live if money were no object.

Multimedia: Internet

Have students search the Internet for an online newspaper in Colombia for rental ads to print out and bring to class.

Pronunciación: See the Laboratory Manual for presentation and practice of the letters *y* and *ll*.

Resources: Transparency 124

Tengo… Necesito… Quiero…

Notes

- This section expands students' vocabulary for describing personal possessions and introduces some vocabulary for the world of work. Students will learn more about the working world in *Cap. 17.*
- It is an understatement to say that it is impossible to keep up with or completely reflect the variety of vocabulary used for technology in the Spanish-speaking world in a textbook. Supplement the vocabulary in this section as needed.

Suggestions

- Model vocabulary in sentences about yourself and communicative exchanges with the students.
- Optional vocabulary (some of it especially for older students): *la bicicleta de montaña, el estéreo, la videocasetera*
- Have students give sentences about the kinds of vehicles they associate with the following circumstances or people.
  1. *una persona muy dedicada a los deportes*
  2. *un adolescente que vive en el centro y no tiene coche*
  3. *una familia con tres hijos*
  4. *una tarde calurosa* (new) *de verano*
- Bring and/or have students bring mounted photos from magazines related to the chapter topic. Present as many items as possible. Periodically go back to a photo and ask questions such as: *¿Qué es esto, una grabadora o una cámara?*
- Point out that *conseguir* (*consigo*) is conjugated like *seguir.*
- Remind students that *la moto* and *la foto* are short for (and more commonly used than) *la motocicleta* and *la fotografía.*
- Point out that *el trabajo* has several meanings: *work; job* (position); *schoolwork* (such as a written report or term paper).
- Emphasize that *funcionar* expresses whether a machine of any kind works well, badly, or not at all. *Trabajar* is never used in that context.

Reciclado

- Review transportation words students have already learned: *el coche = el carro, el tren, el autobús, el avión, el barco.*

	CIERTO	FALSO
4. Mi alquiler incluye los gastos de electricidad, gas y calefacción.	☐	☐
5. Mi apartamento tiene una vista magnífica.	☐	☐
6. Vivo en uno de los mejores barrios de la ciudad.	☐	☐
7. En el futuro, me gustaría vivir en una zona residencial en las afueras.	☐	☐
8. Los vecinos ideales son como yo.	☐	☐

Paso 2. Ahora, en parejas, túrnense para entrevistarse sobre su vivienda actual, usando las ideas del **Paso 1.**

MODELO: ¿Tu familia vive en una casa de dos pisos?

Paso 3. Digan a la clase lo que Uds. tienen en común en cuanto a su vivienda actual.

Tengo… Necesito… Quiero… (Part 3)

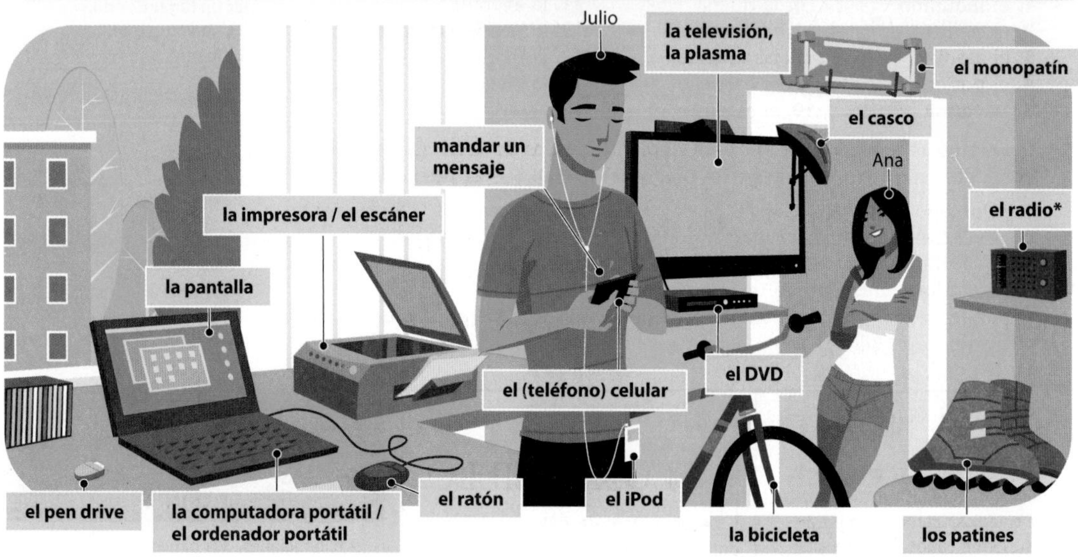

La electrónica

el archivo	file
la arroba	@
el buzón de voz	voice mailbox
la contraseña	password
el correo electrónico	e-mail
el disco duro	hard drive
la electrónica	electronic equipment
el equipo	equipment
la grabadora	(tape) recorder/player
la pantalla (grande/plana)	(big/flat) screen (monitor)
la red social	social networking site

Cognados: el app (*f.*)**, el blog, la cámara digital, el CD-ROM, el control remoto, el disco compacto (el CD), el hard drive, el DVD(-ROM), el e-mail, Facebook** (*m.*)**, el fax, la fotocopia, la fotocopiadora, el GPS, el Internet, la memoria, el módem, Twitter** (*m.*)**, el video**

En el trabajo

el aumento	raise
el jefe / la jefa	boss
el sueldo	salary

Los verbos

almacenar	to store, save
bajar/descargar (gu)	to download
buscar (qu) en el Internet	to look up on the Internet

*El radio *is the apparatus;* la radio *is the medium.*

NATIONAL STANDARDS: Communication

Have students work in groups of three to four to list what they consider to be the five most important machines or objects for the average student. Compare lists and create a master list on the board. Poll the class to see how many students have the items listed on the board. Have them discuss how these things affect their daily lives.

Resources: Transparency 125

cambiar (de canal, de ropa...)	to change (channels, clothing . . .)
conseguir (*like* **seguir**)	to get, obtain
copiar/hacer (foto)copia	to copy
entrar/estar en el Internet	to go/be online
entrar/estar en Facebook	to go/be on Facebook
fallar	to "crash" (*computer*)
funcionar	to work, function; to run (*machines*)
grabar	to record; to tape
guardar	to keep, to save (*documents*)
imprimir	to print
instalar	to install
mandar	to send
manejar	to drive; to operate (*a machine*)
obtener (*like* **tener**)	to get, obtain

Los vehículos

la camioneta	station wagon
el carro/coche (descapotable)	(convertible) car
la moto(cicleta)	motorcycle

Conversación

A. Lo que tengo. Haga una lista de todo el equipo de **Vocabulario: Preparación** que Ud. tiene. Luego haga una lista de las cosas que necesita.

B. Asociaciones. ¿Qué cosas asocia Ud. con los siguientes verbos?

1. mandar
2. fallar
3. conseguir
4. grabar
5. guardar
6. cambiar
7. imprimir
8. instalar

C. Definiciones

Paso 1. ¿Qué palabras corresponden a estas definiciones? **¡OJO!** Puede haber (*There can be*) más de un aparato que hace estas funciones o puede haber más de un verbo en algunos casos.

1. Es un aparato que sirve para mandar documentos inmediatamente. el fax
2. Es un aparato que hace copias de un documento. la fotocopiadora
3. Es lo que usamos para cambiar el programa de televisión sin levantarnos del sofá. el control remoto
4. Este sistema recibe mensajes cuando no podemos (o no queremos) contestar el teléfono. el buzón de voz
5. Es lo que usamos para escuchar música sin hacer ruido. el iPod
6. Esto se hace cuando hay en la tele una película que queremos ver pero que ahora mismo no podemos verla. grabar
7. Es un sinónimo de guardar, como guardar un documento en el disco duro. almacenar

Paso 2. Ahora le toca a Ud. darles las definiciones a sus compañeros de clase, siguiendo el modelo del **Paso 1.** Ellos van a adivinar (*guess*) cuál es la palabra definida.

D. La tecnología y yo

Paso 1. Complete las siguientes oraciones para describir su relación con la tecnología.

1. (No) Soy bueno/a para la tecnología porque...
2. Me encanta la tecnología y por eso...
3. No puedo imaginar la vida sin ________ (aparato) porque...
4. Estoy conectado/a al Internet ________ (¿con qué frecuencia?) porque...
5. Entro en el Internet sobre todo (*especially*) para...

Paso 2. Ahora, en parejas, comparen sus respuestas. ¿Son muy similares sus preferencias y hábitos con relación a la tecnología?

Así se dice

mandar = enviar (envío)
el Internet = la Internet
el monopatín = el skateboard (*Sp.*)
el (teléfono) celular = el (teléfono) móvil (*Sp.*)
el video (*L.A.*) = el vídeo (*Sp.*)

Mundo interactivo

You should now be prepared to work with Scenario 6, Activity 3 in Connect Spanish (**www.connectspanish.com**).

- Review house/possessions vocabulary from *Cap. 5* and *Cap. 10*.
- Review the names of places in the house by asking which place students associate with the following: *la bicicleta, la computadora, la moto, la televisión, hacer ejercicio, jugar a los videojuegos, mirar la televisión, oír la radio, sacar fotos,* and so on.

Pronunciación: See Pronunciation Notes, IM.

Bright Idea

Con. A: Suggestion

Students may ask for additional words: *la identificación de llamadas* (caller ID), *el desvío de llamadas* (call forwarding), *el bloqueo de llamadas* (call block), *el sistema de devolución automática de llamadas* (call back), *la llamada en espera* (call-waiting), *la línea de teléfono* (land line), *el Tivo.*

Con. A: Reciclado

After students have completed their lists, ask them to count the number of items on each list. Ask the students with the longest lists to read their lists to the class so that students can compare what they have. As students read the lists, other students should respond appropriately with direct object pronouns: *Ya lo/la tengo, Lo/La tengo también, También lo/la necesito,* and so on. Model an appropriate response for the first few items, to get the back and forth going.

Con. B: Extension

9. *copiar* **10.** *manejar* **11.** *funcionar*

Con. C: Suggestion

Once again, emphasize the importance of giving good definitions. It is one of the language skills that students will need the most as they start interacting with native speakers. It is also important for students to be active recipients of definitions and to know how to form the questions necessary to help the person who is trying to define a word.

Con. D: Suggestions

- Assign *Paso 1* as written homework so that students are well prepared for pair work followed by a whole-class discussion.
- Use these topics to stimulate a whole-class discussion about technology: *Las ventajas y desventajas de la tecnología. ¿Estamos demasiado conectados? ¿Presenta peligros el uso de la tecnología?*

Heritage Speakers

Hay varios términos para referirse al *ordenador.* La palabra *ordenador* se usa en España. Hay hispanohablantes de Latinoamérica que dicen *el computador* (masculino) y otros que prefieren decir *la computadora* (femenino). Anime a los hispanohablantes a indicar qué término prefieren.

Con. E: Suggestions

- Ask students to figure out what the following information from the ad means: *Mensamanía* (= *mensaje* + *manía*), *la tarifa plana* (students know *la pantalla plana*), 2€ (€ = euros).
- Put the messages created in *Paso 2* on an overhead and have the whole class try to decipher them.
- Have students share their answers to *Paso 3* with the class. Tally responses and have a discussion about at least one item.
- Introduce additional computer-related vocabulary.

  el buscador (search engine)
  el ciberespacio (cyberspace)
  cliquear / hacer clic / clicar (to click on the mouse)
  la memoria virtual (virtual memory)
  la página web or el sitio web (web page).

- Write the words *el buscapersonas* and *el localizador*. Tell students they mean the same thing and have them try to guess the meaning (beeper). Point out that in some areas of this country, Spanish speakers might call it *el bíper*.

Nota cultural

Suggestions

- OLPC (in Spanish, *Un portátil por niño*) is a complex project involving the support of major companies whose objective is to bring a rugged, low-cost, low-power, connected laptop to each child. These laptops are available to governments at a cheaper than usual rate. You can find more information at www.one.laptop.org.
- *El Plan Ceibal* is named for the national tree/flower of Uruguay, *el ceibo*, known in English as the cockspur coral. The name *CEIBAL* (*Conectividad Educativa de Informática Básica para el Aprendizaje en Línea*) was chosen for its symbolic connection to *el ceibo*. More information on this Uruguayan initiative is available at www.ceibal.org.uy.
- Other countries, such as Argentina, are considering adopting a plan similar to OLPC.

Comprensión

1. *En los países hispanos, ¿es la norma tener un teléfono celular?* (*Sí, casi todos tienen uno.*)
2. *¿Es barata la tecnología en los países hispanos?* (*No, es muy cara.*)
3. *¿En qué área de la tecnología se puede ver claramente la desigualdad de su acceso entre los países ricos y los pobres?* (*el acceso al Internet*)

E. Los mensajes

Paso 1. En parejas, traten de descifrar (*try to decipher*) la pregunta del anuncio de VODAFONE. ¿Los fines de semana mandas mensajes para quedar o quedas para mandar mensajes?

Estrategia

Xa representa una preposición muy común (Pista [*Hint*]: **X** = **por**).

Vocabulario para leer

podrás you'll be able
SMS el servicio de mensajes cortos
MMS el sistema de mensajes de multimedia
apúntate sign up
cuanto antes as soon as possible
disfrutarás de you'll enjoy
quedar con alguien to have a planned meeting with someone

La vida es móvil. Móvil es Vodafone.
Mensamanía Fin de Semana
¿Ls fins d smana mands mnsajs xa qdar o qdas xa mndar mnsajs?
Con la tarifa plana Mensamanía Fin de Semana de Vodafone podrás enviar los fines de semana de abril todos los SMS y MMS que quieras a móviles Vodafone por sólo 2€. Apúntate cuanto antes, llamando o enviando gratis FINDE ON al 136, y disfrutarás de hasta cinco fines de semana de Mensamanía.
vodafone

Paso 2. Ahora inventen un mensaje para la clase, usando un código similar al (*to that*) del anuncio.

Nota cultural

El acceso a la tecnología en el mundo hispano

La tecnología está presente en todo el mundo hispano, donde se puede ver y adquirir[a] todos los aparatos electrónicos que uno pudiera[b] desear. Pero estos son muy caros a veces y su mayor o menor presencia depende del poder adquisitivo[c] del individuo.

- Hoy día, por ejemplo, casi todo el mundo tiene un teléfono celular.
- El acceso al Internet es más problemático y muestra[d] un panorama de desigualdad.[e]

Un ejemplo, según datos[f] recientes: España (17) y México (18) aparecen en la lista de los 20 países mundiales con más usuarios.[g] Pero para analizar estos datos, es importante saber que España tiene 46,5 millones de habitantes mientras que México tiene 112 millones, o sea que[h] el porcentaje de usuarios mexicanos es muy bajo en comparación.

Los gobiernos[i] hispanos son conscientes de la brecha[j] digital y hay gran interés por mejorar[k] la situación. Por ejemplo, en el Uruguay existe el Plan Ceibal, por el cual[l] todos los niños de edad escolar en el sistema público reciben una computadora portátil, bajo el proyecto mundial OLPC (*One Laptop Per Child*).

[a]*acquire* [b]*could* [c]*poder... purchasing power* [d]*it shows* [e]*inequality* [f]*data* [g]*users* [h]*o... so* [i]*governments* [j]*gap* [k]*por... in improving* [l]*por... through which*

Una niña que ya sabe entrar en el Internet

¿Existe en su ciudad o estado un plan para darle a cada niño o niña una computadora?

NATIONAL STANDARDS: Connections

Latin America is one of the fastest areas of growth for the Internet. Brazil has one of the most highly developed computer networks in the world with satellite access to these networks even from the Amazon. Web surfers can access major newspapers, such as *El Espectador* and *El Tiempo* from Bogota, Colombia, as well as other reputable periodicals from other Latin American nations. For example, those who are interested in learning about Peru can do so through on the Internet, accessing documents in English, Spanish, and even in Quechua.

GRAMÁTICA

¿Recuerda Ud.?

In **Gramática 20 (Cap. 7)** you learned how to form **Ud.** and **Uds.** (formal) commands with the "opposite" vowel. Remember that object pronouns (direct, indirect, reflexive) must follow and be attached to affirmative commands; they must precede negative commands.

AFFIRMATIVE:	Hábl**e**le Ud.	Duérm**an**se.	Díg**a**selo Ud.
NEGATIVE:	No le habl**e** Ud.	No se duerm**an**.	No se lo dig**a** Ud.

¿Cómo se dice en español?

1. Give me the book. **(Uds.)**
2. Don't give it (*m.*) to her. **(Uds.)**
3. Sit here, please. **(Ud.)**
4. Don't sit in that chair! **(Ud.)**
5. Tell them the truth. **(Uds.)**
6. Tell it (*f.*) to them now! **(Uds.)**
7. Never tell it (*f.*) to her. **(Uds.)**
8. Take care of yourself. **(Ud.)**
9. Listen to me. **(Ud.)**

You'll learn how to form informal commands in **Gramática 33.**

33 Influencing Others (Part 2)
Tú (Informal) Commands

Grammar Tutorial 33
connect SPANISH
www.connectspanish.com

Gramática en acción: Mandatos de la adolescencia

- Guarda la ropa limpia en tu cómoda.
- Pon la ropa sucia en el cesto.
- No te pongas esos pantalones para ir a la escuela.
- No dejes los zapatos por todas partes.
- Deja de mandar mensajes mientras te hablo.
- Quítate el iPod: te estoy hablando.

¿Y Ud.?

¿Oía Ud. esos mandatos cuando era adolescente? ¿Sí o no? ¿Quién se los daba? (Me los daba mi…)

Informal commands (**Los mandatos informales**) are used with persons whom you would address as **tú.** Spanish has different forms for formal and informal commands. And unlike **Ud.** and **Uds.** commands, whose form is the same whether affirmative or negative, the negative **tú** commands have different forms than the affirmative commands.

a command or imperative / **un mandato** = a verb form used to tell someone to do something

Commands from adolescence • *Put your clean clothes away in your dresser.* • *Put your dirty clothes in the laundry hamper.* • *Don't put on those pants to go to school.* • *Don't leave your shoes everywhere.* • *Stop texting while I'm talking to you.* • *Take off your iPod: I'm talking to you.*

Resources: Transparency 126

Gramática 33
¿Recuerda Ud.?: Suggestion

Note the recycling of object pronouns and their position with commands. You may wish to review direct and indirect object pronouns at this time.

Extension

11. Wake up earlier. (*Ud.*)
12. Get dressed quickly. (*Uds.*)
13. Enjoy yourself with your friends. (*Ud.*)
14. Don't give it (*m.*) to them now. (*Uds.*)

¿Recuerda Ud.?: Answers

1. *Denme el libro.* **2.** *No se lo den a ella.* **3.** *Siéntese aquí, por favor.* **4.** *No se siente en esa/aquella silla.* **5.** *Díganles la verdad.* **6.** *Dígansela ahora.* **7.** *No se la digan nunca a ella. / Nunca se la digan a ella.* **8.** *Cuídese.* **9.** *Escúcheme.*

Tú (Informal) Commands

Note

If you have been using *tú* commands all along, start by having students list the ones they already know.

Suggestion

Have students give the infinitive form of each command in the *GEA.*

Reciclado: As you continue practice of preterite vs. imperfect, have students who heard each phrase as a teenager explain why their mother (or father) said that. *¿Le dijo su madre eso solo una vez o se lo decía con frecuencia? ¿Por qué?*

Negative *tú* Commands

Suggestions

- Point out to students all of the forms for negative *tú* commands, and that the position of the object pronouns is identical to the pronoun position used in formal commands.
- You may wish to treat the material in this section for passive recognition only. Have students learn only high-frequency irregular *tú* commands.
- Explain to students that the command system in Spanish (although easy to understand when someone gives you a command) is difficult to master in speaking. They should not be discouraged if complete control does not come easily.

Preliminary Exercise

Have students respond to statements with negative commands. Write the following example on the board, then give them additional statements.

No quiero cantarlo. → Pues, no lo cantes.
No quiero… comprarlo, mirarlo, leerlo, beberlo, escribirlo, decidirlo

Affirmative *tú* Commands

Suggestions

- Remind students of the impoliteness implied in any command, particularly with *tú*. Even with friends, they should use questions instead of commands.

  ¿Me pasas la sal, por favor?
  ¿Me prestas tu suéter?
  ¿Me cierras la puerta?

- Have students give affirmative commands to a friend who says he/she should do the following things. Write the following example on the board, then give the additional statements.

  Debo hacer la cama. → Haz la cama. (Hazla.)
  Debo…
  decir la verdad
  hacer más tacos
  ir a la biblioteca
  poner los libros en la mesa
  salir ahora
  ser buen(a) estudiante
  tener más paciencia
  venir a clase todos los días

Negative **tú** Commands / **Los mandatos informales negativos**

Las terminaciones regulares
-ar → -es
-er/-ir → -as

-ar verbs		**-er/-ir verbs**	
No hables.	Don't speak.	**No comas.**	Don't eat.
No toques.	Don't play.	**No escribas.**	Don't write.
No juegues.	Don't play.	**No pidas.**	Don't order.
No empieces.	Don't start.	**No salgas.**	Don't leave.
		No vayas.	Don't go.

1. **Formation of Negative Informal Commands**
   Negative **tú** commands are basically the same as **Ud./Uds.** commands but with the characteristic **-s** of **tú** forms. They use the "opposite" vowel, and all of the irregularities that you learned for **Ud./Uds.** commands.
   - Stem-changing verbs show the stem change.
   - Verbs that end in **-car, -gar,** and **-zar** have a spelling change.
   - Verbs with irregular **yo** forms show the irregularity in the command.
   - A few verbs have irregular **tú** commands (the **Ud.** command with a final **-s**).

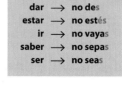

dar → no des
estar → no estés
ir → no vayas
saber → no sepas
ser → no seas

No cantes tú tan fuerte.
*Don't **you** sing so loudly.*

¡OJO!
The pronoun **tú** is used only for emphasis.

2. **Position of Pronouns**
   As with negative **Ud./Uds.** commands, object pronouns—direct, indirect, and reflexive—precede negative **tú** commands.

No lo mires.
Don't look at him.
No les escribas.
Don't write to them.
No te levantes.
Don't get up.

Affirmative **tú** Commands / **Los mandatos informales afirmativos**

Las terminaciones regulares
-ar → -a
-er/-ir → -e

-ar verbs		**-er/-ir verbs**	
Habla.	Speak.	**Come.**	Eat.
Toca.	Play.	**Escribe.**	Write.
Juega.	Play.	**Pide.**	Order.
Empieza.	Start.	**Oye.**	Listen.

1. **Formation of Regular Informal Affirmative Commands**
   Unlike **Ud./Uds.** commands and the negative **tú** commands, most affirmative **tú** commands have the same form as the third person singular (**Ud.**) form of the present indicative.* Stem changes occur, but there are no changes for verbs ending in **-car/-gar/-zar.**

2. **Irregular Informal Affirmative Commands**
   Some verbs have irregular affirmative **tú** command forms.

decir → di	**salir** → sal
hacer → haz	**ser** → sé
ir → ve	**tener** → ten
poner → pon	**venir** → ven

*As you know, there are two different moods in Spanish: the indicative mood (the one you have been using, which is used to state facts and ask questions) and the subjunctive mood (which is used to express more subjective actions or states). Beginning with **Gramática 34,** you will learn more about the subjunctive mood.*

NATIONAL STANDARDS: Communication

In many Hispanic countries it is not uncommon to see the infinitive used for impersonal commands, especially on signs in public places.

No pisar el césped.
No fumar.
Guardar silencio.

¡OJO!

Sé, the informal affirmative command of **ser,** has an accent mark to distinguish it from the pronoun **se.** Other one-syllable commands don't have accent marks (**di, ve, ten…**).

Sé puntual, pero **ten** cuidado.
Be there on time, but be careful.

¡OJO!

The affirmative **tú** commands for **ir** and **ver** are identical: **ve.** Context will clarify meaning. The command form of **ver** is rarely used.

¡**Ve** esa película!
See that movie!

Ve a casa ahora mismo.
Go home right now.

3. Position of Pronouns
As with affirmative **Ud./Uds.** commands, object and reflexive pronouns follow affirmative **tú** commands and are attached to them. Accent marks are necessary except when a single pronoun is added to a one-syllable command.

Léela, por favor.
Read it, please.

Póntelos.
Put them on.

Dile la verdad.
Tell him the truth.

Autoprueba

Choose the correct command form for each sentence.

1. ______me qué quieres.
2. No ______ al parque sola.
3. No le ______ nada de la fiesta.
4. ______ te un abrigo.
5. ______ a la tienda.
6. No ______ eso en mi cama.

a. di
b. digas
c. pon
d. pongas
e. vayas
f. ve

Answers: **1.** a **2.** e **3.** b **4.** c **5.** f **6.** d

Summary of Informal Commands

NEGATIVE:	-ar ⟶ -es	-er/-ir ⟶ -as
AFFIRMATIVE:	-ar ⟶ -a	-er/-ir ⟶ -e

AFFIRMATIVE: *command* + *pronoun* (1 word)
NEGATIVE: **no** + *pronoun* + *command* (3 words)

Nota **comunicativa**

Los mandatos con *vosotros*

In **Capítulo 2,** you learned about the pronoun **vosotros/as** that is used in Spain as the plural of **tú.** Here is how **vosotros** commands are formed, for recognition only.

- Affirmative **vosotros** commands are formed by substituting **-d** for the final **-r** of the infinitive. There are no irregular affirmative **vosotros** commands.

hablar ⟶ hablad
comer ⟶ comed
escribir ⟶ escribid

- Negative **vosotros** commands for most verbs are formed by adding the "opposite" vowel + **-is** to the infinitive stem (the infinitive minus its **-ar** or **-er/-ir** ending). **-ar** and **-er** stem-changing verbs *do not* show the change, but **-ir** stem-changing verbs and spelling change verbs *do.* Verbs with irregular **yo** forms show the **yo** irregularity, and there are a few irregular verbs. (You will learn more about this in **Gramática 34.**)

No habléis.
No comáis.
No escribáis.
No volváis.
No durmáis.
No toquéis.
No digáis.

- Placement of object pronouns is the same as for all other command forms.

Decídmelo.
No me lo digáis.

Note

Point out that *sé* (from *ser*) can also be mistaken for *sé* (first person singular of the present indicative) of the verb *saber.* Context will clarify the meaning.

Nota comunicativa

Suggestions

- Remind students that *vosotros/as* is primarily used in Spain.
- Model and practice the *vosotros/as* commands for students, especially if you are a Spaniard, if you use *vosotros/as* forms, and/or if your students are likely to study in Spain.

Heritage Speakers

Pregúnteles a los hispanohablantes si saben usar o si usan las formas de *vosotros/as*. También es posible que haya hispanohablantes en su clase que usen el *voseo,* que se oye en Colombia, el Ecuador, Costa Rica, la Argentina, el Uruguay y otros países. Revise con la clase los mandatos con *vos.*

Hablá vos. *No hablés vos.*
Acostate vos. *No te acostés vos.*

Preliminary Exercises

- Have students make the following commands or questions more polite.
  1. To the teacher: *Repita.*
  2. To a classmate: *Repite lo que dijo la profesora.*
  3. To a housemate: *Lava los platos. / Compra leche hoy.*
  4. To a middle-aged woman in the street: *¿Dónde está la parada del autobús?*
  5. To a young man in the street: *¿Qué hora es?*
- Have students work in groups to get advice from each other, e.g., what kind of computer to buy, which kind of exercise to do to lose weight, where to study, what movie to see, and so on. Students should try to use as many commands as possible.

Prác. A: Note

Active vocabulary: *la mentira*

Prác. A: Suggestion

Have students give the infinitive on which each command form is based. Note: *Paso 2,* item 1: *cruzar* will be new for students. You may wish to give them the infinitive and focus on the *z* → *c* change. The item is included because of its high frequency of use as a negative command for children.

Prác. B: Suggestion

Encourage students to give additional related commands for each item. Some suggested commands are included in parentheses with the answers.

Prác. B: Answers

Note: Answers in parentheses are related to *Con. B: Suggestion.*

Por favor,… **1.** *quítate el abrigo.* (*Pero no te quites el suéter.*) **2.** *saca tu merienda de la mochila.* (*Empieza a comer. Cómete la merienda.*) **3.** *siéntate en el círculo.* (*No uses la computadora ahora.*) **4.** *come algo.* (*Y bébete la leche también.*) **5.** *sal a jugar con los otros niños.* (*Pero no corras mucho.*) **6.** *duérmete ahora.* (*No cantes más.*) **7.** *abre el cuaderno.* (*Haz los ejercicios.*) **8.** *pon tus libros en el estante.* (*No los dejes en el piso.*) **9.** *no llores.* (*Piensa en la lección. No pienses en tu mamá.*) **10.** *no digas palabras feas.* (*Di solo palabras bonitas.*)

Prác. B: Follow-up

- Have students give commands that children would like to give to others.
- Ask students: *¿Qué mandatos oye Ud. con frecuencia ahora? ¿Qué mandatos da Ud. con frecuencia y a quién se los da?*

Estrategia

Note the use of the reflexive pronoun with the verbs **comer** and **beber** in items 2 and 5. This use of the reflexive means *to eat up* and *to drink up*, respectively.

Cómete las zanahorias.
Eat up your carrots.

No **te bebas** la leche tan rápido.
Don't drink up your milk so fast.

Práctica

A. ¡Anticipemos! Recuerdos de la niñez

Paso 1. Indique los mandatos que le daban a Ud. con frecuencia cuando era niño/a. Después de leerlos todos, indique los dos que le daban más. ¿Qué mandato no oyó Ud. nunca?

	CON FRECUENCIA	LOS MÁS COMUNES
1. Limpia tu cuarto.	☐	☐
2. Cómete el desayuno.	☐	☐
3. Haz la tarea.	☐	☐
4. Cierra la puerta.	☐	☐
5. Bébete la leche.	☐	☐
6. Lávate las manos.	☐	☐
7. Dime la verdad.	☐	☐
8. Quítate el iPod.	☐	☐
9. Guarda tu bicicleta en el garaje.	☐	☐
10. Sé bueno/a.	☐	☐

Paso 2. Ahora indique lo que con frecuencia le prohibían a Ud. hacer. Indique también los dos mandatos que le daban más. ¿Qué mandato no le daban nunca?

	CON FRECUENCIA	LOS MÁS COMUNES
1. No cruces (*Don't cross*) la calle solo/a.	☐	☐
2. No juegues con mis cosas.	☐	☐
3. No comas dulces antes de cenar.	☐	☐
4. No me digas mentiras (*lies*).	☐	☐
5. No les des tanta comida a los peces.	☐	☐
6. No hables con personas desconocidas (*strangers*).	☐	☐
7. No dejes el monopatín en el jardín.	☐	☐
8. No cambies los canales tanto.	☐	☐
9. No seas malo/a.	☐	☐

B. Mandatos en una clase preescolar (*preschool*)

Paso 1. Dé un mandato lógico para niños pequeños en cada una de las siguientes situaciones típicas. Siga los modelos, usando los verbos entre paréntesis para formar los mandatos.

MODELOS: Un niño está saliendo del salón de clase. (salir) → Por favor, **no salgas** del salón de clase.

Una niña siempre deja sus lápices en el piso. (dejar) → Por favor, **no dejes** tus lápices en el piso.

1. Un niño no se quita el abrigo en clase. (quitarse)
2. Una niña debe sacar su merienda de la mochila. (sacar)
3. Es hora de sentarse en círculo, pero un niño está usando la computadora. (sentarse)
4. Es hora de la merienda, pero una niña no come nada. (comer)
5. Es la hora del recreo (*recess*), pero una niña no sale a jugar. (salir)
6. Es hora de dormir la siesta, pero una niña está cantando. (dormirse)
7. Es hora de hacer los ejercicios de matemáticas, pero un niño no quiere abrir su cuaderno. (abrir)
8. Una niña debe poner sus libros en el estante, pero no quiere. (poner)
9. Una niña está llorando porque quiere ver a su mamá. (llorar)
10. Una niña dice palabras feas. (decir)

Paso 2. Ahora dé otros tres mandatos que se les dan mucho a los niños pequeños.

Conversación

A. La importancia de una carrera universitaria

Paso 1. En parejas, lean el anuncio y contesten las preguntas.

Vocabulario para leer

el logro achievement
la beca scholarship
el título degree

mejorar to improve
desarrollar to develop

favor de + *inf.* please (*do something*)

30 AÑOS DE LOGROS
13,421 BECAS PARA ESTUDIOS DE MEDICINA Y ASISTENCIA SANITARIA
12,770 BECAS PARA ESTUDIOS DE ADMINISTRACIÓN COMERCIAL
10,196 BECAS PARA ESTUDIOS DE CIENCIA
73,000 BECAS EN TOTAL
Asiste a la universidad. Obtén un título. Mejora tu vida.
Nosotros del Hispanic Scholarship Fund hemos ayudado a miles de
estudiantes hispanos a obtener un título universitario y a llegar a
desarrollar plenamente su potencial. Te podemos ayudar a ti, también.
Favor de visitar www.hsf.net para mayor información o para solicitar una beca.
30TH
HISPANIC SCHOLARSHIP FUND
www.hsf.net

1. Busquen los mandatos informales que se usan en el anuncio. ¿Qué significan en inglés? Asiste (*Attend*), Obtén (*Get*), Mejora (*Improve*).
2. ¿A quiénes va dirigido (*directed*) este anuncio, a la gente (*people*) joven o a la gente mayor? ¿Por qué creen eso? A la joven. Porque los anima a asistir a la universidad y usa la forma **tú.**
3. ¿Qué tipo de estudios se destacan (*stand out*) en el anuncio? medicina, asistencia sanitaria, administración comercial, ciencia

Paso 2. Es muy común usar mandatos en los anuncios. Creen Uds. (*Create*) un anuncio para hacerle publicidad a su universidad. Deben usar por lo menos seis mandatos, dos de ellos negativos.

B. Entre compañeros de casa. En parejas, hagan una lista de los cinco mandatos que se oyen con más frecuencia en su casa (apartamento, residencia). Piensen no solo en los mandatos que Uds. oyen sino (*but*) también en los que Uds. les dan a los demás (*others*).

Vocabulario útil

apagar (gu) (*to turn off*)
la computadora
contestar el teléfono
lavar los platos
no hacer ruido

no ser...
así (like that), **bobo/a** (dumb),
impaciente, impulsivo/a,
loco/a, pesado/a,
precipitado/a (hasty), **tonto/a**

poner la tele
prestarme dinero
sacar (qu) la basura

Con. A: Note

Active vocabulary: *la gente*

Con. A, Paso 2: Redacción

- Have students work in small groups.
- Ask at least one group to work at the board.
- Have students write out their ads to hand in.
- Correct the ads, then share them with the whole class and ask students to vote for the best ad.

Con. B: Suggestions

- Have students complete this activity in groups of three, then discuss the results with the class.
- Have students write down, in infinitive form, five activities that can be performed in class (e.g., *cerrar la puerta*). Then have the class select five people (or have five students volunteer) to carry out the commands. The other students exchange lists, then form commands based on the phrases on their lists. They should give the commands to one of the selected students or volunteers, who, in turn, tries to do what he/she is told.

Con. B: Note

Active vocabulary: *los/las demás*

Con. B: Variation

Have students make up informal commands for the following situations.

1. *para cuando sale para una entrevista para un trabajo*
2. *para cuando conoce a los padres de un nuevo amigo / una nueva amiga*
3. *para cuando su amigo/a quiere comprar una nueva computadora*
4. *para un(a) estudiante de primer año en esta universidad*

Bright Ideas

- Have students indicate if they should use the formal or informal commands with the following people.
  1. *su hermano/a*
  2. *su profesor(a)*
  3. *su médico/a*
  4. *su jefe/a*
  5. *su mejor amigo/a*
  6. *un compañero o una compañera de clase*
- *Consejos a una amiga. Roberta quiere mantenerse sana. Conteste sus preguntas usando los mandatos informales.*
  1. *¿Debo comer papas fritas tres veces a la semana?*

(← Cont.)

2. *¿Debo hacer ejercicio todos los días?*
3. *¿Debo fumar más?*
4. *¿Debo tomar más vino?*
5. *¿Debo pedir dos postres en los restaurantes?*
6. *¿Debo acostarme temprano por la noche?*

Con. C: Suggestion

After doing *Paso 1*, have students share their commands with the whole class. Write particularly unique or interesting commands on the board, as models for students to use in *Paso 2*.

Con. C: Extension

4. *A Celia le encanta ir al cine, especialmente los viernes por la noche. Pero su novio siempre está muy cansado todos los viernes después de una larga semana de trabajo. Celia, en cambio* (new), *quiere salir a divertirse.*

Con. C: Optional

Have students write a letter to a columnist for a popular magazine for their age group. Have them present serious or complex problems in their letters. Have students complete the letters as homework, then have them read their letters to the class so that others can offer advice using *tú* commands.

Grammar 34
Present Subjunctive: An Introduction

Suggestions

- Students should be able to read and understand the *GEA* with little difficulty. Note that the footnoted translation gives not only a good English translation but a literal one at times. *Comprensión* allows students to use the subjunctive structure. You may wish to allow them to answer just *sí* or *no*.
- Ask students to tell you what kinds of information are highlighted in the *GEA*. For this *GEA*, some words are in boldface (the verb in the independent clause) and some are in red (the subjunctive verb). Students will not be able to use that vocabulary to describe these features, but they should be able to find them and tell you something about them. Ask what additional feature is in all of the sentences: the use of the word *que*. Ask if there is anything else that is common about the sentences: two of them involve influence of some kind (*quiero, es muy importante*), one involves emotion (*espero*), a fourth probability (*es probable*). Finally, ask students to tell you about the verbs used after *que*, both in the *GEA* and in *Comprensión*. They should be able to see that the "opposite" vowel is used. Now you can summarize the main characteristics

C. Situaciones

Paso 1. Imagine que estas personas son sus amigos. Déles consejos en forma de mandatos informales.

1. El señor Valderrama es un anciano que vive en el edificio de apartamentos donde vive Ud. Tiene que comprarse una televisión nueva y tiene muchas preguntas. También le gustaría tener una computadora, pero no tiene mucha experiencia en aparatos electrónicos.
2. Su amiga Mariana trabaja demasiado. Duerme poco y bebe muchísimo café. Jamás hace ejercicio. Siempre está mirando su iPhone.
3. Su prima Sara vive sola en una casa grande en la mejor zona de la ciudad, con dos perros y dos gatos. Tiene demasiados gastos para su sueldo. Antes, sus abuelos le mandaban dinero, pero ahora ellos viven en una residencia de ancianos y no pueden seguir mandándoselo.

Paso 2. Ahora, en parejas, inventen una situación como las del **Paso 1.** Luego, léanla a la clase. Sus compañeros van a dar los consejos.

34 Expressing Subjective Actions or States
Present Subjunctive (Part 1): An Introduction

Grammar Tutorial 34
connect SPANISH
www.connectspanish.com

Gramática en acción: Manuela busca apartamento

—Por supuesto, **quiero que** esté en un buen barrio.
—Claro, por eso **es muy importante que** haya una parada del autobús cerca.
—Sí, ¡**espero que** mi sueldo sea suficiente para el alquiler y todos los gastos mensuales!
—¿El depósito? **Es probable que** mis padres me den el dinero para pagarlo.

Comprensión

Según lo que dice Manuela por teléfono, ¿es probable que…

1. Manuela esté hablando con su mejor amiga? sí
2. Manuela tenga un perro? no
3. Manuela no tenga coche? sí
4. Manuela viva en una ciudad grande? sí
5. los padres de Manuela estén preocupados por la situación económica de su hija? sí

Present Subjunctive / El presente de subjuntivo

1. Indicative Mood

Except for **Ud./Uds.** and negative **tú** commands, all the verb forms you have learned so far in *Puntos de partida* are part of the *indicative mood* (**el modo indicativo**). In both English and Spanish, the indicative is used to state facts and to ask questions; it objectively expresses what the speaker considers to be true.

El modo indicativo

Prefiero llegar temprano a casa.
I prefer getting home early.

¿**Vienes** a la fiesta, ¿verdad?
You're coming to the party, right?

Manuela is looking for an apartment *—"Naturally, I want it to be (lit., that it be) in a good neighborhood." —"Of course, that's why it's really important for there to be (lit., that there be) a bus stop nearby." —"Yes, I hope (that) my salary will be enough for the rent and all the monthly expenses!" —"The deposit? It's probable that my parents will give me the money to pay it."*

Heritage Speakers

Invite a los hispanohablantes a inventar el otro lado de la conversación telefónica. Luego invite a dos estudiantes a dramatizar el *GEA* para la clase.

2. Subjunctive Mood

Both English and Spanish have another verb system called the *subjunctive mood* (**el modo subjuntivo**). The subjunctive is used to express the speaker's desires or opinions, as well as ideas that are not a reality. These include things that the speaker

- wants to happen or wants others to do
- reacts to emotionally
- does not yet know to be true

To sum up:

- indicative = objective reality (speaker knows it)
- subjunctive = subjective or conceptual actions or states (that is, in the mind of the speaker)

El modo subjuntivo

Prefiero que llegues temprano a casa.
I prefer for you to be (that you be) home early.

Espero que vengas a la fiesta.
I hope (that) you're coming to the party.

Es probable que vengas a la fiesta, ¿no?
You're probably coming (It's probable that you will come) to the party, aren't you?

3. Simple vs. Complex Sentences

In English and in Spanish, sentences may be simple or complex.

- a *simple sentence* (**una oración simple**) has one conjugated verb
- a *complex sentence* (**una oración compleja**) has two or more *clauses* (**las cláusulas**), each with a conjugated verb

There are two types of clauses: main and subordinate.

- *Main clauses* (**Las cláusulas principales**) (① in the sentences to the right) express an idea that controls the subordinate clause. These are also called independent clauses.
- *Subordinate clauses* (**Las cláusulas subordinadas**) (② in the sentences to the right) contain an incomplete thought and cannot stand alone. They require a main clause to form a complete sentence. Because they depend on the main clause, they are also called dependent clauses. In English, they can begin with the introductory word *that*, but the introductory word is often omitted in English. In Spanish they begin with **que**, which is *never optional*.

a clause / **una cláusula** = a group of words that contains a subject and a verb

Oraciones simples

Vienes a la fiesta. *You are coming to the party.*	Alicia **está** en casa. *Alicia is at home.*

Oraciones complejas
El indicativo

①		②
Ella **sabe** *She knows*	**que** *(that)*	**vienes** a la fiesta. *you're coming to the party.*
Miguel **piensa** *Miguel thinks*	**que** *(that)*	Alicia **está** en casa. *Alicia is at home.*

El subjuntivo

①		②
Quiere *She wants*	**que** *(for)*	vengas a la fiesta. *you to come to the party.*
Miguel **espera** *Miguel hopes*	**que** *(that)*	Alicia esté en casa. *Alicia is at home.*
Duda *She doubts*	**que** *(that)*	vengas a la fiesta. *you're coming to the party.*

4. Use of the Subjunctive in Subordinate Clauses

When the subjects of the clauses in a complex sentence are different, the subjunctive is often used in the subordinate clause in Spanish.

①		②
first subject = indicative	**que**	second subject = subjunctive

of the subjunctive on the board or on an overhead, as a general introduction to the topic: two-clause sentences, the word *que*, indicative (influence, emotion, probability) in the first clause, a change of subject in the second clause, where the verb is in the subjunctive.

- Ask students to invent the other half of the telephone conversation.

Gramática 34 Present Subjunctive: An Introduction

Present Subjunctive

Note

The subjunctive is a difficult concept for native speakers of English, and most will need years of practice and immersion to master it. Aim at conceptual awareness and partial control at the elementary level. Partial control means that students are aware of the existence of the subjunctive and know the rules of use and the forms, but that, in general, they only produce it in well-guided contexts.

Emphasis 2: Suggestion

Point out that the subjunctive also exists in English and offer examples.

God bless you.
I suggest you be there at one.
If I were a rich man, . . .

Emphasis 3: Suggestions

- Emphasize the use of the circled numbers to indicate the main and subordinate clauses respectively in examples. The main clause verb will be in boldface, the subordinate clause verb (when it is subjunctive) will be in red. This system will be used throughout the rest of the text.
- Emphasize that in English, the conjunction *that* is often optional, but *que* is required in Spanish. It can never be omitted.

Emphasis 4: Suggestions

- Emphasize the syntactic requirements for the subjunctive.
  1. two clauses
  2. a different subject in each clause
- To illustrate the sentence structure, use the diagram at the bottom of the page that points out the different subjects and their corresponding verbs in the indicative and subjunctive.

Heritage Speakers

Pregúnteles a los hispanohablantes si su familia usa normalmente la expresión «Que Dios te/lo/la bendiga». Es comúnmente usada por los adultos en Puerto Rico para despedir a los jóvenes.

Emphasis 6: Suggestions

- Ask students to give you the first and second subjects in the paradigm sentences in this point. They are the same in all four sentences: *yo, mis padres*.
- Point out that these uses of the subjunctive were shown in the *GEA* at the beginning of this section. Go back to the *GEA* and reread it with students, pointing out the syntactic and lexical features of the subjunctive again.
- Emphasize that students will practice all three uses of the subjunctive (doubt/denial being one use) in this grammar section. Ask them always to be alert to the verb in the main clause (that is, the subjunctive-causing verb) and to ask themselves into which of the three uses the verb falls.

Forms of the Present Subjunctive

Suggestions

- Emphasize the relationship of the *Ud./Uds.* and negative *tú* commands to the subjunctive.
- Emphasize that the personal endings in this tense of the subjunctive mood are the same as those of the present indicative (*-s, -mos,* and so on).
- Using brief sentences, present the subjunctive forms of *trabajar*. Write the forms on the board as they are produced.

  Yo quiero que Uds. trabajen mucho.
  ¿Quieren Uds. que yo trabaje mucho?
  ¿Quiero que John trabaje mucho?, and so on.

  Present additional sentences with *beber* and *recibir.*
- Provide some common expressions with the subjunctive.

  Que te vaya bien.
  Que Dios te bendiga.
- Emphasize the forms of the subjunctive only for student production, but use full syntax in your input.
- Use simple subjunctive-causing phrases such as *Quiero que…* and *Espero que…* when having students practice forming the subjunctive so they will associate the mood with expressions of influence, emotion, and doubt/denial, or introduce *Ojalá que…*

5. Same Subject ⟶ Infinitive
As you already know, when there is no change of subject in the sentence, the infinitive follows the conjugated verb and no conjunction is necessary. In this type of sentence, the infinitive is the direct object of the conjugated verb.

Quiero ir a la fiesta.
I want to go to the party.

6. Common Uses of the Subjunctive
In Spanish, the subjunctive is commonly used in the subordinate clause when the main clause verb expresses *influence, emotion,* or *doubt* or *denial,* ***and*** when there is a different subject in the main and subordinate clauses. You will practice all of these uses of the subjunctive in this grammar section, and you will learn more about each of them in **Gramática 38, 39,** and **40.**

Influencia: **Necesito** que mis padres me den más dinero.
Emoción: **Espero** que mis padres me den más dinero.
Duda: **Dudo** que mis padres me den más dinero.
Negación: **No creo** que mis padres me den más dinero.

Forms of the Present Subjunctive / Las formas del presente de subjuntivo

The **Ud./Uds.** and negative **tú** command forms that you have already learned are part of the subjunctive system. They are shaded in the following box. What you have learned about forming those commands will help you learn the forms of the present subjunctive.

	hablar: habl-	**comer: com-**	**escribir: escrib-**	**volver: vuelv-**	**decir: dig-**
Singular	hable hables hable	coma comas coma	escriba escribas escriba	vuelva vuelvas vuelva	diga digas diga
Plural	hablemos habléis hablen	comamos comáis coman	escribamos escribáis escriban	volvamos volváis vuelvan	digamos digáis digan

1. Present Indicative *yo* Stem + Present Subjunctive Endings
The personal endings of the present subjunctive are formed with the "opposite" vowel. They are added to the first person singular (**yo**) of the present indicative, minus its **-o** ending: **habl-, com-, escrib-, vuelv-, dig-,** as shown in the preceding chart.

Terminaciones del presente de subjuntivo
-ar: **-e, -es, -e, -emos, -éis, -en**
-er/-ir: **-a, -as, -a, -amos, -ais, -an**

¡OJO!
present subjunctive stem = present indicative **yo** form minus **-o**

2. *-ar* and *-er* Stem-changing Verbs
These verbs follow the stem-changing pattern of the present indicative.

pensar (pienso):	**piense** **pienses** **piense**	**pensemos** **penséis** **piensen**
poder (puedo):	**pueda** **puedas** **pueda**	**podamos** **podáis** **puedan**

3. *-ir* Stem-changing Verbs

The present subjunctive of **-ir** stem-changing verbs has the same stem change as that of the present indicative when the stem vowel is stressed.

- **preferir: e ⟶ ie**
- **pedir: e ⟶ i**
- **dormir: o ⟶ ue**

In addition, these verbs show a second stem change in the **nosotros** and **vosotros** forms.

- e ⟶ i
- o ⟶ u

This is *the same change* that happens in the present participle (**-ndo**) and in the third person singular and plural of the preterite of **-ir** stem-changing verbs, so you have already learned to make it.

- **preferir (prefiero) (i)**

prefiera	**prefiramos**
prefieras	**prefiráis**
prefiera	**prefieran**

prefiriendo / prefirió, prefirieron

Remember that when infinitives appear in vocabulary lists, the stem changes are always indicated. All you have to do is remember where they occur.

- **pedir (pido) (i)**

pida	**pidamos**
pidas	**pidáis**
pida	**pidan**

pidiendo / pidió, pidieron

- **dormir (duermo) (u)**

duerma	**durmamos**
duermas	**durmáis**
duerma	**duerman**

durmiendo / durmió, durmieron

4. Verbs Ending in *-car, -gar,* and *-zar*

These verbs have a spelling change in all persons of the present subjunctive to preserve the **c, g,** and **z** sounds. This is the same change that happens in the **Uds./Uds.** commands, in the negative **tú** commands, and in the first person singular of the preterite of these verbs.

- **-car: c ⟶ qu**
- **-gar: g ⟶ gu**
- **-zar: z ⟶ c**

buscar (qu)		**pagar (gu)**		**empezar (c)**	
busque	**busquemos**	**pague**	**paguemos**	**empiece**	**empecemos**
busques	**busquéis**	**pagues**	**paguéis**	**empieces**	**empecéis**
busque	**busquen**	**pague**	**paguen**	**empiece**	**empiecen**
busque(n), no busques, busqué		**pague(n), no pagues, pagué**		**empiece(n), no empieces, empecé**	

5. Verbs with Irregular *yo* Forms

Since the present subjunctive stem is the **yo** form of the present indicative (minus **-o**), verbs with irregular **yo** forms in the present indicative show that irregularity in *all* persons of the present subjunctive.

conocer:	**conozca,...**	salir:	**salga,...**
decir:	**diga,...**	tener:	**tenga,...**
hacer:	**haga,...**	traer:	**traiga,...**
oír:	**oiga,...**	venir:	**venga,...**
poner:	**ponga,...**	ver:	**vea,...**

6. Irregular Verbs

A few verbs have irregular present subjunctive forms.

dar:	**dé, des, dé, demos, deis, den**
estar:	**esté,...**
ir:	**vaya,...**
saber:	**sepa,...**
ser:	**sea,...**

7. Present Subjunctive of *haber*

Remember that the infinitive form of **hay** is **haber.** The present subjunctive of **hay** is **haya.**

Espero que no **haya** mucha contaminación en la ciudad.
I hope there won't be a lot of pollution in the city.

No creo que **haya** clases mañana.
I don't think that there are any classes tomorrow.

Emphasis 3: Suggestions

- Continue to use simple subjunctive-causing phrases such as *Quiero que…* as semantic cues when having students practice forming the subjunctive so they will associate the mood with expressions of influence, emotion, and doubt/denial.
- Emphasize the second stem-change and its connection to the present participle and preterite forms.

Emphasis 4: Suggestions

- Emphasize the connection of the subjunctive forms of spelling-change verbs to the command forms shown and to the first person preterite.
- Briefly present *-ar* and *-er* spelling change verbs, pointing out that the spelling changes occur in all persons of the subjunctive.

Emphasis 5, 6: Suggestion

Briefly model the subjunctive forms of irregular verbs in communicative exchanges with students, asking one or two questions using each verb. Continue to use only *Quiero que…* as the semantic cue or introduce *Ojalá que.*

Emphasis 7: Suggestions

- Emphasize that the subjunctive of *hay* is *haya* and that, like *hay* and *había,* it is impersonal and does not change to the plural form before a plural noun.
- The full conjugation of *haber* as an auxiliary verb is presented in *Cap. 15,* with the present perfect (indicative and subjunctive).

Heritage Speakers

En el español estándar, la forma aceptada del presente de subjuntivo del verbo *haber* es *haya*. Sin embargo, algunos hispanohablantes dicen *haiga* en vez de *haya*. Este fenómeno es del habla cotidiana. No es una forma aceptada en la lengua formal.

Preliminary Exercises

- Read each verb form and have students tell whether it is in the present indicative or present subjunctive.

-ar:	*baile*	*hablemos*
	cena	*miramos*
	lleguemos	*buscan*
	pago	*te olvides*
	recuerde	
-er/-ir:	*aprende*	*recibo*
	aprenda	*beban*
	lea	*digo*
	leemos	*pongamos*
	escribamos	*traigan*
	coma	*sabe*
	asisten	*sepan*

- Use the following chain drill to practice the subjunctive forms:

1. *En clase: El profesor no quiere que Uds. se duerman.* (*yo, nosotros, tú, los estudiantes, Lupe, vosotros*)
2. *En casa, el día antes de la fiesta, es necesario que alguien llame a nuestros amigos.* (*comprar las bebidas, buscar los CDs, invitar a María, traer la salsa*)

Prác. A, B: Note

Both activities call for passive recognition of subjunctive forms and structures.

Prác. A: Suggestions

- After students have read the items on their own, ask them to identify the sentences that have the subjunctive in them (items 3, 4, 7, and 8), then to identify the subjunctive verb forms and the other elements of the subjunctive (two clauses, two subjects, subjunctive-causing verb in the main clause, *que*).
- Ask for a show of hands for each item to see which students agree with each statement. Ask students to explain their reasons and/or encourage whole-class discussion of each topic, as appropriate.

Prác. A: Note

Active vocabulary: *el teléfono fijo*

Prác. B: Suggestions

- Ask students which column contains the main clause and which has the subordinate clause.
- Ask students which of the three uses of the subjunctive (influence, emotion, doubt/denial) each of the main clause verbs represents.

Prác. B: Note

Active vocabulary: *dudar, esperar* (to hope), *prohibir*

Endings of the Present Subjunctive

-ar → -e
-er/-ir → -a

Autoprueba

Complete each verb form with the correct letters to form the subjunctive.

1. conocer: cono_____amos
2. decir: di_____an
3. sacar: sa_____es
4. entregar: entre_____en
5. conseguir: consi_____an
6. morir: m_____ramos

Answers: 1. cono**zc**amos 2. di**g**an 3. sa**qu**es 4. entre**gu**en 5. consi**g**an 6. m**u**ramos.

Práctica

A. ¡Anticipemos! ¿Están todos de acuerdo? Diga si Ud. está de acuerdo o no con las siguientes declaraciones.

	ESTOY DE ACUERDO	NO ESTOY DE ACUERDO
Para buscar una vivienda		
1. Es importante informarse sobre las zonas de una ciudad antes de alquilar un apartamento.	☐	☐
2. Se recomienda leer los anuncios clasificados de viviendas.	☐	☐
3. Todos esperan que sus vecinos sean buenas personas y no hagan ruido.	☐	☐
4. A mucha gente no le importa que la calle tenga mucho tráfico y sea ruidosa (*noisy*).	☐	☐
Sobre la tecnología		
5. Todo el mundo desea tener muchos amigos en Facebook.	☐	☐
6. No es necesario tener un teléfono fijo (*land line*) si uno tiene un celular.	☐	☐
7. Me molesta que algunos estudiantes manden mensajes cuando estamos en clase.	☐	☐
8. Dudo que haya mucha gente sin acceso al Internet en este país.	☐	☐

B. El mundo del trabajo. Use frases de la lista de la derecha para completar las oraciones de modo (*in such a way*) que se refieran a su situación en el trabajo. (Siempre hay más de una respuesta posible.) Si Ud. no trabaja ahora, no importa. ¡Invéntese una respuesta!

1. La jefa quiere que _____.
2. También espera (*she hopes*) que _____.
3. Y duda que _____.
4. Prohíbe (*She forbids*) que _____.
5. En el trabajo, es importante que _____.
6. Yo espero que _____.
7. No me gusta que _____.
8. Es difícil que _____.

a. a veces trabajemos los sábados
b. todos lleguemos a tiempo
c. hablemos por teléfono con los amigos
d. me den un aumento de sueldo
e. nos paguen más a todos
f. no usemos el escáner para asuntos (*matters*) personales
g. me den un trabajo de tiempo completo algún día
h. no perdamos tiempo charlando (*chatting*) con los demás
i. escribamos e-mails personales en la oficina
j. me den otro proyecto (*project*)
k. ¿ ?

Prác. B: Variation

Change the context to *los estudiantes de la clase de español.* Have students make all other necessary changes, keeping the main clause verbs.

Conversación

A. ¿Puede Ud. substituir a su profesor(a) en el salón de clase? Demuéstrele a su profesor(a) que Ud. lo/la conoce bien, haciendo oraciones como las que dice él/ella en clase. (Solo tiene que cambiar el infinitivo.)

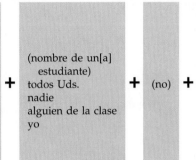

quiero que espero que prohíbo que dudo que es necesario que me alegro de (*I'm glad*) que no creo que recomiendo que	+	(nombre de un[a] estudiante) todos Uds. nadie alguien de la clase yo	+	(no)	+	copiar en un examen dormirse en clase entrar en el Internet estar en Facebook estudiar hacer la tarea llegar a tiempo saber el subjuntivo sacar notas mejores tener un blog ¿ ?

B. Cómo dar una buena fiesta

Paso 1. Haga una lista de las cosas que hay que hacer para dar una fiesta exitosa (*successful*), en su opinión. Use infinitivos en su lista.

MODELOS: llamar a los amigos con anticipación (*ahead of time*)
comprar…

Paso 2. En parejas, comparen sus listas del **Paso 1** y hagan una sola lista de por lo menos diez acciones.

Paso 3. Luego conviertan la lista en una serie de recomendaciones para dar una buena fiesta.

MODELO: Recomendamos que llamen a los amigos con anticipación.

Vocabulario útil

Es necesario/bueno/importante/esencial que…
Recomendamos que…
Sugerimos que…
} + *subjuntivo*

¿Recuerda Ud.?

In **Gramática 35** and in the grammar sections of **Capítulo 13,** you will learn more about the three major uses of the subjunctive. Review what you have learned so far by answering the following questions.

1. How many clauses are in a sentence that contains the subjunctive in Spanish? two
2. In which clause does the subjunctive appear? subordinate (dependent) clause
3. In which clause does the indicative appear? main (independent) clause
4. What word must always appear? *que*
5. What do you know about the subjects in each clause? They are different.

Con.: Note

No partner/pair activities (except for *Con. B, Pasos 2–3*) are provided for this section, although you could easily transform all of *Con. A* and *B* into pair work, if you think your students are ready for that challenge. Otherwise, do *A* and *B* as whole-class activities so that you can monitor students' use of the subjunctive at this early stage.

Con. A: Note

Active vocabulary: *alegrarse de*

Con. A: Variation

Have students dictate what professors must do, using the phrases in *Con. A* as models and providing their own ending phrases.

Con. B: Suggestion

If your class is small enough, have students do this activity in small groups, working at the board. Conclude by having students read aloud all of the lists, critique them, and vote for the best list.

Con. B: Follow-up

Have students tell what advice their family and friends give them on a regular basis, e.g., *Mis padres recomiendan que yo consiga trabajo en la librería.*

Redacción: Assign *Con. B* as a composition, allowing students to submit their lists as a pair or, if they have worked in groups, as a group activity.

Con. B: Optional

Do the activity in the same sequence of *Pasos* but with *Cómo comprar y usar una computadora* as the topic. Give students these possible infinitive phrases for the dependent clause.

hablar con un amigo que entiende la tecnología
leer revistas especializadas / los anuncios en los periódicos
ir a (name of a local computer store)
comprar (*marca, modelo*)
no usar (*marca, tipo de software*)
poner la computadora en (*lugar*)

Gramática 35
Use of the Subjunctive: Influence

GEA: Follow-up

Ask students the following questions about the pairs of sentences that introduce this section.

¿Qué diferencia hay entre el significado de las oraciones en cada par?
¿Cuál es la diferencia lingüística?

Emphasis 2: Suggestions

- Point out that when an expression of influence is followed by a subject change, the subjunctive is required.

  La madre quiere que los niños estén contentos.
  Ask who wants (→ *la madre*).
  Ask who should be happy (→ *los niños*).
- Point out that when there is no subject change, the infinitive is used, just as in English.

  Quiero estar contento.
  Ask who wants (→ *yo*).
  Ask who would like to be happy (→ *yo*).
- Point out that influence implies that the speaker wants (expects/hopes/dreams) to affect somebody's behavior or even his/her own. The influence can be exerted from a power position (using verbs such as *ordenar, insistir en, pedir, mandar, exigir,* and *prohibir*) to the humblest position (*suplicar* [new] and *desear*).

Emphasis 3: Note

- *Decir* and *insistir en* are verbs of both information and influence, depending on the context. When the verbs are informative, they trigger the indicative in subordinate clauses.

  Carolina nos dice que llegan a las siete. = Carolina tells (informs) us that they will arrive at 7:00.
  Insisto en que son amigos. = I insist (maintain) that they are friends (not enemies).

  When the verbs imply influence, they trigger the subjunctive.

  Carolina nos dice que lleguemos a las siete. = Carolina tells us to arrive at 7:00.
  Insisto en que sean amigos. = I insist that they be(come) friends.

Emphasis 3, 4: Suggestion

Point out that there are many other verbs and impersonal expressions of influence that can trigger the use of the subjunctive in the subordinate clause.

35 Expressing Desires and Requests
Use of the Subjunctive (Part 2): Influence

Grammar Tutorial 35
connect SPANISH
www.connectspanish.com

Gramática en acción: ¿Quién debe hacerlo?

Comprensión

Escoja la oración que describa cada dibujo.

1. __b__ **a.** Quiero aprender las formas del subjuntivo.
   b. Quiero que aprendamos juntos las formas del subjuntivo.

2. __b__ **a.** Insisto en hablar con Jorge.
   b. Insisto en que hables con Jorge.

3. __a__ **a.** Es necesario arreglar esta habitación.
   b. Es necesario que arregles esta habitación.

1. Features of the Subjunctive

So far, you have learned to identify the subjunctive by the features listed at the right.

- appears in a subordinate clause
- has a different subject from the one in the main clause
- is preceded by **que**

In addition, the subjunctive is associated with three concepts or conditions that "trigger" the use of it in the subordinate clause: influence, emotion, and doubt or denial.

2. The Concept of Influence

①		②
first subject = indicative	**que**	second subject = subjunctive
INFLUENCE		

One trigger for the use of the subjunctive in the subordinate clause is the concept of *influence* (**la influencia**). The subject of the main clause *wants, prefers, insists,* and so on, that the subject of the subordinate clause do something, expressed by a verb in the subjunctive. The verb in the main clause is always in the indicative.

La influencia

①		②
Yo **quiero** *I want*	**que**	tú **pagues** la cuenta. *you to pay the bill.*
La profesora **prefiere** *The professor prefers*	**que** *that*	los estudiantes no **lleguen** tarde. *students don't arrive late.*

Resources: Transparency 83

3. Verbs of Influence

There are many other verbs of influence, some very strong and direct, some very soft and polite.

STRONG(ER)	SOFT(ER)
insistir en	**desear**
mandar (*to order*)	**pedir (pido) (i)**
permitir (*to permit, allow*)	**preferir (prefiero) (i)**
prohibir (prohíbo)	**recomendar (recomiendo)**
querer (quiero)	**sugerir (sugiero) (i)** (*to suggest*)

4. Impersonal Expressions of Influence

An impersonal generalization (**es** + *adjective*) can also be the main clause that triggers the subjunctive. There are many of these expressions in Spanish. The subject of the impersonal expression of influence is *it* (expressed by the verb **es**), and the subjunctive is used when there is another subject in the sentence.

Es necesario que / **Es urgente** que / **Es mejor** que } Paco **estudie** español.

¡OJO!

As you know, when there is no second subject, the infinitive follows impersonal expressions in Spanish: **Es bueno estudiar** español.

Práctica

A. ¡Anticipemos! ¿Cierto o falso?

Paso 1. Diga si las siguientes ideas son ciertas o falsas para Ud.

	CIERTO	FALSO
1. Siempre insisto en que mis compañeros de cuarto bajen (mi esposo/a, novio/a baje) el volumen de la música.	☐	☐
2. No quiero que nadie use mi computadora.	☐	☐
3. Prohíbo que mi compañero de cuarto (esposo/a, novio/a) toque mis cosas.	☐	☐
4. No es necesario que me pidan permiso antes de usar algo mío (*of mine*).	☐	☐
5. Prefiero que alguien me baje las nuevas apps en la computadora, porque soy muy torpe (*clumsy*) en asuntos de la tecnología.	☐	☐
6. Deseo que se prohíba el uso de los celulares en los edificios de la universidad, porque interrumpen las clases.	☐	☐

Paso 2. Ahora, en parejas, entrevístense sobre las ideas del **Paso 1.**

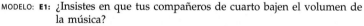

MODELO: **E1:** ¿Insistes en que tus compañeros de cuarto bajen el volumen de la música?

E2: Yo nunca insisto en que mis compañeros de cuarto bajen el volumen de la música.

Paso 3. Digan a la clase lo que Uds. tienen en común.

Autoprueba

Indicate the sentences that have subordinate clauses with the subjunctive.

1. ☐ Quiero ir a la tienda
2. ☐ Prohíben que los estudiantes usen calculadoras.
3. ☐ Es urgente que vayas ahora.
4. ☐ Sé que estudias mucho.
5. ☐ ¿Quieres que te lo diga todo?

Answers: 2, 3, 5

Emphasis 4: Suggestions

- Students have used impersonal expressions + *inf.* since the beginning of this text. Emphasize the need for the second subject after expressions of generalization for the subjunctive to be used.
- Tell students that it is impossible to provide a list of *all* impersonal expressions of influence that can trigger the subjunctive. Students should be alert to the concept of influence in a generalization.
- Either the subjunctive construction or the infinitive may be used with the verbs *mandar, permitir,* and *prohibir.*

  Mi padre prohíbe que yo vaya al cine solo.
  Mi padre me prohíbe ir al cine solo.

  Other similar verbs are *aconsejar, dejar, hacer,* and *impedir.*

Prác A: Note

Examples and activities in this and subsequent sections avoid the use of indirect object pronouns in the main clause (*… me recomiendan que…*) except in very guided situations.

Preliminary Exercises

- Have students express the following in Spanish.
  1. It's important to do it.
  2. It's important for Alice to do it.
  3. It's necessary to leave now.
  4. It's necessary that we leave now.
- Have students work in groups to make a list of five things that they would like other people to do. Then have them present requests to someone in class, who must either do it or give a good excuse for not doing it.

  Queremos que Roberto nos traiga donuts mañana. → Lo siento. No les puedo traer donuts porque no tengo dinero.

Prác. A: Suggestion

Ask students to analyze the elements of each sentence: 2 clauses, 2 subjects, indicative verb, *que,* subjunctive verb.

Prác. A: Reciclado

Have students give formal commands for these situations. If it is a request, encourage them to use *por favor* and an appropriate tone.

Prác. C: Suggestions

- Ask students to tell which subjunctive concept (influence, emotion, or doubt/denial) the main clauses represent.
- Add additional items to expand the activity.

Prác.: Optional

Give students commands, and have them report what you want them to do.

¡No fume Ud.! → Ud. no quiere que yo fume.

1. *Grabe el programa.*
2. *No crea eso.*
3. *No cambie de canal.*
4. *Tráigame el control remoto.*
5. *No diga eso.*
6. *No me llame.*
7. *Escúchela.*
8. *Espérelo.*
9. *No nos busque.*
10. *Sírvalos.*

Con. A: Note

This is the first activity in which the word *que* is not explicitly provided (although it is included in the model) and in which students are not given instructions about where to use the subjunctive (although, again, the usage is modeled). If your students are struggling with this concept, you may wish to review the structure provided in the model, emphasizing main clause = indicative, *que*, subordinate clause = subjunctive.

Bright Idea

Con. A: Suggestion

Have students give sentences that describe what you, the instructor, want / insist on / permit, and so on from them, and vice versa.

Prác. B: Answers: 1. *Los profesores quieren que los estudiantes lleguen a clase a tiempo.* **2.** *Los profesores prohíben que los estudiantes traigan comida y bebidas a clase.* **3.** *Los profesores insisten en que entreguemos la tarea a tiempo.* **4.** *Los estudiantes piden que los profesores no les den mucho trabajo.* **5.** *También quieren que haya más vacaciones.* **6.** *Los padres insisten en que sus hijos saquen buenas notas.*

B. Expectativas (*Expectations*) **de la educación**

Paso 1. ¿Qué esperan durante el año académico los profesores, los estudiantes y los padres de los estudiantes? Haga oraciones según las indicaciones. Añada (*Add*) todas las palabras necesarias, conjugue los infinitivos de los verbos y use el subjuntivo en la cláusula subordinada.

MODELO: padres / querer / que / hijos / estudiar →
Los padres **quieren** que **sus** hijos **estudien.**

1. profesores / querer / que / estudiantes / llegar a clase / a tiempo
2. profesores / prohibir / que / estudiantes / traer comida y bebidas / clase
3. profesores / insistir en / que / (nosotros) entregar la tarea / a tiempo
4. estudiantes / pedir / que / profesores / no darles / mucho trabajo
5. también / (ellos) querer / que / haber más vacaciones
6. padres / insistir en / que / hijos / sacar buenas notas

Paso 2. Y Ud., ¿qué quiere que hagan los profesores? Invente otras tres oraciones para indicar sus deseos.

C. Una mudanza (*move*). Imagine que Ud. y sus compañeros de casa o su familia se van a mudar a otra casa o apartamento. ¿Dónde van a poner las siguientes cosas? Explique por qué las ponen en ese sitio.

MODELO: **Queremos que** la televisión de pantalla plana **esté** en la sala, porque nos gusta mirar la tele allí.

queremos que… es mejor que… es necesario que… es buena idea que… nos gusta que…	+	la televisión de pantalla plana la impresora el teléfono fijo las bicicletas el equipo de música el sofá el radio	+	una de las alcobas el baño la cocina el comedor el estudio el garaje el patio la sala

Conversación

A. ¿Qué quiere Ud.?

Paso 1. En parejas, hablen de afectar las acciones de otras personas.

MODELO: E1: ¿Qué quieres que haga tu padre?
E2: **Quiero que** mi padre me **compre** una computadora.

querer preferir insistir en mandar permitir prohibir recomendar	+	padre/madre amigos/as hermana profesor(a) novio/a esposo/a compañero/a de cuarto hijo/a, hijos ¿ ?	+	comprarme… (una televisión, rosas, ¿ ?) visitarme… (mañana, el jueves, ¿ ?) invitarme… (al cine, a cenar, ¿ ?) (no) dar tarea… (hoy, mañana, ¿ ?) ayudarme… (en los quehaceres, a hacer la tarea, ¿ ?) salir con… (otra persona, mi amigo, ¿ ?) llamarme… (todos los días, el viernes, ¿ ?) explicarme… (la gramática, ¿ ?) ¿ ?

Paso 2. Ahora hablen de las cosas que otras personas quieren, prefieren, permiten, etcétera, que Uds. hagan.

MODELO: E1: ¿Qué quieren tus hijos que hagas?
E2: Quieren que yo compre una computadora nueva.

B. El programa *Te escucho*. *Te escucho* es un programa de radio que da consejos sobre todo tipo de problemas. En esta ocasión son problemas relacionados con el uso y abuso de la tecnología. En parejas, imaginen que Uds. son los presentadores del programa y preparen las respuestas a las siguientes preguntas de algunos radioyentes. Lean lo que dicen las siguientes personas y preparen las respuestas que Uds. creen que los moderadores del programa deben darles.

1. **Habla Hortensia:** «Soy una chica de 20 años. Acabo de mudarme a esta ciudad y tengo pocos amigos aquí. Pero no me siento sola porque siempre estoy conectada en el Internet. Mi madre dice que no es normal que yo pase tantas horas en la computadora y que no salga con los amigos. ¿Qué piensan Uds.? ¿Qué me recomiendan?»
2. **Habla la Sra. Silva:** «Mi esposo es un hombre bueno y responsable. Pero la mayor parte del tiempo que pasa en casa, está en el estudio, en el Internet. Yo no comprendo por qué pasa tanto tiempo en eso. Estoy preocupada y también aburrida. ¿Qué me recomiendan que haga? ¿Qué le debo decir a mi esposo?»
3. **Habla Guillermo, un joven de 17 años:** «Mi hermano de 13 años está en Facebook, lo que es normal. Pero ayer descubrí que pone fotos de él y de toda la familia en el Internet. Yo no quiero que ponga fotos de nosotros, pero él dice que las fotos son de él. Hay una foto horrible de mi madre. No quiero decírselo a mis padres porque tengo miedo de que le quiten la computadora a mi hermano. Pero no sé qué otra cosa puedo hacer. ¿Cuáles son mis opciones? ¿Es mejor que no haga nada?»

Un café de Internet, en Bogotá

Paso 2. Ahora piensen en un problema que se relacione con la tecnología que sea similar a los del **Paso 1.** Descríbanlo por escrito (*in writing*). El resto de la clase les va a hacer sugerencias sobre cómo resolverlo.

Estrategia

Empiecen sus consejos con cláusulas como las siguientes.

Te/Le recomendamos/ sugerimos que...
Es importante/urgente/ necesario que...
Dudamos que...

C. Intercambios

Paso 1. Complete las siguientes oraciones lógicamente... ¡y con sinceridad!

1. Mis padres (hijos, abuelos,...) insisten en que (yo) ____.
2. Mi mejor amigo/a (esposo/a, novio/a,...) desea que (yo) ____.
3. Prefiero que mis amigos ____.
4. No quiero que mis amigos ____.
5. Es urgente que (yo) ____.
6. Es necesario que mi mejor amigo/a (esposo/a, novio/a,...) ____.

Paso 2. Ahora pregúntele a un compañero o compañera cómo completó las oraciones del **Paso 1** para saber algo de su vida.

MODELO: ¿En qué insisten tus padres?

Mundo interactivo

You should now be prepared to work with Scenario 6, Activity 4 in Connect Spanish (**www.connectspanish.com**).

Con. B: Note

The *Estrategia* provides models for using indirect object pronouns in the main clause. You may wish to model several pieces of advice using those pronouns.

Con. B: Suggestions

- Point out that some of the recommendations could be in the form of direct commands. A combination of these with suggestions using the subjunctive is typical for advice.
- Have students decide between *tú* and *Ud.* for each of the two cases. Remind them to think of the issue of formal vs. informal when they get to *Paso 2.*
- *Paso 1.* Have students work in small groups or pairs, then share their findings with the rest of the class.
- *Paso 2.* Assign as written homework for the next class.

Con. C: Follow-up

Have students share and compare their sentences. Write inclusive categories on the board that can be used to tally answers. Ask students if they see any patterns.

NATIONAL STANDARDS: Communities

Point out that call-in talk and advice shows are popular in Spanish-speaking countries as well as among the U.S. Hispanic population. One advice show is broadcast by The Hispanic Network, Inc. (*La Red Hispana*). Have students go to this organization's website to find out what kinds of information their programming offers. Encourage them to look for information on call-in radio shows in Spain and Latin America as well.

Un poco de todo

A: Follow-up

- *Paso 1.* Ask students: *Si Ud. tiene hijos, ¿qué otros mandatos les da a ellos? Si no tiene hijos, ¿qué mandatos recuerda que le daban a Ud. en su niñez?*
- *Paso 2.* Ask students: *¿Qué cosas quieren sus padres, sus hijos o sus amigos que Ud. haga este año? Explique por qué y diga si piensa hacerlo o no.*
- Have students work in small groups. Each member will complete two of the following sentences.

Queremos que el/la líder de este país...
Recomendamos que el/la líder de este país...
Es importante que el/la líder de este país...
Sugerimos que el/la líder de este país...

Have the groups select and then write their three best sentences on the board. Then have students work individually to select sentences from the board and use them to write a letter to the president or prime minister. Have volunteers read their letters and have the class vote for the best letter. The final version can be assigned as homework. For the next day, have them exchange and correct each other's letters.

B: Note

The following grammar topics are included in *Lengua y cultura:* adjective agreement, apocopation of adjectives, superlatives, *ser* vs. *estar* vs. *haber, saber* vs. *conocer,* present indicative and present subjunctive of regular and irregular verbs, imperfect.

Un poco de todo

A. Un niño que no se porta bien

Paso 1. Eduardo Suárez es un niño típico de 8 años: Con frecuencia hace lo que no debe. Lea el mandato que le da su madre (la primera oración de cada par). Luego complete la segunda oración con el mandato opuesto.

MODELO: Eduardo, siéntate en la silla. No ____ (sentarse) en el piso. ⟶ No **te sientes** en el piso.

1. Eduardo, no escuches la radio ahora. Escúchame (Escucharme) a mí cuando te hablo.
2. Niño, por favor, haz tu tarea. No hagas (hacer) eso.
3. ¡Ay, no juegues con la pelota (*ball*) dentro de la casa. Sal (Salir) a jugar afuera.
4. Eduardo, no cantes en la mesa. Canta (Cantar) después de comer.
5. Hijo, dame a mí tu almuerzo. No se lo des (dárselo) al perro.
6. Por favor, pon los pies en el piso. No los pongas (ponerlos) en el sofá.

Paso 2. ¿Qué más quiere la Sra. Suárez que haga Eduardo o que no haga? Indique sus deseos, haciendo dos oraciones para cada situatión del **Paso 1.**

MODELO: La Sra. Suárez prefiere que Eduardo **se siente** en una silla. No quiere que **se siente** en el piso.

Estrategia

Use verbos como los siguientes en la cláusula principal.

desear
esperar
insistir en
permitir
preferir (prefiero) (i)
prohibir (prohíbo)
querer

B. Lengua y cultura: La ciudad de Cartagena, Colombia. Complete the following passage with the correct forms of the words in parentheses, as suggested by context. When two possibilities are given, select the correct word. **¡OJO!** As you conjugate the verbs in this activity, put the infinitives preceded by *I:* in the imperfect. Other verbs will be present indicative, present subjunctive, or infinitive as determined by the context.

Unos edificios de apartamentos muy modernos en Bocagrande

B: Answers: 1. *son* **2.** *gran* **3.** *está* **4.** *vivía* **5.** *de la* **6.** *tiene* **7.** *más* **8.** *mismas* **9.** *que*

Mayra y Joaquín son dos colombianos que llegaron recientemente a este país. Los dos (ser/estar[1]) de Cartagena, una (grande[2]) ciudad colombiana, y también puerto,[a] que (ser/estar[3]) en el mar Caribe. De niña, Mayra (*I:* vivir[4]) en la parte más antigua (en la / de la[5]) ciudad, el Centro Amurallado[b] colonial. La familia de Joaquín (tener[6]) un apartamento en Bocagrande, la zona (más/mejor[7]) moderna de Cartagena. Sin embargo, los dos les hacen las (mismo[8]) recomendaciones a sus amigos (que/quienes[9]) desean visitar la ciudad.

[a]*a port* [b]Centro... *Walled Center*

NATIONAL STANDARDS: Cultures

Cartagena, officially *Cartagena de Indias* (Cartagena of the [West] Indies), to differentiate it from the city of Cartagena in Spain, is located on the northern coast of Colombia, on the Caribbean. It is the 5th largest urban area of Colombia, with a metro population of over 1.2 million inhabitants. It is a common tourist destination, famous for its 16th century fortress, *San Felipe de Barajas.*

Multimedia: Internet

Have students search the Internet for more information on Cartagena, Colombia, including places they would like to visit in and around the city. Have them share their findings with the rest of the class.

Mayra y Joaquín (ser/estar[10]) de acuerdo en que el Centro Amurallado tiene (mucho[11]) cosas que ver. Por eso, los dos recomiendan (que / lo que[12]) sus amigos, turistas en Cartagena, (dar[13]) un paseo por ese centro histórico de la ciudad. También es necesario (que/—[14]) vean y admiren las fortalezas y las murallas.[c] ¿(Saber/Conocer[15]) Uds. que algunas miden veinte metros de ancho[d]? ¡(Ser/Estar[16]) impresionantes! Además[e] (ser/haber[17]) playas muy chéveres, como la playa de La Boquilla* y el Parque Natural Corales del Rosario, en la isla Barú.† Por la noche Mayra y Joaquín (sugerir[18]) que sus amigos visiten un restaurante en la Boquilla y que (pedir[19]) mariscos. Luego deben (ir[20]) a un club a bailar cumbia.

[c]fortalezas... *forts and walls* [d]miden... *are 20 meters thick* [e]*In addition*

10. *están* **11.** *muchas* **12.** *que* **13.** *den* **14.** *que* **15.** *Saben* **16.** *Son* **17.** *hay* **18.** *sugieren* **19.** *pidan* **20.** *ir*

Comprensión

1. ¿De qué ciudad son Mayra y Joaquín? Cartagena, Colombia
2. ¿Qué es lo que distingue la geografía de esta ciudad? Tiene costa en el mar Caribe.
3. ¿En qué partes de la ciudad vivían los dos de niños? Mayra: el centro colonial, el Centro Amurallado; Joaquín: la zona más moderna, Bocagrande
4. ¿Qué recomiendan Mayra y Joaquín que hagan sus amigos que visitan Cartagena? Recomiendan que visiten el centro histórico, admiren las for talezas y murallas, vayan a la playa, pidan mariscos en un restaurante y bailen cumbia.

C. Un mundo ruidoso (*noisy*)

Paso 1. En parejas, contesten las siguientes preguntas.

1. En el mundo de hoy, ¿qué cosas causan ruido?
2. ¿Qué ruidos les molestan más a Uds.?
3. ¿Cuáles son los lugares que Uds. consideren más ruidosos?

Paso 2. Ahora, con otro compañero o otra compañera imaginen que Uds. están a cargo (*in charge*) de hacer una presentación sobre el tema del ruido en el Departmento de Salud Pública. Usando mandatos de **tú,** hagan una lista de reglas (*rules*) sobre las cosas que se deben o no se deben usar y cuándo y dónde.

MODELO: Apaga tu celular antes de entrar en clase.

Vocabulario útil

apagar (gu) to turn off
bajar el volumen to lower the volume
hablar en voz alta/baja to speak loudly/softly
poner

En su comunidad

Entreviste a una persona hispana de su universidad o ciudad sobre su ciudad donde de origen y el barrio donde vivía en su país.

PREGUNTAS POSIBLES

- ¿Qué tipo de ciudad es? ¿Es grande o pequeña? ¿vieja o moderna?
- ¿Hay buenas vistas desde algún punto de la ciudad? ¿Hay un buen sistema de transporte público, como autobuses o metro?
- ¿Dónde vivía su familia? ¿En el centro o en las afueras? ¿en un barrio histórico o moderno? ¿en una casa individual o en un apartamento?
- ¿Cómo es (o era) la vida del barrio? (Pida detalles.)

*La Boquilla *is a fishing village outside of Cartagena; it has a long, secluded beach with restaurants and bars.*
†La isla Barú *is about ten minutes by motorboat from Cartagena. It has white sand beaches, crystal clear water, and big coral reefs.*

Redacción: Using the model of the paragraphs in *B*, ask students to write a similar "article" about attractions in a place they know well, such as the city where your college or university is located, their home town, or a foreign place they have visited. Allow students to use as much of the structure of *B* as they can, and set reasonable expectations for length (something shorter than the text's paragraphs).

After you have corrected the paragraphs, ask a few students to read their paragraphs in class, omitting the place names. The class will try to guess the place that is described in the reader's composition.

En su comunidad

Suggestions

- Remind students to get the following basic information: the informant's country of origin, how long he or she has lived in this country, and if the informant visits his or her country of origin frequently.
- This activity could instead be assigned as an online research project on a country of the student's choice or assigned by you.
- See the IM for additional suggestions and guidelines.

Resources: Desenlace

In the *Cap. 12* segment of "Chapter-by-Chapter Supplementary Materials" in the IM, you will find a chapter-culminating activity. You can use this activity to consolidate and review the vocabulary and grammar skills students have acquired.

TelePuntos

Note

Pages 374–379 are optional. You may cover some, all, or none of this material in class, or assign it to students—as a group or individually—for homework or extra credit. Pages 380–381 (*En resumen: En este capítulo*) are a summary of all of the chapter's active material.

Suggestions

- If you are using the video in class, show it once, ask brief comprehension questions, then show it again.
- Even if you plan to ask students to watch the video in your campus media center or on their own, it is a good idea to continue to stress the need to watch the shows as many times as they want or need to in order to complete the *Después de mirar* activities.

Antes de mirar

Note

In 2011, according to *Forbes* magazine, the 10 richest people in the world were (from top down): Carlos Slim Helú (*Mex.*), Bill Gates (*U.S.*), Warren Buffett (*U.S.*), Bernard Arnault (*France*), Larry Ellison (*U.S.*), Lakshmi Mittal (*India*), Amancio Ortega (*Sp.*), Eike Batista (*Brazil*), Mukesh Ambani (*India*), and Christy Walton (*U.S.*). These ratings can change from year to year.

Suggestion

Ask students to be as precise as possible in answering the first two questions: *¿Creen que en todos los países hay personas que usan la tecnología como Uds. la usan? ¿Cómo son esos usuarios? ¿A qué clase socioeconómica pertenecen? ¿Qué edad y qué nivel educativo tienen?*

Programa 12

Note

Students will find this show to be easily accessible due to the topic and the large amount of cognate vocabulary.

Suggestion

Emphasize to students that the more carefully they study the preliminary activities (*Antes de mirar, Vocabulario de este programa,* and *Fragmento del guion*), the more they will understand. Scanning *Después de mirar* before viewing is also an excellent strategy.

TELEPUNTOS

SALU2

México: América Móvil lanza oferta por Telmex
F. Figueroa Fagandini en Economía, Internet hace 1 año
33 comentarios
Avisos Google
Márcale a tu familia
Habla a Mexico sin limites tarifa fija mensual pruébalo gratis mexico.telehispanic.com
Aunque ambas empresas tienen como accionista mayoritario al grupo Carso, y el grupo Carso es mayoritariamente de Carlos Slim, hasta hoy Telmex y América Móvil (más conocido por sus marcas Claro y Telcel) se han mantenido como empresas independientes, pero eso está a punto de cambiar. Supimos que América Móvil lanzó una oferta de compra de acciones para hacerse con el control de Telmex y Telmex International, que aparentemente ya había sido

América Móvil es la compañía de telefonía móvil más grande de América Latina y la cuarta (*fourth*) en el mundo, con 170 millones de usuarios.

Antes de mirar

¿Qué sabe Ud. del uso de la tecnología en los países de habla española? ¿Cree que su uso en esos países es similar al (*to that*) que tiene en este país? Muchas personas han ganado (*have made*) muchísimo dinero de la tecnología. ¿Sabe Ud. quién es la persona más rica del mundo?

PROGRAMA 12: ¡No sin mi celular!

Este programa trata de la presencia de las nuevas tecnologías en Latinoamérica. Incluye reportajes sobre la compañía América Móvil y sobre los hábitos tecnológicos de unos estudiantes universitarios ecuatorianos.

Vocabulario de este programa

¿Qué tal han estado?	How have you been?	**el uso**	**el hábito**
inconcebible	inconceivable	**la investigación**	research
el teléfono fijo	land line	**el buscador**	search engine
tercero/a	third	**¡claro!**	of course!
por todas partes	all over	**crear**	to create
libanés/libanesa	Lebanese	**la prueba**	proof
las calles estrechas	narrow streets	**el beso**	kiss
a pesar de	in spite of	**el texteo**	texting
han decidido	have decided	**anticuado/a**	out-of-date

Fragmento del guion

CHICO: Las más frecuentes son YouTube, Facebook y Google para hacer los deberes,[a] buscar investigación. También entro en la universidad en la base de datos de JSTOR.

CHICA: No, Twitter, no. No me agrada[b] esa red social.

[…]

CHICO: Yo me conecto a Internet en mi casa y en la universidad.

[…]

CHICO: Yo creo que falta desarrollar[c] un poco lo que es el Wi-Fi aquí en Quito. Pero ha incrementado[d] bastantísimo[e] el uso del Wi-Fi en todo lo que son lugares públicos: restaurantes, aeropuertos, terminales de bus… Sí, básicamente sí.

[…]

CHICO: El mundo ha sufrido[f] un gran cambio tecnológico desde que… o sea,[g] desde los últimos veinte años. Ahora nos podemos comunicar con cualquier[h] persona en el mundo en cuestión de segundos.[i] Podemos hacer videosllamadas[j] con cualquier persona al otro lado del Atlántico, podemos hablar con gente en Europa, con gente en África… Y hace diez, quince años[k] eso era casi imposible, o costaba mucho hacer una llamada internacional. Ahora es gratuito.[l]

[a]*homework* [b]No… No me gusta [c]falta… *it's necessary to develop* [d]ha… *has grown* [e]*a lot* [f]ha… *has experienced* [g]o… *I mean* [h]*any* [i]en… *in a matter of seconds* [j]*videocalls* [k]hace… *ten, fifteen years ago* [l]*free*

—¿Entras con frecuencia en Facebook?
—¡Siempre, siempre, siempre, siempre! ¡Ya es como costumbre (*habit*)!

Mundo interactivo

Continue your work as an intern at HispanaVisión with Laura Sánchez Tejada, the roving reporter of *Salu2*, as you complete Scenario 6, Activities 3 and 4 in Connect Spanish (**www.connectspanish.com**).

Al mirar

Va a oír los siguientes nombres en este programa. ¿Los pronuncian en inglés o en español los entrevistados?

Facebook	iPhone	Twitter
Google	iPod	Wi-Fi
Hotmail	JSTOR	YouTube

Answer: While some native speakers will put a Spanish spin on technology words, it is quite prevalent for Spanish-speakers to pronounce such names in English, as happens in the program.

Después de mirar

A. ¿Está claro? ¿Cierto o falso? Corrija las oraciones falsas.

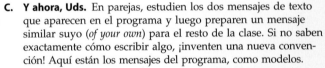

	CIERTO	FALSO
1. Carlos Slim Helú es mexicano de origen libanés.	☑	☐
2. Telmex es una compañía de computadoras.	☐	☑
3. En México, los teléfonos celulares solo son comunes en el D.F.	☐	☑
4. Los jóvenes entrevistados trabajan en la Universidad de San Francisco.	☐	☑
5. Sarita, la hija de Víctor, ya tiene un iPhone y una página de Facebook.	☐	☑
6. Facebook es la red social más popular entre los jóvenes ecuatorianos.	☑	☐
7. Víctor lee los textos con facilidad (*easily*).	☐	☑

Act. A, Answers: 2. *Falso: Es una compañía de telefonía móvil.* **3.** *Falso: Son populares en todo el país.* **4.** *Falso: Son estudiantes.* **5.** *Falso: Ana dice que los va a tener antes de los 10 años. Hoy Sara solo tiene 5 años.* **7.** *Falso: Para Víctor es difícil. Ana los lee con facilidad.*

B. Un poco más. Complete las siguientes oraciones con información del video.

1. Carlos Slim Helú es ______.
2. Los sitios de Internet que más visitan los estudiantes del programa son ______.
3. En el Ecuador, hay acceso Wi-Fi en ______.

Act. B, Answers: 1. *el hombre más rico del mundo / un mexicano de origen libanés / el dueño de América Móvil* **2.** *Facebook, Twitter, Google, Hotmail y YouTube* **3.** *casa, la universidad, el trabajo, los lugares públicos (restaurantes, aeropuertos, terminales de bus)*

C. Y ahora, Uds. En parejas, estudien los dos mensajes de texto que aparecen en el programa y luego preparen un mensaje similar suyo (*of your own*) para el resto de la clase. Si no saben exactamente cómo escribir algo, ¡inventen una nueva convención! Aquí están los mensajes del programa, como modelos.

- Ola, q tal? q acs ste finde? Yamam pq es el qmple d mi hno ste finde y kiero acr 1 fiesta. Bsossssss. = *Hola, ¿qué tal? ¿Qué haces este fin de semana? Llámame porque es el cumpleaños de mi hermano este fin de semana y quiero hacer una fiesta. Muchos besos* (kisses).
- Hsta ntoncs salu2 muy cordials d td el ekipo d ste programa. = *Hasta entonces* (then), *saludos muy cordiales de todo el equipo de este programa.*

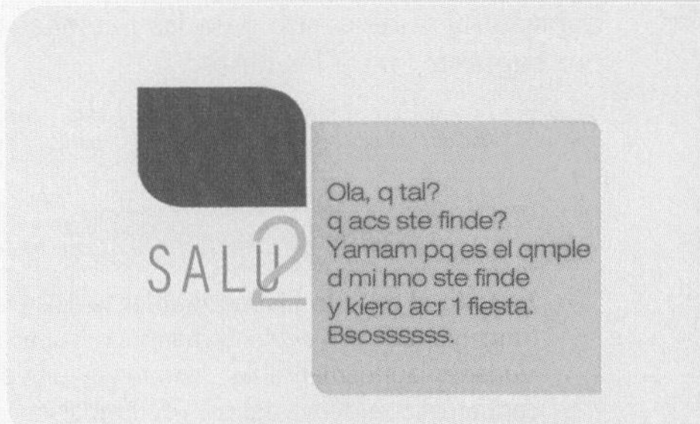
SALU2
Ola, q tal?
q acs ste finde?
Yamam pq es el qmple
d mi hno ste finde
y kiero acr 1 fiesta.
Bsossssss.

La prueba final para ver a qué generación Ud. pertenece (*belong*): ¿Lee los textos con facilidad?

Sobre el programa

En realidad, la experta en texteos de *Salu2* es Laura. ¿Por qué? Porque lo hace con mucha más frecuencia, como toda la gente joven. Ella es capaz de[a] escribir mensajes con una sola mano. Lo que ya no hace[b] es mandar ni mirar mensajes mientras maneja.[c] Eso lo hacía hasta el año pasado, pero un día se salió de la carretera[d] mientras miraba sus mensajes. Pero ni a ella, ni[e] a su prima, que iba con ella, les pasó nada. Pero el susto[f] fue tremendo y Laura y su prima aprendieron la lección.

[a]*capaz... able to* [b]*Lo... What she no longer does* [c]*mientras... while she drives* [d]*se... she went off the road* [e]*ni... ni neither . . . nor* [f]*scare*

Producción personal

Filme dos entrevistas con estudiantes o personal (*personnel*) de habla española de su universidad en las que (*which*) los entrevistados hablan de los usos que hacen de la tecnología, como lo hicieron los estudiantes ecuatorianos de este programa.

Fragmento del guion

Suggestions

- Point out that in this chapter, the script excerpt is actually a selection of interviewees' statements from Laura's report.
- Ask students to indicate all of the words and expressions in the *Fragmento* they find useful for talking about technology.
- Point out the frequent use of *Internet* without the article (*Yo me conecto a Internet…*).

Después de mirar

B: Suggestions

- Ask students to guess the type of students who attend *la Universidad de San Francisco de Quito* (*USFQ*) and have them explain their answers. You may also wish to have some students do research about the university (*www.usfq.edu.ec*). USFQ is a private liberal arts institution.
- Have students come up with possible questions for the answers heard in the program. These questions can be the basis for their interviews in *Producción personal.*

C: Suggestions

- Rather than having students work in groups in class, assign this activity as homework. Suggest that students find a website with texting conventions and vocabulary.
- Whether done as homework or in class, ask students to share their messages with the whole class, and have other students try to decipher them.
- Discuss students' new conventions: What prompted them? What did they use as basis for their invention of abbreviations?

Sobre el programa

Optional

1. *¿Es Ud. más como Víctor o como Laura en cuanto a (as far as) la tecnología? Explique.*
2. *¿Puede escribir mensajes con una sola mano?*
3. *¿Manda mensajes mientras maneja?*

Producción personal

Note

See the IM for additional suggestions for this chapter's assignment as well as for general guidelines and suggestions for video assignments.

Lectura cultural

Notes

- The Instructor's Edition on this page offers some additional information on the country of focus. For more information about the country of focus, see the chapter's opening pages and the IM.
- See the IM for some expressions used in Colombia.

First Reading: Suggestion

Point out that Hispanics often identify themselves with the name of their *barrio*.

Exploración lingüística

Ask students to find the following in the reading. Some of these words are glossed and some are not.

- *Las palabras que se usan para hablar del plan de una ciudad (la plaza, urbanístico, central, el plan de fundación, el edificio, la Catedral)*
- *Las palabras relacionadas con instituciones sociales o gubernamentales (el poder, la Catedral, la iglesia, el gobernador, el ejército, el rey, el municipio, el gobierno)*
- *Las palabras relacionadas con el metro (pasajeros, las estaciones)*

Comprensión: Answers

1. *Porque los vecinos de un barrio tienen una relación muy estrecha y todos se conocen bien.* **2.** *Porque la plaza era parte del plan de fundación de la ciudad de los españoles.* **3.** *El más antiguo es el de Buenos Aires. El más impresionante es el de México, D.F.*

En otros países hispanos

Suggestions

- In Mexico, main plazas are usually called *el Zócalo*.
- There are many truly spectacular *plazas* in the major cities of the Hispanic world. Here are some of them. Spain: *la Plaza Mayor* (Salamanca and Madrid), *la Plaza de España* (Sevilla); Latin America: *la Plaza de Armas* (Lima and Cuzco, Peru; Santiago, Chile), *la Plaza de Bolívar* (Bogotá, Colombia), *la Plaza de Mayo* (Buenos Aires, Argentina).
- Other Latin American and Spanish cities with subway systems include: Santiago (Chile), Guadalajara (Mexico), Caracas (Venezuela), Lima (Peru), Madrid, Barcelona, Valencia, and Seville (Spain)

A LEER

Lectura cultural

Colombia

Es común que los vecinos de un barrio colombiano lleguen a tener[a] un trato estrecho[b] y que hasta organicen juntos fiestas y celebraciones en el barrio para fechas especiales. Es normal saber los nombres de muchos de los vecinos del barrio, no solo los[c] del edificio o de la calle donde uno vive. Con frecuencia, la gente habla de los amigos del barrio como un grupo distinto,[d] parecido[e] a los amigos del colegio,[f] de la universidad o del trabajo. En el barrio, es normal ver grupos de personas que charlan[g] juntas, en la plaza o en una esquina[h] o simplemente en la puerta de un edificio o tienda. Por eso el barrio es un lugar de intensa vida social, especialmente para las personas que no trabajan fuera de casa o para las personas mayores. Y, por supuesto,[i] para los niños.

¿Hay un sentido (*sense*) de comunidad en el barrio o zona residencial donde Ud. vive?

[a]lleguen… *come to have* [b]trato… *very close relationship* [c]*those* [d]*distinct, separate* [e]*similar* [f]*school* [g]*are chatting* [h]*corner* [i]por… *of course*

En otros países hispanos

- **En todo el mundo hispanohablante** Las plazas son fundamentales en el plan urbanístico hispano. En las ciudades latinoamericanas siempre hay una plaza central, que se deriva del plan de fundación[a] de la ciudad de los españoles. En esas plazas, frecuentemente llamadas la Plaza Mayor o la Plaza de Armas, había edificios donde estaban presentes los poderes[b] más importantes de la organización social de aquel entonces:[c] la Catedral (es decir, la Iglesia Católica), el edificio del gobernador[d] o del ejército[e] (como representantes del rey[f]) y el municipio (el gobierno[g] de la ciudad).
- **En México y la Argentina** Varias ciudades hispanas tienen metro, pero los de México y la Argentina son notables. El de Buenos Aires es el más antiguo del Hemisferio Sur: Su construcción comenzó en 1913. Pero el más impresionante es sin duda el metro de la Ciudad de México. Es el segundo metro en longitud[h] de Norteamérica y el mayor de Latinoamérica. Por el número de pasajeros, es el quinto[i] del mundo. Su sistema para nombrar las estaciones es muy colorido y eficiente: Usa palabras y dibujos, para que las personas analfabetas[j] también puedan saber dónde están.

[a]plan… *original plan* [b]*powers* [c]aquel… *back then* [d]*governor* [e]*army* [f]*king* [g]*government* [h]*length* [i]*fifth* [j]para… *so that people who can't read*

Un lugar perfecto para dar un paseo: La Plaza de los Coches (*carriages*), en Cartagena

Tres símbolos colombianos

- **La orquídea** La flor nacional colombiana, la orquídea, se encuentra por todo el país en gran variedad de formas y colores. Las orquídeas se consideran entre las flores más hermosas[a] del mundo.
- **Juan Valdez** No existe un verdadero Juan Valdez; es un personaje[b] ficticio que representa al campesino cafetero[c] colombiano. Ha llegado a ser[d] el ícono del café de Colombia a nivel mundial.
- **La cumbia** La música más distintivamente colombiana es sin duda la cumbia, que tiene influencias musicales africanas, indígenas y europeas. La cumbia se caracteriza por el sonido de los tambores.[e]

[a]bonitas [b]*character* [c]campesino… *coffee-growing peasant* [d]Ha… *He has become* [e]*drums*

Una cita

«Colombianos, las armas os han dado[a] la independencia, pero solo las leyes[b] os darán[c] la libertad.»

Francisco de Paula Santander (1792–1840), uno de los padres de la independencia colombiana

[a]os… *have given you* [b]*laws* [c]os… *will give you*

COMPRENSIÓN

1. ¿Por qué es importante el barrio en la vida de una ciudad hispana?
2. ¿Por qué hay una plaza central en las ciudades latinoamericanas?
3. ¿Cuál es el metro más antiguo de Latinoamérica? ¿Y el más impresionante?

Tres símbolos colombianos

Notes

- Juan Valdez appeared frequently in television ads in the 20th century.
- *Totó* is a very well known *cumbia* singer. You may wish to download his song «*Yo soy la cumbia*».

Una cita

Note

Francisco de Paula Santander was one of the political and military leaders during Colombia's war of independence (1810–1819). He was president of *la República de Nueva Granada*, which was the republic that united Colombia as well as other Latin American countries when they first became independent from Spain.

Del mundo hispano

Antes de leer

Haga una lista de los aparatos que Ud. usa diariamente, sin los cuales no podría (*without which you couldn't*) vivir. ¿Qué aparatos no existen todavía que le gustaría tener y usar? (**¡OJO!** Para describirlos, solo tiene que describir su uso, por ejemplo: una máquina que contesta el e-mail.)

Lectura: «Apocalipsis, I», de Marco Denevi

La extinción de la raza de los hombres se sitúa aproximadamente a fines del siglo XXXI.[a] La cosa sucedió así:[b] las máquinas habían alcanzado[c] tal perfección que los hombres no necesitaban comer, ni dormir, ni leer, ni escribir, ni siquiera[d] pensar. Les bastaba apretar[e] un botón y las máquinas lo hacían todo por ellos.

Gradualmente fueron desapareciendo las mesas, los teléfonos, los Leonardo da Vinci, las rosas té, las tiendas de antigüedades,[f] los discos con las nueve sinfonías de Beethoven, el vino de Burdeos, las golondrinas,[g] los cuadros[h] de Salvador Dalí, los relojes, los sellos[i] postales, los alfileres,[j] el Museo del Prado, la sopa de cebolla,[k] los transatlánticos, las pirámides de Egipto, las Obras Completas de don Benito Pérez Galdós.[l] Sólo había máquinas.

Después, los hombres empezaron a notar que ellos mismos iban desapareciendo paulatinamente[m] y que en cambio[n] las máquinas se multiplicaban. Bastó poco tiempo para que el número de los hombres quedase reducido a la mitad[ñ] y el[o] de las máquinas aumentase al doble y luego al décuplo.[p] Las máquinas terminaron[q] por ocupar todo el espacio disponible.[r] Nadie podía dar un paso, hacer un simple ademán[s] sin tropezarse con[t] una de ellas. Finalmente los hombres se extinguieron.[u]

Como[v] el último se olvidó de desconectar las máquinas, desde entonces[w] seguimos funcionando.

[a]a… *at the end of the 31st century* [b]La… *It happened like this* [c]habían… *had achieved* [d]ni… *not even* [e]Les… *It was enough* [f]*antiques* [g]*swallows* [h]*paintings* [i]*stamps* [j]*pins* [k]*onion* [l]*19th century Spanish novelist* [m]*quietly* [n]en… *in contrast* [ñ]Bastó… *It only took a little while for the number of men to be reduced to half* [o]*that (the number)* [p]*tenfold* [q]*ended up* [r]*available* [s]*gesture* [t]sin… *without running into* [u]se… *died out* [v]*Since* [w]desde… *since then*

Comprensión

A. ¿Cierto o falso? Corrija las oraciones falsas.

	CIERTO	FALSO
1. Las máquinas llegaron a ser perfectas.	☑	☐
2. Los hombres lo hacían todo por las máquinas.	☐	☑
3. A las máquinas les gustaban las cosas más finas y artísticas del mundo y por eso conservaban el vino de Burdeos, las pirámides de Egipto, etcétera.	☐	☑
4. El número de hombres incrementaba mientras disminuía el número de máquinas.	☐	☑
5. Finalmente no hubo más máquinas.	☐	☑
6. El narrador de este microcuento es una máquina.	☑	☐

A: Answers: 2. *Falso: Las máquinas lo hacían todo por los hombres.* **3.** *Falso: A las máquinas no les gustaban esas cosas. Por eso esas cosas desaparecieron.* **4.** *Falso: El número de máquinas incrementaba mientras disminuía el número de hombres.* **5.** *Falso: Finalmente no hubo más hombres.*

B. «Gradualmente fueron desapareciendo… » Conteste las siguientes preguntas.

1. ¿Cuáles de las cosas que fueron desapareciendo (segundo [*second*] párrafo del cuento) reconoce Ud.? Answers will vary.
2. ¿Qué tienen en común esas cosas? Answers will vary.
3. ¿Para quiénes son más importantes esas cosas, para los hombres o para las máquinas? ¿Por qué? Answers will vary.

Del mundo hispano

Note

See the IM for optional follow-up, writing, and Internet activities.

Antes de leer

Suggestions

- Have students brainstorm both questions at home or in groups in class. Remind students to think of all *aparatos*, not just electronics.
- Conduct a whole class discussion about students' answers. Ask students to justify the importance of the appliances they have named.

Lectura

Note

The term *microcuento* is often used to describe extremely short stories, like this one. Denevi was a master of the genre.

Estrategia: The meaning of progressive forms

This text includes some progressive forms that students probably have not actively used, but they should be able to understand them in context. Ask students to find the three progressive verb forms (*fueron desapareciendo, iban desapareciendo, seguimos funcionando*) and guess their meaning from context. Students should easily recognize *seguir* + present participle, as it is presented in (*Cap. 6*).

Optional Writing Activity

Option 1: Ask students to choose a form of technology that they use frequently and write a description of their relationship with it. Is it a useful tool? Does it dominate their life? Could they do without it? How would their life change if they could no longer use it?

Option 2: Ask students to choose a form of technology and write a creative description of it. They should be playful, perhaps narrating from the tool's perspective (or any other perspective they like), telling why and when it might have been invented, describing it without ever naming it, and so on.

A ESCUCHAR

Vocabulario para escuchar

emitimos	we air
se trata del	we're talking about
la bienvenida	welcome
los radioyentes	radio listeners
los detalles	details
cómo no	of course
una pandemia	pandemic
la máquina	machine
conocida	known
monitorizar	to monitor
mejorar	to improve

Antes de escuchar

Empareje cada término médico con su definición.

1. __a__ un componente necesario para el funcionamiento del cuerpo que es regulado (*regulated*) por la insulina
2. __c__ un órgano del cuerpo humano
3. __b__ una hormona que produce el páncreas

a. la glucosa
b. la insulina
c. el páncreas

Escuche

Medicina y tecnología: El proyecto de creación de un páncreas artificial

Un doctor habla en la radio de la diabetes y de un proyecto tecnológico. Escuche según las indicaciones de su profesor(a).

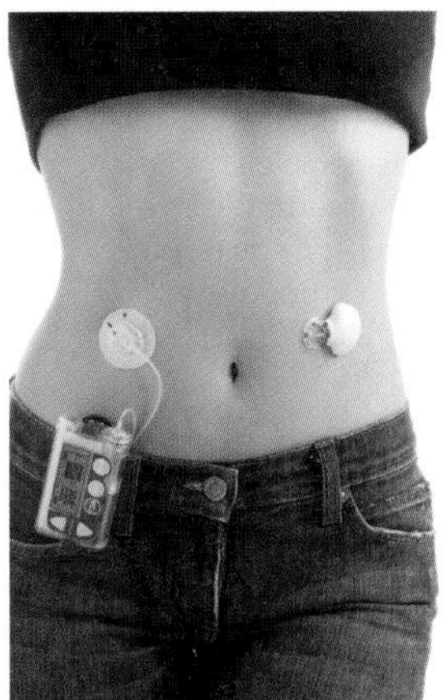

Dos herramientas (*tools*) útiles en la lucha contra (*struggle against*) la diabetes: Un monitor continuo de glucosa [izquierda] y una bomba (*pump*) de insulina

Go to the iMix section in Connect Spanish (**www.connectspanish.com**) to access the iTunes playlist *"Puntos9,"* where you can purchase "La cartera" by Carlos Vives.

Después de escuchar

A. La diabetes. Empareje la información de las dos columnas.

1. __e__ la característica de diabetes tipo 1
2. __b__ el porcentaje de la población adulta mundial que va a sufrir de diabetes en el futuro
3. __d__ el nombre común de la diabetes tipo 1
4. __c__ el porcentaje de pacientes diabéticos que sufren de diabetes tipo 1
5. __a__ el porcentaje de la población adulta mundial que sufre de diabetes en la actualidad

a. casi el 7%
b. casi el 8%
c. el 10%
d. la diabetes juvenil
e. la ausencia total de insulina

B. Más detalles. Conteste las siguientes preguntas.

1. ¿Dónde ocurre esta conversación? ¿Cómo se llama el programa?
2. ¿Qué es el páncreas artificial? ¿Qué tipo de personas lo necesitan?
3. ¿Existe ya esa máquina?
4. ¿Por qué es un gran proyecto?

¡Música!

El colombiano Carlos Vives es muy conocido[a] en todo el mundo hispano como interprete[b] de vallenato[c] y de música que fusiona ritmos típicamente colombianos con la música pop/rock. Su canción «La cartera» es del álbum *El amor de mi tierra.*[d]

[a]*known* [b]*singer* [c]*Colombian musical genre* [d]*homeland*

Carlos Vives, durante un concierto, en Bogotá, Colombia

Antes de escuchar

Suggestion

Point out that students may not know the answers immediately, but there are internal clues to how to make the matches.

Follow-up

Ask the following general questions: *¿La tecnología está mejorando* (new) *la vida de muchos pacientes? ¿Puede dar ejemplos? ¿Qué sabe de la diabetes? ¿A quién conoce que sufre de esta enfermedad?*

Escuche

Notes

- In this chapter students can listen to a radio interview with a doctor who engages in high-level medical research.
- If the listening is assigned as homework, ask students to listen to the passage at least twice.
- See the IM for the Audioscript and more information about music in Colombia.

Después de escuchar

B: Answers

1. *Ocurre en la radio. El programa se llama «Medicina y tecnología».* **2.** *Es una máquina. La necesitan las personas que sufren de diabetes.* **3.** *No existe todavía.* **4.** *Mejora la calidad de la vida de los diabéticos.*

B. Follow-up

- Ask students to listen again (or replay the tape yourself) and pay attention to the greetings and formulaic expressions of courtesy used by the hostess (*la presentadora*) and the guest (*el invitado*).
- Have students brainstorm about and discuss the possible bad effects of technology in the field of medicine. Are the bad effects worth the use of technology in that field?

¡Música!

Note

- *Carlos Vives Restrepo* (1961–) started his career as an actor in the 80s. He recorded his first musical hit in the early 90s, when he reoriented his musical career to the *vallenato,* a Colombian musical genre. He divides his time between Colombia and Miami. He is the recipient of numerous awards for his music.
- For helpful tips on using songs in the classroom, see the IM.

A ESCRIBIR

El tema

La educación universitaria: ¿presencial o a distancia?

Preparar

Paso 1. Piense en las opciones que existen hoy para obtener un título universitario: presencial (es decir, asistiendo a una universidad, según la manera tradicional) o a distancia, gracias al Internet. ¿Cuál es el método más usado? ¿Qué ventajas y desventajas tiene cada opción? ¿Cuál fue la opción que Ud. eligió (*chose*)? ¿Está contento/a con su decisión?

Paso 2. En parejas, hagan una lista de argumentos a favor y en contra de cada una de las dos opciones para obtener un título universitario: de forma presencial o a distancia. Deben incluir ejemplos específicos para apoyar (*support*) sus argumentos.

Redactar

Usando las ideas de **Preparar,** escriba un ensayo contrastivo sobre las opciones que existen hoy día para conseguir un título universitario. Ud. puede presentar varios argumentos, pero también puede optar por defender una opción desde el principio o mantener una actitud neutral en el ensayo. No se olvide de incluir un párrafo de conclusión.

Editar

Revise el ensayo para comprobar (*to check*):

- la ortografía y los acentos
- el uso correcto de las formas del presente de indicativo
- el uso del imperfecto (si describe cómo era tradicionalmente la educación antes del Internet)
- el uso del subjuntivo para expresar influencia

Finalmente, prepare su versión final para entregarla.

Preparar

Suggestions

- Present vocabulary for expressing some *títulos universitarios: la licenciatura* (Bachelor's degree, whether a B.A. or a B.S.), *el masters* or *la maestría*, el *doctorado* (Ph.D.).
- Discuss with students the difference between a contrastive essay that defends a particular point of view, and one that merely aims to present both sides of a topic.
- Students may need generalizations such as the following to express important ideas in this essay: *Es bueno/mejor/peor/importante/conveniente…* Remind students that if they introduce a specific subject after these phrases, they must use the subjunctive. Example: *Es bueno tener opciones* vs. *Es bueno que los estudiantes tengan diferentes opciones.*
- Suggest that students use the following phrases (and others you might think of) in their essay.
  - to contrast ideas: *sin embargo, no obstante* (new)
  - to transition ideas: *además* (new), *por un lado / por otro lado* (new), *en primer lugar, en resumen*
  - to express facts: *los expertos afirman que, los estudios muestran que*
- Suggest that students avoid the use of the first person singular in the first paragraphs of the essay.
- You may wish to discuss the various pros and cons about this topic as a whole-class activity.

Redactar

Suggestions

- Suggested length for this writing assignment: approximately 150–200 words
- Suggested structure: 3 paragraphs

  P. 1. Presentation of the main idea of the essay, to get the reader's attention

  P. 2. Presentation of various arguments, with explanation followed by evidence

  P. 3. Conclusion that summarizes the argument and also presents the author's opinion and/or recommendations

Editar

Follow-up

Where do students see education heading in the future with regard to technology?

En resumen: En este capítulo

Vocabulario

Suggestions

- Give definitions or descriptions and have students name the item.

  El dinero que a uno le pagan cada una o dos semanas por el trabajo que hace. → el sueldo

- Divide students into two teams and have them play Password. Clues must be a single word in Spanish and must not be a variation of the answer (*grabar/grabadora*). Allow only one clue and attempt per turn.
- Bring or have students bring images of *Vocabulario* activities and items. Use these to elicit descriptions, ask/answer questions, and play games.
- Ask questions using words from *Vocabulario.*
  1. *Además del teléfono tradicional, ¿qué otros tipos de teléfonos hay?*
  2. *Para mandar documentos, fotos, etcétera, ¿qué aparato resulta muy rápido?*
  3. *¿Qué se necesita para comunicarse por correo electrónico?*

Note

In Spain, *la radio* is always feminine.

Word Families

En este capítulo

- *alquilar, el alquiler, el/la inquilino/a*
- *la bicicleta, la moto(cicleta)*
- *copiar, hacer* (*foto*)*copia*
- *el disco duro, el disco compacto* (*el CD*)
- *la electrónica, el correo electrónico*
- *grabar, la grabadora*
- *imprimir, la impresora*
- *el monopatín, los patines*
- *la vecindad, el/la vecino/a*

Entre capítulos

- *las afueras* = *afuera* (6)
- *alegrarse* (*de*) = *alegre* (6)
- *almacenar* = *el almacén* (4)
- *el/la dueño/a* = *el/la dueño/a* (owner) (7)
- *el edificio de apartamentos* = *el edificio* (2)
- *el equipo* (equipment) = *el equipo* (team) (10)
- *esperar* (to hope) = *esperar* (to wait for, expect) (7)
- *el gasto* = *gastar* (9)
- *guardar* (to keep; to save) = *guardar* (to save files) (8)
- *el monopatín, los patines* = *patinar* (10)
- *obtener* = *tener* (4)
- *el ordenador* = *ordenado/a* (6)

EN RESUMEN En este capítulo

LearnSmart

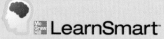

Visit **www.connectspanish.com** to practice the vocabulary and grammar points covered in this chapter.

Gramática en breve

33. *Tú* Commands

Negative **tú** commands = "opposite" vowel

-ar → -es

-er/-ir → -as

Affirmative **tú** commands = **Ud.** form of the present indicative

-ar → -a

-er/-ir → -e

34. Present Subjunctive: An Introduction

Endings: "opposite" vowel

-ar: -e, -es, -e, -emos, -éis, en

-er/-ir: -a, -as, -a, -amos, -áis, -an

Structure:

①		②
first subject = indicative	**que**	second subject = subjunctive

35. Uses of the Subjunctive: Influence

①		②
first subject = indicative INFLUENCE	**que**	second subject = subjunctive

Vocabulario

Los verbos

alegrarse (de)	to be happy (about)
dudar	to doubt
esperar	to hope
haber (*inf. of* **hay**)	(there is, there are)
insistir (en)	to insist (on)
mandar	to order
permitir	to permit, allow
prohibir (prohíbo)	to prohibit, forbid

Repaso: desear, pedir (pido) (i), preferir (prefiero) (i), querer, recomendar (recomiendo), sugerir (sugiero) (i)

Los vehículos

el carro (descapotable)	(convertible) car
el casco	helmet
el monopatín	skateboard
la moto(cicleta)	motorcycle; moped
los patines	(roller/inline) skates

Repaso: la bicicleta, la camioneta, el coche

La electrónica

el archivo	(computer) file
la arroba	@
el buzón de voz	voice mailbox
el canal	channel
la contraseña	password
el correo electrónico	e-mail
el disco duro	hard drive
la electrónica	electronic equipment
el equipo	equipment
la grabadora	(tape) recorder/player
la impresora	printer
el ordenador (portátil) (*Sp.*)	(laptop) computer
la pantalla (grande/plana)	(big/flat) screen (monitor)
el pen drive	memory stick
el ratón	mouse
la red social	social network
el teléfono fijo	land line

Cognados: el app (*f.*), **el blog, la cámara digital, el CD-ROM, el control remoto, el disco compacto (el CD), el DVD (-ROM), el e-mail, el escáner, Facebook** (*m.*), **el fax, la fotocopia, la fotocopiadora, el GPS, el hard drive, el Internet, el iPod, la memoria, el módem, la plasma, Twitter** (*m.*), **el video**

Repaso: la computadora (portátil), el teléfono (celular), la televisión

almacenar	to store, save
bajar	to download
buscar (qu) en el Internet	to look for on the Internet
entrar en Facebook / el Internet	to go into Facebook / on the Internet
cambiar (de)	to change
descargar (gu)	to download
fallar	to "crash" (*computer*)
funcionar	to work, function; to run (*machines*)
grabar	to record; to tape
guardar	to keep; to save (*documents*)
hacer (foto)copia	to copy
imprimir	to print
manejar	to drive; to operate (a *machine*)
obtener (*like* **tener**)	to get, obtain

Cognados: copiar, instalar

Repaso: buscar (qu), conseguir (*like* **seguir**), **entrar, estar, mandar un mensaje, sacar (qu) fotos**

En el trabajo

el aumento	raise
el/la jefe/a	boss
el sueldo	salary
el trabajo	work; job

La ciudad y el barrio

las afueras	outskirts; suburbs
el alquiler	rent
el ascensor	elevator
la avenida	avenue
el barrio	neighborhood
la calefacción	heating
la calle	street
el *campus*	(university) campus
el/la dueño/a	landlord, landlady
el edificio de apartamentos	apartment building
la electricidad	electricity
el gas	gas (*not for cars*)
el gasto	expense
el/la inquilino/a	tenant; renter
la parada del autobús	bus stop
la parada del metro	subway stop
el piso	floor (*of a building*)
el primer piso	first floor (second story)
el segundo piso	second floor (third story)
la planta baja	ground floor
el/la portero/a	building manager; doorman
la residencia	residence
la residencia de ancianos	nursing home
el/la vecino/a	neighbor
la vista	view
la vivienda	housing
la zona	zone, area

Repaso: el apartamento, la casa, el centro, la ciudad, la dirección, el/la dueño/a (*owner*)**, la plaza, la residencia (de estudiantes)**

alquilar	to rent
mudarse	to move (*residences*)

Otros sustantivos

los/las demás	others
la gente	people
la mentira	lie

Vocabulario personal

- *la parada del autobús/metro* = *la parada* (8)
- *los patines* = *el patinaje* (10), *patinar* (10), *patinar en línea* (10)
- *la planta baja* = *bajo/a* (3)
- *el piso* = *el piso* (10)
- *el/la portero/a* = *la puerta* (2)
- *el primer piso* = *primero* (*adv.*) (5)
- *la vista* = *ver* (5)
- *la vivienda* = *vivir* (3)

¡OJO!

el carro ≠ *caro/a*

Suggestions

- Have students restate the following sentences to make them reflect their own situations.
  1. *Vivo en el centro.*
  2. *Mis vecinos son muy simpáticos.*
  3. *Tengo una vista magnífica de la ciudad.*
  4. *Alquilo un apartamento cerca de la universidad.*
  5. *El dueño de la casa de apartamentos paga la electricidad y el gas.*
  6. *En mi casa de apartamentos hay portero.*
- Have students describe their living situation, then have them tell how it compares to their previous situations. For some, it may be worse (from family home to dorm), for others it may be better.

Chapter Opening Photo and Chapter Theme

Chapter Theme–Related Questions

Write the following on the board or on an overhead transparency. Have students take turns putting the activities in the order of their appeal or naming their favorite.

- _____ *Ir a un museo*
- _____ *Ir al cine*
- _____ *Ir a un concierto de música clásica*
- _____ *Ver un ballet o un espectáculo de baile*
- _____ *Leer una novela*
- _____ *Ir al teatro a ver una obra*
- _____ *Crear algo (una pintura, una escultura…)*
- _____ *Componer una canción*
- _____ *Mirar la televisión*
- _____ *Ver un partido deportivo*
- _____ *Navegar el Internet*

Then ask students the following questions.

1. *¿Hay alguna actividad más interesante para Ud. que todas las que están en la lista? ¿Cuál es?*
2. *¿Hay en su ciudad ferias o mercados de arte y artesanía? ¿Compra Ud. a veces algunas cosas allí? ¿Qué cosas compra?*
3. *¿Qué le gusta más mirar en esos sitios, las pinturas, las esculturas o las artesanías?*
4. *¿Hay algún tipo de artesanía que sea típico de su ciudad o estado? ¿Cuál es? ¿Le gusta a Ud.?*

El Ecuador y Bolivia

Datos esenciales

EL ECUADOR

Nombre oficial: *República del Ecuador*
Lema: *«Dios, Patria y Libertad»*
Capital: *Quito*
Otras ciudades: *Guayaquil, Cuenca, Machala*
Composición étnica: *65% mestizos, 25% indígenas, 7% blancos, 3% negros*
Jefe de estado: *el Presidente Rafael Correa, desde 2007*
Forma de gobierno: *República unitaria democrática*
Lengua oficial: *el español; en muchas regiones también se habla el quechua*
Moneda: *el dólar estadounidense (desde 2000; antes se circulaba el sucre)*
Religión: *95% católicos, 5% otros (especialmente evangélicos)*

BOLIVIA

Nombre oficial: *Estado Plurinacional de Bolivia*
Lema: *«La unión es la fuerza»*
Capital: *La Paz (capital administrativa), Sucre (capital constitucional)*

13 El arte y la cultura

Una pintora que vende sus cuadros (*paintings*), en el Ecuador

- ¿Le interesa el arte en general? ¿Qué tipo de expresión artística le interesa más? ¿Le fascina la pintura, la escultura, la arquitectura, la danza, el cine, el teatro, la música, el diseño de moda (*fashion design*) o la literatura? ¿O prefiere otro tipo de expresión artística?
- ¿Hay museos en su ciudad? ¿De qué tipo? ¿Hay teatros y cines?
- ¿Le gusta la artesanía (*arts and crafts*)? ¿Hay algún tipo de artesanía típica de su región, como la cerámica o la elaboración de objetos de cuero, metal, madera (*wood*) o cristal?

connect SPANISH

www.connectspanish.com

Resources

For Students

- Connect Spanish (**www.connectspanish.com**), which contains all content from the following resources, as well as the *Mundo interactivo* scenarios, the LearnSmart adaptive learning system, and more!
- **Physical Resources:** Workbook / Laboratory Manual, Laboratory Audio Program, DVD

For Instructors

- Connect Spanish (**www.connectspanish.com**), which contains access to all student sections of Connect Spanish, as well as helpful time-saving tools and resources such as an integrated gradebook, Instructor's Manual, Testing Program, digital transparencies, Audioscript, Videoscript, and more!

El Ecuador

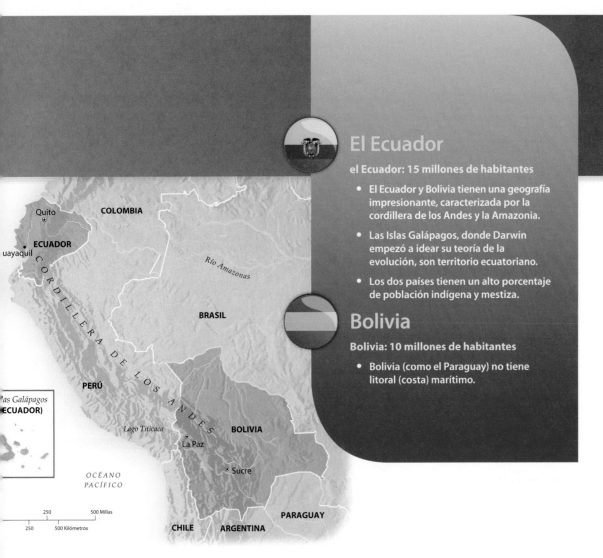

el Ecuador: 15 millones de habitantes

- El Ecuador y Bolivia tienen una geografía impresionante, caracterizada por la cordillera de los Andes y la Amazonia.
- Las Islas Galápagos, donde Darwin empezó a idear su teoría de la evolución, son territorio ecuatoriano.
- Los dos países tienen un alto porcentaje de población indígena y mestiza.

Bolivia

Bolivia: 10 millones de habitantes

- Bolivia (como el Paraguay) no tiene litoral (costa) marítimo.

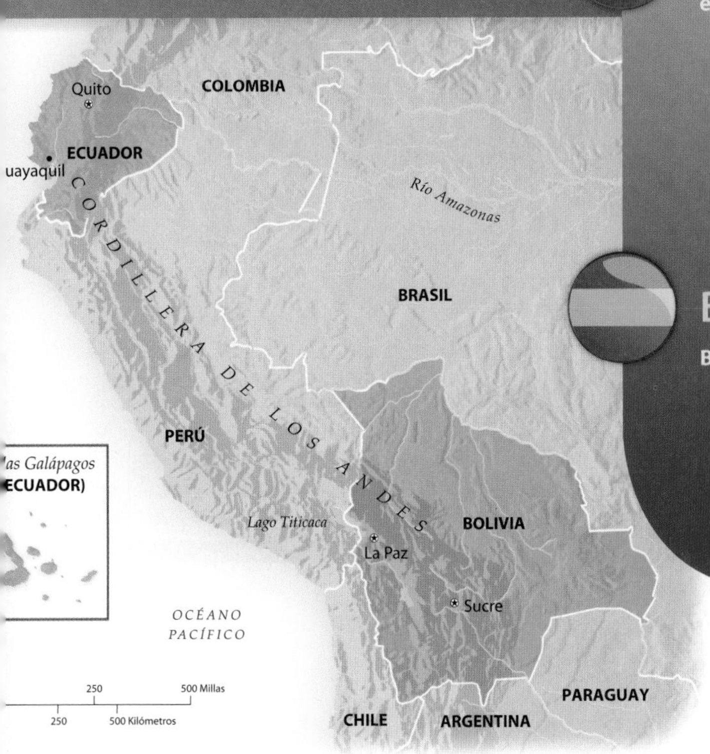

En este capítulo

CONTENT / **CONTENIDO**	OBJECTIVES / **OBJETIVOS**
The Arts 384	To talk about artistic preferences and talents
Ordinals 388	To express numerical order
The Subjunctive: Emotion 389	To express emotional reactions in complex sentences
The Subjunctive: Doubt and Denial 394	To express uncertainty in complex sentences
The Subjunctive: A Summary 398	To review all of the uses of the subjunctive
El Ecuador and **Bolivia 406**	To learn about two Andean countries where the influence of indigenous people is notable

Otras ciudades: *Santa Cruz de la Sierra, Cochabamba*
Composición étnica: *30% quechuas, 30% mestizos, 25% aymaras, 15% blancos*
Jefe de estado: *el Presidente Juan Evo Morales*
Forma de gobierno: *República presidencialista*
Lenguas oficiales: *el español, el quechua y el aymara; también se hablan el guaraní y otras lenguas indígenas*
Moneda: *el peso boliviano*
Religión: *95% católicos, 5% evangélicos*

Point Out

- *La Amazonia* is the name for the region crossed by *el río Amazonas*. This region, which is enormously important to the ecology of the planet, is shared by nine countries: Peru, Brazil (the two countries with the most territory in *la Amazonia*), Bolivia, Ecuador, Venezuela, Colombia, Guyana, Surinam, and French Guiana (*la Guayana Francesa*).
- Bolivia has two official capitals. The government resides in La Paz, while judicial power resides in Sucre. At 3,660 meters, La Paz is the highest capital in the world.

Note

While some examples of art from Ecuador and Bolivia will be presented in this chapter, the authors have chosen *not* to limit examples of art and culture to those two countries in order to expose students to works of art and culture from all over the Spanish-speaking world.

Suggestion

See the IM for more information and suggestions.

Multimedia

The IM provides suggestions for using the multimedia materials in the classroom.

Resources: Transparency 128

Vocabulario: Preparación

Las artes

Note

See the model for vocabulary presentation and other material in the *Cap. 13 Vocabulario: Preparación* section of "Chapter-by-Chapter Supplementary Materials" in the IM.

Suggestions

- Emphasize the dual gender of the following words: *el/la artista, el/la cantante, el/la guía, el/la poeta.* Point out that *la guía* can refer to a guidebook or to a female guide.
- Point out the spelling differences between English and Spanish: *escultura* vs. sculpture, *arquitectura* vs. architecture.
- Help students relate the following words: scene → *escena* → *escenario.*
- Point out that a play is called *una obra de teatro.*
- Optional vocabulary: *artesanal, artístico/a, diseñar, el/la diseñador(a), el/la rapero/a.*
- Have students look at the art and vocabulary. Then describe the art scene using as many words from the list as possible, and have students repeat them.
- Have students tell whether the following sentences about traditional culture are *cierto* or *falso.*
  1. *Se puede comprar artesanías en un supermercado.*
  2. *La cerámica es una de las artesanías más conocidas* (new) *de este país.*
  3. *En este país no hay ruinas de ningún tipo de civilizaciones anteriores a la nuestra.*
  4. *Los tejidos no son una forma de creación artística.*
  5. *Cada región de este país tiene sus canciones típicas.* (*Dé ejemplos.*)
- Present the following questions to establish a class discussion.

  ¿Cree que todas las personas son artistas de alguna manera?
  ¿Cree que es fácil que una persona viva de su arte si tiene mucho talento?

Suggestion

Have students answer the following questions.

1. *¿Hay algún pintor o pintora que sea su favorito/a? ¿Quién es? Describa su estilo de pintura. ¿Es abstracto o figurativo?*
2. *¿Qué es más importante para Ud., que un edificio sea elegante o que sea práctico? ¿Le gusta la arquitectura de su universidad? Explique.*

VOCABULARIO **Preparación**

Las artes*

La expresión artística	Las personas	Los verbos	
la arquitectura	**el arquitecto / la arquitecta**	**diseñar**	to design
el baile / la danza	**el bailarín / la bailarina**	**bailar**	
el cine / el teatro / la ópera	**el actor / la actriz**	**actuar (actúo)**	
	el director / la directora	**dirigir (dirijo)**	to direct
la escultura	**el escultor / la escultora**	**esculpir**	to sculpt
la literatura	**el escritor / la la escritora**	**escribir**	
la pintura / el dibujo	**el pintor / la pintora**	**pintar**	
		dibujar	to draw

The word* **arte *is both masculine and feminine. The masculine articles and adjectives are normally used with* **arte** *in the singular while the feminine ones are used in the plural. Note that* **las artes** *often refers to "the arts" in general:* **Guillermo es estudiante** *de arte moderno.* **Me gustan mucho** *las artes gráficas.*

Resources: Transparency 129

NATIONAL STANDARDS: Connections

- ***La Catedral de Quito*** (1562, finished in 1567) is one of the oldest cathedrals in Latin America. Built in Gothic-Mudejar style, it is distinctive for its white walls and interior tile work.
- ***El lago de los cisnes*** (1877), a ballet set to music by Peter Ilyich Tchaikovsky (Russia, 1840–1893), tells the story of a woman who turns into a swan.

Las obras artísticas

la canción	song
el cuadro	painting
el edificio	building
el espectáculo	show
el guion	script
el papel	role
la película	movie
la obra (de arte)	work (of art)
la obra de teatro	play
la obra maestra	masterpiece

Cognados: el ballet, la comedia, el concierto, el drama, la fotografía, el mural, la música, la novela, el poema

Otras personas

el dramaturgo / la dramaturga	playwright
el/la guía	guide

Cognados: el/la artista, el/la novelista, el/la poeta

Otros verbos

crear	to create
tejer	to weave

La tradición cultural

la artesanía	arts and crafts
la cerámica	pottery; ceramics
las ruinas	ruins
los tejidos	woven goods
folclórico/a	traditional

Conversación

A. Obras de arte

Paso 1. ¿Qué clase de arte representan las siguientes obras y qué son?

1. la catedral de Quito y la de Santiago de Compostela
2. Diego Rivera y los artistas (a veces anónimos) del barrio
3. la Venus de Milo y la Estatua de la Libertad
4. *El lago de los cisnes* (*Swan Lake*) y *El amor brujo* (*Love, the Magician*)
5. *El laberinto del fauno* y *El Mago de Oz*
6. *La Bohème* y *La Traviata*
7. las pirámides aztecas y mayas
8. *Don Quijote* y *Cien años de soledad*
9. *Las Meninas*, por Diego Velázquez (página 400)
10. «*El cuervo* (*The Raven*)», por Edgar Allan Poe
11. las imágenes de Ansel Adams
12. «La Bamba», los boleros, los corridos

Con. A: Answers: 1. *la arquitectura; edificios* **2.** *la pintura; murales* **3.** *la escultura; esculturas* **4.** *la música; ballets* **5.** *el cine; películas* **6.** *la música, el teatro; óperas* **7.** *la arquitectura; ruinas* **8.** *la literatura; novelas* **9.** *la pintura; cuadro* **10.** *la literatura; poema* **11.** *la fotografía; fotografías* **12.** *la música; canciones*

Paso 2. Ahora dé otros ejemplos de obras en cada una de las categorías artísticas que Ud. mencionó en el **Paso 1.**

Así se dice

Some Spanish speakers use **el/la comediante** to express *actor/actress*, but usually in reference to people who act on the stage. Use **el cómico / la cómica** to refer explicitly to a *comedian/comedienne.*

An alternative spelling of **folclórico/a** is **folklórico/a.**

Nota **comunicativa**

Más sobre los gustos y preferencias

You already know a number of verbs for talking about what you like and don't like: **gustar, encantar, interesar, molestar.** As you know, these verbs are used with indirect object pronouns, and the verb always agrees with the thing or things liked or disliked, not with the person whose preferences are being described.

Here are some additional verbs that are used like **gustar.**

- **aburrir** — **Me aburre** el baile moderno. *Modern dance is boring to me (bores me).*
- **atraer** — A Juan **le atraen** las ruinas incas. *Juan is drawn to (attracted by) Incan ruins.*
- **fascinar** — **Nos fascinan** las artesanías indígenas. *We're fascinated by indigenous handicrafts.*

3. *Para Ud., ¿qué es más importante en una película: el guión, la dirección o la actuación? ¿Quiénes son sus actores favoritos? ¿Hay algún director o directora de cine que sea su favorito/a? ¿Quién?*

Con. A, Paso 2: Suggestion

Ask for works of art by Hispanic artists. This can be assigned as homework.

Reciclado: Before presenting the material in the *Nota comunicativa,* review the use of *gustar* and other verbs like it that students already know (*encantar, interesar, molestar*). Emphasize the following points: 1) obligatory use of the indirect object pronoun, even when a noun is expressed; 2) agreement with the thing(s) liked; 3) infinitive as singular subject. No *¿Recuerda Ud.?* feature is provided here, as verbs of this type were recently reviewed.

Nota comunicativa

Suggestions

- Review *odiar* (transitive).
- Present *apreciar* (also transitive).
- ***Las pirámides aztecas y mayas*** were built by Mesoamerican civilizations. They are found in the area that is today Mexico, Guatemala, Belize, Honduras, and El Salvador.
- ***Don Quijote de la Mancha*** (1605, 1615) is a novel published in two volumes a decade apart. It was written by the Spanish author Miguel de Cervantes (1547–1616), who many consider to be the creator of the modern novel.
- ***Gabriel García Márquez:*** See the note on p. 29.
- ***Diego Velázquez*** (1599–1660): See the reproduction of *Las Meninas* and the Culture note on p. 400.
- ***Edgar Allan Poe*** (1809–1849) was the master of the horror tale and is considered by many to be the inventor of the detective story.
- ***"La Bamba"*** is a folk song from the state of Veracruz, Mexico. It was made popular in the United States by Ritchie Valens in 1958. Valens (1941–1959), the first Mexican-American crossover success in pop music.
- ***Boleros*** are a type of slow, romantic song good for slow dancing.
- ***Corridos*** are a type of Mexican song that narrates a story about topics such as immigration, love, work, oppression, and feuds.
- ***El amor brujo*** is a ballet written in 1915 by the Spanish composer Manuel de Falla (1876–1946).
- ***El laberinto del fauno*** (*Pan's Labyrinth*, 2006) is a movie written and directed by the Mexican filmmaker Guillermo del Toro. It garnered enormous critical praise worldwide and won three Academy Awards.
- ***El mago de Oz*** (*The Wonderful Wizard of Oz,* 1900), written by L. Frank Baum (1856–1919), an American journalist, playwright, and author of juvenile stories, was made into a movie in 1938.
- ***La Bohème*** is an opera by Puccini (1858–1924) that depicts the lives of artists in Paris in the mid-1800s.
- ***La Traviata,*** an opera written by Giuseppe Verdi (1813–1901), mounts a romantic attack on conventional bourgeois morality.

Con. B: Note

Active vocabulary: *clásico/a, moderno/a*

Con. B: Suggestion

Do this activity as a whole-class discussion according to the following steps.

- Ask a basic question about each art form mentioned (*¿Les gusta…*), asking students to raise their hands if they like the art form.
- Ask follow-up questions, as appropriate, especially about attendance at the arts activities mentioned (*¿Fue Ud. alguna vez a la ópera?*).
- Tally responses as you go. Then guide students toward expressing valid generalizations about the class's opinion of the arts activities mentioned.

Con. B: Follow-up

Have each student write another cultural cue on a piece of paper. Collect all papers and write the cultural cues on the board so that students can answer them. Encourage both silly and serious cues.

Nota cultural

Suggestions

- Point out that the term *colombino* refers to Columbus, which is *Cristóbal Colón's* last name in Latin and the name by which he is known in English.
- Point out that Catholic cathedrals are often among the most magnificent monuments in Hispanic cities, since Catholicism was the Spanish Empire's religion. Impressive churches were an obvious way to attract indigenous people to the faith and convert them.
- Ask students if they can name some well-known buildings from Spanish-speaking countries. They may have heard of Frank Geary's *Museo de arte moderno* in Bilbao, Spain, of Gaudí's buildings in Barcelona, or of some of the many museums or cathedrals in large cities.

Comprensión

1. *¿Desde cuándo hay obras impresionantes de arquitectura en Latinoamérica?* (*desde la época precolombina*)
2. *¿Qué evento histórico marca un cambio muy importante en el desarrollo de la arquitectura latinoamericana?* (*la conquista de América por los españoles*)
3. *¿Qué ocurre hoy día con los edificios antiguos?* (*Se renuevan y se modifican.*)

B. Entrevista: ¿Te gustan los eventos culturales?

Paso 1. Haga por lo menos cinco preguntas usando las siguientes ideas como base. Use verbos de la **Nota comunicativa** de la página 385.

MODELO: la ópera ⟶ ¿Te aburre la ópera?

1. el ballet clásico
2. los museos de arte moderno
3. las obras de teatro
4. los grandes museos como *The Smithsonian* o *The Natural History Museum*
5. los conciertos de música clásica
6. los recitales de poesía en algún café
7. las películas extranjeras
8. la ópera
9. ¿ ?

Paso 2. Ahora use las preguntas para entrevistar a cinco compañeros de clase para saber su opinión sobre las manifestaciones artísticas mencionadas en sus preguntas. ¿Qué puede Ud. decir sobre las tendencias culturales de la clase?

Nota **cultural**

La arquitectura en el mundo hispano

Los países de habla española tienen una larga tradición arquitectónica, con edificios de las tradiciones indígena, europea, colonial y ultramoderna.

- **La América indígena:** Aquí hay obras arquitéctonicas impresionantes[a] que tienen su origen en la época precolombina,[b] es decir, desde mucho antes de la llegada de Cristóbal Colón a territorio americano. Las civilizaciones azteca, maya e inca, que fueron los grandes imperios[c] de su tiempo, dejaron construcciones fascinantes y complejas[d] que todavía[e] se conservan y se pueden visitar hoy día. Los complejos[f] arquitectónicos de Machu Picchu en el Perú, Tikal en Guatemala y Teotihuacán en México —inca, maya y azteca respectivamente— están entre los ejemplos más sobresalientes[g] de esas grandes culturas.
- **La América colonial:** La conquista de América y el imperio español trajeron los estilos artísticos europeos a América. Desde el siglo[h] XVI las nuevas ciudades se llenaron[i] rápidamente de magníficos edificios religiosos y civiles, como las catedrales de Quito (1567) en el Ecuador y de la Ciudad de México (1571). El esplendor de la arquitectura latinoamericana de esta época es paralelo a lo que ocurría en España durante el mismo siglo, cuando se construyeron catedrales y palacios magníficos en muchas ciudades.
- **Las ciudades modernas:** En la actualidad, la arquitectura sigue transformando ciudades a ambos[j] lados del Atlántico. La Ciudad de México, Santiago de Chile, Buenos Aires y Madrid son los ejemplos más sobresalientes de las grandes ciudades modernas, en donde los rascacielos[k] conviven[l] con edificios representativos de la larga historia de cada país. Los viejos edificios se renuevan[m] y se modifican para darles nuevos usos, de tal manera[n] que siguen siendo parte activa en la vida de cada ciudad.

La Casa de la Moneda de Potosí, Bolivia: originalmente una fábrica de monedas (*mint*), ahora un museo y un ejemplo precioso de la arquitectura colonial boliviana

¿Cuáles son los edificios o complejos arquitéctonicos más sobresalientes en su estado o ciudad?

[a]*impressive* [b]*pre-Columbian* [c]*empires* [d]*complex* [e]*still* [f]*complexes, groups of buildings* [g]*outstanding* [h]*century* [i]*se… filled up* [j]*both* [k]*skyscrapers* [l]*coexist* [m]*se… are being renovated* [n]*de… so that*

Multimedia: Internet

Have students choose a Spanish-speaking country and do an Internet search about some of its architectural landmarks.

C. ¿Qué hacen?

Paso 1. Haga oraciones completas, usando una palabra o frase de cada columna. **¡OJO!** Hay más de una posibilidad en algunos casos.

la compositora	+	bailar	+	novelas
la artesana		componer		canciones
la actriz		dirigir		en el ballet
el director		diseñar		cerámica
el músico		escribir		edificios y casas
el bailarín		esculpir		papeles en la televisión
el dramaturgo		hacer		guiones
la pintora		interpretar		tejidos
el escritor		mirar		con actores
la arquitecta		pintar		obras de teatro
el poeta		tocar		cuadros
		trabajar		instrumentos musicales
				poesía

Paso 2. Ahora, con dos o tres compañeros, dé nombres de artistas (del sexo femenino o masculino) en cada categoría. ¿Cuántos artistas hispanos pueden nombrar?

D. Entrevista

Paso 1. Complete las siguientes declaraciones de manera que sean ciertas para Ud.

Vocabulario útil

el country
el *hip hop*
el *jazz*
la música de los años 50 (60,…)
el pop
el *rap*
el rock (clásico)
el *tecno*

1. Me gusta mucho _____ (una actividad relacionada con el arte).
2. El arte que más me interesa como espectador(a) es _____.
3. (No) Tengo talento artístico para _____.
4. (No) Me gusta ir a mercados y ferias de artesanía. Allí (no) compro _____.
5. En la universidad, los espectáculos que más me interesan son _____.
6. En cuanto a (*As for*) música, prefiero _____. Mi canción/artista/cantante favorito/a es _____.

Paso 2. Ahora, en parejas, hablen de sus preferencias artísticas, usando como base las declaraciones del **Paso 1.**

Paso 3. Digan a la clase las preferencias que Uds. tienen en común.

Con. C, Paso 2: Suggestion

Do this *paso* as a contest. Have each group write their answers on the board so that everyone can see what they came up with. Provide the following names after completing the activity.

el cine: *Robert Rodríguez, Pedro Almodóvar, Antonio Banderas, Luis Buñuel, Salma Hayek, Gabriel García Bernal, Penélope Cruz, Javier Bardem, Isabel Croixet, América Ferrera, Rosario Dawson, Selena Gómez, Jessica Alba*

la literatura: *Isabel Allende, Laura Esquivel, Gabriel García Márquez, Octavio Paz, Carlos Fuentes*

la música: *Manuel de Falla, Pablo Casals, Gloria Estefan, Julio Iglesias, Tito Puente, Carlos Santana, Los Lobos, Ricky Martin, Jennifer López*

la pintura: *Frida Kahlo, Diego Rivera, José Clemente Orozco, Salvador Dalí, Pablo Picasso, Fernando Botero*

la arquitectura: *Antoni Gaudí, Santiago Calatrava, Rafael moneo*

Con. D: Preliminary Exercise

Use the following questions to generate whole-class discussion in preparation for *Con. D.* Volunteer information about yourself about each question as appropriate and to model useful vocabulary. Write useful or new vocabulary on the board as you work through the questions.

1. *¿Tienen Uds. talento artístico? ¿Qué aptitudes tienen? ¿Qué les gusta crear? ¿Cuándo empezaron a cultivar esa aptitud? ¿Hay alguien en la clase que tenga aspiraciones de dedicarse al arte profesionalmente? ¿Cuáles son las ventajas y desventajas?*
2. *¿Sienten algún interés en el arte en general? ¿Qué tipo de arte les interesa? ¿Por qué?*
3. *¿Les gusta ir a mercados y ferias de artesanía? ¿Qué cosas se venden allí? ¿Qué les gusta comprar? ¿Hay alguien en la clase que coleccione obras de artesanía? ¿Qué colecciona? ¿Cuántos objetos tiene en su colección?*
4. *¿Qué obras teatrales les gustan? ¿Hay muchas actividades culturales y artísticas en esta ciudad? Si las hay, ¿asisten a espectáculos de baile, música o drama? ¿Qué les gustan más? ¿Qué clase de música prefieren?*

Con. D: Pronunciation

All these musical terms are pronounced in Spanish in a manner close to their original pronunciation in English: *country = /cantri/, hip hop = /jipjop/,* jazz *= /yas/, rock = /roc/.*

Con. D: Follow-up

Ask students what they know about Latin America music.

Redacción: After students have completed *Con. D,* assign either a self-portrait or a description of their partner as a writing assignment. (This activity will be especially successful if you've done the preliminary exercise.) Suggest that students "illustrate" their composition with photos or visuals taken from magazines, as appropriate. Share interesting compositions with the class, concealing the name of the writer. Ask the class to guess who wrote each composition.

Ranking Things: Ordinals

Suggestions

- Select a row of students and identify the first ten using ordinal numbers, e.g.: *Juan es el primer estudiante, Isabel es la segunda estudiante, Susana es la tercera,* and so on.
- **Reciclado:** Remind students that they have used *el primero* with dates, and in *Cap. 12* they used a few ordinal numbers to refer to floors of a building.
- Point out that in Spanish, cardinal numbers are more commonly used than ordinal numbers above *tenth: Alfonso XIII (trece), el siglo XII (doce).*

Preliminary Exercise

Have students respond *cierto* or *falso* to the following sentences.

1. *El (lunes) es el (primer) día de la semana.* (Vary days, creating some incorrect items.)
2. *(Enero) es el (primer) mes del año.* (Vary months, creating some incorrect items.)
3. *Bob es el (quinto) estudiante en esta fila.*

Con.: Optional

Have students rank in order of importance to them the following characteristics in each category.

- ***Los cursos para el próximo semestre/trimestre***

  la hora de la clase
  el profesor / la profesora
  la materia
  la posibilidad de sacar buenas notas
  el costo de los libros
  si incluye laboratorio o no
  el edificio donde se da la clase
  el tamaño (new) *de la clase*

- ***La selección de un trabajo***

  el sueldo
  el prestigio de la compañía
  la ciudad
  la posibilidad de ascenso (new)
  la personalidad del jefe / de la jefa
  las condiciones físicas de la oficina
  si le van a dar una oficina privada o no

Note

See the Laboratory Manual for presentation and practice of the letters *x* and *n*.

Ranking Things: Ordinals

primer(o/a)	first	**cuarto/a**	fourth	**sexto/a**	sixth	**noveno/a**	ninth
segundo/a	second	**quinto/a**	fifth	**séptimo/a**	seventh	**décimo/a**	tenth
tercer(o/a)	third			**octavo/a**	eighth		

- Ordinal numbers are adjectives and must agree in number and gender with the nouns they modify. Ordinals usually precede the noun: **la cuarta lección, el octavo ejercicio.**
- Like **bueno,** the ordinals **primero** and **tercero** shorten to **primer** and **tercer,** respectively, before masculine singular nouns: **el primer niño, el tercer mes.**
- Ordinal numbers are frequently abbreviated with superscript letters that show the adjective ending: **las 1as lecciones, el 1er grado, el 5° estudiante.** When agreement is not needed, the ordinals are abbreviated simply as **1°, 2°,** and so on.

Conversación

A. ¿Cultura, yo?

Paso 1. Veamos (*Let's see*) si Ud. tiene interés en la cultura o no. Ordene las siguientes actividades según sus preferencias y hábitos, empezando por **1°.**

_____ ir al cine a ver las últimas películas en inglés
_____ ver películas extranjeras dobladas (*dubbed*) o subtituladas
_____ visitar museos, preferentemente en visitas guiadas
_____ comprar o sacar de la biblioteca libros de ficción
_____ ver obras de teatro
_____ bailar en clubes y fiestas
_____ ver programas de la tele
_____ ir a conciertos de música clásica/*jazz*
_____ ir a conciertos de música pop/rock/*country*
_____ leer o escribir poesía

Paso 2. Ahora, en parejas, entrevístense sobre sus cinco actividades favoritas. Usen números ordinales.

MODELO: Mi actividad favorita es ir a ver películas extranjeras subtituladas. Mi segunda actividad favorita es…

B. Autorretrato (*Self-portrait*) **de un(a) estudiante.** Complete las declaraciones.

1. Soy estudiante de _____ año.
2. Estoy en mi _____ semestre/trimestre de español.
3. Los lunes, mi primera clase es la de _____, a las _____. Mi segunda clase es la de _____, a las _____.
4. Con frecuencia, soy la _____ persona en llegar a la clase de español.
5. Soy la _____ persona de mi familia que asiste a una universidad. Y soy la _____ persona de mi familia que asiste a *esta* universidad.

Mundo interactivo

You should now be prepared to work with Scenario 7, Activity 1 in Connect Spanish (**www.connectspanish.com**).

Resources: Transparency 130

GRAMÁTICA

¿Recuerda Ud.?

In **Capítulo 12,** you learned the forms of the present subjunctive and the basics of how and when it is used. Review what you learned by answering the following questions.

1. Is the subjunctive used in one- or two-clause sentences?
2. Is the it used in the main (independent) or subordinate (dependent) clause?
3. Is it used before or after the word **que**?
4. What is the relationship between the subject of the main and the subordinate clauses when the subjunctive is used?
5. What verb form follows an impersonal expression when there is no change of subject?
6. Influence is one "cause" of the subjunctive. What are two more subjunctive "triggers"?

You will learn about those two subjunctive "triggers" in **Gramáticas 36** and **37.**

36 Expressing Feelings

Use of the Subjunctive (Part 3): Emotion

Grammar Tutorial 36
connect | SPANISH
www.connectspanish.com

Gramática en acción: Diego y Lupe oyen tocar a los mariachis

México, D.F.

DIEGO: Ay, ¡cómo me encanta esta música!

LUPE: **Me alegro de que** te guste.

DIEGO: Y **yo me alegro de que** estemos aquí. ¿Sabes el origen de la palabra **mariachi**?

LUPE: No… ¿Lo sabes tú?

DIEGO: Bueno, una de las teorías es que viene del siglo XIX, cuando los franceses ocuparon México. Ellos contrataban a grupos de músicos para tocar en las bodas. Y como los mexicanos no podían pronunciar bien la palabra francesa *mariage,* pues acabaron por decir **mariachi.** Y de allí viene el nombre de los grupos.

LUPE: ¡Qué fascinante! **Me sorprende que** sepas tanto de nuestra historia.

DIEGO: Pues, todo buen antropólogo debe saber un poco de historia también, ¿no?

Comprensión

1. Lupe se alegra de que ______. a Diego le guste la música de los mariachis.
2. Y Diego se alegra de que ______. estén allí.
3. A Lupe le sorprende que ______. Diego sepa tanto de la historia de México.

Diego and Lupe hear a mariachi group play *DIEGO: Oh, how I love this music! LUPE: I'm glad you like it. DIEGO: And I'm glad we're here. Do you know the origin of the word **mariachi**? LUPE: No . . . Do you? DIEGO: Well, one of the theories is that it comes from the nineteenth century, when the French occupied Mexico. They used to hire musical groups to play at weddings. And because the Mexicans couldn't correctly pronounce the French word* mariage*, they ended up saying **mariachi.** And so that's where the name of the groups comes from. LUPE: How fascinating! I'm surprised (that) you know so much about our history. DIEGO: Well, all good anthropologists should also know a little bit of history, shouldn't they?*

¿Recuerda Ud.?: Suggestion

In addition to reviewing the answers to the brief exercise, you may wish to review the use of the subjunctive with influence in brief conversational exchanges with students.

Answers

1. in two-clause sentences **2.** in the subordinate clause **3.** after **4.** The subject is different in each clause. **5.** the infinitive **6.** emotion, doubt/denial

Gramática 36

Use of the Subjunctive: Emotion

Suggestion

Have students pick out the subjunctive and subjunctive cues in the *GEA.* Ask: What do the cues have in common? (emotional responses)

Follow-up

Ask students the following questions.

*¿Le sorprende a Ud. que la palabra **mariachi** venga del francés?*
¿De qué cosas se alegra Ud.?
¿Qué le molesta que haga su compañero/a de cuarto/casa (esposo/a, etcétera)?
¿Qué le sorprende de la clase de español?

Multimedia: Internet

Have students search the Internet for music clips of *mariachi* music. If possible, bring a video or CD of a *mariachi* performance to class.

Heritage Speakers

Anime a los hispanohablantes a describir a los mariachis. ¿Qué tipo de ropa llevan? ¿Dónde suelen cantar? ¿Qué temas predominan en sus canciones?

NATIONAL STANDARDS: Cultures

The *mariachi* is essentially a mixture of European and indigenous musical cultures that probably began in the 16th century. There is no mention, however, of the *mariachi* until the 19th century. The origin of the word *mariachi* is a mystery, but there are two principal theories. Most scholars believe that *mariachi* is a derivation of an indigenous word related to music. A widely circulated theory, although less supported by scholars, is that *mariachi* is a corruption of the French word *mariage.* This theory is the one explained in the dialogue.

Emphasis 1: Suggestion

Point out that a change of subject is required for the subjunctive with emotional statements, just as with expressions of influence.

Emphasis 2, 3, 4: Notes

- Many of these verbs and generalizations are also value judgments (*es bueno/malo/necesario/extraño*). They are reactions that imply a personal opinion, which may differ from one person to another.
- Emphasize the use of the infinitive, not the subjunctive, after expressions and generalizations of emotion when there is no change of subject.

  Siento estar tan cansado. vs. *Siento que estés tan cansado.*

  Es mejor esperar. vs. *Es mejor que esperen.*
- Point out that there are many other verbs and impersonal expressions of emotion that can trigger the use of the subjunctive in the subordinate clause.

Emphasis 4: Optional Generalizations

Generalizations of emotion: *es estupendo / fenomenal / inconcebible / inexplicable / una pena que... ; ¡qué pena que... !*

Emphasis 4: Suggestions

- Students have used impersonal expressions + *inf.* since the beginning of this text. Emphasize the need for the second subject after expressions of generalization for the subjunctive to be used.
- Tell students that it is impossible to provide a list of *all* impersonal expressions of emotion that can trigger the subjunctive. Students should be alert to the concept of emotion in a generalization.

Preliminary Exercises

- Use the following chain drill to practice forms.
  1. *Espero que tú sepas el número correcto.* (*Ud., ella, nosotros, Uds.*)
  2. *Los padres temen que seamos malos estudiantes.* (*yo, tú, ellos, Elvira*)
  3. *Es una lástima que no podamos ir al museo.* (*yo, Uds., él, vosotras*)
- Have students express the following ideas in Spanish.
  1. *I'm afraid that they're not coming / that he can't do it.*
  2. *It surprises me that you can't do it / that he won't permit it.*
  3. *I'm sorry that your daughter is sick.*

①		②
first subject = indicative	**que**	second subject = subjunctive
EMOTION		

1. The Concept of Emotion

Another "trigger" for the use of the subjunctive in the subordinate clause is the concept of *emotion* (**la emoción**). The subject of the main clause *is glad, fears, hopes*, and so on, that the subject of the subordinate clause does something, expressed by a verb in the subjunctive. The verb in the main clause is always in the indicative.

Esperamos que Ud. **pueda** asistir.
We hope (that) you'll be able to come.

Tengo miedo de que mi abuelo **esté** muy enfermo.
I'm afraid (that) my grandfather is very ill.

Es una lástima que no **den** conciertos.
It's a shame (that) they're not putting on any concerts.

2. Verbs of Emotion

Here are some common expressions of emotion.

alegrarse de	to be happy about
esperar	to hope
lamentar	to regret; to feel sorry
sentir (siento) (i)	to regret; to feel sorry
temer	to fear, be afraid

Temo que María **se caiga** mientras baila.
I'm afraid that María will fall while she's dancing.

3. Verbs of Emotion Like *gustar*

Gustar and similar verbs are frequently used to express emotion. If there is a change of subject in the subordinate clause, the subjunctive will be used.

¡OJO!

Remember that these verbs are used with indirect object pronouns in Spanish. They are expressed in English in a number of different ways.

me (te/le...) encanta/fascina/gusta/molesta/sorprende que...
I'm (you're/he's . . .) very glad/fascinated/pleased/annoyed/surprised that . . .
It really pleases/fascinates/pleases/bothers/surprises me (you/him . . .) that . . .

encantar	**molestar**	
fascinar	**sorprender**	to surprise
gustar		

Me molesta que las entradas del museo **sean** tan caras.
It bothers me that museum entrance fees are so expensive.

Nos sorprende que este cantante **tenga** tanto éxito.
I'm surprised that this singer is so successful.

4. Impersonal Expressions of Emotion

When a new subject is introduced after a generalization of emotion, it is followed by the subjunctive in the subordinate clause. Here are some general expressions of emotion.

¡OJO!

Remember to use the infinitive after impersonal expressions of emotion when there is no change of subject. Compare these sentences.

Es mejor estudiar mucho.
Es mejor que **estudiemos** mucho.

es absurdo que...	it's absurd that . . .
es extraño que...	it's strange that . . .
¡qué extraño que... !	how strange that . . . !
es increíble que...	it's incredible that . . .
es mejor/bueno/malo que...	it's better/good/bad that . . .
es normal que...	it's normal that . . .
es terrible que...	it's terrible that . . .
es una lástima que...	it's a shame that . . .
¡qué lástima que... !	what a shame that . . . !
es urgente que...	it's urgent that . . .

Heritage Speakers

Note que los hispanohablantes a veces retienen la cláusula dependiente a pesar de que no haya cambio de sujeto.

Espero que (yo) saque una nota buena en el examen.
Siento que (yo) lo haya ofendido.

Anime a los hispanohablantes a describir la diferencia estructural o gramatical entre los siguientes pares de oraciones.

Me alegro de que (yo) haya sacado una buena nota.
Me alegro de haber sacado una buena nota.

Espero que (yo) pueda asistir a la boda.
Espero poder asistir a la boda.

Resources: Transparency 131

Autoprueba

Identify the sentences that require the subjunctive when expressed in Spanish.

1. ☐ I'm surprised you're here.
2. ☐ We're happy about the prize.
3. ☐ They're afraid of the director.
4. ☐ It's good that they want all of your paintings.
5. ☐ I hope to attend the concert.

Answers: **1, 4**

Práctica

A. ¡Anticipemos! Opiniones sobre el cine

Paso 1. Diga si las siguientes declaraciones son ciertas o falsas para Ud.

	CIERTO	FALSO
1. Me molesta que muchas películas sean tan violentas.	☐	☐
2. Es absurdo que algunos actores ganen (*earn*) tanto dinero.	☐	☐
3. Espero que presenten a más actores asiáticos, hispanos y de origen africano en las películas.	☐	☐
4. Es una lástima que no haya muchos papeles para las actrices maduras.	☐	☐
5. Es increíble que gasten millones de dólares en hacer películas.	☐	☐
6. Me sorprende que Jessica Simpson sea tan famosa.	☐	☐

Paso 2. Ahora haga oraciones sobre cómo Ud. quiere o no quiere que sean las cosas con respecto al cine. Use las oraciones del **Paso 1** como base.

MODELO: **1.** Quiero que las películas **no sean tan violentas.**

B. Comentarios sobre el arte

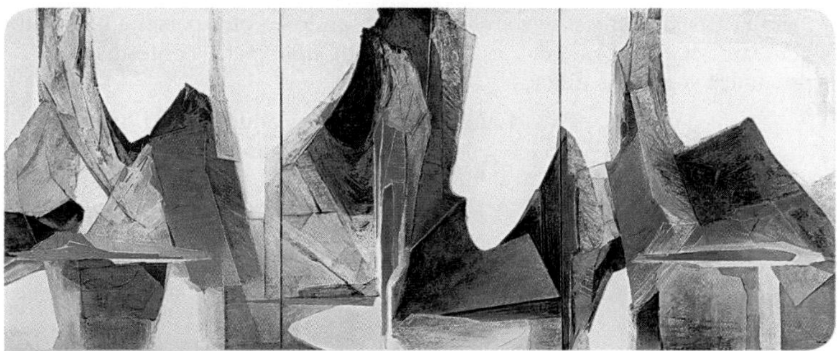

***Catavi*, por la pintora boliviana María Luisa Pacheco (1919–1982)**

Paso 1. Complete las siguientes opiniones sobre esta pintura de María Luisa Pacheco. Use la forma apropiada de los verbos entre paréntesis.

1. Dicen que esta pintora es famosa. Me sorprende que su pintura le (gustar) a la gente. Temo que sus obras (ser) demasiado abstractas para mí. Es una lástima que (haber) tantas obras de arte que yo no comprendo. guste, sean haya
2. ¡Me encanta esta pintura! ¡Qué lástima que (haber) gente que no entiende el arte abstracto. Me alegro de que esta pintura (estar) en este libro, porque no yo conocía la obra de Pacheco. Me sorprende que (ella) no (tener) más fama fuera de Bolivia. haya, esté, tenga

Paso 2. Ahora, en parejas, entrevístense sobre sus opiniones de esta pintura. Deben explicar lo que les gusta más y lo que les gusta menos.

Multimedia: Internet

Have students search the Internet for Spanish language newspapers (*El Comercio,* for example). Based on current news events, students should prepare five statements expressing their emotions and using the subjunctive, for example: *Es increíble que haya tanto turismo en el Ecuador.*

Heritage Speakers

En algunos dialectos del español, hay hispanohablantes que tienden a eliminar la conjunción *que* antes de la cláusula subordinada. Por consiguiente, a veces se oye decir: «Espero haya contestado tu pregunta» o «Espero no se vaya ningún jugador». Aunque haya personas que hablan así, se recomienda evitar este uso popular.

4. *It's incredible that Johnny is already 12 years old!*
5. *What a shame that Julio isn't feeling well!*
6. *How strange that Jorge never calls you!*
7. *I'm glad that you're going to get the painting for your grandmother.*

Prác. A: Suggestions

- Ask students to analyze the elements of each sentence: 2 clauses, 2 subjects, indicative verb, *que,* subjunctive verb.
- After students have completed *Pasos 1* and *2* working on their own, ask for a show of hands for those who answered *cierto* for each item in *Paso 1.* Then ask for volunteers to restate the items (as modeled in *Paso 2*).
- Give a few original items of your own, then ask for items from the class.

Prác. A: Note

Active vocabulary: *ganar* (to earn)

Prác. B: Suggestions

- Have students explain the choice of mood in all the sentences in the activity.
- Have students invent similar situations and present them to the class.

Redacción: As a follow-up to *Prác. B,* ask students to describe in writing one of their favorite works of art or a craft that they particularly like. Define art broadly so that students can write about music or film as well as about painting, sculpture, or arquitecture. Encourage students to choose works by Hispanic artists if possible. (One way to facilitate this is to bring to class books that have reproductions of art by Hispanic artists and allow students to write about one of the works of art in those books.) The description should include:

- what the piece of art is
- who made it, when, and where
- a description of the work itself
- one or several personal reactions to the piece (using the subjunctive, if appropriate)

After you have corrected students' compositions, ask several students to present their paragraphs to the class, using a copy of the piece of art (or the actual piece, if it is something that they own). Students can also do presentations of this kind in small groups.

Prác. B: Note

Catavi is a mining town in the Bolivian highlands.

Nota comunicativa

Suggestions

- Emphasize that *ojalá* is invariable in form and is always followed by the subjunctive. *Ojalá* itself is not conjugated.
- *Ojalá* comes from the Arabic expression that means *Allah (God) willing* or *may Allah want.* Point out that Arabs lived in most of what is today Spain and Portugal for eight centuries (8th–15th). Their influence was great in the Iberian Peninsula; their language, especially, influenced Spanish vocabulary. Other commonly used Spanish words that come from Arabic include *el álgebra, el aceite, la almohada* (new), *la aceituna* (new).

Prác. C: Follow-up

Ask students: *¿A Ud. le interesa la ópera? ¿Le fascina, le aburre o no tiene opinión?*

Con. A: Suggestions

- Show the drawings on an overhead transparency and have students close their books. Ask questions and have volunteers answer.
- Have students work in groups to react to the following situations, and then resolve them by giving advice or making a request, for example:

  Situación: Su profesor(a) de español les da muchos exámenes. → Opinión: (No) *Me gusta eso. Quiero que nos dé más/menos exámenes. Solución: Profesor(a), dénos más/menos exámenes, por favor.*

1. *Yo les hablo demasiado rápido en español.*
2. *En un restaurante, no hay asientos en la sección de no fumar y Ud. se sienta al lado de un señor que fuma mucho.*
3. *Su vecino/a pone el estéreo por la mañana mientras Ud. trata de estudiar.*
4. *Sus padres (amigos) siempre van de vacaciones al mismo sitio todos los veranos.*

Resources: Transparencies 132, 133

Nota **comunicativa**

Cómo expresar los deseos con *ojalá*

Ojalá is one way to express *I hope* in Spanish. As with the verbs of emotion, it is followed by the present subjunctive. **Ojalá** is invariable in form and the use of **que** with it is optional.

¡Ojalá (que) yo **gane** la lotería algún día!
I hope (that) I win the lottery some day!
¡Ojalá (que) haya paz en el mundo algún día!
I hope (that) there will be peace in the world some day!

Ojalá (que) no **pierdan** tu equipaje.
I hope (that) they don't lose your luggage.

Ojalá can also be used alone as an interjection in response to a question.

—¿Te va a ayudar Julio a estudiar para el examen?
—**¡Ojalá!**

Prác. C: Answers: *Ojalá (que)…* **1.** *los escenarios sean fantásticos.* **2.** *haya subtítulos en inglés.* **3.** *el director esté preparado.* **4.** *los músicos toquen bien.* **5.** *nuestros asientos no estén lejos del escenario.* **6.** *lleguemos a tiempo.*

C. Una noche en la ópera. Dos amigos van a la ópera. Diga lo que temen y lo que esperan. Use **ojalá.**

MODELO: las entradas (*tickets*) / no costar mucho →
Ojalá (que) las entradas no **cuesten** mucho.

1. los escenarios / ser / fantásticos
2. haber / subtítulos en inglés
3. el director (*conductor*) / estar / preparado
4. los músicos / tocar bien
5. nuestros asientos / no estar / lejos del escenario
6. (nosotros) llegar / a tiempo

Conversación

A. Situaciones

Paso 1. Las siguientes personas están pensando en otra persona o en algo que van a hacer. ¿Qué emociones sienten? ¿Qué temen? Conteste las preguntas según los dibujos.

1. Jorge piensa en su amiga Estela. ¿Por qué piensa en ella? ¿Dónde está? ¿Qué siente Jorge? ¿Qué espera? ¿Qué espera Estela? ¿Espera que la visiten los amigos? ¿que le manden algo?

2. ¿Dónde quiere pasar las vacaciones Mariana? ¿Espera que alguien la acompañe? ¿Dónde espera que estén juntos? ¿Qué teme Mariana? ¿Qué espera?

Paso 2. Ahora, en parejas, hagan y contesten preguntas basadas en los dibujos y en sus respuestas del **Paso 1.** ¿Tuvieron los/las dos la misma impresión de los dibujos?

Heritage Speakers

Algunos hispanohablantes eliminan *que* después de *ojalá*. Varios tiempos verbales, además del presente de subjuntivo, aparecen después de esta expresión impersonal. Anime a los hispanohablantes a explicar la diferencia entre las siguientes oraciones.

Ojalá que llueva hoy.
Ojalá que lloviera hoy.
Ojalá que haya llovido.
Ojalá que hubiera llovido ayer.

B. ¿Cómo es nuestra sociedad? Diga lo que Ud. opina de las siguientes declaraciones respecto a algunos de los valores de nuestra sociedad. Empiece sus opiniones con las **Expresiones** indicadas o con cualquier (*any*) otra.

Expresiones

es bueno/malo que **es extraño/increíble que** **es normal que** **es una lástima que** **lamento que** **me sorprende que**	+ *subjuntive*	**es obvio que** **es verdad que** **la realidad es que** **(yo) sé que**	+ *indicative*

Estrategia

Use el subjuntivo con las expresiones de la izquierda. Use el indicativo con las (*those*) de la derecha.

MODELO: Los futbolistas profesionales ganan sueldos fenomenales ⟶ **Es increíble que** los futbolistas **ganen** sueldos fenomenales.

1. Muchas personas viven para trabajar. No saben descansar.
2. La nuestra es una sociedad de consumidores.
3. Juzgamos (*We judge*) a los otros por las cosas materiales que tienen.
4. Las personas ricas tienen mucho prestigio en esta sociedad.
5. Las mujeres generalmente no ganan tanto dinero como los hombres por hacer igual trabajo.
6. Algunas obras de arte cuestan millones de dólares.
7. Para la gente joven la televisión es más atractiva que los libros.
8. Hay discriminación contra la gente mayor en ciertas profesiones.

C. Esta universidad. Diga lo que Ud. opina de las siguientes declaraciones respecto a lo que ocurre en esta universidad. Use frases como: **Me gusta que… , Me molesta que… , Es terrible que…**

MODELO: Gastan mucho/poco dinero en construir nuevos edificios. ⟶ **Me molesta que gasten** mucho dinero en construir nuevos edificios.

1. Se les da mucha importancia a los deportes.
2. El precio de la matrícula es exagerado / muy bajo.
3. Se ofrecen muchos/pocos cursos en mi especialización.
4. Es necesario estudiar ciencias/lenguas para graduarse.
5. Hay muchos/pocos requisitos (*requirements*) para graduarse.
6. En general, hay mucha/poca gente en las clases.

D. Tres deseos. En parejas, piensen en tres deseos: uno que se relacione con Uds. personalmente, otro con algún amigo o miembro de su familia y otro con su país, con el mundo o con la humanidad en general. Expresen sus deseos con **Ojalá (que).**

MODELO: Ojalá que **no haya otra guerra.**

Vocabulario útil

las elecciones
la gente que no tiene hogar (casa)
la guerra war
el hambre hunger
el partido

la pobreza poverty

resolver (resuelvo) to solve; to resolve
terminar to end

Con. B: Note

The expressions that take the indicative preview aspects of the use of the subjunctive or indicative with expressions of doubt and denial (*Gram. 37*). In this case, students will use the indicative after expressions that affirm the truth of what follows.

Con. B: Suggestion

Do this activity with the whole class. Ask students to indicate whether the feelings they expressed were positive or negative or whether they simply affirmed the truth of the statements given. Where there are sharp differences of opinion, lead class discussion on the topics if they are of interest to students, providing vocabulary, as needed.

Con. B: Extension

Follow up with items that use real-world statements related to students.

9. (Estudiante) *está enfermo/a hoy.*
10. *No tenemos clase el sábado.*
11. (Estudiante) *se gradúa en junio.*
12. *El coche de _____ no funciona bien.*
13. *Llueve mucho/poco este año.*

Con. C: Suggestion

Have students complete the activity in groups of four to six. Have one student act as the secretary, taking notes on general reactions. Later he/she will summarize the comments of his/her group with sentences like: *Nuestro grupo piensa/opina/dice* (*no está de acuerdo en*) *que…* General results from all groups can serve as a starting point for a simple discussion or a debate.

Gramática 37
Use of the Subjunctive: Doubt and Denial

Suggestion
Have students explain the uses of the subjunctive in the *GEA* sentences.

Note
While students will probably be aware of the effects of the sun at high altitudes, they may not associate such heights with extreme weather conditions, especially cold. Tell them that the average temperature on the *altiplano* is below 10 °C (50 °F) and that there are great differences between the average day temperature of 25 °C (77 °F) and the night of below 0 °C (32 °F).

Follow-up
Select another photo from the text or bring in photos of your own and create similar statements about them. Allow students to express their own opinions by using the subjunctive "triggers" from the *GEA*.

Emphasis 1: Suggestion
Point out the similarity of this pattern (two verbs, a second subject) to that of the subjunctive after expressions of influence/emotion.

37 Expressing Uncertainty
Use of the Subjunctive (Part 4): Doubt and Denial

Grammar Tutorial 37
connect SPANISH
www.connectspanish.com

Gramática en acción: El traje tradicional de las bolivianas

Unas mujers bolivianas con su ropa tradicional, en La Paz

¿Cuánto sabe Ud. de la ropa que llevan las indígenas bolivianas? ¿Cree que son ciertas o falsas las siguientes declaraciones? Las respuestas están al pie de la página.

1. **Es verdad que** los sombreros hongo son una parte del traje tradicional de las indígenas del altiplano boliviano.
2. **Es probable que** sea muy frecuente ver a bolivianas que llevan sombrero hongo.
3. **Dudo que** los pantalones sean parte del traje tradicional de las bolivianas del altiplano.
4. **No creo que** el uso de los sombreros hongo sea una tradición inca.
5. En Bolivia, **es obvio que** llevar sombrero es una buena protección contra el sol.

¿Y Ud.?
¿Le gusta el traje tradicional de las mujeres bolivianas? ¿Cree que es hermoso (*beautiful*) y práctico? ¿Le sorprende que las bolivianas indígenas lleven sombrero?

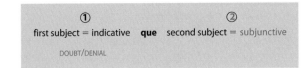

①		②
first subject = indicative	**que**	second subject = subjunctive
DOUBT/DENIAL		

1. **The Concepts of Doubt and Denial**
The concepts of *doubt* (**la duda**) and *denial* (**la negación**) are also "triggers" for the use of the subjunctive in the subordinate clause. The subject of the main clause *doubts, does not believe, denies,* and so on, that the subject of the subordinate clause does something, expressed by a verb in the subjunctive. The verb in the main clause is always in the indicative.

No creo que **sean** cuadros de Goya.
I don't believe (that) they're paintings by Goya.

Es imposible que la actriz **salga** al escenario ahora.
It's impossible for the actress to go on (stage) now.

The traditional costume of Bolivian women *How much do you know about the clothing that indigenous Bolivian women wear? Do you think that the following statements are true or false? The answers are at the bottom of the page.* **1.** *It's true that bowler hats are a part of the traditional costume of indigenous women of the Bolivian high plateau.* **2.** *It's likely that one frequently sees Bolivian women who are wearing bowler hats.* **3.** *I doubt that pants are part of the traditional costume of women from the high plateau.* **4.** *I don't think that the use of bowler hats is an Inca tradition.* **5.** *In Bolivia, it's obvious that wearing a hat is good protection from the sun.*

Respuestas: **1.** *cierto: Muchas indígenas bolivianas lo llevan.* **2.** *cierto: Bolivia tiene el porcentaje más alto de población indígena en toda América. Por eso es muy normal ver a mujeres que llevan ropa tradicional.* **3.** *cierto: La pollera, un tipo de falda con mucho vuelo* (flare) *y colores, es la ropa típica de las indígenas bolivianas.* **4.** *cierto: Es una tradición colonial.* **5.** *cierto: La región del altiplano boliviano está tan alta que la exposición a los rayos solares es un problema serio. Por eso, el sombrero es una protección ideal para la cara, y también protege a los habitantes del frío.*

NATIONAL STANDARDS: Comparisons
Expressions of certainty (not doubt) are used with the subjunctive by some native speakers to convey that they are not absolutely sure or do not necessarily believe the statement. For example, *No dudo que Juan tenga suerte* or *Creo que los vecinos hayan llegado.* Have students think about ways that doubt is cast on statements in English (tone of voice, intonation, tag statements such as *not!,* and so on).

2. Verbs of Doubt and Denial
Here are some verbs that express doubt and denial. Not all Spanish expressions of doubt are given here. Remember that any expression of doubt is followed by the subjunctive in the subordinate clause.

no creer	to disbelieve
dudar	to doubt
negar (niego) (gu)	to deny
no estar seguro/a (de)	to be unsure (of)

¡OJO!
Creer and **estar seguro/a** are followed by the indicative in affirmative statements because they do not express doubt, denial, or negation. Compare these examples.

Estamos seguros de que el concierto **es** hoy.
We're sure that the concert is today.

No creemos que el concierto **sea** hoy.
We don't believe that the concert is today.

¡OJO!
When there is no change of subject, these verbs can be followed either by the infinitive or by the indicative or subjunctive, as needed.

Creo que **sé** la respuesta. / **Creo saber** la respuesta. } *I believe (that) I know the answer.*

No creo que (yo) **sepa** la respuesta. / **No creo saber** la respuesta. } *I don't believe (that) I know the answer.*

¡OJO!
In questions with **creer,** the use of the indicative or the subjunctive reflects what the speaker thinks: indicative = believes so, subjunctive = doubts it.

¿**Crees** que **sea** auténtica la pieza?
Do you think that the piece is authentic? (I don't.)

¿**Crees** que **es** auténtica la pieza?
Do you think that the piece is authentic? (I do.)

3. Impersonal Expressions of Doubt and Denial
When a new subject is introduced after a generalization of doubt or denial, the subjunctive is used in the subordinate clause. Here are some generalizations of doubt and denial.

es posible que...	it's possible that . . .
es imposible que...	it's impossible that . . .
es probable que...	it's probable (likely) that . . .
es improbable que...	it's improbable (unlikely) that . . .
no es cierto que...	it's not certain that . . .
no es seguro que...	it's not a sure thing that . . .
no es verdad que...	it's not true that . . .

¡OJO!
Generalizations that express certainty are not followed by the subjunctive but rather by the indicative.

Es verdad que Julio **cocina** bien.
No hay duda de que Julio **cocina** bien.

Es posible que **veamos** el Ballet Nacional de Cuba esta semana.
It's possible (that) we'll see the National Ballet of Cuba this week.

Es imposible ver el Ballet Nacional de Cuba esta semana porque no hay entradas.
It's impossible to see the National Ballet of Cuba this week because there aren't any tickets.

Emphasis 2: Suggestions

- Point out that there are many other verbs and impersonal expressions of doubt and denial that can trigger the use of the subjunctive in the subordinate clause.
- Contrast and model *no creer* and *dudar* (subjunctive) with *creer,* which usually implies affirmation and is therefore followed by the indicative.
- Point out that an easy rule is that *all* negated verbs take subjunctive in the subordinate clause. *No niego* and *no dudo* are the only exceptions. They can take either the subjunctive or the indicative, depending on the meaning the speaker wishes to convey. Most students are not ready for these subtleties, and the use of *no niego* and *no dudo* should be restricted for now.
- Verbs of doubt and denial are usually followed by the infinitive when there is no subject change: *Dudo que Juan tenga el dinero. Dudo tener el dinero.* However, as the examples with *creer* show, it is also possible to use either the indicative or the subjunctive (depending on the "trigger") when there is no change of subject: *Dudo que* (*yo*) *tenga el dinero.* At first, it may seem that it is needless to introduce this detail with verbs of doubt or denial, but students will naturally generate sentences like the *creer* paradigms. Unless this distinction is made, such sentences would technically be incorrect.
- Emphasize that the use of the indicative or subjunctive in subordinate clauses reflects the opinion of the person asking the question. Indicative: *¿Crees que los Ramírez son ricos?* (The speaker believes they are.) Subjunctive: *¿Crees que los Ramírez sean ricos?* (The speaker doubts that they are.)

Emphasis 3: Suggestions

- Students have used impersonal expressions + *inf.* since the beginning of this text. Emphasize the need for the second subject after expressions of generalization for the subjunctive to be used.
- Tell students that it is impossible to provide a list of *all* impersonal expressions of doubt and denial that can trigger the subjunctive. Students should be alert to the concept of emotion in a generalization.

Preliminary Exercises

- Have students indicate whether the following expressions would require the indicative (I) or the subjunctive (S).
  1. *Es cierto que…* (I)
  2. *No estamos seguros de que…* (S)
  3. *No es verdad que…* (S)
  4. *Dudo que…* (S)
  5. *No creo que…* (S)
  6. *Es imposible que…* (S)
  7. *Es probable que…*(S)
  8. *Estamos seguros de que…* (I)
  9. *No es cierto que…* (S)
  10. *Es improbable que…*(S)
- Have students tell whether the following sentences would require the indicative (I) or the subjunctive (S) in Spanish.
  1. I'm sure she's right. (I)
  2. I doubt we'll get there on time. (S)
  3. I don't think they know. (S)
  4. It's impossible that he knows. (S)
  5. We believe she's at home. (I)
  6. It's unlikely that they will go. (S)
  7. It's true that Susan always arrives on time. (I)
  8. They don't believe I know how to cook. (S)

Prác. A: Suggestion

- Before students start *Paso 1,* ask them whether the sentences contain the subjunctive (no) and why not.
- In preparation for *Paso 2,* asks students to analyze what will happen to the *Paso 1* sentences when the suggested phrases are added to them.

Prác. B: Preliminary Exercises

Have students express the following ideas in Spanish.

1. I doubt that they are rich / that they are coming.
2. I don't believe that they are rich / that they are coming.
3. I believe that they are rich / that they are coming.

Prác. B: Suggestion

Emphasize the need to decide between the indicative or subjunctive when conjugating the second verb, as indicated in *Estrategia*.

Prác. B: Note

The civilization of *los tihuanacos* (in Quechua) or *los tiwanaku* (in Aymara) is considered the oldest in South America, up to 3,000 years old by some estimates. It developed near *el lago Titicaca* (altitude 3,820 meters, or 12,532 feet), on the border between Bolivia and Peru. As the Tihuanaco culture declined, the Aymara people took over, and eventually the whole region was dominated by the Inca Empire.

Autoprueba

Identify the phrases that express doubt or denial.

1. ☐ dudamos
2. ☐ estoy segura
3. ☐ niegas
4. ☐ es cierto
5. ☐ es posible
6. ☐ no cree

Answers: 1, 3, 5, 6

Práctica

A. ¿Qué opina Ud.?

Paso 1. Diga lo que Ud. opina de las siguientes declaraciones.

	ES CIERTO	NO ES CIERTO
1. A la mayoría de la gente le gusta ir a los museos.	☐	☐
2. Todos mis amigos prefieren el teatro al cine.	☐	☐
3. Conozco a muchas personas que se interesan en la arquitectura.	☐	☐
4. En esta clase hay mucha gente con talento artístico.	☐	☐
5. La expresión artística más popular entre los jóvenes es la música.	☐	☐
6. Me encanta regalar objetos de cerámica.	☐	☐
7. Voy a conciertos de música clásica con frecuencia.	☐	☐
8. *El cascanueces* (*The Nutcracker*) es un ballet típico del mes de mayo.	☐	☐

Paso 2. Ahora repita las declaraciones del **Paso 1,** empezando con **Es cierto que…** o **No es cierto que… ,** según sus respuestas. **¡OJO!** Hay que usar el subjuntivo después de **No es cierto que…**

Prác. B: Answers: 1. *«Creo que es una vasija… »* **2.** *«Es obvio que está… »* **3.** *«Es posible que las figuras representen… »* **4.** *«¿Cree que es/sea… ?»* **5.** *«No creo que sea… »* **6.** *«Es probable que sea… »* **7.** *«Dudo que las figuras simbolicen… »* **8.** *«Es más probable que sean… »*

Una vasija incaica

B. Una vasija (*vessel*) **en el museo.** Haga oraciones completas para expresar las especulaciones de dos antropólogos sobre una nueva pieza que está en el museo.

Habla el profesor Martín:

1. «creer / que / ser una vasija de la civilización inca»
2. «ser obvio / que / estar hecha de barro (*made of clay*)»
3. «ser posible / que / el diseño (*design*) representar algo en especial»
4. «¿creer / que / ser una pieza auténtica?»

Habla la profesora Figueroa:

5. «no creer / que / ser una vasija inca»
6. «ser probable / que / ser una pieza auténtica de la civilización tihuanaco»
7. «dudar / que / el diseño simbolizar algo en especial»

Estrategia

primer verbo = indicativo
segundo verbo = ¿indicativo o subjuntivo?

Conversación

A. En un mercado de artesanía. ¿Cómo puede reaccionar un turista en un mercado como el de (*that in*) la foto de la página 397? Complete las oraciones, pensando en los precios y en los regalos que a los turistas les gusta comprar para llevar de recuerdos (*as souvenirs*).

Una turista, que busca un sombrero en el mercado de Otavalo, Ecuador

1. ¡Es fantástico (que)… !
2. No creo que los precios del mercado…
3. Dudo mucho que estos vendedores…
4. Estoy seguro/a de que…
5. No es muy probable que…

Vocabulario útil

la muñeca doll
el poncho de mujer
la figurita de cerámica ceramic figurine

Nota comunicativa

Los verbos que requieren preposiciones

You learned in earlier chapters that when two verbs occur in a series (one right after the other), the second verb is usually in the infinitive.

Prefiero cenar a las siete.	*I prefer to eat at seven.*

Some Spanish verbs, however, require that a preposition or other word be placed before the second verb (still in the infinitive). You have already used many of the important Spanish verbs that have this feature.

- The following verbs require the preposition **a** before an infinitive.

aprender a	**empezar (empiezo) (c) a**	**invitar a**	**venir a**
ayudar a	**enseñar a**	**ir a**	**volver (vuelvo) a**

Mis padres me **enseñaron** a **bailar.**	*My parents taught me to dance.*

- These verbs or verb phrases require **de** before an infinitive.

acabar de	**dejar de**	**tener ganas de**
acordarse (me acuerdo) de	**olvidarse de**	**tratar de** (*to try to*)

Siempre **tratamos** de **llegar** puntualmente.	*We always try to arrive on time.*

- **Insistir** requires **en** before an infinitive.

Insisten en **venir** esta noche.	*They insist on coming over tonight.*

- Two verbs require **que** before an infinitive: **haber que, tener que.**

Hay que **ver** el nuevo museo.	*It's necessary to see the new museum.*

Con. A: Suggestions

- Set up an "open-air market" in the classroom and have students take turns role-playing exchanges in different "booths."
- You may want to review and/or introduce vocabulary associated with purchasing prior to completing this activity.

  cobrar (new) *costar* *regatear*
  comprar *pagar*

- Ask students personalized questions regarding items in the classroom.

  Esta camisa me costó doscientos cincuenta dólares. ¿Es posible?
  ¿Cuánto costó esta calculadora? ¿Setenta y cinco dólares?

Nota comunicativa

Note

Students have used most of the verbs presented here, along with their respective prepositions and other words. Treat the material as a summary, not as new information.

Suggestions

- Point out the use of *a* + *inf.* with verbs of motion, e.g., *salir a bailar, llegar a entender, ir a cenar,* and so on.
- Contrast and model *olvidar* + *inf.* vs. *olvidarse de* + *inf.; acordarse de* (new) + *inf.* vs. *recordar* + *inf.; pensar* + *inf.* vs. *pensar de/en/que.*
- Point out that *hay que* is an impersonal verb form equivalent to the English *one should/must. Tener que,* however, is more personal and can be conjugated in all persons.

Optional

- Have students express the following ideas in Spanish.
  1. He's learning to read. (to write, to play tennis)
  2. She helps me wash the dishes. (dust, cook)
  3. We're beginning to understand it. (to read it, to explain it)
  4. They always invite us to go to the theater. (to the movies, to the museum)
  5. They're coming to eat. (to visit us, to see us)
  6. He's trying to help. (to cook, to see)
  7. I just ate. (arrived, called)
  8. He insists on doing it. (bringing it, listening to it)
- Have students complete these sentences in as many ways as they can.
  1. *Mis padres/hijos deben…*
  2. *Mis padres me ayudan a…*
  3. *Mis amigos me invitan a…*
  4. *Mis amigos quieren…*

Gramática 38

The Subjunctive: A Summary

Suggestion

Before asking students to form sentences, go through the list of sentence starters alongside the photo, making sure that students understand when to use the subjunctive or the infinitive with the first set and also reviewing why the indicative and the subjunctive are used in each set.

Then go through the list of items, making sure that students understand the grammatical needs of each: infinitive (that is, no *que*), indicative sentence starter, or subjunctive sentence starter.

Finally, allow students to form sentences.

Reciclado: Review the names of colors by asking students to tell what colors they see in the textiles in the photo.

Note

This is primarily a summary section. The only new material presented is the concept of noun clauses and the use of indirect object pronouns with verbs like *decir.*

B. En los próximos cinco años…

En parejas, hagan oraciones con una palabra o frase de cada columna para expresar lo que Uds. creen que les puede ocurrir en el futuro próximo (*near*). ¿Cuántas respuestas similares tienen Uds.?

¿INDICATIVO O SUBJUNTIVO?

(no) creo que… (no) dudo que… es (im)posible que… (no) estoy seguro/a de que… (no) es cierto que… tengo que…	+	(yo) { aprender a dejar de empezar a ir a tratar de volver a	+	ser famoso/a estar casado/a (*married*) ganar la lotería jugar a la lotería pintar cuadros fumar tener hijos terminar mis estudios esculpir ¿ ?

38 Expressing Influence, Emotion, Doubt, and Denial

The Subjunctive (Part 5): A Summary

Grammar Tutorial 38
connect SPANISH
www.connectspanish.com

Gramática en acción: Los tejidos de Otavalo, Ecuador

Textiles en un mercado de Otavalo, Ecuador

+ Subjuntivo/Infinitivo

- Quiero (que)…
- Espero (que)…
- Ojalá (que)…
- No me sorprende (que)…
- Dudo (que)…

+ Indicativo

- Dicen que…
- Sé que…
- No hay duda que…
- Creo que…

¿Y Ud.?

Haga oraciones gramaticalmente correctas y verdaderas para Ud.

1. … (yo) pueda visitar el mercado de Otavalo algún día.
2. … visitar el Ecuador algún día.
3. … el mercado de Otavalo está en las montañas del Ecuador.
4. … haya mucho turismo porque es una zona muy bonita y tiene artesanía típica muy fina.
5. … los otavaleños hacen hermosos (bonitos) tejidos.
6. … Otavalo es un lugar muy interesante para visitar.
7. … los otavaleños no pierdan sus ricas tradiciones.
8. … haya mucha información sobre Otavalo en el Internet.

¿Y Ud.? Possible Answers: 1. *Ojalá (que) pueda…* **2.** *Quiero visitar…* **3.** *Sé que el mercado de Otavalo está…* **4.** *No me sorprende que haya…* **5.** *Dicen que los otavaleños hacen…* **6.** *No hay duda que Otavalo es…* **7.** *Espero que los otavaleños no pierdan…* **8.** *Ojalá (que) haya…*

Multimedia: Internet

Have students search the Internet for official websites dedicated to the open-air market in Otavalo, Ecuador. They can find images of the market and view handmade *artesanías* of the Otavalo people online.

①	El subjuntivo	②
first subject = indicative	**que**	second subject = subjunctive
INFLUENCE		
EMOTION		
DOUBT OR DENIAL		

①	El indicativo	②
first subject = indicative	**que**	second subject = indicative
INFORMATION		
CERTAINTY, BELIEF		

This section will help you review what you have already learned about using the subjunctive. If you need more details, review **Gramáticas 35–37.**

1. **The Subjunctive in Two-clause Sentences**
Remember that, in Spanish, the subjunctive occurs primarily in the second clause of two-clause sentences, with a different subject in each clause. If there is no change of subject, an infinitive follows the first verb.

Quiero / **Es necesario** } sacar una nota buena.
I want / *It's necessary* } *to get a good grade.*

Quiero / **Es necesario** } que **los estudiantes** saquen una buena nota.
I want / *It's necessary for* } ***the students*** *to get a good grade.*

2. **Subjunctive "Trigger"**
The main clause, in addition to fulfilling the preceding conditions, must contain an expression of *influence, emotion,* or *doubt* or *denial* in order for the subjunctive to occur in the subordinate clause. If there is no such expression, the indicative is used.

¡OJO!

Remember to look for the "triggers," not just for specific verbs. For example, when you see the verbs **decir** or **creer** in the main clause of a sentence, you need to be aware of how they are used.

The verb **decir** is a subjunctive "trigger" (as in first sentence to the right) when it conveys an order. When **decir** conveys information rather than influence (as in the second sentence), it triggers the indicative.

Similarly, **creer** conveys certainty or belief (as in the third sentence) but **no creer** conveys denial (as in the fourth sentence). When **creer** affirms rather than denies information, it is followed by the indicative.

Dicen que cante Carlota.
They say that Carlota should sing.

Dicen que Julio **canta** muy mal; por eso quieren que cante Carlota.
They say that Julio sings very badly; that's why they want Carlota to sing.

Yo creo que Julio **canta** muy bien.
I think that Julio sings very well.

No creo que Carlota cante mejor que él.
I don't think that Carlota sings better than he (does).

3. **Influence** + *indirect object pronoun*
Some expressions of influence are frequently used with indirect object pronouns. The indirect object pronoun in the main clause indicates the subject of the subordinate clause, as in the sample sentences: **Nos ⟶ (nosotros) vayamos.**

Nos dicen / **Nos** piden / **Nos** recomiendan } que vayamos al concierto.
They tell us to / *They ask us to* / *They recommend that we* } *go to the concert.*

Bright Idea

Suggestions

- Point out to students that they should be able to do the following.
    1. identify the main clause
    2. identify the subordinate clause
    3. locate expressions of influence, emotion, and doubt or denial in the main clause that require the use of the subjunctive in the subordinate clause
- Have students provide expressions of influence, desire, requesting, emotion, and doubt or denial that require the use of the subjunctive in the subordinate clause.

Emphasis 2: Suggestions

- Emphasize and model the use of subjunctive or indicative after certain verbs, depending on the particular connotations of the verb. Here *decir* is followed by both indicative and subjunctive in subordinate clauses depending on the meaning conveyed: *decir* = to say ⟶ indicative; *decir* = to tell, order ⟶ subjunctive.
- Help students categorize other verbs that require the indicative.
    1. *verbos de información: decir, informar, contar*
    2. *verbos de percepción: ver, observar, saber*
    3. *verbos de pensamiento: pensar, creer, opinar*

Emphasis 3: Suggestion

Point out that the indirect object pronouns in these Spanish sentences are used to restate the subject, especially when the subject of the subordinate clause is omitted.

Emphasis 4: Suggestions

- Be sure that students understand that this grammar point is merely descriptive of what they already know, not new information.
- Emphasize and model that noun clauses function as nouns; nouns are typically:
  1. subjects: *Me gusta el chocolate / comer bien.*
  2. objects: *Odio el café / tener hambre.*
  3. objects of a preposition: *Nos reunimos en el café. / Insisto en ir al café.*

Prác. A: Suggestion

Have students comment critically on the painting: *En su opinión, ¿qué hace que esta pintura sea única?*

Heritage Speakers

Anime a los hispanohablantes a describir en voz alta el cuadro de Velázquez.

4. Noun Clauses

All of the uses of the subjunctive that you have learned so far, summarized on the preceding page, fall into the general category of the use of the subjunctive in *noun clauses* (**las cláusulas nominales**).* The noun clause is the second (subordinate) clause in the sentence, the one that contains the subjunctive. It is called a noun clause because it functions like a noun in the sentence, usually as the direct object of the verb in the main clause but sometimes (especially with **gustar**) as the subject.

In the first two pairs of sentences to the right, the subordinate clause is the direct object of the main verb, answering the question *what?*

He wants *what?* ⟶ that they stop playing
They want *what?* ⟶ for the concert to be well attended

In the third pair of sentences, the subordinate clause is the subject of the verb **gustar.**

High ticket prices are not pleasing to the spectators.

Note that a subordinate clause is viewed as a singular subject in Spanish, so **gusta** (not **gustan**) is used in the sentence.

cláusula subordinada = complemento

—¿Qué quiere el director de la orquesta?
—Quiere **que los músicos dejen de tocar.**
"What does the orchestra director want?"
"He wants the musicians to stop playing."

—¿Qué esperan los músicos?
—Esperan **que haya muchos espectadores en el concierto.**
"What do the musicians want?"
"They want the concert to be well attended (that there be many spectators)."

cláusula subordinada = sujeto

—¿Qué no les gusta a los espectadores?
—No les gusta **que las entradas sean muy caras.**
"What don't the spectators like?"
"They don't like tickets to be (that ticket prices are) so expensive."

Autoprueba

Identify the sentences that would require the subjunctive when expressed in Spanish.

1. ☐ What does the director want?
2. ☐ The sculptor insists that we see his new piece.
3. ☐ I want to go to the opera with you.
4. ☐ It's strange that the fans booed.
5. ☐ We doubt the singer will perform tonight.
6. ☐ Paco says that the party is on Sunday.

Answers: **2, 4, 5**

***Las meninas,* por Diego Velázquez (español, 1599–1660)**

Práctica

A. En el Museo del Prado. Siempre es buena idea tener la ayuda de un guía cuando uno visita un museo.

Paso 1. ¿Qué quiere Ud. que haga su guía?

Quiero que el guía…

1. enseñarme los cuadros más famosos de Velázquez me enseñe
2. explicarme algunos detalles de los cuadros me explique
3. saber mucho sobre la vida del pintor sepa

Paso 2. ¿Qué le sorprende de los cuadros de Velázquez?

Me sorprende que muchos cuadros de Velázquez…

1. tener como tema la vida cotidiana (*everyday*) tengan
2. estar en otros museos fuera de España estén
3. ser de la familia real (*royal*) de Felipe IV sean

**Knowing this will help you to describe how the subjunctive works, but it doesn't change anything about how you have learned to use it.*

Culture

From 1621 to 1665, Felipe IV was the king of Spain. He was also the sovereign of the Spanish Netherlands and the king of Portugal (as Filipe III) until 1640. Felipe IV was an avid supporter of the arts and of particular artists such as the Spanish painter Diego Velázquez.

Las meninas (1656) is probably the most famous painting by Velázquez. The title refers to the women, one of whom is a dwarf, who tend to princess Margarita (center). In the shadows, we see Velázquez painting a portrait of the King and Queen, who are reflected in a mirror on the back wall. Their reflected image implies that they are standing in the viewers' place. Have students comment on this use of space. Ask students to speculate on why the painting is named *Las meninas* and not *La Infanta Margarita,* the center of attention.

Paso 3. Ud. todavía quiere saber algo más sobre la vida y el arte de Velázquez.

Es posible que el guía…

1. recomendarme algunos libros sobre la vida y el arte del pintor me recomiende
2. preguntarle a un colega si sabe algo más sobre Velázquez le pregunte
3. no tener más tiempo para hablar conmigo tenga

B. ¡Qué maravilla de robot! Imagine que Ud. tiene un robot último modelo que va a hacer todo lo que Ud. le diga, especialmente las cosas que Ud. detesta o le cuestan hacer (*are hard for you to do*). ¿Qué le va a mandar al robot que haga? Haga oraciones completas.

le voy a decir que… le voy a mandar que…	+	escribirme el informe para la clase de literatura hacerme la crítica de una película para la clase de composición poner la mesa asistir por mí a todas las clases que tengo en la universidad pagar mis cuentas trabajar por mí en la oficina todas las tardes ¿ ?

Conversación

El lugar ideal para vivir

Paso 1. Piense en el lugar ideal para vivir. ¿Es una casa o un apartamento? ¿Está en una ciudad grande o pequeña? ¿Qué actividades culturales ofrece la ciudad? Lea la siguiente lista de factores e indique los que son indispensables para Ud., más otros dos que no estén en la lista.

- ☐ casa con jardín grande
- ☐ apartamento grande
- ☐ apartamento con vista
- ☐ buenos museos
- ☐ cerca de una universidad importante
- ☐ buena orquesta y teatros
- ☐ muchos cines
- ☐ cerca de un gran centro comercial
- ☐ parques
- ☐ zonas naturales cerca de Ud.
- ☐ ¿ ?
- ☐ ¿ ?

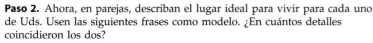

Paso 2. Ahora, en parejas, describan el lugar ideal para vivir para cada uno de Uds. Usen las siguientes frases como modelo. ¿En cuántos detalles coincidieron los dos?

MODELOS: Deseo que mi casa/apartamento…
No quiero vivir en…
(No) Me importa (mucho) (que)…
Es importante que la casa / el apartamento…
(No) Es absolutamente necesario que…
Espero (que)…

Mundo interactivo

You should now be prepared to work with Scenario 7, Activity 2 in Connect Spanish (**www.connectspanish.com**).

Multimedia: Internet

- Have students search the Internet for more Velázquez paintings, periods of his work, and/or different Hispanic artists. Have students give presentations based on their findings.
- Have students search the Internet for the official website of the Prado Museum in Madrid. They can find information about visiting, as well as images of some of the masterpieces housed there.

Prác. B: Follow-up

- Ask students: *¿Cuáles son las ventajas y desventajas (lo bueno y lo malo) de los robots?*
- Have students imagine that they have a house with the latest technology and the most advanced robot. Have them complete the following sentences with this in mind.
  1. *Me alegro de que el robot* ______ (*ayudarme tanto, funcionar bien casi siempre, no quejarse nunca, no pedirme un aumento de sueldo, ¿ … ?*).
  2. *Me sorprende que el robot* ______ (*hablar tan bien y tan lógicamente, ser tan inteligente, parecer tan humano, saberlo todo, ¿ … ?*).
  3. *Dudo que los robots* ______ *algún día.* (*reemplazar* [to replace] *a los seres humanos, controlarlo todo, ¿ … ?*).

Con.: Suggestions

- This can easily be done as a pair or group exercise.
- Before students start the exercise, go through the items in *Paso 1* with the whole class, forming questions (based on the items) that use the subjunctive when possible; e.g.: *¿Quiere que su casa tenga jardín?*
- Before starting *Paso 2*, go through the models with students to determine whether the indicative, subjunctive, or the infinitive should be used with each cue.

Reciclado: Add other housing-related vocabulary to the list of possibilities in *Paso 1*. For example: ______ *alcobas*, ______ *baños, piscina, aire acondicionado, lavaplatos, lavadora y secadora…*

Bright Idea

Con.: Suggestion

After students have completed the activity, have them work in groups to "develop" ideal housing for students at the university. Then have them develop a flyer for advertising their development. They can draw floor plans of individual dorms, apartments, or houses, as well as building and grounds layout. They should label their drawings in Spanish. They should also list features of the development in Spanish. Finally, they should remember to name their development (in Spanish!). Have the groups present their developments to the class. Have the class vote for the most appealing development.

Redacción: Assign *Conversación* as written homework. Specify the number of sentences that you expect students' paragraphs to contain.

Un poco de todo

A: Suggestions

- Use the following transformation drill to review the subjunctive structure prior to beginning *Paso 1*. Write the following model on the board.

  Marcos nunca llega a casa temprano. Dudo que… → Dudo que Marcos llegue a casa temprano hoy.

  1. *Marcos nunca ayuda a limpiar la casa. Dudo que…*
  2. *Nunca se acuesta temprano. Es probable…*
  3. *Casi nunca hace su cama por la mañana. No creo que…*
  4. *Con frecuencia no se despierta hasta las once. Dudo que…*
  5. *Usa mi coche y lo deja sin gasolina. Estoy seguro/a de que…*
- Assign this in groups of five to six students so that they can have a discussion. Remind them to be polite in their disagreement.

A: Variations

- Make up statements about yourself, your family, or class members to which students can react using the phrases provided in *A*. Some statements should be false, even outrageous.
- Substitute more controversial statements for those given in the text.

  Creo que el aborto debe ser legal.
  Se debe permitir el uso de la marihuana.

Un poco de todo

A. Reacciones

Paso 1. Las siguientes declaraciones se refieren a temas importantes en el mundo de hoy. ¿Qué opinan Uds.? Expresen sus opiniones, usando algunas de las siguientes expresiones.

Expresiones

Dudo que…	Es probable que…
Es absurdo que…	Es terrible que…
Es bueno/malo que…	(No) Es verdad que…
Es increíble que…	No hay duda que…
Es una lástima que…	(No) Me gusta que…

MODELO: Hay mucha pobreza en el mundo. →
Es una lástima que **haya** mucha pobreza en el mundo.

1. Los niños miran la televisión muchas horas al día.
2. Hay mucha pobreza (*poverty*) en el mundo.
3. En este país gastamos mucha energía.
4. Hay muchas escenas sexuales y violentas en la televisión y en el cine.
5. En muchas partes del mundo se come poco y mal.
6. Los temas de la música *rap* son demasiado violentos.
7. Hay mucho interés en la exploración del espacio.
8. Fumar no es malo para la salud.
9. No se permite el uso de la marihuana.
10. Los vehículos que consumen mucha gasolina son más populares cada día.

Paso 2. Indiquen Uds. soluciones para algunos de los problemas que se mencionan en el **Paso 1.** Empiece las soluciones con las siguientes expresiones.

Expresiones

Es importante que…	Insisto en que…
Es mejor que…	Quiero que…
Es necesario que…	Recomiendo que…
Es urgente que…	

MODELO: Es urgente que **ayudemos** a los pobres.

B. Lengua y cultura: En el Museo Nacional Centro de Arte Reina (*Queen*) **Sofía.** As part of a tour group, two friends are at **el Museo Nacional Centro de Arte Reina Sofía,** and their tour guide is talking about *Guernica*, by Pablo Picasso. Complete the following dialogue with the correct form of the words in parentheses, as suggested by context. When two possibilities are given in parentheses, select the correct word or phrase. Conjugate the verbs in the present indicative, the **Uds.** command form, the present subjunctive, or the preterite, or leave them in the infinitive, if appropriate.

***Guernica*, por Pablo Picasso (español, 1881–1973)**

Culture

- The *Museo Nacional Centro de Arte Reina Sofía* in Madrid was declared a full-time national museum in 1992. The building this museum occupies was begun as a hospital in the mid 1700s but was never completed. After surviving movements to have it demolished, the building was repaired, restored, and finished by several different architects. Before becoming a national museum, it was a cultural center called *el Centro de Arte Reina Sofía,* in which temporary exhibits and events were held.
- The town of Guernica, also known as Guernica y Luno, is located in north-central Spain, twelve miles northeast of Bilbao. The town was destroyed in 1937 during the Spanish Civil War by German and Italian aircraft in the first mass bombing. Picasso's work depicts the pain and suffering that resulted from the attack.

GUÍA: (Pasar[1]) Uds. por aquí, por favor. También les pido que (dejar[2]) suficiente espacio para todos. Y bien, aquí estamos (delante/detrás[3]) de *Guernica,* la obra maestra pintada por Picasso. (Ser/Estar[4]) obvio que el cuadro (representar[5]) los horrores de la guerra,[a] ¿no? En 1937 Picasso (pintar[6]) este cuadro como reacción al bombardeo[b] (del / de la[7]) ciudad de Guernica durante la Guerra Civil Española. Por razones políticas, (durante / encima de[8]) la dictadura[c] de Franco,[d] el cuadro (fue/estuvo[9]) muchos años en el Museo de Arte Moderno de Nueva York. Pero por deseo expreso del pintor, el cuadro (trasladarse[e10]) a España después de la muerte de Franco…

Pasen / dejen; delante; Es / representa; pintó; de la; durante; estuvo; se trasladó

BETO: Yo dudo que (este/esto[11]) cuadro (ser[12]) una obra maestra. No creo que (tener[13]) nada de bonito. ¡No tiene colores!

este / sea; tenga

ANA: Yo no (creer[14]) que todos los cuadros (tener[15]) que (ser[16]) bonitos. Para mí, la falta de color (servir[17]) para expresar el dolor y el desastre… (Por/Para[18]) eso se (poder[19]) percibir el mensaje de la destrucción de la guerra en la pintura.

creo / tengan / ser; sirve; Por / puede

[a]*war* [b]*bombing* [c]*dictatorship* [d]Francisco Franco (1892–1975), dictador de España desde 1939 hasta su muerte [e]*to move*

Comprensión. ¿Quién pudo haber dicho (*could have said*) lo siguiente, el guía, Beto o Ana?

	EL GUÍA	BETO	ANA
1. «Yo prefiero los cuadros en colores.»	☐	☑	☐
2. «Ahora voy a mostrarles una obra maestra de la pintura española.»	☑	☐	☐
3. «No me molesta que esta pintura esté pintada en blanco y negro.»	☐	☐	☑
4. «Quiero que todos me sigan y que se pongan delante del cuadro.»	☑	☐	☐

En su comunidad

Entreviste a una persona hispana de su universidad o ciudad sobre el arte y la artesanía de su país de origen.

PREGUNTAS POSIBLES

- ¿Cuáles son los artistas más conocidos de su país? ¿A qué tipo de arte se dedican?
- ¿Qué tipo de artesanía se hace en su país? ¿y en su ciudad o región? ¿Tiene muestras (*examples*) de esta artesanía en su casa?
- ¿Hay muchas oportunidades de asistir a eventos culturales (por ejemplo, exposiciones en museos, conciertos, espectáculos de danza, teatro o cine) en su país? Por lo general, ¿son baratas o caras las entradas para los eventos culturales?
- ¿Cuáles son los eventos culturales que Ud. prefiere? ¿Asiste a ellos con frecuencia?

B: Follow-up

Ask the following questions to personalize the activity.

¿Expresa algo para Ud. el cuadro de Guernica? ¿Qué expresa?
¿Por qué (no) le gusta?
¿Cree Ud. que el arte se debe usar para transmitir un mensaje o solo para producir un placer estético?

B: Note

The following grammar topics are included in *Lengua y cultura:* gender, demonstratives, use of prepositions, formal commands, subjunctive vs. indicative, preterite forms, *ser* vs. *estar,* lexical item (*por eso*).

En su comunidad

Suggestions

- Remind students to get the following basic information: the informant's country of origin, how long he or she has lived in this country, and if the informant visits his or her country of origin frequently.
- This activity could instead be assigned as an online research project on a country of the student's choice or assigned by you.
- See the IM for additional suggestions and guidelines.

Multimedia: Internet

Have students search the Internet for more of Pablo Picasso's works, including *Guernica.* The *Museo Nacional Centro de Arte Reina Sofía* in Madrid has its own website and features some of his works. Have students look up this museum and research its relationship to *el Museo del Prado.*

Resources: Desenlace

In the *Cap. 13* segment of "Chapter-by-Chapter Supplementary Materials" in the IM, you will find a chapter-culminating activity. You can use this activity to consolidate and review the vocabulary and grammar skills students have acquired.

TelePuntos

Note

Pages 404–409 are optional. You may cover some, all, or none of this material in class, or assign it to students—as a group or individually—for homework or extra credit. Pages 410–411 (*En resumen: En este capítulo*) are a summary of all of the chapter's active material.

Antes de mirar

Suggestion

Have students share their answers in a whole-class discussion. If your town or state has architectural works of particular note, be sure to mention them during the discussion.

Fragmento del guion

Note

For some native speakers, the Spanish spoken by *Pilar Castillo* may not be completely standard, as in, for example, the expression *cada otra noche* not included in the *Fragmento. Castillo* is a Heritage Speaker of Spanish, and her Spanish shows the influence of English in some expressions. This type of influence is typical wherever two languages coexist.

Programa 13

Note

The language in this program is relatively simple, but the concepts are sophisticated.

Suggestions

- Before showing the program, you may wish to point out that many of the names, proper and common, that appear in the Gaudí report are *catalán: Antoni* (*Antonio*), *Gaudí, parc* (*parque*), *Güell, Batlló, Milà*. Spaniards tend not to translate *catalán* names into Spanish, and thus would speak of *el Parque Güell* as *el Parc Güell*. Laura does not follow that convention.
- For students not familiar with Catholic customs, you may wish to point out that names like *la Sagrada Familia* and *Nuestra Señora de…* are common names for Catholic cathedrals and churches.
- You may wish to preview the name of the organization featured in the program called *SPARC = el Centro Social y Público de Recursos Artísticos*. Help students guess what *SPARC* stands for in English = Social and Public Art Resource Center.
- Emphasize to students that the more carefully they study the preliminary activities (*Antes de mirar, Vocabulario de este programa*, and *Fragmento del guion*), the more they will understand.

TELEPUNTOS SALU2

El Tempo de la Sagrada (*Sacred*) Familia, la obra inacabada (*unfinished*) de Antoni Gaudí: «Su construcción, que comenzó en 1882, todavía no ha terminado (*hasn't ended*). Se espera que esté terminada para el año 2026.»

Antes de mirar

¿Le interesa a Ud. la arquitectura en general? ¿Conoce la obra de algún arquitecto importante del siglo (*century*) XX? ¿Y qué sabe de los murales como expresión artística? ¿Los asocia con el arte abstracto o con el arte con mensaje político y social?

PROGRAMA 13: Arte angelino° de Los Ángeles

Este programa presenta unos reportajes sobre la obra de importantes arquitectos españoles del siglo XX y XXI, y sobre el fascinante movimiento muralista en la ciudad de Los Ángeles.

Vocabulario de este programa

principios de	the beginning of	**el/la compatriota**	fellow country person
reconocido/a	renowned, well-known	**la muestra**	example
catalán, catalana	from **Cataluña** (Catalonia, Spain)	**la concientización**	consciousness-raising
pertenecer (pertenezco)	to belong	**proteger (protejo)**	to protect
fines de	the end of	**quisiéramos**	we wish
la naturaleza	nature	**el motivo de orgullo**	source of pride
fijarse en	to notice, pay attention to	**se nos acabó el tiempo**	our time is up
la iglesia	church		

Fragmento del guion

PILAR CASTILLO: Los temas más representados en los murales de Los Ángeles tienen que ver[a] con las historias de cada comunidad, quién está pintando los murales, sea[b] chino o coreano, sea afroamericano, mexicano, chicano. Esas comunidades tienen su propia[c] historia, de su cultura y de sus historias viviendo aquí en Los Ángeles.

LAURA: Este mural se llama *La Ofrenda*[d] y es de otra artista chicana, Yreina Cervantes. Fue pintado en 1988.

PILAR CASTILLO: Y es un tributo a la fuerza[e] y la lucha[f] de los campesinos[g] en el movimiento United Farm Workers. En particular enfoca a[h] la líder Dolores Huerta, quien es un ejemplo del papel[i] de la mujer en el movimiento.

LAURA: Este mural se titula[j] *El Gran Muro* y representa la historia de California y de Los Ángeles más concretamente, desde tiempos prehistóricos. Es el mural más largo del mundo: mide media milla.[k] Para este mural, Baca trabajó con otros muchos artistas y 400 jóvenes. Tardaron[l] cinco veranos en terminarlo.

[a]tienen… *have to do* [b]*whether* [*he*] *is* [c]*own* [d]*Offering* [e]*strength* [f]*struggle* [g]*farm workers* [h]a… *it focuses on* [i]*role* [j]se… se llama [k]mide… *it's a half mile long* [l]*It took them*

Segmento de *El Gran Muro* (*Wall*), el mural más largo del mundo, de la artista chicana Judith Baca

Scanning *Después de mirar* before viewing is also an excellent strategy.

Al mirar

Suggestion

- It is particularly important for students to have read Al mirar before watching this show, as doing so will familiarize them with the names and concepts they will hear.
- You may want to suggest that students complete this activity after watching, to see if they can remember the information.

Mundo interactivo

Continue your work as an intern at HispanaVisión with Laura Sánchez Tejada, the roving reporter of *Salu2*, as you complete Scenario 7, Activities 1 and 2 in Connect Spanish (**www.connectspanish.com**).

Al mirar

Identifique cada artista con su género (*genre*) y movimiento.

ARTISTAS

1. __a,d__ Judith Baca
2. __a,e__ Santiago Calatrava
3. __b,d__ Yreina Cervantes
4. __a,c__ Antoni Gaudí
5. __a,e__ Rafael Moneo
6. __b,c__ Diego Rivera
7. __b,d__ David Alfaro Siqueiros

GÉNERO

a. arquitectura
b. pintura

MOVIMIENTO

c. modernista
d. muralista
e. vanguardista

Una terraza con banco (*bench*) en forma de serpiente, en el Parc Güell, Barcelona: Un lugar de fantasía y color diseñado por Antoni Gaudí

Después de mirar

A. ¿Está claro? ¿Cierto o falso? Corrija las oraciones falsas.

	CIERTO	FALSO
1. Gaudí solo construyó edificios en Barcelona.	☐	☑
2. Calatrava diseñó la Catedral católica de Los Ángeles.	☐	☑
3. SPARC, el Centro Social y Público de Recursos Artisticos, está en Los Ángeles.	☑	☐
4. Pilar Castillo es una muralista angelina.	☐	☑
5. El movimiento muralista es exclusivo de la comunidad chicana/mexicana de Los Ángeles.	☐	☑
6. Baca trabajó sola en la creación de su mural *El Gran Muro*.	☐	☑

A: Answers: 1. *Falso: También construyó edificios en otras ciudades españolas.* **2.** *Falso: La construyó Rafael Moneo.* **4.** *Falso: Ella trabaja para SPARC.* **5.** *Falso: El muralismo viene de México.* **6.** *Falso: Baca trabajó con otros artistas y 400 jóvenes.*

B. Un poco más. Conteste las siguientes preguntas.

1. ¿Qué tienen en común Gaudí, Calatrava y Moneo?
2. ¿Qué elementos se destacan (*stand out*) en los edificios de Gaudí?
3. ¿De dónde viene la influencia original del movimiento muralista angelino? ¿Cómo se adapta esta influencia a la realidad de Los Ángeles?
4. ¿Qué serio problema enfrentan (*face*) los murales? ¿Qué es necesario hacer para que esta situación se resuelva?

B: Answers: 1. *Son arquitectos españoles.* **2.** *las formas geométricas de la naturaleza, mosaicos multicolores.* **3.** *La influencia viene del movimiento muralista mexicano, de Rivera y Siqueiros. Los temas de los murales angelinos tienen que ver con las comunidades étnicas de Los Ángeles.* **4.** *Hay mucho vandalismo. Los jóvenes tienen que entender que los murales representan su historia.*

C. Y ahora, Uds. En parejas, escriban un poema basado en una de las obras que ven en este programa. ¡Usen su creatividad!

ESTRUCTURA	MODELO:
nombre de la obra / edificio	Parc Güell
adjetivo	colorida (*colorful*)
otro nombre o sustantivo	fantasía
verbo	juega
adjetivo, adjetivo, adjetivo	divertido, espectacular, infantil
verbo del tipo gustar o reacción personal	me atrae

Sobre el programa

Laura disfrutó[a] mucho haciendo este programa sobre el arte. Su madre es profesora de Historia de México en la Universidad de Nuevo León (México), y para una historiadora las expresiones artísticas son imposibles de ignorar. Y por si eso fuera poco,[b] su padre es arquitecto. Así que[c] Laura creció[d] oyendo hablar de arte y contemplando obras arquitectónicas y de todo tipo de arte. De hecho,[e] fue ella misma la que[f] sugirió el reportaje de la Catedral de Los Ángeles, porque por[g] su padre sabía que era obra de un arquitecto español.

[a]*enjoyed* [b]*Y... And as if that was not enough* [c]*Así... So* [d]*grew up* [e]*De... In fact* [f]*la... the one who* [g]*through*

Producción personal

Haga un fotomontaje con voz en off (*voice over*) sobre la obra de un(a) artista hispano/a cuya (*whose*) obra le interesa mucho a Ud.

Al mirar

Note

Students will have to listen carefully to link *Calatrava* with *Moneo* and conclude that *Calatrava* is associated with *el vanguardismo.*

Después de mirar

A: Note

Outside of Barcelona, Gaudí's works are found in *Santander* (*El Capricho de Comillas*), *León* (*Casa Botines*), *Astorga* (*el Palacio episcopal*), and *Mallorca* (*restauration of the Cathedral*).

C: Suggestions

- Allow students to choose any piece of art (whether in the program or not) and to play with the arrangement of the structure as well. The objective is to create artistic language, not follow the model exactly.
- Encourage students to use the dictionary to find words that express their ideas better than their limited vocabulary can.
- In the model, point out the gender of the first adjective (*colorida*), which agrees with *fantasía,* not with *Parc Güell.*
- You may also wish to have the whole class brain storm words that they associate with a few of the buildings shown in the program, as a model for their work in pairs.
- This activity can easily be assigned as homework if you do not wish to spend class time on it.

Sobre el programa

Suggestion

The word *historiadora* has not been glossed on purpose, as students should be able to guess its meaning. Make sure that students understand it. Point out that the ending *-dor(a)* is a common suffix for professions in Spanish: *aviador(a), vendedor(a), limpiador(a), trabajador(a), contador(a),* etc.

Sobre el programa: Optional

1. *A Laura le gusta mucho...* (*el arte*)
2. *La madre de Laura es...* (*historiadora*)
3. *El padre de Laura es...* (*arquitecto*)
4. *La persona que sugirió al reportaje sobre la Catedral de Los Ángeles fue...* (*Laura*)
5. *Laura sabía de la Catedral por...* (*su padre*)

Producción personal

See the IM for additional suggestions for this chapter's assignment as well as for general guidelines and suggestions for video assignments.

Lectura cultural

Notes

- The Instructor's Edition on this page offers some additional information on the country of focus. For more information about the country of focus, see the chapter's opening pages and the IM.
- See the IM for some expressions used in Ecuador and Bolivia.

First Reading: Suggestions

- Other Ecuadorian museums of note include the following: *el Museo del Banco Central* and *el Museo de la Ciudad* (Quito), and *el Museo Antropológico y de Arte Contemporáneo* (*Guayaquil*)
- *El Museo del Barrio* has been in existence for over 40 years.

Exploración lingüística

Ask students to find the following in the reading. Some of these words are glossed and some are not.

- *Una expresión equivalente a la palabra* y (*tanto… como*)
- *Algunos verbos que se asocian con la cultura* (*apoyar, promover, preservar, fomentar, investigar, difundir*)
- *Un sinónimo de* dinero *en Latinoamérica* (*plata*)

Comprensión: Answers

1. *la Casa de la Cultura Ecuatoriana*
2. *Son libros de escritores locales, con tapas de cartón y que se venden por poco dinero.*
3. *la Capilla del Hombre* (*Quito*), *el Museo del Prado* (*Madrid*), *el Museo Nacional de Antropología* (*México, D.F.*), *el Museo del Barrio* (*Nueva York*)

Tres símbolos ecuatorianos y bolivianos

Suggestions

- Refer to statistics about ethnic make-up (chapter-opening pages).
- Students may be familiar with Bolivian and Ecuadorian music from the Simon and Garfunkle song *El cóndor pasa*. Music from this region is available online.
- *El lago Titicaca* the cradle of Andean civilization, is the highest navegable lake in the world.
- *Las Islas Galápagos* are 960 kilometers (596 miles) to the west of the Ecuadorian mainland. They were discovered in 1859 by Tomás de Berlanga.
- See the IM for more information.

A LEER

Lectura cultural

El Ecuador y Bolivia

Tanto el Ecuador como Bolivia son países multiculturales, donde diferentes grupos étnicos contribuyen a las artes en general.

En el Ecuador, la institución encargada de apoyar y promover[a] la cultura es La Casa de la Cultura Ecuatoriana Benjamín Carrión (CCE), una red nacional de bibliotecas, cines, museos, teatros y publicaciones, con sede[b] en Quito. Su misión es de «[p]reservar, promover,[c] fomentar,[d] investigar y difundir[e] el arte, ciencia y patrimonio cultural ecuatoriano» para fortalecer[f] la identidad nacional del país. Entre los muchos museos del Ecuador, La Capilla[g] del Hombre es visita obligada. Es un museo dedicado a las obras de un solo pintor ecuatoriano, Oswaldo Guayasamín, que representa la historia del pueblo latinoamericano.

¿Qué sitios culturales de su ciudad o estado/provincia les recomienda Ud. a los turistas que visiten?

En Bolivia, la editorial[h] Yerba Mala[i] Cartonera es una iniciativa a destacar.[j] «Publican» las obras de todo tipo de escritores locales, en libros impresos[k] en papel ordinario y con tapas[l] recicladas de las cajas de cartón que se botan[m] en los supermercados. Los autores mismos[n] venden sus libros en lugares públicos, al precio de un boliviano ($0,30, aproximadamente). Y si alguien no tiene plata,[ñ] se lo regalan, para difundir[o] la cultura.

[a]encargada… *in charge of supporting and promoting* [b]*headquarters* [c]*to promote* [d]*to encourage* [e]*to spread* [f]*strengthen* [g]*Chapel* [h]*publishing house* [i]Yerba… *Weeds* [j]*highlight* [k]*printed* [l]*covers* [m]cajas… *cardboard boxes that are thrown away* [n]*themselves* [ñ]dinero

En otros países hispanos

- **En España y México** Uno de los museos de arte más importantes del mundo es el Museo del Prado, en Madrid. Allí se puede admirar las obras de Velázquez y Goya, entre otros muchos artistas españoles y europeos anteriores al siglo[a] XX. El Museo Nacional de Antropología, en México, D.F., es uno de los mejores del mundo en su género.[b] En este museo se puede admirar y apreciar la excelencia de la artesanía y arquitectura de los pueblos indígenas mesoamericanos.
- **En los Estados Unidos** En Nueva York está el Museo del Barrio, dedicado a la obra de artistas latinos, con énfasis en el arte puertorriqueño.

[a]*century* [b]*category, genre*

Una de las islas Galápagos, donde Charles Darwin estudió las especies de flora y fauna del lugar

Tres símbolos ecuatorianos y bolivianos

- **La diversidad étnica y lingüística** El Ecuador y Bolivia son países que han logrado[a] preservar un gran porcentaje de su población indígena. Esto es sin duda una gran parte de la riqueza cultural y orgullo[b] nacional de ambos países.
- **El mestizaje**[c] El encuentro entre los españoles y los indígenas dio como resultado una mezcla[d] racial que hoy es el sustrato[e] más grande de la población de estos dos países (y de latinoamericana en general).
- **La naturaleza** La variedad geográfica del Ecuador y Bolivia es simplemente espectacular, desde los picos[f] más altos de los Andes hasta la selva[g] amazónica, pasando por el Lago Titicaca en Bolivia y las Islas Galápagos en el Ecuador.

[a]han… *have succeeded in* [b]*pride* [c]*mixture of indigenous and European peoples* [d]*mixture* [e]*subsection* [f]*peaks* [g]*jungle*

Una cita

«La cultura ya no es más[a] sinónimo de las "bellas artes"[b] (literatura, pintura y música…), es todo un amasijo[c] que supone[d] los signos propios, subjetivos y físicos (materialidad), intelectivos y afectivos que cuajan[e] a una nación. […] La cultura ha ido acumulando[f] casi todo: las conductas, los derechos axiales[g] de los seres humanos, los prontuarios de valores,[h] tradiciones, usos y costumbres[i] de los pueblos.»

Marco Antonio Rodríguez, Presidente de la La Casa de la Cultura Ecuatoriana

[a]ya… *is no longer* [b]bellas… *fine arts* [c]*hodgepodge* [d]*includes* [e]*give meaning* [f]ha… *has come to include* [g]derechos… *basic rights* [h]prontuarios… *codes of conduct or values* [i]usos… *customs and habits*

COMPRENSIÓN

1. ¿Qué institución está encargada de fomentar la cultura ecuatoriana?
2. ¿Cómo son los libros de la editorial Yerba Mala Cartonera?
3. ¿Cuáles son algunos de los museos famosos del mundo hispanohablante? ¿Cuál es la especialidad de cada una?

Una cita

Suggestions

- Have a whole-class discussion about this definition of the term *cultura*. Ask students to give specific examples of what *culture* means to them in this country, and to reflect on how learning culture affects language learning.
- Have students visit the official website of *la Casa de la Cultura Ecuatoriana:* www.cce.org.ec.

Del mundo hispano

Antes de leer

En su opinión, ¿son algunos árboles más bellos (*beautiful*) o más feos que otros? ¿más útiles o menos útiles? ¿Le parece una señal de belleza (*sign of beauty*) que un árbol produzca flores y frutos comestibles? ¿Hay un árbol que sea su favorito? ¿Cuál es? (Puede decir los nombres en inglés si no los sabe en español.)

Lectura: «La higuera»,° de Juana Fernández de Ibarbourou

°La... *The fig tree*

Porque es áspera[a] y fea;
Porque todas sus ramas[b] son grises,
Yo le tengo piedad[c] a la higuera.

En mi quinta[d] hay cien árboles bellos:
Ciruelos redondos,[e]
Limoneros rectos[f]
Y naranjos de brotes[g] lustrosos.

En las primaveras,
Todos ellos se cubren[h] de flores
En torno a[i] la higuera.

Y la pobre[j] parece tan triste
Con sus gajos torcidos[k] que nunca
De apretados capullos[l] se visten...
Por eso,
Cada vez que yo paso a su lado
Digo, procurando[m]
Hacer dulce y alegre mi acento:
—Es la higuera el más bello
De los árboles todos del huerto.[n]

Si ella escucha,
Si comprende el idioma en que hablo,
¡Qué dulzura tan honda hará nido[ñ]
En su alma sensible[o] de árbol.

Y tal vez, a la noche,
Cuando el viento abanique su copa,[p]
Embriagada de gozo[q] le cuente:
—Hoy a mí me dijeron hermosa.[r]

[a]*rough* [b]*branches* [c]*pity* [d]*country house* [e]Ciruelos... *Round plum trees* [f]Limoneros... *Straight lemon trees* [g]*shoots* [h]se... *are covered* [i]En... *All around* [j]la... la pobre higuera [k]gajos... *twisted branches* [l]apretados... *tight buds* [m]*trying* [n]*orchard* [ñ]¡Qué... *How deep the sweetness that will make a nest* [o]alma... *sensitive soul* [p]abanique... *fans her upper branches* [q]Embriagado... *Drunk with joy* [r]*beautiful*

Comprensión

A. Descripciones

Paso 1. Haga una lista de los adjetivos y frases que describen la higuera y otra lista de las palabras que describen los otros árboles.

1. la higuera **2.** los otros árboles (los ciruelos, los limoneros, los naranjos)

Paso 2. Ahora explique con sus propias (*own*) palabras cómo es la higuera en comparación con los otros árboles de la quinta.

B. Emoción y opinión. Conteste las siguientes preguntas.

1. ¿Qué emoción siente la poeta frente a la higuera?
2. ¿Cómo desea la poeta ayudar a la higuera?
3. ¿Cómo espera la poeta que la higuera se sienta por la noche?
4. ¿Cree Ud. que los árboles sienten emociones?
5. ¿Por qué cree Ud. que la poeta le da una personalidad a la higuera pero no a los otros árboles?
6. En su opinión, ¿cómo es la poeta? Piense en su reacción frente a la higuera.
7. ¿Cree Ud. que este poema contiene un mensaje o lección moral? ¿Cuál es?

Comprensión Answers

A, Paso 1: 1. *áspera, fea, ramas grises, triste, gajos torcidos, alma sensible, embriagada de gozo* **2.** *bellos, redondos, rectos, brotes lustrosos, se cubren de flores, de apretados capullos se visten* **Paso 2.** Answers will vary.

B: Answers will vary.

Del mundo hispano

Note

See the IM for optional follow-up, writing, and Internet activities.

Antes de leer

Suggestions

- You may wish to do *Antes de leer* as a whole-class discussion, as it is a challenging topic.
- Students will not know the names for specific trees, so focus on characteristics. Scan the poem for vocabulary that will aid the discussion (*recto, redondo, brote, gajos torcidos, apretados capullos*, and so on). But do end the discussion by asking students to name their favorite tree, if they have one. If you are not a native speaker of Spanish, come to class prepared to help students with the names of trees, especially those of trees that are typical of your area.
- Although these words are glossed in the poem, it is a good idea to present tree-related vocabulary to facilitate the comprehension. Use an image or drawing of a tree and label these parts: *ramas, brotes, flor, gajo, capullo, nido, copa*. You may also wish to present the two place words that appear in the poem: *quinta, huerto*.

Estrategia

Coping with Unusual Syntax

While it also occurs in prose, inverted syntax is quite common in poetry, and it can easily trip up students. Point out that the fourth and fifth stanzas have syntactically complex sentences, in which there is inversion of subject/verb and of the usual adjective-noun word order. Help students decipher the meaning of these sentences by rearranging the chunks into a more traditional word order.

Con sus gajos torcidos que nunca de apretados capullos se visten... → *Sus gajos torcidos nunca se visten de apretados capullos.*

—Es la higuera el más bello De los árboles todos del huerto. → *La higuera es el más bello de todos los árboles del huerto.*

Comprensión B

Suggestion

You may wish to have students discuss these questions in groups, then share answers with the rest of the class. Each group can discuss some or all of these questions before the whole-class discussion begins.

Antes de escuchar

Suggestions

- Survey the movie-going habits of the class by asking for a show of hands.
- Ask students which Spanish-language movies they have seen and enjoyed.
- Help students anticipate the information they will hear by asking them which aspects of a film are usually reviewed.

Escuche

Notes

- In this chapter students can listen to a radio show with two hosts who review movies . . . and rarely agree on any of them!
- If the listening is assigned as homework, ask students to listen to the passage at least twice.
- See the IM for the Audioscript and more information about music in Bolivia and Ecuador.

Después de escuchar

A: Follow-up

En su opinión, ¿es mejor ver una película antes de leer el libro en el que se basa la película o después? Dé unos ejemplos.

B: Follow-up

Ask students to write a brief review of a movie they've seen recently. The goal of the review is to help people not familiar with the movie decide whether or not they want to see it.

¡Música!

Notes

- *Los Kjarkas* (pronounce the *j* like the English *h* and pronounce *K* and the *j* simultaneously: *Khar-kas*) started their career in the 1960s as a quartet consisting of three brothers and a friend. The name *kjarka,* which is a Quechua word, means strength (*fortaleza*). Today the group has six members. The song "*Llorando por ti*" was a great hit in the 1980s for a Brazilian group, *La Lambada*. In fact, the Brazilian version was a plagiarism of the song by *los Kjarkas*.
- *El charango* is a small string instrument, similar to a lute. It is made from the shell of an armadillo.
- For helpful tips on using songs in the classroom, see the IM.

A ESCUCHAR

Vocabulario para escuchar

el punto de vista	point of view
trata de	deals with
inesperada	unexpected
el argumento	plot
increíble	unbelievable
la actuación	performance
cursi	in poor taste, trite
al elegir	when she chose
recrea	it recreates

Antes de escuchar

¿Le gusta el cine? ¿Tiene un género (*genre*) preferido de películas: las de acción, de artes marciales, de aventura, de ciencia ficción, de horror, de suspenso, de guerra (*war*), las comedias, los dramas, las musicales? En su opinión, ¿qué características necesita tener una película para que (*so that*) sea interesante y/o buena? ¿Lee Ud. en el periódico o en el Internet reseñas (*reviews*) de las películas antes de verlas? ¿Las lee después de verlas? ¿O no las lee nunca?

Escuche

Cuestión de estrellas:° *Una reseña de La vida de Susana Jiménez*

°Cuestión... *About the stars*

En la radio dos críticos hacen la reseña de una película. Escuche según las indicaciones de su profesor(a).

Después de escuchar

A. ¿Cierto o falso? ¿Qué dicen los críticos de la película? Corrija las oraciones falsas.

	CIERTO	FALSO
1. El hombre piensa que es una película que se debe ver.	☑	☐
2. La mujer piensa que es una película recomendable.	☐	☑
3. Los dos críticos piensan que la actriz principal es buena.	☑	☐
4. Los críticos están de acuerdo: el guión es bueno.	☐	☑

A: Answers
2. *Dice que es increíble y superficial, para ver en casa.* **4.** *La mujer dice que es superficial y cursi.*

B. Más detalles. Conteste las siguientes preguntas.

1. Según la mujer, ¿cuál es el problema principal de la película?
2. ¿Cuáles son unos aspectos positivos de la película, según los críticos?

B: Answers
1. *El guion es superficial y cursi.* **2.** *Son buenos el director, la actuación de la actriz y la cinematografía.*

El grupo foclórico Los Kjarkas

¡Música!

Los Kjarkas son un grupo boliviano de música folclórica que tiene seis miembros. Uno de ellos es un músico japonés que toca el charango.[a] La canción «Llorando se fue[b]» es del álbum *Lo mejor de Bolivia*.

[a]*stringed instrument* [b]se... *she went away*

Go to the iMix section in Connect Spanish (**www.connectspanish.com**) to access the iTunes playlist *"Puntos9,"* where you can purchase "Llorando se fue" by Los Kjarkas.

A ESCRIBIR

El tema

Las formas de arte en las escuelas públicas

Preparar

Paso 1. Piense en los siguientes aspectos de la importancia del arte.

1. ¿Qué significa la palabra **arte**? ¿Cómo puede afectar el arte la vida de una persona?
2. ¿Cómo/Dónde se debe aprender las diversas formas de arte? ¿En la escuela o en el tiempo libre?
3. En general, ¿qué formas de arte se promueven (*are promoted*) y se enseñan en las escuelas públicas?

Paso 2. Con un compañero o compañera de clase, haga una lista de argumentos a favor de la idea de apoyar (*supporting*) y enseñar las artes en la escuelas públicas y otra de argumentos en contra.

Unos niños, en una clase de arte, en el Ecuador

Redactar

Usando las ideas de **Preparar,** escriba un ensayo a favor o en contra de la enseñanza (*teaching*) de las artes en las escuelas públicas. Tenga en cuenta (*Keep in mind*) el clima de austeridad económica en el que (*which*) vive el país. Haga referencia a la importancia de los fondos necesarios para apoyar la enseñanza de las artes y explique si es una buena manera de usar fondos públicos o no.

Editar

Revise el ensayo para comprobar:

- la ortografía y los acentos
- la organización de las ideas y la cohesión de los párrafos
- el uso de oraciones complejas y del subjuntivo en contextos de influencia, emoción y duda
- el uso del indicativo después de verbos de opinión e información

Finalmente, prepare su versión final para entregarla.

Preparar

Suggestions

- Ask students to review the uses of the subjunctive (*Caps. 12, 13*).
- Remind students to vary their vocabulary to express their likes and dislikes. Verbs of this type that they know include: *gustar, encantar, interesar, molestar* (*Gram.* 22), *aburrir, atraer, fascinar* (*Nota comunicativa*, p. 335).
- Suggest that students use the following phrases and others like them to present facts: *es evidente que, los expertos afirman que,* and *no hay duda que.*
- Tell students to avoid anecdotal examples to support their points. They should base their arguments on facts.

Redactar

Suggestions

- Suggested length for this writing assignment: approximately 200 words
- Suggested structure: 3 paragraphs

P. 1. Presentation of the main idea of the essay, to gain the reader's attention.

P. 2. Presentation of the arguments: explanation followed by evidence.

P. 3. A conclusion that summarizes the arguments and also presents the author's opinion about the debate.

Editar

Follow-up

What do the arts and entertainment of a country have to say about the culture of that nation?

En resumen: En este capítulo Vocabulario

Suggestions

- Read the following definitions and have students give the words defined.
  1. *Es una actividad artística en la que unas personas representan la vida de otras personas imaginarias o reales.*
  2. *Picasso, O'Keeffe y Van Gogh son ejemplos de este tipo de artistas.*
  3. *Esta persona diseña y dibuja casas o edificios.*
  4. *En este lugar se representan obras de teatro.*
  5. *Gloria Estefan y Julio Iglesias tienen esta profesión.*
  6. *El sinónimo de crear una escultura.*
  7. *Los artistas hacen esto antes de pintar un cuadro, generalmente.*
- Bring or have students bring images of fine and performing arts. Use the images to elicit descriptions and ask/answer questions.
- Make statements about the images displayed in class or about aspects of university life on your campus to which students can react with the following expressions: *No, no creo…*, *No, dudo que…*, *No, niego que…*

Word Families

En este capítulo

- *la arquitectura, el/la arquitecto/a*
- *las artes, el/la artista, la artesanía, la obra de arte*
- *la canción, el/la cantante*
- *dibujar, el dibujo*
- *el drama, el/la dramaturgo/a*
- *la escultura, esculpir, el/la escultor(a)*
- *el espectáculo, el/la espectador(a)*
- *el guion, el/la guía*
- *la música, el musical, el/la músico/a*
- *la novela, el/la novelista*
- *la obra de teatro, la obra de arte, la obra maestra*
- *la pintura, pintar, el/la pintor(a)*
- *los tejidos, tejer*

Entre capítulos

- *aburrir = aburrido/a* (6), *ser aburrido/a* (10), *aburrirse* (10)
- *las artes, el/la artista, la artesanía, la obra de arte = el arte* (2)
- *atraer = traer* (5)
- *el bailarín, la bailarina = bailar* (2)
- *la canción, el/la cantante = cantar* (2)
- *el/la escritor(a) = escribir* (3), *el escritorio* (2)
- *la fotografía* (photography) *= la foto(grafía)* (photograph) (10)
- *hay que = hay* (1)
- *la obra de teatro = el teatro* (10)

EN RESUMEN En este capítulo

LearnSmart

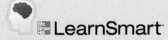

Visit **www.connectspanish.com** to practice the vocabulary and grammar points covered in this chapter.

Gramática en breve

36. Uses of the Subjunctive: Emotion

①		②
first subject = indicative EMOTION	**que**	second subject = subjunctive

37. Uses of the Subjunctive: Doubt and Denial

①		②
first subject = indicative DOUBT AND DENIAL	**que**	second subject = subjunctive

38. The Subjunctive: A Summary

①		②
influence / emotion / doubt or denial	**que**	subjunctive
information / certainty or belief	**que**	indicative

Vocabulario

Los verbos

aburrir (*like* **gustar**)	to bore
acordarse (me acuerdo) (de)	to remember
atraer (*like* **traer**) (*like* **gustar**)	to draw, attract
fascinar (*like* **gustar**)	to fascinate
ganar	to earn (*income*)
lamentar	to regret; to feel sorry
negar (niego) (gu)	to deny
sentir (siento) (i)	to regret; to feel sorry
sorprender (*like* **gustar**)	to surprise
temer	to fear, be afraid
tratar de + *inf.*	to try to (*do something*)

Repaso: alegrarse de, creer, dudar, encantar, esperar, estar seguro/a de, gustar, molestar, tener miedo de

La expresión artística

el baile	dance
la canción	song
el cuadro	painting (*specific piece*)
la danza	dance
el dibujo	drawing
el escenario	stage; scenery
la escultura	sculpture
el espectáculo	show
la fotografía	photography
el guion	script
la obra de arte	work of art
la obra de teatro	play
la obra maestra	masterpiece
el papel	role
la pintura	painting (*general*)

Cognados: la arquitectura, las artes (*pl.*), **el ballet, la comedia, el drama, el mural, la música, el musical, la novela, la ópera, el poema**

Repaso: el arte, el cine, el concierto, el edificio, la fotografía, la literatura, la película, el teatro

actuar (actúo)	to act
componer (compongo) (*like* **poner**)	to compose
crear	to create
dibujar	to draw
dirigir (dirijo)	to direct
diseñar	to design
esculpir	to sculpt
tejer	to weave

Cognado: pintar

Repaso: bailar, cantar, escribir, pintar

Las personas

el actor, la actriz	actor, actress
el bailarín, la bailarina	dancer
el/la cantante	singer
el/la compositor(a)	composer
el/la director(a)	director; conductor
el/la dramaturgo/a	playwright
el/la escritor(a)	writer
el/la escultor(a)	sculptor
el/la espectador(a)	spectator; *pl.* audience
el/la guía	guide
el/la músico	musician
la orquesta	orchestra
el/la pintor(a)	painter

Cognados: el/la arquitecto/a, el/la artista, el/la novelista, el/la poeta, el público

La tradición cultural

la artesanía	arts and crafts
la cerámica	pottery; ceramics
los tejidos	woven goods

Cognado: la ruina

Heritage Speakers

El uso de la palabra *poetisa* es anticuado. Ahora tiene cierto sentido peyorativo, y se prefiere la palabra *la poeta.*

Los adjetivos

artístico/a	artistic
clásico/a	classic(al)
folclórico/a	traditional
moderno/a	modern

Los números ordinales

primer(o/a)	**sexto/a**
segundo/a	**séptimo/a**
tercer(o/a)	**octavo/a**
cuarto/a	**noveno/a**
quinto/a	**décimo/a**

Palabras adicionales

es extraño que	it's strange that
¡qué extraño que... !	how strange that . . . !
es...	it's . . .
absurdo que	absurd that
cierto que	certain that
(im)posible que	(im)possible that
(im)probable que	(un)likely, (im)probable that
increíble que	incredible that
normal que	normal that
seguro que	a sure thing that
terrible que	terrible that
urgente que	urgent that
es una lástima que	it's a shame that
¡qué lástima que... !	what a shame that . . . !
hay que + *inf.*	it is necessary to (*do something*)
ojalá (que)	I hope (that)

Repaso: es mejor/bueno/malo que, es verdad que

Vocabulario personal

- *el papel* (role) = *el papel* (paper) (2)
- *primero/a* = *el primero de* (6), *el primer piso* (12)
- *sentir* = *sentirse* (9)

¡OJO!

- *crear* ≠ *creer*
- *el cuadro* ≠ *el cuaderno*

Suggestion

Write the expressions from *Palabras adicionales* on the board. Make statements about people in the class, university, state, or national events, or other people and events that students should know about. Have them respond to each statement using one of the expressions.

Muchos estudiantes estudian el arte. → *Me sorprende que tantos estudiantes estudien el arte.*

Chapter Opening Photo and Chapter Theme

Note

Road rage happens not only in this country but in Spanish-speaking countries as well. The terms used to refer to road rage vary from country to country and include: *la rabia rutera, la furia caminera, la furia al volante, la ira al manejar, la conducción colérica o agresiva.*

Chapter Theme–Related Questions

1. *¿Quiénes lo/la ayudan más en los momentos difíciles de la vida, sus amigos o su familia?*
2. *¿Qué institución social le da más ayuda en esos momentos? ¿la iglesia? ¿el gobierno* (new)*? ¿alguna otra institución? ¿o ninguna?*
3. *¿Cómo se siente Ud. cuando tiene que prepararse para un examen difícil o presentar un informe* (new) *importante? ¿Se siente frustrado/a? ¿nervioso/a? ¿intimidado? ¿impaciente?*
4. *¿Creen Uds. que hay muchos estudiantes que sufren estrés en esta universidad? En su opinión, ¿quiénes están más estresados, los profesores o los estudiantes?*

Reciclado: Review forms of the preterite, which will be used often in this chapter, by asking students what they did in these situations.

- *para terminar un informe* (new)
- *cuando se sintieron muy estresados*
- *para estudiar para un examen muy importante*
- *para ayudar a un amigo o amiga que necesitaba dinero*
- *para preparar una cena elegante*
- *para prepararse para una cita muy importante*

14 Las presiones° de la vida moderna

Las... *Pressures*

La hora punta (*rush hour*) en Lima, Perú

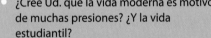

- ¿Cree Ud. que la vida moderna es motivo de muchas presiones? ¿Y la vida estudiantil?
- En su opinión, ¿tenemos hoy más presiones en la vida diaria que hace 50 años (*than 50 years ago*)? Explique su respuesta.
- ¿Qué hace Ud. para calmarse cuando se siente muy estresado/a?

connect SPANISH

www.connectspanish.com

Resources

For Students

- Connect Spanish (**www.connectspanish.com**), which contains all content from the following resources, as well as the *Mundo interactivo* scenarios, the LearnSmart adaptive learning system, and more!
- **Physical Resources:** Workbook / Laboratory Manual, Laboratory Audio Program, DVD

For Instructors

- Connect Spanish (**www.connectspanish.com**), which contains access to all student sections of Connect Spanish, as well as helpful time-saving tools and resources such as an integrated gradebook, Instructor's Manual, Testing Program, digital transparencies, Audioscript, Videoscript, and more!

El Perú

30 millones de habitantes

- El Perú es otro de los países andinos que tienen costa en el océano Pacífico y territorio amazónico.
- Lima, la capital del Perú, es una inmensa ciudad de más de 8 millones de habitantes. Es la quinta entre las ciudades más grandes de Latinoamérica y una de las veinte ciudades más grandes del mundo.
- Los incas, los indígenas del Perú, crearon el imperio más grande de toda América hasta la llegada de los españoles. La presencia inca todavía se siente en todo el país.

En este capítulo

CONTENT / **CONTENIDO**	OBJECTIVES / **OBJETIVOS**
Pressures of Student Life 414, Accidents 417	To talk about things that cause stress, including accidents
Using Expressions with **hace...** 420	To express how long something has been happening and how long ago something happened
Accidental **se:** Another Use of **se** 423	To express unplanned or unexpected events
Por or **para**? 427	To learn about the contexts in which these prepositions are used
El Perú 436	To learn about the South American country that was home to the vast Inca Empire

413

El Perú

Datos esenciales

Nombre oficial: *República del Perú*
Lema: *«Firme y feliz por la unión»*
Capital: *Lima*
Otras ciudades: *Arequipa, Trujillo, Chiclayo, Cusco*
Composición étnica*: 45% indígenas (quechuas y aymaras), 37% mestizos, 15% blancos, 3% negros, chinos, japoneses y otros*
Jefe de estado actual: *el Presidente Ollanta Humala, desde 2011;*
Forma de gobierno: *República presidencialista*
Lenguas oficiales: *el español y el quechua; además se hablan el aymara y otras lenguas indígenas amazónicas*
Moneda: *el nuevo sol*
Religión: *81% católicos, 13% evangélicos, 3% otros, 3% ninguna religión*

Point Out

- Peru was the center of the Inca Empire (*el Imperio inca o incaico*), which greatly expanded during the 15th and early 16th centuries. It was the largest of the Pre-Columbian empires, covering parts of what is today Ecuador, Colombia, Chile, Argentina, Bolivia, and Peru. However, when the Spanish conqueror Francisco Pizarro arrived in 1532, the empire was engaged in a debilitating civil war.
- Lima was founded in 1535 as *la Ciudad de los Reyes.* It was the capital of *el Virreinato del Perú*, one of the four major government regions of the Spanish Empire in America. (The others are *el Virreinato de Nueva España* (*México*), *el Virrenato del Río de la Plata* (*la Argentina*), and *el Virreinato de Nueva Granada* (*Colombia*).
- The last Inca emperor (called *El Inca*) was Túpac Amaru. He was captured and executed by the Spanish in 1572.
- The capital of the Inca Empire was Cuzco (now more frequently spelled *Cusco*), which became a beautiful colonial city during the Spanish era. It has been designated the Historical Capital of the country. Machu Picchu, the sacred city of the Incas, is further up in the Andes.

Suggestion

Have students list their ideas about Peru, including information on geography, politics, economy, culture, music, and cuisine. When you finish the chapter, return to the students' lists and ask what ideas they would change and/or add.

NATIONAL STANDARDS: Communication

Have groups of six or more students have a round table discussion about the stresses students suffer, strategies to avoid stress, and ways to alleviate stress. Have students pinpoint major causes of stress. As you study *Cap. 14,* have the groups organize their ideas and create a pamphlet in Spanish that could be distributed to university students. The pamphlets can be presented as you finish the chapter.

Multimedia

The IM provides suggestions for using the multimedia materials in the classroom.

Resources: Transparency 134

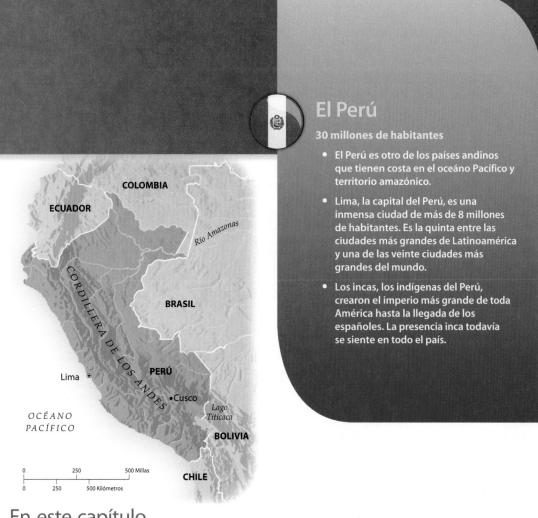

Vocabulario: Preparación
Las presiones de la vida académica
Suggestions

- **Reciclado:** Review classroom vocabulary (*Cap. 2*) before or while you are presenting the vocabulary in this section.
- Emphasize that the first person singular of *recoger* is *recojo.*
- Emphasize that *devolver* means *to return something to someone*, not *to return to a place* (= *regresar*).
- Optional vocabulary: *bromear, decir algo en broma, la tranquilidad* (the opposite of *el estrés*), *estar tranquilo/a.*
- Model vocabulary, using it in sentences about yourself and in exchanges with students. Explain some expressions in Spanish.
  1. Acordarse *es un verbo reflexivo. Uds. conocen un verbo sinónimo, ¿verdad? ¿Cuál es?* (recordar, del *Cap. 9*) *¿Cuál es un antónimo? El verbo* acordarse, *como* recordar, *sufre un cambio en la radical (o → ue):* me acuerdo, te acuerdas, nos acordamos. *¿Se acuerda Ud. de quién era el presidente de los Estados Unidos en 1995?*
  2. *El verbo* entregar *es sinónimo de* ______ (students answer). (dar) *¿Qué se puede entregar? ¿Entregaron alguna tarea ayer para alguna clase?*
  3. *Estacionar el coche es un gran problema en muchas ciudades (en esta universidad). ¿Uds. tienen dificultades cuando necesitan estacionar su coche? ¿Dónde? ¿Cuándo?*
- Read the following definitions and descriptions and have students give the correct words.
  1. *Muchos estudiantes sufren esto.*
  2. *Es una prueba que se hace para demostrar la comprensión de los estudios.*
  3. *Es un aparato que nos despierta por la mañana.*
  4. *Con estas se abren las puertas.*
  5. *Estas expresiones se usan para pedir disculpas.*
  6. *Uno escribe esto para planear las cosas que tiene que hacer cada día* (*clases, citas, otras actividades, etcétera*).
  7. *Es poner el coche en un lugar cuando no lo conducimos.*
  8. *Es sinónimo de* dar, *en el sentido de* darle una tarea al profesor.
- **Reciclado:** Review the subjunctive by asking questions about the people in the drawing. For example: *¿Qué es urgente que haga la profesora? ¿Qué es necesario que compre Lina?*
- **Follow-up:** Ask: *¿Están bajo muchas presiones solo los estudiantes? ¿Tienen también muchas presiones los profesores? ¿Cuáles son las presiones que pueden sufrir los profesores?*

Resources: Transparency 135

VOCABULARIO Preparación

Las presiones de la vida académica

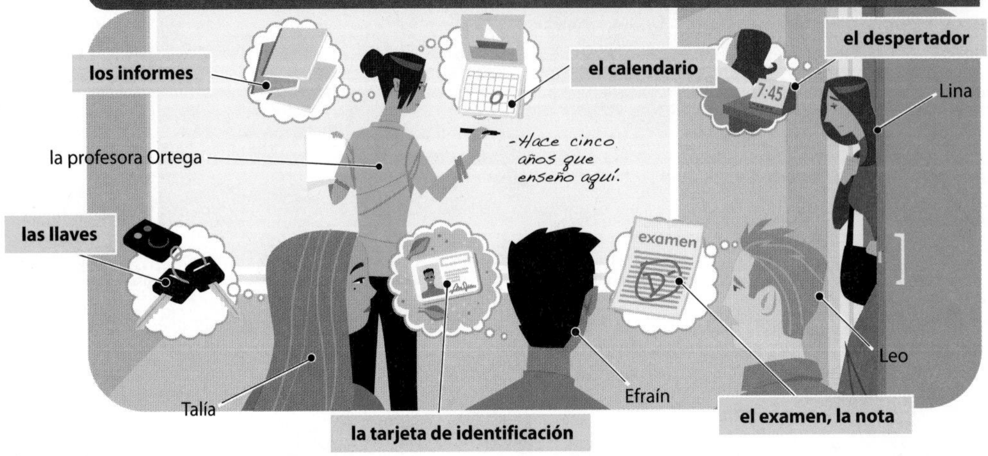

la ansiedad	anxiety
el estrés	stress
el horario	schedule
el informe (oral/escrito)	(oral/written) report
el plazo	deadline
el programa (del curso)	(course) syllabus
la prueba	quiz; test
la tarea	homework
el trabajo	job, work; report, (piece of) work
el trabajo de tiempo completo/parcial	full-time/parttime job
acordarse (me acuerdo) (de)	to remember
devolver (devuelvo)	to return (*something to someone*)
entregar (gu)	to turn/hand in
estacionar	to park
estar (muy) estresado/a	to be (very) stressed, be under (a lot of) stress
llegar (gu) a tiempo / tarde	to arrive on time/late
olvidarse (de)	to forget (about)
pedir (pido) (i) disculpas	to apologize
recoger (recojo)*	to collect; to pick up
sacar (qu) buenas/malas notas	to get good/bad grades
ser (in)flexible	to be (in)flexible
sufrir (de)	to suffer (*from*)
tener/estar bajo muchas presiones	to have/be under a lot of pressure
tomar apuntes	to take notes
Disculpa. Discúlpame.	Pardon me. I'm sorry. (*fam.*)
Disculpe. Discúlpeme.	Pardon me. I'm sorry. (*form.*)
Lo siento (mucho).	I'm (very) sorry.
Perdón.	Pardon me. I'm sorry.

Así se dice

la nota = la calificación
el plazo = la fecha límite
estacionar = aparcar (*Sp.*), parquear (*Mex.*)

la tarjeta de identificación = el carnet de identificación (*Peru*), el carnet de identidad (*Sp.*), la cédula (*Col.*)

The word **nota** does not mean *note* as in *to take notes* **(tomar apuntes)** or as in *a written note* **(un recado).** But it can mean *note* as in the phrase **tomar nota de** (*to take note of*).

Note the present indicative conjugation of* **recoger: recojo, recoges, recoge, recogemos, recogéis, recogen.

Conversación

A. Asociaciones

Paso 1. ¿Qué palabras asocia Ud. con los siguientes verbos? Pueden ser sustantivos, o verbos antónimos o sinónimos.

1. estacionar	**5.** sacar
2. recoger	**6.** sufrir
3. acordarse	**7.** pedir
4. entregar	**8.** llegar

Paso 2. ¿Qué palabras o situaciones asocia Ud. con los siguientes sustantivos?

1. el calendario	**8.** las llaves
2. el despertador	**9.** la tarjeta de identificación
3. las notas	**10.** las disculpas
4. las pruebas	**11.** las presiones
5. el plazo	**12.** la inflexibilidad
6. el horario	**13.** los apuntes
7. los informes	**14.** el trabajo

B. Situaciones

Paso 1. En parejas, empareje las preguntas o comentarios con las respuestas apropiadas.

PREGUNTAS/COMENTARIOS

1. __c__ —Anoche no me acordé de poner el despertador.
2. __b__ —No puede estacionar el coche aquí sin permiso.
3. __e__ —¿Sacaste buena nota en la prueba?
4. __f__ —Ramiro se ve fatal. Algo le causa mucho estrés.
5. __d__ —Discúlpeme, profesor, pero aquí tiene mi trabajo escrito sobre la Unión Europea.
6. __a__ —Disculpa, pero no puedo hablar contigo ahora. Tengo que terminar el programa de curso para el semestre que viene y corregir (*grade, correct*) todos estos trabajos finales.

RESPUESTAS

a. —Siento que tengas tanto trabajo. ¿Qué crees que es más urgente que hagas en este momento?
b. —Ya lo sé, pero lo voy a dejar aquí. Estoy cansado de buscar estacionamiento por todo el *campus*.
c. —¡No te puedo creer! ¿Otra vez? ¿A qué hora llegaste al trabajo entonces (*then*)?
d. —¿Pero no se acordó de que el plazo era ayer? Es la última (*last*) vez que le acepto un informe atrasado (*late*).
e. —Muy buena, pero es una sorpresa. No tuve tiempo de estudiar.
f. —¡Pero, hombre! Si el pobre tiene un trabajo de tiempo completo, y además (*besides*) toma tres cursos este semestre…

Paso 2. Ahora, inventen un contexto para cada diálogo. ¿Dónde están las personas que hablan? ¿En una oficina? ¿en clase? ¿Quiénes son?

MODELO: **1.** ⟶ Las personas que hablan están en el trabajo (la oficina). Probablemente están almorzando. Son compañeros de trabajo; se conocen, pero no son amigos…

Con. A, Paso 1: Possible Answers

1. *el carro, el coche* **2.** *el papel, la basura* **3.** *recordar, olvidarse* **4.** *la tarea; devolver* **5.** *fotos, la basura, la lengua, un diente / una muela, buenas/malas notas; poner* **6.** *el estrés; tener* **7.** *disculpas, permiso; contestar* **8.** *salir*

- Ask students the following questions to personalize the vocabulary.
  1. *¿Está Ud. contento/a con su horario de este semestre/trimestre? ¿Por qué? ¿Tiene Ud. que entregar algún informe esta semana? ¿Cuál es el plazo? ¿Tiene pruebas o exámenes? ¿Tuvo algún examen o informe importante la semana pasada?*
  2. *¿Viene Ud. en coche a la universidad? ¿Es difícil para Ud. encontrar estacionamiento? ¿Dónde estaciona?*
  3. *¿Saca Ud. buenas notas este semestre/trimestre? ¿Son mejores o peores que las del semestre pasado?*
  4. *¿Le gusta el calendario de esta universidad (cuando empieza y termina el semestre [trimestre] / cuando hay vacaciones)? ¿Por qué?*
  5. *Normalmente, ¿es Ud. una persona que llega tarde o temprano a las citas / las clases? ¿Necesita un despertador por la mañana o puede Ud. despertarse por si solo/a?*
  6. *¿Se acuerda Ud. de sus citas sin mirar la agenda? ¿Se acuerda Ud. de escribir sus citas en la agenda y de mirarla después?*
- **Reciclado:** Note use of preterite in many of this chapter's *Vocabulario: Preparación* activities. Ask students why preterite is used in each case (to emphasize use of preterite for completed actions).

Con. A: Extension

Have students give all the antonyms and synonyms they know for the following words.

9. *abrir*	**12.** *llegar a tiempo*
10. *perder*	**13.** *ser flexible*
11. *ser feliz*	**14.** *la tranquilidad*

Con. A: Variation

Use a game format to get synonyms and antonyms. Divide the class into teams. Allow teams to work on each word for only 1 minute; the team with the most correct associations wins the round.

Con. B: Suggestion

Model the appropriate tone or intonation for the *Respuestas*. Then have students practice the exchanges aloud.

Con. B: Note

Active vocabulary: *último/a*

Heritage Speakers

- Por la influencia del inglés en algunos dialectos del español del suroeste de los Estados Unidos, se oye decir *grado* en vez de *nota* o *calificación*, que son las palabras aceptadas. Otra expresión influida por el inglés es la palabra *notas* para expresar *apuntes*.
- Algunos hispanohablantes de los Estados Unidos usan la palabra *alarma* para referirse al *despertador*.
- El término *parquear* (*estacionar*) que se oye en México también se usa en algunos países latinoamericanos y en los Estados Unidos. Algunas derivaciones son *el parqueadero* (*estacionamiento*). En España, donde dicen *aparcar*, usan la palabra *aparcamiento*.

Con. C: Suggestions

- Allow students a few minutes to prepare their statements for *Paso 2;* then have them share their ideas with the class.
- Have a class discussion beginning with these questions.

  ¿Qué cursos universitarios son más importantes en la preparación para su carrera?

  ¿Cree Ud. que los triunfos en la vida son una combinación de la buena preparación y la suerte?

Con. C: Note

Active vocabulary: *universitario/a*

Con. D: Reciclado

Item 2 asks students to use ordinal numbers to rank the causes of their stress.

Con. D: Suggestions

- Ask pairs of students to relate back the causes of stress in their lives, in the order they have chosen. Write answers on the board or on an overhead and determine what are the two or three most stressful things in students' lives.
- **Reciclado:** Ask how students can solve or resolve the stresses they feel by completing sentences like these: *Para aliviar ______, es necesario que (nosotros)… Para ______, es urgente que…*

Redacción: Assign *Con. D* as a composition before allowing students to talk about it in pairs or in groups. Tell students how long you want the composition to be and establish other guidelines as well. The day the composition is due, have students discuss the four questions in pairs or in groups. Make different pairs or groups responsible for giving feedback on one question to the whole class.

C. La educación universitaria

Paso 1. Lea lo que dicen Luis Miguel y Edward James Olmos sobre la vida y la educación.

S
O *para*
L *ganadores*[a]
O

«El destino es un mezcla[e] de la preparación y la suerte.[f]»

Luis Miguel, cantante mexicano

Ellos han logrado[b] triunfar. ¡Y cada frase que dicen es una lección gratuita[c] para el éxito[d]!

Les digo con todo mi corazón, con toda mi vida. Yo no tengo talento natural. No soy un genio. Pero mis padres a pesar de[g] ser tan humildes[h] me dieron educación.»

Edward James Olmos, actor mexicoamericano

[a]*winners* [b]han… *have been able to* [c]*free* [d]*success* [e]*mix* [f]*luck* [g]a… *in spite of* [h]*poor*

Paso 2. ¿Cree Ud. que estos dos artistas tienen razón? Conteste las siguientes preguntas.

1. ¿Qué cree Ud. que es más importante para triunfar en la vida, tener talento natural o preparación?
2. ¿Cree que va a ayudarle a encontrar un buen trabajo la educación que está recibiendo Ud.?
3. ¿Son importantes las buenas notas para conseguir un buen trabajo? ¿O cree que es suficiente obtener un título universitario, no importa con qué notas?

D. La vida universitaria. Con frecuencia se oye a las personas mayores hablar de los años universitarios con nostalgia: años de libertad, sin responsabilidades, sin las presiones de la vida que vienen después. ¿Ve Ud. así la época universitaria? En parejas, comenten (*discuss*) este tema. Usen las siguientes preguntas como guía.

1. ¿Tienen muchas presiones los estudiantes universitarios?
2. ¿Qué les causa estrés a Uds.? Ordenen las causas de su estrés, empezando por 1ª. (La primera causa de nuestro estrés es…)
3. ¿Son más divertidos los años universitarios que los años de la escuela secundaria?
4. ¿Les preocupa a Uds. el costo de la matrícula? ¿Es difícil para Uds. o para su familia pagarla?
5. ¿Creen Uds. que la vida va a ser mejor después de graduarse en la universidad? Expliquen su respuesta.

Multimedia: Internet

Have students search the Internet for information on Luis Miguel and Edward James Olmos. They should be able to find photos, biographical information, fan clubs, and music clips to report to the class.

NATIONAL STANDARDS: Cultures

In Spanish *tener educación* not only means to have intellectual preparation but also to be courteous (*ser cortés*) and to have good manners (*tener buenos modales*). Someone who is *mal educado/a* does not know how to behave in public and does not show enough respect for other people, especially his or her elders. *Bien educado/a* is one of the most valued qualities in Hispanic cultures.

¡Qué mala suerte!°

¡Que... *What bad luck!*

Los accidentes

doler (duele) (*like* **gustar**)	to hurt, ache
equivocarse (qu) (de)	to make a mistake (about/with)
levantarse con el pie izquierdo	to get up on the wrong side of the bed
pegar (gu)	to hit, strike
pegar(se) (gu) con/contra	to run/bump into/against
tener buena/mala suerte	to have good/bad luck; to be (un)lucky

¡Qué + *adjective***!**	How . . . !
distraído/a	absent-minded, distracted
¡Qué distraído!	How absent-minded!
torpe	clumsy
¡Qué torpe!	How clumsy!
¡Qué + *noun***!**	What (a) . . . !
¡Qué desastre!	What a mess! What a disaster!
Fue sin querer.	I didn't mean (to do) it.

Así se dice

chocar con/contra = darse con/contra
distraído/a = despistado/a
hacerse daño en = lastimarse en
romperse = quebrarse

Note that the first person singular of **caer** *is irregular:* **caigo.** *The present participle is* **cayendo.**

†**Romper** *means* to break. *It is generally used with* **se: Se rompió la ventana.** *And it is very frequently used in the accidental* **se** *construction:* **Se le rompió el brazo.** *You will learn about that usage in* **Gramática 40** *in this chapter.*

¡Qué mala suerte!

Suggestions

- **Reciclado:** Review body parts (*Cap. 11*) with the new vocabulary.
  ¿Qué partes del cuerpo pueden dolerle a uno?
  ¿Qué partes del cuerpo se pueden romper?
  ¿Con qué partes del cuerpo se puede uno pegar o chocar contra una cosa dura (new)*?*
- Point out that *equivocarse* can be a synonym for *no tener razón*. Another common option: *estar equivocado/a.*
- Emphasize the *¡qué* + adjective/noun*!* It is likely that you have been using this structure in your discourse since the beginning the course. The structure is made explicit and active here.
- Emphasize that *doler* is like *gustar.*
- Model vocabulary in sentences about yourself and in communicative exchanges with the students.
- Have students give the corresponding word.
  1. *Es sinónimo de no tener razón.*
  2. *Tomo esto cuando me duele la cabeza.*
  3. *Es un adjetivo que significa no estar atento a lo que pasa.*
  4. *Es una persona que tiene accidentes frecuentes.*
- Ask students the following questions to personalize the vocabulary.
  1. *¿Le duele la cabeza con frecuencia? ¿Qué hace cuando le duele? ¿En qué situaciones es común que a una persona le duela la cabeza?* (Point out: subjunctive)
  2. *Las personas distraídas, ¿se olvidan de todo o se acuerdan de muchas cosas? ¿Pierden objetos? ¿Qué tipo de objetos? ¿Es Ud. distraído/a? ¿Por qué? Dé algunos ejemplos.*
  3. *¿Es Ud. torpe? ¿Choca con los muebles con frecuencia? ¿con los pies de otras personas? ¿Deja caer* (new) *cosas? ¿Qué personas son típicamente torpes? ¿los futbolistas? ¿los payasos* (new)*?*

Heritage Speakers

Muchos hispanohablantes dicen *Casi me caigo* o *Por poco me caigo;* es decir, usan el presente con *casi* para expresar *I almost fell* (el pasado).

Resources: Transparency 136

Con. A: Suggestion

Ask students the following questions to personalize the information.

¿Qué tipos de seguros conoce Ud.?
¿Cuáles tiene Ud.?
¿Cuál es el más importante, en su opinión?

Reciclado: Recycle the subjunctive. Have students respond *cierto* or *falso*.

1. *Si alguien choca contra una puerta, es lógico que le duela algo.*
2. *Si una persona tiene muchas presiones, es posible que también tenga más accidentes.*
3. *Es cierto que todos trabajamos mal cuando estamos bajo muchas presiones.*
4. *Es probable que la vida moderna cause más problemas que beneficios.*

Con. B: Reciclado

- Note the recycling of some affirmative and negative words.
- Review the use of the preterite and imperfect for the telling of a story. Have students work in pairs to tell each other about accidents they have had. Then have students report to the class their partner's accidents, including when it happened, where, with whom, how the person felt, what he/she did afterward.

Con. B: Note

Active vocabulary: *las escaleras*

Heritage Speakers

Pregúnteles a los hispanohablantes cuáles son algunas de las expresiones más corrientes en español para expresar dolor, sorpresa, compasión o para dar ánimo.

Nota cultural

Suggestions

- Point out that in Spanish as in English, many expressions emerge and fade. An expression will often become associated with a specific time period.
- Remember that the IM offers a number of expressions for the country of focus of each chapter in the section that corresponds to *A leer: Lectura cultural.*
- If you live in a predominantly Mexican or Mexican-American area, you may wish to present some of the most common Mexican expressions, such as *¡Órale!/¡Híjole!* (Come on!).
- Optional expressions:

¡Venga!	Come on!
¡Vamos!	Come on! Let's go!
¡Anímese! ¡Anímate!	Cheer up!

Con. A: Possible Answers
1. *Patina en la calle o en un parque.* **2.** *Puede caerse y romperse un brazo o una pierna.* **3.** *Porque tiene seguro / está asegurado.* **4.** Answers will vary.

Conversación

A. Un anuncio para un seguro. La palabra **seguro** no solo significa *sure*. También quiere decir *insurance*. Este es un anuncio de un seguro de accidentes.

1. ¿Dónde patina el hombre?
2. ¿Qué le puede ocurrir?
3. ¿Por qué tiene buena suerte?
4. ¿Tiene Ud. un seguro de accidentes?

B. Accidentes y tropiezos (*mishaps*)

Paso 1. ¿Le pasaron a Ud. alguna de las siguentes cosas en los últimos meses? Modifique las declaraciones, usando palabras afirmativas y negativas, para que sean (*so that they are*) verdaderas para Ud.

MODELOS: Me caí **una vez** por las escaleras (*stairs*) de mi casa.
Nunca me caí por las escaleras de mi casa.

1. Me caí por las escaleras de mi casa.
2. No me acordé de hacer la tarea para la clase de ____.
3. Me equivoqué al contestar (*when I answered*) una pregunta en clase.
4. El despertador sonó, pero no me desperté.
5. Soy un poco torpe. Rompí sin querer algo que no era mío (*mine*).
6. Choqué con algo y me hice daño.
7. Me olvidé del plazo para entregar un informe.
8. Me olvidé de devolverle algo a alguien.
9. Iba un poco distraído/a y me equivoqué de puerta.

Paso 2. Ahora, usando las oraciones del **Paso 1** como guía, pregúntele a un compañero o compañera cómo le fue ayer. También puede preguntarle si le pasaron otros desastres.

MODELO: ¿Te caíste por las escaleras? ¿Te hiciste daño?

Nota **cultural**

Reacciones emocionales

En español hay muchas expresiones que expresan la reacción de una persona. Estas expresiones pueden variar según el país o región. Las siguientes son de uso generalizado.

- Para expresar dolor, sorpresa o compasión

¡Ay!	Ouch! Oops!	**¡No puede ser!**	It can't be! No way!
¡Uy!	Oops! Oh!	**¡No me diga(s)!**	No! No way!
		¿Qué le vamos a hacer?	What can you do (about it)?

¡Cuánto lo siento!	**¡Qué maravilla!** (*How wonderful!*)
¡Qué bonito/feo/bien!	**¡Qué pena/lástima** (*shame*)**!**
¡Qué horror!	**¡Qué terrible/triste!**

- Con referencia a la suerte

¡Buena suerte!	Good luck!	**¡Qué mala suerte!**	Such bad luck!
¡Que te/le vaya bien!	Hope it goes well!		

- Después de un estornudo (*sneeze*): **¡Salud!**

También es importante notar que en español es costumbre generalizada invocar el nombre de Dios (*God*). Esto ocurre frecuentemente en expresiones de tristeza (*sadness*), esperanza (*hope*) y compasión: **¡Dios mío! ¡Por Dios! Que Dios te bendiga** (*bless you*)**. Si Dios quiere.**

¿Cuál de esas expresiones es su favorita?

Comprensión

Answers will vary.

1. *¿Qué le dice Ud. a un amigo que está triste o deprimido?*
2. *¿Qué dice Ud. cuando se hace daño en la mano?*
3. *¿Qué puede decirle a un amigo que le cuenta algo increíble?*

C. ¿Qué le vamos a hacer? Indique lo que puede pasar o algo que una persona puede hacer en cada una de las siguientes situaciones. También indique algunas de las expresiones que una persona hispanohablante podría (*might*) decir en cada caso.

MODELO: Una estudiante choca contra el escritorio de un compañero de clase. ⟶
Lo que pasa: La estudiante se hace daño en la pierna o el pie y se cae. Las cosas del escritorio de su compañero también se caen.
Se puede decir: ¡Ay¡ ¡Qué torpe soy! ¡Perdón! ¡Fue sin querer!

1. A alguien le duele mucho la cabeza.
2. Una persona que va distraída choca con otra en la cafetería.
3. Una persona torpe rompe la cámara de un amigo.
4. Un compañero de clase se equivocó en muchas preguntas en el último examen.
5. Una amiga se hizo daño mientras jubaga a su deporte favorito.
6. Un amigo se levantó con el pie izquierdo.

Nota **comunicativa**

Más sobre los adverbios: *adjetivo* + **-mente**

You already know the most common Spanish adverbs: words like **bien/mal, mucho/poco, siempre/nunca...**

Adverbs that end in *-ly* in English usually end in **-mente** in Spanish. The suffix **-mente** is added to the feminine singular form of adjectives. Note that the accent mark on the stem word (if there is one) is retained.

ADJECTIVO	ADVERBIO	INGLÉS
rápida	**rápidamente**	*rapidly*
fácil	**fácilmente**	*easily*
paciente	**pacientemente**	*patiently*

D. Intercambios

Paso 1. Modifique las siguientes acciones con un adverbio basado en los adjetivos de **Vocabulario útil. ¡OJO!** Hay más de una opción en algunos casos.

MODELO: esperar ⟶ esperar pacientemente

1. esperar
2. trabajar
3. llegar
4. hacer algo
5. relajarse (*to relax*)
6. estudiar
7. empezar algo
8. estar confundido/a

Vocabulario útil

constante	**posible**
directo/a	**puntual**
fácil	**rápido/a**
inmediato/a	**total**
paciente	**tranquilo/a**

Paso 2. Ahora, en parejas, túrnense para entrevistarse sobre las frases del **Paso 1.** Deben obtener información interesante y personal de su compañero/a.

MODELOS: esperar pacientemente ⟶ ¿Sabes esperar pacientemente? ¿A quién esperas pacientemente? ¿Cuándo esperas pacientemente?

Paso 3. Digan a la clase por lo menos un detalle interesante de su compañero/a.

Con. D: Preliminary Exercise
Have students give the corresponding adverb (rapid response).

1. *práctico*
2. *especial*
3. *perfecto*
4. *triste*
5. *alegre*
6. *feliz*
7. *final*
8. *típico*
9. *personal*
10. *rápido*
11. *leal*
12. *elegante*
13. *cariñoso*
14. *tranquilo*
15. *directo*

Mundo interactivo
You should now be prepared to work with Scenario 7, Activity 3 in Connect Spanish (**www.connectspanish.com**).

Con. D: Follow-up

- Have students tell what actions they associate with the following adverbs. Have them create sentences about themselves.

  ¿Qué hace Ud. de la siguiente manera?

  1. *infrecuentemente*
  2. *lentamente* (new)
  3. *tristemente*
  4. *felizmente*
  5. *fielmente*
  6. *fabulosamente*

- Have students complete the following sentences. Model your own answer for each sentence, then follow up with a question.

  Yo ______ rápidam ente, pero no ______ rápidamente. ⟶ *Yo leo rápidamente, pero no escribo rápidamente. ¿Y Ud.? ¿Qué hace rápidamente?*

  1. *Yo ______ rápidamente, pero no ______ rápidamente.*
  2. *Yo siempre ______ tranquilamente.*
  3. *Yo ______ mejor que mis padres.*
  4. *Yo ______ peor que mi mejor amigo/a.*

- Ask students the following questions.

  1. *¿Habla Ud. solamente en español en esta clase?*
  2. *¿Llega Ud. puntualmente a todas sus clases?*
  3. *En la librería, ¿espera Ud. pacientemente en cola cuando paga los libros?*
  4. *Cuando recibe correo electrónico de un amigo o amiga, ¿le contesta inmediatamente?*

Pronunciación: See the Workbook / Laboratory Manual for presentation and practice of the letters *ñ* and *ch*.

Nota comunicativa

Suggestions

- Point out that when two *-mente* adverbs are used together, joined by a conjunction in a single sentence, the first adverb is shortened to the feminine singular adjective and only the second adverb includes the *-mente* suffix: *Carlos hizo la lección rápida y fácilmente.*
- Remind students that *mucho* and *poco* are invariable when used as adverbs: *Isabel tiene muchas* (adjective) *clases; por eso estudia mucho* (adverb).
- Point out that when an adjective does not end in *-o,* there is no *-a* before *-mente* to form the adverb: *fácilmente, totalmente.*
- Some students may inquire about the accent mark on *rápidamente* and *fácilmente,* noting that the word is stressed on the next-to-last (penultimate) syllable. If the adjective has a written accent mark, it is retained in the adverbial form. It is purely an orthographic, not a phonemic, convention.

Gramática 39
Hace... que: Another Use of *hacer*

GEA: Notes

- *Cusco* is now the official Spanish spelling, but the city's name is still often spelled as *Cuzco.*
- *Cusco,* a Quechua name, is often called the Rome of the Americas because of the number of historic sites found there. It was the last capital of the Incas. Today, the city has over 500,000 inhabitants, making it one of the largest cities in Peru. Its cathedral and *la Plaza de Armas* are considered among the most beautiful of the Hispanic world. The city, designated as a World Heritage Site by UNESCO, is one of Peru's main tourist destinations.

GEA: Suggestions

- Read the *GEA* with students and call their attention to the use of a present tense verb in item 1 and a preterite verb in item 2.
- For each question in *¿Y en los Estados Unidos?,* write the relevant dates on the white board or overhead: **1.** 1776 **2.** 1959 **3.** 1776 **4.** 2008 or 2012. Use the phrase *más de 200 años* for the independence questions.
- Note that *los Estados Unidos* is viewed as a plural subject in this text because the article is consistently used with it. It is also correct to use it as a singular subject when it is used without the article.
- **Possible Answers: 1.** *Hace más de 200 años que los Estados Unidos son un país independiente.* **2.** *Hace ______ años que los Estados Unidos tienen 50 estados.* **3.** *Los Estados Unidos se independizaron de Inglaterra hace más de 200 años.* **4.** *En los Estados Unidos hubo elecciones presidenciales hace ______ años.*

Emphasis 1: Suggestions

- Use the *hace... que* + present tense structure as frequently as possible in your speech. Some (but not all) students will begin to use it spontaneously if they hear it enough. You may wish to treat this grammar topic for recognition only.
- Explain and model these expressions: *hace mucho tiempo, hace muchos días.*
- Emphasize that students should never change the form of *hace* in this construction.
- When the *hace* phrase follows a present tense verb, some native speakers prefer to use just *hace* rather than *desde hace: Estudio español hace un año.* While both usages

GRAMÁTICA

39 Telling How Long Something Has Been Happening or How Long Ago Something Happened

Hace... que: Another Use of **hacer**

Grammar Tutorial 39
connect SPANISH
www.connectspanish.com

Gramática en acción: Una lección de historia

La bella (*beautiful*) ciudad de Cusco, Perú

Cusco, una ciudad histórica, fue la capital del imperio de los incas. Luego, durante la dominación española, fue una importante ciudad colonial.

1. La ciudad de Cusco continúa habitada desde hace más de 3.000 años. Esto la hace la ciudad más antigua de Sudamérica.
2. Hace aproximadamente 500 años que los conquistadores españoles llegaron a Cusco por primera vez. La convirtieron en una ciudad importante de su imperio.

¿Y los Estados Unidos?

¿Cuánto tiempo hace que... ?

1. son un país independiente
2. tienen cincuenta estados
3. se independizaron de Inglaterra
4. hubo elecciones presidenciales

El presente: *has/have been (happening) for + time*

- **hace** + *time* + **que** + *present tense verb*
  Hace un año **que** estudio español.
- *present tense verb* + **desde hace** + *time*
  Estudio español **desde hace** un año.

I've been studying Spanish for one year.

El pretérito: *ago*

- **hace** + *time* + **que** + *preterite tense verb*
  Hace un año **que** empecé a estudiar español.
- *preterite tense verb* + **hace** + *time*
  Empecé a estudiar español **hace** un año.

I started studying Spanish a (one) year ago.

1. ***Hace*** + *time*
   In Spanish, a phrase with **hace** + *time* is used to express two very different perspectives on time.
   - With the *present* tense, the **hace** phrase tells how long something *has been happening*. (English uses the present perfect progressive tense for this: *has/have been* verb + *-ing for . . .*)

A history lesson *Cuzco, a historic city, was the capital of the Inca Empire. Then, during the Spanish occupation, it was an important colonial city.* **1.** *The city of Cuzco has been continually inhabited for more than 3,000 years. That makes it the oldest city in South America.* **2.** *The Spanish conquistadors arrived in Cuzco for the first time about 500 years ago. They made it into an important city in their empire.*

Heritage Speakers

- En algunos dialectos del español, hay hispanohablantes que usan *hacen* cuando el período de tiempo a que se refieren es plural, por ejemplo, *Hacen tres días que...* o *Hacen varios minutos que...* , etcétera. Pregúnteles a los hispanohablantes si usan esta construcción o si la han oído antes. A pesar de este uso popular de *hacen,* la forma impersonal, *hace,* es la preferida.
- Pregúnteles a los hispanohablantes si usan esta u otra estructura para expresar *cuánto tiempo.*

- With the *preterite*, the **hace** phrase tells how long *ago* something *happened.*

Note that the **hace** + *time* phrase can come before or after the verb. When it comes before, the word **que** is also used with it. When it comes after the verb to express *has/have been . . .* , the phase **desde hace** is used.

Hace dos años **que** **estudio** en esta universidad.
Estudio en esta universidad **desde hace** dos años.
I've been studying at this university for two years.

Hace dos años **que** **me gradué** en la escuela secundaria.
Me gradué en la escuela secundaria **hace** dos años.
I graduated from high school two years ago.

¡OJO!

The form of the word **hace** never varies in this structure, whether it is used with a present tense or a preterite tense verb.

2. Questions with *hace*

Use the question **¿Cuánto tiempo hace que... ?** with both structures. The tense of the verb you use indicates your meaning.

- + *present tense* = to ask how long something *has been happening*
- + *preterite tense* = to ask how long *ago* something *happened*

You can answer a question of this kind just by saying the time.

—**¿Cuánto tiempo hace que** vives aquí?
—Dos meses.
"How long have you been living here?"
"(For) Two months."

—**¿Cuánto tiempo hace que** te mudaste aquí?
—Dos meses.
"How long ago did you move here?"
"Two months ago."

Práctica

hace + *time* + **que** + *present* / *present* + **desde hace** + *time* } = *has/have been doing*
hace + *time* + **que** + *preterite* / *preterite* + **hace** + *time* } = ago

A. ¡Anticipemos! ¿Qué tiene ganas de hacer?

Paso 1. ¿Qué tiene Ud. ganas de hacer en las siguientes situaciones?

MODELO: Ud. está en clase. Son las 12:30 de la tarde. Hace cinco horas que no come nada. → Tengo muchas ganas de almorzar.

1. Ud. está en casa. Hace tres horas que escribe ejercicios de español.
2. Hace dos meses que Ud. vive en una residencia estudiantil. Sus compañeros siempre hacen mucho ruido.
3. Hace diez años que Ud. tiene un coche viejo que no funciona bien.
4. Ud. está en una discoteca. Hace media hora que baila y tiene mucho calor.
5. Hace tres días que llueve y Ud. está aburrido/a de estar sin salir de la casa tanto tiempo.

Práctica A, Paso 1: Possible Answers
1. *Tengo ganas de mirar la tele.* 2. *Tengo ganas de mudarme a otra residencia.* 3. *Tengo ganas de comprar un nuevo coche.* 4. *Tengo ganas de beber algo.* 5. *Tengo ganas de salir a correr.*

Paso 2. Ahora, en parejas, túrnense para preguntarse qué tienen ganas de hacer en las situaciones del **Paso 1.**

MODELO: E1: Estás en clase. Son las 12:30 de la tarde. Hace cinco horas que no comes nada.
E2: Tengo muchas ganas de comer una hamburguesa con papas fritas.

Autoprueba

Match each sentence with the corresponding idea.

a. for *x* years **b.** *x* years ago

1. ______ Hace dos años que te conozco.
2. ______ Te conocí hace dos años.
3. ______ Hace tres años que tomé cálculo.
4. ______ Hace tres años que estudio español.

Answers: 1. a 2. b 3. b 4. a

B. Eventos históricos. ¿Cuánto tiempo hace que pasaron los siguientes eventos? Haga oraciones completas con las palabras indicadas. ¿Sabe Ud. todas las respuestas? Los años en que pasaron estos eventos aparecen abajo.

MODELO: el primer hombre / llegar a la luna →
Hace más de cuarenta años que el primer hombre **llegó** a la luna.

1. Cristóbal Colón / llegar a América
2. la Segunda Guerra (*War*) Mundial / terminar
3. Michael Jackson / morir
4. el presidente (el primer ministro) actual / ser elegido (*to be elected*)
5. el profesor / la profesora de español / empezar a enseñar en esta universidad

Los años: MODELO: 1969 1. 1492 2. 1945 3. 2009 4. ¿ ? 5. ¿ ?

Prác. B: Possible Answers
1. *Hace más de 500 años que Cristóbal Colón llegó a América.* 2. *Hace más de sesenta años que terminó la Segunda Guerra Mundial.* 3. *Hace ______ años que murió Michael Jackson.* 4. *Hace más de ______ años que fue elegido el presidente (el primer ministro) actual.* 5. *Hace más de ______ años que el profesor / la profesora de español empezó a enseñar en esta universidad.*

NATIONAL STANDARDS: Connections

- **Cristóbal Colón** (1451–1506): Born in Genoa, Italy, *Colón* (*Cristoforo Colombo,* in Italian) was a navigator who sailed west across the Atlantic Ocean in search of a route to Asia. *Colón* achieved fame by making landfall on a Caribbean island instead.
- **World War II:** This global conflict lasted from 1939 to 1945.
- **Michael Jackson** (1958–2009): Known as the King of Pop, he was a singer, songwriter, and dancer.

are possible, *hace* alone is viewed as very informal, if not actually incorrect.

- There are other ways to express the *has/have been . . .* concept of time; the choice is often a matter of dialectal variation. Here are two common structures.

llevar + *time* (Spain): *Llevo 20 años en este país.*
tener + *time* (Guatemala, Mexico, and others): *Tengo 20 años de estar en este país.*

Preliminary Exercises

- Give the following dictation.
  1. *Hace tres años que vivo aquí.*
  2. *Hace un año que no vemos a los nietos.*
  3. *Hace una semana que no hablo con mis padres.*
  4. *Hace cinco meses que estudiamos español.*
  5. *Hace dos años que llegué a esta universidad.*
  6. *Hace quince años que aprendí a esquiar.*

  Follow up the dictation with questions to check comprehension.

  ¿Cuántos años hace que vivo aquí?
- Have students use the following cues to form sentences that express how long someone has been doing something.

  MODELO: *Julio / trabajar / una hora → Hace una hora que Julio trabaja.*
  1. *yo / descansar / una hora*
  2. *tú / cocinar / media hora*
  3. *Jaime / estudiar / dos horas*
  4. *nosotros / leer / hora y media*
  5. *niños / escribir cartas / dos horas*
  6. *Tina / hablar por teléfono / veinte minutos*
- Have students tell how long ago they did the following things.
  1. you were born (*nacer: nací*)
  2. you moved (*mudarse*) to this town
  3. you met your best friend
  4. you handed in your last major paper

Prác. A, B: Note

Prác. A focuses on the use of *hace* with the present tense; *Prác. B* focuses on the use of *hace* with the preterite.

Prác. A: Suggestions

- Ask students to find the *hace* phrase plus the present tense verb.
- You may also wish to ask students to translate the *hace* sentence into English.

Prác. A: Note

Active vocabulary: *estudiantil*

Con. A, B: Note

Con. A provides complete scaffolding for students, while *Con. B* requires students to come up with *hace* structures on their own.

Con. B: Suggestions

- Go through the items with the class as a whole before students work on their own.
- If you wish, tell students that items 1–5 require the present, while items 7–10 require the preterite.
- Point out that item 1, *conocer a su mejor amigo/a,* can be asked and answered in both the present and the preterite. Ask students to explain the meaning, depending on the tense of *conocer* that is used.

Redacción: Assign the preparation of questions for both *Pasos 1* and *2* as a written assignment. Ask students to create one additional question for each item. For example, *Paso 1*, question 1: *¿Cuánto tiempo hace que vives en esta ciudad? ¿Te gustó la ciudad cuando llegaste?*

Conversación

A. Información personal

Paso 1. Complete las siguientes oraciones con información personal.

1. Hace ____ que mi familia vive en el estado / la provincia de ____.
2. Hace ____ que yo vivo en este estado / esta provincia.
3. Hace ____ que comí pizza por última vez.
4. Me duché / Me bañé hace ____.
5. Vi a mi mejor amigo/a hace ____.
6. Hace ____ que practico/hago ____ (deporte o pasatiempo).

Paso 2. Ahora, en parejas, comparen sus oraciones del **Paso 1.** Digan a la clase por lo menos una cosa que tienen en común.

B. Intercambios

Paso 1. Haga preguntas basadas en las siguientes ideas. **¡OJO!** Algunas requieren un verbo en el presente y otras un verbo en el pretérito.

MODELOS: vivir en esta ciudad →
¿Cuánto tiempo hace que **vives** en esta ciudad?
visitar a sus abuelos la última vez →
¿Cuánto tiempo hace que **visitaste** a tus abuelos la última vez?

1. vivir en esta ciudad
2. asistir a esta universidad
3. vivir en su apartamento/casa/residencia
4. estudiar español
5. manejar
6. conocer a su mejor amigo/a
7. visitar a sus abuelos (a sus padres, a ¿ ?) la última vez
8. sacar una mala nota
9. escribir el último trabajo para una de sus clases
10. llegar tarde a clase

Paso 2. Ahora use las preguntas del **Paso 1** para entrevistar a un compañero o compañera de clase. Luego digan a la clase un detalle interesante de su pareja.

¿Recuerda Ud.?

You know how to use the Spanish verb **gustar** and other verbs like it (**molestar, doler...**). Review what you know by completing these sentences.

1. No me gusta / gustan los exámenes.
2. No me gusta / gustan tomar pruebas tampoco.
3. ¿Te molesta / molestan los perros?
4. Al abuelo le duele / duelen las piernas.

You have also learned a number of uses for the word **se.** Match each function of **se** with the appropriate sentence.

1. __c__ Los niños tienen que bañarse ahora.
2. __d__ Los amigos se quieren mucho.
3. __b__ ¿El regalo? Se lo di a Ana ayer.
4. __a__ Aquí se habla español.

a. to express *one* or *you*
b. to replace the indirect object pronoun **le** or **les** before **lo/la/los/las**
c. to express a reflexive action
d. to express a reciprocal action

In **Gramática 40** you will learn another use for the word **se** in a structure that is similar to **gustar** and other verbs like it.

40 Expressing Unplanned or Unexpected Events

Another Use of **se**

Grammar Tutorial 40
connect SPANISH
www.connectspanish.com

Gramática en acción: Un día fatal

1. A Diego se le cayó la taza de café.

2. A Antonio se le olvidaron los libros.

3. A Antonio y a Diego se les olvidó apagar las luces del coche.

¿Y Ud.?

¿También pasó un día fatal ayer? Indique si las siguientes oraciones son ciertas o falsas para describir su día.

	CIERTO	FALSO
1. Se me perdió algo.	☐	☐
2. Se me olvidó hacer algo importante.	☐	☐
3. Se me cayeron algunas cosas.	☐	☐
4. Se me rompió algo de valor (*value*).	☐	☐

Accidental **se** / **El *se* accidental**

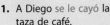

a + Noun (a + Pronoun)	se	Indirect Object Pronoun	Verb	Subject
A Antonio	se	le	**olvid**aron	los apuntes.
(A mí)	Se	me	**cay**ó	la taza de café.
¿(A ti)	Se	te	**perdi**ó	la cartera?

1. **Using *se* to Express Accidental Events**
   Unplanned or unexpected events (*I dropped . . . , We lost . . . , You forgot . . .*) are frequently expressed in Spanish with **se** and a third person form of the verb. The event is viewed as happening *to* someone—the unwitting "victim" of the action.

   Se me cayó el papel.
   I dropped the paper. (The paper was dropped by me.)

   Se le olvidaron las llaves.
   He forgot the keys. (The keys were forgotten by him.)

   Se te olvidó llamar a tu hija.
   You forgot to call your daughter. (Calling your daughter was forgotten by you.)

An awful day ***1.*** *Diego dropped a cup of coffee.* ***2.*** *Antonio forgot his books.* ***3.*** *Antonio and Diego forgot to turn off the headlights on their car.*

Gramática 40
Another Use of *se*

Note

You may wish to aim only for students to have partial control of this structure. This can include a few fixed or memorized phrases (*se me olvidó, se me perdió*, and so on).

GEA: Suggestions

- Focus on each drawing and describe the circumstances that led up to each event (using preterite and imperfect in your discourse). Then read the drawing's caption.
- Ask students if these sentences remind them of another verb that they have used frequently (= *gustar*).
- Help students analyze pronoun use (singular in sentences 1 and 2, plural in 3) and verb use (singular in sentences 1 and 3, plural in 2).

GEA: Note

Active vocabulary: *apagar, la luz, la taza*

Extension

Provide additional situations for the *¿Y Ud.?* follow-up.

5. *Se me acabó el dinero mientras estaba de vacaciones.*
6. *Se me olvidó hacer una tarea importante.*
7. *Se me perdieron unos apuntes de clase.*
8. *Se me rompió el brazo.*
9. *Se me olvidó la cartera en casa.*
10. *Se me quedaron los libros en la biblioteca.*
11. *Se me perdió todo el dinero que tenía.*
12. *Se me cayeron los lentes.*

Suggestion

Have students convert the following into *se* structures.

1. *Jaime perdió las llaves.*
2. *Carlos rompió la lámpara.*
3. *Susana y Roberto olvidaron sus libros.*

Emphasis 1: Suggestions

- Point out that the subject of the English sentence becomes the indirect object pronoun in the Spanish equivalent: I = *se* ***me,*** Antonio = *se* ***le.*** The structure is similar to that of *gustar*.
- Point out the option of emphasizing or clarifying the indirect object with the corresponding prepositional phrase: *a mí, a él,* and so on.

Heritage Speakers

En ocasiones, tanto en América como en España, se oye *me se* y *te se* en vez de *se me* y *se te* en esta construcción. La construcción aceptada, sin embargo, es *se me* y *se te*.

Resources: Transparency 137

Emphasis 2: Suggestions

- Point out that the use of the singular vs. the plural verb depends on the direct object from the English sentence.
- Remind students that *a* + *el* ⟶ *al* (first pair of sentences).

Emphasis 3: Suggestion

This section concentrates on the use of this structure with *me, te,* and *le*. You might expand the activities in this section to cover *nos, os,* and *les* if you want students to practice these forms.

Emphasis 4: Note

The following verbs are new to students: *acabar, caer, quedar*. Note that students are familiar with *acabar* and *quedar* in other expressions: *acabar de* + inf., *caerse, quedarse*.

Emphasis 5: Suggestion

Asociaciones. Ask students what words they associate with the following verbs. Give them hints, as needed.

1. *acabar* (liquids, supplies)
2. *caer* (objects)
3. *perder* (objects)
4. *quedar* (things one leaves behind / at home)
5. *romper* (dishware)
6. *olvidar* (objects)

Preliminary Exercises

- Ask students to identify the indirect object pronoun they hear in the following sentences.
  1. *Se me olvidó el bolígrafo.*
  2. *Se le rompieron los platos.*
  3. *Se te cayeron las flores.*
  4. *Se te acabó la gasolina.*
  5. *Se le quedaron en casa los boletos.*
- Give the following dictation.
  1. *Se me cayeron las llaves.*
  2. *Se te rompieron los vasos.*
  3. *A Pepe se le rompió el despertador.*
  4. *A María se le olvidaron las aspirinas.*

  Follow up the dictation with questions to check comprehension or by having students provide the English equivalents.
- Have students do the following chain drill to practice the structure.

  ¡Qué distraídos estuvimos todos ayer! Dé oraciones nuevas según las indicaciones.
  1. *A Pablo se le olvidó la cartera.* (*mí, Inés, ti, el chico*)
  2. *Se te perdieron las llaves otra vez.* (*Ernesto, Ud., la niña, mí*)
  3. *María fue la más distraída de todos. Se le olvidó/olvidaron…* (*desayunar, los lentes, estudiar para el examen, los cheques, venir a clase*)
- Have students give the Spanish equivalents.
  1. I dropped my glasses/plate/books.
  2. Robert lost his book / keys / alarm clock.

Resources: Transparency 138

2. Agreement with the Subject

In these kinds of sentences, as with **gustar** and similar verbs, the subject of the sentence is the thing that is dropped, forgotten, and so on. The subject usually follows the verb.

- When the subject is singular, the verb will be singular, even if the "victim" is plural.
- When the subject is plural, the verb will be plural, even if the "victim" is singular.

A los niños **se les olvidó el cumpleaños** de su madre.
The children forgot their mother's birthday.

Al niño **se le olvidó el cumpleaños** de su madre.
The child forgot his mother's birthday.

A Antonio **se le olvidaron los apuntes.**
Antonio forgot his notes.

A Antonio y Diego **se les olvidaron los apuntes.**
Antonio and Diego forgot their notes.

¡OJO!
Remember that an infinitive is viewed as a singular subject in Spanish: **A los niños se les olvidó llamar a su madre.**

3. Parts of the Sentence

Here are the components of these kinds of sentences.

- The "victim" must always be indicated by an indirect object pronoun, which follows the word **se.**
- When the "victim" is overtly stated, he/she/it is expressed with an **a** + *noun* phrase.
- When the "victim" is not overtly stated, meaning can be clarified or emphasized with an optional **a** + *pronoun* phrase.
- The word **no** always comes before the word **se.**

Se le rompió el brazo.
He/She broke his/her arm.

A Ana / A la niña se **le** rompió el brazo.
Ana / The child broke her arm.

(A ella) Se **le** rompió el brazo.
She broke her arm.

A Ana **no se** le rompió el brazo.
Ana didn't break her arm.

4. Verbs Frequently Used with *se*

Here are some verbs frequently used in this construction.

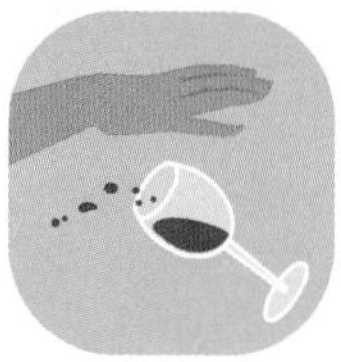
caer

romper

quedar

acabar	to finish; to run out of
caer	to fall; to drop
olvidar	to forget
perder (pierdo)	to lose
quedar	to remain, be left
romper	to break

5. Accident Versus Intent

This structure is used to emphasize the accidental nature of an event. When the speaker wishes to emphasize *who* committed the act, or that the act was intentional, that person becomes the subject of the verb and the **se** structure is not used.

Se me rompió el plato.
The plate broke on me. (accidentally)

(Yo) Rompí el plato.
I broke the plate. (emphasizes either who broke the plate or the intentionality of the act)

El *se* accidental

a + *noun* + **se** + *indirect object pronoun* + *verb* + *subject*
(**a** + *pronoun*) **se** + *indirect object pronoun* + *verb* + *subject*

Práctica

A. ¿Accidental o deliberada? Lea las siguientes pares de oraciones e indique si las acciones que se describen son accidentales o deliberadas.

	ACCIDENTAL	DELIBERADA
1. a. Se me rompieron los lentes.	☑	☐
b. Estaba furiosa, tiré (*I threw*) mis lentes al piso y los rompí.	☐	☑
2. a. La comida no me gustaba para nada y la tiré a la basura.	☐	☑
b. Se me cayó la comida en mi nueva blusa blanca.	☑	☐
3. a. Se me quemó (*burned*) en un incendio (*fire*) todo lo que tenía.	☑	☐
b. Quemé todas las cartas y fotos de mi novio cuando nos separamos.	☐	☑

B. ¡Anticipemos! ¡Qué mala memoria! Hortensia es tan distraída que, cuando se fue de vacaciones al Perú, se le olvidó hacer muchas cosas importantes antes de salir. Empareje los olvidos (*lapses*) de Hortensia con las consecuencias.

OLVIDOS

1. __d__ Se le olvidó cerrar la puerta de su casa.
2. __c__ Se le olvidó pagar las cuentas.
3. __e__ Se le olvidó pedirle a alguien que cuidara a (*to take care of*) su perro.
4. __g__ Se le olvidó cancelar el periódico.
5. __a__ Se le olvidó pedirle permiso a su jefa.
6. __b__ Se le olvidó llevar el pasaporte.
7. __f__ Se le olvidó hacer reserva en un hotel.

CONSECUENCIAS

a. Va a perder el trabajo.
b. No la van a dejar subir al avión.
c. Le van a suspender el servicio de la electricidad y del gas... ¡y cancelar sus tarjetas de crédito!
d. Alguien le va a robar el televisor.
e. ¡«King» se va a morir de hambre!
f. Si llega al Perú, no va a tener dónde alojarse (*to stay*).
g. Todos van a saber que no está en casa.

C. Una mañana fatal

Paso 1. Complete la siguiente descripción de lo que le pasó a Pablo ayer. **¡OJO!** Use el **se** accidental.

Pablo tuvo una mañana fatal. Primero (olvidar[1]) poner el despertador. Se levantó tarde y se vistió rápidamente. No cerró bien su maletín;[a] por eso (caer[2]) unos papeles importantes. Recogió los papeles y subió al coche, pero después de cinco minutos, (acabar[3]) la gasolina y se le paró[b] el coche. Dejó el coche en la calle y decidió ir a pie. Llevaba el maletín en una mano y las llaves y un documento urgente en la otra. Desgraciadamente, en el camino,[c] (perder[4]) el documento. Cuando llegó a la oficina, buscó a su jefe para entregarle el documento pero no podía encontrarlo entre sus papeles. Cansado y enojado, cerró el maletín sin cuidado y (romper[5]) los lentes.

[a]*briefcase* [b]se... *(the car) stopped on him* [c]en... *on the way*

Paso 2. Ahora descríbale a un compañero o compañera una mañana o un día fatal que Ud. tuvo. **¡OJO!** Use el **se** accidental.

MODELO: El primer día de clases, se me olvidó poner el despertador y llegué tarde a clase. Luego...

Autoprueba

Match the following sentences.

1. _____ No encuentro las llaves.
2. _____ Tu calculadora no funciona.
3. _____ Paco no entregó la tarea.
4. _____ Necesito comprar leche.

a. Se te rompió.
b. Se me acabó.
c. Se me perdieron.
d. Se le olvidó.

Answers: **1.** c **2.** a **3.** d **4.** b

Prác. C: Answers
1. *se le olvidó* **2.** *se le cayeron* **3.** *se le acabó* **4.** *se le perdió* **5.** *se le rompieron*

Prác. A: Suggestions

- Emphasize to students that this activity deals with the concept behind the accidental *se* structure: accidents vs. things over which we exercise deliberate control.
- Ask students to identify the "victim" in the accidental *se* options.
- Have students translate both options.

Prác. C, Paso 2: Follow-up

Ask students:

¿Qué más le pasaba a Ud.? ¿Qué ha cambiado (new)*?*

Have students give sentences with actions that used to happen to them but do not happen anymore.

Antes se me perdían los lentes. Ahora se me pierden los suéteres.

Con. A, B: Suggestion

Emphasize the tense used in each: *A, Paso 1* = present, *Paso 2* = imperfect, *B, Paso 2* = preterite.

Con. A: Follow-up

- Have volunteers answer this question. *¿Recuerda Ud. alguno de los días más desastrosos de su vida? ¿Qué le pasó?*
- Have students work in groups to discuss their most recent *día fatal.*

Con. C: Notes

- You may wish to review the meaning of the *dichos* as a whole-class activity before asking students to match them to the *situaciones.*
- The *dichos* are given in the correct tense to be matched with the *situaciones*. All students need to do is find the correct match.
- Approximate English equivalents of *los dichos:*

  a. to make one's mouth water
  b. to become late
  c. to have a sinking feeling, have one's heart sink
  d. to let the cat out of the bag
  e. to lose one's patience
  f. to be wild about someone or something

Conversación

A. ¡Desastres por todas partes (*everywhere*)**!**

Paso 1. ¿Es Ud. una persona distraída o torpe? Indique las oraciones que describen lo que le pasa a Ud. Puede cambiar algunos de los detalles de las oraciones si es necesario. **¡OJO!** Se usa el presente para hablar de acciones típicas.

1. ☐ Con frecuencia se me caen los libros (los platos,...).
2. ☐ Se me pierden constantemente las llaves (los calcetines,...).
3. ☐ Se me olvida apagar la computadora (la electricidad,...).
4. ☐ Siempre se me rompen los lentes (las lámparas,...).
5. ☐ De vez en cuando (*From time to time*) se me quedan los libros (los cuadernos,...) en la clase.
6. ☐ Se me olvida fácilmente mi horario (el teléfono de algún amigo,...).

Paso 2. ¿Es Ud. igual ahora que cuando era más joven? Complete cada oración del **Paso 1** para describir cómo era de niño/a. **¡OJO!** Use el imperfecto.

MODELO: De niño/a, (no) se me caían los libros con frecuencia.

Paso 3. Ahora compare sus respuestas con las de un compañero o compañera. ¿Quién es más distraído/a o torpe ahora? ¿Quién era así de niño/a?

B. Encuesta (*Poll*)**: Accidentes de la semana**

Paso 1. Haga una lista de cinco accidentes o cosas que ocurren con frecuencia en la vida diaria y que a nosotros nos parecen desastres. Debe usar por lo menos tres verbos diferentes.

MODELO: perder las llaves de la casa o apartamento

Paso 2. Ahora hágales cinco preguntas a cinco personas de la clase sobre los accidentes o desastres que Ud. apuntó en el **Paso 1.**

MODELO: perder las llaves de la casa o apartamento ⟶
La semana pasada, ¿se te perdieron las llaves de la casa o apartamento?

Paso 3. Diga a la clase cuál fue el accidente o desastre más común de los cinco y quién fue la persona que sufrió más accidentes entre sus encuestados (*interviewees*).

C. Unos dichos (*colloquial expressions*) **hispanos.** El **se** accidental se usa en muchos dichos en español. En parejas, traten de adivinar (*guess*) el significado de los siguientes dichos o den su equivalente en inglés. Luego emparejen los dichos con la situación apropiada.

DICHOS

a. Se le hace agua la boca.
b. Se le hacía tarde.
c. Se le fue el alma (*soul*) a los pies.
d. Se le fue la lengua.
e. Se le acabó la paciencia.
f. Se le cae la baba (*drool*) por (algo o alguien).

SITUACIONES

1. La clase empezaba a las dos. Eran las dos menos veinte y Raúl todavía estaba en la ducha. A Raúl __b__

2. Ramón le contó a María un secreto, pero María se lo dijo a Luisa y ahora todo el mundo (*everybody*) en la residencia lo sabe. Ramón está furioso. A María __d__

3. La hija de Carmen es preciosa. A Carmen __f__

4. Julio tiene muchísimas ganas de comer la comida de su madre. ¡Qué rica! Solo de pensarlo, a Julio __a__

5. «¡Ya no más! (*Enough already!*)», gritó (*screamed*) la madre. «Vete a tu cuarto ahora mismo.» A la madre __e__

6. Del hospital llamaron al padre para decirle que su hija había tenido (*had had*) un grave accidente. Al padre __c__

¿Recuerda Ud.?

Before beginning **Gramática 41,** remember what you learned in **Capítulo 6** about prepositional pronouns. The first and second person singular pronouns differ from subject pronouns; the rest are identical to subject pronouns. Give the prepositional pronouns that correspond to the following persons.

1. Pepe: de __él__
2. Lisa y yo: detrás de __nosotros/as__
3. tú: para __ti__
4. yo: de __mí__
5. Ud.: con __Ud.__
6. Juan y Olga: para __ellos__

41 *¿Por o para?*
A Summary of Their Uses

Grammar Tutorial 41
connect | SPANISH
www.connectspanish.com

Gramática en acción: ¿Qué se representa?

Comprensión

Empareje cada dibujo con la oración que le corresponde.

Ⓐ

1. __b__

2. __a__

a. Caminan por el parque.
b. Caminan para el parque.

Ⓑ

3. __a__

4. __b__

a. El regalo que mandó la abuela es para Eduardo.
b. La madre de Eduardo compró el regalo por la abuela.

Ⓒ

5. __b__

6. __a__

a. Camila está nerviosa por la entrevista.
b. Camila se viste para la entrevista.

Gramática 41: *¿Por o para?*

Reciclado: Students already know the most important uses of these prepositions.

GEA: Suggestions

- The items in *Comprensión* contain sentences that are very similar. The drawings themselves will help students match the sentences correctly.
- Go over the answers to *Comprensión* with students.
- No translations are provided for this *GEA*. Ask students to translate each pair of sentences. They should be able to do so based on what they already know about *por* and *para*.

Follow-up

After completing *¿Qué se representa?,* read the following sentences and have students make drawings based on what they hear.

Haga un dibujo que ilustre cada una de las siguientes oraciones.

1. *Pedro trabaja para una familia muy rica.*
2. *Pedro va a trabajar por su compañero esta tarde.*
3. *Es una escultura demasiado pequeña y fea para ese precio.*
4. *Teresa va a hacer algo especial mañana para el cumpleaños de su mejor amiga.*

To follow up, ask *¿Quién es el/la mejor dibujante de la clase?*

Resources: Transparency 139

You have been using **por** and **para** since you started to study Spanish. Each preposition has some English equivalents that are unique to it, making it easy to decide between them in those cases. However, both **por** and **para** can mean *for*, depending on the context. You already know much of the information in this section.

Por

1. Unique Meanings of *por*
The preposition **por** has a number of English equivalents that are only expressed with **por,** never with **para.**

• *by / by means of*	El libro fue escrito **por** Mario Vargas Llosa. *The book was written by Mario Vargas Llosa.* Nos hablamos **por teléfono** mañana. *We'll talk by (on the) phone tomorrow.*
• *through/along*	Me gusta pasear **por el parque** y **por la playa.** *I like to stroll through the park and along the beach.*
• *during/in* (time of day)	Trabajo **por la mañana.** *I work in the morning.*
• *because of / due to*	Estoy nervioso **por la entrevista.** *I'm nervous because of the interview.*

2. *Por* = *For*
When it expresses *for,* **por** looks back at the *reason* or *cause* for something. To remember this, think of the interrogative **¿por qué?** = *why?*

• *for = in exchange for*	Piden **1.000 dólares por el coche.** *They're asking $1,000 for the car.* **Gracias por todo.** *Thanks for everything.*
• *for = for the sake of, on behalf of*	Lo hago **por ti.** *I'm doing it for you (for your sake).*
• *for = period of time* (often omitted)	Vivieron allí (**por**) **un año.** *They lived there for a year.*

3. Fixed Expressions with *por*
Por is used in the expressions to the right, some of which (like **por eso** and **por si acaso**) express the *reason* or *cause* of something.

por Dios	for heaven's sake
por ejemplo	for example
por eso	that's why
por favor	please
por fin	finally
por lo general	generally, in general
por lo menos	at least
por primera/última vez	for the first/last time
por si acaso	just in case
¡por supuesto!	of course!
por todas partes	everywhere

Por

Suggestions

- Have students say the following in Spanish (the items are coordinated with the presentation of the uses of *por*).
  - by the painter/writer; by phone/letter
  - through the campus/plaza; along the beach/street
  - in the afternoon/evening; at 2:00 in the afternoon (**¡OJO!** *de la tarde*)
  - because of the test/accident
  - Thanks for the book/pen/money.
  - I'm doing it for you/him/us.
  - I studied for four hours / two days.
- Point out that *in order to get* or *in search of* is expressed with *por: Van por pan.*
- Have students use fixed expressions with *por* to respond to these questions or comments.
  1. *¿Es necesario estudiar treinta minutos cada día para la clase de español?*
  2. *Creo que va a llover hoy. ¿Debo llevar impermeable?*
  3. *¿Le paso la carne? ¿la ensalada?*
  4. *Me dicen que Ud. toma ocho clases este semestre/trimestre.*
  5. *Empecé a leer este libro el año pasado; lo terminé esta mañana.*
  6. *¡Me robaron el coche anoche!*
  7. *¿Le gusta viajar?*
  8. *¿Por qué llegué tarde? Pues hay mil razones.*

Bright Idea

Suggestion

Offer the following expressions as well.

por ahora	*por desgracia*
por amor	*por gusto*
por casualidad	*por nada*
por cierto	*por tonto/a*

Heritage Speakers

En algunos dialectos del español y especialmente en los de España, es muy común oír que se usa la preposición *a* antes de *por,* mayormente cuando *por* se encuentra después de un verbo de movimiento. Por ejemplo: *Carlos fue **a** por pan; Fuimos **a** por gasolina.* A pesar de que hay quienes usen *a por,* se recomienda simplemente el uso de *por* sin la preposición *a*.

NATIONAL STANDARDS: Cultures

Mario Vargas Llosa (1938–): This Peruvian author is one of the best known and most respected living Spanish-language writers. He is the author of many novels and books about history, all of which provide insightful reflections on the diverse reality of Latin America. Vargas Llosa is also an essayist and a journalist, and he has pursued a political career as well. He was awarded the Nobel Prize in Literature in 2010.

Para

1. Unique Meaning of *para*

The preposition **para** has one English equivalent that is only expressed with **para,** never with **por.**

- *in order to + infinitive*

Regresaron pronto **para estudiar.**
They returned soon (in order) to study.

Estudian **para conseguir** un buen trabajo.
They're studying (in order) to get a good job.

2. *Para* = *For*

When it expresses *for,* **para** looks ahead, toward the *goal, purpose,* or *destination* of something. To remember this, think of the interrogative **¿para qué?** = *for what purpose?*

- *for = destined for / to be given to*

Todo esto es **para ti.**
All this is for you.

Le di un libro **para su hijo.**
I gave her a book for her son.

- *for = by* (deadline, specified future time)

Para mañana, estudien ***por*** y ***para.***
*For tomorrow, study **por** and **para**.*

La composición es **para el lunes.**
The composition is for Monday.

- *for = toward / in the direction of*

Salió **para el Perú** ayer.
She left for Peru yesterday.

- *for = to be used for*

El dinero es **para la matrícula.**
The money is for tuition.

Es un vaso **para agua.**
It's a water glass.

¡OJO!
Compare the second example to **un vaso de agua** = *a glass (full) of water.*

- *for = as compared with / in relation to others*

Para mí, el español es fácil.
For me, Spanish is easy.

Para (ser) **extranjera,** habla muy bien el inglés.
For (being) a foreigner, she speaks English very well.

- *for = in the employ of*

Trabajan para el gobierno.
They work for the government.

Autoprueba

Indicate whether you would use **por** or **para.**

1. ______ to travel to a place
2. ______ to travel through a place
3. ______ to tell by whom something was created
4. ______ to work for someone (a company)
5. ______ to work for someone (on behalf of)
6. ______ to last for a period of time
7. ______ to be due by a certain time

Answers: **1.** *para* **2.** *por* **3.** *por* **4.** *para* **5.** *por* **6.** *por* **7.** *para*

Por and para Summary

por: reason, cause
para: goal, purpose, destination

Para

Bright Idea

Suggestion

Point out that some uses of *por* and *para* can be understood "directionally." *Por* normally refers *back* to something, while *para* refers to a forward point or purpose.

Salí para comprar pan.
I went out to buy bread. (purpose)
No salí por la lluvia.
I didn't go out because of the rain. (reason)

por ↔	**para**
reason	destination
cause	purpose

Suggestions

- Emphasize that *para* is *for* with the concept of destination.
  - Destined for whom? → *para su hijo*
  - Destined for what point in time? → *para mañana*
  - Geographical destination, in space? → *Salieron para Lima.*
  - Destined for what use? → *un vaso para agua.*
- Have students give the English equivalents (the items are coordinated with the order of presentation of the uses of *para*).
  - They came back to eat lunch / to rest.
  - It's for her/me.
  - The exercise is for Monday/Friday.
  - They left for Bolivia / Costa Rica.
  - It's a wine/beer glass.
  - For an American/German, he speaks French well.
  - She works for Ramón / Mr. Jiménez. (**¡OJO!** *el Sr. Jiménez*)

Heritage Speakers

Una expresión con *para* es *estar para* (*to be about to* [do something]). En algunos dialectos, especialmente en México, se dice *estar por* en vez de *estar para*. Por ejemplo, *Carlota está por llegar* significa *Carlota está a punto de llegar*. También se oye *estar al* en algunos países caribeños. Pregúnteles a los hispanohablantes qué expresión prefieren usar.

Preliminary Exercise

Have students respond *por* or *para* to indicate the correct prepositions for the following sentences.

1. We stayed for three days. (*por*)
2. We drove through the park. (*por*)
3. The report is for Monday. (*para*)
4. They left for Alaska. (*para*)
5. The money is for his mom. (*para*)
6. Math is hard for me. (*para*)
7. We canceled the trip for two reasons. (*por*)
8. This class is for advanced students. (*para*)

Bright Idea
Prác. A: Extension

Have students explain the difference between the following pairs of sentences.

Vamos por el edificio.
(through the building)
Vamos para el edificio.
(to/toward the building)
Le di un euro por el pan.
(in exchange for the bread)
Le di un euro para el pan.
(in order to buy/get bread)

Prác. B: Note

The purpose of this activity is to focus students' attention on the most frequent uses of *por* and *para*, with emphasis on contrastive uses when such exist. Note that these associations or paraphrases can be used in *Prác. C* and *D* to "explain" why *por* or *para* is used in a given sentence. You may also wish to go back to *Prác. A* and ask students to use the phrases to explain the use of *por* or *para* in the items in that activity.

Prác. C: Suggestions

- After students complete each question, ask them to explain their use of *por* or *para*, using phrases from *Prác. B*.
- Have students use the questions to interview you. Use *por* or *para* in your responses, and try to extend each exchange, turning the questions back to students, as appropriate.

Práctica

A. ¡Anticipemos! Situaciones. Escoja una respuesta para cada pregunta o situación. Luego invente un contexto para cada diálogo. ¿Dónde están las personas que hablan? ¿Quiénes son? ¿Por qué dicen lo que dicen?

PREGUNTAS/SITUACIONES

1. __g__ ¡Uf! Vengo de jugar un partido de basquetbol. ¡Jugamos por dos horas!
2. __h__ ¿Por qué quieres que llame a Pili y Adolfo? Nunca están en casa por la noche, mucho menos (*especially*) a estas horas.
3. __e__ ¿No vas a comer nada? Por lo menos un sándwich.
4. __c__ ¡Cuánto lo siento, don Javier! Sé que llegué tarde a la cita. Discúlpeme.
5. __f__ Es imposible que tome el examen hoy, por muchas razones.
6. __d__ ¿No lo oíste? Juana acaba de tener un accidente horrible.
7. __b__ ¡Pero, papá, quiero ir!
8. __a__ Ay, Mariana, ¿no sabías que hubo un ciclón? Murieron más de cien personas.

RESPUESTAS

a. ¡Por Dios! ¡Qué desgracia!
b. Te digo que no, por última vez.
c. No se preocupe. Lo importante es que por fin está aquí.
d. ¡Por Dios! ¿Qué pasó? ¿Está bien?
e. No, gracias. No tengo mucha hambre y además (*besides*) tengo que irme en seguida.
f. ¿Por ejemplo? Dígame…
g. Ah, por eso tienes tanto calor.
h. Llámalos de todas formas, por si acaso están en casa esta noche.

B. Asociaciones. *¿Por* o *para*? ¿Con qué preposición asocia Ud. las siguientes frases?

1. gracias por
2. una fecha en el futuro para
3. un período de tiempo por
4. durante por
5. la persona que hizo algo por
6. con cierto destino (*destination*) para
7. con el propósito (*purpose*) de para
8. en lugar de otra persona por
9. con el fin (*goal*) de ayudar a una persona por
10. a causa de por
11. en medio (*middle*) de, a lo largo de (*along*) por
12. trabajar en una compañía para
13. pagar dinero por
14. en comparación con otros para

C. Preguntas. Complete las siguientes preguntas con **por** o **para**.

1. ¿__Para__ quién trabaja Ud.? ¿Trabaja __por__ la mañana o __por__ la tarde?
2. ¿__Por__ dónde tiene que pasar __para__ llegar a la universidad?
3. ¿Cuánto pagó Ud. __por__ su carro?
4. ¿__Para__ qué sirve la llave grande que Ud. tiene en la mano?
5. ¿__Para__ qué profesión estudió Ud.? ¿__Por__ cuántos años tuvo que estudiar?
6. ¿__Para__ qué día de esta semana necesita Ud. la tarea?

D. *¿Por o para?* Complete los siguientes diálogos y oraciones con **por** o **para.**

1. Los Sres. Arana salieron para el Perú ayer. Van en avión, claro, pero luego piensan viajar en coche por todo el país. Van a estar allí por dos meses. Va a ser una experiencia extraordinaria para toda la familia.
2. Mi prima Graciela quiere estudiar para (ser) doctora. Por eso trabaja para un médico por la mañana; tiene clases por la tarde.
3. —¿Por qué están Uds. aquí todavía? Yo pensaba que iban a dar un paseo por el parque.
—Íbamos a hacerlo, pero no fuimos por la nieve.
4. Este cuadro fue pintado (*painted*) por Picasso para expresar los desastres de la guerra (*war*). Para muchos críticos de arte, es la obra maestra de este artista.
5. La Asociación «Todo por Ellos» trabaja por las personas mayores, para ayudarlos cuando lo necesitan. ¿Trabaja Ud. para alguna asociación de voluntarios? ¿Qué tuvo que hacer para inscribirse (*sign up*)?

Conversación

A. Entreviste a su profesor(a). Hágale preguntas a su profesor(a) para saber la siguiente información.

1. la tarea para mañana y para la semana que viene
2. lo que hay que estudiar para el próximo examen
3. si para él/ella son interesantes o aburridas las ciencias
4. lo que piensa de la pronunciación de Uds., para ser principiantes
5. qué deben hacer Uds. para mejorar su pronunciación del español
6. cuánto tiempo deben Uds. dedicar todos los días a practicar el español

B. Preguntas con *por* y *para*

Paso 1. Complete las siguientes ideas con **por** o **para.**

1. prepararse para una profesión
2. estar nervioso por algo
3. trabajar para una compañía
4. hablar por teléfono con frecuencia
5. tener algo que hacer para mañana
6. pasear por el *campus*
7. tener algo que comprar para su casa/apartamento/cuarto
8. la idea de pagar mil dólares por un abrigo
9. tener algo que hacer por alguien
10. la idea de vivir en un sitio por toda la vida

Paso 2. Ahora, en parejas, hagan y contesten preguntas, usando las frases del **Paso 1.**

MODELO: prepararse _____ una profesión →
¿Sabes para qué profesión estás preparándote?

Mundo interactivo

You should now be prepared to work with Scenario 7, Activity 4 in Connect Spanish (**www.connectspanish.com**).

Prác. D: Suggestions

- Have students give the reason for each use of *por* or *para*. Expand items with personal questions.
- Note that item 5 is coordinated with the ad for the *Asociación Todo por Ellos*.
- For item 5, ask students: *¿Qué se puede hacer por las personas mayores?*

Con. B: Follow-up

Ask students the following questions to personalize uses of *por* and *para*.

1. *¿Para qué (profesión) estudia Ud.?*
2. *¿Para qué compañía trabaja Ud. (su padre/madre, su esposo/a)?*
3. *¿Cuáles son más difíciles para Ud., los exámenes escritos o los orales? ¿los exámenes de matemáticas o los de historia?*
4. *¿Tiene Ud. mucho que hacer para mañana? ¿mucho que leer? ¿mucho que escribir?*
5. *¿Tiene que comprar algo esta noche? ¿algo para Ud. para su casa/apartamento/cuarto? ¿algo para un amigo? ¿algo para la familia?*

Culture

Most older people in the Hispanic world end up living with their grown-up children and their grandchildren when they can no longer take care of themselves. At this point family members will take care of them until they die. Being too old or sick is not the only reason for older people to live with their children. This may also happen after the loss of a spouse. In any case, grandparents have an important role in the upbringing of their grandchildren, often taking care of them while the parents work. For this reason, there are relatively few *residencias de ancianos* in Hispanic countries, although they are not as rare as they used to be.

Un poco de todo

Suggestions

- Have students give possible reactions to the following situations. Compare their answers and take a vote on the most original ones.

  ¿Cómo se pone uno o qué se puede hacer en estas situaciones?

  1. *Son las seis de la mañana. Ud. oye el despertador pero todavía tiene sueño.*
  2. *Ud. quiere despedirse, pero la persona con quien está hablando quiere seguir hablando.*
  3. *Ud. está en Buenos Aires. Pierde su cartera y con ella todo su dinero y el pasaporte.*
  4. *Su vecino dejó el coche delante del garaje de Ud. y ahora Ud. no puede sacar su coche.*
  5. *Ud. sufre muchas presiones a causa de los exámenes finales.*

- Have students identify which of the following experiences they have had and explain the problems that resulted. How did they resolve the problems?

  Una vez…

  1. *se me perdió la tarjeta de identificación de la universidad.*
  2. *se me cayó un vaso de vino tinto en la ropa.*
  3. *se me perdieron los lentes de contacto.*
  4. *se me rompió un objeto caro.*
  5. *se me quedó en casa un trabajo para la clase.*

A: Reciclado: Note review of the preterite and subjunctive.

A: Redacción: Assign *Paso 2* as written homework, asking students to create a written dialogue. Set expectations about length and content, and stress that students will need to pay particular attention to the use of the preterite, imperfect, and subjunctive. After students have created their dialogues, collect them and make the necessary corrections. Ask 2–3 pairs of students to perform their dialogues for the class. Then ask simple comprehension questions and discuss the dialogues, as appropriate.

A, Paso 1: Answers
*BENÍTEZ: ¿Cuánto tiempo hace **que le duele** la cabeza? ORTEGA: Hace una semana **que me duele. Tengo** que corregir muchos exámenes y **es** necesario **que lea** mucho. BENÍTEZ: ¿**Tuvo** algún accidente? ¿**Chocó** contra algo? ORTEGA: No. BENÍTEZ: ¿Cuánto tiempo hace **que fue** / no va al oculista? ORTEGA: No **me acuerdo.** La verdad es **que se me olvidó** hacer una cita. BENÍTEZ: Entonces **le recomiendo que vaya** al oculista en seguida. También **le sugiero que deje** de leer tanto **por** unos días y **que tome** aspirinas **para** el dolor de cabeza.*

A: Comprensión:
1. *Tiene dolor de cabeza y tiene que leer muchos exámenes. Trabaja mucho.*
2. *No dice, pero cree que debe ir al oculista.*
3. *Porque se le olvidó hacer una cita.*
4. *Le recomienda que vaya al oculista, que deje de leer tanto y que tome unas aspirinas.*

Un poco de todo

A. A la profesora Ortega le duele la cabeza.

Paso 1. Haga oraciones completas con las siguientes ideas. Los verbos pueden estar en el presente de indicativo, el presente de subjuntivo o el pretérito. Añada (*Add*) pronombres y las palabras **que** y **se** cuando sea necesario y use **por** o **para,** según el contexto.

DOCTORA BENÍTEZ: ¿Cuánto tiempo hace / doler[1] la cabeza?
PROFESORA ORTEGA: Hace una semana / doler[2]. Tener[3] que corregir muchos exámenes y ser[4] necesario / (yo) leer[5] mucho.
DOCTORA BENÍTEZ: ¿Tener[6] algún accidente? ¿Chocar[7] contra algo?
PROFESORA ORTEGA: No.
DOCTORA BENÍTEZ: ¿Cuánto tiempo hace / ir[8] al oculista[a]?
PROFESORA ORTEGA: No acordarse.[9] La verdad es / olvidarme[10] hacer una cita.
DOCTORA BENÍTEZ: Entonces[b] recomendarle[11] / ir[12] al oculista en seguida. También sugerirle[13] / dejar[14] de leer tanto (por/para)[15] unos días y / tomar[16] aspirinas (por/para)[17] el dolor de cabeza.

[a]*eye doctor* [b]*Then*

Comprensión. Conteste las siguientes preguntas.

1. ¿Qué problemas tiene la profesora Ortega?
2. ¿Qué cree la doctora Benítez que está causando el dolor de cabeza de su paciente?
3. ¿Por qué no fue al oculista la profesora Ortega?
4. ¿Que recomienda la doctora Benítez que haga la profesora?

Paso 2. Ahora, en parejas, inventen un diálogo similar sobre uno de los personajes de las páginas 414 y 417.

B. Lengua y cultura: De turismo por el Perú. Complete the following passage with the correct form of the words in parentheses, as suggested by context. When two possibilities are given in parentheses, select the correct word. **¡OJO!** As you conjugate the verbs in this activity, use the **tú** command when you see *comm:* in front of the infinitive. For other verbs, you will decide whether to use the present indicative or subjunctive, the preterite or imperfect, or simply the infinitive. Context will indicate which forms to use.

Machu Picchu, la ciudad imperial de los incas durante el siglo XV (1400–1500)

¿Te interesa la historia? ¿Te (gusta/gustan[1]) los lugares espirituales? Entonces,[a] (*comm:* ir[2]) a Machu Picchu. (Son/Están[3]) las ruinas de una antigua ciudad inca que (es/está[4]) en (el/la[5]) corazón de los Andes, cerca de Cusco. No es fácil (llegue/llegar[6]) a ese lugar. (Por/Para[7]) eso (se/la[8]) llaman «la ciudad perdida[b] de los incas.» En el pasado, (ser[9]) a la vez[c] lugar de refugio y de vacaciones de los reyes[d] y nobles incas. Después de la llegada de los españoles, esta ciudad fue ignorada y (estar[10]) oculta[e] hasta que Hiram Bingham, un profesor y explorador estadounidense, la (encontrar[11]) en 1911. (Hacer[12]) un siglo[f] que Machu Picchu es un sitio famoso y un atractivo destino[g] turístico (por/para[13]) muchas personas de todas partes del mundo.

Pero Machu Picchu no (es/está[14]) el único lugar interesante que se puede visitar en el Perú. Si visitas (el/la[15]) país con tiempo suficiente, te recomendamos que (hacer[16]) una excursión (por/para[17]) la selva.[h] También (*comm:* viajar[18]) al desierto de Atacama, el lugar más árido (en el / del[19]) mundo. Además,[i] (*comm:* pasar[20]) unos días en las playas de Mancora y Cabo Blanco. (*Comm:* Hacer[21]) un viaje fabuloso que (nunca/siempre[22]) vas a olvidar. Esperamos que (*tú:* poder[23]) ir con alguien muy especial para (ti/tú[24]). (Sabemos/Conocemos[25]) que el Perú (les/los[26]) va a fascinar.

[a]*Then* [b]*lost* [c]*a... at the same time* [d]*kings* [e]*hidden* [f]*century* [g]*destination* [h]*jungle* [i]*In addition*

Comprensión. Las siguientes oraciones son falsas. Corríjalas con información de la lectura.

1. El actual rey del Perú vive en Machu Picchu.
2. Es fácil llegar a Machu Picchu.
3. Hiram Bingham fue un explorador español.
4. Machu Picchu es el único sitio de interés turístico en el Perú.
5. Para los turistas no es nada atractivo viajar al Perú.

En su comunidad

Entreviste a una persona hispana de su universidad o ciudad sobre lo que más les causa estrés a él y a otras personas de su comunidad.

PREGUNTAS POSIBLES

- ¿Cuáles son los problemas que más les preocupan a Ud. y a su familia o a sus amigos? ¿Hay alguno que les cause más estrés que las otras?
- Si vive en una ciudad grande, ¿son el tráfico y el estacionamiento problemas para Ud.?
- ¿Qué presiones tiene la gente joven de su familia o comunidad? ¿Les preocupa su acceso a la universidad? ¿Por qué?
- ¿Qué actividades hace Ud. para relajarse (*relax*)?
- ¿Es Ud. una persona torpe o distraída? ¿Se le olvida hacer unas cosas o pierde cosas con bastante frecuencia? ¿Tiene accidentes relacionados con el estrés?

A: Answers: 1. *gustan* **2.** *ve* **3.** *Son* **4.** *está* **5.** *el* **6.** *llegar* **7.** *Por* **8.** *la* **9.** *era* **10.** *estuvo* **11.** *encontró* **12.** *Hace* **13.** *para* **14.** *es* **15.** *el* **16.** *hagas* **17.** *por* **18.** *viaja* **19.** *del* **20.** *pasa* **21.** *Haz* **22.** *nunca* **23.** *puedas* **24.** *ti* **25.** *Sabemos* **26.** *los*

B, Comprensión: Answers
1. *Los reyes incas pasaban las vacaciones y buscaban refugio en Machu Picchu.* **2.** *No es fácil llegar a ese lugar porque está en el corazón de los Andes.* **3.** *Bingham fue un profesor y explorador estadounidense.* **4.** *Los turistas también deben hacer una excursión por la selva, viajar al desierto de Atacama y pasar unos días en la playa.* **5.** *A los turistas les fascina ir al Perú.*

B: Note

The following grammar topics are included in *Lengua y cultura:* gender, *gustar* and similar verbs, negative words, *por* vs. *para*, *ser* vs. *estar*, preterite vs. imperfect, indicative vs. subjunctive, *tú* command forms, direct and indirect object pronouns, *hace* + time.

En su comunidad

Suggestions

- Remind students to get the following basic information: the informant's country of origin, how long he or she has lived in this country, and if the informant visits his or her country of origin frequently.
- This activity could instead be assigned as an online research project on a country of the student's choice or assigned by you.
- See the IM for additional suggestions and guidelines.

Resources: Desenlace

In the *Cap. 14* segment of "Chapter-by-Chapter Supplementary Materials" in the IM, you will find a chapter-culminating activity. You can use this activity to consolidate and review the vocabulary and grammar skills students have acquired.

NATIONAL STANDARDS: Cultures

Hiram Bingham (1875–1956) was an American academic, explorer, and politician. He rediscovered Machu Picchu in 1911 with the help of local indigenous farmers.

TelePuntos

Note

Pages 434–439 are optional. You may cover some, all, or none of this material in class, or assign it to students—as a group or individually—for homework or extra credit. Pages 440–441 (*En resumen: En este capítulo*) are a summary of all of the chapter's active material.

Antes de mirar

Suggestion

Have a whole-class discussion about both of the suggested topics and write causes of stress and superstitions on the board (including vocabulary, as needed) as preparation for viewing. Ask students to predict which of the topics on the board will appear in the program.

Fragmento del guion

Suggestions

- You may wish to explore the concept of *exámenes extraordinarios* with students. They are, in a way, an alternative to this country's option of incompletes. What do students think about them? You may want to tell students that failing is a much more common occurrence in the Hispanic educational system than it is in this country.
- Ask students to find instances of the subjunctive in the *Fragmento* and to explain all of them that they can. An example that students should be able to explain: *...espero que sea positivo y pase.* An example that students might be able to explain: *...depende en dónde vivan / de la situación económica que tengan.* Examples that will be beyond students' reach: *...va a ser el grado de estrés que tengan, siempre va a haber algo que perturbe, ya sea...* Note with the latter example that the translation of *ya sea,* be it, is evidence of the use of the subjunctive in English.
- Ask students to analyze the use of the verb *estresar.* They should be able to figure out that it is like *gustar.*
- Students may note that the verb *depender* is followed both by *de* and *en* in the *Fragmento.* While *depender de* is the norm, *depender* is often followed by *en* to refer to a place (*depende en dónde vivan*).

TELEPUNTOS SALU2

«Sí estoy un poco supersticiosa, porque cuando pasa un gato negro... es lo más común. Y también cuando pasas abajo de una escalera (*stepladder*) también es una superstición muy fuerte (*strong*) aquí.»

Antes de mirar

¿Cree Ud. que, en general, los estudiantes de su universidad sufren de mucho estrés? ¿Cuáles son las causas de estrés más frecuentes entre Uds.? ¿Sufren más de estrés en algunas épocas del año que en otras? ¿Es Ud. supersticioso/a? Si lo es, ¿en qué situaciones lo demuestra (*do you show it*)?

PROGRAMA 14: ¡Ay, qué estrés!

El programa de hoy presenta entrevistas con dos estudiantes universitarios de la Ciudad de México, una sobre las causas de estrés y la otra sobre si son supersticiosos.

Vocabulario de este programa

ojalá	I hope	**las horas punta**	rush hour
restar	to take away (from)	**dispuesto/a**	ready and willing
la calidad	quality	**invertir (invierto) (i)**	to invest
¿cómo anda... ?	how is . . . ?	**prevenir** (*like* **venir**)	to prevent
la edad	age	**encomendarse a Dios (me encomiendo)**	to entrust (oneself) to God
provocar (qu)	to cause	**entre comillas**	in quotation marks
presentar	to take (*as an exam*)	**percatarse**	to notice
los parciales	mid-terms (*exams*)	**tener cariño**	to feel love, affection
quedar fuera	to be out, put out	**sin darse cuenta**	without realizing it
la temporada	season, period	**le pedí que me mandara uno**	I asked her to send me one
la carga	load		
la calificación	la nota		
podría hacerse rico/a	he/she could become rich		

Fragmento del guion

ESTUDIANTE: Mi preocupación de esta semana, principalmente,[a] es que acabo de presentar un extraordinario.* Entonces,[b] me estuve preparando todo, este, los días anteriores. Hoy lo presenté y espero mi resultado el jueves. Entonces[c] espero que sea positivo y pase. Ese es mi único estrés. [...]

ESTUDIANTE: Bueno, de vivir en la ciudad lo que más me estresa es el tráfico, porque igual[d] salgo una hora antes de mi casa para llegar a la escuela y siempre, siempre hay tráfico. O las distancias, que también son muy largas y con el tráfico, entonces ya haces[e] máximo como tres horas para llegar a un lugar. [...]

PROFESOR: Yo opino que depende de la situación, depende en dónde vivan, depende de la posición económica que tengan va a ser el grado[f] de estrés que tengan. Pero siempre va a haber[g] algo que perturbe[h] su mente,[i] ya sea[j] de lo cotidiano,[k] o sea, este... no sé, algo externo.

[a]*mainly* [b]*That's why* [c]*Then* [d]*it's always the same* [e]*ya... it can take you* [f]*degree* [g]siempre... *there's always going to be* [h]*disturbs* [i]*mind* [j]*ya... whether it be* [k]*daily*

En las cadenas (*chains*) de este estudiante se mezclan símbolos religiosos personales y amuletos. ¡Protección contra (*against*) todo!

*Public universities in Mexico (and in other countries) offer "extraordinary" exams: exams that offer a second chance to pass the course. Students may take these **extraordinarios** if they did not pass or did not even take the final the first time around.

Mundo interactivo

Continue your work as an intern at HispanaVisión with Laura Sánchez Tejada, the roving reporter of *Salu2*, as you complete Scenario 7, Activities 3 and 4 in Connect Spanish (**www.connectspanish.com**).

Al mirar

Mientras mira el programa, indique las causas de estrés y las supersticiones y creencias (*beliefs*) que se mencionan en el programa.

CAUSES DE ESTRÉS	SUPERSTICIONES Y CREENCIAS
☑ el tráfico	☑ los amuletos
☐ los novios	☑ un gato negro
☑ los exámenes	☐ un trébol (*clover*) de cuatro hojas
☑ el dinero	☑ un santo (*saint*)
☑ los profesores	☑ una escalera
☑ el trabajo	☐ cruzarse los dedos
☑ las notas	
☐ los padres	

« ...es el tránsito (*traffic*), es la seguridad (*safety*), es, este, el hecho (*fact*) de estar preocupado por sus estudios, es conseguir dinero para poder pagarse sus estudios, conseguir un poco de apoyo (*support*) por parte de la familia, el mismo (*very*) tránsito de la ciudad, la misma presión que ejercen, nosotros, los profesores, hacia los estudiantes... »

Después de mirar

A. ¿Está claro? ¿Cierto o falso? Corrija las oraciones falsas.

	CIERTO	FALSO
1. La única presión que sufre Víctor tiene que ver (*has to do*) con el tráfico.	☐	☑
2. Ningún estudiante cree que el tráfico sea una causa de estrés.	☐	☑
3. Un profesor opina que conseguir dinero para poder pagarse los estudios genera estrés.	☑	☐
4. La mayoría de los estudiantes entrevistados es supersticiosa.	☐	☑
5. Ninguno de los estudiantes entrevistados es religioso.	☐	☑
6. Es obvio que Víctor es supersticioso.	☐	☑

B. Un poco más. Conteste las siguientes preguntas.

1. ¿En qué es comparable la Ciudad de México con Los Ángeles?
2. ¿En qué época del año académico tuvieron lugar (*took place*) las entrevistas? ¿Cómo lo sabe Ud.?
3. ¿Qué presiones mencionan los estudiantes y los profesores?
4. ¿Qué objetos o amuletos para la buena suerte usan los estudiantes supersticiosos?

C. Y ahora, Uds. En parejas, comparen las respuestas de los jóvenes mexicanos con la realidad de los estudiantes en su universidad. ¿En qué son semejantes y en qué son diferentes? ¿Sufren los estudiantes de su universidad algún tipo de presiones que no se menciona en el programa?

Sobre el programa

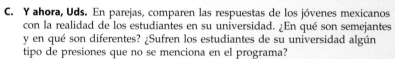

Víctor no exagera cuando dice que lo que más le estresa es el tráfico en Los Ángeles. Vive en una casa muy cómoda en una zona muy agradable, pero tarda[a] al menos una hora en llegar al estudio de *Salu2*. Para Víctor es ideal que su trabajo en el estudio termine muy temprano del día: empiezan a las cinco de la mañana y terminan a eso de[b] las doce. Esto le permite ir en la tarde por Sarita, su hija, a la escuela. Marina, la madre de ella, que enseña en una universidad muy cerca de la casa, la lleva a la escuela por la mañana.

[a]*it takes him* [b]*a... around*

Act. A, Answers: 1. *Falso: Víctor sufre otras presiones: la enfermedad de su padre y la seguridad económica de su familia.* **2.** *Falso: Varios estudiantes mencionan el tráfico como causa de estrés.* **4.** *Falso: De 8 estudiantes, 5 declaran que son supersticiosos.* **5.** *Falso: Realmente no se sabe si los estudiantes son religiosos, pero 4 de los 8 entrevistados mencionan algo relacionado con la religión. Una de ellas dice específicamente que «se encomienda a Dios».* **6.** *Falso: No es obvio que Víctor sea supersticioso. Ana sí es supersticiosa.*

Act. B, Answers: 1. *Hay mucho tráfico en las dos ciudades.* **2.** *En la temporada de exámenes. Varios estudiantes hablan de exámenes «esta semana».* **3.** *el tráfico, la carga del trabajo, el horario, trabajar y estudiar al mismo tiempo, la situación económica* **4.** *un rosario, una imagen de San Miguel Arcángel, diferentes símbolos de varias religiones*

Producción personal

Filme dos entrevistas con estudiantes de su universidad sobre el estrés que sufren y las causas principales de su estrés.

Programa 14

- Unfamiliar vocabulary will be the biggest challenge for students in this program.
- The superstitions report, which is well supported by visuals in the show, will be the easiest portion of the show for students to understand.
- For students unfamiliar with Catholic customs, you may wish to discuss the concept of religious objects such as *amuletos* and *rosarios* as well as the veneration of saints (*San Miguel Arcángel*).
- Ask students what they think Ana's *amuleto* is and to discuss what kinds of things people use as *amuletos* in general.
- Emphasize to students that the more carefully they study the preliminary activities (*Antes de mirar, Vocabulario de este programa*, and *Fragmento del guion*), the more they will understand. Scanning *Después de mirar* before viewing is also an excellent strategy.

Al mirar

Suggestion

Have students try to do this activity after watching, to test their memories.

Después de mirar

C: Suggestion

Follow-up pair or group work with a whole class discussion. Ask one student to act as the class "secretary" and write answers on the board.

Sobre el programa

Optional

1. *¿Cuánto tiempo tarda Víctor en llegar al estudio desde su casa? (una hora por lo menos.)*
2. *¿Qué le gusta a Víctor de su horario? (Le gusta que termina muy temprano del día. Por eso puede ir por su hija a la escuela por la tarde.)*
3. *¿Quién lleva a Sarita a la escuela por la mañana? (Marina, su mamá)*

Producción personal

See the IM for additional suggestions for this chapter's assignment as well as for general guidelines and suggestions for video assignments.

A LEER

Lectura cultural

El Perú

Como ocurre ahora en todos los países, hay múltiples cuestiones[a] que también les causan ansiedad a los peruanos. El tema de la educación es una de estas cuestiones. La educación pública requiere una mayor inversión[b] de dinero para que[c] el sistema sea más efectivo y sirva a todos. Además,[d] se necesita que los maestros[e] tengan mejores salarios.

El tema de los salarios es otra de las serias preocupaciones de muchos peruanos. En el Perú existe la Remuneración Mínima, que es el salario mínimo establecido[f] por la ley.[g] Es el salario que recibe gran parte de los trabajadores[h] peruanos, pero que para muchos de ellos no resulta suficiente para cubrir[i] sus gastos cotidianos.[j]

¿Qué cuestiones sociales son motivo de ansiedad entre la gente de su estado/provincia o país?

[a]*topics* [b]*investment* [c]para... *so that* [d]*In addition* [e]*teachers* [f]*established* [g]*law* [h]*workers* [i]*cover* [j]*daily*

La Universidad Nacional Mayor de San Marcos (Lima, Perú), la primera universidad en Sudamérica, fundada en 1551

En otros países hispanos

- **En las grandes ciudades del mundo hispano** El tráfico y el estacionamiento son causa diaria de estrés para muchas personas, considerando que en los países hispanos hay un buen número de megalópolis.[a] Afortunadamente, muchas ciudades tienen estupendas redes de transporte público, como ocurre, por ejemplo, en Madrid, México, D.F. y Buenos Aires.
- **En todo el mundo hispanohablante** En la cultura popular hispana, existen algunas supersticiones comunes a muchos países. Según las creencias populares, los siguientes acontecimientos[b] traen mala suerte.
  - romper un espejo[c] (¡Esto significa siete años de mala suerte!)
  - pasar por debajo de una escalera[d]
  - derramar[e] sal (Hay un «antídoto»: tirar[f] un poco de la sal derramada por encima del hombro[g] izquierdo.)
  - cruzarse con un gato negro en el camino[h]
  - el martes 13 (Cuando el día decimotercero[i] del mes cae en martes.)

Otra de las supersticiones es el mal de ojo,[j] que se refiere al daño que la mirada[k] de algunas personas puede causar, particularmente en los niños.

[a]*huge cities* [b]*events* [c]*mirror* [d]*ladder* [e]*to spill* [f]*to throw* [g]por... *over the shoulder* [h]*path* [i]*thirteenth* [j]mal... *evil eye* [k]*look*

Tres símbolos peruanos

- **El cajón** Es un instrumento de percusión similar a una caja,[a] creado por los descendientes de los esclavos africanos en la zona costera[b] peruana. Hoy es un instrumento muy popular que se utiliza no solo en la música afroperuana sino[c] también en otros tipos de música en diferentes países, incluyendo el flamenco en España.
- **El pisco** Este exquisito licor de uva[d] se fabrica[e] en la costa sur del Perú desde hace más de tres siglos.[f] La demanda internacional por esta bebida ha aumentado[g] significativamente en los últimos diez años.
- **La marinera** Esta es la danza nacional por excelencia del Perú. Es un baile de cortejo,[h] en el que el hombre intenta seducir a su pareja. En la ciudad de Trujillo hay un concurso[i] anual, muy popular, de la marinera.

[a]*box* [b]*coastal* [c]*but* [d]*grape* [e]se... *is made* [f]*centuries* [g]ha... *has increased* [h]*courting* [i]*competition*

Una cita

«Hay, hermanos, muchísimo que hacer.»

César Vallejo (1892–1938), poeta peruano

Esta es una frase conocida[a] por todos los peruanos. Su interpretación varía, pero todos los peruanos coinciden en interpretarla como una tarea urgente: trabajar por el Perú.

[a]*known*

COMPRENSIÓN

1. ¿Qué cuestiones les causan ansiedad a los peruanos?
2. ¿Qué es la Remuneración Mínima?
3. ¿Cuáles son tres de las supersticiones que en el mundo hispano se asocian con la mala suerte?

Lectura cultural

Notes

- The Instructor's Edition on this page offers some additional information on the country of focus. For more information about the country of focus, see the chapter's opening pages and the IM.
- See the IM for some expressions used in Peru.

First Reading: Note

In other countries, the term *salario mínimo* is used.

En otros países hispanos: Suggestions

- You may wish to present this *refrán: Trece y martes, ni te cases ni te embarques.* (On Tuesday the 13th, don't get married and don't take a trip.)
- Ask students to compare these superstitions to those of this country or of their own culture. Most of the superstitions listed have exact equivalents in this country.

Exploración lingüística

Ask students to find the following in the reading. Some of these words are glossed and some are not.

- *Un sinónimo de* salario (*remuneración*)
- *Una palabra que se aplica a una ciudad muy grande y extendida* (*megalópolis*)
- *Un cognado falso que significa* matter (*cuestión*)

Comprensión

Answers

1. *los temas de la educación y de los salarios* **2.** *el salario más bajo que permite la ley* **3.** *romper un espejo, pasar por debajo de una escalera, derramar sal, cruzarse con un gato negro, el día martes 13, el mal de ojo*

Tres símbolos peruanos

Suggestions

- Ask students if they have seen or heard the *cajón,* and if so, in which kind of music.
- Ask students to name other types of music and dances typical of other countries they have read about so far. Is there a type of music typically associated with their country, culture, or state?

Una cita

Notes

- César Vallejo is considered one of the world's greatest and most revolutionary poets of the 20th century. In his short life, he lived in France and Spain, and traveled to what was then Soviet Russia several times. He greatly influenced 20th century international vanguard movements in poetry.
- The quote is a line from the poem *«Los nueve monstruos»,* from the collection *Poemas humanos,* published posthumously.
- Vallejo can be a particularly difficult poet to read. His prose is viewed as similar to that of James Joyce. His poetry often deals with human misery and the sadness he feels because of it. Some lines and stanzas of his poems can be linguistically accessible to the students if you provide glosses.
- Vallejo's poetry can be found at www.poemas-del-alma.com/cesar-vallejo.htm.

Del mundo hispano

Antes de leer

¿Qué opina su profesor(a) de su trabajo en la universidad? Lea las siguientes preguntas y contéstelas como Ud. cree que su profesor(a) las contestaría (*would answer*). Luego, hágale las preguntas a su profesor(a), tratando de obtener más información para cada pregunta.

1. ¿Qué aspecto de su trabajo le gusta más? ¿Cuál le gusta menos?
2. ¿Qué es lo más aburrido de su trabajo? ¿Lo más interesante?
3. ¿Se siente frustrado/a con su trabajo a veces? ¿Qué hace entonces (*then*)?
4. ¿Le gustaría tener otro tipo de trabajo?
5. ¿Qué otro trabajo no le gustaría hacer para nada?

Lectura: «OH», de Mario Benedetti

Comprensión

A. Para comprender el poema. Seleccione la opción correcta y explique su respuesta.

1. Este poema fue escrito por/para un jefe.
2. Este jefe trabaja con cuentas/niños.
3. Al jefe le gusta / no le gusta su trabajo.
4. En la segunda estrofa (*stanza*) del poema, el poeta dice que la actitud del jefe es visible/invisible.
5. En la tercera estrofa, el poeta dice que la actitud del jefe es visible/invisible.
6. El poeta le recomienda al jefe que exprese sus sentimientos en privado / enfrente de sus empleados.
7. El poeta muestra hacia el jefe una actitud de intolerancia/compasión.

B. Para interpretar el poema. Conteste las siguientes preguntas según su opinión.

1. ¿Son contradictorias las estrofas 2 y 3?
2. ¿Cree Ud. que todas las personas que hacen el mismo trabajo por veintiocho años vayan a sentirse tan aburridas como este jefe? ¿Por qué sí o por qué no?
3. Si uno no está contento con su trabajo o con otro aspecto de su vida, ¿es bueno expresar su descontento de la manera que recomienda el poeta en la cuarta estrofa? Si Ud. cree que no es nada bueno expresarse así (*in that way*), es decir, en público, ¿cree que es mejor hacerlo en privado?
4. ¿Por qué cree Ud. que el poeta le habla al jefe usando la forma **usté** en vez de **usted**?

OH

Jefe
usté está aburrido
aburrido de veras[a]
hace veintiocho años
que sabe sus asientos[b]
que comprueba los
saldos[c]
y revuelve[d] el café.

Está aburrido
jefe
se le nota en los ojos[e]
en la voz[f]
en las órdenes
en el paso[g]
en las mangas[h]
en los setenta rubros[i]
de letra redondilla.[j]

Jefe
usté está aburrido
nadie lo sabe
nadie.

Pero ahora que está
solo
ahora que no ven Ellos
desahóguese[k]
grite[l]
discuta[m]
diga mierda[n]
dé golpes[ñ] en la mesa
vuélvase insoportable[o]
por favor
diga no
diga no muchas veces
hasta quedarse ronco.[p]

No cuesta nada[q]
jefe
haga la prueba.[r]

[a]de… *truly* [b]*ledger entries* [c]comprueba… *you check the balance sheets* [d]*stir* [e]se… *it's obvious* [f]*voice* [g]el… *your way of walking* [h]*little errors* [i]*headings (in a spreadsheet)* [j]*rounded* [k]*let it out* [l]*scream* [m]*argue* [n]*shit* [ñ]dé… *slam your fist* [o]vuélvase… *became unbearable* [p]quedarse… *you get hoarse* [q]No… *You can do it (lit. It doesn't cost anything.)* [r]haga… *give it a try*

Del mundo hispano

Note

See the IM for optional follow-up, writing, and Internet activities.

Antes de leer

Suggestions

- Ask students to add more questions to the list before they interview you. You may want to ask students to work in groups to create the additional questions.
- Have students work in pairs to predict your answers. Ask for their predictions in written form. Then offer a prize to the pair of students whose predictions come closest to your answers.
- Think about your answers to these questions before you allow students to ask them. It's a good idea to try to answer in a lighthearted way, as well as to project a positive attitude toward your profession and your students. (If you're not comfortable answering the questions, tell students that you will assume the identity of another person—the president / prime minister of this country, the CEO of a large corporation—and have them address their questions to that person.)

Estrategia

The Use of Repetition and Rhythm

The use of repetition to create a certain rhythm and to emphasize ideas or concepts is a frequent poetic strategy. Benedetti uses these strategies in "*OH*." Ask students to look for examples of repetition in the three longest stanzas of the poem. The repetition in the first two stanzas might reflect the tedium of the boss's job. In the first stanza, the same simple *verb + direct object* syntactic structure is used as his boring tasks are enumerated: *que sabe sus asientos / que comprueba los saldos / y revuelve el café.* In the second stanza, repetition emphasizes the different ways in which the boss displays his bored affect: via phrases that begin with *en* and are followed by an article and a noun. There is also repetition in the fourth stanza: the list of commands about how the boss should relieve his stress.

Comprensión, B: Answers

1. Many students will say that they are contradictory, but one could reason that they are not. The boss's behavior might just show that he is cranky, mean, or depressed, not that he hates his job. **2, 3.** Answers will vary. **4.** It is more colloquial to pronounce *usted* in this way in informal contexts, dropping the /d/ at the end of the word. The informal pronunciation emphasizes the personal tone used by the writer, even though he uses form al (*usted*) address rather than *tú.*

Antes de escuchar

You may wish to conduct this as a whole-class discussion. You may also prefer to name a person in the news who suffers from depression, so that students can talk about that person rather than about someone they know personally. That said, some students *are* willing to discuss personal issues like this in class, so let the class be your guide as to what is possible.

Escuche

Notes

- In this chapter students can listen to a radio interview with a psychiatrist who specializes in treating adolescents with depression.
- If the listening is assigned as homework, ask students to listen to the passage at least twice.
- See the IM for the Audioscript and more information about music in Peru.

B: Follow-up

Ask students to write a short "self-help" article for the university newspaper to bring awareness about depression on campus. The goal of the article is to help people become familiar with the symptoms of depression and where they can be treated on campus.

¡Música!

Notes

- Susana Baca (1944–) is a Peruvian singer and songwriter. She is well-known outside of Peru as a musician who mixes traditional and modern musical trends. She is very respected for her work in preserving the musical traditions of Peruvians of African descent. Baca is the recipient of a Latin Grammy award.
- Baca's song "*María Landó*" became famous outside Peru when it was included in David Byrne's compilation album, *The Soul of Black Peru*.
- For helpful tips on using songs in the classroom, see the IM.

A: Answers

1. *Todos tienen momentos tristes, pero no todos sufren de depresión.* **2.** *La depresión tiene muchas causas.* **3.** *Las personas deprimidas no quieren estar cerca de sus amigos y familiares.* **4.** *Es una de las enfermedades más tratables.*

B: Answers

1. Answers will vary but may include: *el divorcio de los padres, problemas de aprendizaje, el abuso de las drogas y el alcohol, cambios hormonales, enfermedad física…* **2.** Answers will vary but may include: *la tristeza, la desesperanza, la ansiedad, sentirse inútil, automutilación…* **3.** *Hablar con un médico o con un terapeuta.*

Go to the iMix section in Connect Spanish (**www.connectspanish.com**) to access the iTunes playlist "*Puntos9*," where you can purchase "Luna llena" by Susana Baca.

A ESCUCHAR

Antes de escuchar

Piense en una persona que Ud. conoce (o en una persona famosa) que sufre o ha sufrido (*has suffered*) de depresión. ¿Cómo se siente o sentía? ¿Qué hizo para mejorarse?

Escuche

Medicina y tecnología: La depresión entre los adolescentes

Un doctor habla de la depresión en la radio. Escuche según las indicaciones de su profesor(a).

Vocabulario para escuchar

la tristeza	sadness	**deprimido/a**	depressed
el estado de ánimo	mood	**la desesperanza**	hopelessness
el comportamiento	behavior	**emocionar**	to get (*someone*) excited about (*something*)
enfrentarse a	to face		
hacer frente a	to face up to	**el peso**	weight
el aprendizaje	learning	**evitar**	to avoid
el acoso	harassment, bullying	**tratable**	treatable

Después de escuchar

A. Hablando de la depresión. ¿Qué dice el Dr. Carvajal sobre la depresión? Todas de las siguientes oraciones son falsas. Corríjalas.

1. Todo el mundo (*Everyone*) sufre de depresión.
2. La depresión tiene solo una causa.
3. Uno de los síntomas de la depresión es querer estar siempre con los amigos y la familia.
4. La depresión es una de las enfermedades menos tratables.

B. Más detalles. Conteste las siguientes preguntas.

1. ¿Cuáles son tres de las causas de la depresión?
2. ¿Cuáles son tres de los síntomas de la depresión?
3. Según el Dr. Carvajal, ¿qué es lo primero que se debe hacer cuando un joven está deprimido?

¡Música!

Susana Baca (1944–) es una cantante afroperuana que mezcla[a] la música tradicional y la contemporánea en sus canciones. La canción «Luna llena[b]» es del álbum *Susana Baca*.

[a]*mixes* [b]*Luna… Full moon*

Susana Baca, en un concierto

A ESCRIBIR

El tema

Las presiones de la vida estudiantil

Preparar

Paso 1. Muchos estudiantes universitarios se encuentran bajo muchas presiones durante su primer año en la universidad. Llene (*Fill in*) la siguiente tabla con las presiones que Ud. cree que lo/la afectan más. Luego entreviste a dos compañeros para saber las opiniones de ellos.

Las presiones…	académicas	sociales	financieras	familiares
Ud.				
compañero/a 1				
compañero/a 2				

Paso 2. ¿Cómo es que las presiones pueden afectar los estudios y la vida de un estudiante? ¿Qué debe hacer un estudiante para prepararse para estas presiones universitarias?

Redactar

Usando toda la información de **Preparar,** escriba un artículo para el periódico de su universidad dirigido (*aimed*) a los estudiantes recién llegados (*newly arrived*). Antes de empezar a escribir, piense en el tono que quiere emplear. ¿Va a ser un artículo serio? ¿humorístico? ¿satírico? También determine si va a dirigirse (*address*) directamente a sus lectores (*readers*) o no. Si se dirige directamente a los lectores, ¿va a usar la forma de **tú** o de **Ud.**?

Editar

Revise el ensayo para comprobar:

- la ortografía y los acentos
- la organización y la secuencia de las ideas
- el tiempo y la forma de los verbos
- el tono del ensayo

Finalmente, prepare su versión final para entregarla.

Preparar

Suggestions

- Ask students to review the uses of the subjunctive for making recommendations (*Caps. 12, 13*).
- Suggest that students incorporate some of the expressions presented in *Nota cultural* (p. 418), depending on the tone that they use.
- Remind students to use adverbs to provide smooth transitions.

Redactar

Suggestions

- Suggested length for this writing assignment: approximately 200 words
- Discuss the possible tones that can be used with students.
- In addition to deciding how to address their readers, students need to decide what narrative voice to use: *yo, nosotros, el* se *impersonal,* among others.
- Suggested structure: 3 paragraphs

  P. 1. Establishing the topic
  P. 2. Description of various student pressures followed by suggestions on how to handle them
  P. 3. Conclusion that summarizes the article and offers a general recommendation

Editar

Follow-up

After students turn in their articles, have a whole-class discussion about the pressures that students feel. Do the pressures encountered at the university help students prepare for the real world that they will face after graduation? Why or why not?

En resumen: En este capítulo

Vocabulario

Suggestions

- Remind students about the first person preterite spelling change for *apagar* (*gu*) and *sacar* (*qu*).
- Remind students that the plural of *luz* is *luces*.
- Have students use vocabulary words to narrate a round-robin *un día fatal*. As a class, they can establish the subject (an individual, real or imaginary). Each student gives a sentence that describes the subject's terrible day.

Word Families

En este capítulo

- *caer, caerse*
- *el estrés, estresado/a*
- *pedir disculpas, discúlpame, discúlpeme*

Entre capítulos

- *acabar* = *acabar de* (7)
- *el despertador* = *despertarse* (5)
- *escrito/a* = *el escritorio* (2), *escribir* (3)
- *estacionar* = *la estación* (8)
- *estudiantil* = *estudiar* (2) *el/la estudiante* (2)
- *fue sin querer* = *querer* (4), *sin* (5)
- *el horario* = *la hora* (1)
- *levantarse con el pie izquierdo* = *levantarse* (5)
- *¡lo siento mucho!* = *sentir* (9)
- *pegarse* = *pegar* (10)
- *la tarjeta de identidad* = *la tarjeta* (8), *la tarjeta de crédito* (7), *la tarjeta de embarque* (8), *la tarjeta postal* (8)
- *el trabajo* = *trabajar* (2), *trabajador(a)* (3)
- *universitario/a* = *la universidad* (2)

¡OJO!

- *apagar* ≠ *pagar*
- *el plazo* ≠ *la plaza*

EN RESUMEN En este capítulo

LearnSmart

Visit **www.connectspanish.com** to practice the vocabulary and grammar points covered in this chapter.

Gramática en breve

33. Hace + *time*

hace = has/have been doing
hace + *time* + **que** + *present*
present + **desde hace** + *time*

hace = ago
hace + *time* + **que** + *preterite*
preterite + **hace** + *time*

34. Accidental *se*

a + *noun* + **se** + *indirect object pronoun* + *verb* + *subject*
(**a** + *pronoun*) **se** + *indirect object pronoun* + *verb* + *subject*

35. *¿Por o para?*

por = reason, cause

by / by means of — *through/along*
because of / due to — *during/in* (time of day)

for = in exchange for, for the sake of / on behalf of, for (*period of time*)

para = goal, purpose, destination
in order to + *inf.*

for = destined for / to be given to, by (*future time*), toward / in the direction of, to be used for, as compared with / in relation to others, in the employ of

Vocabulario

Los verbos

acabar	to finish; to run out of
apagar (gu)	to turn off
quedar	to remain, be left

Repaso: olvidar, perder (pierdo)

Las presiones de la vida académica

la ansiedad	anxiety
los apuntes	notes (*academic*)
el despertador	alarm clock
el estrés	stress
el horario	schedule
el informe (oral/escrito)	(oral/written) report
la nota	grade (*academic*)
el plazo	deadline
la presión	pressure
el programa (del curso)	(course) syllabus
la prueba	quiz; test
la tarjeta de identificación	identification card
el trabajo	report, (piece of) work
el trabajo de tiempo completo/parcial	full-time/parttime job

Cognado: el calendario

Repaso: el examen, la llave, la tarea, el trabajo (*work; job*), **la vida**

devolver (devuelvo)	to return (*something to someone*)
estacionar	to park
estar bajo muchas presiones	to be under a lot of pressure
recoger (recojo)	to collect; to pick up
sacar (qu)	to get (*grades*)
sufrir (de)	to suffer
tener muchas presiones	to have a lot of stress

Repaso: acordarse (me acuerdo) (de), entregar (gu), llegar (gu) a tiempo / tarde, olvidar(se) de, tomar

Los accidentes

caer (caigo)	to fall; to drop
caerse	to fall down
chocar (qu) con/contra	to run into, bump against
equivocarse (qu) (de)	to make a mistake (about)
hacerse daño	to hurt oneself
hacerse daño en	to hurt one's (*body part*)
ir distraído/a	to be distracted
levantarse con el pie izquierdo	to get up on the wrong side of the bed
pedir (pido) (i) disculpas	to apologize
pegarse (gu) con/contra	to run, bump into/against
romper(se)	to break
tener buena/mala suerte	to have good/bad luck, be (un)lucky

Repaso: doler (duele), pegar (gu)

Discúlpame. Disculpa.	Pardon me. I'm sorry. (*fam.*)
Discúlpeme. Disculpe.	Pardon me. I'm sorry. (*form.*)
Fue sin querer.	I didn't mean (to do) it.
Lo siento (mucho).	I'm (very) sorry.

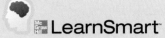

Repaso: perdón

Los adjetivos

distraído/a	absentminded, distracted
escrito/a	written
estresado/a	stressed out, under stress
estudiantil	(of) student(s)
torpe	clumsy
último/a	last, final
universitario/a	(of the) university

Cognados: académico/a, (in)flexible, oral

Otros sustantivos

el desastre	disaster
las escaleras	stairs
la luz (*pl.* **luces**)	light
la taza	cup

Palabras adicionales

hace + *time* + **que** + *preterite* / *preterite* + **hace** + *time*	ago
hace + *time* + **que** + *present* / *present* + **desde hace** + *time*	to have been (*doing something*) for (*time*)
-mente	-ly (*adverbial suffix*)
por	by
por Dios	for heaven's sake
por ejemplo	for example
por primera/última vez	for the first/last time
por si acaso	just in case
¡por supuesto!	of course!
por todas partes	everywhere
¡qué + *adj.***!**	how + *adj.*!
¡qué + *noun***!**	what (a) + *noun*!

Repaso: gracias por, para, por (about; because of; through; in; for)**, por eso, por favor, por fin, por la mañana/tarde/noche, por lo general, por lo menos, por teléfono**

Vocabulario personal

Suggestions

- Have students complete sentences such as:
  1. *Por primera vez en mi vida, yo…*
  2. *Por supuesto que yo…*
  3. *Por si acaso hay…*
  4. *En esta clase, por lo menos…*

  Encourage them to be creative and humorous in their responses. Ask them to compose new sentences that use the new *Palabras adicionales.*
- Have students give the opposite expressions for the following verbs.

  acabar *entregar* *sacar*
  acordarse *quedar* *ser flexible*
  caerse *recoger*

15 La naturaleza y el medio ambiente°

°*La... Nature and the environment*

La Pampa, la inmensa pradera (*grassland*) que se extiende por varias provincias de la Argentina, el Uruguay y el Brasil

- ¿Qué sabe Ud. de la Pampa? ¿Es similar a alguna región de su país?
- ¿Le gusta a Ud. estar en contacto con la naturaleza? ¿Qué actividades hace cuando está fuera de (*outside*) la ciudad?
- ¿Hay mucha contaminación en el área donde Ud. vive? ¿Es la contaminación un problema que le preocupa?

Connect | SPANISH

www.connectspanish.com

Chapter Opening Photo and Chapter Theme

Note

Point out that the phrase *el medio ambiente* is made up of two distinct words that have independent meanings when they are used alone: *el medio* = environment, and also medium (as in *los medios de comunicación*); *el ambiente* = ambiance, and also environment. The adjective derived from the noun phrase is *medioambiental* (written as one word).

Chapter Theme–Related Questions

- Have students tell whether the following statements are true or false for them.
  1. *Es absolutamente necesario tener mi propio* (new) *coche.*
  2. *Es importante tener un coche que no gaste demasiada gasolina.*
  3. *Los daños que se le han hecho* (new) *a la capa de ozono no afectan mi vida diaria.*
  4. *Tenemos que explotar nuestros recursos naturales si queremos mantener un buen nivel de vida.*
  5. *El medio ambiente, hay que protegerlo.*
  6. *Es mejor usar energía nuclear porque es más eficiente.*

Reciclado: Review the indicative vs. the subjunctive, since the forms of the present perfect indicative and subjunctive will be presented in this chapter. Ask students to list some of the environmental concerns they have; they will not know all of the vocabulary needed, but you can provide it, writing new vocabulary on the board or on an overhead. Then ask questions about each topic, beginning with impersonal expressions such as: *¿Es posible que resolvamos ______ en un futuro próximo* (new)*? ¿Es necesario que... ? ¿Es urgente que... ?*

NATIONAL STANDARDS

Connections

The Southern Cone (*El Cono Sur*) is the part of South America that is located south of the Tropic of Capricorn (*el Trópico de Capricornio*). The next three chapters of *Puntos* will focus on the four Spanish-speaking countries that are included in that region: Argentina and Uruguay (*Cap. 15*), Chile (*Cap. 16*), and Paraguay (*Cap. 17*). (The southern part of Brazil is also included in the region, of course.) Except for Paraguay, the countries in the region enjoy a high standard of living compared with the rest of Latin America. Literacy rates are comparable to those of the most developed nations, and there is a lot of industry, a long life expectancy, and good medical and educational systems. In Argentina, Chile, and Uruguay, the majority of the population is of European descent, while most of the population of Paraguay is *mestizo*.

La Argentina

41 millones de habitantes

- La Argentina y el Uruguay son dos países del Cono Sur, el triángulo de territorio sudamericano que está al sur del Trópico de Capricornio.
- La Argentina es un país que, por su gran extensión, tiene variedad de climas y una geografía que incluye desde la selva (*jungle*) tropical al norte, hasta la Antártida al sur.

El Uruguay

3,5 (tres y medio) millones de habitantes

- El Uruguay y la Argentina están separados por el inmenso estuario del Río de la Plata. Pero también están unidos por la historia y la cultura.

En este capítulo

La Argentina y el Uruguay

Datos esenciales

LA ARGENTINA

Nombre oficial: *República Argentina*
Lema: *«En unión y libertad»*
Capital: *Buenos Aires*
Otras ciudades: *Córdoba, Mendoza, Santa Fe*
Composición étnica: *97% blancos, 3% mestizos e indígenas (La Argentina tiene la mayor población caucásica de toda América.)*
Jefe de estado actual: *Cristina Fernández de Kirchner, desde 2007*
Forma de gobierno: *República federal democrática*
Lengua oficial: *el español; el guaraní se reconoce como la segunda lengua oficial en la provincia de Corrientes; hay otras lenguas indígenas en la provincia de Misiones.*
Moneda: *el peso argentino*
Religión: *92% católicos, 2% protestantes, 2% judíos, 4% otros*

EL URUGUAY

Nombre oficial: *República Oriental del Uruguay*
Lema: *«Libertad o Muerte»*
Capital: *Montevideo*
Otras ciudades: *Colonia del Sacramento, Artigas, Salto*
Composición étnica: *88% blancos, 8% mestizos, 4% negros*
Jefe de estado actual: *José Mujica, desde 2010*
Forma de gobierno: *República presidencialista*
Lengua oficial: *el español*
Moneda: *el peso uruguayo*
Religión: *47% católicos, 11% protestantes, 23% sin denominación, 17% ateos/agnósticos (El Uruguay es el país más secular de todo el hemisferio.)*

Suggestions

- Remind students that seasons are reversed in this part of the Southern Hemisphere. Buenos Aires and Montevideo are mild in the fall (March through May) and spring (September through November) and relatively hot in the summer (December through February), making Christmas a summer holiday. The winter months are June through August.
- See the IM for more suggestions and information.

Resources

For Students

- Connect Spanish (**www.connectspanish.com**), which contains all content from the following resources, as well as the *Mundo interactivo* scenarios, the LearnSmart adaptive learning system, and more!
- **Physical Resources:** Workbook / Laboratory Manual, Laboratory Audio Program, DVD

For Instructors

- Connect Spanish (**www.connectspanish.com**), which contains access to all student sections of Connect Spanish, as well as helpful time-saving tools and resources such as an integrated gradebook, Instructor's Manual, Testing Program, digital transparencies, Audioscript, Videoscript, and more!

Resources: Transparency 140

Vocabulario: Preparación

La naturaleza y el medio ambiente

Note

See the model for vocabulary presentation and other material in the *Cap. 15 Vocabulario: Preparación* section of "Chapter-by-Chapter Supplementary Materials" in the IM.

Suggestions

- Point out that *la fábrica* and *la falta* are false cognates.
- Emphasize the spelling changes in the conjugations of *destruir* and *construir: destruyo, destruyes,…* and *construyo, construyes,…* Also point out the first person singular of *proteger: protejo.*
- **Reciclado:** Model the use of *acabar* in *se nos acabó* and *se nos acabaron.*
- Optional vocabulary: *echarle la culpa (a alguien), lento/a, tener la culpa.*
- Model the pronunciation of the words as well as the use of selected words. Integrate them in statements about yourself, your community, and/or the university.

Optional Vocabulary Topic

Many students like to learn the names of animals, as well as the sounds they make in Spanish. Here are some of the most common.

- *la gallina: clo-cló*
- *el gallo: qui-qui-ri-quí*
- *el gato: miau*
- *la oveja: be*
- *el pato: cua-cuá*
- *el pavo: glu-glú*
- *el perro: guau*
- *los polluelos (pollitos): pío-pío*
- *la vaca / el toro: mu*
- *la rana: croac-croac*

Optional

- Read the following definitions and have students give the corresponding word from the vocabulary.
  1. *bonito o hermoso, muy atractivo* (*bello*)
  2. *cuando no hay suficiente cantidad de algo* (*la falta*)
  3. *lo opuesto de destruir* (*construir*)
  4. *puede ser de varios tipos, depende de dónde viene: si del agua, del sol, etcétera* (*la energía*)
  5. *un sistema político* (*el gobierno*)
  6. *el grupo de personas que vive en una ciudad o estado* (*la población*)

VOCABULARIO Preparación

La ciudad y el campo°

countryside

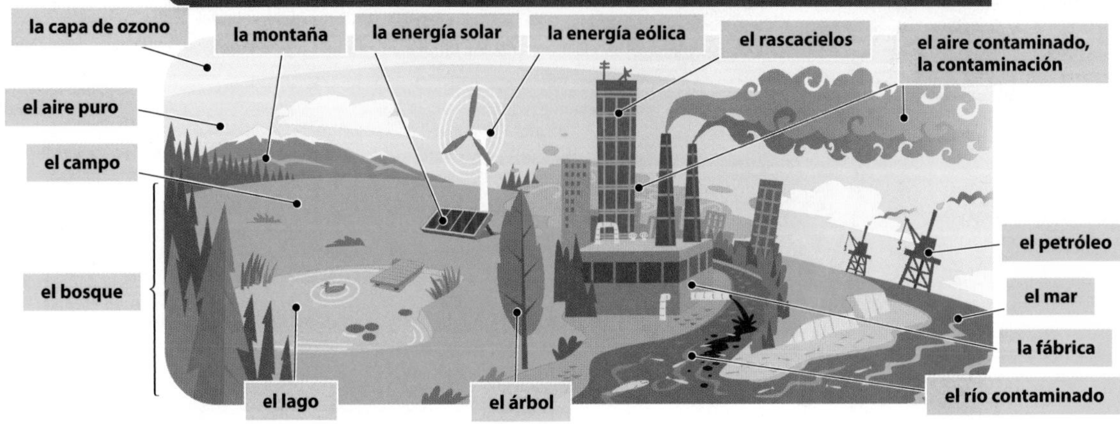

Los recursos naturales°	Los… *Natural resources*
la energía	energy
eólica	wind
renovable	renewable
el medio ambiente	environment
la naturaleza	nature
el reciclaje	recycling
la Tierra	Earth

Cognados: la energía eléctrica/nuclear/solar, el planeta

bello/a	beautiful
contaminado/a	contaminated, polluted
puro/a	pure

Los animales

la ballena	whale
el caballo	horse
la especie (en peligro de extinción)	(endangered) species
el gato	cat
el pájaro	bird
el perro	dog
el pez (*pl.* **peces**)	fish
el toro	bull
la vaca	cow

Cognados: el elefante, el gorila

doméstico/a	domesticated, tame
salvaje	wild

El desarrollo°	El… *Development*
el agricultor / la agricultora	farmer
la agricultura	farming, agriculture
el campesino / la campesina	peasant
el delito	crime
la falta	lack; absence
la finca	farm
el gobierno	government
la población	population
el ritmo de la vida	pace of life
el servicio	service
el transporte	transportation
acelerado/a	fast, accelerated
denso/a	dense
público/a	public
acabar	to finish, run out (of); to use up completely
conservar	to save, conserve
construir*	to build
contaminar	to pollute
desarrollar	to develop
destruir (*like* **construir**)	to destroy
fabricar (qu)	to manufacture
proteger (protejo)	to protect
reciclar	to recycle

Note the present indicative conjugation of* construir: **construyo, construyes, construye, construimos, construís, construyen.

- Have students imagine that they have a Hispanic friend who does not know what the following are. Have them explain the meaning of each.
  1. the EPA
  2. the Secretary of the Interior
  3. the welfare system
  4. the National Parks system and park rangers
  5. a parole officer
  6. the inner city

Resources: Transparency 141

Conversación

A. ¿En la ciudad o en el campo?

	LA CIUDAD	EL CAMPO
1. El aire es más puro; hay menos contaminación.	☐	☑
2. La naturaleza es más bella.	☐	☑
3. El ritmo de la vida es más acelerado.	☑	☐
4. Hay más delitos.	☑	☐
5. Los servicios profesionales (financieros, legales…) son más accesibles.	☑	☐
6. Hay pocos medios de transporte públicos.	☐	☑
7. La población es menos densa.	☐	☑
8. Hay falta de viviendas.	☑	☐

Así se dice

la fábrica = la factoría
la finca = la granja, el rancho, la estancia

El árbol is also called **el palo** in Mexico, Central America, and the Caribbean. The names of at least two California cities contain the word **palo:** Palo Alto and Palos Verdes.

B. Definiciones. Defina las siguientes palabras en español.

MODELO: el agricultor ⟶ Es el dueño de una finca.

1. la fábrica **2.** el campesino **3.** la falta **4.** la finca **5.** la naturaleza **6.** la población **7.** el río **8.** el rascacielos **9.** el agricultor

Con. B: Possible Answers: 1. *Es el lugar donde se fabrican automóviles y otros productos.* **2.** *Es una persona que vive en una zona rural y trabaja en el campo.* **3.** *Es no tener algo que necesitamos.* **4.** *Allí vive el agricultor y allí trabajan los campesinos.* **5.** *Es lo contrario de las ciudades.* **6.** *Incluye a todas las personas que viven en un país.* **7.** *Lleva agua.* **8.** *Es un edificio altísimo.* **9.** *Cultiva una finca con la ayuda de los campesinos.*

Nota cultural

Programas medioambientales

Muchos países del mundo se encuentran en la situación de equilibrar[a] la protección del medio ambiente con los objetivos del desarrollo económico. En muchos casos, la explotación de recursos naturales es la mayor fuente de ingreso[b] para la economía de un país. Los gobiernos latinoamericanos están conscientes de la necesidad de proteger el medio ambiente y de conservar los recursos naturales, y están haciendo lo posible por hacerlo. Los siguientes son algunos de los muchos programas medioambientales que existen en los países hispanohablantes.

- En las grandes ciudades de varios países (Bolivia, Chile, Colombia, el Ecuador, Honduras, México y Venezuela, entre otros) se han establecido[c] programas de restricción vehicular, que tratan de regular la cantidad de tráfico en determinadas horas o días. Se basan en un sistema que limite el uso de un vehículo según su placa.[d] Además de[e] reducir el tráfico diario en la ciudad, estos programas pueden mejorar[f] la calidad del aire.
- En muchos países hispanohablantes (la Argentina, el Uruguay, España y México, entre otros) existen programas de reciclaje, basados en sistemas de separación de basura. Es decir que, según su clase, los materiales se depositan en contenedores[g] de colores diferentes: el papel y el cartón[h] en un contenedor; el vidrio,[i] el metal y el plástico en otro; y en algunos casos los desperdicios de materia orgánica,[j] en otro.

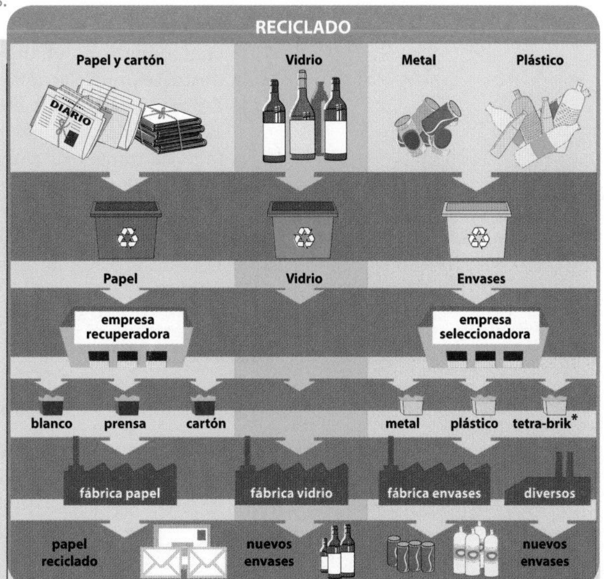

¿Qué programas medioambientales hay en su ciudad o estado?

[a]*needing to balance* [b]fuente… *source of income* [c]se… *have been established* [d]*license plate* [e]Además… *Besides* [f]*improve* [g]*containers, receptacles* [h]*cardboard*

[i]*glass* [j]los… *organic waste matter*

__Tetra-brik__ is a type of carton packaging used for beverages such as milk and fruit juices. It is a regional term, used in Spain, Argentina, and other parts of the Spanish-speaking world.

Preliminary Exercise

Ask students the following questions to personalize the vocabulary.

1. *¿Hay mucha contaminación en esta ciudad?*
2. *¿Cómo es el ritmo de vida en (ciudad), acelerado o lento? ¿Qué ritmo de vida prefiere Ud.? ¿Le gusta caminar por la ciudad de noche?*
3. *¿Trata Ud. de conservar la energía? ¿Hay ahora una crisis con la energía? Si una persona realmente quiere conservar energía, ¿qué puede hacer?*
4. *¿Hay muchos delitos y crímenes en esta ciudad? ¿Qué lugares son famosos por la frecuencia de sus delitos? ¿Tiene Ud. miedo de visitar estos lugares?*
5. *¿Va Ud. al campo con frecuencia? ¿Tiene su familia una finca en el campo? ¿La visita Ud.? ¿Cuándo? Descríbala. ¿Le gustaría vivir en una finca? Por lo general, ¿cómo es el ritmo de vida en una finca?*

Con. A: Follow-up

Have students tell if they agree with the following statements about their city.

1. *Hay un buen sistema de transporte público.*
2. *Hay parques y zonas verdes por todas partes.*
3. *Ocurren muy pocos delitos.*
4. *Hay poca contaminación.*
5. *El ritmo de la vida es demasiado lento* (new).
6. *Hay demasiadas fábricas.*
7. *La población es muy densa.*
8. *No hay falta de viviendas.*

Nota cultural

Suggestion

- The art has no glosses. Students should be able to understand terms such as *recuperadora* (recycling), *Envases* (Containers), *seleccionadora* (sorting), and *prensa* (newsprint), with the visual support of the piece.

Comprensión

1. *¿Qué aspecto económico dificulta la protección del medio ambiente en algunos países hispanos?* (*Tienen que equilibrar el desarrollo económico con la protección del medio ambiente.*)
2. *¿En qué países hay un programa para limitar el uso de los coches?* (*en Bolivia, Chile, Colombia, el Ecuador, Honduras, México y Venezuela, entre otros*)
3. *¿Cuáles son algunos de los materiales que se reciclan en muchos países?* (*el papel, el cartón, el vidrio, el metal, el plástico, la materia orgánica*)

NATIONAL STANDARDS: Communication

Divide the class into three groups. One will defend life in the city, another life in the country, and a third will prepare a list of questions to ask each group. Give students 10–15 minutes to prepare their arguments supporting their position and to prepare questions. The city and country groups should then give a simple opening statement, after which the third group will pose its first question. Provide specific time limits for the debating groups to answer, and allow time at the end for final arguments.

Resources: Transparency 142

Con. C: Suggestions

- Ask each group to put the four headings at the top of four columns on a sheet of paper before they start to classify the animals.
- Students should also come up with the names of animals presented for the first time or reviewed in *Vocabulario: Preparación.* The following animals from previous chapters are not reviewed: *la langosta, el cerdo, el pollo, el camarón, el atún, el pavo, el ratón.*
- This activity will work well if you put a time limit on *Paso 1.*

Con. C: Extension

After you have determined who won the first phase of this activity, give students the following words, accompanying them with verbal or pantomimed clues and award points for the group that is the first to classify the species correctly.

MODELO: *la tortuga = un animal que camina muy lentamente* (pantomine)

Possible items: *la ardilla* (squirrel; students encountered this word in *Cap.* 11), *el gallo* (rooster), *el mapache* (racoon), *la mosca* (fly), *el lagarto* (the origin of the English word *alligator*), *el tiburón* (shark), *la oveja* (sheep), *el pato* (duck)

Bright Idea

Con. D: Preliminary Exercise

Ask students the following questions.

¿Qué hacen para conservar la energía?
¿Qué productos destruyen la capa de ozono?
¿Usa Ud. mucha agua y energía en su casa?
¿Qué cosas recicla Ud.? ¿periódicos? ¿botellas? ¿latas?

Con. D: Suggestion

Have pairs rank the problems in order of importance to their city, state, and country, or at least indicate the top two or three problems in each area. Then tally the results for the whole class to see if there is agreement or disagreement about what our problems are.

Redacción: Assign *Con. D, Paso 2,* as an individual or partner composition.

- Paragraph 1: Name and describe the three most serious problems in your area.
- Paragraph 2: Offer suggestions for solving them. Remind students to use the subjunctive, as appropriate.

Set expectations for length and other usages.

C. ¿Cuánto sabe de los animales?

Paso 1. En grupos, clasifiquen los siguientes animales en cuatro grupos: los insectos, los animales domésticos, los animales salvajes y las especies en peligro de extinción. **¡OJO!** Algunos nombres van a ir en más de un grupo. Luego añadan los nombres de otros animales o insectos que saben los miembros del grupo.

el águila	la cucaracha	la jirafa	la ostra
el camello	el delfín	el león	la rata
el cocodrilo	el hipopótamo	el mosquito	el rinoceronte
el cóndor	el jaguar	el orangután	el tigre

Paso 2. Presenten la lista de su grupo a la clase. ¡Un premio (*prize*) para el grupo que puso el mayor número de nombres de animales en la categoría apropiada!

D. Problemas medioambientales

Paso 1. En parejas, indiquen cuáles de los siguientes problemas y temas afectan a su ciudad, estado o país, o si creen que algunos afectan a los tres. Deben añadir por lo menos un tema que Uds. consideren que es importante.

AFECTA A...	MI CIUDAD	MI ESTADO	MI PAÍS
1. la contaminación del aire	☐	☐	☐
2. la destrucción de la capa de ozono	☐	☐	☐
3. la deforestación de los bosques	☐	☐	☐
4. el desarrollo de energías renovables	☐	☐	☐
5. la falta de transporte público adecuado	☐	☐	☐
6. el ritmo acelerado de la vida	☐	☐	☐
7. la proliferación de fábricas que contaminan el aire y el agua	☐	☐	☐
8. la falta de protección de los espacios naturales	☐	☐	☐
9. ¿ ?	☐	☐	☐

Paso 2. Ahora elijan (*choose*) uno o dos de estos temas y prepárense para explicar lo que se está haciendo ahora para resolver el problema y lo que, en su opinión, es necesario hacer. Presenten sus ideas a la clase.

E. Opiniones. En parejas, comenten las siguientes opiniones. Pueden usar las siguientes expresiones para aclarar (*clarify*) su posición con respecto a cada tema. **¡OJO!** Todas las expresiones requieren el uso del subjuntivo.

Vocabulario útil

Es / Me/Nos parece { **necesario/esencial que...** / **importantísimo que...** / **absurdo que...** }
Me opongo / Nos oponemos a que... I am / We are against . . .
No creo/creemos que...

1. Para conservar energía debemos reciclar todo lo posible.
2. Es mejor calentar (*to heat*) las casas con estufas de leña (*wood stoves*) que con gas o electricidad.
3. Se debe crear más parques urbanos, estatales/provinciales y nacionales.
4. La protección del medio ambiente no debe impedir la explotación de los recursos naturales.
5. Para evitar la contaminación urbana, debemos limitar el uso de los coches a ciertos días de la semana.
6. El gobierno debe ponerles multas (*fines*) muy graves a las compañías e individuos que causan la contaminación.

NATIONAL STANDARDS: Communication

Have students interview their classmates to find out what they do to help conserve our natural resources. Students should then share their findings with the rest of the class.

Write key words on the board and remind students to try to use them in their interviews.

el reciclaje
apagar/poner las luces
caminar
pasear en bicicleta

F. Un recurso natural importante

Paso 1. Lea el siguiente anuncio de una empresa colombiana y luego conteste las preguntas.

En ECOPETROL tenemos conciencia ambiental y social. Nuestra planeación incluye siempre los estudios de localización e impacto ambiental, buscando no perturbar la naturaleza y la vida de las poblaciones vecinas a nuestras futuras operaciones. En esta planeación el trabajo con la comunidad es indispensable.

Nuestro propósito: Una mejor convivencia

EMPRESA COLOMBIANA DE PETROLEOS
ECOPETROL

1. ¿Qué tipo de negocio cree Ud. que tiene la Empresa Ecopetrol? ¿Qué produce?
2. ¿Qué asuntos (*matters*) son de mayor interés para esta empresa? ¿El tráfico? ¿la deforestación? ¿las poblaciones humanas? ¿otros asuntos?
3. ¿Cree que la foto del anuncio es buena para la imagen de la empresa? ¿Por qué?
4. El sustantivo **convivencia** se relaciona con el verbo **vivir** y contiene la preposición **con.** ¿Qué cree Ud. que significa **convivencia**?
5. ¿Sabe Ud. cuál es otro país latinoamericano que produce lo mismo que Ecopetrol?

Paso 2. Ahora, en parejas, creen un anuncio para el periódico de su universidad, sugiriendo ideas para conservar energía y reciclar en su *campus*.

Con. F: Answers
1. *Produce y vende petróleo.* **2.** *el medio ambiente y el impacto social de sus operaciones* **3.** Answers will vary. **4.** living together **5.** Answers will vary. The top five petroleum-producing countries in Latin America are: Mexico, Venezuela, Brazil, Colombia, Argentina.

Con. E: Extension

7. *El desarrollo de la tecnología fomenta el ritmo tan acelerado de nuestra vida.*
8. *Los países desarrollados están destruyendo los recursos naturales de los países más pobres.*
9. *Los países menos desarrollados tienen el derecho* (new) *de usar sus recursos naturales como quieran, sin preocuparse de los problemas ambientales del mundo.*

Con. F: Suggestion

Have students look through Spanish-language magazines and newspapers to locate ads with environmental statements or themes. Are there many? What kinds of messages do they convey?

Bright Idea

Con. F: Follow-up

Have students create a poster in Spanish to motivate others to conserve energy and to reduce pollution. Give them the following suggestions.

la conservación de la energía
la contaminación del agua/aire
la promoción de otras formas de energía
el reciclaje

Have students present their posters in class.

Optional

¿A qué tipo de energía corresponden las siguientes descripciones, energía hidráulica, solar, nuclear, eólica o eléctrica?

1. *Es la energía más usada en los hogares* (new).
2. *Según los expertos, es la forma de energía más limpia; es decir, es la que produce menos contaminación.*
3. *Puede ser la forma de energía más eficiente, pero también es la más peligrosa* (new).
4. *Esta energía viene del viento; por eso solo se puede desarrollar en lugares específicos.*
5. *Para producir esta forma de energía son necesarios los ríos y las cataratas* (new).

Heritage Speakers

- Invite a un hispanohablante a leer el anuncio en voz alta.
- Anime a los hispanohablantes a hablar de los esfuerzos de conservación que se hacen en su país de origen. ¿Reciclan? ¿Se promueven otras formas de energía tales como la energía solar o la energía eólica?

Vocabulario Preparación ■ **447**

Los autos

Suggestions

- Ask students what vocabulary words they associate with the following.

  ¿Con qué asocia Ud...

  1. *los colores rojo, amarillo y verde?*
  2. *a los mecánicos?*
  3. *la contaminación?*
  4. *parar?*
  5. *una llanta?*
  6. *arrancar?*
  7. *la carretera?*
- Remind students that *gastar dinero* means *to spend money*.
- Optional vocabulary: *la avería* (breakdown), *la bocacalle* (entrance to a street), *el cruce de peatones* (crosswalk), *el camino* (path, road), *el pinchazo* (flat tire)
- Emphasize the spelling changes in *conducir* (*zc*), *arrancar* (*qu*), *chocar* (*qu*), *obedecer* (*zc*), and *tocar* (*qu*).

Preliminary Exercises

- Read the following statements and have students respond *cierto* or *falso*.
  1. *El tanque del coche contiene aceite.*
  2. *Si el semáforo está en rojo, es necesario parar.*
  3. *Un Cadillac gasta poca gasolina.*
  4. *Es necesario tener licencia para conducir.*
- Ask students the following questions.
  1. *En esta clase, ¿cuántos tienen coche? ¿Es viejo o nuevo su coche? ¿grande o pequeño? ¿Gasta mucha gasolina o poca? ¿mucho aceite o poco? ¿Cuánto le cuesta llenar el tanque?*
  2. *En general, ¿funciona bien su coche? Cuando no funciona, ¿lo arregla Ud. o se lo arregla un mecánico? ¿un amigo? ¿Es vieja la batería o nueva? ¿Le es difícil hacer arrancar el coche por la mañana? ¿Le es difícil arrancar cuando hace frío?*
  3. *¿Tuvo Ud. alguna vez una llanta desinflada? ¿Dónde y cómo ocurrió? ¿Quién la cambió? ¿Tuvo Ud. que llamar para pedir ayuda? ¿Siempre lleva Ud. una llanta de repuesto (llanta de recambio / una quinta llanta)?*
  4. *¿Viene Ud. en coche al* campus? *¿Es fácil estacionarse aquí? ¿Es necesario pagar para poder estacionarse en el* campus? *¿Cuánto se paga? ¿Quiénes encuentran estacionamiento con más facilidad, los profesores o los estudiantes?*

Los autos

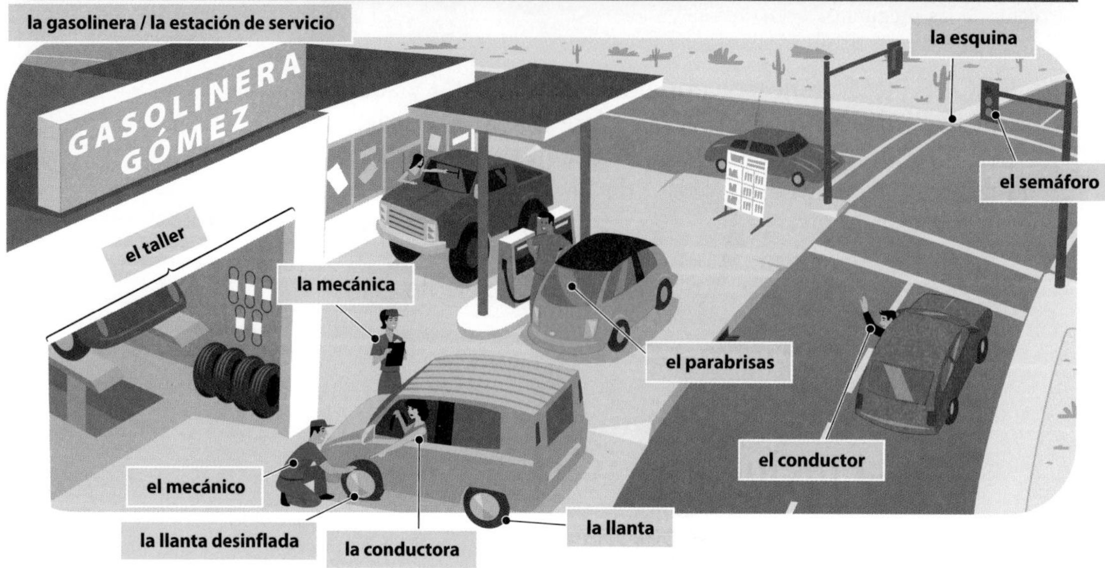

la acera	sidewalk
la autopista	freeway, interstate
la avenida	avenue
la calle	street
la camioneta	van
la carretera	highway
la circulación, el tránsito	traffic
el coche/carro (descapotable, híbrido, todoterreno)	(convertible, hybrid, all-terrain) car
el estacionamiento	parking place/lot
los frenos	brakes
la licencia de manejar/conducir	driver's license
el tanque	tank

Cognados: la gasolina, el SUV, el tráfico

arrancar (qu)	to start up (*a car*)
arreglar	to fix, repair
chocar (qu) con	to run into, collide (with)
estacionar	to park
gastar (mucha/poca gasolina)	to use (a lot/little of gas)
llenar	to fill (up)
manejar, conducir (conduzco)*	to drive
obedecer (obedezco)*	to obey
parar	to stop
revisar el aceite	to check the oil
tocar (qu) la bocina	to honk the horn

Cognado: reparar

Así se dice

el estacionamiento = el aparcamiento, el parking
la llanta = la rueda
arrancar = encender el motor
estacionar = aparcar (*Sp.*), parquear (*Col., Mex.*)
la licencia de manejar/conducir = el carnet de conducir, el permiso de manejar

There are many ways to express *car* in Spanish. You already know **el coche** and **el carro. El automóvil,** or simply **el auto,** is perhaps the most generic word, understood in all parts of the Spanish-speaking world.

Like the verb* **conocer, conducir *and* **obedecer** *have a spelling change in the* **yo** *form of the present indicative:* **conozco, conduzco, obedezco.** *This spelling change is also used in all forms of the present subjunctive.*

Heritage Speakers

En algunos países latinoamericanos, como Colombia por ejemplo, se dice *pase* en vez de *licencia de conducir*. Otro término usado principalmente en España es *el carnet de conducir*. También hay varios términos para expresar *to park: estacionar(se), aparcar* (Esp.) y *parquear*. Para referirse a *parking lot* o *parking place,* se puede decir *estacionamiento* o *parqueadero*. Pregúnteles a los hispanohablantes de la clase qué palabras usan y por qué.

Resources: Transparency 143

Conversación

A. Definiciones

Paso 1. Empareje las definiciones con las palabras y frases.

DEFINICIONES	PALABRAS Y FRASES
1. __g__ Se pone en el tanque.	**a.** los frenos
2. __h__ Se llenan de aire.	**b.** la esquina
3. __i__ Lubrica el motor.	**c.** la carretera
4. __d__ Es necesaria para arrancar el motor.	**d.** la batería
5. __b__ Sitio donde dos calles se encuentran, formando un ángulo recto (*square*).	**e.** el taller
6. __f__ Es necesario cambiarla cuando no tiene aire suficiente.	**f.** una llanta desinflada
7. __c__ Es una calle pública ancha (*wide*) donde los coches circulan rápidamente.	**g.** la gasolina
8. __a__ Se usan para parar el coche.	**h.** las llantas
9. __j__ El policía nos la pide cuando nos para el coche.	**i.** el aceite
10. __e__ Allí se revisan y se arreglan los coches.	**j.** la licencia

Paso 2. Ahora, siguiendo el modelo de las definiciones del **Paso 1,** dé una definición de las siguientes palabras.

1. el semáforo **3.** estacionar **5.** la gasolinera
2. la circulación **4.** gastar gasolina **6.** la autopista

B. Entrevista: Un conductor responsable

Paso 1. Entreviste a un compañero o compañera para saber con qué frecuencia hace las siguientes cosas.

1. dejar la licencia en casa cuando va a manejar
2. acelerar (*to speed up*) cuando ve a un policía
3. tomar bebidas alcohólicas y después manejar
4. respetar el límite de velocidad o excederlo
5. estacionar el coche donde dice «Prohibido estacionar»
6. revisar el aceite y la batería
7. seguir todo derecho (*straight*) a toda velocidad cuando no sabe llegar a su destino (*destination*)
8. rebasar (*to pass*) tres carros a la vez (*at the same time*)
9. mandar mensajes electrónicos mientras maneja
10. no parar cuando el semáforo está en rojo

Paso 2. Ahora, con el mismo compañero o compañera, haga una lista de diez de las cosas que debe hacer —o no debe hacer— un conductor responsable. Pueden usar frases del **Paso 1,** si quieren.

MODELOS: Es importante que el conductor **respete** el límite de velocidad.
No exceda el límite de velocidad.
Respetar / **No exceder** el límite de velocidad.

Paso 3. Ahora analice Ud. sus propias (*own*) costumbres y cualidades como conductor(a). ¡Diga la verdad! ¿Es Ud. un conductor o conductora responsable?

Con. A, Paso 2: Possible Answers: 1. *Es lo que indica que se debe parar en una esquina.* **2.** *Son todos los autos que están en las calles o en las carreteras.* **3.** *Es poner el coche, por tiempo limitado, en una zona autorizada.* **4.** *El carro hace esto cuando manejamos.* **5.** *Allí se compra la gasolina.* **6.** *Es un tipo de calle muy grande donde los autos circulan rápidamente.*

5. *¿Sabe Ud. manejar? ¿Cuántos años hace que aprendió a manejar? ¿Cuántos años tenía? ¿Quién le enseñó a manejar? ¿Tuvo Ud. algún accidente mientras aprendía? ¿Qué es lo mejor de manejar? ¿y lo peor?*

Con. A: Note

Active vocabulary: *la batería*

Con. A: Variation

Have students work in pairs, one covering the first column and the other the second.

Con. B: Suggestions

- Have students rank items in order of importance.
- Tell students what forms you would like them to use to create their lists. The models show a complex sentence with the subjunctive, an *Ud.* command, and commands with the infinitive (which will be introduced in *Cap. 16*).

Con. B: Optional

Ask students the following questions.

¿Es símbolo de mucho prestigio social tener un Ferrari? ¿un Volkswagen? ¿un Hyundai? ¿un BMW? ¿un Toyota? ¿una camioneta? ¿un pickup*?*
¿Cómo es el típico dueño / la típica dueña de cada uno de estos coches?

Con. B: Note

Active vocabulary: *el límite de velocidad, el/la policía*

NATIONAL STANDARDS: Connections

In order to drive in many foreign countries, drivers from this country are required to have a valid International Driver's License (IDL) or an International Driver's Permit (IDP). AN IDP translates your state-issued driver's license into ten languages so that you can show it to officials in foreign countries to help them interpret your driver's license. IDPs are not valid for driving in the country in which they were issued. There are only two organizations authorized to issue IDPs to U.S. residents. The American Automobile Association (AAA) and the America Auto Touring Alliance (AATA) are permitted to issue IDPs only to people who have a valid U.S. driver's license and who are at least 18 years of age. An IDP costs $15.00. Beware of Internet sites for companies that charge considerably more but are not authorized to issue these documents!

Reciclado: Note the recycling of formal and informal command forms in *Con. C* and *D.*

Con. C: Suggestion

Using the map of Montevideo on an overhead, model several sets of *Ud.* command directions before asking students to do this activity on their own. No answers are given, as there are various ways to give directions.

Con. D: Suggestions

- Adapt all of the destinations given to your campus or city.
- Model directions again (this activity asks for *tú* commands) before allowing students to work in pairs.

Pronunciación: See the Workbook / Laboratory Manual for review and practice of cognates.

Nota **comunicativa**

Frases para indicar cómo llegar a un lugar

Since you know how to form informal (**tú**) and formal (**Ud./Uds.**) commands, you should be able to give simple directions in Spanish.

doblar	to turn
seguir (sigo) (i)	to keep on going; to continue
a la derecha/izquierda	to the right/left
por (la calle/avenida…)	on, through (. . . street/avenue)
(todo) derecho/recto	straight ahead
¿Cómo se llega a… ?	How do you get to . . . ?

C. En el centro de Montevideo. En parejas, usen el siguiente mapa del centro de Montevideo para dar direcciones a los lugares indicados. Usen mandatos con **Ud.**

MODELOS: **Empiece** doblando / por doblar… en…
Siga todo derecho hasta llegar…
Doble en…

1. del Museo Histórico Nacional al Mercado del Puerto
2. del Mercado del Puerto al Hospital Maciel
3. del Hospital Maciel al Teatro Solís

[a]*Port* [b]*Dock* [c]*Pier*

D. ¿Cómo se llega a… ?

Paso 1. En parejas, escriban o den verbalmente direcciones para ir desde su *campus* a los siguientes lugares. Usen mandatos con **tú.**

1. a un cine que está cerca del *campus*
2. al centro de la ciudad
3. a un centro comercial popular
4. a un restaurante bien conocido (*well-known*)

Paso 2. Ahora lean las direcciones del **Paso 1** a la clase pero sin dar el nombre del destino (*destination*). La clase va a tratar de adivinar (*guess*) el destino.

E. Intercambios. En parejas, hagan y contesten preguntas sobre los siguientes temas. Si alguno de Uds. no tiene coche, debe hablar del coche que le gustaría tener.

1. la marca (*make*) y el modelo de su coche y la placa (*license plate*) que tiene
2. dónde lo estaciona
3. cuánto tiempo hace que lo tiene y cuánto tiempo más piensa tenerlo
4. si el coche expresa su personalidad o si es solo un medio de transporte para Ud.
5. si el coche tiene nombre

Mundo interactivo

You should now be prepared to work with Scenario 8, Activity 1 in Connect Spanish (**www.connectspanish.com**).

Resources: Transparency 144

GRAMÁTICA

¿Recuerda Ud.?

You have already learned to form and use the present participle (**el gerundio**) in Spanish. The present participles are indicated in boldface in the following sentences. Give their English equivalents and tell how they are formed in Spanish.

1. Carlota, ¡vas **manejando** demasiado rápido!
2. Los niños están **durmiendo** en este momento.

There is another kind of participle in English and in Spanish: the past participle. A number of adjectives that you have learned to use with **estar** are actually past participles. Can you tell how the following adjectives are derived from their infinitives?

1. **-ar** verbs: **cansado/a, cerrado/a, encantado/a, pasado/a, resfriado/a**
2. **-er/-ir** verbs: **aburrido/a, divertido/a, querido/a**
3. irregular verbs: **abierto/a, escrito/a**

You will learn more about past participles and how they are used in **Gramática 42** and **43.**

42 *Más descripciones*

Past Participle Used As an Adjective

Grammar Tutorial 42
connect | SPANISH
www.connectspanish.com

Gramática en acción: Algunos refranes y dichos en español

a. En boca cerrada no entran moscas.

b. Estar tan aburrido como una ostra.

c. Cuando está abierto el cajón, el más honrado es ladrón.

Comprensión

Empareje estas oraciones con el refrán o dicho que explican.

1. __c__ Es posible que una persona honrada caiga en la tentación de hacer algo malo si la oportunidad se le presenta.
2. __a__ Hay que ser prudente. A veces es mejor no decir nada para evitar (*avoid*) problemas.
3. __b__ Ejemplifican el aburrimiento (*boredom*) porque llevan una vida tranquila… siempre igual.

A few Spanish proverbs and sayings ***a.*** *Into a closed mouth no flies enter.* ***b.*** *To be as bored as an oyster.* ***c.*** *When the drawer is open, the most honest person is (can become) a thief.*

¿Recuerda Ud.?

The adjectives given in *¿Recuerda Ud.?* are past participle adjectives for which students also know the corresponding infinitive.

Gramática 42 Past Participle Used As an Adjective

GEA: Suggestion

Ask students what *cerrada, aburrido,* and *honrado* have in common. (→ *-do/a* ending)

GEA: Note

Active vocabulary: *evitar*

Follow-up

After reviewing the *refranes*, ask students the following questions.

1. *¿Es mejor no decir nada? ¿Qué le puede pasar a uno cuando tiene la boca abierta?*
2. *¿Llevan una vida muy interesante las ostras? ¿Por qué cree que no se divierten? ¿Sufren muchas presiones?*
3. *¿Son criminales todos los que cometen delitos? ¿Es posible que una persona honrada llegue a cometer un crimen? ¿Cree que hay demasiadas tentaciones en el mundo moderno?*

Forming the Past Participle (p. 452)

Emphasis 1: Suggestions

- Model the past participle forms, e.g.: *cerrar, cerrado → La puerta está cerrada.*
- Use the following rapid response drill to practice the forms. Have students give the past participle for each verb you say.

comprar	*invitar*	*perder*
pagar	*arreglar*	*comer*
mandar	*visitar*	*recibir*
terminar	*vender*	*pedir*
preparar	*conocer*	*dormir*
llamar	*leer*	*seguir*

- Model the pronunciation of irregular past participles. Say the participle and have students give the corresponding infinitive. Then reverse the procedure.

Heritage Speakers

El dicho *aburrido como una ostra* se presenta aquí con el verbo *estar* y expresa la idea *as bored as an oyster*. Sin embargo, algunos hispanohablantes prefieren la idea *as boring as an oyster*. En este caso sería necesario emplear el verbo *ser*. Pregúnteles a los hispanohablantes qué dirían: *Está tan aburrido/a como una ostra* o *Es tan aburrido/a como una ostra*. Pídales que compartan otros dichos y refranes que se usan en su familia con la clase.

Resources: Transparency 145

Emphasis 2: Suggestions

- Have students express the following in Spanish.

broken	returned	made
seen	written	done
covered	said	open(ed)
discovered	dead	put

- Emphasize that compound verbs that have an irregular root verb, with few exceptions, have the same irregularity as the root verb *in the past participle*.

  *decir → pre**decir:** pre**dicho***
  *poner → com**poner:** com**puesto***
  *hacer → des**hacer:** des**hecho***

  Have students give the past participle for the following verbs and also give their English equivalent.

revolver	*deponer*	*describir*
exponer	*envolver*	*reponer*
prescribir	*oponer*	*rever*
presuponer	*prever*	*redecir*
recubrir	*encubrir*	*subscribir*
imponer	*rehacer*	*suponer*

The Past Participle As Adjective

Emphasis 1: Suggestions

- Emphasize that the past participle used as an adjective must agree in gender and number with the noun it modifies.
- Use the following rapid response drill to practice agreement. Have students change the participle to agree with the nouns indicated.
  1. *hecho: bolsas, vestidos, camisa*
  2. *escrito: carta, ejercicio, libros*
  3. *roto: tazas, silla, disco*

Emphasis 2: Suggestion

Emphasize the use of the past participle with *estar* to describe resulting conditions. Point out that students learned many *-ado/-ido* adjectives in *Cap. 5* with *estar* expressions.

- **Reciclado:** Here are the past participle adjectives that are active vocabulary but for which students have *not* learned the corresponding infinitive. Go through the list of adjectives, asking students to give the corresponding infinitive, which students should be able to do easily, with the exception of the irregular participle *frito/a* (*freír*). Then use the adjectives in conversational exchanges with students. Here is the list: *asado/a, atrasado/a, avergonzado/a, casado/a, congelado/a, desordenado/a, distraído, estresado/a, frito/a, mareado/a, ocupado/a, ordenado/a, pesado/a, preocupado/a, tostado/a.*

The Past Participle / **El participio pasado**		
verbos en *-ar*	**verbos en *-er/-ir***	
hablar → hablado spoken	**comer → comido** eaten	**vivir → vivido** lived

the past participle / **el participio pasado** = the form of a verb used with *to have* in English to form the perfect tenses (*I have written*)

Forming the Past Participle / **Cómo se forma el participio pasado**

1. Regular Forms

The past participle of most English verbs ends in *-ed: to walk → walked, to close → closed.* Many, however, are irregular: *to sing → **sung**, to write → **written.***

In Spanish, the *past participle* (**el participio pasado**) is formed by adding **-ado** to the stem of **-ar** verbs, and **-ido** to the stem of **-er** and **-ir** verbs.

An accent mark is used on the past participle of **-er/-ir** verbs with stems ending in **-a, -e,** or **-o.**

El participio pasado
-ar → -ado
-er/-ir: → -ido

Pronunciation hint: **-d-** = [đ], like English *th*

caer → caído	**oír → oído**
creer → creído	**(son)reír → (son)reído**
leer → leído	**traer → traído**

2. Irregular Forms

Some Spanish verbs have irregular past participles.

¡OJO!

The past participle of most compound verbs (such as **descubrir**) that have an irregular root verb (in this case, **cubrir**) have the same irregularity in the past participle: **(des)cubierto.**

abrir:	abierto	**morir:**	muerto
cubrir:*	cubierto	**poner:**	puesto
decir:	dicho	**resolver:***	resuelto
descubrir:*	descubierto	**romper:**	roto
escribir:	escrito	**ver:**	visto
hacer:	hecho	**volver:**	vuelto

The Past Participle As an Adjective / **El participio pasado como adjetivo**

1. Used As an Adjective

In both English and Spanish, the past participle can be used as an adjective to modify a noun. Like other Spanish adjectives, the past participle must agree in number and gender with the noun modified.

Viven en **una casa construida** en 1920.
They live in a house built in 1920.

El español es una de **las lenguas habladas** en los Estados Unidos y en el Canadá.
Spanish is one of the languages spoken in the United States and in Canada.

2. With *estar*

The past participle is frequently used with **estar** to describe conditions that are the result of a previous action.

El lago **está** contaminado.
The lake is polluted.

Todos los peces **estaban** cubiertos de crudo.
All the fish were covered with crude oil.

¡OJO!

English past participles often have the same form as the past tense.

*I **closed** the book.*
*The thief stood behind the **closed** door.*

The Spanish past participle is never identical in form or use to a past tense.

Cerré la puerta. Ahora la puerta está cerrada.
*I **closed** the door. Now the door is **closed.***

Resolvieron el problema. Ahora el problema está resuelto.
*They **solved** the problem. Now the problem is **solved.***

*__cubrir__ = *to cover*, **descubrir** = *to discover*, **resolver (resuelvo)** = *to solve, resolve*

Práctica

A. ¡Anticipemos! En este momento…

Paso 1. En este momento, ¿son ciertas o falsas las siguientes declaraciones con relación a su salón de clase?

	CIERTO	FALSO
1. La puerta está abierta.	☐	☐
2. Las luces están apagadas.	☐	☐
3. Las ventanas están cerradas.	☐	☐
4. Algunos libros están abiertos.	☐	☐
5. Los estudiantes están sentados.	☐	☐
6. Hay algo escrito en el pizarrón blanco.	☐	☐
7. Una silla está rota.	☐	☐
8. Un aparato está enchufado.	☐	☐

Paso 2. Ahora describa el estado de las siguientes cosas en su casa (cuarto, apartamento).

1. las luces **3.** la televisión **5.** la puerta
2. la cama **4.** las ventanas **6.** las cortinas (*curtains*)

B. ¿Cuánto sabe de la Argentina y del Uruguay? Para saber más, complete las siguientes oraciones con el participio pasado de uno de los siguientes infinitivos.

VERBOS: acelerar, celebrar, conquistar (*to conquer*), desarrollar, escribir, establecer (*to establish*), preferir, reconocer (*to recognize*), separar, traer

1. La Argentina y el Uruguay son dos países muy ________. desarrollados
2. Los dos países están ________ por el estuario del Río de la Plata. separados
3. El gaucho es una figura ________ como símbolo nacional. reconocida
4. En la Pampa, hay grandes fincas ________ en la época colonial. establecidas
5. El mate es la bebida ________ de los argentinos y uruguayos. preferida
6. Los guaraníes son un pueblo indígena ________ por los españoles. conquistado
7. Los guaraníes murieron a causa de enfermedades ________ por los europeos. traídas
8. «El Aleph» es un cuento ________ por el famoso escritor argentino Jorge Luis Borges. escrito
9. El carnaval de Montevideo, ________ por cuarenta días, es una de las celebraciones de más duración en el mundo. celebrado
10. En Buenos Aires y Montevideo, el ritmo de la vida es muy ________. acelerado

C. Comentarios sobre el mundo de hoy. Complete cada párrafo con el participio pasado de los verbos de cada lista.

VERBOS: desperdiciar (*to waste*), destruir, hacer, reciclar

Todos los días, Ud. tira[a] a la basura aproximadamente media libra[b] de papel. Todo ese papel ____[1] constituye un gran número de árboles ____.[2] Esto es un buen motivo para que Ud. empiece un proyecto de recuperación de papeles hoy en su oficina. Ud. puede completar el ciclo del reciclaje únicamente si compra productos ____[3] con materiales ____.[4]

[a]*throw* [b]media… *half a pound*

(Continúa.)

Autoprueba

Give the infinitive of these past participles as adjectives.

1. estudiadas
2. leído
3. vistos
4. dicha
5. abiertas
6. bebido

Answers: **1.** *estudiar* **2.** *leer* **3.** *ver* **4.** *decir* **5.** *abrir* **6.** *beber*

Vocabulario útil

colgar (cuelgo) (gu)	to hang
enchufar	to plug in

El mate, una tradición en la Argentina y el Uruguay

Prác. C, Answers:
1. *desperdiciado* **2.** *destruidos* **3.** *hechos* **4.** *reciclados*

- Past participles are also related to many nouns that students already know. Follow a similar procedure with these nouns: *el/la aficionado/a, el estado, el helado, el/la invitado/a, la llegada, el pescado, el puesto, el resfriado, la salida, el vestido, la vista.*
- Provide additional examples to contrast the English simple past and past participle with the Spanish, e.g., *I did the homework. The homework is done.* vs. *Hice la tarea. La tarea está hecha.*
- Explain that another common structure with the past participle is *tener + object + past participle.*

  Tengo los ejercicios preparados.

  This construction is equivalent to the present perfect (presented in the next grammar section) but emphasizes the completion and recentness of the action. Notice that *estar + past participle* is impersonal. The *tener + object + past participle* tells who did the action.

Preliminary Exercises

Have students express the following ideas in Spanish.

¿Cómo se dice en español?

1. a game won
2. the lost luggage
3. a repeated sentence
4. the tired child
5. dead animals
6. the broken cup

Prác. A: Suggestions

- In *Paso 1,* ask students to supply the infinitives from which each past participle adjective is derived.
- Have students invent additional sentences to describe the classroom. Others respond *cierto* or *falso.* Write on the board verbs that are useful for describing the classroom.

Prác. B: Note

There is more information about *mate* in *A leer: Lectura cultural.*

Prác. C: Note

These passages are adapted, slightly simplified, from authentic materials from Mexico and Spain. Have students read completely through each paragraph before completing it.

Multimedia: Internet

Have students search the Internet to find out what Latin American countries are doing to conserve natural resources and to limit the amount of contaminants released into the environment. Encourage students to use Spanish and English search words to find websites. You may want to assign specific topics, areas, or countries to groups of students and have them prepare a brief oral presentation based on their findings.

Con.: Optional

Situaciones. *¿Cuál es la situación en este momento? Conteste según el modelo.*

MODELO: *Natalia les tiene que* ***escribir*** *una tarjeta a sus abuelos.* →
La tarjeta no está ***escrita*** *todavía.*

1. *Los Sres. García deben* ***abrir*** *la tienda más temprano.*
2. *Pablo tiene que* ***cerrar*** *las ventanas; entra un aire frío.*
3. *Los niños siempre esperan que la tierra se* ***cubra*** *de nieve para la Navidad.*
4. *Delia debe* ***poner*** *la mesa. Los invitados llegan a las nueve.*
5. *Claro está que la contaminación va a contribuir a la* ***destrucción*** *de la capa de ozono.*
6. *Es posible que los ingenieros* ***descubran*** *el error en la construcción del reactor nuclear.*
7. *Se debe* ***resolver*** *pronto el problema de la falta de energía.*

Con. A: Possible Answers

En el dibujo A,… En el dibujo B,…
1. *la cocina está desordenada. / está ordenada.* **2.** *el grifo está abierto. / está cerrado.* **3.** *la puerta del refrigerador está abierta. / está cerrada.* **4.** *la mesa no está puesta. / está puesta.* **5.** *el pan no está cortado. / está cortado.* **6.** *el patio está cubierto de nieve. / no hay nieve.* **7.** *el perro está agitado. / el gato está dormido.*

Con. A: Variation

Have students use the preterite and the imperfect to create stories based on the drawings. Ask questions to help them get started: *¿Qué hora es en el dibujo? ¿Cuántas personas hay en la casa? ¿Quiénes son?*, and so on.

Con. B: Suggestion

Review the meaning of *ya* and *todavía*.

Con. C: Suggestion

Have students work in groups and compete with each other to see which group can find the most associations for a given item.

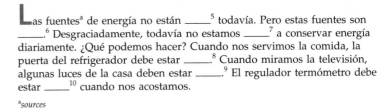

VERBOS: acostumbrar, agotar (*to use up*), apagar, bajar, cerrar, limitar

5. agotadas 6. limitadas 7. acostumbrados 8. cerrada 9. apagadas 10. bajado

Las fuentes[a] de energía no están ___[5] todavía. Pero estas fuentes son ___.[6] Desgraciadamente, todavía no estamos ___[7] a conservar energía diariamente. ¿Qué podemos hacer? Cuando nos servimos la comida, la puerta del refrigerador debe estar ___.[8] Cuando miramos la televisión, algunas luces de la casa deben estar ___.[9] El regulador termómetro debe estar ___[10] cuando nos acostamos.

[a]*sources*

Conversación

A. ¡Ojo alerta! Las cocinas de los dibujos A y B se diferencian (*differ*) en por lo menos siete aspectos. En parejas, encuéntrenlas todas. Usen participios pasados como adjetivos si pueden.

Vocabulario útil

el grifo faucet
agitar
cortar
(des)ordenar

B. ¿Hecho o por hacer todavía (*yet to be done*)**?**

Paso 1. Haga oraciones completas que sean verdaderas para Ud. Use un participio pasado como adjetivo, según el modelo. Si Ud. no tiene ninguna de estas cosas, diga «No tengo… », según el modelo.

MODELOS: una tarea para la clase de ___ (escribir) →
Mi tarea para la clase de inglés ya está **escrita.**
Mi tarea para la clase de inglés no está **escrita** todavía.
No tengo que hacer ninguna tarea **escrita** para ninguna clase.

1. un informe (oral/escrito) para la clase de ___ (organizar)
2. una presentación oral para la clase de ___ (preparar)
3. los problemas para la clase de matemáticas (resolver)
4. ¿ ?

Paso 2. Ahora, en parejas, comparen sus respuestas. Digan a la clase algo que tienen en común.

C. ¡Rápidamente! Dé Ud. el nombre de…

1. algo contaminado
2. una persona muy/poco organizada
3. un programa de computadora bien diseñado
4. un edificio bien/mal construido
5. algo que puede estar cerrado o abierto
6. un servicio necesitado por muchas personas
7. un tipo de transporte usado por muchas personas a la vez
8. algo deseado por muchas personas

Resources: Transparency 146

43 ¿Qué has hecho?

Perfect Forms: Present Perfect Indicative and Present Perfect Subjunctive

Grammar Tutorial 43
connect SPANISH
www.connectspanish.com

Gramática en acción: Una llanta desinflada

¿Qué ha pasado? ¡Ay, no! ¡Una llanta desinflada! ¡Nunca he cambiado una llanta desinflada!

¿Y Ud.? Alguna vez…

1. ¿le ha cambiado una llanta desinflada a un carro?
2. ¿le ha revisado el aceite al coche?
3. ¿le ha reparado otras cosas al coche?
4. ¿ha tenido un accidente automovilístico?
5. ¿ha excedido el límite de velocidad en la autopista?

Present Perfect Indicative / El presente perfecto de indicativo

haber + *past participle* (-ado/-ido)			
he **habl**ado	I have spoken	hemos **habl**ado	we have spoken
has **habl**ado	you have spoken	habéis **habl**ado	you have spoken
ha **habl**ado	you have spoken, he/she has spoken	han **habl**ado	you/they have spoken

1. Present Perfect Indicative

In English, to say *I have* (*written, spoken* . . .), you use a present tense form of *to have* plus the past participle. This compound tense is called the *present perfect*. The Spanish equivalent, **el presente perfecto,** is formed with present tense forms of **haber** plus the past participle.

In general, the Spanish present perfect tense is used just like the English present perfect.

No **hemos estado** aquí antes.
We haven't been here before.

Me he divertido mucho.
I've had a very good time.

Ya le **han escrito** la carta.
They've already written her the letter.

¡OJO!

Haber, an auxiliary verb, is never interchangeable with **tener** when forming the present perfect.

2. Form and Placement

Note the following about **el presente perfecto.**

- The form of the past participle never changes.
- **Haber** and the past participle are never separated and their order never changes.

Ella **ha cambiado llantas** varias veces.
She's changed tires several times.

¿Por qué **has estacionado** tú allí?
Es el estacionamiento del jefe.
*Why have **you** parked there?*
It's the boss's parking spot.

A flat tire *What has happened? Oh, no! A flat tire! I've never changed a flat tire!*

Gramática 43
Perfect Forms: Present Perfect Indicative and Present Perfect Subjunctive

GEA: Suggestion

After reading the drawing's caption, students should be able to answer the questions. Model the response to the first question yourself, making your use of *he* very obvious in your answer and writing *he* on the board. Be sure to model both positive (*Sí, alguna vez* [*le*] *he…*) and negative (*No, nunca* [*le*] *he…*) answers.

GEA: Follow-up

Ask the following questions after completing the *GEA.*

1. *Si su coche tiene una llanta desinflada, ¿le pide a alguien que lo/la ayude a cambiarla?*
2. *¿Le dice Ud. al mecánico que le revise el aceite al coche o lo hace Ud. mismo/a?*
3. *¿Puede Ud. reparar algunos problemas o necesita siempre que se lo haga un mecánico?*

Present Perfect Indicative

Emphasis 1: Suggestions

- Model the present tense of *haber* and the formation of the present perfect.
- Emphasize that only the form that resembles the masculine singular of the past participle is used in the present perfect tense. In this construction, the past participle is not an adjective.

Emphasis 2: Suggestion

Emphasize that the object pronouns must precede the conjugated *haber* form; they are never placed after the conjugated form of *haber* nor attached to the end of the participle: *Ya la he llamado.* (*a María*) *Ya se lo he dado.* (*el trabajo a María*)

Reciclado: Students will often try to use the present perfect indicative instead of the *hace* + time + *que* construction, due to interference from English. For example, instead of *Hace un año que estudio español,* students might say **He estudiado español por un año.* Remind students regularly that Spanish speakers prefer the *hacer* construction to express time passed. Reenter this construction now.

¿Cómo se dice en español?

1. How long have you been at this university? / I have been here for two years.
2. How long have you studied Spanish? / I have studied it for only one year.
3. How long ago did you move to this town? / I moved here one year ago.

Heritage Speakers

Explíqueles a los hispanohablantes que en España se usa consistentemente el presente perfecto en lugar del pretérito para hablar de algo que ha ocurrido muy recientemente. *¿A qué hora has desayunado?* en vez de *¿A qué hora desayunaste?*

Resources: Transparency 147

← (Cont.)

Emphasis 3: Suggestion

Remind students that *hay* is a special third person (impersonal) form of *haber* meaning *there is/are.*

Preliminary Exercises

- Read the following phrases and have students give the corresponding subject pronoun: *he corrido, hemos caminado, han perdido, has dormido, habéis dicho, ha visto.*
- *¿Cómo se dice en español?*
  1. I have studied/eaten/read/gotten up.
  2. He/She has answered/promised/lived/opened.
  3. We have called/lost/written.
  4. They have traveled/run/discovered.

Present Perfect Subjunctive

Suggestions

- Review the basic concept and uses of the subjunctive (influence, emotion, doubt).
- Present the subjunctive forms of *haber.*
- Emphasize that these forms are the subjunctive counterparts of the present indicative (*he hablado, has hablado, ha hablado,* and so on).
- Point out that the first and third person singular forms (*yo, Ud./él/ella*) are the same.

Prác. A: Preliminary Exercises

Use this chain drill to practice the forms in sentences.

¿Qué hemos hecho hoy?

1. *José se ha preparado muy bien para la clase.* (*tú, el profesor, los estudiantes, Luis, Carmen y Pilar, vosotros*)
2. *Yo he empezado la lección para hoy.* (*leer, escribir, estudiar, comprender, aprender*)
3. *Lidia se ha despertado.* (*levantarse, bañarse, vestirse, desayunar, correr al* campus, *leer en la cafetería, reírse de un chiste con los amigos, ir a su primera clase*)

Prác. A: Suggestions

- Have students report what they have done or not done by saying *ya lo he hecho* or *no lo he hecho todavía.*
- Ask students to locate the present perfect tense verbs and give the infinitive.
- If students have done one of these things, ask them follow-up questions, using the preterite and imperfect.

- **No** and object pronouns always come before the form of **haber.**

Todavía **no** han escrito la carta.
They haven't written the letter yet.

Todavía **no le** han escrito la carta al presidente.
They haven't written the letter to the president yet.

¡OJO!

Remember that **acabar** + **de** + *infinitive*—not the present perfect tense—is used to state that something *has just occurred.*

Acabo de mandar la carta.
I've just mailed the letter.

3. Present Perfect of *hay*

The present perfect form of **hay** is **ha habido.** It is invariable, and it expresses both *there has been* and *there have been.*

[Práctica A–B]

Ha habido mucha discusión sobre este tema.
There has been a lot of discussion about this topic.

Ha habido muchos accidentes en esta esquina.
There have been many accidents at this corner.

Present Perfect Subjunctive / **El presente perfecto de subjuntivo**

To express *I have written* (*spoken . . .*) in a context that requires the subjunctive, use the present subjunctive forms of **haber** to form the *present perfect subjunctive* (**el presente perfecto de subjuntivo**).

The English equivalent of the Spanish present perfect subjunctive will vary according to the context, as shown in the examples on the right.

[Práctica C–D]

haya **habl**ado	hayamos **habl**ado
hayas **habl**ado	hayáis **habl**ado
haya **habl**ado	hayan **habl**ado

Es bueno que lo **hayan construido.**
It's good (that) they built (have built) it.

Me alegro de que **hayas venido.**
I'm glad (that) you've come (you came).

Es posible que lo **haya hecho.**
It's possible (that) he may have done (he did) it.

Autoprueba

Give the correct form of **haber.**

INDICATIVO	SUBJUNTIVO
1. yo ____	4. tú ____
2. Uds. ____	5. Ud. ____
3. nosotros ____	6. ellos ____

Answers: **1.** he **2.** han **3.** hemos **4.** hayas **5.** haya **6.** hayan

Práctica

A. ¡Anticipemos! El pasado y el futuro

Paso 1. Indique cuáles de las siguientes experiencias Ud. ha tenido.

1. ☐ He hecho un viaje a Europa.
2. ☐ He montado a camello (*camel*).
3. ☐ He buceado (*gone scuba diving*).
4. ☐ He ido de safari a África.
5. ☐ He comprado un auto.
6. ☐ He preparado un plato mexicano.
7. ☐ He ocupado un puesto político.
8. ☐ He tenido una mascota.
9. ☐ He escrito un poema.
10. ☐ He visto una película de Almodóvar.
11. ☐ He leído un periódico en español.
12. ☐ Me he roto el brazo o la pierna.

Heritage Speakers

- Recuérdeles a los hispanohablantes que, en el español estándar, la forma aceptada del presente de subjuntivo del verbo *haber* es *haya.* Sin embargo, hay algunos hispanohablantes que usan *haiga* en vez de *haya* en el habla diaria. Deben acordarse de que la forma apropiada es *haya* y que se recomienda evitar decir o escribir *haiga.* ¿Cuántos estudiantes hispanohablantes dicen o han oído decir *haiga* en vez de *haya*?
- Recuérdeles a los hispanohablantes que la forma *ha habido* es impersonal y que siempre se usa en la forma singular: *Ha habido muchos accidentes en esta carretera.*

Paso 2. Ahora, en parejas, hagan y contesten las siguientes preguntas. Luego digan a la clase cuál de Uds. dos es el más «atrevido» (*daring*).

1. ¿Cuál es el lugar más raro (*strange*) que has visitado en tu vida?
2. ¿Cuál es el plato o ingrediente más exótico que has comido?
3. ¿Cuál es el libro más extraordinario que has leído?
4. ¿Cuál es la cosa más peligrosa (*dangerous*) que has hecho?

B. El auto de Carmina. Carmina acaba de comprarse un auto usado. Describa lo que le ha pasado a Carmina, según el modelo.

MODELO: ir a la agencia de compra-venta →
Ha ido a la agencia de compra-venta.

1. pedirle ayuda a un amigo Le ha pedido…
2. ver diferentes coches y compararlos Ha visto… y los ha comparado.
3. mirar uno baratísimo Ha mirado…
4. revisarle las llantas Le ha revisado…
5. conducirlo para probarlo Lo ha conducido…
6. pensarlo y regresar a la agencia Lo ha pensado… y ha regresado…
7. decidir comprarlo Ha decidido…
8. comprarlo Lo ha comprado.
9. volver a casa Ha vuelto…
10. llevar a sus amigas al cine en su coche Ha llevado…

C. ¡No lo creo! ¿Tienen espíritu aventurero sus compañeros de clase? ¿Llevan una vida interesante? ¿O viven tan aburridos como una ostra? ¡A ver!

Paso 1. Indique cuál de las oraciones de cada par expresa su opinión acerca de los estudiantes de esta clase.

Vocabulario útil

escalar	to climb
hacer **autostop**	to hitchhike
el paracaidismo	skydiving

1. ☐ Creo que alguien en esta clase ha visto las pirámides de Egipto.
   ☐ Es dudoso que alguien haya visto las pirámides de Egipto.
2. ☐ Estoy seguro/a de que por lo menos uno de mis compañeros ha escalado una montaña alta.
   ☐ No creo que nadie haya escalado una montaña alta.
3. ☐ Creo que alguien ha viajado haciendo autostop.
   ☐ Dudo que alguien haya hecho autostop en un viaje.
4. ☐ Creo que alguien ha practicado el paracaidismo.
   ☐ Es improbable que alguien haya practicado el paracaidismo.
5. ☐ Estoy seguro/a de que alguien ha tomado el metro en Nueva York a medianoche.
   ☐ No creo que nadie haya tomado el metro neoyorquino a medianoche.

Paso 2. Ahora escuche las respuestas mientras su profesor(a) pregunta si alguien ha hecho estas actividades. ¿Tenía Ud. razón en el **Paso 1**?

Prác. A: Follow-up

Ask students the following questions to personalize the activity.

1. *¿Qué ha hecho Ud. hoy? ¿Ha hablado con un amigo / una amiga? ¿Ha estudiado? ¿Ha comido?*
2. *¿Qué ha hecho Ud. esta semana? ¿Ha ido a una fiesta? ¿Ha bailado? ¿Ha cantado? ¿Ha tomado Coca-Cola/cerveza/vino? ¿Ha visto alguna película?*
3. *¿Ha escrito una carta este mes? ¿Ha visitado un museo? ¿Ha salido de la ciudad? ¿Se ha levantado antes de las seis? ¿antes de las cinco? ¿Por qué tan temprano?*
4. *¿Ha depositado dinero en el banco? ¿Ha vendido o comprado algo?*

Prác. B: Optional

¿Lo ha hecho? *Responda a los siguientes mandatos usando el presente perfecto de indicativo. Use los pronombres de complemento directo e indirecto para evitar la repetición.*

MODELO: *Limpia tu cuarto.* →
Ya lo he limpiado.

1. *Arranca el coche.*
2. *Llamen Uds. al mecánico.*
3. *Abra el mapa.*
4. *Revise Ud. los frenos, por favor.*
5. *Siga las direcciones.*

Reciclado: Note the use of formal command forms in the Optional activity.

Heritage Speakers

También se dice *echar dedo* o *ir de aventón* para expresar *hacer autostop*. Pregúnteles a los hispanohablantes qué expresión usan. Si son de un país hispanohablante, pregúnteles si es común que la gente haga autostop en su país y qué tipo de persona lo haría.

Prác. C: Follow-up

Have students suggest other things that they think no one in class has ever done, for example, *No creo que nadie haya… ; Creo que nadie ha…*

D. Opiniones sobre el medio ambiente

Paso 1. ¿Qué se ha hecho en los últimos años para proteger el medio ambiente? Haga oraciones completas en el presente perfecto de indicativo. Sus oraciones pueden ser afirmativas o negativas, según su opinión.

MODELO: este país: desarrollar nuevas formas de energía renovable →
Este país (no) **ha desarrollado** nuevas formas de energía renovable.

1. este país: desarrollar la energía eólica
2. la población de esta ciudad: reciclar el papel, el plástico y el vidrio (*glass*) con regularidad
3. los seres humanos (*humans*): proteger muchas especies de animales
4. varios países: destruir zonas naturales para construir más viviendas
5. el aire de esta ciudad: contaminarse más
6. este estado: construir muchas carreteras nuevas

Paso 2. Ahora añada un comentario personal a sus oraciones del **Paso 1.** Puede ser una explicación (con el indicativo) o una reacción personal (con el subjuntivo).

MODELOS: Este país (no) ha desarrollado nuevas formas de energía renovable. →
Este país no ha desarrollado nuevas formas de energía renovable **porque tenemos mucho petróleo.**
Es terrible que este país no **haya desarrollado** nuevas formas de energía renovable todavía.

El obelisco, en la Plaza de la República (entre las avenidas Corrientes y 9 de Julio), en Buenos Aires

Conversación

A. Entrevista: ¿Lo has hecho o no?

Paso 1. Indique si Ud. ha hecho o no las siguientes cosas, según el modelo. También añada a la lista una cosa que ha hecho esta semana y una cosa que debería haber hecho (*you should have done*).

MODELOS: visitar la Argentina o el Uruguay →
He visitado la Argentina una vez.
Nunca **he visitado** la Argentina, pero sí **he visitado** el Uruguay.

1. correr en un maratón
2. manejar un Alfa Romeo
3. escribir un poema
4. actuar en una obra teatral
5. conocer a una persona famosa
6. romperse la pierna alguna vez
7. ¿ ?
8. ¿ ?

Paso 2. Ahora, usando como base algunas de las actividades del **Paso 1** que Ud. ha hecho o no, complete las siguientes oraciones con referencia a sus compañeros de clase o a su profesor(a). Nombre a una persona diferente en cada oración. **¡OJO!** Tiene que decidir si va a usar el indicativo o el subjuntivo en estas oraciones.

MODELO: Creo que… → Creo que **la profesora ha manejado** un Alfa Romeo.

1. Creo que…
2. Dudo que…
3. Es probable que…
4. Estoy seguro/a de que…
5. Ojalá que…

Paso 3. Lea sus oraciones del **Paso 2** a la clase entera. La persona nombrada en su oración va a decir si la oración es cierta o falsa. ¿Quién acertó más (*guessed most accurately*)?

Prác. D: Preliminary Exercises

- Read the following sentences and have students tell whether the present perfect indicative or the present perfect subjunctive is used.
  1. *Dice que ha hablado con ella.*
  2. *Es posible que haya hablado con ella.*
  3. *No, no han repetido las palabras.*
  4. *No creo que hayan repetido las palabras.*
  5. *Me alegro de que me hayas escrito.*
  6. *No vengas a menos que me hayas escrito antes.*
- Have students give the subjunctive equivalents: *he hablado, he repetido, has comido, has manejado, ha mandado, ha venido, hemos podido, hemos alquilado, han comprendido, se han acostado.*

Prác. D, Paso 1: Answers

1. *…(no) ha desarrollado…* **2.** *…(no) ha reciclado…* **3.** *…(no) han (hemos) protegido…* **4.** *…(no) han destruido…* **5.** *…(no) se ha contaminado…* **6.** *…(no) ha construido…*

Con. A: Suggestions

- *Paso 1.* Model one or two series of sentences about yourself.
- *Paso 2.* Model some possible reactions to the sentences: (No) *Dudo que…, Es imposible que…, Estoy seguro/a de que…, Es obvio que…*

Con. A: Follow-up

- Have students complete *Paso 1.* Then, for each item, ask one student to respond, making sure that students use the present perfect indicative in their responses.
- After students have completed *Paso 2,* ask several students to read their sentences. The person named should tell whether the statement is true or false.

Con.: Optional

Ask the following questions.

¿Qué es posible que hayan hecho las siguientes personas?

1. *Un hombre con máscara sale corriendo de un banco, con una bolsa en la mano.*
2. *Un joven está saliendo de una lavandería con un montón de ropa limpia.*
3. *Un sábado de otoño, a las cuatro y media de la tarde, muchas personas están saliendo de un estadio.*
4. *Unos turistas están hablando ansiosamente con un policía. La mujer no lleva bolsa.*
5. *Una familia está saliendo de McDonald's.*

B. ¿Verdad o mentira?

Paso 1. Invente Ud. tres declaraciones sobre cosas que ha hecho y no ha hecho en su vida. Dos de las declaraciones deben ser verdaderas y una debe ser mentira.

MODELO: **He hecho** un viaje a Sudamérica.
Nunca **he conocido** a nadie famoso.
He visto muchas películas en español.

Paso 2. Lea sus declaraciones a un compañero o compañera. Él/Ella va a tratar de encontrar la mentira.

MODELO: **Creo** que **has hecho** un viaje a Sudamérica y que **has visto** muchas películas en español. **Dudo** que no **hayas conocido** a nadie famoso.

Nota **comunicativa**

El pluscuamperfecto: *había* + *participio pasado*

Use the past participle with the imperfect form of **haber** (**había, habías,...**) to talk about what you had—or had not—done before a given time in the past. This form, called the *past perfect* (**el pluscuamperfecto**), is used like its English equivalent.

Antes de graduarme en la escuela secundaria, no **había estudiado** español.	*Before graduating from high school, I hadn't studied Spanish.*
Antes de 1995, **habíamos vivido** en Kansas todo el tiempo.	*Before 1995, we had always lived in Kansas.*

C. Intercambios. En parejas, hagan y contesten preguntas basadas en las siguientes frases. Inventen por lo menos una pregunta original.

MODELO: ¿qué cosa? / no haber aprendido a hacer antes del año pasado →
E1: ¿Qué cosa no **habías aprendido** a hacer antes del año pasado?
E2: Pues… no **había aprendido** a nadar. Aprendí a nadar este año en la clase de natación.

1. ¿qué cosa? / no haber aprendido a hacer antes de ahora
2. ¿qué materia? / no haber estudiado antes de venir a esta universidad
3. ¿qué deporte? / (no) haber practicado mucho antes de llegar a los 12 años
4. ¿qué viaje? / haber hecho varias veces antes de ahora
5. ¿qué libro clásico o importante? / no haber leído antes de venir a esta universidad
6. ¿qué decisión? / no haber tomado antes de cumplir 18 años
7. ¿ ?

Mundo interactivo

You should now be prepared to work with Scenario 8, Activity 2 in Connect Spanish (**www.connectspanish.com**).

Con. B: Suggestion

Do *Paso 2* as a whole-class activity.

Con. C: Follow-up

- Have students describe what they had already done or not done by the time they turned 18 years old: *Antes de cumplir 18 años, ¿qué había hecho? ¿Qué no había hecho?*
- Have students complete the following sentences logically using the past perfect tense.
  1. *Antes de 1492, Cristóbal Colón no ______.*
  2. *Antes de 1938, la Segunda Guerra Mundial no ______.*
  3. *Antes de 1990, mis padres/hijos (no) ______.*
  4. *Antes de 2000, yo (no) ______.*
- Have students talk about things they had done or had not done before the year 2012. Have them begin with the cues given, then invent their own.

  ¿Qué cosas habían hecho, o no habían hecho, Uds. antes del año 2012? Dé oraciones nuevas según las indicaciones.
  Antes de 2012, (todavía no) habíamos… estudiar español, asistir a esta universidad, graduarnos en la escuela superior, escuchar un concierto, ver una comedia española, comer flan, ¿ ?
- Use the following cues for additional practice.

  ¿Qué cosas no habían hecho… y no han hecho todavía?
  No habíamos…
  visitar la Patagonia
  viajar a Moscú
  aprender ruso
  conocer a Ricky Martin
  ¿ ?
  Y no lo hemos hecho todavía.

Redacción: Have students complete the items in *Con. C,* taking notes about their partner's activities. Then assign *Con. C* for written homework. Students should write at least 10 sentences (2 sentences for 5 of the 7 items). The first sentence should be what their partner had or had not done. The second should be about themselves. Suggest that students use phrases such as: *Pero yo sí había… Yo tampoco había…*

Nota comunicativa

Suggestion

The past perfect is presented here and practiced in *Con. C.* Use additional activities, such as the following, if you prefer to stress this tense.

Jaimito es un acusón (new). *Siempre le dice a su madre las cosas que ha hecho Laura, su hermana mayor. ¿Qué le dijo a su madre ayer?*

MODELO: *Jaimito le dijo que Laura había dicho una mentira.*
mirar la televisión toda la tarde
no estudiar
perder sus libros
romper un plato
faltar a clase
comer todo el pastel
pegarle
¿ ?

Un poco de todo

Bright Idea

Preliminary Exercises

- Review with students the formation of the past participles in Spanish, starting with regular *-ar, -er,* and *-ir* verbs.
- Have students give you the irregular past participle forms for the following verbs.

abrir	*hacer*	*romper*
cubrir	*morir*	*ver*
decir	*poner*	*volver*
escribir		

- Have students provide the past participles for the following verbs and then give the English equivalents. Remind them to identify the root verb first.

componer	*devolver*	*prescribir*
contradecir	*predecir*	*suponer*
descubrir		

- Write the following model on the board and have students work in pairs to ask and answer questions using the cues.

MODELO: *escribir la carta* →

E1: *¿Ya está* escrita *la carta?*

E2: *No, no la* he escrito.

E1: *¡Hombre! Es imposible que no la* hayas escrito *todavía.*

1. *hacer las maletas*
2. *comprar los boletos*
3. *hacer la cena*
4. *facturar el equipaje*
5. *sacudir los muebles*
6. *poner la mesa*
7. *comprar el fax*
8. *salvar la información en la computadora*
9. *apagar la computadora*
10. *entregarle el trabajo al profesor / a la profesora*

A: Suggestion

Bring or have students bring additional pieces that make commentaries about modern life. The pieces can be in English or in Spanish. Use them to elicit discussion in Spanish.

Un poco de todo

A. Dos dibujos, un punto de vista. Los dibujos A y B comentan aspectos del mismo tema.

Vocabulario útil

el arado plow	**la flor**	**la mecanización**	**el tractor**
el burro	**la gente**	**la mula**	
la deshumanización			

(A)

(B)

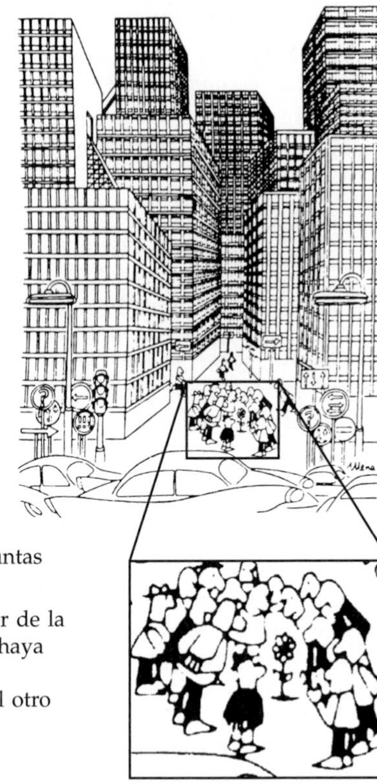

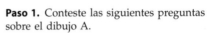

Cartoon by Mena, ALI Brussels.

Paso 1. Conteste las siguientes preguntas sobre el dibujo A.

1. ¿Qué se ha comprado el agricultor de la izquierda? ¿Qué es probable que haya vendido para comprarlo?
2. ¿Qué es «más moderno», según el otro agricultor?
3. ¿Qué desventaja tiene el tractor?

Paso 2. Conteste las siguiente preguntas sobre el dibujo B.

1. Describa la ciudad que se ve en el dibujo.
2. ¿Qué ha descubierto la gente? ¿Por qué mira con tanto interés?
3. ¿Qué hicieron primero antes de construir esta ciudad? ¿Qué destruyeron?

Paso 3. Ahora explique su opinión personal sobre estos dos dibujos. ¿Son chistosos (*funny*)? ¿serios? ¿Es probable que los dos artistas estén de acuerdo sobre algunos aspectos del mundo de hoy? ¿Sobre qué aspectos?

B. Lengua y cultura: El Parque Nacional los Glaciares. Complete the following paragraphs with the correct form of the words in parentheses, as suggested by context. When two possibilities are given, select the correct word. Form adverbs with **-mente,** as needed. **¡OJO!** *PP:* = present perfect (indicative or subjunctive) *P/I:* = preterite or imperfect. Other infinitives are either present subjunctive or must remain in the infinitive form.

Algunos aspectos de la cultura y de la geografía de la Argentina son bien conocidos por todos. Seguro que Uds. (*PP:* ver[1]) bailar el tango, porque es un baile que se (*PP:* hacer[2]) muy popular (reciente[3]) entre los bailes de salón.[a] Y casi todos (saben/conocen[4]) qué es la Pampa y quiénes (son/estar[5]) los gauchos.

B: **Answers: 1.** *han visto* **2.** *ha hecho* **3.** *recientemente* **4.** *saben* **5.** *son*

El Cerro (*Mt.*) Fitz Roy, en la Patagonia

Pero es fácil (olvidar[6]) que la Argentina es un país larguísimo que se extiende desde la selva[b] tropical en la frontera[c] con el Brasil hasta la Antártida. Por eso (el/la[7]) país tiene una increíble variedad climática y geográfica.

Si Ud. es aficionado/a al ecoturismo, (se/le[8]) aconsejamos que (visitar[9]) el Parque Nacional los Glaciares, en (el/la[10]) región de la Patagonia, al sur del país. El gobierno argentino (*P/I:* crear[11]) el parque en 1937, y en 1982 la UNESCO (lo/la[12]) (*P/I:* declarar[13]) Patrimonio Natural de la Humanidad. Allí, en las 600.000 hectáreas[d] del parque, los visitantes pueden explorar impresionantes glaciares. Es posible (escalar[14]) montañas de hielo[e] con grandes precipicios, que es un desafío[f] aun[g] para los (mejor[15]) escaladores.[h]

6. *olvidar* **7.** *el* **8.** *le* **9.** *visite* **10.** *la* **11.** *creó* **12.** *lo* **13.** *declaró* **14.** *escalar* **15.** *mejores*

[a]bailes... *ballroom dances* [b]*jungle* [c]*frontier* [d]*hectares (1 hectare = 2.47 acres)* [e]*ice* [f]*challenge* [g]*even* [h]*climbers*

Comprensión. Conteste las siguientes preguntas.

1. ¿Qué aspectos de la cultura argentina son bien conocidos?
2. ¿Por qué hay gran variedad climática y geográfica en la Argentina?
3. ¿En qué región está el Parque Nacional Los Glaciares?
4. ¿Por qué es tan bueno el Parque para el alpinismo (*mountain climbing*)?

En su comunidad

Entreviste a una persona hispana de su universidad o ciudad sobre cuestiones medioambientales relacionados con su país de origen.

PREGUNTAS POSIBLES

- ¿Hay problemas de contaminación en su ciudad o país de origen? ¿Qué los causa?
- ¿Qué está haciendo el país para preservar los recursos naturales? ¿Y para disminuir la contaminación?
- ¿Ve un cambio en la actitud de las personas de su país o ciudad con relación a la conservación de los recursos naturales?
- ¿Hay programas de reciclaje? ¿Cree que son efectivos?

B: Suggestion

Call students' attention to *la Antártida*, the correct way to express Antarctica in standard Spanish.

B: Note

The following grammar topics are included in *Lengua y cultura:* apocopation of adjectives, adverb formation with *-mente*, object pronouns, use of the infinitive, present perfect, subjunctive vs. indicative, preterite and imperfect, *ser* vs. *estar, que* vs. *lo que.*

B, Comprensión: Answers

1. *el tango, la Pampa, los gauchos* **2.** *Porque el país es larguísimo.* **3.** *Está en la Patagonia.* **4.** *Porque tiene montañas de hielo con grandes precipicios.*

Redacción: Using the *Lengua y cultura* paragraphs as a model, ask students to write a similar description of this country. Allow students to use as much of the structure of the text's paragraphs as they need to. Set expectations about length.

After students have handed in their compositions, tally the places mentioned in them and share that information with the whole class to start a discussion. Is there consensus about the tourist attractions or features of this country that were mentioned? Why or why not?

En su comunidad

Suggestions

- Remind students to get the following basic information: the informant's country of origin, how long he or she has lived in this country, and if the informant visits his or her country of origin frequently.
- This activity could instead be assigned as an online research project on a country of the student's choice or assigned by you.
- See the IM for additional suggestions and guidelines.

Resources: Desenlace

In the *Cap. 15* segment of "Chapter-by-Chapter Supplementary Materials" in the IM, you will find a chapter-culminating activity. You can use this activity to consolidate and review the vocabulary and grammar skills students have acquired.

Multimedia: Internet

Have students search the Internet for information about *la Patagonia, la Pampa,* and *los gauchos.* Then have them present a written or oral report on one of the topics.

TelePuntos

Note

Pages 462–467 are optional. You may cover some, all, or none of this material in class, or assign it to students—as a group or individually—for homework or extra credit. Pages 468–469 (*En resumen: En este capítulo*) are a summary of all of the chapter's active material.

Antes de mirar

Suggestion

Have a whole-class discussion about these topics. Write *medidas* on the board and ask students to predict how many of them they will see in the show.

Programa 15

- This show will be relatively accessible to students.
- You may wish to focus students' attention on the variety of ways to express concepts related to *waste* and *recycling* in Spanish: *la basura, los desperdicios, los desechos, el reciclaje, el reciclado.*
- Laura's pronunciation of the word *páneles* (i.e. *panels*) is the standard in México, but not in other countries, where the preferred stress for these words is *panel* and *paneles.*
- Emphasize to students that the more carefully they study the preliminary activities (*Antes de mirar, Vocabulario de este programa,* and *Fragmento del guion*), the more they will understand. Scanning *Después de mirar* before viewing is also an excellent strategy.

Fragmento del guion

Note

Virtually all of the first segment of the show is given to students in this format.

Al mirar

Suggestion

Make sure that students read the options in both columns before they start watching. This will serve as an advance organizer for viewing.

TELEPUNTOS

SALU2

«Por ende (*Therefore*), nuestros modelos a seguir son exactamente aquellos establecidos por la EPA y la jerarquía del manejo de desperdicios sólidos (*solid waste management*) que ellos presentan.»

Antes de mirar

Piense en las medidas (*actions*) que se pueden tomar para proteger el medio ambiente a distintos niveles (*levels*): a nivel personal, a nivel gubernamental (*government*) local y a nivel gubernamental nacional. En su opinión, ¿son suficientes las medidas que Ud., su ciudad y su país están tomando? ¿Qué otras se deberían tomar (*should be taken*)?

PROGRAMA 15: EcoSalu2

En este programa se muestran reportajes de tres países diferentes que presentan diversas maneras de proteger el medio ambiente.

Vocabulario de este programa

encantador(a)	charming	**el desecho**	refuse, waste
en la actualidad	currently	**prensado/a**	compacted, flattened
la factura	bill, invoice	**el neumático, la goma**	**la llanta**
a la larga	in the long run	**a corto plazo**	short term
el/la ingeniero/a	engineer	**la red vial**	road system
único/a	only	**quedarse atrás**	to be left behind
la ranita	little frog	**experimentar**	to experience
promover (promuevo)	to promote	**por muy buen camino**	on the right track
la sigla	initial		
el vidrio	glass		

Fragmento del guion

LAURA: Hoy estamos en una casa en la que[a] se han hecho muchos cambios para lograr[b] más eficiencia medioambiental. Es una casa del año de 1929, pero está totalmente remodelada. Las casas viejas con frecuencia son de construcción sólida, pero poco eficientes en cuanto a[c] conservación de energía.

La primera decisión fue poner páneles solares en el techo.[d] Como en California hay tanto sol, las necesidades de energía de la familia quedan cubiertas[e] con energía solar exclusivamente.

Esta familia no ha pagado ni un centavo[f] a la compañía eléctrica desde que instalaron los páneles solares. La casa también cuenta con[g] páneles solares para el agua caliente. Con estos páneles, la temperatura del agua puede llegar hasta 140 grados Fahrenheit, es decir, 60 grados centígrados. Incluso hasta hay[h] páneles solares para la calefacción de la alberca.[i]

Para asegurar el ahorro[j] de energía, en la casa se usan ventanas y puertas eficientes, bombillas[k] y aparatos eléctricos de bajo consumo.

[a]la... *which* [b]*achieve* [c]en... *regarding* [d]*roof* [e]quedan... *are met* [f]ni... *not one cent* [g]cuenta... tiene [h]Incluso... *There are even* [i]piscina [j]asegurar... *ensure the saving* [k]*light bulbs*

«Con todas estas medidas, los habitantes de la casa dejan un impacto medioambiental mucho menor al que (*than that which*) se deje la mayoría de los hogares (*homes*) de los países ricos.»

Mundo interactivo

Continue your work as an intern at HispanaVisión with Laura Sánchez Tejada, the roving reporter of *Salu2*, as you complete Scenario 8, Activities 1 and 2 in Connect Spanish (**www.connectspanish.com**).

Al mirar

Mientras mira el programa, empareje las siguientes iniciativas ecológicas con las ciudades o países correspondientes.

INICIATIVAS

1. __b__ una casa vieja de gran eficiencia medioambiental
2. __f__ el reciclado de neumáticos
3. __a__ el Departamento de Administración de Desperdicios Sólidos, regulado por la agencia EPA
4. __e__ Bicing
5. __d__ Ecobici
6. __c__ iniciativas similares de bicicleta

LUGARES

a. Puerto Rico
b. Los Ángeles
c. Berlín y París
d. México, D.F.
e. Barcelona (España)
f. China

Después de mirar

A. ¿Está claro? Complete las siguientes oraciones según el programa.

1. Los habitantes de la casa remodelada no pagan mucho dinero / ni un centavo a la compañía de electricidad.
2. En Puerto Rico hay solo un centro / muchos centros de reciclaje.
3. Los materiales reciclados se convierten en nuevos materiales en Puerto Rico / otros países.
4. Bicing es una iniciativa en España / en España y en otros países de Europa también.
5. Ecobici es un programa de comprar / alquilar bicicletas a bajo precio.
6. La Avenida de la Reforma se cierra al tráfico todos los fines de semana / domingos.

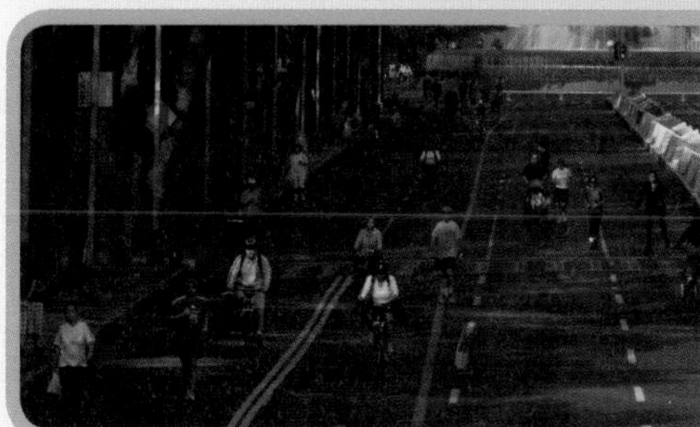

«En México hay muy pocos carriles (*lanes*) especiales para bicis. Pero los domingos, una de las arterias principales de la ciudad, la Avenida de la Reforma, se cierra a los autos por varios kilómetros y se prestan las bicis gratis.»

B. Un poco más. Haga listas de los siguientes detalles del programa.

1. las reformas que se han hecho en la casa remodelada
2. los materiales que se reciclan en Puerto Rico
3. los países a los que (*which*) Puerto Rico exporta el material reciclado
4. dos iniciativas ecológicas en México, D.F.

B: Answers: 1. *páneles solares en el techo, ventanas eficientes, bombillas y aparatos eléctricos de bajo consumo* **2.** *basura, vidrio, papel, metal, plástico* **3.** *los Estados Unidos, China* **4.** *Ecobici; cerrar la Avenida de la Reforma a los autos los domingos*

C. Y ahora, Uds. En grupos, hablen sobre las iniciativas para la reducción de tráfico que presenta el último reportaje del programa de hoy. ¿Hay alguna iniciativa similar en su país? ¿Creen Uds. que estos programas son necesarios en su ciudad? ¿Creen que son prácticos? Justifiquen sus respuestas.

Sobre el programa

Para este programa, Laura no tuvo que ir muy lejos para encontrar una «ecocasa». La casa del reportaje es la[a] de la productora[b] de *Salu2*, una argentina que llegó a California hace más de una década, atraída[c] por la meca del cine, como tantas personas de todo el mundo. Como pasa con frecuencia, las cosas no salieron tal como ella lo había pensado[d] y ha terminado[e] como productora de televisión, un trabajo que cada vez le gusta más.[f]

[a]*that* [b]*producer* [c]*attracted* [d]*tal… as she thought (they would)* [e]*ended up* [f]*cada… she likes more and more (each day)*

Producción personal

Filme un corto (*short segment*) en defensa de su propia (*own*) posición sobre un tema de interés ecológico. Puede ser a favor o en contra de alguna medida o iniciativa. Para su corto, puede entrevistar a algunos expertos y/o tomar datos de otras fuentes (*sources*) y usar su voz en off.

Después de mirar

B: Suggestion

Have a contest to see which student can get the most correct answers.

C: Suggestions

- Ask students to research some of these initiatives online, as homework, so that they come to class ready to discuss the topic.
- Encourage students to disagree and to voice their views strongly. Introduce phrases for doing so, such as: *Lo siento, pero no estoy de acuerdo. Creo que estás muy equivocado/a. No creo que tengas todos los datos necesarios. ¡No se puede sostener esa opinión con datos!* And so on.

Sobre el programa

Optional

1. *¿Cómo puede uno referirse a una casa medioambientalmente eficiente?* (*ecocasa*)
2. *¿De quién es la casa?* (*de la productora de* Salu2)
3. *¿Cuánto tiempo hace que ella vive en California?* (*más de una década*)
4. *¿Por qué llegó a California esta mujer?* (*Quería trabajar en el cine.*)

Producción personal

See the IM for additional suggestions for this chapter's assignment as well as for general guidelines and suggestions for video assignments.

Lectura cultural

Notes

- The Instructor's Edition on this page offers some additional information on the country of focus. For more information about the country of focus, see the chapter's opening pages and the IM.
- See the IM for some expressions used in Argentina and Uruguay.

First Reading: Notes

- The Iguazu River has 275 waterfalls along 2.7 kilometers (1.7 miles) of the river.
- The *Río de la Plata* is considered by some actually to be a sea, just off the Atlantic Ocean; others see it as the widest river on Earth. The estuary reaches a width of 220 kilometers (140 miles) at its mouth. It is the location of the two largest cities and capitals of both countries, Buenos Aires and Montevideo.
- *El ombú*, known in English only as the shady tree, is a large tree with a wide top (which creates a lot of shade below it) and a trunk of soft wood. The trees can live to be hundreds of years old.

En otros países hispanos

Suggestion

Brazil, another megadiverse country, is also a member of the group.

Exploración lingüística

Ask students to find the following in the reading. Some of these words are glossed and some are not.

- *Cognados relacionados con la geografía (la diversidad, el glaciar, el pico, el monte, el estuario, etcétera)*
- *Otras palabras nuevas relacionadas con la geografía (los límites, las cataratas, la frontera, la cordillera, el río, la pampa, etcétera)*
- *Adjetivos que describen la naturaleza (natural, formidable, impresionante, interminable)*

Tres símbolos argentinos y uruguayos

Notes

- *Yerba mate* is made of the leaves of the *mate* shrub. It is popular not only in Argentina and Uruguay but also in Brazil and Paraguay. Traditionally, *mate* is drunk out of a dry gourd shell (also called *el mate*), into which the *mate* leaves are placed and water is poured. The drink is sipped through a *bombilla*, a straw-like instrument that allows one to drink without getting leaves in one's mouth. As the tea is drunk, more hot water is poured over the leaves.
- Because of the availability of the Pampa as a range for cattle, Argentina has excellent cattle and beef. A common meal is *el asado*, the Argentine version of a barbecue. *El bife* is a standard beef cut, a type of steak.

Una cita

Notes

- Uruguay's official name is *la República Oriental del Uruguay*. The adjective *oriental* comes from *el oriente*, literally, the east.
- Education is of great importance to Uruguayans; the country's literacy rate (98%) is one of the highest in Latin America.

A LEER

Lectura cultural

La Argentina y el Uruguay

Tanto el Uruguay como la Argentina son países orgullosos[a] de la belleza[b] y la diversidad de su naturaleza. De norte a sur y de este a oeste, la Argentina tiene formidables atracciones naturales. Al norte, donde convergen los límites[c] con el Brasil y el Paraguay, están las cataratas[d] del Iguazú, una de las maravillas del mundo natural. Al sur se encuentra el impresionante glaciar Perito Moreno. Al oeste, en la frontera con Chile, la cordillera[e] de los Andes ostenta[f] el pico[g] más alto de todo el continente americano: el monte Aconcagua, de 6.962 metros (22.841 pies) de altura. Al este, el río Uruguay, que marca la totalidad de la frontera[h] entre el país del mismo nombre y la Argentina, se une con el río Paraná para formar el estuario del Río de la Plata. Y en el centro, en un territorio también compartido[i] con el Uruguay, se encuentran la Pampa, una interminable planicie[j] de tierras para el ganado[k] y el cultivo de granos. Al sur profundo, la Argentina continúa más allá del Estrecho de Magallanes[l] hasta la misma Antártida.

¿Se sienten orgullosos (*proud*) de la belleza natural de su zona las personas de su estado/provincia?

Por su parte, el Uruguay contiene los Humedales de Santa Lucía y del Este. Son tierras cubiertas de agua que mantienen ecosistemas de gran valor[m] medioambiental y el mayor parque de ombúes[n] del mundo.

[a]*proud* [b]*beauty* [c]*borders* [d]*waterfalls* [e]*mountain range* [f]*is proud to show off* [g]*summit* [h]*border* [i]*shared* [j]*plain* [k]*cattle* [l]Estrecho... *Straight of Magellan* [m]*value* [n]*large shade trees*

En otros países hispanos

- **En Costa Rica, Colombia, el Ecuador, México, el Perú y Venezuela** Estas naciones están entre los diecisiete países megadiversos identificados por el Centro de Monitoreo de Conservación Ambiental, un organismo[a] del Programa de las Naciones Unidas para el Medio Ambiente (el PNUMA). Los países megadiversos, en su mayoría tropicales, son países que tienen el mayor porcentaje de biodiversidad en el planeta.
- **En España** En la actualidad, este país europeo está invirtiendo[b] en el desarrollo de las energías eólica y solar, ya que[c] el país disfruta de[d] innumerables horas de sol y buenas zonas de viento.

[a]*agency* [b]*investing* [c]ya... *since* [d]disfruta... *enjoys*

La Garganta del Diablo (*Devil's Throat*), en las Cataratas del Iguazú

Tres símbolos argentinos y uruguayos

- **El mate** También conocido como la yerba mate, es una hierba de la que[a] se hace un tipo de té, inmensamente popular en el Uruguay y la Argentina. La tradición de tomar mate en un grupo de amigos es muy uruguaya.
- **El tango** Este baile se originó en la Argentina y desarrolló su propia[b] forma en el Uruguay también. Se ha hecho popular en todo el mundo no solo como baile de pareja, sino[c] también como un estilo musical.
- **La Pampa** Este inmenso territorio abarca[d] partes de la Argentina, el Uruguay y el Brasil. Es la tierra del gaucho, el *cowboy* sudamericano, quien ahora es solo un personaje[e] folclórico. Para ver a un gaucho hoy día, es necesario visitar una estancia[f] modelo.

[a]hierba... *herb from which* [b]*own* [c]*but rather* [d]*spreads over* [e]*character* [f]finca argentina

Una cita

«Sean los Orientales[a] tan ilustrados[b] como valientes.»

José Gervasio Artigas (1764–1850), héroe nacional y padre de la independencia uruguaya

Es el ideal de la cultura uruguaya. Significa que es necesario luchar[c] por lo que uno quiere, pero también es necesario tener conocimiento[d] para actuar sabiamente.[e]

[a]Sean... *May people from Uruguay be* [b]*educated* [c]*to fight* [d]*knowledge* [e]*wisely*

COMPRENSIÓN

1. ¿Qué destino turístico se destaca (*stands out*) en la Argentina? las cataratas del Iguazú
2. ¿Qué región es parte tanto de la Argentina como del Uruguay? la Pampa
3. ¿Qué países hispanos se clasifican como megadiversos? ¿Por qué lo son? Col., C.R., Ecu., Méx., Perú y Ven. Tienen mucha biodiversidad.
4. ¿Qué tipos de energías renovables son importantes en España ahora? eólica y solar

Del mundo hispano

Antes de leer

1. ¿En qué ambiente vive Ud. ahora o ha vivido la mayor parte de su vida? ¿En una ciudad? ¿en las afueras de una ciudad? ¿en un pueblo pequeño? ¿en un ambiente rural?
2. ¿De qué manera(s) ha influido en Ud. el ambiente en que ha vivido en cuanto a (*as far as*) las siguientes ideas?
    - sus preferencias en cuanto a la comida
    - la manera en que se viste
    - cómo pasa su tiempo libre
    - cómo se relaciona con otras personas
    - sus necesidades materiales
    - sus ideas políticas y sociales

Lectura: «Cuadrados° y ángulos», de Alfonsina Storni

°Squares

Casas enfiladas,[a] casas enfiladas,
casas enfiladas.
Cuadrados, cuadrados, cuadrados.
Casas enfiladas.
Las gentes ya tienen el alma[b] cuadrada,
ideas en fila[c]
y ángulos en la espalda.[d]
Yo misma he vertido[e] ayer una lágrima,[f]
Dios mío, cuadrada.

[a] *in a straight row* [b] *soul* [c] en... *in single file* [d] la... *their backs* [e] Yo... *I myself shed* [f] *tear*

Comprensión

A. Elementos del poema. Identifique los siguientes aspectos del poema.

1. las palabras y frases que se repiten
2. los versos (*lines*) que describen las casas
3. el tipo de lugar descrito (*described*) en el poema
4. los versos que describen a las personas
5. los versos que se refieren a la poeta misma

B. Comentario. Conteste las siguientes preguntas para expresar su opinión como lector(a) (*reader*).

1. ¿Qué efecto tiene la repetición en este poema?
2. ¿Qué relación existe entre las personas y las casas?
3. ¿Qué tipo de persona es la poeta? ¿Qué efecto tiene en ella el ambiente que describe?
4. ¿Cree Ud. que la poeta se refiere solo a un lugar determinado? ¿O cree que se refiere a un problema más grande?
5. ¿Cree Ud. que la poeta podría (*could*) ser más feliz en un ambiente diferente? ¿En cuál?

Comprensión

A: Answers

1. *casas enfiladas, cuadrados/cuadrada* **2.** *versos 1–4* **3.** *una ciudad o las afueras de una ciudad en donde la arquitectura es muy monótona* **4.** *versos 5–7* **5.** *versos 8–9*

B: Answers

Answers will vary, but the following concepts may be useful.

1. There may be an effect of bombardment or an oppressive sense of monotony and uniformity.
2. The people reflect the sharpness and monotony of their environment.
3. She seems sensitive and injured by this hostile environment. The words *Dios mío* show her surprise and dismay. That she cries shows that she has something to cry about; that the tear is square only increases her sadness.
4. Storni died in 1938, so she was not referring to the post-WWII suburbs of North America, so often cited as boring and monotonous. But she is definitely referring to neighborhoods in which both the homes and their residents are too conformist for her comfort. There is no reference to a specific place, which may mean she is writing about this problem in general.
5. Perhaps she would be happy in a more natural place or somewhere with more diverse people and architecture.

Del mundo hispano

Note

See the IM for optional follow-up, writing, and Internet activities.

Antes de leer

Suggestions

- Do item 1 as an all-class survey, with results recorded on the board or overhead. Alternative: Have students conduct the survey themselves by asking several classmates for their answers.
- The questions in item 2 might be difficult for students who have never thought about them before. Provide a model by first giving a personal example of your own. Example: *Yo soy de una ciudad donde la población es muy diversa y hay restaurantes de todos tipos. Por eso me encanta la comida de diferentes partes del mundo.* Then have students work through the items in pairs or in small groups.
- Alternately, you may wish to ask students to group themselves according to the environment in which they live or have lived, then, as a group, identify the effect of this environment on them. You might also ask groups to speculate about the effect of other types of environments. Have groups share their ideas about other groups, then ask the students from those environments to react to these characterizations.

Estrategia

Working with Unfamiliar Words

Focus on the key words *enfiladas* and *cuadrados,* explaining that they are adjectives that are the past participle of verbs and that in both cases they are related to nouns as well. Write *enfiladas* and *cuadrados* on the board, underline the roots in them (*en<u>fila</u>das*, *<u>cuadr</u>ados*), and ask students if they recognize or can guess the meanings of the roots and the verbs as well: *enfilar* = to line up, *cuadrar* = to square. In this context, *cuadrados* just refers to the shape of the houses, while *enfiladas* refers to the arrangement of the houses.

B: Suggestion

Read (or have a student read) the first four lines of the poem. Have students comment on the effect that hearing the sound of the *ados/ada* suffixes over and over has on them.

Escuche

Notes

- In this chapter students can listen to a radio program about environmental issues, broadcast on a campus radio station.
- If the listening is assigned as homework, ask students to listen to the passage at least twice.
- Explain that *vos* is used in many countries, although in most of them *tú* and *vos* alternate, depending on relationships or regions. However, most Argentines and Uruguayans are consistent *vos* users.
- *Vos* has distinct forms for the present tense and the commands. Here are a few examples, with verbs that appear in the listening passage.

  ayudar: vos ayudás, ayudá
  defender: vos defendés, defendé
  unir: vos unís, uní
  hacer: vos hacés, hacé

- Greenpeace is a nongovernmental environmental organization whose goal is to "ensure the ability of the Earth to nuture life in all its diversity." Greenpeace evolved from the peace movements and antinuclear protests in British Columbia in the 1970s. It does not accept or solicit government or corporate donations, nor does it endorse political candidates.
- See the IM for the Audioscript and more information about music in Argentina and Uruguay.

Después de escuchar

A. Answers

2. *No recibe dinero de ningún gobierno.* **3.** *Se preocupa por todo tipo de problemas medioambientales, incluyendo la protección de los animales.* **4.** *También busca voluntarios.*

B: Answers

1. *Vida natural. Es una estación de radio universitaria.* **2.** *Para jóvenes universitarios, porque usa la forma de* vos *y su tono es muy informal.* **3.** *Porque todos necesitan aire limpio y agua limpia y es necesario dejar el planeta en buenas condiciones para los hijos.* **4.** *los bosques, la selva, la contaminación, las ballenas, la basura, los residuos eléctricos y electrónicos* **5.** *Se puede mirar la página Web de Greenpeace.*

A ESCUCHAR

Vocabulario **para escuchar**

hacer campaña	to have a campaign
el partido político	political party
pilas	bateries

En la Argentina y el Uruguay, así como en muchos países centroamericanos, se usa el pronombre personal **vos** en vez del (*instead of the*) pronombre **tú.** Los mandatos informales con **vos** tienen formas diferentes de los mandatos con **tú.** En el programa de radio, Ud. va a escuchar algunos de estos mandatos.

escuchá = escucha
pensá = piensa
unite = únete
hacete = hazte
ayudá = ayuda
andá = anda (*go*)
defendé = defiende

Antes de escuchar

¿Qué problemas medioambientales le preocupan a Ud.? ¿Le preocupan más los problemas locales o los internacionales? ¿Es Ud. miembro/a de alguna organización dedicada a la protección del medio ambiente?

Escuche

Vida natural, de Radio Universidad

En una estación de radio hay un programa que hace una campaña para la organización Greenpeace. Escuche según las indicaciones de su profesor(a).

Después de escuchar

A. ¿Cierto o falso? Indique si las siguientes oraciones son ciertas o falsas. Corrija las falsas.

	CIERTO	FALSO
1. Greenpeace tiene una organización en la Argentina.	☑	☐
2. Greenpeace recibe dinero de varios gobiernos.	☐	☑
3. Greenpeace solo se preocupa de los problemas de la contaminación del aire y el agua.	☐	☑
4. Greenpeace solo busca miembros que contribuyan con dinero a la organización.	☐	☑

B. Más detalles. Conteste las siguientes preguntas.

1. ¿Cómo se llama el programa? ¿En qué tipo de estación de radio se presenta?
2. ¿Para qué tipo de oyentes es este programa? ¿Por qué piensa Ud. eso?
3. ¿Cómo trata de convencer el locutor (*host*) del programa a sus oyentes de que es importante hacerse miembro de Greenpeace?
4. ¿Cuáles son dos de los temas que preocupan a Greenpeace?

¡Música!

Mercedes Sosa (1935–2009) fue una de las grandes damas de la música latinoamericana, famosa en todo el mundo. Cantaba música folclórica y tradicional no solo de la Argentina sino[a] de todo el continente sudamericano. Su canción «Todo cambia» se basa en la letra de un poema del poeta chileno Julio Numhauser. Es del álbum *30 años*.

[a]*but rather*

La famosa cantante argentina Mercedes Sosa

Go to the iMix section in Connect Spanish (**www.connectspanish.com**) to access the iTunes playlist "*Puntos9*," where you can purchase "Todo cambia" by Mercedes Sosa.

¡Música!

Notes

- Mercedes Sosa, one of the most beloved voices of the Hispanic world, was of French and *mestizo* descent. She was part of the *Nueva Canción* movement, which happened all over Latin America in the late 1950s and 1960s. She sang songs from all over the Spanish-speaking world and Brazil. She was also an activist, and was exiled in the late 1970s when Argentina was under the cruel dictatorship of Jorge Videla. She was the recipient of numerous awards, including several Grammys.
- For helpful tips on using songs in the classroom, see the IM.

A ESCRIBIR

El tema

Los efectos del cambio climático

Preparar

Paso 1. En parejas, piensen en el tema del cambio (*change*) climático. ¿Hay más de una posición con respecto al tema? Según algunos científicos, ¿cuáles son las causas del cambio climático? ¿Cuáles son sus efectos? ¿Qué opinan las personas que no están de acuerdo con la idea del cambio climático?

Hagan una lista de cuatro o cinco efectos del cambio climático que, en su opinión, son más problemáticos. También hagan una lista de los argumentos de los defensores del cambio climático, y otra, de los que se oponen a este concepto.

Paso 2. Ahora, de forma independiente, defina su postura (*position*) personal con respecto a este tema. Esto lo/la va a ayudar a escoger el enfoque (*focus*) y la tesis (*argument*) de su ensayo.

Redactar

Ud. va a escribir un ensayo de exposición de causa/efecto usando la información de la sección **Preparar.** En este caso, su propia (*own*) opinión es fundamental para estructurar su texto, ya que (*since*) Ud. tiene que tomar una postura sobre un tema que es controversial. Debe dar detalles y ejemplos que apoyen (*support*) su tesis.

Editar

Revise el ensayo para comprobar:

- la ortografía y los acentos
- la organización y la secuencia de las ideas (causa y efecto)
- el tiempo y la forma de los verbos (el presente perfecto para indicar acciones del pasado que son relevantes en el presente; el subjuntivo para expresar su reacción personal a las circunstancias que describe en el ensayo)
- el tono del ensayo

Finalmente, prepare su versión final para entregarla.

Preparar

Suggestions

- Ask students to review the forms and uses of the past participle and the present perfect (presented in this chapter).
- Suggest that students try to incorporate past participles used as adjectives.
- Suggest that students use the following to express facts: *los expertos / algunos estudios científicos afirman / muestran que*, and so on.
- Suggest that students use the following expressions to state cause and effect: *a causa de, puesto que, provocar, resultar en, por consiguiente, por este motivo, como consecuencia, como resultado*, and so on. All of them are new.

Redactar

Suggestions

- Suggested length for this writing assignment: minimum of 200 words
- Suggested structure: 3 paragraphs

P. 1. Presentation of the topic, including the writer's point of view

P. 2. Description of the various climate changes, possible causes, and their effects on the environment and human life

P. 3. Conclusion that summarizes the essay and offers a general recommendation

Editar

Follow-up

After students turn in their essays, have a whole-class discussion based on their positions on the topic.

En resumen: En este capítulo

Vocabulario

Suggestions

- Bring or have students bring magazine clippings of images related to the vocabulary words. Use the images for quick comprehension checks (*¿Qué es esto? → Es una llanta desinflada.*) and as a springboard for questions and short discussions.
- Remind students that *conducir* and *obedecer* are conjugated like *conocer,* with a *-zc-* in the first person singular: *conduzco, obedezco.* They should also remember the spelling changes for *construir* (*y*), *destruir* (*y*), *proteger* (*j*), *arrancar* (*qu*), *chocar* (*qu*), and *seguir* (*g*).
- Remind students that *cubrir, descubrir,* and *resolver* all have irregular past participles: *cubierto, descubierto, resuelto.*

Bright Idea

Suggestion

Remind students that most verbs in the present subjunctive follow the pattern of the first person singular (*yo*) form of the present indicative; therefore, verbs with first person spelling changes in the present indicative will have the same spelling change in the present subjunctive.

construir: construyo → construya, construyas, constuya, and so on
destruir: destruyo → destruya, destruyas, destruya, and so on
proteger: protejo → proteja, protejas, proteja, and so on
conducir: conduzco → conduzca, conduzcas, conduzca, and so on
obedecer: obedezco → obedezca, obedezcas, obedezca, and so on
seguir: sigo → siga, sigas, siga, and so on

Orthographic changes that occur in the first person singular preterite are also used in the subjunctive.

arrancar: arranqué → arranque, arranques, arranque, and so on
chocar: choqué → choque, choques, choque, and so on

Word Families

En este capítulo

- *la agricultura, el/la agricultor(a)*
- *el auto, la autopista*
- *el campo, el/la campesino/a*
- *conducir, la licencia de conducir, el/la conductor(a)*
- *cubrir, descubrir*

EN RESUMEN En este capítulo

LearnSmart

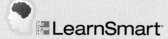

Visit **www.connectspanish.com** to practice the vocabulary and grammar points covered in this chapter.

Gramática en breve

42. Past Participle Used As Adjective

Regular Past Participles
-ar → -ado/a
-er/-ir → -ido/a

Irregular Past Participles
abierto/a, descubierto/a, dicho/a, escrito/a, hecho/a, muerto/a, puesto/a, roto/a, visto/a, vuelto/a

43. Present Perfect Indicative and Subjunctive

Present Perfect Indicative		***Present Perfect Subjunctive***	
indicative of **haber** + *past participle*		subjuntive of **haber** + *past participle*	
he	**hemos**	**haya**	**hayamos**
has	**habéis**	**hayas**	**hayáis**
ha	**han**	**haya**	**hayan**

Vocabulario

Los verbos

cubrir	to cover
descubrir	to discover
evitar	to avoid
resolver (resuelvo)	to solve, resolve

Los recursos naturales

el bosque	forest
la energía (eólica, renovable)	(wind, renewable) energy
el lago	lake
el medio ambiente	environment
el reciclaje	recycling
el recurso natural	natural resource
el río	river
la naturaleza	nature
la Tierra	Earth

Cognados: el aire, la energía eléctrica/nuclear/solar, el petróleo, el planeta

Repaso: el árbol, el mar, la montaña

conservar	to save, conserve
construir	to build
contaminar	to pollute
desarrollar	to develop
destruir (*like* **construir**)	to destroy
fabricar (qu)	to manufacture
proteger (protejo)	to protect
reciclar	to recycle

Repaso: acabar

El desarrollo

el/la agricultor(a)	farmer
la agricultura	farming, agriculture
el/la campesino/a	peasant
el campo	field; countryside
la capa de ozono	ozone layer
el delito	crime
el desarrollo	development
la fábrica	factory
la falta	lack; absence
la finca	farm
el gobierno	government
la población	population
el rascacielos	skyscraper
el ritmo de la vida	pace of life
el servicio	service

Repaso: la ciudad, la contaminación, el transporte

Los animales

la ballena	whale
la especie (en peligro de extinción)	(endangered) species
el pez (*pl.* **peces**)	fish
el toro	bull
la vaca	cow

Cognados: el elefante, el gorila

Repaso: el caballo, el gato, el pájaro, el perro

Los autos

la estación de servicio	gas station
los frenos	brakes
la gasolinera	gas station
la llanta (desinflada)	(flat) tire
el/la mecánico/a	mechanic
el parabrisas	windshield
el taller	(repair) shop
el tanque	tank

Cognados: la batería, la gasolina, el SUV

Repaso: el aceite, la camioneta, el carro, el coche

arrancar (qu)	to start up (*a car*)
arreglar	to fix, repair
gastar	to use (*gas*)
llenar	to fill (up)
revisar	to check

Cognado: reparar

En la carretera

la acera	sidewalk
la autopista	freeway, interstate
la bocina	horn (*car*)
la carretera	highway
la circulación	traffic
el/la conductor(a)	driver
la esquina	(street) corner
el estacionamiento	parking place/lot
la licencia de manejar/conducir	driver's license
el límite de velocidad	speed limit
el/la policía	police officer
el semáforo	traffic signal
el tránsito	traffic

Cognado: el tráfico

Repaso: la calle

conducir	to drive
doblar	to turn
obedecer (obedezco)	to obey
parar	to stop
seguir (sigo) (i)	to keep on going
tocar (qu)	to honk

Repaso: chocar (qu) (con), estacionar, manejar

(todo) derecho/recto	straight ahead

Repaso: a la derecha, a la izquierda, por (through)

¿cómo se llega a... ?	how do you get to ... ?

Los adjetivos

acelerado/a	fast, accelerated
bello/a	beautiful
contaminado/a	contaminated, polluted
domesticado/a	domesticated, tame
renovable	renewable
salvaje	wild
todoterreno (*inv.*)	all-terrain

Cognados: denso/a, híbrido/a, público/a, puro/a

Repaso: descapotable

Vocabulario personal

- *el desarrollo, desarrollar*
- *el estacionamiento, la estación de servicio*
- *la fábrica, fabricar*
- *la gasolina, la gasolinera*
- *la naturaleza, natural*
- *el servicio, la estación de servicio*

Entre capítulos

- *la autopista* = *el autobús* (8)
- *el caballo* = *montar a caballo* (10)
- *contaminar, contaminado/a* = *la contaminación* (6)
- *domesticado/a* = *doméstico/a* (10)
- *eléctrico/a* = *la electricidad* (12), *la electrónica* (12)
- *la estación de servicio, el estacionamiento* = *la estación de autobuses / de trenes* (8), *estacionar* (14)
- *la falta* = *faltar a* (9)
- *la gasolina, la gasolinera* = *el gas* (12)
- *gastar* (to use [gas]) = *gastar* (to spend) (9)
- *la licencia de manejar* = *manejar* (12)
- *parar* = *la parada* (8), *la parada del metro/autobús* (12)
- *el parabrisas* = *para* (3)
- *el pez* = *el pescado* (7)
- *público/a* = *el público* (13)
- *seguir* (to keep on going; to go) = *seguir* (to continue) (6)
- *el servicio* = *servir* (5)
- *tocar* (to honk) = *tocar* (to play) (2)

¡OJO!

- (*todo*) *derecho* ≠ *a la derecha*

Suggestions

- Have students regroup the words under new categories, for example, *negativo* vs. *positivo* or *infraestructura* vs. *naturaleza* vs. *mecanismos.*
- Play a word association game. Begin each round with one of the five adjectives. After each round write the first and last word on the board.

Chapter Opening Photo and Chapter Theme

Chapter Theme–Related Questions

- Have students respond *cierto* or *falso* to the following sentences.
  1. *Es necesario casarse / tener hijos para tener una vida feliz y completa.*
  2. *Se debe prohibir que la gente se case antes de los veinte años, ya que inevitablemente el resultado de casarse joven es el divorcio.*
  3. *Los padres deben vivir con sus hijos en la vejez.*
  4. *Está bien que los adolescentes de 12 años tengan novio o novia.*
  5. *En orden de importancia, la familia es lo primero; segundo, los amigos; y tercero, es decir, por último, el trabajo.*
  6. *El matrimonio es una institución religiosa. Por eso el matrimonio debe ser entre un hombre y una mujer.*
  7. *Según los votos nupciales, el matrimonio es perdurable, es decir, que es eterno, que dura para siempre. Por eso el divorcio debe prohibirse.*
- Have students work in groups to list a few rules that people should follow before getting married. For example: *Las parejas deben consultar con un consejero / una consejera de matrimonio por unos meses antes de casarse.*

Reciclado: Review the structure of the subjunctive by asking students to complete the following sentences. As you do the items, review the syntactic and "trigger" requirements for the subjunctive.

1. *Para que un matrimonio sea perdurable, es necesario que la pareja…*
2. *Mis padres (no) quieren que…*
3. *Mis hijos (no) quieren que…*
4. *Es improbable que se prohíba el divorcio porque…*
5. *A veces los hijos temen que sus padres…*

16 La vida social y afectiva

¡Viva el amor! (en Asunción, Paraguay)

- ¿Tiene Ud. pareja? ¿Tiene novio o novia? ¿esposo o esposa? ¿O solamente sale con alguien? ¿Sale con varias personas a la vez (*at the same time*)?
- En este momento, ¿cuál es la relación social más importante de su vida? ¿Es su relación con su novio/novia o con su esposo/esposa? ¿O es su relación con sus amigos? ¿con sus compañeros de casa/cuarto? ¿con los «hermanos» o «hermanas» de su *fraternity* o *sorority*?
- ¿Cree Ud. en el amor a primera vista? ¿Y en el amor para toda la vida? En su opinión, ¿qué es necesario para que (*so that*) haya una relación feliz y duradera (*lasting*) entre una pareja?

connect SPANISH

www.connectspanish.com

Resources

For Students

- Connect Spanish (**www.connectspanish.com**), which contains all content from the following resources, as well as the *Mundo interactivo* scenarios, the LearnSmart adaptive learning system, and more!
- **Physical Resources:** Workbook / Laboratory Manual, Laboratory Audio Program, DVD

For Instructors

- Connect Spanish (**www.connectspanish.com**), which contains access to all student sections of Connect Spanish, as well as helpful time-saving tools and resources such as an integrated gradebook, Instructor's Manual, Testing Program, digital transparencies, Audioscript, Videoscript, and more!

Paraguay

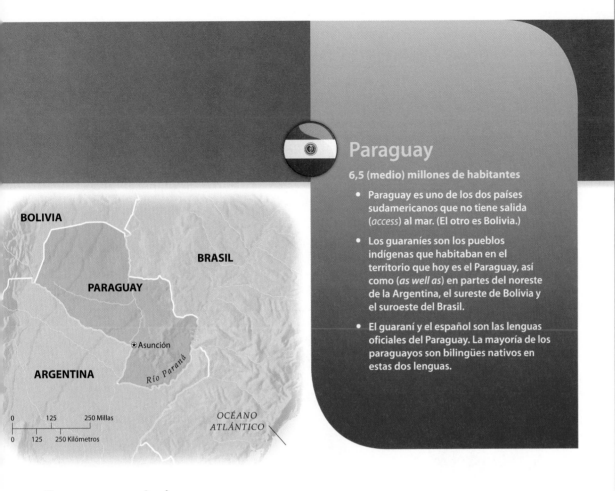

6,5 (medio) millones de habitantes

- Paraguay es uno de los dos países sudamericanos que no tiene salida (*access*) al mar. (El otro es Bolivia.)
- Los guaraníes son los pueblos indígenas que habitaban en el territorio que hoy es el Paraguay, así como (*as well as*) en partes del noreste de la Argentina, el sureste de Bolivia y el suroeste del Brasil.
- El guaraní y el español son las lenguas oficiales del Paraguay. La mayoría de los paraguayos son bilingües nativos en estas dos lenguas.

En este capítulo

CONTENT / **CONTENIDO**	OBJECTIVES / **OBJETIVOS**
Relationships 472, the Stages of Life 474	To talk about one's life
Subjunctive after Nonexistent and Indefinite Antecedents 476	To describe people, places, and things
Subjunctive after Conjunctions of Contingency and Purpose 480	To express actions that depend on each other
El Paraguay 488	To learn about a South American country that is largely **mestizo** and bilingual

471

El Paraguay

Datos esenciales

Nombre oficial: *República de Paraguay*
Lema: *«Paz y Justicia»*
Capital: *Asunción*
Otras ciudades: *San Lorenzo, Ciudad del Este*
Composición étnica: *95% mestizo, 5% otros*
Jefe de estado actual: *Fernando de Lugo, desde 2008*
Forma de gobierno: *República presidencialista*
Lenguas oficiales: *el español y el guaraní*
Moneda: *el guaraní*
Religión: *90% católicos, 7% protestantes, 3% otros*

Notes

- Paraguay is sometimes called *el corazón de América* because of its location in the South American continent.
- The Guarani language is still spoken by about 5 million people who live in Paraguay, Argentina and Brazil. Guarani is third only to Latin and Greek for the number of plants and animals named in the language. See *A leer: Lectura cultural,* p. 488.
- The origin of the name of Paraguay is not clear. Some think that it is derived from a Guarani word meaning *sea water*, which could be a reference to *el Gran Pantanal*, the huge alluvial plain that Paraguay shares with Bolivia and Brazil.
- Paraguay is viewed as a landlocked country, but it does have access to the sea through the Paraguay River, which empties into the Paraná River, which in turn flows into the *Río de la Plata*.
- The Paraguay River divides the country into two parts, and most of the population lives in the eastern half. The western half is *el Chaco,* a largely inhospitable tropical plain.

Suggestion

Have students list their ideas about Paraguay including information on geography, politics, economy, culture, music, and cuisine. When you finish the chapter, return to the lists and ask students what ideas they would change and/or add. The success of this activity will depend not only on the content about Paraguay presented in the text but also on the extent to which you have time to supplement that content with your own knowledge and experiences and also with information given in this Instructor's Edition and the IM.

NATIONAL STANDARDS: Communication

Have students work in small groups to discuss the modern family. Are all families *familias típicas*? How has our idea of the traditional family changed over the last decade? Ask students: *¿Hay alguien en esta clase que conozca a una familia que no sea la familia típica tradicional? ¿Cómo es esa familia?*

Multimedia

The IM provides suggestions for using the multimedia materials in the classroom.

Resources: Transparency 148

Vocabulario: Preparación

Las relaciones sentimentales

Suggestions

- Optional vocabulary: *el compromiso matrimonial, estar prometido/a, separado/a.*
- Emphasize that *un matrimonio* means *a married couple* as well as *a marriage.*
- Point out that the term *novio/a* usually connotes a more serious relationship in Hispanic cultures than that implied by the English words *boyfriend/girlfriend.* See the *Nota cultural* on page 473.
- Have students write down four adjectives to describe their ideal mate. Then, on the board, write the adjectives in separate columns, one for *el esposo ideal* and the other for *la esposa ideal.* Use this information as a springboard for a class discussion. *¿Hay diferencias entre las dos columnas? ¿Cree Ud. que los hombres buscan ciertas cualidades y que las mujeres buscan otras? ¿Qué es más importante, la belleza física o la belleza espiritual?,* and so on.
- Remind students that the first person singular of *salir* is *salgo.*
- Remind students that *to have a good time* cannot be translated directly from English to Spanish. The correct verb is *divertirse.*
- The listing of adjectives with *ser* or *estar* is an approximate rendering of their use, designed to give students a rule of thumb for using them. You may wish to review the uses of *ser* and *estar* with adjectives. Remind students that, although they would say *está divorciado/a, ser* would be used in phrases like *es un hombre divorciado* (in which *divorciado* is an adjective modifying the noun *hombre*).

Reciclado

- Note the use of the reciprocal *se* (*Gram. 32, Cap. 11*) in the verbs introduced in this section.
- Words for in-laws were introduced in a *Vocabulario útil* section in *Cap. 3.* Reenter those as well as other family words now. Use the family tree in that chapter to help model them.

VOCABULARIO Preparación

Las relaciones sentimentales

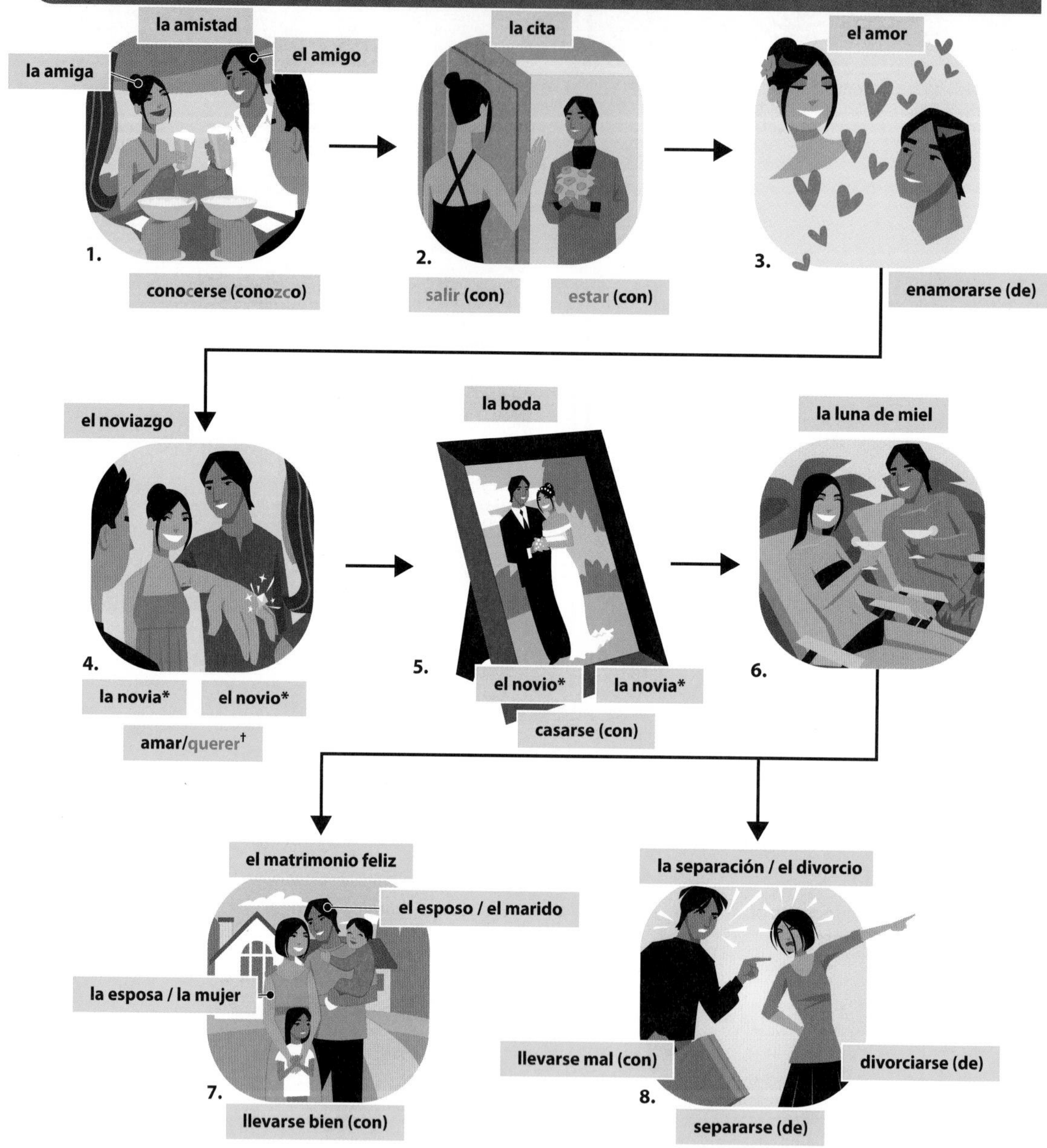

*El novio / La novia *can mean* boyfriend/girlfriend, fiancé(e), *or* groom/bride.

†**Amar** *and* **querer** *both mean* to love, *but* **amar** *can imply more passion in some dialects of Spanish.*

Heritage Speakers

Pídales a los hispanohablantes que hablen de la importancia de las relaciones entre familiares y amigos y las diferencias y semejanzas entre los hispanos y los no hispanos en cuanto a las relaciones con la familia.

Resources: Transparency 149

el matrimonio	marriage; married couple
la pareja	(married) couple; partner
el viudo / la viuda	widower/widow
pelear (con)	to fight (with)
romper (con)	to break up (with)
ser...	
amistoso/a	friendly
cariñoso/a	affectionate
casado/a	a married person
recién casado/a	recently married
soltero/a	single
estar...	
casado/a (con)	married (to)
divorciado/a (de)	divorced (from)
enamorado/a (de)	in love (with)
separado/a (de)	separated (from)

Así se dice

la boda = el casamiento

Conversación

A. ¡Usemos la lógica! Complete las siguientes oraciones lógicamente.

1. Mi abuelo es el _____ de mi abuela, es decir, está _____ con ella.
2. Muchos novios tienen un _____ bastante (*rather*) largo antes de la boda.
3. María y Julio tienen una _____ el viernes para comer en un restaurante. Luego van a bailar.
4. La _____ de Juan y Pati es el domingo a las dos de la tarde, en la iglesia (*church*) de San Martín.
5. La _____ entre ex esposos es imposible. No pueden ser amigos.
6. ¡El _____ es ciego (*blind*)!
7. Para algunas personas, el _____ es un concepto anticuado. Prefieren vivir juntos, sin casarse.
8. Algunas personas no quieren gastar su dinero en una _____ después de la boda.

esposo / casado
noviazgo
cita
boda
amistad
amor
matrimonio
luna de miel

Nota cultural

Expresiones familiares de cariño° *°affection*

En el mundo hispano se usan muchas palabras y frases para referirse a las personas queridas y para expresar cariño. Estas pueden ser diferentes en cada país. Las siguientes palabras son de uso común, aunque[a] algunas de ellas no se usan en todos los países.

- Entre personas unidas romántica o familiarmente: **mi amor, amorcito/a, mi vida, cielo,[b] corazón, querido/a, cariño, gordo/a, viejo/a, flaco/a,[c] negro/a**
- De hijos a padres: **viejo/a, mis viejos** (la Argentina, el Uruguay)
- Para referirse a una pareja con quien no se está casado: **mi compañero/a**
- Para referirse a los padrinos[d] de un niño o niña: **compadre/comadre**

La gente joven siempre tiene su propia jerga[e] en cada país, pero no siempre son palabras que se usan para dirigirse[f] a las personas mayores.

- **cuate:** una palabra del náhuatl, la lengua de los aztecas (México, Centroamérica, Bolivia)
- **pana:** significa **compañero/a** (Venezuela, Colombia, la República Dominicana y otros países)
- **compa:** derivado de **compañero**
- **negro/a:** se usa entre amigos en varios países
- **tío/a** (España)
- **buey** (México)

[a]*although* [b]*heaven* [c]*skinny* [d]*godparents* [e]*slang* [f]*address*

En un bautizo en una iglesia católica, los padres sujetan (*hold*) al bebé. (México, D.F.)

Como se nota en la lista anterior,[g] una de las grandes diferencias entre el español y el inglés es el hecho de usar[h] como palabras cariñosas adjetivos que describen características físicas: **gordo/a, flaco/a, negro/a, viejo/a.** Estos adjetivos se aplican indistintamente[i] a cualquier[j] persona, es decir, no es necesario que la persona sea gorda o delgada, blanca o negra, joven o vieja.

¿Con qué palabras se dirige Ud. a sus amigos? ¿y a las personas que ama?

[g]*preceding* [h]*el... the use* [i]*indiscriminately* [j]*any*

Preliminary Exercises

- Ask students the following questions to check comprehension and personalize the vocabulary.
  1. *¿Qué palabras asocia Ud. con la amistad? ¿el amor? ¿una boda? ¿la luna de miel? ¿el novio? ¿la esposa?*
  2. *¿Le gusta estar con sus amigos? ¿Qué hacen? ¿Siempre se llevan bien? ¿Tienen sus amigos los mismos intereses que Ud.?*
  3. *¿Cree que un matrimonio debe tener intereses parecidos? ¿Es importante que los esposos sean amigos? ¿Cuál es la edad ideal para casarse?*
- *¿De qué tipo de relación se habla?*
  1. *Es una relación cariñosa entre dos personas. A veces empieza cuando somos niños. (la amistad)*
  2. *El posible resultado de un matrimonio que no se lleva bien. (el divorcio)*
  3. *Una relación sentimental que puede llegar al matrimonio. (el amor)*
  4. *Una ceremonia religiosa o civil que formaliza la relación entre dos personas que quieren vivir juntas. (la boda)*

Con. A: Note

Active vocabulary: *bastante, la iglesia*

Nota cultural

Suggestions

- Impress upon students the diversity of Spanish word choices for expressing love relationships. Ask students if they think the same is true in this country.
- Explain the concept of being the godparent of the child of good friends, a custom that is taken very seriously in Spanish-speaking countries.
- Introduce the concept of *el apodo* and discuss how physical characteristics are often the source of Spanish nicknames.

Comprensión

1. *¿Qué adjetivos se usan en español para referirse a una persona querida? (querido/a, gordo/a, viejo/a, flaco/a, negro/a)*
2. *¿Con qué relación están relacionadas las palabras* compadre *y* comadre*? (con los padrinos)*
3. *¿Qué gran diferencia hay entre el español y el inglés en cuanto a algunas palabras cariñosas? (el uso de adjetivos que describen características físicas)*

NATIONAL STANDARDS: Connections

Traditional couples now appear to be only one of many relationship options, not only in this country but in other countries as well. In recent years we have witnessed an increase in interracial couples, single mothers and fathers, and couples who live together without ever marrying. Marriage between people of the same sex has been legal in Spain since 2005 and in Argentina since 2010.

Con. C: Suggestions

- Before students start *Paso 1*, suggest that they think about their own marriage (if they are married), about the marriage of their parents, grandparents, or good friends, or about the marriage of a famous couple.
- Do *Paso 3* as a whole-class activity. Tally the five most important elements on the board, then discuss the results. What do they reveal about the class's values?

Las etapas de la vida

Suggestions

- Offer the following optional vocabulary: *el nacimiento, la pubertad, la tercera edad, criar* (*crío*). Point out and model the difference between *crecer* (to grow up) and *criar* (to raise).
- Remind students that the past participle of *morir* is *muerto* and that *muerto* can also be used as an adjective.
- Emphasize and model the conjugations of *nacer* and *crecer*, which are similar to *conocer: nazco, crezco, conozco.*

Reciclado

- Have students make associations with stages of life: *¿Qué colores/estaciones del año asocia Ud. con cada una de las etapas de la vida? ¿Qué actividades asocia con ellas?*
- Ask students the following questions to personalize the vocabulary.
  1. *¿Cuál es la fecha de su nacimiento? ¿Dónde creció Ud.?*
  2. *En su opinión, ¿cuál es la mejor/peor etapa de la vida de una persona? ¿Por qué?*
  3. *¿Le tiene Ud. miedo a la muerte? ¿Cree Ud. que hay otra vida después de esta?*

B. Preguntas impertinentes

Paso 1. Use las siguientes palabras para hacer preguntas muy personales. Las preguntas pueden ser sobre el presente o el pasado.

MODELOS: ¿**Has roto** alguna vez con un novio / una novia?
¿De quién **estás enamorado/a** ahora mismo?

1. romper con	**5.** amar
2. salir con	**6.** la luna de miel
3. una cita	**7.** llevarse mal con
4. estar enamorado/a	**8.** estar divorciado/a

Paso 2. Ahora, en parejas, hagan y contesten las preguntas del **Paso 1.** Si creen que alguna pregunta es demasiado personal, pueden contestar cortésmente: «**Prefiero no contestar esa pregunta.**» También pueden contestar sin cortesía: «**¿Y a ti qué te importa?**»

Paso 3. Digan a la clase las cosas que Uds. tienen en común.

Nota **comunicativa**

Cómo expresar los mandatos con el infinitivo

You have already learned how to use formal (**Ud./Uds.**) and informal (**tú**) commands in Spanish. Another very common way to communicate a command in Spanish, especially in lists, written instructions, and recipes, is to use the infinitive. Object pronouns always follow the infinitive in an infinitive command.

No estacionar. **No pisar** el césped (*grass*). **Llamar** a los padres. **Invitarlos** a cenar.

You will use infinitive commands in **Paso 1** of **Conversación C.**

C. Receta para unas buenas relaciones. En su opinión, ¿cuáles son los ingredientes necesarios para un buen matrimonio o una buena amistad?

Paso 1. Haga una lista de los cinco ingredientes esenciales en forma de mandatos con el infinitivo.

Paso 2. Compare su lista con las (*those*) de otros tres estudiantes. ¿Han seleccionado algunos de los mismos ingredientes? Hablen de todos los ingredientes y hagan una lista de los cinco más importantes.

Paso 3. Ahora comparen los resultados obtenidos por todos los grupos.

Las etapas° de la vida

°Las... *Stages*

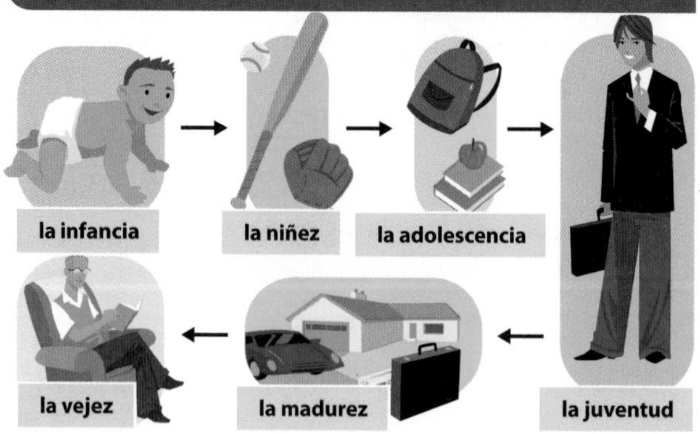

la muerte	death
nacer (nazco)	to be born
crecer (crezco)	to grow
morir (muero) (u)	to die

Heritage Speakers

Pídales a los hispanohablantes que den otras expresiones de cariño que usan. Pregúnteles a quién(es) se las dicen y en qué circunstancias.

Resources: Transparency 150

Conversación

A. Etapas de la vida

Paso 1. Relacione las siguientes palabras y frases con las distintas etapas de la vida de una persona. **¡OJO!** Hay más de una relación posible en algunos casos.

1. el amor
2. los nietos
3. los juguetes (*toys*)
4. no poder comer sin ayuda
5. los hijos en la universidad
6. los granos (*pimples*)
7. la universidad
8. la boda

Paso 2. Ahora dé una definición o descripción de las siguientes etapas de la vida. Pueden ser descripciones serias o divertidas.

MODELOS: La infancia es cuando una persona tiene menos de dos años.
La infancia es la etapa de la vida en que solo te importa comer, dormir y jugar.

1. la niñez **2.** la adolescencia **3.** la madurez **4.** la vejez

B. La vida de Ud. por etapas

Paso 1. Describa las acciones que Ud. hacía, hace o va a hacer en cada etapa de la vida. **¡OJO!** Ud. va a usar diferentes tiempos verbales para cada etapa: el pretérito y el imperfecto para el pasado, el presente para la etapa actual y el futuro (**ir** + **a** + *infinitivo*) para las etapas posteriores (*later*).

MODELOS: En mi infancia, **viví** en Oklahoma. Mis padres no **estaban** divorciados todavía.
En el momento actual **estoy** en la madurez. **Vivo** en... **Me preocupa** mucho...
En el futuro, **voy** a estudiar...

Paso 2. Ahora, en parejas, comparen sus descripciones. Digan a la clase lo que Uds. tienen en común.

¿Recuerda Ud.?

Before studying **Gramática 44,** review the indefinite and negative words that you learned in **Gramática 19 (Cap. 7).** Remember that **alguien** and **nadie** take the personal **a** when they are used as direct objects.

Busco **a alguien** de la familia.	*I'm looking for someone from the family.*
No veo **a nadie** en el salón de baile.	*I don't see anyone in the dance hall.*

Give the opposite of the following words. **1.** nada algo **2.** algunos ningún/ninguno **3.** alguien nadie

Mundo interactivo

You should now be prepared to work with Scenario 8, Activity 3 in Connect Spanish (**www.connectspanish.com**).

Con. A: Answers
1. *la adolescencia, la juventud, la madurez*
2. *la madurez, la vejez*
3. *la infancia, la niñez*
4. *la infancia, la vejez*
5. *la madurez*
6. *la adolescencia*
7. *la juventud*
8. *la juventud, la madurez*

Con. A: Extension

9. *dos coches y un perro* (*la madurez*)
10. *pasarlo bien* (*la niñez, la adolescencia, la juventud*)
11. *los amigos íntimos* (*la adolescencia, la juventud*)
12. *un coche con cuatro puertas* (*la madurez*)

Con. B: Reciclado

Note the review of most indicative tenses that students have learned so far in *Con. B.* Follow up students' responses by using subjunctive-generating questions in your conversational exchanges with students, as well as the present perfect (indicative and subjunctive).

Con. B: Redacción

- Assign *Paso 1* as a composition assignment. After you have corrected the compositions, read several to the class, asking them to guess who wrote each one.
- Ask students to write a description of their family, including at least twelve words from the lists in *Vocabulario: Preparación* in this chapter as well as previously learned vocabulary. Tell students that, while they may have written a description of their family when studying *Cap. 3,* now they can write a much more complete and detailed description because they have much more language to work with.

Pronunciación: See the Laboratory Manual for review and practice of cognates.

NATIONAL STANDARDS: Communities

Have students work in groups to write three questions that they would ask someone about their concept of family and friends. Have the groups share and "pool" the questions they wrote. Encourage them to use these to interview people in the community. They should try to include someone from each stage of life, people from both genders, and at least one or more persons, especially Hispanics, who are not from the U.S. or Canada. Have them share their findings with their classmates, and use the results to make generalizations about the importance of family and friends to different genders, age groups, and nationalities.

Gramática 44

The Subjunctive After Nonexistent and Indefinite Antecedents

Note

El Día del Padre (*de los Padres*) is not celebrated on the same day in all Hispanic countries. In Spain and Bolivia, it's on March 19, and in Guatemala and El Salvador it's on June 17. The celebration of *el Día de la Madre* (*de las Madres*) also varies from country to country. In Spain, it's the first Sunday in May, while in Argentina it's the third Sunday in October. Most other countries celebrate it on different days in May.

Suggestion

Students should be able to figure out this use of the subjunctive by analyzing the examples given in *GEA* and by looking at the summary chart below.

Follow-up

- Have students complete the following sentences.
  1. *Mi padre/madre es una persona que...*
  2. *Un padre o madre ideal es una persona que...*
- Ask the following questions.

  Los lunes por la mañana, ¿hay algo que lo/la haga feliz? ¿que lo/la haga sonreír?

  ¿Y los viernes por la mañana? ¿los domingos por la mañana?

Help students with negative answers.

No, no hay nada que me haga sonreír.

Bright Idea

Suggestions

- As a class, briefly review the formation and uses of the subjunctive.
- At this point, students should be able to identify independent and dependent clauses, as well as expressions of 1) influence, 2) emotion and feeling, and 3) doubt and denial, which require the use of subjunctive in the dependent clause.

Emphasis 1: Suggestion

Emphasize and model the relationship between adjectives and adjective clauses (to modify a noun), for example, *Veo una casa blanca / que tiene ventanas.* Draw parallels with noun clauses and their relationship to nouns.

GRAMÁTICA

44 ¿Hay alguien que... ? ¿Hay un lugar donde... ?

The Subjunctive (Part 6): The Subjunctive After Nonexistent and Indefinite Antecedents

Grammar Tutorial 44
connect SPANISH
www.connectspanish.com

Gramática en acción: Los buenos padres

¡Feliz Día del Padre, papá!
¡Te quiero mucho!

- Un buen padre, así como una buena madre, es alguien que quiere a sus hijos de manera incondicional, se preocupa por su formación y les enseña a ser personas útiles en la vida.
- Todos los niños **necesitan** padres **que** los quieran incondicionalmente, los eduquen y los cuiden.

¿Y Ud.?

Complete las siguientes oraciones.

1. No hay nadie que me quiera más que mi(s) _____.
2. Mi padre/madre es la persona que me enseñó a _____.
3. La persona que se preocupa más por mí es mi _____.

the antecedent / **el antecedente** = a word or phrase modified by an adjective clause

	①		②
	definite/existent antecedent	**que**	indicative
	indefinite/nonexistent antecedent	**que**	subjunctive

1. Adjective Clauses and Antecedents

As you know, noun clauses function like nouns in a sentence. Adjective clauses function like adjectives: they modify a noun or a pronoun. In the sentences to the right, the nouns *car* and *house* (*for sale*) are modified by dependent adjective clauses. The noun that is modified is called the *antecedent* (**el antecedente**) of the dependent clause.

I have a car **that gets good gas mileage.**

Is there a house for sale **that is closer to the city**?

Good parents • *A good father, just like a good mother, is someone who loves his/her children unconditionally, worries about their education, and teaches them to be useful in life.* • *All children need parents who love them unconditionally, educate them, and take care of them.*

Heritage Speakers

Pídales a los hispanohablantes que expliquen la diferencia entre las siguientes oraciones.

Quiero alquilar la casa a una familia que no ***tiene*** *niños.*
Quiero alquilar la casa a una familia que no ***tenga*** *niños.*

2. Subjunctive with Nonexistent and Indefinite Antecedents
Sometimes the antecedent of an adjective clause is something that does not exist from the point of view of the speaker, or something whose existence is indefinite or uncertain. In these cases, the subjunctive must be used in the adjective (dependent) clause in Spanish.

EXISTENT ANTECEDENT
There is *nothing* that you can do.

NONEXISTENT ANTECEDENT
We need *a car* that will last for years. (We don't have one yet.)

EXISTENT ANTECEDENT: INDICATIVE
Hay algo aquí que me **interesa.**
There is something here that interests me.

NONEXISTENT ANTECEDENT: SUBJUNCTIVE
No veo nada que me **interese.**
I don't see anything that interests me.

3. Adjective Clauses That Describe a Place
When the adjective clause describes a place, the word **donde** (rather than **que**) introduces the adjective clause.

INDEFINITE ANTECEDENT: SUBJUNCTIVE
Buscamos un restaurante donde sirvan comida chilena auténtica.
We're looking for a restaurant where they serve authentic Chilean food.

4. Questions Versus Answers with Adjective Clauses
The *subjunctive* is used in the dependent clause in a question about something that the speaker does not know exists for certain. However, the indicative *or* the subjunctive may be used in the answer, depending on whether the person who answers the question is sure of the existence of the antecedent or not.

QUESTION: SUBJUNCTIVE
—¿**Hay algo** aquí que te **guste**?
"Is there anything here that you like?"

DEFINITE ANTECEDENT: INDICATIVE
—Sí, **hay varios bolsos** que me **gustan.**
"Yes, there are several purses that I like."

NEGATIVE ANTECEDENT: SUBJUNCTIVE
—No, **no hay nada** aquí que me **guste.**
"No, there's nothing here that I like."

5. Use of the Personal *a*
Remember that the personal **a** is used only before specific persons or animals. It is not used before unknown or nonspecific persons.

UNKNOWN PERSON: SUBJUNCTIVE
Busco **un señor** que **sepa** francés.
I'm looking for a man who knows French. (I don't know of any.)

KNOWN PERSON: INDICATIVE
Busco **al señor** que **sabe** francés.
I'm looking for the man who knows French. (I know there's one in our office, for example.)

¡OJO!
The personal **a** is always used before **alguien** and **nadie** when they are direct objects.

DIRECT OBJECT
¿Conoces **a alguien** que sepa francés?
Do you know someone who speaks French?

No conozco **a nadie** que sepa francés.
I don't know anyone who knows French.

NOT DIRECT OBJECT
No hay **nadie** aquí que sepa francés.
There's no one here who speaks French.

Emphasis 2: Suggestions

- Give students the following formulas and models to help them conceptualize the use of subjunctive with adjective clauses.

  experience = knowledge of the existence of the object

  - − experience = + subjunctive: *Quiero salir con un muchacho que tenga interés en la política internacional. (No lo conozco todavía.)*
  - + experience = − subjunctive: *Quiero salir con un muchacho que tiene interés en la política internacional. (Ya lo conozco.)*
- Relate the uses of the subjunctive in adjective clauses to the general use of the subjunctive to express conceptual states/actions.

Emphasis 3: Suggestion

Emphasize and model the use of *donde* to introduce the adjective clause: *Queremos trabajar en una ciudad donde haya una comunidad intercultural. Viven en un barrio donde los niños pueden jugar en la calle.*

Emphasis 4: Suggestion

Model, in brief exchanges with students, more examples of the question/answer series.

1. *¿Hay estudiantes en esta clase que tengan hijos?* →
   No, no hay ningún estudiante en esta clase que tenga hijos.
   Sí, hay un (dos) estudiante(s) en esta clase que tiene(n) hijos.
2. *¿Hay profesores en esta universidad que vivan en residencias estudiantiles?* →
   No, no hay ningún profesor en esta universidad que viva en una residencia estudiantil.
   Sí, hay profesores en esta universidad que viven en residencias estudiantiles.

Prác.: Preliminary Exercises

- Read each English sentence and have students tell whether the antecedent is existent or nonexistent. Then give the beginning of each sentence in Spanish and ask students to finish the translation.
  1. There's nothing here that I like. / *No hay nada aquí que me guste.*
  2. Here's something that you will like. / *Aquí hay algo que te va a gustar.*
  3. I don't know anyone who can do it. / *No conozco a nadie que lo pueda hacer.*

(Cont.)

NATIONAL STANDARDS: Connections

- Another use of *donde* in a declarative statement is to mean *in the house of.* For example, *Estoy donde José* means *I'm at José's house.* Other Romance languages have similar structures, such as the French, *Je suis chez Jacques* (*I'm at Jacques' house*).
- Have students make lists of hypothetical situations, possessions, and so on, for each other. Then have them use these lists to interview each other. List the following examples on the board.

  ¿Hay alguien aquí que viva en una mansión? ¿que sepa hablar otro idioma? ¿que tenga un Mercedes u otro coche de lujo? ¿que viaje a México todos los años? ¿que quiera ser médico algún día?

4. I know many people who can do it. / *Conozco a muchas personas que lo pueden hacer.*
5. There's no car that is economical. / *No hay ningún coche que sea económico.*

- Read each English sentence and ask students whether the antecedent is definite or indefinite. Then give the beginning of each sentence in Spanish and ask students to finish the translation.

1. I have a book that is interesting. / *Tengo un libro que es interesante.*
2. I want to buy a book that is interesting. / *Quiero comprar un libro que sea interesante.*
3. I'm looking for a secretary who speaks Spanish. / *Busco un secretario que hable español.*

Prác. A: Suggestions

- Before students start *Paso 1*, call their attention to the two sentence fragments that start out each set of phrases. Point out the verbs in each set. Ask what mood the verbs in the first set are in and why, then ask the same question for the second set.
- Point out that adjectives in each group are masculine because they agree with *alguien* and *nadie*, which are viewed as masculine in Spanish for purposes of agreement.
- Allow students to do *Paso 1* silently.
- Go through the items, asking students who have checked a given characteristic to raise their hands. Ask follow-up questions, as appropriate: *¿Quién es? ¿Cuándo se divorció?*, and so on.
- Take items in each set and convert them to the opposite point of view: *Conozco a alguien que… → No conozco a nadie que… ; No conozco a nadie que… → Conozco a alguien que…* Ask students to raise their hands if the item fits them and ask follow-up questions.

Prác. A: Additional Items

- *…es/sea feliz en su matrimonio.*
- *…solo quiere/quiera estar con su novio (esposo).*

Prác. A: Extension

- Ask students: *¿Tiene parientes que hagan algo «especial»? Descríbalo/a.*
- Give students one minute to form a question about some unusual activity they like, then have them ask the class if anyone else shares their hobby.

Autoprueba

Indicate which of the following sentences expresses an indefinite or nonexistent antecedent.

1. We need the counselor who works with this couple.
2. They are looking for a minister who will perform the wedding on the beach.
3. I met a man who has thirteen children.

Answer: 2

Práctica

A. ¡Anticipemos! Hablando de gente que conocemos

Paso 1. Indique las características que Ud. ha visto en personas que conoce. Añada una característica más a cada lista.

Conozco a alguien que…

1. □ está separado/divorciado.
2. □ está recién casado.
3. □ se lleva mal con sus padres (hijos).
4. □ acaba de tener un bebé.
5. □ va a casarse pronto.
6. □ está locamente (*madly*) enamorado.
7. □ ¿ ?

No conozco a nadie que…

8. □ sea viudo.
9. □ no crea en el matrimonio.
10. □ esté en su luna de miel ahora.
11. □ salga con una persona famosa.
12. □ esté separado de su esposo o esposa.
13. □ haya roto con su novio/a (esposo/a) esta semana.
14. □ ¿ ?

Paso 2. Ahora, en parejas, comparen sus respuestas. ¿Cuál es la coincidencia más interesante que tienen?

B. Hablando de bodas

Paso 1. Complete las oraciones de la página 479, según lo que se ve en el siguiente dibujo.

Resources: Transparency 151

1. Hay un hombre que está/esté sacando una foto.
2. Hay una persona que está/esté llorando.
3. Hay un hombre que está/esté sonriendo.
4. Hay dos niñas que están/estén peleando.
5. No hay nadie que está/esté cantando.
6. ¿Hay alguien que está/esté tirando (*throwing*) arroz?

Paso 2. Ahora complete las siguientes oraciones según su experiencia. Use el indicativo o el subjuntivo, según el caso.

En las bodas que yo he visto,...

1. hay / no hay mucha gente de otros estados que... (asistir)
2. hay alguien / no hay nadie que... (dar un buen regalo)
3. hay / no hay una ceremonia que... (ser en la iglesia)
4. hay gente / no hay nadie que... (tirar arroz)
5. siempre hay alguien / nunca hay nadie que... (llorar)
6. ¿ ?

Conversación

A. Una encuesta (*poll*). ¿Qué sabe Ud. de los compañeros de su clase de español? Pregúnteles si saben hacer lo siguiente o a quién le ocurre lo siguiente. Deben levantar la mano solo los que puedan contestar afirmativamente. Luego la persona que hizo la pregunta debe hacer un comentario apropiado. Siga el modelo.

MODELO: hablar chino ⟶
En esta clase, ¿hay alguien que **hable** chino?
(*Nadie levanta la mano.*) No hay nadie que **hable** chino.
(*Alguien levanta la mano.*) Hay una (dos) persona(s) que **habla(n)** chino.

1. hablar ruso / japonés
2. saber tocar la viola / el violín
3. conocer a un actor / una actriz
4. saber preparar comida vietnamita/tailandesa
5. celebrar su cumpleaños hoy / nunca celebrar su cumpleaños
6. cantar en la ducha/ópera
7. bailar tango/salsa
8. ¿ ?

B. Intercambios

Paso 1. Complete las siguientes declaraciones de acuerdo con su vida real y sus deseos.

1. Tengo un amigo / una amiga que...
2. No conozco a nadie que...
3. Este verano quiero tener un trabajo que...
4. Este verano no quiero hacer nada que...
5. Busco un compañero / una compañera en la vida que...
6. En este mundo, no hay nada que sea más importante que...
7. Este semestre/trimestre tengo cursos que...
8. El próximo semestre/trimestre quiero tomar cursos que...

Paso 2. Ahora, en parejas, hagan y contesten preguntas basadas en las declaraciones del **Paso 1.**

Paso 3. Digan a la clase las coincidencias o diferencias más interesantes que Uds. tienen.

Prác. B: Suggestions

- Make sure that students understand the choices they need to make in each *Paso*. In *Paso 1*, the choice is between an indicative or subjunctive form. In *Paso 2*, students need to choose the option that expresses their experience, then provide the appropriate verb form, either in the indicative or in the subjunctive.
- In *Paso 1*, ask follow-up questions about each item: *¿Quién es el hombre que está tomando una foto? ¿Es fotógrafo?*, and so on.
- In *Paso 2*, if students have not attended a wedding, ask them to think about an ideal wedding.
- As follow-up for *Paso 2*, ask at least one student to share all of his/her sentences with the class.

Con. A: Suggestions

- Ask individual students to ask questions of the class based on the suggested items. (There are two possible questions for each item.) Ask other students to comment on the show of hands, as in the model. Then ask the remaining students in the class to invent similar items.
- If you have a very large class, model several questions for the whole class, then allow students to work in groups.

Con. B, Paso 2: Suggestion

Encourage students to use conversation-extending techniques to elicit more information.

Con. B: Extension

Write these sentences on the board. Have students supply their own details to form questions to use in an interview situation.

9. *¿Tienes algún amigo que... ?*
10. *¿Tienes alguna clase que... ?*
11. *En mi opinión, no hay nada/nadie que...*

Gramática 45
The Subjunctive After Conjunctions of Purpose and Contingency

Note

Students may not know the meaning of the term *contingency*. Explain that it refers to a possible but unlikely future event or to an event that is dependent on something else.

Follow-up

Ask students the following question.

¿Han estado Uds. en situaciones similares a las de los dibujos?

Encourage students to give details.

Emphasis 1: Suggestions

- The acronyms *A SPACE* or *ESCAPA* can be introduced to help students remember this list of conjunctions.
- Emphasize and model the relationship of the adverbial clauses to adverbs (they function as an adverb): *Llega mañana / antes de que salgamos.*
- In *Cap. 17,* students will be introduced to temporal adverbial conjunctions (*cuando, tan pronto como, hasta que,* and so on). The subjunctive is used only when they introduce future, incomplete actions or states.
- Although *antes de que* is categorized here as an obligatory adverbial conjunction, it is truly a temporal conjunction because the expression, by its very nature, sets up a time relationship between two events. That said, we have included it with this group of prepositions because the subjunctive is *always* used after *antes de que*, as is the case with the other conjunctions in the group.

45 *Lo hago para que tú…*

The Subjunctive (Part 7): The Subjunctive After Conjunctions of Purpose and Contingency

Grammar Tutorial 45
connect SPANISH
www.connectspanish.com

Gramática en acción: Relaciones familiares y sociales

a.

b.

c.

¿A qué dibujo corresponde cada una de las siguientes oraciones? ¿Quién las dice?

1. __b__ «Aquí tienes la tarjeta de crédito, pero úsala solo **en caso de que** haya una emergencia, ¿eh?»
2. __a__ «Deja ya de jugar. No te permito que juegues en la computadora **antes de que** termines la tarea. ¿Me entiendes?»
3. __c__ «Quiero casarme contigo **para que** estemos siempre juntos y no salgas más con Raúl.»

Comprensión

1. En el dibujo **a,** es obvio que el niño ____. Es natural que la madre ____.
2. En el dibujo **b,** está claro que la nieta ____. Por eso el abuelo ____.
3. En el dibujo **c,** creo que el joven ____. No estoy seguro/a de que la joven ____. Esta pareja es muy joven para ____.

① indicative — conjunction of contingency or purpose — ② subjunctive

Las conjunciones de propósito y contingencia

a conjunction / **una conjunción** = a word or phrase that connects other words, phrases, or clauses

1. **Conjunctions of Purpose and Contingency**
The subjunctive is *always* used in the dependent clause after the conjunctions listed at the right. These conjunctions express *purpose* (**el propósito**) or *contingency* (**la contingencia**) (when one action depends on another = *I'll do X unless Y occurs*). These dependent clauses function as adverbs in the sentence.

a menos que	unless
antes (de) que	before
con tal (de) que	provided (that)
en caso de que	in case
para que	so that
sin que	without; unless

Family and social relationships *To which drawing does each of the following sentences correspond? Who is saying them?* **1.** *"Here's the credit card, but use it only in case there's an emergency, OK?"* **2.** *"Stop playing right now. I don't allow you to play with the computer before you finish your homework. Do you understand me?"* **3.** *"I want to marry you so that we can always be together and (so that) you don't go out with Raúl again."*

Resources: Transparency 152

Note that each conjunction contains the word **que.**

Voy **con tal (de) que** ellos me **acompañen.**
I'm going, provided (that) they go with me.

En caso de que llegue Juan, dile que ya salí.
In case Juan arrives, tell him that I already left.

No voy a la fiesta **sin que** tú me **acompañes.**
I won't go to the party unless you go with me.

2. **Same Subject** = *preposition + infinitive*
When there is no change of subject, a *preposition + infinitive* phrase is often used to express purpose or contingency, rather than a *conjunction + subjunctive.* The prepositional forms are: **antes de, con tal de, en caso de, para, sin.** Only **a menos que** does not have a prepositional equivalent.

para Estoy aquí **para aprender.** (subject = **yo**)
but: Estoy aquí **para que** Uds. **aprendan.** (subjects = **yo, Uds.**)

antes de Coma Ud. algo **antes de salir.** (subject = **Ud.**)
but: Coma Ud. algo **antes de que salgamos.** (subjects = **Ud., nosotros**)

con tal de Podemos salir **con tal de tener** tiempo. (subject = **nosotros**)
but: Podemos salir **con tal de que tengas** tiempo. (subjects = **nosotros, tú**)

sin Es difícil salir con los amigos **sin gastar** dinero. (subject = impersonal)
but: Es difícil salir con los amigos **sin que gastemos** dinero. (subjects = impersonal, **nosotros**)

Autoprueba

Match each conjunction with its correct meaning in English.

1. ______ **para que** a. unless
2. ______ **antes de que** b. before
3. ______ **con tal de que** c. provided that
4. ______ **a menos que** d. in case
5. ______ **en caso de que** e. so that

Answers: **1.** e **2.** b **3.** c **4.** a **5.** d

Práctica

A. ¡Anticipemos! ¿Es Ud. un buen amigo o buena amiga? La amistad es una de las relaciones más importantes de la vida. Lea las siguientes declaraciones e indique si es cierto o falso que eso le pasa a Ud. con sus amigos. **¡OJO!** No todo lo que se dice es bueno. Hay que leer las declaraciones con cuidado.

	CIERTO	FALSO
1. Les hago muchos favores a mis amigos con tal de que después ellos me ayuden a mí.	☐	☐
2. Les doy consejos a mis amigos para que ellos luego tomen buenas decisiones.	☐	☐
3. Les presto dinero a mis amigos a menos que yo sepa que no me lo van a devolver.	☐	☐
4. Les traduzco el menú en los restaurantes mexicanos en caso de que no sepan leer español.	☐	☐
5. Los llevo a casa cuando beben bebidas alcohólicas para que no tengan ningún accidente.	☐	☐

Emphasis 2: Suggestion

Emphasize the difference between the *preposition + inf.* structure (*Nota comunicativa, Cap. 13,* p. 397) and the *conjunction + subjunctive* structure. The latter has a second subject (*Van al cine antes de que llegue Raúl.*), and the former does not (*Van al cine antes de cenar.*).

Preliminary Exercises

- Have students express the following ideas in Spanish.
  1. unless you go with me / call me / write to me
  2. in case they arrive/leave/come
  3. provided that they go / eat dinner / have lunch
  4. in order for us to go / be there / arrive on time

  Remind students that these are conjunctions (with subjunctive), not prepositions (with infinitives).
- Have students complete the following sentences with their own ideas.
  1. *Nunca bailo en una fiesta a menos que…*
  2. *Cuando salgo con mis amigos, siempre llevo la licencia de conducir en caso de que…*
  3. *No me voy a casar/divorciar a menos que…*
  4. *Estoy preparado/a en caso de que…*
  5. *Voy a estudiar ______ para que…*

Prác. A: Suggestions

- Ask students to find the conjunction in each sentence, then the subjunctive verb form.
- Have students add at least two more characteristics of a good (or bad) friend and read them to the class.

Prác. B: Follow-up

- Write the conjunctions on the board. Have students use them as appropriate to complete the following sentences.
  1. *El cielo está muy nublado hoy. Voy a llevar impermeable…*
  2. *Es fácil sacar una nota buena en esta clase…*
  3. *Nunca pienso casarme/divorciarme…*
  4. *Vamos a las montañas este fin de semana…*
- Have students complete the following sentences with information about themselves.
  1. *Voy a graduarme en… a menos que…*
  2. *Este verano voy a… a menos que…*
  3. *Voy a seguir viviendo en esta ciudad con tal que…*
  4. *Voy a comprar… en caso de que…*

Nota comunicativa

Reciclado: *Por* and *para* were presented in *Gram. 41* (*Cap. 14*). Remind students that a general rule of thumb is that *por* looks back at causes while *para* looks forward at purpose and goals. Ask students to tell whether *por* or *para* would be used in the following sentences and to indicate why.

1. My parents left for Mexico this morning. (*para* = geographical destination)
2. It's a wine glass. (*para* = intended use or purpose)
3. She's nervous because of the exam. (*por* = because of, due to)
4. For an American, she speaks Spanish well. (*para* = implied comparison)
5. The homework is for Monday. (*para* = specified future time)

Prác. C: Suggestions

- Note that both meaning and grammar need to be considered when the fragments are matched.
- After doing the activity as written, encourage students to create their own endings for the sentences.

Prác. B, Paso 1: Answers
1. *No voy a menos que podamos…* **2.** *Vamos solos a las montañas para que pasemos… (para pasar)* **3.** *Esta vez voy a aprender a esquiar con tal de que tú me enseñes.* **4.** *Vamos a salir temprano por la mañana a menos que nos acostemos…* **5.** *Es urgente que lleguemos a la estación de esquí antes de que empiece…* **6.** *Deja la dirección y el teléfono del hotel en caso de que tus padres nos necesiten.* **7.** *No vamos a regresar antes de que nos hayamos cansado…*

B. Un fin de semana de esquí

Paso 1. Manolo y Lola están haciendo planes para un fin de semana de esquí. Use la conjunción entre paréntesis para unir las oraciones, haciendo todos los cambios necesarios.

1. No voy. Podemos dejar a la niña con los abuelos. (a menos que)
2. Vamos solos a las montañas. Pasamos un fin de semana romántico. (para que)
3. Esta vez voy a aprender a esquiar. Tú me enseñas. (con tal de que)
4. Vamos a salir temprano por la mañana. Nos acostamos tarde esta noche. (a menos que)
5. Es urgente que lleguemos a la estación (*resort*) de esquí. Empieza a nevar. (antes de que)
6. Deja la dirección y el teléfono del hotel. Tus padres nos necesitan. (en caso de que)
7. No vamos a regresar. Nos hemos cansado de esquiar. (antes de que)

Paso 2. Diga si las siguientes oraciones son ciertas o falsas o si no se menciona la infomación, según el **Paso 1.**

	CIERTO	FALSO	NO SE MENCIONA
1. Manolo y Lola acaban de casarse.	☐	☐	☑
2. Casi siempre salen de vacaciones con su hija.	☐	☐	☑
3. Los dos son excelentes esquiadores.	☐	☑	☐
4. Van a dejar a la niña con los abuelos.	☑	☐	☐

Nota **comunicativa**

¿Para qué?* / *para* (*que*)… and *¿por qué?* / *porque…

These words are all close in meaning, but they are used for different purposes. Their use is similar to the use of their English equivalents.

¿Para qué?	What for? For what purpose?	**¿Por qué?**	Why? For what reason?
Para (que)…	(In order) To . . . So that . . .	**Porque…**	Because . . .

Compare the use of these words in the following sentences.

—¿**Para qué** necesitas ahora la lista de invitados a la boda?
—**Para** confirmar el número de invitados que van a asistir. Y **para que** el dueño del restaurante sepa exactamente cuántos invitados van a venir.

—¿**Por qué** estás tan nervioso?
—¡**Porque** me caso en una semana!

¡OJO!
¿Por qué… ? / Porque… ⟶ *indicative*
Para… + *infinitive*
Para que… ⟶ *subjunctive*

C. Razones para hacer las cosas que hacemos. Empareje las frases de las dos columnas para hacer oraciones completas.

1. __c__ Las universidades tienen cursos que son requisitos para…
2. __d__ Los profesores corrigen (*correct*) tareas para…
3. __b__ Estudiamos español para…
4. __e__ Trabajamos en parejas en clase para…
5. __a__ Los profesores organizan actividades en grupo en clase para que…

a. los estudiantes tengan más oportunidad de hablar español.
b. poder comunicarnos con mucha más gente.
c. que los estudiantes tengan un conocimiento amplio del mundo.
d. darles a los estudiantes más ayuda.
e. hablar más en clase.

D. Relaciones sociales. Hay relaciones sociales de muchos tipos en donde unos dependen de otros. Complete las siguientes oraciones con el presente de subjuntivo para describir algunas de ellas.

1. Los abuelos miman (*spoil*) a sus nietos con tal de que los padres... (permitirlo)
2. Los padres esperan que los padrinos (*godparents*) cuiden a sus hijos en caso de que ellos... (morirse)
3. Los buenos amigos siempre saben lo que uno necesita antes de que... (decírselo)
4. Los amigos paraguayos se reúnen afuera para tomar el té paraguayo con tal de que... (hacer buen tiempo)
5. Los estudiantes no estudian sin que los profesores... (darles tarea)
6. Los esposos se llevan bien a menos que... (haber entre ellos una gran diferencia de opiniones)
7. Los padres trabajan para que sus hijos... (tener lo que necesitan)

Una mujer que toma su tereré (*Paraguayan version of Argentine* mate)

Prác. D: Answers: 1. *lo permitan* **2.** *se mueran* **3.** *se lo diga* **4.** *haga buen tiempo* **5.** *les den tarea* **6.** *haya entre ellos una gran diferencia de opiniones* **7.** *tengan lo que necesitan*

Conversación

A. Situaciones. Cualquier acción puede justificarse. En parejas, den una explicación para las siguientes situaciones. Luego comparen sus explicaciones con las de otra pareja.

1. Los padres trabajan mucho para (que) / porque...
2. Los profesores les dan tarea a los estudiantes para (que) / porque...
3. Los dueños de los equipos deportivos profesionales les pagan mucho a algunos jugadores para (que) / porque...
4. Las películas extranjeras se doblan (*are dubbed*) para (que) / porque...
5. Los padres castigan (*punish*) a los niños para (que) / porque...
6. Las parejas se divorcian para (que) / porque...
7. Los jóvenes forman pandillas (*gangs*) para (que) / porque...

Estrategia

No se olvide: **porque** ⟶ *indicative*
para + *infinitive*
para que ⟶ *subjunctive*

B. Intercambios

Paso 1. Complete las siguientes ideas usando una conjunción de contingencia o propósito o una preposición: **a menos que, antes de (que), con tal de (que), en caso de (que), para (que), sin (que).**

MODELO: Voy a graduarme en esta universidad... ⟶ Voy a graduarme en esta universidad en dos años **a menos que saque malas notas en varias clases.**

1. Voy a graduarme en esta universidad...
2. (No) Voy a casarme con mi novio/a actual... (Mi hijo/a [no] va a casarse con su novio/a actual...)
3. Espero tener un buen trabajo en dos o tres años...
4. Deseo tener hijos/nietos...
5. Voy a quedarme en este estado...

Paso 2. Ahora, en parejas, comparen sus oraciones y digan a la clase cuáles de sus ideas son muy similares o muy diferentes.

Mundo interactivo

You should now be prepared to work with Scenario 8, Activity 4 in Connect Spanish (**www.connectspanish.com**).

Con: A: Extension

8. *Estudiamos para (que) / porque...*
9. *Reciclamos para (que) / porque...*
10. *Votamos para (que) / porque...*

Bright Idea

Con. B: Follow-up

Bring magazine clippings or printed images from the Internet. Display the images and encourage students to ask appropriate questions using *¿Por qué?* and *¿Para qué?* For example, for a pain relief advertisement, students might ask: *¿Para qué es ese producto?* (For what is that product used?) and *¿Por qué necesita el señor tomar ese producto?* (Why does the man need to take that product?)

Redacción: Assign 2–3 of the *Con. B* items as a writing assignment. Set expectations about the length of each answer (short paragraph).

Optional

Ask students to complete the following sentences to create reasons to break up with someone. They should use conjunctions of purpose or contingency or prepositions.

1. *No puedo continuar contigo...*
2. *Quiero que dejemos de vernos...*
3. *Es necesario que terminemos...*
4. *Tengo que romper contigo...*
5. *Debo decirte que esto se acabó...*

Then ask students to invent sentences to convince another person to go out with them or marry them. Be prepared for humorous responses.

MODELOS: *Quiero que salgas conmigo para que yo te pueda ayudar con el español.*
Quiero que te cases conmigo para que nos hagan muchos regalos de boda.

Un poco de todo

A: Reciclado

Recycle the weekend activities vocabulary. Have students express the following ideas in Spanish.

1. We go there to have fun.
2. We also go so that the kids can play baseball.
3. They're going to swim before eating (they eat).
4. Are they going to swim before we eat?
5. Don't go without talking to your mother.
6. And don't leave without your father giving you money.

B: Note

The following grammar topics are included in *Lengua y cultura:* adjective agreement, demonstratives, object pronouns, use of verbs like *gustar, se + verb*, subjunctive vs. indicative, preterite and imperfect, present perfect, *ser* vs. *estar, por* vs. *para.*

B: Suggestion

Point out that *pelaos* and *pelaas* are contractions of *pelados* and *peladas.* In Colombia, in Spain, and in many other countries, the intervocalic *-d-* is often not pronounced in everyday speech.

Redacción: Assign *¿Cómo se divierten Ud. y sus amigos?* as a composition topic. Allow students to use as much of the structure of the *Lengua y cultura* passage as needed. However, they must, in addition, cover at least two if not all of the following *etapas de la vida* in their composition: *la niñez, la adolescencia, en esta etapa de mi vida, en el futuro* (*cuando me gradúe*).

Un poco de todo

A. Situaciones de la vida. En parejas, hagan y contesten preguntas según el modelo. Deben justificar sus respuestas.

MODELO: compañero/a de cuarto / tener coche →

E1: ¿**Buscas** un compañero de cuarto que **tenga** coche?
E2: No, ya tengo coche. (Sí, **para que** yo no **tenga** que manejar tanto. / Sí, **en caso de que** mi coche viejo no **funcione.**)

1. marido/mujer / ser médico/a
2. amigo/a / no haber roto recientemente con su pareja
3. casa / estar lejos de la ciudad
4. ciudad / haber un buen sistema de transporte público
5. amistad / estar basada en la confianza (*trust*)
6. coche / arrancar en seguida, sin dificultad
7. computadora / tener más memoria
8. teléfono celular / poder recibir correo electrónico y fotos

B. Lengua y cultura: ¿Cómo se divierten los hispanos? Complete the following description of the favorite pastimes of Hispanic youths. Give the correct form of the words in parentheses, as suggested by context. When two possibilities are given in parentheses, select the correct word. **¡OJO!** Context will help you choose what to do with the infinitives. If they don't remain in the infinitive form, these are your choices.

Indicativo: el presente, el presente perfecto, el pretérito, el imperfecto
Subjuntivo: el presente, el presente perfecto

Unos jóvenes paraguayos en Asuncíon

Como es obvio, hay algunas diferencias entre las culturas norteamericana e hispana. Pero en cuanto a[a] la manera en que los jóvenes se divierten, la verdad es que hay (mucho[1]) puntos en común. A los jóvenes hispanohablantes, que se (*ellos:* llamar[2]) chicos y chicas en el Paraguay, gallos y gallas en Chile, patojos y patojas en Guatemala, pelados y peladas en Colombia, (les/se[3]) (encantar[4]) la música. (Por/Para[5]) eso, no es extraño que (*ellos:* ir[6]) a las discotecas donde (bailar[7]) hasta el amanecer.[b] (A los / Los[8]) muchachos en especial (le/les[9]) (interesar[10]) los eventos deportivos.

En los últimos años, el concepto del centro comercial se (desarrollar[11]) en las ciudades hispanas. Como en este país, (a menos / con tal de[12]) que (haber[13]) tiendas de moda juvenil y electrónica, así como[c] restaurantes económicos, (este[14]) centros atraen[d] (a/–[15]) los jóvenes. También puede haber[e] cines y hasta[f] supermercados en los centros comerciales.

Una cosa que sí distingue[g] a los países hispanos es la costumbre[h] del paseo, que consiste en (caminar[16]) por distracción.[i] Es una manera de pasar un rato con amigos o familiares y es una actividad (por/para[17]) personas de cualquier[j] edad. Es importante (recordar[18]) que el paseo no se considera una actividad deportiva sino social. En este sentido, no es comparable de ninguna forma con el *hiking* en la cultura angloparlante.

[a]en... *as far as* [b]*dawn* [c]así... *as well as* [d]*to attract (like* traer) [e]puede... *there can be* [f]*even* [g]*differentiates* [h]*custom, tradition* [i]*amusement* [j]*any*

B: Answers: 1. *muchos* **2.** *llaman* **3.** *les* **4.** *encanta* **5.** *Por* **6.** *vayan* **7.** *bailan* **8.** *A los* **9.** *les* **10.** *interesan* **11.** *ha desarrollado* **12.** *con tal de* **13.** *haya* **14.** *estos* **15.** *a* **16.** *caminar* **17.** *para* **18.** *recordar*

Comprensión. Conteste las siguientes preguntas.

1. Según la información en los párrafos, ¿cuáles son algunas de las semejanzas en la forma de divertirse entre los jóvenes hispanos y norteamericanos?
2. ¿Qué palabras se usan para expresar «muchachos y muchachas» en varios países hispanos?
3. ¿Qué es el paseo?
4. ¿Qué ventajas y desventajas ve Ud. en la costumbre hispana del paseo?

Comprensión, Answers: 1. *la música, bailar, los deportes, ir al centro comercial, ir a tiendas y restaurantes y al cine* **2.** *chicos y chicas, gallos y gallas, patojos y patojas, pelados y peladas* **3.** *Es una actividad social que consiste en caminar por distracción.* **4.** Answers will vary.

En su comunidad

Entreviste a una persona hispana de su universidad o ciudad sobre las relaciones afectivas en su país.

PREGUNTAS POSIBLES

- ¿Qué palabras cariñosas se usan con más frecuencia entre padres e hijos en su país de origen? ¿Y entre esposos o novios? ¿entre amigos?
- ¿Cómo se celebra una boda típica en su país?
- ¿Cuál es el porcentaje de divorcios? ¿Es más alto que el de este país o más bajo? Comparado con lo que era hace veinte o treinta años, ¿ha cambiado recientemente?

En su comunidad

Suggestions

- Remind students to get the following basic information: the informant's country of origin, how long he or she has lived in this country, and if the informant visits his or her country of origin frequently.
- This activity could also be assigned as an online research project on a country of the student's choice or assigned by you.
- See the IM for additional suggestions and guidelines.

Optional

Have students complete the following sentences. Write them on the board or on an overhead transparency. You might prompt the sentences with questions.

MODELO: *¿En qué tipo de restaurante prefiere Ud. comer? → Prefiero comer en restaurantes donde ofrezcan una gran selección de vinos.*

1. *Prefiero comer en restaurantes donde ______.*
2. *No me gusta que los programas de televisión ______.*
3. *Voy a graduarme en ______ a menos que ______.*
4. *Me gusta que los profesores ______.*
5. *Deseo tener algún día un coche que ______.*
6. *Este verano voy a ______ a menos que ______.*
7. *Me gustan las personas que ______.*
8. *En el futuro, quiero tener ______ hijos con tal de que ______.*
9. *No conozco ninguna familia que ______.*
10. *Necesito amigos que ______.*
11. *Mis amigos y yo buscamos ______ que ______.*
12. *No voy a ______ antes de que ______.*

Resources: Desenlace

In the *Cap. 16* segment of "Chapter-by-Chapter Supplementary Materials" in the IM you will find a chapter-culminating activity. You can use this activity to consolidate and review the vocabulary and grammar skills students have acquired.

TelePuntos

Note

Pages 486–491 are optional. You may cover some, all, or none of this material in class, or assign it to students—as a group or individually—for homework or extra credit. Pages 492–493 (*En resumen: En este capítulo*) are a summary of all of the chapter's active material.

Antes de mirar

Suggestion

Have a whole class discussion about the topics raised in the questions.

Programa 16

- This show will be relatively accessible to students, and it will probably be one of the ones that they will like the most.
- The winner of the contest will not be announced on the next show (*Programa 17*), as *Salu2* is a daily show and only certain episodes of it are included in *Telepuntos*. Students can vote for (and defend) one of the two contestants in the *Y ahora, Uds.,* *activity.*
- Emphasize to students that the more carefully they study the preliminary activities (*Antes de mirar, Vocabulario de este programa,* and *Fragmento del guion*), the more they will understand. Scanning *Después de mirar* before viewing is also an excellent strategy.

Fragmento del guion

Suggestion

Point out use of the diminutive in *cerquita*. This diminutive is used not only in Mexico but in other parts of the Spanish-speaking world as well.

TELEPUNTOS SALU2

«¿Qué les parecen (*How do you feel about*) estas imágenes? ¿Románticas? Las parejas latinas tienden a demostrar (*to show*) su afecto abiertamente en los lugares públicos… »

Antes de mirar

¿Qué piensa Ud. de las demostraciones de afecto (*affection*) de las parejas en público? ¿Le molestan o no? ¿Conoce Ud. a alguien que haya encontrado pareja a través de (*through*) un servicio de Internet? ¿Ha usado Ud. este tipo de servicio alguna vez? ¿Lo usaría? (*Would you use it?*)

PROGRAMA 16: Cosas del amor

En este programa se muestran reportajes sobre la tolerancia en los países hispanos hacia (*toward*) las demostraciones de afecto de las parejas en público. También se reporta cómo varias parejas se conocieron. Por fin se ven los vídeos de tres personas que buscan pareja. Se pide a los telespectadores que elijan entre dos hombres al que (*the one who*) va a salir con la mujer.

Vocabulario de este programa

sensible	sensitive	**hacer de cupidos**	to be a match maker, act as Cupid	**¿A qué esperas?**	What are you waiting for?
la costumbre	habit, custom	**el sueño**	dream	**Uds. tendrán que**	you will have to
importarle	to be important to one	**no me falta trabajo**	I don't lack work	**dedicarse (qu) (a)**	to work (as)
Uds. se preguntarán	you'll wonder	**reconocer (reconozco)**	to recognize	**formar un hogar**	to settle down
por lo tanto	therefore	**la ropa interior**	underwear	**disponible**	available
¡qué asco!	how disgusting!	**cansarse de**	to grow tired of	**diremos**	we will tell
¿cuántos años tienen ya de casados?	how long have you been married?				

Fragmento del guion

LAURA: ¡Hola! ¿Cómo se conocieron?
HOMBRE: Ah, bueno, nosotros nos conocimos en una fiesta. En un baile que acudimos casualmente.[a] Coincidimos[b] en esa fiesta y ahí[c] nos conocimos.
[…]
LAURA: ¿Cómo conociste a tu pareja?
MUJER: Lo conocí en una librería, aquí cerquita[d] de donde yo nací y crecí. Y… nos fue… él estaba viendo la computadora y yo entré a la librería a hacer copias.
LAURA: ¿Y fue amor a primera vista[e]?
MUJER: Yo creo que sí, porque fue como algo inesperado[f] donde los dos nos dimos la mirada[g] y hubo una conexión.
LAURA: Oooh… ¿y cómo es el tipo de persona ideal para tu vida?
MUJER: Para mi vida, una persona así como él.
LAURA: Ah, muy bien. Perfecto.

[a]*que… that we went to by chance* [b]*we were there at the same time* [c]allí [d]*very close by* [e]*a… at first sight* [f]*unexpected* [g]*nos… looked at each other*

« …él siempre me apoya (*supports*) en todo lo que yo quiera hacer. Y sin él, la verdad,… ya no soy completa.»

Mundo interactivo

Continue your work as an intern at HispanaVisión with Laura Sánchez Tejada, the roving reporter of *Salu2*, as you complete Scenario 8, Activities 3 and 4 in Connect Spanish (**www.connectspanish.com**).

Al mirar

En este episodio hay mucho humor, lo cual (*which*) se debe especialmente a Ana, la presentadora. Indique las ocasiones en que Ana dice algo claramente cómico y/o irónico.

1. ☑ Al principio (*At the beginning*), cuando les dice a los hombres que no se vayan porque hay contenido cultural en el programa.
2. ☑ Cuando les pide perdón a los hombres sensibles.
3. ☐ Cuando dice que en Panamá es normal ver a la gente besarse.
4. ☐ Cuando felicita (*she congratulates*) a Víctor por su matrimonio.
5. ☑ Cuando al final les dice a las chicas telespectadoras que piensen en Yolanda, no en sí mismas (*themselves*).

«Nuestros tres participantes (*contestants*) colocaron sus perfiles (*posted their profiles*) en un sitio de Internet para buscar pareja y los tres nos dieron permiso para mostrar sus videos y participar en este programa.»

Después de mirar

A. ¿Está claro? Complete las siguientes oraciones según el programa.

1. Se ven demostraciones de afecto en _____. todos los países hispanos
2. Las parejas que se ven en el segundo reportaje viven en _____. California
3. Hace _____ años que Víctor está casado. diez
4. *El juego del amor* es la versión en español de _____. The Dating Game
5. Los participantes en *El juego del amor* se llaman _____. Yolanda, Ronnie y Pedro
6. _____ va(n) a elegir una pareja. Los telespectadores van

B. Un poco más. Conteste las siguientes preguntas.

1. ¿Qué explicación ofrece el reportaje sobre la costumbre de las demostraciones románticas en público en los países hispanos?
2. ¿Cómo se conocieron las personas de cada pareja? ¿Fue amor a primera vista entre algunos de ellos? ¿Entre quiénes?
3. ¿Está casada Ana? ¿Por qué cree Ud. eso?
4. ¿Cuál es la profesión de los tres participantes que buscan pareja?
5. ¿Qué observación sobre Víctor les hace Ana a las telespectadoras, a manera de chiste (*as a joke*)?

C. Y ahora, Uds. En grupos de 4 o 5, debatan sobre cuál de los hombres es mejor para Yolanda. Después voten y presenten sus resultados al resto de la clase, ofreciendo argumentos a favor y en contra de los dos hombres.

Act. B, Answers: 1. *Los jóvenes hispanos viven un tiempo más largo con sus familias y tienen menos espacio privado para sus relaciones amorosas.* **2.** *La primera pareja se conoció en una fiesta y no dicen si fue amor a primera vista. La segunda se conoció en una librería y sí fue amor a primera vista. La tercera se conoció en un baile y también fue amor a primera vista.* **3.** *No, porque, cuando Víctor dice que hace diez años que está casado, Ana dice: «ojalá que yo pueda decir lo mismo un día».* **4.** *Yolanda trabaja en el área de los medios de comunicación, Ronnie es actor y Pedro es dentista.* **5.** *Les dice que Víctor no está disponible, porque está casado.*

Sobre el programa

¿Y qué hay de la vida romántica de Laura? Tiene un novio estadounidense en San Francisco. Cuando llegó a los Estados Unidos, Laura tenía tres años de ser novia de un compañero de universidad de Nuevo León (México). Pero la distancia entre ellos pudo más que[a] el amor. En su primer viaje a San Francisco, solo dos meses después de llegar a California, conoció a un veterinario mientras hacía entrevistas en un refugio de animales. Fue un flechazo instantáneo[b] para los dos, aunque estaban hablando a través de c un traductor. Y ahora, ¡acumulan millas aéreas todos los fines de semana!

[a]pudo… *was stronger than* [b]flechazo… amor a primera vista [c]a… *through*

Producción personal

Filme una entrevista con una pareja en la que (*which*) hablen de cuándo y cómo se conocieron y cuánto tiempo hace que están juntos.

Después de mirar

C: Suggestion

Follow up this activity with a similar *Juego del amor* in class. Ask students to prepare similar profiles as homework. In class, choose some of them to act as contestants, and have the rest of the class vote, as in *Salu2*.

Sobre el programa

Optional: Comprensión

1. *¿Cuándo y cómo conoció Laura a su novio actual?* (*cuando hacía una entrevista en San Francisco, dos meses después de llegar a California*)
2. *¿Es este su primer novio?* (*No, tuvo un novio mexicano por tres años.*)
3. *¿Cuál es la profesión del novio de Laura?* (*Es veterinario.*)
4. *¿Habla español el novio?* (*no*)

Producción personal

See the IM for additional suggestions for this chapter's assignment as well as for general guidelines and suggestions for videotape assignments.

Lectura cultural

Notes

- The Instructor's Edition on this page offers some additional information on the country of focus. For more information about the country of focus, see the chapter's opening pages and the IM.
- See the IM for some expressions used in Paraguay.

First Reading: Notes

- Introduce optional vocabulary for discussing the reading: *comprometerse* = to get engaged; *estar comprometido/a* = to be engaged.
- It is not common to give an engagement ring in all Spanish-speaking countries, although a boyfriend may give a girlfriend a ring as a gift for other reasons. Wedding bands are the norm, for women and, increasingly, for men, and they are called *anillos* or *alianzas*.

En otros países hispanos

Notes

- Public displays of affection between *novios* are especially common in city parks, but they occur in other public places as well. Hispanics pay no attention to the couples.
- It is also worth noting that Hispanics in general display their affection for others very physically, as has been noted in the context of greetings, where it is common to hug and kiss.

Exploración lingüística

Ask students to find the following in the reading. Some of these words are glossed and some are not.

- *Un sinómino de* tener novio/a (*estar de novio/a*)
- *Dos significados de la palabra* pareja (pair, partner)
- *Dos sinónimos de* salir con (*andar con, tener amigo*)

Comprensión

Answers

1. *El concepto de novio/a es más serio. Las palabras* novio *y* novia *se usan también para referirse a* bride *y* groom. **2.** *pareja* **3.** *Porque con frecuencia los jóvenes hispanos viven con su familia y no tienen mucha privacidad.* **4.** *el concepto de la cita romántica*

Tres símbolos paraguayos

Notes

- *El Gran Chaco* covers 250,000 square miles (about 650.000 km²), making it six times larger than Yosemite National Park. Only 2% of Paraguayans live in *el Chaco,* which is largely covered with low shrubs and marshes. There are several national parks in the region.
- The Guarani language has given the Spanish language names such as *piraña, jaguar, tapir,* and *petunia.*

Un lugar especial

Notes

The Itaipu Dam is an impressive structure. It was built with enough concrete to construct 210 stadiums for 100,000 spectators each and enough steel to erect 380 Eiffel Towers.

A LEER

Lectura cultural

El Paraguay

En el Paraguay, como en casi todo el mundo hispanohablante, el concepto de noviazgo es un poco diferente del de[a] este país. Tener novio/a o estar de novio/a indica que una relación es seria y formal, con miras al[b] futuro. **Novio** y **novia,** además,[c] son los términos que se aplican a las personas que se casan o que se acaban de casar. Como el noviazgo ya señala un compromiso,[d] no es tan frecuente usar la palabra **prometido/a**[e] para referirse a los novios que van a casarse. Cuando las relaciones entre dos personas son informales, se dice que **andan**[f] o **salen** juntos,[g] o simplemente que la persona tiene un amigo o amiga. Con frecuencia se usa la palabra **pareja** para referirse a una persona que convive[h] con otra sin casarse. Por ejemplo, se dice: «Te presento a mi pareja.»

¿Qué expresiones en inglés usa Ud. para referirse a los diferentes tipos de relaciones entre parejas?

[a]del... *from that of* [b]con... *(one that is) looking ahead to the* [c]*in addition* [d]señala... *indicates a commitment* [e]*fiancé/fiancée* [f]*lit., are walking* [g]*together* [h]*cohabits*

En otros países hispanos

- **En todo el mundo hispanohablante** Es cosa común ver demostraciones de afecto entre una pareja en parques, plazas y calles, lo cual[a] a veces resulta chocante[b] a algunas personas de otras culturas. Pero es conveniente recordar que la mayoría de los jóvenes vive con su familia y no tiene muchas oportunidades de intimidad.[c]
- **En España y otros países** El concepto de la cita no es común entre los jóvenes. En términos generales, muchos jóvenes españoles asocian la idea de tener una cita con alguien con costumbres pasadas de moda[d] o les suena[e] demasiado formal. Desde que[f] los chicos empiezan a salir sin sus padres, lo típico es salir en grupos, en los cuales[g] se forman parejas. Pero todavía prefieren salir en grupo a tomar algo en un bar por la noche o a tomar un café por la tarde.

[a]lo... *which* [b]*shocking* [c]*privacy* [d]costumbres... *old-fashioned traditions* [e]les... *it sounds to them* [f]Desde... *From the time that* [g]en... *in which*

Tres símbolos paraguayos

- **El Gran Chaco** Es una altiplanicie aluvial[a] formada por los ríos Paraguay y Pilcomayo y sus afluentes.[b] Es un inmenso territorio que comprende[c] el 60 por ciento del Paraguay, además de[d] gran parte de Bolivia, así como del norte de la Argentina y una parte del Brasil. En el Chaco ha habido colonias de menonites desde los años 20, pero solo hasta ahora la mayoría del territorio está empezando a desarrollarse para la agricultura.
- **La cultura guaraní** Esta cultura indígena continúa muy presente en el Paraguay, especialmente a través de[e] su lengua, que es hablada por más del 80 por ciento de la población. El Paraguay es uno de los países más homogéneos de Latinoamérica precisamente porque la población es mestiza, parte de ascendencia guaraní y parte española.
- **El té paraguayo** Esta bebida es la base de la yerba mate, como en la Argentina y el Uruguay. En el Paraguay se prepara el mate con agua fría o jugo de fruta, y a esto se le llama **tereré.** El tipo de taza[f] en que se bebe el tereré, que es la guampa, tradionalmente está hecha de una calabaza,[g] pero se hacen de otros materiales hoy en día también.

[a]una... *a high alluvial (that is, formed from river deposits) plateau* [b]*tributaries* [c]*makes up* [d]además... *besides* [e]a... *through* [f]*cup* [g]*gourd*

La Represa de Itaipú

Un lugar especial

La Represa[a] de Itaipú es la represa hidroeléctrica más grande del mundo. Es el resultado de un proyecto binacional entre los gobiernos del Paraguay y el Brasil y se encuentra en la frontera[b] entre esos dos países. La represa, que se abrió en 1984, provee[c] casi toda la energía que necesita el Paraguay y un cuarto de la energía que consume el Brasil.

[a]*Dam* [b]*border* [c]*provides*

COMPRENSIÓN

1. ¿En qué es diferente el concepto de novio/a del (*from that*) de *boyfriend/girlfriend?*
2. ¿Qué palabra se usa para referirse a una persona que convive con otra en una relación amorosa sin que estén casados?
3. ¿Por qué es normal que los jóvenes demuestren su cariño en público?
4. ¿Qué costumbre de este país no es común entre los jóvenes españoles?

Del mundo hispano

Antes de leer

Imagine que Ud. ve a una persona que no conoce e inmediatamente se enamora de ella. De las siguientes cosas que Ud. podría (*could*) hacer en esta situación, ¿cuáles son apropiadas socialmente? Explique cada respuesta.

	¿APROPIADAS SOCIALMENTE? SÍ	NO
1. mirar a esa persona	☐	☐
2. hablar con esa persona	☐	☐
3. pedirle el número de teléfono a esa persona	☐	☐
4. escribir un poema sobre esa persona	☐	☐
5. darle a esa persona un poema que Ud. escribió	☐	☐
6. decirle a esa persona que quiere tocarla	☐	☐
7. tocar a esa persona	☐	☐

Lectura: «Palomas»,° de Gloria Fuertes

°*Doves*

Mis manos son dos aves,[a]
a lo mejor[b] palomas.
Que buscan por el aire
una luz en la sombra.[c]
Mis manos, al mirarte,[d]
quedaron pensativas,[e]
yo temo que enloquezcan[f]
si es que en ti no se posan.[g]

[a]*birds* [b]a… *maybe* [c]*shadows, darkness* [d]al… *when they looked at you* [e]*thoughtful* [f]*they'll go crazy* [g]es… *if they don't come to rest on you*

Comprensión

A. Ideas y versos. En este poema cada par de versos (*lines*) expresa una idea independiente. Es decir, los versos 1 y 2 expresan una idea, los versos 3 y 4 expresan otra, etcétera. Empareje las siguientes oraciones con los dos versos que resumen.

1. v. 5–6 Cuando te vi, me quedé inmóvil por la sorpresa.
2. v. 7–8 Siento ganas inmensas de tocarte.
3. v. 3–4 Busco algo especial.
4. v. 1–2 Yo ando por el mundo como un pájaro.

B. Comprensión y análisis. Conteste las siguientes preguntas.

¿Por qué cree Ud. que la poeta…

1. usa como sujeto «Mis manos» en vez de «Yo»?
2. usa la palabra **palomas** para referirse a sus manos?
3. usa el verbo **posar** en el verso final?

Del mundo hispano

Note

See the IM for optional follow-up, writing, and Internet activities.

Antes de leer

Suggestions

- Do as a whole-class survey, after giving students a few minutes to answer individually or in pairs. Compare students' opinions and elicit debate about disagreements.
- Give students the following information about *palomas* before they begin to read: *Las palomas son un tipo de pájaro. Son pájaros con instintos muy fuertes, fáciles de domesticar. En español no se distingue entre* dove *y* pigeon. *La palabra* paloma *tiene una buena connotación.*

Estrategia

Dividing Poems into Parts

To help students decode the poem, tell them that it can be divided into four short sections (as is done in *Comprensión A*). Ask them to try to find the sections before they read *Comprensión A*. The first section simply describes *mis manos*, the second tells that they're looking for *luz en la sombra* (i.e., something special), the third describes the moment they become aware of "you" (the person to whom the poet is speaking), the fourth describes what will happen if they can't touch "you."

Comprensión B: Possible Answers

1. *Mis manos* allows the poet to use the images of birds, air, light, and shadow to describe their search. By using them as subject the poet can give them their own animal-like personality: *buscan, mirar, quedaron pensativas, enloquezcan, se posan.* We touch and explore the world actively with our hands, which are the most mobile part of our bodies. **2.** The subject varies between *mis manos* and *palomas*. While *mis manos* are not separate beings and cannot really *mirarte, quedar pensativas,* or *enloquecer,* because they don't have their own will, *las palomas* potentially can do all of those things. *Las palomas* are also known as gentle, sociable birds that are attracted to humans. People domesticate and use carrier pigeons; doves are known for their plaintive coo and are often said to be lonely if alone. **3.** Hands can touch softly, like the landing of a dove.

Escuche

Notes

- In this chapter students can listen to a radio ad for an online dating service.
- If the listening is assigned as homework, ask students to listen to the passage at least twice.
- See the IM for the Audioscript and more information about music in Paraguay.

Después de escuchar

B: Follow-up

Ask students to write an online ad for a dating service. Before students start on this task, have a whole-class discussion about the kind of information it is important to include and what information is best left out.

¡Música!

Note

- *Los Paraguayos* played until the mid seventies. Their leader was *Luis Alberto del Paraná.*
- For helpful tips on using songs in the classroom, see the IM.

A ESCUCHAR

Antes de escuchar

¿Cómo se puede encontrar a la pareja ideal? Según su experiencia, ¿es difícil conocer a personas que podrían (*could*) ser su pareja? ¿Qué es necesario o fundamental para que haya una buena relación entre una pareja?

Escuche

Un anuncio para Naranjas

En la radio hay un anuncio de un servicio *online* de búsqueda (*search*) de parejas. Escuche según las indicaciones de su profesor(a).

Vocabulario para escuchar

la media naranja	better half	**lograr**	to achieve
el éxito	success	**duradero/a**	long-lasting
el cuestionario	questionnaire	**los valores**	values
los pilares	pillars, bases	**la afinidad**	compatibility
cualquier	any	**elegir**	to select
los terapeutas	therapists	**inscríbete gratis**	register for free
los investigadores	researchers	**el perfil**	profile
los compatibles	**las personas compatibles**	**la soledad**	loneliness
comprobado/a	demonstrated		

A: Answers
1. *Se hace online.* 2. *Está basado en su cuestionario.* 3. *La afinidad es muy importante.* 4. *Se inscribe gratis. Se paga solo por la suscripción.*

B: Answers
1. *el cuestionario y la mayor red de personas* 2. *Porque está basado en numerosos estudios y en el trabajo de un dedicado equipo de psicólogos que trabaja exclusivamente para Naranjas.* 3. *Es gratis inscribirse y son gratis también el perfil de personalidad y la lista preseleccionada.* 4. *Por el precio de seis meses ofrece doce meses de servicio.* 5. *Porque ayuda a la gente a buscar su media naranja.*

Después de escuchar

A. La información correcta. Las siguientes oraciones son falsas. Corríjalas.

1. El cuestionario de Naranjas se hace con papel y lápiz.
2. El éxito de este sitio está basado en las reuniones con los terapeutas.
3. La afinidad de valores e intereses no es importante para una buena relación entre dos personas.
4. Es necesario pagar para inscribirse.

B. Más detalles. Conteste las siguientes preguntas.

1. ¿Qué ventajas ofrece Naranjas sobre otros sitios?
2. ¿Por qué es importante el cuestionario de Naranjas?
3. ¿Qué ofrece gratis Naranjas?
4. ¿Cuál es la oferta para los nuevos miembros?
5. ¿Por qué cree Ud. que este sitio se llama Naranjas?

Los Paraguayos

¡Música!

El grupo Los Paraguayos interpreta música folclórica que incorpora[a] el arpa p araguaya. «Galopera*» es una canción tradicional de su álbum *Malagueña*.

[a]usa

*La galopera, o el galope (*gallop*), es un baile folclórico del Paraguay.

Go to the iMix section in Connect Spanish (**www.connectspanish.com**) to access the iTunes playlist *"Puntos9,"* where you can purchase "Galopera" by Los Paraguayos.

A ESCRIBIR

El tema

Columna de consejos sentimentales

Preparar

Elija un tipo de relaciones personales sobre el que (*which*) quiere escribir un ensayo:

- las relaciones entre parejas
- las relaciones puramente amistosas

Ahora, usando como base su lista de ideas del **Paso 1** de la **Actividad C** (página 474), piense en lo que puede ocurrir en una relación cuando estos requisitos no existen. ¿Cuáles son los problemas más comunes que enfrentan (*face*) una pareja o unos buenos amigos? Haga una lista de tales (*such*) problemas.

Finalmente, piense en lo que Ud. y otras personas hacen cuando tienen problemas en una relación. ¿Con quién se debe hablar? ¿Con quién se puede consultar la situación? ¿Qué es preferible *no* hacer?

Redactar

A base de las ideas de **Preparar,** escriba Ud. una columna sobre las relaciones personales para el periódico estudiantil de su universidad. Empiece por ponerle título a la columna. Luego elija un tono que sea compatible con las ideas que quiere expresar. El tema de las relaciones personales se presta (*lends itself*) a varios tonos: humorístico, confesional, de ayuda personal (*self-help*), etcétera.

Editar

Revise el ensayo para comprobar:

- la ortografía y los acentos
- la organización y la secuencia de las ideas
- el tiempo y la forma de los verbos, especialmente el uso del subjuntivo
- el tono del ensayo

Finalmente, prepare su versión final para entregarla.

Preparar

Suggestions

- Ask students to review the uses of the subjunctive, especially the new structures in *Cap. 16.*
- Ask students to use the following to express facts with the indicative: *la experiencia nos muestra/enseña que… ; todo el mundo sabe / ha experimentado… ; no hace falta saber mucho para que… .*

Redactar

Suggestions

- Suggested length for this writing assignment: approximately 200 words
- Suggested structure: 3 paragraphs

  P. 1. Presentation of the topic
  P. 2. Description of the various characteristics of a good relationship, followed by suggestions about what to do when these characteristics are missing
  P. 3. Conclusion that summarizes the points made in the essay and offers at least one general recommendation

Editar

Follow-up

Have a whole-class discussion about the following topic: How can the suggestions students offered in their essays about personal relationships be applied to achieving peaceful relationships between countries that are at odds with each other?

En resumen: En este capítulo

Vocabulario

Suggestions

- Point out the first person singular of *conocer* (*conozco*), *crecer* (*crezco*), and *nacer* (*nazco*).
- Have students describe a relationship in their family, for example, that of their parents, and tell when and how they met, how long they dated, and so on. Model a description for them.
- Write the stages of life in Spanish on the board. Have students write at least two sentences for each stage of life. Have them write sentences describing a typical activity for the stages of life, for example:

  Llora a menos que esté cerca de su mamá. (*infancia*)

  Está muy solo y deprimido porque ya no trabaja y sus hijos están muy ocupados con propias obligaciones. (*vejez*)

  Está muy contento porque por fin tiene tiempo para viajar y trabajar en el jardín. (*vejez*)

  Have students read sentences to the class. The class should identify the stage of life.

Word Families

En este capítulo

- *la amistad, amistoso/a*
- *el amor, amar*
- *casarse, casado/a*
- *el divorcio, divorciarse, divorciado/a*
- *enamorarse, enamorado/a*
- *el noviazgo, el/la novio/a*
- *la separación, separarse, separado/a*

Entre capítulos

- *a menos que* = *menos* (1)
- *a primera vista* = *primero* (13), *la vista* (12)
- *la amistad, amistoso/a* = *el/la amigo/a* (2)
- *antes* (*de*) *que* = *antes de* (5)
- *casarse, casado/a* = *la casa* (2)
- *con tal* (*de*) *que* = *con* (2)
- *la juventud* = *joven* (3)
- *llevarse bien/mal con* = *llevar* (4)
- *la muerte* = *morir* (9)
- *la mujer* (wife) = *la mujer* (woman) (2)
- *el/la novio/a* (fiancé[e]; bride/groom) = *el/la novio/a* (boy/girlfriend) (6)
- *para que* = *para* (3)
- *querer* (to love) = *querer* (to want) (4)
- *romper con* = *romper* (14)
- *sin que* = *sin* (5)
- *la vejez* = *viejo/a* (3)

EN RESUMEN En este capítulo

LearnSmart

Visit **www.connectspanish.com** to practice the vocabulary and grammar points covered in this chapter.

Gramática en breve

44. The Subjunctive After Nonexistent and Indefinite Antecedents

①		②
definite/existent antecedent	**que**	indicative

Hay alguien/algo que…

①		②
indefinite/nonexistent antecedent	**que**	subjunctive

No hay nadie/nada que…
¿Hay alguien/algo que… ?

45. The Subjunctive After Conjunctions of Purpose and Contingency

①		②
indicative	conjunction of purpose or contingency	subjunctive

Conjunctions: **a menos que, antes (de) que, con tal (de) que, en caso de que, para que, sin que**

Vocabulario

Las relaciones sentimentales

amar	to love
casarse (con)	to marry
conocerse (conozco)	to meet
divorciarse (de)	to get divorced (from)
enamorarse (de)	to fall in love (with)
llevarse bien/mal (con)	to get along well/poorly (with)
querer	to love
romper (con)	to break up (with)
separarse (de)	to separate (from)

Repaso: estar (con), pelear con, salir (con)

la amistad	friendship
el amor	love
la boda	wedding (*ceremony*)
la iglesia	church
la luna de miel	honeymoon
el marido	husband
el matrimonio	marriage; married couple
la mujer	wife
la novia	fiancée; bride
el noviazgo	engagement
el novio	fiancé; groom
la pareja	(married) couple; partner
el/la viudo/a	widower/widow

Cognados: el divorcio, la separación

Repaso: el/la amigo/a, la cita, el/la esposo/a, el/la novio/a (*boy/girlfriend*)

amistoso/a	friendly
divorciado/a (de)	divorced (from)
enamorado/a (de)	in love (with)
recién casado/a (con)	newlywed (to)
separado/a (de)	separated (from)
soltero/a	single
estar casado/a (con)	to be married (to)
ser casado/a	to be a married person

Repaso: cariñoso/a, feliz (*pl.* felices)

Las etapas de la vida

la etapa	stage, phase
la juventud	youth
la madurez	middle age
la muerte	death
la vejez	old age

Cognados: la adolescencia, la infancia

Repaso: la niñez, la vida

crecer (crezco)	to grow
nacer (nazco)	to be born

Repaso: morir (muero) (u)

Las conjunciones

a menos que	unless
antes (de) que	before
con tal (de) que	provided (that)
en caso de que	in case
para que	so that
sin que	without; unless

Las preposiciones

con tal de	provided
en caso de	in case

Repaso: antes de, para, sin

Palabras adicionales

bastante	rather, sufficiently; enough
¿para qué… ?	for what purpose?, what for?

Repaso: conmigo, contigo, ¿por qué?, porque

Multimedia: Internet

Have students search the Internet for more information on weddings in Latin America and Spain. There are several websites in Spanish that describe different ways of planning civil and religious weddings. Encourage students to talk about differences and similarities between weddings in Spain and/or Latin America and weddings in the U.S. and/or Canada.

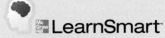

Vocabulario personal

En resumen En este capítulo ■ **493**

Chapter Opening Photo and Chapter Theme

Chapter Theme–related Questions

- Have students put the following phrases in order of importance to them (1 to 8).

  ______ *Pasar la mayor parte del tiempo al aire libre*
  ______ *Trabajar independientemente o sin supervisión constante*
  ______ *Viajar con frecuencia*
  ______ *Leer y escribir mucho*
  ______ *Ganar mucho dinero y jubilarme joven*
  ______ *Tener muchas posibilidades de mejorar y de tener aumentos de sueldo*
  ______ *Hacer mucho trabajo físico*
  ______ *Tomar muchas decisiones*

- Have students list specific professions or jobs they associate with the phrases listed above.
- Ask students the following questions.

  ¿Cree Ud. que las características del trabajo ideal cambian según las circunstancias de la vida?
  ¿En qué circunstancias pueden cambiar?
  ¿Cuáles son las características más importantes de un trabajo en cualquier momento de la vida?

Reciclado: Review the *ir* + *a* + *inf.* structure for expressing the future by asking the following questions.

1. *¿Cuándo va a graduarse en esta universidad?*
2. *¿Qué va a hacer después de graduarse? ¿Va a buscar un trabajo en seguida o va a descansar por un tiempo? ¿O piensa seguir estudiando?*
3. *Si piensa trabajar, ¿qué tipo de trabajo va a buscar? ¿En qué ciudad, estado o país piensa trabajar?*
4. *Si piensa descansar, ¿qué va a hacer en ese tiempo? ¿Va a viajar? ¿Va a quedarse en casa?*

17 ¿Trabajar para vivir o vivir para trabajar?

Durante la cosecha (*harvest*) de uvas Chardonnay, en Chile

- Piense en el título de este capítulo. Si Ud. ya tiene un trabajo de tiempo completo, ¿lo hace para vivir? ¿O vive para su trabajo? Si no trabaja todavía, ¿cuál cree que va a ser su actitud cuando ya trabaje?
- ¿Qué tipo de condiciones y beneficios espera Ud. tener en un trabajo? ¿Es importante para Ud. tener un horario flexible? ¿tener más de dos semanas de vacaciones? ¿tener seguro (*insurance*) médico? Si Ud. ya trabaja, ¿tiene a su disposición estas condiciones y beneficios?

Mc Graw Hill connect SPANISH

www.connectspanish.com

Resources

For Students

- Connect Spanish (**www.connectspanish.com**), which contains all content from the following resources, as well as the *Mundo interactivo* scenarios, the LearnSmart adaptive learning system, and more!
- **Physical Resources:** Workbook / Laboratory Manual, Laboratory Audio Program, DVD

For Instructors

- Connect Spanish (**www.connectspanish.com**), which contains access to all student sections of Connect Spanish, as well as helpful time-saving tools and resources such as an integrated gradebook, Instructor's Manual, Testing Program, digital transparencies, Audioscript, Videoscript, and more!

Chile

16,5 (y medio) millones de habitantes

- Chile es un país muy largo y angosto (*narrow*) que tiene casi todos los tipos de climas, con excepción del tropical. Se extiende desde el desierto de Atacama, el lugar más seco (*driest*) del mundo, hasta la Antártida.
- La minería, especialmente del cobre (*copper*), representa una gran parte del Producto Nacional Bruto (*Gross National Product*) de Chile.
- Los vinos chilenos, producidos en la zona central del país, están entre los mejores del mundo. De hecho (*In fact*), Chile ocupa el cuarto lugar entre los mayores exportadores de vino a los Estados Unidos.

En este capítulo

CONTENT / **CONTENIDO**	OBJECTIVES / **OBJETIVOS**
Professions 496, the Working World 498	To talk about all aspects of work
Money Matters 500	To talk about aspects of money management
The Future 502	To express future plans in a new way
The Subjunctive in Time Clauses 503	To express pending actions
Chile 516	To learn about a modern South American country with one of the continent's strongest economies

Chile

Datos esenciales

Nombre oficial: *República de Chile*
Lema: *«Por la razón o la fuerza»*
Capital: *Santiago de Chile*
Otras ciudades: *Valparaíso, Antofagasta, Temuco, Concepción, Punta Arenas*
Composición étnica: *95% blancos y mestizos, 4% mapuches, 1% otros indígenas (aymaras, rapanuis, etcétera)*
Jefe de estado actual: *Sebastián Piñera Echenique, desde 2009*
Forma de gobierno: *República democrática presidencial*
Lengua oficial: *el español; se habla también el mapudungun (la lengua de los mapuches)*
Moneda: *el peso chileno*
Religión: *70% católicos, 15% evangélicos, 8% ninguna, 5% otros (cristianos y no cristianos)*

Notes

- Chile has become an important regional and international player in recent years, thanks to its stable economy and democracy.
- The country has a life expectancy of almost 81 years for women and 74 for men. Its birth rate is below 1.9 per woman.
- Chile is the number one exporter of copper in the world.
- Chile has several islands, but its most famous one is *la Isla de Pascua* (Easter Island), home of the *rapanui* people and the famous *moai* statues.

Suggestions

- Ask students to look at the map of Chile and name two geographical features that determine the country's climate and geography, despite great latitudinal variation. The expected answers are the Andes to the east and the Pacific Ocean to the west.
- Have students list their ideas about Chile, including information on geography, politics, economy, culture, music, and cuisine. When you finish the chapter, return to the lists and ask students what ideas they would change and/or add. The success of this activity will depend not only on the content about Chile presented in the text but also on the extent to which you have time to supplement that content with your own knowledge and experiences and also with information given in this Instructor's Edition and the IM.

Multimedia

The IM provides suggestions for using the multimedia materials in the classroom.

Resources: Transparency 153

Vocabulario: Preparación

Las profesiones y los oficios

Suggestions

- This chapter offers a relatively large vocabulary load, in three different *Vocabulario: Preparación* sections. That said, much of the chapter's vocabulary is related to previously active vocabulary (see the Word Families list on p. 520), so it should be easy for students to master. To reduce the load of active vocabulary, suggest to students that they learn only the words for *Las profesiones y los oficios* that apply to them.
- Optional vocabulary: *el/la atleta profesional, el/la cirujano/a, el/la criado/a, el/la gerente, el/la niñero/a.*
- Optional: Introduce *dedicarse a* for speaking about professions: *¿A qué se dedica Ud.? / ¿Cuál es su profesión? → Me dedico a la enseñanza. / Soy profesor(a).*
- Use the following questions to check comprehension.
  1. *¿Quién gana más dinero, un plomero o un enfermero? ¿un obrero o un siquiatra?*
  2. *¿Quién tiene el trabajo más aburrido y por qué? ¿un siquiatra o un peluquero? ¿un comerciante o un abogado? ¿un plomero o un vendedor?*
  3. *¿Quién tiene más responsabilidades y por qué? ¿un maestro de escuela o un ingeniero? ¿un abogado o un plomero?*
  4. *¿Para qué profesiones es necesaria una educación universitaria? ¿De cuántos años?*
  5. *¿Cuál de estos trabajos le gusta más/menos? Explique por qué, dando las ventajas y desventajas.*
- Point out that there is little consensus in the Spanish-speaking world about words used for females practicing certain professions. Names given here should be acceptable to most Spanish speakers, but there is considerable discussion about terms such as *la pilota, la médica,* and so on. Have students review the *Nota cultural* on page 497.
- Remind students why the article *el* is used before *amo/a* (because *amo/a* begins with a stressed *a*). Ask students if they know another word with which this happens (*el agua*).
- Note that some Spanish speakers use the words *psicología / psicólogo/a* and *psiquiatría / psiquiatra* or *psiquíatra*. These alternate spellings and pronunciations are less favored today.

VOCABULARIO **Preparación**

Las profesiones y los oficios°

°trades

el maestro (la maestra) (de escuela)

1.

la médica (el médico)

2.

el plomero (la plomera)

3.

la cocinera (el cocinero)

4.

el peluquero (la peluquera)

5.

la mujer soldado (el soldado)

6.

Las profesiones

el abogado / la abogada	lawyer
el bibliotecario / la bibliotecaria	librarian
el consejero / la consejera	counselor
el contador / la contadora	accountant
el enfermero / la enfermera	nurse
el hombre / la mujer de negocios	businessperson
el ingeniero / la ingeniera	engineer
el/la periodista	journalist
el sicólogo / la sicóloga	psychologist
el/la siquiatra	psychiatrist
el trabajador social / la trabajadora social	social worker
el traductor / la traductora	translator

¡OJO!

If the vocabulary needed to describe your career goal is not listed here, look it up in a dictionary or ask your instructor.

Los oficios

el amo/ama de casa	housekeeper, homemaker
el cajero / la cajera	cashier; teller
el dependiente / la dependienta	clerk
el obrero / la obrera	worker, laborer
el técnico / la técnica	technician
el vendedor / la vendedora	salesperson

Cognados: el/la analista de sistemas, el/la artista, el/la asistente de vuelo, el/la astronauta, el/la dentista, el/la electricista, el fotógrafo / la fotógrafa, el mecánico / la mecánica, el/la militar, el profesor / la profesora, el programador / la programadora, el secretario / la secretaria, el veterinario / la veterinaria

NATIONAL STANDARDS: Communication

Have students interview each other about professions in their families. Have them find out what they do or want to do professionally, what their parents or children do, and if they have any relatives that have interesting or unique professions. Have students report their findings to the class and use the information to make generalizations about the class.

Resources: Transparency 154

Conversación

A. ¿A quién necesita Ud.?

Paso 1. ¿A quién se debe llamar o con quién se debe consultar en estas situaciones? **¡OJO!** Hay más de una respuesta posible en algunos casos.

1. La tubería del agua (*plumbing*) de la cocina no funciona bien. el/la plomero/a
2. Ud. acaba de tener un accidente automovilístico; el conductor del otro coche dice que Ud. tuvo la culpa (*blame*). el/la abogado/a
3. Por las muchas presiones de su vida profesional y personal, Ud. tiene serios problemas afectivos. el/la sicólogo/a, el/la siquiatra
4. Ud. es el dueño o la dueña de un restaurante y necesita a alguien que haga la comida. el/la cocinero/a
5. Ud. quiere que alguien le construya un muro (*wall*) en el jardín. el/la obrero/a
6. Ud. conoce los detalles de un escándalo local y quiere divulgarlos. el/la periodista

Paso 2. Ahora, en parejas, inventen situaciones como las del **Paso 1.** Luego léanlas a otros estudiantes para que ellos digan a quién deben consultar.

B. Asociaciones. ¿Qué profesiones u oficios asocian Uds. con estas frases? Consulten la lista de profesiones y oficios y usen el **Vocabulario útil.**

1. creativo/rutinario
2. muchos/pocos años de preparación o experiencia
3. buen sueldo / sueldo regular
4. mucha/poca responsabilidad
5. mucho/poco prestigio
6. flexibilidad / «de nueve a cinco»
7. mucho/poco tiempo libre
8. peligroso (*dangerous*) / seguro
9. en el pasado, solo para hombres/mujeres
10. todavía, solo para hombres/mujeres

Así se dice

el/la contador(a) = el/la contable (*Sp.*)
el/la periodista = el/la reportero/a
el/la plomero/a = el/la fontanero/a (*Sp.*)

Vocabulario **útil**

actor/actriz
arquitecto/a
camarero/a
cantinero/a (*bartender*)
carpintero/a
chófer
detective
niñero/a
pintor(a)
poeta
policía / mujer policía
político/a
presidente/a
sacerdote (*priest*), **pastor(a), rabino/a**
senador(a)

Nota **cultural**

Nuevas tendencias del español para evitar el sexismo lingüístico

Con el incremento de posiciones y cargos[a] ocupados por mujeres en todos los ámbitos[b] profesionales y de poder,[c] el debate por eliminar el sexismo en la lengua española se ha intensificado.

- Hay una clara tendencia por evitar el uso de la forma masculina o la palabra «hombre» para incluir en su designación a personas de los dos sexos, especialmente cuando hay sustantivos colectivos mixtos.

  el estudiantado[d] = estudiantes (hombres y mujeres)
  el profesorado[e] = profesores y profesoras
  la infancia = niños y niñas
  la tercera edad, las personas mayores = ancianos y ancianas

- En muchos ambientes laborales, se evita dar el tratamiento de «señorita» a todas las mujeres y se prefiere el de «señora», para no hacer distinción entre las mujeres solteras y las casadas, al igual que[f] esta distinción no se hace entre los hombres.
- La aplicación de la forma femenina a algunos cargos importantes, títulos y profesiones se ha estabilizado a medida que[g] las mujeres han conquistado estos puestos: **jefa, médica, ministra, presidenta.**

[a]*posts* [b]*arenas* [c]*power* [d]*student body, the students* [e]*faculty, the professors* [f]al... *just as* [g]a... *as*

Michelle Bachelet, ex Presidenta y ex Ministra de Salud y de Defensa de Chile

- Para integrar en una sola[h] palabra las formas masculina y femenina, se ha empezado a usar el símbolo de la arroba: @. Por ejemplo, **chic@s = chicos y chicas.** La limitación de esta forma es que es solo un recurso gráfico.[i]

Aunque[j] queda mucho por hacer para eliminar el sexismo en la lengua española, se han dado grandes pasos en todos los países y a todos los niveles.

¿Conoce Ud. algún ejemplo de sexismo en su lengua materna?

[h]*single* [i]un... *a graphic symbol* [j]*Although*

Con. A: Suggestion

Do *Con. A* as listening comprehension.

Bright Idea

Con. A: Extension

7. *En la escuela, su hijo no se lleva bien con los otros niños.*
8. *A Ud. le duele una muela o un diente.*
9. *Ud. está en un avión que va volando hacia Miami y tiene sed.*
10. *Su computadora no funciona.*

Con. B: Variations

- Have students keep a list of their first association for each item, then report back to the class. Tally the first associations for all students on the board. Do patterns emerge? Discuss them as a whole-class activity.
- Ask students to invent definitions of various professions.

Nota cultural

Notes

- This change of professional roles is also occurring in the inverse: professions that were once reserved for women are now being exercised by men as well: *enfermero, amo de casa, secretario,* and so on.
- Many jobs have always had masculine (*-o*) and feminine (*-a*) forms. As women have entered professions previously held mostly by men, the pattern of changing *-o* to *-a* or adding *-a* has been followed: *arquitecto/a, cajero/a, ingeniero/a, maestro/a, profesor(a), sicólogo/a, traductor(a), vendedor(a),* and so on.
- The names of a few professions do not follow the *-o* → *-a* rule: *el/la soldado (la mujer soldado), el/la piloto.*
- For professions that end in *-a*, the article shows the gender of the person: *el/la dentista, el/la policía, el/la siquiatra, el/la terapeuta,* and so on.

Comprensión

1. *¿Cuáles son algunas de las palabras que pueden incluir en su designación a personas de uno y otro sexo? (el estudiantado, el profesorado, la infancia, la tercera edad, las personas mayores)*
2. *¿Qué tratamiento femenino se usa menos en la actualidad en el mundo laboral? (señorita)*
3. *¿Cuáles son algunas de las nuevas formas femeninas que se aplican a cargos y profesiones importantes? (jefa, médica, ministra, presidenta)*
4. *¿Qué uso se le da ahora al símbolo de la arroba? (indicar en una palabra las formas masculina y femenina)*

NATIONAL STANDARDS: Cultures

Michelle Bachelet Jeria (1951–), the first woman president of Chile (2006–2010), is a pediatric physician who also studied military strategy. A self-declared agnostic, she ran for and served as president as a single woman (separated from her husband). This mother of three speaks Spanish, French, German, and Portuguese. She is the first Latin American female president to have won the post without being associated with a previous male president or leading male political figure in the country. She is clearly an outstanding example of how women are advancing in Spanish-speaking countries on their own terms, despite the perception (and reality) of *machismo* that is often associated with these countries.

Con. C: Suggestions

- Model several recommendations before allowing students to begin the activity. Demonstrate subjunctive syntax.
- Have students work in pairs to role-play an advisor and a student who is seeking advice about his/her future. Have students discuss a variety of topics including summer jobs, time management, experience, preferences, and money. Have students report their findings to the class.

Con. D: Reciclado

Note the use of past (imperfect), present indicative, and present subjunctive forms in this activity's items.

El mundo laboral

Suggestions

- Have students respond *cierto* or *falso* to the following statements and then correct the false ones.
  1. *Una persona que busca un puesto se llama un aspirante.* (C)
  2. *Si a Ud. no le gusta su trabajo, debe despedirlo.* (F)
  3. *Si a Ud. le gustaría renunciar a su trabajo, debe conseguir una solicitud.* (F)
  4. *Para llenar una solicitud, se puede usar bolígrafo o lápiz.* (C)
- Point out that *compañía* is frequently used in company names, but *empresa* is the general word for *corporation* and *company.*
- Point out that *renunciar* (or *dimitir*) means *to resign from a job. Resignar* is a false cognate and is never used to express *to resign from a job.*
- Point out to students the distinction made by many native speakers of Spanish between *el salario* (a false cognate for *salary*) and *el sueldo.* The former is what hourly or manual laborers earn, the latter is for white collar professionals.
- Optional vocabulary: *caerle* (*caigo*) *bien/mal a alguien, la dirección de personal, el/la director(a) de personal.*

NATIONAL STANDARDS

Communication

Have students work together to prepare their own *currículum vitae* in Spanish. Encourage them to include information about their education, previous employment, and so on.

Resources: Transparency 155

Vocabulario útil

las comunicaciones
la contabilidad accounting
el derecho law
la gerontología
la ingeniería
el *marketing*/mercadeo
la organización administrativa
la pedagogía/enseñanza
la retórica speech
la sociología

C. ¿Qué preparación se necesita para ser… ? Imagine que Ud. es consejero universitario / consejera universitaria. Explíquele a un(a) estudiante qué cursos debe tomar para prepararse para las siguientes carreras. Use el **Vocabulario útil** y la lista de cursos académicos del **Capítulo 2.** Piense también en el tipo de experiencia que debe obtener.

1. traductor(a) en la ONU (Organización de las Naciones Unidas)
2. reportero deportivo / reportera deportiva en la televisión
3. contador(a) para un grupo de abogados
4. periodista para una revista de ecología
5. trabajador(a) social, especializado/a en los problemas de los ancianos
6. maestro/a de primaria, especializado/a en la educación bilingüe

D. Intercambios

Paso 1. En parejas, túrnense para hacer y contestar preguntas para averiguar (*find out*) la siguiente información.

1. lo que hacían sus abuelos
2. la profesión u oficio de sus padres
3. si tienen un amigo o pariente que tenga una profesión extraordinaria o interesante y el nombre de esa profesión
4. lo que sus padres (su esposo/a) quiere(n) que Uds. sean (lo que Uds. quieren que sean sus hijos)
5. lo que Uds. quieren ser (lo que sus hijos quieren ser)
6. la carrera que estudian muchos de sus amigos (los hijos de sus amigos)

Paso 2. Ahora digan a la clase dos detalles interesantes sobre su compañero/a.

El mundo laboral

el empleo	job; position	**el gerente / la gerente**	manager
bien/mal pagado	well-/poorly paying	**el puesto**	position
de tiempo completo/ parcial	full-/part-time	**el salario**	pay, wages (*often per hour*)
		la solicitud	job application
la empresa	corporation; business	**el sueldo**	salary

*S.A. = **Sociedad Anónima** (*Incorporated, Inc.*)

Heritage Speakers

- Algunos hispanohablantes usan la palabra *aplicación* en vez de *solicitud.* Esta forma es un anglicismo, y es preferible usar *solicitud,* especialmente en situaciones formales. Pregúnteles a los hispanohablantes qué término usan. Pídales que nombren otros anglicismos comunes entre los hispanohablantes que viven en este país.
- Pregúnteles a los hispanohablantes qué formas usan para referirse a las mujeres en las siguientes profesiones: *jefe, juez, mecánico, médico, piloto, policía, presidente, soldado*. Pregúnteles si sus padres y abuelos o sus hijos usan las mismas formas que ellos usan o si prefieren otras formas.

conseguir (*like* **seguir**) **un empleo**	to get a job	**graduarse (me gradúo) (en)**	to graduate (from)
dejar un puesto	to leave a position	**llenar**	to fill out (*a form*)
despedir (*like* **pedir**)	to let (*someone*) go; to fire (*someone*) (*from a job*)	**renunciar (a)**	to resign (from)
		solicitar	to apply for (*a job*)

Así se dice

el trabajo de tiempo parcial = la jornada de tiempo parcial
el empleo = el puesto, el trabajo

Conversación

A. En busca de un empleo

Paso 1. Ponga en orden del 1 al 7 las siguientes acciones típicas de la búsqueda (*search*) de un empleo. Algunas acciones pueden ser simultáneas.

a. 1/2 Escribir el currículum.
b. 7 Hacer preguntas sobre los beneficios que ofrece la empresa.
c. 1/2 Leer los avisos (*ads*) clasificados sobre trabajos en un periódico o en el Internet.
d. 5 Esperar que lo/la llamen para una entrevista.
e. 3/4 Llenar la solicitud y mandarla con el currículum.
f. 6 Tener una entrevista con el gerente.
g. 3/4 Pedirle a alguien que le escriba una carta de recomendación.

Paso 2. Ahora añada por lo menos dos acciones más a la secuencia del **Paso 1.**

Paso 3. Finalmente, narre en el pasado y en primera persona (**yo**) la secuencia completa (**Pasos 1** y **2**). Explique su propia experiencia de buscar un trabajo.

MODELO: Yo necesitaba un trabajo para el próximo verano. Por eso, primero fui a la oficina de empleos de la universidad…

B. Definiciones. Defina las siguientes palabras y frases en español.

MODELO: la empresa →
una compañía grande, como la IBM o Ford

1. el currículum
2. dejar un empleo
3. la aspirante
4. el gerente
5. el sueldo
6. llenar una solicitud

Con. B: Possible Answers

1. *la lista de puestos y preparación académica que uno ha tenido*
2. *decirle al jefe que uno no quiere seguir en el puesto*
3. *una persona que solicita un puesto*
4. *la persona que manda en la oficina o el departamento*
5. *el dinero que uno gana*
6. *contestar las preguntas de un cuestionario con el fin de trabajar para una empresa*

Preliminary Exercise

Ask students the following questions to check comprehension and to personalize the vocabulary.

1. *¿Cómo se siente Ud. durante una entrevista? ¿Tranquilo/a?*
2. *¿Cuáles son algunas de las razones más comunes para dejar un puesto? ¿Cuáles son algunas de las razones más comunes para despedir a un empleado?*
3. *¿Quién estudia comercio? ¿Quiere trabajar en una gran empresa algún día? ¿En qué tipo de empresa? ¿Quiere entrar como gerente o como empleado/a? ¿Cuáles son las cualidades necesarias para ser un(a) buen (a) gerente?*
4. *¿Trabaja Ud. ahora o solo estudia? ¿Dónde trabaja? ¿Tiene buen sueldo? ¿Le gustaría cambiar de puesto? ¿Por qué?*
5. *¿Es un buen empleado / una buena empleada o es perezoso/a?*

Con. A: Suggestion

Encourage students to read all items before beginning the activity.

Con. A: Follow-up

Have students work in groups to write brief dialogues that illustrate the different parts of the sequence. Then have them present their sections to the class.

Redacción: Ask students to describe in writing the job they want to have in the future: *Mi empleo ideal.* They must include:

- the title and a brief description of the job
- the qualifications it requires (a college degree, for example)
- why they want to have that job
- if they personally know someone who has a similar job or know of a famous person who has it
- why that person is an inspiration to them

NATIONAL STANDARDS: Communication

Have students work in pairs to write the following types of questions. Have them imagine that the interviewer would be from an international computer company with offices and branches in Latin America and Europe.

1. *preguntas que un entrevistador va a hacer*
2. *preguntas que un entrevistador no debe hacerle al aspirante*
3. *preguntas que el aspirante puede o debe hacer*

Have each pair of students exchange questions with another pair of students. Then have the original partners role-play an interview using the questions they received.

Una cuestión de dinero

Note

The area of finances and investments is one in which a substantial amount of English has entered the Spanish language: *los híbridos, switchear, tomar posiciones en un bear market, stop loss, spreads,* and so on.

Suggestions

- Point out that *cobrar un cheque* means *to cash a check,* but for cashing traveler's checks *cambiar un cheque de viajero* is used. Explain and model the differences between *ahorrar* (to save money or time), *guardar* (to save, keep something), and *salvar* (to save, rescue someone). Contrast and model the difference between *gastar* (to spend money) and *pasar* (to spend time).
- Explain that vocabulary for financial and banking transactions varies a good deal in the Spanish-speaking world. Introduce other terms you might prefer or hear, for example, *depositar* vs. *ingresar* and *libreta* (*de ahorros*) vs. *cartilla.*
- Optional vocabulary: *el dinero en efectivo, los ingresos* (income), *hacer una transferencia / un giro.*

Preliminary Exercise

Have students respond *cierto* or *falso* to the following statements.

1. *El préstamo es dinero que recibimos del banco.* (C)
2. *Si uno quiere ahorrar dinero, es necesario ponerlo en una cuenta corriente.* (F)
3. *El presupuesto es un sistema para organizar la manera de gastar dinero.* (C)
4. *Si Ud. paga con tarjeta de crédito, carga algo a su cuenta.* (C)
5. *Un cajero automático se usa para recibir dinero.* (C)
6. *Visa y MasterCard son ejemplos de facturas.* (F)
7. *Sacar es el antónimo de depositar.* (C)

Con. A: Suggestions

- Have students complete this as a pair activity, turning the items into questions.
- *Paso 2.* Have students complete this as written homework.

Con. A: Note

Active vocabulary: *al principio de*

Una cuestión de dinero

el billete	bill (*money*)
la caja	cashier window
la cuenta corriente	checking account
la cuenta de ahorros	savings account
el efectivo	cash
el interés	interest
el préstamo	loan
el presupuesto	budget
el recibo	receipt
ahorrar	to save (*money*)
cobrar	to cash (*a check*); to charge (*someone for an item or service*)
compartir	to share
depositar	to deposit
devolver (*like* **volver**)	to return (*something*)
economizar (c)	to economize
ganar	to earn
gastar	to spend (*money*)
pagar (gu) a plazos / con cheque / en efectivo	to pay in installments / by check / in cash
pedir (pido) (i) prestado/a	to borrow

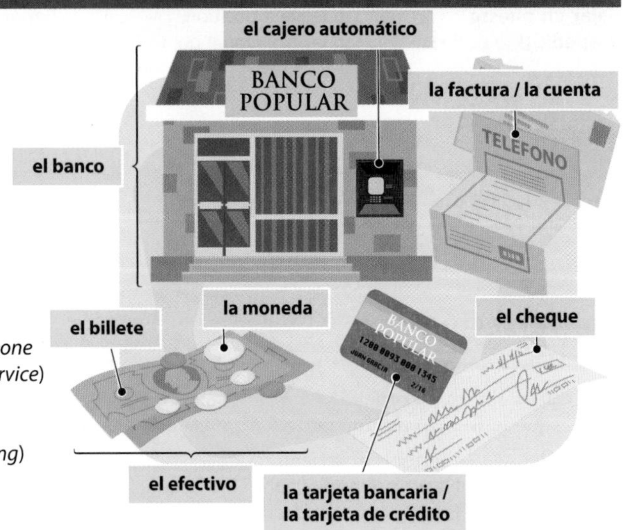

prestar	to lend
sacar (qu)	to withdraw, take out

Así se dice

depositar dinero = ingresar dinero, poner dinero en una cuenta
pagar en efectivo = pagar al contado

Conversación

A. El mes pasado. Piense en sus finanzas personales del mes pasado. ¿Fue un mes típico? ¿Tuvo dificultades al final del mes o todo le salió bien?

Paso 1. Indique las respuestas apropiadas, según su experiencia.

	SÍ	NO
1. Hice un presupuesto al principio (*beginning*) del mes.	☐	☐
2. Deposité más dinero en el banco del que (*than what*) saqué.	☐	☐
3. Saqué dinero del cajero automático más de tres veces.	☐	☐
4. Pagué todas mis cuentas a tiempo.	☐	☐
5. Les pedí un préstamo a mis padres.	☐	☐
6. Preparé mis almuerzos en casa para economizar un poco.	☐	☐
7. Gasté mucho dinero en divertirme.	☐	☐
8. Le presté dinero a un amigo.	☐	☐
9. Usé la tarjeta de crédito solo un par de veces.	☐	☐
10. Dejé de comprar café.	☐	☐

Paso 2. Pensando todavía en sus respuestas, diga tres cosas que Ud. debe hacer para mejorar su situación económica.

MODELO: Debo hacer un presupuesto mensual.

Resources: Transparency 156

B. Diálogos

Paso 1. Empareje las preguntas de la izquierda con las respuestas de la derecha.

1. __c__ ¿Cómo prefiere Ud. pagar?
2. __d__ ¿Hay algún problema con la cuenta?
3. __e__ Me da una identificación, por favor. Necesito verla para que pueda cobrar su cheque.
4. __a__ ¿Va a depositar este cheque en su cuenta corriente o en su cuenta de ahorros?
5. __b__ ¿Le pongo el recibo en la bolsa (*bag*)?

a. En la cuenta de ahorros, por favor.
b. No, mejor me lo da a mí.
c. Voy a pagar en efectivo.
d. Sí, señora. Ud. me cobró demasiado por el postre.
e. Aquí tiene mi licencia de manejar.

Paso 2. Ahora, en parejas, inventen un contexto posible para cada diálogo. ¿Dónde están las personas que hablan? ¿en un banco? ¿en una tienda? ¿Qué hacen? ¿Quiénes son? ¿Clientes? ¿cajeros? ¿dependientes?

C. Situaciones. En parejas, describan lo que pasa en los dibujos de la derecha. Usen las siguientes preguntas como guía.

- ¿Quiénes son estas personas?
- ¿Dónde están?
- ¿Cómo van a pagar?
- ¿Qué van a hacer después?

1.

2.

Nota **comunicativa**

Más pronombres posesivos

In Spanish, as in English, *stressed possessives* (**las formas tónicas de los posesivos**) are used after a noun that is preceded by a definite or indefinite article. Stressed possessives can also be used when the noun is not expressed.*

mío/a(s)	my, (of) mine
tuyo/a(s)	your, (of) yours
suyo/a(s)	your, (of) yours, his, of (his), her, (of) hers
nuestro/a(s)	our, (of) ours
vuestro/a(s)	your, (of) yours
suyo/a(s)	your, (of) yours their, (of) theirs

¡OJO!

The **nosotros/as** and **vosotros/as** forms are identical to the possessives you already know.

Esta es **la** maleta **mía** y esa es **la suya.**
This is my suitcase and that one is his (hers, yours, theirs).

Es **un** amigo **mío.**
He's a friend of mine.

—¿De quién es este libro?
—Es **mío.**
"Whose book is this?"
"It's mine."

D. Mis finanzas personales. En parejas, túrnense para hacer y contestar preguntas, usando posesivos en sus respuestas según el modelo.

MODELO: Mi banco es… ⟶ Mi banco es University Bank. **¿Y el tuyo?**

1. Mi banco es…
2. Mi préstamo del banco para la matrícula de la universidad (no) es muy alto.
3. Mis facturas mensuales para los gastos de vivienda (no) son muy altas.
4. Hoy (no) tengo mucho dinero en mi cuenta corriente.
5. Este mes (no) debo usar más mi tarjeta de crédito.
6. Mi presupuesto para este mes (no) es un desastre.

Mundo interactivo

You should now be prepared to work with Scenario 9, Activity 1 in Connect Spanish (**www.connectspanish.com**).

See Appendix 3 for more information about using the stressed possessive forms.

Con. B: Suggestion

Have students role-play this activity. You or a native speaker can take the role of the Spanish-speaking clerk (left-hand column).

Con. C: Variations

- Ask students to read their descriptions aloud to the class, which must guess which drawing is being described.
- Have students do this as a written activity.

Pronunciación: See the Laboratory Manual for review and practice of stress and the written accent mark.

Nota comunicativa

Suggestions

- If you have been using the stressed forms of the possessives in your input, students will be familiar with them.
- Present the following examples, then give the Spanish equivalents: *He's my friend.* ⟶ *He's a friend of mine.* / *It's her dog.* ⟶ *It's a dog of hers.*
- Point out the ambiguity of meaning of the third person form *suyo*.
- Have students give the Spanish equivalents for the following ideas:
  1. She's a friend of mine / of ours / of his / of theirs.
  2. We have some books of yours / of his / of theirs.
- Emphasize that more information about these possessives is given in Appendix 3.

Resources: Transparency 157

¿Recuerda Ud.?

Suggestion

Point out to students that, in a given context, the present subjunctive can also express the future: *Espero que Juan trabaje conmigo mañana.*

Gramática 46 Future Verb Forms

GEA: Suggestions

- Ask students: *¿Son típicos de una niña de diez años los sueños* (new) *de Alicia? ¿Qué sueños tenía Ud. a los 10 años? ¿Se han realizado algunos de ellos?*
- Use the items to introduce the *Ud.* forms of the future by asking follow-up questions for each item: **1.** *Dentro de diez años, ¿dónde vivirá Ud.? ¿En otra ciudad? ¿en otro estado? ¿en otro país?*
- As shown in the preceding point, ask expansion questions for each item to help students express themselves. Here are some useful prompts: **2.** *soltero/a, viudo/a* (new) **3.** *sobrinos, nietos* **4.** *la residencia, el apartamento* **5.** *en este país / con toda la familia* **6.** *nombre de profesión* **7.** *mucho/poco dinero*
- Finally, introduce the *tú* form by giving students the *-ás* ending and allowing them to ask follow-up questions of other students: **1.** *Dentro de diez años, ¿dónde vivirás?*

Note

The future of probability is presented as a *Nota comunicativa* on p. 506.

Multimedia: Internet

Have students search the Internet for a Spanish language horoscope site. Students should print out and bring in their horoscope to share with the class. Have students rewrite their horoscope in the future tense if it is not already in the future.

GRAMÁTICA

¿Recuerda Ud.?

Before studying the future tense in **Gramática 46,** review **Gramática 3 (Cap. 2)** and **Gramática 11 (Cap. 4),** where you learned ways of expressing future actions. Then indicate which of the following sentences can be used to express a future action.

1. ☐ Trabajé hasta las dos.
2. ☑ Trabajo a las dos.
3. ☑ Voy a trabajar a las dos.
4. ☐ Trabajaba a las dos.
5. ☐ Estoy trabajando.
6. ☐ He trabajado a las dos.

46 Talking About the Future

Future Verb Forms

Grammar Tutorial 46
connect SPANISH
www.connectspanish.com

Gramática en acción: ¿Cómo será su futuro?

Alicia, 10 años

- Viviré en otra ciudad.
- Me casaré con un hombre muy guapo.
- Tendremos dos hijos.
- Viviremos en una casa magnífica.
- Viajaré a muchos países.
- Seré maestra de escuela, y mi marido también.
- Ganaremos mucho dinero.

¿Y Ud.?

¿Cómo será su vida dentro de diez años? Modifique las declaraciones de **Gramática en acción** para describirla.

So far, you have been expressing future actions in Spanish mostly with the present tense or with **ir** + **a** + *infinitive.* But Spanish also has a future tense, like English (*I will . . . , you will . . .*). In Spanish the *future* (**el futuro**) is used to express strong intentions and dreams.

Future of Regular Verbs / **El futuro**					
hablar		**comer**		**vivir**	
hablaré	hablaremos	comeré	comeremos	viviré	viviremos
hablarás	hablaréis	comerás	comeréis	vivirás	viviréis
hablará	hablarán	comerá	comerán	vivirá	vivirán

What will your future be like? *• I'll live in another city. • I'll marry a very handsome man. • We'll have two children. • We'll live in a magnificent house. • I'll travel to many countries. • I'll be a school teacher, and my husband (will be one) too. • We'll earn a lot of money.*

Heritage Speakers

En español las palabras *a* y *ha* se confunden fácilmente porque se pronuncian de la misma manera. Por lo tanto, los hispanos pueden tener dificultades en distinguir entre *va a haber / va a ver* y *va a ser / va a hacer.* El futuro evita la confusión: *habrá, verá, será* y *hará,* respectivamente. Anime a los hispanohablantes a explicar la diferencia entre estas cuatro formas y dar ejemplos de su uso en oraciones.

Resources: Transparency 158

1. **Future Tense Endings**
   In English the *future* (**el futuro**) is a compound tense, formed with the auxiliary (helping) verbs *will* or *shall: I **will** speak, you **shall** do what I say,* and so on. The Spanish future is a simple verb form (only one word). It is formed by adding the identical set of future endings to **-ar, -er,** and **-ir** infinitives. No auxiliary verbs are needed.

Las terminaciones del futuro

infinitivo +	-é	-emos
	-ás	-éis
	-á	-án

2. **Irregular Future Forms**
   Here are the most common Spanish verbs that are irregular in the future. The future endings are attached to their irregular stems.

   Note that the future of **hay (haber)** is **habrá** (*there will be*).*

decir: **diré, dirás, dirá, diremos, diréis, dirán**

decir:	**dir-**	
haber (hay):	**habr-**	
hacer:	**har-**	**-é**
poder:	**podr-**	**-ás**
poner:	**pondr-**	**-á**
querer:	**querr-**	**-emos**
saber:	**sabr-**	**-éis**
salir:	**saldr-**	**-án**
tener:	**tendr-**	
venir:	**vendr-**	

3. **Ways to Express the Future**
   As you know, the future tense is not the only way to express future actions in Spanish. Other ways to express the future, especially the near future, include:

   - the simple present indicative
   - **ir** + **a** + *infinitive*
   - the simple present subjunctive

   The Spanish future tense is mostly used to express serious goals and projects farther into the future, as when expressing dreams and aspirations, as seen in **Gramática en acción.**

Nos vemos mañana a las ocho.
We'll see each other tomorrow at 8:00.

Voy a llevar una chaqueta para la entrevista.
I will wear (am going to wear) a jacket to the interview.

No creo que **consiga** ese puesto.
I don't think (that) she'll get that job.

Trabajaré mucho y **me haré** rico.
I'll work very hard, and I'll get rich.

4. **Expressing Willingness**
   When the English *will* refers not to future time but to the *willingness* of someone to do something, Spanish does not use the future but rather the verbs **querer** or **poder,** or simply the present tense of any verb. In this context, **querer** has almost the force of a command.

¿**Quieres/Puedes** cerrar la puerta, por favor?
Will/Could you please close the door?

¿**Cierras** la puerta, por favor?
Can you close the door, please?

The future forms of the verb* **haber *are used to form the* future perfect tense (**el futuro perfecto**), *which expresses what* will have *occurred at some point in the future:* **Para mañana, ya *habré hablado* con Miguel.** (*By tomorrow,* I will have *already* spoken *with Miguel.*) *You will find a more detailed presentation of these forms in Appendix 4, Additional Perfect Forms (Indicative and Subjunctive).*

Emphasis 1: Suggestions

- Model the future of regular verbs.
- Ask students brief questions using the future of *comprar, beber,* and *escribir.*
- Read the following forms and have students give the corresponding subject pronoun: *tomaré, regresarán, mandará, necesitarás, llevarán, viajaremos, entrará, compraré, celebraremos, aprenderán, comprenderás, leeré, creerán, vivirá.*

Emphasis 2: Suggestions

- Model the irregular futures and *habrá* in sentences about yourself and in brief communicative exchanges with students.
- Point out the similarities among irregular stems.
  1. drop a vowel: *haber, poder, querer, saber*
  2. drop two letters: *decir, hacer*
  3. replace the theme vowel with *-d-: poner, salir, tener, venir*

Note

The future perfect is presented only in the footnote on this page. Active production is not required in the activities.

Emphasis 3: Suggestions

- Emphasize that in Spanish and English, the future is most often expressed with present indicative and subjunctive rather than with the future tense. The future tense implies strong intention: *I'm going to study tonight* vs. *I will study tonight,* and *Voy a estudiar esta noche* vs. *Estudiaré esta noche.*
- Point out that the future can also be used to command: *No matarás* (the Ten Commandments, *los Diez Mandamientos*).

Emphasis 4: Suggestion

Model the difference between the English *will* for future vs. *will* for expressing willingness. *Querer* is used for willingness, but makes very strong requests. Point out that other verbs such as *importar* can be used to soften the request.

¿Te importa cerrar la puerta, por favor? (Do you mind closing the door, please?)

Preliminary Exercises

- Use a rapid response drill.

Dé el futuro.
yo: cantar, visitar, acostarse, vender, asistir, escribir
tú: estudiar, casarse, ayudar, aprender, recibir, divertirse
Ud./él/ella: pagar, terminar, guardar, correr, pedir, dormir
nosotros: regresar, esperar, gastar, comer, insistir, servir
Uds./ellos/ellas: dejar, leer, abrir, vivir

- Use the following chain drill to practice forms. Have students imagine that it is payday.

Son las tres de la tarde de un viernes, y todos han recibido el cheque semanal (new). *¿Qué harán? Algunos comprarán comestibles. Otros…*

pagar las cuentas
volver a hacer un presupuesto
depositar algo de dinero en la cuenta de ahorros
quejarse porque nunca tienen dinero suficiente
decir que ya no usarán las tarjetas de crédito
¿ ?

Prác. A: Suggestion

Ask students to find the future verb form(s) in each sentence and give the corresponding infinitive.

Prác. A: Follow-up

- Ask students the following questions about what they will do this evening.
  1. *¿A qué hora llegará Ud. a casa esta noche?*
  2. *¿A qué hora cenará?*
  3. *¿A qué hora empezará a estudiar?*
  4. *¿Irá a la biblioteca?*
  5. *¿Mirará la televisión?*
  6. *¿Hablará por teléfono?*
  7. *¿Leerá mucho?*
  8. *¿Se bañará antes de acostarse?*
  9. *¿A qué hora se acostará?*
  10. *¿Se dormirá fácilmente?*
- *Paso 2.* Have students explain why they related a category to a certain person. That person says whether he/she agrees with the association. *Eso será verdad. / Eso nunca ocurrirá.*
- **Reciclado:** Have students give sentences about themselves and their classmates by starting with (*No*) *Es probable/posible que…* (→ *yo sea profesora de idiomas*) to review the subjunctive.

Autoprueba

Complete the verbs with the correct future endings.

1. yo vivir_____
2. ella dir_____
3. ellos saldr_____
4. Uds. vendr_____
5. nosotros comer_____
6. tú querr_____

Answers: **1.** viv*iré* **2.** dir*á* **3.** sald*rán* **4.** vend*rán* **5.** come*remos* **6.** quer*rás*

Prác. B: Answers
1. *Hablaré… , Pasaré… , Escribiré… , Enseñaré… : profesor(a) de español* **2.** *Trabajarás… , Ganarás… , Tendrás… , Cobrarás… : abogado/a* **3.** *Verá… , Resolverá… , Leerá… , Le hará… : siquiatra* **4.** *Pasarán… , Usarán… , Inventarán… , Les mandarán… : técnico/a de computadoras, programador(a) de computadoras*

Práctica

A. ¡Anticipemos! Mis compañeros de clase. ¿Cree Ud. que conoce bien a sus compañeros de clase? ¿Sabe lo que les va a pasar en el futuro?

Paso 1. Indique si las siguientes declaraciones serán realidad para Ud. algún día.

	SÍ	NO
1. Seré profesor(a) de idiomas.	☐	☐
2. Me casaré (Me divorciaré) dentro de tres años.	☐	☐
3. Viviré en un país hispanohablante.	☐	☐
4. Compraré un coche deportivo.	☐	☐
5. Tendré una familia muy grande.	☐	☐
6. Haré estudios superiores (*graduate*).	☐	☐
7. Participaré activamente en la vida política de mi ciudad o del país.	☐	☐
8. No tendré que trabajar porque seré rico/a.	☐	☐

Paso 2. Ahora, usando las declaraciones del **Paso 1,** indique el nombre de una persona de la clase para quien Ud. cree que la declaración es cierta. La persona nombrada debe contestar.

MODELO: **ESTUDIANTE:** La profesora Martínez no **tendrá** que trabajar porque **será** rica.
PROFESORA: Degraciadamente, **seguiré** trabajando, ¡porque nunca **seré** rica!

B. ¿Qué harán? Explique lo que harán las siguientes personas en su trabajo futuro. Luego, para cada grupo, diga qué profesión se describe.

MODELO: yo / darles consejos a los estudiantes →
Les **daré** consejos a los estudiantes.

1. yo
- hablar bien el español
- pasar mucho tiempo en la biblioteca
- escribir artículos sobre la literatura latinoamericana
- enseñar clases en español

2. tú
- trabajar en una oficina y en la corte
- ganar mucho dinero
- tener muchos clientes
- cobrar por muchas horas de trabajo

3. Felipe
- ver a muchos pacientes
- resolver muchos problemas mentales
- leer a Freud y a Jung
- hacerle un sicoanálisis a un paciente

4. Susana y Juanjo
- pasar mucho tiempo sentados
- usar el teclado (*keyboard*) constantemente
- inventar nuevos programas
- mandarles mensajes electrónicos a todos los amigos

C. Este mes

Paso 1. Describa lo que Ud. hará o no hará este mes en cuanto a (*as far as*) sus finanzas.

MODELO: (no) gastar menos este mes ⟶ (No) **Gastaré** menos este mes.

1. (no) gastar más este mes Gastaré
2. (no) pagar a tiempo todas mis cuentas Pagaré
3. (no) hacer un presupuesto y/pero (no) seguirlo Haré / lo seguiré
4. (no) depositar mucho/poco dinero en mi cuenta de ahorros Depositaré
5. (no) cobrar un cheque de mi empleo / un pariente Cobraré
6. (no) seguir usando mis tarjetas de crédito Seguiré
7. (no) pedirles dinero a mis amigos/padres/hijos Les pediré
8. (no) buscar un trabajo de tiempo completo/parcial Buscaré

Paso 2. Ahora, en parejas, comparen sus respuestas. Digan a la clase si Uds. son responsables en cuanto a asuntos de dinero, siguiendo los modelos. También digan a la clase las cosas que tienen en común.

MODELOS: Dylan y yo somos muy responsables con nuestro dinero porque…
Dylan es muy responsable con su dinero, pero yo tengo que aprender a ser más responsable con el mío porque…

Conversación

A. Soluciones extremas para casos extremos. Diga cuáles son las ventajas y desventajas de las siguientes opciones para conseguir más dinero.

MODELO: dejar de tomar tanto café ⟶
Si dejo de tomar tanto café, **ahorraré** solo unos pocos dólares. **Estaré** menos nervioso/a, pero creo que **tendré** más dificultad en despertarme por la mañana.

Un billete de la Lotería Nacional de España

1. dejar de fumar / tomar tanto café
2. pedirles dinero a mis amigos o parientes
3. cometer un robo
4. alquilar unos cuartos de mi casa
5. buscar un trabajo de tiempo parcial
6. comprar muchos billetes de lotería
7. estudiar más y divertirme menos
8. invertir mi dinero en bonos y acciones (*stocks and bonds*)

Vocabulario útil

la cárcel	jail
invertir (invierto) (i)	to invest

Con. A: Suggestion

Have students do this activity with a partner or in groups. Then have pairs or groups read their comments for each strategy. Finally, have the class vote for the best and worst strategies for getting money quickly.

Con.: Optional

- Have students name the following.
  1. *tres cosas que harán hoy*
  2. *tres cosas que harán mañana*
  3. *tres cosas que harán este fin de semana*
  4. *tres cosas que harán durante las vacaciones*
  5. *tres cosas que harán después de graduarse*
- Put the following sentence-builder items on the board or on an overhead and ask students to make predictions about what the following people will be doing in 10 years.

  Las personas:
  yo, tú, nosotros (los estudiantes de esta clase), el profesor / la profesora, mi padre/madre, mis padres/hijos, mi mejor amigo/a

  Las acciones:
  tener uno o dos hijos
  jubilarse (new)
  querer cambiar de trabajo
  ganar mucho/poco dinero
  saber hablar español perfectamente
  asistir a esta universidad
  poder hacer lo que quiera
  dar clases de…
  decir que…
  trabajar en…
  ser dueño/a de…
  ir/viajar a…
  poner mucho dinero en su cuenta bancaria mensualmente
  ¿ ?

Resources: Transparency 159

Con. B: Preliminary Exercise

Have students think about the world today and what it might be like in 25 years. Then have them answer these questions.

1. *¿Habrá una mujer presidenta / primera ministra?*
2. *¿Eliminaremos las armas nucleares?*
3. *¿Colonizaremos la luna?*
4. *¿Tendrá computadora todo el mundo?*
5. *¿Seremos todos bilingües?*
6. *¿Limpiaremos el medio ambiente?*
7. *¿Manejaremos coches todavía?*
8. *¿Se oirá la música* rap *todavía?*
9. *¿Existirá el matrimonio todavía como institución social?*
10. *¿Eliminaremos las enfermedades como el cáncer y el SIDA?*

Con. B: Suggestion

Have students do this activity in groups. If you assign it for written homework (see next annotation), allow students to turn in one composition for each pair or group.

Redacción

- Assign *Con. B* as a composition activity. Set reasonable expectations for length.
- After you have collected and corrected compositions, hand them back and ask students to read them to the class.
- Have the class vote for the following categories: *el ensayo más… optimista, pesimista, probable, creativo.*

Nota comunicativa

Suggestions

- Use visuals with the future of probability to speculate about the individuals in the drawings.

  ¿Quién será la mujer que espera?
  ¿Dónde estará esperando?
  ¿A quién estará esperando?

- Emphasize that this use of the future is very frequent in Spanish, possibly even more frequent than the use of the standard future (the future of intention).
- Point out that the future of probability in English can also be expressed with *must* and *will: Cecilia must* (*will*) *be on her way by now.*
- Point out that another word for *lío* is *embotellamiento.*

B. El mundo del año 2100

Paso 1. ¿Cómo será el mundo del futuro? En parejas, hagan una lista de cosas que Uds. creen que van a ser diferentes para el año 2100 (por ejemplo: el transporte, la comida, la vivienda). Piensen también en temas globales: la política, los problemas que presenta la capa de ozono, etcétera.

Paso 2. Ahora, a base de su lista, hagan una serie de predicciones para el futuro.

MODELO: La gente **comerá** (**Comeremos**) comidas sintéticas.

Vocabulario útil

la colonización
el espacio
los OVNIs (Objetos Voladores No Identificados)
la pobreza poverty
el robot
el satélite
el transbordador espacial space shuttle
la vida artificial

diseñar
eliminar

intergaláctico/a
interplanetario/a
sintético/a

Nota comunicativa

Cómo expresar la probabilidad con el futuro

Estela, en el aeropuerto

Cecilia, en la carretera

—¿Dónde **estará** Cecilia? ¿Qué le **pasará**?
"I wonder where Cecilia is." (*"Where can Cecilia be?"*) *"I wonder what's up with her."* (*"What can be wrong?"*)

—**Estará** en un lío de tráfico.
"She's probably (*must be*) *in a traffic jam."* (*"I bet she's in a traffic jam."*)

In Spanish, the future can also be used to express probability or conjecture about what is happening now. This use of the future is called the *future of probability* (**el futuro de probabilidad**). Note in the preceding examples that the English cues for expressing probability (*probably, I bet, must be, I wonder, Where can . . . ?,* and so on) are not directly expressed in Spanish. Their sense is conveyed in Spanish by the use of the future form of the verb.

Heritage Speakers

Note que, en español, cuando el futuro se usa para expresar probabilidad en el presente, equivale a *to wonder* y *probably* en inglés. Anime a los hispanohablantes a dar la forma del futuro de probabilidad para las siguientes oraciones.

¿Quién está a la puerta?
¿Cuántos años tiene esa señora?

También pídales que expliquen con sus propias palabras el significado de cada oración.

NATIONAL STANDARDS: Cultures

- *La Isla de Pascua:* The *moai* (which means *structure* in the indigenous language) are monoliths carved out of volcanic rock by the original inhabitants of the island, *los rapanuis.* There are about 900 *moai*, carved between 1250 and 1500, some 20 feet high and

(Cont. —›)

C. Predicciones. ¿Quiénes serán las siguientes personas? ¿Qué estarán haciendo? ¿Dónde estarán? En parejas, usen lo que saben de Chile e inventen todos los detalles que puedan sobre las siguientes fotos.

Vocabulario útil

la bodega	wine cellar
la cata de vino	wine tasting
la Isla de Pascua	Easter Island
el moai	*monolithic statue on Easter Island*
probar (pruebo)	to taste
los rapanuis	*inhabitants of Easter Island*
la viña	root stock (*of wine*)

1.

2.

¿Recuerda Ud.?

In **Gramática 45 (Cap. 16),** you learned about a series of adverbial conjunctions that always require the use of the subjunctive in the dependent clause. There are five such conjunctions. Complete the following phrases to name them all.

1. a menos que
2. antes (de) que
3. con tal (de) que
4. en caso de que
5. para que

You will learn more about using one of these conjunctions and about others like them in **Gramática 47.**

Reciclado: Have students change the following sentences to express probability and conjecture with the future. The first set of sentences reenters travel and money vocabulary, the second set reenters health vocabulary.

DE VIAJE

1. *Todo es caro en aquella tienda, ¿no crees?*
2. *¿Cuál es el precio de aquella estatua?*
3. *Podemos usar las tarjetas de crédito aunque estamos en el extranjero.*
4. *¡Las facturas llegan a casa antes de que lleguemos nosotros!*
5. *¿Tengo suficiente dinero para pagarlas?*

LA SALUD

6. *Julito está enfermo.*
7. *¿Cuántos grados de temperatura tiene?*
8. *La doctora viene más tarde.*
9. *Le da un antibiótico.*
10. *Le pone una inyección.*

Con. C: Preliminary Exercises

- Have students express the following ideas in Spanish using the future of probability.
  1. He's probably a teacher, and she must be a doctor.
  2. I wonder where she works.
  3. I wonder which one earns more money.
  4. They're probably from a big city.
  5. They probably have a lot of kids.
  6. They must be asking questions about (*acerca de*) us, too!
- Have students explain the following situations and actions using the future of probability.
  1. *Un amigo está en la sala de emergencias de un hospital.*
  2. *Un amigo ha hecho una cita con el profesor / la profesora de español.*
  3. *Un amigo está entrando en el banco.*
  4. *Un amigo hace las maletas.*
  5. *Un amigo necesita llamar a sus padres.*
  6. *Un amigo está vestido elegantísimamente.*

Resources: Transparency 160 (p. 506)

NATIONAL STANDARDS (Cont.)

weighing 20 tons. Although the *moai* are whole-body statues, they are commonly referred to as Easter Island heads, because they are famous for their large heads, broad noses and chins, and their enigmatic expressions. *Los rapanuis*, natives of what is now called Polynesia, have been able to preserve their language and culture. They depend primarily on tourism and fishing.

- *Las viñas chilenas:* The Spanish introduced the first root stock into Chile in the 16th century. In the 18th century, the French sent Cabernet and Merlot root stock to Chile, starting a long wine-growing tradition in the country. Today, Chilean wines are popular throughout the world.

Gramática 47

Subjunctive and Indicative After Conjunctions of Time

GEA: Notes

- **Reciclado:** The mix of tenses in this *GEA* provides a good opportunity for reviewing many of the tenses that students have learned so far.
- Active vocabulary: *jubilarse*

Follow-up

- Ask students to identify the tense/mood used in each verb in the *GEA.*
- Ask students what mood is used in the subordinate (dependent) clauses shown in color (→ subjunctive).
- Ask students if they see any similarities between the conjunctions that introduce the clauses (→ time).
- Help students relate this use of the subjunctive with other uses they have already studied, for example, when the action has not yet happened.

Emphasis 1: Suggestion

Remind students that a conjunction is a word or phrase that connects other words, phrases, or clauses.

47 Expressing Future or Pending Actions

The Subjunctive (Part 8): The Subjunctive and Indicative After Conjunctions of Time

Grammar Tutorial 47
connect SPANISH
www.connectspanish.com

Gramática en acción: Planes para el futuro

1. Después de graduarme, tendré que buscar trabajo. **Tan pronto como** tenga trabajo, ganaré mucho dinero y pagaré los préstamos de la universidad.

2. **En cuanto** me jubile, jugaré al golf por lo menos tres veces por semana. ¡Pero desgraciadamente quedan quince años **hasta que** me jubile!

3. Cuando trabajaba, siempre estaba cansado. Ahora me siento mejor que nunca. ¡Y voy a jugar al golf **hasta que** tenga 100 años!

¿Y Ud.?

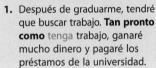

1. ¿Buscará trabajo antes de graduarse o después de graduarse?
2. Cuando Ud. se gradúe, ¿piensa empezar a trabajar en seguida? ¿Ganará mucho dinero?
3. ¿Tendrá que pagar préstamos cuando se gradúe?
4. Cuando tenga un trabajo, ¿estará más cansado/a que ahora?
5. ¿Practicará algún deporte hasta que tenga 90 años?

①		②
FUTURE/PENDING ACTION: indicative	adverbial conjunction of time	subjunctive
①		②
HABITUAL/COMPLETED ACTION: indicative	adverbial conjunction of time	indicative

1. **Adverbial Conjunctions of Time**
   Future events are often expressed in Spanish in two-clause sentences in which the dependent clause is introduced by a conjunction of time. The most common ones are listed at the right.

Las conjunciones de tiempo

antes (de) que	before	**en cuanto**	as soon as
cuando	when	**hasta que**	until
después (de) que	after	**tan pronto como**	as soon as

Plans for the future *1. After I graduate, I'll have to look for a job. As soon as I have a job, I'll earn lots of money, and I'll pay off my university loans. 2. As soon as I retire, I'll play golf at least three times a week. But unfortunately it'll be fifteen more years until I retire! 3. When I was still working, I was always tired. Now I feel better than ever. And I'm going to play golf until I'm 100 (years old)!*

Heritage Speakers

Pídales a los hispanohablantes que representen la GEA frente a la clase.

Resources: Transparency 161

2. Use of the Subjunctive After Time Conjunctions

The subjunctive is used when the dependent clause introduced by a time conjunction describes an event that hasn't happened yet or that is pending in some way. This use of the subjunctive is very frequent in Spanish in clauses that begin with **Cuando...**

¡OJO!

When the present subjunctive is used in this way to express pending future actions, the *main-clause* verb is in the present indicative or future.

Cuando sea grande/mayor...
When I'm older . . .

Cuando tenga tiempo...
When I have the time . . .

Cuando me gradúe...
When I graduate . . .

MAIN CLAUSE: PRESENT INDICATIVE OR FUTURE

Debo depositar el dinero **tan pronto como** lo **reciba.**
I should deposit the money as soon as I get it.

Pagaré las cuentas **en cuanto reciba** mi cheque.
I'll pay the bills as soon as I get my check.

---

3. Use of the Indicative After Time Conjunctions

The indicative is used when the dependent clause introduced by a time conjunction describes a habitual action (present or past) or a completed event in the past.

HABITUAL ACTIONS: INDICATIVE

Siempre pago las cuentas **en cuanto recibo** mi cheque.
I always pay bills as soon as I get my check.

Siempre depositaba el dinero **tan pronto como** lo **recibía.**
I always deposited the money as soon as I got it.

COMPLETED PAST ACTION: INDICATIVE

El mes pasado pagué las cuentas **en cuanto recibí** mi cheque.
Last month I paid my bills as soon as I got my check.

Cuando era adolescente, mis padres me pagaban por hacer algunos quehaceres domésticos.
When I was a teenager, my parents used to pay me for doing some household chores.

---

4. *Antes (de) que* + *subjunctive*

As you know, the subjunctive is always used after the time conjunction **antes (de) que.** You can review this usage in **Gramática 45 (Cap. 16).**

¡Claro que no puedo depositar el dinero **antes de que reciba** el cheque!
Of course I can't deposit the money before I receive the check!

	Future/Pending	Habitual/Past
MOST CONJUNCTIONS OF TIME:	subjunctive	indicative
antes (de) que:	subjunctive	subjunctive

Autoprueba

Indicate which sentences express a pending action and thus require the subjunctive in Spanish.

1. I'll call as soon as I get home.
2. We interview applicants only after we contact their references.
3. Many students apply for graduate school as soon as they begin their senior year.
4. They won't deposit this check until you sign it.

Answers: **1, 4**

Emphasis 2: Suggestion

Remind students that they learned certain conjunctions that always require the subjunctive in *Gram. 45* (conjunctions of purpose and contingency). Emphasize that with conjunctions of time (with the exception of *antes de que*), the subjunctive is used only when they introduce future, uncompleted actions or states.

Emphasis 3: Suggestion

Model and contrast a future action, a habitual action, and a past action.

Emphasis 4: Suggestions

- Emphasize that the subjunctive is always used after *antes de que,* even though it is a time conjunction. **¡OJO!** Due to its meaning, it is always followed by a future uncompleted action.
- Point out that the subjunctive is used with most time conjunctions even without a change of subject in the subordinate clause.

  Vamos a salir tan pronto como terminemos.

Después de, ante de, and *hasta,* however, are followed by an infinitive when there is no change in subject.

Saldremos después de comer.
Lavaré los platos antes de salir.
No vamos a salir hasta terminar la tarea.

Preliminary Exercise

Have students tell whether the following sentences express future (uncompleted), habitual, or past actions.

1. I'll do it when he gets here. (F)
2. They always write when they are abroad. (H)
3. We'll study until they arrive. (F)
4. As soon as I have the time, I'll do it. (F)
5. He studied until he fell asleep. (P)
6. She'll give us the answers after we hand in the test. (F)
7. We turn off the lights when we leave the house. (H)

Prác. A: Notes

- Students need to focus on habitual (indicative) vs. future (subjunctive) actions.
- Active vocabulary: *propiola*

Prác. A: Suggestions

- *Paso 1.* After students have decided whether the sentences refer to habitual or future actions, ask them to determine whether the verb in each choice is indicative (*b*) or subjunctive (*a*). Ask students to explain their answers.
- *Paso 2.* Although scaffolding is provided to ensure students' success with this part of the activity, you may still wish to model answers before allowing students to complete the activity.

Prác. B: Note

This activity reviews the use of many tenses and moods.

Prác. B: Follow-up

Have students respond *cierto* or *falso* to the following statements about Mariana.

1. *Mariana estudia en la universidad ahora.* (C)
2. *En la universidad, es probable que haya seguido muchos cursos de economía.* (F)
3. *Mariana es muy responsable en cuanto al dinero.* (C)

Práctica

A. Decisiones económicas

Paso 1. Lea las siguientes oraciones sobre Rigoberto y determine primero si se trata de (*each is about*) una acción habitual (**H**) o de una acción futura (**F**), algo que no ha ocurrido todavía). Luego escoja la frase que complete mejor cada oración.

H	F	
☐	☑	**1.** __a__ Rigoberto se va a comprar un auto en cuanto… **a.** ahorre suficiente dinero. **b.** ahorra suficiente dinero.
☑	☐	**2.** __b__ Siempre usa su tarjeta de crédito cuando… **a.** no tenga dinero en efectivo. **b.** no tiene dinero en efectivo.
☐	☑	**3.** __a__ Piensa pagar su préstamo para la universidad tan pronto como… **a.** consiga un trabajo. **b.** consigue un trabajo.
☐	☑	**4.** __a__ No puede pagar sus cuentas este mes hasta que… **a.** su hermano le devuelva el dinero que le prestó. **b.** su hermano le devuelve el dinero que le prestó.

Estrategia

Use un sustantivo en las oraciones 1 y 2. Use un infinitivo en las oraciones 3 y 4. En las oraciones 5 y 6, debe usar o el indicativo o el subjuntivo.

Paso 2. Ahora diga cómo maneja Ud. sus propios (*own*) asuntos económicos. Determine primero si la oración describe una acción habitual (**H**) o una acción futura (**F**). Luego complete la oración de una manera apropiada y personal.

H	F	
☐	☑	**1.** En cuanto el banco me dé un préstamo, voy a comprarme ____.
☑	☐	**2.** Cuando no tengo dinero en efectivo, siempre uso ____.
☐	☑	**3.** Tan pronto como consiga un trabajo, voy a ____.
☐	☑	**4.** Este mes, voy a ____ antes de que se me olvide.
☑	☐	**5.** Generalmente no le presto más dinero a un amigo hasta que me ____ el dinero que me debe.
☐	☑	**6.** En cuanto ____, empezaré a buscar un trabajo de tiempo completo.

Prác. B: Answers

1. *se graduó, le dieron, se gradúe, le darán (le van a dar)*
2. *era, quería, tenía, decidió, termine, podrá (va a poder)*
3. *pagaba, paga, depositan*
4. *tiene, devuelva, prestó*

B. Cosas de la vida. Las siguientes oraciones describen algunos aspectos de la vida de Mariana en el pasado, en el presente y en el futuro. Léalas para tener una idea general del contexto. Luego dé la forma apropiada de los infinitivos.

1. Hace cuatro años, cuando Mariana (graduarse) en la escuela secundaria, sus padres (darle) un reloj. El año que viene, cuando (graduarse) en la universidad, (darle) un carro.
2. Cuando (ser) niña, Mariana (querer) ser actriz. Luego, cuando (tener) 18 años, (decidir) que estudiaría[a] enfermería. Cuando (terminar) su carrera este año, yo creo que (poder) encontrar un buen empleo como enfermera.
3. Antes Mariana siempre (pagar) sus cuentas con cheque. Ahora las (pagar) por el Internet en cuanto le (*ellos:* depositar) el sueldo en su cuenta.
4. Este mes Mariana (tener) que comprar un regalo para la boda de unos buenos amigos. No puede comprarlo hasta que su hermana le (devolver) el dinero que Mariana le (prestar).

[a]*she would study*

Heritage Speakers

En este capítulo los estudiantes aprendieron que el presente de subjuntivo se usa después de *cuando* con acciones no realizadas. Sin embargo, a veces es posible encontrar el imperfecto de subjuntivo después de *cuando*.

ROBERTO: Me dicen que mi carro estará en el aeropuerto cuando aterrice el avión.
SUSANA: ¿Qué te dijeron?
ROBERTO: Me dijeron que mi carro estaría en el aeropuerto cuando *aterrizara* el avión.

Anime a los hispanohablantes a explicar lo que pasa en este diálogo, o sea, la cita indirecta de sus palabras.

C. Hablando de dinero: Planes para el futuro. Complete las siguientes oraciones con el presente de subjuntivo de los verbos indicados. Luego invente una terminación original para cada oración.

1. Voy a ahorrar más dinero en cuanto...
   (ellos) darme un aumento de sueldo / (yo) dejar de gastar tanto / ¿ ?
2. Pagaré todas mis cuentas tan pronto como...
   tener el dinero para hacerlo / ser absolutamente necesario / ¿ ?
3. El semestre/trimestre que viene, pagaré la matrícula después de que...
   cobrar mi cheque en el banco / (¿quién?) mandarme un cheque / ¿ ?
4. No podré pagar el alquiler hasta que...
   sacar dinero de mi cuenta de ahorros / depositar el dinero en mi cuenta corriente / ¿ ?
5. No voy a jubilarme hasta que mis hijos...
   terminar sus estudios universitarios / casarse / ¿ ?

Prác. C: Answers

1. *me den, deje*
2. *tenga, sea*
3. *cobre, me mande(n)*
4. *saque, deposite*
5. *terminen, se casen*

Conversación

A. Descripciones. Describa los dibujos, completando las oraciones e inventando un contexto para las escenas. Luego describa su propia vida.

1. Esta noche, Pablo va a estudiar hasta que...
   Contexto: _______
   ¿Y Ud.?
   - Esta noche, voy a estudiar hasta que...
   - Siempre estudio hasta que...
   - Anoche estudié hasta que...

2. Los Sres. Castro van a cenar tan pronto como...
   Contexto: _____
   ¿Y Ud.?
   - Esta noche, voy a cenar tan pronto como...
   - Siempre ceno tan pronto como...
   - Anoche cené tan pronto como...

Bright Idea

Prác. C: Preliminary Exercise

Have students complete the following statements using the future tense.

1. *Cuando yo me gradúe, yo...*
2. *Para celebrar mi cumpleaños, mi amigo/a y yo...*
3. *En cuanto tenga suficiente dinero, yo...*
4. *Cuando termine este año escolar, mi familia y yo...*
5. *Cuando vuelva a casa hoy, yo...*

Prác. C: Suggestion

Personalize each set of activity items by asking questions of individual students. Encourage detailed answers only if students are comfortable revealing this kind of information.

Con. A: Note

The drawing next to each paired set indicates a future uncompleted action.

Con. A: Extension

Have students complete the following sentences with personal information.

1. *Voy a... en cuanto...*
2. *Siempre... en cuanto...*
3. *De niño/a,... en cuanto...*

Resources: Transparency 162

Con. B: Suggestions

- You may wish to have students work in groups for this activity.
- Bring in Spanish language magazines with ads for various high tech products and services and share them with the groups.
- Give a prize for the best ad.

Con.: Optional

Opiniones. *¿Qué pensará Ud. o qué hará cuando ocurran los siguientes acontecimientos? Complete las oraciones con el futuro.*

1. *Cuando colonicemos otro planeta,…*
2. *Cuando descubran algo para curar el cáncer,…*
3. *Cuando haya una mujer presidenta / primera ministra,…*
4. *Cuando me jubile,…*
5. *Cuando yo sea anciano/a,…*
6. *Cuando me gradúe,…*
7. *Antes de graduarme,…*
8. *Después de conseguir mi primer/próximo trabajo,…*
9. *En cuanto tenga suficiente dinero,…*
10. *Antes de tener hijos…*

NATIONAL STANDARDS

Cultures

- Pablo Neruda (1907–1973): Chilean poet, essayist, and politician, Neruda was the recipient of the Nobel Prize for Literature in 1971. He is one of the most famous poets of the 20th century, especially for his romantic poetry. His three houses in Chile (one in Santiago, one in Valparaíso, and the third in Isla Negra, a little seaside town that is not an island) have become museums.
- Places in Chile: Valparaíso is a beautiful coastal city, the second largest in Chile and an important port. Concepción is south of Santiago. Chiloé is a big island in the south of Chile, home of rain forests that are much like those of the U.S. Pacific Northwest.

B. Publicidad

Paso 1. Diga si las siguientes declaraciones son ciertas o falsas según el anuncio y su conocimiento (*knowledge*) general. Corrija las declaraciones falsas.

	C	F
1. Hay muchas razones para usar el Internet cuando estamos de vacaciones.	☑	☐
2. No es lógico que uno quiera usar el Internet durante las vacaciones.	☐	☑
3. Con el plan movistar, se puede tener acceso al Internet desde cualquier (*from any*) lugar.	☑	☐
4. Este plan es ideal para que uno use el Internet antes de salir de vacaciones.	☐	☑
5. Es mejor que uno tome este plan antes de que se vaya de vacaciones.	☐	☑
6. Este plan solo sirve para que uno lea su e-mail.	☐	☑

Mundo interactivo

You should now be prepared to work with Scenario 9, Activity 2 in Connect Spanish (**www.connectspanish.com**).

Paso 2. Ahora, en parejas, inventen un anuncio para uno de los aparatos o servicios que Uds. tienen, electrónicos o no. Deben escoger un aparato o servicio que sea su favorito y muy necesario en su vida diaria. Antes de escribir, piensen en un público específico: la gente joven, los niños, una persona mayor, los estudiantes universitarios, etcétera.

Un poco de todo

A. Los planes de Alicia

Paso 1. Alicia está a punto de (*about to*) graduarse en la Universidad Católica de Chile, en Santiago. Use las conjunciones indicadas para unir las ideas de cada oración, haciendo todos los cambios necesarios.

MODELO: (yo) esperar encontrar un buen trabajo / tan pronto como / graduarse
→ **Espero** encontrar un buen trabajo tan pronto como **me gradúe.**

1. (yo) buscar apartamento / tan pronto como / ahorrar dinero
2. David, mi novio español: poder visitarme / en cuanto / yo: tener un apartamento propio
3. cuando David: estar aquí / (nosotros) visitar las casas de Pablo Neruda en Valparaíso e Isla Negra
4. después de ir a Valparaíso / (nosotros) ir a Concepción y a la isla de Chiloé
5. es posible que / David: querer quedarse en Chile / cuando conocer el país
6. David y yo: poder pasar las vacaciones en España con su familia / cuando casarse
7. mis padres: estar muy contentos con nuestra boda futura / porque a ellos: encantar David.
8. pero antes de conseguir un trabajo / ¡(yo) tener que preparar el currículum y pedir recomendaciones!

Estrategia

Use el presente de indicativo o subjuntivo, el futuro o el infinitivo. También es posible usar el presente perfecto de subjuntivo en uno de los casos.

Paso 2. Ahora en parejas, hablen de sus planes para después de graduarse, usando como modelo las oraciones apropiadas del **Paso 1.**

MODELO: Yo espero encontrar un buen trabajo tan pronto como me gradúe en esta universidad. Después de encontrar un buen trabajo,…

A: Answers

1. *Buscaré apartamento tan pronto como ahorre dinero.* **2.** *David, mi novio español, podrá (puede) visitarme en cuanto yo tenga un apartamento propio.* **3.** *Cuando David esté aquí, visitaremos las casas de Pablo Neruda en Valparaíso e Isla Negra.* **4.** *Después de ir a Valparaíso, iremos a Concepción y a la isla de Chiloé.* **5.** *Es posible que David quiera quedarse en Chile cuando conozca (haya conocido) el país.* **6.** *David y yo podremos (podemos) pasar las vacaciones en España con su familia cuando nos casemos.* **7.** *Mis padres están muy contentos con nuestra boda futura porque a ellos les encanta David.* **8.** *Pero antes de conseguir un trabajo, ¡tengo (tendré) que preparar el currículum y pedir recomendaciones!*

B. Lengua y cultura: Trabajos para estudiantes universitarios. Complete the following paragraphs with the correct form of the words in parentheses, as suggested by context. When two possibilities are given in parentheses, select the correct word. *P/I:* will show you when to use the preterite or the imperfect. Conjugate all other infinitives in the future, present indicative, or subjunctive, or leave them in the infinitive form.

Universidad de Chile, en Santiago

La necesidad de dinero es un problema para muchos estudiantes en todas partes del mundo. En la mayoría de los países hispanohablantes, (el/la[1]) sistema universitario es gratuito. Además,[a] es natural que los estudiantes (vivir[2]) con sus familias, (por qué / porque[3]) la mayoría no (irse[4]) a (estudiar[5]) a otras ciudades. (*Ellos:* Estudiar[6]) en (el/la[7]) universidad más cercana.[b]

Sin embargo, muchos estudiantes no buscan trabajo hasta que (*ellos:* terminar[8]) sus estudios universitarios. Y, así como en este país, hay estudiantes que (conseguir[9]) trabajo de tiempo parcial antes de (terminar/terminen[10]) la escuela secundaria. A continuación se puede leer las experiencias laborales de algunos estudiantes durante la época universitaria.

Una joven paraguaya: «Desde los 16 años, (*yo:* trabajar[11]) en una oficina. Así puedo (cobrar/pagar[12]) la matrícula en la universidad y mi ropa y gastos personales y también (*yo:* poder[13]) colaborar un poquito con la economía familiar.»

Un joven chileno: «Cuando (*P/I: yo:* ser/estar[14]) estudiante universitario, (*P/I:* trabajar[15]) como fotógrafo. (*P/I: Yo:* Sacar[16]) fotos en bodas, bautizos y primeras comuniones. Era un (bueno[17]) trabajo (por/para[18]) un estudiante, porque (*P/I: yo:* tener[19]) (de/que[20]) trabajar los fines de semana pero casi nunca los días de clase.»

Una estudiante uruguaya de la escuela secundaria: «Tan pronto como las clases (terminar[21]) este verano, (*yo:* empezar[22]) a trabajar en la tienda de mi tía y (ganar[23]) un poco de dinero. No quiero que mis padres (tener[24]) que pagarlo todo cuando yo (estar[25]) en la universidad.»

[a]*Besides* [b]*más… nearest*

Comprensión. Conteste las siguientes preguntas.

1. ¿Qué necesidad comparten los estudiantes de todo el mundo?
2. ¿Es caro o barato el sistema universitario de los países hispanos?
3. ¿Dónde vive la mayoría de los estudiantes hispanos?
4. ¿Qué trabajos se describen en estos párrafos?

A: Answers: **1.** *el* **2.** *vivan* **3.** *porque* **4.** *se va* **5.** *estudiar* **6.** *Estudian* **7.** *la* **8.** *terminan* **9.** *consiguen* **10.** *terminar* **11.** *trabajo* **12.** *pagar* **13.** *puedo* **14.** *era* **15.** *trabajaba* **16.** *Sacaba* **17.** *buen* **18.** *para* **19.** *tenía* **20.** *que* **21.** *terminen* **22.** *empezaré / voy a empezar* **23.** *ganaré / voy a ganar* **24.** *tengan* **25.** *esté*

B, Comprensión: Answers **1.** *la necesidad de dinero* **2.** *Es barato porque es gratuito.* **3.** *con sus familias* **4.** *trabajar en una oficina, fotógrafo, maestra*

En su comunidad

Entreviste a una persona hispana de su universidad o ciudad sobre algunos temas laborales.

PREGUNTAS POSIBLES

- ¿A qué se dedica? (¿Cuál es su trabajo?) ¿Cuánto tiempo hace que se dedica a eso? ¿Le gusta su trabajo? ¿Por qué?
- ¿Vino a este país por razones de trabajo?
- ¿Cómo es la situación laboral en su país de origen?
- ¿Qué piensa de la situación laboral en este país hoy día? ¿Cree que es mejor que cuando llegó a este país o peor?

B: Notes

- Note that this chapter's *Lengua y cultura* requires a number of uses of the present indicative. Once they have learned the subjunctive (and especially when working in chapters that focus on the subjunctive), some students tend to overuse it. This activity can provide a vehicle for reminding students to use the indicative appropriately.
- The following grammar topics are included in *Lengua y cultura:* gender, apocopation of adjectives, use of the infinitive, future, subjunctive vs. indicative, preterite and imperfect, *ser* vs. *estar, por* vs. *para, porque* vs. *por qué,* other lexical items.

B: Follow-up

Ask students: *¿Qué harán Uds. para conseguir trabajo este verano? ¿Cómo piensan buscarlo? Y cuando se gradúen, ¿que harán?*

B: Redacción

Using the *Lengua y cultura* paragraphs as a model, ask students to write a similar description of aspects of university life in this country. Allow students to use as much of the structure of the text's paragraphs as they need to. Suggest that they interview a few students in the class to get information about their work life. Set expectations about length.

En su comunidad

Suggestions

- Remind students to get the following basic information: the informant's country of origin, how long he or she has lived in this country, and if the informant visits his or her country of origin frequently.
- This activity could instead be assigned as an online research project on a country of the student's choice or assigned by you.
- See the IM for additional suggestions and guidelines.

Resources: Desenlace

In the *Cap. 17* segment of "Chapter-by-Chapter Supplementary Materials" in the IM, you will find a chapter-culminating activity. You can use this activity to consolidate and review the vocabulary and grammar skills students have acquired.

NATIONAL STANDARDS: Communication

Have students interview each other or students from another Spanish class about whether or not they work, and why, where, and how many hours per week they work. Students can work as a class to brainstorm possible questions. Have them conduct their interviews outside class if possible and summarize their findings in a brief paragraph. In class, have them work in small groups to share their results. Then discuss the results as a class. Encourage them to characterize students at your university based on their findings and have them debate whether or not their student body is typical compared to other universities in the country.

TelePuntos

Note

Pages 514–519 are optional. You may cover some, all, or none of this material in class, or assign it to students—as a group or individually—for homework or extra credit. Pages 520–521 (*En resumen: En este capítulo*) are a summary of all of the chapter's active material.

Antes de mirar

Suggestions

- Poll the class to see if students admire any of the same people.
- Conduct a whole-class discussion about today's heroes and whether they are people close to us or media celebrities.

Programa 17

- This program will be relatively accessible to students. The conditional verb forms will be unfamiliar, but they are all previewed or glossed.
- In the interview with Dr. Zaragoza-Kaneki, note the non-standard use of *haber* to mean *we have* or *there are: en esta comunidad **habemos** muchas personas de habla hispana.* This usage is typical of heritage speakers of Spanish.
- Although it is not specified in the segment, Nico is from Argentina, and his accent in Spanish reveals his origin. It will be particularly easy for students to hear his accent (light but typical) when he pronounces words with *ll* or *y*, like *llevando, llamo,* and *yo.*
- Emphasize to students that the more carefully they study the preliminary activities (*Antes de mirar, Vocabulario de este programa,* and *Fragmento del guion*), the more they will understand. Scanning *Después de mirar* before viewing is also an excellent strategy.

Fragmento del guion

Suggestion

If you can, show students images of *un cajón, un bombo legüero,* and *unas castañuelas.* Most students will not be familiar with these instruments. There are many photos on the Internet.

TELEPUNTOS SALU2

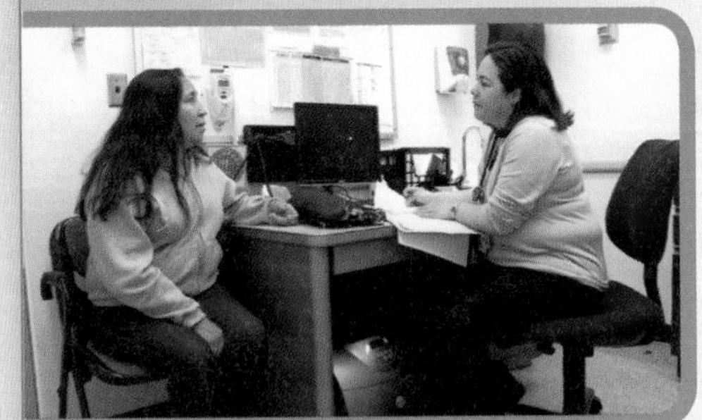

«Nos da mucho orgullo (*pride*) estar aquí y poder dar este servicio a los pacientes.»

Antes de mirar

¿A qué personas admira Ud.? ¿Qué hacen (o han hecho) esas personas para ganar su admiración? ¿Qué profesiones o tipos de personas cree Ud. que son las más admiradas en el mundo de hoy? ¿Científicos, maestros, deportistas profesionales… ? ¿A quiénes admiramos más: a las personas famosas o las personas muy cercanas (*close*) a nosotros?

PROGRAMA 17: Hispanos que admiramos

El programa está dedicado a personas hispanas que son admiradas; incluye entrevistas con dos personas de diferentes profesiones.

Vocabulario de este programa

en respuesta a nuestra petición	responding to our request	**tanto para… como para…**	for both … and for …	**el seguro**	insurance
efectivamente	actually	**el compromiso**	commitment	**ponerle una cara a**	to put a face to
dedicado/a	who works as/in	**si no estuviéramos**	if we weren't	**suceder**	to take place
los seres queridos	loved ones	**acudirían**	they would go	**montuno**	*rhythmic coda of many Cuban songs*
acudir	**venir**	**dar gusto**	to give pleasure		
proporcionar	to provide	**disfrutar**	to enjoy	**vas llevando**	[with it] you carry
la gente necesitada	the needy	**los recursos federales**	federal funding	**relleno/a**	filled with
atender (atiendo)	to serve; to receive (*clientes*)	**como es de imaginar**	as you can imagine	**los termino reemplazando**	I end up replacing them
diriá	I would say				

Fragmento del guion

ANA: Nico compone música para programas de video y televisión, como *Salu2.* Lo que nos fascina de Nico es su habilidad para crear música apropiada para distintos temas y países.

VÍCTOR: A ver,[a] Nico, cuéntales a los telespectadores un poco de tu trabajo como compositor.

NICO: Como compositor, para la música, especialmente para *Salu2,* hay tantos países, lo que hago es investigar la música autóctona[b] de cada país. Ver qué instrumentos folclóricos usan, qué ritmos usan. Y, bueno, también tengo una colección muy grande de instrumentos en mi estudio. Y… por ejemplo, en el caso de España, lo que haría[c] es… Obviamente, el flamenco es la música, parte de la música autóctona de España. Usaría[d] muchas guitarras españolas; como percusión usaría el cajón,[e] o las castañuelas.[f] O en países como… totalmente diferentes, como Perú, usaría mucho el charango, que es más andino. Los ritmos, usaría muchísimos de los ritmos andinos; usaría más flautas, o bombos legüeros,[g] que son unos bombos muy grandes hechos con piel de vaca.[h] Y bueno así. O sea, es muy divertido.

[a]A… *Let's see* [b]*native* [c]*I would do* [d]*I would use* [e]*percussion instrument shaped like a box* [f]*castanets* [g]bombos… *bass drums* [h]piel… *cowhide*

Nico Barry en su estudio, con su charango: «Los instrumentos, los toco todos yo… »

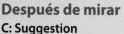

Mundo interactivo

Continue your work as an intern at HispanaVisión with Laura Sánchez Tejada, the roving reporter of *Salu2,* as you complete Scenario 9, Activities 1 and 2 in Connect Spanish (**www.connectspanish.com**).

Al mirar

Mientras mira el programa, indique las profesiones y oficios que se mencionan en el programa.

1. ☐ actor/actriz
2. ☑ personal médico diverso
3. ☑ maestro/a
4. ☑ compositor(a)
5. ☑ astronauta
6. ☑ deportista
7. ☐ abogado/a
8. ☑ ama de casa

«Obtener atención médica para toda persona en nuestro país es una de nuestras más grandes metas (*goals*). Tengo confianza (*I'm confident*) de que lo vamos a lograr (*achieve*).»

Después de mirar

A. ¿Está claro? Complete las siguientes oraciones con información del programa.

1. Los telespectadores nombraron a las personas que admiran por medio de (*via*) ____. mensajes
2. El programa recibió ____ de nombres de personas admiradas. cientos
3. La Dra. Zaragoza-Kaneki es una angelina de origen ____. mexicano
4. En su clínica, más del 65 por ciento de los pacientes es de origen hispano, y el 40 por ciento de todos los pacientes no habla inglés.
5. Su deseo para la clínica es obtener recursos federales para ____. poder atender a más personas en la comunidad
6. De pequeños, Ana quería ser ____ y Víctor, ____. astronauta, médico
7. Ana y Víctor entrevistan a Nico en ____. el estudio de *Salu2*

B. Un poco más. Conteste las siguientes preguntas.

1. ¿Entre qué horas está abierta la clínica?
2. ¿Por qué eligió la Dra. Zaragoza-Kaneki su profesión?
3. ¿Cuál es una de las metas importantes para la doctora?
4. ¿Por qué admiran Ana y Víctor a Nico Barry?
5. ¿Qué hace Nico Barry para componer la música de *Salu2*?

B, Answers: 1. *de las ocho de la mañana a las cinco de la tarde* **2.** *Viene de una familia de doctores.* **3.** *obtener atención médica para toda persona en nuestro país* **4.** *Porque Nico compone la música para Salu2. Tiene una gran habilidad para crear música apropiada para distintos temas y países.* **5.** *Investiga la música, los instrumentos y los ritmos de cada país.*

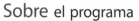

C. Y ahora, Uds. En parejas, imaginen que tienen la oportunidad de entrevistar a la Dra. Zaragoza-Kaneki y al compositor Nico Barry para hacer un reportaje más extenso sobre ellos. Hagan una lista de cinco preguntas que les gustaría hacerle a cada uno.

Sobre el programa

¿A quiénes admiran Ana, Laura y Víctor? Ana siente especial admiración por su abuela materna, una indígena kuna* que le enseñó a cocinar y a usar remedios naturales. Lo que más admira Ana de su abuela es que fue capaz[a] de integrarse en la vida de la capital sin perder sus valores[b] y tradiciones indígenas.

Laura tiene un gran respeto por su madre, una profesora universitaria de historia. Es una mujer muy culta[c] que les ha trasmitido a sus hijas la idea de que es posible tener una familia y ser profesionista a la vez.[d]

Víctor admira a su padre y se siente muy orgulloso[e] de él. Su padre emigró a California siendo niño, y tuvo que trabajar bien duro[f] no solo para ayudar a su familia, sino también[g] para educarse. Tomaba cursos universitarios mientras trabajaba turnos de diez horas o más. Llegó a ser maestro bilingüe en las escuelas públicas de Los Ángeles, trabajo del que se jubiló recientemente después de treinta años.

[a]*able* [b]*values* [c]*educated, very knowledgeable* [d]*a… at the same time* [e]*proud* [f]*bien… very hard* [g]*but also*

Producción personal

Filme tres entrevistas en las que (*which*) los entrevistados hablan de las personas que más admiran. Los entrevistados deben explicar por qué admiran a esas personas.

The kuna *are an indigenous people from* Panamá *and* Colombia. *Kuna women produce* molas (*hand-crafted textile panels*), *which are well-known in this country. The beautifully colored and patterned* molas *are part of women's dresses.*

Después de mirar

C: Suggestion

After students have prepared their questions, follow-up with mock interviews. Choose two of your most fluent students to act as the doctor and the composer.

Sobre el programa

Suggestions

- Point out the use of *culto/a* to refer to a person of great general knowledge. Hispanics in general place great value on this personal trait.
- Point out the use of the term *profesionista,* used in Mexico and a few other countries. *Profesional* is the more widely used term.

Optional: Comprensión

1. *¿A quién admira Ana y por qué? (Admira a su abuela materna. Le enseñó a cocinar y a usar remedios naturales.)*
2. *¿A quién admira Laura y por qué? (Admira a su madre, porque es una persona muy culta y porque ha podido ser profesionista y tener una familia a la vez.)*
3. *¿Cuál fue la profesión del padre de Víctor? ¿Por qué es un hombre admirable? (Fue maestro de escuela. Trabajó muy duro para ayudar a su familia y educarse.)*

Producción personal

Suggestion

See the IM for additional suggestions for this chapter's assignment as well as for general guidelines and suggestions for video assignments.

Lectura cultural
Notes
See the IM for more information on Chile and for some expressions used there.

First Reading: Note
Chile has experienced spectacular economic development from the 1980s on. By most measures, it's one of the most stable and strongest economies in Latin America, along with Brazil and Argentina.

En otros países hispanos
Suggestions
- Ask students to discuss the term *trabajólico/a*. Is it considered a good or a bad characteristic in this country?
- Remind students about the title of this chapter and engage them in a whole-class discussion on how they perceive the topic in this country as compared to the Hispanic world.

Exploración lingüística
Ask students to find the following in the reading. Some of these words are glossed and some are not.
- *Un sinónimo de* campesinos (*trabajadores agrícolas*)
- *Un adjetivo derivado de* salario (*salarial*)
- *Dos adverbios que se usan de manera consecutiva* (*afanosa y compulsivamente* [Explain that the first of two adverbs in sequence does not have the -*mente* ending.])

Comprensión: Answers
1. *Algunos tienen salarios muy altos, mientras que los salarios de otros son muy bajos.* **2.** *Se refiere a una persona que trabaja afanosa y compulsivamente.* **3.** *un mes de vacaciones, la licencia por maternidad o paternidad, un sistema nacional de salud*

Tres símbolos chilenos
Notes
- *Los mapuches* were the only indigenous group that the Spanish could not subjugate. In fact, the Incas (who dominated the area before the arrival of the Spanish) couldn't conquer them either.
- *A cultrún* is used by a *machi*, a female shaman, in religious and cultural rituals such as the *Nguillatún* prayer used in a healing ritual called the *Machitún* as well as in the *We Tripantu* (the Mapuche New Year's festival).

A LEER

Lectura cultural
Chile

Chile es uno de los países del mundo en donde la gente más trabaja. Como ocurre en otras partes del mundo, parte del problema es que algunos necesitan más de un trabajo para sobrevivir.[a] Pero existe también una minoría que tiene salarios altos. La realidad es que hay una brecha[b] salarial en el país: Según un reciente Informe de Salarios de la Organización Internacional del Trabajo, un trabajador chileno que cobra un sueldo alto gana 7,86 veces más que un trabajador que cobra un sueldo bajo. Los abogados, médicos, ingenieros, empresarios, ejecutivos de bancos y congresistas[c] tienen las profesiones mejor pagadas. Y los obreros, profesores, trabajadores agrícolas y empleados públicos están entre las ocupaciones que no tienen buena remuneración.

¿Hay una gran brecha salarial en el sistema laboral de este país?

[a]*survive* [b]*gap* [c]*congressional representatives*

Unos cultrunes mapuches con los símbolos que en esa cultura representan las cuatro estaciones

En otros países hispanos

- **En algunos países hispanohablantes** En la actualidad se empieza a oír la palabra **trabajólico/a,** que la Real Academia Española de la Lengua define como «Que trabaja afanosa[a] y compulsivamente». Curiosamente, la Real Academia identifica este adjetivo como una expresión chilena. En general, el hecho[b] de trabajar mucho o en exceso, de ser una persona trabajólica o creer que trabajar mucho es una buena cualidad son contrarios a la manera de pensar de los hispanos. Para la mayoría de estos, hay que trabajar para vivir, pero nunca al revés.[c]
- **En España** En este país, como en muchos otros países europeos, los trabajadores disfrutan de[d] buenos beneficios laborales que están establecidos por la ley.[e] Por ejemplo, un mes de vacaciones al año es el mínimo legal. Otro ejemplo es la licencia[f] por maternidad o paternidad, que la ley garantiza[g] con cuatro meses, además de otros beneficios asociados. Finalmente, España tiene un sistema nacional de salud que cubre prácticamente a toda la población.

[a]*eagerly* [b]*act* [c]al… *the other way around* [d]disfrutan… tienen [e]*law* [f]*leave* [g]*guarantees*

Tres símbolos chilenos

- **El cultrún** Es un tambor[a] ceremonial del pueblo mapuche, en cuya superficie[b] está representada gráficamente toda su cosmovisión. Los mapuches, una cultura milenaria[c] de Sudamérica, son el pueblo indígena más importante de Chile.
- **Los Andes** Esta gran cordillera[d] es una imagen constante en la diversa geografía chilena y representa su frontera natural con Bolivia y la Argentina. Los Andes son muy distintivos porque el territorio de Chile es tan angosto[e] que en su punto más ancho[f] de este a oeste solo mide 180 kilómetros.[g]
- **«Gracias a la vida»** Esta canción, de la cantautora[h] y folclorista chilena Violeta Parra, es un himno a la vida y a los pequeños y grandes logros[i] de la humanidad, entre ellos el amor entre parejas. Esta canción es conocida no solo por la inmensa mayoría de los hispanohablantes, sino[j] por muchas personas de todos los países. Muchos cantantes la han cantado.

[a]*drum* [b]cuya… *whose surface* [c]*thousand-year-old* [d]*mountain range* [e]*narrow* [f]más… *widest* [g]180… *111.85 miles* [h]*singer-songwriter* [i]*achievements* [j]*but rather*

Una cita

«Trabajadores de mi Patria:[a] tengo fe[b] en Chile y su destino.[c] […] Sigan ustedes sabiendo que, mucho más temprano que tarde, de nuevo se abrirán las grandes alamedas[d] por donde pase el hombre libre, para construir una sociedad mejor.»

Salvador Allende (1903–1973), presidente de Chile: «Último Discurso[e]», 11 de septiembre de 1973

[a]*Homeland* [b]*faith* [c]*destiny* [d]*boulevards* [e]*Speech*

COMPRENSIÓN

1. ¿Cómo es la brecha salarial en Chile?
2. ¿Qué significa la palabra **trabajólico/a**?
3. ¿De qué beneficios disfrutan los trabajadores españoles por ley?

Una cita
Note
The quote is from the end of Allende's last speech, just before he died during the bombing of the presidential palace. People use this last line to refer to it: "*se abrirán las grandes alamedas…*" The sentence offers a visual image of people free to demonstrate and associate (in contrast with the censorship that a dictatorship imposes) and of the idea that people will build a better and more just society.

Del mundo hispano

Antes de leer

La Real Academia Española de la Lengua da varias definiciones de la palabra **camino.** Aquí están las dos principales. ¿Puede Ud. dar una traducción al inglés de cada una? ¿Cuál de las definiciones describe un camino de forma física? ¿Cuál es más metafórica?

- «Tierra hollada (marcada por los pies) por donde se transita habitualmente»
- «Dirección que ha de seguirse (*is to be followed*) para llegar a algún lugar»

Lectura: «XXIX», de Antonio Machado

Caminante,[a] son tus huellas[b]
el camino,[c] y nada más;
caminante, no hay camino:
se hace camino al andar.[d]
Al andar se hace el camino,
y al volver la vista atrás[e]
se ve la senda[f] que nunca
se ha de volver a pisar.[g]
Caminante, no hay camino,
sino estelas[h] en la mar.

[a]*Traveler (person who travels on foot)* [b]*footprints* [c]*path, road* [d]al... *as you walk* [e]al... *when you look back* [f]*path* [g]nunca... *will never be tread upon again* [h]*wakes (of boats)*

Comprensión

A. En el texto. Conteste las siguientes preguntas relacionadas con el poema.

1. Identifique las palabras y expresiones del poema que son sinónimos o metáforas de las palabras **caminar** y **camino.**
2. En este poema hay mucha repetición, tanto de (*as much of*) versos como de ideas. Identifique la repetición que se encuentra en el poema.
3. ¿Qué frases usa el poeta para describir el camino? Explíquelas con sus propias palabras.

B. Interpretación. Conteste las siguientes preguntas, según su propia interpretación del poema.

1. El poeta se dirige a (*addresses*) un **caminante.** En su opinión, ¿quién es ese caminante?
2. ¿Qué simboliza **el camino** en este poema?
3. La última representación del camino en este poema es la imagen de **estelas en la mar.** ¿Qué pueden simbolizar las estelas, en el contexto del poema?
4. ¿Cuál de las siguientes afirmaciones representa mejor el mensaje del poema? Identifique el verso que explica su respuesta.
   - **a.** El caminante selecciona un camino definido y visible y lo sigue.
   - **b.** El camino se hace visible solo después de que el caminante ha caminado por él.
5. ¿Que filosofía de la vida expone el poema? ¿Está Ud. de acuerdo? Explique su respuesta.
   - **a.** Es necesario que encontremos nuestro camino en la vida y que lo sigamos con determinación.
   - **b.** Vamos descubriendo nuestro camino en la vida a medida que (*as*) vivimos.

A: Answers

1. *caminar: andar, pisar / camino; huellas, senda, estelas en la mar* **2.** *caminante, no hay camino, se hace camino al andar / al andar se hace el camino; volver* **3.** *son tus huellas, se hace camino al andar, la senda que nunca se ha de volver a pisar, estelas en la mar.* Explanations will vary.

B: Answers

Answers will vary, but here are some possibilities.
1. The *caminante* could be any of us. **2.** The *camino* is one's path through life. **3.** The *estelas* signify one's impact on one's community. **4.** b; explanations will vary. **5.** b; explanations will vary.

Del mundo hispano

Note

See the IM for optional follow-up, writing, and Internet activities.

Antes de leer

Answers

- Allow for creative interpretations if students' meaning is clear.
- Example translations: Ground that has been trod upon (worn down by feet), used habitually for travel. Directions that must be followed in order to arrive somewhere.
- The first definition is a description of a physical path. The second is more metaphorical. It describes the manner in which one lives and the decisions one makes; it describes a path through time and through life.

Estrategia

Repetition

Repetition is a key element in this poem, and it is apparent in the repetition of words, variants of words, and alternate ways to express the same idea. Be sure that students know the difference between *caminar, camino,* and *caminante*. *Comprensión A* items 1 and 2 lead students to focus on the various ways in which repetition is used to convey the message of the poem.

Escuche

Notes

- In this chapter students can listen to a specialist describing how to prepare for and have a great job interview.
- If the listening is assigned as homework, ask students to listen to the passage at least twice.
- See the IM for the Audioscript and more information about music in Chile.

A: Follow-up

Ask students to come up with examples of bad interviewing techniques from the point of view of the interviewer (not the job candidate).

B: Follow-up

Ask students to write a pamphlet to distribute at a student job fair. The suggestions will be about how to have a great job interview.

¡Música!

Notes

- Violeta Parra (1917–1967) was a famous Chilean folk singer and one of the founders of the Chilean *Nueva canción* movement. She came from a distinguished and prolific artistic family; her brother Nicanor is also considered one the great Chilean and Latin American poets of the 20th century.
- This song is a hymn to life, despite the fact that Parra's life ended in suicide. Many artists have sung it over the years, notably the Argentine folk singer Mercedes Sosa and Joan Baez, who is Parra's counterpart in the United States.
- For helpful tips on using songs in the classroom, see the IM.

A ESCUCHAR

Antes de escuchar

¿Qué debe o puede hacer una persona para prepararse para una entrevista de trabajo? ¿Es normal que alguien se ponga nervioso cuando sabe que tiene una entrevista?

Escuche

Mundo laboral

En la radio hay un programa que hace sugerencias para las entrevistas laborales. Escuche según las indicaciones de su profesor(a).

Vocabulario para escuchar

la petición	request	**averigüe**	find out
cualquier	any	**asegúrese**	be sure
la formación	education, training	**la cartera**	portfolio, folder
la carrera	career	hacer **falta**	to need
acerca de	about	**el agradecimiento**	thanks

Después de escuchar

A. Sugerencias específicas. Haga por lo menos una sugerencia para cada momento del proceso de una entrevista laboral.

1. varios días antes de la entrevista
2. el día antes de la entrevista
3. el mismo día, antes de la entrevista
4. durante la entrevista
5. después de la entrevista

A: Answers

1. *preparar respuestas a las preguntas «estándar», saber algo de la empresa, aprender los nombres de los entrevistadores* **2.** *preparar la ropa y la cartera* **3.** *no llegar tarde* **4.** *relajarse, mantenerse con calma, mantener contacto visual, escuchar bien las preguntas, contestar sin prisa.* **5.** *mandar nota de agradecimiento*

B. El programa de radio. Conteste las siguientes preguntas.

1. ¿Por qué se repite la programación de la semana anterior?
2. Según el programa, ¿cuál es la mejor manera de reducir el estrés de una entrevista?
3. ¿Dónde se puede encontrar el texto del programa?

B: Answers

1. *Porque muchos radioyentes la pidieron.* **2.** *estar preparado* **3.** *en la página Web del programa*

¡Música!

Violeta Parra es un ícono musical de Chile, a pesar de que[a] murió hace cerca de[b] cuarenta años. Era una folclorista musical y también una artista visual. Su canción «Gracias a la vida» es una de las canciones más conocidas en todo el mundo hispanohablante. Es del álbum *Violeta Parra: Las últimas composiciones.*

[a]*a… in spite of the fact that* [b]cerca… *about*

Violeta Parra, en concierto

Go to the iMix section in Connect Spanish (**www.connectspanish.com**) to access the iTunes playlist *"Puntos9,"* where you can purchase "Gracias a la vida" by Violeta Parra.

A ESCRIBIR

El tema

Mi futuro

Preparar

Paso 1. Llene la tabla con información sobre cinco o seis de las características que tendrá o de las actividades que serán parte de su vida en el futuro. El futuro es el verbo más apropiado para esta lista.

Plano profesional	Plano personal

Paso 2. Ahora describa las circunstancias que harán posibles sus planes futuros y las contingencias que podrían prevenir que sus planes futuros se realizaran (*could prevent your plans for the future from being realized*).

Redactar

Utilice la información de **Preparar** para desarrollar un ensayo sobre sus planes personales y profesionales para el futuro. Piense bien antes de decidir el tono de su ensayo. Incorpore un comentario indicando si sus metas (*goals*) son típicas de las personas de su edad o no.

Editar

Revise el ensayo para comprobar:

- la ortografía y los acentos
- la organización y la secuencia de las ideas
- el tiempo y la forma de los verbos, especialmente el uso del futuro y del subjuntivo
- el tono del ensayo

Finalmente, prepare su versión final para entregarla.

Preparar

Suggestions

- Ask students to think about what might be considered to be realistic life goals vs. goals that may be out of their reach. Ask them to focus on their true goals in life for this writing assignment.
- Suggest that students include some topics that aren't typically listed for future goals (childcare for children, free-time activities, relationship with parents, health, what type of parents they will be, and so on).
- Suggest that students include some conjunctions of time from *Gram. 47* in their essay.

Redactar

Suggestions

- Suggested length for this writing assignment: approximately 200 words
- Suggested structure: 3 paragraphs
  - **P. 1.** Introduction with general personal and professional goals for the future
  - **P. 2.** A more specific description of the writer's personal and professional goals, with examples in the future. Examples from the student writer will be in the first person. Students can also discuss whether these goals are typical or atypical by comparing themselves to others.
  - **P. 3.** A brief summary of the student's future

Editar

Follow-up

Have a whole-class discussion about the following topic: How do a person's goals for the future affect that person's present and his or her future? How does a person's present environment and upbringing affect who he or she will be when he or she is older?

En resumen: En este capítulo

Vocabulario

Suggestions

- Read the following descriptions and have students tell what professions they associate with each: *¿Qué profesión asocia Ud. con cada descripción?*
  1. *Recibe muchas invitaciones para comer en buenos restaurantes. Es muy susceptible a los ataques al corazón. Viaja mucho.* (*el hombre / la mujer de negocios*)
  2. *Compra y vende cosas. Pone anuncios de sus productos en la televisión, en los periódicos, etcétera. Está contento cuando los empleados venden mucho.* (*el/la gerente*)
  3. *Tiene que leer mucho. Tiene un puesto de mucho prestigio. A veces no sabe si su cliente es inocente o no.* (*el/la abogado/a*)
- Play a game to identify professions. Make individual cards with the names of professions in Spanish. Tape a card on each student's back without allowing the student to see it. Have students circulate to ask *sí/no* questions about themselves. After each question, they should move to another classmate. Classmates may only respond *Sí* or *No;* they should not elaborate. The first student to figure out what he or she is wins. Continue until everyone is successful. Model exchanges before they begin.

  ¿Trabajo en una oficina? → *No.*
  ¿Manejo mucho? → *No.*
  ¿Enseño? → *Sí.*
  ¿Soy maestro/a? → *Sí.*
- The first person singular of *graduarse* is *me gradúo*. Remind students of the spelling changes for *economizar* (*c*) and *sacar* (*qu*).

Word Families

En este capítulo

- *el banco, la tarjeta bancaria*
- *la caja, el cajero automático, el/la cajero/a*
- *el cheque, con cheque*
- *la cuenta corriente, la cuenta de ahorros*
- *la cuenta de ahorros, ahorrar*
- *la entrevista, el/la entrevistado/a, el/la entrevistador(a), entrevistar*
- *el préstamo, pedir prestado/a*
- *solicitar, la solicitud*

Entre capítulos

- *a plazos* = *el plazo* (14)
- *el billete* = *el billete (de ida y vuelta)* (8)
- *el cheque, con cheque* = *el chequeo* (11)
- *el/la cocinero/a* = *la cocina* (5), *cocinar* (7)
- *con cheque* = *con* (2)
- *conseguir* = *conseguir* + inf. (9)
- *la cuenta corriente, la cuenta de ahorros* = *la cuenta* (7)
- *dejar* = *dejar (en)* (10), *dejar de* + inf. (11)
- *despedir* = *despedirse (de)* (9)
- *después (de) que* = *después de* (5)
- *devolver* = *volver* (5)
- *economizar* = *la economía* (2)
- *el/la electricista* = *la electricidad* (12), *eléctrico/a* (15), la *electrónica* (12)
- *la factura* = *facturar* (8)

EN RESUMEN En este capítulo

LearnSmart

Visit **www.connectspanish.com** to practice the vocabulary and grammar points covered in this chapter.

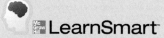

Gramática en breve

46. The Future

Infinitive + **-é, -ás, -á, -emos, -éis, -án**

Irregular forms: **dir-, habr-, har-, podr-, pondr-, querr-, sabr-, saldr-, tendr-, vendr-** + *future endings*

47. The Subjunctive After Conjunctions of Time

	Future/ Pending	Habitual/ Past
most conjunctions of time	subjunctive	indicative
antes (de) que	subjunctive	subjunctive

Conjunctions: **antes (de) que, cuando, después (de) que, en cuanto, hasta que, tan pronto como**

Vocabulario

Las profesiones y los oficios

el/la abogado/a	lawyer
el amo/ama de casa	housekeeper
el/la cajero/a	cashier; teller
el/la cocinero/a	cook; chef
el/la contador(a)	accountant
el hombre / la mujer de negocios	businessperson
el/la ingeniero/a	engineer
el/la maestro/a (de escuela)	schoolteacher
el/la obrero/a	worker, laborer
el/la peluquero/a	hairstylist
el/la periodista	journalist
el/la plomero/a	plumber
el/la sicólogo/a	psychologist
el/la siquiatra	psychiatrist
el soldado / la mujer soldado	soldier
el/la técnico/a	technician
el/la trabajador(a) social	social worker
el/la traductor(a)	translator
el/la vendedor(a)	salesperson

Cognados: el/la analista de sistemas, el/la astronauta, el/la electricista, el/la fotógrafo/a, el/la programador(a), el/la veterinario/a

Repaso: el/la artista, el/la asistente de vuelo, el/la bibliotecario/a, el/la consejero/a, el/la dentista, el/la dependiente/a, el/la enfermero/a, el/la mecánico/a, el/la médico/a, el/la profesor(a), el/la secretario/a

El mundo laboral

el/la aspirante	candidate; applicant
el currículum	resumé
el empleo	job, position
bien/mal pagado	well-/poorly paid
de tiempo completo/ parcial	full-/part-time
la empresa	corporation; business
la entrevista	interview
el/la entrevistado/a	interviewee
el/la entrevistador(a)	interviewer
el/la gerente	manager
el oficio	trade (*profession*)
el salario	pay, wages (*often per hour*)
la solicitud	application (*form*)

Cognado: el/la recepcionista

Repaso: el puesto, el sueldo, el teléfono, el trabajo

dejar	to quit
despedir (*like* **pedir**)	to let (*someone*) go; to fire (*someone*) (*from a job*)
graduarse (me gradúo) (en)	to graduate (from)
jubilarse	to retire
llenar	to fill out (*a form*)
renunciar (a)	to resign (from)
solicitar	to apply for (*a job*)

Repaso: conseguir (*like* **seguir**), **contestar**

Una cuestión de dinero

el banco	bank
el billete	bill (*money*)
la caja	cashier window
el cajero automático	automatic teller machine (ATM)
el cheque	check
la cuenta corriente	checking account
la cuenta de ahorros	savings account
el efectivo	cash
la factura	bill
el interés	interest
la moneda	coin
el préstamo	loan
el presupuesto	budget
el recibo	receipt
la tarjeta bancaria	debit card

Repaso: la cuenta, el dinero, la tarjeta de crédito

ahorrar	to save (*money*)
cobrar	to cash (*a check*); to charge (*someone for an item or service*)
compartir	to share
pedir (pido) (i) prestado/a	to borrow
sacar (qu)	to withdraw, take out

Cognados: depositar, economizar (c)

Repaso: devolver (*like* volver), ganar, gastar, pagar (gu), prestar

a plazos	in installments
con cheque	by check
en efectivo	in cash

Los adjetivos

laboral	work, work-related
propio/a	own, one's own

Las formas posesivas

mío/a(s)
tuyo/a(s)
suyo/a(s)
nuestro/a(s)
vuestro/a(s)

Las conjunciones de tiempo

después (de) que	after
en cuanto	as soon as
hasta que	until
tan pronto como	as soon as

Repaso: antes (de) que, cuando

Palabras adicionales

al principio de	at the beginning of

Vocabulario personal

- *el/la fotógrafo/a = la foto(grafía)* (8), *la fotografía* (13), *sacar fotos* (8)
- *ganar* (to earn) = *ganar* (to win) (8)
- *graduarse (en) = el grado* (10)
- *hasta que = hasta luego* (1), *hasta* (5)
- *el hombre / la mujer de negocios = el hombre* (2), *la mujer* (2)
- *el interés = interesar* (8)
- *llenar* (to fill out [a form]) = *llenar* (to fill up) (15)
- *el/la maestro/a (de escuela) = la obra maestra* (13), *la escuela* (10)
- *la mujer soldado = la mujer* (2)
- *el/la obrero/a = la obra* (13), *la obra de teatro* (13), *la obra maestra* (13)
- *el/la periodista = el periódico* (3)
- *el préstamo, pedir prestado/a = prestar* (8)
- *la profesión = el/la profesor(a)* (2)
- *el recibo = recibir* (3)
- *sacar = sacar la basura* (10), *sacar fotos* (8), *sacar notas* (14)
- *el/la sicólogo/a = la sicología* (2)
- *tan pronto como = tan… como* (6)
- *la tarjeta bancaria = la tarjeta de crédito* (7), *la tarjeta de identificación* (14)
- *el/la trabajador(a) social = trabajar* (2), *trabajador(a)* (3), *el trabajo* (12,14)
- *el/la vendedor(a) = vender* (3)

¡OJO!

- *el/la aspirante ≠ la aspiradora*
- *el gerente ≠ la gente*
- *en cuanto ≠ ¿cuánto/a?*
- *el presupuesto ≠ por supuesto*

Suggestions

- Have students list on the board different work-related and bank-related situations; for example, an office manager giving an employee a bad work review, a student asking for a loan. Have students take turns role-playing different situations without indicating which one. The class should guess the situation.
- Ask students the following questions to review the vocabulary.
  1. *¿Tiene Ud. una cuenta de ahorros? ¿En qué banco? ¿Ha ahorrado mucho dinero este año? ¿Es posible que ahorre más el año que viene? ¿Tiene también una cuenta corriente? ¿Escribe muchos cheques? ¿Tiene siempre suficiente dinero en su cuenta? ¿Qué ocurre cuando no lo tiene?*
  2. *En esta clase, ¿cuántos de Uds. tienen tarjetas de crédito?* (to one student) *¿Son tarjetas nacionales como Visa o son tarjetas para tiendas locales? ¿Las usa con mucha frecuencia? ¿Las usa demasiado? ¿Tiene muchas facturas que pagar ahora?*
  3. *En general, ¿tienen muchas facturas los estudiantes? ¿Cuáles son los gastos típicos de un estudiante? ¿Tiene Ud. todos estos gastos? ¿Tiene también un presupuesto? ¿Qué porcentaje de su presupuesto es para el alquiler?*
  4. *¿Cuánto paga de alquiler? ¿Lo paga siempre el primero del mes o a veces lo paga más tarde? ¿Qué pasa si lo paga tarde?*
  5. *¿Gasta Ud. mucho dinero en ropa? ¿Cómo la paga, con tarjetas de crédito, al contado o con cheque? ¿Se queja Ud. del precio de la ropa?*

← (Cont.)

Chapter Opening Photo and Chapter Theme

Chapter Theme–related Questions

- Have students give one example from recent media, events, or history for each of the following categories. Help them with new or unfamiliar vocabulary by paraphrasing the vocabulary, as needed.

  una guerra
  un desastre natural
  un reportero
  un evento social importante
  un derecho y una obligación de un ciudadano de este país
  una democracia
  un imperio
  una dictadura
  un reino

- Ask students:
  1. *¿Cree Ud. que está bien informado/a de lo que pasa? ¿Por qué?*
  2. *¿Piensa Ud. que es importante estar bien informado/a? Explique.*

Reciclado: In preparation for the presentation of the past subjunctive, review the syntax of the subjunctive and its "triggers" by asking students to complete the following sentences. Depending on the interests of students in your class, the context for these questions can easily be changed to include politics and government, personal relations, family relations, and so on.

1. *En esta clase, el profesor / la profesora quiere que…*
2. *Los estudiantes esperan que el profesor / la profesora…*
3. *El profesor / La profesora duda que…*
4. *No hay nadie en esta clase que…*
5. *Vamos a salir bien en este curso con tal de que…*
6. *Vamos a seguir estudiando español hasta que…*

España

Datos esenciales

Nombre oficial: *Reino de España*
Lema: *«Plus Ultra» (Mas Allá, [latín])*
Capital: *Madrid*
Otras ciudades: *Barcelona, Segovia, Sevilla, Toledo*
Composición étnica: *una población muy homogénea resultado de una mezcla de diferentes grupos europeos; 1,5% gitanos (un grupo que llegó a la Península Ibérica en el siglo XV). Actualmente, la diversidad racial está aumentando mucho debido a la intensa inmigración de los últimos 30 años.*

18 La actualidad

Manifestación (*Demonstration*) en la Puerta del Sol, Madrid

- ¿Es importante para Ud. estar al día (*up to date*) en cuanto a (*as far as*) lo que pasa en el mundo?
- ¿Qué medios de comunicación usa principalmente para mantenerse informado/a? ¿La radio y la televisión? ¿la prensa (*press*)? ¿el Internet?
- ¿Votó en las últimas elecciones? ¿Cree que es importante votar?

connect SPANISH

www.connectspanish.com

NATIONAL STANDARDS: Connections

This last chapter of *Puntos de partida* plus the essay with which the book concludes (page 552) will focus on Spain and on the global community of Hispanics. The history of Spain is characterized by the number of cultures that passed through the Peninsula: Phoenicians, Romans, Visigoths, Arabs, Jews, Gypsies. Today's Spain is no different, as the country is experiencing intense and growing immigration from Latin America, North and sub-Saharan Africa, Eastern Europe, and other areas. While Spain was clearly involved in the destruction of indigenous cultures in the Western Hemisphere, its actions also gave rise to new cultural mixes, the blend of *lo español* with *lo indígena* that is seen in the majority of Latin America and in parts of Africa (*la Guinea Ecuatorial*) and the Pacific (*las Islas Filipinas*). In turn, immigrants from Spanish-speaking areas have brought their language and cultures to the United States and Canada.

España

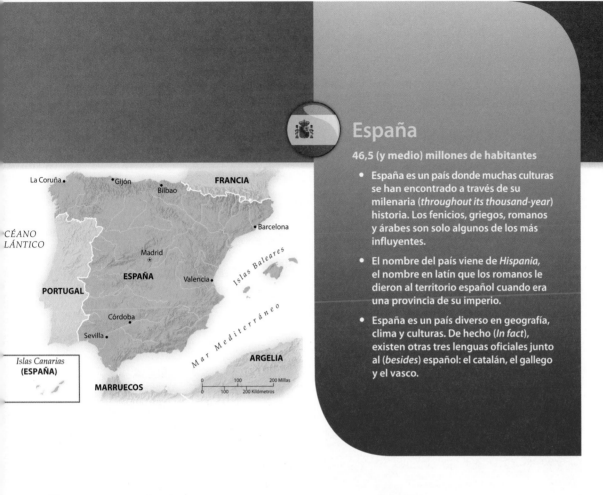

46,5 (y medio) millones de habitantes

- España es un país donde muchas culturas se han encontrado a través de su milenaria (*throughout its thousand-year*) historia. Los fenicios, griegos, romanos y árabes son solo algunos de los más influyentes.
- El nombre del país viene de *Hispania*, el nombre en latín que los romanos le dieron al territorio español cuando era una provincia de su imperio.
- España es un país diverso en geografía, clima y culturas. De hecho (*In fact*), existen otras tres lenguas oficiales junto al (*besides*) español: el catalán, el gallego y el vasco.

En este capítulo

CONTENT / **CONTENIDO**	OBJECTIVES / **OBJETIVOS**
The News 524, Government 526	To talk about current events in the country and the world
The Past Subjunctive 529	To express past actions and conditions that require the subjunctive
The Conditional 536	To express what you would do
España 546	To learn about a European country in the Iberian Peninsula that has been a crossroad of civilizations for centuries

Jefe de estado actual: *Juan Carlos I, rey, desde 1975; y José Luis Rodríguez Zapatero, Presidente del Gobierno, desde 2004*
Forma de gobierno: *monarquía parlamentaria*
Lenguas: *el castellano o español y otras tres lenguas que se hablan en sus respectivas regiones: el catalán, el gallego y el vasco*
Moneda: *el euro*
Religión: *mayoritariamente católica, aunque el 15% se declara no creyente; 2% otras religiones*

Notes

- Spain's system is similar to that of England, having a king who has ceremonial functions and a democratically elected government.
- *Juan Carlos I de Borbón* (1938–) became king after the death of the dictator Francisco Franco, who ruled Spain from 1939 until 1975. Franco had planned for the restoration of the monarchy upon his death.
- See the IM for more historical information on Spain.

Suggestions

- Show a world map and ask students to focus on Spain's geographical position. Ask what advantages and disadvantages such a position has and how that would affect the country's history.
- Ask students to reflect on the words that are derived from Spain's name under the Romans, *Hispania* → *hispano/a*.
- Have students list their ideas about Spain, including information on geography, politics, economy, culture, music, and cuisine. When you finish the chapter, return to the lists and ask students what ideas they would change and/or add.

Multimedia: Internet

Have students look for the official CNN website online where they can read and watch video clips of today's news headlines in Spanish.

Resources: Transparency 163

Resources

For Students

- Connect Spanish (**www.connectspanish.com**), which contains all content from the following resources, as well as the *Mundo interactivo* scenarios, the LearnSmart adaptive learning system, and more!
- **Physical Resources:** Workbook / Laboratory Manual, Laboratory Audio Program, DVD

For Instructors

- Connect Spanish (**www.connectspanish.com**), which contains access to all student sections of Connect Spanish, as well as helpful time-saving tools and resources such as an integrated gradebook, Instructor's Manual, Testing Program, digital transparencies, Audioscript, Videoscript, and more!

Vocabulario: Preparación
Las noticias
Note

See the model for vocabulary presentation and other material in the *Cap. 18 Vocabulario: Preparación* section of "Chapter-by-Chapter Supplementary Materials" in the IM.

Suggestions

- Emphasize that the first person singular of *ofrecer* is like that of *conocer* (*ofrezco*) and that *mantener* is like *tener* (*mantengo*).
- Point out that *testigo* does not change the ending for the feminine form: *el testigo* and *la testigo*.
- Have students provide names from current events that correspond to the following categories.
- **Reciclado:** Note the use of subjunctive in some of the following cues. Ask students why the subjunctive is used in some of the cues, and ask what mood they will use in their answers. Model one cue/response sequence.

  ¿Está Ud. bien informado/a? Dé un nombre de la vida real para cada una de las siguientes categorías.
  1. *un reportero famoso en la tele*
  2. *una guerra que esté ocurriendo ahora mismo*
  3. *un desastre actual que le haya impresionado*
  4. *un acuerdo de paz que se haya firmado recientemente*
  5. *un asesinato reciente que haya sido objeto de mucha publicidad*
- Give students the following *dictado*.
  1. *Merecemos salarios más altos, pero el jefe no quiere darnos un aumento.*
  2. *Es necesario que nos declaremos en huelga.*
  3. *Pero el jefe va a despedir a todos los obreros que protesten.*
  4. *No te preocupes: unidos podremos conseguir lo que pedimos.*

Resources: Transparency 164

VOCABULARIO **Preparación**

Las noticias° — Las... *The News*

1.

2.

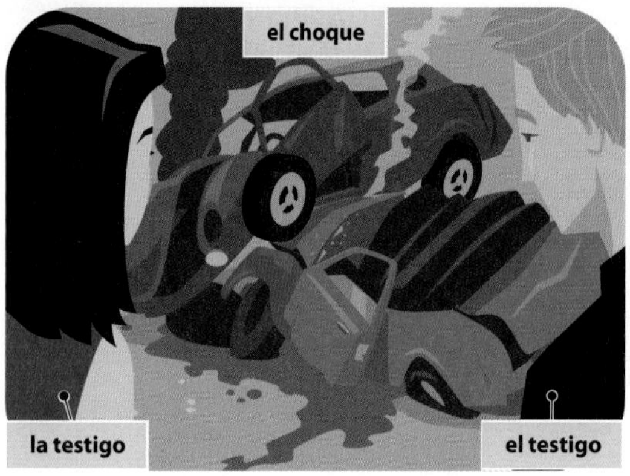

3.

4.

Los acontecimientos°	Los... *Events*
el asesinato	assassination
asesinar	to assassinate
matar	to kill
el desastre (natural)	(natural) disaster
la esperanza	hope
mantener (*like* **tener**) **la esperanza**	to maintain, keep up hope
la guerra	war
la lucha	fight, struggle
luchar	to fight
el medio de comunicación	medium of communication (*pl.* mass media)
la muerte	death

el periódico	newspaper
la prensa	press
la revista	magazine

Cognados: el ataque (terrorista), el blog, la bomba, la erupción, la radio, la televisión, el terrorismo, el/la terrorista

El noticiero°	El... *Newscast*
comunicar(se) (qu) (con)	to communicate (with)
enterarse (de)	to find out, learn (about)
estar al día	to be up to date
informar	to inform
ofrecer (ofrezco)	to offer

NATIONAL STANDARDS: Cultures

The unprecedented growth in the Hispanic population in the U.S. has fueled the increase in Spanish-language media. Three major Hispanic television networks in the U.S. are *Telemundo, Univisión*, and *Televisa*. *CNN en español* is the Spanish equivalent of CNN, with 24/7 reporting on news, sports, economy, and finance in Spanish.

NATIONAL STANDARDS: Communication

- Give students 5–10 minutes to prepare their own news reports. Assign specific topics to different students or groups: headlines, weather, local, international, sports, and so on. Have students select an order of presentation, and begin the news program.
  If possible, videotape the presentation.

(Cont. →)

Conversación

A. Las noticias: ¿qué y cómo?

Paso 1. ¿Qué tipo de noticias le interesan más a Ud.? Indique todas las que siempre o casi siempre atraen su interés.

1. ☐ las noticias sobre la política internacional
2. ☐ las noticias locales de su ciudad
3. ☐ las noticias de su estado o provincia
4. ☐ las noticias sobre los desastres o las tragedias
5. ☐ las noticias de interés humano
6. ☐ las noticias sobre los deportes
7. ☐ las noticias financieras o sobre los negocios
8. ☐ las noticias sobre el arte y la cultura
9. ☐ ¿ ?

Paso 2. Ahora, en parejas, comparen sus preferencias noticieras. ¿Hay más coincidencias (*similarities*) o más diferencias entre sus preferencias?

Paso 3. Hagan una lista de los medios de comunicación que se usan hoy en día, en orden de preferencia personal.

B. ¿Quién está más al día? En grupos de tres o cuatro, den un ejemplo de las siguientes cosas o personas.

MODELO: un reportero ⟶ Jorge Ramos Ávalo

1. un reportero / una reportera
2. un asesinato
3. una huelga o una lucha
4. una guerra
5. un desastre natural
6. otro tipo de desastre (por ejemplo, un accidente)
7. un ataque terrorista
8. un canal de televisión o estación de radio

C. Definiciones

Paso 1. Dé las palabras definidas.

1. un programa que nos informa diariamente de lo que pasa en el mundo el noticiero
2. una muerte violenta causada intencionadamente el asesinato
3. un medio de comunicación que presenta la información por escrito el periódico, la revista
4. la persona que investiga y presenta una noticia el/la reportero/a
5. una persona que emplea la violencia para causar pánico el/la terrorista
6. cuando los obreros dejan de trabajar para protestar por su situación laboral o por su salario la huelga
7. una persona que está presente cuando ocurre algo y lo ve todo el/la testigo

Paso 2. Ahora, en parejas, definan las siguientes palabras en español.

1. la guerra
2. la muerte
3. el terrorismo
4. ofrecer
5. luchar
6. estar al día

Paso 3. Lean a la clase las definiciones que crearon en el **Paso 2** para que sus compañeros adivinen (*guess*) la palabra definida.

Así se dice

el acontecimiento = el evento, el hecho, el suceso
estar al día = estar al tanto, estar al corriente
la huelga = el paro

Con. C, Paso 2: Possible Answers: 1. *la lucha entre dos o más países* **2.** *cuando una persona deja de vivir* **3.** *un movimiento que trata de causar pánico o miedo* **4.** *darle algo a alguien* **5.** *usar la violencia contra alguien* **6.** *saber lo que está pasando*

Con. A: Follow-up

Use the activity to find out the favorite newspapers, magazines, Net servers, and so on of the students in the class.

Con. B: Suggestion

Set a time limit for this activity. Ask students to hand in the answers from their group, check them for accuracy, and give a prize to the group that had the most right answers within the time limit.

Culture

The *tertulia,* a common custom in many parts of the Spanish-speaking world, is a get-together in a bar or café of a group of friends and/or colleagues who like to spend time talking about current issues, religion, literature, the economy, and so on. The two most popular topics of conversation are sports and politics. Some groups gather every day at the same time and place, usually in the afternoon or evening. Others may get together once a week or once a month. Some groups will continue to get together for many years.

NATIONAL STANDARDS (Cont.)

- Have students watch the evening television newscast on a Spanish-language channel and hand in a two- or three-paragraph report on it the next day.

Con. D: Suggestions

- Model three to four responses, using the *Vocabulario útil* and emphasizing the indicative/subjunctive usage patterns that students will have to follow.
- Have students select one item and report their opinions back to the class.
- Use this activity as a written assignment.

Con. D: Follow-up

- Ask each pair to come up with one provocative statement to read to the class. Their classmates will react as a whole-class activity.
- Have students contrast or debate what ultraconservative and ultra-liberal people might say about the following topics: **1.** *la libertad de prensa* **2.** *un país bajo una dictadura* **3.** *la pena* (new) *de muerte* **4.** *las huelgas* **5.** *el aborto* **6.** *la eutanasia* **7.** *los sindicatos* (new) **8.** *el sistema de asistencia social*

El gobierno y la responsabilidad cívica

Suggestions

- Emphasize that the first person singular of *obedecer* is like that of *conocer* and *ofrecer: obedezco.*
- Point out the difference in meaning between *el derecho* (right; law) and *la derecha* (the conservative right, right-hand side). Review other meanings of *derecho,* for example, *todo derecho* (straight ahead).
- Emphasize the various possible meanings of *la política*, according to context: *politics, a policy, a female politician.*
- Give students the names of major political parties; for example: *el Partido Republicano* (*los republicanos*), *el Partido Demócrata* (*los demócratas*). Point out the difference in Spanish between *democrático/a* (practicing democracy) and *demócrata* (referring to the specific party).
- Ask students the following questions to personalize the vocabulary.
  1. *En este país, ¿hay una ley que proteja la libertad de prensa? ¿Qué derechos individuales se garantizan en la constitución?* (Write *la libertad de* ______ on the board.)

Resources: Transparency 165

D. Ud. y los medios de comunicación. En parejas, expresen y justifiquen su opinión sobre las siguientes ideas.

1. El interés por los *reality shows* demuestra (*shows*) que el público se interesa en la realidad del mundo.
2. La prensa de los países democráticos es con frecuencia irresponsable y parcial.
3. Ver la televisión es una pérdida (*waste*) de tiempo.
4. Hay demasiado sexo y violencia en los programas de televisión.
5. El Internet es una fuente (*source*) de información tan buena como los otros medios de comunicación.
6. Los niños no deben poder ver la televisión hasta que tengan diez años.

Vocabulario útil

creer que + *indicative*
no creer que + *subjunctive*
dudar que + *subjunctive*
no dudar que + *indicative*
esperar que + *subjunctive*
estar de acuerdo con/en que + *indicative*
no estar de acuerdo con/en que + *subjunctive*
es una lástima / probable / increíble que + *subjunctive*

El gobierno y la responsabilidad cívica

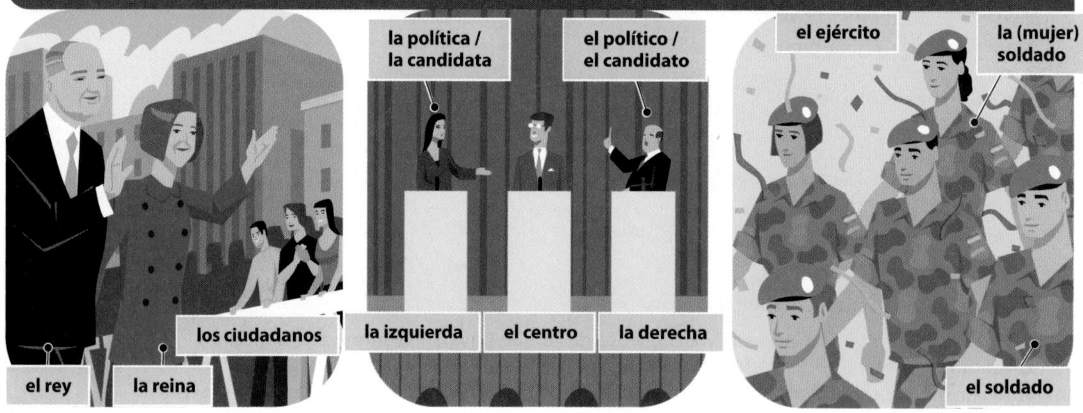

1. 2. 3.

Las personas

el ciudadano / la ciudadana	citizen
los/las demás	others
el dictador / la dictadora	dictator
el rey / la reina	king/queen

Los conceptos

el deber	responsibility; obligation
el derecho	right
la (des)igualdad	(in)equality
la dictadura	dictatorship
la discriminación	discrimination
la ley	law
el partido (político)	(political) party
la política	politics; policy
el servicio militar	miltary service

Las acciones

durar	to last
ganar	to win
obedecer (obedezco)	to obey
perder (pierdo)	to lose
postularse (para un cargo / como candidato/a)	to run (for a position / as a candidate)
votar	to vote

Heritage Speakers

Pregúnteles a los hispanohablantes si en su casa se oyen las noticias en español o en inglés. Si las oyen en español, pregúnteles en qué canal de televisión o estación de radio. Pídales que comparen los noticieros hispanos con los noticieros norteamericanos. ¿Son diferentes? ¿En qué aspectos son diferentes o similares?

Culture

The concept of dual citizenship means that a person is a citizen of two countries at the same time. Each country has its own laws governing dual citizenship. Some people may have dual citizenship automatically under two different laws rather than by choice. For example, a child who is born of U.S. parents in a foreign country may be both a

(Cont. →)

Conversación

A. ¿Quién sabe más de la política?

Paso 1. ¿Cuánto sabe Ud. de la política? Si puede, dé un ejemplo de las siguientes categorías.

1. un país con un rey o una reina
2. un país que tenga o haya tenido una dictadura
3. un dictador o una dictadora
4. un cargo político que dure cuatro años
5. el mes típico para votar en este país
6. un político o una política muy conocido/a hoy en día
7. un partido político de este país
8. un derecho esencial de todos los ciudadanos de este país
9. una causa de la desigualdad social o política

Paso 2. En parejas, comparen sus respuestas del **Paso 1.** Luego digan a la clase cuál de Uds. pudo dar ejemplos en más categorías y qué respuestas tienen en común.

Así se dice

postularse (para un cargo político como candidato/a) = presentarse (como candidato/a a un cargo político)

Nota cultural

El panorama social y político en el mundo hispano

Aquí hay algunos datos de interés sobre los países de habla española.

- **La mayoría de edad:** En el mundo hispano en general se llega a la mayoría de edad a los 18 años, que es la edad en que la ley permite consumir bebidas alcohólicas y obtener el permiso de manejar.
- **El servicio militar:** Hoy día el servicio militar es voluntario en España y la Argentina y obligatorio en la mayoría de los otros países. Sin embargo, «obligatorio» no significa que todo el mundo lo haga o que todo el mundo lo haga de manera igual.
- **Las mujeres en el ejército:** Las mujeres pueden ser militares en la Argentina, Colombia, Chile, México y España.
- **Las mujeres en la política:** A pesar de[a] la fama del machismo que existe en la cultura hispana y aunque[b] no hay igualdad en la representación de cargos del gobierno, las mujeres han llegado a ser presidentas de su país en varios países (Chile, la Argentina, Costa Rica y Panamá) y también vicepresidentas y primeras ministras, incluso ministras de Defensa aun[c] siendo civiles (Michelle Bachelet en Chile y Carme Chacón en España). Además[d] hay numerosas juezas[e] mujeres que ocupan otros cargos políticos.

¿En cuáles de estos datos hay grandes similaridades entre su país y los países hispanohablantes?

[a]A... *In spite of* [b]*although* [c]*even* [d]*Besides* [e]*judges*

Sonia Sotomayor, primera jueza hispana de la Corte Suprema de los Estados Unidos

2. *¿Vota Ud. en todas las elecciones? ¿Votó en las últimas elecciones para presidente o primer ministro? ¿en las últimas elecciones municipales? ¿Cree Ud. que el votar es un deber? ¿Bajo qué tipo de gobierno no es posible votar con libertad?*
3. *¿Cree Ud. que siempre debemos obedecer la ley? ¿Hay leyes que sean más importantes que otras? ¿Siempre obedece Ud. las leyes de tránsito? ¿Qué castigos* (new) *hay para los delitos menores? ¿y para los delitos más graves?*

- Point out that having rights also means respecting others' rights and liberties. Others are entitled to the same rights that you enjoy, and their needs and priorities may be quite different from your own. Have students list on the board the responsibilities that also imply rights. Discuss specific rights that have led to conflicts, for example, freedom of speech and flag burning or musical expression.

Preliminary Activity

Ask students the following questions to personalize the vocabulary.

1. *¿Qué canal de televisión prefiere Ud. para enterarse de las noticias? ¿Cree Ud. que en ese canal presentan mejor información? ¿O es que le gusta el locutor / la locutora que presenta las noticias? ¿Le interesan a Ud. mucho las noticias del estado o de la provincia de* (your state/province) *o no le interesan tanto? Diga por qué.*
2. *¿Le importan más a Ud. su autonomía e individualismo o los sentimientos de los demás? En una tienda, ¿hace cola con paciencia o trata de pasar antes de los demás? En una parada de autobús, ¿hace cola o trata de subir primero?*
3. *Para Ud., ¿cuáles son los derechos más elementales de los que todos debemos gozar? ¿Cuáles son los deberes de un buen ciudadano? ¿Es importante que todos votemos en todas las elecciones, sean nacionales o locales? ¿Por qué cree Ud. que muchas personas no votan?*

Nota cultural

Comprensión

1. *¿Cuál es la mayoría de edad en los países hispanohablantes, en general? (los 18 años)*
2. *¿Es obligatorio el servicio militar en todos los países hispanohablantes? (no)*
3. *¿En qué países ha habido presidentas de gobierno? (en Chile, la Argentina, Costa Rica y Panamá)*

Culture (Cont.)

U.S. citizen and a citizen in his or her birth country. People with dual citizenship can hold two valid passports.

Heritage Speakers

Pregúnteles a los hispanohablantes que han vivido en otro país si el servicio militar es obligatorio allí.

Con. B: Suggestion

Even though most students will not know much information about the government in Spain, they should be able to do this activity relatively easily. After working through the items, ask simple true/false questions to test comprehension and review the information. Ask students to correct false statements.

1. *España tiene una dictadura.*
2. *España tiene un presidente.*

And so on.

Con. B: Answers

1. *igualdad* **2.** *gobierno* **3.** *monarquía* **4.** *rey* **5.** *reina* **6.** *vota* **7.** *los demás* **8.** *políticos* **9.** *ejército* **10.** *servicio obligatorio* **11.** *ciudadano*

Con. C: Follow-up

- Have students report their opinions back to the class. Tally the responses on the board and have a whole-class discussion about the results.
- Assign the following topic for discussion in small groups or discuss it as a whole class: *¿Cuáles son los derechos básicos de todos los ciudadanos? ¿Y los deberes?*
- **Redacción:** Assign *Con. C* as a written assignment. Set reasonable expectations for length and other specifications (tense usage, specific examples, and so on).

Pronunciación: See the Laboratory Manual for presentation and practice of intonation, punctuation, and rhythm.

¿Recuerda Ud.?
Bright Idea
Suggestion

Review with students the formation of the preterite, starting with regular *-ar, -er,* and *-ir* forms, followed by the irregular verbs. Special attention should be given to *-ir* stem-changing verbs that require an additional change in the third persons singular and plural.

Optional: You may also wish to review the imperfect, which is often used in the independent clauses that trigger the use of the past subjunctive in the dependent clause.

- Ask students to conjugate *hablar, comer,* and *vivir* in the imperfect.
- Ask them which three verbs are irregular in the imperfect (*ir, ser,* and *ver*), then ask for their first person singular and plural forms.

El Presidente de España, José Luis Rodríguez Zapatero, y la Ministra de Defensa, Carmen Chacón

Vocabulario útil

Aunque...	Although . . .
De hecho,...	In fact . . .
En mi opinión...	
Por un lado...	On the one hand . . .
Por otro lado...	On the other hand . . .
Sin embargo...	

¿Recuerda Ud.? Answers:
1. *hablaron* **2.** *comieron* **3.** *vivieron* **4.** *jugaron* **5.** *perdieron* **6.** *durmieron* **7.** *rieron* **8.** *leyeron* **9.** *estuvieron* **10.** *tuvieron* **11.** *destruyeron* **12.** *mantuvieron* **13.** *trajeron* **14.** *dieron* **15.** *supieron* **16.** *se vistieron* **17.** *dijeron* **18.** *creyeron* **19.** *fueron* **20.** *pudieron*

B. El gobierno de España. Complete el siguiente párrafo sobre España con las palabras de la lista.

ciudadano	los demás	rey
ejército	monarquía	servicio militar
gobierno	políticos	vota
igualdad	reina	

España es un país democrático, con principios de _____[1] muy similares a los que existen en países con democracias bien establecidas, como los Estados Unidos y el Canadá. Sin embargo, una diferencia es el tipo de _____[2]. En España existe una _____[3] parlamentaria, lo que significa que hay un _____[4] y una _____[5]. Los reyes son figuras representativas, sin poder ejecutivo. Nadie _____[6] por el rey, pero sí se vota para elegir al presidente y todos _____[7] cargos _____[8].

España tiene un _____[9] voluntario; es decir, que no hay _____[10] obligatorio para ningún _____[11].

C. ¿Qué opina Ud.? En parejas, den su opinión sobre las siguientes ideas.

1. En este país, se permite que consumamos demasiado petróleo (energía, carne).
2. Votar es un deber, no un privilegio.
3. En este país, la igualdad de todos no es una realidad todavía.
4. Es posible que una dictadura sea una buena alternativa a la democracia en algunos casos.
5. El personal a cargo de los servicios básicos de un país (por ejemplo, del agua) no debe tener derecho a declararse en huelga.

¿Recuerda Ud.?

The forms of the past subjunctive, which you will learn in **Gramática 48,** are based on the third person plural of the preterite. Here is a brief review of that preterite form.

- regular **-ar** verbs: **-ar** → **-aron**
- regular **-er/-ir** verbs: **-er/-ir** → **-ieron**
- **-ir** stem-changing verbs: **e** → **i, o** → **u** in the stem: **pidieron, durmieron**
- verbs whose stem ends in a vowel (**leer, construir,** and so on): **-ieron** → **-yeron**: **leyeron, construyeron**
- irregular preterite stems: **quisieron, hicieron, dijeron,** and so on
- four totally irregular verbs: **ser/ir** → **fueron, dar** → **dieron, ver** → **vieron**

Give the third person plural of the preterite for these infinitives.

1. hablar	**5.** perder	**9.** estar	**13.** traer	**17.** decir
2. comer	**6.** dormir	**10.** tener	**14.** dar	**18.** creer
3. vivir	**7.** reír	**11.** destruir	**15.** saber	**19.** ir
4. jugar	**8.** leer	**12.** mantener	**16.** vestirse	**20.** poder

Mundo interactivo

You should now be prepared to work with Scenario 9, Activity 3 in Connect Spanish (**www.connectspanish.com**).

GRAMÁTICA

48 *Queríamos que todo el mundo votara*

The Subjunctive (Part 9): The Past Subjunctive

Grammar Tutorial 48
connect SPANISH
www.connectspanish.com

Gramática en acción: Las últimas elecciones

BORICUA[a]
¡INSCRIBETE[b] Y VOTA!
QUE NADA
NOS DETENGA[c]
1-800-596-VOTA

Indique las ideas que son verdaderas para Ud. sobre las últimas elecciones en su país, estado o provincia.

En las últimas elecciones…

1. ☐ yo no tenía edad para votar.
2. ☐ yo tenía edad para votar, pero no voté.
3. ☐ para mí era importante que votara mucha gente.
4. ☐ yo dudaba que ganara uno de los candidatos que yo apoyaba, ¡pero sí ganó!
5. ☐ no se postuló ningún candidato que me convenciera o me entusiasmara de verdad.
6. ☐ en mi estado/provincia no hubo clases para los niños, para que las escuelas primarias sirvieran de lugares de votación.

[a]Puertorriqueño/a [b]*Register* [c]Que… *Let nothing stop us*

Although Spanish has two simple indicative past tenses (preterite and imperfect), it has only one simple subjunctive past tense, the *past subjunctive* (**el imperfecto de subjuntivo**). Generally speaking, this tense is used in the same situations as the present subjunctive but to talk about past events. The exact English equivalent depends on the context in which it is used.

Past Subjunctive of Regular Verbs / El imperfecto de subjuntivo

hablar: hablar~~on~~		comer: comier~~on~~		vivir: vivier~~on~~	
hablara	habláramos	comiera	comiéramos	viviera	viviéramos
hablaras	hablarais	comieras	comierais	vivieras	vivierais
hablara	hablaran	comiera	comieran	viviera	vivieran

The last elections *Indicate the ideas that are true for you about the last elections in your country, state, or province. In the last elections…* **1.** *I wasn't old enough to vote.* **2.** *I was old enough to vote, but I didn't vote.* **3.** *it was important to me that many people vote.* **4.** *I doubted that one of the candidates that I supported would win, but he did win!* **5.** *no candidate ran who won me over or about whom I got really enthusiastic.* **6.** *in my state/province there were no classes for children, so that elementary schools could serve as voting sites.*

Gramática 48 The Past Subjunctive

Suggestion

Teach this grammar topic for recognition only. Most first-year students will not acquire productive control of the past subjunctive in speaking.

GEA: Follow-up

- Have students do the *GEA* silently, then call on selected students or ask for a show of hands for each item, to get a sense for typical answers.
- Ask students to make sentences they did not select true for them.
- Discuss the results, especially those for items 2 and 5. Take advantage of the opportunity to discuss with students why it is important that everyone, especially college students, vote in all elections.

Heritage Speakers

Note que a veces algunos hispanohablantes añaden una *i* en la tercera persona plural de algunos verbos irregulares; por ejemplo, *dijieran, trajieran* y *produjieran*. A pesar de que existan estas formas en el habla común y corriente, la forma aceptada de cada verbo es *dijeran, trajeran* y *produjeran*.

Forms of the Past Subjunctive

Note

The pluperfect subjunctive is not presented in *Puntos de partida,* (although it is included in Appendix 4), since it is beyond the expectations and ability of beginning students for control and production. If you wish to present this grammar point, you can introduce it in this section and reintroduce it in Gram. 49 with *si* clauses.

Emphasis 1: Suggestions

- Have students give the third person plural preterite forms.

caminar	*nadar*	*leer*
terminar	*ofrecer*	*creer*
usar	*resolver*	*abrir*
pensar	*correr*	*escribir*
esperar	*prometer*	*subir*
cerrar	*volver*	*admitir*

- Present the formation of the past subjunctive and emphasize that all forms, without exception, are based on the third person plural of the preterite.
- Model the past subjunctive in sentences about yourself or communicative exchanges. Use the verbs *trabajar, volver,* and *abrir*.
- Auditory discrimination practice: To highlight the importance of verb endings, give students listening comprehension practice with the third person plural forms of *-ar* verbs. 1) As you say a series of verb forms, ask students to tell which tense they heard: preterite, past subjunctive, or future. Examples: *bailaran / bailaron / bailarán; cantarán / cantaran / cantaron*. 2) Do the same for *-er/-ir* verbs. 3) After doing this for a number of verbs, write verb forms for different verbs on the board (or on an overhead), in columns according to the tense. Ask students to select and say a verb form; the class will identify the tense.

Emphasis 4: Suggestions

- Have students give the third person plural preterite forms.

dar	*poder*	*venir*
hacer	*poner*	*divertirse*
ser	*querer*	*servir*
ir	*saber*	*dormir*
decir	*tener*	*jugar*
estar	*traer*	*pedir*

- Model the past subjunctive forms of *servir, sentir, dar, decir, hacer, ir,* and *venir* in sentences about yourself and communicative exchanges with students.

Forms of the Past Subjunctive / **Las formas del imperfecto de subjuntivo**

1. Past Subjunctive Endings

As you can see in the chart on page 529, the past subjunctive endings are identical for **-ar, -er,** and **-ir** verbs. Those endings are added to the past subjunctive stem: the third person plural of the preterite minus **-on.** For this reason, the forms of the past subjunctive reflect all of the irregularities of the third person preterite (points 2–4, below).

Las terminaciones del imperfecto de subjuntivo*

-a	**-amos**
-as	**-ais**
-a	**-an**

2. The Past Subjunctive of Stem-changing Verbs

- **-ar** and **-er** verbs: no change

empezar: empezar~~on~~ ⟶ **empezara, empezaras,... empezara,**
volver: volvier~~on~~ ⟶ **volviera, volvieras,...**

- **-ir** verbs: All persons of the past subjunctive have the vowel change of the third person plural of the preterite.

Remember that the stem change for the third person preterite of **-ir** verbs is shown in parentheses in vocabulary lists. It is this change that occurs in *all* persons of the past subjunctive.

pedir (pido) (i): pidier~~on~~ ⟶

pidiera	**pidiéramos**
pidieras	**pidierais**
pidiera	**pidieran**

dormir (duermo) (u): durmier~~on~~ ⟶

durmiera	**durmiéramos**
durmieras	**durmierais**
durmiera	**durmieron**

3. The Past Subjunctive of Verbs with Spelling Changes

All persons of the past subjunctive reflect the change from **i** to **y** between two vowels.

i ⟶ y (caer, construir, creer, destruir, leer, oír)

Other preterite spelling changes (**c ⟶ qu, g ⟶ gu, z ⟶ c**) do not occur in the past subjunctive because those changes do not appear in the third person plural of the preterite: **buscaron, pagaron, empezaron.**

creer: creyer~~on~~ ⟶

creyera	**creyéramos**
creyeras	**creyerais**
creyera	**creyeran**

4. The Past Subjunctive of Verbs with Irregular Preterites

dar: dier~~on~~ ⟶

diera	**diéramos**
dieras	**dierais**
diera	**dieran**

dar:	dier~~on~~ ⟶ **diera,...**	**venir:**	vinier~~on~~ ⟶ **viniera,...**
decir:	dijer~~on~~ ⟶ **dijera,...**	**poner:**	pusier~~on~~ ⟶ **pusiera,...**
estar:	estuvier~~on~~ ⟶ **estuviera,...**	**querer:**	quisier~~on~~ ⟶ **quisiera,...**
haber:	hubier~~on~~ ⟶ **hubiera,...**	**saber:**	supier~~on~~ ⟶ **supiera,...**
hacer:	hicier~~on~~ ⟶ **hiciera,...**	**ser:**	fuer~~on~~ ⟶ **fuera,...**
ir:	fuer~~on~~ ⟶ **fuera,...**	**tener:**	tuvier~~on~~ ⟶ **tuviera,...**
poder:	pudier~~on~~ ⟶ **pudiera,...**		

An alternative form of the past subjunctive ends in* **-se: hablase, hablases, hablase, hablásemos, hablaseis, hablasen. *This form will not be practiced in* Puntos de partida.

Heritage Speakers

- Pregúnteles a los hispanohablantes si usan o no las terminaciones en *-se, -ses, -se, -semos, -seis, -sen* del pasado de subjuntivo. Si las usan, pregúnteles cuándo y por qué.
- En algunos países y regiones hispanohablantes, es muy común oír que se usa el condicional cuando, por lo general, se recomienda el uso del imperfecto de subjuntivo en cláusulas condicionales con *si*. Por ejemplo, es posible oír *Si yo tendría el dinero para ir a España, iría* en vez de *Si yo tuviera el dinero para ir a España, iría.* A pesar del uso popular del condicional en cláusulas con *si*, se recomienda usar el imperfecto

(Cont. ⟶)

Uses of the Past Subjunctive / **Los usos del imperfecto de subjuntivo**

1. Expressing Past Events

The past subjunctive usually has the same uses as the present subjunctive, but for talking about the past. Compare the pairs of sentences at the right. The first sentence in each pair is in the present tense, the second in the past.

Quiero que **se enteren** esta tarde.
I want them to find out this afternoon.
Quería que **se enteraran** por la tarde.
I wanted them to find out in the afternoon.

Siente que no **puedan** allí esta noche.
He's sorry (that) they can't be there tonight.
Sintió que no **pudieran** allí anoche.
He was sorry (that) they couldn't be there last night.

Dudamos que **mantengan** la paz.
We doubt that they will keep the peace.
Dudábamos que **mantuvieran** la paz.
We doubted that they would keep the peace.

2. Subjunctive "Triggers"

Remember that the subjunctive is used after:

(1) expressions of influence, emotion, and doubt

(1) ¿**Era necesario** que **regatearas**?
Was it necessary for you to bargain?

(1) **Sentí** que no **tuvieran** tiempo para ver Granada.
I was sorry that they didn't have time to see Granada.

(1) **No creía** que **hubiera** tiempo para hacerlo.
I didn't think that there would be time to do it.

(2) nonexistent and indefinite antecedents

(2) **No había nadie** que **pudiera** resolverlo.
There wasn't anyone who could (might have been able to) resolve it.

(3) conjunctions of contingency and purpose, as well as those of time

(3) Los padres **trabajaron** mucho **para que** sus hijos **asistieran** a la universidad.
The parents worked hard so that their children could (might) go to the university.

(3) Anoche, **íbamos** a salir **en cuanto llegara** Felipe.
Last night, we were going to leave as soon as Felipe arrived.

3. Past Subjunctive of *querer* to Express Requests

The past subjunctive of the verb **querer** is often used to make a request sound more polite.

Quisiéramos hablar con Ud. en seguida.
We would like to speak with you immediately.

Quisiera un café, por favor.
I would like a cup of coffee, please.

Autoprueba

Change the following verbs from the present subjunctive to the past subjunctive.

1. quiera	**3.** salgan	**5.** esté
2. tengamos	**4.** sepas	**6.** traigas

Answers: **1.** *quisiera* **2.** *tuviéramos* **3.** *salieran* **4.** *supieras* **5.** *estuviera* **6.** *trajeras*

Uses of the Past Subjunctive

Emphasis 1: Suggestions

- Point out that the past subjunctive is used to describe past events in grammatical contexts that require the subjunctive.
- Emphasize that when a verb in the independent clause is in the past, the past (never the present) subjunctive is used in the dependent clause (past → past).
- Tell students that when the verb in the main clause is in the present, the verb in the subordinate clause *can* be in the past: *Siento que no pudieran estar allí. Sé que no estaban allí.* Help students develop simple logic about time sequence (*I'm sorry now about something that happened yesterday*).

Emphasis 2: Reciclado

Note that Emphasis 2 reviews all of the uses of the subjunctive that students will learn in this text. You may wish to review these uses systematically.

Emphasis 3: Suggestions

- Emphasize that this tense is used to form polite requests. This is similar to the English *really should* and *would like you to* softened requests.
- Point out that the verbs *deber* and *poder* are used by some Spanish speakers in softened requests: *Debieras estudiar más. ¿Pudieras darme el libro?*
- Remind students of the importance of tone whenever requests of any kind are made. The most polite words, said in a harsh way, can be offensive.

Heritage Speakers (Cont.)

de subjuntivo. Anime a los hispanohablantes a indicar qué tiempo verbal prefieren usar con cláusulas con *si*.

- Los hispanohablantes también usan el imperfecto de subjuntivo de los verbos *poder* y *deber* (*pudieras, debieras*) para pedirle o sugerirle algo a alguien con mucha cortesía. Pregúnteles a los hispanohablantes en qué situaciones usarían las formas más corteses de *poder* y *deber*. También anímelos a pedirles favores cortésmente a sus compañeros de clase usando las formas *pudieras, debieras* y *yo quisiera que…*

Reciclado: Note the use of the preterite/imperfect and present/past subjunctive through all of the activities in *Práctica* and *Conversación*.

Preliminary Exercise

Use the following chain drill to practice forms.

Dé oraciones nuevas según las indicaciones.
Cuando Ud. estudiaba en la secundaria, ¿qué le gustaba?
Me gustaba que nosotros…
estudiar idiomas
leer libros interesantes
ver películas en la clase de historia
hacer experimentos en la clase de física
bailar después de los partidos
divertirnos después de la clase
¿ ?

Prác. A, B: Note

Note that two *¡Anticipemos!* activities are provided for this section, as sentences containing the past subjunctive tend to be long and at times complex. *Prác. A* is the harder of the two activities. You may prefer to begin with *Prác. B*, which is thematically linked to *Prác. C*.

Prác. A: Suggestions

- Tell students that the language in this activity is relatively close to authentic, which may make the activity harder for them to do than later activities. That said, this is the kind of language students will encounter in authentic readings in second-year/intermediate classes, so it is a good idea for them to get used to it.
- Ask students to read the *titulares* silently as you read them aloud. Ask them to which general topic each refers or in which section of the newspaper it might be found. Then do the same with the excerpts from the articles and, again, ask students to give the general topic. Then ask students to indicate the past subjunctive verb forms in each one. (Note that in *Paso 2* students are asked to give the reason for the use of the subjunctive.) Doing this should make it possible for students successfully to complete the activity, even though they may not understand every word of the *titulares* or the *noticias*.

Prác. A: Follow-up

- Ask students to summarize each *noticia* in a brief and simple sentence in Spanish, using their own language. Example: *Un aficionado del club de fútbol está (estaba) muy contento de que ganara su equipo.*

Práctica

A. ¡Anticipemos! Las noticias en la prensa

Paso 1. Empareje los siguientes titulares (*headlines*) con las noticias correspondientes (abajo y en la página 533).

LOS TITULARES

Ⓐ **Final de la Copa UEFA:[a] triunfo del Sevilla F.C.[b]**

Ⓑ **Miles de ecuatorianos votan en España**

Ⓒ **Industria de la fresa[c] se recupera**

Ⓓ **Presidente recibe a representantes de Oriente Medio[d]**

Ⓔ **Maestra de origen marroquí[e] recibe el premio[f] estatal a la excelencia educativa**

Ⓕ **Almodóvar vuelve a trabajar con sus musas más famosas**

[a]*United European Football Association* [b]Fútbol Club [c]*strawberry* [d]Oriente… *Middle East* [e]*Moroccan* [f]*prize*

LAS NOTICIAS

1. __A__ Un aficionado del club de fútbol sevillano, bromeando,[a] dijo que no creía que hubiera nadie que estuviera tan contento como él, «excepto sus hijos, sus vecinos y el resto de los sevillistas[b]».

2. __F__ El cineasta español esperaba que su nueva película fuera bien recibida, pero no esperaba tanto éxito.[c]

3. __E__ La educadora expresó públicamente su deseo de que el honor que le daban fuera «una pequeña prueba[d] del valor de la integración de los emigrantes en la sociedad del país».

4. __B__ El gobierno del país sudamericano le pidió al gobierno español que facilitara el proceso electoral de sus ciudadanos, en unas elecciones que prometían un índice[e] de participación sin precedentes entre sus emigrantes.

[a]*joking* [b]*Sevilla soccer team fans* [c]*success* [d]*proof* [e]*rate*

Resources: Transparency 166

5. __C__ Los agricultores mostraron su satisfacción por el buen invierno de lluvia. Además[f], indicaron que no se esperaba que hubiera serios problemas meteorológicos este año, según el Instituto Meteorológico Nacional.

6. __D__ Los diferentes emisarios, que deseaban una nueva reunión[g] para que se discutiera un plan alternativo, expresaron unánimemente el compromiso[h] de sus gobiernos a encontrar una solución final y satisfactoria para todos. «Es la hora de la paz», declaró el Ministro de Asuntos Exteriores después de la reunión.

[f]*Besides* [g]*meeting* [h]*commitment*

Paso 2. Identifique la razón del uso del subjuntivo en cada noticia.

B. ¡Anticipemos! En la escuela secundaria

Paso 1. Lea las siguientes declaraciones e indique las que reflejan su propia experiencia. Cambie las oraciones falsas para que también expresen su experiencia.

Cuando yo estaba en la escuela secundaria…

1. ☐ era obligatorio que yo asistiera a todas mis clases.
2. ☐ mis padres insistían en que yo no saliera con mis amigos sin terminar la tarea antes.
3. ☐ era necesario que yo trabajara para que pudiera asistir a la universidad algún día.
4. ☐ no había ninguna clase que me interesara.
5. ☐ tenía que sacar buenas notas para que mis padres me dieran dinero.
6. ☐ era necesario que volviera a casa a una hora determinada.
7. ☐ mis padres me exigían que limpiara mi cuarto cada semana.
8. ☐ mis padres no permitían que saliera con cierta persona.

Paso 2. Ahora, en parejas, comparen sus respuestas del **Paso 1.** Luego digan a la clase algo que tenían en común y algo que era muy diferente en cuanto a (*regarding*) sus experiencias de adolescentes.

C. Y ahora, la niñez. ¿Qué quería Ud. de la vida cuando era niño/a? ¿Y qué querían los demás que Ud. hiciera? Conteste, haciendo oraciones completas con una frase de cada columna.

mis padres (no) querían que yo… mis maestros me pedían que… yo buscaba amigos que… me gustaba mucho que nosotros…	+	ir a la iglesia / al templo con ellos portarse bien, ser bueno/a estudiar mucho, hacer la tarea todas las noches, sacar buenas notas ponerse ropa vieja para jugar, jugar en la calle, pelear con mis amigos mirar mucho la televisión, leer muchas tiras cómicas, comer muchos dulces vivir en nuestro barrio, asistir a la misma escuela, tener muchos juguetes (*toys*), ser aventureros ir a cierto lugar de vacaciones en verano, pasar todos juntos los días feriados, poner un árbol de Navidad muy alto

- Ask students to tell what they have learned about Spain by reading the headlines and *noticias*. Examples: *Hay muchos emigrantes marroquíes en España.* Provide additional information about Spanish history and culture, as appropriate.

Prác. B, C: Suggestion

If you have a multi-generational class, compare the answers of students of different generations.

Prác. B: Suggestions

- Ask students to identify the past subjunctive verb in each sentence.
- Ask students to give the reasons for the use of the past subjunctive in each sentence.

Prác. C: Follow-up

Include the following questions as well.

1. *¿Qué cosa no le gustaba para nada?*
2. *¿Qué quería Ud. que sus padres (sus hermanos) hicieran?*
3. *¿Qué quería que sus abuelos le regalaran para su cumpleaños?*
4. *¿Adónde quería Ud. que sus padres lo/la llevaran de vacaciones cuando era más joven?*
5. *¿Le permitían sus padres que tomara bebidas alcohólicas cuando tenía 15 años?*

Prác. C: Extension

Have students describe a friend from their youth.

Yo tenía un amigo / una amiga que…

¡OJO! Students will use the indicative in this initial sentence.

Heritage Speakers

Invite a algunos hispanohablantes a hablar de lo que sus padres, abuelos o hermanos mayores querían que hicieran o que no hicieran cuando eran niños o niñas.

Prác. D: Suggestion

Ask students to give the reason for the use of the subjunctive in each sentence.

Prác. D: Follow-up

Bring a Spanish-language newspaper or have students look for one on the Internet. Have students identify three to five instances of the past subjunctive. Then have them explain why the past subjunctive was used in each case.

Prác. D: Optional

Preguntas

Encourage students to use clauses with *para que, con tal que,* and so on.

1. *¿A qué le tenía miedo cuando era pequeño/a? ¿Era probable que ocurrieran las cosas que temía? ¿Temía a veces que sus padres lo/la castigaran* (new)*? ¿Lo merecía a veces? ¿Era necesario que siempre los obedeciera? ¿Qué le prohibían que hiciera?*
2. *¿Qué tipo de clases buscaba para este semestre/trimestre? ¿Clases que fueran fáciles? ¿interesantes? ¿Las encontró? ¿Han sido las clases tal como las esperaba? ¿Qué tipos de clases va a buscar para el semestre/trimestre que viene?*
3. *¿Qué buscaban los primeros inmigrantes que vinieron a los Estados Unidos / el Canadá? ¿Buscaban un lugar donde pudieran practicar su religión? ¿un lugar donde hubiera abundantes recursos naturales? ¿menos restricciones? ¿más libertad política y personal? ¿más respeto por los derechos humanos? ¿menos población? ¿más espacio?*

Cuando Ud. era niño/a,…

1. *¿dónde le prohibían sus padres que jugara?*
2. *¿qué alimentos era obligatorio que comiera?*
3. *¿temía que sus padres se enteraran de algo? ¿De qué? ¿Era un secreto?*

Con. A, Paso 2: Suggestions

- Make sure that students do not fixate on the specific details of their questions. For example, the model refers to someone's older sibling. Students should not ask other students about their older siblings (other students may not have any) but about the concept of being allowed to play with their elders' videogames.
- Set an approximate time limit.

La Princesa Letizia de Asturias, probablemente la futura reina de España por su matrimonio con el Príncipe Felipe de Borbón

D. El noticiero de las seis. Cuando dan las noticias, los reporteros presentan los acontecimientos del día, pero a veces también ofrecen sus propias opiniones.

Paso 1. Lea las siguientes declaraciones y cámbielas al pasado. Debe usar el imperfecto del primer verbo en cada oración y luego el imperfecto de subjuntivo en la segunda parte.

MODELO: «Los obreros quieren que les den un aumento de sueldo.» →
«Los obreros **querían** que les **dieran** un aumento de sueldo.»

1. «Es posible que los trabajadores sigan en huelga hasta el verano.»
2. «Es necesario que las víctimas reciban atención médica.»
3. «Es una lástima que no haya espacio para todos allí.»
4. «Los terroristas piden que los oficiales no los persigan.»
5. «Parece imposible que el gobierno acepte sus demandas.»
6. «Es necesario que el gobierno informe al público del desastre.»
7. «Dudo que la paz mundial esté fuera de nuestro alcance (*reach*).»
8. «Los directores prefieren que la nueva fábrica se construya en México.»
9. «Temo que el número de votantes sea muy bajo.»
10. «El Príncipe Felipe quiere que la periodista Letizia Ortiz Rocasolano sea su esposa.»

Paso 2. Ahora indique si las oraciones del **Paso 1** representan un hecho o si son una opinión.

Conversación

A. Una encuesta (*poll*)

Paso 1. Haga cinco oraciones completas con elementos de cada columna. Trate de no repetir muchos elementos.

MODELO: Cuando yo era niña, mi hermana mayor no permitía que yo jugara con sus videojuegos.

cuando yo era niño/a cuando yo era adolescente (13 o 14 años) cuando yo estaba en el último año de la escuela secundaria	+	(yo) mi madre/padre mis padres mi mejor amigo/a mi hermano/a mis hermanos (no) era necesario/imposible ¿ ?	+	tener miedo de (que)… (no) querer (que)… necesitar un trabajo para (que)… prohibir que… (no) permitir que… (no) gustar (que)… ¿ ?

Prác. D: Answers: ***Paso 1*** **1.** *«Era posible que… siguieran… .»* **2.** *«Era necesario que… recibieran… .»* **3.** *«Era una lástima que no hubiera… allí.»* **4.** *«Los terroristas pedían que… no los persiguieran.»* **5.** *«Parecía imposible que… aceptara… .»* **6.** *«Era necesario que… informara… .»* **7.** *«Dudaba que… estuviera… .»* **8.** *«Los directores preferían que… se construyera… .»* **9.** *«Temía que… fuera… .»* **10.** *«El Príncipe Felipe quería que… fuera… .»* ***Paso 2*** **1.** *una opinión* **2.** *un hecho* **3.** *una opinión* **4.** *un hecho* **5.** *una opinión* **6.** *una opinión* **7.** *una opinión* **8.** *un hecho* **9.** *una opinión* **10.** *un hecho*

Discussion Questions

Hace diez años…

1. *¿era difícil que Ud. hablara con sus padres (hijos) sobre algún tema? ¿De qué tema?*
2. *¿con quién era imposible que Ud. se pusiera de acuerdo?*
3. *¿contra qué orden de sus padres (acción o actividad de sus hijos) era común que Ud. protestara?*

NATIONAL STANDARDS: Connections

Have students work in small groups or assign as homework: Write two to three sentences similar to the ones *in Prác. D,* based on other historical events or on current news events.

Paso 2. Ahora convierta sus oraciones de **Paso 1** en preguntas generales sobre los temas que Ud. escogió. Use las preguntas para encuestar a cinco compañeros de clase para ver si tuvieron experiencias similares cuando eran niños o adolescentes.

MODELO: Cuando eras niño, ¿te permitían tus hermanos mayores que jugaras con sus videojuegos?

Paso 3. Diga a la clase por lo menos dos detalles interesantes de su encuesta.

B. Con mucha cortesía. El niño del dibujo sabe que está molestando a sus padres cuando los despierta para pedirles un favor. Por eso les habla muy cortésmente: «**quisiera un vaso de agua... quisiera saber...** ». ¿Cómo podrían Uds. (*could you*) pedir de una forma muy cortés lo que necesitan en las siguientes situaciones? ¿Qué dirían (*would you say*) para conseguirlo?

1. Ud. quiere el número de teléfono de una persona que acaba de conocer. Habla con un amigo de él/ella.
2. Uds. quieren saber cuándo es el examen final en esta clase y qué va a comprender (*include*).
3. Ud. necesita una prórroga (*extension*) para el próximo examen de español.
4. Ud. necesita una carta de recomendación del profesor / de la profesora.
5. Ud. quiere invitar personalmente al rector o a la rectora de la universidad a cenar en su residencia con motivo de una ocasión especial.

Cartoon by Antonio Mingote

—Verás, quisiera un vaso de agua. Pero no te molestes, porque ya no tengo sed. Solo quisiera saber si, en el caso de que tuviese otra vez sed, podría (*I could*) venir a pedirte un vaso de agua.

Nota **comunicativa**

Cómo expresar deseos imposibles

In **Capítulo 13,** you learned to use **ojalá (que)** + *present subjunctive* to express hopes that can become a reality.

ojalá + *present subjunctive* = *I hope*

Ojalá que saque una buena nota en este curso.

Ojalá que encuentre trabajo tan pronto como me gradúe.

Ojalá (que) can also be used with the *past subjunctive* to express wishes about things that are not likely to occur or that are impossible.

ojalá + *past subjunctive* = *I wish*

Ojalá que pudiera ir a la playa este fin de semana. (*You can't because the semester/quarter isn't over yet. And, unless you live on the East or West Coast, the beach may be far away.*)

Ojalá que todos los estudiantes **pudieran** pasar el verano en un país hispanohablante. (*It's obvious that that's not possible for everyone.*)

The expression **ojalá** comes from the Arabic meaning *if Allah wishes.* It is similar to English *God willing* and Spanish **si Dios quiere.**

C. ¡Ojalá! Complete las siguientes oraciones lógicamente.

1. Ojalá que (yo) tuviera...
2. Ojalá que (yo) pudiera...
3. Ojalá inventaran una máquina que...
4. Ojalá solucionaran el problema de...
5. Ojalá que en esta universidad fuera posible...

Redacción: Ask students to turn the questions plus poll results into a brief composition that compares their experiences growing up with those of one or two of the people they interviewed. Give them a general structure for the composition and set reasonable length expectations.

- First paragraph: Their experiences
- Second paragraph: The experiences of their partner
- Third paragraph: A brief comparison of their lives growing up

Con. B: Optional

Practice comprehension of the past subjunctive in the following context.

Imagine que su bisabuela (great-grandmother), *quien asistió a la universidad en los años cincuenta, le ha explicado a Ud. las normas de conducta de esa época. ¿Qué es diferente hoy día? ¿Hay algunas normas antiguas que a Ud. le parezcan mejores que las modernas? ¿Por qué?*

1. *Era obligatorio que los hombres y las mujeres vivieran en residencias separadas.*
2. *Todos cenaban a la misma hora. Para entrar en el comedor, era necesario que los hombres llevaran corbata y las mujeres, falda.*
3. *Había «hora de visita» en las residencias. Los hombres solo podían visitar a sus amigas durante esas horas y viceversa.*
4. *Era necesario que las mujeres estuvieran en su residencia a una hora determinada de la noche. Pero no había ninguna restricción semejante para los hombres.*

Con. B: Follow-up

Have students tell what they would say in the following situations.

¿Qué diría Ud. en las siguientes situaciones?

1. *Ud. ha llamado a un amigo a las diez de la noche para invitarlo a salir, pero él ya estaba dormido y Ud. lo ha despertado.*
2. *Ud. llega a casa muy enfermo/a, con tos y fiebre. El médico le ha aconsejado guardar cama para que descanse. Pero su compañero/a de cuarto (esposo/a, etcétera) le ha preparado una fiesta sorpresa de cumpleaños. Todos sus amigos lo/la saludan cuando entra.*

Nota comunicativa

Reciclado: Suggestions

- Remind students that *ojalá* (*que*) + present subjunctive means *I hope* (*something will happen*). *Ojalá* (*que*) + past subjunctive means *I wish*. Wishes with the past subjunctive are unlikely or impossible to happen.
- Remind students that the use of *que* after *ojalá* is optional.
- Remind students that *¡ojala!* can be used alone (as in the title of *Con. C*) to express *I wish!*

¿Recuerda Ud.?

Review all of the future forms, starting with regular verbs, then the irregulars (*decir, haber, hacer, poder, poner, querer, saber, salir, tener, venir*).

Gramática 49
Conditional Verb Forms

Suggestions

- Before beginning *Gram. 49;* lead into the *GEA* with *le gustaría* + inf. questions, which have been active since *Cap. 8.*
- Preview this section by asking the following kinds of questions.

  Si Ud. tuviera un millón de dólares, ¿qué haría?
  Si Ud. pudiera hacerle una sola pregunta al presidente de los Estados Unidos / al primer ministro del Canadá, ¿qué le preguntaría?
  Si pudiera cambiar cualquier cosa en el mundo, ¿qué cambiaría?
- Using the conditional, ask students what their ideal vacation would be.

  ¿Irían a la playa? ¿a las montañas?
  ¿Qué país visitarían?
  ¿Preferirían alojarse en un hotel de lujo o en un hotel de menos categoría?
  ¿Qué harían durantes sus vacaciones ideales?

¿Recuerda Ud.?

In **Gramática 46 (Cap. 17)** you learned the forms and uses of the future tense. Can you provide the correct future forms of the following verbs?

1. (yo) viajar viajaré **3.** (tú) ir irás **5.** (nosotros) hacer haremos
2. (ellos) beber beberán **4.** (Ud.) venir vendrá **6.** (ella) poner pondrá

Review all of the future forms before studying the conditional in **Gramática 49.** Also note that you learned a conditional expression in **Capítulo 8: me gustaría.** What is the English equivalent of the following sentence?

Me gustaría visitar el museo esta tarde. I would like to visit the museum this afternoon.

49 Expressing What You Would Do
Conditional Verb Forms

Grammar Tutorial 49
connect SPANISH
www.connectspanish.com

Gramática en acción: Un mundo utópico

En un mundo ideal…

- Habría paz en todos los países.
- El medio ambiente no estaría contaminado.
- Todas las personas tendrían los mismos derechos y libertades.
- Nadie cometería ningún acto criminal.
- Ningún niño sufriría de hambre ni de enfermedades.

¿Y Ud.?

¿Cómo sería un mundo ideal si Ud. pudiera efectuar los cambios? ¿Qué más características **añadiría** Ud.? Los verbos deben terminar en **-ía** o **-ían,** como los verbos en **Gramática en acción.**

The phrase **me gustaría** expresses what you *would like* to (do, say, and so on). The verb **gustaría** is a conditional form. You will learn to form the *conditional* (**el condicional**) of all verbs in this section.

Conditional of Regular Verbs / El condicional					
hablar		**comer**		**vivir**	
hablaría	hablaríamos	comería	comeríamos	viviría	viviríamos
hablarías	hablaríais	comerías	comeríais	vivirías	viviríais
hablaría	hablarían	comería	comerían	viviría	vivirían

A perfect world *In an ideal world . . . • There would be peace in all countries. • The environment would not be polluted. • Everyone would have the same rights and freedoms. • No one would engage in any criminal acts. • No child would be hungry or sick.*

Resources: Transparency 167

1. Conditional Endings

In English the conditional (like the future) is a compound tense, formed with the auxiliary (helping) verb *would: I **would** speak, you **would** do,* and so on.

The Spanish conditional (like the future) is a simple verb form (only one word). It is formed by adding the identical set of conditional endings to **-ar, -er,** and **-ir** infinitives. No auxiliary verb is needed.

Las terminaciones del condicional

infinitivo +	-ía	-íamos
	-ías	-íais
	-ía	-ían

2. Irregular Conditional Forms

Verbs that form the future on an irregular stem use the same stem to form the conditional.

Note that the conditional of **hay (haber)** is **habría** (*there would be*).*

decir: diría, dirías, diría, diríamos, diríais, dirían

decir:	**dir-**	-ía
haber (hay):	**habr-**	-ías
hacer:	**har-**	-ía
poder:	**podr-**	-íamos
poner:	**pondr-**	-íais
querer:	**querr-**	-ían
saber:	**sabr-**	
salir:	**saldr-**	
tener:	**tendr-**	
venir:	**vendr-**	

3. Uses of the Conditional

- to express what you *would* do in a particular situation or given a particular set of circumstances

—Manuel, ¿**hablarías** español en Portugal?
—No, **hablaría** portugués.
—¿**Irías** a la playa en las Islas Canarias?
—Sí, claro. Me **gustaría** nadar allí.
"Would you speak Spanish in Portugal?"
"No, I would speak Portuguese."
"Would you go to the beach in the Canary Islands?"
"Yes, of course. I would like to swim there."

- to express the future from the point of view of the past (. . . *said that he would* . . .)

MANUEL: —Iré a Madrid en enero. → Manuel dijo que **iría** a Madrid en enero.
MANUEL: *"I'll go to Madrid in January." → Manuel said that he would go to Madrid in January.*

4. Another Way to Express *would*

Remember that *would* = *used to* (a habitual action) is expressed with the imperfect tense in Spanish.

Manuel **iba** a España todos los veranos.
Manuel would (used to) go to Spain every summer.

The conditional forms of the verb* **haber *are used to form the* conditional perfect tense (**el condicional perfecto**)*, which expresses what* would have occurred *at some point in the past:* **Habríamos tenido** que buscarla en el aeropuerto. (***We would have had*** *to pick her up at the airport.*) *You will find a more detailed presentation of these forms in Appendix 4, Additional Perfect Forms (Indicative and Subjunctive).*

Emphasis 1: Suggestions

- Point out that the infinitive is used as the stem, as with the future.
- Remind students that context and pronouns will distinguish the *yo* and *Ud./él/ella* forms (which are the same).
- Present the *-ía* endings for infinitives to enable students to complete the *GEA* follow-up.
- Help students identify the endings for the conditional: they are the same as the imperfect indicative endings for *-er* and *-ir* verbs.
- Model conditional forms in brief communicative exchanges with students. Try to use high frequency verbs.

beber	*hacer*
comprar	*salir*
decir	*tener*
escribir	

Emphasis 2: Suggestion

Emphasize that the future and conditional have the same set of irregular verbs.

Reciclado: Review irregular verbs by giving students the *yo* form of the present indicative and asking them to give you the future *yo* form, followed by the conditional *yo* form.

Emphasis 3: Suggestion

Model the use of future vs. conditional in quoting people: *Estela dice que vendrá* vs. *Estela dijo que vendría.*

Emphasis 4: Suggestion

Remind students that when *would* refers to a habitual action (*I would study in the library every afternoon.*), the imperfect indicative, not the conditional, is required.

Preliminary Exercises

- Use the following rapid response drill to practice the forms.

Dé el condicional.
yo: mandar, necesitar, aprender, decir
tú: llevar, viajar, leer, hacer
Ud./él/ella: entrar, comprar, vivir, poner
nosotros: celebrar, comprender, ir, poder
Uds./ellos/ellas: regresar, creer, tener, venir

(Cont.)

NATIONAL STANDARDS: Cultures

The Canary Islands are a group of islands off the western coast of Africa that are part of Spain. They are of volcanic origin, and the active Mount Teide is the tallest Spanish peak. The islands enjoy mild weather the year round, making them an ideal spot for Spanish as well as European tourists.

- Ask students the following questions to contextualize the conditional.
  1. *¿Qué lengua hablaría una persona de Pekín? ¿Cuál sería su nacionalidad? ¿Y una persona de Moscú? ¿del Canadá? ¿de Lisboa? ¿de Guadalajara? ¿Podría Ud. hablar con todos ellos? ¿Qué lengua(s) tendría que aprender?*
  2. *¿Qué haría Ud. para obtener mucho dinero? ¿Y para ahorrar mucho dinero? ¿y para gastar mucho dinero? ¿Siempre ha tenido Ud. mucho dinero? Como consecuencia, ¿qué tipo de vida ha llevado Ud. en cuanto al aspecto económico?*

Prác. A: Suggestion

Ask students to find the conditional verb form(s) in each sentence and give the corresponding infinitive.

Redacción: Assign *Prác. A* as the basis for a research paper. Students should choose a travel destination in Spain and research some specific details of the trip. Specify all of the details that you would like them to include, for example: how to get there, how to travel from one city to another inside the country, major sites to visit, and so on. Set reasonable expectations about length and tell students that they will use the conditional in most of their sentences.

Prác. B: Follow-up

- Have students retell the passage using *nosotros* as the subject.
- Use the conditional verb forms in personalized questions to students about what they would do on an ideal vacation. Ask students: *¿Adónde irían Uds. (si pudieran) este fin de semana? ¿Qué pasaría después de su escapada?* Try to avoid other contrary-to-fact statements that would require the use of the imperfect subjunctive.

Autoprueba

Provide the missing letters for the following verbs in the conditional.

1. salir: sal__ía	**3.** querer: que__ías	**5.** tener: ten__ía
2. hacer: ha__íamos	**4.** decir: d__ían	**6.** poder: po__ía

Answers: **1.** *saldría* **2.** *haríamos* **3.** *querrías* **4.** *dirían* **5.** *tendría* **6.** *podría*

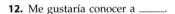

El Parque Güell, diseñado por el famoso arquitecto español Antoni Gaudí, en Barcelona

Práctica

A. ¡Anticipemos! ¿Qué haría Ud. en España?

Paso 1. Complete las siguientes declaraciones para describir un viaje ideal a España. Mire las fotos de este capítulo para ideas sobre algunos sitios que visitar.

Vocabulario útil

churros y chocolate
el jerez sherry
la paella

1. Viajaría a España porque _____.
2. Yo haría el viaje con _____.
3. Hablaría _____.
4. Comería _____ y bebería _____.
5. Iría a _____ y allí vería _____.
6. No podría terminar el viaje sin antes visitar _____.
7. Me compraría _____ y usaría _____.
8. Me divertiría mucho _____. (**¡OJO!** Use un gerundio: **-iendo** o **-ando.**)
9. Tendría que sacar muchas fotos para mostrárselas a _____.
10. Le(s) mandaría tarjetas postales a _____.
11. Querría _____ durante el viaje, pero probablemente no lo haría.
12. Me gustaría conocer a _____.

Paso 2. Ahora, en parejas, comparen sus viajes. Luego digan a la clase los detalles más interesantes de su conversación.

Prác. B: Answers
1. *gustaría* **2.** *trabajaría* **3.** *Podría* **4.** *Tomaría* **5.** *Bebería* **6.** *Vería* **7.** *sería* **8.** *tendría* **9.** *Podría* **10.** *tendría*

Comprensión: 2. *Le gusta nadar.* **3.** *Tiene que pagar con tarjeta de crédito.*

B. ¿Es posible escapar? Cuente la siguiente fantasía, dando la forma condicional de los verbos.

Necesito salir de todo esto… Creo que me (gustar[1]) ir al Caribe… No (trabajar[2])… (Poder[3]) nadar todos los días… (Tomar[4]) el sol en la playa… (Beber[5]) el agua de un coco… (Ver[6]) bellos lugares naturales… El viaje (ser[7]) ideal…

Pero… , tarde o temprano, (tener[8]) que volver a lo de siempre… a los rascacielos de la ciudad… al tráfico… al medio ambiente contaminado… al trabajo… (Poder[9]) usar mi tarjeta de crédito, como dice el anuncio —pero ¡(tener[10]) que pagar después!

Comprensión. ¿Cierto, falso o no lo dice? Corrija las oraciones falsas.

	CIERTO	FALSO	NO LO DICE.
1. Esta persona trabaja en una ciudad grande.	☑	☐	☐
2. No le interesan los deportes acuáticos.	☐	☑	☐
3. Puede pagar este viaje de sueños al contado.	☐	☑	☐
4. Tiene un novio / una novia con quien quisiera hacer el viaje.	☐	☐	☑

NATIONAL STANDARDS: Cultures

Antoní Gaudí (1852–1926): A Catalan architect whose unique style combines Gothic elements with Modernism, Gaudí's structures are full of movement based on natural images. His most famous works are in Barcelona: *el Parc Güell, la Iglesia de la Sagrada Familia*, and a number of private homes that are museums today.

C. ¿Qué haría Ud. si pudiera?

Paso 1. En parejas, hagan y contesten preguntas, según el modelo. Pueden cambiar los detalles, si quieren.

MODELO: estudiar árabe/japonés →
E1: ¿Estudiarías **árabe**?
E2: No. Estudiaría **japonés**.

1. estudiar italiano/chino
2. renunciar a un puesto sin avisar / con dos semanas de anticipación
3. hacer un viaje a España / la Argentina
4. salir de casa sin apagar el estéreo / las luces
5. tener un presupuesto rígido / uno flexible
6. gastar menos en ropa/libros
7. poner el aire acondicionado en invierno/verano
8. alquilar un coche de lujo / uno económico

Paso 2. Ahora sigan con el mismo modelo del **Paso 1,** pero inventen los detalles.

1. dejar de estudiar / ¿ ?
2. vivir en otra ciudad / ¿ ?
3. ser presidente/a de los Estados Unidos / primer ministro (primera ministra) del Canadá / ¿ ?
4. gustarle conocer a una persona famosa / ¿ ?

D. ¡Entendió mal! En parejas, hagan y contesten preguntas usando el futuro y el condicional, según el modelo.

MODELO: llegar el trece de junio / tres →
E1: **Llegaré** el trece de junio.
E2: ¿No dijiste que **llegarías** el tres?
E1: ¡Que no! Te dije que **llegaría** el trece. Entendiste mal.

1. estar en el café a las dos / doce
2. estudiar con Juan / Juana
3. ir de vacaciones a Madrid en julio / junio
4. verte en casa / en clase
5. comprar la blusa rosada / roja

Nota **comunicativa**

Cláusulas con *si*

To express hypothetical situations, Spanish uses sentences with **si** (*if*) clauses, just like English.*

if CLAUSE	RESULT
si + *past subjunctive*	*conditional*
Si yo **pudiera,**	**iría** a España de vacaciones.
If I could,	*I would go to Spain on vacation.*
Si yo **fuera** tú,	no **haría** eso.
If I were you,	*I wouldn't do that.*

You are already familiar with **si** clauses with the present indicative. They present actions that are habitual in the present or likely to happen.

Si ahorro suficiente dinero, iré de vacaciones a España.
If I save enough money, I'll go to Spain on vacation.

¡OJO!
The present subjunctive is never used after **si.**

*These contrary-to-fact situations express speculations about the present and the future. The perfect forms of the conditional and the past subjunctive are used to speculate about the past; that is, what would have happened if a particular event had occurred: Si **hubiera tenido** el dinero, **habría hecho** el viaje. (*If **I had had** the money, **I would have made** the trip.*) You will find a more detailed presentation of this structure in Appendix 4, Additional Perfect Forms (Indicative and Subjunctive).

Prác. C: Answers
Paso 1. 1. *estudiaría(s)* 2. *renunciaría(s)* 3. *haría(s)* 4. *saldría(s)* 5. *tendría(s)* 6. *gastaría(s)* 7. *pondría(s)* 8. *alquilaría(s)*

Paso 2. 1. *dejaría(s)* 2. *viviría(s)* 3. *sería(s)* 4. *te/me gustaría*

Prác. D: Answers
1. *Estaré/estarías/estaría* 2. *Estudiaré/estudiarías/estudiaría* 3. *Iré/irías/iría* 4. *Te veré / te verías / te vería* 5. *Compraré/comprarías/compraría*

Prác. C: Suggestions

- Have students complete the items in the future. Contrast the difference in meaning when the future is used.
- Have students add two questions of their own to each group.

Prác D: Extension

6. *haber un examen el viernes / la semana que viene*
7. *ser el examen en el laboratorio / en la clase*
8. *costar el libro $20 / $30*

Nota comunicativa

Point out the tenses that can be used in the independent clause in each structure:

- *si* + present indicative → present indicative, command, future
- *si* + imperfect subjunctive → conditional

Prác. E: Preliminary Exercises

- Have students tell whether the following sentences are contrary to fact or not.
  1. *Si estoy en el centro, siempre almuerzo en Barney's.* (no)
  2. *Si lloviera, no iríamos.* (yes)
  3. *Si estamos cansados, descansamos una hora por la tarde.* (no)
  4. *Habla como si* (new) *fuera argentina.* (yes)
  5. *Si yo tuviera esa clase, tendría que estudiar mucho.* (yes)
  6. *Si te veo mañana, te lo daré.* (no)
- Use the following pattern drill to practice forms.

  Pablo tiene que decidir si acepta o no un puesto que paga bastante bien, pero que está en un pueblo pequeño y algo aislado (new). *¿Qué le diría Ud.?*

  —Si yo…, no lo haría. (*ser tú, tener ese problema, no poder decidir*).
  —Si yo…, me volvería loco/a. (*estar allí, vivir allí*)

Prác. E: Variation

Have students provide interesting or provocative situations. Have the class react, completing the phrase: *Si yo fuera…*

Prác. F: Reciclado

Ask students to invent background details for each drawing and situation, using the present to tell who the people depicted are. Then ask them to speculate about the details that led up to each drawing, using the preterite and imperfect. Finally, have them speculate as to what will happen, using the future.

E. ¿Qué haría Ud.?

Paso 1. Complete las siguientes declaraciones lógicamente.

1. Si yo quisiera comprar comida, iría a ____.
2. Si necesitara comprar un libro, iría a ____.
3. Si necesitara consultar un libro, iría a ____.
4. Si tuviera sed en este momento, tomaría ____.
5. Si tuviera que emigrar, iría a ____.
6. Si fuera a ____, tendría que viajar en ____.
7. Si tuviera suficiente dinero, compraría ____.
8. Si pudiera, me gustaría ____.

Paso 2. Ahora, en parejas, túrnense para comparar sus declaraciones ya completas. Luego digan a la clase lo que Uds. tienen en común.

F. Situaciones

Paso 1. Empareje las oraciones con el dibujo apropiado.

a.

b.

c.

d.

e.

1. __e__ Los Martínez quieren usar su coche.
2. __a__ A Mariana le encanta ese traje.
3. __d__ Simón quiere encender (*to turn on*) la luz.
4. __c__ Julia no tiene ganas de levantarse.
5. __b__ La Sra. Blanco tiene miedo de viajar en avión.

Paso 2. Ahora haga una oración con **si** para cada situación. Use su imaginación para añadir detalles.

MODELO: Mariana se compraría ese traje si…

Heritage Speakers

Los hispanohablantes de algunas regiones usan el condicional en cláusulas con *si*. El tiempo aceptado es el imperfecto de subjuntivo. Compare las siguientes oraciones: USO RECOMENDADO: *Si yo **tuviera** dinero, iría a España.* VARIACIÓN REGIONAL: *Si yo **tendría** dinero, iría a España.*

Resources: Transparency 168

Conversación

A. Una encuesta (*poll*)

Paso 1. Prepare cinco preguntas sobre temas universales, como son la vida sentimental y familiar, el trabajo, el medio ambiente, etcétera.

MODELOS: ¿Por cuánto tiempo **vivirías** con alguien sin casarte?
¿**Vivirías** con alguien que no creyera en el matrimonio?

Vocabulario útil

casarse / vivir juntos sin casarse
tener (número de) hijos / adoptar
vivir permanentemente en esta ciudad / este estado / esta provincia / otro país
ganar mucho dinero o tener mucho tiempo libre
proteger (protejo) el medio ambiente
poder vivir sin la televisión / el Internet / el teléfono celular

Paso 2. Use sus preguntas del **Paso 1** para entrevistar a cinco compañeros de clase. Luego prepare un breve informe para toda la clase con los resultados de su encuesta.

B. ¿En qué circunstancias... ? En parejas, hagan y contesten preguntas sobre los siguientes temas.

MODELO: comprar un coche nuevo →
E1: ¿En qué circunstancias **comprarías** un coche nuevo?
E2: **Compraría** un coche nuevo si tuviera más dinero.

1. dejar de estudiar en esta universidad
2. emigrar a otro país
3. estudiar otro idioma
4. no obedecer a tus padres / a tu jefe/a
5. votar por ____ para presidente/a / primer ministro (primera ministra)
6. ser candidato/a para presidente/a / primer ministro (primera ministra)
7. casarse / divorciarse
8. no decirle la verdad a un amigo / una amiga

C. ¿Qué haría si... ?

Paso 1. En parejas, inventen soluciones para los siguientes dilemas.

1. Si su mejor amigo/a le pidiera 500 dólares para algo muy urgente.
2. Si uno de sus profesores o profesoras le dijera: «Ud. me cae muy bien (*I think you're really nice*). Por eso no tiene que tomar el examen final».
3. Si su novio/a le propusiera que se casaran inmediatamente. (O si su esposo/a le propusiera que se divorciaran en seguida.)
4. Si de pronto tuviera un millón de dólares hoy.

Paso 2. Ahora inventen dos situaciones bien difíciles de resolver que la clase tiene que solucionar. ¡Sean imaginativos!

Mundo interactivo

You should now be prepared to work with Scenario 9, Activity 4 in Connect Spanish (**www.connectspanish.com**).

Con. B: Answers
1. *dejaría(s)* **2.** *emigraría(s)* **3.** *estudiaría(s)* **4.** *obedecería(s)* **5.** *votaría(s)* **6.** *sería(s)* **7.** *te casarías / me casaría; te divorciarías / me divorciaría* **8.** *no le diría(s)*

Bright Idea

Optional

¿Qué harías con mil dólares? (Saving is not an option.)

¿Qué no harías ni por un millón de dólares? (Refer to reality television programming.)

Con. A: Redacción

Assign *Con. A* as a written + oral presentation assignment. Students should present their questions, then the answers, then analyze the results. Suggest that they focus on the most controversial or surprising answers.

Con. C: Follow-up

- Have students tell what they would do in exchange for a favor that their roommates or housemates did for them.

  Si mi compañera de apartamento no dejara platos sucios por todos lados, yo limpiaría la cocina con más gusto.

  ¡OJO! Have students use the subject pronoun for emphasis.

- Have students complete the following sentences.
  1. *Si yo fuera presidente/a (primer ministro / primera ministra), yo...*
  2. *Si yo estuviera en... ,...*
  3. *Si tuviera un millón de dólares,...*
  4. *Si yo pudiera... ,...*
  5. *Si yo fuera... ,...*
  6. *Si... , estaría contentísimo/a.*
  7. *Si... , estaría enojadísimo/a.*

- Have half of the class write *si* clauses using past subjunctive; the other writes result clauses using the conditional. Collect *si* clauses in one box, result clauses in another. Draw a clause from each box and read the resulting sentence aloud.

Un poco de todo

A: Suggestions

- *Paso 2.* Expand each item with questions about the historical situation in the question. Focus on the imperfect/preterite in the questions, not necessarily on the use of the imperfect subjunctive. For example, for item 1 you might ask:

  ¿En qué año llegaron al Nuevo Mundo los primeros colonizadores?
  ¿Había muchos indígenas aquí en aquel entonces (new)*?*
  ¿Qué hicieron los colonizadores tan pronto como llegaron?
  ¿Les tenían miedo a los indígenas?

A: Follow-up

Discuss with students examples of how U.S. history is intimately connected to the Hispanic world. You may wish to ask a few students to prepare a short oral presentation on the Spanish and Mexican historical presence on what today is U.S. soil: the arrival of Spaniards in Florida and California, *la compra de la Luisiana, el Tratado de Guadalupe Hidalgo, la Guerra Hispanoamericana,* and so on.

B: Suggestion

Have students write their own *si* clauses for classmates to complete. Encourage creativity and humor.

Bright Idea

B: Extension

For item 2, have students imagine they will have no electricity, but they can take (have) three things. What would they want to have?

C: Notes

- Note that this chapter's *Lengua y cultura* requires a number of uses of the present indicative/subjunctive and of commands. The future and conditional are explicitly reviewed in *A–B*.
- The following grammar topics are included in *Lengua y cultura*: gender, adjective agreement, demonstratives, use of the infinitive, subjunctive vs. indicative, present perfect, commands, *ser* vs. *estar*, *por* vs. *para*, *porque* vs. *por qué*.

A: Answers

Paso 1 (Possible answers) **1.** *los primeros colonizadores, los cuáqueros* **2.** *los españoles, los portugueses* **3.** *los primeros colonizadores de Australia* **4.** *muchos grupos asiáticos y del Medio Oriente* **5.** *los irlandeses, algunos grupos de África y de Asia*

Paso 2 **1.** *Inglaterra deseaba que los colonos consiguieran más tierras en Norteamérica.* **2.** *Los indígenas americanos temían que los colonos les quitaran sus tierras.* **3.** *El rey de Inglaterra quería que los colonos pagaran impuestos.* **4.** *Los estadounidenses fueron a la guerra para que México les diera parte de su territorio.* **5.** *A los estados del sur no les gustaba que los estados del norte controlaran las leyes.* **6.** *Los abolicionistas deseaban que todas las personas del país tuvieran los mismos derechos.* **7.** *Era necesario que este país participara en dos guerras mundiales.*

Un poco de todo

A. Escenas históricas

Paso 1. La gente emigra por razones diversas. Complete las siguientes oraciones con la forma correcta del imperfecto de subjuntivo de uno de los verbos de la lista. Luego, si puede, nombre un grupo al que puede referirse cada oración.

haber poder practicar seguir tener

1. Las leyes del país de origen de este grupo no permitían que _______ libremente su religión. practicara
2. Algunas personas esperaban que _______ oro y plata en América. hubiera
3. El rey no quería que estos criminales _______ viviendo en este país. siguieran
4. Estos inmigrantes buscaban un país donde _______ encontrar paz, esperanza y seguridad personal. pudieran
5. Los miembros de este grupo buscaban un país donde no _______ que pasar hambre. tuvieran

Paso 2. Ahora exprese algunos acontecimientos de la historia de los Estados Unidos, haciendo oraciones completas con los siguientes elementos. **¡OJO!** Esto ocurrió en el pasado; por eso la primera cláusula debe tener un verbo en el pasado.

1. Inglaterra: desear / que / los colonos: conseguir más tierras en Norteamérica
2. los indígenas americanos: temer / que / los colonos: quitarles sus tierras
3. el rey de Inglaterra: querer / que / los colonos: pagar impuestos (*taxes*)
4. los estadounidenses: ir a la guerra / para que / México: darles parte de su territorio
5. los estados del sur: no gustarles / que / los estados del norte: controlar las leyes
6. los abolicionistas: desear / que / todas las personas del país: tener los mismos derechos

B. Si el mundo fuera diferente... Adaptarse a un nuevo país o nuevas circunstancias es difícil, pero también es una aventura interesante. ¿Qué ocurriría si el mundo fuera diferente?

MODELO: Si yo fuera la última persona en el mundo... →
- tendría que aprender a hacer muchas cosas.
- sería la persona más importante —y más ignorante— del mundo.

1. Si yo pudiera tener solamente un amigo o amiga, ____.
2. Si yo tuviera que pasar un año en una isla desierta, ____.
3. Si yo fuera ____ (otra persona), ____.
4. Si el presidente fuera presidenta, ____.
5. Si yo viviera en (nombre de país), ____.

C. Lengua y cultura: Maneras de practicar el español fuera de clase. Complete the following paragraphs with the correct form of the words in parentheses, as suggested by context. When two possibilities are given, select the correct word. **¡OJO!** As you conjugate verbs, decide whether to use the subjunctive (present, present perfect, or past) or the indicative (present, present perfect, future, preterite, or imperfect). For items flagged with *comm.*, use a command. Start out in the present.

C: Answers
1. *hable* **2.** *vea*

Claro está que Ud. habla español en clase. También es probable que lo (hablar[1]) con su profesor(a) cada vez que lo/la (ver[2]) en el *campus* de la universidad.

Culture

Use the theme of immigration from activity A to discuss Hispanics in the United States and the history of their presence.

The majority of Hispanics in the U.S. are found in three geographical areas.

1. south Florida (Cubans)
2. the Southwest: Texas, New Mexico, Arizona, and California (Mexicans)
3. New York (Puerto Ricans)

Although one can generalize in terms of which Hispanics are located in a particular region of the United States, Hispanics from all areas of Spain and Latin America live in every major metropolitan city throughout the United States.

Pero (por/para[3]) hablar español con soltura,[a] Ud. tiene que practicar más.

«¡Ojalá que (*yo:* poder[4]) practicar español fuera de clase!» ¿(*pres. perf.:* Decir[5]) Ud. eso alguna vez? Pues hay muchas maneras de hacerlo. Por ejemplo, los compañeros de una misma clase de español siempre pueden hablar español cuando (verse[6]) para no (perder[7]) (ninguno[8]) oportunidad de practicar. Otra idea es (mirar[9]) una telenovela[b] o (un/una[10]) programa de noticias en español. También puede escuchar la radio cuando (manejar[11]). Lo importante es dedicar un rato[c] a escuchar español auténtico con frecuencia.

Jorge Ramos y María Elena Salinas, presentadores del noticiero de Univisión

Muchas personas (sentirse[12]) muy frustradas con esta actividad (por qué/porque[13]) no pueden comprenderlo todo. Pero (haber[14]) que recordar que no es necesario entender cada una de las palabras que se oyen. Para los estudiantes principiantes,[d] es suficiente identificar (el/la[15]) tema y (alguno[16]) palabras y expresiones. Si Ud. (escuchar[17]) español habitualmente en los medios de comunicación, (aprender[18]) mucho… y rápidamente.

Otra actividad útil es leer el periódico o una revista de actualidad en español. Puesto que[e] hay muchos hispanohablantes en (este/ese[19]) país, es relativamente fácil conseguir algo que leer en español. Y si esto no (ser/estar[20]) fácil en el lugar donde Ud. vive, (*comm., Ud.:* buscar[21]) en el Internet. (Por/Para[22]) ejemplo, si le gusta viajar, (*comm., Ud.:* consultar[23]) las páginas relacionadas con el turismo en los países donde se habla español.

Finalmente, (*comm., Ud.:* recordar[24]) su propia comunidad. Es muy posible que Ud. (vivir[25]) en una ciudad o estado que tiene una comunidad hispana. Le sugerimos que (*Ud.:* visitar[26]) tiendas o supermercados hispanos para que (*Ud.:* ver[27]) las cosas que se venden allí. ¡Leer la lista de los ingredientes de cualquier producto es ya[f] un ejercicio de lectura!

[a]con… *fluently* [b]*soap opera* [c]un… *a bit of time* [d]*beginning* [e]Puesto… *Since* [f]*actually*

3. para 4. pudiera (pueda) 5. Ha dicho 6. se ven 7. perder 8. ninguna 9. mirar 10. un 11. maneja 12. se sienten 13. porque 14. hay 15. el 16. algunas 17. escuchara 18. aprendería 19. este 20. es 21. busque 22. Por 23. consulte 24. recuerde 25. viva 26. visite 27. vea

Comprensión. Conteste las siguientes preguntas.

1. Además de (*Besides*) hablar español con sus compañeros de clase, ¿qué cosas puede Ud. hacer para practicar el idioma fuera de la clase?
2. ¿Es buena o mala la idea de mirar la televisión en español? ¿Qué tipos de programas se recomienda ver?
3. ¿Es necesario que un estudiante entienda cada una de las palabras de lo que oye o mira en los medios de comunicación en español?
4. ¿Qué tipos de lecturas puede Ud. conseguir en español para practicar más?
5. ¿Qué posibilidades de hablar español existen en la comunidad?

C: Comprensión: Answers:
1. mirar la televisión y escuchar la radio 2. Es buena idea. Se recomienda ver una telenovela o un programa de noticias. 3. No es necesario. 4. un periódico o una revista 5. Answers will vary.

En su comunidad

Entreviste a una persona hispana de su universidad o ciudad sobre el gobierno de su país de origen y sobre sus preferencias políticas.

PREGUNTAS POSIBLES

- ¿Qué tipo de gobierno hay su país? ¿Ha habido algún cambio grande en la estructura del gobierno en los últimos años? ¿Y en las últimas decadas?
- ¿Quién es el presidente o la presidenta del país? ¿Hay un congreso y un senado?
- ¿Cuáles son los partidos políticos más importantes? Si hay más de dos partidos, ¿se forman coaliciones de partidos para gobernar?
- ¿Estaba afiliado/a a algún partido en su país? ¿Votó alguna vez? ¿En qué elecciones?

C: Follow-up

- Working in groups, ask students to make lists of places (businesses, cafés, movie theaters, and so on) in their community where they could speak Spanish.
- Ask students to make a list of resolutions: five things they will do in the future to practice Spanish.

En su comunidad

Suggestions

- Remind students to get the following basic information: the informant's country of origin, how long he or she has lived in this country, and if the informant visits his or her country of origin frequently.
- This activity could instead be assigned as an online research project on a country of the student's choice or assigned by you.
- See the IM for additional suggestions and guidelines.

Resources: Desenlace

In the *Cap. 18* segment of "Chapter-by-Chapter Supplementary Materials" in the IM, you will find a chapter-culminating activity. You can use this activity to consolidate and review the vocabulary and grammar skills students have acquired.

TelePuntos

Note

Pages 544–549 are optional. You may cover some, all, or none of this material in class, or assign it to students—as a group or individually—for homework or extra credit. Pages 550–551 (*En resumen: En este capítulo*) are a summary of all of the chapter's active material.

Antes de mirar

Suggestion

Students should be able to answer these questions easily, as these topics are well covered in the chapter. You may wish to list the *medios de comunicación* cited by your students on the board, then ask students which ones they think that people in the show will mention.

Programa 18

Notes

- The structures of program will be accessible to students but the vocabulary will be challenging. In this chapter, it is particularly important that students scan *Al mirar* before viewing, as doing so will preview much of the show's content.
- In the first segment, the interview questions are presented on-screen, which will greatly aid students' comprehension.

Suggestion

Emphasize to students that the more carefully they study the preliminary activities (*Antes de mirar, Vocabulario de este programa,* and *Fragmento del guion*), the more they will understand. Scanning *Después de mirar* before viewing is also an excellent strategy.

Fragmento del guion

Suggestion

Be certain that students from a non-Western background understand what *un hermano* (*religioso*) is.

Después de mirar

A: Answers:

1. *Le encanta a Víctor.* **2.** *No cree que estén bien informados.* **3.** *Cree que si hicieran la misma encuesta en los Estados Unidos, recibirían respuestas similares.* **4.** *El primero es de México y el segundo de Guatemala.* **5.** *Solo se ofrece el almuerzo.* **6.** *Víctor y su esposa acaban de adoptar a una niña como hija.* **7.** *Ana trabaja allí.*

B: Answers:

1. *los medios electrónicos, especialmente el Internet* **2.** *en enviar a Guatemala a personas que quieren ayudar y mejorar su español* **3.** *ancianos con pocos recursos económicos, personas sin hogar.* **4.** *Aprenden a valorar lo que tienen y que la pobreza no es una cosa mala, pero que sí es injusta.* **5.** *Se llama Gabriela, nació en Guatemala, tiene año y medio y acaba de llegar a su familia (es adoptada).*

TELEPUNTOS

Como estudia comunicación, esta joven mexicana desea verse inmersa en información sobre la política y la sociedad, para saber a qué atenerse (*to pay attention to*).

Antes de mirar

¿Por qué medios de comunicación se entera Ud. de las noticias? ¿Cree Ud. que está al día de lo que pasa en el mundo? ¿Qué tipo de noticias son de mayor interés para Ud.?

¿Trabaja Ud. de voluntario/a en alguna organización? ¿Por qué lo hace?

PROGRAMA 18: ¡Noticias!

Este programa trata del acceso a las noticias a través de una serie de entrevistas con estudiantes universitarios mexicanos. También hay un reportaje sobre el tema del voluntariado (*volunteering*) que incluye un programa para voluntarios extranjeros en Guatemala.

Vocabulario de este programa

la encuesta	poll	**la belleza**	beauty
disfrutar	to enjoy	**regir (rijo) (i)**	to rule, matter
la fuente	source	**suponer(se)** (*like* **poner**)	to suppose
por medio de	through	**sin fines de lucro**	non-profit
estar suscrito/a	to be enrolled	**el colegio**	school
la cadena	channel	**sumo/a**	great
los medios impresos	print media	**mejorar**	to improve
prender	to turn on (*an appliance*)	**antiguo/a**	former
más que nada	mainly	**la pobreza**	poverty
los adelantos	advances	**conmovedor(a)**	moving (*in an emotional way*)
el afán	interest	**las personas sin hogar**	homeless people
la facilidad	ease	**enriquecedor(a)**	enriching
estar al corriente	estar al día		

Fragmento del guion

CODIRECTORA: Tenemos muchísimas organizaciones en Guatemala. Pero algunas de ellas tienen toda la buena intención de atender[a] niños, de atender ancianos,[b] pero no tienen los fondos[c] suficientes para poder pagar… al personal que se necesita. Entonces, es ahí donde llegamos.[d] A las organizaciones donde realmente no tienen el recurso[e] económico para pagar al personal que necesita y que nosotros podemos ser un alivio[f] para poder atender a esa población que ellos tienen.

LAURA: CCS recibe entre dos y treinta y cinco voluntarios a la vez[g] durante todo el año y los coloca[h] en más de dieciocho organizaciones en toda la Ciudad de Guatemala. Puede ser en un colegio para niños pequeños… en una clínica… o en un comedor[i] para gente sin casa o sin recursos económicos.

HERMANO[j] LUVÍN: Diario[k] atendemos noventa a cien ancianos, en los cuales les damos alimentación que consta[l] de un almuerzo, que para ellos es desayuno, almuerzo y cena, porque no tienen dónde más comer.[m] Fuera de eso,[n] les prestamos el servicio de baño.[ñ] Ellos vienen de la calle, sucios, vueltos nada.[o] Y les damos ropa, les damos el baño para que cambien y para que se bañen y queden distintos. También le[s] damos la parte espiritual, como motivación para que su autoestima[p] se eleve un poco y piensen que son importantes para la sociedad, aunque vivan en las circunstancias que viven.

[a]*assisting* [b]*the elderly* [c]*funds* [d]Entonces… *Therefore, that's where we go.* [e]*resources* [f]*relief* [g]a… *at one time* [h]*places* [i]*soup kitchen* [j]*brother (in a religious order)* [k]*On a daily basis* [l]alimentación… *nourishment that consists* [m]no… *they have no where else to eat* [n]Fuera… *In addition* [ñ]les… *we provide them with bathing facilities* [o]vueltos… *reduced to nothing* [p]*self-esteem*

Mundo interactivo

Continue your work as an intern at HispanaVisión with Laura Sánchez Tejada, the roving reporter of *Salu2*, as you complete Scenario 9, Activities 3 and 4 in Connect Spanish (**www.connectspanish.com**).

Al mirar

Empareje las siguientes citas (*quotes*) con las personas que las dicen.

CITAS

1. __a__ «Yo apenas (*hardly ever*) leo la prensa en papel ya.»
2. __e__ «Y aparte (*besides*), yo creo que la edad no es como para estarte preocupando (*at this age I don't think we should be worrying*) por las noticias.»
3. __d__ «Igual nada más (*Usually*) hablamos de las noticias cuando pasa algo como muy relevante, por ejemplo, un temblor (*earthquake*)… »
4. __c__ «Sus problemas son endémicos: desempleo (*unemployment*) alto, infraestructuras deficientes, bajo nivel de vida y un alto índice de analfabetismo (*illiteracy rate*).»
5. __f__ «Aprenden a valorar (*value*) lo que tienen en su casa, a valorar su familia, que la vida simple no es mala… »
6. __g__ «Y aquí me lleno (*I fill myself up*). Aquí, tranquila porque me voy bien satisfecha (*satisfied*) conmigo misma… »
7. __b__ «Súper bién. Con sus seis añitos (*Just 6 years old*), es como una mini mamá.»

PERSONAS

a. Ana
b. Víctor
c. Laura
d. una estudiante que está sentada
e. una estudiante de chaqueta morada
f. una de las codirectoras de CCS
g. una señora que está en el comedor

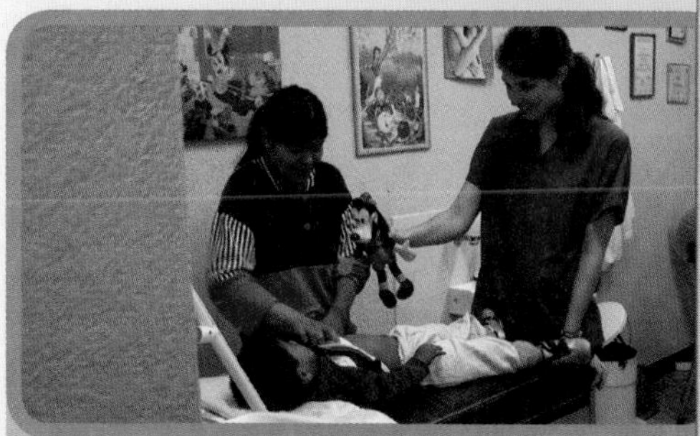

«Y al final, ¿ellos qué es lo que se llevan (*they [the volunteers] take away*)? Se llevan la sensación de haber ayudado (*having helped*), pero la mayoría se van con la idea de que ellos aprendieron más de lo que dieron.»

Después de mirar

A. ¿Está claro? Las siguientes oraciones son falsas. Corríjalas.

1. A Ana le encanta leer el periódico los domingos.
2. El profesor cree que los estudiantes están bien informados de las noticias políticas y económicas.
3. Víctor cree que los jóvenes estadounidenses son muy diferentes de los mexicanos con respecto a estar al día de lo que pasa en el mundo.
4. Los dos reportajes son de México.
5. En el comedor se ofrecen el desayuno y el almuerzo.
6. Ana acaba de adoptar a una niña como hija suya.
7. Víctor trabaja de voluntario en un comedor para personas sin hogar.

B. Un poco más. Conteste las siguientes preguntas.

1. ¿Qué medios usan más los jóvenes para enterarse de las noticias?
2. ¿En qué se especializa Cross Cultural Solutions (CCS)?
3. ¿A qué tipo de personas se atiende en el comedor que se ve en el programa de hoy?
4. Según una codirectora de CCS, ¿qué aprenden los voluntarios?
5. ¿Qué se sabe de la nueva hija de Víctor?

C. Y ahora, Uds. Usen las mismas preguntas que se usaron en el programa para entrevistar a cinco compañeros de clase. Luego comparen sus respuestas con las (*those*) de los jóvenes mexicanos entrevistados en el programa. ¿Tenía Víctor razón cuando dijo que las respuestas serían similares en los dos países? ¿Cómo se explica esto?

Producción personal

Filme una entrevista que le hace a una persona que trabaja de voluntaria en alguna organización local o de la universidad.

Sobre el programa

La familia de Víctor ha aumentado con la llegada de una nueva hija, Gabriela Marina, a quien llaman Gaby. Hace tres años que Víctor y Marina decidieron adoptar a otra niña y finalmente su sueño[a] se ha hecho realidad con la llegada de Gaby. La niña es muy bonita, y lo que importante es que es muy sana y se ha adaptado a su nuevo hogar de la noche a la mañana.[b]

Sarita está feliz con su nueva hermanita y está claro que, para Gaby, Sarita es la persona más interesante de la familia. Se pasa el día diciendo «Tita», que es su manera de pronunciar Sarita. El bautizo de Gaby es el próximo mes y los padrinos[c] serán Ana y el hermano de Marina. ¡Y habrá una gran fiesta en casa de los abuelos!

[a]*dream* [b]*de… immediately* [c]*godparents*

C: Suggestions

- Note the two parts in this activity: the whole-class interview, then the analysis of the responses given in the show. You could have students draw lots to determine who will be interviewed.
- Alternatively, you could divide the class into groups of 4-5 students each for this activity. Have groups rotate 2-3 times so that each student in a group gets to interview and is interviewed by a student from another group. Students will accumulate 2-3 sets of interview questions. After the rotations, ask groups to tally their answers and tackle the comparison with the answers given by Mexican students.

Sobre el programa

Suggestions

- Before assigning the reading, ask students what they remember about Víctor's family.
- Ask students what the children's full names would be in Mexico, as the daughters of *Víctor Gutiérrez Castillo* and *Marina Flores Martín*.

Optional: Comprensión

1. *¿Cuántos hijos tienen Víctor y su esposa?* (*Tienen dos hijas, Sarita y Gabriela o Gaby.*)
2. *¿Dónde nació su nueva hija?* (*en Guatemala*)
3. *¿Qué palabra dice Gaby constantemente? ¿Qué significa?* (*Dice «Tita», que significa Sarita.*)
4. *¿Cómo se siente Sarita con la llegada de su nueva hermana?* (*Está muy feliz.*)
5. *¿Quiénes van a ser los padrinos de Gaby?* (*Ana y el hermano de Marina*)

Producción personal

See the IM for additional suggestions for this chapter's assignment as well as for general guidelines and suggestions for video assignments.

Lectura cultural

Note

See the IM for more information and some expressions used in Spain.

First Reading: Notes

- The autonomous communities are diverse in size and geography, much as U.S. states and Canadian provinces are different from one another.
- In addition to the autonomous communities, there are two autonomous cities, Ceuta and Melilla, which are on the North African coast. They are currently claimed by Morocco.
- Gibraltar, a small city on a big rock at the southernmost point of Spain, has been under British rule since the 1700s. Ownership of it is constantly a question of negotiation between Spain and England.

En todo el mundo hispano

Note

While most of Latin America had become independent from Spain by 1925, the Caribbean countries did not become independent from Spain until much later. The Dominican Republic became independent in 1844, after having been a part of Haiti since 1822. Cuba did not become independent until 1902, gaining its independence from the U.S., which took control of the island from Spain following the Spanish-American War (1898). Puerto Rico has actually never become independent, something that is a topic of much discussion and debate there. (See *Cap. 10.*)

Exploración lingüística

Ask students to find the following in the reading. Some of these words are glossed and some are not.

- *Un sinónimo de* región (*autonomía*)
- *Un sinónimo de* encantar (*entusiasmar*)
- *Un sinónimo de* aproximadamente (*alrededor de*)

Comprensión

Answers

1. *en diecisiete autonomías* **2.** *cuatro: el castellano, el gallego, el vasco y el catalán* **3.** *el bicentenario de la independencia de los países americanos de España* **4.** *el Mercado Común del Sur*

Tres símbolos españoles

Notes

- There are many other icons of Spanish culture: *la tortilla de patatas,* bullfighting, . . .
- Spain is home to an amazing amount of art and architecture from all ages,

A LEER

Lectura cultural

España

España es un país de una gran diversidad geográfica y cultural. Si bien[a] hay bastante homogeneidad racial, en el país conviven[b] regiones con identidades bien definidas y arraigadas[c] en una historia milenaria.[d] Algunas de estas regiones tienen su propia lengua: el gallego en Galicia, el vasco en el País Vasco y el catalán en Cataluña. Otras regiones tienen dialectos del castellano claramente distintivos, como el andaluz en Andalucía y el canario en las Islas Canarias.

¿Cuáles son las ventajas y desventajas de un sistema federativo como el (*that*) de los Estados Unidos?

Con la Constitución de 1978, España reconoce[e] esta diversidad, constituyéndose[f] como un Estado de Autonomías: diecisiete regiones que funcionan de manera descentralizada, no muy diferente del sistema federativo estadounidense.

La diversidad de España y su realidad en múltiples autonomías es una fuente[g] de innumerables tensiones lingüísticas, políticas, presupuestarias,[h] etcétera. Pero también es motivo de orgullo[i] general, porque con un territorio del tamaño[j] de Texas, España es un país de intensos contrastes que entusiasman incluso a los mismos españoles que abogan por su propia región autonómica.[k]

[a]*Si... Although* [b]*coexist* [c]*rooted* [d]*thousand-year* [e]*recognizes* [f]*organizing itself* [g]*source* [h]*budgetary* [i]*pride* [j]*size* [k]*que... about which even the very Spaniards who defend the autonomy of their own region are enthusiastic*

En todo el mundo hispano

- **En todos los países americanos hispanohablantes** En 2010, estos países celebraron el bicentenario del proceso de su independencia de España. Esa lucha, que empezó en la mayoría de los casos en el siglo[a] XIX, duró alrededor de[b] quince años y culminó con la creación de los nuevos estados americanos.
- **En la Argentina, el Paraguay y el Uruguay** Junto con el Brasil, estos países formaron el Mercado Común del Sur, o MERCOSUR, en 1991 por el Tratado[c] de Asunción. Es un acuerdo[d] que fomenta[e] la libre circulación de productos y servicios a fin de[f] crear mejores condiciones económicas para los países miembros. En la actualidad hay cinco países más asociados con MERCOSUR: Bolivia, Chile, Colombia, el Ecuador y el Perú.

[a]*century* [b]*alrededor... about* [c]*Treaty* [d]*agreement* [e]*encourages* [f]*a... para*

Un bar de tapas, en Valencia

Tres símbolos españoles

- **La Constitución Española de 1978** En un país fragmentado por diferentes identidades locales y regionales, la Constitución es uno de los pocos conceptos sobre los que[a] se fundamenta[b] hoy día la cohesión y unidad españolas.
- **Las tapas** Estos son pequeños platos de comida que se toman como aperitivos o como almuerzo o cena. Es una manera distintivamente española no solo de comer sino[c] de socializar en los muchos bares que existen en cualquier[d] ciudad del país. El concepto de las tapas ha alcanzado[e] ahora cierta popularidad en los Estados Unidos, el Canadá y otros países.
- **El flamenco** Aunque[f] no es la música típica de todas las autonomías de España, el flamenco es sin duda la música que el resto del mundo asocia con el país. Tiene su origen en Andalucía y lleva la marca indeleble del pueblo gitano.[g]

[a]*sobre... upon which* [b]*se... is based* [c]*but also* [d]*any* [e]*ha... has reached* [f]*Although* [g]*gypsy*

Una cita

«En un lugar de la Mancha,[a] de cuyo[b] nombre no quiero acordarme,... »

Así comienza la novela *El ingenioso hidalgo*[c] *Don Quijote de la Mancha*, de Miguel de Cervantes (1547–1616), obra maestra de la literatura mundial. Su protagonista es un símbolo universal de la lucha por las batallas[d] perdidas y su imagen es uno de los grandes íconos españoles.

[a]*la... geographical area of central Spain characterized by its high golden plains* [b]*whose* [c]*gentleman* [d]*battles*

COMPRENSIÓN

1. ¿Cómo está dividida España administrativamente?
2. ¿Cuántas lenguas se hablan en España?
3. ¿Qué se celebró en 2010?
4. ¿Qué es MERCOSUR?

simply impossible to list here. Velázquez, Picasso, and Dalí are probably artists that should be mentioned. *El acueducto de Segovia* and *el complejo romano de Mérida* are excellent examples of the Roman presence in Spain. Major works of the Muslim culture include *la Alhambra de Granada, la Mezquita de Córdoba*, and *la Giralda de Sevilla.*

Una cita

Notes

- You may wish to compare Cervantes to Shakespeare in terms of his importance in world literature (although the playwright Lope de Vega is generally called the Spanish Shakespeare).
- Spanish is sometimes called *la lengua de Cervantes.*

Del mundo hispano

Antes de leer

El Uruguay estuvo bajo una dictadura militar desde 1973 hasta 1985. Durante esta época, muchos uruguayos opuestos a ese régimen sufrieron persecución. ¿Qué sabe Ud. de la vida bajo una dictadura? ¿Qué derechos se pierden cuando no hay democracia?

Lectura: «Celebración de la voz° humana/2», de Eduardo Galeano

°*voice*

1 Tenían las manos atadas,[a] o esposadas,[b] y sin embargo los dedos danzaban, volaban, dibujaban palabras. Los presos[c] estaban encapuchados;[d] pero inclinándose alcanzaban a ver[e] algo, alguito, por abajo. Aunque[f] hablar estaba prohibido, ellos conversaban con las manos.

2 Pinio Ungerfeld me enseñó el alfabeto de los dedos, que en prisión aprendió sin profesor:

3 —*Algunos teníamos mala letra*— me dijo—. *Otros eran unos artistas de la caligrafía.*

4 La dictadura uruguaya quería que cada uno fuera nada más que uno, que cada uno fuera nadie: en cárceles[g] y cuarteles,[h] y en todo el país, la comunicación era delito.

5 Algunos presos pasaron más de diez años enterrados[i] en solitarios calabozos[j] del tamaño[k] de un ataúd,[l] sin escuchar más voces que el estrépito[m] de las rejas[n] o los pasos de las botas por los corredores. Fernández Huidobro y Mauricio Rosencof, condenados a esa soledad, se salvaron porque pudieron hablarse, con golpecitos,[ñ] a través de la pared. Así se contaban sueños y recuerdos, amores y desamores; discutían, se abrazaban, se peleaban; compartían certezas[o] y bellezas y también compartían dudas y culpas[p] y preguntas de esas que no tienen respuesta.

6 Cuando es verdadera, cuando nace de la necesidad de decir, a la voz humana no hay quien la pare.[q] Si le niegan la boca, ella habla por las manos, o por los ojos, o por los poros, o por donde sea. Porque todos, toditos, tenemos algo que decir a los demás, alguna cosa que merece ser por los demás celebrada o perdonada.

[a]*tied* [b]*handcuffed* [c]*prisoners* [d]*in hoods* [e]alcanzaban… podían ver [f]*Although* [g]*jails* [h]*type of jail* [i]*buried* [j]*cells* [k]*size* [l]*coffin* [m]*racket, noise* [n]*bars* [ñ]*little taps* [o]*certainties* [p]*feelings of guilt* [q]no… *no one can stop it*

Comprensión

A. Los detalles. Busque los siguientes detalles en el texto de Galeano.

1. las condiciones en que estaban los presos
2. los sistemas que usaban para comunicarse
3. una comparación entre uno de esos sistemas de comunicación y la palabra escrita (*writing*)
4. los temas de que hablaban

B. Interpretación. Explique con sus propias palabras las siguientes ideas del texto.

1. «La dictadura uruguaya quería que cada uno fuera nada más que uno, que cada uno fuera nadie: en cárceles y cuarteles, y en todo el país, la comunicación era delito.»
2. «Cuando es verdadera, cuando nace de la necesidad de decir, a la voz humana no hay quien la pare.»

Comprensión

A: Possible Answers

1. *«con las manos atadas, o esposadas»; «encapuchados»; «hablar estaba prohibido»; «la dictadura uruguaya quería que… cada uno fuera nadie»; «enterrados en solitarios calabozos»* **2.** *«el alfabeto de los dedos», «con golepecitos»* **3.** *«Algunos teníamos mala letra… Otros eran unos artistas de la caligrafía.»* **4.** *«sueños y recuerdos, amores y desamores», «certezas y bellezas», «dudas y culpas», «preguntas de esas que no tienes respuestas».*

Del mundo hispano

Note

See the IM for optional follow-up, writing, and Internet activities.

Antes de leer

Suggestions

- This story will be hard for students to understand if they don't know its context: who the protagonists might be (political prisoners) and why they are in jail (supposed crimes against the dictatorship). You may wish to ask several students to research the Uruguyan dictatorship and present their findings to the class.
- The language in this story is fairly simple, but its concepts are sophisticated. Help students with the first paragraph by giving them this hint: The three sentences of the first paragraph each have a conjunction or connector of opposition: *sin embargo, pero, aunque*. Each sentence describes a restriction on the freedom of the prisoners, then how the prisoners get around it.

Estrategia

Summarizing Paragraphs

One way better to understand a dense text is to summarize the contents of each paragraph. Ask students to try to do this on their own or present the following summaries of paragraphs (paragraphs 2 and 3 are described in one sentence) and ask them to match the summaries with the appropriate paragraph from the story.

Descripción del lenguaje de las manos (2, 3)
Elogio de la voz humana (6)
Descripción del estado de los presos en general y cómo se comunicaban a pesar de las restricciones (1)
Descripción de la relación entre dos presos en particular (5)
Las intenciones de los militares (4)

B: Answers

Answers will vary but the basic ideas are: **1.** *La dictadura no quería que los ciudadanos se organizaran ni (que) se comunicaran.* **2.** *Los humanos por naturaleza quieren comunicarse con otros.*

Antes de escuchar

Suggestion

Ask students what they know about Spain and what kind of image they have of the country. If they have visited the country, ask them to share what surprised them the most, and what they liked the most.

Escuche

Note

See the IM for the Audioscript and more information about music in Spain.

Después de escuchar

Follow-up

Ask students to prepare mini presentations on one of the following topics: the Iberian people, the Romans in Spain, the Arabs in Spain, the Catholic Kings, the Spanish Empire, the Civil War, Franco's Regime, King Juan Carlos I.

¡Música!

Notes

- Sanz (1968–) has won eighteen Grammys and has sung with many famous artists, including Shakira and Juanes.
- For helpful tips on using songs in the classroom, see the IM.

A ESCUCHAR

El acueducto de Segovia, construido por los romanos y que todavía funciona

Antes de escuchar

¿Qué sabe Ud. de la historia de España? Seguro que sabe que tuvo un gran imperio, pero ¿sabía que en ese país hubo una guerra civil, como en los Estados Unidos? ¿Cómo cree que es el país en la actualidad, pobre o rico? ¿moderno o tradicional?

Escuche

Una breve historia de España

Va a escuchar una conferencia (*lecture*) sobre la historia de este país. Escuche según las indicaciones de su profesor(a).

Vocabulario para escuchar

el siglo	century	**el reino**	kingdom
entonces	then	**tras**	after
autóctono/a	**indígena**	**listo/a**	ready
la huella	trace, mark	**pasar de ser**	to go from being
la caída	fall	**creciente**	growing
el imperio	empire	**milenario/a**	thousand-year
a lo largo de	throughout	**acoger**	to welcome

Estrategia

- Para indicar los siglos en español se usan los números romanos. Por ejemplo, el siglo XV = el siglo quince (*1400s*).
- a.C. = antes de Cristo
  d.C. = después de Cristo

B: Answers: 1. *una democracia* **2.** *un país muy desarrollado* **3.** *un país de inmigrantes, una población multiracial y multilingüe*

Go to the iMix section in Connect Spanish (**www.connectspanish.com**) to access the iTunes playlist *"Puntos9,"* where you can purchase "No es lo mismo" by Alberto Sanz.

Después de escuchar

A. Una breve historia. Escriba el siglo a que corresponde los eventos.

1. Los griegos, fenicios y otros pueblos se establecieron en la Península Ibérica antes del siglo __I__ d.C.
2. Los romanos dominaron la Península Ibérica desde el siglo __II a.C.__ hasta el siglo __V d.C.__.
3. La invasión de los árabes ocurrió en el siglo __VIII__.
4. Los árabes fueron expulsados de la Península Ibérica en el siglo __XV__.
5. El país que hoy se conoce como España comenzó en el siglo __XV__.
6. El final del gran imperio español ocurrió en el siglo __XIX__.
7. España tuvo una guerra civil en el siglo __XX__.

B. La España de hoy. ¿Cómo es España hoy? Use palabras de la conferencia y sus propias palabras para describir la España de hoy.

1. el gobierno
2. la economía
3. la población

Alberto Sanz, en concierto

¡Música!

Alejandro Sanz es un cantante madrileño y compositor de canciones románticas y poéticas. Tiene fama mundial y ha sido ganador de numerosos premios.[a] La canción «No es lo mismo» es del álbum del mismo nombre.

[a] *awards*

A ESCRIBIR

El tema

La ley que determina la mayoría de edad para los jóvenes: ¿Algo que modificar?

Preparar

Paso 1. Haga una lista de las diversas actividades que son restringidas por la ley hasta llegar a una determinada edad.

- ¿Qué edad se requiere que tenga un(a) joven para poder hacer cada una? ¿Cuáles coinciden con la mayoría de edad que fija (*sets*) la ley de este país?
- ¿Cómo se justifican estas restricciones? ¿Está Ud. de acuerdo con ellas?
- ¿Piensa Ud. que se podría modificar la ley que fija la mayoría de edad? ¿Por qué sí o por qué no?

El documento que cada ciudadano español tiene que tener

Redactar

Utilizando la información de **Preparar,** escriba un ensayo persuasivo en defensa o en contra de las actuales restricciones que, con base en la edad, se imponen en los jóvenes de su país. Utilice suficientes argumentos para defender su postura (*position*). No se olvide de incluir un párrafo de conclusión.

Editar

Revise el ensayo para comprobar:

- la ortografía y los acentos
- la variedad del vocabulario
- la organización y la secuencia de las ideas
- el uso correcto de los verbos (tiempos, modos y terminaciones)

Finalmente, prepare su versión final para entregarla.

Preparar

Suggestions

- Have students discuss the effects on the reader of an offensive tone and a neutral tone when writing a persuasive essay.
- Help students develop ideas for an effective closing paragraph. Is there a middle ground between the two positions suggested (*en defensa o en contra*) that students can offer as a recommendation?

Redactar

Suggestions

- Review with students the basic content of a persuasive essay. The writer needs to convince the reader with acceptable arguments and conclusions.
- Suggest that students use the following words and phrases in their essay:
  - to contrast ideas: *sin embargo, no obstante*
  - to transition ideas: *además, por otro lado, en primer lugar, en resumen*
- Suggest that students use the following to express facts: *los expertos afirman que, los estudios muestran que.*
- Suggest that students use the *Vocab. útil* (p. 528) to express opinions.
- Suggested length for this writing assignment: approximately 300 words
- Suggested structure: 4–5 paragraphs

  Introduction: Presentation of the main idea of the essay to get the reader's attention

  Body (2-3 paragraphs): Presentation of various arguments, with an explanation followed by evidence

  Final Paragraph: Summary of the argument(s) and the author's opinion and/or recommendation(s)

Editar

Follow-up

Have a whole-class discussion about the following topic: If you were to hold a *tertulia* with a group of friends, what other political topics/laws would you want to discuss changing?

En resumen: En este capítulo Vocabulario

Suggestions

- Have students write in Spanish definitions for the words in the list. Then have them create crossword puzzles and use their definitions as cues. Have them exchange and solve each other's puzzles.
- Have students choose one word from the list and use this as the title for a brief composition.
- Ask students the following questions to review the vocabulary.
  1. *¿Cómo se entera Ud. de las noticias? ¿Lee el periódico o mira el noticiero en la tele u oye las noticias en la radio?*
  2. *¿Cree todo lo que lee en la prensa? ¿Cree que los medios de información informan bien al público, por lo general?*

Bright Idea

Suggestion

Have students give words based on the following definitions.

1. *una persona que nace en un país o que se establece permanentemente en un país (el/la ciudadano/a)*
2. *lo que hacían los obreros cuando no están contentos con las condiciones de trabajo (la huelga, la manifestación)*
3. *lo que deben hacer los ciudadanos cuando hay elecciones (votar)*
4. *una pelea armada entre dos o más países (la guerra)*
5. *un sinónimo de responsabilidad u obligación (el deber)*
6. *una frase que se refiere a la radio, la televisión y los periódicos en conjunto (los medios de comunicación)*
7. *las otras personas de nuestra comunidad (los/las demás)*
8. *la acción de aceptar una ley, una regla o una orden (obedecer)*
9. *una persona que representa o gobierna un país de forma hereditaria, no por votación pública (el rey / la reina)*
10. *el grupo de personas que defiende a un país en caso de guerra (el ejército)*

Word Families

En este capítulo

- *el asesinato, asesinar*
- *comunicarse, el medio de comunicación*
- *la dictadura, el/la dictador(a)*
- *la lucha, luchar*
- *las noticias, el noticiero*
- *la política, el/la político/a*
- *el terrorismo, el/la terrorista, el ataque terrorista*

Entre capítulos

- *el choque = chocar (14)*
- *el/la ciudadano/a = la ciudad (3)*
- *comunicarse (con) = las comunicaciones (2), la comunidad (12)*
- *el deber = deber (3)*
- *el derecho = a la derecha de (6)*
- *durar = durante (5)*
- *el ejército = el ejercicio (5)*
- *enterarse (de) = entero (10)*
- *la esperanza = esperar (12, 17)*
- *la estación de radio = la estación de autobuses/trenes (8), la estación de servicio (15)*
- *informar = el informe (14)*
- *el medio de comunicación = el medio de transporte (8)*
- *el servicio militar = servir (5), el servicio (15)*

EN RESUMEN En este capítulo

LearnSmart

Visit **www.connectspanish.com** to practice the vocabulary and grammar points covered in this chapter.

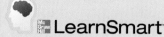

Gramática en breve

48. The Past Subjunctive

Third person plural preterite minus **-on + -a, -as, -a, -amos, -ais, -an**

49. The Conditional

Infinitive + **-ía, -ías, -ía, -íamos, -íais, -ían**
Irregular forms: **dir-, habr-, har-, podr-, pondr-, querr-, sabr-, saldr-, tendr-, vendr-** + *conditional endings*

Vocabulario

Las noticias

el acontecimiento	event, happening
el asesinato	assassination
el choque	collision, crash
la esperanza	hope, wish
la estación de radio	radio station
la guerra	war
la huelga	strike (*labor*)
la lucha	fight, struggle
la manifestación	demonstration, march
el medio de comunicación	medium of communication (*pl.* mass media)
las noticias	news
el noticiero	newscast
la paz (*pl.* **paces**)	peace
la prensa	(print) press; news media
el/la reportero/a	reporter
el/la testigo	witness

Cognados: el ataque (terrorista), la bomba, la erupción, el terrorismo, el/la terrorista, la víctima

Repaso: el blog, el canal (de televisión), el desastre, el Internet, la muerte, el periódico, la radio, la revista, la televisión

asesinar	to assassinate
comunicarse (qu) (con)	to communicate (with)
enterarse (de)	to find out, learn (about)
estar al día	to be up to date
informar	to inform
luchar	to fight
mantener (*like* **tener**)	to maintain, keep
matar	to kill

Repaso: ofrecer (ofrezco), vivir

El gobierno y la responsabilidad cívica

el cargo	(political) office
el centro	center
el/la ciudadano/a	citizen
el deber	responsibility; obligation
el derecho	right
la (des)igualdad	(in)equality
el/la dictador(a)	dictator
la dictadura	dictatorship
el ejército	army
la ley	law
el partido	political party
la política	politics; policy
el/la político/a	politician
el rey / la reina	king/queen
el servicio militar	military service

Cognado: el/la candidato/a, la discriminación

Repaso: los/las demás, la derecha, el gobierno, la izquierda, el soldado / la mujer soldado

durar	to last
postularse (para un cargo / como candidato/a)	to run (for a position / as a candidate)

Cognado: votar

Repaso: ganar, obedecer (obedezco), perder (pierdo)

Vocabulario personal

En resumen En este capítulo ■ 551

La Guinea Ecuatorial

Datos esenciales

Nombre oficial: *República de Guinea Ecuatorial*

Lema: *«Unidad, Paz, Justicia»*

Capital: *Malabo (antiguamente conocida como Santa Isabel), situada en la isla de Bioko (que antes se conocía como Fernando Po)*

Población: *68.200 habitantes*

Composición étnica: *86% fang, 6% bubi, 8% otros*

Jefe de estado actual: *Presidente Teodoro Obiang Nguema Mbasogo, desde 1979*

Forma de gobierno: *república presidencialista dentro de un marco dictatorial*

Lenguas oficiales: *el español, el francés, el portugués; también se hablan lenguas étnicas, como el fang, el bubi y el annobonés*

Moneda: *el franco CFA (Comunidad Francesa de África), la moneda oficial de unos catorce países africanos, la mayoría de los cuales eran colonias francesas (los otros eran colonias españolas y portuguesas)*

Religión: *80% católicos, 4% musulmanes, 7% protestantes, 9% otros*

Las Islas Filipinas

Datos esenciales

Nombre oficial: *República de las Filipinas*

Lema: *«Maka-Diyos, Maka-Tao, Makakalikasan at Makabansa» (Por el amor de Dios, el Hombre, la Naturaleza y el País [filipino])*

Capital: *Manila*

Población: *101 millones de habitantes*

Composición étnica: *28% tagalog, 13% cebuano, muchos otros grupos (primariamente mongoloides)*

Jefe de estado: *Benigno Aquino III, desde 2010, hijo de la primera presidenta del país, Corazón Aquino*

Forma de gobierno: *república presidencialista*

Lenguas oficiales: *el filipino (basado en el tagalog) y el español; se hablan también 170 lenguas locales, incluyendo el cebuano, el pampango y el chabacano (una lengua criolla variante del español)*

Moneda: *el peso filipino*

Religión: *83% católicos, 9% musulmanes, 5% budistas, 3% otros*

LECTURA CULTURAL FINAL

El español en el resto del mundo

Introducción

A lo largo de[a] dieciocho capítulos, se ha presentado en *Puntos de partida* el inmenso y variado mundo hispanohablante, desde[b] los Estados Unidos hasta el Cono Sur, en América, y España, en Europa.

Pero el español es una lengua importante en otros países también. En África, sobrevive[c] bien arraigado[d] en la Guinea Ecuatorial, así como[e] en las ciudades norte-africanas de Ceuta y Melilla, que son territorio español. En Oceanía,* en las islas Filipinas, la lengua española es parte de su herencia[f] colonial, aunque[g] ya no es una lengua oficial en ese país. Y también hay que mencionar al Canadá, país donde hay una creciente[h] inmigración hispanohablante.

[a]*A... Throughout* [b]*from* [c]*it survives* [d]*established* [e]*así... as well as* [f]*heritage* [g]*although* [h]*growing*

The term* **Oceanía *refers to the islands of the tropical Pacific Ocean, including Polynesia, Australia, and New Zealand, as well as the Philippines and other island groups.*

LA GUINEA ECUATORIAL

La Guinea Ecuatorial es uno de los países más pequeños de África, pero también es uno de los más prósperos, debido a los yacimientos[a] de petróleo que se encuentran en su territorio. Fue colonia española desde[b] 1778 hasta 1968, y desde 1844 el español es una de sus lenguas oficiales, además del[c] francés y el portugués.

Aunque[d] tradicionalmente el país no se considera un país hispano, la realidad es que la mayoría de la población habla español, especialmente en la capital, Malabo. El español es también la lengua de varios escritores ecuatoguineanos, que se están abriendo camino[e] en el mundo literario hispanohablante.

La influencia de España en la Guinea Ecuatorial, así como[f] pasó en los países americanos de habla española, fue mucho más allá[g] de lo lingüístico. Es evidente en la religión (ya que[h] en el país existe una inmensa mayoría católica), en el sistema de apellidos que se usa (dos apellidos: primero el[i] del padre y luego el de la madre) y hasta[j] en la comida (entre otros platos, las empanadas).

[a]debido... *due to the fields* [b]*from* [c]además... *in addition to* [d]*Although* [e]que... *who are making a name for themselves* [f]así... *as* [g]más... *beyond* [h]ya... *since* [i]*that* [j]*even*

Una plaza de Malabo, la capital de la Guinea Ecuatorial

LAS ISLAS FILIPINAS

La Universidad de Santo Tomás, fundada por los dominicanos (*Dominican friars*) en 1611

Las islas Filipinas son un archipiélago formado por más de 7000 islas en el Océano Pacífico. Fueron territorio español por más de 300 años. El fin de la colonización española ocurrió en 1898, cuando España cedió[a] el control de las Filipinas a los Estados Unidos, como consecuencia de la Guerra Hispanoamericana. Aunque[b] el español era la primera lengua oficial del país, el uso del español disminuyó[c] con la ocupación estadounidense y se perdió en la gran mayoría de la población. Sin embargo, los nombres y apellidos de muchos filipinos, así como[d] los nombres de muchos lugares y cosas de uso cotidiano[e] son españoles, testimonio de la gran influencia de la lengua española en el país.

La herencia de España ha quedado reflejada[f] también en la cocina filipina, en la que se combinan las influencias española, china y del sudeste asiático. En las islas Filipinas se preparan muchos platos que mantienen el nombre en español y que son adaptaciones de recetas españolas tradicionales, como la paella, el cocido,[g] el lechón asado[h] y la torta, similar a la españolísima tortilla de patatas, por solo nombrar algunos.

[a]*gave up* [b]*Although* [c]*declined* [d]así... *just like* [e]*everyday* [f]ha... *can still be seen reflected* [g]*stew* [h]lechón... *roasted suckling pig*

EL CANADÁ

Cartel (*Poster*) para la *Hispanic Fiesta* de 2010

Se estima que en el Canadá vive hoy entre medio millón y un millón de hispanohablantes, cuya mayoría[a] se concentra en la zona de las ciudades de Toronto y Hamilton. También hay comunidades hispanas importantes en el oeste del país, porque a finales[b] del siglo[c] XIX hubo una ola[d] inmigratoria de argentinos y chilenos a la provincia de Alberta.

Los hispanocanadienses disfrutan de[e] acceso a numeroso medios de comunicación en español. Además,[f] hay en el Canadá varios festivales y eventos que conmemoran la presencia hispana en el país. Uno de los más importantes es la *Hispanic Fiesta*, que se celebra anualmente en el mes de agosto en Toronto. Allí se encuentra comida de todas partes del mundo hispanohablante, se puede escuchar música andina y mexicana, entre otras formas musicales, y ver demostraciones de tango, flamenco y otros bailes.

[a]cuya... *the majority of whom* [b]a... *at the end* [c]*century* [d]*wave* [e]disfrutan... *enjoy* [f]*Besides*

COMPRENSIÓN

1. ¿En qué continentes y regiones del mundo se habla español como lengua oficial?
2. ¿En qué países tiene el español una presencia actual o histórica muy importante, aunque (*although*) no es la lengua oficial?
3. ¿Qué colonia española se independizó de España en el siglo (*century*) XX?
4. En general, ¿en qué se nota la influencia española en la Guinea Ecuatorial, las Filipinas y el Canadá?

El Canadá

Datos esenciales

Nombre oficial: *Canadá*
Lema: *«Desidereantes Meiorem Patriam» (Ellos desean una patria mejor, en latín)*
Capital: *Ottawa*
Población: *34 millones de habitantes*
Composición étnica: *28% de origen británico; 23% de origen francés; 15% de otros países europeos; 2% indígenas americanos; 44% otros*
Jefe de estado: *Isabel II de Inglaterra, desde 1952, representada por el gobernador general David Johnston, desde 2010*
Jefe de gobierno: *Primer Ministro Stephen Harper, desde 2006*
Forma de gobierno: *democracia parlamentaria y monarquía constitucional, cuya cabeza es la reina de Inglaterra*
Lenguas oficiales: *el inglés y el francés; se hablan también otras lenguas indígenas y lenguas traídas por inmigrantes*
Moneda: *el dólar canadiense*
Religión: *43% católicos, 23% protestantes, 16% ninguna, 12% sin especificar, 4% otros cristianos, 2% musulmanes*

Comprensión

Answers

__1.__ en América del Norte y del Sur, Europa, África y Oceanía __2.__ en las islas Filipinas y el Canadá __3.__ la Guinea Ecuatorial, en 1968 __4.__ en la literatura, la religión, los nombres de las personas y de cosas de uso cotidiano, la comida, la música

Multimedia: Internet

Have students choose a country from those presented in this section and investigate it more in depth on the Internet. Then have them report their findings to the class or submit a brief report to you in writing.

APPENDIX 1 Glossary of Grammatical Terms

ADJECTIVE A word that describes a noun or pronoun.	una casa **grande** *a **big** house* *Ana* es **inteligente.** *Ana is **smart.***
Demonstrative adjective An adjective that points out a particular noun.	**este** chico, **esos** libros, **aquellas** personas ***this** boy, **those** books, **those** people* (*over there*)
Interrogative adjective An adjective used to form questions.	¿**Qué** cuaderno? ***Which** notebook?* ¿**Cuáles** son los carteles que buscas? ***What* (*Which*)** *posters are you looking for?*
Possessive adjective (unstressed) An adjective that indicates possession or a special relationship.	**sus** coches ***their** cars* **mi** hermana ***my** sister*
Possessive adjective (stressed) An adjective that more emphatically describes possession.*	Es **una** amiga **mía.** *She's **my** friend. / She's a friend **of mine.*** Es **un** coche **suyo.** *It's **her** car. / It's a car **of hers.***
ADVERB A word that describes an adjective, a verb, or another adverb.	Roberto es **muy** alto. *Roberto is **very** tall.* María escribe **bien.** *María writes **well.*** Van **demasiado** rápido. *They are going **too** quickly.*
ARTICLE A determiner that sets off a noun. **Definite article** An article that indicates a specific noun.	**el** país ***the** country* **la** silla ***the** chair* **las** mujeres ***the** women*
Indefinite article An article that indicates an unspecified noun.	**un** chico ***a** boy* **una** ciudad ***a** city* **unas** zanahorias (***some***) *carrots*

*See Appendix 3 on page A-7 for more information.

CLAUSE A construction that contains a subject and a verb.

Main (Independent) clause A clause that can stand on its own because it expresses a complete thought.

Busco una muchacha.
I'm looking for a girl.

Si yo fuera rica, **me compraría una casa.**
If I were rich, ***I would buy a house.***

Subordinate (Dependent) clause A clause that cannot stand on its own because it does not express a complete thought.

Busco a la muchacha **que juega al tenis.**
I'm looking for the girl ***who plays tennis.***

Si yo fuera rica, me compraría una casa.
If I were rich, *I would buy a house.*

COMPARATIVE The form of adjectives and adverbs used to compare two nouns or actions.

Luis es **menos hablador que** Julián.
Luis is ***less talkative than*** *Julián.*

Luis corre **más rápido que** Julián.
Luis runs ***faster than*** *Julián.*

CONJUGATION The different forms of a verb for a particular tense or mood. A present indicative conjugation:

(yo) **hablo**	(nosotros/as) **hablamos**
(tú) **hablas**	(vosotros/as) **habláis**
(Ud.) **habla**	(Uds.) **hablan**
(él/ella) **habla**	(ellos/as) **hablan**
I speak	*we speak*
you (fam. sing.) speak	*you (fam. pl.) speak*
you (form. sing.) speak	*you (pl. fam., form.) speak*
he/she speaks	*they speak*

CONJUNCTION An expression that connects words, phrases, or clauses.

Cristóbal **y** Diana
Cristóbal ***and*** *Diana*

Hace frío, **pero** hace buen tiempo.
It's cold, ***but*** *it's nice out.*

DIRECT OBJECT The noun or pronoun that receives the action of a verb.

Veo **la caja.**
I see ***the box.***

La veo.
I see ***it.***

GENDER A grammatical category of words. In Spanish, there are two genders: masculine and feminine.

	MASCULINE	FEMININE
ARTICLES AND NOUNS:	**el** disco compacto	**la** cinta
PRONOUNS:	**él**	**ella**
ADJECTIVES:	bonit**o**, list**o**	bonit**a**, list**a**
PAST PARTICIPLES:	El informe está **escrito.**	La composición está **escrita.**

IMPERATIVE *See* Mood.

IMPERFECT (*IMPERFECTO*) In Spanish, a verb tense that expresses a past action with no specific beginning or ending.

Nadábamos con frecuencia.
We ***used to swim*** *often.*

IMPERSONAL CONSTRUCTION One that contains a third person singular verb but no specific subject in Spanish. The subject of English impersonal constructions is generally *it.*	**Es importante** que... ***It is important*** *that...* **Es necesario** que... ***It is necessary*** *that...*
INDICATIVE *See* Mood.	
INDIRECT OBJECT The noun or pronoun that indicates *for who(m)* or *to who(m)* an action is performed. In Spanish, the indirect object pronoun must always be included, even when the indirect object is explicitly stated as a noun.	Marcos **le** da el suéter **a Raquel.** / Marcos **le** da el suéter. *Marcos gives the sweater* ***to Raquel.*** */ Marcos gives* ***her*** *the sweater.*
INFINITIVE The form of a verb introduced in English by *to: to play, to sell, to come.* In Spanish dictionaries, the infinitive form of the verb appears as the main entry.	Luisa va a **comprar** un periódico. *Luisa is going* ***to buy*** *a newspaper.*
MOOD A set of categories for verbs indicating the attitude of the speaker toward what he or she is saying.	
Imperative mood A verb form expressing a command.	¡**Ten** cuidado! ***Be*** *careful!*
Indicative mood A verb form denoting actions or states considered facts.	**Voy** a la biblioteca. ***I'm going*** *to the library.*
Subjunctive mood A verb form, uncommon in English, used in Spanish primarily in subordinate clauses after expressions of desire, doubt, or emotion. Spanish constructions with the subjunctive have many possible English equivalents.	Quiero que **vayas** inmediatamente. *I want you* ***to go*** *immediately.*
NOUN A word that denotes a person, place, thing, or idea. Proper nouns are capitalized names.	**abogado, ciudad, periódico, libertad, Luisa** ***lawyer, city, newspaper, freedom, Luisa***
NUMBER	
Cardinal number A number that expresses an amount.	**una** silla, **tres** estudiantes ***one*** *chair,* ***three*** *students*
Ordinal number A number that indicates position in a series.	la **primera** silla, el **tercer** estudiante *the* ***first*** *chair, the* ***third*** *student*
PAST PARTICIPLE The form of a verb used in compound tenses (*see* Perfect Tenses). Used with forms of *to have* or *to be* in English and with **ser, estar,** or **haber** in Spanish.	**comido, terminado, perdido** ***eaten, finished, lost***

PERFECT TENSES Compound tenses that combine the auxiliary verb **haber** with a past participle.

Present perfect indicative This form uses a present indicative form of **haber.** The use of the Spanish present perfect generally parallels that of the English present perfect.

No **he viajado** nunca a México.
I've *never* ***traveled*** *to Mexico.*

Past perfect indicative This form uses **haber** in the imperfect tense to talk about something that had or had not been done before a given time in the past.

Antes de 2008, **no había estudiado** español.
Before 2008, ***I hadn't studied*** *Spanish.*

Present perfect subjunctive This form uses the present subjunctive of **haber** to express a present perfect action when the subjunctive is required.

¡Ojalá que Marisa **haya llegado** a su destino!
I hope (that) Marisa ***has arrived*** *at her destination!*

PERSON The form of a pronoun or verb that indicates the person involved in an action.

	SINGULAR	PLURAL
FIRST PERSON:	***I*** **/ yo**	***we*** **/ nosotros/as**
SECOND PERSON:	***you*** **/ tú, Ud.**	***you*** **/ vosotros/as, Uds.**
THIRD PERSON:	***he, she*** **/ él, ella**	***they*** **/ ellos, ellas**

PREPOSITION A word or phrase that specifies the relationship of one word (usually a noun or pronoun) to another. The relationship is usually spatial or temporal.

a la escuela
to *school*

cerca de la biblioteca
near *the library*

con él
with *him*

antes de la medianoche
before *midnight*

PRESENT PARTICIPLE The verb form that ends in *-ing* in English. Used with forms of *to be* in English and with **estar** in Spanish to form the progressive.

hablando, comiendo, pidiendo
speaking, eating, asking

PRETERITE (*PRETÉRITO*) In Spanish, a verb tense that expresses a past action with a specific beginning and ending.

Salí para Roma el jueves.
I left *for Rome on Thursday.*

PROGRESSIVE The verb that expresses continuing or developing action.

Julio **está durmiendo** ahora.
Julio ***is sleeping*** *now.*

Anita **estaba comiendo** cuando sonó el teléfono.
Anita ***was eating*** *when the phone rang.*

PRONOUN A word that refers to a person (I, you) or that is used in place of one or more nouns.

Demonstrative pronoun A pronoun that singles out a particular person, place, thing, or idea.

Aquí están dos libros. **Este** es interesante, pero **ese** es aburrido.
Here are two books. ***This one*** *is interesting, but* ***that one*** *is boring.*

Interrogative pronoun A pronoun used to ask a question.

¿**Quién** es él?
Who *is he?*

¿**Qué** prefieres?
What *do you prefer?*

Object pronoun A pronoun that replaces a direct object noun or an indirect object noun. Both direct and indirect object pronouns can be used together in the same sentence.	Si **me** llamas más tarde, **te** doy el número de teléfono de David. *If you call **me** later, I'll give **you** David's phone number.*
	Veo a **Alejandro. Lo** veo. *I see **Alejandro.** I see **him.***
However, when the pronouns **le** or **les** appear before **lo, la, los,** or **las, le** or **les** changes to **se.**	**Le** doy **el libro a Juana.** *I give the book **to Juana.***
	Se lo doy (a ella). *I give **it** to **her.***
Reflexive pronoun A pronoun that represents the same person as the subject of the verb.	**Me** miro en el espejo. *I look at **myself** in the mirror.*
Relative pronoun A pronoun that introduces a dependent clause and denotes a noun already mentioned.	El hombre con **quien** hablaba era mi vecino. *The man with **whom** I was talking was my neighbor.*
	Aquí está el bolígrafo **que** buscas. *Here is the pen (**that**) you're looking for.*
Subject pronoun A pronoun representing the person, place, thing, or idea performing the action of a verb.	**Lucas y Julia** juegan al tenis. ***Lucas and Julia** are playing tennis.*
	Ellos juegan al tenis. ***They** are playing tennis.*
SUBJECT The word(s) denoting the person, place, thing, or idea performing an action or existing in a state.	**Sara** trabaja aquí. ***Sara** works here.*
	¡**Buenos Aires** es una ciudad magnífica! ***Buenos Aires** is a great city!*
	Mis **libros** y mi **computadora** están allí. *My **books** and my **computer** are over there.*
SUBJUNCTIVE *See* Mood.	
SUPERLATIVE The form of adjectives or adverbs used to compare three or more nouns or actions. In English, the superlative is marked by *most, least,* or *-est.*	Escogí **el vestido más caro.** *I chose **the most expensive** dress.*
	Ana es **la persona menos habladora** que conozco. *Ana is **the least talkative person** I know.*
TENSE The form of a verb indicating time: present, past, or future.	Raúl **era, es** y siempre **será** mi mejor amigo. *Raúl **was, is,** and always **will be** my best friend.*
VERB A word that reports an action or state.	Maribel **llegó.** *Maribel **arrived.***
	La niña **estaba** cansada. *The child **was** tired.*
Auxiliary verb A verb in conjuction with a participle to convey distinctions of tense and mood. In Spanish, one auxiliary verb is **haber.**	**Han** viajado por todas partes del mundo. *They **have** traveled everywhere in the world.*
Reflexive verb A verb whose subject and object are the same.	Juan **se corta** la cara cuando **se afeita.** *Juan **cuts himself** when he **shaves** (**himself**).*

APPENDIX 2 Using Adjectives as Nouns

Nominalization means using an adjective as a noun. In Spanish, adjectives can be nominalized in a number of ways, all of which involve dropping the noun that accompanies the adjective, then using the adjective in combination with an article or other word. One kind of adjective, the demonstrative, can simply be used alone. In most cases, these usages parallel those of English, although the English equivalent may be phrased differently from the Spanish.

Article + Adjective

Simply omit the noun from an *article + noun + adjective* phrase.

el **libro** azul ⟶ **el azul** (*the blue one*)
la **hermana** casada ⟶ **la casada** (*the married one*)
el **señor** mexicano ⟶ **el mexicano** (*the Mexican one*)
los **pantalones** baratos ⟶ **los baratos** (*the inexpensive ones*)

You can also drop the first noun in an *article + noun +* **de** *+ noun* phrase.

la **casa** de Julio ⟶ **la de Julio** (*Julio's*)
los **coches** del Sr. Martínez ⟶ **los del Sr. Martínez** (*Mr. Martínez's*)

In both cases, the construction is used to refer to a noun that has already been mentioned. The English equivalent uses *one* or *ones,* or a possessive without the noun.

— ¿Necesitas el **libro** grande?
— No. Necesito **el pequeño.**
"Do you need the big book?"
"No. I need the small one."

— ¿Usamos el **coche** de Ernesto?
— No. Usemos **el de Ana.**
"Shall we use Ernesto's car?"
"No. Let's use Ana's."

Note that in the preceding examples the noun is mentioned in the first part of the exchange (**libro, coche**) but not in the response or rejoinder.

Note also that a demonstrative can be used to nominalize an adjective: **este rojo** (*this red one*), **esos azules** (*those blue ones*).

Lo + Adjective

As seen in **Capítulo 11, lo** combines with the masculine singular form of an adjective to describe general qualities or characteristics. The English equivalent is expressed with words like *part* or *thing.*

lo mejor	*the best thing* (*part*), *what's best*
lo mismo	*the same thing*
lo cómico	*the funny thing* (*part*), *what's funny*

Article + Stressed Possessive Adjective

The stressed possessive adjectives—but not the unstressed possessives—can be used as possessive pronouns: **la maleta suya** ⟶ **la suya.** The article and the possessive form agree in gender and number with the noun to which they refer.

Este es mi **banco.** ¿Dónde está **el suyo**?
This is my bank. Where is yours?

Sus **bebidas** están preparadas; **las nuestras,** no.
Their drinks are ready; ours aren't.

No es la **maleta** de Juan; es **la mía.**
It isn't Juan's suitcase; it's mine.

Note that the definite article is frequently omitted after forms of **ser: ¿Esa maleta? Es suya.**

Demonstrative Pronouns

The demonstrative adjective can be used alone, without a noun. An accent mark can be added to the demonstrative pronoun (**éste, ése, aquél**) to distinguish it from the demonstrative adjectives if context does not make meaning clear.

Necesito este diccionario y **ese** (**ése**).
I need this dictionary and that one.

Estas señoras y **aquellas** (**aquéllas**) son las hermanas de Sara, ¿no?
These women and those (*over there*) *are Sara's sisters, aren't they?*

It is acceptable in modern Spanish, according to the **Real Academia Española,** to omit the accent on demonstrative pronouns when context makes the meaning clear and no ambiguity is possible.

APPENDIX 3 More About Stressed Possessives

When in English you would emphasize the possessive with your voice or with *of mine* (*of yours, of his*, and so on), you will use the *stressed possessives* (**las formas tónicas de los posesivos**) in Spanish. As the term implies, they are more emphatic than the *unstressed forms* (**las formas átonas de los posesivos**).

The stressed forms follow the noun, and the noun *must* be preceded by a definite or indefinite article or by a demonstrative adjective. The stressed forms agree with the noun modified in number and gender. In the following examples, boldface italic type in the English translations indicates voice stress.

Es **su** perro.	*It's her dog.*

But:

Es **un** perro **suyo.**	*It's **her** dog (i.e., not ours). It's a dog of hers.*
El perro **suyo** se llama King.	***Her** dog is named King.*
Ese perro **suyo** es bravo.	*That dog of hers is fierce.*

Es **su** maleta.	*It's **his** suitcase.*

But:

Es **una** maleta **suya.**	*It's **his** suitcase.*
La maleta **suya** está perdida.	***His** suitcase (i.e., not ours) is lost.*
Esa maleta **suya** está perdida.	*That suitcase of his is lost.*

The stressed possessives are often used as nouns. See **Appendix 2: Using Adjectives as Nouns.**

APPENDIX 4 Additional Perfect Forms (Indicative and Subjunctive)

As you know, some indicative verb tenses have corresponding perfect forms in the indicative and subjunctive moods. Here is the present tense system.

el presente:	yo hablo, como, pongo
el presente perfecto:	yo he hablado, comido, puesto
el presente perfecto de subjuntivo:	yo haya hablado, comido, puesto

Other indicative forms that you have learned also have corresponding perfect indicative and subjunctive forms. Here are the most important ones, along with examples of their use. In each case, the tense or mood is formed with the appropriate form of **haber.**

El pluscuamperfecto de subjuntivo

yo:	hubiera hablado, comido, vivido, *and so on.*
tú:	hubieras hablado, comido, vivido, *and so on.*
Ud./él/ella:	hubiera hablado, comido, vivido, *and so on.*
nosotros:	hubiéramos hablado, comido, vivido, *and so on.*
vosotros:	hubierais hablado, comido, vivido, *and so on.*
Uds./ellos/ellas:	hubieran hablado, comido, vivido, *and so on.*

These forms correspond to **el presente perfecto de indicativo** (**Capítulo 15**). These forms are most frequently used in **si** clause sentences, along with the conditional perfect. See examples in the second column.

El futuro perfecto

yo:	habré hablado, comido, vivido, *and so on.*
tú:	habrás hablado, comido, vivido, *and so on.*
Ud./él/ella:	habrá hablado, comido, vivido, *and so on.*
nosotros:	habremos hablado, comido, vivido, *and so on.*
vosotros:	habréis hablado, comido, vivido, *and so on.*
Uds./ellos/ellas:	habrán hablado, comido, vivido, *and so on.*

These forms correspond to **el futuro** (**Capítulo 17**) and are most frequently used to tell what *will have already happened* at some point in the future. (In contrast, the future is used to tell what *will happen.*)

Mañana **hablaré** con Miguel.
I'll speak with Miguel tomorrow.

Para las tres, ya **habré hablado** con Miguel.
By 3:00, I'll already have spoken to Miguel.

El año que viene **visitaremos** a los nietos.
We'll visit our grandchildren next year.

Para las Navidades, ya **habremos visitado** a los nietos.
We'll already have visited our grandchildren by Christmas.

El condicional perfecto

yo:	habría hablado, comido, vivido, *and so on.*
tú:	habrías hablado, comido, vivido, *and so on.*
Ud./él/ella:	habría hablado, comido, vivido, *and so on.*
nosotros:	habríamos hablado, comido, vivido, *and so on.*
vosotros:	habríais hablado, comido, vivido, *and so on.*
Uds./ellos/ellas:	habrían hablado, comido, vivido, *and so on.*

These forms correspond to **el condicional** (**Capítulo 18**). These forms are frequently used to tell what *would have happened* at some point in the past. (In contrast, the conditional tells what one *would do.*)

Yo **hablaría** con Miguel.
I would speak with Miguel (if I were you, at some point in the future).

Yo **habría hablado** con Miguel.
I would have spoken with Miguel (if I had been you, at some point in the past).

***Si* Clause: Sentences About the Past**

You have learned (**Capítulo 18**) to use the past subjunctive and conditional to speculate about the present in **si** clause sentences: what *would happen* if a particular event *were* (or *were not*) to occur.

Si **tuviera** el tiempo, **aprendería** francés.
If I had the time, I would learn French.

The perfect forms of the past subjunctive and the conditional are used to speculate about the past: what *would have happened* if a particular event *had* (or *had not*) occurred.

En la escuela superior, si **hubiera tenido** el tiempo, **habría aprendido** francés.
In high school, if I had had the time, I would have learned French.

APPENDIX 5 Verbs

A. Regular Verbs: Simple Tenses

Infinitive Present Participle Past Participle	INDICATIVE					SUBJUNCTIVE		IMPERATIVE
	Present	Imperfect	Preterite	Future	Conditional	Present	Imperfect	
hablar hablando hablado	hablo hablas habla hablamos habláis hablan	hablaba hablabas hablaba hablábamos hablabais hablaban	hablé hablaste habló hablamos hablasteis hablaron	hablaré hablarás hablará hablaremos hablaréis hablarán	hablaría hablarías hablaría hablaríamos hablaríais hablarían	hable hables hable hablemos habléis hablen	hablara hablaras hablara habláramos hablarais hablaran	habla tú, no hables hable Ud. hablemos hablad, no habléis hablen
comer comiendo comido	como comes come comemos coméis comen	comía comías comía comíamos comíais comían	comí comiste comió comimos comisteis comieron	comeré comerás comerá comeremos comeréis comerán	comería comerías comería comeríamos comeríais comerían	coma comas coma comamos comáis coman	comiera comieras comiera comiéramos comierais comieran	come tú, no comas coma Ud. comamos comed, no comáis coman
vivir viviendo vivido	vivo vives vive vivimos vivís viven	vivía vivías vivía vivíamos vivíais vivían	viví viviste vivió vivimos vivisteis vivieron	viviré vivirás vivirá viviremos viviréis vivirán	viviría vivirías viviría viviríamos viviríais vivirían	viva vivas viva vivamos viváis vivan	viviera vivieras viviera viviéramos vivierais vivieran	vive tú, no vivas viva Ud. vivamos vivid, no viváis vivan

B. Regular Verbs: Perfect Tenses

INDICATIVE										SUBJUNCTIVE			
Present Perfect		Past Perfect		Preterite Perfect		Future Perfect		Conditional Perfect		Present Perfect		Past Perfect	
he		había		hube		habré		habría		haya		hubiera	
has	hablado	habías	hablado	hubiste	hablado	habrás	hablado	habrías	hablado	hayas	hablado	hubieras	hablado
ha	comido	había	comido	hubo	comido	habrá	comido	habría	comido	haya	comido	hubiera	comido
hemos	vivido	habíamos	vivido	hubimos	vivido	habremos	vivido	habríamos	vivido	hayamos	vivido	hubiéramos	vivido
habéis		habíais		hubisteis		habréis		habríais		hayáis		hubierais	
han		habían		hubieron		habrán		habrían		hayan		hubieran	

C. Irregular Verbs

Infinitive Present Participle Past Participle	INDICATIVE					SUBJUNCTIVE		IMPERATIVE
	Present	Imperfect	Preterite	Future	Conditional	Present	Imperfect	
andar andando andado	ando andas anda andamos andáis andan	andaba andabas andaba andábamos andabais andaban	anduve anduviste anduvo anduvimos anduvisteis anduvieron	andaré andarás andará andaremos andaréis andarán	andaría andarías andaría andaríamos andaríais andarían	ande andes ande andemos andéis anden	anduviera anduvieras anduviera anduviéramos anduvierais anduvieran	anda tú, no andes ande Ud. andemos andad, no andéis anden
caber cabiendo cabido	quepo cabes cabe cabemos cabéis caben	cabía cabías cabía cabíamos cabíais cabían	cupe cupiste cupo cupimos cupisteis cupieron	cabré cabrás cabrá cabremos cabréis cabrán	cabría cabrías cabría cabríamos cabríais cabrían	quepa quepas quepa quepamos quepáis quepan	cupiera cupieras cupiera cupiéramos cupierais cupieran	cabe tú, no quepas quepa Ud. quepamos cabed, no quepáis quepan

C. Irregular Verbs (*continued*)

Infinitive Present Participle Past Participle	INDICATIVE					SUBJUNCTIVE		IMPERATIVE
	Present	Imperfect	Preterite	Future	Conditional	Present	Imperfect	
caer cayendo caído	caigo caes cae caemos caéis caen	caía caías caía caíamos caíais caían	caí caíste cayó caímos caísteis cayeron	caeré caerás caerá caeremos caeréis caerán	caería caerías caería caeríamos caeríais caerían	caiga caigas caiga caigamos caigáis caigan	cayera cayeras cayera cayéramos cayerais cayeran	cae tú, no caigas caiga Ud. caigamos caed, no caigáis caigan
creer creyendo creído	creo crees cree creemos creéis creen	creía creías creía creíamos creías creían	creí creíste creyó creímos creísteis creyeron	creeré creerás creerá creeremos creeréis creerán	creería creerías creería creeíamos creeríais creerían	crea creas crea creamos creáis crean	creyera creyeras creyera creyéramos creyerais creyeran	cree tú, no creas crea Ud. creamos creed, no creáis crean
dar dando dado	doy das da damos dais dan	daba dabas daba dábamos dabais daban	di diste dio dimos disteis dieron	daré darás dará daremos daréis darán	daría darías daría daríamos daríais darían	dé des dé demos deis den	diera dieras diera diéramos dierais dieran	da tú, no des dé Ud. demos dad, no deis den
decir diciendo dicho	digo dices dice decimos decís dicen	decía decías decía decíamos decíais decían	dije dijiste dijo dijimos dijisteis dijeron	diré dirás dirá diremos diréis dirán	diría dirías diría diríamos diríais dirían	diga digas diga digamos digáis digan	dijera dijeras dijera dijéramos dijerais dijeran	di tú, no digas diga Ud. digamos decid, no digáis digan

C. Irregular Verbs (*continued*)

Infinitive Present Participle Past Participle	INDICATIVE					SUBJUNCTIVE		IMPERATIVE
	Present	Imperfect	Preterite	Future	Conditional	Present	Imperfect	
estar	estoy	estaba	estuve	estaré	estaría	esté	estuviera	está tú,
estando	estás	estabas	estuviste	estarás	estarías	estés	estuvieras	no estés
estado	está	estaba	estuvo	estará	estaría	esté	estuviera	esté Ud.
	estamos	estábamos	estuvimos	estaremos	estaríamos	estemos	estuviéramos	estemos
	estáis	estabais	estuvisteis	estaréis	estaríais	estéis	estuvierais	estad, no
	están	estaban	estuvieron	estarán	estarían	estén	estuviera	estéis
								estén
haber	he	había	hube	habré	habría	haya	hubiera	
habiendo	has	habías	hubiste	habrás	habrías	hayas	hubieras	
habido	ha	había	hubo	habrá	habría	haya	hubiera	
	hemos	habíamos	hubimos	habremos	habríamos	hayamos	hubiéramos	
	habéis	habíais	hubisteis	habréis	habríais	hayáis	hubierais	
	han	habían	hubieron	habrán	habrían	hayan	hubieran	
hacer	hago	hacía	hice	haré	haría	haga	hiciera	haz tú, no
haciendo	haces	hacías	hiciste	harás	harías	hagas	hicieras	hagas
hecho	hace	hacía	hizo	hará	haría	haga	hiciera	haga Ud.
	hacemos	hacíamos	hicimos	haremos	haríamos	hagamos	hiciéramos	hagamos
	hacéis	hacíais	hicisteis	haréis	haríais	hagáis	hicierais	haced, no
	hacen	hacían	hicieron	harán	harían	hagan	hicieran	hagáis
								hagan
ir	voy	iba	fui	iré	iría	vaya	fuera	ve tú, no
yendo	vas	ibas	fuiste	irás	irías	vayas	fueras	vayas
ido	va	iba	fue	irá	iría	vaya	fuera	vaya Ud.
	vamos	íbamos	fuimos	iremos	iríamos	vayamos	fuéramos	vayamos
	vais	ibais	fuisteis	iréis	iríais	vayáis	fuerais	id, no
	van	iban	fueron	irán	irían	vayan	fueran	vayáis
								vayan

C. Irregular Verbs (*continued*)

Infinitive Present Participle Past Participle	INDICATIVE					SUBJUNCTIVE		IMPERATIVE
	Present	Imperfect	Preterite	Future	Conditional	Present	Imperfect	
oír oyendo oído	oigo oyes oye oímos oís oyen	oía oías oía oíamos oíais oían	oí oíste oyó oímos oísteis oyeron	oiré oirás oirá oiremos oiréis oirán	oiría oirías oiría oiríamos oiríais oirían	oiga oigas oiga oigamos oigáis oigan	oyera oyeras oyera oyéramos oyerais oyeran	oye tú, no oigas oiga Ud. oigamos oíd, no oigáis oigan
poder pudiendo podido	puedo puedes puede podemos podéis pueden	podía podías podía podíamos podíais podían	pude pudiste pudo pudimos pudisteis pudieron	podré podrás podrá podremos podréis podrán	podría podrías podría podríamos podríais podrían	pueda puedas pueda podamos podáis puedan	pudiera pudieras pudiera pudiéramos pudierais pudieran	
poner poniendo puesto	pongo pones pone ponemos ponéis ponen	ponía ponías ponía poníamos poníais ponían	puse pusiste puso pusimos pusisteis pusieron	pondré pondrás pondrá pondremos pondréis pondrán	pondría pondrías pondría pondríamos pondríais pondrían	ponga pongas ponga pongamos pongáis pongan	pusiera pusieras pusiera pusiéramos pusierais pusieran	pon tú, no pongas ponga Ud. pongamos poned, no pongáis pongan
querer queriendo querido	quiero quieres quiere queremos queréis quieren	quería querías quería queríamos queríais querían	quise quisiste quiso quisimos quisisteis quisieron	querré querrás querrá querremos querréis querrán	querría querrías querría querríamos querríais querrían	quiera quieras quiera queramos queráis quieran	quisiera quisieras quisiera quisiéramos quisierais quisieran	quiere tú, no quieras quiera Ud. queramos quered, no queráis quieran

C. Irregular Verbs (*continued*)

Infinitive Present Participle Past Participle	INDICATIVE					SUBJUNCTIVE		IMPERATIVE
	Present	Imperfect	Preterite	Future	Conditional	Present	Imperfect	
saber sabiendo sabido	sé sabes sabe sabemos sabéis saben	sabía sabías sabía sabíamos sabíais sabían	supe supiste supo supimos supisteis supieron	sabré sabrás sabrá sabremos sabréis sabrán	sabría sabrías sabría sabríamos sabríais sabrían	sepa sepas sepa sepamos sepáis sepan	supiera supieras supiera supiéramos supierais supieran	sabe tú, no sepas sepa Ud. sepamos sabed, no sepáis sepan
salir saliendo salido	salgo sales sale salimos salís salen	salía salías salía salíamos salíais salían	salí saliste salió salimos salisteis salieron	saldré saldrás saldrá saldremos saldréis saldrán	saldría saldrías saldría saldríamos saldríais saldrían	salga salgas salga salgamos salgáis salgan	saliera salieras saliera saliéramos salierais salieran	sal tú, no salgas salga Ud. salgamos salid, no salgáis salgan
ser siendo sido	soy eres es somos sois son	era eras era éramos erais eran	fui fuiste fue fuimos fuisteis fueron	seré serás será seremos seréis serán	sería serías sería seríamos seríais serían	sea seas sea seamos seáis sean	fuera fueras fuera fuéramos fuerais fueran	sé tú, no seas sea Ud. seamos sed, no seáis sean
tener teniendo tenido	tengo tienes tiene tenemos tenéis tienen	tenía tenías tenía teníamos teníais tenían	tuve tuviste tuvo tuvimos tuvisteis tuvieron	tendré tendrás tendrá tendremos tendréis tendrán	tendría tendrías tendría tendríamos tendríais tendrían	tenga tengas tenga tengamos tengáis tengan	tuviera tuvieras tuviera tuviéramos tuvierais tuvieran	ten tú, no tengas tenga Ud. tengamos tened, no tengáis tengan

C. Irregular Verbs (*continued*)

Infinitive Present Participle Past Participle	INDICATIVE					SUBJUNCTIVE		IMPERATIVE
	Present	Imperfect	Preterite	Future	Conditional	Present	Imperfect	
traer trayendo traído	traigo traes trae traemos traéis traen	traía traías traía traíamos traíais traían	traje trajiste trajo trajimos trajisteis trajeron	traeré traerás traerá traeremos traeréis traerán	traería traerías traería traeríamos traeríais traerían	traiga traigas traiga traigamos traigáis traigan	trajera trajeras trajera trajéramos trajerais trajeran	trae tú, no traigas traiga Ud. traigamos traed, no traigáis traigan
venir viniendo venido	vengo vienes viene venimos venís vienen	venía venías venía veníamos veníais venían	vine viniste vino vinimos vinisteis vinieron	vendré vendrás vendrá vendremos vendréis vendrán	vendría vendrías vendría vendríamos vendríais vendrían	venga vengas venga vengamos vengáis vengan	viniera vinieras viniera viniéramos vinierais vinieran	ven tú, no vengas venga Ud. vengamos venid, no vengáis vengan
ver viendo visto	veo ves ve vemos veis ven	veía veías veía veíamos veíais veían	vi viste vio vimos visteis vieron	veré verás verá veremos veréis verán	vería verías vería veríamos veríais verían	vea veas vea veamos veáis vean	viera vieras viera viéramos vierais vieran	ve tú, no veas vea Ud. veamos ved, no veáis vean

D. Stem-Changing and Spelling Change Verbs

Infinitive Present Participle Past Participle	INDICATIVE					SUBJUNCTIVE		IMPERATIVE
	Present	Imperfect	Preterite	Future	Conditional	Present	Imperfect	
pensar (pienso) pensando pensado	pienso piensas piensa pensamos pensáis piensan	pensaba pensabas pensaba pensábamos pensabais pensaban	pensé pensaste pensó pensamos pensasteis pensaron	pensaré pensarás pensará pensaremos pensaréis pensarán	pensaría pensarías pensaría pensaríamos pensaríais pensarían	piense pienses piense pensemos penséis piensen	pensara pensaras pensara pensáramos pensarais pensaran	piensa tú, no pienses piense Ud. pensemos pensad, no penséis piensen
volver (vuelvo) volviendo vuelto	vuelvo vuelves vuelve volvemos volvéis vuelven	volvía volvías volvía volvíamos volvíais volvían	volví volviste volvió volvimos volvisteis volvieron	volveré volverás volverá volveremos volveréis volverán	volvería volverías volvería volveríamos volveríais volverían	vuelva vuelvas vuelva volvamos volváis vuelvan	volviera volvieras volviera volviéramos volvierais volvieran	vuelve tú, no vuelvas vuelva Ud. volvamos volved, no volváis vuelvan
dormir (duermo) (u) durmiendo dormido	duermo duermes duerme dormimos dormís duermen	dormía dormías dormía dormíamos dormíais dormían	dormí dormiste durmió dormimos dormisteis durmieron	dormiré dormirás dormirá dormiremos dormiréis dormirán	dormiría dormirías dormiría dormiríamos dormiríais dormirían	duerma duermas duerma durmamos durmáis duerman	durmiera durmieras durmiera durmiéramos durmierais durmieran	duerme tú, no duermas duerma Ud. durmamos dormid, no durmáis duerman
sentir (siento) (i) sintiendo sentido	siento sientes siente sentimos sentís sienten	sentía sentías sentía sentíamos sentíais sentían	sentí sentiste sintió sentimos sentisteis sintieron	sentiré sentirás sentirá sentiremos sentiréis sentirán	sentiría sentirías sentiría sentiríamos sentiríais sentirían	sienta sientas sienta sintamos sintáis sientan	sintiera sintieras sintiera sintiéramos sintierais sintieran	siente tú, no sientas sienta Ud. sintamos sentid, no sintáis sientan
pedir (pido) (i) pidiendo pedido	pido pides pide pedimos pedís piden	pedía pedías pedía pedíamos pedíais pedían	pedí pediste pidió pedimos pedisteis pidieron	pediré pedirás pedirá pediremos pediréis pedirán	pediría pedirías pediría pediríamos pediríais pedirían	pida pidas pida pidamos pidáis pidan	pidiera pidieras pidiera pidiéramos pidierais pidieran	pide tú, no pidas pida Ud. pidamos pedid, no pidáis pidan

D. Stem-Changing and Spelling Change Verbs (*continued*)

Infinitive Present Participle Past Participle	INDICATIVE					SUBJUNCTIVE		IMPERATIVE
	Present	Imperfect	Preterite	Future	Conditional	Present	Imperfect	
reír (río) (i) riendo reído	río ríes ríe reímos reís ríen	reía reías reía reíamos reíais reían	reí reíste rio reímos reísteis rieron	reiré reirás reirá reiremos reiréis reirán	reiría reirías reiría reiríamos reiríais reirían	ría rías ría riamos riáis rían	riera rieras riera riéramos rierais rieran	ríe tú, no rías ría Ud. riamos reíd, no riáis rían
seguir (sigo) (i) siguiendo seguido	sigo sigues sigue seguimos seguís siguen	seguía seguías seguía seguíamos seguíais seguían	seguí seguiste siguió seguimos seguisteis siguieron	seguiré seguirás seguirá seguiremos seguiréis seguirán	seguiría seguirías seguiría seguiríamos seguiríais seguirían	siga sigas siga sigamos sigáis sigan	siguiera siguieras siguiera siguiéramos siguierais siguieran	sigue tú, no sigas siga Ud. sigamos seguid, no sigáis sigan
construir (construyo) construyendo construido	construyo construyes construye construimos construís construyen	construía construías construía construíamos construíais construían	construí construiste construyó construimos construisteis construyeron	construiré construirás construirá construiremos construiréis construirán	construiría construirías construiría construiríamos construiríais construirían	construya construyas construya construyamos construyáis construyan	construyera construyeras construyera construyéramos construyerais construyeran	construye tú, no construyas construya Ud. construyamos construid, no construyáis construyan
conducir (conduzco) conduciendo conducido	conduzco conduces conduce conducimos conducís conducen	conducía conducías conducía conducíamos conducíais conducían	conduje condujiste condujo condujimos condujisteis condujeron	conduciré conducirás conducirá conduciremos conduciréis conducirán	conduciría conducirías conduciría conduciríamos conduciríais conducirían	conduzca conduzcas conduzca conduzcamos conduzcáis conduzcan	condujera condujeras condujera condujéramos condujerais condujeran	conduce tú, no conduzcas conduzca Ud. conduzcamos conducid, no conduzcáis conduzcan

VOCABULARIES

This **Spanish-English Vocabulary** contains all the words that appear in the text, with the following exceptions: (1) most close or identical cognates that do not appear in the chapter vocabulary lists; (2) most conjugated verb forms; (3) diminutives ending in **-ito/a;** (4) absolute superlatives in **-ísimo/a;** (5) most adverbs ending in **-mente,** and (6) words listed or glossed in the **Vocabulario de este programa, Fragmento del guión,** and **Sobre el programa** features of the **TelePuntos** sections. Active vocabulary is indicated by the number of the chapter in which a word or given meaning is first listed (**1** = **Capítulo 1**); vocabulary that is glossed in the text is not considered to be active vocabulary and is not numbered. Only meanings that are used in the text are given. The **English-Spanish Vocabulary** is based on the chapter lists of active vocabulary.

The gender of nouns is indicated, except for masculine nouns ending in **-o** and feminine nouns ending in **-a.** Because **ch** and **ll** are no longer considered separate letters, words beginning with **ch** and **ll** are found as they would be found in English. The letter **ñ** follows the letter **n: añadir** follows **anuncio,** for example.

Irregular verbs found in the verb charts of Appendix 5 are set all in color: **andar.** Verbs with stem changes or spelling changes in the *present tense* show the **yo** form of the present tense in parentheses with the stem-vowel or spelling changes indicated in color: **sentarse (me siento); conocer (conozco); escoger (escojo); actuar (actúo).** Verbs with stem changes in the third person *preterite* and the *present participle* show the stem vowel (**i** or **u**) in parentheses after the present tense **yo** form: **preferir (prefiero) (i); morirse (me muero) (u).** Verbs with any other spelling changes in the first person *preterite* or *present subjunctive* show the change in parentheses: **buscar (qu); pagar (gu); empezar (empiezo) (c); averiguar (ü).**

The following abbreviations are used:

adj.	adjective	*interj.*	interjection
adv.	adverb	*inv.*	invariable form
Arg.	Argentina	*L.A.*	Latin America
C.A.	Central America	*m.*	masculine
Carib.	Caribbean	*Mex.*	Mexico
Col.	Colombia	*n.*	noun
conj.	conjunction	*obj.* (*of prep.*)	object (of a preposition)
def. art.	definite article	*pl.*	plural
d.o.	direct object	*poss.*	possessive
f.	feminine	*p.p.*	past participle
fam.	familiar	*prep.*	preposition
form.	formal	*pron.*	pronoun
gram.	grammatical term	*refl. pron.*	reflexive pronoun
Guat.	Guatemala	*s.*	singular
ind. art.	indefinite article	*sl.*	slang
inf.	infinitive	*Sp.*	Spain
i.o.	indirect object	*sub. pron.*	subject pronoun

Spanish-English Vocabulary

A

a to; at (*with time*) (1); **a base de** based on; **a bordo** on board; **a causa de** because of; **a continuación** following; **a este respecto** in this regard; **a la derecha de** to the right of (6); **a la izquierda de** to the left of (6); **a la moda** in fashion, in a stylish way; **a la(s)...** at . . . (*time of day*) (1); **a menos que** unless (16); **a partir de** beyond (4); **a pesar de** in spite of; **a plazos** in installments (17); **¿a qué hora... ?** at what time . . . ? (1); **a solas** alone; **a tiempo** on time (8); **a través de** across, through; throughout; **¿a usted le gusta... ?** do you (*form. s.*) like . . . ? (1); **a veces** sometimes, at times (3); **a ver** let's see
abacería grocery store
abajo below; underneath
abanicar (qu) to fan
abarcar (qu) to cover (*a topic*)
abecedario alphabet
abierto/a (*p.p. of* **abrir**) open (6)
abogado/a lawyer (17)
abogar (gu) to advocate
abolicionista *m., f.* abolitionist
abrazarse (c) to embrace (11)
abrazo hug, embrace
abreviatura abbreviation
abrigo coat (4)
abril *m.* April (6)
abrir (*pp.* **abierto**) to open (3)
absoluto/a absolute
abstracto/a abstract
absurdo/a absurd; **es absurdo que** it's absurd that (13)
abuelo/a grandfather/grandmother (3); *m. pl.* grandparents (3)
abundante abundant
aburrido/a bored (6); **ser aburrido/a** to be boring (10)
aburrimiento boredom
aburrir (*like* **gustar**) to bore (13); **aburrirse** to get bored (10)
abuso abuse
acabar to finish (14); to run out of (14); **acabar de** + *inf.* to have just (*done something*) (7)
academia academy
académico/a *adj.* academic (14); **año académico** school year; **vida académica** academic life (14)
acampar to camp; **tienda de acampar** tent
acaso: por si acaso just in case (14)
acceso access
accidente *m.* accident (14)
acción *f.* action; **Día** (*m.*) **de Acción de Gracias** Thanksgiving
aceite *m.* oil (7)
acelerado/a fast, accelerated (15)
acelerar to accelerate, speed up
acento accent; **acento diacrítico** diacritical mark
acentuado/a accentuated
aceptable acceptable
acera sidewalk (15)
acerca de *prep.* about, concerning, regarding
acercarse (qu) (a) to come near to
acertar (acierto) to guess correctly
ácido acid
acompañar to accompany
acondicionado: aire (*m.*) **acondicionado** air conditioning
aconsejar to advise
acontecimiento event, happening (18)
acordarse (me acuerdo) (de) to remember (13)
acordeón *m.* accordion
acoso harassment, bullying
acostarse (me acuesto) to go to bed (5)
acostumbrarse (a) to become accustomed (to), get used (to)
acrílico/a acrylic
actitud *f.* attitude
actividad *f.* activity
activo/a active
acto act
actor *m.* actor (13)
actriz *f.* (*pl.* **actrices**) actress (13)
actuación *f.* performance
actual *adj.* current, present-day
actualidad: de/en la actualidad currently, right now (10)
actuar (actúo) to act (13)
acuario aquarium; **Acuario** Aquarius
acuático/a aquatic
acudir (a) to go (to)
acueducto aqueduct
acuerdo agreement; **(no) estar de acuerdo** to (dis)agree (3)
acumular to accumulate
adaptación *f.* adaptation
adaptarse (a) to adapt (to)
adecuado/a appropriate
adelante forward
adelgazar (c) to lose weight
además *adv.* moreover; **además de** *prep.* besides
adicional additional (1)
adiós good-bye (1)
adivinar to guess (9)
adjetivo *gram.* adjective (3); **adjetivo de nacionalidad** adjective of nationality (3); **adjetivo posesivo** possessive adjective (3)
administración *f.* administration; **administración de empresas** business administration (2)
administrar to administer, manage, run
admiración *f.* admiration
admirar to admire
admitir to admit
adolescencia adolescence (16)
adolescente *m., f.* adolescent, teenager
¿adónde? where (to)? (4)
adoptar to adopt
adoquinado/a cobblestoned
adorar to adore
adquirir to acquire
adquisitivo: poder (*m.*) **adquisitivo** purchasing power
aduana customs (*at a border*) (8); **pasar por la aduana** to go/pass through customs (8)
adulto/a adult
adverbio *gram.* adverb
aeróbico: hacer ejercicios aeróbicos to do aerobics (11)
aerolínea airline
aeropuerto airport (8)
afanoso/a laborious, hard
afectar to affect
afectivo/a: estado afectivo emotional state (9)
afecto affection
afeitarse to shave (5)
afición *f.* hobby (10)
aficionado/a fan; **ser aficionado/a (a)** to be a fan (of) (10)
afiliación *f.* affiliation
afiliado/a (a) affiliated (with)
afinidad *f.* compatibility
afirmación *f.* statement
afluente affluent
afortunado/a fortunate, lucky
africano/a *n., adj.* African
afroamerindo/a *n., adj.* Afro-Amerindian
afroperuano/a Afro-Peruvian
afuera *adv.* outdoors (6)
afueras *n. pl.* outskirts (12); suburbs (12)
agencia agency; **agencia de compraventa (de coches)** used car dealership; **agencia de viajes** travel agency
agenda agenda; date book
agente *m., f.* agent; **agente de viajes** travel agent
ágil agile
agitar to agitate
agnóstico/a agnostic
agobiado/a overwhelmed
agosto August (6)
agotar to empty; to drain
agradable agreeable, pleasant
agradar to please
agradecimiento *n.* thanks
agregar (gu) to add
agresivo/a aggressive
agrícola *adj. m., f.* agricultural

agricultor(a) farmer (15)
agricultura farming, agriculture (15)
agrio/a bitter
agroturismo agritourism
agroturista *m., f.* agritourist
agrupar to group
agua *f.* (*but* **el agua**) **(mineral)** (mineral) water (7)
aguacate *m.* avocado
aguar (ü) to dilute, water down
agudo/a sharp
águila *f.* (*but* **el águila**) eagle
agujero hole
ahí there
ahijado/a godson/goddaughter
ahora now (2); **ahora mismo** right now (6)
ahorrar to save (*money*) (17)
ahorros: cuenta de ahorros savings account (17)
airado/a angry, annoyed
aire *m.* air (15); **aire acondicionado** air conditioning
ajedrez *m.* chess; **jugar (juego) (gu) al ajedrez** to play chess (10)
ajo garlic
al (*contraction of* **a** + **el**) to the (4); **al** + *inf.* while (*doing something*) **al alcance** within reach; **al lado de** alongside of (6); **al menos** at least; **al principio de** at the beginning of (17)
alameda tree-lined avenue
alberca swimming pool (*Mex.*)
álbum *m.* album
alcance: al alcance within reach
alcanzar (c) to reach; to achieve
alce *m.* elk; moose
alcoba bedroom (5)
alcohol *m.* alcohol
alcohólico/a alcoholic; **bebida alcohólica** alcoholic beverage
alegrarse (de) to be happy (about) (12)
alegre happy (6)
alemán *m.* German (*language*) (2)
alemán, alemana *n., adj.* German (3)
Alemania Germany
alérgico/a allergic
alerta: ojo alerta eagle eye
alfabeto alphabet
alfombra rug (5)
algo something; anything (7)
algodón *m.* cotton; **de algodón** *adj.* cotton (4)
alguien someone, anyone (7)
algún (alguna/os/as) some, any (7); **alguna vez** once; ever
allá (way) over there (4)
allí there (4)
almacén *m.* department store (4)
almacenar to store, save (12)
almohada pillow
almorzar (almuerzo) (c) to have lunch (5)
almuerzo lunch (7)
¿aló? hello? (*telephone greeting*)
alojarse to lodge
alpinismo mountain climbing; **practicar (qu) el alpinismo** to mountain climb
alquilar *v.* to rent (12)
alquiler *m.* rent (12)
alrededor (de) around
alternar to take turns
alternativa *n.* alternative
alternativo/a *adj.* alternative
altiplano high plateau
altitud *f.* height, altitude
alto/a tall (3); **de alta costura** high fashion **de alto riesgo** high risk
altura altitude
alucinante incredible
alumno/a student
aluvial alluvial
amable kind; nice (3)
amanecer *m.* dawn
amar to love (16)
amarillo/a yellow (4)
amasijo dough; mixture
Amazonas *m. s.* Amazon (River)
amazónico/a *adj.* Amazonian; **Selva Amazónica** Amazon Jungle
ambiental environmental
ambiente *m.* atmosphere; environment; **medio ambiente** environment (15)
ambos/as both
América: América Latina Latin America; **Estados Unidos de América** United States of America
americano/a American; **fútbol** (*m.*) **americano** football
amerindo/a *n., adj.* Amerindian
amigo/a friend (2)
amistad *f.* friendship (16)
amistoso/a friendly (16)
amo/a (*f. but* **el ama**) **de casa** housekeeper (17)
amor *m.* love (16)
ampliación *f.* expansion
amplio/a wide; large, spacious
amueblado/a furnished
amueblar to furnish
amuleto charm, amulet
amurallado/a walled
analfabeto/a illiterate
análisis *m. inv.* analysis
analista *m., f.* analyst; **analista de sistemas** systems analyst (17)
analizar (c) to analyze
ananá *m.* pineapple
anaranjado/a orange (4)
ancho/a wide
anciano/a *n.* old person; *adj.* old; ancient; **residencia de ancianos** nursing home (12)
Andalucía Andalusia
andaluz (a) *n., adj.* Andalusian
andar to walk; **andar en bicicleta** to ride a bicycle; **cinta de andar** treadmill
anécdota anecdote
anémico/a anemic
anfitrión, anfitriona host (*of an event*) (9)
ángel *m.* angel
angelino/a from Los Angeles
anglosajón, anglosajona Anglo Saxon
angosto/a narrow
ángulo angle
anillo ring
ánima soul
animación *f.* animation
animado/a lively; animated; **dibujos animados** cartoons
animal *m.* animal (15); **animal doméstico** pet
animarse to cheer up; **animarse a** to encourage someone (*to do something*)
ánimo: estado de ánimo state of mind
aniversario anniversary
annobonés *m. language of African origin spoken in Equatorial Guinea*
anoche *adv.* last night (11)
anónimo/a anonymous
ansiedad *f.* anxiety (14)
Antártida Antarctica
ante *prep.* before; in front of
anteayer *adv.* the day before yesterday (5)
antecedente *m. gram.* antecedent
anteojos *m. pl.* glasses (11)
antepenúltimo/a third from the end
anterior previous, preceding
antes *adv.* before; **antes de** *prep.* before (5); **antes de Cristo (a.C.)** before Christ (B.C.); **antes (de) que** *conj.* before (16)
antibiótico antibiotic (11)
anticipar to anticipate
antídoto antidote
antiguo/a old; ancient; former
Antillas Mayores Greater Antilles
antipático/a unpleasant (3)
antojo appetizer
antónimo antonym
antropología anthropology
antropólogo/a anthropologist
anualmente annually
anunciar to announce (8)
anuncio announcement; advertisement
añadir to add
año year (6); **año académico** school year; **año bisiesto** leap year; **año entrante** next year; **Año Nuevo** New Year; **año pasado** last year; **año que viene** next year; **cumplir años** to have a birthday (9); **este año** this year; **fin** (*m.*) **de año** end of the year (9); **tener... años** to be . . . years old (3)
apagar (gu) to turn off (14)

apagón *m.* blackout
aparato appliance; **aparato doméstico** home appliance (10)
aparcamiento parking place; parking lot
aparcar (qu) to park
aparecer (aparezco) to appear
apartamento apartment (2)
aparte also
apellido surname
apenas barely
aperitivo appetizer
apetecer (apetezco) (*like* **gustar**) to appeal to
apio celery
aplicación *f.* application
aplicar (qu) to apply
apóstol *m., f.* apostle
apoyar to support
apoyo support; help
app *f.* (*but* **el app**) app(lication) (12)
apreciar to appreciate
aprender to learn (3); **aprender a** + *inf.* to learn how to (*do something*) (3)
aprendizaje *m.* learning
apretado/a tight
apropiado/a appropriate
aproximadamente approximately
apuntar to write down; **apuntarse** to enroll; to add one's name to the list
apuntes *m. pl.* notes (*academic*) (14)
aquel, aquella that ([way] over there) (4)
aquello that ([way] over there) (4)
aquellos/as those ([way] over there) (4)
aquí here (2)
árabe *m.* Arabic (*language*); *n., adj. m., f.* Arab
Arabia Saudita Saudi Arabia
arado *n.* plow
araña spider
árbol *m.* tree (9); **árbol genealógico** family tree
archipiélago archipelago
archivo (computer) file (12)
arco arch
ardilla squirrel
área *f.* (*but* **el área**) area, region
arena sand
arepa *patty made of cornmeal and flour and stuffed with different foods*
aretes *m. pl.* earrings (4)
argentino/a *n., adj.* Argentine
argumento argument; plot
árido/a arid, dry
armado/a: fuerzas armadas armed forces
armar un bochinche to throw a (loud) party
armario armoire, free-standing closet (5)
arpa *f.* (*but* **el arpa**) harp
arquitecto/a architect (13)
arquitectónico/a architectural
arquitectura architecture (13)
arraigado/a deeply rooted
arrancar (qu) to start up (*a car*) (15)
arreglar to fix, repair (15)
arrepentido/a sorry; repentant
arroba @ (12)
arrodillarse to kneel
arrogante arrogant
arroz *m.* (*pl.* **arroces**) rice (7)
arruinar to ruin
arte *m.* art (2); **artes** *f. pl.* the arts (13); **bellas artes** fine arts; **obra de arte** work of art (13)
arteria artery
arterial; tension (*f.*) **arterial** blood pressure
artesanía arts and crafts (13)
artesano/a artisan
artículo article; **artículo (in)definido** *gram.* (in)definite article
artista *m., f.* artist (13)
artístico/a artistic (13); **expresión** (*f.*) **artística** artistic expression (13)
arvejas *f. pl.* green peas (7)
asado/a roast(ed) (7); **lechón** (*m.*) **asado** roast suckling pig; **pollo asado** roast chicken (7)
ascendencia ancestry, descent
ascensor *m.* elevator (12)
asegurar to assure; **asegurarse (de que)** to make certain (that)
asesinar to assassinate (18)
asesinato assassination; murder (18)
así thus; so; **asi como** as well as; **así que** therefore, consequently, so
asiático/a *adj.* Asian
asiento seat (8)
asignar to assign
asistencia sanitaria health care
asistente (*m., f.*) **de vuelo** flight attendant (8)
asistir (a) to attend, go to (*a class, function*) (3)
asma *m.* asthma
asociación *f.* association
asociado/a associated; **estado libre asociado** commonwealth
asociar to associate
aspecto aspect
aspiradora vacuum cleaner (10); **pasar la aspiradora** to vacuum (10)
aspirante *m., f.* candidate; applicant (17)
astronauta *m., f.* astronaut (17)
asumir to assume
asunto matter
atacar (qu) to attack
ataque (*m.*) **(terrorista)** (terrorist) attack (18)
atar to tie
Atenas Athens
atención *f.* attention; **poner atención** to pay attention
ateo/a atheist
ático attic
atmosférico/a atmospheric
atracción *f.* attraction
atractivo/a attractive
atraer (*like* **traer**) (*like* **gustar**) to draw, attract (13)
atrás *adv.* back, backward; behind; **de atrás** backwards
atrasado/a (*with* **estar**) late (8)
atún *m.* tuna (7)
audaz (*pl.* **audaces**) bold, daring
audiencia audience
aula *f.* (*but* **el aula**) classroom
aumentar to increase
aumento raise (12)
aun *adv.* even
aún *adv.* still, yet
aunque although
auscultar to listen (*with a stethoscope*)
ausencia absence
ausente absent
austeridad *f.* austerity
auténtico/a authentic
auto auto (15)
autobiográfico/a autobiographical
autobús *m.* bus (8); **estación** (*f.*) **de autobuses** bus station (8); **ir en autobús** to go/travel by bus (8); **parada del autobús** bus stop (12)
autóctono/a indigenous
automático/a automatic; **cajero automático** automatic teller machine (ATM) (17)
automóvil *m.* automobile
automovilístico/a *adj.* automobile
automutilación *f.* self-mutilation
autonomía autonomy; region
autónomo/a autonomous
autopista freeway, interstate (15)
autoprueba self-test
autor(a) author
autorizado/a authorized
autorretrato self-portrait
autostop: hacer autostop to hitchhike
autosuficiencia self-sufficiency
autosuficiente self-sufficient
avanzado/a advanced
ave *f.* (*but* **el ave**) bird
avenida avenue (12)
aventura adventure
aventurero/a adventurous
aventurismo adventure tourism
aventurista *m., f.* adventure tourist
avergonzado/a embarrassed (9)
averiguar (ü) to find out
avión *m.* airplane (8); **ir en avión** to go/travel by plane (8); **volar (vuelo) en avión** to fly, go by plane (8)
avisar to warn
aviso warning
¡ay! *interj.* ah!; ouch!
ayer yesterday; **ayer fue (miércoles…)** yesterday was (Wednesday . . .) (5)

ayuda help (7)
ayudante *m., f.* assistant
ayudar to help (7)
azteca *n., adj. m., f.* Aztec
azúcar *m.* sugar (7)
azul blue (4)

B

baba saliva; **se le cae la baba por** he/she is drooling over
bahía bay
bailar to dance (2)
bailarín, bailarina dancer (13)
baile *m.* dance (13)
bajada ebb; dip
bajar to lower; to download (12); **bajarse (de)** to get down (from) (8); to get off (of) (*a vehicle*) (8)
bajo *prep.* under; **estar bajo muchas presiones** to be under a lot of pressure (14)
bajo/a short (*in height*) (3); low
balcón *m.* balcony
ballena whale (15)
ballet *m.* ballet (13)
baloncesto basketball
banana banana (7)
banano banana tree
bancario/a: tarjeta bancaria debit card (17)
banco bank (17)
bandeja tray
bandera flag
bandoneón *m.* large concertina
bañarse to take a bath (5)
bañera bathtub (5)
baño bathroom (5); **traje** (*m.*) **de baño** swimsuit (4)
bar *m.* bar; **ir a un bar** to go to a bar (10)
barato/a inexpensive (4)
barbacoa barbecue (7)
barcelonés, barcelonesa of Barcelona (Spain)
barco boat, ship (8); **ir en barco** to go/travel by boat, ship (8)
barra bar
barrer (el piso) to sweep (the floor) (10)
barrera barrier
barrio neighborhood (12)
barro mud
basarse en to base one's ideas, opinions on
base *f.* base; **a base de** based on; **base de datos** data base; **con base en** based on
básico/a basic
basquetbol *m.* basketball (10)
bastante rather, sufficiently; enough (16)
bastar to be enough
basura trash; **sacar (qu) la basura** to take out the trash (10)
bata robe
batalla battle
batería drum set (15)
bautizo baptism
bebé *m., f.* baby
beber to drink (3)
bebida drink (5); **bebida alcohólica** alcoholic beverage
beca scholarship
béisbol *m.* baseball (10)
beisbolista *m., f.* baseball player
Bélgica Belgium
belleza beauty
bello/a beautiful (15); **bellas artes** (*f. pl.*) fine arts
bendecir (*like* **decir**) to bless; **que Dios te bendiga** God bless you
bendito/a blessed
beneficio benefit
besarse to kiss each other (11)
beso kiss
bestia beast
biblioteca library (2)
bibliotecario/a librarian (2)
bicentenario bicentennial
bicicleta bicycle; **andar en bicicleta** to ride a bicycle; **pasear en bicicleta** to ride a bicycle (10)
bien *adv.* well (1); **caerle bien a alguien** to make a good impression on someone; **empleo bien pagado** well-paid job/position (17); **está bien** it's fine, OK (6); **estar bien** to be well; to be comfortable (*temperature*) (6); **llevarse bien (con)** to get along well (with) (16); **muy bien** fine, very well (1); **pasarlo bien** to have a good time (9); **portarse bien** to behave (9); **salir bien** to come/turn out well (5); to do well (5)
bienes raíces *m. pl.* real estate
bienestar *m.* well-being (11)
bienvenida *n.* welcome
bienvenido/a *adj.* welcome
bife *m.* beef
bilingüe bilingual
billete *m.* bill (*money*) (17); ticket (*Sp.*) (8); **billete de ida y vuelta** round-trip ticket (8); **billete de ida** one-way ticket (8); **billete electrónico** e-ticket (8)
binacional binational
biodiversidad *f.* biodiversity
biografía biography
biología biology
bisiesto: año bisiesto leap year
bisonte *m.* bison
bistec *m.* steak (7)
blanco/a white (4); **pizarrón** (*m.*) **blanco** whiteboard (2); **vino blanco** white wine (7)
blando/a soft
blog *m.* blog (12)
bluejeans *m., pl.* jeans
blusa blouse (4)
boca mouth (11)
bocadillo sandwich (*Sp.*)
bochinche: armar un bochinche to throw a (loud) party
bocina horn (*car*) (15)
boda wedding (*ceremony*) (16)
bodega grocery store (*Carib.*)
bola ball
bolero love song
boleto ticket (*L.A.*) (8); **boleto de ida** one-way ticket (8); **boleto de ida y vuelta** round-trip ticket; **boleto electrónico** e-ticket (8)
bolígrafo pen (2)
boliviano/a *n., adj.* Bolivian
bolso purse (4)
bomba bomb (18)
bombardeo bombing
bombilla light bulb
bonito/a pretty (3)
bordo: a bordo on board
boricua *n., adj. inv.* Puerto Rican
Borinquen *indigenous name of Puerto Rico*
borrador *m.* draft
borrasca storm
bosque *m.* forest (15); **bosque tropical lluvioso** tropical rain forest
botanas *f. pl.* (*Mex.*) appetizers (9)
botánico/a botanical
botar to throw out
botas *f. pl.* boots (4)
botella bottle
botón *m.* button
boxeador(a) boxer
brasileño/a *n., adj.* Brazilian
brazo arm (11)
brecha gap; **brecha digital** digital gap; **brecha salarial** wage gap
Bretaña: Gran Bretaña Great Britain
breve brief
brindar to toast, celebrate
británico/a British
bromear to joke
bronce bronze
bruja witch
brujo wizard; warlock
bruto/a: producto nacional bruto gross national product
bucear to scuba dive; to snorkel
budista *n., adj. m., f.* Buddhist
buen, bueno/a good (3); **buenas noches** good night (1); **buenas tardes** good afternoon (1); **buenos días** good morning (1); **lo bueno** the good news/thing (11); **muy buenas** good afternoon/evening (1); **tener buena suerte** to have good luck, be lucky (14)
buey *sl.* dude (*Mex.*)
buscar (qu) to look for (2); **buscar en el Internet** to look for on the Internet (12)
búsqueda search
buzón (*m.*) **de voz** voice mailbox (12)

C

caballo horse (10); **montar a caballo** to ride a horse (10)
caber to fit
cabeza head (11); **dolor** (*m.*) **de cabeza** headache
cabina cabin (*on a ship*) (8)
cacerola casserole dish
cacique, cacica chief
cada *inv.* each, every (5); **cada vez más** increasingly; **cada vez mayor** greater and greater
cadena chain
caer to fall; to drop (14); **caer en** to fall on (*day of the week*); **caerle bien/mal a alguien** to make a good/bad impression on someone; **caerse** to fall down (14); **se le cae la baba por** he/she is drooling over
café *m.* coffee (2)
cafeína caffeine
cafetera coffeemaker (10)
cafetería cafeteria (2)
cafetero coffee plantation
caída fall
caimán *m.* alligator
caja cashier window (17)
cajero/a cashier; teller (17); **cajero automático** automatic teller machine (ATM) (17)
cajón *m.* drawer
calabaza pumpkin; squash
calabozo prison cell
calcetines *m. pl.* socks (4)
calculadora calculator (2)
calcular to calculate
cálculo calculus
calefacción *f.* heating (12)
calendario calendar (14)
calentar (caliento) to warm
calidad *f.* quality
cálido/a hot
caliente hot (*temperature*) (7)
calificación *f.* grade
caligrafía calligraphy; handwriting
calle *f.* street (12)
callejero *adj.* (of the) street
calma calm
calmarse to calm down
calor *m.* heat; **hacer (mucho) calor** to be very hot (6); **tener (mucho) calor** to be (very) warm, hot (6)
caloría calorie
caluroso/a hot
cama bed (5); **guardar cama** to stay in bed (11); **hacer la cama** to make the bed (10); **tender (tiendo) la cama** to make the bed
cámara (digital) (digital) camera (12)
camarero/a waiter/waitress (7)
camarones *m. pl.* shrimp (7)
cambiar (de) to change (12)
cambio change; **cambio climático** climate change
caminadora treadmill (11)
caminante *m., f.* walker, hiker
caminar to walk (10)
caminata: dar una caminata to hike; to go for a hike (10)
caminero/a: furia caminera road rage
camino road; path
camión *m.* truck
camioneta station wagon (8); van (8)
camisa shirt (4)
camiseta T-shirt (4)
campaña campaign; **tienda de campaña** tent (8)
campeón, campeona champion
campesino/a peasant (15)
camping *m.* campground (8); **hacer *camping*** to go camping (8)
campo field; countryside (15)
campus *m.* (university) campus (12)
Canadá Canada; **Día** (*m.*) **del Canadá** Canada Day
canadiense *n., adj. m., f.* Canadian
canal *m.* channel (12)
canario canary
cancelar to cancel
cáncer *m.* cancer
cancha field, court (tennis)
canción *f.* song (13)
candidato/a candidate (18); **postularse (para un cargo) como candidato/a** to run (for a position) as a candidate (18)
cansado/a tired (6)
cansancio fatigue
cansarse to get tired (11)
cantante *m., f.* singer (13)
cantar to sing (2)
cantautor(a) singer, songwriter
cantidad *f.* quantity
cantinero/a bartender
caña sugar cane
capa layer; **capa de ozono** ozone layer (15)
Caperucita Roja Little Red Ridinghood
capilla chapel
capital *f.* capital city (6)
capitán, capitana captain
capítulo chapter
Capricornio Capricorn
capullo bud
caracola large shell
característica *n.* characteristic
característico/a *adj.* characteristic
caracterizar (c) to characterize
caramañola *torpedo-shaped meat pie of Colombia and Panama*
cárcel *f.* jail
cardinal: punto cardinal cardinal point (6)
cargo (political) office (18); **postularse para un cargo (como candidato/a)** to run for a position (as a candidate) (18)
Caribe *m.* Caribbean; **mar** (*m.*) **Caribe** Caribbean Sea
caribeño/a Caribbean
caricatura caricature
cariño affection
cariñoso/a affectionate (6)
carnaval *m.* carnival
carne *f.* meat (7)
carnet (*m.*) **de identificación / de identidad** identification card
caro/a expensive (4)
carpa tent
carpintero/a carpenter
carrera career
carreta cart, wagon
carretera highway (15)
carro (descapotable) (convertible) car (12)
carta letter (3); card; **jugar (juego) (gu) a las cartas** to play cards (10)
cartera wallet; handbag (4)
cartón *m.* cardboard
casa house, home (3); **amo/a** (*but* **el ama**) **de casa** housekeeper (17) **casa natal** house where someone was born; **en casa** at home (2); **limpiar la casa** to clean (the) house (10); **regresar a casa** to go home (2)
casabe *m.* *tortilla-type bread made of cassava*
casado/a married; **estar casado/a (con)** to be married (to) (16); **recién casado/a (con)** newlywed (to) (16); **ser casado/a** to be a married person (16)
casarse (con) to marry (16)
cascanueces *m. inv.* nutcracker
casco helmet (12)
caserío hamlet; farmhouse
casi *inv.* almost (3); **casi nunca** almost never (3)
caso case; **en caso de (que)** in case (16)
castaño/a brown
castellano Spanish (language) (*Sp.*)
castigar (gu) to punish
catalán *m.* Catalan (*language*)
Cataluña Catalonia
catarata waterfall
catarro cold (*health condition*)
catedral *f.* cathedral
categoría category
católico/a *n., adj.* Catholic
catorce fourteen (1)
caucásico/a Caucasian
causa cause; **a causa de** because of
causar to cause
cava cellar
cazador(a) hunter
cazar (c) to hunt
CD *m.* CD (compact disc) (12)
CD-ROM *m.* CD-ROM (12)
cebolla onion

cebuano *Austronesian language spoken in the Philippines*
cédula identity card
celda cell (*prison*)
celebración *f.* celebration
celebrar to celebrate (6)
celta *n., adj. m., f.* Celtic
celular: (teléfono) celular *m.* cell phone (2)
cementerio cemetery
cena dinner, supper (7)
cenar to have (eat) dinner, supper (7)
Cenicienta Cinderella
centavo cent
centígrado Celsius
centro center (18); downtown (4); **centro comercial** shopping mall (4)
Centroamérica Central America
centroamericano/a Central American
cepillarse los dientes to brush one's teeth (5)
cerámica pottery; ceramics (13)
cerca *adv.* near, nearby, close; **cerca de** close to (6)
cercano/a *adj.* close, near
cerdo pork; **chuleta de cerdo** pork chop (7)
cereal *m.* cereal (7)
cerebro brain (11)
ceremonia ceremony
cero zero (1)
cerrado/a closed (6)
cerrar (cierro) to close (5)
cerro hill
certeza certainty
cerveza beer (7)
cesárea C-section
césped *m.* lawn; grass
cesto basket
ceviche *m.* *raw fish dish*
chabacano *Spanish-based Creole language spoken in the Philippines*
champán *m.* champagne (9)
champiñones *m. pl.* mushrooms (7)
chanclas *f. pl.* flip-flops (4)
chaqueta jacket (4)
charango *stringed instrument*
charlar to chat
chauchas *f. pl.* green beans
cheque *m.* check (17); **con cheque** by check (17)
chequeo check-up (11)
chévere *sl.* cool
chibcha *n., adj. m., f.* *indigenous people of the Colombian Andes*
chicha *natural fruit soft drink*
chico/a guy/girl (4)
chileno/a *n., adj.* Chilean
chino Chinese (*language*)
chino/a *n., adj.* Chinese
chirriar to squeal
chisme *m.* gossip
chiste *m.* joke (8)
chocante shocking
chocar (qu) con/contra to run into, bump against (14)
chocolate *m.* chocolate
chofer *m., f.* driver
choque *m.* collision, crash (18)
chuleta (de cerdo) (pork) chop (7)
churro *strip of fried dough*
ciclismo bicycling (10)
ciclo cycle
ciclón *m.* cyclone
ciego/a blind
cien one hundred (3)
ciencia science (2); **ciencia ficción** science fiction; **ciencias** *f. pl.* **naturales** natural sciences (2); **ciencias** *f. pl.* **políticas** political science (2); **ciencias** *f. pl.* **sociales** social sciences (2)
ciento one hundred (*used with* 101–199) (4); **ciento dos** one hundred two (4); **ciento noventa y nueve** one hundred ninety-nine (4); **ciento uno** one hundred one (4)
cierto/a true; **es cierto que** it's certain that (13)
ciervo deer; stag
cigarrillo cigarette
cinco five (1)
cincuenta fifty (3)
cine *m.* movies (5); movie theater (5)
cineasta *m., f.* filmmaker
cinematográfico/a *adj.* movie, film
cinta: cinta de andar/correr treadmill; **cinta rodante** treadmill
cinturón *m.* belt (4)
circulación *f.* traffic (15)
circular to circulate
círculo circle
circunstancia circumstance
ciruelo plum tree
cirugía surgery
cisne *m.* swan
cita date; appointment (11)
citar to cite
ciudad *f.* city (3)
ciudadano/a citizen (18)
cívico/a civic; **responsabilidad** (*f.*) **cívica** civic duty (18)
civil civil; **guerra civil** civil war
civilización *f.* civilization
claro/a clear
clase *f.* class (*of students*) (2); class, course (*academic*) (2); **compañero/a (de clase)** classmate (2); **dar clases** to teach class; **salón** (*m.*) **de clase** classroom (2)
clásico/a classic(al) (13)
clasificar (qu) to classify
cláusula *gram.* clause
clave *f. n., adj.* key
cliente/a client (2)
clima *m.* climate (6)
climático/a *adj.* climate; **cambio climático** climate change
clínica clinic
clóset *m.* closet
coalición *f.* coalition
cobrar to cash (*a check*) (17); to charge (*someone for an item or service*) (17)
cobre *m.* copper
coche *m.* car (3); **agencia de compra-venta (de coches)** used car dealership
cochera garage; carport
cocina kitchen (5); cuisine (7)
cocinar to cook (7)
cocinero/a cook; chef (17)
coco coconut
cocodrilo crocodile
codiciado/a coveted
código code
codo elbow
coexistir to coexist
coger (cojo) to take (*things*) (*Sp.*)
cognado *gram.* cognate
coherente coherent
cohesión *f.* cohesion
coincidencia coincidence
coincidir to coincide
cola line (*of people*) (8); **hacer cola** to stand in line (8)
colaborar to collaborate
colección *f.* collection
colectivo bus
colega *m., f.* colleague
colegio school
colérico/a furious
colesterol *m.* cholesterol
coletilla tag (as in tag question)
Colgar (cuelgo) (gu) to post (*on the Internet*)
collar *m.* necklace
colmado small grocery store (*Carib.*)
colocar (qu) to place
colombiano/a Colombian
colonia colony
colonización *f.* colonization
colono/a settler
color *m.* color (4)
colorido/a colorful
columna column
comadre *f.* godmother
combatir to combat
combinar to combine
comedia comedy (13)
comediante *m., f.* comedian
comedor *m.* dining room (5)
comentario comment
comentarista *m., f.* commentator
comenzar (comienzo) (c) to begin; **comenzar a** + *inf.* to begin to + *inf.*
comer to eat (3)
comercial: centro comercial shopping mall (4)

comercio business, commerce; **libre comercio** free trade
comestibles *m. pl.* groceries, foodstuff (7)
cometer to commit
cómico/a funny; **tira cómica** comic strip
comida food (7); meal (7); **comida rápida** fast food
como like; as; **así como** as well as; **tan… como** as . . . as (6); **tanto como** as much as (6)
¿cómo? how?; what? (1); **¿cómo es usted?** what are you (*form. s.*) like? (1); **¿cómo está?** how are you (*form. s.*)? (1); **¿cómo estás?** how are you (*fam. s.*)? (1); **¿cómo se llama usted?** what is your (*form. s.*) name? (1); **¿cómo se llega a… ?** how do you get to . . . ? (15); **¿cómo te llamas?** what is your (*fam. s.*) name? (1)
cómoda bureau; dresser (5)
comodidad *f.* convenience
cómodo/a comfortable (4)
compacto/a: disco compacto (**CD** *m.*) compact disc (CD) (12)
compadre *m.* godfather
compañero/a companion; friend; **compañero/a (de clase)** classmate (2); **compañero/a de cuarto** roommate (2)
compañía company
comparación *f.* comparison (6)
comparar to compare
comparativo/a comparative
compartir to share (17)
compasión *f.* compassion
competencia competition
competición *f.* competition
complejo/a complex
complemento (in)directo *gram.* (in)direct object
completar to complete
completo/a complete; **trabajo de tiempo completo** full-time job (14)
complicación *f.* complication
componer (*like* **poner**) to compose (13)
comportamiento behavior
composición *f.* composition
compositor(a) composer (13)
compostero composter
compra-venta: agencia de compra-venta (de coches) used car dealership
comprar to buy (2)
compras: de compras shopping (4); **ir de compras** to go shopping (4)
comprender to understand (3)
comprensible understandable
comprensión *f.* understanding; comprehension
comprensivo/a *adj.* understanding
comprobar (compruebo) to prove
comprometido/a committed
compromiso engagement
compulsivo/a compulsive
computación *f.* computer science (2)
computadora computer (2); **computadora portátil** laptop (computer) (2)
común common
comunicación *f.* communication; *pl.* communication (*subject*) (2); **medio de comunicación** medium of communication (18)
comunicativo/a communicative
comunidad *f.* community
comunión *f.* communion
comunitario/a *adj.* community
con with (2); **chocar (qu) con** to run into, bump against (14); **comunicarse (qu) (con)** to communicate (with) (18); **con base en** based on; **con cheque** by check (17); **con cuidado** carefully; **con frecuencia** frequently (2); **con permiso** excuse me (1); **¿con qué frecuencia… ?** how often . . . ? (3); **con respecto a** regarding; **con tal de** *prep.* provided (16); **con tal (de) que** *conj.* provided (that) (16); **darse con** to run into; **pegarse (gu) con** to run, bump into (14)
concentración *f.* concentration
concentrar to concentrate
concepto concept
conciencia conscience
concierto concert; **ir a un concierto** to go to a concert (10)
conciso/a concise
conclusión *f.* conclusion
concordancia *gram.* agreement
concurso contest
condenado/a condemned
condición *f.* condition
condicional *gram.* conditional
cóndor *m.* condor
conducción *f.* driving
conducir (conduzco) to drive (15); **licencia de conducir** driver's license (15)
conductor(a) driver (15)
conectar to connect
conector *m.* connector
conexión *f.* connection
conferencia lecture
confesional confessional
confianza confidence
confiar (confío) to trust
confirmar to confirm
confundido/a confused
congelado/a frozen; very cold (6)
congelador *m.* freezer (10)
congresista *m., f.* congress member
conjugación *f.* conjugation
conjugar (gu) *gram.* to conjugate
conjunción *f. gram.* conjunction (16); **conjunción de tiempo** conjunction of time (17)
conjunto group
conmemorar to commemorate
conmigo with me (6)
Cono Sur Southern Cone
conocer (conozco) to know, be acquainted, familiar with (7); to meet (7); **conocerse** to meet (16)
conocimiento knowledge
conquista conquest
conquistador(a) conqueror
consciente conscious, aware
consecuencia consequence
consecutivo/a consecutive
conseguir (*like* **seguir**) to get, obtain (9); **conseguir** + *inf.* to succeed in (*doing something*) (9)
consejero/a advisor (2)
consejo (piece of) advice (7)
conservación *f.* conservation
conservacionista conservationist
conservador(a) conservative
conservar to save, conserve (15)
considerar to consider
consigo with himself, herself, themselves
consiguiente: por consiguiente as a result
consistencia consistency
consistir (en) to consist (of)
constante constant
constitución *f.* constitution
constituir (*like* **construir**) to constitute
construcción *f.* construction
construir (construyo) to build (15)
consulta consultation
consultorio (medical) office (11); consultation
consumidor(a) consumer
consumir to consume
consumo consumption
contabilidad *f.* accounting
contable *m., f.* accountant (*Sp.*)
contacto contact; **lentes** (*m. pl.*) **de contacto** contact lenses (11); **mantenerse** (*like* **tener**) **en contacto** to stay in touch
contador(a) accountant (17)
contaminación *f.* pollution (6)
contaminado/a contaminated, polluted (15)
contaminar to pollute (15)
contar (cuento) to tell, narrate (8)
contemplación *f.* contemplation
contemplar to contemplate
contemporáneo/a contemporary
contenedor *m.* container
contener (*like* **tener**) to contain
contenido contents
contento/a content, happy (6)
contestar to answer (7)
contexto context
contigo with you (*fam.*) (6)
continente *m.* continent
contingencia contingency
continuación: a continuación following
continuar (continúo) to continue (6)

contra against; **chocar (qu)/pegarse (gu) contra** to run, bump against (14); **darse contra** to run into
contraseña password (12)
contrastar to contrast
contraste *m.* contrast
contrastivo/a contrasting
contribuir (*like* **construir**) to contribute
control *m.* control; **control de seguridad** security (check) (8); **control remoto** remote control (12); **pasar por el control de seguridad** to go/pass through security (check) (8)
controlar to control
convencer (convenzo) to convince
convención convention, system
conversación *f.* conversation
conversar to converse
convertir (convierto) to convert
convivencia cohabitation; living together
convivir to live together
coordinar to coordinate
copa (wine) glass; **Copa del Mundo** World Cup (*soccer*); **Copa Mundial** World Cup (*soccer*)
copia copy; **hacer copia** to copy
copiar to copy (12)
copioso/a copious
coquí *m.* *small frog of Puerto Rico*
corazón *m.* heart (11)
corbata tie (4)
cordillera mountain range
coreano/a *n., adj.* Korean
coro chorus
corona crown
corporación *f.* corporation
correcto/a correct
corregir (corrijo) to correct
correr to run (10); **cinta de correr** treadmill
correspondencia correspondence
corresponder (a) to correspond (to)
correspondiente *m., f.* correspondent; *adj.* corresponding
corrido *Mexican folk song*
corriente: cuenta corriente checking account (17); **estar al corriente** to be up to date
cortar to cut
cortejo courting
cortés *m., f.* polite
cortesía courtesy; **expresión** (*f.*) **de cortesía** pleasantry (1)
cortijo country house
cortina curtain
corto *n.* short segment
corto/a short (*in length*) (3); **pantalones** (*m. pl.*) **cortos** shorts (4)
cosa thing (5)
cosecha harvest; crop
cosechar to harvest
cosmético/a cosmetic
cosmopolita *m., f.* cosmopolitan
cosmovisión *f.* world view
costa coast
costar (cuesto) to cost
costarricense *n., adj. m., f.* Costa Rican
costero/a coastal
costo cost
costoso/a expensive
costumbre *f.* custom
costura; de alta costura high fashion
cotidiano/a daily
country *m.* country music
creación *f.* creation
crear to create (13)
creatividad *f.* creativity
creativo/a creative
crecer (crezco) to grow (16)
crédito credit; **tarjeta de crédito** credit card (7)
creencia belief
creer (en) to think; to believe (in) (3)
creíble believable
creyente *m., f.* believer
criatura child
cristal *m.* glass
cristianismo Christianity
cristiano/a *n., adj.* Christian
Cristo Christ; **antes de Cristo (a.C.)** before Christ (B.C.); **después de Cristo (a.D.)** Anno Domini (A.D.)
crítica criticism
criticar (qu) to criticize
crítico/a critic
crónica chronicle
cronológico/a chronological
crucero cruise (ship) (8)
cruz *f.* (*pl.* **cruces**) cross; **Día** (*m.*) **de la Cruz** Day of the Cross
cruzar (c) to cross; **cruzarse con** to cross paths with
cuaderno notebook (2)
cuadrado *n.* square
cuadrado/a *adj.* square
cuadro painting (*specific piece*) (13); **de cuadros** plaid (4)
cuajar to fit in
cual; el/la cual, lo cual, los/las cuales which
¿cuál(es)? what? (2); which? (2); **¿cuál es la fecha de hoy?** what's today's date? (6); **¿cuál es tu onda?** what's your style?
cualidad *f.* quality
cualquier *adj.* any
cuando when
¿cuándo? when? (2)
cuanto: en cuanto as soon as (17); **en cuanto a** regarding
¿cuánto? how much? (2); **¿cuánto cuesta(n)?** how much does it (do they) cost? (4); **¿cuánto tiempo hace que… ?** how long has it been since . . . ?
¿cuántos/as? how many? (2)
cuarenta forty (3)
Cuaresma Lent
cuartel *m.* barracks
cuarto room (2); one-fourth; quarter (of an hour); **compañero/a de cuarto** roommate (2); **menos cuarto** a quarter to (*hour*) (1); **y cuarto** a quarter (fifteen minutes) after (*the hour*) (1)
cuarto/a *adj.* fourth (13)
cuate *sl. m., f.* buddy, pal
cuatro four (1)
cuatrocientos/as four hundred (4)
cubano/a *n., adj.* Cuban
cubanoamericano/a *n., adj.* Cuban American
cubierto/a (*p.p. of* **cubrir**) covered
cubiertos *m. pl.* cutlery
cubrir (*p.p.* **cubierto**) to cover (15)
cucaracha cockroach
cuchara spoon
cucharada spoonful
cuchillo knife
cuenta check, bill (7); **cuenta corriente** checking account (17); **cuenta de ahorros** savings account (17)
cuento story
cuero leather; **de cuero** leather (4)
cuerpo (humano) (human) body (11)
cuervo crow
cuestión *f.* issue, matter (17)
cuestionario questionnaire
cuidado care; *interj.* careful!; **con cuidado** carefully; **tener cuidado** to be careful
cuidar a to care for; **cuidarse** to take care of oneself (11)
culebra snake
culinario/a culinary
culminar to culminate
culpa fault; **tener la culpa** to be at fault
cultivo cultivation
culto cult
cultura culture
cultural cultural; **tradición** (*f.*) **cultural** cultural tradition (13)
cumbia *Colombian folk dance now popular throughout Latin America*
cumpleaños *m. inv.* birthday (6); **pastel** (*m.*) **de cumpleaños** birthday cake (9)
cumplir años to have a birthday (9)
cuñado/a brother-in-law, sister-in-law
cupo quota; capacity (room)
cupón *m.* coupon
curación *f.* cure
curar to cure
curativo curing, curative
curioso/a curious
currículum *m.* résumé (17)
cursi in poor taste, trite
curso course; **programa** (*m.*) **del curso** course syllabus (14)
cuyo/a whose

D

dama lady
danza dance (13)
daño: hacerse daño to hurt oneself (14); **hacerse daño en** to hurt one's (*body part*) (14)
dar to give (8); **dar clases** to teach class; **dar un paseo** to take a walk (10); **dar una caminata** to hike; to go for a hike (10); **dar una fiesta** to throw a party (9); **darse con/contra** to run into; **darse la mano** to shake hands (11)
dato piece of information; *pl.* data; **base** (*f.*) **de datos** data base
de of (1); from (1); **de algodón** *m.* cotton (4); **de alta costura** high fashion; **de alto riesgo** high risk; **de atrás** backwards; **de compras** shopping (4); **de cuadros** plaid (4); **de cuero** leather (4); **¿de dónde eres (tú)?** where are you (*fam. s.*) from? (1); **¿de dónde es usted?** where are you (*form. s.*) from? (1); **de estatura mediana** of medium height; **de exposición** expository; **de forma presencial** in person; **de joven** as a youth (10); **de la actualidad** currently, right now (10); **de la mañana** in the morning, A.M. (1); **de la noche** in the evening, P.M. (1); **de la tarde** in the afternon, P.M. (1); **de lana** wool (4); **de lunares** polka-dot (4); **de manera que** so that, in such a way that; **de modo que** in such a way that; **de nada** you're welcome (1); **de niño/a** as a child (10); **de oro** gold (4); **de plata** silver (4); **¿de quién?** whose? (3); **de rayas** striped (4); **de remate** hopeless(ly); **de repente** suddenly (11); **de seda** silk (4); **de todo** everything (4); **de todo tipo** of all kinds; **de vacaciones** on vacation (8); **¿de veras?** really?; **de viaje** on a trip, traveling (8); **es de…** it is made of . . . (4)
debajo de below (6)
debate *m.* debate
debatir to debate
deber *n. m.* responsibility (18); obligation (18)
deber *v.* + *inf.* should, must, ought to (*do something*) (3)
debido/a a due to; because of
década decade
decadencia decadence
decente decent
decidir to decide
décimo/a tenth (13)
decimotercer(o/a) thirteenth
decir to say; to tell (8); **eso quiere decir…** that means . . . (11)
declaración *f.* statement
declarar to state
decoración *f.* decoration
decorar to decorate
dedicarse (qu) (a) to dedicate oneself (to)
dedo (de la mano) finger (11); **dedo del pie** toe (11)
deducir (deduzco) to deduce
defender (defiendo) to defend
defensa defense
defensor(a) defender
deficiencia deficiency
deficiente deficient
definición *f.* definition
definido: artículo definido *gram.* definite article
definir to define
degustar to taste
dejar to leave; to let, allow; to quit (17); **dejar de** + *inf.* to stop (*doing something*) (11); **dejar (en)** to leave behind (in [*a place*]) (10); **dejar sin hacer** to leave undone (10)
del (*contraction of* **de** + **el**) of the, from the (3)
delante de in front of (6)
delegación *f.* delegation
delfín *m.* dolphin
delgado/a thin, slender (3)
deliberado/a deliberate
delicioso/a delicious
delito crime (15)
demanda demand
demás: los/las demás the rest, others (12)
demasiado *adv.* too (9)
demasiado/a *adj.* too much (9); too many (9)
demócrata *m., f.* democrat
demonio demon, devil
demora delay (8)
demostración *f.* demonstration
demostrar (demuestro) to demonstrate
demostrativo/a *gram.* demonstrative (4)
denominación *f.* denomination
densidad *f.* density
denso/a dense (15)
dentista *m., f.* dentist (11)
dentro inside; **dentro de** inside; within, in (*time*)
departamento department
depender (de) to depend (on)
dependiente/a clerk (2)
deporte *m.* sport (10); **practicar (qu)** to play (*a sport*)
deportista *m., f.* athlete
deportivo/a *adj.* sporting, sports; sports-loving (10)
depositar to deposit (17)
depósito deposit
depresión *f.* depression
deprimido/a depressed
derecha *n.* right side; **a la derecha de** to the right of (6)
derecho right (18); **(todo) derecho** straight ahead (15)
derivarse (de) to derive (from)
derramar to spill
desacuerdo disagreement
desafío challenge
desahogarse (gu) to let off steam; to vent
desamor *m.* lack of affection
desaparecer (desaparezco) to disappear
desarrollar to develop (15)
desarrollo development (15)
desastre *m.* disaster (14)
desastroso/a disastrous
desayunar to have (eat) breakfast (7)
desayuno breakfast (7)
descansar to rest (5)
descanso rest
descapotable: carro descapotable (convertible) car (12)
descargar (gu) to download (12)
descendiente *m., f.* descendent
descentralizado/a decentralized
descifrar to decipher, figure out
desconectar to unplug, disconnect
desconocido/a unknown
descontento/a unhappy
descortés *m., f.* rude, impolite
describir (*p.p.* **descrito**) to describe
descripción *f.* description
descriptivo/a descriptive
descrito/a (*p.p. of* **describir**) described
descubierto/a (*p.p. of* **descubrir**) discovered
descubrimiento discovery
descubrir (*p.p.* **descubierto**) to discover (15)
desde *prep.* from; since
desear to want (2)
deseo wish
desequilibrio imbalance
desértico/a *adj.* desert
desesperanza desperation
desfile *m.* parade
desgracia misfortune; disgrace
desgraciadamente unfortunately (11)
deshacer (*like* **hacer**) **(el equipaje)** to unpack (one's luggage)
deshumanización *f.* dehumanization
desierto desert
designación *f.* designation
desigualdad *f.* inequality (18)
desilusión *f.* disillusion
desinflado/a: llanta desinflada flat tire (15)
desocupado/a empty; available
desordenado/a messy (6)
despacio *adv.* slowly
despedir (*like* **pedir**) to let (*someone*) go (17); to fire (*someone*) (*from a job*) (17); **despedirse (de)** to say good-bye (to) (9)
despejado/a clear (*sky*)
desperdiciar to waste
desperdicio waste
despertador *m.* alarm clock (14)

despertarse (me despierto) (*p.p.* **despierto**) to wake up (5)
despierto/a (*p.p. of* **despertar**) awake
despistado/a absent-minded; forgetful
después *adv.* afterwards (5); **después de** *prep.* after (5); **después de Cristo (a.D.)** Anno Domini (A.D.); **después (de) que** *conj.* after (17)
destacar (qu) to emphasize
destino destination; destiny
destrucción *f.* destruction
destruir (*like* **construir**) to destroy (15)
desventaja disadvantage
detalle *m.* detail (9)
detective *m., f.* detective
detenerse (*like* **tener**) to stop
determinación *f.* determination
determinado/a specific
determinar to determine
detestar to detest
detrás de behind (6)
deuda debt
devolver (*like* **volver**) to return (*something to someone*) (14)
devoto/a devout
día *m.* day (2); **buenos días** good morning (1); **Día de Acción de Gracias** Thanksgiving; **Día de la Cruz** Day of the Cross; **Día de la Madre** Mother's Day; **Día de los Difuntos** Day of the Dead; **Día de los Muertos** Day of the Dead; **Día de San Patricio** St. Patrick's Day; **Día de San Valentín** St. Valentine's Day; **Día del Canadá** Canada Day; **Día del Padre** Father's Day; **día festivo** holiday (9); **Día Internacional de la No Violencia Contra la Mujer** International No Violence Against Women Day; **días de la semana** days of the week (5); **estar al día** to be up to date (18); **¿qué día es hoy?** what day is today? (5); **todos los días** every day (2)
diabetes *f.* **(juvenil)** (childhood) diabetes
diabético/a diabetic
diacrítico/a: acento diacrítico diacritical mark
diagnosticar (qu) to diagnose
diágrafo group of letters that represent a single sound
dialecto dialect
diálogo dialogue
diamante *m.* diamond
diariamente daily
diario/a daily (5)
dibujante *m., f.* comic strip artist
dibujar to draw (13)
dibujo drawing (13); **dibujos animados** cartoons
diccionario dictionary (2)
dicho saying
diciembre *m.* December (6)
dictador(a) dictator (18)
dictadura dictatorship (18)
diecinueve nineteen (1)
dieciocho eighteen (1)
dieciséis sixteen (1)
diecisiete seventeen (1)
diente *m.* tooth (5); **cepillarse los dientes** to brush one's teeth (5)
dieta diet; **estar a dieta** to be on a diet (7)
dietético/a *adj.* diet
diez ten (1)
diferencia difference; **a diferencia de** unlike
diferenciado/a differentiated
diferente different
difícil hard, difficult (6)
dificultad *f.* difficulty
difundir to disseminate
difunto/a dead; **Día** (*m.*) **de los Difuntos** Day of the Dead
digestión *f.* digestion
digital digital; **brecha digital** digital gap; **cámara digital** digital camera (12)
dígito digit
dignidad *f.* dignity
dilema *m.* dilemma
diligente diligent
dimensión *f.* dimension
Dinamarca Denmark
dinero money (2); **sacar (qu) dinero** to withdraw money
dinoflagelado *type of marine plankton*
dios *m. s.* god; **Dios** God; **por Dios** for heaven's sake (14); **que Dios te bendiga** God bless you
diosa goddess
diptongo *gram.* diphthong
dirección *f.* address (7)
directo direct; **complemento directo** *gram.* direct object
director(a) director; conductor (13)
dirigir (dirijo) to direct (13)
disco disc; **disco compacto (CD** *m.*) compact disc (CD) (12); **disco duro** hard drive (12)
discoteca discotheque; **ir a una discoteca** to go to a disco (10)
discriminación *f.* discrimination (18)
disculpa apology, excuse; **pedir disculpas** to apologize (14)
disculpar to excuse, pardon; **disculpa, discúlpame** pardon me (*fam. s.*) (14); I'm sorry (*fam. s.*) (14); **disculpe, discúlpeme** pardon me (*form. s.*) (14); I'm sorry (*form. s.*) (14)
discurso speech
discusión *f.* argument; discussion
discutir (con/sobre) to argue (with/about) (9)
diseñador(a) designer
diseñar to design (13)
diseño design
disfraz *m.* (*pl.* **disfraces**) costume, disguise
disfrutar de to enjoy
disminuir (*like* **construir**) to diminish
disparar to shoot
dispensario clinic
disponible available
disposición *f.* disposition
dispuesto/a ready, prepared
distancia distance
distante distant
distinción *f.* distinction
distintivo/a distinctive
distinto/a different
distracción *f.* distraction
distraído/a absentminded, distracted (14); **ir distraído/a** to be distracted (14)
distribuido/a distributed
distrito district
diversidad *f.* diversity
diversión *f.* fun activity (10)
diverso/a diverse
divertido/a fun; **ser divertido/a** to be fun (10)
divertirse (me divierto) to have a good time, enjoy oneself (5)
divorciado/a (de) divorced (from) (16)
divorciarse (de) to get divorced (from) (16)
divorcio divorce (16)
divulgar (gu) to divulge
doblar to turn (15)
doble *m.* double
doce twelve (1)
dócil docile
doctor(a) doctor
doctorado doctorate
documental *m.* documentary
documento document
dólar *m.* dollar
doler (duele) (*like* **gustar**) to hurt, ache (11)
dolor (*m.*) **(de)** pain, ache (in) (11); **dolor de cabeza** headache; **tener dolor de** to have a pain/ache in (11)
domesticado/a domesticated, tame (15)
doméstico/a domestic, related to the home (10); **animal** (*m.*) **doméstico** pet; **aparato doméstico** home appliance (10); **tarea doméstica** household chore
dominación *f.* domination
dominar to control; to dominate
domingo Sunday (5)
dominicano/a *n., adj.* Dominican
dominio control
don *m.* *title of respect used with a man's first name*
donar to donate
donde where
¿dónde? where? (1); **¿de dónde eres (tú)?** where are you (*fam. s.*) from? (1); **¿de dónde es usted?** where are you (*form. s.*) from? (1)

doña *title of respect used with a woman's first name*
dormir (duermo) (u) to sleep (5); **dormir la siesta** to take a nap (5); **dormirse** to fall asleep (5)
dormitorio bedroom
dos two (1); **dos veces** twice (11)
doscientos/as two hundred (4)
drama *m.* drama (13)
dramático/a dramatic
dramaturgo/a playwright (13)
droga drug
dromedario dromedary
ducha *n.* shower
ducharse to take a shower (5)
duda *n.* doubt
dudar to doubt (12)
dudoso/a doubtful
duelo duel
dueño/a landlord, landlady (12); owner (7)
dulces *m. pl.* sweets; candy (7)
dulzura sweetness
duración *f.* duration
duradero/a lasting
durante during (5)
durar to last (18)
duro/a hard; **disco duro** hard drive (12)
DVD(-ROM) *m.* DVD(-ROM) (12)

E

e and (*used instead of* **y** *before words beginning with stressed* **i** *or* **hi,** except **hie-**)
e-mail *m.* e-mail (12)
ecocasa ecological house
ecología ecology
ecologista *m., f.* ecologist
economía economy; *s.* economics (2)
económico/a economical
economista *m., f.* economist
economizar (c) to economize (17)
ecoturismo ecotourism
ecoturista *m., f.* ecotourist
ecoturístico/a *adj.* ecotourist
ecuador *m.* equator
ecuatoguineano/a of or from Equatorial Guinea
ecuatoriano/a Ecuadoran
edad *f.* age
edificio building (2); **edificio de apartamentos** apartment building (12)
editar to edit
editorial *f.* publishing house
educación *f.* education
educador(a) educator
educarse (qu) to be educated
educativo/a educational
efectivo cash (17); **en efectivo** in cash (17)
efectivo/a effective
efecto effect
efectuar to carry out, execute
eficiencia efficiency
eficiente efficient
Egipto Egypt
egoísta *m., f.* selfish
ejecutivo/a *n., adj.* executive
ejemplificar (qu) to exemplify
ejemplo example; **por ejemplo** for example (14)
ejercer (ejerzo) to apply, exercise
ejercicio exercise (5); **hacer ejercicio** to exercise (5); **hacer ejercicios aeróbicos** to do aerobics (11)
ejército army (18)
el *def. art. m. s.* the; **el cual** which; **el lunes (martes...)** on Monday (Tuesday . . .) (5); **el primero de** the first of (*month*) (6); **el próximo (martes...)** next (Tuesday . . .) (5)
él *sub. pron.* he (2)
elaboración *f.* elaboration
elaborar to elaborate
elección *f.* choice; *pl.* election
electricidad *f.* electricity (12); electric bill (12)
electricista *m., f.* electrician (17)
eléctrico/a electrical; **energía eléctrica** electrical energy (15)
electrónica electronic equipment (12)
electrónico/a electronic; **billete** (*m.*) (*Sp.*) / **boleto** (*L.A.*) **electrónico** e-ticket (8)
elefante *m.* elephant (15)
elegante elegant
elegir (elijo) to select; to elect
elemento element
elevado/a high
elevador *m.* elevator
eliminar to eliminate
ella *sub. pron.* she (2)
ellos/as *sub. pron.* they (2); *obj.(of prep.)* them (2)
embarazada pregnant
embarazo pregnancy
embargo: sin embargo nevertheless
embarque: puerta de embarque boarding gate (8); **tarjeta de embarque** boarding pass (8)
emblema *m.* emblem
embotellamiento traffic jam
embriagado/a intoxicated, drunk
embutido sausage
emergencia emergency
emigrante *m., f.* emigrant
emigrar to emigrate
emisario/a emissary
emitir to emit
emoción *f.* emotion (9)
emocionado/a excited
emocional emotional
emocionante exciting
emocionarse to get excited about
empanada *turnover pie or pastry*
emparedado sandwich
emparejar to match
empezar (empiezo) (c) to begin, start (5); **empezar a** + *inf.* to begin to (*do something*) (5) +
empleado/a employee
empleador(a) employer
empleo job, position (17); **empleo bien/mal pagado** well-/poorly paid job/position (17); **empleo de tiempo completo/parcial** full-/part-time job/position (17)
empresa corporation (17); business (17); **administración** (*f.*) **de empresas** business administration (2)
empresario/a businessman/woman
en in (1); on (1); at (1); **en casa** at home (2); **en caso de** *prep.* in case (16); **en caso de que** *conj.* in case (16); **en cuanto** as soon as (17); **en efectivo** in cash (17); **en la actualidad** currently, right now (10); **en negrilla** boldface; **en onda** in style; **en punto** on the dot (*time*) (1); **en rebaja** on sale; **en resumen** in summary; **en seguida** immediately (5); **en vez de** instead of
enamorado/a (de) in love (with) (16)
enamorarse (de) to fall in love (with) (16)
enano/a dwarf
encantado/a pleased to meet you (1); enchanted
encantar (*like* **gustar**) to like very much, love (8)
encanto charm
encapuchado/a hooded
encarcelado/a incarcerated
encargado/a in charge
encender (enciendo) to turn on (*appliance*); to light
encerado blackboard
encima de on top of (6)
encontrar (encuentro) to find (9); **encontrarse (con)** to meet (*someone somewhere*) (11)
encuentro encounter
encuesta survey
encuestar to survey
endémico/a endemic
enemigo enemy
energético/a energetic
energía energy (15); **energía eléctrica** electrical energy (15); **energía eólica** wind energy (15); **energía nuclear** nuclear energy (15); **energía renovable** renewable energy (15); **energía solar** solar energy (15)
enérgico/a energetic
enero January (6)
enfado anger
énfasis *m.* emphasis
enfático/a emphatic
enfatizar (c) to emphasize
enfermarse to become sick (9)
enfermedad *f.* illness, sickness (11)

enfermero/a nurse (11)
enfermo/a sick (6)
enfilado/a in a line
enfocar (qu) to focus
enfoque *m.* focus
enfrentarse a to face
enfrente de *prep.* in front of
engordar to gain weight; to fatten
enhorabuena congratulations
enloquecerse (me enloquezco) to go crazy
enojarse (con) to get angry (with) (9)
ensalada salad (7)
ensayista *m., f.* essayist
ensayo essay
enseñanza teaching
enseñar to teach (2); **enseñar a** + *inf.* to teach to (*do something*)
entender (entiendo) to understand (5)
enterarse (de) to find out, learn (about) (18)
entero/a entire
enterrado/a buried
entonces then, next
entrada entrance
entrante: año entrante next year
entrar to enter; **entrar en el Internet** to go on the Internet (12); **entrar en Facebook** to go into Facebook (12)
entre *prep.* between, among (6)
entregar (gu) to hand in (8)
entrenador(a) trainer, coach
entrenar to practice, train (10)
entresemana during the week
entretenimiento entertainment
entrevista interview (17)
entrevistado/a interviewee (17)
entrevistador(a) interviewer (17)
entrevistar to interview
entusiasmar to enthuse
envase *m.* container
enviar (envío) to send
eólico/a: energía eólica wind energy (15)
epitafio epitaph
época era, time (*period*)
equilibrar to balance
equipaje *m.* baggage, luggage (8); **deshacer** (*like* **hacer**) **el equipaje** to unpack; **facturar el equipaje** to check baggage (8)
equipar to equip
equipo team (10); equipment (12)
equivalente *m.* equivalent
equivaler (*like* **salir**) to equal
equivocarse (qu) (de) to make a mistake (about) (14)
eructar to burp, belch
erupción *f.* eruption (18)
escala stop (8); **hacer escalas** to make stops (8)
escalador(a) climber
escalar to climb
escalera staircase; *pl.* stairs (14)
escándalo scandal
escáner *m.* scanner (12)
escapar to escape
escaparate *m.* store (display) window
escaso/a scarce
escena scene
escenario stage (13); scenery (13)
esclavo/a slave
escoger (escojo) to choose, select
escolar *adj.* school
Escorpión *m.* Scorpio
escribir (*p.p.* **escrito**) to write (3)
escrito/a (*p.p. of* **escribir**) written (14); **informe** (*m.*) **escrito** written report (14)
escritor(a) writer (13)
escritorio desk (2)
escuálido/a scrawny
escuchar to listen (to) (2)
escuela school (10); **escuela primaria** elementary school; **escuela secundaria** high school; **maestro/a de escuela** schoolteacher (17)
esculpir to sculpt
escultor(a) sculptor (13)
escultura sculpture (13)
ese/a *adj.* that (4)
esencial essential
esfuerzo effort
eso *adj.* that (4); **eso quiere decir…** that means . . . (11); **por eso** for that reason (3)
esos/as *adj.* those (4)
espacial *adj.* space; **nave** (*f.*) **espacial** spaceship; **transbordador** (*m.*) **espacial** space shuttle
espacio space
espacioso/a spacious
espalda back
espantapájaros *m. inv.* scarecrow
español *m.* Spanish (*language*) (2)
español(a) *n.* Spaniard; *adj.* Spanish (3)
espárragos asparagus (7)
especial special
especialidad *f.* specialty
especialización *f.* major (*academic*); specialization
especializarse (c) (en) to major (in)
especie (*f.*) species (15); **especie en peligro de extinción** endangered species (15)
especificar (qu) to specify
específico/a specific
espectacular spectacular
espectáculo show (13)
espectador(a) spectator (13); *pl.* audience (13)
especulación *f.* speculation
espejo mirror
espera wait; **llamada de espera** call-waiting; **sala de espera** waiting room (8)
esperanza hope, wish (18)
esperar to wait (for) (7); to expect (7); to hope (12)
espinaca spinach
espíritu *m.* spirit
espiritual spiritual
esplendor *m.* splendor
esposado/a handcuffed
esposo/a husband/wife (3)
esqueleto skeleton
esquema *m.* outline
esquí *m.* skiing (10)
esquiador(a) skier
esquiar (esquío) to ski (10)
esquina (street) corner (15)
esta noche tonight (6)
estación *f.* station (8); season (6); **estación de autobuses** bus station (8); **estación de radio** radio station (18); **estación de servicio** gas station (15); **estación del tren** train station/(8)
estacionamiento parking place/lot (15)
estacionar to park (14)
estadístico/a statistical
estado state (3); **estado afectivo** emotional state (9); **estado de ánimo** state of mind; **estado libre asociado** commonwealth; **Estados Unidos de América** United States of America
estadounidense *n., adj.* of the United States of America (3)
estancia stay (*in a hotel*)
estante *m.* bookshelf (5)
estar to be (2); **¿cómo está?** how are you (*form. s.*)? (1); **¿cómo estás?** how are you (*fam. s.*)? (1); **está bien** it's fine, OK (6); **está de moda** it's trendy (hot) (4); **está (muy) nublado** it's (very) cloudy, overcast (6); **estar a dieta** to be on a diet (7); **estar al corriente** to be up to date; **estar al día** to be up to date (18); **estar bajo muchas presiones** to be under a lot of pressure (14); **estar bien** to be comfortable (*temperature*) (6); **estar casado/a (con)** to be married (to) (16); **estar de acuerdo** to agree (3); **estar de vacaciones** to be on vacation (8); **(no) estar de acuerdo** to (dis)agree (3)
estatal *adj.* state
estatua statue
estatura height; **de estatura mediana** of medium height
este *m.* east (6)
este/a *adj.* this (3)
éstereo stereo
estereotipo stereotype
estilo style
estimar to estimate
esto this (3)
estómago stomach (11)
estornudo sneeze
estos/as *adj.* these (3)

estrategia strategy
estrecho *n.* straight; **Estrecho de Magallanes** Strait of Magellan
estrépito crashing
estrés *m.* stress (14)
estresado/a stressed out, under stress (14)
estresante stressful
estresar to cause stress
estricto/a strict
estrofa verse (*poem*)
estructura structure
estructurar to structure
estuario estuary
estudiantado student body
estudiante *m., f.* student (2)
estudiantil *adj.* (of) student(s) (14)
estudiar to study (2)
estudio office (*in a home*) (5); studio (TV); *pl.* studies (*education*)
estufa stove (10)
estupendo/a stupendous
etapa stage, phase (16)
etcétera etcetera
eterno/a eternal
ético/a ethical
etnia ethnicity
étnico/a ethnic
etnolingüístico/a ethnolinguistic
Europa Europe
europeo/a *n., adj.* European
evangélico/a *n., adj.* evangelical
evangelista *m., f.* evangelist
evento event
evitar to avoid (15)
evolución *f.* evolution
exacto/a exact
exagerado/a exaggerated
examen *m.* exam, test (4)
examinar to examine (11)
exceder to exceed
excelencia excellence
excelente excellent
excepción *f.* exception
excepto except
excesivo/a excessive
exclusivo/a exclusive
excursión *f.* excursion
excusa excuse
exigir (exijo) to demand
exiliarse to go into exile
existencia existence
existir to exist
éxito success; **tener éxito** to be successful
exitoso/a successful
exótico/a exotic
expandir to expand
expectativa expectation
expedición *f.* expedition
experiencia experience
experto/a expert
explicación *f.* explanation
explicar (qu) to explain (8)
exploración *f.* exploration
explorador(a) explorer
explotación *f.* exploitation
explotar to exploit
exponer (*like* **poner**) (*p.p.* **expuesto**) to display; to propose
exportador(a) exporter
exportar to export
exposición *f.* exposition; **de exposición** expository
expresar to express
expresión *f.* expression; **expresión artística** artistic expression (13); **expresión de cortesía** pleasantry (1)
expulsar to expel
expulsión *f.* expulsion
exquisito/a exquisite
extender (extiendo) to extend
extensión *f.* extension
externo/a external
extinción *f.* extinction, **especie** (*f.*) **en peligro de extinción** endangered species (15)
extracto extract
extranjero/a *n.* foreigner (2); *adj.* foreign; **ir al extranjero** to go abroad (8); **lengua extranjera** foreign language (2)
extraño/a strange; **es extraño que** it's strange that (13); **¡qué extraño que…!** how strange that . . . ! (13)
extrovertido/a extrovert(ed)

F

fábrica factory (15)
fabricar (qu) to manufacture (15)
fabuloso/a fabulous
Facebook *m.* Facebook (12); **entrar en Facebook** to go into Facebook (12)
fácil easy (6)
facilitar to facilitate
factor *m.* factor
factoría factory
factura bill (17)
facturar el equipaje to check baggage (8)
falda skirt (4)
fallar to crash (*computer*) (12)
falta lack (15); absence (15)
faltar (a) to be absent (from), not attend (9)
fama fame
familia family (3)
famoso/a famous
fantasía fantasy
fantástico/a fantastic
farmacéutico/a pharmacist (11)
farmacia pharmacy
faro lighthouse
fascinante fascinating
fascinar (*like* **gustar**) to fascinate (13)
fatal *sl.* bad, awful
fatalista *m., f.* fatalist
fauno faun
favor *m.* favor; **a favor de** in favor of; **por favor** please (1)
favorito/a favorite
fax *m.* FAX (12)
febrero February (6)
fecha date (*calendar*) (6); **¿cuál es la fecha de hoy?** what's today's date? (6); **fecha límite** deadline; **¿qué fecha es hoy?** what's today's date? (6)
federación *f.* federation
federativo/a federative
felicidades *f. pl.* congratulations
felicitaciones *f. pl.* congratulations
feliz (*pl.* **felices**) happy (9)
femenino/a feminine
fenicio/a Phoenician
fénix *m.* phoenix
fenomenal phenomenal
fenómeno phenomenon
feo/a ugly (3)
feria fair
feriado: día (*m.*) **feriado** holiday
fertilidad *f.* fertility
festivo/a festive, celebratory (9); **día** (*m.*) **festivo** holiday (9)
ficción *f.* fiction; **ciencia ficción** science fiction
fiebre *f.* fever (11); **tener fiebre** to have a fever
fiel faithful (3)
fiesta party (2); **dar una fiesta** to throw a party (9); **hacer una fiesta** to throw a party (9)
figura figure
fijo/a set, fixed; **precio fijo** fixed, set price (4); **teléfono fijo** landline (12)
fila line
Filadelfia Philadelphia
Filipinas Philippines
filipino/a *n., adj.* Philippine
filmar to film, record
filosofía philosophy (2)
filosófico/a philosophical
fin *m.* end; **a fines de** at the end of; **fin de año** end of the year (9); **fin de semana** weekend (2); **por fin** finally (5)
final *m.* end
finalmente finally (5)
financiar to finance
financiero/a financial
finanzas *f. pl.* finances
finca farm (15)
Finlandia Finland
fino/a fine
firmar to sign
física physics (2)
físico/a physical
flaco/a skinny
flamenco flamingo; *music and dance form of southern Spain*

flan *m.* (baked) custard (7)
flauta flute
flexibilidad *f.* flexibility
flor *f.* flower (8)
flota fleet
folclórico/a traditional (13)
folclorista *m., f.* folklorist
folklórico/a traditional
fomentar to encourage, promote
fondo background; fund; bottom
fontanero/a plumber (*Sp.*)
forma form, shape (4); way; **de forma presencial** in person
formación *f.* formation; education, training
formar to form
formidable tremendous
fórmula formula
formulario form
fortalecer (fortalezco) to strengthen
fortaleza fort
fosforescente phosphorescent
foto(grafía) photo(graph) (8); **sacar (qu) fotos** to take photos (8)
fotocopia photocopy (12); **hacer fotocopia** to copy (12)
fotocopiadora copy machine (12)
fotografía photography (13)
fotógrafo/a photographer (17)
fotomontaje *m.* photo montage
fraccionamiento neighborhood
fragmentado/a fragmented
fragmento fragment, excerpt
francés *m.* French (*language*) (2)
francés, francesa *n.* French person; *adj.* French
Francia France
franja stripe, band; border, fringe
frase *f.* phrase; sentence
frecuencia frequency; **con frecuencia** frequently (2); **¿con qué frecuencia...?** how often . . . ? (3)
frecuente frequent
frecuentemente frequently (11)
frenos *m. pl.* brakes (15)
frente *f.* forehead
frente a facing; **hacer frente a** to face up to
fresa strawberry
fresco: hace fresco it's cool (weather) (6); **fresco/a** fresh (7)
frigorífico refrigerator
frijoles *m. pl.* beans (7)
frío cold(ness); *adj.* cold; **hace (mucho) frío** it's (very) cold (*weather*); **tener (mucho) frío** to be (very) cold (6)
frito/a fried (7); **papa/patata frita** French fried potato (7)
frituras *f. pl.* fried food
frontera border
frustración *f.* frustration
frustrado/a frustrated
fruta fruit (7); **jugo de fruta** fruit juice (7)
frutilla strawberry
fruto fruit
fuego fire
fuente *f.* source; fountain; serving dish
fuera *adv.* outside
fuerzas (*f. pl.*) **armadas** armed forces
fumador(a) smoker; **sala de fumadores** smoking area (8)
fumar to smoke (8); **sala de fumar** smoking area (8)
funcionamiento *n.* functioning, working
funcionar to work, function (12); to run (*machines*) (12)
fundación *f.* foundation
fundar to found
furia rage; **furia al volante** road rage; **furia caminera** road rage
furioso/a furious, angry (6)
fútbol *m.* soccer (10); **fútbol americano** football (10)
futbolista *m., f.* soccer player
futuro *n.* future
futuro/a *adj.* future

G

gabinete *m.* cabinet
gafas *f. pl.* glasses
gallego Galician (*language*)
galleta cookie (7)
gallo/a rooster, hen; **misa del gallo** midnight mass
galope *m.* *traditional dance of Paraguay*
galopera *traditional dance of Paraguay*
gambas *f. pl.* shrimp
ganacia earning
ganador(a) winner
ganar to win (10); to earn (*income*) (13)
ganas: tener ganas de + *inf.* to feel like (*doing something*) (4)
gandules *m. pl.* pigeon peas
ganga bargain (4)
garaje *m.* garage (5)
garantizar (c) to guarantee
garganta throat (11)
garifunas Black Caribs (*descendents of Carib indigenous people and African slaves in Honduras*)
gas *m.* gas (*not for cars*) (12)
gaseosa soft drink
gasolina gasoline (15)
gasolinera gas station (15)
gastar to spend (*money*) (9); to use (*gas*) (15)
gasto expense (12)
gastronomía gastronomy
gastronómico/a gastronomic
gato cat (3)
gaucho Argentine cowboy
gazpacho *cold tomato soup of southern Spain*
gemelo/a twin
genealógico/a: árbol (*m.*) **genealógico** family tree
generación *f.* generation
general general; **en general** in general; **por lo general** generally (5)
generar to generate; to create
genérico/a generic
género genre; gender
generoso/a generous
gente *f. s.* people (12)
genuinamente genuinely
geografía geography
geográfico/a geographic
geología geology
gerente *m., f.* manager (17)
gerundio *gram.* gerund
gimnasio gym(nasium)
gitano/a *n., adj.* gypsy
glaciar *m.* glaciar
gobernador(a) governor
gobierno government (15)
gol *m.* goal (*soccer*)
golf *m.* golf (10)
golpe *m.* blow; **golpe de estado** coup d'état
gordo/a fat (3)
gorila gorilla (15)
gorra baseball cap (4)
GPS *m.* GPS (12)
grabadora (tape) recorder/player (12)
grabar to record (12); to tape (12)
gracias thank you (1); **Día** (*m.*) **de Acción de Gracias** Thanksgiving; **gracias por** + *noun/inf.* thanks for (9); **muchas gracias** thank you very much (1)
grado grade, year (*in school*) (10); degree (*temperature*)
graduarse (me gradúo) (en) to graduate (from) (17)
graffiti *m.* graffiti
gráfico/a graphic
gramática grammar
gramo gram
gran, grande large, big; great (3); **Gran Bretaña** Great Britain; **pantalla grande** big screen (monitor) (12)
granizo hail
granja farm
grano grain
grasa fat
gratis *inv.* free (of charge)
gratuito/a free (of charge)
grave serious
Grecia Greece
griego/a *n., adj.* Greek
grifo faucet
gripa flu (*Mex.*)
gripe *f.* flu (11)
gris gray (4)
gritar to shout
grito shout; cry
grueso/a thick
grupo group; band
guagua bus (*Carib.*)

guaguanco *subgenre of rumba*
guampa *cup made from a hollowed bull's horn used to drink* mate; *cup used to drink* tereré
guanábana soursop (*tropical fruit*)
guancasco *traditional dance of the Lenca of Honduras*
guante *m.* glove
guapo/a handsome; good-looking (3)
guaraní *m. indigenous language of South America*
guardar to keep (12); to save (*documents*) (12); **guardar cama** to stay in bed (11); **guardar un puesto** to save a place (*in line*) (8)
guatemalteco/a *n., adj.* Guatemalan
gubernamental governmental
guerra war (18); **guerra civil** civil war
guía *m., f.* guide (13)
guiado/a guided
guion *m.* script (13)
gustar to be pleasing (8); **¿a usted le gusta... ?** do you (*form. s.*) like . . . ? (1); **me gustaría (mucho)...** I would (really) like . . . (8); **(no,) no me gusta** (no,) I don't like . . . (1); **(sí,) me gusta...** (yes), I like . . . (1); **¿te gusta... ?** do you (*fam. s.*) like . . . ? (1)
gusto like preference; *pl.* likes (1); **mucho gusto** nice to meet you (1)

H

haber (*inf. of* **hay**) there is, there are (12)
habichuelas *f. pl.* beans
habitante *m., f.* inhabitant
habitar to inhabit
hábito habit
hablar to speak; to talk (2); **hablar con soltura** to speak fluently; **hablar por teléfono** to talk on the phone (2)
hacer to do; to make (5); **hace** + *time* + **que** + *present* to have been (*doing something*) for (*time*) (14); **hace** + *time* + **que** + *preterite* ago (14); *present* + **desde hace** + *time* to have been (*doing something*) for (*time*) (14); *preterite* + **hace** + *time* ago (14); **hace (muy) buen/mal tiempo** it's very good/bad weather (6.); **hace (mucho) calor** it's (very) hot (weather) (6.); **hace fresco** it's cool (weather) (6.); **hace (mucho) frío** it's (very) cold (*weather*); **hacer *camping*** to go camping (8); **hacer cola** to stand in line (8); **hacer copia** to copy; **hacer (el método) Pilates** to do Pilates (11); **hacer (el) yoga** to do yoga (11); **hacer (foto) copia** to copy (12); **hacer autostop** to hitchhike; **hacer ejercicio** to exercise (5); **hacer ejercicios aeróbicos** to do aerobics (11); **hacer escalas** to make stops (8); **hacer frente a** to face up to; **hacer la cama** to make the bed (10); **hacer la(s) maleta(s)** to pack one's suitcase(s) (8); **hacer paradas** to make stops (8); **hacer planes para** + *inf.* to make plans to (*do something*) (10); **hacer reserva** to make a reservation; **hacer *surfing*** to surf (10); **hacer un *picnic*** to have a picnic (10); **hacer un viaje** to take a trip (5); **hacer una fiesta** to throw a party (9); **hacer una juerga** to throw a party; **hacer una pregunta** to ask a question (5); **hacerse daño** to hurt oneself (14); **hacerse daño en** to hurt one's (*body part*) (14); **¿qué tiempo hace?** what's the weather like? (6)
hallaca *Venezuelan meat pastry*
hamaca hammock
hambre *f.* hunger; **pasar hambre** to go hungry; **tener (mucha) hambre** to be (very) hungry (7)
hamburguesa hamburger (7)
hard drive *m.* hard drive (12)
hasta *adv.* until; even; *prep.* until; **hasta luego** see you later (1); **hasta mañana** see you tomorrow (1); **hasta pronto** see you soon; **hasta que** until (17)
hay there is/are (1); **hay (mucho/a)** there's (lots of) (6); **hay que** + *inf.* it is necessary to (*do something*) (13); **no hay** there is/are not (1); **no hay de qué** you're welcome (1)
hecho *n.* fact, event (9)
hecho/a (*p.p. of* **hacer**) made
hectárea *land measure equal to 2.5 acres*
helado ice cream (7)
heliconia *flowering tropical plant*
hemisferio hemisphere
heredar to inherit
herencia inheritance
hermanastro/a stepbrother, stepsister
hermano/a brother/sister (3); *m. pl.* siblings (3)
hermoso/a beautiful
héroe *m.* hero
hervir (hiervo) (i) to boil
híbrido/a hybrid (15)
hidroeléctrico/a hydroelectric
hielo ice
hierba grass
hígado liver
hijastro/a stepson, stepdaughter
hijo/a son/daughter (3); *m. pl.* children (3)
himno hymn; **himno nacional** national anthem
hipopótamo hippopotamus
hispánico/a Hispanic
hispano/a Hispanic (3)
Hispanoamérica Hispanic America
hispanohablante *adj. m., f.* Spanish-speaking
hispanonorteamericano/a Hispanic North American
historia history (2)
historiador (a) historian
histórico/a historical
hockey *m.* hockey (10)
hogar *m.* home
hoja leaf
¡hola! hi!; hello!
Holanda Holland
hombre *m.* man (2); **hombre de negocios** businessman (17)
homeopático/a homeopathic
homogeneidad *f.* homogeneity
homogéneo/a homogenous
hondureño/a *n., adj.* Honduran
hongo mushroom; toadstool; fungus; **sombrero hongo** bowler hat, derby
honor *m.* honor
honrado/a honest; honorable
hora hour; time; **¿a qué hora... ?** at what time . . . ? (1); **es hora de...** it's time to . . . ; **¿qué hora es?** what time is it? (1)
horario schedule (14)
hormona hormone
horno oven; **horno de microondas** microwave oven (10)
horror *m.* horror
hospital *m.* hospital
hospitalidad *f.* hospitality
hospitalización *f.* hospitalization
hotel *m.* hotel
hoy today (1); **¿cuál es la fecha de hoy?** what's today's date? (6); **¿qué día es hoy?** what day is today? (5); **¿qué fecha es hoy?** what's today's date? (6)
huelga strike (*labor*) (18)
huella mark; (finger)print
huerto orchard
huevo egg (7)
huipil *m. traditional Mayan blouse*
huir (*like* **construir**) to flee
humanidad *f.* humanity; *pl.* humanities (2)
humanista *n., adj.* humanist
humanitario/a humanitarian
humano/a human; **cuerpo humano** human body (11)
humorístico/a humorous

I

ibérico/a *adj.* Iberian
íbero/a *n.* Iberian
ícono icon
icónico/a iconic
ida: billete (*m.*) (*Sp.*) / **boleto** (*L.A.*) **de ida** one-way ticket (8); **billete** (*m.*) (*Sp.*) / **boleto** (*L.A.*) **de ida y vuelta** round-trip ticket (8)
idealista *m., f.* idealistic
idear to think up, conceive (*idea*)
idéntico/a identical
identidad *f.* identity; **carnet** (*m.*) **de identidad** identification card

identificación *f.* identification; **carnet** (*m.*) **de identificación** identification card; **tarjeta de identificación** identification card (14)
identificar (qu) to identify (oneself)
idioma *m.* language
ídolo idol
iglesia church (16)
ignorante ignorant
ignorar to ignore
igual same; equal
igualdad *f.* equality (18)
igualmente likewise, same here (1)
ilimitado/a unlimited
ilustrar to illustrate
ilustrativo/a illustrative
imagen *f.* image
imaginación *f.* imagination
imaginar(se) to imagine
imaginativo/a imaginative
imitar to imitate
impaciente impatient
impacto impact
impedir (*like* **pedir**) to impede
imperfecto *gram.* imperfect
imperio empire
impermeable *m.* raincoat (4); *adj.* impermeable
impertinente impertinent
imponer (*like* **poner**) to impose
importancia importance
importante important
importar (*like* **gustar**) to matter, be important
imposible impossible; **es imposible que** it's impossible that (13)
impresión *f.* impression
impresionante impressive
impresionar to impress
impreso/a printed
impresora printer (12)
imprimir to print (12)
improbable unlikely; **es improbable que** it's unlikely, improbable that (13)
improvisar to improvise
impuesto tax
impulsivo/a impulsive
inca *n. m., f.* Inca; *adj. m., f.* Incan
incendio fire
incidente *m.* incident
incienso incense
inclinación *f.* inclination
inclinarse to lean
incluir (*like* **construir**) to include
incómodo/a uncomfortable
inconveniencia inconvenience
inconveniente *m.* inconvenient
incorporar to incorporate, include
incorrecto/a incorrect
increíble incredible; **es increíble que** it's incredible that (13)
incrementar to increase
incremento increment
indefinido/a indefinite; **artículo indefinido** *gram.* indefinite article; **palabra indefinida y negativa** *gram.* indefinite and negative word (7)
independencia independence
independiente independent
independizarse (c) to become independent
indescriptible indescribable
indicación *f.* instruction; direction
indicar (qu) to indicate
indicativo *gram.* indicative
índice *m.* index
indiferente indifferent
indígena *n. m., f.* indigenous person; *adj. m., f.* indigenous
indigenista *m., f. pertaining to indigenous topics and themes*
indio/a *n., adj.* Indian
indirecto/a indirect; **complemento indirecto** *gram.* indirect object
indiscreto/a indiscreet
indispensable indispensible, essential
indistinto/a indistinct
individuo *n.* individual
individuo/a *adj.* individual
industria industry
inesperado/a unexpected
infancia infancy (16)
infantil *adj.* child, children's
infección *f.* infection
infinitivo *gram.* infinitive
inflexibilidad *f.* inflexibility
influencia influence
influir (*like* **construir**) to influence
información *f.* information
informar to inform (18)
informática computer science
informativo/a informative
informe *m.* **(oral/escrito)** (oral/written) report (14)
infraestructura infrastructure
infrecuente infrequent
ingeniería engineering
ingeniero/a engineer (17)
ingenioso/a ingenious
Inglaterra England
inglés *m.* English (*language*) (2)
inglés, inglesa *n., adj.* English (3)
ingrediente *m.* ingredient
ingreso income
inicial initial
iniciativa initiative
inicio beginning
inmediato/a immediate
inmenso/a immense
inmerso/a immersed
inmigración *f.* immigration
inmobiliario/a *adj.* real estate, property
inmóvil unmoving
innecesario/a unnecessary
innovador(a) innovative
innumerable countless
inocente innocent
inolvidable unforgettable
inquieto/a restless
inquilino/a tenant (12); renter (12)
inscribir(se) (*p.p.* **inscrito**) **(en)** to sign up, register (for)
inscripción *f.* inscription
inscrito/a (*p.p. of* **inscribir**) registered
insecto insect
insistir (en) to insist (on) (12)
insoportable unbearable
inspiración *f.* inspiration
instalación *f.* facility
instalar to install (12)
instantáneo/a instantaneous
institución *f.* institution
instituto institute
instructor(a) instructor
instrumento instrument
insulina insulin
integrarse to integrate oneself
intelectivo/a cognitive
inteligente intelligent (3)
intención *f.* intention
intencionadamente intentionally
intensidad *f.* intensity
intensificar (qu) to intensify
intenso/a intense
interacción *f.* interaction
intercambiar to exchange
intercambio exchange
interés *m.* interest (17)
interesante interesting
interesar (*like* **gustar**) to interest (*someone*) (8)
intergaláctico/a intergalactic
interior interior; inner; **ropa interior** underwear (4)
interminable endless
internacional international; **Día** (*m.*) **Internacional de la No Violencia Contra la Mujer** International No Violence Against Women Day
Internet *m.* Internet (12); **buscar (qu) en el Internet** to look for on the Internet (12); **entrar en el Internet** to go on the Internet (12)
interno/a internal
interplanetario/a interplanetary
interpretación *f.* interpretation
interpretar to interpret
interrogativo/a *gram.* interrogative (1)
interrumpir to interrupt
intimidad *f.* intimacy
íntimo/a intimate; close
intolerancia intolerance
intranquilidad *f.* restlessness
introducción *f.* introduction
introducir (*like* **conducir**) to introduce
inundación *f.* flood

inútil useless
invadido/a invaded
invasión *f.* invasion
inventar to invent
inversión *f.* investment
invertir (invierto) (i) to invest
investigación *f.* investigation; research
investigador(a) researcher
investigar (gu) to investigate; to research
invierno winter (6)
invitación *f.* invitation
invitado/a guest (9)
invitar to invite (7)
invocar (qu) to invoke
inyección *f.* injection (11); **ponerle una inyección** to give (*someone*) a shot (11)
iPod *m.* iPod (12)
ir to go (4); **ir a** + *inf.* to be going to (*do something*) (4); **ir a un bar** to go to a bar (10); **ir a un concierto** to go to a concert (10); **ir a una discoteca** to go to a disco (10); **ir al extranjero** to go abroad (8); **ir de compras** to go shopping (4); **ir de safari** to go on a safari; **ir de vacaciones a...** to go on vacation in/to . . . (8); **ir distraído/a** to be distracted (14); **ir en...** to go/travel by . . . (8); **ir en autobús** to go/travel by bus (8); **ir en avión** to go/travel by plane (8); **ir en barco** to go/travel by boat, ship (8); **ir en tren** to go/travel by train (8); **vamos** let's go (4)
ira al manejar road rage
iraní (*pl.* **iraníes**) *n., adj.* Iranian
iraquí (*pl.* **iraquíes**) *n., adj.* Iraqi
iridiscencia iridescence
Irlanda Ireland
ironía irony
irónico/a ironic
irresponsable irresponsible
isla island (6)
Islandia Iceland
islote *m.* islet
israelí (*pl.* **israelíes**) *n., adj.* Israeli
Italia Italy
italiano Italian (*language*) (2)
italiano/a *n., adj.* Italian
itinerario itinerary
izquierda *n.* left-hand side; **a la izquierda de** to the left of (6)
izquierdo/a *adj.* left; **levantarse con el pie izquierdo** to get up on the wrong side of the bed (14)

J

jaguar *m.* jaguar
jamás never (7)
jamón *m.* ham (7)
Japón Japan
japonés *m.* Japanese (*language*)
japonés, japonesa *n., adj.* Japanese
jarabe *m.* (cough) syrup (11)
jardín *m.* garden (5)
jazz *m.* jazz
jeans *m. pl.* blue jeans (4)
jefe/a boss (12)
jerarquía hierarchy
jersey *m.* sweater, pullover
jirafa giraffe
jornada de tiempo parcial part-time job
joropo *folkloric music of Venezuela*
joven *n. m., f.* youth; *adj.* young (3); **de joven** as a youth (10)
joyería jewelry
jubilarse to retire (17)
juego game; **Juegos Olímpicos** Olympic Games
juerga party; **hacer una juerga** to throw a party
jueves *m.* Thursday (5)
jugador(a) player (10)
jugar (juego) (gu) (a, al) to play (*a game, sport*) (5); **jugar a las cartas / al ajedrez** to play cards/chess (10)
jugo (de fruta) (fruit) juice (7)
juguete *m.* toy
julio July (6)
junio June (6)
juntos/as together (8)
jurar to swear (*oath*)
justicia justice
justificar (qu) to justify
juvenil *adj.* youth; youthful; **diabetes** (*f.*) **juvenil** childhood diabetes
juventud *f.* youth (16)
juzgar (gu) to judge

K

kaki: color (*m.*) **kaki** khaki
kilo(gramo) kilo(gram)
kilómetro kilometer

L

la *def. art. f. s.* the; *d.o. f. s.* you (*form.*); her, it; **a la(s)...** at . . . (*time of day*) (1); **la cual** which
labor *f.* work, job
laboral *adj.* work, work-related (17)
laboratorio laboratory
lado side; **al lado de** alongside of (6); **por el otro lado** on the other hand; **por un lado** on one hand
ladrar to bark
ladrón, ladrona thief
lago lake (15)
lágrima tear
lamentar to regret; to feel sorry (13)
laminado/a laminated
lámpara lamp (5)
lana wool; **de lana** wool (4)
langosta lobster (7)
lapicero pen
lápiz *m.* (*pl.* **lápices**) pencil (2)
largo/a long (3)
las *def. art. s. pl.* the; *d.o. f. pl.* you (*form. pl.*); **a la(s)...** at . . . (*time of day*) (1); **las cuales** which
lástima shame; **es una lástima que** it's a shame that (13); **¡qué lástima que... !** what a shame that . . . ! (13)
lastimarse to injure oneself
lata can
latín *m.* Latin (*language*)
latino/a *adj.* Latin; **América Latina** Latin America
Latinoamérica Latin America
latinoamericano/a *n., adj.* Latin American
lavabo (bathroom) sink (5)
lavadora washing machine (10)
lavaplatos *m. inv.* dishwasher (10)
lavar to wash (10); **lavarse** to wash (oneself)
lección *f.* lesson
leche *f.* milk (7)
lechón *m.* suckling pig; **lechón asado** roast suckling pig
lechuga lettuce (7)
lector(a) reader
lectura reading
leer (*like* **creer**) to read (3)
legislación *f.* legislation
lejos de far from (6)
lema *m.* motto
lempira *currency of Honduras*
lengua language (2); tongue (11); **lenguas extranjeras** foreign languages (2); **sacar (qu) la lengua** to stick out one's tongue (11)
lentes *m. pl.* glasses (11); **lentes de contacto** contact lenses (11)
lentillas *f. pl.* contact lenses (*Sp.*)
león *m.* lion; **león marino** sea lion
letra letter; lyrics (*song*) (7); **letra redondilla** roman font
levantar to raise, lift; **levantar pesas** to lift weights (11); **levantarse** to get up (out of bed) (5); to stand up (5); **levantarse con el pie izquierdo** to get up on the wrong side of the bed (14)
leve *adj.* light
ley *f.* law (18)
libanés, libanesa lebanese
liberar(se) to free (oneself)
libertad *f.* freedom, liberty
libertador(a) liberator
libra pound
libre free, unoccupied (10); **estado libre asociado** commonwealth; **libre comercio** free trade; **ratos** (*m. pl.*) **libres** spare (free) time (10); **tiempo libre** free time (10)
librería bookstore (2)
libro book (2); **libro de texto** textbook (2)

licencia license; **licencia de manejar/ conducir** driver's license (15)
licor *m.* liqueur
licuar to liquefy
liga league
ligero/a light, not heavy (7)
limitación *f.* limitation
limitar to limit
límite *m.* limit; **fecha límite** deadline; **límite de velocidad** speed limit (15)
limón *m.* lemon
limonada lemonade
limonero lemon tree
limosina limousine
limpiar (la casa) to clean (the) house (10)
limpio/a clean (6)
línea line; **patinar en línea** to rollerblade (10)
lingüístico/a linguistic
lío problem; trouble; **meterse en líos** to get into trouble
liquidación *f.* liquidation
líquido liquid
Lisboa Lisbon
lista list
listo/a smart; clever (3)
literario/a literary
literatura literature (2)
litoral *m.* coast
llamada call
llamar to call (7); **¿cómo se llama usted?** what is your (*form. s.*) name? (1); **¿cómo te llamas?** what is your (*fam. s.*) name? (1); **me llamo...** my name is . . . (1); **llamarse** to be called (5)
llanero Venezuelan cowboy
llanero/a of or pertaining to the plains
llanta (desinflada) (flat) tire (15)
llave *f.* key (5)
llegada arrival (8)
llegar (gu) to arrive (3); **¿cómo se llega a... ?** how do you get to . . . ? (15); **llegar a ser** to become
llenar to fill (up) (15); to fill out (*a form*) (17)
llevar to wear (4); to carry (4); to take (4); **llevar una vida sana/tranquila** to lead a healthy/calm life (11); **llevarse bien/mal (con)** to get along well/poorly (with) (16)
llorar to cry (9)
llover (llueve) to rain (6); **llueve** (it's raining) (6)
lluvia rain
lluvioso/a *adj.* rainy; rain; **bosque** (*m.*) **tropical lluvioso** tropical rain forest
lo *d.o. m. s.* you (*form.*); him; it; **lo bueno** the good news/thing (11); **lo cual** which; **lo malo** the bad news/ thing (11); **lo que** what, that which (5); **lo siento (mucho)** I'm (very) sorry (14); **lo suficiente** enough (11); **por lo general** generally (5); **por lo menos** at least (9); **por lo regular** in general
lobo/a wolf
localidad *f.* ticket (*to movie, play*)
localización *f.* location
loco/a crazy (6)
locutor(a) commentator
lógico/a logical
lograr to achieve
logro achievement
Londres London
longitud *f.* longitude
los *def. art. m. pl.* the; *d.o. m. pl.* you (*form. pl.*); **los cuales** which; **los lunes (los martes...)** on Mondays (Tuesdays . . .) (5)
lubricar (qu) to lubricate
lucha fight, struggle (18)
luchar to fight (18)
luego then, afterward, next (5); **hasta luego** see you later (1)
lugar *m.* place (2)
lujo luxury
lujoso/a luxurious
luminiscente luminescent
luna moon; **luna de miel** honeymoon (16)
lunares: de lunares polka-dot (4)
lunes *m.* Monday (5); **el lunes** on Monday (5); **los lunes** on Mondays (5); **lunes que viene** next Monday (5)
lustroso/a shiny
Luxemburgo Luxembourg
luz *f.* (*pl.* **luces**) light (14)

M

madrastra stepmother
madre *f.* mother (3); **Día** (*m.*) **de la Madre** Mother's Day
madrileño/a of or pertaining to Madrid
madrina godmother
madurez *f.* middle age (16)
maduro/a mature
maestro/a (de escuela) schoolteacher (17); *adj.* master; **obra maestra** masterpiece (13)
Magallanes: Estrecho de Magallanes Strait of Magellan
magnífico/a magnificent
mago wizard
mahones *m. pl.* jeans
maíz *m.* (*pl.* **maíces**) corn
mal *adv.* poorly (2); **caerle mal a alguien** to make a bad impression on someone; **empleo mal pagado** poorly paid job/ position (17); **llevarse mal (con)** to get along poorly (with) (16); **pasarlo mal** to have a bad time (9); **portarse mal** to misbehave (9); **salir mal** to come/turn out badly; to do poorly (5)
mal, malo/a *adj.* bad (3); **lo malo** the bad news/thing (11); **tener mala suerte** to have bad luck, be unlucky (14)
maleta suitcase (8); **hacer la(s) maleta(s)** to pack one's suitcase(s) (8)
maletero porter (8)
malvado/a evil
mamá mother, mom (3)
mami mom, mommy
mamífero mammal
mancha stain
mandar to send; to order (*someone to do something*) (12); **mandar un mensaje** to (send a) text (2)
mandato command (7)
manejar to drive (12); to operate (*a machine*) (12); **ira al manejar** road rage; **licencia de manejar** driver's license (15)
manera way, manner; **de manera que** so that, in such a way that
manifestación *f.* demonstration, march (18)
mano *f.* hand (11); **darse la mano** to shake hands (11)
mansión *f.* mansion
mantener (*like* **tener**) to maintain, keep (18); **mantenerse en contacto** to stay in touch
mantequilla butter (7)
manzana apple (7); (city) block
mañana tomorrow (1); **de la mañana** in the morning, A.M. (1); **hasta mañana** see you tomorrow (1); **pasado mañana** the day after tomorrow (5); **por la mañana** in the morning (2)
mapa *m.* map
mapudungun *m.* *language of the Mapuche people*
máquina machine
mar *m.* sea (8); **mar Caribe** Caribbean Sea
maracuyá *m.* passion fruit
maratón *m.* marathon
maravilla wonder, marvel
maravilloso/a marvelous
marca brand; label
marcar (qu) to mark
marcial martial
mareado/a dizzy (11); nauseated (11)
marido husband (16)
marinera *folkloric dance of coastal Peru*
marino/a marine; **león** (*m.*) **marino** sea lion
mariscos *m. pl.* shellfish (7)
marítimo/a maritime; sea, marine
marketing *m.* marketing
marrón *adj., m., f.* brown
martes *m.* Tuesday (5); **los martes** on Tuesdays (5)
Marruecos Morocco
marzo March (6)
más more (2); **cada vez más** increasingly; **más de** + *number* more than + *number* (6); **más... que** more (-er) . . . than (6)
masa mass
máscara mask

mascota pet (3)
masculino/a masculine
masia *country home in Catalonia*
masivo/a massive
masticar (qu) to chew
matar to kill (18)
mate *m.* *traditional drink of Argentina*
matemáticas *f. pl.* math (2)
materia subject area (2)
material *m.* material (4)
materialidad *f.* material aspect; outward appearance
maternidad *f.* maternity
materno/a maternal
matinal *adj.* morning
matriarcado matriarchy
matrícula tuition (2)
matricularse to enroll, register
matrimonio marriage; married couple (16)
máximo/a maximum
maya *n., adj. m., f.* Mayan
mayo May (6)
mayor older (6); oldest; greater; greatest; **Antillas** (*f. pl.*) **Mayores** Greater Antilles; **cada vez mayor** greater and greater
mayoría majority
mayoritariamente primarily
mayúscula capital (letter), uppercase
me *d.o.* me; *i.o.* to/for me; *refl. pron.* myself; **me gustaría (mucho)...** I would (really) like . . . (8); **me llamo...** my name is . . . (1); **(no,) no me gusta** (no,) I don't like . . . (1); **(sí,) me gusta...** (yes), I like . . . (1)
mecánico/a mechanic (15)
mecanización *f.* mechanization
mecanografía typing
medalla medal
mediano/a: de estatura mediana of medium height
medianoche *f.* midnight (6)
medias *f. pl.* stockings (4)
medicamento medicine
medicina medicine (11)
médico/a (medical) doctor (3)
medio *n.* medium; means; *pl.* mass media (18); **medio ambiente** environment (15); **medio de comunicación** medium of communication (18); **medio de transporte** means of transportation (8)
medio/a *adj.* half; middle; average; **media naranja** better half; **y media** half past (*the hour*) (1)
medioambiental environmental
mediodía *m.* noon (6)
mejilla cheek
mejor better; best (6)
mejorar(se) to improve; to get better
mellizo/a fraternal twin
melódico/a melodious
memoria memory (12)
mencionar to mention
menor younger (6); youngest; less; least
menos less; least; minus; **a menos que** *conj.* unless (16); **al menos** at least; **menos cuarto** a quarter to (*hour*) (1); **menos de** + *number* less than + *number* (6); **menos quince** fifteen minutes till (*hour*) (1); **por lo menos** at least (9)
mensaje *m.* message; **mandar un mensaje** to (send a) text (2)
mensual monthly
mentira lie (12)
menú *m.* menu (7)
menudo: a menudo *adv.* often
mercadeo marketing
mercado market(place) (4)
merecer (merezco) to deserve
merendar (meriendo) to have a snack (7)
merengue *m.* *dance from the Dominican Republic*
merienda snack (7)
mes *m.* month (6)
mesa table (2); **poner la mesa** to set the table (10); **quitar la mesa** to clear the table (10)
meseta plateau
mesita end table (5)
mesoamericano/a *n., adj.* Meso-American
mestizaje *m.* mixing of races
meta goal
metáfora metaphor
metal *m.* metal
metálico/a metallic
meteorológico/a *n.* meteorological; *adj.* meteorological
meter to put, place; **meterse en líos** to get into trouble
método method; **hacer (el método) Pilates** to do Pilates (11)
metro subway; **parada del metro** subway stop (12)
metrópoli *f.* metropolis
mexicano/a Mexican (3)
mexicanoamericano/a Mexican American
mezcla mix
mezclar to mix
mezclilla denim
mezquita mosque
mí *obj. of prep.* me (6)
mi(s) *poss. adj.* my (3)
microcuento very short story
microondas: horno de microondas microwave oven (10)
miedo fear; **tener miedo (de)** to be afraid (of) (4)
miel *f.* honey; **luna de miel** honeymoon (16)
miembro/a member
mientras while (10)
miércoles *m.* Wednesday (5); **ayer fue miércoles...** yesterday was Wednesday . . . (5)
mierda shit
mil (one) thousand (4)
milenario/a thousand-year
mililitro milliliter
militar *n. m., f.* soldier; *adj.* military; **servicio militar** military service (18)
milla mile
millón: un millón (de) one million (4)
mineral: agua *f.* (*but* **el agua**) **(mineral)** (mineral) water (7)
minidiálogo minidialogue
mínimo minimum
ministerio ministry
ministro/a minister; **primer(a) ministro/a** prime minister
minoría minority
minuto minute
mío/a(s) *poss. adj.* my; *poss. pron.* (of) mine (17)
mirada look
mirar to look at, watch (3); **mirar la tele(visión)** to watch television (3)
misa mass; **misa del gallo** midnight mass
misión *f.* mission
mismo/a same (6); **ahora mismo** right now (6)
misterioso/a mysterious
mitad *f.* half
mixto/a mixed
mochila backpack (2)
moda fashion; style; **a la moda** in fashion, in a stylish way; **es de última moda** it's trendy (hot) (4); **está de moda** it's trendy (hot) (4)
modales *m. pl.* manners
modelo model, example
módem *m.* modem (12)
moderación *f.* moderation
modernidad *f.* modernity
moderno/a modern (13)
modificar (qu) to modify
modismo idiom
modista dressmaker
modo way, matter; mode; *gram.* mood; **de modo que** in such a way that
molestar (*like* **gustar**) to bother (11)
molesto/a annoyed (6)
molino: rueda de molino treadmill
momento moment
monarquía monarchy
monasterio monastery
moneda coin (17); currency
monedero coin purse
mongoloide *adj. m., f.* Mongoloid
monitor *m.* monitor
monitoreo monitoring
monitorizar (c) to monitor
monoparental *adj.* single-parent
monopatín *m.* skateboard (12)
monótono/a monotonous
monovolumen *m.* minivan
monstruo monster
montaje *m.* montage

montaña mountain (8)
montar to ride; **montar a caballo** to ride a horse (10); **montar en bicicleta** to ride a bicycle
montón *m.*: **un montón** a lot
montuno *traditional hat of Panama*
monumento monument
morado/a purple (4)
moreno/a brunet(te) (3)
morir(se) ([me] muero) (u) (*p.p.* **muerto**) to die (9)
moro/a *n.* Moor; *adj.* Moorish
mosca fly
mostrador *m.* counter
mostrar (muestro) to show (8)
motivo motive
moto(cicleta) motorcycle; moped (12)
motor *m.* motor
móvil mobile
movimiento movement
mucho *adv.* much (2); a lot (2); **lo siento mucho** I'm very sorry (14); **me gustaría mucho...** I would really like . . . (8); **muchísimo** an awful lot (8)
mucho/a a lot (of) (3); *pl.* many (3); **estar bajo muchas presiones** to be under a lot of pressure (14); **muchas gracias** thank you very much (1); **mucho gusto** nice to meet you (1); **tener mucha hambre** to be very hungry (7); **tener mucha sed** to be very thirsty (7); **tener muchas presiones** to be under a lot of stress (14); **tener mucho calor** to be very warm, hot (6); **tener mucho frío** to be very cold (6)
mudanza *n.* move
mudarse to move (*residence*) (12)
mueble *m.* piece of furniture (5); **sacudir los muebles** to dust the furniture
muela molar, back tooth (11); **sacarle (qu) una muela** to extract (*someone's*) molar (11)
muerte *f.* death (16)
muerto/a (*p.p. of* **morir**) dead; **Día** (*m.*) **de los Muertos** Day of the Dead
mujer *f.* woman (2); wife (16); **Día** (*m.*) **Internacional de la No Violencia Contra la Mujer** International No Violence Against Women Day; **mujer de negocios** businesswoman (17); **mujer soldado** female soldier (17)
mula mule
mulato/a mulatto
multa fine
multilingüe multilingual
múltiple multiple
multiplicarse (qu) to multiply, grow in number
multirracial multiracial
mundial *adj.* world; **Copa Mundial** World Cup
mundo world (3); **Copa del Mundo** World Cup (soccer)
municipio municipality
muñeca doll
mural *m.* mural
muralista *m., f.* muralist
muralla city wall
murciélago bat
muro wall
músculo muscle
museo museum; **visitar un museo** to visit a museum (10)
música music (13)
musical musical (13)
músico *m., f.* musician (13)
musulmán, musulmana Muslim
muy very (2); **está muy nublado** it's very cloudy, overcast (6); **muy bien** fine, very well (1); **muy buenas** good afternoon/evening (1)

N

nacer (nazco) to be born (16)
nacimiento birth
nación *f.* nation; **Organización** (*f.*) **de Naciones Unidas (ONU)** United Nations (U.N.)
nacional national; **himno nacional** national anthem; **producto nacional bruto** gross national product
nacionalidad *f.* nationality; **adjetivo de nacionalidad** adjective of nationality (3)
nada nothing, not anything (7); **de nada** you're welcome (1); **para nada...** at all (8)
nadar to swim (8)
nadie no one, nobody, not anybody (7)
nahuatl *m.* Nahuatl (*language of the Aztecs*)
nana *fam.* grandma
naranja orange (7); **media naranja** better half
naranjo orange tree
nariz *f.* (*pl.* **narices**) nose (11)
narración *f.* narration
narrador(a) narrator
narrar to narrate
natación *f.* swimming (10)
natal: casa natal house where someone was born
nativo/a native
natural natural; **ciencias** (*f. pl.*) **naturales** natural sciences (2); **recurso natural** natural resource (15)
naturaleza nature (15)
naturopata *m., f.* naturopath
náufrago shipwreck
nave (*f.*) **espacial** spaceship
navegación *f.* navigation
navegar (gu) to navigate; **navegar la Red** to surf the Internet
Navidad *f.* Christmas (9)
necesario/a necessary (3)
necesidad *f.* need, necessity
necesitar to need (2)
negación *f.* negation
negar (niego) (gu) to deny (13)
negativo/a negative; **palabra indefinida y negativa** *gram.* indefinite and negative word (7)
negociar to negotiate
negocio business; **hombre** (*m.*) **de negocios** businessman (17); **mujer** (*f.*) **de negocios** businesswoman (17)
negrilla: en negrilla boldface
negro/a black (4)
neoyorquino/a *adj.* pertaining to New York
neomático tire (automobile)
nerviosismo nervousness
nervioso/a nervous (6)
neutralizar (c) to neutralize
neutro/a neutral
nevar (nieva) to snow (6); **nieva** it's snowing (6)
nevera refrigerator
ni neither; nor; **ni... ni** neither . . . nor
nicaragüense *n., adj. m., f.* Nicaraguan
nido nest
niebla fog
nieto/a grandson/granddaughter (3)
ningún (ninguna) no, not any (7)
niñero/a baby-sitter (10)
niñez *f.* (*pl.* **niñeces**) childhood (10)
niño/a small child; boy/girl (3); **de niño/a** as a child (10)
no no (1); **no estar de acuerdo** to disagree (3); **no hay** there is/are not (1); **no hay de qué** you're welcome (1); **no tener razón** to be wrong (4); **ya no** no longer
noche *f.* night; **buenas noches** good-night (1); **de la noche** in the evening, P.M. (1); **esta noche** tonight (6); **por la noche** at night, in the evening (2)
Nochebuena *f.* Christmas Eve (9)
Nochevieja *f.* New Year's Eve (9)
nombrar to name
nombre *m.* name (7)
noreste *m.* northeast
norma rule, norm
normal normal; **es normal que** it's normal that (13)
normalidad *f.* normality
noroeste *m.* northwest
norte *m.* north (6)
Norteamérica North America
norteamericano/a North American
nos *d. o. pron.* us; *i. o. pron.* to/for us; *refl. pron.* ourselves; **nos vemos** see you around (1)
nosotros/as *subj. pron.* we (2); *obj.* (*of prep.*) us (2)
nota grade (*academic*) (14); note
notar to note, notice
noticias *f. pl.* news (18)

noticiero newscast (18)
novecientos/as nine hundred (4)
novela novel (13)
novelista *m., f.* novelist (13)
noveno/a ninth (13)
noventa ninety (3)
noviazgo engagement (16)
noviembre *m.* November (6)
novio/a boyfriend/girlfriend (6); fiancé(e) (16); groom/bride (16)
nube *f.* cloud
nublado cloudy; **está (muy) nublado** it's (very) cloudy, overcast (6)
nuclear: energía nuclear nuclear energy (15)
nuestro/a(s) *poss. adj.* our (3); *poss. pron.* our, of ours (17)
nueve nine (1)
nuevo/a new (3); **Año Nuevo** New Year; **Nueva York** New York
número number (1); **número ordinal** ordinal number (13)
numeroso/a numerous
nunca never (3); **casi nunca** almost never (3)
nupcial nuptial; **votos** (*m. pl.*) **nupciales** wedding vows
nutritivo/a nutritious

O

o or (1)
obedecer (obedezco) to obey (15)
objetivo *n.* objective
objeto object (2)
obligación *f.* obligation
obligado/a customary
obligatorio/a obligatory
obra work; **obra de arte** work of art (13); **obra de teatro** play (13); **obra maestra** masterpiece (13); **obra teatral** play
obrero/a worker, laborer (17)
observación *f.* observation
obstáculo obstacle
obtener (*like* **tener**) to get, obtain (12)
ocasión *f.* occasion
ocasionar to cause
océano ocean (8); **océano Pacífico** Pacific Ocean
ochenta eighty (3)
ocho eight (1)
ochocientos/as eight hundred (4)
octavo/a eighth (13)
octillizo/a octuplet
octubre *m.* October (6)
oculista *m., f.* ophthalmologist
oculto/a hidden
ocupación *f.* occupation
ocupado/a busy (6)
ocupar to hold, occupy
ocurrir to occur
odiar to hate (8)
oeste *m.* west (6)
oferta offer, deal
off: voz en off voice over
oficial official
oficina office (2)
oficio trade (*profession*) (17)
ofrecer (ofrezco) to offer (8)
oído inner ear (11)
oír to hear (5); to listen to (*music, the radio*) (5)
ojalá (que) I hope (that) (13)
ojo eye (11); **ojo alerto** eagle eye; *interj.* **¡ojo!** watch out!
olímpico/a: Juegos (*m. pl.*) **Olímpicos** Olympic Games
olor *m.* odor
olvidar(se) (de) to forget (about) (9)
omnipresente omnipresent
once eleven (1)
onda wave; **¿cuál es tu onda?** what's your style? **en onda** in style; **¿qué onda?** what's new/happening?
ONU *f.* **(Organización** [*f.*] **de Naciones Unidas)** U.N. (United Nations)
opción *f.* option
ópera opera (13)
operación *f.* operation
opinar to think; to have, express an opinion
opinión *f.* opinion
oponerse (a) (*like* **poner**) to oppose
oportunidad *f.* opportunity
optar (por) to opt (for)
optimista *m., f.* optimist; *adj.* optimistic
opuesto/a opposite
oración *f.* sentence
oral oral (14); **informe** (*m.*) **oral** oral report (14)
orangután *m.* orangutan
órbita orbit
orden *m.* order
ordenado/a neat (6)
ordenador *m.* **(portátil)** *Sp.* (laptop) computer (12)
ordenar to put in order
ordinal: número ordinal ordinal number (13)
ordinario/a ordinary
oreja (outer) ear (11)
orgánico/a organic
organismo organism
organización *f.* organization
organizar (c) to organize
órgano organ
orgullo pride
orgulloso/a proud
oriental eastern
origen *m.* origin
originario/a native
oriundo/a native
oro gold; **de oro** gold (4)
orquesta orchestra (13)
orquídea orchid
ortogar (gu) to give
ortografía spelling
oso bear
ostra oyster
otavaleno/a *resident of Otavalo* (*Ecuador*)
otoño fall, autumn (6)
otorgar (gu) to grant
otro/a other, another (3); **otra vez** again; **por el otro lado** on the other hand
ozono: capa de ozono ozone layer (15)

P

paciencia patience
paciente *n. m., f.* patient (11); *adj.* patient
pacífico/a Pacific; **océano Pacífico** Pacific Ocean
padrastro stepfather
padre *m.* father (3); *m. pl.* parents (3); **Día** (*m.*) **del Padre** Father's Day
padrino godfather
paella *Spanish dish made with rice, shellfish, and often chicken, and flavored with saffron*
pagado/a: empleo bien/mal pagado well-/poorly paid job/position (17)
pagar (gu) to pay (for) (2)
página page; **página Web** webpage
país *m.* country (3)
pájaro bird (3)
Pakistán Pakistan
pakistaní *m., f.* Pakistani
palabra word (1); **palabra indefinida y negativa** *gram.* indefinite and negative word (7)
palacio palace
palestino/a Palestinian
palma palm tree
palmera palm tree
palo stick
pampa plain (*geography, Arg.*)
pampango *language spoken in the Philippines*
pan *m.* bread (7); **pan tostado** toast (7)
panameño/a *n., adj.* Panamanian
páncreas *m. inv.* pancreas
pandemia pandemic
pandilla gang
pánel (*m.*) **solar** solar panel
panhispano/a Pan-Hispanic
pánico panic
panorama *m.* panorama
pantalla (grande/plana) (big/flat) screen (monitor) (12)
pantalones *m. pl.* pants (4); **pantalones cortos** shorts (4)
papa (frita) (French fried) potato (7)
papá *m.* father, dad (3); *m. pl.* parents
papel *m.* paper (2); role (13)
par *m.* pair
para (intended) for; in order to (3); **para** + *inf.* (*do something*) (10); **para nada…** at all (8); **para que** so that (16)

parabrisas *m. inv.* windshield (15)
paracaidismo skydiving
parada stop (8); **hacer paradas** to make stops (8); **parada del autobús** bus stop (12); **parada del metro** subway stop (12)
paraguayo/a *n., adj.* Paraguayan
parar to stop (15)
parcial partial; **empleo de tiempo parcial** part-time job/position (17); **trabajo de tiempo parcial** part-time job (14)
pardo/a brown
parecer (parezco) (*like* **gustar**) to seem; **parecerse (a)** to resemble
pared *f.* wall (5)
pareja (married) couple; partner (16)
paréntesis *m. inv.* parentheses
pariente *m.* relative (3)
parlamentario/a parliamentary
parque *m.* park
parqueadero parking lot
párrafo paragraph
parrilla grill
parte *f.* part (5); **por todas partes** everywhere (14)
participación *f.* participation
participar to participate
particular particular; unique; **en particular** particularly
partida: punto de partida starting point
partido game, match (10); political party (18)
partir: a partir de beyond (4)
pasado/a past, last (11); **año pasado** last year; **pasado mañana** the day after tomorrow (5)
pasaje *m.* fare, price (*of a transportation ticket*) (8)
pasajero/a passenger (8)
pasaporte *m.* passport (8)
pasar to spend (*time*) (6); to happen (6); **pasar hambre** to go hungry; **pasar la aspiradora** to vacuum (10); **pasar las vacaciones en...** to spend one's vacation in . . . (8); **pasar por la aduana** to go/pass through customs (8); **pasar por el control de seguridad** to go/pass through security (check) (8); **pasarlo bien/mal** to have a good/bad time (9)
pasatiempo pastime (10)
Pascua Easter (9)
pasear to take a walk, stroll; to go for a ride; **pasear en bicicleta** to ride a bicycle (10)
paseo walk, stroll; **dar un paseo** to take a walk (10)
pasillo aisle (8)
paso step
pastel *m.* cake (7); pie (7); **pastel de cumpleaños** birthday cake (9)
pastilla pill (11)
pastor(a) minister
patata (frita) (French fried) potato (7)
paternidad *f.* paternity
patinaje *m.* skating (10)
patinar to skate (10); **patinar en línea** to rollerblade (10)
patines *m. pl.* (roller/inline) skates (12)
patio patio (5); yard (5)
patojo/a *sl.* young man/woman (*Guat.*)
Patricio: Día (*m.*) **de San Patricio** St. Patrick's Day
patrimonio patrimony
patriota *m., f.* patriot
pavo turkey (7)
paz *f.* (*pl.* **paces**) peace (18)
peca freckle
pecho chest
pedazo piece
pedir (pido) (i) to ask for (5); to order (5); **pedir disculpas** to apologize (14); **pedir prestado/a** to borrow (17)
pegar (gu) to hit (10); **pegarse con/contra** to run, bump into/against (14)
peinarse to comb/brush one's hair (5)
Pekín Peking
pelado/a *sl.* young man/woman (*Col.*)
pelear to fight (10)
pelícano pelican
película movie (5)
peligro danger; **especie** (*f.*) **en peligro de extinción** endangered species (15)
peligroso/a dangerous
pelo hair; **teñirse (me tiño) (i) el pelo** to dye one's hair; **tomarle el pelo** to pull someone's leg
pelota ball
pelotero/a baseball player
peluquero/a hairstylist (17)
pen drive *m.* memory stick (12)
pendiente *m.* earring (*Sp.*)
península peninsula
pensar (pienso) (en) to think (about) (5); **pensar** + *inf.* to intend, plan to (*do something*) (5)
pensativo/a pensive
penúltimo/a next to last
peor worse (6)
pequeño/a small (3)
percibir to perceive
perder (pierdo) to lose; to miss (*an event*) (5)
perdón excuse me (1)
perdonar to forgive
perdurable lasting
perezoso/a lazy (3)
perfección *f.* perfection
perfecto/a perfect
pérfido/a treacherous
perfil *m.* profile
perforación *f.* drilling (*well*)
perfume *m.* perfume
periódico newspaper (3)
periodismo journalism
periodista *m., f.* journalist (17)
período period (*of time*)
permanecer (permanezco) to remain, stay
permanente permanent
permiso permission; permit; **(con) permiso** excuse me (1); **permiso de manejar** driving permit
permitir to permit, allow (12)
pero but (1)
perro dog (3)
persecución *f.* persecution
perseguir (*like* **seguir**) to chase; to pursue
persona person (2)
personaje *m.* character (*book, movie*)
personal (*m.*) **médico** medical personnel (11)
personal *adj.* personal; **pronombre** (*m.*) **personal** *gram.* personal pronoun (2)
personalidad *f.* personality
perspectiva perspective
persuasivo/a persuasive
pertenecer (pertenezco) a to belong to
perturbar to perturb, bother
peruano/a *n., adj.* Peruvian
pesado/a boring; difficult (10); heavy
pesar to weigh; **a pesar de** in spite of
pesas: levantar pesas to lift weights (11)
pescado fish (7)
petición *f.* request
petróleo petroleum, oil (15)
petrolero/a *adj.* oil; petroleum
pez *m.* (*pl.* **peces**) fish (15)
picante hot, spicy (7)
picnic:* hacer un *picnic to have a picnic (10)
pico peak
pie *m.* foot (11); **dedo del pie** toe; **levantarse con el pie izquierdo** to get up on the wrong side of the bed (14)
pierna leg (11)
pila battery; **ponerse las pilas** to get one's act together; to energize oneself
pilar *m.* pillar
Pilates: hacer (el método) Pilates to do Pilates (11)
píldora pill
piloto *m., f.* pilot (8)
pimienta pepper (7)
pingüino penguin
pino pine (tree)
pintar to paint (13)
pintor(a) painter (13)
pintura painting (*general*) (13)
piña pineapple
pirámide *f.* pyramid
piraña piranha
Pirineos *m. pl.* Pyrenees
pisar to step on, tread on
piscina swimming pool (5)

Piscis *m.* Pisces
pisco *type of alcoholic beverage of Peru and Chile*
piso floor (*of a building*) (12); **barrer (el piso)** to sweep (the floor) (10); **primer piso** first floor (second story) (12); **segundo piso** second floor (third story) (12)
pizarra chalkboard
pizarrón *m.* (chalk)board (2); **pizarrón blanco** whiteboard (2)
placa license plate
plan *m.* plan; **hacer planes para** + *inf.* to make plans to (*do something*) (10)
planchar to iron (10)
planeación *f.* planning
planeta *m.* planet (15)
planetario/a planetary
plano map; blueprint
plano/a flat; **pantalla plana** flat screen (monitor) (12)
planta plant
planta baja ground floor (12)
plasma *m.* plasma (12)
plástico plastic
plata *n.* silver; **de plata** *adj.* silver (4)
plátano plantain
platino platinum
plato dish (5); plate (5); **plato principal** main course (7)
playa beach (6)
plaza plaza, square (4)
plazo deadline (14); **a plazos** in installments (17)
pleno/a complete; full
plomero/a plumber (17)
pluma pen
plurinacional multinational
población *f.* population (15)
pobre poor (3)
pobreza poverty
poco (a) little (2); few (4); **un poco (de)** a little bit (of) (2)
poder (puedo) to be able, can (4)
poder *m.* power; **poder adquisitivo** purchasing power
poema *m.* poem
poesía poetry
poeta *m., f.* poeta (13)
poético/a poetic
policía *m., f.* police officer (15); *f.* police (*force*); **mujer** (*f.*) **policía** policewoman
política politics; policy (18)
político/a *n.* politician (18); *adj.* political; **ciencias** (*f. pl.*) **políticas** political science (2)
pollera *typical indigenous skirt of the Andes*
pollo chicken (7); **pollo asado** roast chicken (7); **pollo frito** fried chicken
polvo dust
poner to put (5); to place (5); to turn on (*an appliance*) (5); **poner atención** to pay attention; **poner la mesa** to set the table (10); **ponerle una inyección** to give (*someone*) a shot (11); **ponerse** to put on (*an article of clothing*) (5); **ponerse** + *adj.* to become, get + *adj.* (9); **ponerse las pilas** to get one's act together; to energize oneself
popularidad *f.* popularity
por about (6); because of (6); through (8); for (8); by (14); **gracias por** + *noun/inf.* thanks for (9); **por consiguiente** as a result; **por Dios** for heaven's sake (14); **por ejemplo** for example (14); **por el otro lado** on the other hand; **por eso** for that reason (3); **por favor** please (1); **por fin** finally (5); **por la mañana** in the morning (2); **por la noche** at night, in the evening (2); **por la tarde** in the afternoon (2); **por lo general** generally (5); **por lo menos** at least (9); **por lo regular** in general; **por primera/última vez** for the first/last time (14); **por si acaso** just in case (14); **por todas partes** everywhere (14); **por un lado** on one hand
porcentaje *m.* percentage
porción *f.* portion, part
poro pore
porotos *m. pl.* beans
porque because (3)
portarse bien/mal to (mis)behave (9)
portátil portable; **computadora portátil** laptop (computer) (2); **ordenador** (*m.*) **portátil** (*Sp.*) laptop computer (12)
portero/a building manager; doorman (12)
portón *m.* front door, gate
portugués *m.* Portuguese (*language*)
portugués, portuguesa *n., adj.* Portuguese
posar to pose
posesión *f.* possession
posesivo/a possessive (17); **adjetivo posesivo** *gram.* possessive adjective (3)
posibilidad *f.* possibility
posible possible (3); **es posible que** it's possible that (13)
posición *f.* position
positivo/a positive
posponer (*like* **poner**) to postpone
postal: tarjeta postal postcard (8)
posterior later, subsequent
postre *m.* dessert (7)
postularse to run (18); **postularse como candidato/a** to run as a candidate (18); **postularse para un cargo como candidato/a** to run for a position as a candidate (18)
potencia power
potencial *m.* potential; *adj.* potential
práctica practice
practicar (qu) to practice (2); **practicar el alpinismo** to mountain climb; **practicar un deporte** to play a sport
práctico/a practical
preadolescencia preadolescence
precedente *m.* precedent
preceder to precede
precio (fijo) (fixed, set) price (4)
precioso/a precious
precipicio precipice
precipitado/a hasty
precisamente precisely
precolombino/a pre-Columbian
predicción *f.* prediction
predominante predominant
predominar to predominate
preescolar *adj.* preschool
preferencia preference (1)
preferir (prefiero) (*i.*) to prefer (4)
pregunta question (5); **hacer una pregunta** to ask a question (5)
preguntar to ask (*a question*) (8)
prehistórico/a prehistoric
premio prize
prenda article of clothing
prensa (print) press (18); news media (18)
prensado/a pressed
preocupación *f.* worry
preocupado/a worried (6)
preocupar(se) to worry
preparación *f.* preparation
preparar to prepare (7); **prepararse** to prepare oneself; to get ready
preposición *f. gram.* preposition (5)
preseleccionado/a pre-selected
presencia presence
presencial: de forma presencial in person
presentación *f.* presentation
presentador(a) presenter; (television) anchor
presentar to introduce; to present
presente *m.* present (*time*); *gram.* present tense; *adj.* present
preservar to preserve
presidencia precedence
presidencial presidential
presidente/a president
presión pressure (14); **estar bajo muchas presiones** to be under a lot of pressure (14); **tener muchas presiones** to be under a lot of stress (14)
preso/a prisoner
prestado/a: pedir prestado/a to borrow (17)
préstamo loan (17)
prestar to lend (8)
prestigioso/a prestigious
presupuestario/a budgetary
presupuesto budget (17)
pretérito *gram.* preterite
prevenir (*like* **venir**) to warn

primario/a primary; first; elementary; **escuela primaria** elementary school
primavera spring (6)
primer(o/a) first (5); **el primero de** the first of (*month*) (6); **primer piso** first floor (second story) (12); **primer (a) ministro/a** prime minister; **por primera vez** for the first time (14)
primo/a cousin (3); *m. pl.* cousins (3)
princesa princess
principal main; **plato principal** main course (7)
príncipe *m.* prince
principiante *m., f.* beginner; novice
principio beginning; **al principio de** at the beginning of (17)
prisa: tener prisa to be in a hurry (4)
privacidad *f.* privacy
privado/a private
privilegio privilege
probabilidad *f.* probability
probable probable; **es probable que** it's likely, probable that (13)
probar (pruebo) to try, taste
problema *m.* problem
problemático/a problematic
procedimiento procedure
procesión *f.* procession
proceso process
procurar to procure
producción *f.* production
producir (*like* **conducir**) to produce
producto product; **producto nacional bruto** gross national product
productor(a) producer
profesión *f.* profession (17)
profesional *n. m., f.* professional, person with a profession
profesionista *m., f.* professional, person with a profession
profesor(a) professor (1)
profesorado faculty
profundo/a deep
programa *m.* program; **programa (del curso)** (course) syllabus (14)
programación *f.* programming
programador(a) programmer (17)
progresivo/a progressive
prohibir (prohíbo) to prohibit, forbid (12)
proliferación *f.* proliferation
promedio average
prometer to promise (8)
promover (promuevo) to promote
pronombre *m. gram.* pronoun; **pronombre personal** *gram.* personal pronoun (2); **pronombre relativo** *gram.* relative pronoun
pronosticar (qu) to forecast
pronóstico forecast
pronto soon; **hasta pronto** see you soon; **tan pronto como** as soon as (17)
prontuario guide
pronunciación *f.* pronunciation
pronunciar to pronounce
propiedad *f.* property, characteristic
propio/a own, one's own (17)
proponer (*like* **poner**) to propose
proporcionar to provide
propósito purpose
prórroga extension
protagonista *m., f.* protagonist
protección *f.* protection
proteger (protejo) to protect (15)
protestante *n., adj. m., f.* Protestant
protestar to protest
proveer (*like* **creer**) to provide
proverbio proverb
providencia providence
próximo/a next; **el próximo (martes…)** next (Tuesday . . .) (5); **la próxima semana** next week (5)
proyección *f.* projection
proyecto project
prudente prudent
prueba quiz; test (14); proof
publicación *f.* publication
publicar (qu) to publish
publicidad *f.* publicity
público *n.* audience (13)
público/a *adj.* public (15); **transporte** (*m.*) **público** public transportation
pueblo town
puente *m.* bridge
puerta door (2); **puerta de embarque** boarding gate (8)
puerto port (8)
puertorriqueño/a *n., adj.* Puerto Rican
puesto job, position; place (*in line*) (8)
pulmones *m. pl.* lungs (11)
pulpería grocery store (*C.A.*)
punto point; **a punto de** + *inf.* about to + *inf.*; **en punto** on the dot (*time*) (1); **punto cardinal** cardinal point (6); **punto de vista** point of view
puro/a pure (15)
púrpura *n.* purple
purpúreo/a *adj.* purple

Q

que that, which (3); who (3); **así que** therefore, consequently, so; **hasta que** *conj.* until; **que Dios te bendiga** God bless you; **ya que** since
¿qué? what? which?; **¿a qué hora… ?** at what time . . . ? (1); **¿con qué frecuencia… ?** how often . . . ? (3); **¿por qué?** why?
¡qué… ! what . . . !; **¡qué yuca!** how difficult!
quebrarse (me quiebro) to break
quedar to remain, be left (14); to stay, remain (*in a place*) (6)
quehacer (*m.*) **doméstico** household chore (10)
quejarse (de) to complain (about) (8)
querer (quiero) to want (4); to love (16); **eso quiere decir…** that means . . . (11); **fue sin querer** I didn't mean to do it (14); **quererse** to love each other; to be fond of each other (11); **querido/a** dear (6)
querido/a dear (6)
queso cheese (7)
quetzal *currency of Guatemala*
quien who; whom
¿quién(es)? who? whom?; **¿de quién?** whose? (3)
química chemistry (2)
quince fifteen (1); **menos quince** fifteen minutes till (*hour*) (1); **y quince** fifteen minutes after (*the hour*) (1)
quinceañera *young woman's fifteenth birthday party* (9)
quinientos/as five hundred (4)
quinta country house; farm
quintillizo/a quintuplet
quinto/a fifth (13)
quitar to remove; **quitar la mesa** to clear the table (10); **quitarse** to take off (*an article of clothing*) (5)

R

rabia rutera road rage
ración *f.* portion
radiante bright, shining, radiant
radical *m. gram.* root
radio *m.* radio (apparatus); *f.* radio (*medium*); **estación** (*f.*) **de radio** radio station (18)
radioyente *m., f.* radio listener; *m. pl.* radio audience
raíz *f.* (*pl.* **raíces**) root
rama branch
rana frog
ranchera *traditional music of Mexico sung by mariachis*
rancho ranch
rap *m.* rap music
rapanúi *n. m., f.* *indigenous person of Easter Island*
rápido *adv.* quickly
rápido/a fast; **comida rápida** fast food
raqueta racket
raro/a rare; strange
rascacielos *m. inv.* skyscraper (15)
rata rat
rato while, short time; **ratos libres** spare (free) time (10)
ratón *m.* mouse (12)
raya: de rayas striped (4)
raza race (*ethnic*)
razón *f.* reason; **no tener razón** to be wrong (4); **tener razón** to be right (4)
reacción *f.* reaction
reaccionar to react
real royal
realidad *f.* reality
realizar (c) to achieve, attain

rebaja sale, reduction; *pl.* sales, reductions (4); **en rebaja** on sale
rebanada slice
rebasar to pass (*vehicle*)
rebelde *n. m., f.* rebel; *adj.* rebellious
rebelión *f.* rebellion
recado message
recámara bedroom
recepción *f.* reception
recepcionista *m., f.* receptionist (17)
receptor *m.* receiver; recipient
receta recipe (7); prescription (11)
recetar to prescribe
recibir to receive (3)
recibo receipt (17)
reciclaje *m.* recycling (15)
reciclar to recycle (15)
recién recently; **recién casado/a (con)** newlywed (to) (16)
reciente recent
recíproco/a reciprocal
recitar to recite
recoger (recojo) to collect (14); to pick up (14)
recomendable recommendable
recomendación *f.* recommendation
recomendar (recomiendo) to recommend (8)
reconocer (reconozco) to recognize
reconquista reconquest
reconstituido/a remarried: hybrid (*of a family*)
reconstituir (*like* **construir**) to reconstitute; to reconstruct
recordar (recuerdo) to remember (9)
recrear to recreate
recreo recess
recto/a straight; **(todo) recto** straight ahead (15)
rector(a) university president
recuerdo memory
recuperación *f.* recuperation
recuperador(a) recuperative
recuperar to recuperate
recurso resource; **recurso natural** natural resource (15)
red *f.* network; Internet; **navegar (gu) la Red** to surf the Internet; **red social** social network (12)
redacción *f.* editing
redactar to write; to edit
redondillo/a: letra redondilla roman font
redondo/a round
reducción *f.* reduction
reducir (*like* **conducir**) to reduce
referencia reference
referirse (me refiero) (i) (a) to refer (to)
reflejar to reflect
reflexivo/a reflexive; **verbo reflexivo** *gram.* reflexive verb (5)
reforma change
refresco soft drink (7)
refrigerador *m.* refrigerator (10)
refrigeradora refrigerator
refugio refuge
regalar to give (*as a gift*) (8)
regalo present, gift (3)
regatear to haggle, bargain (4)
regateo bartering
reggae *m.* reggae
régimen *m.* regime
región *f.* region
registración *f.* registration
registrar to register
registro register; record
regla rule
regresar to return (*to a place*) (2); **regresar a casa** to go home (2)
regulador(a) regulator
regular *adj.* so-so (1); **por lo regular** in general
regular to regulate
reina queen (18)
reinar to reign
reino kingdom
reír(se) (río) (i) (de) to laugh (about) (9)
reiterar to reiterate
reja bar (*of prison*)
relación *f.* relation; relationship; **relación sentimental** emotional relationship (16)
relacionar to relate
relajado/a relaxed
relativo/a: pronombre (*m.*) **relativo** *gram.* relative pronoun
relevante relevant
religión *f.* religion
religioso/a religious
relleno/a filled
reloj *m.* watch (4)
remate: de remate hopeless(ly)
remedio remedy
remodelado/a remodeled
remoto: control (*m.*) **remoto** remote control (12)
remuneración *f.* remuneration
renovable renewable (15); **energía renovable** renewable energy (15)
renovar (renuevo) to renew
rentar to rent (*Mex.*)
renunciar (a) to resign (from) (17)
reparar to repair (15)
repasar to review
repaso review
repeler to repel
repente: de repente suddenly (11)
repetición *f.* repetition
repetir (repito) (i) to repeat
repetitivo/a repetitive
reportaje *m.* report (*on a news show*)
reportar to report
reportero/a reporter (18)
represa dam
representación *f.* representation
representante *n. m., f.* representative
representar to represent
representativo/a *adj.* representative
república republic
requerir (requiero) (i) to require
requisito requirement
reseña review (*book, movie*)
reserva reserve; reservation (*Sp.*); **hacer reserva** to make a reservation
resfriado *n.* cold (11)
resfriado/a *adj.* congested, stuffed up (11)
resfriarse (me resfrío) to catch/get a cold (11)
residencia dormitory (2); residence (12); **residencia de ancianos** nursing home (12)
residencial *m.* building (*housing*)
residente *m., f.* resident
residuos *m. pl.* waste
resistente resistant, strong
resolver (resuelvo) (*p.p.* **resuelto**) to solve, resolve (15)
respectivo/a respective
respecto: a este respecto in this regard; **(con) respecto a** regarding
respetar to respect
respeto respect
respiración *f.* breathing
respirar to breathe (11)
responsabilidad *f.* responsibility; **responsabilidad cívica** civic duty (18)
responsable responsible
respuesta answer (6)
restablecimiento re-establishment, restoration
restaurante *m.* restaurant (7)
resto rest, remainder
restricción *f.* restriction
resuelto/a (*p.p. of* **resolver**) resolved
resultado result
resumen *m.* summary; **en resumen** in summary
resumir to summarize
resurrección *f.* resurrection
retumbar to resound
reunión *f.* meeting
reunirse (me reúno) (con) to get together (with) (9)
revelar to reveal
revés: al revés backwards
revisar to check (15)
revista magazine (3)
revolucionario/a revolutionary
revolver (*like* **volver**) to stir
rey *m.* king (18)
Ricitos de Oro Goldilocks
rico/a rich (3); tasty, savory; rich (7)
riesgo risk; **de alto riesgo** high risk
rígido/a rigid
rima rhyme
rincón *m.* corner
rinoceronte *m.* rhinoceros
río river (15)
riqueza richness

ritmo rhythm; **ritmo de la vida** pace of life (15)
rito rite; ritual
robar to rob, steal
robo theft; robbery
rodante: cinta rodante treadmill
rodeado/a (de) surrounded (by)
rojo/a red (4)
Roma Rome
romano/a Roman
romántico/a romantic
romper(se) (*p.p.* **roto**) to break (14); **romper (con)** to break up (with) (16)
ropa clothing (4); **ropa interior** underwear (4)
ropero wardrobe
rosa rose; **rosa té** tea rose
rosado/a pink (4)
rosario rosary
rostro face
roto/a (*p.p. of* **romper**) broken
rotulador *m.* felt-tipped pen
rubio/a blond(e) (3)
rueda wheel, tire; **rueda de molino** treadmill
ruido noise (5)
ruidoso/a noisy
ruina ruin (13)
ruso Russian (*language*)
ruso/a *n., adj.* Russian
rutero/a: rabia rutera road rage
rutina routine (5)
rutinario/a *adj.* routine

S

sábado Saturday (5)
saber to know (7); **saber** + *inf.* to know how to (*do something*) (7)
sabiduría wisdom
sabio/a wise
sabroso/a tasty
sacar (qu) to extract (11); get (*grades*) (14); to withdraw, take out (17); **sacar dinero** to withdraw money; **sacar fotos** to take photos (8); **sacar la basura** to take out the trash (10); **sacar la lengua** to stick out one's tongue (11); **sacarle un diente / una muela** to extract (*someone's*) tooth/molar (11)
sacerdote *m.* priest
sacudir los muebles to dust the furniture
safari: ir de safari to go on a safari
Sagitario Sagittarius
sagrado/a sacred
sal *f.* salt (7)
sala living room (5); **sala de espera** waiting room (8); **sala de fumadores/fumar** smoking area (8)
salarial: brecha salarial wage gap
salario pay, wages (*often per hour*) (17)
salchicha sausage; hot dog (7)
salida departure (8)
salir (de) to leave (*a place*) (5); **salir bien/mal** to come/turn out well/badly; to do poorly/well (5); **salir (con)** to go out (with) (5); **salir de vacaciones** to leave on vacation (8); **salir (para)** to leave (for) (*a place*) (5)
salmón *m.* salmon (7)
salón (*m.*) **de clase** classroom (2)
salsa sauce; salsa (*music*)
saltar to jump
salud *f.* health (11)
saludable healthy
saludarse to greet each other (11)
saludo greeting (1)
salvadoreño/a *n., adj.* Salvadoran
salvaje wild (15)
salvar to save
san, santo/a *n.* saint; **Día** (*m.*) **de San Patricio** St. Patrick's Day; **Día** (*m.*) **de San Valentín** St. Valentine's Day
sanador(a) healer
sancocho *stew made with meat, cassava, and plantains*
sandalias *f. pl.* sandals (4)
sándwich *m.* sandwich (7)
sangre *f.* blood (11)
sanitario/a health; **asistencia sanitaria** health care
sano/a healthy (11); **llevar una vida sana** to lead a healthy life (11)
santuario sanctuary
sarcástico/a sarcastic
sartén *f.* skillet
satélite *m.* satellite
satírico/a satirical
satisfacción *f.* satisfaction
satisfactorio/a satisfactory
Saudito/a: Arabia Saudita Saudi Arabia
sazonar to season
secadora clothes dryer (10)
secar(se) (qu) to dry (oneself)
sección *f.* section
seco/a dry
secretario/a secretary (2)
secreto secret
secuencia sequence
secundario/a secondary; **escuela secundaria** high school
sed *f.* thirst; **tener (mucha) sed** to be (very) thirsty (7)
seda silk; **de seda** *adj.* silk (4)
sedentario/a sedentary
seducir (*like* **conducir**) to seduce
seguida: en seguida immediately (5)
seguimiento following
seguir (sigo) (i) to continue (6); to keep on going (15)
según according to (3)
segundo/a second (13); **segundo piso** second floor (third story) (12)
seguridad *f.* security; safety; **control** (*m.*) **de seguridad** security (check) (8); **pasar por el control de seguridad** to go/pass through security (check) (8)
seguro/a sure, certain (6); **es seguro que** it's a sure thing that (13)
segregación *f.* segregation
seis six (1)
seiscientos/as six hundred (4)
selección *f.* selection; choice
seleccionar to select, choose
selva jungle; **Selva Amazónica** Amazon Jungle
semáforo traffic signal (15)
semana week; **días** (*m. pl.*) **de la semana** days of the week (5); **fin** (*m.*) **de semana** weekend (2); **la próxima semana** next week (5); **semana que viene** next week (5); **una vez a la semana** once a week (3)
sembrar (siembro) to sow, plant
semejante similar
semejanza similarity
semestre *m.* semester
senado senate
senador(a) senator
senda path
sendero path
sensación *f.* sensation
sensibilidad *f.* sensitivity
sensible sensitive
sentarse (me siento) to sit down (5)
sentido sense
sentimental: relación (*f.*) **sentimental** emotional relationship (16)
sentimiento feeling, emotion
sentir (siento) (i) to regret; to feel sorry (13); **lo siento (mucho)** I'm (very) sorry (14); **sentirse** to feel (*an emotion*) (9)
señor (Sr.) *m.* man; Mr.; sir (1)
señora (Sra.) woman; Mrs.; ma'am (1)
señorita (Srta.) young woman; Miss; Ms. (1)
separación *f.* separation (16)
separar(se) (de) to separate (from) (16)
septiembre *m.* September (6)
séptimo/a seventh (13)
ser to be (1); **ayer fue (miércoles…)** yesterday was (Wednesday . . .) (5); **¿cómo es usted?** what are you (*form. s.*) like? (1); **¿de dónde eres (tú)?** where are you (*fam. s.*) from? (1); **¿de dónde es usted?** where are you (*form. s.*) from? (1); **de última moda** it's trendy (hot) (4); **eres** you are (1); **es** he/she is, you (*form. s.*) are (1); **es absurdo que** it's absurd that (13); **es cierto que** it's certain that (13); **es de…** it is made of . . . (4); **es extraño que** it's strange that (13); **es (im)posible que** it's (im)possible that (13); **es (im)probable que** it's (un)likely, (im)-probable that (13); **es increíble que** it's incredible that (13); **es la una** it's one o'clock (1); **es normal**

que it's normal that (13); **es seguro que** it's a sure thing that (13); **es terrible que** it's terrible that (13); **es una lástima que** it's a shame that (13); **es urgente que** it's urgent that (13); **fue sin querer** I didn't mean to do it (14); **llegar (gu) a ser** to become; **pasar de ser** to go from being; **¿qué hora es?** what time is it? (1); **ser aburrido/a** to be boring (10); **ser aficionado/a (a)** to be a fan (of) (10); **ser casado/a** to be a married person (16); **ser divertido/a** to be fun (10); **ser en** + *place* to take place in/at (*a place*) (9); **son las...** it's ... o'clock (1); **(yo) soy de...** I am from ... (1)
serie *f.* series
serio/a serious
servicio service (15); **estación** (*f.*) **de servicio** gas station (15); **servicio militar** military service (18)
servilleta napkin
servir (sirvo) (i) to serve (5); **servir para** to be used for (5)
sesenta sixty (3)
sesión *f.* session
setecientos/as seven hundred (4)
setenta seventy (3)
sevillano/a of or pertaining to Seville
sexismo sexism
sexo sex
sextillo/a sextuplet
sexto/a sixth (13)
si if (3); **por si acaso** just in case (14)
sí yes (1); **sí, me gusta...** yes, I like ... (1)
sicología psychology (2)
sicólogo/a psychologist (17)
siempre always (3)
sierra mountain
siesta nap; **dormir la siesta** to take a nap
siete seven (1)
siglo century
significar (qu) to mean
significativo/a significant
signo sign
siguiente following (5)
sílaba syllable
silencio silence
silla chair (2)
sillón *m.* armchair (5)
simbólico/a symbolic
simbolizar (c) to symbolize
símbolo symbol
similaridad *f.* similarity
simpático/a nice, likeable (3)
sin without (5); **fue sin querer** I didn't mean to do it (14); **sin duda** without a doubt; **sin embargo** nevertheless (6); **sin que** *conj.* without; unless (16)
sinceridad *f.* sincerity
sincero/a sincere
sino but (rather); **sino que** *conj.* but (rather)
sinónimo synonym
sintético/a synthetic
síntoma *m.* symptom (11)
siquiatra *m., f.* psychiatrist (17)
sistema *m.* system; **analista** (*m., f.*) **de sistemas** systems analyst (17)
sistemático/a systematic
sitio place, location; **sitio Web** website
situación *f.* situation
situado/a situated
situarse (me sitúo) to situate oneself; to be placed (*in time*)
snowboard *m.* snowboarding
soberano/a sovereign
sobre *prep.* about (4); on; on top of; over
sobremesa after-dinner conversation
sobresaliente outstanding
sobrevivir to survive
sobrino/a nephew/niece (3)
social social; **ciencias** (*f. pl.*) **sociales** social sciences (2); **red** (*f.*) **social** social network (12); **trabajador(a) social** social worker (17)
socialismo socialism
socialista *n., adj. m., f.* socialist
sociedad *f.* society
sociología sociology (2)
sofá *m.* couch (5)
sol *m.* sun; **hace (mucho) sol** it's (very) sunny (6.); **tomar el sol** to sunbathe (8)
solar solar; **energía solar** solar energy (15); **pánel** (*m.*) **solar** solar panel
solas: a solas alone
soldado soldier (17); **mujer** (*f.*) **soldado** female soldier (17)
soleado/a sunny
soler (suelo) to tend to
solicitante *m., f.* applicant
solicitar to apply for (*a job*) (17)
solicitud *f.* application (*form*) (17)
sólido/a solid
solitario/a solitary, lonely
solo *adv.* only (2)
solo/a *adj.* alone (5)
soltero/a single (*not married*) (16)
soltura: hablar con soltura to speak fluently
solución *f.* solution
sombra shadow; shade
sombrero hat (4); **sombrero hongo** bowler hat, derby
sonar (sueno) to ring; to sound (10)
sonido sound
sonreír(se) (*like* **reír**) to smile (9)
sopa soup (7)
sorprender (*like* **gustar**) to surprise (13)
sorpresa surprise
sostenible sustainable
sostenido/a held
su(s) his, hers, its, your (*form. sing.*); their, your (*form. pl.*) (3)
subir (a) to go up; to get on (*a vehicle*) (8)
subjuntivo *gram.* subjunctive
subordinado/a: cláusula subordinada *gram.* subordinate clause
substituir (*like* **construir**) to substitute
subtítulo subtitle
suburbio suburb
suceso happening
sucesor(a) *m.* successor
sucio/a dirty (6)
sudadera sweatshirt (4)
Sudamérica South America
sudamericano/a South American
Suecia Sweden
suegro/a father-in-law, mother-in-law
sueldo salary (12)
suelo floor
sueño dream; **tener sueño** to be sleepy (4)
suerte *f.* luck; **tener buena/mala suerte** to have good/bad luck, be (un)lucky (14)
suéter *m.* sweater (4)
suficiente enough (11); **lo suficiente** enough (11)
sufijo *gram.* suffix
sufrir (de) to suffer (from, with) (14)
sugerencia suggestion
sugerir (sugiero) (i) to suggest (9)
suicidio suicide
sujeto *gram.* subject
superlativo *gram.* superlative
supermercado supermarket
superstición *f.* superstition
supersticioso/a superstitious
supervisor(a) supervisor
suplemento supplement
supuesto: ¡por supuesto! of course! (14)
sur *m.* south (6)
sureste *m.* southeast
surfear to surf
surfing:* hacer *surfing to surf (10)
suroeste *m.* southwest
surrealista *adj. m., f.* surreal
suscripción *f.* subscription
suspenso suspense
sustantivo *gram.* noun (2)
sustrato essence
SUV *m.* SUV (15)
suyo/a(s) *poss. adj.* your (*form.*); his, her, its, their; *poss. pron.* (of) your, yours (*form.*); (of) his, her, its, their; (of) theirs (17)

T

tabaco tobacco
tabla table, chart
tablero chalkboard
tabú *f.* taboo
tailandés, tailandesa Thai
Tailandia Thailand
taíno/a *pre-Columbian culture of the Caribbean*
tal such, such a; **con tal de** provided (16); **con tal (de) que** *conj.* provided (that) (16); **¿qué tal?** how are you? (1); **tal como** just as; **tal vez** perhaps

taladro drill
talento talent
talla size
taller *m.* (repair) shop (15)
tamal *m.* tamale
tamalada *get-together to make and eat tamales*
tamaño size
también also (1)
tambor *m.* drum
tampoco neither, not either (7)
tan *adv.* so; as; **tan... como** as . . . as (6); **tan pronto como** as soon as (17)
tanque *m.* tank (15)
tanto/a *adj.* as much, so much; such a; *pl.* so many; as many; **tanto como** as much as (6); **tanto/a(s)... como** as much/many . . . as (6)
tapas *f. pl.* appetizers (9)
tapir *m.* tapir
taquigrafía shorthand
tarde *adv.* late (2)
tarde *f.* afternoon; **buenas tardes** good afternoon (1); **de la tarde** in the afternon, P.M. (1); **por la tarde** in the afternoon (2)
tarea homework (5); **tarea doméstica** household chore
tarjeta card (8); **tarjeta bancaria** debit card (17); **tarjeta de crédito** credit card (7); **tarjeta de embarque** boarding pass (8); **tarjeta de identidad** identification card; **tarjeta de identificación** identification card (14); **tarjeta postal** postcard (8)
tarta cake
tata *fam.* grandpa
tatuaje *m.* tattoo
taxi *m.* taxi
taza cup (14)
té *m.* tea (7); **rosa té** tea rose
teatral theatrical; **obra teatral** play
teatro theater; **ir al teatro** to go to the theater (10); **obra de teatro** play (13)
techo roof
teclado keyboard
técnico/a technician (17)
tecnología technology
tecnológico/a technological
teja tile
tejer to weave (13)
tejido weave; *pl.* woven goods (13); textiles
tela cloth
tele *f.* T.V.
telefónico/a *adj.* telephone
teléfono phone (2); **hablar por teléfono** to talk on the phone (2); **teléfono celular** cell phone (2); **teléfono fijo** landline (12)
telegrama *m.* telegram
telenovela soap opera
telespectador(a) television viewer
televidente *m., f.* television viewer
televisión *f.* television; **mirar la tele(visión)** to watch television (3)
televisor *m.* television set
tema *m.* theme, topic
temblar to tremble
temer to fear, be afraid (13)
temperatura temperature (11); **tomarle la temperatura** to take someone's temperature (11)
templo temple
temporada season
temporal temporary
temprano *adv.* early (2)
tendencia tendency
tender (tiendo) la cama to make the bed
tenedor *m.* fork
tener to have (4); **no tener razón** to be wrong (4); **tener... años** to be . . . years old (3); **tener buena/mala suerte** to have good/bad luck, be (un) lucky (14); **tener cuidado** to be careful; **tener dolor de** to have a pain/ache in (11); **tener éxito** to be successful; **tener fiebre** to have a fever; **tener ganas de** + *inf.* to feel like (*doing something*) (4); **tener la culpa** to be at fault; **tener miedo (de)** to be afraid (of) (4); **tener (mucha) hambre** to be (very) hungry (7); **tener (mucha) sed** to be (very) thirsty (7); **tener muchas presiones** to be under a lot of stress (14); **tener (mucho) calor** to be (very) warm, hot (6); **tener (mucho) frío** to be (very) cold (6); **tener prisa** to be in a hurry (4); **tener que** + *inf.* to have to (*do something*) (4); **tener razón** to be right (4); **tener sueño** to be sleepy (4)
tenis *m.* tennis (10); *pl.* tennis shoes (4)
tensión *f.* tension; **tensión arterial** blood pressure
tentación *f.* temptation
tentempié *m.* snack
teñirse (me tiño) (i) el pelo to dye one's hair
teoría theory
terapeuta *m., f.* therapist
terapia therapy
tercer(o/a) third (13)
tereré *traditional Paraguayan drink*
terminación *f. gram.* ending
terminal *m.* station, terminal
terminar to finish
término term
termómetro thermometer
ternura tenderness
terraza terrace
terremoto earthquake
terrestre *adj.* earth
terrible terrible; **es terrible que** it's terrible that (13)
territorio territory
terrorismo terrorism (18)
terrorista *m., f.* terrorist (18); **ataque** (*m.*) **terrorista** (terrorist) attack (18)
tertulia get-together
tesis *f. inv.* thesis
testigo *m., f.* witness (18)
testimonio testimony
textil *adj.* textile
texto text; **libro de texto** textbook (2)
ti (*obj. of prep.*) you (*fam.*) (6)
tiempo weather; time (6); *gram.* tense; **a tiempo** on time (8); **conjunción** (*f.*) **de tiempo** conjunction of time (17); **empleo de tiempo completo/parcial** full-/part-time job/position (17); **jornada de tiempo parcial** part-time job; **¿qué tiempo hace?** what's the weather like? (6); **tiempo libre** free time (10); **trabajo de tiempo completo/parcial** full-time / part-time job (14)
tienda shop, store (4); **tienda de acampar** tent; **tienda (de campaña)** tent (8)
Tierra Earth (15)
tigre *m.* tiger
tihuanaco/a Tiwanakan (*of or pertaining to the pre-Columbian Tiwanaku civilization of Bolivia*)
tilma poncho
timbre *m.* doorbell
tímido/a shy
tina bathtub
tinieblas *f. pl.* darkness
tinto: vino tinto red wine (7)
tío/a uncle/aunt (3); *m. pl.* aunts and uncles (3)
típico/a typical
tipo type, kind; **de todo tipo** of all kinds
tira cómica comic strip
tirar to throw
tiritar to shiver
títere *m.* puppet
titular *m.* headline
título title
toalla towel (5)
toallero towel rack
tocar (qu) to touch; to play (*a musical instrument*) (2); to honk (15); **tocarle a uno** to be someone's turn (10)
tocineta bacon
todavía still (6)
todo/a *adj.* all (3); every (3); **por todas partes** everywhere (14); **todo derecho/recto** straight ahead (15); **todos los días** every day (2)
todo *n.* everything; **de todo** everything (4); **de todo tipo** of all kinds
todoterreno *inv.* all-terrain (15)
tolerante tolerant
tomar to take (2); to drink (2); **tomar el sol** to sunbathe (8); **tomar unas vacaciones** to take a vacation (8); **tomarle**

la temperatura to take someone's temperature (11); **tomarle el pelo** to pull someone's leg
tomate *m.* tomato (7)
tono tone
tonto/a silly, foolish (3)
torcido/a twisted
torno: en torno a around
toro bull (15)
torpe clumsy (14)
torre *f.* tower
torta sandwich (*Mex.*)
tortilla potato omelet (*Sp.*); *thin unleavened cornmeal or flour pancake* (*Mex.*)
tortuga turtle
tos *f.* cough (11)
tosco/a rustic; crude
toser to cough (11)
tostado/a toasted (7); **pan** (*m.*) **tostado** toast (7)
tostadora toaster (10)
tostones *m. pl. crispy fried plantain slices*
totalidad *f.* totality
trabajador(a) *adj.* hardworking (3)
trabajador(a) *n.* worker; **trabajador(a) social** social worker (17)
trabajar to work (2)
trabajo work; job (12); report, (piece of) work (14); **trabajo de tiempo completo/parcial** full-time / part-time job (14)
trabajólico/a workaholic
trabalenguas *m. inv.* tongue twister
tractor *m.* tractor
tradición *f.* tradition; **tradición cultural** cultural tradition (13)
tradicional traditional
traducción *f.* translation
traducir (*like* **conducir**) to translate
traductor(a) translator (17)
traer to bring (5)
tráfico traffic (15)
tragedia tragedy
trágico/a tragic
traje *m.* suit (4); **traje de baño** swimsuit (4)
trámite *m.* step, procedure
tranquilo/a calm (11); **llevar una vida tranquila** to lead a calm life (11)
transatlántico *n.* ocean liner
transbordador (*m.*) **espacial** space shuttle
transformar to transform
transición *f.* transition
tránsito traffic (15)
transmitir to pass on, transmit
transporte *m.* transportation; **medio de transporte** means of transportation (8); **transporte público** public transportation
tras *prep.* after
trasero/a back
trasladarse to move
trastienda back room (*of a store*)
tratable treatable
tratado treaty
tratamiento treatment (11)
tratar de + *inf.* to try to (*do something*) (13); **tratar de** + *noun* to deal with + *noun*
través: a través de across; through; throughout
travieso/a mischievous
trayectoria trajectory; path
trece thirteen (1)
treinta thirty (1); **y treinta** thirty minutes past (*the hour*) (1)
tren *m.* train (8); **estación** (*f.*) **del tren** train station (8); **ir en tren** to go/travel by train (8)
trepidar to vibrate
tres three (1)
trescientos/as three hundred (4)
triángulo triangle
tribu *f.* tribe
tributo tribute
trillizo/a triplet
trilogía trilogy
trimestre *m.* trimester
triste sad (6)
tristeza sadness
triunfar to triumph
trofeo trophy
tropical tropical; **bosque** (*m.*) **tropical lluvioso** tropical rain forest
trópico *n.* tropics
tropiezo mistake
trotadora treadmill
trozo piece
trucha trout
trueno thunder
tú *subj. pron.* you (*fam. s.*) (2); **¿de dónde eres (tú)?** where are you (*fam. s.*) from? (1); **¿y tú?** and you (*fam. s.*)? (1)
tu(s) your (*fam. sing.*) (3)
tumba tomb
turismo tourism
turista *n. m., f.* tourist
turístico/a *adj.* tourist
turnarse to take turns
turno shift (*on a job*)
turrón *m. type of candy traditionally eaten at Christmas*
tuyo/a(s) *poss. adj.* your (*fam. s.*); *poss. pron.* of yours (*fam. s.*) (17)
Twitter *m.* Twitter (12)

U

u or (*used instead of* **o** *before words beginning with* **o** *or* **ho**)
ubicación *f.* placement, location
ubicar (qu) to locate
¡uf! *interj.* oof!; whew!
último/a last, final (14); **es de última moda** it's trendy (hot) (4); **por última vez** for the last time (14)
ultramoderno/a ultramodern
un, uno/a one (1); *ind. art.* a, an; **un millón (de)** one million (4); **un poco (de)** a little bit (of) (2); **una vez a la semana** once a week (3)
unánime unanimous
único/a *adj.* only; unique
unido/a united; **Estados** (*m. pl.*) **Unidos de América** United States of America; **Naciones** (*f. pl.*) **Unidas** United Nations; **Organización** (*f.*) **de Naciones Unidas (ONU)** United Nations (U.N.)
unificar (qu) to unify
unión *f.* union
unir to join (together); to unite; **unirse a** to join (*a cause, organization*)
universidad *f.* university (2)
universitario/a (of the) university (14)
urbanístico *n.* urban development
urbanistico/a *adj.* of urban development
urbano/a urban
urgente urgent; **es urgente que** it's urgent that (13)
uruguayo/a *n., adj.* Uruguayan
usar to wear; to use (4)
uso use
usted (Ud., Vd.) *sub. pron.* you (*form. s.*); *obj.* (*of prep.*) you (*form. s.*) (2); **¿a usted le gusta… ?** do you (*form. s.*) like . . . ? (1); **¿cómo es usted?** what are you (*form. s.*) like? (1); **¿cómo se llama usted?** what is your (*form. s.*) name? (1); **¿de dónde es usted?** where are you (*form. s.*) from? (1); **¿y usted?** and you (*form. s.*)? (1)
ustedes (Uds., Vds.) *sub. pron.* you (*form. pl.*); *obj.* (*of prep.*) you (*form pl.*) (2)
usuario/a user
útil useful
utilizar (c) to use, utilize
uva grape
¡uy! *interj.* oh!; ah!

V

vaca cow (15)
vacaciones *f. pl.* vacation; **de vacaciones** on vacation (8); **estar de vacaciones** to be on vacation (8); **ir de vacaciones a…** to go on vacation in/to . . . (8); **pasar las vacaciones en…** to spend one's vacation in . . . (8); **salir de vacaciones** to leave on vacation (8); **tomar unas vacaciones** to take a vacation (8)
vacuna vaccine
vacunación *f.* vaccination
vacunarse to get a shot
vainilla vanilla
Valentín: Día (*m.*) **de San Valentín** St. Valentine's Day
valioso/a valuable
vallenato *Colombian folk music*

valor *m.* value
valorización *f.* appreciation
vals *m.* waltz
vanguardia *n.* vanguard
vapor *m.* mist
vaquero/a cowboy/cowgirl
variación *f.* variation
variante variant
variar (varío) to vary
variedad *f.* variety
varios/as several
vasco/a *n., adj.* Basque
vasija earthenware pot; vessel
vaso (drinking) glass
vasto/a vast
vecindario neighborhood
vecino/a neighbor (12)
vegetariano/a *n., adj.* vegetarian
vehículo vehicle (12)
veinte twenty (1)
veinticinco twenty-five
veinticuatro twenty-four
veintidós twenty-two
veintinueve twenty-nine
veintiocho twenty-eight
veintiséis twenty-six
veintisiete twenty-seven
veintitrés twenty-three
veintiún, veintiuno/a twenty-one
vejez *f.* (*pl.* **vejeces**) old age (16)
vela candle (9)
velocidad *f.* speed; **límite** (*m.*) **de velocidad** speed limit (15)
vena vein
vendedor(a) salesperson (17)
vender to sell (3)
Venecia Venice
venerar to revere, venerate
venezolano/a *n., adj.* Venezuelan
venir to come (4); **año que viene** next year; **lunes** (*m.*) **que viene** next Monday (5); **semana que viene** next week (5)
venta sale
ventaja advantage
ventana window (2)
ventanilla small window (*on a plane*) (8)
ver (*p.p.* **visto**) to see (5); **a ver** let's see; **nos vemos** see you around (1)
verano summer (6)
veras: ¿de veras? really
verbo *gram.* verb (2); **verbo reflexivo** *gram.* reflexive verb (5)
verdad *f.* truth
verdadero/a true; real
verde green (4)
verdura vegetable (7)
verificar (qu) to verify
versión *f.* version
verso verse; line of a poem
verter (vierto) (i) to spill; to shed (*a tear*)
vestido dress (4)
vestir (visto) (i) to dress; **vestirse** to get dressed (5)
veterinario/a veterinarian (17)
vez *f.* (*pl.* **veces**) time; **a veces** sometimes, at times (3); **alguna vez** once; ever; **cada vez más** increasingly; **cada vez mayor** greater and greater; **dos** two (1); **en vez de** instead of; **otra vez** again; **por primera/última vez** for the first/last time (14); **una vez** once; **una vez a la semana** once a week (3); **tal vez** perhaps
viajar to travel (8)
viaje *m.* trip (5); **agencia de viajes** travel agency; **agente de viajes** travel agent; **de viaje** on a trip, traveling (8); **hacer un viaje** to take a trip (5)
vicepresidente/a vice president
víctima victim (18)
victoria victory
vida life (11); **vida académica** academic life (14); **llevar una vida sana/tranquila** to lead a healthy/calm life (11); **ritmo de la vida** pace of life (15)
video video (12)
videojuego videogame
videoturismo videotourism
vidrio glass
viejo/a old (3)
viento wind; **hace (mucho) viento** it's very windy
viernes *m.* Friday (5)
vietnamita *n., adj. m., f.* Vietnamese
vikingo/a Viking
vinagre *m.* vinegar
vino (blanco, tinto) (white, red) wine (7)
violación *f.* violation
violencia violence; **Día** (*m.*) **Internacional de la No Violencia Contra la Mujer** International No Violence Against Women Day
violento/a violent
violín *m.* violin
virus *m. inv.* virus
visión *f.* vision
visita visit
visitante *m., f.* visitor
visitar to visit; **visitar un museo** to visit a museum (10)
víspera eve
vista view (12); **punto de vista** point of view
viudo/a widower/widow (16)
vivienda housing (12)
vivir to live (3)
vivo/a lively; bright (*of colors*)
vocabulario vocabulary
vocal *f.* vowel
voga: en voga in vogue
volante *m.* steering wheel; **furia al volante** road rage
volar (vuelo) to fly; **volar en avión** to fly, go by plane (8)
volcán *m.* volcano
volcánico/a volcanic
voleibol *m.* volleyball (10)
voltear to turn (over)
volumen *m.* volume
voluntario/a volunteer
volver (vuelvo) (*p.p.* **vuelto**) to return (to a place) (5); **volver a** + *inf.* to (do something) again (5)
vos *subj. pron.* you (*fam. s. C.A., S.A.*)
vosotros/as *sub. pron.* you (*fam. pl. Sp.*); *obj.* (*of prep.*) you (*fam. pl. Sp.*) (2)
votación *f.* vote; voting
votante *m., f.* voter
votar to vote (18)
votos (*m. pl.*) **nupciales** wedding vows
voz *f.* (*pl.* **voces**) voice; **voz en off** voice over
vuelo flight (8); **asistente** (*m., f.*) **de vuelo** flight attendant (8)
vuelta: billete *m.* (*Sp.*) / **boleto** (*L.A.*) **de ida y vuelta** round-trip ticket (8)
vuelto/a (*p.p. of* **volver**) returned
vuestro/a(s) your (*fam. pl. Sp.*) (3); *poss. pron.* your (*fam. pl. Sp.*) (17)
vulnerar to violate; to hurt

W

Web *m.*: **página Web** webpage; **sitio Web** website

Y

y and (1); **y cuarto** a quarter (fifteen minutes) after (*the hour*) (1); **y media** half past (*the hour*) (1); **y quince** fifteen minutes after (*the hour*) (1); **y treinta** thirty minutes past (*the hour*) (1)
ya already (9); **ya no** no longer; **ya que** since
yacimiento deposit (*mineral*)
yerno son-in-law
yo *sub. pron.* I (2); **yo soy de…** I am from . . . (1)
yoga *m.* yoga; **hacer (el) yoga** to do yoga (11)
yogur *m.* yogurt (7)
York: Nueva York New York
yuca cassava, manioc; **¡qué yuca!** how difficult!

Z

zampoña *South American panpipe*
zanahoria carrot (7)
zapatería shoe store
zapato shoe; *pl.* shoes (4)
zarzuela *traditional Spanish operetta*
zócalo central plaza (*Mex.*)
zona zone, area (12)
zumo juice (*Sp.*)

VOCABULARIES

English-Spanish Vocabulary

A

@ **arroba** (12)
A.M. **de la mañana** (1)
able: to be able **poder (puedo)** (4)
about **por** (6); **sobre** (4)
abroad: to go abroad **ir al extranjero** (8)
absence **falta** (15)
absent: to be absent (from) **faltar (a)** (9)
absentminded **distraído/a** (14)
absurd: it's absurd that **es absurdo que** (13)
academic **académico/a** (14); academic life **vida académica** (14)
accelerated **acelerado/a** (15)
accident **accidente** *m.* (14)
according to **según** (3)
account: checking account **cuenta corriente** (17); savings account **cuenta de ahorros** (17)
accountant **contador(a)** (17)
ache *n.* (in) **dolor (de)** (11); *v.* **doler (duele)** (*like* **gustar**) (11); to have an ache in **tener dolor de** (11)
acquainted: to be acquainted with **conocer (conozco)** (7)
act *v.* **actuar (actúo)** (13)
activity: fun activity **diversión** *f.* (10)
actor **actor** *m.* (13)
actress **actriz** *f.* (*pl.* **actrices**) (13)
additional **adicional** (1)
address **dirección** *f.* (7)
adjective *gram.* **adjetivo** (3); adjective of nationality **adjetivo de nacionalidad** (3); possessive adjective **adjetivo posesivo** (3)
administration: business administration **administración** (*f.*) **de empresas** (2)
adolescence **adolescencia** (16)
advice (piece of) **consejo** (7)
advisor **consejero/a** (2)
aerobics: to do aerobics **hacer ejercicios aeróbicos** (11)
affectionate **cariñoso/a** (6)
afraid: to be afraid (of) **tener miedo (de)** (4), **temer** (13)
after **después de** (5), **después (de) que** (17)
afternoon: good afternoon **buenas tardes** (1); **muy buenas** (1); in the afternoon **de la tarde** (1), **por la tarde** (2)
afterward **luego** (5); afterwards **después** (5)
ago **hace** + *time* + **que** + *preterite* (14); *preterite* + **hace** + *time* (14)
agree **estar de acuerdo** (3)
agriculture **agricultura** (15)
ahead: straight ahead **(todo) derecho** (15), **todo recto** (15)
air **aire** *m.* (15)
airplane **avión** *m.* (8)
airport **aeropuerto** (8)
aisle **pasillo** (8)
alarm clock **despertador** *m.* (14)
all **todo/a** (3)
all-terrain **todoterreno** *inv.* (15)
allow **permitir** (12)
almost **casi** *inv.* (3); almost never **casi nunca** (3)
alone **solo/a** (5)
alongside of **al lado de** (6)
already **ya** (9)
also **también** (1)
always **siempre** (3)
America: of the United States of America *n., adj.* **estadounidense** (3)
among *prep.* **entre** (6)
analyst: systems analyst **analista** (*m., f.*) **de sistemas** (17)
and **y** (1); and you? **¿y tú?** *fam. s.* (1), **¿y usted?** *form. s.* (1)
angry **furioso/a** (6); to get angry (with) **enojarse (con)** (9)
animal **animal** *m.* (15)
announce **anunciar** (8)
annoyed **molesto/a** (6)
another **otro/a** (3)
answer **respuesta** (6); to answer **contestar** (7)
antibiotic **antibiótico** (11)
anxiety **ansiedad** *f.* (14)
any **algún (alguna/os/as)** (7)
anybody: not anybody **nadie** (7)
anyone **alguien** (7)
anything **algo** (7); not anything **nada** (7)
apartment **apartamento** (2); apartment building **edificio de apartamentos** (12)
apologize **pedir disculpas** (14)
app(lication) **app** *f.* (*but* **el app**) (12)
appetizers **botanas** (*Mex.*) (9); **tapas** (9)
apple **manzana** (7)
appliance: home appliance **aparato doméstico** (10)
applicant **aspirante** *m., f.* (17)
application (*form*) **solicitud** *f.* (17)
apply for (*a job*) **solicitar** (17)
appointment **cita** (11)
April **abril** *m.* (6)
architect **arquitecto/a** (13)
architecture **arquitectura** (13)
area **zona** (12); smoking area **sala de fumadores/fumar** (8)
argue (with/about) **discutir (con/sobre)** (9)
arm **brazo** (11)
armchair **sillón** *m.* (5)
armoire **armario** (5)
army **ejército** (18)
arrival **llegada** (8)
arrive **llegar (gu)** (3)
art **arte** *m.* (2); arts and crafts **artesanía** (13); the arts **artes** *f. pl.* (13); work of art **obra de arte** (13)
artist **artista** *m., f.* (13)
artistic **artístico/a** (13); artistic expression **expresión** (*f.*) **artística** (13)
as: as . . . as **tan... como** (6); as a child **de niño/a** (10); as a youth **de joven** (10); as much as **tanto como** (6); as much/many . . . as **tanto/a(s)... como** (6); as soon as **en cuanto** (17), **tan pronto como** (17)
ask (a question) **hacer una pregunta** (5), **preguntar** (8); to ask for **pedir (pido) (i)** (5)
asleep: to fall asleep **dormirse (me duermo)** (5)
asparagus **espárragos** (7)
assassinate **asesinar** (18)
assassination **asesinato** (18)
astronaut **astronauta** *m., f.* (17)
at **en** (1); at . . . (*time of day*) **a la(s)...** (1); at all **para nada** (8); at home **en casa** (2); at least **por lo menos** (9); at the beginning of **al principio de** (17); at times **a veces** (3); at what time . . . ? **¿a qué hora... ?** (1)
attack: terrorist attack **ataque** (*m.*) **terrorista** (18)
attend (*class, function*) **asistir (a)** (3); to not attend **faltar (a)** (9)
attendant: flight attendant **asistente** (*m., f.*) **de vuelo** (8)
attract **atraer** (*like* **traer**) (*like* **gustar**) (13)
audience **espectadores** *m. pl.* (13); **público** (13)
August **agosto** (6)

aunt **tía** (3); aunts and uncles **tíos** *m. pl.* (3)
auto **auto** (15)
automatic teller machine (ATM) **cajero automático** (17)
autumn **otoño** (6)
avenue **avenida** (12)
avoid **evitar** (15)
awful: an awful lot **muchísimo** (8)

B

baby-sitter **niñero/a** (10)
backpack **mochila** (2)
bad **mal, malo/a** (3); (very) bad (weather) out **(muy) mal tiempo** (6); the bad news/thing **lo malo** (11); to have a bad time **pasarlo mal** (9); to have bad luck **tener mala suerte** (14)
badly: to come/turn out badly **salir mal** (5)
baggage **equipaje** *m.* (8); to check baggage **facturar el equipaje** (8)
baked custard **flan** *m.* (7)
ballet **ballet** *m.* (13)
banana **banana** (7)
bank **banco** (17)
bar: to go to a bar **ir a un bar** (10)
barbecue **barbacoa** (7)
bargain *n.* **ganga** (4); *v.* **regatear** (4)
baseball **béisbol** *m.* (10); baseball cap **gorra** (4)
basketball **basquetbol** *m.* (10)
bath: to take a bath **bañarse** (5)
bathroom **baño** (5); bathroom sink **lavabo** (5)
bathtub **bañera** (5)
be **estar** (2); **ser** (1); to be . . . years old **tener... años** (3); to be a fan (of) **ser aficionado/a (a)** (10); to be a married person **ser casado/a** (16); to be able **poder (puedo)** (4); to be absent (from) **faltar (a)** (9); to be afraid **temer** (13); to be afraid (of) **tener miedo (de)** (4); to be born **nacer (nazco)** (16); to be (very) cold **tener (mucho) frío** (6); to be comfortable (*temperature*) **estar bien** (6); to be distracted **ir distraído/a** (14); to be fond of each other **quererse (me quiero)** (11); to be fun **ser divertido/a** (10); to be happy (about) **alegrarse (de)** (12); to be (very) hungry **tener (mucha) hambre** (7); to be in a hurry **tener prisa** (4); to be left **quedar** (14); to be lucky **tener buena suerte** (14); to be married (to) **estar casado/a (con)** (16); to be on a diet **estar a dieta** (7); to be on vacation **estar de vacaciones** (8); to be right **tener razón** (4); to be sleepy **tener sueño** (4); to be (very) thirsty **tener (mucha) sed** (7); to be under a lot of pressure **estar bajo muchas presiones** (14); to be unlucky **tener mala suerte** (14); to be up to date **estar al día** (18); to be used for **servir (sirvo) (i) para** (5); to be (very) warm, hot **tener (mucho) calor** (6); to be wrong **no tener razón** (4)
beach **playa** (6)
beans **frijoles** *m. pl.* (7)
beautiful **bello/a** (15)
because **porque** (3); because of **por** (6)
become + *adj.* **ponerse** + *adj.* (9)
bed **cama** (5); to get out of bed **levantarse** (5); to get up on the wrong side of the bed **levantarse con el pie izquierdo** (14); to go to bed **acostarse (me acuesto)** (5); to make the bed **hacer la cama** (10); to stay in bed **guardar cama** (11)
bedroom **alcoba** (5)
beer **cerveza** (7)
before **antes de** (16), **antes (de) que** (16)
begin **empezar (empiezo) (c)** (5); to begin to (*do something*) **empezar a** + *inf.* (5)
beginning: at the beginning of **al principio de** (17)
behave **portarse bien** (9)
behind **detrás de** (6); to leave behind (in [*a place*]) **dejar (en)** (10)
believe (in) **creer (en)** (3)
below **debajo de** (6)
belt **cinturón** *m.* (4)
best **mejor** (6)
better **mejor** (6)
between *prep.* **entre** (6)
beyond **a partir de** (4)
bicycle: to ride a bicycle **pasear en bicicleta** (10)
bicycling **ciclismo** (10)
big **gran, grande** (3); big screen (monitor) **pantalla grande** (12)
bill **cuenta** (7); **factura** (17); electric bill **electricidad** *f.* (12); (*money*) **billete** *m.* (17)
bird **pájaro** (3)
birthday **cumpleaños** *m. s.* (6); birthday cake **pastel** (*m.*) **de cumpleaños** (9); to have a birthday **cumplir años** (9)
black **negro/a** (4)
blog **blog** *m.* (12)
blond(e) **rubio/a** (3)
blood **sangre** *f.* (11)
blouse **blusa** (4)
blue **azul** (4)
blue jeans ***jeans*** *m. pl.* (4)
board **pizarrón** *m.* (2)
boarding: boarding gate **puerta de embarque** (8); boarding pass **tarjeta de embarque** (8)
boat **barco** (8); to go/travel by boat **ir en barco** (8)
body: human body **cuerpo humano** (11)
bomb **bomba** (18)
book **libro** (2)
bookshelf **estante** *m.* (5)
bookstore **librería** (2)
boots **botas** *f. pl.* (4)
bore **aburrir** (*like* **gustar**) (13)
bored **aburrido/a** (6); to get bored **aburrirse** (10)
boring **pesado/a** (10); to be boring **ser aburrido/a** (10)
borrow **pedir prestado/a** (17)
boss **jefe/a** (12)
bother **molestar** (*like* **gustar**) (11)
boy **niño** (3); **chico** (4)
boyfriend **novio** (6)
brain **cerebro** (11)
brakes **frenos** *m. pl.* (15)
bread **pan** *m.* (7)
break **romper(se)** (14); to break up (with) **romper (con)** (16)
breakfast **desayuno** (7); to have (eat) breakfast **desayunar** (7)
breathe **respirar** (11)
bride **novia** (16)
bring **traer** (5)
brother **hermano** (3)
brown **(de) color café** (4)
brunet(te) **moreno/a** (3)
brush one's teeth **cepillarse los dientes** (5)
budget **presupuesto** (17)
build **construir (construyo)** (15)
building **edificio** (2); apartment building **edificio de apartamentos** (12); building manager **portero/a** (12)
bull **toro** (15)
bump against/into **chocar (qu) contra/con** (14); **pegarse (gu) con** (14)
bureau **cómoda** (5)
bus **autobús** *m.* (8); bus station **estación** (*f.*) **de autobuses** (8); bus stop **parada del autobús** (12); to go, travel by bus **ir en autobús** (8)
business **empresa** (17); business administration **administración** (*f.*) **de empresas** (2)
businessman **hombre** (*m.*) **de negocios** (17)
businesswoman **mujer** (*f.*) **de negocios** (17)
busy **ocupado/a** (6)
but **pero** (1)
butter **mantequilla** (7)
by **por** (14); by check **con cheque** (17)

C

cabin (*on a ship*) **cabina** (8)
cafeteria **cafetería** (2)
cake **pastel** *m.* (7); birthday cake **pastel de cumpleaños** (9)
calculator **calculadora** (2)
calendar **calendario** (14)
call **llamar** (7); to be called **llamarse** (5)
calm **tranquilo/a** (11); to lead a calm life **llevar una vida tranquila** (11)

camera: digital camera **cámara digital** (12)
campground ***camping*** *m.* (8)
camping: to go camping **hacer *camping*** (8)
campus (university) ***campus*** *m.* (12)
candidate (*for a job*) **aspirante** *m., f.* (17); (*political*) **candidato/a** (18); to run as a candidate **postularse como candidato/a** (18); to run for a position as a candidate **postularse para un cargo como candidato/a** (18)
candle **vela** (9)
candy **dulces** *m. pl.* (7)
cap (baseball) **gorra** (4)
capital city **capital** *f.* (6)
car **coche** *m.* (3); **carro** (12); convertible car **carro descapotable** (12)
card: credit card **tarjeta de crédito** (7); debit card **tarjeta bancaria** (17); identification card **tarjeta de identificación** (14); to play cards **jugar (juego) (gu) a las cartas** (10)
cardinal point **punto cardinal** (6)
care: to take care of oneself **cuidarse** (11)
carrot **zanahoria** (7)
carry **llevar** (4)
case: in case **en caso de (que)** (16); just in case **por si acaso** (14)
cash (*a check*) **cobrar** (17); in cash **en efectivo** (17)
cashier **cajero/a** (17); cashier window **caja** (17)
cat **gato** (3)
catch a cold **resfriarse (me resfrío)** (11)
CD (compact disc) **CD** *m.* (12)
CD-ROM **CD-ROM** *m.* (12)
celebrate **celebrar** (6)
celebratory **festivo/a** (9)
cell phone **teléfono celular** (2)
center **centro** (18)
ceramics **cerámica** (13)
cereal **cereal** *m.* (7)
certain **seguro/a** (6); it's certain that **es cierto que** (13)
chair **silla** (2)
champagne **champán** *m.* (9)
change **cambiar (de)** (12)
channel **canal** *m.* (12)
charge (*someone for an item or service*) **cobrar** (17)
check (*bank*) **cheque** *m.* (17); (*restaurant*) **cuenta** (7); by check **con cheque** (17); *v.* **revisar** (15); to check baggage **facturar el equipaje** (8)
check-up **chequeo** (11)
checking account **cuenta corriente** (17)
cheese **queso** (7)
chef **cocinero/a** (17)
chemistry **química** (2)
chess: to play chess **jugar (juego) (gu) al ajedrez** (10)
chicken **pollo** (7); roast chicken **pollo asado** (7)
child: as a child **de niño/a** (10)
childhood **infancia** (16); **niñez** *f.* (10)
children **hijos** *m. pl.* (3)
chop: (pork) chop **chuleta (de cerdo)** (7)
chore: household chore **quehacer** (*m.*) **doméstico** (10)
Christmas **Navidad** *f.* (9)
Christmas Eve **Nochebuena** *f.* (9)
church **iglesia** (16)
citizen **ciudadano/a** (18)
city **ciudad** *f.* (3)
civic duty **responsabilidad** (*f.*) **cívica** (18)
class (*of students*) **clase** *f.* (2); (*academic*) **clase** *f.* (2)
classic(al) **clásico/a** (13)
classmate **compañero/a (de clase)** (2)
classroom **salón** (*m.*) **de clase** (2)
clean *adj.* **limpio/a** (6); to clean (the) house **limpiar (la casa)** (10)
clear the table **quitar la mesa** (10)
clerk **dependiente/a** (2)
clever **listo/a** (3)
client **cliente/a** (2)
climate **clima** *m.* (6)
clock: alarm clock **despertador** *m.* (14)
close **cerrar (cierro)** (5)
close to *prep.* **cerca de** (6)
closed **cerrado/a** (6)
closet (*free-standing*) **armario** (5)
clothes dryer **secadora** (10)
clothing **ropa** (4)
cloudy: it's (very) cloudy **está (muy) nublado** (6)
clumsy **torpe** (14)
coat **abrigo** (4)
coffee **café** *m.* (2)
coffeemaker **cafetera** (10)
coin **moneda** (17)
cold (*illness*) **resfriado** *n.* (11); it's (very) cold **hace (mucho) frio** (6); to be (very) cold **tener (mucho) frío** (6); to catch/get a cold **resfriarse (me resfrío)** (11)
collect **recoger (recojo)** (14)
collision **choque** *m.* (18)
color **color** *m.* (4)
come **venir** (4); to come out badly **salir mal** (5); to come out well **salir bien** (5)
comedy **comedia** (13)
comfortable **cómodo/a** (4); to be comfortable (*temperature*) **estar bien** (6)
command **mandato** (7)
communicate (with) **comunicarse (qu) (con)** (18)
communication (*subject*) **comunicaciones** *f. pl.* (2); medium of communication **medio de comunicación** (18)
compact disc (CD) **disco compacto** (**CD** *m.*) (12)
comparison **comparación** *f.* (6)
complain (about) **quejarse (de)** (8)
compose **componer** (*like* **poner**) (13)
composer **compositor(a)** (13)
computer **computadora** (2); computer file **archivo** (12); computer science **computación** *f.* (2); laptop (computer) **computadora portátil** (2)
concert: to go to a concert **ir a un concierto** (10)
conductor **director(a)** (13)
congested (*cold*) *adj.* **resfriado/a** (11)
congratulations! **¡felicitaciones!** (9)
conjunction *gram.* **conjunción** *f.* (16); conjunction of time **conjunción** (*f.*) **de tiempo** (17)
conserve **conservar** (15)
contact lenses **lentes** (*m. pl.*) **de contacto** (11)
contaminated **contaminado/a** (15)
content *adj.* **contento/a** (6)
continue **seguir (sigo) (i)** (6); **continuar (continúo)** (6)
control: remote control **control** (*m.*) **remoto** (12)
convertible car **carro descapotable** (12)
cook **cocinero/a** (17)
cookie **galleta** (7)
cool: it's cool (weather) **hace fresco** (6)
copy *n.:* copy machine **fotocopiadora** (12); *v.* **copiar** (12); **hacer fotocopia** (12)
corner (*street*) **esquina** (15)
corporation **empresa** (17)
cost: how much does it (do they) cost? **¿cuánto cuesta(n)?** (4)
cotton **de algodón** *adj.* (4)
couch **sofá** *m.* (5)
cough *n.* **tos** *f.* (11); cough syrup **jarabe** *m.* (11); *v.* **toser** (11)
country **país** *m.* (3)
countryside **campo** (15)
couple (*married*) **pareja** (16); **matrimonio** (16)
course (*academic*) **clase** *f.* (2); (*of a meal*) **plato** (7); course syllabus **programa del curso** (14); main course **plato principal** (7); of course! **¡por supuesto!** (14)
cousin **primo/a** (3); *pl.* **primos** (3)
cover **cubrir** (*p.p.* **cubierto**) (15)
cow **vaca** (15)
craft: arts and crafts **artesanía** (13)
crash *n.* **choque** *m.* (18); *v.* (*computer*) **fallar** (12)
crazy **loco/a** (6)
credit card **tarjeta de crédito** (7)
crime **delito** (15)
cruise (ship) **crucero** (8)
cuisine **cocina** (7)
cultural tradition **tradición** (*f.*) **cultural** (13)
cup **taza** (14)
currently **de/en la actualidad** (10)
customs (*at a border*) **aduana** (8); to go/pass through customs **pasar por la aduana** (8)

D

dad **papá** *m.* (3)
daily **diario/a** (5)
dance *n.* **baile** *m.* (13); **danza** (13); *v.* **bailar** (2)
dancer **bailarín, bailarina** (13)
date **cita** (11); (*calendar*) **fecha** (6); to be up to date **estar al día** (18); what's today's date? **¿cuál es la fecha de hoy?** (6), **¿qué fecha es hoy?** (6)
daughter **hija** (3)
day **día** *m.* (2); day after tomorrow **pasado mañana** (5); days of the week **días** (*m. pl.*) **de la semana** (5); every day **todos los días** (2); the day before yesterday **anteayer** (5); what day is today? **¿qué día es hoy?** (5)
deadline **plazo** (14)
dear **querido/a** (6)
death **muerte** *f.* (16)
debit card **tarjeta bancaria** (17)
December **diciembre** *m.* (6)
delay **demora** (8)
demonstration **manifestación** *f.* (18)
demonstrative *gram.* **demostrativo/a** (4)
dense **denso/a** (15)
dentist **dentista** *m., f.* (11)
deny **negar (niego) (gu)** (13)
department store **almacén** *m.* (4)
departure **salida** (8)
deposit **depositar** (17)
desk **escritorio** (2)
dessert **postre** *m.* (7)
destroy **destruir** (*like* **construir**) (15)
detail **detalle** *m.* (9)
develop **desarrollar** (15)
development **desarrollo** (15)
dictator **dictador(a)** (18)
dictatorship **dictadura** (18)
dictionary **diccionario** (2)
die **morir(se) ([me] muero) (u)** (9)
diet: to be on a diet **estar a dieta** (7)
difficult **difícil** (6); **pesado/a** (10)
digital camera **cámara digital** (12)
dining room **comedor** *m.* (5)
dinner **cena** (7); to have (eat) dinner **cenar** (7)
direct **dirigir (dirijo)** (13)
director **director(a)** (13)
dirty **sucio/a** (6)
disagree **no estar de acuerdo** (3)
disaster **desastre** *m.* (14)
disc: compact disc (CD) **disco compacto** (**CD** *m.*) (12)
disco: to go to a disco **ir a una discoteca** (10)
discover **descubrir** (*p.p.* **descubierto**) (15)
discrimination **discriminación** *f.* (18)
dish **plato** (5)
dishwasher **lavaplatos** *m.* (10)
distracted **distraído/a** (14); to be distracted **ir distraído/a** (14)
divorce **divorcio** (16)
divorced (from) **divorciado/a (de)** (16)
dizzy **mareado/a** (11)
do **hacer** (5); do you like . . . ? **¿a usted le gusta. . . ?** *form. s.* (1); to (do something) again **volver (vuelvo) a** + *inf.* (5); to do aerobics **hacer ejercicios aeróbicos** (11); to do Pilates **hacer (el método) Pilates** (11); to do poorly **salir mal** (5); to do well **salir bien** (5); to do yoga **hacer (el) yoga** (11)
doctor (medical) **médico/a** (3)
dog **perro** (3)
domestic (*related to the home*) **doméstico/a** (10)
domesticated **domesticado/a** (15)
door **puerta** (2)
dormitory **residencia** (2)
dot: on the dot (*time*) **en punto** (1)
doubt **dudar** (12)
download **bajar** (12); **descargar (gu)** (12)
downtown **centro** (4)
drama **drama** *m.* (13)
draw **dibujar** (13); (*attract*) **atraer** (*like* **traer**) (*like* **gustar**) (13)
drawing **dibujo** (13)
dress **vestido** (4)
dressed: to get dressed **vestirse (me visto) (i)** (5)
dresser **cómoda** (5)
drink **bebida** (5); *v.* **beber** (3); **tomar** (2)
drive *n.*: hard drive **disco duro** (12); **hard drive** *m.* 12; *v.* **manejar** (12); **conducir (conduzco)** (15)
driver **conductor(a)** (15); driver's license **licencia de conducir/manejar** (15)
drop **caer** (14)
drum set **batería** (15)
during **durante** (5)
duty: civic duty **responsabilidad** (*f.*) **cívica** (18)
DVD(-ROM) **DVD(-ROM)** *m.* (12)

E

e-mail **e-mail** *m.* (12)
e-ticket **billete** (*m.*) (*Sp.*) / **boleto** (*L.A.*) **electrónico** (8)
each **cada** *inv.* (5)
ear **oreja** (11); inner ear **oído** (11)
early *adv.* **temprano** (2)
earn (*income*) **ganar** (13)
earrings **aretes** *m. pl.* (4)
Earth **Tierra** (15)
east **este** *m.* (6)
Easter **Pascua** (9)
easy **fácil** (6)
eat **comer** (3); to eat breakfast **desayunar** (7); to eat dinner, supper **cenar** (7); to eat lunch **almorzar (ue) (c)** (5)
economics **economía** (2)
economize **economizar (c)** (17)
economy **economía** (2)
egg **huevo** (7)
eight **ocho** (1)
eight hundred **ochocientos/as** (4)
eighteen **dieciocho** (1)
eighth **octavo/a** (13)
eighty **ochenta** (3)
either: not either **tampoco** (7)
electric bill **electricidad** *f.* (12)
electrical energy **energía eléctrica** (15)
electrician **electricista** *m., f.* (17)
electricity **electricidad** *f.* (12)
electronic equipment **electrónica** (12)
elephant **elefante** *m.* (15)
elevator **ascensor** *m.* (12)
eleven **once** (1)
embarrassed **avergonzado/a** (9)
embrace **abrazarse (c)** (11)
emotion **emoción** *f.* (9)
emotional: emotional relationship **relación** (*f.*) **sentimental** (16); emotional state **estado afectivo** (9)
end of the year **fin** (*m.*) **de año** (9)
end table **mesita** (5)
endangered species **especie** (*f.*) **en peligro de extinción** (15)
energy **energía** (15); electrical energy **energía eléctrica** (15); nuclear energy **energía nuclear** (15); renewable energy **energía renovable** (15); wind energy **energía eólica** (15)
engagement **noviazgo** (16)
engineer **ingeniero/a** (17)
English (*language*) **inglés** *m.* (2); *n., adj.* **inglés, inglesa** (3)
enjoy oneself **divertirse (me divierto) (i)** (5)
enough **bastante** (16), **suficiente** (11); **lo suficiente** (11)
environment **medio ambiente** (15)
equality **igualdad** *f.* (18)
equipment **equipo** (12); electronic equipment **electrónica** (12)
eruption **erupción** *f.* (18)
evening: good evening **buenes noches** (1); **muy buenas** (1); in the evening **de la noche** (1); **por la noche** (2)
event **acontecimiento** (18); **hecho** (9)
every **cada** *inv.* (5); **todo/a** (3); every day **todos los días** (2)
everything **de todo** (4)
everywhere **por todas partes** (14)
exam **examen** *m.* (4)
examine **examinar** (11)
excuse me **(con) permiso** (1), **perdón** (1)
exercise *n.* **ejercicio** (5); *v.* **hacer ejercicio** (5)
expect **esperar** (7)
expense **gasto** (12)
expensive **caro/a** (4)
explain **explicar (qu)** (8)

expression: artistic expression **expresión** (*f.*) **artística** (13)
extract **sacar (qu)** (11); to extract (*someone's*) tooth/molar **sacarle (qu) un diente / una muela** (11)
eye **ojo** (11)

F

Facebook **Facebook** *m.* (12); to go into Facebook **entrar en Facebook** (12)
fact **hecho** (9)
factory **fábrica** (15)
faithful **fiel** (3)
fall (*season*) *n.* **otoño** (6); *v.* **caer** (14); to fall asleep **dormirse** (5); to fall down **caerse** (14); to fall in love (with) **enamorarse (de)** (16)
familiar: to be familiar with **conocer (conozco)** (7)
family **familia** (3)
fan: to be a fan (of) **ser aficionado/a (a)** (10)
far from **lejos de** (6)
fare **pasaje** *m.* (8)
farm **finca** (15)
farmer **agricultor(a)** (15)
farming **agricultura** (15)
fast **acelerado/a** (15)
fat **gordo/a** (3)
father **padre** *m.* (3), **papá** *m.* (3)
FAX **fax** *m.* (12)
fear **temer** (13)
February **febrero** (6)
feel **sentir** (13); (*an emotion*) **sentirse (me siento) (i)** (9); to feel like (*doing something*) **tener ganas de** + *inf.* (4); to feel sorry **lamentar** (13)
female housekeeper **ama** (*f.*) (*but* **el ama**) **de casa** (17)
female soldier **mujer** (*f.*) **soldado** (17)
festive **festivo/a** (9)
fever **fiebre** *f.* (11)
few **poco/a** (4)
fiancé **novio** (16)
fiancée **novia** (16)
field **campo** (15)
fifteen **quince** (1); fifteen minutes till (*hour*) **menos quince** (1); young woman's fifteenth birthday party **quinceañera** (9)
fifth **quinto/a** (13)
fifty **cincuenta** (3)
fight *n.* **lucha** (18); *v.* **luchar** (18)
file (*computer*) **archivo** (12)
fill (up) **llenar** (15); to fill out (*a form*) **llenar** (17)
final **último/a** (14)
finally **por fin** (5), **finalmente** (5)
find **encontrar (encuentro)** (9); to find out **enterarse (de)** (18)
fine **muy bien** (1); it's fine **está bien** (6)
finger **dedo (de la mano)** (11)
finish **acabar** (14)
fire (*someone*) (*from a job*) **despedir** (*like* **pedir**) (17)
first **primero** (5); **primer(o/a)** (13); first floor (second story) **primer piso** (12); for the first time **por primera vez** (14); the first of (*month*) **el primero de** (6)
fish (*cooked*) **pescado** (7); (*live*) **pez** *m.* (*pl.* **peces**) (15)
five **cinco** (1)
five hundred **quinientos/as** (4)
fix **arreglar** (15)
fixed price **precio fijo** (4)
flat: flat screen (*monitor*) **pantalla plana** (12); flat tire **llanta desinflada** (15)
flexible **flexible** (14)
flight **vuelo** (8); flight attendant **asistente** (*m., f.*) **de vuelo** (8)
flip-flops **chanclas** *f. pl.* (4)
floor (*of a building*) **piso** (12); first/second floor (second/third story) **primer/segundo piso** (12); ground floor **planta baja** (12); to sweep the floor **barrer el piso** (10)
flower **flor** *f.* (8)
flu **gripe** *f.* (11)
fly by plane **volar (vuelo) en avión** (8)
following **siguiente** (5)
fond: to be fond of each other **quererse (me quiero)** (11)
food **comida** (7)
foodstuff **comestibles** *m. pl.* (7)
foolish **tonto/a** (3)
foot **pie** *m.* (11)
football **fútbol** (*m.*) **americano** (10)
for **para** (3); **por** (8); for example **por ejemplo** (14); for heaven's sake **por Dios** (14); for that reason **por eso** (3); for what purpose? **¿para qué... ?** (16); what for? **¿para qué... ?** (16)
forbid **prohibir (prohíbo)** (12)
foreign language **lengua extranjera** (2)
foreigner **extranjero/a** (2)
forest **bosque** *m.* (15)
forget (about) **olvidar(se) (de)** (9)
form **forma** (4)
forty **cuarenta** (3)
four **cuatro** (1)
four hundred **cuatrocientos/as** (4)
fourteen **catorce** (1)
fourth *adj.* **cuarto/a** (13)
free (*unoccupied*) **libre** (10); free time **ratos** (*m. pl.*) **libres** (10), **tiempo libre** (10)
freeway **autopista** (15)
freezer **congelador** *m.* (10)
French (*language*) **francés** *m.* (2); French fried potato **papa/patata frita** (7)
frequently **con frecuencia** (2), **frecuentemente** (11)
fresh **fresco/a** (7)
Friday **viernes** *m.* (5)
fried **frito/a** (7); French fried potato **papa/patata frita** (7)
friend **amigo/a** (2)
friendly **amistoso/a** (16)
friendship **amistad** *f.* (16)
from **de** (1); from the **del** (3); I am from . . . **(yo) soy de...** (1); where are you from? **¿de dónde eres (tú)?** *fam. s.* (1); **¿de dónde es usted?** *form. s.* (1)
front: in front of **delante de** (6)
frozen **congelado/a** (6)
fruit **fruta** (7); fruit juice **jugo de fruta** (7)
full-time job **empleo de tiempo completo** (17)
fun activity **diversión** *f.* (10); to be fun **ser divertido/a** (10)
function **funcionar** (12)
furious **furioso/a** (6)
furniture (*piece*) **mueble** *m.* (5)

G

game **partido** (10)
garage **garaje** *m.* (5)
garden **jardín** *m.* (5)
gas (*not for cars*) **gas** *m.* (12)
gas station **estación** (*f.*) **de servicio** (15), **gasolinera** (15)
gasoline **gasolina** (15)
gate: boarding gate **puerta de embarque** (8)
generally **por lo general** (5)
German (*language*) **alemán** *m.* (2); *n., adj.* **alemán, alemana** (3)
get **obtener** (*like* **tener**) (12); how do you get to . . . ? **¿cómo se llega a... ?** (15); to get **conseguir** (*like* **seguir**) (9); to get (*grades*) **sacar (qu)** (14); to get a cold **resfriarse (me resfrío)** (11); to get along poorly (with) **llevarse mal (con)** (16); to get along well (with) **llevarse bien (con)** (16); to get angry (with) **enojarse (con)** (9); to get down (from) **bajarse (de)** (8); to get off (of) (*a vehicle*) **bajarse (de)** (8); to get on (*a vehicle*) **subir (a)** (8); to get tired **cansarse** (11); to get together (with) **reunirse (me reúno) (con)** (9); to get up (out of bed) **levantarse** (5); to get up on the wrong side of the bed **levantarse con el pie izquierdo** (14)
gift **regalo** (3)
girl **chica** (4), **niña** (3)
girlfriend **novia** (6)
give **dar** (8); to give (*as a gift*) **regalar** (8); to give (*someone*) a shot **ponerle una inyección** (11)
glasses **anteojos** *m. pl.* (11), **lentes** *m. pl.* (11)
go **ir** (4); let's go **vamos** (4); to be going to (*do something*) **ir a** + *inf.* (4); to go abroad **ir al extranjero** (8); to go by boat/ship **ir en barco** (8); to go by bus **ir en autobús** (8); to go by plane **ir/volar (vuelo) en avión** (8); to go

camping **hacer *camping*** (8); to go for a hike **dar una caminata** (10); to go home **regresar a casa** (2); to go into Facebook **entrar en Facebook** (12); to go on the Internet **entrar en el Internet** (12); to go on vacation in/to . . . **ir de vacaciones a...** (8); to go out (with) **salir (con)** (5); to go through customs **pasar por la aduana** (8); to go through security (check) **pasar por el control de seguridad** (8); to go to (*a class, function*) **asistir (a)** (3); to go to a concert **ir a un concierto** (10); to go to a disco **ir a una discoteca** (10); to go to bed **acostarse (me acuesto)** (5); to go to the theater **ir al teatro** (10); to go up **subir (a)** (8); to go/travel by train **ir en tren** (8)
gold *adj.* **de oro** (4)
golf **golf** *m.* (10)
good **buen, bueno/a** (3); good afternoon **buenas tardes** (1); good afternoon/evening **muy buenas** (1); good morning **buenos días** (1); good night **buenas noches** (1); the good news/thing **lo bueno** (11); to have a good time **pasarlo bien** (9), **divertirse (me divierto) (i)** (5); to have good luck **tener buena suerte** (14)
good-bye **adiós** (1); to say good-bye (to) **despedir(se)** (*like* **pedir**) **(de)** (9)
good-looking **guapo/a** (3)
goods: woven goods **tejidos** *m. pl.* (13)
gorilla **gorila** *m.* (15)
government **gobierno** (15)
GPS **GPS** *m.* (12)
grade (*academic*) **nota** (14); (*year in school*) **grado** (10)
granddaughter **nieta** (3)
grandfather **abuelo** (3)
grandmother **abuela** (3)
grandparents **abuelos** *m. pl.* (3)
grandson **nieto** (3)
gray **gris** (4)
great **gran, grande** (3)
green **verde** (4)
green peas **arvejas** *f. pl.* (7)
greet each other **saludarse** (11)
greeting **saludo** (1)
groceries **comestibles** *m. pl.* (7)
groom **novio** (16)
ground floor **planta baja** (12)
guess **adivinar** (9)
guest **invitado/a** (9)
guide **guía** *m., f.* (13)

H

haggle **regatear** (4)
hairstylist **peluquero/a** (17)
half past (*the hour*) **y media** (1)
ham **jamón** *m.* (7)
hamburger **hamburguesa** (7)
hand **mano** *f.* (11); to shake hands **darse la mano** (11)
hand in **entregar (gu)** (8)
handbag **cartera** (4)
handsome **guapo/a** (3)
happen **pasar** (6)
happening **acontecimiento** (18)
happy **alegre** (6), **contento/a** (6); **feliz** (*pl.* **felices**) (9); to be happy (about) **alegrarse (de)** (12)
hard **difícil** (6)
hard drive **disco duro** (12), **hard drive** *m.* (12)
hardworking **trabajador(a)** (3)
hat **sombrero** (4)
hate **odiar** (8)
have **tener** (4); to have a bad time **pasarlo mal** (9); to have a birthday **cumplir años** (9); to have a good time **divertirse (me divierto) (i)** (5), **pasarlo bien** (9); to have a pain/ache in **tener dolor de** (11); to have a picnic **hacer un *picnic*** (10); to have a snack **merendar (meriendo)** (7); to have bad luck **tener mala suerte** (14); to have been (*doing something*) for (*time*) **hace** + *time* + **que** + *present* (14); *present* + **desde hace** + *time* (14); to have breakfast **desayunar** (7); to have dinner, supper **cenar** (7); to have good luck **tener buena suerte** (14); to have just (*done something*) **acabar de** + *inf.* (7); to have lunch **almorzar (almuerzo) (c)** (5); to have to (*do something*) **tener que** + *inf.* (4)
he *sub. pron.* **él** (2)
head **cabeza** (11)
health **salud** *f.* (11)
healthy **sano/a** (11); to lead a healthy life **llevar una vida sana** (11)
hear **oír** (5)
heart **corazón** *m.* (11)
heating **calefacción** *f.* (12)
heaven: for heaven's sake **por Dios** (14)
hello! **¡hola!** (1)
helmet **casco** (12)
help *n.* **ayuda** (7); *v.* **ayudar** (7)
her *poss. adj.* **su(s)** (3); her, (of) her *poss. adj., poss. pron.* **suyo/a(s)** (17)
here **aquí** (2)
hi! **¡hola!** (1)
highway **carretera** (15)
hike: to go for a hike **dar una caminata** (10)
his *poss. adj.* **su(s)** (3); his, of his *poss. adj., poss. pron.* **suyo/a(s)** (17)
Hispanic **hispano/a** (3)
history **historia** (2)
hit **pegar (gu)** (10)
hobby **afición** *f.* (10)
hockey **hockey** *m.* (10)
holiday **día** (*m.*) **festivo** (9)
home *n.* **casa** (3); at home **en casa** (2); nursing home **residencia de ancianos** (12); to go home **regresar a casa** (2); *adj.* (*related to the home*) **doméstico/a** (10)
home appliance **aparato doméstico** (10)
homework **tarea** (5)
honeymoon **luna de miel** (16)
honk **tocar (qu)** (15)
hope **esperanza** (18); I hope (that) **ojalá (que)** (13); to hope **esperar** (12)
horn (*car*) **bocina** (15)
horse: to ride a horse **montar a caballo** (10)
host (*of an event*) **anfitrión, anfitriona** (9)
hot (*spicy*) **picante** (7); (*temperature*) **caliente** (7); it's (very) hot **hace (mucho) calor** (6); it's hot (trendy) **está de moda** (4); **es de última moda** (4); to be (very) hot **tener (mucho) calor** (6)
hot dog **salchicha** (7)
house **casa** (3)
household chore **quehacer** (*m.*) **doméstico** (10)
housekeeper: female housekeeper **ama** (*f.*) (*but* **el ama**) **de casa** (17); male housekeeper **amo de casa** (17)
housing **vivienda** (12)
how + *adj.*! **¡qué** + *adj.*! (14); how strange that . . . ! **¡qué extraño que... !** (13)
how? **¿cómo?** (1); how are you ? **¿cómo está(s)?** (1); **¿qué tal?** (1); how do you get to . . . ? **¿cómo se llega a... ?** (15); how many? **¿cuántos/as?** (2); how much? **¿cuánto?** (2); how much does it (do they) cost? **¿cuánto cuesta(n)?** (4); how often . . . ? **¿con qué frecuencia... ?** (3)
human body **cuerpo humano** (11)
humanities **humanidades** *f. pl.* (2)
hungry: to be (very) hungry **tener (mucha) hambre** (7)
hurry: to be in a hurry **tener prisa** (4)
hurt **doler (duele)** (*like* **gustar**) (11)
husband **esposo** (3), **marido** (16)
hybrid **híbrido/a** (15)

I

I *sub. pron.* **yo** (2); I am **soy** (1); I am from . . . **(yo) soy de...** (1); I didn't mean to do it **fue sin querer** (14); I hope (that) **ojalá (que)** (13); I would (really) like . . . **me gustaría (mucho)...** (8); I'm sorry **disculpa, discúlpame** *fam. s.* (14); **disculpe, discúlpeme** *form. s.* (14); I'm (very) sorry **lo siento (mucho)** (14)
ice cream **helado** (7)
identification card **tarjeta de identificación** (14)
if **si** (3)

illness **enfermedad** *f.* (11)
immediately **en seguida** (5)
impossible: it's impossible that **es imposible que** (13)
improbable: it's improbable that **es improbable que** (13)
in **en** (1); in case **en caso de (que)** (16); in cash **en efectivo** (17); in front of **delante de** (6); in love (with) **enamorado/a (de)** (16); in order to (*do something*) **para** + *inf.* (10); in the afternoon **de la tarde** (1); in the evening **de la noche** (1); in the morning **por la mañana** (2), **de la mañana** (1)
incredible: it's incredible that **es increíble que** (13)
indefinite and negative word *gram.* **palabra indefinida y negativa** (7)
inequality **desigualdad** *f.* (18)
inexpensive **barato/a** (4)
inflexible **inflexible** (14)
inform **informar** (18)
injection **inyección** *f.* (11)
inner ear **oído** (11)
insist (on) **insistir (en)** (12)
install **instalar** (12)
installments: in installments **a plazos** (17)
intelligent **inteligente** (3)
intended for **para** (3)
interest *n.* **interés** *m.* (17); *v.* to interest (*someone*) **interesar** (*like* **gustar**) (8)
Internet **Internet** *m.* (12); to go on the Internet **entrar en el Internet** (12); to look for on the Internet **buscar (qu) en el Internet** (12)
interrogative *gram.* **interrogativo/a** (1)
interstate **autopista** (15)
interview **entrevista** (17)
interviewee **entrevistado/a** (17)
interviewer **entrevistador(a)** (17)
invite **invitar** (7)
iPod **iPod** *m.* (12)
iron **planchar** (10)
island **isla** (6)
issue **cuestión** *f.* (17)
Italian (*language*) **italiano** (2)
its *poss. adj.* **su(s)** (3); (of) its *poss. adj., poss. pron.* **suyo/a(s)** (17)

J

jacket **chaqueta** (4)
January **enero** (6)
job **empleo** (17), **trabajo** (12); full-time job **empleo de tiempo completo** (17), **trabajo de tiempo completo** (14); part-time job **empleo de tiempo parcial** (17), **trabajo de tiempo parcial** (14); poorly paid job **empleo mal pagado** (17); well-paid job **empleo bien pagado** (17)
joke **chiste** *m.* (8)
journalist **periodista** *m., f.* (17)
juice **jugo** (7); fruit juice **jugo de fruta** (7)
July **julio** (6)
June **junio** (6)
just in case **por si acaso** (14)

K

keep **guardar** (12); **mantener** (*like* **tener**) (18); to keep on going **seguir (sigo) (i)** (15)
key **llave** *f.* (5)
kill **matar** (18)
kind **amable** (3)
king **rey** *m.* (18)
kiss: to kiss each other **besarse** (11)
kitchen **cocina** (5)
know **conocer (conozco)** (7); **saber** (7); to know how to (*do something*) **saber** + *inf.* (7)

L

laborer **obrero/a** (17)
lack **falta** (15)
lake **lago** (15)
lamp **lámpara** (5)
landlady **dueña** (12)
landline **teléfono fijo** (12)
landlord **dueño** (12)
language **lengua** (2); foreign language **lengua extranjera** (2)
laptop (computer) **computadora portátil** (2), **ordenador** (*m.*) **portátil** *Sp.* (12)
large **gran, grande** (3)
last **pasado/a** (11); **último/a** (14); for the last time **por última vez** (14); last night *adv.* **anoche** (11)
late **atrasado/a** (8); *adv.* **tarde** (2)
later: see you later **hasta luego** (1)
laugh (about) **reír(se) (río) (i) (de)** (9)
law **ley** *f.* (18)
lawyer **abogado/a** (17)
layer: ozone layer **capa de ozono** (15)
lazy **perezoso/a** (3)
lead a calm/healthy life **llevar una vida tranquila/sana** (11)
learn (about) **enterarse (de)** (18); to learn how to (*do something*) **aprender a** + *inf.* (3)
least: at least **por lo menos** (9)
leather *adj.* **de cuero** (4)
leave (*a place*) **salir (de)** (5); to leave behind (in [*a place*]) **dejar (en)** (10); to leave on vacation **salir de; vacaciones** (8); to leave undone **dejar sin hacer** (10);
left: to the left of **a la izquierda de** (6)
leg **pierna** (11)
lend **prestar** (8)
lenses: contact lenses **lentes** (*m. pl.*) **de contacto** (11)
less . . . than **menos... que** (6); less than + *number* **menos de** + *number* (6)
let (*someone*) go **despedir** (*like* **pedir**) (17)
letter **carta** (3)
lettuce **lechuga** (7)
librarian **bibliotecario/a** (2)
library **biblioteca** (2)
license: driver's license **licencia de conducir/manejar** (15)
lie **mentira** (12)
life **vida** (11); academic life **vida académica** (14); pace of life **ritmo de la vida** (15)
lift weights **levantar pesas** (11)
light *n.* **luz** *f.* (*pl.* **luces**) (14); *adj.* light (not heavy) **ligero/a** (7)
like *n.* **gusto** (1); do you like . . . ? **¿te gusta... ?** *fam. s.* (1); **¿a usted le gusta... ?** *form. s.* (1); I would (really) like . . . **me gustaría (mucho)...** (8); (no,) I don't like . . . **(no,) no me gusta** (1); to like very much **encantar** (*like* **gustar**) (8); what are you like? **¿cómo es usted?** *form. s.* (1); yes, I like . . . **sí, me gusta...** (1)
likeable **simpático/a** (3)
likely: it's likely that **es probable que** (13)
likewise **igualmente** (1)
limit: speed limit **límite** (*m.*) **de velocidad** (15)
line (*of people*) **cola** (8); to stand in line **hacer cola** (8)
listen to (*music, the radio*) **oír** (5); to listen (to) **escuchar** (2)
literature **literatura** (2)
little *n.* (a) little **poco** (2); a little bit (of) **un poco (de)** (2); *adj.* **poco/a** (4)
live **vivir** (3)
living room **sala** (5)
loan **préstamo** (17)
lobster **langosta** (7)
long **largo/a** (3)
look at **mirar** (3); to look for **buscar (qu)** (2); to look for on the Internet **buscar (qu) en el Internet** (12)
lose **perder (pierdo)** (5)
lot: a lot *adv.* **mucho** (2); a lot (of) **mucho/a** (3); an awful lot **muchísimo** (8); there's lots of **hay mucho/a** (6)
love *n.* **amor** *m.* (16); *adj.* in love (with) **enamorado/a (de)** (16); *v.* **amar** (16); **querer (quiero)** (16); **encantar** (*like* **gustar**) (8); to fall in love (with) **enamorarse (de)** (16); to love each other **quererse** (11)
luck: to have bad/good luck **tener mala/buena suerte** (14)
lucky: to be lucky **tener buena suerte** (14)
luggage **equipaje** *m.* (8)
lunch *n.* **almuerzo** (7); to have lunch **almorzar (almuerzo) (c)** (5)
lungs **pulmones** *m. pl.* (11)
-ly (adverbial suffix) **-mente** (14)
lyrics **letra** (7)

M

ma'am **señora (Sra.)** (1)
machine: automatic teller machine (ATM) **cajero automático** (17)
made: it is made of . . . **es de...** (4)
magazine **revista** (3)
mailbox: voice mailbox **buzón** (*m.*) **de voz** (12)
main course **plato principal** (7)
maintain **mantener** (*like* **tener**) (18)
make **hacer** (5); to make a mistake (about) **equivocarse (qu) (de)** (14); to make plans to (*do something*) **hacer planes para** + *inf.* (10); to make stops **hacer escalas/paradas** (8); to make the bed **hacer la cama** (10)
male housekeeper **amo de casa** (17)
mall: shopping mall **centro comercial** (4)
man **hombre** *m.* (2); **señor (Sr.)** *m.* (1)
manager **gerente** *m., f.* (17)
manufacture **fabricar (qu)** (15)
many **muchos/as** (3); as many . . . as **tanto/a(s)... como** (6); how many? **¿cuántos/as?** (2)
march **manifestación** *f.* (18)
March **marzo** (6)
market(place) **mercado** (4)
marriage **matrimonio** (16)
married: to be a married person **ser casado/a** (16); to be married (to) **estar casado/a (con)** (16)
marry **casarse (con)** (16)
mass media **medios** *m. pl.* (18)
masterpiece **obra maestra** (13)
match (*game*) **partido** (10)
material **material** (4)
math **matemáticas** *f. pl.* (2)
matter **cuestión** *f.* (17)
May **mayo** (6)
me *obj. of prep.* **mí** (6)
meal **comida** (7)
mean: I didn't mean to do it **fue sin querer** (14); that means . . . **eso quiere decir...** (11)
means of transportation **medio de transporte** (8)
meat **carne** *f.* (7)
mechanic **mecánico/a** (15)
medical: medical office **consultorio** (11); medical personnel **personal** (*m.*) **médico** (11)
medicine **medicina** (11)
medium of communication **medio de comunicación** (18)
meet **conocerse** (16); nice to meet you **mucho gusto** (1); to meet (*someone somewhere*) **encontrarse (me encuentro) (con)** (11)
memory **memoria** (12)
memory stick **pen drive** *m.* (12)
menu **menú** *m.* (7)
messy **desordenado/a** (6)
Mexican **mexicano/a** (3)
microwave oven **horno de microondas** (10)
middle age **madurez** *f.* (16)
midnight **medianoche** *f.* (6)
military service **servicio militar** (18)
milk **leche** *f.* (7)
million: one million **un millón (de)** (4)
mine, (of) mine *poss. adj., poss. pron.* **mío/a(s)** (17)
mineral water **agua** (*f.;* but **el agua**) **mineral** (7)
minute: fifteen minutes till (*hour*) **menos quince** (1); thirty minutes past (*the hour*) **y treinta** (1)
misbehave **portarse mal** (9)
miss (*an event*) **perder (pierdo)** (5)
Miss **señorita (Srta.)** (1)
mistake: to make a mistake (about) **equivocarse (qu) (de)** (14)
modem **módem** *m.* (12)
modern **moderno/a** (13)
molar **muela** (11)
mom **mamá** (3)
Monday **lunes** *m.* (5); next Monday **lunes que viene** (5); on Monday **el lunes** (5); on Mondays **los lunes** (5)
money **dinero** (2)
monitor **pantalla** (12); big screen monitor **pantalla grande** (12); flat screen monitor **pantalla plana** (12)
month **mes** *m.* (6)
moped **moto(cicleta)** (12)
more **más** (2); more . . . than **más... que** (6); more than + *number* **más de** + *number* (6)
morning: good morning **buenos días** (1); in the morning **por la mañana** (2); **de la mañana** (1)
mother **madre** *f.* (3); **mamá** (3)
motorcycle **moto(cicleta)** (12)
mountain **montaña** (8)
mouse **ratón** *m.* (12)
mouth **boca** (11)
move (*residence*) **mudarse** (12)
movie **película** (5); movie theater **cine** *m. s.* (5); movies **cine** *m. s.* (5)
Mr. **señor (Sr.)** *m.* (1)
Mrs. **señora (Sra.)** (1)
Ms. **señorita (Srta.)** (1)
much **mucho** (2); as much . . . as **tanto/a(s)... como** (6); as much as **tanto como** (6); how much? **¿cuánto?** (2); how much does it (do they) cost? **¿cuánto cuesta(n)?** (4)
museum: to visit a museum **visitar un museo** (10)
mushrooms **champiñones** *m. pl.* (7)
music **música** (13)
musical **musical** (13)
musician **músico** *m., f.* (13)
must (*do something*) **deber** + *inf.* (3)
my *poss. adj.* **mi(s)** (3); **mío/a(s)** (17)

N

name **nombre** *m.* (7); my name is . . . **me llamo...** (1); what is your name? **¿cómo se llama usted?** *form. s.* (1); **¿cómo te llamas?** *fam. s.* (1)
nap: to take a nap **dormir la siesta** (5)
narrate **contar (cuento)** (8)
nationality: adjective of nationality **adjetivo de nacionalidad** (3)
natural: natural resource **recurso natural** (15); natural sciences **ciencias** (*f. pl.*) **naturales** (2)
nature **naturaleza** (15)
nauseated **mareado/a** (11)
neat **ordenado/a** (6)
necessary **necesario/a** (3); it is necessary to (*do something*) **hay que** + *inf.* (13)
need **necesitar** (2)
negative: indefinite and negative word *gram.* **palabra indefinida y negativa** (7)
neighbor **vecino/a** (12)
neighborhood **barrio** (12)
neither **tampoco** (7)
nephew **sobrino** (3)
nervous **nervioso/a** (6)
network: social network **red** (*f.*) **social** (12)
never **jamás** (7), **nunca** (3); almost never **casi nunca** (3)
nevertheless **sin embargo** (6)
new **nuevo/a** (3)
New Year's Eve **Nochevieja** *f.* (9)
newlywed **recién casado/a** (16)
news **noticias** (18); news media **prensa** (18); the bad news **lo malo** (11); the good news **lo bueno** (11)
newscast **noticiero** (18)
newspaper **periódico** (3)
next *adv.* **luego** (5); *adj.* next (Tuesday . . .) **el próximo (martes...)** (5); next Monday **lunes** (*m.*) **que viene** (5); next week **próxima semana** (5)
nice **amable** (3), **simpático/a** (3); nice to meet you **mucho gusto** (1); (very) nice out **(muy) buen tiempo** (6)
niece **sobrina** (3)
night: at night **por la noche** (2); last night *adv.* **anoche** (11)
nine **nueve** (1)
nine hundred **novecientos/as** (4)
nineteen **diecinueve** (1)
ninety **noventa** (3)
ninth **noveno/a** (13)
no **no** (1); **ningún (ninguna)** (7); no, I don't like . . . **(no,) no me gusta** (1)
no one **nadie** (7)
nobody **nadie** (7)
noise **ruido** (5)
noon **mediodía** *m.* (6)

normal: it's normal that **es normal que** (13)
north **norte** *m.* (6)
nose **nariz** *f.* (*pl.* **narices**) (11)
not any **ningún (ninguna)** (7)
notebook **cuaderno** (2)
notes (*academic*) **apuntes** *m., pl.* (14)
nothing **nada** (7)
noun *gram.* **sustantivo** (2)
novel **novela** (13)
novelist **novelista** *m., f.* (13)
November **noviembre** *m.* (6)
now **ahora** (2); right now **ahora mismo** (6)
nuclear energy **energía nuclear** (15)
number **número** (1); ordinal number *gram.* **número ordinal** (13)
nurse **enfermero/a** (11)
nursing home **residencia de ancianos** (12)

O

o'clock: it's . . . o'clock **son las...** (1)
obey **obedecer (obedezco)** (15)
object **objeto** (2)
obligation **deber** *m.* (18)
obtain **obtener** (*like* **tener**) (12); **conseguir** (*like* **seguir**) (9)
ocean **océano** (8)
October **octubre** *m.* (6)
of **de** (1); of course! **¡por supuesto!** (14); of the **del** (3)
off: to turn off **apagar (gu)** (14)
offer **ofrecer (ofrezco)** (8)
office **oficina** (2); (*in a home*) **estudio** (5); (*medical*) **consultorio** (11); (*political*) **cargo** (18)
often: how often . . . ? **¿con qué frecuencia... ?** (3)
oil **aceite** *m.* (7); **petróleo** (15)
OK: it's OK **está bien** (6)
old **viejo/a** (3); old age **vejez** *f.* (16)
older (than) **mayor (que)** (6)
on **en** (1); on a trip **de viaje** (8); on Monday **el lunes** (5); on the dot (*time*) **en punto** (1); on top of **encima de** (6); on Tuesdays **los martes** (5); on vacation **de vacaciones** (8)
one **uno** (1); it's one o'clock **es la una** (1)
one hundred **cien** (3); (*used with* 101–199) **ciento** (4)
one hundred ninety-nine **ciento noventa y nueve** (4)
one hundred one **ciento uno** (4)
one hundred two **ciento dos** (4)
one million **un millón (de)** (4)
one thousand **mil** (4)
only *adv.* **solo** (2)
open *v.* **abrir** (*p.p.* **abierto**) (3); *adj.* **abierto/a** (6)
opera **ópera** (13)
operate (*a machine*) **manejar** (12)
or **o** (1)
oral **oral** (14); oral report **informe** (*m.*) **oral** (14)
orange *n.* **naranja** (7); *adj.* **anaranjado/a** (4)
orchestra **orquesta** (13)
order **mandar** (12); (*in a restaurant*) **pedir (pido) (i)** (5)
ordinal number *gram.* **número ordinal** (13)
other **otro/a** (3); others **los/las demás** (12)
ought to (*do something*) **deber** + *inf.* (3)
our *poss. adj.* **nuestro/a(s)** (3); our, of ours *poss. adj., poss. pron.* **nuestro/a(s)** (17)
outdoors *adv.* **afuera** (6)
outer ear **oreja** (11)
outskirts **afueras** *f. pl.* (12)
overcast: it's (very) overcast **está (muy) nublado** (6)
own, one's own **propio/a** (17)
owner **dueño/a** (7)
ozone layer **capa de ozono** (15)

P

P.M. **de la noche** (1); **de la tarde** (1)
pace of life **ritmo de la vida** (15)
pack one's suitcase(s) **hacer la(s) maleta(s)** (8)
paid: poorly paid job/position **empleo mal pagado** (17)
pain (in) **dolor** *m.* **(de)** (11); to have a pain in **tener dolor de** (11)
paint **pintar** (13)
painter **pintor(a)** (13)
painting (*general*) **pintura** (13); (*specific piece*) **cuadro** (13)
pants **pantalones** *m. pl.* (4)
paper **papel** *m.* (2)
pardon me **disculpa, discúlpame** *fam. s.* (14); **disculpe, discúlpeme** *form. s.* (14)
parents **padres** *m. pl.* (3)
park **estacionar** (14)
parking lot/place **estacionamiento** (15)
part **parte** *f.* (5)
part-time job/position **empleo de tiempo parcial** (17), **trabajo de tiempo parcial** (14)
partner **pareja** (16)
party **fiesta** (2); political party **partido** (18); to throw a party **dar una fiesta** (9); **hacer una fiesta** (9)
pass: boarding pass **tarjeta de embarque** (8)
pass through customs **pasar por la aduana** (8); to pass through security (check) **pasar por el control de seguridad** (8)
passenger **pasajero/a** (8)
passport **pasaporte** *m.* (8)
password **contraseña** (12)
past **pasado/a** (11)
pastime **pasatiempo** (10)
patient **paciente** *n. m., f.* (11)
patio **patio** (5)
pay *n.* (*often per hour*) **salario** (17); *v.* to pay (for) **pagar (gu)** (2)
pea: green peas **arvejas** *f. pl.* (7)
peace **paz** *f.* (*pl.* **paces**) (18)
peasant **campesino/a** (15)
pen **bolígrafo** (2)
pencil **lápiz** *m.* (*pl.* **lápices**) (2)
people **gente** *f. s.* (12)
pepper **pimienta** (7)
permit **permitir** (12)
person **persona** (2)
personal pronoun *gram.* **pronombre** (*m.*) **personal** (2)
personnel: medical personnel **personal** (*m.*) **médico** (11)
pet **mascota** (3)
petroleum **petróleo** (15)
pharmacist **farmacéutico/a** (11)
phase **etapa** (16)
philosophy **filosofía** (2)
phone **teléfono** (2); cell phone **teléfono celular** (2); to talk on the phone **hablar por teléfono** (2)
photo(graph) **foto(grafía)** (8); to take photos **sacar (qu) fotos** (8)
photocopy **fotocopia** (12)
photographer **fotógrafo/a** (17)
photography **fotografía** (13)
physics **física** (2)
pick up **recoger (recojo)** (14)
picnic: to have a picnic **hacer un *picnic*** (10)
pie **pastel** *m.* (7)
piece: piece of advice **consejo** (7); piece of furniture **mueble** *m.* (5)
Pilates: to do Pilates **hacer (el método) Pilates** (11)
pill **pastilla** (11)
pilot **piloto** *m., f.* (8)
pink **rosado/a** (4)
place *n.* **lugar** *m.* (2); (*in line*) **puesto** (8); parking place **estacionamiento** (15); *v.* **poner** (5)
plaid **de cuadros** (4)
plan: to make plans to **hacer planes** (10)
plane: to fly, go/travel by plane **volar (vuelo) en avión** (8); **ir en avión** (8)
planet **planeta** *m.* (15)
plasma **plasma** *m.* (12)
plate **plato** (5)
play (*dramatic*) *n.* **obra de teatro** (13); (*a game, sport*) *v.* **jugar (juego) (gu) (a, al)** (5); (*a musical instrument*) **tocar (qu)** (2); to play cards **jugar (juego) (gu) a las cartas** (10); to play chess **jugar (juego) (gu) al ajedrez** (10)
player **jugador(a)** (10)
playwright **dramaturgo/a** (13)
plaza **plaza** (4)
pleasantry **expresión** (*f.*) **de cortesía** (1)

please **por favor** (1)
pleased to meet you **encantado/a** (1)
pleasing: to be pleasing **gustar** (8)
plumber **plomero/a** (17)
poet **poeta** *m., f.* (13)
point: cardinal point **punto cardinal** (6)
police officer **policía** *m., f.* (15)
policy **política** (18)
political: political office **cargo** (18); political party **partido** (18); political science **ciencias** (*f. pl.*) **políticas** (2)
politician **político/a** (18)
politics **política** *s.* (18)
polka-dot **de lunares** (4)
pollute **contaminar** (15)
polluted **contaminado/a** (15)
pollution: there's (lots of) pollution **hay (mucha) contaminación** *f.* (6)
poor **pobre** (3); poorly paid job/position **empleo mal pagado** (17); to do poorly **salir mal** (5); to get along poorly (with) **llevarse mal (con)** (16)
population **población** *f.* (15)
pork chop **chuleta (de cerdo)** (7)
port **puerto** (8)
porter **maletero** (8)
position **empleo** (17); part-time position **empleo de tiempo parcial** (17), **trabajo de tiempo parcial** (14); poorly paid position **empleo mal pagado** (17); to run for a position (as a candidate) **postularse para un cargo (como candidato/a)** (18); well-paid position **empleo bien pagado** (17)
possessive **posesivo/a** (17); possessive adjective *gram.* **adjetivo posesivo** (3)
possible **posible** (3); it's possible that **es posible que** (13)
postcard **tarjeta postal** (8)
potato: French fried potato **papa/patata frita** (7)
pottery **cerámica** (13)
practice **practicar (qu)** (2); **entrenar** (10)
prefer **preferir (prefiero)** (4)
preference **preferencia** (1)
prepare **preparar** (7)
preposition *gram.* **preposición** *f.* (5)
prescription **receta** (11)
present **regalo** (3)
press **prensa** (18)
pressure **presión** (14); to be under a lot of pressure **estar bajo muchas presiones** (14)
pretty **bonito/a** (3)
price (*of a transportation ticket*) **pasaje** *m.* (8); fixed, set price **precio fijo** (4)
print **imprimir** (12)
printer **impresora** (12)
probable: it's probable that **es probable que** (13)
profession **profesión** *f.* (17)
professor **profesor(a)** (1)
programmer **programador(a)** (17)
prohibit **prohibir (prohíbo)** (12)
promise **prometer** (8)
pronoun: personal pronoun *gram.* **pronombre** (*m.*) **personal** (2)
protect **proteger (protejo)** (15)
provided **con tal de** (16); provided (that) **con tal (de) que** (16)
psychiatrist **siquiatra** *m., f.* (17)
psychologist **sicólogo/a** (17)
psychology **sociología** (2)
public **público/a** (15)
pure **puro/a** (15)
purple **morado/a** (4)
purpose: for what purpose? **¿para qué... ?** (16)
purse **bolso** (4)
put **poner** (5); to put on (*an article of clothing*) **ponerse** (5)

Q

quarter: a quarter (fifteen minutes) after (*the hour*) **y cuarto** (1); a quarter to (*hour*) **menos cuarto** (1)
queen **reina** (18)
question **pregunta** (5); to ask a question **hacer una pregunta** (5)
quit **dejar** (17)
quiz **prueba** (14)

R

radio station **estación** (*f.*) **de radio** (18)
rain **llover (llueve)** (6); it's raining **llueve** (6)
raincoat **impermeable** *m.* (4)
raise **aumento** (12)
rather **bastante** (16)
read **leer** (*like* **creer**) (3)
reason: for that reason **por eso** (3)
receipt **recibo** (17)
receive **recibir** (3)
receptionist **recepcionista** *m., f.* (17)
recipe **receta** (7)
recommend **recomendar (recomiendo)** (8)
record **grabar** (12)
recycle **reciclar** (15)
recycling **reciclaje** *m.* (15)
red **rojo/a** (4); red wine **vino tinto** (7)
reflexive verb *gram.* **verbo reflexivo** (5)
refrigerator **refrigerador** *m.* (10)
regret **lamentar** (13), **sentir (siento) (i)** (13)
relationship: emotional relationship **relación** (*f.*) **sentimental** (16)
relative **pariente** *m., f.* (3)
remain (*in a place*) **quedarse** (6); to remain, be left **quedar** (14)
remember **acordarse (me acuerdo) (de)** (13); **recordar (recuerdo)** (9)
remote control **control** (*m.*) **remoto** (12)
renewable **renovable** (15); renewable energy **energía renovable** (15)
rent *n.* **alquiler** *m.* (12); *v.* to rent **alquilar** (12)
renter **inquilino/a** (12)
repair **arreglar** (15), **reparar** (15); repair shop **taller** *m.* (15)
report **trabajo** (14); oral report **informe** (*m.*) **oral** (14); written report **informe** (*m.*) **escrito** (14)
reporter **reportero/a** (18)
residence **residencia** (12)
resign (from) **renunciar (a)** (17)
resolve **resolver (resuelvo)** (15)
resource: natural resource **recurso natural** (15)
responsibility **deber** *m.* (18)
rest **descansar** (5)
restaurant **restaurante** *m.* (7)
résumé **currículum** *m.* (17)
retire **jubilarse** (17)
return (*something to someone*) **devolver** (*like* **volver**) (14); (*to a place*) **regresar** (2), **volver (vuelvo)** (5)
rice **arroz** *m.* (7)
rich (*wealthy*) **rico/a** (3); (*tasty*) **rico/a** (7)
ride: to ride a bicycle **pasear en bicicleta** (10); to ride a horse **montar a caballo** (10)
right (*legal*) **derecho** (18); right? **¿no?** (4), **¿verdad?** (4); right now **ahora mismo** (6); right now (*currently*) **de/en la actualidad** (10); to be right **tener razón** (4); to the right of **a la derecha de** (6)
ring **sonar (suena)** (10)
river **río** (15)
roast(ed) **asado/a** (7); roast chicken **pollo asado** (7)
role **papel** *m.* (13)
rollerblade **patinar en línea** (10)
room **cuarto** (2); waiting room **sala de espera** (8)
roommate **compañero/a de cuarto** (2)
round-trip ticket **billete** *m.* (*Sp.*) **/ boleto** (*L.A.*) **de ida y vuelta** (8)
routine **rutina** (5)
rug **alfombra** (5)
ruin **ruina** (13)
run **correr** (10); to run against/into **chocar (qu) contra/con** (14); **pegarse (gu) con** (14); to run as a candidate **postularse como candidato/a** (18); to run for a position **postularse para un cargo** (18); (*machines*) **funcionar** (12); to run out of **acabar** (14)

S

sad **triste** (6)
sake: for heaven's sake **por Dios** (14)
salad **ensalada** (7)
salary **sueldo** (12)
sales **rebajas** *f. pl.* (4)
salesperson **vendedor(a)** (17)

salmon **salmón** *m.* (7)
salt **sal** *f.* (7)
same **mismo/a** (6); same here **igualmente** (1)
sandals **sandalias** *f. pl.* (4)
sandwich **sándwich** *m.* (7)
Saturday **sábado** (5)
sausage **salchicha** (7)
save **conservar** (15); (*a place in line*) **guardar un puesto** (8); (*documents*) **almacenar** (12), **guardar** (12); (*money*) **ahorrar** (17)
savings account **cuenta de ahorros** (17)
savory **rico/a** (7)
say **decir** (8); to say good-bye (to) **despedir(se)** (*like* **pedir**) **(de)** (9)
scanner **escáner** *m.* (12)
scenery **escenario** (13)
schedule **horario** (14)
school **escuela** (10)
schoolteacher **maestro/a de escuela** (17)
science **ciencia** (2); computer science **computación** *f.* (2); natural sciences **ciencias** (*f. pl.*) **naturales** (2); political science **ciencias** (*f. pl.*) **políticas** (2); social sciences **ciencias** (*f. pl.*) **sociales** (2)
screen **pantalla** (12); big screen (monitor) **pantalla grande** (12); flat screen (monitor) **pantalla plana** (12)
script **guión** *m.* (13)
sculptor **escultor(a)** (13)
sculpture **escultura** (13)
sea **mar** *m.* (8)
season **estación** *f.* (6)
seat **asiento** (8)
second **segundo/a** (13); second floor (third story) **segundo piso** (12)
secretary **secretario/a** (2)
security (check) **control** (*m.*) **de seguridad** (8); to go/pass through security (check) **pasar por el control de seguridad** (8)
see **ver** (5); see you around **nos vemos** (1); see you later **hasta luego** (1); see you tomorrow **hasta mañana** (1)
sell **vender** (3)
send a text **mandar un mensaje** (2)
separate (from) **separarse (de)** (16)
separated from **separado/a (de)** (16)
separation **separación** *f.* (16)
September **septiembre** *m.* (6)
serve **servir (sirvo) (i)** (5)
service **servicio** (15); military service **servicio militar** (18)
set price **precio fijo** (4)
set the table **poner la mesa** (10)
seven **siete** (1)
seven hundred **setecientos/as** (4)
seventeen **diecisiete** (1)
seventh **séptimo/a** (13)
seventy **setenta** (3)
shake hands **darse la mano** (11)
shame: it's a shame that **es una lástima que** (13); what a shame that . . . ! **¡qué lástima que... !** (13)
shape **forma** (4)
share **compartir** (17)
shave **afeitarse** (5)
she *sub. pron.* **ella** (2)
shellfish **mariscos** *m. pl.* (7)
ship **barco** (8); cruise ship **crucero** (8); to go/travel by ship **ir en barco** (8)
shirt **camisa** (4)
shoes **zapatos** *m. pl.* (4)
shop **tienda** (4); repair shop **taller** *m.* (15)
shopping **de compras** (4); shopping mall **centro comercial** (4); to go shopping **ir de compras** (4)
short (*in height*) **bajo/a** (3); (*in length*) **corto/a** (3)
shorts **pantalones** (*m. pl.*) **cortos** (4)
shot: to give (*someone*) a shot **ponerle una inyección** (11)
should (*do something*) **deber** + *inf.* (3)
show *n.* **espectáculo** (13); *v.* **mostrar (muestro)** (8)
shower: to take a shower **ducharse** (5)
shrimp **camarones** *m., pl.* (7)
siblings **hermanos** *m. pl.* (3)
sick **enfermo/a** (6); to become sick **enfermarse** (9)
sickness **enfermedad** *f.* (11)
sidewalk **acera** (15)
silk *adj.* **de seda** (4)
silly **tonto/a** (3)
silver *adj.* **de plata** (4)
sing **cantar** (2)
singer **cantante** *m., f.* (13)
single (*not married*) **soltero/a** (16)
sink: bathroom sink **lavabo** (5)
sir **señor (Sr.)** *m.* (1)
sister **hermana** (3)
sit down **sentarse (me siento)** (5)
six **seis** (1)
six hundred **seiscientos/as** (4)
sixteen **dieciséis** (1)
sixth **sexto/a** (13)
sixty **sesenta** (3)
skate *n.* (*roller/inline*) **patines** *m. pl.* (12); *v.* **patinar** (10)
skateboard **monopatín** *m.* (12)
skating **patinaje** *m.* (10)
ski **esquiar (esquío)** (10)
skiing **esquí** *m.* (10)
skirt **falda** (4)
skyscraper **rascacielos** *m. inv.* (15)
sleep **dormir (duermo) (u)** (5)
sleepy: to be sleepy **tener sueño** (4)
slender **delgado/a** (3)
small **pequeño/a** (3); small child **niño/a** (3)
smart **listo/a** (3)
smile **sonreír(se)** (*like* **reír**) (9)
smoke **fumar** (8)
smoking area **sala de fumadores/fumar** (8)
snack **merienda** (7); to have a snack **merendar (meriendo)** (7)
snow **nevar (nieva)** (6); it's snowing **nieva** (6)
so that **para que** (16)
so-so **regular** (1)
soccer **fútbol** *m.* (10)
social: social network **red** (*f.*) **social** (12); social sciences **ciencias sociales** (2); social worker **trabajador(a) social** (17)
socks **calcetines** *m. pl.* (4)
soft drink **refresco** (7)
solar energy **energía solar** (15)
soldier **soldado** (17); female soldier **mujer** (*f.*) **soldado** (17)
solve **resolver (resuelvo)** (15)
some **algún (alguna/os/as)** (7)
someone **alguien** (7)
something **algo** (7)
sometimes **a veces** (3)
son **hijo** (3)
song **canción** *f.* (13)
soon: as soon as **en cuanto** (17), **tan pronto como** (17)
sorry: to feel sorry **lamentar** (13), **sentir (siento) (i)** (13); I'm (very) sorry **lo siento (mucho)** (14)
sound **sonar (suena)** (10)
soup **sopa** (7)
south **sur** *m.* (6)
Spanish (*language*) **español** *m.* (2); *n., adj.* **español(a)** (3)
spare (free) time **ratos** (*m. pl.*) **libres** (10)
speak **hablar** (2)
species: species **especie** *f.* (15); endangered species **especie** (*f.*) **en peligro de extinción** (15)
spectator **espectador(a)** (13)
speed limit **límite** (*m.*) **de velocidad** (15)
spend (*money*) **gastar** (9); (*time*) **pasar** (6); to spend one's vacation in . . . **pasar las vacaciones en...** (8)
spicy **picante** (7)
sport **deporte** *m.* (10)
sporting **deportivo/a** (10)
sports, sports-loving *adj.* **deportivo/a** (10)
spring **primavera** (6)
square **plaza** (4)
stage **escenario** (13); (*phase*) **etapa** (16)
stairs **escaleras** *f. pl.* (14)
stand up **levantarse** (5); to stand in line **hacer cola** (8)
start **empezar (empiezo) (c)** (5); to start up (*a car*) **arrancar (qu)** (15)
state **estado** (3); emotional state **estado afectivo** (9)
station **estación** *f.* (8); bus station **estación de autobuses** (8); gas station **estación de servicio** (15); radio

station **estación de radio** (18); station wagon **camioneta** (8)
stay **quedarse** (6); to stay in bed **guardar cama** (11)
steak **bistec** *m.* (7)
stick out one's tongue **sacar (qu) la lengua** (11)
still **todavía** (6)
stockings **medias** *f. pl.* (4)
stomach **estómago** (11)
stop *n.* **escala** (8), **parada** (8); bus stop **parada del autobús** (12); subway stop **parada del metro** (12); to make stops **hacer escalas** (8), **hacer paradas** (8); to stop **parar** (15); to stop (*doing something*) **dejar de** + *inf.* (11)
store *n.* **tienda** (4); *v.* **almacenar** (12)
stove **estufa** (10)
straight ahead **(todo) derecho** (15), **todo recto** (15)
strange: how strange that . . . ! **¡qué extraño que... !** (13); it's strange that **es extraño que** (13)
street **calle** *f.* (12)
street corner **esquina** (15)
stress **estrés** *m.* (14); to be under a lot of stress **tener muchas presiones** (14); under stress, stressed out **estresado/a** (14)
strike (*labor*) **huelga** (18)
striped **de rayas** (4)
struggle **lucha** (18)
student *n.* **estudiante** *m., f.* (2); *adj.* **estudiantil** (14)
study **estudiar** (2)
stuffed up **resfriado/a** *adj.* (11)
subject area **materia** (2)
suburbs **afueras** *f. pl.* (12)
subway stop **parada del metro** (12)
succeed in (*doing something*) **conseguir** (*like* **seguir**) + *inf.* (9)
suddenly **de repente** (11)
suffer **sufrir (de)** (14)
sufficiently **bastante** (16)
sugar **azúcar** *m.* (7)
suggest **sugerir (sugiero) (i)** (9)
suit **traje** *m.* (4)
suitcase **maleta** (8); to pack one's suitcase(s) **hacer la(s) maleta(s)** (8)
summer **verano** (6)
sunbathe **tomar el sol** (8)
Sunday **domingo** (5)
sunny: it's (very) sunny **hace (mucho) sol** (6)
supper **cena** (7); to have (eat) supper **cenar** (7)
sure **seguro/a** (6); it's a sure thing that **es seguro que** (13)
surf **hacer *surfing*** (10)
surprise **sorprender** (*like* **gustar**) (13)
SUV **SUV** *m.* (15)
sweater **suéter** *m.* (4)
sweatshirt **sudadera** (4)
sweep (the floor) **barrer (el piso)** (10)
sweets **dulces** *m. pl.* (7)
swim **nadar** (8)
swimming **natación** *f.* (10); swimming pool **piscina** (5)
swimsuit **traje** (*m.*) **de baño** (4)
syllabus **programa del curso** (14)
symptom **síntoma** *m.* (11)
systems analyst **analista** (*m., f.*) **de sistemas** (17)

T

T-shirt **camiseta** (4)
table **mesa** (2); to clear the table **quitar la mesa** (10); to set the table **poner la mesa** (10)
take **tomar** (2); **llevar** (4); to take a bath **bañarse** (5); to take a nap **dormir la siesta** (5); to take a shower **ducharse** (5); to take a trip **hacer un viaje** (5); to take a vacation **tomar unas vacaciones** (8); to take a walk **dar un paseo** (10); to take care of oneself **cuidarse** (11); to take off (*an article of clothing*) **quitarse** (5); to take out **sacar (qu)** (17); to take out the trash **sacar (qu) la basura** (10); to take photos **sacar (qu) fotos** (8); to take place at/in (*a place*) **ser en** + *place* (9); to take someone's temperature **tomarle la temperatura** (11)
talk **hablar** (2); to talk on the phone **hablar por teléfono** (2)
tall **alto/a** (3)
tame **domesticado/a** (15)
tank **tanque** *m.* (15)
tape **grabar** (12)
tape player/recorder **grabadora** (12)
tasty **rico/a** (7)
tea **té** *m.* (7)
teach **enseñar** (2)
team **equipo** (10)
technician **técnico/a** (17)
television: to watch television **mirar la tele(visión)** (3)
tell **contar (cuento)** (8); **decir** (8)
teller **cajero/a** (17); automatic teller machine (ATM) **cajero automático** (17)
temperature **temperatura** (11); to take someone's temperature **tomarle la temperatura** (11)
ten **diez** (1)
tenant **inquilino/a** (12)
tennis **tenis** *m.* (10)
tennis shoes **tenis** *m. pl.* (4)
tent **tienda de campaña** (8)
tenth **décimo/a** (13)
terrible: it's terrible that **es terrible que** (13)
terrorism **terrorismo** (18)
terrorist **terrorista** *m., f.* (18); terrorist attack **ataque** (*m.*) **terrorista** (18)
test **examen** *m.* (4); **prueba** (14)
text: to (send a) text **mandar un mensaje** (2)
textbook **libro de texto** (2)
than: less . . . than **menos... que** (6); less than + *number* **menos de** + *number* (6); more . . . than **más... que** (6); more than + *number* **más de** + *number* (6); older than **mayor que** (6); younger than **menos que** (6)
thank you (very much) **(muchas) gracias** (1); thanks for **gracias por** + *inf./noun* (9)
that *conj.* **que** (3); that *adj.* **ese/a** (4); *pron.* **eso** (4); that ([way] over there) *adj.* **aquel, aquella** (4); that ([way] over there) *pron.* **aquello** (4); that means . . . **eso quiere decir...** (11); that which **lo que** (5)
theater: to go to the theater **ir al teatro** (10)
their *poss. adj.* **su(s)** (3); (of) theirs *poss. adj., poss pron.* **suyo/a(s)** (17)
them *obj.* (*of prep.*) **ellos/as** (2)
then **luego** (5)
there **allí** (4)
there: (way) over there **allá** (4)
there is/are **hay** (1); is there / are there? **¿hay?** (1); there is/are not **no hay** (1); there's (lots of) **hay (mucho/a)** (6)
these *adj., pron.* **estos/as** (3)
they *sub. pron.* **ellos/as** (2)
thin **delgado/a** (3)
thing **cosa** (5); the bad thing **lo malo** (11); the good thing **lo bueno** (11)
think **creer (en)** (3); to think (about) **pensar (pienso) (en)** (5)
third **tercer(o/a)** (13)
thirsty: to be (very) thirsty **tener (mucha) sed** (7)
thirteen **trece** (1)
thirty **treinta** (1); thirty minutes past (*the hour*) **y treinta** (1)
this *adj., pron.* **este/a** (3); *pron.* **esto** (3)
those *adj., pron.* **esos/as** (4); those ([way] over there) *adj., pron.* **aquellos/as** (4)
three **tres** (1)
three hundred **trescientos/as** (4)
throat **garganta** (11)
through **por** (8)
throw: to throw a party **dar/hacer una fiesta** (9)
Thursday **jueves** *m.* (5)
ticket **billete** *m.* (*Sp.*) **/ boleto** (*L.A.*) (8); round-trip ticket **billete/boleto de ida y vuelta** (8)
tie **corbata** (4)
time **tiempo** (6); at what time . . . ? **¿a qué hora... ?** (1); conjunction of time **conjunción** (*f.*) **de tiempo** (17); for the first/last time **por primera/última vez** (14); free time **tiempo libre** (10); on

time **a tiempo** (8); spare (free) time **ratos** (*m. pl.*) **libres** (10); to have a bad time **pasarlo mal** (9); to have a good time **divertirse (me divierto)** (5); **pasarlo bien** (9); what time is it? **¿qué hora es?** (1)
tire: flat tire **llanta desinflada** (15)
tired **cansado/a** (6); to get tired **cansarse** (11)
to **a** (1); to the **al** (4); to the right of **a la derecha de** (6)
toast **pan tostado** (7)
toasted **tostado/a** (7)
toaster **tostadora** (10)
today **hoy** (1); what day is today? **¿qué día es hoy?** (5); what's today's date? **¿cuál es la fecha de hoy?** (6), **¿qué fecha es hoy?** (6)
toe **dedo del pie** (11)
together **juntos/as** (8)
tomato **tomate** *m.* (7)
tomorrow **mañana** (1); see you tomorrow **hasta mañana** (1)
tongue **lengua** (11); to stick out one's tongue **sacar (qu) la lengua** (11)
tonight **esta noche** (6)
too much **demasiado** *adv.* (9)
tooth **diente** *m.* (5); back tooth **muela** (11); to brush one's teeth **cepillarse los dientes** (5)
top: on top of **encima de** (6)
towel **toalla** (5)
trade (*profession*) **oficio** (17)
tradition: cultural tradition **tradición** (*f.*) **cultural** (13)
traditional **folclórico/a** (13)
traffic **circulación** *f.* (15), **tráfico** (15), **tránsito** (15); traffic signal **semáforo** (15)
train **tren** *m.* (8); to go/travel by train **ir en tren** (8); to train **entrenar** (10); train station **estación** (*f.*) **del tren** (8)
translator **traductor(a)** (17)
transportation: means of transportation **medio de transporte** (8)
trash: to take out the trash **sacar (qu) la basura** (10)
travel **viajar** (8); to travel by bus **ir en autobús** (8); to travel by boat/ship **ir en barco** (8); to travel by plane **ir en avión** (8)
traveling **de viaje** (8)
treadmill **caminadora** (11)
treatment **tratamiento** (11)
tree **árbol** *m.* (9)
trendy: it's trendy **está de moda** (4), **es de última moda** (4)
trip **viaje** *m.* (5); on a trip **de viaje** (8); to take a trip **hacer un viaje** (5)
try to (*do something*) **tratar de** + *inf.* (13)
Tuesday **martes** *m.* (5); on Tuesdays **los martes** (5)
tuition **matrícula** (2)
tuna **atún** *m.* (7)
turkey **pavo** (7)
turn **doblar** (15); to be someone's turn **tocarle (qu) a uno** (10); to turn on (*an appliance*) **poner** (5); to turn off **apagar (gu)** (14); to turn out badly **salir mal** (5); to turn out well **salir bien** (5)
twelve **doce** (1)
twenty **veinte** (1)
twice **dos veces** (11)
Twitter **Twitter** *m.* (12)
two **dos** (1)
two hundred **doscientos/as** (4)

U

ugly **feo/a** (3)
uncle **tío** (3); aunts and uncles **tíos** *m. pl.* (3)
under stress **estresado/a** (14); to be under a lot of stress **tener muchas presiones** (14)
understand **comprender** (3); **entender (entiendo)** (5)
underwear **ropa interior** (4)
undone: to leave undone **dejar sin hacer** (10)
unfortunately **desgraciadamente** (11)
United States: of the United States of America *n., adj.* **estadounidense** (3)
university *n.* **universidad** *f.* (2); *adj.* **universitario/a** (14)
unless **a menos que** (16); **sin que** (16)
unlikely: it's unlikely that **es improbable que** (13)
unlucky: to be unlucky **tener mala suerte** (14)
unoccupied **libre** (10)
unpleasant **antipático/a** (3)
until **hasta que** (17)
up: to be up to date **estar al día** (18)
urgent: it's urgent that **es urgente que** (13)
us *obj.* (*of prep.*) **nosotros/as** (2)
use **usar** (4); (*gas*) **gastar** (15); to be used for **servir (sirvo) (i) para** (5)

V

vacation: on vacation **de vacaciones** (8); to be on vacation **estar de vacaciones** (8); to go on vacation in/to . . . **ir de vacaciones a…** (8); to leave on vacation **salir de vacaciones** (8); to spend one's vacation in . . . **pasar las vacaciones en…** (8); to take a vacation **tomar unas vacaciones** (8)
vacuum cleaner **aspiradora** (10); to vacuum **pasar la aspiradora** (10)
van **camioneta** (8)
vegetables **verduras** (7)
vehicle **vehículo** (12)
verb *gram.* **verbo** (2); reflexive verb *gram.* **verbo reflexivo** (5)
very *adv.* **muy** (2); very very **-ísimo** (9); very well **muy bien** (1)
veterinarian **veterinario/a** (17)
victim **víctima** (18)
video **video** (12)
view **vista** (12)
visit a museum **visitar un museo** (10)
voice mailbox **buzón** (*m.*) **de voz** (12)
volleyball **voleibol** *m.* (10)
vote **votar** (18)

W

wages (*often per hour*) **salario** (17)
wait (for) **esperar** (7)
waiter/waitress **camarero/a** (7)
waiting room **sala de espera** (8)
wake up **despertarse (me despierto)** (5)
walk **caminar** (10); to take a walk **dar un paseo** (10)
wallet **cartera** (4)
want **desear** (2); **querer (quiero)** (4)
war **guerra** (18)
wash **lavar** (10)
washing machine **lavadora** (10)
watch *n.* **reloj** *m.* (4); *v.* **mirar** (3); to watch television **mirar la tele(visión)** (3)
water **agua** *f.* (*but* **el agua)** (7)
way over there **allá** (4)
we *sub. pron.* **nosotros/as** (2)
wear **llevar** (4), **usar** (4)
weather **tiempo** (6); what's the weather like? **¿qué tiempo hace?** (6); it's (very) good/bad weather **hace (muy) buen/mal tiempo** (6)
weave **tejer** (13)
wedding (*ceremony*) **boda** (16)
Wednesday **miércoles** *m.* (5)
week: days of the week **días** (*m. pl.*) **de la semana** (5); next week **la próxima semana** (5), **la semana que viene** (5); once a week **una vez a la semana** (3)
weekend **fin** (*m.*) **de semana** (2)
weight: to lift weights **levantar pesas** (11)
welcome: you're welcome **de nada** (1), **no hay de qué** (1)
well: very well **muy bien** (1); to come/turn out well **salir bien** (5); to do well **salir bien** (5)
well-being **bienestar** *m.* (11)
well-paid job/position **empleo bien pagado** (17)
west **oeste** *m.* (6)
whale **ballena** (15)
what **lo que** (5)
what? **¿cómo?** (1); **¿cuál?** (2); **¿qué?** (1); at what time? **¿a qué hora… ?** (1); for what purpose? **¿para qué… ?** (16); what (a) + *noun*! **¡qué** + *noun*! (14); what

a shame that . . . ! **¡qué lástima que… !** (13); what are you like? **¿cómo es usted?** *form. s.* (1); what day is today? **¿qué día es hoy?** (5); what for? **¿para qué… ?** (16); what is your name? **¿cómo se llama usted?** *form. s.*; **¿cómo te llamas?** *fam. s.* (1); what time is it? **¿qué hora es?** (1); what's the weather like? **¿qué tiempo hace?** (6); what's today's date? **¿cuál es la fecha de hoy?** (6), **¿qué fecha es hoy?** (6)
when? **¿cuándo?** (2)
where? **¿dónde?** (1); where (to)? **¿adónde?** (4); where are you from? **¿de dónde eres (tú)?** *fam. s.* (1); **¿de dónde es usted?** *form. s.* (1)
which **que** (3)
which? **¿cuál?** (2)
while **mientras** (10)
white **blanco/a** (4); white wine **vino blanco** (7)
whiteboard **pizarrón** (*m.*) **blanco** (2)
who **que** (3)
who? **¿quién?** (1)
whose? **¿de quién?** (3)
why? **¿por qué?** (3)
widow **viuda** (16)
widower **viudo** (16)
wife **esposa** (3), **mujer** *f.* (16)
wild **salvaje** (15)
win **ganar** (10)
wind energy **energía eólica** (15)
window **ventana** (2); small window (*on a plane*) **ventanilla** (8)
windshield **parabrisas** *m. inv.* (15)
windy: it's (very) windy **hace (mucho) viento** (6)
wine (white, red) **vino (blanco, tinto)** (7)
winter **invierno** (6)
wish **esperanza** (18)
with **con** (2); with me **conmigo** (6); with you *fam. s.* **contigo** (6)
withdraw **sacar (qu)** (17)
without **sin** (5); **sin que** (16)
witness **testigo** *m., f.* (18)
woman **mujer** *f.* (2); **señora (Sra.)** (1)
wool **de lana** (4)
word **palabra** (1); indefinite and negative word *gram.* **palabra indefinida y negativa** (7)
work (labor) **trabajo** (12); (piece of) **trabajo** (14); to work **funcionar** (12); **trabajar** (2); work of art **obra de arte** (13); *adj.* **laboral** (17)
worker **obrero/a** (17)
world **mundo** (3)
worried **preocupado/a** (6)
worse **peor** (6)
woven goods **tejidos** *m. pl.* (13)
write **escribir** (*p.p.* **escrito**) (3)
writer **escritor(a)** (13)
written **escrito/a** (*p.p. of* **escribir**) (14); written report **informe** (*m.*) **escrito** (14)
wrong: to be wrong **no tener razón** (4); to get up on the wrong side of the bed **levantarse con el pie izquierdo** (14)

Y

yard **patio** (5)
year **año** (6); (*in school*) **grado** (10); end of the year **fin** (*m.*) **de año** (9); to be . . . years old **tener… años** (3)
yellow **amarillo/a** (4)
yes **sí** (1)
yesterday was . . . **ayer fue…** (5); the day before yesterday *adv.* **anteayer** (5)
yoga: to do yoga **hacer (el) yoga** (11)
yogurt **yogur** *m.* (7)
you *sub. pron.* **tú** *fam. s.* (2); **usted** *form. s.* (2); **vosotros/as** *fam. pl.* (*Sp.*) (2); **ustedes (Uds.)** *pl.* (2); *obj. of prep.* **ti** *fam. s.* (6); **usted** *form. s.* (6); and you? **¿y tú?** *fam. s.* (1); **¿y usted?** *form. s.* (1); how are you? **¿cómo está(s)?** (1), **¿qué tal?** (1)
you're welcome **de nada** (1), **no hay de qué** (1)
young **joven** (3); young woman **señorita (Srta.)** (1)
younger (than) **menor (que)** (6)
your *poss. adj.* **tu(s)** *fam. s.* (3); **su(s)** *form. s., pl.* (3); **vuestro/a(s)** *fam. pl.* (*Sp.*) (3); your, (of) yours *poss. adj., poss. pron.* **tuyo/a(s)** *fam. s.* (17); **suyo/a(s)** *form. s., pl.* (17); **vuestro/a(s)** *fam. pl.* (*Sp.*) (17)
youth **juventud** *f.* (16); as a youth **de joven** (10)

Z

zero **cero** (1)
zone **zona** (12)

CREDITS

Grateful acknowledgment is made for use of the following:

Photographs: *Page 2 top* © Corbis/photolibrary; *2 bottom* © Sandra Raccanello/Grand Tour/Corbis; *4 top right* Siri Stafford/Getty Images; *4 bottom left* © Frederico Gil; *5* Beathan/Corbis; *7* dynamicgraphics/Jupiterimages; *8 left* Kevin Peterson/Getty Images; *8 right* Andersen Ross/Getty Images; *10* America/Alamy; *12* © Michael Newman/PhotoEdit; *14* © JAVIER SORIANO/AFP/Getty Images; *20 top* © Pictor Images/ImageState; *20 bottom* © Glowimages/Punchstock; *21 top* © Ulrike Welsch; *21 bottom* © José Fuste Raga/photolibrary; *24* © Simon Jarratt/Corbis/photolibrary; *28* © UNMSM; *30* © Lifesize/Getty Images; *42* © BananaStock/Punchstock; *44 left* Tetra images RF/Getty Images; *44 right* Digital Vision/Getty Images; *45* © Digital Vision; *48* Photography by Marsha Miller, Courtesy of University of Texas at Austin; *52* "La Memoria de Nuestra Tierra: California" 1996 © Judith F. Baca, Courtesy of SPARC, www.sparcmurals.org; *54* © Kevin Winter/Getty Images; *55* © Pixtal/age fotostock; *58* Hill Street Studios/Blend Images/Getty Images; *60 top, left to right* Michael Prince/TAXI/Getty Images; Jose Luis Pelaez Inc./Blend Images/Getty Images; *60 middle, left to right* © Seth Joel/Getty Images; Jose Luis Pelaez Inc./Blend Images/Getty Images; Jose Luis Pelaez Inc./Blend Images/Getty Images; John Henley/Blend Images/Getty Images; *60 bottom left to right* Glow Images/Superstock; Getty Images/Digital Vision; © Blend Images/PunchStock; G.K. & Vikki Hart/Getty Images; Ryan McVay/Getty Images; Michael Matisse/Getty Images; *63* Jose Luis Pelaez, Inc./Getty Images; *66* © Pictor Images/ImageState; *72 left* Corbis/Superstock; *72 right* Lifesize/Getty Images; *82* Pixtal/age fotostock; *84* © 1987 Carmen Lomas Garza; Photo credit: Wolfgang Dietze; Collection of Leonila Ramirez, Don Ramon's Restaurant, San Francisco, California; *87* Collection SFMOMA, Albert M. Bender Collection, Gift of Albert M. Bender, © Banco de Mexico Diego Rivera & Frida Kahlo Museums Trust, Mexico, D.F./Artists Rights Society (ARS), New York; *90* Fernando Castillo/LatinContent/Getty Images; *92* Kevin Winter/Getty Images; *96* © Danny Lehman/Corbis; *98 left* Rubberball/Getty Images; *98 right* Stockbyte/Getty Images; *99 left to right* Ryan McVay/Getty Images; Imagestate Media (John Foxx)/Imagestate; Rubberball Productions; *101 top* © Nicemonkey/Alamy; *101 bottom* Artwork courtesy of La Antigua Galería de Arte Antigua Guatemala, www.artintheamericas.com; *102* The McGraw-Hill Companies, Inc./Barry Barker, photographer; *111* Ingram Publishing; *116* © Diego Lezama/Lonely Planet Images; *118* UncorneredMarket.com/Getty Images; *122* Photo courtesy of Paul Soberanis Letona; *123 top* Courtesy of Exofficio; *124* Photo by Rodrigo Varela/WireImage/Getty Images; *128* © Egon Bömsch/age fotostock; *132* © Tomàs Badia/Flickr; *140* © Thomas Stargardter/LatinFocus.com; *153* © EPA/Roberto Escobar/Corbis; *156* Courtesy of Francesca Tabone; *158* Festival of World Cultures, 2007; *162* © JUAN CARLOS ULATE/Reuters/Landov; *166* Bill Brooks/Alamy; *167* DEA/S. BUONAMICI/Getty Images; *170* Janis Christie/Getty Images; *175 left* Stockbyte/Getty Images; *175 right* © PhotoLibrary; *178* BananaStock/PictureQuest; *179* Courtesy Jennifer Kirk; *182 top* © Image Source/PunchStock; *182 bottom* © Radius Images/PhotoLibrary; *187* Jack Hollingsworth/Getty Images; *188* © Alamy; *192* Courtesy Jennifer Kirk; *194* © Newscom; *198* ELMER MARTINEZ/AFP/Getty Images; *202* © Nicholas Gill/Alamy; *216* © Purestock/Getty Images; *220* © JJM Stock Photography/Alamy; *224* © Norberto Lauria/Alamy; *225* © Certified Angus Beef LLC. All rights reserved; *226* John Parra/Getty Images; *230* © Christian Kober/photolibrary; *235* © Michael J. Doolittle/The Image Works; *236* © Stuart Cohen; *252* Tetra Images/Getty Images; *255* © MedioImages; *258* © age fotostock/SuperStock; *260* © Michael Caulfield/WireImage/Getty Images; *261* © Terry Harris/Alamy; *264* © Don Tremain/Getty Images; *267* ADALBERTO ROQUE/AFP/Getty Images; *268* © A. Garcia/LatinFocus.com; *273* © LatinFocus; *275* © C Bockermann/CHROMOR/age fotostock; *283* © A. Garcia/LatinFocus.com; *286* © Christopher Pillitz/Getty Images; 287 *top left to right* Ingram Publishing/SuperStock; © Comstock/PunchStock; Masterfile/Royalty Free; *287 bottom left to right* © Ingram Publishing/Fototsearch; © Image Club; *288* Lucy Nicholson/AFP/Getty Images; *292* © José Francisco Salgado, PhD; *294 top, left to right* Comstock Images/Alamy; © Ingram Publishing/age fotostock; Photodisc/Getty Images; Ben Blankenburg/Corbis; *294 bottom, left to right* TRBfoto/Getty Images; Mark Andersen/Getty Images; Brand X Pictures; *295* © AP Photo/Ricardo Arduengo; *307 left to right* © Stephane Cardinale/Corbis Sygma; Focus on Sport/Getty Images; Stefanie Keenan/WireImage/Getty Images; *311* Courtesy of William Vazquez; *314* Medioimages/Photodisc/Getty Images; *316* MICHAEL BUSH/UPI/Landov; *317* © Hola Images/Getty Images; *320* © Rolf Becker; *325 top left* © Royalty Free/Corbis; *325 top right* © Mike Watson/moodboard/Corbis; *325 bottom* © David R. Frazier Photolibrary, Inc./Alamy; *327* © Marty Granger; *331 top* © Imagesource/photolibrary; *331 bottom* © Pixtal/age fotostock; *332 top* Dosfotos/photolibrary; *332 bottom* © Blend Images/age fotostock; *338* © Corbis Cusp/Alamy;

341 © Jacques Jangoux/Alamy; *344* Paula Bronstein/Getty Images; *346* Michael Caulfield/WireImage/Getty Images; *350* © Radius/SuperStock; *356* Jack Hollingsworth/Getty Images; *362* Glow Images/Superstock; *371* © Jenny Matthews/Alamy; *372* © Dave G. Houser/Corbis; *376* © age fotostock/SuperStock; *378 left MiniMed Paradigm® REAL-Time Insulin Pump and Continuous Glucose Monitoring System Manufactured by the diabetes division of Medtronic, Inc.; 378 right* FREDY BUILES/Reuters/Landov; *382* Courtesy of Bernai Velvarde; *386* © Ralf Heinze/photolibrary; *389* ©Joe Sohm/The Image Works; Courtesy of The Blanton Museum of Art and the Pacheco Family; *394* Melanie Stetson Freeman/The Christian Science Monitor via Getty Images; *396* Aryballos-shaped vessel (ceramic), Incan/Museo Regional de Cuzco, Peru/Bildarchiv Steffens Henri Stierlin/The Bridgeman Art Library; *397* John Warburton-Lee Photography/photolibrary; *398* © Tibor Bogner; *400* The Granger Collection, NYC—All rights reserved; *402* ullstein bild/The Granger Collection, NYC—All rights reserved; *406* © Jimmy Dorantes/Latin Focus; *408* Courtesy of Los Kjarkas; *409* © SuperStock/age footstock; *412* © Mariana Bazo/Reuters/Corbis; *420 Top* Photo Corporation/photolibrary; *432* Photographer's Choice/Getty Images; *436* © Toño Labra/age fotostock; *438* © Philip Ryalls/Redferns; *442* © Corbis; *453* © Viviane Ponti/Lonely Planet Images; *458* © Glowimages/age fotostock; *461* © Digital Vision/Getty Images; *464* © Royalty-Free/Corbis; *466* © Stefan M. Prager/Redferns/Getty Images; *470* © JORGE ADORNO/Reuters/Corbis; *473* © Frans Lemmens/SuperStock; *476* © BananaStock/PunchStock; *483* © svmma/Flickr/Getty Images; *484* © mike disney/Alamy; *488* © Mike Goldwater/Alamy; *490 top* © pulp/Getty Images; *490 bottom* Tony Russell/Redferns/Getty Images; *494* © Paul Harris/photolibrary; *497* Marcelo Hernandez/LatinContent/Getty Images; *507 left* © Michael Snell/Robert Harding Travel/photolibrary; *507 right* © Lee Foster/Alamy; *513* © Jon Arnold Images Ltd/Alamy; *516* Courtesy of Carla Venegas Bashman; *518* © Newscom; *522* © KOTE RODRIGO/epa/Corbis; *527* Steve Petteway, Collection of the Supreme Court of the United States; *528* Chema Moya/EFE/Newscom; *534* Fotonoticias/WireImage/Getty Images; *538* © age fotostock/SuperStock; *543* Courtesy of Univision Network; *546* © Greg Elms/Lonely Planet Images; *548 top* © Royalty Free/Corbis; *548 bottom* Marcelo Hernadez/LatinContent/Getty Images; *549* © FELIX ORDONEZ AUSIN/Reuters/Corbis; *552* Siegfried Heckötter, bona dea production; *553 top* Courtesy of Huno Garces; *553 bottom* Hispanic Fiesta, Toronto, Canada.

Realia: *Page 18* Ansa International; *53* Courtesy of Cincilingua International Language Center, Cincinnati, Ohio; *62* Courtesy of Marcela Carolina & Alberto Andrés; *91* Photo and caption used by permission of EFE News Services (U.S.) Inc.; *104* CREDIT LINE: *Quo,* HF Revistas; *123* "Algo más que ropa" by Gregori Dolz used courtesy of American Airlines *NEXOS* American Airlines Publishing Group; *192* Adapted from LAU.KAMPUSSIA.COM; *253* David Sebastian Ojeda, Buenos Aires, artepiero@hotmail.com; *259* Used courtesy of Iberocruceros, a division of Costa Crociere, S.p.A.; *287* Adapted from *La Voz de Nuevo México,* December 29, 2005; *315* Courtesy of Grupo Senda; *337* © Quino/Quipos; *460 left* © Quino/Quipos; *460 right* Cartoon by MENA; *535* Cartoon by Antonio Mingote.

Literature: *Page 345* "Epitafio" by Nicanor Parra from *Poemas y antipoemas* © Nicanor Parra, 1954. Used by permission; *377* "Apocalipsis, I" by Marco Denevi from *Falsificaciones*, Corregidor 2007. Used by permission of the publisher; *407* "La higuera" by Juana Fernández Ibarbourou. Used by permission; *437* "Oh" from *Poemas de la oficina* © Fundación Mario Benedetti c/o Guillermo Schavelzon & Asociados, Agencia Literaria www.schavelzon.com. Used by permission; *465* "Cuadrados y ángulos" by Alfonsina Storni in *El dulce daño*. Editorial Losada S.A., Buenos Aires, 1997; *489* "Palomas" by Gloria Fuertes. Used by permission of Luzmaría Jiménez Faro, Heredera Universal de Gloria Fuertes; *517* "XXIX" in *Proverbios y cantares* by Antonio Machado. Used by permission of the heirs of Antonio Machado; *547* From *Celebración de la voz humana/2* in *El libro de los abrazos,* Eduardo Galeano, Siglo Veintiuno Editors, 1990, p. 11 by Eduardo Galeano. Used by permission.

INDEX

D

E

V

W

Y

Z

MANDATOS° Y FRASES COMUNES EN EL SALÓN DE CLASE

°*Commands*

Los estudiantes

Practice saying these sentences aloud. Then try to give the Spanish as you look at the English equivalents.

Tengo una pregunta (que hacer).	*I have a question* (*to ask*).
¿Cómo se dice *page* en español?	*How do you say "page" in Spanish?*
Otra vez, por favor. No entiendo.	(*Say that*) *Again, please. I don't understand.*
¿Cómo?	*What* (*did you say*)?
¡(Espere,) Un momento, por favor! No sé (la respuesta).	(*Wait,*) *Just a minute, please! I don't know* (*the answer*).
(Sí,) Cómo no.	(*Yes,*) *Of course.*

Los profesores

After you read these Spanish sentences, cover the English equivalents and say what each expression means.

¿Hay preguntas?	*Are there any questions?*
¿Qué opina/cree Ud.?	*What do you think?*
Escuche. Repita.	*Listen. Repeat.*
Lea (en voz alta).	*Read* (*aloud*).
Escriba/Complete (la siguiente oración).	*Write/Complete* (*the next sentence*).
Conteste en español.	*Answer in Spanish.*
Prepare (el ejercicio) para mañana.	*Prepare* (*the exercise*) *for tomorrow.*
Abra el libro en la página ______.	*Open your book to page ______.*
Cierre el cuaderno.	*Close your notebook.*
Saque (un papel).	*Take out* (*a sheet of paper*).
Levante la mano si...	*Raise your hand if...*
Vaya a la pizarra.	*Go to the board.*
Pregúntele a otro estudiante ______.	*Ask another student ______.*
Déle ______ a ______.	*Give ______ to ______.*
Busque un compañero.	*Look for a partner.*
Haga la actividad con dos compañeros.	*Do the activity with two classmates.*
Formen grupos de cinco estudiantes.	*Get into groups of five students.*
En parejas...	*In pairs...*

SELECTED VERB FORMS

Regular Verbs | Simple Tenses and Present Perfect (Indicative)

	PRESENT	PRETERITE	IMPERFECT	PRESENT PERFECT
hablar	hablo	hablé	hablaba	he hablado
comer	como	comí	comía	he comido
vivir	vivo	viví	vivía	he vivido

Common Irregular Verbs | Present and Preterite (Indicative)

caer	caigo	caí
dar	doy	di
decir	digo	dije
estar	estoy	estuve
hacer	hago	hice
ir	voy	fui
oír	oigo	oí
poder	puedo	pude
poner	pongo	puse
querer	quiero	quise
saber	sé	supe
ser	soy	fui
tener	tengo	tuve
traer	traigo	traje
venir	vengo	vine
ver	veo	vi

Irregular Verbs | Imperfect (Indicative)

ir	iba	**ser**	era	**ver**	veía

Regular Verbs | Simple Tenses and Present Perfect (Subjunctive)

	PRESENT	IMPERFECT	PRESENT PERFECT
hablar	hable	hablara	haya hablado
comer	coma	comiera	haya comido
vivir	viva	viviera	haya vivido

Regular and Irregular Verbs | Future and Conditional

hablar	hablaré	hablaría
comer	comeré	comería
vivir	viviré	viviría

decir	diré	diría
hacer	haré	haría
poder	podré	podría
poner	pondré	pondría
querer	querré	querría
saber	sabré	sabría
tener	tendré	tendría
venir	vendré	vendría

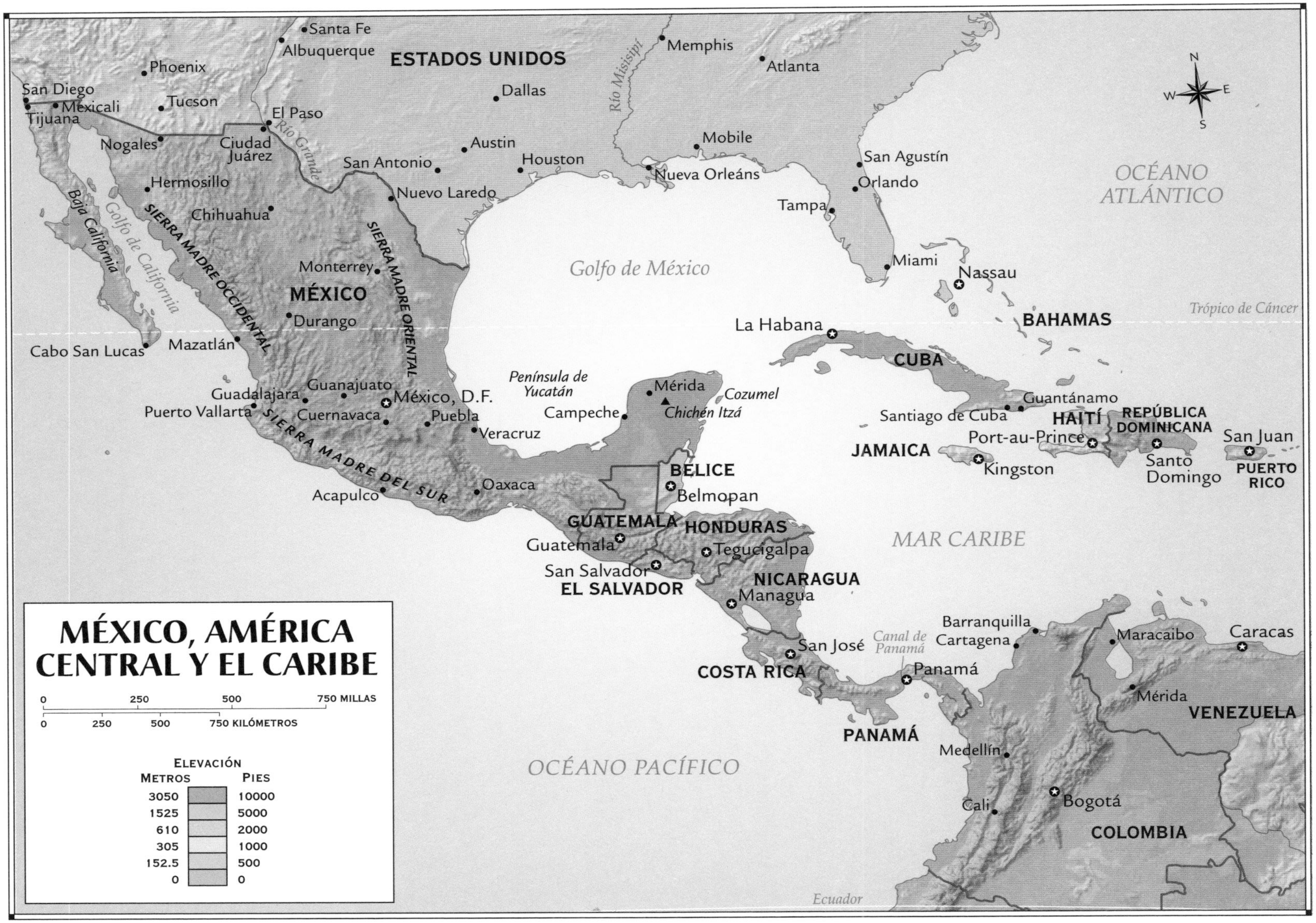

MÉXICO, AMÉRICA CENTRAL Y EL CARIBE
0
250
500
750 MILLAS
0
250
500
750 KILÓMETROS
ELEVACIÓN
METROS
PIES
3050
10000
1525
5000
610
2000
305
1000
152.5
500
0
0
ESTADOS UNIDOS
Santa Fe
Albuquerque
Phoenix
Tucson
San Diego
Mexicali
Tijuana
El Paso
Nogales
Ciudad Juárez
Río Grande
San Antonio
Austin
Dallas
Houston
Nuevo Laredo
Memphis
Río Misisipí
Atlanta
Mobile
Nueva Orleáns
San Agustín
Orlando
Tampa
Miami
OCÉANO ATLÁNTICO
Hermosillo
Chihuahua
Baja California
Golfo de California
SIERRA MADRE OCCIDENTAL
SIERRA MADRE ORIENTAL
Monterrey
MÉXICO
Durango
Cabo San Lucas
Mazatlán
Golfo de México
Nassau
BAHAMAS
Trópico de Cáncer
La Habana
CUBA
Península de Yucatán
Mérida
Cozumel
Chichén Itzá
Campeche
Guadalajara
Guanajuato
México, D.F.
Puerto Vallarta
Cuernavaca
Puebla
Veracruz
SIERRA MADRE DEL SUR
Acapulco
Oaxaca
BELICE
Belmopan
GUATEMALA
HONDURAS
Guatemala
Tegucigalpa
San Salvador
EL SALVADOR
NICARAGUA
Managua
Santiago de Cuba
Guantánamo
HAITÍ
REPÚBLICA DOMINICANA
JAMAICA
Port-au-Prince
Kingston
Santo Domingo
San Juan
PUERTO RICO
MAR CARIBE
San José
COSTA RICA
Canal de Panamá
Panamá
PANAMÁ
Barranquilla
Cartagena
Maracaibo
Caracas
Mérida
VENEZUELA
Medellín
Bogotá
Cali
COLOMBIA
OCÉANO PACÍFICO
Ecuador

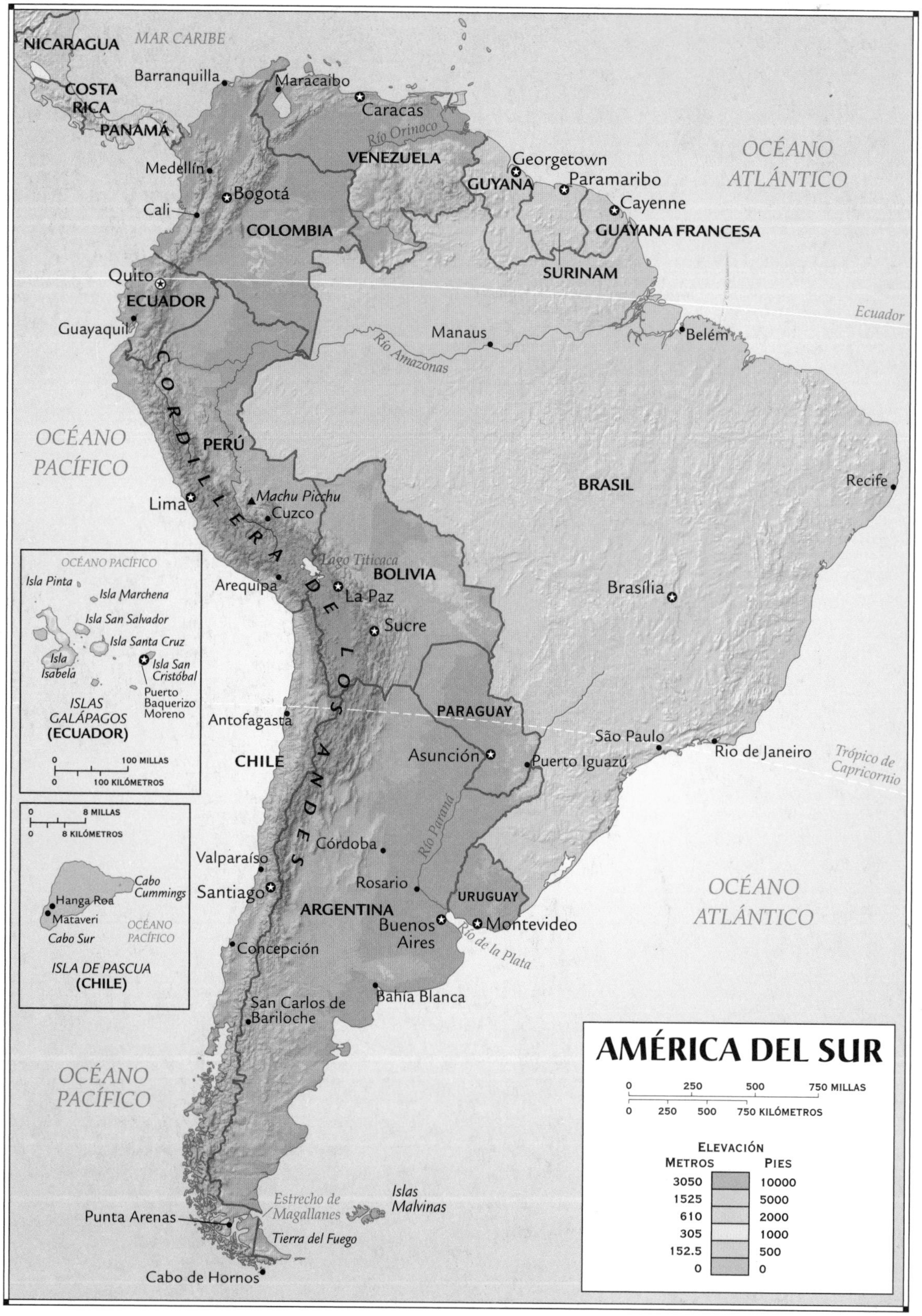
AMÉRICA DEL SUR
NICARAGUA
MAR CARIBE
COSTA RICA
PANAMÁ
Barranquilla
Maracaibo
Caracas
Río Orinoco
VENEZUELA
Medellín
Bogotá
Cali
COLOMBIA
Georgetown
Paramaribo
Cayenne
GUYANA
GUAYANA FRANCESA
SURINAM
OCÉANO ATLÁNTICO
Quito
ECUADOR
Guayaquil
Ecuador
Manaus
Río Amazonas
Belém
CORDILLERA DE LOS ANDES
OCÉANO PACÍFICO
PERÚ
BRASIL
Recife
Lima
Machu Picchu
Cuzco
Lago Titicaca
BOLIVIA
Arequipa
La Paz
Sucre
Brasília
OCÉANO PACÍFICO
Isla Pinta
Isla Marchena
Isla San Salvador
Isla Santa Cruz
Isla Isabela
Isla San Cristóbal
Puerto Baquerizo Moreno
ISLAS GALÁPAGOS
(ECUADOR)
0 100 MILLAS
0 100 KILÓMETROS
PARAGUAY
Antofagasta
São Paulo
Rio de Janeiro
Trópico de Capricornio
CHILE
Asunción
Puerto Iguazú
0 8 MILLAS
0 8 KILÓMETROS
Cabo Cummings
Hanga Roa
Mataveri
Cabo Sur
OCÉANO PACÍFICO
ISLA DE PASCUA
(CHILE)
Córdoba
Río Paraná
Valparaíso
Santiago
Rosario
URUGUAY
ARGENTINA
Buenos Aires
Montevideo
Río de la Plata
OCÉANO ATLÁNTICO
Concepción
Bahía Blanca
San Carlos de Bariloche
OCÉANO PACÍFICO
0 250 500 750 MILLAS
0 250 500 750 KILÓMETROS
ELEVACIÓN
METROS PIES
3050 10000
1525 5000
610 2000
305 1000
152.5 500
0 0
Estrecho de Magallanes
Islas Malvinas
Punta Arenas
Tierra del Fuego
Cabo de Hornos